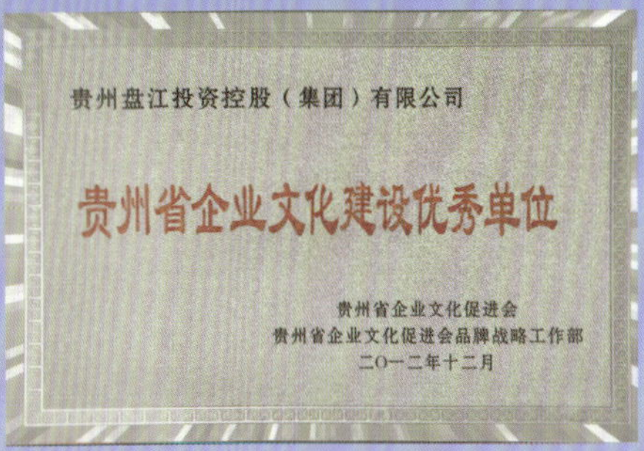

贵州省企业文化建设优秀单位

Outstanding Unit of Enterprise Culture construction of Guizhou Province

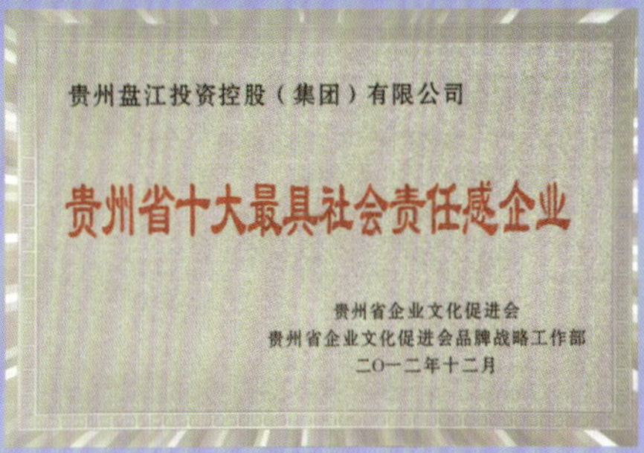

贵州省十大最具社会责任感企业

Top Ten Most Socially Responsible Enterprise of Guizhou Province

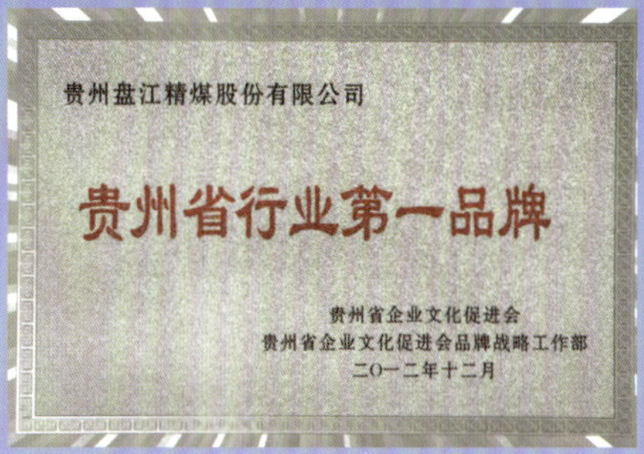

贵州省行业第一品牌

The First Brand in the Industry of Guizhou Province

The Guizhou Panjiang Investment Holdings (Group) Co.,Ltd .is a provincial state-owned enterprises, its predecessor was Panjiang Bureau of Mines,which belonged to the former Ministry of Coal .In 1997, the corporate got reformed and changed its name to Panjiang Coal Power (Group) Co., Ltd.. In 2010, Guizhou Province SASAC approved business transformation and the corporate changed its name to Guizhou Panjiang Investment Holdings (Group) Co., Ltd., and moved its headquarters from Pan County, Guizhou to Guiyang City.

项目建设现场

Project construction site

Panjiang Group is among the country’s 520 key state-owned enterprises, the 100 enterprises of China's coal enterprises, the top ten enterprises in Guizhou Province. The Group owns more than 50 of the wholly-owned subsidiaries,branch companies and holding companies. One of them, the Panjiang Fine Coal Corporation (sh.600395) is the first listed company in Guizhou province’s coal industry. In recent years, the company adhere to the“coal-based, multi-industry, scientific-development” strategy, the Group's business achieved successful transformation of production and management to capital management, industrial expansion and strategic control. Currently, the eight industrial clusters, sixteen industry segments of “coal and related industries, clean energy industry, stone resources industry, equipment manufacturing industries, specialty agriculture, modern service industry, urban development, finance and trade”initially formed. Among them, the coal industry is No.1 in the south of the Yangtze River, the scale of utilization of medium low-density gas in the coalbed methane industry ranks first in China, cement and other industries have become the region’s corporate champions.

In 2012, the Group continued to maintain a strong momentum of development, producted 20.25 million tons of raw coal, 3.91 millions tons of coke, 6.61 millions tons of cement, generated 990 million kwh of power; achieved the total production and operation value of 26 billion yuan, up 80% over the previous year; taxes and fees for 2.47 billion yuan, up 28% over the previous year; total assets reached 34.2 billion yuan,with year-on-year growth of 31.5%; net assets reached 14.5 billion yuan, with year-on-year growth of 23.9%.

晚霞.竖井

Sunset. Shaft

成立观山湖区
The establishment of Guanshanhu district

观山湖区召开第一次党代会
Guanshanhu district held its first congress

观 山 湖 区
Guanshanhu District

观山湖区召开一届一次人代会
Guanshanhu district held a session of a National People's Congress

观山湖区召开一届一次政协会议
Guanshanhu district held a session of a Political Consultative Conference

观山湖区面积307平方公里，下辖金华镇、朱昌镇、百花湖乡及碧海、世纪城、金华园、新世界、逸景、金源、金麦、金岭8个社区服务中心。2012年末，常住总人口21.46万人。

2012年，全年生产总值90.23亿元，全年完成财政总收入38.36亿元，同比增长21%，公共财政预算收入完成27.8亿元，同比增长13.5%；完成固定资产投资380.2亿元，同比增长51.4%；完成社会消费品零售总额54.08亿元，同比增长18.1%。全年招商引资内资实际到位资金168.2亿元，同比增长84%，其中省外到位资金102.87亿元，同比增长109%，实际利用外资5688万美元，同比增长72%

产业培育优化取得新进展，加大结构调整，产业培育发展成效明显；积极抓好农业生产；积极稳妥发展工业，规模以上工业增加值完成11.93亿元；突出重点发展三产，三次产业结构优化为2.1：35.3：62.6。城市开发建设再上新台阶，完成总投资32.8亿元的重大基础设施项目19个，基础设施建设拓展至307平方公里规划范围。生态文明建设提升新档次。民生事务工作迈出新步伐。社会管理创新呈现新活力。改革发展事业迎来新跨越。

观山湖公园
Guanshanhu Park

贵阳市二环四路城市带金阳新区火车北站功能区骨干路网开建
Guiyang city two rings four roads city belt Jinyang new district North train station with a ribbon CAPE backbone road construction

Guanshanhu District has an area of 307 square kilometers, under the jurisdiction of Jinhua town, Zhuchang town, Baihuahu village and Bihai, Shiji City, Jinhua Park, New World, Yijing, Jinyuan, Jinmai, Jinling eight community service centers. By the end of 2012, the total resident population of 214,600 people.

In 2012, the annual GDP of 9.023 billion yuan, the annual fiscal revenue 3.836 billion yuan, an increase of 21%, the public budget revenue of 2.78 billion yuan, an increase of 13.5%; fixed assets investment 38.02 billion yuan, an increase of 51.4%; complete the total retail sales of social consumer goods 5.408 billion yuan, an increase of 18.1%. Annual investment funded the actual funds 16.82 billion yuan, an increase of 84%, of which the province capital in place of 10.287 billion yuan, an increase of 109%, the actual utilization of foreign capital 56,880,000 dollars, an increase of 72%.

Optimization of industrial training has made new progress, intensify structural adjustment, industrial foster development effectiveness significantly; actively promote agricultural production; actively and steadily develop industry, above-scale industrial added value reached 1.193 billion yuan; prominent focus on the development of tertiary, three industrial structure optimization of 2.1:35.3:62.6. Urban development to a new level, a total investment of 3.28 billion yuan to complete the 19 major infrastructure projects, infrastructure expanded to 307 square kilometers planning area. Enhance ecological civilization construction of new grade. Livelihood affairs take new steps. Social management innovation presents a new vitality. Reform and usher in a new career leap.

贵阳市二环四路金阳新区火车北站功能区招商引资项目集中签约
Guiyang city two rings four roads city belt Jinyang new district North train station functional areas investment projects focused on signing

2013观山湖灯会——欢聚
2013 Guanshanhu Lantern Festival - togetherness

GUIZHOU STATISTICAL YEARBOOK

贵州统计年鉴

2013

贵州省统计局　国家统计局贵州调查总队　编

Compiled by Guizhou Provincial Bureau of Statistics　NBS Survey Office in Guizhou

GUIZHOU STATISTICAL YEARBOOK

图书在版编目（CIP）数据

贵州统计年鉴．2013：汉英对照／贵州省统计局，国家统计局贵州调查总队编．-- 北京：中国统计出版社，2013.9

ISBN 978-7-5037-6973-3

Ⅰ．①贵… Ⅱ．①贵… ②国… Ⅲ．①统计资料－贵州省－2013－年鉴 Ⅳ．① C832.73-54

中国版本图书馆 CIP 数据核字 (2013) 第 220515 号

贵州统计年鉴 -2013
作　　者／贵州省统计局　国家统计局贵州调查总队

责任编辑／佘竞雄
出版发行／中国统计出版社
地　　址／北京市丰台区西三环南路甲 6 号　邮政编码／100073
电　　话／邮购（010）63376909 书店（010）68783171
网　　址／http://csp.stats.gov.cn
印　　刷／贵州新华印务有限责任公司
经　　销／新华书店
开　　本／890mm × 1240mm　1/16
字　　数／1629 千字
印　　张／56 印张
印　　数／1600 册
版　　别／2013 年 9 月第 1 版
版　　次／2013 年 9 月第 1 次印刷
书　　号／ISBN 978-7-5037-6973-3
定　　价／330.00 元

本书附同版本 CD-ROM 一张，光盘内容以书面文字为准。
如有印装错误，本社发行部负责调换。

编 者 说 明

一、《贵州统计年鉴 -2013》系统收录了2012年贵州省国民经济和社会发展等各方面的统计数据，改革开放以来特别是2007年以来的主要统计数据，以及2012年全国、各省（区、市）主要统计数据，是反映贵州省情的重要工具书。

二、本年鉴包括29个部分: 综合; 国民经济核算; 人口; 就业人员和职工工资; 固定资产投资; 对外经济贸易; 能源; 财政税收; 价格指数; 人民生活; 城市概况; 资源和环境; 农业; 工业; 建筑业; 运输和邮电; 批发和零售业; 住宿、餐饮业和旅游业; 金融业; 教育和科技; 文化、体育和卫生; 社会服务及其他; 民营经济; 民族自治地方; 经济强县; 扶贫与开发; 市（州）、县（市、区、特区）资料; 全国各省（区、市）资料; 历年资料。为便于读者使用统计数据，在每部分之后附有主要统计指标解释。

三、本年鉴中，凡由有关部门（单位）提供的数据都在表式的注释中说明了数据来源; 部分统计指标的范围以及口径变化在表下均有注释，使用时请读者注意。

四、本年鉴中部分数据合计数或相对数由于计算单位或取舍不同而产生的计算误差，均未作机械调整。

五、本年鉴表中的符号使用说明: “…”表示数据不足最小计量单位; “空格”表示该统计指标数据不详或无数据; “#”表示该指标的其中项。

本年鉴在编辑、出版、发行过程中，得到了有关部门（单位）的大力支持和帮助，在此谨致衷心感谢!

Editor's Notes

I. Guizhou Statistical Yearbook 2013 is an annual statistical publication, which reflects comprehensively the economic and social development of Guizhou Province. It covers data for 2012, key statistical data for the years since Reform and Opening-up especially the year 2007, and Main Statistics of Province (autonomous regions, municipalities)as well as the whole country. It is a useful reference book to thoroughly know Guizhou.

II. The Yearbook contains 29 chapters: General Survey; National Accounts; Population; Employment and Wages; Investment in Fixed Assets; Foreign Trade and Economic Cooperation; Energy; Government Finance and Taxation; Price Indices; People's Living Conditions; General Survey of Cities; Resources and Environment; Agriculture; Industry; Construction; Transport, Postal and Telecommunication Services; Wholesale and Retail Trades; Hotel, Catering Services and Tourism; Financial Intermediation; Education, Science and Technology; Culture, Sports and Public Health; Social Services and Others; Private Economy; Minority Nationality Autonomous Areas; Economically Strong Counties; Anti-poverty and Development; Main Statistics of Prefectures and Counties; Main Statistics of Provinces(autonomous regions, municipalities)in the Whole Country; Historical Statistics. Explanatory Notes on Main Statistical Indicators is attached to the end of each chapter to help the readers to use the statistical data in this book.

III. Notes are taken under the data tables in which the data are provided by relative departments other than statistical divisions, or the statistical coverage has been changed. Please pay attention when you use it.

IV. Statistical discrepancies due to rounding are not adjusted in the yearbook.

V. Notations used in the yearbook: "…"indicates that the figure is not large enough to be measured with the smallest unit in the table; "blank space" indicates that data are unknown or are not available; "#"indicates a major breakdown of the total.

Thanks for enthusiastic of many relational departments and individuals to the editing, publication and distribution of the Yearbook!

《贵州统计年鉴－2013》编辑委员会

徐　圻（省广电局局长）
黄定承（省新闻出版局局长）
蔡国祥（省体育局局长）
李尚宽（省安全监管局局长）
郑　华（省知识产权局局长）
傅迎春（省旅游局局长）
沈　健（省粮食局局长）
叶　韬（省扶贫办主任）
薛建英（省国税局局长）
赵广忠（省气象局局长）
李德明（省通信管理局局长）
王　平（人民银行贵阳中心支行行长）
张卫民（贵阳海关关长）
李再勇（贵阳市市长）
周　荣（六盘水市市长）
王秉清（遵义市市长）
曾永涛（安顺市代市长）
夏庆丰（铜仁市市长）
陈昌旭（毕节市市长）
杨永英（黔西南州州长）
廖　飞（黔东南州州长）
向红琼（黔南州州长）

Editorial Board

Xu Qi: Director of the Provincial Radio and TV Administration

Huang Dingcheng: Director of the Provincial Press and Publication Administration

Cai Guoxiang: Director of the Provincial Sport Administration

Li Shangkuan: Director of the Provincial Safety Production Supervision and Management

Zheng Hua: Director of the Provincial Intellectual Property Right Bureau

Fu Yingchun: Director of the Provincial Tourism Administration

Shen Jian: Director of the Provincial Grain Administration

Ye Tao: Director of the Provincial Anti-poverty Office

Xue Jianying: Director of the Provincial National Taxation Administration

Zhao Guangzhong: Director of Guizhou Meteorological Bureau

Li Deming: Director of Guizhou Communication

Wang Ping: Director of the People's Bank of China Guiyang Branch

Zhang Weimin: Director of Guiyang Customs of the People's Republic of China

Li Zaiyong: Mayor of Guiyang City

Zhou Rong: Mayor of Liupanshui City

Wang Bingqing: Mayor of Zunyi City

Zeng Yongtao: Deputy Mayor of Anshun City

Xia Qingfeng: Mayor of Tongren City

Chen Changxu: Mayor of Bijie City

Yang Yongying: Chief Executive of Qianxinan State

Liao Fei: Chief Executive of Qiandongnan State

Xiang Hongqiong: Chief Executive of Qiannan State

《贵州统计年鉴－2013》编辑人员

Editorial Staff of Guizhou Statistical Yearbook 2013

Editor-in-chief: Tao Mouli Zhu Xinwu Zhong Saimei

Deputy Editor-in-chief:

Feng Yuyi Zhang Beiping Wang Xianzhu Yang Dakun He Youcai
Xiao Yunhui Wang Wenzhong Dong Anna Zhang Guiping Liu Daichun
Pan Kang Wang Zhengchao Tang Xiaochuan Yang Tianlu Liao Jinchang
Liu Wenhua Yuan Jinfa Wang Yu

Directors of Editorial Department:

Peng Long Liu Jie

Vice Directors of Editorial Department:

Wang Ying Wang Lianlian

Editor-in- chief by Section(in order of strokes of chinese surname):

Mao Min Wang Zhaohui Bai Wenying Zhang Xiaofang Zhang Xuejin
Li Shigang Yang Zhaoshun Shen Xianfa Xiao Yao Shao Wei
Chen Yingfang Zhou Rong Hu Gang Ni Ming Gong Yong
Liao Jianwei

Editorial Staff(in order of strokes of chinese surname):

Wan Zhaohui Yi Wenjun Deng Weiqing Feng Lu Liu Qiang
Zhang Shiying Du Tianzhu Yang Boyun Wang Mingfeng Xiao Gaoping
Zhou Lian Zhou Huiyun Hu Guoyang Zhao Shiling Zhao Yuanyuan
Xia Renguo You Taoying Dong Jianwei

English Translators: Hou Jiajia

Computer Typesetting: Wei Bo Huang He

目 录

CONTENTS

一 综 合
General Survey

二 国民经济核算
National Accounts

三 人口
Population

四 就业人员和职工工资
Employment and Wages

五 固定资产投资
Investment in Fixed Assets

六 对外经济贸易
Foreign Trade and Economic Cooperation

九 价格指数
Price Indices

十 人民生活
People's Living Conditions

十一 城市概况
General Survey of Cities

十二 资源和环境
Resources and Environment

十四 工 业
Industry

十七 批发和零售业
Wholesale and Retail Trades

十八 住宿、餐饮业和旅游业
Hotel, Catering Services and Tourism

二十一 文化、体育和卫生
Culture, Sports, and Public Health

二十二 社会服务及其他
Social Services and Others

二十三 民营经济
Private Economy

二十四　民族自治地方
Minority Nationality Autonomous Areas

二十五　经济强县
Economically Strong Counties

二十六　扶贫与开发
Anti-poverty and Development

二十七 市(州)、县(市、区、特区)资料
Main Statistics of City(State,Prefecture) and County(City,District,Special Region)

二十八 全国各省（区、市）资料
Main Statistics of Provinces (autonomous regions, municipalities) in the Whole Country

二十九 历年资料
Historical Statistics

机构风采

Institutions Highlights

贵州省经济和信息化委员会

Guizhou Province Economic and Information Technology Commission

2011年8月17日，中国贵州首届酒博览会期间，省经信委主任王江平陪同赵克志省长参观装备制造馆

August 17, 2011, during China Guizhou first wine Expo, Guizhou Province Economic and Information Technology Commission director, Wang Jiangping accompanied by the governor Zhao Kezhi visited museum equipment manufacturing

2011年5月4日，省经信委陪同副省长谢庆生参观贵州在香港举办的商品展览会

May 4, 2011, Guizhou Province Economic and Information Technology Commission accompanied by Vice Governor Xie Qingsheng visit Guizhou Trade Fair held in Hong Kong

2012年11月7日，在京出席中国共产党第十八次全国代表大会的代表王江平接受了中央驻黔媒体及贵州媒体的集中采访

November 7, 2012, Wang Jiangping attended the eighteenth National Congress of Chinese Communist Party in Beijing to accept the interview in the central Guizhou Focus Media and Guizhou media

2012年，面对复杂多变的世界经济形势和我国经济增速减缓的严峻态势，及全省工业克服产成品价格下降、市场需求减少等不利影响，以要素保障为重点、强化经济运行调度，以项目建设为重点、扩大工业投资规模，以园区建设为重点、加快产业集聚发展，以节能和资源综合利用为重点、推进工业绿色发展，以创新能力建设为重点、推动企业技术进步，以打造服务环境为重点、加快民营经济和中小企业发展，全省工业经济全面完成预定目标，呈现出提速增效、位次前移、结构趋优、活力增强的良好发展态势。

工业经济高速增长。2012年全省工业总产值达到7172亿元，工业经济占GDP的比重达到35%。全年累计完成规模以上工业增加值2254亿元（500万元口径，下同），首次突破2000亿元大关，同比增长21.3%。2000万元口径规模以上工业增速16.2%，分别高于全国、西部6.2和3.4个百分点，在全国与西部均位列第三，在全国的位次较上年前移两位。工业经济占GDP的比重达到35%，比上年提高了2.9个百分点。月度走势保持平稳，工业增速呈逐季上扬态势。

主要行业发展良好。其中，煤炭产业完成工业增加值555.6亿元，同比增长28.4%，对全省规模以上工业经济增长

2012年4月9日，“东西合作 阳光牵手”江苏•贵州IT产业战略合作协议签约仪式在贵阳举行。副省长孙国强出席签约仪式并讲话，省经信委主任王江平参加签约仪式
April 9, 2012, “East-West collaboration sun in hand”, Jiangsu, Guizhou IT industry strategic cooperation agreement signing ceremony held in Guiyang. Sun Guoqiang, vice governor attended the ceremony and delivered a speech,Guizhou Province Economic and Information Technology Commission director, Wang Jiangping attended the signing ceremony

2012年1月30日，省经信委召开贯彻落实国发2号文件精神座谈会。副省长孙国强出席会议并讲话
January 30, 2012, Guizhou Province Economic and Information Technology Commission convening implement national spirit of the document issued on the 2nd symposium. Sun Guoqiang, vice governor attended the meeting and delivered a speech

2012年4月26日，省经信委与中国工商银行贵州省分行签署战略合作备忘录April 26, 2012, Guizhou economic and Information Technology Commission and Commercial Bank of China Guizhou Province branch signed a strategic cooperation memorandum

In 2012, facing the complex world economic situation and China’s economic growth has slowed down the grim situation, and to overcome the province’s industrial finished products prices, market demand and other adverse effects, in order to focus on elements of security, strengthen economic operation scheduling, project construction as the focus, expand the industrial scale of investment, construction of the park as the focus, accelerate industrial agglomeration development, energy conservation and comprehensive utilization of resources, focusing on promoting green industry development, innovation and capacity building as the focus, to promote technological progress, and to create services focus on the environment, accelerate the development of private economy and SMEs, the province’s industrial economy has fully completed the intended target, showing speed efficiency, ranking forward, structural increasingly excellent, enhanced vitality good momentum of development.

Industrial economic growth. In 2012 the province’s industrial output value reached 717.2 billion yuan, industrial economy to GDP reached 35%. Annual above-scale industrial added value totaled 225.4 billion yuan (5 million yuan caliber, the same below), mark the first time exceeded 200 billion yuan, an increase of 21.3%. 20 million yuan caliber scale industrial growth rate of 16.2%, respectively, higher than the national 6.2 and 3.4 percentage points from the west, both in the country and the western third place, in the country’s ranking compared to last year forward two. Industrial economy to GDP reached 35%, compared with last year increased by 2.9 percentage points. Monthly trend remained stable, rising trend of industrial growth was a quarterly basis.

Major industries developed well. Among them, the coal industry, the industrial added value 55.56 billion yuan, an increase of 28.4%, made contribution for the province’s industrial economic growth rate reached 33.7 percent, ranking first in the province; tobacco industry to achieve industrial added value of 61.7 billion yuan, total industrial added value and profits ranking first in the province’s industrial top

的贡献率达到33.7%，位居全省第一；烟酒工业实现工业增加值617亿元，工业增加值和利税总额居全省工业十大产业之首，是拉动工业经济增长的重要支柱。从比重看，排前五位的行业分别是煤、白酒、电力、烟草、化工。

工业投资全面完成。全年完成工业投资3126.2亿元（含工业园区基础设施投资），突破3000亿元，同比增长35%，高于全国15个百分点。其中，更新改造投资完成969.9亿元，同比增长21.8%；基本建设投资完成2058.1亿元，同比增长50.4%。全年规模以上工业企业实现利润总额466亿元，同比增长47.4%。

长征电气有限公司直驱永磁风力发电机生产基地
Changzheng Electric Co.,Ltd. direct-drive permanent magnet wind turbine production base

2012年9月15日，调研组一行在贵州鸿基伟业新能源有限公司调研
September 15, 2012, the research group research at Guizhou Hongji Weiye New Energy Co., Ltd.

贵州中烟工业有限责任公司新搬迁的生产车间
Guizhou Tobacco Industry Co., Ltd. the new production plant relocation

建设中的盘南电厂
The construction of Pannan Power Plant

区域经济齐头并进。各地工业发展速度不断加快，经济总量进一步壮大，支柱产业带动作用进一步增强，产业集聚发展程度进一步提高，规模工业增加值占生产总值的比重均明显提升。全省9个市州工业增加值均超过21%，毕节市增速最高达到29.5%。

民营经济加快发展。全年规模以上非公有制控股企业、私营企业分别完成工业增加值949.6亿元、624.1亿元，同比分别增长29.4%、32.6%，增速分别超出全省规模以上工业平均增速8.1个百分点、11.3个百分点。全省民营经济市场主体共计104.3万户，占全省工商注册企业数达99%以上，民营经济占GDP比重达40%。

先进的大型火电装置

Advanced large-scale thermal power unit

ten industries, is an important pillar of driving the industry economic growth. From looking at the proportion, the top five industries are coal, liquor, electricity, tobacco, chemicals.

Industrial investment completed. Annual industrial investment 312.62 billion yuan (including industrial park infrastructure investment), exceeded 300 billion yuan, an increase of 35%, higher than the national 15 percent. Among them, the renovation investment completed 96.99 billion yuan, an increase of 21.8%; capital investment completed 205.81 billion yuan, an increase of 50.4%. Annual above-scale industrial enterprises realized a total profit of 46.6 billion yuan, an increase of 47.4%.

Regional economy go hand in hand. Around the industrial development continues to accelerate further growth of the total economy, to further enhance the leading role of the pillar industries, to further improve the level of development of industrial agglomeration, the scale of industrial added value accounted for the proportion of GDP were significantly improved. The province's nine cities and prefectures of industrial added value of more than 21%, Bijie City, up to 29.5% growth rate.

Accelerate the development of private economy. Annual large-scale non-public owned enterprises, private enterprises industrial added value of 94.96 billion yuan,62.41 billion yuan, respectively, an increase of 29.4%, 32.6%, the growth rate exceeded the province's industrial growth rate from an average of 8.1 percentage points, 11.3 percentage points. The province's private economy, market players totaling 1.043 million, accounting for the province's industrial and commercial registration number of enterprises in more than 99%, the private economy accounted for 40% of GDP.

自建的新磷酸装置，比原引进装置净增产能50%

The new manufacturing phosphoric acid plant,, than the original imported equipment net capacity of 50%

西电东送重点工程——索风营电站

The power transmission from west to East Project - Suofengying Hydropower Station

贵州省民委

Guizhou Provincial Ethnic Affairs Commission

2012年2月28日，贵州省委副书记、省长赵克志在副省长刘晓凯的陪同下到省民委调研
February 28, 2012, Guizhou Provincial Committee vice secretary, Governor Zhao Kezhi, accompanied by Vice Governor Liu Xiaokai to have investigation of Provincial Ethnic Affairs Commission

2012年，贵州省民委突出抓好国发2号文的贯彻落实，强化民族事业发展十大推进计划的深入实施，不断加强和巩固民族团结的成果，努力推动了民族团结进步事业全面发展，省民委领导班子被评为“省直机关十佳领导班子”。

一是紧紧依靠党委、政府的领导和国家民委的支持，着力推动民族工作取得突破。一年来，省政府先后召开了第五次民族工作联席会议、全省扶持人口较少民族发展工作会议，对全省各级各部门贯彻落实好国发2号文件精神，全力做好全省的民族工作作出了全面的安排部署，提出了按照“两个优先”做好扶持人口较少民族发展工作的要求。

二是抓住贯彻国发2号文件的契机，着力破解事关民族地区跨越发展的难题。

三是精心组织实施民族事业发展十大推进计划，着力推动民族地区经济社会发展取得成效。

四是深入民族团结宣传教育和创建活动，着力巩固民族团结和谐的大好局面。

五是实施民族文化“七个一”工程，着力推动民族文化繁荣发展。

六是加大少数民族干部队伍的培训力度，着力提高干部的素质。

2012年3月26日，贵州省政府副省长刘晓凯在省民委主任吴军的陪同下，到贵州省民族研究院调研
March 26, 2012, Guizhou Provincial Vice Governor Liu Xiaokai accompanied by Provincial Ethnic Affairs Commission Director Wu Jun to research into Guizhou Ethnic Institute

2012年3月，贵州省民委主任吴军在六盘水市调研时了解民族工艺品生产情况
March 2012, Guizhou Ethnic Affairs Commission Director Wu Jun understood and had research in Liupanshui ethnic handicrafts production

2012年5月30日，全省人口较少民族发展工作会议在平塘县召开
May 30, 2012, the province's small population of national development work conference held in Pingtang County

In 2012, Guizhou Ethnic Affairs Commission grasped the implementation of State Issued No.2 Document, and strengthen national career development program to promote the further implementation of the top ten, continue to strengthen and consolidate the results of national unity, and strive to promote the comprehensive development of the cause of national unity and progress, provincial Ethnic Affairs Commission leadership was named "Top Ten provincial organs of leadership".

First, closely rely on party committees and government leadership and the support of State Ethnic Affairs Commission, efforts to promote the nation's breakthrough work. Over the past year, the provincial government has convened a joint meeting of the fifth national work, the province's small population to support the development of national work conference on the province's departments at all levels to implement the spirit of the Stat Issued No.2 Document, to make the province comprehensive national work arrangements, in accordance with the "two first" good to support small populations of national development job requirements.

Second, is to seize the implementation of the Stat Issued No.2 Document opportunity to focus on crack across ethnic areas related to development problems.

Third, carefully organized and implemented ten national career development promotion plan, efforts to promote national economic and social development has achieved results.

Fourth, in-depth publicity and education of national unity and to create activities, efforts to consolidate national unity and harmony of the excellent situation.

Fifth, the implementation of national culture "seven one" project, efforts to promote the prosperity and development of national culture.

Sixth, is to increase the training of minority cadres, and efforts to improve the quality of cadres.

贵州省公安厅

Guizhou Province Public Security Department

省领导参观阳光工程建设

The provincial leaders to visit the Sunshine project construction

贵州省全国公安系统英雄模范立功集体代表座谈会

Guizhou Province Public Security System of national hero meritorious represent the collective Forum

2012年，是全省公安工作和队伍建设取得突出进步的一年，也是公安工作能力和水平取得较大提高的一年。一年来，全省公安机关在省委、省政府和公安部的坚强领导下，以维护社会和谐稳定、增强人民群众安全感为目标，以“三项重点工作”为重要工作抓手，深入开展“三项建设”，全面推进“三基”工程建设，扎实开展保持党的纯洁性教育试点活动，基层基础实力不断增强，公安工作和队伍建设取得了可喜的进步，为维护全省国家安全和社会稳定，促进“和谐贵州”建设做出了突出的贡献。

2012年，全省共破刑事案件77428起，同比上升47.2%；共查处治安案件202564起，同比上升9%；破获各类毒品案件7091起，同比上升34.6%；道路交通事故四项指数全面下降，火灾事故死亡人数下降43.6%。全省公安机关紧紧抓住队伍建设这个根本，以省公安厅被确定为“保持党的纯洁性”主题教育活动试点为契机，深入推进队伍建设，队伍纪律作风、精神面貌明显转变，执法能力、执法水平明显提高，警民关系更加和谐，人民群众安全感、满意度分别较2011年上升了3.51、2.87个百分点，实现了连续5年提升。

倾听民意

To listen to public opinion

整装待发

Be ready to go

抢险救援
Emergency rescue and relief work

抗凝冻，保民生
Anti-Freezing, ensure livelihood

In 2012, is the year that province's public security work and team building achieved outstanding progress, but also the ability and level of public security work to achieve greater increase of the year. Over the past year, the province's public security organs under the strong leadership of the provincial committee, provincial government and the Ministry of Public Security, in order to maintain social harmony and stability, enhance people's sense of security as the goal, "three priorities" for the important work of the starting point, carry out "three-building", comprehensively promote the "three bases" construction, solid education campaign to maintain the purity of the party pilot activities, grassroots foundation strength, security work and team building made encouraging progress, to safeguard national security and the province social stability and promote "harmonious Guizhou" construction made outstanding contributions.

In 2012, the province's 77,428 criminal cases were broken up, an increase of 47.2%; were investigated and security cases 202,564, an increase of 9%; cracked drug cases 7,091, an increase of 34.6%; Overall decline in road traffic accident of "four indices", fire deaths dropped 43.6%. The province's public security organs to seize the team building of the fundamental, Provincial Public Security Department was identified as "maintaining the Party's purity" theme educational activities in the pilot as an opportunity, to further promote team building, team discipline, morale significantly change, the ability of law enforcement , significantly improve the level of law enforcement, public and police relations more harmonious, the people's sense of security, satisfaction, respectively, compared with 2011 increased by 3.51,2.87 percentage points, to achieve the fifth consecutive year.

安全防范
Security prevention

警察妈妈与被拐儿童
Police mum and abducted children

贵州省民政厅

Guizhou Province Civil Affairs Department

2012年2月8日，全省民政工作会召开
February 8, 2012, the province's civil affairs work was held

2012年9月8日，戴司长赴黔调研
September 8, 2012, the Secretary Dao went to Guizhou to have research

杨亚军书记在贵定烈士陵园给烈士扫墓
Yang Yajun secretary to Guiding the martyrs park to broom martyrs cemetery grave

丁治学厅长在贵定减灾演练现场
Director Ding Zhixye at the Guiding disaster drill site

2012年，贵州民政工作紧紧围绕“加速发展、加快转型、推动跨越”的主基调，围绕保障和改善民生、加强和创新社会管理、服务经济社会发展、促进社会和谐的工作主线，以改革创新的精神大力推动民政工作的制度建设、项目建设和能力建设，全面完成全年的各项工作目标任务，民政事业发展取得新成绩。

基本民生保障水平稳步提高。减灾救灾工作成效显著，2011-2012年度受灾群众冬春救助工作列为省委、省政府2012年保障和改善民生“十六件民生实事”之首，投入资金12.44亿元，发放粮食19.47万吨，创贵州省近年款物投入、救助人数、救助标准“三个之最”；社会救助体系建设深入推进，城乡低保提标工作全面完成。

社会管理创新持续推进。基层群众自治实践不断深化；社会组织服务管理体制不断创新。

服务国防和军队现代化建设有力有效。拥军优抚政策全面落实；安置改革措施稳步推行。

专项社会事务服务管理显著增强。区划地名管理积极推进；社会事务管理服务水平不断提高。

民政综合能力不断增强。民政事业发展思路更加清晰；民政事业发展支撑更加有力；民政人才队伍建设进一步加强；民政信息化建设稳步推进；民政系统党风廉政建设深入推进。

2012年6月5日，刘忠平副厅长出席民政视频会议系统推进会
June 5, 2012, Liu Zhongping, deputy director attended the video civil affairs conference system promote will

马天云副厅长慰问老同志
Deputy director Ma Tianyun had condolences of old comrades

In 2012, Guizhou civil affairs work closely around the “accelerated development, speed up transformation and promote across” main tone, focusing on protecting and improving people’s livelihood, strengthen social innovation management, services, economic and social development, promote social harmony main line of work, reform and innovation vigorously promote the spirit of the system of civil work construction projects and capacity-building, complete objectives and tasks of the work for the year, the Civil Affairs career development to achieve new results.

Basic livelihood security level has increased steadily. Disaster mitigation and relief work with remarkable achievement, 2011-2012 winter affected people relief work as the first of the provincial committee, provincial government 2012 to protect and improve people’s livelihood “sixteen practical livelihood matters”, invested 1.244 billion yuan, 194,700 tons of food distributed , the highest in recent years, Guizhou Province, money and material inputs, the number of rescue, relief standard “three of the most”; further promote the social assistance system, urban and rural low insurance work completed.

Continue to promote social management innovation. Deepening grassroots autonomous practice; social organization services management system constantly had innovation.

Service of national defense and army modernization powerful and effective. Support army special care policy is fully implemented; placement of the steady implementation of the reform measures.Special social affairs service management significantly enhanced. Divided district name management actively promote; social affairs management services continues to increase.

Civil affairs administrative comprehensive capacity is growing. Development of civil affairs ideas more clearly; civil affairs career development support more effective; civil affairs to further strengthen the development of qualified personnel; civil affairs information technology pushed steadily; civil system to further promote clean government.

2012年7月6日，杨春兴副厅长在白石岩乡调研
July 6, 2012, Yang Chunxing Shiyan deputy director to have research in Baiyan Township

甄燕驰副厅长在凯里看望散居孤儿
Zhen Yanchi, deputy director to visit the diaspora orphans in Kaili

贵州省司法厅

Guizhou Provincial Department of Justice

司法部部长吴爱英、时任贵州省省长赵克志、时任省委政法委书记崔亚东视察基层监狱

Minister of the Department of Justice Wu Aiying, when he was governor of Guizhou Province, Zhao Kehi, Provincial Politics and Law Committee secretary Cui Yadong had inspections of the grassroots prison

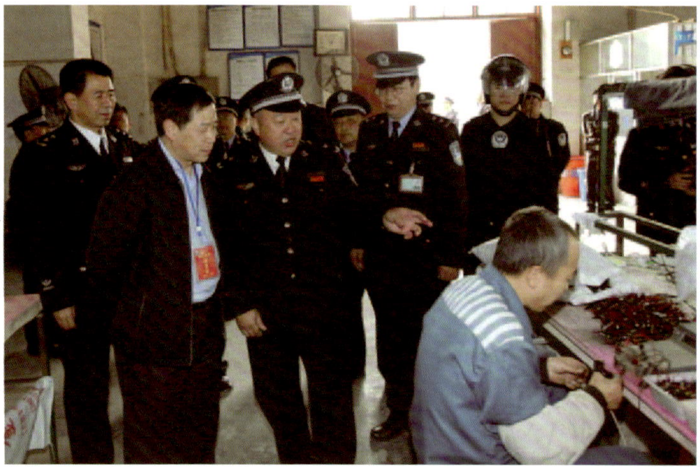

吴跃厅长、曹云平副厅长视察基层监狱

Director Wu Yue, deputy director Cao Yunping had inspection of grassroots prison

2012年，全省司法行政系统坚持抓班子、带队伍、保稳定、促工作，着力加强班子建设、制度建设、作风建设，努力提高工作的制度化、规范化、精细化、信息化水平，全面履行司法行政职能，各项工作取得了新进展、新成效。

全年全省律师共办理各类案件115451件，其中刑事案件6291件，民商事案件15800件，行政案件682件，其他非诉、调解、仲裁、咨询案件67612件，为政府、企事业、社会团体等担任法律顾问5001家。为非公经济提供法律顾问559家，筹融资29.5亿元，挽回经济损失1.07亿元。公证机构共办理公证87135件，其中涉外公证13220件。办理各类法律援助案件27018件，接待咨询94974人次。审核登记的司法鉴定机构共完成司法鉴定检案26269件，采信率98%。各级人民调解组织排查纠纷179221件，调处纠纷192038件，防止纠纷激化7495件，防止群体性事件发生4199件。累计接收社区矫正人员24076人，解除矫正7790人，社区矫正工作在全国综合排名跃升至第5位。全年衔接刑释解教人员19571人，协助安置14656人，帮教26844人。监狱劳教工作认真贯彻“首要标准”，落实宽严相济刑事司法政策，教育改造质量不断提高。监狱管理体制改革目标全面实现，全系统首次实现真正意义上的“四无”，监所安全创历史最好水平。

新任律师执业宣誓

New solicitor practicing sworn

In 2012, the province's administration of justice system persist in grasping the team, leading the team, maintaining stability and promoting work, efforts to strengthen the team-building, institution building, work style construction, and strive to improve the institutionalization, standardization, refinement, the level of information, the full implementation of judicial and administrative functions, the work has made new progress, new results.

The whole year, the province lawyers handled a total of 115,451 of the various cases, including 6,291 criminal cases, civil and commercial cases 15,800, 682 administrative cases, other non-litigation, mediation, arbitration, consulting 67,612 cases, for the government, enterprises, social groups such as the legal adviser 5,001. Legal advisor for 559 the non-public economy, to raise financing of 2.95 billion yuan, avoided economic losses of 107 million yuan. A notary public for notarization 87,135, which foreign notarized 13,220. 27,018

法制宣传进校园

Legal system propaganda into the campus

举办法制宣传活动

Law publicity and activities

企业管理干部学法用法考试

Business administration study and apply laws exam

服刑人员墙内就业推介现场

The inmates employment recommend site inside walls

for all kinds of legal aid cases, reception consulting 94,974 people. Forensic examination and registration completed forensic inspection case 26,269, 98% of the admissible rate. People's mediation organizations at all levels of investigation and dispute 179,221, 192,038 mediating disputes, to prevent the intensification of the dispute of 7,495, to prevent mass incidents occurred 4,199. Accumulated 24,076 personnel receive community corrections, lift the correction of 7,790, community corrections in the national ranking jumped to No. 5. Annual convergence through-labor, 19,571, to assist in the resettlement of 14,656 people, admonishing 26,844 people. Prison inmates work conscientiously implement the “primary criterion”, the implementation of the Criminal Justice Policy temper justice with mercy, and continuously improve the quality of education and reform. Prison management system targets got the full realization, the system-wide for the first time realized the “four noes” in the true sense, the security of the prison was the best in history.

贵州省人力资源和社会保障厅

Guizhou Provincial Human Resources and Social Security Department

2012年3月31日，国家外专局与省政府签署合作协议框架
March 31, 2012, the State Foreign Experts Bureau and the provincial government signed a cooperation framework agreement

2012年，全省人力资源社会保障战线干部职工改革创新、奋力拼搏，促进全省人力资源社会保障事业实现创新突破。

一是贯彻落实国发2号文件精神呈现新气象。促成人社部、国家外专局分别与省政府签订了合作协议备忘录，获得15项政策支持，争取到中央资金79.15亿元。

二是就业创业工作取得新突破。大力实施就业优先战略，着力助推产业园区发展，推动创业带动就业，全年共发放就业小额担保贷款35亿元，实现城镇新增就业42万人，促进失业人员再就业13万人，促进就业困难人员就业6万人，实现农村劳动力转移就业63万人，城镇新增就业增长率排名全国第一。

三是社会保障体系建设实现新跨越。推进覆盖城乡的社会保障体系建设，实现城乡居民社会养老保险制度全覆盖，率先在西部地区出台被征地农民就业和社会保障政策，五项社会保险基金征缴收入达到221.8亿元。

2012年6月26日，人社部与省政府签订合作备忘录
June 26, 2012, Human Resources and Social Department and the provincial government signed a memorandum of cooperation

四是人才队伍建设跨上新台阶。修订完善27个专业技术职称系列评审条件，坚持职称评审工作向基层一线和高学历人才倾斜，率先在全国向各市州下放副高级专业技术资格评审权限，大力组织开展专业技术人员继续教育培训和专家服务基层活动；启动实施高技能人才振兴计划，加大引进国外智力工作力度。

五是公务员管理工作开创新局面。研究并实施公务员招考取消一般岗位专业限制、规范年龄计算方式、取消笔试科目分类、改进体检标准和

发放创业补贴现场

Subsidies paid entrepreneurial scene

In 2012, the province's human resources and social security reform and innovation front cadres and workers, worked hard to promote the province's human resources and social security undertakings to achieve breakthrough innovation.

First, implement the spirit of the document on the 2nd National Development presents new atmosphere. Facilitator and Social Affairs, National Bureau respectively signed a cooperation agreement with the provincial government memorandum, obtained 15 policy support, to secure central funds 7.915 billion yuan.

Second, employment and entrepreneurship has made new breakthroughs. Vigorously implement the strategy of giving priority to employment, efforts to boost industrial park development, and promote entrepreneurship to create jobs, a total employment of small loans issued 3.5 billion yuan, 420,000 new jobs in cities and towns to promote the re-employment of 130,000 people unemployed, and promote 60,000 people experiencing employment difficulty, the rural labor force employed 630,000 people, urban employment growth rate ranked first in the country.

Third, the social security system to achieve a new leap forward. Promote the social security system covering urban and rural construction, urban and rural social endowment insurance system full coverage, the introduction of the first in the western region of landless farmers employment and social security policies, five social insurance fund collection revenue reached 22.18 billion yuan.

Fourth, the development of qualified personnel reached new heights. Amendments to improve the 27 professional titles series

农村老年人领取基本养老金存折

Rural elderly receive the basic pension passbook

全省人力资源社会保障政策宣传活动现场

The province's human resources and social security policy advocacy activities at the scene

贵州万名专家下基层启动仪式
Guizhou ten thousand experts go to the grassroots launch ceremony

复检方法、取消顺延递补等六项改革措施，考录工作更加体现社会公平正义；实施贵州“千人赴港培训计划”，积极推进创先争优，有效加强公务员队伍建设；圆满完成军转干部安置任务，军转工作在全国被称为“贵州模式”予以推广。

六是机关事业单位人事制度改革取得新进展。完成事业单位岗位设置管理和人员聘用制度实施工作；完善机关津贴补贴和艰苦边远地区津贴制度，深入推进全省事业单位实施绩效工资工作，有效维护了广大事业单位职工合法合规的收入。

七是和谐劳动关系建设取得新成效。加强和谐劳动关系建设，全省仲裁机构实体化建设覆盖率达到100%；企业职工劳动合同签订率、群众举报投诉案件结案率、劳动人事争议仲裁案件结案率均保持在90%以上；为70余万农民工追讨工资近5亿元，切实维护了广大劳动者合法权益。

八是干部队伍建设呈现新面貌。积极推进全省人社系统干部培训，推行中层领导干部竞争上岗和交流轮岗工作，着力建设一支凝聚力强、有思想、敢创新、能吃苦、打硬仗的干部职工队伍，努力形成干事创业、创先争优、聚力发展的良好氛围。

企业职工送锦旗
Enterprise workers to send a banner

高技能人才培训
Highly skilled personnel training

农民工慰问演出
Performance for Migrant workers

selection criteria, adhere to the basic line RAE titles and highly educated people tilt, the first in the country to the cities and states delegated deputy senior professional and technical qualifications assessment authority, vigorously organized continuing education and training of professional and technical personnel and experts services grassroots activities; start the implementation of highly skilled personnel revitalization plan, increase the introduction of foreign intelligence efforts.

Fifth, work and create new civil service management. Research and implementation of civil service recruitment professional positions cancellation general restrictions, the age standardized calculation method, the abolition written subjects classification methods to improve medical standards and reverification canceled postponed replacement and other six reform measures examination and admission embody social justice; implementation of Guizhou "thousands of training programs to Hong Kong", and actively promote struggling the superiority and first, effectively strengthen civil construction; successful completion of resettlement task demobilized cadres, demobilized working in the country known as the "Guizhou mode" be promoted.

Sixth, is the organs and institutions of the personnel system reform has made new progress. Completed post setting management institutions and personnel employment system implementation; perfect bodies subsidies and allowances and hardship allowance system in remote areas, to further promote the province's institutions to implement pay for performance, effectively safeguarding the legitimate institutions of the majority of the income of compliance.

Seventh, is a harmonious labor relations to achieve new results. Strengthen the building of harmonious labor relations, the province's arbitration body construction entities reach 100% coverage; enterprise workers labor contract rate, clearance rate of complaints reported by the masses, labor and personnel dispute arbitration case clearance rate were maintained at above 90%; 700,000 migrant workers recover wages nearly 500 million yuan, and earnestly safeguard the legitimate rights and interests of the majority of workers.

为农民工追回拖欠工资
Recover unpaid wages for migrant workers

Eighth, is the new face of cadres presented. Actively promote the province's system of cadres training in human society, the implementation of mid-level leadership cadres competition and exchange rotation work, focus on building a cohesive, thinking, and the courage to innovate, hardworking, tough fight cadres and workers, efforts to form a good atmosphere for general business, struggling the superiority and first, the development of cohesion.

贵州省住房和城乡建设厅

Guizhou Provincial Housing and Urban-Rural Construction Department

2013年3月28日，省委常委、常务副省长谌贻琴（右二）参观贵州省住房和城乡建设厅展馆
March 28, 2013, provincial Party Standing Committee, executive vice governor Chen Yiqin (second from right) visit the Guizhou Provincial Housing and Urban-Rural Department Construction Exhibition

2013年3月29日，全省促进100个城市综合体健康发展现场推进会议在贵阳召开，图为慕德贵副省长（右二）及与会代表参观贵阳市花果园城市综合体项目
March 29, 2013, the province to promote the 100 city complex health development promoting conference at the sopt held in Guiyang, the picture is vice governor Mu Degui (second from right) and delegates to visit Guiyang city flower garden city complex project

贵州省住房和城乡建设厅党组书记、厅长张鹏（左二）在剑河县调研城镇建设
Guizhou Provincial housing and urban-rural construction department party secretary, director Zhang Peng (second from left) researched the urban construction in Jianhe County

2012年，贵州省住房和城乡建设厅深入落实“两加一推”主基调，积极推进“两大战略”和实施“三化同步”，住房城乡建设事业取得了新突破。

“国发2号文件”精神深入落实，争取中央支持成效显著。省政府与住房城乡建设部签订《共同推进贵州住房城乡建设事业又好又快发展合作协议》，以合作协议为依托，以项目为载体，争取中央补助资金历年最多，达到105.04亿元，比上年增加35.8亿元，增长51.68%；住房城乡建设部确定贵州省为“中国南方喀斯特”第二期世界自然遗产申报牵头单位。

规划引领作用充分发挥，“城镇化带动”战略大力实施。《贵州省城镇体系规划（2012-2030年）》经住房城乡建设部组织专家评审通过，《黔中经济区核心区空间发展战略规划》实施；《贵安新区总体规划》编制有序推进，“三横两纵”骨干路网全面开工；100个城市综合体建设前期工作深入推进；重点打造100个示范小城镇，预计城镇化率提高1.5个百分点，达到36.5%。

市政基础设施建设力度加大，城镇综合承载能力不断增强。预计城建投资完成1000亿元，超年度目标320亿元，同比增长86%；在全国率先启动省级数字化综合监管平台建设，推行数字化城市管理系统建设“以奖代补”，协助铜仁市、六盘水市等地开展国家智慧城市试点申报；结合信息化建设，城市服务功能得到积极提升。

保障性安居工程建设进度滞后的局面彻底扭转，超额完成目标任务。彻底扭转5月份开工率全国排名靠后的局

2012年国庆节期间，省住房和城乡建设厅厅长张鹏（左三）一行在丹寨县扬武乡调研

During the 2012 national day, the Provincial Housing and Urban-Rural Development Department Director Zhang Peng (third from left) and the team had investigation in Yangwu township Danzhai county

2013年2月18日，省住房和城乡建设厅与工商银行贵州省分行、建设银行贵州省分行、农业银行贵州省分行、交通银行贵州省分行签订《金融支持贵州住房城乡建设事业政银合作备忘录》，副省长慕德贵出席签字仪式

February 18, 2013, Provincial housing and urban-rural development department and the industrial and commercial bank of China Guizhou branch, China Construction Bank Guizhou branch, Agricultural Bank of China Guizhou branch, the Bank of communications Guizhou branch signed a "financial support of the Guizhou housing and urban-rural development government-bank cooperation memorandum", vice governor Mu Degui attended the signing ceremony

In 2012, the Guizhou Provincial Housing and Urban-Rural Construction Department to further implement the "two plus one push" main tone, actively promote the "two strategies" and the implementation of the "three simultaneous", the cause of urban and rural housing construction has made new breakthroughs.

The spirit of "State No. 2 document" had in-depth implementation, for the central support with remarkable results. The provincial government and the ministry of housing and urban-rural construction signed the "to promote the cause of Guizhou urban housing construction good and fast development cooperation agreement", to the cooperation agreement as the basis, to the project as a carrier, strive for the central subsidy funds up to the highest in the past years, reached 10.504 billion yuan, an increase of 3.58 billion yuan, an increase of 51.68%; the Ministry of housing and urban-rural development approved that Guizhou Province was the second world natural heritage declaration of the lead unit of "China [southern Karst".

Planning and leading role into full play, "urbanization driven" vigorously implement the strategy. "Guizhou province urban planning (2012-2030)" was approved by the Ministry of housing and urban-rural space experts, the implementation of "the core area of Central Guizhou Economic Zone Development Strategy Planning", "the overall planning of Gui'an new district" in an orderly way, "three vertical and two horizontal" backbone network got overall work; further promote the 100 city complex construction of the preliminary work; focus on creating 100 demonstration of small towns, the urbanization rate is expected to increase by 1.5 percentage points, to 36.5%.

Municipal infrastructure construction is strengthened, the overall carrying capacity of cities is growing. Urban construction investment is expected to 100 billion yuan, surpass the annual target of 32 billion yuan, an increase of 86%; the first in the

贵阳花溪农村危房改造点

Rural reconstruction of housing Guiyang Huaxi point

毕节市黔西县素朴镇已建成廉租房
Supu town Qianxi county of Bijie city have built low rent housing

大方县六龙镇依托古镇特色加快旅游观光型小城镇建设
Dafang County Liulong town rely on the ancient town characteristic to speed up the construction of small town tourism and sightseeing

黔西南州普安县青山镇——30个省级示范小城镇之一，路网改造后，交通便捷
Qianxinan state Pu'an county Qingshan town -- one of the 30 provincial demonstration of small towns, after road network renovation, traffic is convenient

面，比国家要求提前4个月实现全面开工；开展“居有所乐”试点，公平分配深入推进，工程质量切实保证，后续运营逐步规范。

住房公积金监管不断强化，积极开展贷款支持保障性安居工程建设试点。

农村危房改造工程大力实施，村庄整治试点工作继续推进，农村面貌不断改观。

市场监管进一步加强，房地产业和建筑业持续健康发展。房地产市场运行态势总体平稳，房地产开发投资预计完成1400亿元，超年度目标400亿元，同比增长59.33%。

建筑节能和标准工作取得新进展，墙体材料革新加速推进。

风景园林工作积极开展，世界固体自然遗产申报牵头作用切实发挥。

依法行政工作深入落实，建设行业人才队伍建设有序推进。出台重大决策程序规定，《关于加快开放型经济发展的实施意见》出台，废止规范性文件13项。

党风廉政建设责任制进一步落实，精神文明建设推进作风转变取得积极成效。

村庄整治和农村危房改造相结合后漂亮的黔北民居
Villages and rural reconstruction combined with the beautiful northern Guizhou dwellings

country to start the construction of provincial integrated digital control platform, to carry out the construction of digital city management system "take award replace the implement", assist Tongren city, Liupanshui city and other places to carry out the national wisdom city pilot declaration; combined with the informatization construction, city service function actively promote.

Progress in the construction of affordable housing lag situation completely reversed, overfulfilled the target task. Reverse operating rate in May national ranking by the situation, 4 months ahead of schedule required by the nation to achieve a comprehensive construction; carry out the "happy with housing" pilot, equitable distribution of advancing, project quality guarantee, the follow-up operation and standardization.

Housing provident fund supervision strengthened, actively carry out loans to support low-income housing construction pilot.

Projects to upgrade rural reconstruction vigorously implement, village renovation pilot work continues to advance, the rural landscape has changed.

To further strengthen market supervision, the sustained and healthy development of the real estate industry and building industry. The operation of the real estate market situation is stable on the whole, the development of real estate investment is expected to be completed 140 billion yuan, surpass the objectives for the year 40 billion yuan, grow 59.33% compared to the same period.

Building energy saving and standard work has made new progress, wall materials innovation to accelerate.

Landscape work carried out actively,to play the solid lead role of the world natural heritage declaration.

毕节市赫章县六曲河镇改造后的广场一角

A corner of Liuquhe town Hezhang county Bijie city after the transformation of the square

毕节市赫章县六曲河镇。小城镇建设与美丽乡村建设有效衔接

Liuquhe town Hezhang county Bijie city. Effective connection between the construction of small towns and beautiful village construction

Administrative work in-depth implementation, the construction industry talent team construction pushed in an orderly way. Introduction of major decision-making procedures, "opinions on accelerating the development of open economy" appearing, abolished normative documents 13.

The responsibility to further implement the construction of the party conduct and honesty, spiritual civilization construction promote the style change achieved positive results.

贵州省农委

Guizhou Province Agricultural Committee

副省长刘远坤到农业示范园区调研
Vice Governor Liu Yuankun research to agricultural demonstration park

2012年，贵州省农业生产全面向好，农村经济亮点突出，农民收入快速增长，为保障城乡农产品供给、维护社会和谐稳定、促进“三化同步”发展提供了重要支撑，做出了重要贡献。

农业增加值和农民收入快速增长。第一产业增加值比上年增长8.5%，是近四年来增幅最大的一年；农民人均纯收入达到4753元，比上年实际增长11.5%，连续六年增幅在8%以上，连续三年高于城镇居民收入增幅。

粮油肉菜等主要农产品全面丰收。粮食总产量1079.5万吨，比上年增长23.1%，实现恢复性增产；油菜籽产量78.18万吨，增长8.9%，创历史新高；蔬菜产量1375.63万吨，增长10%；肉类总产量192.07万吨，禽蛋产量14.65万吨，奶类产量5.1万吨，同比分别增长5.7%、7.3%和5.2%。

省政府党组成员、省农工委党组书记、省农委党组书记黄家培到基层调研
Party members of the provincial government, the Province Agricultural and Industry Committee secretary, Province Agricultural Committee party secretary Huang Jiapei to the grass-root to have research

省农委主任刘福成到基层调研旱情
Province Agricultural Committee director Liu Fucheng to research the drought situation in the grass-root

农业结构调整和产业发展成效突出。经济作物比重大幅提升，粮经作物面积比调整到51∶49；全省蔬菜面积1161.47万亩，茶园386.57万亩，果园289.31万亩，中药材面积112.03万亩，年末大鲵存池43.5万尾，均保持较快增长；规模化种养比重提升，优质特色农产品总量增加，草地畜牧业稳步发展；休闲农业与乡村旅游经营主体2825个，全年营业收入20.8亿元。

农产品加工业和产业化经营加快发展。全省规模以上农产品加工业总产值645亿元，食品加工等行业比重提高；251家省级以上龙头企业年末资产总额200亿元，全年销售收入230亿元，利润13亿元；农民专业合作社1.28万家，省级农民专业合作社联合会成立；农产品电子商务快速发展。

In 2012, Guizhou Province to the good overall agricultural production, the rural economy highlights outstanding, farmer income growth, for the protection of urban and rural supply of agricultural products to maintain social harmony and stability, promoting the "three synchronization" development has provided important support, has made important contributions.

Added value of agriculture and farmers' income got growth. The first industry increased by 8.5% over the previous year, the largest increase in nearly four years rural per capita net income reached 4,753 yuan, the actual increase of 11.5% over the previous year, an increase of 8% for six consecutive years or more, for three consecutive years higher than urban residents' income growth.

大鲵养殖

Giant salamander breeding

Meat and other major agricultural comprehensive grain got harvest. Grain output 10.795 million tons, an increase of 23.1% over the previous year, have resumed production; rapeseed production 781,800 tons, an increase of 8.9%, a record high; vegetable production 13,756,300 tons, an increase of 10%; meat output 1,920,700 ton, egg production 146,500 tons, milk production 51,000 tons, an increase of 5.7%, 7.3% and 5.2%, respectively.

肉牛养殖场

Beef cattle farms

Agricultural structure adjustment and industrial development effectiveness prominent. Significantly improved the proportion of cash crops, grain crop area ratio adjusted to 51:49; province's vegetable area 11,614,700 acres, 3,865,700 acres of tea plantations, orchards 2,893,100 acres, 1,120,300 acres of Chinese herbal medicine area, at the end of the year, salamander memory pools 435,000, maintained rapid growth; enhance the proportion of large-scale breeding and quality characteristics of agricultural products increased overall steady development of grassland animal husbandry; leisure agriculture and rural tourism business entities 2,825, annual revenue 2.08 billion yuan.

Agro-industrial and industrial management to accelerate development. The province's above-scale industrial output value of 64.5 billion yuan agricultural product processing, food processing and other industries increased proportion; 251 leading enterprises above the provincial total assets of 20 billion yuan at the end of the year, the annual sales income of 23 billion yuan, profits of 1.3 billion yuan; farmer cooperatives 12,800, the provincial federation of farmer cooperatives established; produce rapid development of e-commerce.

农产品深加工车间

Agricultural products deep processing workshop

The quality and safety of agricultural products and brand building higher level. Vegetables, tea, fruits, aquatic products and livestock quality sampling the overall pass rate of 97.6%,

早熟马铃薯种植基地
Precocious potato base

脱毒马铃薯播期对晚疫病及产量影响试验
Potato late blight and sowing dates on yield trials

无性繁殖脱毒马铃薯育苗
Potato breeding asexual reproduction

农产品质量安全和品牌建设再上台阶。蔬菜、茶叶、水果和畜禽水产品质量抽检总体合格率97.6%，农产品质量安全水平继续提升；创建农业标准化示范县（区）6个、园艺作物标准园55个，建成省级以上畜禽标准化规模养殖场98家、水产健康养殖示范场11家；累计认定无公害农产品1281个、绿色食品68个、有机食品6个、地理标志保护产品7个，8个农产品晋级“贵州自主创新品牌100强”。

农业科技服务和装备水平继续提升。在85个县实施基层农技推广体系改革与建设补助项目，在1071个乡镇实施农技推广机构条件建设，基本建成乡镇农技推广、动植物防疫、农产品质量监管等服务体系；新增农机具 28.7万台套，农机总动力2102万千瓦，全省耕种收综合机械化水平达15.5%。完成阳光工程培训10.8万人。

农业农村基础建设进一步加强。新农村建设18个“整乡推进”试点深入实施，重点村寨基础设施、支柱产业和社会事业全面发展；农业生产条件逐步改善；农业资源区划、农村能源与生态建设取得新进展；现代农业园区建设开始起步。

何首乌饮片
Polygonum Pieces

何首乌种植基地
Polygonum planting base

无土栽培

Soilless cultivation

大棚花卉种植

Greenhouse Floriculture

continue to enhance the quality and safety of agricultural products; creation of agricultural standardization demonstration counties (district) 6, 55 standard garden horticultural crops, livestock and poultry built above the provincial standard 98 scale farms, aquaculture demonstration farm 11; cumulative identified pollution-free agricultural 1,281, 68 green food, organic food 6, geographical indications protection products 7, 8 agricultural promotion "Guizhou independent innovation brand 100".

Agricultural science and technology continue to improve the level of services and equipment. In the 85 counties of the grassroots agricultural extension system reform and construction grant program, implemented in 1,071 the township agricultural extension building of institutional conditions, basically built the township agricultural extension, animal and plant quarantine, quality control of agricultural service system; new farm machinery 287,000 sets of gross agricultural machinery 21.02 million kilowatts, the province's integrated farming mechanization level of 15.5%. Sunshine Project training completed 108,000.

Further strengthening agriculture and rural infrastructure. New rural construction 18 "whole village to promote" pilot-depth implementation, focusing on village infrastructure, pillar industries and the development of social undertakings; agricultural production conditions gradually improved; agricultural resources, rural energy and ecological construction made new progress; modern agricultural park construction started.

贵州省商务厅

Guizhou Provincial Industrial and Commercial Bureau

贵州省委书记赵克志一行参加昆交会开幕式
Guizhou provincial party committee secretary Zhao Kezhi and the team took part in Kunming Trade Fair opening ceremony

贵州省委书记赵克志巡视昆交会贵州馆
Guizhou provincial Party committee secretary Zhao Kezhi visited Guizhou Museum in Kunming Trade Fair

贵州省委书记赵克志出席中国贵州•美国经贸交流会，并与美国工商界人士亲切交谈
Guizhou provincial party committee secretary Zhao Kezhi attended the China Guizhou•the United States economic and trade exchange, and had a cordial conversation with the American business community

贵州省人大常委会副主任周忠良、省商务厅申晓庆厅长一行到黎阳高新技术园区调研
Deputy director of Guizhou Provincial People's Congress Standing Committee Zhou Zhongliang, Director of Provincial Industrial and Commercial Bureau Shen Xiaoqing had research to Liyang High-tech Park

2012年，全省社会消费品零售总额达2005.25亿元，同比增长16%。从经营地看，城镇社会消费品零售额1644.96亿元，同比增长16.1%；乡村社会消费品零售额360.29亿元，增长15.3%。从商品形态看，商品零售额1809.40亿元，同比增长16.2%；餐饮收入额195.85亿元，同比增长13.4%。从行业划分看，批发业226.17亿元，同比增长36.1%；零售业1580.71亿元，同比增长13.9%；住宿业17.12亿元，同比增长24.7%；餐饮业181.25亿元，同比增长12.4%。

2012年，全省对外贸易逆势增长，再创历史新高，跨入60亿新台阶，进出口总值达66.3亿美元，同比增长35.8%，较全国平均水平高出29.6个百分点。

2012年，全省共批准外商直接投资项目53个，同比减少19.7%，合同外资金额合计57383万美元，同比减少66.40%，实际利用外资金额合计104582.27万美元，同比增长55.35%。外资主要投向房地产业，电力、燃气及水的生产和供应业，建筑业，制造业，批发和零售业，实际投资金额为22484万美元、8188万美元、5328万美元、5179万美元、2526万美元。

2012年9月9日，第二届中国(贵州)国际酒类博览会隆重开幕

September 9, 2012, the second China (Guizhou) International Wine Fair grand opening

2012贵州•香港投资贸易活动周启动仪式

2012 Guizhou•Hongkong investment and trade activities week launch ceremony

In 2012, the province's total retail sales of social consumer goods reached 200.525 billion yuan, an increase of 16%. From the business perspective, the urban social consumer goods retail sales of 164.496 billion yuan, an increase of 16.1%; rural retail sales of social consumer goods 36.029 billion yuan, an increase of 15.3%. From the form of commodity, commodity retail sales of 180.94 billion yuan, an increase of 16.2%; catering income 19.585 billion yuan, an increase of 13.4%. From the industry perspective, the wholesale industry 22.617 billion yuan, an increase of 36.1%; retail industry 158.071 billion yuan, an increase of 13.9%; accommodation industry 1.712 billion yuan, an increase of 24.7%; catering industry 18.125 billion yuan, an increase of 12.4%.

第二届中国（贵州）国际酒类博览会现场

The second China (Guizhou) International Wine Fair site

2012年度中美法律交流座谈会在贵阳举行

The 2012 annual US-China legal exchange forum held in Guiyang

In 2012, the province's foreign trade showed the growing trend, made a new record high, got into the 6 billion yuan step, import and export value of $6.63 billion, an increase of 35.8%, higher 29.6 percentage points than the national average.

In 2012, the province has approved 53 foreign direct investment projects, a decrease of 19.7%, contracted foreign investment amounted to $573,830,000, a decrease of 66.40%, the amount of foreign capital actually used amounted to $1,045,822,700, an increase of 55.35%. Foreign capital is mainly invested in real estate, electric power, gas and water production and supply industry, construction industry, manufacturing, wholesale and retail trade, the actual amount of investment of $224,840,000, $81,880,000, $53,280,000, $51,790,000, $25,260,000.

贵州省商务厅与密西根州经济发展署签订《贵州省与密西根州经济合作备忘录》

Guizhou Provincial Industrial and Commercial Bureau and Michigan Economic Development Agency signed the "Guizhou province and Michigan Economic cooperation Memorandum"

贵州省工商局

Guizhou Provincial Industrial and Commercial Bureau

2012年3月21日，贵州省省长赵克志到贵州省工商局调研
March 21, 2012, Guizhou provincial governor Zhao Kezhi had investigation of Guizhou Province industrial and commercial bureau

2012年，全省工商系统抢抓落实国发2号文件的机遇，积极主动争取国家工商总局出台了《关于支持贵州经济社会又好又快发展意见》，认真贯彻落实“两加一推”主基调，强力推进工业强省、城镇化带动两大战略，按照“12345”总体工作思路，履行职能，扎实工作，开拓创新，服务发展，为全省经济社会又好又快、更好更快发展做出了积极贡献。

各类市场主体发展实现历史性突破。2012年，全省工商系统大力实施“市场主体增量工程”，坚持“非禁即允”准入原则，下放审批权限、优化“三通”服务，落实“一审一核”、限时办结等制度和措施，促进了各类市场主体加速发展。全省市场主体总量首次突破 100万户大关。截止2012年12月底，全省市场主体总量达到1099293户，注册资本总量8842.43亿元，同比分别增长21.98%、47.34%。其中：内资企业41090户，注册资本4515.76亿元；私营企业143935户，注册资本3532.51亿元；个体工商户899111户，注册资本373.79亿元；农民专业合作社13465户，注册资本158.50亿元；外商投资企业1692户，注册资本419657.10万美元。

扶持微型企业发展实现良好开局。2012年，全省工商系统认真履行牵头职责，推动形成了“各级政府为主、工商

《贵州省著名商标认定和保护办法》于2012年5月1日起实行
“Guizhou province famous trademark recognition and protection measures”put into practice on May 1, 2012

2012年7月3日，来自利比里亚等21个国家的38名“发展中国家计算机软硬件及网络技术培训班”学员到贵州省工商局参观学习
July 3, 2012, “the developing country of computer hardware and network training class” 38 students from 21 countries such as Liberia to the Guizhou Province industrial and commercial bureau to visit and study

2012年11月21日，六盘水工商局率先创建"无传销城市"
November 21, 2012, the Liupanshui industrial and commercial bureau took the lead in establishing the "without pyramid city"

2012年3月29日，全省扶持微型企业发展工作动员会议在贵阳召开，安排部署全省微型企业工作任务
March 29, 2012, the province's support micro enterprise development conference held in Guiyang, arrangements task for the miniature enterprise

In 2012, the province's industrial and commercial system to seize the implementation of Document No. 2 opportunities, actively seek the State Administration for Industry and Commerce promulgated the "opinions on the support of the Guizhou sound and rapid economic and social development", earnestly implement the "two plus one push" main tone, promoting industrial strong province, urbanization driven of two strategies, in accordance with the "12345" the whole idea of work, to perform its functions, do solid work, innovation, service development, and make positive contribution to the province's economic and social good and fast, better and faster development.

All kinds of market main body development to achieve a historic breakthrough. In 2012, the province's industrial and commercial system vigorously implement the "market incremental Engineering", adhere to the "non-cut that allow" access principle, delegated approval authority, optimization of "three pass" service, the implementation of "investigate and check" time-bound applications systems and measures, to accelerate the development of all types of market entities. The province's total market for the first time in 1,000,000 households. At the end of December, 2012, the province's total market reached 1,099,293 households, the total registered capital of 884.243 billion yuan, year-on-year growth of 21.98%, 47.34%, respectively. Among them: the domestic enterprises 41,090 households, 451,576 billion yuan of registered capital; private enterprise 143,935 households, the registered capital of 353.251 billion yuan; 899,111 individual industrial and commercial households, the registered capital of 37.379 billion yuan; professional farmers cooperatives 13,465, the registered capital of 15.85 billion yuan; 1,692 foreign-invested enterprises, registered capital of 4,196,571,000 dollars.

2012年8月20日，贵州工商系统300多名执法人员签名，郑重向社会作出庄严承诺
August 20, 2012, the signature of Guizhou industrial and commercial system more than 300 law enforcement personnel, solemnly to the society and to make a solemn commitment

Support micro enterprise development to achieve a good start. In 2012, the province's industrial and commercial system to perform the lead role, promote the formation of the "all levels of government, industrial and commercial system coordinated services, the relevant departments coordinated, the social parties to participate in" work pattern, formed a "Provincial People's Government views on the vigorously support micro enterprise development", "Guizhou Province general program support micro enterprise development implementation measures" to supporting, departments at all levels of support measures to complement the policy framework, a quarter of early completion of the provincial government issued the annual support the establishment of 20,600 households micro enterprise task, micro enterprises registered capital of 2,482,460,000 yuan, driven 114,984 people in employment.

2012年3月2日，安顺市镇宁县工商局为微型企业颁发营业执照
March 2, 2012, Zhenning county, Anshun city industrial and commercial bureau issued a business license for micro enterprises

协调服务、相关部门协同、社会各方参与”的工作格局，形成了以《省人民政府关于大力扶持微型企业发展的意见》为总纲、《贵州省扶持微型企业发展实施办法》为配套、各级各部门扶持措施为补充的政策框架，提前一个季度完成了省政府下达的全年扶持设立20600户微型企业任务，微型企业注册资金 248246万元，带动 114984人就业。

实施商标战略取得新成效。2012年，全省工商系统强力推进“一分局一商标”、“一县（市）一品牌”工作，积极引导企业、农民专业合作社、个体工商户注册商标、争创著名商标和驰名商标。全年新增注册商标7079件，同比增长37.8%。截至2012年12月底，全省累计注册商标36960件。

2012年7月9日，贵州省工商局向困难群众捐赠洗衣机
July 9, 2012, Guizhou Province industrial and commercial bureau donated washing machine to the difficulties of the masses

广告市场监管力度加大。2012年省政府办公厅转发了省工商局等部门《关于促进贵州广告业又好又快发展的指导意见》，明确了广告业在市场准入政策扶持等方面的优惠政策，为贵州广告业加速发展提供了措施保障。

服务新农村建设取得新成效。食品安全监测体系作用彰显，全年全省流通环节没有发生重特大食品安全事故。依法监管扎实有效。打击传销和规范直销工作深入推进。各类市场监管强力推进。市场诚信体系基本建成。参与社会管理能力明显提升。12315行政执法体系“四个平台”建设强力推进。流通领域商品质量监管水平明显提升。法治工商建设上迈上新台阶。队伍建设和基层基础建设上迈出新步伐。信息化建设深入推进。党风廉政建设扎实开展。

2012年4月5日，毕节市黔西县工商局成立全省首支工商女子维权队
April 5, 2012, Qianxi County, Bijie City industrial and commercial bureau established the first women's rights team

2012年8月23日，六盘水市六枝特区工商局开展“述职述廉”活动
August 23, 2012, Liupanshui City industrial and commercial bureau to carry out a “debriefing work and clean and honest” activities

New progress has been made in the implementation of brand strategy. In 2012, the province's industrial and commercial system promoting "a branch of a trademark", "a county (city) a brand" work, and actively guide the enterprises, farmers professional cooperatives, individual industrial and commercial households registered trademarks, and striving for well-known trademark and famous trademark. The new 7,079 registered trademarks, year-on-year growth of 37.8%. At the end of December, 2012, the province has 36,960 registered trademarks.

Supervision of advertising market increase. In 2012, the office of the provincial government forwarding the provincial Trade and Industry Bureau and other departments "guiding opinions on promoting sound and rapid development of the advertising industry in Guizhou", the advertising industry in the market access policy support and preferential policies, provides measures of protection for the Guizhou advertising industry to accelerate the development.

2012年8月9日，全省工商系统专项整治"霸王条款"
August 9, 2012, the province's industrial and commercial system of special rectification "despot clause"

2012年1月10日，遵义市红花岗区工商局加强春节食品市场监管
January 10, 2012, Honghuagang District of Zunyi City industrial and commercial bureau to strengthen the spring festival food market supervision

2012年10月30日，贵阳市观山湖区工商局查获100多件广州军区特供酒
October 30, 2012, Guanshanhu, Guiyang city industrial and commercial bureau seized more than 100 pieces of Guangzhou military region for wine

2012年2月24日，贵定县工商局联合质监部门开展农资打假专项行动
February 24, 2012, Guiding County industrial and commercial bureau and quality supervision departments to carry out agricultural crackdown special action

Serving the new rural construction has made new achievements. Highlight the food safety monitoring system, the total circulation without the occurrence of major food safety accidents. According to the regulation of solid and effective. To further promote the fight against pyramid schemes and regulating direct selling. All kinds of market supervision management significantly promote. The integrity of the market system has been basically completed. Participation in social management ability significantly improved. 12315 administrative law enforcement system of "four platform" construction vigorously promote. Circulating levels of commodity quality supervision significantly promote. Building the rule of law and business to a new level. Team building and infrastructure construction on a new step. Informatization construction get further push. Construction of a clean and honest government carry out solidly.

贵州省新闻出版（版权）局

Guizhou Provincial Press and Publication (Copyright) Bureau

局长：黄定承

Secretary：Huang Dingcheng

2012年，在各级各部门的共同努力下，全省新闻出版和版权工作取得了较好成绩。

一是舆论引导和精品生产能力明显增强。全省图书报刊出版单位全方位宣传国发2号文件和党的十八大精神，做好十八大报告、党章等十八大文献的印刷发行工作；围绕迎接学习宣传十八大，策划推出了系列主题出版物。

二是新闻出版体制改革成效显著。全省音像出版单位转企改制工作任务基本完成；32家非时政类报刊出版单位成功转企改制。

三是新闻出版产业取得新发展。全年共争取中央各类补贴资金1.25亿元，争取省级文化产业发展专项资金640万元。全年共完成总产出70.32亿元，比上年同期增长19%；实现增加值20.74亿元，比上年同期增长22.50%。

四是农家书屋建设取得新成果。完成了3177个农家书屋和232个数字农家书屋建设任务。

五是版权管理与服务迈上新台阶。95家省级机关和9个市（州）政府机关共投入资金4650万元，采购软件96469套，全面完成了省、市两级政府机关软件正版化整改工作任务，并初步形成了工作长效机制。

六是“扫黄打非”工作成效明显。全省共出动执法人员51392人（次），收缴非法出版物261.2万件，公开销毁非法出版物237.9万件，办理行政处罚案件109起，移送刑事案件15起，刑事处罚13人。

七是行政管理和服务水平得到新提升。升级了行政审批系统；全年共受理许可申请264件，办结率为100%。

八是党的建设和党风廉政建设呈现新面貌。

In 2012, under the joint efforts of the departments at all levels, the province's press and publication and copyright work has achieved good results.

First, the public opinion to guide and the boutique production capacity significantly enhanced. The province's books and periodicals publishing unit full range of key words through the State Issued document NO.2 promulgated and the spirit of 18th CPC National Congress, to do 18th CPC National Congress reports, the party constitution literature printed and distributed work about the 18th CPC National Congress; around to meet the study and publicize the 18th CPC National Congress, large plan launched a series of thematic publications.

Second, the reform of the press and publishing system with remarkable results. The province's audio-video publishing units transformed into enterprises tasks basically completed; 32 non-political newspapers publishing units transformed into enterprises successfully.

Third, the news publishing industry to achieve new development. Total for central subsidies of 125 million yuan of funds, for the provincial cultural industry development funds 640 million. Completed a total of 7.032 billion yuan of total output, an increase of 19% over the same period of last year; the added value of 2.074 billion yuan, an increase of 22.50% over the same period of last year.

Fourth, Farm Book House building got new achievements. The completion of the 3,177 Farm Book House and 232 digital Farm BOOK House construction tasks.

Fifth, copyright management and service to a new level. 95 provincial authorities and the 9 city (state) government agencies invested 46.5 million yuan, 96,469 sets of procurement software, complete the provincial and municipal government agencies genuine software rectification work tasks, and initially formed a working long-term mechanism.

Sixth, the "anti-pornography" achieved remarkable success. The province dispatched a total of 51,392 law enforcement officers (times), the collection of illegal publications 2,612,000, 2,379,000 public destruction of illegal publications, handle administrative penalty cases 109 cases, 15 cases transferred to criminal cases, criminal penalties for 13 people.

Seventh, administrative and service levels to get the new upgrade. Upgrade the administrative examination and approval system; accepted a total of 264 applications for leave to 100% completion rate.

Eighth, party building and clean government presented a new look.

2013年全省新闻出版（版权）工作会议

In 2013, the whole Province Press and Publication (Copyright) work conference

贯彻落实2号文件　促进体育事业发展
为贵州经济社会跨越发展提供正能量

The implementation of NO. 2 documents　to promote sports development

Supply the positive energy for Guizhou's economic and social development

第五届亚洲体操锦标赛男团冠军

Fifth Asian Gymnastics Championships men's team title

2012年，贵州体育工作在省委、省政府的领导和国家体育总局的指导下，坚持以科学发展观为统领，以贯彻落实国发2号文件为工作中心，围绕贵州体育事业"十二五"规划，全面落实各项工作任务，成果显著。

认真贯彻落实国发2号文件精神。（一）积极"跑部"，加强汇报。2012年总局共下拨支持贵州省项目资金6691万元，较去年增加70.45%。（二）积极推进"实行项目化、实物化落实"工作。编制《非标准体育场地指标体系研究方案》、《国家（贵州）生态型多梯度高原运动训练示范基地项目规划》和《中国贵州山地户外运动大省专项建设规划》。完成"贵州老王山多梯度运动训练示范基地"地形图测绘工作。（三）加快推进山地户外体育旅游休闲基地建设。

竞技体育再创佳绩。（一）邹市明在伦敦奥运会上为中国代表团夺得第38枚金牌，成功卫冕。贵州省列全国31个省（区、市）奖牌积分第21位。贵州体操队在2012年全国体操锦标赛中勇夺男子团体金牌。（二）全力备战第十二届全运会。（三）成功举办了第十一届亚洲越野锦标赛、第十届全国越野跑锦标赛、全国皮划艇激流回旋青少年锦标

第四届职工运动会（一）

Fourth workers Games(One)

第四届职工运动会（二）

Fourth workers Games(Two)

In 2012, Guizhou sports work in the provincial committee, provincial government's leadership and under the guidance of the State Sports General Administration, adhere to the scientific development concept as a guide to the implementation of State Issued No.2 document as the work centers, around Guizhou sports "Twelfth Five-Year"plan, the full implementation of all tasks, with remarkable results.

Conscientiously implement the spirit of State Issued No.2 document. (A) Positive "run the ministries" to strengthen reporting. In 2012, General Administration of Guizhou Province, supported by project funds allocated 66.91 million yuan, an increase of 70.45%. (B) To actively promote "the implementation of the project, dematerialisation implement" work. Preparation of "non-standard stadium index system research programs", "national (Guizhou) over a gradient plateau ecological demonstration sports training base project planning" and "China's Guizhou province mountain outdoor sports specific plans for construction". Finish "Guizhou Laowang mountainous gradient sports training base" topographic mapping work. (C) To accelerate the mountain outdoor sports tourism and leisure bases.

CBA季前赛贵阳赛区比赛
CBA preseason Guiyang Contest

亚洲越野跑锦标赛在清镇举行
Asian cross-country running championships held in Qingzhen

全民健身日太极拳展示
National Fitness Day Taijiquan show

Sports to new heights. (A) Zou Shiming won 38 gold medals in the London Olympics for the Chinese delegation, successfully defended. Guizhou Province out of the 31 provinces (autonomous regions and municipalities) Section 21 medals Credits. (B) Fully prepare for the Twelfth National Games. (C) Successfully hosted the 11th Asian Cross Country Championships, the Tenth National Cross Country Championships, National Canoe Slalom Junior Championships. (D) Guiyang City bid for and obtain the right to host the 2015 World Cross Country Championships.

贵阳国际山地自行车邀请赛（一）
Guiyang International Mountain Bike Invitational(One)

贵阳国际山地自行车邀请赛（二）
Guiyang International Mountain Bike Invitational(Two)

赛。（四）贵阳市申办并获得2015年世界越野锦标赛举办权。（五）积极开展恢复举办省运会工作。编印《贵州省第九届运动会竞赛规程总则（讨论稿）》，完成竞赛规程的修订工作。

群众体育稳步推进。（一）投入体育彩票公益金4400万元在全省城乡社区建设了2个“雪炭工程”、300条健身路径、400个村级工程、50个乡镇工程，新增体育场地面积521600平方米，完成省政府“50项重点工作”中的体育工作事项。（二）出台《贵州省全民健身实施计划（2011-2015年）》。（三）广泛开展全民健身活动。（四）召开全省社会体育指导员培训工作会议，全省共培训各级社会体育指导员人数2000余名。

打造品牌，挖掘特色赛事，促进体育产业大发展。（一）成功举办全国山地自行车冠军赛百里杜鹃分站赛、贵阳国际山地自行车邀请赛、紫云格凸国际攀岩交流大会等赛事活动。（二）参加“2012中国体育旅游博览会”，贵州万峰林的徒步、南江大峡谷的漂流、百里杜鹃山地自行车被评为全国体育旅游精品线路。（三）全省体彩销售实现历史性突破，体育彩票销售总额为13.1588亿元，提取公益金近4亿元。

体育宣传工作跨新台阶。（一）央视《焦点访谈》首次赴贵州采访镇远龙舟节。（二）中央媒体民族体育文化采访小分队首次赴黔采访。（三）央视新闻频道首次对安顺坝陵河大桥跳伞国际挑战赛进行直播。（四）央视体育频道对2012年中华龙舟大赛第四站（铜仁•碧江站）进行全程直播。

安顺坝陵河大桥跳伞（一）
Anshun Baling River Bridge Parachuting(One)

安顺坝陵河大桥跳伞（二）
Anshun Baling River Bridge Parachuting(Two)

晴隆24道拐汽车爬坡赛

Qinglong 24 turn automobile climbing competition

(E) And actively carry out restoration work organized by the Provincial Games. Published "Guizhou Province the Ninth sports competition general rules (discussion paper)" to complete the revision of competition rules.

Mass Sports pushed steadily. (A) Put sports lottery 44 million yuan investment in the province's urban and rural communities of the two "Snow carbon projects", 300 fitness trails, 400 village-level projects, 50 township projects, new sports area of 521,600 square meters, complete the provincial government "50 key work" in the sports work matters. (B) Promulgated the "National Fitness Implementation Plan in Guizhou Province (2011-2015)". (C) Carry out extensive fitness activities. (D) Held a provincial social sports instructor training session, the province at all levels of social sports instructor training more than 2,000 persons.

Brand building, mining feature event, to promote the development of sports industry. (A) Successfully held the national mountain bike Championships Baili Rhododendron race, Guiyang international mountain bike Invitational, Ziyun Getu international rock climbing conventions events. (B) To participate in the "2012 China Sports Tourism Expo", Guizhou Wanfeng forest hiking, South River Grand canyon rafting, Baili Rhododendron mountain bike was named the national sports tourism products line. (C) The sports lottery sales to achieve a historic breakthrough, total sales of sports lottery public welfare funds for 1.31588 billion yuan, nearly 400 million yuan for public welfare fund.

Sports propaganda across the new stage. (A) the CCTV "Focus" for the first time to Guizhou to interview the Zhenyuan dragon boat festival. (B) The central media national sports culture interview team first interview to Guizhou. (C) The CCTV news channel in Anshun for the first time live the Balinghe bridge jump international challenge. (D) The CCTV sports channel on 2012 Chinese dragon boat contest fourth station (Tongren Bijiang station) for the entire live broadcast.

全国农运会贵州代表团

National Peasant Sports Guizhou Delegation

百灵杯世界围棋公开赛

Bailing Cup World Go Open

贵州省扶贫开发办公室

Guizhou Provincial Office of Poverty Alleviation and Development

全国扶贫开发工作电视电话会议
National television and telephone conference poverty alleviation and development

2013年3月5日，中国减贫与发展研究院签约暨揭牌仪式，国务院扶贫办副主任王国良、省人大常委会副主任周忠良、省政协副主席陈海峰出席
March 5, 2013, Chinese Academy of poverty reduction and development-cum-signing ceremony, Wang Guoliang, deputy director of the State Council Poverty Alleviation Office, Zhou Zhongliang, deputy director of Provincial People's Congress, the provincial CPPCC Vice Chairman Chen Haifeng attend

2013年5月9日，国务院扶贫办郑文凯副主任在贵州考察对口帮扶项目
May 9, 2013, the State Council Poverty Alleviation Office Deputy Director Zheng Wenkai inspect the aid to projects in Guizhou

2012年，贵州省坚持把扶贫开发作为第一民生工程来抓，深入实施片区区域发展与扶贫攻坚规划，大力培育“十大扶贫产业”，着力打造“十大扶贫攻坚示范县”，扶贫工作取得明显成效。

一是扶贫资金投入高位增长。共争取到中央财政扶贫资金29.79亿元，其中，财政扶贫发展资金25.498亿元，净增6.38亿元，增长33.8%。省财政列入扶贫科目的资金为14.1亿元，其中，由省扶贫办组织实施的有6.238亿元。

二是农村贫困人口大幅下降。全省农村贫困人口从2011年的1149万人减少到923万人，减少226万人，为全国减少贫困人口最多的省份；贫困发生率从33.4%下降到26.8%，下降了6.6个百分点。5个县128个乡镇实现“减贫摘帽”。

三是重点县农民人均纯收入快速增长。50个重点县农民人均纯收入4469元，比上年增长16.3%，高于全省农民人均纯收入增幅1.7个百分点。三大片区农民人均纯收入4688元，增幅16%。

2013年5月8日，上海市副市长时光辉一行到对口帮扶的遵义市调研
May 8, 2013, Shanghai Vice Mayor Shi Guanghui and the team to survey the helping of their counterparts in Zunyi City

2013年5月7日，全省对口帮扶会议
May 7, 2013, meeting of the aid to the province

2013年1月7日，贵州省核桃产业化扶贫现场推进会
January 7, 2013, Guizhou walnut industry promote pro-poor will site

In 2012, Guizhou adhere to poverty alleviation and development of livelihood projects as the first task, in-depth implementation of area development and poverty alleviation plan, vigorously cultivate “Ten poverty industry”, focused on creating the “Top Ten Anti-Poverty demonstration counties”, poverty reduction achieved significant results.

First, funding for poverty alleviation got high growth. To secure a total of 2.979 billion yuan central financial funds, which finance pro-poor development funds 2,549,800,000 yuan, a net increase of 638 million yuan, an increase of 33.8%. Subjects included in the provincial finance poverty alleviation funds 1.41 billion yuan, of which there are organized and implemented by the Poverty Alleviation 623.8 million yuan.

Second, the rural poor population dropped significantly. The province’s rural poor people from 11,490,000 in 2011 was reduced to 9,230,000, reducing 2,260,000 people, for the country to reduce poverty in the most populous province; incidence of poverty declined from 33.4 percent to 26.8 percent, down 6.6 percentage points. Five counties 128 towns to achieve “ put off the hat of poverty”.

Third, key counties rapid growth in per capita net income of farmers. 50 key counties farmers per capita net income of 4,469 yuan, an increase of 16.3% over the previous year, higher than the province’s per capita net income of farmers increased by 1.7 percentage points. Three areas farmers per capita net income 4,688 yuan, an increase of 16%.

2013年5月9日，国务院扶贫办郑文凯副主任在贵州考察对口帮扶项目
May 9, 2013, the State Council Poverty Alleviation Office Deputy Director Zheng Wenkai inspect the aid to projects in Guizhou

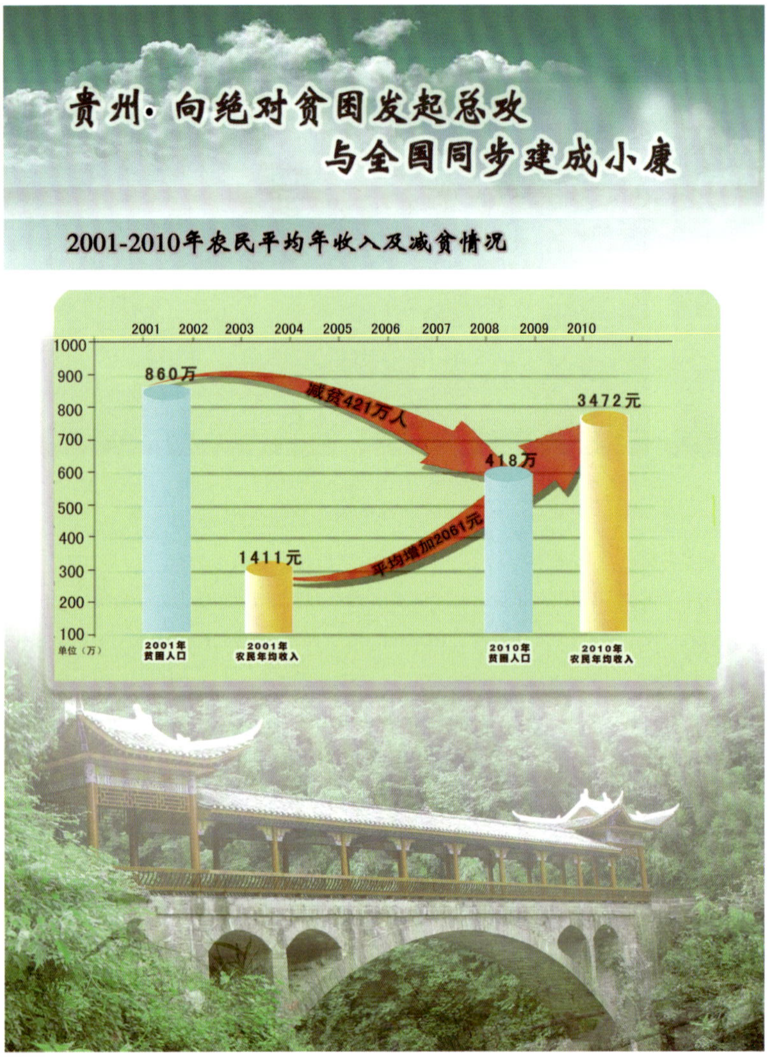

成就图
Achievement Figure

四是扶贫产业稳步推进。规划建设了核桃、中药材、草地生态畜牧、茶叶、蔬菜、马铃薯、油茶、烤烟、乡村旅游和农产品加工等十大扶贫产业，投入资金26.54亿元，实施项目10096个。

五是基础设施状况明显好转。连片特困地区和重点县安全饮水人口比重达到81%。农村居民实现户户通电，农村电网网改率达到98%。实现了100%的乡镇通油路，100%的村通公路，行政村通客车率达到70.76%。实现了乡乡通宽带、行政村通电话。已完成生态移民搬迁10.13万人。

六是农村劳动力素质进一步提高。完成圆梦行动、助学工程、“三位一体”培训、产业化扶贫技能培训等22万人，转移农业劳动力63万人。

侗族姑娘采茶
Dong girl picking tea

Fourth, the poverty industry pushed steadily. Planning and construction of walnuts, herbs, grassland animal husbandry, tea, vegetables, potatoes, tea, tobacco, rural tourism and agro-processing industries and other ten poor alleviation industries, invested 2.654 billion yuan, the implementation of the project 10,096.

Fifth, significant improvement of infrastructure construction. Poverty-stricken areas and key counties contiguous to safe drinking water proportion of the population reached 81%. Rural residents to achieve household electricity, rural power network reconstruction rate of 98%. Achieved 100% of the township pass circuit, 100% of the village roads, administrative village bus pass rate of 70.76%. Achieve a broadband townships, administrative villages on the phone. Ecological relocation has been completed 101,300 people.

大格局发展

Pattern of development

石漠化治理

Rocky desertification control

Sixth, to further improve the quality of the rural labor force. Dream completed action, student supported projects, "Trinity" training, industrial skills training for poverty alleviation and other 220,000 people, the transfer of agricultural labor force 630,000 people.

贵州省民营经济发展局（贵州省中小企业局）

Guizhou Province Private Economic Development Bureau (Guizhou Provincial SME Bureau)

2012年11月22日，省委副书记陈敏尔（前排右二）出席2012多彩贵州旅游商品两赛一会开幕式，并与参会的民族民间能工巧匠亲切交谈

November 22, 2012, the provincial deputy secretary Chen Miner (second from right in the front row) attended the 2012 Colorful Guizhou Tourist Commodities two race one meeting opening ceremony, and had cordial conversation with the participation of folk craftsmen

2012年12月3日，省经济和信息化委副主任、省民营经济发展局（省中小企业局）局长龙超亚与香港国际金融管理学院董事长王中英女士会面，商洽开展中小企业赴港培训事宜

December 3, 2012, deputy director of the Provincial Economic and Information Technology Committee, director of the provincial private Economic Development Bureau(provincial SME Bureau) Long Yachao and the Hong Kong Institute of International Finance Management Ms. Wang Zhongying met to negotiate to Hong Kong to carry out training for SMEs matters

毕节市小微企业第二创业园已有30家小微企业入驻

Bijie City, small and micro enterprises second Pioneer Park for more than 30 small and micro enterprises settled

2012年，全省中小企业民营经济大力实施“民营经济三年倍增计划”，取得长足进步，综合实力迅速迈上新台阶，成为活跃经济、增加就业、稳定社会的主力军。

经济总量稳步提升，整体实力明显增强。近年来，贵州省民营经济名义增速持续以每年高出全省GDP平均增速8-12个百分点的趋势迅猛增长，“十二五”开局以来的年平均增速达到29.5%。至2012年全省民营经济增加值首次突破2000亿元大关，达到2700亿元，增长28.3%，占全省生产总值比重为40%。其他各项主要指标也取得长足进步，个体、私营等民营经济市场主体达到104.3万户，超过企业总数的99.98%以上，上缴税金600.73亿元，占全省税收45%以上。2012年全省民间投资3400亿元，增长67%，占全省的比重47.1%。

县域经济焕发活力，空间布局逐步优化。2012年，贵州民营经济排名前3的地区是贵阳、遵义、毕节，分别为810亿元、651亿元和410亿元，按可比口径计算合计占全省的比例为57.7%，充分体现了“金三角”的战略意义。从县区布局分析，规模较大县和比重较

安顺镇宁顺立达纺织有限公司年产1亿米高档仿真丝化纤面料项目一期建成投产
Anshun town Ningshun Lida Textile Co., Ltd. Annually produce 100 million meters of silk fiber fabrics upscale projects I phase put into operation

安顺黄果树铝业公司生产现场
Anshun Huangguoshu Aluminum Company production site

2012, the province's small and medium private economy vigorously implement the "three-year plan to double the private economy", has made great progress, the overall strength rapidly to a new level and become active economy, increase employment, the main force of social stability.

2012年，贵定金象实业公司的益肝草二期技改竣工并投产，生产能力达到年产5万吨益肝草凉茶饮品
In 2012, Guiding Golden Elephant Industrial Company Yigan grass two technical transformation completed and put into production, production capacity will reach an annual output of 50,000 tons of Yigan grass tea drinks

Steady improvement in the total economy, the overall strength has increased markedly. In recent years, Guizhou Province the private economy continued at an annual nominal growth rate higher than the provincial average GDP growth rate of 8-12 percent of the rapid growth trend, since the beginning of the "Twelfth Five-Year" annual average growth rate reached 29.5%. To 2012, the province's private economic value added for the first time exceeded 200 billion yuan mark, reaching 270 billion yuan, up 28.3%, accounting for the province's GDP accounted for 40%. Other main indicators also made great progress, individual, private and other private economic market players reached 1.043 million, more than 99.98% of the total number of enterprises, taxes 60.073 billion yuan, accounting for more than 45% of the province's tax revenue. In 2012, the province's private investment 340 billion yuan, an increase of 67%, accounting for 47.1% of the proportion of the province.

Rejuvenated county economy, spatial layout gradually optimized. In 2012, Guizhou private economy is the top three areas of Guiyang, Zunyi, Bijie, respectively, 81 billion yuan, 65.1 billion yuan and 41 billion yuan, calculated at comparable prices together accounted for 57.7% of the proportion of the province, fully embodies the "Golden Triangle" of strategic significance. From the county layout analysis, a larger proportion of the larger counties and counties are still too few. A large number of counties in the 1-3 billion yuan of private economic scale,3-5 billion yuan of the small body mass range, more than 10 billion yuan of only Nanming District Guiyang City, Zunyi County Zunyi City, Renhuai City, Liupanshui Ciy Panxian, County Zhongshan Area and other six regions, more than 20 billion yuan is only one Yunyan District of Guiyang City region. Zunyi County, Tongzi County, Meitan County, Dafang County, Jiangkou County, Huishui County and seven counties accounted for more than 70% of the private economy.

Promote economic restructuring and upgrading, the combined effect of increasingly significant. Overall, the private economy gradually three industrial structure optimization, the first industry production decline in the proportion, the secondary industry, tertiary industry's

2012年11月22日，2012多彩贵州旅游商品两赛一会总决赛暨展销大会在贵阳举行。陈敏尔等省领导出席活动，并巡视展馆

November 22,2012, 2012 Colorful Guizhou Tourist Commodities two race one meeting tournament finals and exhibition will be a meeting held in Guiyang. Chen Miner and other provincial leaders attended the event, and toured pavilion

大县仍然数量过少。大量县区的民营经济规模处于10-30亿元、30-50亿元的小体量区间，超过100亿元的仅贵阳市南明区、遵义市遵义县、仁怀市、六盘水市盘县、钟山区等6个地区，超过200亿元仅贵阳市云岩区1个地区。遵义县、桐梓县、湄潭县、大方县、江口县、惠水县等7个县的民营经济占比超过70%。

促进经济转型升级，集聚效应日益显著。总体来说，民营经济三次产业结构逐渐优化，一产比重下降，二产、三产实力增强，从2004年的15.4：44.2：40.4，调整为2012年的9.4：43.3：47.3。民营经济对工业的贡献加强，全省民营规模以上工业企业2916户，占全省规上工业户数的80%，增加值786.48亿元，占全省规上工业的45.6%。民营经济成为建筑业支撑，全省资质以上建筑企业中65.1%为民营企业，民营建筑企业从业人员10.83万人，占全部建筑从业人员的1/3。民营经济是“五张名片”特色轻工产业的主要载体，省内绝大多数的白酒企业、医药企业、茶叶企业、食品企业、旅游商品企业都是民营经济和中小企业。

龙头企业加速推进，引领作用不断增强。老干妈公司用16年时间从小型食品加工厂发展成为全国调味品行业的领军企业，2012年营业收入超过30亿元。朗玛信息在深圳创业板成功上市，市值达到40亿元。一批本地成长起来的重点民营企业规模不断扩大，发展后劲增强。省外民营资本成为贵州省引进投资的重要来源和拉动投资增长的强劲力量。2012年贵州民间投资项目新开工807个，新投产277个。

2012年2月20日，省经济和信息化委员会、中国银行贵州省分行签订战略合作协议，共同致力于促进民营经济和中小企业加快发展

February 20, 2012, the Provincial Economic and Information Technology Committee, Bank of China Guizhou Branch signed a strategic cooperation agreement to work together to promote the accelerated development of private economy and SMEs

2012年8月，贵州省中小企业服务年活动邀请到工业和信息化部中小企业司副司长许科敏作中小企业政策大讲堂巡讲

August 2012, Guizhou SME service activities invited to Deputy Director Xu Kemin of the Ministry of Industry and Information Technology for SME to have the speaking tour of SME policy auditorium

2012年9月22日至25日，第九届中国国际中小企业博览会在广州举办。贵州省共有56家企业参展
September 22 to 25, 2012, the Ninth China International SME Fair held in Guangzhou. Guizhou Province has a total of 56 exhibiting companies

strength, from 2004 15.4:44.2:40.4, adjusted to 2012 9.4:43.3:47.3. The contribution of the private economy to strengthen the industrial province, the private industrial enterprises above designated size 2,916, representing the province's regulations on industrial households 80% of the added value of 78.648 billion yuan, accounting for the province's regulations on industry 45.6%. The private economy as the support construction industry, the province qualified building enterprises 65.1% of private enterprises, private construction enterprises employed 108,300 people, accounting for all construction employees 1/3. The private economy is a "five card" features the main carrier of light industry, the vast majority of the province's liquor companies, pharmaceutical companies, tea companies, food companies, travel goods companies are private economy and SMEs.

Leading enterprises to accelerate, leading role is growing. Laoganma company with 16 years from small food processing plants to become a national condiment industry leader, in 201,2 revenues of more than 3 billion yuan. Langma information successfully listed on GEM in Shenzhen, the market value reached 4 billion yuan. Grew up in a number of local private enterprises have been expanding focus of development to enhance stamina. Foreign private capital of Guizhou Province to become an important source of attracting investment and stimulating investment growth strong force. In 2012, Guizhou folk started 807 new investment projects, the new production 277.

东西部合作的典范——红星发展公司生产现场
Eastern and western cooperation model - Hongxing Development Co. production site

贵州百灵制药生产现场
Guizhou Bailing pharmaceutical production site

贵州省水利厅

Department of Water Resources of Guizhou Province

2012年全省共解决309万农村群众的饮水安全问题。图为苗族村寨用上自来水
2012 the province has solved drinking water security issues for 3.09 million rural people. The picture shows Miao village piped water

2012年是水利改革发展乘势而上、治水兴水取得显著成效的一年。各级水利部门以贯彻落实中央1号文件和国发2号文件为抓手，突出抓好骨干水源工程建设、民生水利建设和水利重点薄弱环节建设，贵州水利改革发展取得明显成效。

水利投资再创历史新高，2012年共完成水利投资170.97亿元。水利规划体系不断完善。“三位一体”规划水利项目全面推进，2012年开工建设“三位一体”规划内骨干水源工程达21个。重点骨干水源工程建设取得新突破。防汛抗旱夺取全面胜利。民生水利建设取得新成绩。最严格的水资源管理制度逐步落实。依法治水管水能力不断增强。水文与水利科技应用扎实推进。党的建设和干部队伍建设成果丰硕。

黔中水利枢纽工程到2012年底累计完成投资45亿元。图为一期工程输水渡槽
By the end of 2012, Guizhou Hydro Project completed a total investment 4.5 billion yuan. The picture shows a canal aqueduct project

2012年全省共实施中小河流治理项目101个。图为治理后焕然一新的涟江惠水县城段
2012 the province implemented a total of 101 small river control projects. The picture shows a new look after the treatment of the Lian River Huishui county segment

2012 is the development of water reform momentum, flood control and water achieved remarkable results of the year. Water conservancy departments at all levels to implement the Central Document No. 1 and No. 2 National Development document as the starting point, focus on key water projects, livelihood water conservancy construction and water conservancy construction of key weaknesses, Guizhou development of water reform achieved significant results.

Water conservancy investment hit a record high, in 2012, completed a total of 17.097 billion yuan investment in water. Water Resources Planning system has improved constantly. “Trinity” plan comprehensively promote water conservancy projects, in 2012, started construction of the “trinity” planning for main water resources up to 21 key projects. Construction of key water projects to achieve new breakthroughs. Flood Control and drought got total victory. Livelihood water conservancy construction has made new achievements. The most stringent water management system progressively implemented. Administering the mains water capacity is growing. Hydrology and Water Science & Technology Applications solid progress. Party building and cadres construction got fruitful result.

贵州省文化厅

Guizhou Provincial Department of Culture

贵州省文化厅与国开行贵州省分行签署发展合作协议
Guizhou Provincial Department of Culture and Guizhou Province Branch of China Development Bank signed a development cooperation agreement

第七届北京文博会贵州展区
The Seventh Beijing Cultural Expo Guizhou Pavilion

2012年，贵州省文化厅提出了新建省美术馆、贵安新区省级文化中心等项目建设初步方案；全省公共图书馆、文化馆（站）和归口管理的博物馆（纪念馆）全部实现免费开放；完成县级“两馆”维修改造22个，实施“数字图书进农家”工程300户。

舞剧《天蝉地傩》在第四届全国少数民族文艺会演中获“音舞类剧目”金奖及6个单项奖；遵义海龙屯土司遗址、黔东南苗族村寨、侗族村寨和铜仁万山汞矿遗址入选《中国世界文化遗产预备名单》；黔东南国家级民族文化生态保护实验区申报成功，《贵州省非物质文化遗产保护条例》颁布实施。

黎平堂安侗族生态博物馆资料信息中心开工仪式
The Liping Tangan Dong eco-museum data information center groundbreaking ceremony

中国•雷山苗年暨鼓藏节开幕式
China • Leishan Miao Year that is drum of the Tibetan Festival opening ceremony

“华盛顿中国文化节•贵州文化周”开幕式演出
“Chinese Cultural Festival in Washington• Guizhou Cultural Week” Opening Ceremony

话剧《天地文通》剧照
Drama”Heaven and Earth”stills

赴德江县宣传贯彻党的十八大精神文艺演出
Went to Dejiang to publicize and implement the spirit of 18th CPC National Congress theatrical performances

In 2012, the Guizhou Provincial Department of Culture to build the initial program of the Provincial New Art Gallery, Guiding new district provincial cultural center and other projects; Museum of the province's public libraries, cultural centers (stations) and centralized management (Memorial) are all free opened; completed at the county level “two museums” repair and renovation of 22, the implementation of the 300 “digital books into their homes” project.

Dance drama “The cicada and Nuo day”won “Gold Award”Song and Dance class repertoire in the fourth National Ethnic Arts Festival and 6 individual awards; the Zunyi Hailong Tuntusi sites, Qiandongnan Miao village, Dong village and Tongren Wanshan mercury mine sites appeared in the “World Heritage Tentative List”; Qiandongnan National Ethnic Culture Ecology experimental zone to declare success, “Guizhou Province Intangible Cultural Heritage Protection Ordinance” promulgated and implemented.

贵州省林业厅

Forestry Department of Guizhou Province

2012年，全省林业系统深入贯彻落实国发2号文件精神，牢牢把握“稳中求进，提速转型”总基调和“两加一推”主基调，全面完成了年度各项工作任务。

林业发展政策环境不断优化，国发2号文件出台后，省林业厅积极争取国家林业局出台了关于支持贵州省加快林业发展的意见；林业支撑保障能力继续提升，林业投入保持稳步增长，2012年累计落实林业投资38亿元，林木种苗补贴、造林补贴、森林抚育经营等补贴政策得到较好落实，公益林补偿范围扩大；森林资源总量持续增长，全省完成营造林面积420.4万亩；林业产业发展提质增效；集体林权制度改革继续深化；森林抚育经营稳步推进；资源管理保护工作切实加强；机关党建和党风廉政建设深入推进。

In 2012, the province's forestry system thoroughly implement the spirit of the document on the 2nd National Development, firmly grasp the "maintaining stability, speed transformation" overall tone and the "two plus one push" the main tone, complete various tasks of the year.

Environment to optimize the development of forestry policy, after the publishment of the document on the 2nd National Development, the Provincial Forestry Department to actively seek support of the State Forestry Administration on the views of Guizhou Province introduces the development of forestry; continue to enhance the support capability of forestry, forestry investment to maintain steady growth, in 2012, total investment 3.8 billion yuan to implement forestry, forest seedling subsidies, subsidies for afforestation, forest management and other tending subsidy policy was implemented well, expand the scope of forest compensation; forest resources continues to grow, the province completed afforestation area of 4,204,000 mu; development of forestry industry quality and efficiency; collective forest right system reform continued to deepen; forest tending operations steadily; resource management to strengthen protection; party building y and party conduct clearance construction further promote.

贵州省国资委

Guizhou Province SASAC (State-owned Assets Supervision and Administration Commission of the State Council)

省国资委主任、党委书记韩先平到企业调研

Provincial SASAC director and party secretary Han Xianping to research in the enterprises

2012年，贵州省国资委及监管企业紧紧围绕省委、省政府的部署要求，扎实落实国发2号文件，充分发挥经济建设主力军作用，为全省经济提速增效做出突出贡献。2012年监管企业累计实现营业收入1946亿元，同比增长32.4 %；利润总额240亿元，同比增长35.3 %；上交税金223.1亿元，同比增长20.2 %；年末资产总额3234.5亿元，同比增长20.2%。

生产经营较快增长，2012年监管企业收入和利润增速居全国各省区市国资委第2位和第1位。改革重组强力推进。发展能力不断增强，加强创新体系建设，提升企业核心竞争力。监管体系不断完善。

2012年7月12日，全省深化国资国企改革工作会议在贵阳召开

July 12, 2012, the province's deepening state owned enterprise reform work conference held in Guiyang

盘江煤电厂区全景

The Panjiang Coal plant panoramic

In 2012, Guizhou Province SASAC and regulatory corporate tightly around the provincial committee, provincial government's deployment requirements, solid implementation of the State Issued document NO.2 , give full play to the role as the main force of economic construction, made outstanding contributions to the province's economic speed efficiency. In 2012, regulatory enterprises realized a total operating income of 194.6 billion yuan, an increase of 32.4%; total profit of 24 billion yuan, an increase of 35.3%; taxes paid 22.31 billion yuan, an increase of 20.2%; 323.45 billion yuan of total assets at the end of the year, an increase of 20.2%.

Production and operation of rapid growth, in 2012, the regulatory corporate income and profit growth in the second and first of the provinces and municipalities SASAC. Strongly promote the reform and reorganization. Development capabilities continue to increase, strengthen the innovation system, to enhance the core competitiveness of enterprises. The regulatory system has improved constantly.

截止2012年12月，贵阳机场二期扩建工程完成90%，二号航站楼主体工程完工99.2%。图为施工中的二号航站楼

As of December 2012, the second phase of the Guiyang airport expansion project is completed 90%, 99.2% completion of the main project of Terminal II. The picture shows the construction of Terminal II

贵州省国家税务局

Guizhou Provincial State Taxation Bureau

省委常委、常务副省长谌贻琴（左二）慰问基层国税干部职工
Provincial Standing Committee, Vice Governor Chen Yiqin (second from left) had condolences of the tax grassroots cadres and workers

国家税务总局党组成员、副局长宋兰（中）与贵州税务12366干部职工亲切交谈
State Administration of Taxation Party members, the Deputy Secretary Song Lan (middle) had cordial conversation with Guizhou tax 12,366 cadres and workers

2012年，全省国税系统共组织税收收入684.35亿元，同比增长17.8%，增收103.44亿元；落实各项税收优惠政策减免退税105.05亿元，增长21.6%，顺利实现税收增收额和减免退税额“双超百亿”目标。同时，大力落实国发2号文件，千方百计争取更大范围、更深层次的政策支持；开展“送政策、优服务、明税情、助发展”主题活动，开通运行全省统一门户网站集群和省局集中的12366纳税服务热线，推广“免填单”办税服务；持续规范执法行为和税收秩序，取消、合并非行政许可类审批项目27项，查处百万元以上案件44件；深入开展创先争优，10个单位荣获“全省创先争优先进基层党组织”和全省“五好基层党组织”称号。

省国税局薛建英局长（前排左二）到道真县扶贫点调研
Provincial State Taxation Bureau director Xue Jianying (second from left in the front row)to research in the Daozhen county Poverty Alleviation point

省国税局党组学习贯彻党的十八大和省委十一届二次全会精神
Provincial State Taxation Bureau organized the study and implement of 18th CPC National Congress and provincial secondary Eleventh Plenary Session

In 2012, the province’s tax system were organized tax revenue 68.435 billion yuan, an increase of 17.8%, income 10.344 billion yuan; implementation of the various tax incentives Tax Credit 10.505 billion yuan, an increase of 21.6%, increase the amount and the smooth realization of tax relief tax rebate “Double over 10 billion yuan” goal. At the same time, Vigorously implement the State Issued No.2 document,do everything possible to fight for broader and deeper policy support; carry out “sending policy, excellent service, clear tax situation, facilitate the development” theme activities, open to run the province's unified portal clusters and the provincial bureau focused tax service hotline 12366, promotion of “not required to fill the table” tax service; continuing standardize law enforcement activities and the taxation order, cancel, merge non-administrative licensing examination and approval items 27 categories, more than one million yuan investigate cases 44; depth carry out the fighting for excellence and first, 10 units awarded “the province’s fighting for excellence and first advanced grassroots party organizations” and the province’s “five-good grass-roots party organizations” title.

贵阳海关

Guiyang Customs

2012年12月7日，张卫民关长带队前往茅台酒厂考察调研，并与贵州茅台集团公司总经理刘自力进行座谈

December 7, 2012, Zhang Weimin Commissioner led a team to the Maotai factory to have inspections and investigations, and informal discussion with the Guizhou Maotai Group Company general manager Liu Zili

2012年，贵阳海关坚持“以人为本，文化兴关，基础强关，建设特色海关”的工作思路，贯彻全国海关关长会议精神，落实海关总署党组提出的“把好国门，搞好服务，防好风险，带好队伍”的要求，完成全年各项工作任务，努力推动地方开放型经济跨越式发展。

2012年，贵阳海关共监管进出口货物257万吨，总值11.35亿美元；征收关税和进口环节税6.71亿元人民币；审批减免税8464万美元；加工贸易合同备案140个，备案金额3.78亿美元；监管进出境旅客11.15万人次，监管行李物品28万件。

In 2012, Guiyang Customs adhere to the “people-oriented, culture prospers the Customs, foundation strong the Customs, building characteristics Customs” idea of the work, to implement the spirit of the National Conference of Customs and Excise, the implementation of the General Administration of Customs of the party group requirement of“guard the country gate, good service, anti risk, lead team”, to complete various tasks throughout the year, efforts to promote local open economy development with leaps and bounds.

In 2012, Guiyang Customs supervision of import and export goods of 2.57 million tons, with a total value of $ 1.135 billion; tariffs and import-related taxes 671 million yuan; approval of tax relief of $ 84,640,000; processing trade contracts for the record of 140, a record amount of $ 378 million; monitoring the entry and exit passengers 111,500 people, 280,000 of regulatory baggage.

2012年9月19日，张卫民关长带队赴黔南州考察调研，先后前往贵定、独山、都匀、福泉四个外向型经济较为发达的市县

September 19, 2012, Zhang Weimin Commissioner led a team to the Qiannan to have inspections and investigations, have visited Guiding, Dushan, Duyun, Fuquan, four export-oriented economy more developed cities and counties

2012年11月24日，张卫民关长前往桐梓县视察工作，在桐梓县领导及遵义海关负责人的陪同下，张卫民关长来到该县重庆工业园现场观摩（一）

November 24, 2012, Zhang Weimin Commissioner went the Tongzi county to have inspections, accompanied by Tongzi county leaders and Zunyi Customs person in charge, Zhang Weimin Commissioner came to the county's Chongqing industrial park to observe the scene(One)

2012年11月24日，张卫民关长前往桐梓县视察工作，在桐梓县领导及遵义海关负责人的陪同下，张卫民关长来到该县重庆工业园现场观摩（二）

November 24, 2012, Zhang Weimin Commissioner went the Tongzi county to have inspections, accompanied by Tongzi county leaders and Zunyi Customs person in charge, Zhang Weimin Commissioner came to the county's Chongqing industrial park to observe the scene(Two)

贵州省物价局

Guizhou Provincial Price Bureau

2012年，全省物价部门坚持以科学发展观为指导，综合施策、多措并举，着力构建保供稳价安民长效机制，积极营造有利的价格环境，努力使物价工作更加亲民近民惠民、更好服务于贵州经济社会发展。

全力以赴稳物价，2012年全省CPI累计同比上涨2.7%，明显低于年初确定的4%左右的调控目标。积极稳妥推改革，从2012年7月1日起在全省试行居民生活用电阶梯电价制度，严格执行差别电价政策，促进节能减排。有力有效强监管。实实在在惠民生。

2012年4月26日，省物价局在都匀市召开全省稳定物价暨推进平价商店建设工作现场会

April 26, 2012, the Provincial Price Bureau held a provincial price stability in Duyun cum promote the construction of fair-price shops work on the spot in Duyun

贵阳市建成平价商店和平价生鲜直销平价点152个

Guiyang City built affordable shops and cheap fresh direct parity of 152

铜仁市签约农副产品产销对接单位109家

Tongren City contracted agricultural production and marketing docking unit 109

2012年11月2日，贵阳市正式启动“平价早餐工程”

November 2, 2012, Guiyang City officially launched the “cheap breakfast project”

In 2012, the province's price department adhere to the scientific development concept as a guide, comprehensive facilities strategy, take measures to focus on building a guarantee stable prices for people’s livelihood long-term mechanism, and actively create a favorable price environment, efforts to make prices more close to the people benefit the people, to better serve the economic and social development in Guizhou.

Go all out to price stability, in 2012, the province's CPI accumulated rose 2.7%, significantly lower than the beginning of the year about 4% of the control objectives. Actively and steadily push reform, pilot ladder system of residential electricity consumption in the province since July 1, 2012, the strict implementation of differential pricing policy, promote energy conservation. Strong and effective strong supervision. Really benefit people's livelihood.

黔南州充分利用价格调节基金扶持建设的生姜种植基地

Qiannan state take full advantage of the price adjustment fund to support the construction of ginger planting base

贵州省公路局

Guizhou Provincial Highway Bureau

2012年，贵州省公路局按照省委、省政府和省交通运输厅部署，全力贯彻“交通优先发展”战略和“两加一推、交通先行”理念，凝心聚力、真抓实干、攻坚克难，全面完成全年目标任务。

固定资产投资创历史新高，共完成固定资产投资249.84亿元，占年度目标任务的106.1%，同比增加53亿元，增幅近27%，为历年之最。高速公路建设顺利推进。国省干线改造力度加大。农村公路建设实现“双百”目标。公路技术状况持续提升。路网结构不断优化。路政管理依法开展。安全管理狠抓落实。

《黔中新衢》普（定）安（顺）高速公路新貌
“Qianzhong Xinqu” Pu(Ding) An(Shun) highway new look

In 2012, the Guizhou Provincial Highway Bureau in accordance with the provincial party committee, the provincial government and the provincial transportation department deployment, fully implement the “traffic priority development” strategy and “two plus one push, traffic priority” ideas, unify the mass and strength, work hard and be practical, overcome difficulties, to complete the objectives and tasks throughout the year.

Investment in fixed assets reached a record high, a total of completed investment in fixed assets 24.984 billion yuan, accounting for 106.1% of the annual target task, an increase of 5.3 billion yuan, an increase of nearly 27%, as most of the calendar year. To promote the construction of highway. National and provincial trunk reconstruction intensified. Rural road construction to achieve the “double hundred” target. Highway technical conditions continue to improve. Road network to optimize the structure. Road administration in accordance with law. Safety management and implementation.

省道308线凯里至雷山二级公路
Highway 308 line Kaili to Leishan secondary roads

遵义凤冈农村公路
Zunyi Fenggang rural roads

贵州省监狱管理局

Guizhou Provincial Prison Administration Bureau

司法部吴爱英部长（左二）、时任贵州省省长赵克志（左一）、贵州省监狱管理局局长曹云平（左三）视察贵州省羊艾监狱服刑人员习艺车间

Department of Justice Wu Aiying Minister(second from left), when he was governor of Guizhou Province Zhao Kezhi(first from left), Guizhou Provincial Prison Authority director Cao Yunping(third from left) visited Guizhou Province YangAi prison inmates apprenticeship workshop

2012年，全省监狱工作努力服务“加快发展、加快转型、推动跨越”主基调，按照“干警队伍引领、安全稳定为先、刑罚执行为重、改造质量立监”的工作思路，以扎实开展政法干警核心价值观教育实践活动、基层基础建设年和百日安全隐患排查整治活动为抓手，深化监狱体制改革、不断强化监狱职能，夯实基层基础、全力抓好安全稳定，创新教育改造手段、努力提高改造质量，着力加强刑罚执行工作、促进依法公正文明执法，提高罪犯生活卫生保障水平、切实维护罪犯合法权益，稳步推进监狱布局调整和监狱企业改革改制、优化监狱发展环境，深入开展“打非治违”活动、强化安全生产基础，大力加强干警队伍建设、不断提升履职能力，使监狱各项工作跃上新台阶，连续实现了无罪犯脱逃、无狱内重大案件、无重大疫情、无重大安全生产事故的“四无”目标，确保了全省监狱的持续安全稳定，为促进贵州经济社会科学发展、后发赶超做出了应有的贡献。

In 2012, the province prison work made efforts to serve service the “to accelerate development, speed up transformation and promote leapfrog”the main tone, according to “the team of police officers to lead, the security and stability for the first, penalty execution of punishment as the key point, the transformation of the quality of legislation monitoring” the work of thinking, in order to carry out educational practice of police officers and men core values, grassroots infrastructure years and the Hundred Days safety hazards investigation and remediation activities as the starting point, deepen the reform of the prison system, prison functions continue to strengthen, reinforce the grass-roots level, to do a good job of security and stability, innovative means of education and reform, efforts improve the quality of transformation, efforts to strengthen the penalty execution work, to promote in accordance with the law fair and civilized law enforcement, improve offender living health protection level, effectively maintain the legitimate rights and interests of criminals, and steadily push forward the prison layout adjustment and prison enterprise reform and restructuring, optimize the environment of prison development, depth “fighting governance violations” activities, to strengthen producing safety basis, vigorously strengthen police officers team building and improve the ability to perform their duties, so that the work of the prison to a new level, criminals escape prison major cases in a row, no major epidemic, no significant production safety accidents “four noes”objectives, to ensure the continued security and stability of the province's prisons, and to promote economic and social scientific development in Guizhou, after catching up to do its due contribution.

黄康生副省长在白云监狱医院向院长方宇同志了解医院有关工作情况

Vice Governor Huang Kangsheng in Baiyun prison hospital to know about the work of the hospital to the Dean of Comrade Chang Fangyu

颁奖

Medal Presentation

贵州省劳动教养管理局

Reeducation through Labor Administration of Guizhou Province

2012年6月21日，司法部吴爱英部长（左二），时任贵州省省长赵克志（左三）在时任省委常委、省委政法委书记崔亚东（右二），省劳教局党委书记、局长李京强（左一）陪同下视察省未教所

June 21, 2012, the Department of Justice Wu Aiying Minister (second from left), when he was governor of Guizhou Province Zhao Kezhi (third from left), accompanied by when he was Provincial Committee and Provincial Politics and Law Committee secretary of the Cui Yadong (second from right), Provincial Reeducation Through Labor Party secretary Li Jingjiang (first from left), to have inspection of the provincial juvenile reformatory

2012年，全省劳教（戒毒）系统紧紧围绕“追比进位、提速增效”的指导思想，强化劳动教养和强制隔离戒毒工作职能，切实把贯彻落实“首要标准”和维护场所安全稳定作为首要的政治任务和第一责任，切实加强场所安全稳定工作，努力提升教育矫治质量，积极创新社会管理，各项工作均取得历史最好成绩。

2012年，全省劳教（戒毒）场所以开展“基层基础建设年”活动为契机，狠抓基层基础建设。同时，加大资金投入力度，切实推进场所文化建设。年内，省女子劳教所党委被中组部评为全国创先争优先进基层党组织，被省直机关工委确定为基层组织建设示范点，全省10个劳教（戒毒）所全部被司法部劳教局评为“四无”劳教（戒毒）所，省劳教局被司法部劳教局评为“四无”劳教局。

In 2012, the province's labor camp (detoxification) system closely around the “chase than binary, speed efficiency” the guiding ideology, strengthen the job functions of reeducation through labor and Compulsory isolation detoxification, earnestly implement the “primary standards” and maintain the stability of the workplace safety as the primary political task and responsibility, and earnestly strengthen workplace safety and stability, efforts to improve the quality of education and correction, a positive innovation of social management, the work to obtain the best results in history.

In 2012, the province's labor camp (detoxification) spaces to carry out the activities of the “grass-roots building year” as an opportunity, pay close attention to grass-roots infrastructure. At the same time, intensified funding, and promote the building of workplace culture. During the year, the Provincial Women's Forced Labor Camp Party Central Organization Department as the national the excel advanced grass-roots party organizations, and provincial organs identified as the building of grassroots organizations demonstration sites, the province's 10 labor camp (detoxification) was awarded as the “four noes” reeducation through labor (detoxification) by the Department of Justice Reeducation through Labor, the Provincial Reeducation Through Labor was titled as the “four noes” Reeducation Through Labor by the Reeducation Through Labor of the Ministry of Justice.

2012年6月13日，黄康生副省长深入省中八劳教所检查调研

June 13, 2012, Vice Governor Huang Kangsheng had a depth inspection and investigation of provinces Zhongba labor camp

2011年12月31日，全省劳教（强戒）工作会议在贵阳召开

December 31, 2011, the province's labor camp (detoxification) work conference held in Guiyang

贵州储备物资管理局

Guizhou Material Reserve Authority

国家物资储备局党组成员、副局长芮执多（前排中）到贵州储备物资管理局调研专用线建设工作
State Reserves Bureau committee member, deputy director Rui Zhiduo(the middle in the front row) to Guizhou Material Reserve Authority to have research of the dedicated line construction work

局党组书记、局长张映芳（中）主持召开全局学习贯彻党的十八精神报告会
Bureau Party Secretary, Director Zhang Yingfang (middle) chaired a global study and implement the spirit of 18th CPC National Congress report

局党组书记、局长张映芳（中）与设计院专家就贵州储备物资管理局油库扩建工作开展现场办公
Bureau Party Secretary, Director Zhang Yingfang (middle) and the Design Institute experts on Guizhou Material Reserve Authority depot expansion work carried out on-site office

2012年，贵州储备物资管理局牢牢把握“稳中求进”的总基调，按照局党组确定的“稳中求进、进中保好、好中求快”要求，推进贵州储备事业科学发展。

参与宏观调控，服务地方经济。紧急收储贵州企业价值数亿元金属材料数万吨，与省内企业实现国储物资企业代储合作；为中石油、中石化提供商业应急储备服务，缓解成品油供应紧张。

切实加强基础管理。安全有效完成国储物资收储、动用、轮换等任务并强化日常保管保养工作；以安全审计为抓手，夯实安全管理基础工作；推进流程化和“5S”现场管理。

认真做好规范管理体制与运行机制工作，为事业单位改革铺垫基础。组建贵州国储物流有限公司，事企界面得到清晰界定，管理局全面监管职责得到加强；事业单位公益性职能进一步明确；公司负责经营管理、物流仓储业务安全生产、规范经营性活动、调整升级业务结构、提高经营效益，2012年实现物流收入3000余万元。

努力推进项目建设。完成五三一处安改后续工程；努力争取油库扩建项目；积极推进资产置换，优化储备结构；六三一处铁路专用线建设在安顺市西秀区的支持下顺利开工建设。

局党组书记、局长张映芳（右一）在挂帮点铜仁市万山区茶店镇调研农村经济、社会、文化等建设情况

Bureau Party Secretary, Director Zhang Yingfang (first from right) in Gaubangdian Tongren City Wanshan district Chadian town to have the research of the rural economic, social, cultural and other construction

贵州储备物资管理局承办国家物资储备系统安全审计工作座谈会并作经验交流发言

Guizhou Material Reserve Authority undertook the state material reserve system security contractor audits forum and speak for the exchange of experience

In 2012, Guizhou Material Reserve Authority firmly grasp the "maintaining stability" the general tone, determined in accordance with the Party Group "while maintaining stability, into mediator good, good in quickly" requirement, to promote the scientific development of reserves in Guizhou .

Participation in macro-control, serve the local economy. Emergency purchasing and storage enterprises worth hundreds of millions of Guizhou number of tons of metallic materials, and the province of enterprises on behalf of reserves State Reserve Material Enterprises cooperation; as PetroChina, Sinopec contingency reserve to provide commercial services to ease the tight supply of refined oil.

Strengthen basic management. Safe and effective completion of the State Reserve materials purchasing and storage, utilization, rotation and strengthen routine tasks such as keeping maintenance work; to security audit as the starting point, consolidate security management infrastructure work; promote streamlined and "5S" site management.

Serious efforts to standardize the management system and operation mechanism work, for the reform of public institutions bedding foundation. Established Guizhou State Reserve Logistics Co., Ltd., things get clearly defined corporate interface, the Authority has been strengthened comprehensive regulatory responsibilities; public functions and institutions to further clarify; company responsible for management, logistics and warehousing operations safety, regulate business activities, adjustment and upgrade business structure, improve operational efficiency, logistics revenue by 2012 more than 30 million yuan.Efforts to promote the project. On completion of Five-Three-One change follow-up project; strive depot expansion project; actively promote the replacement of assets, optimize the structure of reserves; in support of Anshun City Xixiu district, the Six-Three-One special railway line construction had smooth construction.

贵州储备物资管理局组织贵州、四川、云南、湖南等四省国储物流企业洽谈区域合作

Guizhou Material Reserve Authority organized Guizhou, Sichuan, Yunnan, Hunan and other four provinces State Reserve logistics enterprises to discuss regional cooperation

贵州储备物资管理局紧急收储贵州企业产品数万吨

Guizhou Material Reserve Authority had emergency purchasing and storage number of tons of product of the enterprises in Guizhou

贵州省烟草专卖局（公司）

Guizhou Province Tobacco Monopoly Bureau (company)

国家局姜成康局长（右二）在贵州调研烟叶生产
National Bureau Jiang Chengkang Secretary (second from right) researched the tobacco production in Guizhou

国家局何泽华副局长（中）一行视察铜仁。图为在思南县许家坝烟叶工场烟叶分级情况
National Bureau deputy director He Zehua (middle) and his entourage visited Tongren. The picture shows in Sinan County Xu Jia Ba tobacco plant tobacco grading case

中国烟叶公司副总经理张玉征（前排左一）到贵阳市检查验收烟叶生产基础设施建设项目
Chinese tobacco company deputy general manager Zhang Yuzheng (first from left in the front row) to have inspection and acceptance of Guiyang tobacco production infrastructure projects

贵州省烟草专卖局组建于1983年9月，中国烟草总公司贵州省公司组建于1981年11月。1986年6月，贵州省烟草公司上划中国烟草总公司。贵州省烟草专卖局、贵州省公司下设九个市级烟草专卖局（公司）及中国烟草贵州进出口有限责任公司、贵州烟草科学研究院、贵州烟草投资管理有限公司，控股管理贵州烟叶复烤有限责任公司。截至2012年底，公司拥有总资产222亿元。

全省共落实种烟县64个、种烟乡（镇）776个、种烟村5470个、烟农21.37万户，移栽356.1万亩。收购烟叶34.82万吨（696.42万担），销售烟叶34.92万吨（698.45万担）。

全省销售卷烟677.5亿支（135.5万箱），同比增长2.2%。全年实现卷烟销售收入298.28 亿元，同比增长19.9%。实现卷烟税利56.9亿元，同比增长15.27%。

全年实现营业总收入405亿元，同比增长23.2%。上缴国家财政收入63亿元，增长18%。

全年查处假烟案件807起，破获涉烟网络案件22起，15起达到国家局标准。全年查获假冒卷烟1387万支，烟叶、烟丝2056吨。

2012年，省公司被贵州省企业联合会、贵州省企业家协会评为“2012贵州企业100强”第二名。

Guizhou Provincial Tobacco Monopoly Bureau was established in September 1983, China National Tobacco Corporation, Guizhou Province company was established in November 1981. June 1986, Guizhou Tobacco Company zoned China National Tobacco Corporation. Guizhou Provincial Tobacco Monopoly Bureau, Guizhou Province company consists of nine municipal Tobacco Monopoly Bureau (company) and the China Tobacco Import & Export Co., Ltd. Guizhou, Guizhou Tobacco Research Institute, Guizhou Tobacco Investment Management Limited, the controlling management in Guizhou tobacco redrying limited liability company. By the end of 2012, the company has total assets of 22.2 billion yuan.

The province to implement the kinds of tobacco county 64, planted tobacco township (town) 776, kinds of tobacco village 5,470, 213,700 farmers transplanting 3,561,000 mu. Buy tobacco 348,200 tons (6,964,200 dan), sales of tobacco 349,200 tons (6,984,500 dan).

The province's sale of cigarettes 67,750,000,000 (1,355,000 boxes), an increase of 2.2%. Realize an annual sales income of 29.828 billion yuan of cigarettes, an increase of 19.9%. To achieve cigarette taxes of 5.69 billion yuan, an increase of 15.27%.

Realize an annual total revenue of 40.5 billion yuan, an increase of 23.2%. Turned over to the state revenue 6.3 billion yuan, an increase of 18%.

Year investigated 807 cases of counterfeit cigarettes, the tobacco-related network uncovered 22 cases, 15 cases reached the national Bureau of Standards. Year seized counterfeit cigarettes 13,870,000, tobacco 2,056 tons.

In 2012, the provincial company was awarded the second prize by Guizhou Province Enterprises Association, Guizhou Entrepreneurs Association as "2012 Guizhou 100 strong enterprise".

省局（公司）召开烟叶服务品牌建设及服务烟农"十个一"经验交流现场会

Provincial Bureau (company) held a tobacco brand building services and services to farmers, "ten one" exchange of experience on the spot

贵州烟草商业举办"2353"主题教育实践活动论坛。图为"我来谈我践行我弘扬"全省烟草商业"2353"主题教育实践活动论坛现场

Guizhou tobacco business held "2353" theme of educational practice forum. The picture shows "I talk about my practice I promote" the province's tobacco business, "2353" theme of educational practice forum site

毕节市烟区规模化种植基地

Bijie City smoke-scale planting base area

贵州电网公司

Guizhou Power Grid Corporation

8月，2012年度贵州电网公司新员工开班典礼
August, 2012 Guizhou Power Grid Corporation opening ceremony of new employees

贵州电网公司是中国南方电网有限责任公司的全资子公司，负责贵州电网的统一规划、建设、管理和调度，承担着省内电力供应和西电东送双重任务。供电面积17万平方公里，供电服务人口4238万，供电户数1073余万户。2012年，实现售电量1219亿千瓦时，资产总额达637亿元，员工53663人。贵州电网公司先后荣获全国五一劳动奖状、中央企业先进基层党组织、贵州省和谐企业先进单位、"四好"领导班子先进集体等荣誉，并连续蝉联贵州省百强企业榜首。

截至2012年底，贵州电网统调装机3145.8万千瓦，其中，火电装机1884.0万千瓦，占59.90%；水电装机1165.4万千瓦，占37.05%；风电96.4万千瓦，占3.05%。贵州电网已拥有110千伏及以上变电站451座，变电容量6426万千伏安，35千伏及以上线路长度38493千米。并已实现各市州500千伏电网全覆盖，形成环网结构为中心的220千伏坚强地区骨干网架，并通过500千伏兴安直流、高肇直流、500千伏天金线、山河双回、黎桂双回"五交两直"通道与南方主网并联运行。黔电送粤能力达到950万千瓦以上，加上外送周边省区，外送能力已超过1000万千瓦。

2012年9月14日，贵州电网IT运维服务中心揭牌
September 14, 2012, Guizhou Power Grid IT operation and maintenance service center opening

2012年10月24日，位于贵州省威宁县的乌江源风电场项目132台风机全部并网发电，标志着贵州省最大的风电场正式运营
October 24, 2012, is located in Weining County, Guizhou Province, Wujiangyuan wind power plant 132 wind turbines into the grid and start power generation, marking the largest wind power plant in Guizhou Province formal operation

高考期间，贵州电网公司积极为考试场所提供全天候服务
During the college entrance examination, Guizhou Power Grid to actively provide all-day service for the examination place

2012年6月7日，贵州电网公司举办“喜迎十八大，建功促发展”职工乒乓球赛
une 7, 2012, Guizhou Power Grid Corporation held “celebrate 18th CPC National Congress, accomplishment and promote development” workers table tennis

2012年5月16日，社会责任日活动当天，贵州电网遵义供电局为市民演示带电作业流程
May 16, 2012, the day of Social Responsibility Day, Zunyi, Guizhou Power Grid Power Supply Bureau processes live demonstration for the public

Guizhou Power Grid Corporation is a wholly owned subsidiary of China Southern Power Grid Co., Ltd., is responsible for the Guizhou Power Grid of unified planning, construction, management and scheduling, to bear the supply of electricity in the province and west to east the dual task. Supply electricity area of 170,000 square km, power supply serving a population of 42,380,000, the number of households supply more than 10,730,000. In 2012, electricity sales of 121.9 billion kwh, the total assets of 63.7 billion yuan, employs 53,663 people. Guizhou Power Grid Corporation has won the National Labor Award, the central advanced grassroots party organizations, Guizhou Province advanced unit of harmonious enterprise, “four goods” leading groups advanced group and other honors. Consecutive reelection of the top 100 enterprises of Guizhou Province.

By the end of 2012, Guizhou Power Grid transfer system installed capacity of 31.458 million kilowatts, of which thermal power installed capacity of 18.84 million kilowatts, accounting for 59.90%; hydropower installed capacity of 11.654 million kilowatts,accounting for 37.05%; and 964,000 kilowatts of wind power, accounting for 3.05%. Guizhou Power Grid has 451 substations of 110 kV and above, transformer capacity of 64.26 million kilovolt, line length of 38,493 km above 35 kV. And cities and states have achieved full coverage of 500-kilovolt power grid to form a ring structure as the center of a strong regional 220 kV backbone network, and 500 kV Xing'an DC, Gaozhao DC ,500 kV Tianjin line, back to Qinghe Double DC, Li Gui for Double “five cross two straight” channel and the South of the main network operating in parallel. The Qian power to send Guangdong ability to reach more than 9.5 million kilowatts, plus neighboring provinces delivery, delivery capacity has exceeded 10 million kilowatts.

2012年6月10日，主题为“科学发展，安全发展”的贵州省2012年安全生产月宣传咨询日活动在贵阳市筑城广场举行
June 10, 2012, the theme of “scientific development, security and development” 2012 Guizhou Province on production safety month publicity and consultation activities held in Guiyang City fortification square

为配合2012年全国节能宣传周活动，6月16日，贵州电网贵阳供电局纪念塔节能展示中心向市民免费开放
In line with the 2012 National Energy Conservation Week activities, 16 June, Guizhou Guiyang Power Supply Bureau monument energy grid demonstration center open to the public free of charge

中国电信贵州公司

China Telecom Guizhou company

2012年8月14日，中国电信集团公司董事长王晓初到贵阳分公司调研
August 14, 2012, China Telecom Group Chairman Mr Wang Xiaochu to Guiyang Branch have research

中国电信贵州公司下辖9个市（州）分公司，90个县级分公司，3个专业分公司，1家控股公司。截止2012年，中国电信贵州公司移动用户数达到378万户，宽带用户达到194.3万户。2012年经营收入完成44.38亿元，同比增长9.4%。

深入推进信息化建设。与省政府签订贵州“智慧城市”战略合作协议；签订了省委通信指挥系统、省审计厅审计专用指挥系统、省司法厅司法行政执法指挥调度系统、中天城投“智慧地产”等22个信息化战略合作及移动信息化协议。

加强客户服务保障。落实六部委专项行动等活动，对四方面12类45项热难点问题进行改进；扎实开展为民服务创先争优活动；组织落实47项3G服务标准，3G标准达标率达到100%；成立天翼手机省级维修服务中心。

提升通信网络能力。启动宽带普及提速工程相关工作，坚持推进以FTTH为主的“宽带中国•光网城市”战略，推进光纤迅速向用户端延伸；IP网出省带宽扩容到600Gbps，城域网总带宽扩容到800Gbps，FTTH 建设用户端口达到43万，FTTH 实装率为17.9%。

加强农村基础设施建设。建设农村光缆4000公里，新建农村移动基站461个，完成802个自然村开通电话，698个行政村通宽带；移动网络能力稳步提升，重点区域、高速公路等区域覆盖进一步加强。

2012年12月15日，贵州三网融合试点业务正式启动，副省长孙国强、省政协副主席谢晓尧、省经信委主任王江平及省通管局、广电局、三大通信运营企业等省市相关部门和单位领导出席仪式
December 15, 2012, Guizhou triple play pilot service was officially launched, Sun Guoqiang, vice governor, provincial CPPCC Vice Chairman Xie Xiaoyao, Provincial Commission by letter and the provincial director Wang Jiangping, and the provincial communication administration, radio and television bureau, three large communication enterprises, relevant departments and unit leaders attended the ceremony

2012年8月14日，中国电信集团公司与贵州省人民政府在贵阳签署战略合作框架协议。副省长孙国强和副总经理李平分别代表贵州省政府和中国电信集团公司签署协议
August 14, 2012, China Telecom Group and Guizhou Provincial People's Government signed a strategic cooperation framework agreement in Guiyang. Sun Guoqiang, vice governor and deputy general manager Li Ping represent the Guizhou provincial government and China Telecom Group signed the agreement

2012年6月28日，贵州公司与中天城投携手共建“智慧地产”
June 28, 2012, Guizhou company and the Zhongtian city construction investment company work together to build “smart real estate”

2012年3月15日，贵州公司“天翼省级手机维修中心”开业
March 15, 2012, Guizhou company “Tianyi provincial mobile phone repair center” opened

China Telecom Guizhou Company administered 9 city (state) branches, 90 county-level branches, 3 specialized branches, 1 holding company. As of 2012, China Telecom Guizhou company reached 3.78 million mobile subscribers, broadband subscribers reached 1,943,000. In 2012, operating revenue of 4.438 billion yuan, an increase of 9.4%.

Further promote the information construction. Signed with the provincial government of Guizhou “smart city” strategic cooperation agreement; signed a provincial communication and command system, Provincial Audit Department auditing special command system, the Provincial Justice Department of Justice law enforcement dispatching system, the Zhongtian city construction investment “smart real estate” and other 22 information strategic cooperation, and mobile information agreement.

Enhance customer service guarantee. Implementation of the six ministries and special operations and other activities, on four aspects of 12v classes 45 hot and difficult issues to improve; solidly carry out public service excel activities; organizations to implement the 47 standard 3G services, 3G standards compliance rate of 100%; founded Tianyi phone provincial service center.

Enhance communication network capabilities. Start broadband penetration acceleration project related work, persist in advancing to FTTH based “broadband China• Optical Network City” strategy, to promote the fiber quickly to the client-side extension; IP network bandwidth expansion out of the province to 600Gbps, metro expansion to 800Gbps total bandwidth , FTTH build user port reached 430,000, FTTH mounting rate of 17.9%.

Strengthening rural infrastructure construction. Construction of rural cable 4,000 km, the new rural mobile base stations 461, 802 villages to complete the opening call, 698 administrative villages broadband; mobile network capacity improved steadily, key areas, highways and other regional coverage further strengthened.

2012年12月15日，贵州公司信息服务运营中心协同贵阳分公司在金阳新世界小区设立宽带电视体验区，吸引了众多小区业主前来参观体验
December 15, 2012, Guizhou company information services operating center cooperated with Guiyang Branch in Jinyang New World district established residential broadband TV experience zone, attracting many residential property owners, visitors experience

2012年12月12日，贵阳分公司社会渠道之文昌南路天翼卖场盛大开业
December 12, 2012, Guiyang Branch social channels of Wenchang Road Tianyi store grand opening

贵州盐业集团

Guizhou Province Salt Industry Group

贵州盐业集团于2000年11月8日挂牌成立，是省管国有大型企业之一。集团现有成员单位85个，职工3872人。集团组建以来在维护食盐专营、履行社会责任、强化企业管理、深化企业改革、实施“十二五”规划、推动实施市场网络、房地产业、酒店旅游和资本运作“四大板块”业务、推动企业调整转型等方面取得了明显成效。

2012年，集团资产总额31.05亿元，增长42.24%；净资产10.63亿元，增长9.14%；销售收入16.68亿元，增长38.42%；利润总额5401万元，完成目标任务的108.01%。国有资产保值增值率109%。非盐收入7亿元，占总收入比重的42.24%。

集团党委书记、董事长、省盐务管理局局长刘仰瑞（左一）为贵盐集团第六届“黔盐风采”职工文艺汇演获得一等奖的节目颁奖

Group party secretary, chairman, Provincial Salt Administration Bureau Liu Yang Rui (first from left) awarded for Guizhou Province Salt Industry Group the sixth “Guizohu salt style” art show workers who won the first prize program

2013年全省盐业工作会议在贵阳召开

2013 Salt province working conference held in Guiyang

贵州盐业集团参加2013年贵州省企业社会责任报告发布会

Guizhou Province Salt Industry Group to participate in 2013 Guizhou Province Corporate Social Responsibility Report conference

Guizhou Province Salt Industry Group formally established in November 8, 2000, is the province one of large state-owned enterprises. Group of the existing 85 unit members, 3,872 people of worker. Since the group is established in the maintenance of salt monopoly, to fulfill their social responsibilities, and strengthen enterprise management, deepen enterprise reform, the implementation of the “Twelfth Five-Year Plan”, achieved remarkable results in promoting the implementation of the market network, the real estate industry, hotel and tourism and capital operation “four plate” business, promote enterprise restructuring, etc.

In 2012, the Group’s total assets was 3.105 billion yuan, an increase of 42.24%; net assets of 1.063 billion yuan, an increase of 9.14%; sales revenue of 1.668 billion yuan, an increase of 38.42%; total profit of 54.01 million yuan to complete the objectives and tasks of 108.01%. 109% state-owned assets. Non-salt income 700 million yuan, the proportion of 42.24% of total revenue.

贵州盐业集团执行落实现场会在安顺召开

Guizhou Province Salt Industry Group executive implementation held a spot in Anshun

1 One

综　合

General Survey

1-1 行政区划(2012)
Divisions of Administrative Areas

单位:个 (unit)

市(州)名称	City (State,Prefecture)	地级单位 Units at Prefectural Level	#市 Cities	县级单位 Units at County Level	县 Counties	自治县 Autonomous Counties	县级市 Cities at County Level	市辖区 Districts under the Jurisdiction of City
全省合计	**Total**	**9**	**6**	**88**	**56**	**11**	**7**	**13**
贵 阳 市	Guiyang	1	1	10	3		1	6
六盘水市	Liupanshui	1	1	4	2			1
遵 义 市	Zunyi	1	1	14	8	3	2	2
安 顺 市	Anshun	1	1	6	2	2		1
毕 节 市	Bijie	1	1	8	6	1		1
铜 仁 市	Tongren	1	1	10	4	4		2
黔西南布依族苗族自治州	Qianxinan	1		8	7		1	
黔东南苗族侗族自治州	Qiandongnan	1		16	15		1	
黔南布依族苗族自治州	Qiannan	1		12	9	1	2	

注：资料来源于省民政厅(下表同)。
Note:Date in the table are obtained from the department of civil affairs(the same applies to the next table).

1-1 续表 continued

市(州)名称	City (State,Prefecture)	特区 Special District	镇 Town	街道办事处 Urban Subdistrict Office	乡 Township	#民族乡 Ethnic Community Township	城市社区居民委员会 Neighbourhood Committees	村民委员会 Village Committees
全省合计	**Total**	**1**	**729**	**79**	**710**	**236**	**1818**	**18099**
贵 阳 市	Guiyang		31		46	18	494	1156
六盘水市	Liupanshui	1	38	7	56	44	150	1019
遵 义 市	Zunyi		167	20	58	8	322	1689
安 顺 市	Anshun		44	7	36	11	106	1837
毕 节 市	Bijie		101	10	142	77	152	3557
铜 仁 市	Tongren		79	5	85	46	176	2775
黔西南布依族苗族自治州	Qianxinan		74	14	49	3	117	1097
黔东南苗族侗族自治州	Qiandongnan		94	7	110	17	168	3308
黔南布依族苗族自治州	Qiannan		101	9	128	12	133	1661

1-2 各市(州)、县(市、区、特区)名称(2012)

Name of Each City(State,Prefecture) and County(City,District,Special Region)

市(州)名称 City(State,Prefecture)	县(市、区、特区)名称 County(City,District,Special Region)
贵阳市 Guiyang	南明区 云岩区 花溪区 乌当区 白云区 观山湖区 清镇市 开阳县 息烽县 修文县 Nanming Yunyan Huaxi Wudang Baiyun guanshanhu Qingzhen Kaiyang Xifeng Xiuwen
六盘水市 Liupanshui	钟山区 六枝特区 盘县 水城县 Zhongshan Liuzhi Panxian Shuicheng
遵义市 Zunyi	红花岗区 汇川区 赤水市 仁怀市 遵义县 桐梓县 绥阳县 正安县 Honghuagang Huichuan Chishui Renhuai Zunyi Tongzi Suiyang Zhengan 凤冈县 湄潭县 余庆县 习水县 道真仡佬族苗族自治县 务川仡佬族苗族自治县 Fenggang Meitan Yuqing Xishui Daozhen Wuchuan
安顺市 Anshun	西秀区 平坝县 普定县 关岭布依族苗族自治县 镇宁布依族苗族自治县 Xixiu Pingba Puding Guanling Zhenning 紫云苗族布依族自治县 Ziyun
毕节市 Bijie	七星关区 大方县 黔西县 金沙县 织金县 纳雍县 赫章县 威宁彝族回族苗族自治县 Qixingguan Dafang Qianxi Jinsha Zhijin Nayong Hezhang Weining
铜仁市 Tongren	碧江区 万山区 江口县 石阡县 思南县 德江县 沿河土家族自治县 松桃苗族自治县 Bijiang Wanshan Jiangkou Shiqian Sinan Dejiang Yanhe Songtao 玉屏侗族自治县 印江土家族苗族自治县 Yuping Yinjiang
黔西南布依族苗族自治州 Qianxinan	兴义市 兴仁县 普安县 晴隆县 安龙县 望谟县 贞丰县 册亨县 Xingyi Xingren Puan Qinglong Anlong Wangmo Zhenfeng Ceheng
黔东南苗族侗族自治州 Qiandongnan	凯里市 黄平县 施秉县 三穗县 镇远县 岑巩县 天柱县 锦屏县 Kaili Huangping Shibing Sansui Zhenyuan Cengong Tianzhu Jinping 剑河县 台江县 黎平县 榕江县 从江县 雷山县 麻江县 丹寨县 Jianhe Taijiang Liping Rongjiang Congjiang Leishan Majiang Danzhai
黔南布依族苗族自治州 Qiannan	都匀市 福泉市 荔波县 贵定县 瓮安县 平塘县 罗甸县 长顺县 龙里县 惠水县 Duyun Fuquan Libo Guiding Wengan Pingtang Luodian Changshun Longli Huishui 独山县 三都水族自治县 Dushan Sandu

注：2012年贵阳市部分行政区划调整，表中行政区划名称为调整后行政区划名称，以下相关表中统计数据为行政区划调整前数据。

Note:The names in this table indicate the names of the current administrative districts which of Guiyang city were adjusted in 2012. The data in related tables indicats the data of the previous administrative districts.

1-3 社会经济主要指标

指标	Item	总量指标 1978	2000	2006
人口与就业	**Population and Employment**			
人口	**Population**			
年末常住人口(万人)	Total Population at the Year-end (10000 persons)	2686.40	3755.72	3690
#城镇人口	Urban Population	323.97	896.49	1013.27
乡村人口	Rural Population	2362.43	2859.23	2676.73
#男性人口	Male	1364.82	1968.00	1908.85
女性人口	Female	1321.58	1787.72	1781.15
年平均人口(万人)	Annual Average Population(10000 persons)	2663.27	3732.89	3710
就业	**Employment**			
就业人员(万人)	Year-end Employees (10000 persons)	1053.67	1866.28	1953.24
#非私营单位职工人数	Staff and Workers	171.19	193.96	201.87
城镇登记失业人数（万人）	Urban Registeration Unemployment (10000 persons)		10.23	12.12
宏观经济	**Macro Economy**			
国民经济核算	**National Accounting**			
生产总值(亿元)	Gross Domestic Product (100 million yuan)	46.62	1029.92	2338.98
第一产业	Primary Industry	19.42	271.20	382.06
第二产业	Secondary Industry	18.73	391.20	967.54
工业	Industry	15.24	328.73	839.13
建筑业	Construction	3.49	62.47	128.41
第三产业	Tertiary Industry	8.47	367.52	989.38
固定资产投资	**Investment in Fixed Assets**			
全社会固定资产投资(亿元)	Total Investment in Fixed Assets in the Whole Province (100 million yuan)	10.93	402.50	1197.68
消费	**Consumption**			
社会消费品零售总额(亿元)	Total Retail Sales of Consumer Goods(100 million yuan)	21.23	355.58	710.00
对外贸易	**Foreign Trade**			
进出口总额（亿美元）	Total Value of Imports and Exports(USD 100 million)	0.16	6.60	16.17
#出口额	Total Exports	0.03	4.21	10.39
利用外资	**Utilization of Foreign Capital**			
签订合同项目(个)	Projects of Agreements and Contracts(unit)		59	59
实际利用外资金额(万美元)	Foreign Capital Actually Absorbed(USD 10000)	※148	19545	18413
财政	**Government Finance**			
财政总收入(亿元)	Total Financial Revenue(100 million yuan)	14.20	153.04	448.88
#公共财政收入(亿元)	Local Financial Revenue (100 million yuan)	6.26	85.23	226.82
公共财政支出(亿元)	Financial Expenditure (100 million yuan)	12.30	201.57	610.64
价格指数(上年=100)	**Price Indices(preceding year=100)**			
居民消费价格总指数	Consumer Price Index	100.3	99.5	101.7
商品零售价格总指数	Retail Price Index	100.3	97.3	100.9
农业生产资料价格总指数	General Price Index of Means of Agricultural Production	△102.1	100.6	105.4
工业生产者出厂价格指数	Ex-Factory Price Index of Industrial Producer		100.4	104.3
工业生产者购进价格指数	Purchasing Price Index of Industrial Producer		102.9	107.3

Major Social and Economic Indicators

Aggregate Indicators						速度指标（%） Indices and Growth Rates (%)					
						指数（2012为以下各年） Index (2012as Percentage of the Following Years)				平均增长速度 Average Annual Growth Rate	
2007	2008	2009	2010	2011	2012	1978	2000	2007	2011	1979–2012	2001–2012
3632	3596	3537	3479	3469	3484	129.7	92.8	95.9	100.4	0.8	-0.6
1025.68	1046.79	1057.21	1176.25	1212.76	1268.52	391.6	141.5	123.7	104.6	4.1	2.9
2606.32	2549.21	2479.79	2302.75	2256.24	2215.48	93.8	77.5	85.0	98.2	-0.2	-2.1
1879.70	1868.73	1827.56	1797.43	1801.21	1818.61	133.2	92.4	96.8	101.0	0.8	-0.7
1752.30	1727.27	1709.44	1681.57	1667.79	1665.39	126.0	93.2	95.0	99.9	0.7	-0.6
3661	3614	3566.50	3508	3474	3477	130.5	93.1	95.0	100.1	0.8	-0.6
1872.64	1867.20	1841.92	1770.90	1792.80	1825.82	173.3	97.8	97.5	101.8	1.6	-0.2
207.53	199.76	206.44	210.67	225.91	249.67	145.8	128.7	120.3	110.5	1.1	2.1
12.13	12.56	12.34	12.18	12.51	12.56		122.8	103.5	100.4		1.7
2884.11	3561.56	3912.68	4602.16	5701.84	6852.20	2574.3	387.9	182.7	113.6	10.0	12.0
446.38	539.19	550.27	625.03	726.22	891.91	481.4	165.9	128.2	108.6	4.7	4.3
1124.79	1370.03	1476.62	1800.06	2194.33	2677.54	4275.6	448.5	194.6	116.8	11.7	13.3
978.86	1195.30	1252.67	1516.87	1829.20	2217.06	4624.6	439.8	188.6	115.6	11.9	13.1
145.93	174.73	223.95	283.19	365.13	460.48	2637.8	502.3	234.2	123.3	10.1	14.4
1312.94	1652.34	1885.79	2177.07	2781.29	3282.75	5420.8	485.1	191.7	112.1	12.5	14.1
1488.80	1864.45	2450.99	3186.28	4234.44	5717.80						
858.15	1075.24	1247.25	1482.68	1751.62	2027.64	9550.8	570.2	236.3	115.8	14.4	15.6
22.73	33.70	23.07	31.47	48.88	66.32	40313.4	1004.8	291.8	135.7	19.3	21.2
14.65	19.01	13.59	19.20	29.85	49.52	173762.5	1177.4	338.0	165.9	24.5	22.8
51	50	39	42	70	53		89.8	103.9	75.7		-0.9
15333	17379	18027	34026	71674	109805		561.8	716.1	153.2		15.5
556.98	674.58	779.59	969.57	1329.99	1644.48	11580.9	1074.5	295.2	123.6	15.0	21.9
285.14	349.55	416.48	533.73	773.08	1014.05	16199.0	1189.8	355.6	131.2	16.1	22.9
795.40	1055.39	1372.27	1631.48	2249.40	2755.68	22403.9	1367.1	346.5	122.5	17.3	24.4
106.4	107.6	98.7	102.9	105.1	102.7						
104.2	107.2	97.6	103.0	105.5	102.0						
105.1	113.4	96.2	101.1	111.1	100.7						
105.0	112.4	95.1	104.7	105.4	101.0						
107.5	112.5	93.5	109.8	115.0	102.3						

1-3 续表1

指 标	Item	总量指标		
		1978	2000	2006
能源生产与消费	**Total Production and Consumption of Energy**			
一次能源生产总量（万吨标准煤）	Total Production of Primary Energy(10000 tons of SCE)	1204.51	3288.83	8089.39
能源消费总量(万吨标准煤)	Total Energy Consumption(10000 tons of SCE)	674.50	4278.60	6172.45
产 业	**Industry**			
农业	**Agriculture**			
主要农产品产量(万吨)	Output of Major Farm Products(10000 tons)			
粮 食	Grain	643.36	1161.30	1038.00
油 料	Oil-bearing Crops	9.89	74.34	68.24
#油菜籽	Rapeseed	7.34	66.20	63.18
烤 烟	Flue-cured Tobacco	8.11	31.09	30.71
肉类总产量	Meat	12.80	124.06	163.70
水产品	Aquatic Products	0.37	6.24	6.71
工业	**Industry**			
规模以上工业企业	Industrial Enterprises above Designated Size			
增加值（亿元）	Added Value(100 million yuan)		216.99	747.38
#轻工业	Light Industry		82.16	218.52
重工业	Heavy Industry		134.83	528.86
主营业务收入(亿元)	Revenue from Principal Business(100 million yuan)		593.80	1948.57
利税总额(亿元)	Total Profits(100 million yuan)		87.44	299.09
主要工业产品产量	Output of Major Industrial Products			
原煤(万吨)	Coal(10000 tons)	1669	3677	11817
发电量(亿千瓦小时)	Electricity(100 million kwh)	41.43	404.70	974.66
铝(万吨)	Aluminum(10000 tons)	2.32	27.19	56.28
成品钢材(万吨)	Rolled Steel(10000 tons)	4.95	150.93	256.57
水泥(万吨)	Cement(10000 tons)	130.93	783.88	1799.40
磷矿石(万吨)	Phosphorite(10000 tons)	169.02	588.70	1034.60
茅台酒(吨)	Mao-Tai Chiew(ton)	1067	5397	9719
卷烟(万箱)	Cigarettes(10000 cases)	31.60	187.40	211.73
建筑业	**Construction**			
建筑业总产值(亿元)	Gross Output Value of Construction(100 million yuan)	4.40	109.06	312.34
房屋建筑施工面积(万平方米)	Floor Space of Buildings under Construction(10000 sq.m)	313	1792	3369
房屋建筑竣工面积(万平方米)	Floor Space of Buildings Completed(10000 sq.m)	164	824	1108
交通运输业	**Transportation**			
运输线路长度(公里)	Length of Transportation Routes(km)			
铁路营业里程	Length of Railways	1365	1641	2014
公路线路里程	Length of Highways in Operation	25954	34643	113278
客运量(万人)	Passenger Traffic(10000 persons)	3294	53032	69270
旅客周转量(亿人公里)	Passenger-Kilometers(100 million passenger-km)	25.50	238.36	349.82
货运量(万吨)	Freight Traffic(10000 tons)	3467	15615	24709
货物周转量(亿吨公里)	Freight Ton-Kilometers(100 million ton-km)	79.60	404.07	680.96

continued

Aggregate Indicators						速度指标（%） Indices and Growth Rates (%)					
						指数（2012为以下各年） Index (2012 as Percentage of the Following Years)				平均增长速度 Average Annual Growth Rate	
2007	2008	2009	2010	2011	2012	1978	2000	2007	2011	1979–2012	2001–2012
8480.62	9262.34	11070.09	13100.00	12739.97	14932.17	1239.7	454.0	176.1	117.2	7.7	13.4
6799.72	7083.99	7566.33	8175.43	9067.85	9878.38	1464.5	230.9	145.3	108.9	8.2	7.2
1100.86	1158.00	1168.27	1112.30	876.90	1079.50	167.8	93.0	98.1	123.1	1.5	-0.6
69.66	68.39	78.68	60.34	78.85	87.38	883.5	117.5	125.4	110.8	6.6	1.4
64.59	60.38	70.40	51.62	71.81	78.18	1065.1	118.1	121.0	108.9	7.2	1.4
31.22	37.71	36.92	37.02	32.50	37.31	460.0	120.0	119.5	114.8	4.6	1.5
150.60	161.46	169.60	179.09	179.97	190.27	1486.5	153.4	126.3	105.7	8.3	3.6
7.68	7.80	8.03	8.79	10.88	13.47	3640.5	215.9	175.4	123.8	11.2	6.6
890.48	1051.26	1170.29	1227.17	1715.06	2055.46		584.8	231.6	116.2		15.9
267.87	302.25	352.38	413.99	571.20	773.04		555.5	242.3	117.6		15.4
622.61	749.01	817.91	813.18	1143.86	1282.42		588.3	226.4	115.5		15.9
2430.62	2922.35	3234.59	3926.01	5022.11	5966.52		1004.8	245.5	118.8		21.2
403.49	453.53	470.60	671.39	901.36	1172.15		1340.5	290.5	130.0		24.1
10864	11798	10001	12656	13033	15031	900.6	408.8	138.4	115.3	6.7	12.4
1166.32	1192.08	1363.09	1358.69	1344.14	1548.44	3737.5	382.6	132.8	115.2	11.2	11.8
75.07	58.15	80.27	88.79	90.36	104.35	4497.8	383.8	139.0	115.5	11.8	11.9
328.14	337.52	337.62	391.04	462.36	560.22	11317.6	371.2	170.7	121.2	14.9	11.5
1943.10	2048.94	2664.78	3694.84	5000.19	6100.45	4659.3	778.2	314.0	122.0	12.0	18.6
1198.83	1317.18	1360.66	1579.21	2052.82	2281.95	1350.1	387.6	190.3	111.2	8.0	12.0
10789	11308	12161	12911	15523	15806	1481.3	292.9	146.5	101.8	8.3	9.4
220.71	226.74	232.24	239.24	245.23	249.35	789.1	133.1	113.0	101.7	6.3	2.4
348.79	393.88	523.91	622.96	824.72	1039.95	23635.2	953.6	298.2	126.1	17.4	20.7
3813	4230	4953	5756	6779	8254	2640.4	460.5	216.5	121.8	10.1	13.6
1204	1216	1244	1350	1530	1863	1136.4	226.1	154.7	121.8	7.4	7.0
2012	1962	1983	2002	2070	2058	150.8	125.4	102.3	99.4	1.2	1.9
123247	125365	142561	151644	157820	164542	634.0	475.0	133.5	104.3	5.6	13.9
74440	80056	84981	97793	120554	142809	4335.4	269.3	191.8	118.5	11.7	8.6
369.20	407.59	430.56	514.41	631.74	718.22	2816.5	301.3	194.5	113.7	10.3	9.6
26788	33576	34844	40310	44890	52765	1521.9	337.9	197.0	117.5	8.3	10.7
721.26	809.93	897.38	1012.20	1060.69	1177.78	1479.6	291.5	163.3	111.0	8.2	9.3

1-3　续表2

指　　标	Item	总量指标 1978	2000	2006
邮电通信业	**Post and Telecommunication**			
邮路总长度(公里)	Number of Postal Routes(km)		63538	62936
函件(万件)	Number of Letters(10000 pcs)	3880	6943	6859
交换机容量(万门)	Capacity of Telephone Exchanges(10000 lines)	8.95	260.46	1639.41
年末固定电话用户(万户)	Number of Telephones Subscribers at the Year-end(10000 subscribers)	3.80	153.70	493.91
移动电话用户(万户)	Number of Mobile Telephones Subscribers(10000 subscribers)		79.70	646.20
互联网宽带接入端口(万个)	Number of Subscribers of Internet Service(10000 subscribers)			67.44
旅游业	**Tourism**			
旅游总人数(万人次)	Total Number of Visitors(10000 persons)		1998.39	4747.89
#入境旅游人数	Number of International Tourists Inbound		18.39	32.14
旅游总收入(亿元)	Total Tourism Income(100 million yuan)		62.94	387.05
#国际旅游外汇收入(万美元)	International Earnings from Tourism (USD 10000)		6092	11516
金融业	**Financial Intermediatio**			
全部金融机构人民币存款余额(亿元)	Total Savings Deposit Balancen(100 million yuan)	18.05	1106.64	3300.08
#储蓄存款	Savings Deposit	1.84	539.49	1596.86
全部金融机构人民币贷款余额(亿元)	Total Loan Balance (100 million yuan)	21.62	1064.82	2696.11
教育、文化	**Education and Culture**			
教育	**Education**			
专任教师数	Full-time Teachers			
普通高等学校(万人)	Regular Institutions of Higher Education (10000 persons)	0.28	0.72	1.54
普通中学(万人)	Regular Secondary Schools (10000 persons)	5.42	8.12	12.83
小学(万人)	Primary Schools(10000 persons)	15.59	17.48	18.88
在校学生数	Students Enrollmen			
普通高等学校(万人)	Regular Institutions of Higher Education (10000 persons)	1.33	7.55	22.15
普通中学(万人)	Regular Secondary Schools(10000 persons)	137.17	157.20	256.31
小学(万人)	Primary Schools(10000 persons)	423.60	500.21	474.38
学龄儿童入学率(%)	Enrollment Rate of School-age Children (%)	89.5	98.5	98.6
文化	**Culture**			
图书总印数(万册)	Number of Books Printed Copies (10000 copies)	5842	10289	9402
杂志总印数(万册)	Number of Magazines Printed Copies(10000 copies)	69	994	1380
报纸总印数(万份)	Number of Newspapers Printed Copies(10000 copies)	11930	28799	32026
家庭生活	**Family and People's Living Conditions**			
家庭	**Household**			
城镇居民平均每户常住家庭人口(人)	Average Persons Per Urban Household(person)	5.41	3.11	3.02
农村居民平均每户常住人口(人)	Average Persons Per Rural Household(person)	5.80	4.52	4.43
婚姻	**Marital**			
准予登记结婚(万对)	Marriage Registration Permitted(10000 households)	△7.02	28.02	21.31
离婚人数(万人)	Divorce(10000 persons)	△0.38	1.54	8.43
居住	**Residence**			
城镇人均住宅建筑面积(平方米)	Per Capita Building Space in Urban Areas(sq.m)	5.45	17.60	26.42
农村居民人均住房面积(平方米)	Per Capita Living Space in Rural Areas(sq.m)		19.75	23.84
生活	**Per Capita Standard of Living**			
城镇居民人均可支配收入(元)	Per Capita Annual Disposable Income of Urban Households(yuan)	261	5121	9117
农村居民人均纯收入(元)	Per Capita Annual Net Income of Rural Residents(yuan)	109	1374	1985

continued

Aggregate Indicators						速度指标 (%) Indices and Growth Rates (%)					
						指数 (2012为以下各年) Index (2012 as Percentage of the Following Years)				平均增长速度 Average Annual Growth Rate	
2007	2008	2009	2010	2011	2012	1978	2000	2007	2011	1979–2012	2001–2012
60747	65236	61854	96174	99155	136429		214.7	224.6	137.6		6.6
5735	6566	6768	5939	5041	6036	155.6	86.9	105.2	119.7	1.3	-1.2
2334.67	2858.70	3182.88	3673.01	4838.00	5026.53	56162.3	1929.9	215.3	92.7	20.5	28.0
521.19	499.61	451.13	432.61	403.96	380.00	10000.0	247.2	72.9	94.1	14.5	7.8
834.05	1185.84	1583.28	1964.40	2175.22	2515.00		3155.6	301.5	115.6		33.3
96.65	119.89	163.63	231.69	437.87	435.79			450.9	99.5		
6262.89	8190.23	10439.95	12913.02	17019.36	21401.18		1070.9	341.7	125.7		21.8
43.00	39.54	39.95	50.01	58.51	70.50		383.4	164.0	120.5		11.8
512.28	653.13	805.23	1061.23	1429.48	1860.16		2955.4	363.1	130.1		32.6
12918	11697	11044	12958	13507	16894		277.3	130.8	125.1		8.9
3826.37	4736.93	5898.26	7363.92	8742.79	10540.06	58393.7	952.4	275.5	120.6	20.6	20.7
1790.14	2237.05	2676.09	3244.99	3934.48	4806.09	261200.4	890.9	268.5	122.2	26.0	20.0
3128.63	3569.27	4656.50	5747.53	6841.92	8274.78	38273.7	777.1	264.5	120.9	19.1	18.6
1.70	1.80	1.96	2.04	2.19	2.28	828.3	315.0	134.4	104.3	6.4	10.0
13.11	13.54	13.93	14.25	14.74	15.63	288.3	192.6	119.3	106.1	3.2	5.6
19.20	20.00	19.92	19.79	19.71	19.80	127.0	113.2	103.1	100.5	0.7	1.0
24.17	26.75	29.91	32.33	34.41	38.38	2885.8	508.4	158.8	111.5	10.4	14.5
256.00	261.78	269.45	275.68	282.71	287.38	209.5	182.8	112.3	101.7	2.2	5.2
466.31	469.79	456.87	433.50	408.74	380.08	89.7	76.0	81.5	93.0	-0.3	-2.3
98.6	97.2	98.4	97.9	98.6	99.3	111.0	100.9	100.7	100.7	0.3	0.1
8626	10457	9263	8069	8492	7304	125.0	71.0	84.7	86.0	0.7	-2.8
1376	1420	1358	1300	1413	1485	2152.2	149.4	107.9	105.1	9.4	3.4
34676	35110	36286	37004	44931	45032	377.5	156.4	129.9	100.2	4.0	3.8
3.02	3.07	3.04	3.03	2.98	3.01	55.6	96.8	99.7	101.0	-1.7	-0.3
4.43	4.40	4.38	4.34	4.32	4.31	74.3	95.4	97.3	99.8	-0.9	-0.4
23.49	26.32	30.79	37.51	37.34	41.78		149.1	177.9	111.9		3.4
9.17	10.24	11.59	12.79	14.44	16.25		1053.3	177.2	112.5		21.7
27.52	26.95	27.57	27.42	27.83	27.86	511.2	158.3	101.2	100.1	4.9	3.9
24.54	25.27	26.43	27.26	29.63	29.75		150.6	121.2	100.4		3.5
10678	11759	12863	14143	16495	18701	1080.0	270.7	149.4	110.4	7.3	8.7
2374	2797	3005	3472	4145	4753	780.3	251.1	170.2	111.5	6.2	7.9

1–3 续表3

指　标	Item	总量指标		
		1978	2000	2006
社会保险	**Social Insurance**			
社会保险基金收入(亿元)	Revenue of Social Insurance Fund (100 million yuan)		22.87	73.72
社会保险基金支出(亿元)	Expenses of Social Insurance Fund (100 million yuan)		23.41	67.77
卫生	**Health Care**			
医院、卫生院(个)	Number of Hospitals and Health Centers(unit)	4510	1878	1855
执业(助理)医师(万人)	Number of Licensed (Assistant) Doctors (10000 persons)	2.12	4.57	4.11
医院、卫生院床位数(万张)	Number of Beds(10000 beds)	3.75	5.51	6.26
城市市政建设	**City Construction**			
供水总量(万立方米)	Volume of Tap Water Supply(10000 cu.m)	5389	45693	71568
城市排水管道长度(公里)	Length of Sewer Pipelines(km)	214	1665	4485
人工煤气供应量(万立方米)	Volume of Coal Gas Supply(10000 cu.m)			21650
出租汽车(辆)	Taxi(unit)	☆33	7352	13540
年末公共交通运营数(辆)	Number of Public Vehicles under Operation at Year-end (Buses and Trolley Buses, etc.)(unit)	●326	●4144	3687
年末实有道路长度(公里)	Length of Paved Roads at Year-end(km)	184	1679	3474
城市园林绿地面积(公顷)	Area of Parks and Green Land (hectare)	1037	9939	40682
环境	**Environment**			
环保资金投入(亿元)	Environment Protection Investment(100 million yuan)	☆0.17	10.98	32.79
环境污染事故(起)	Accident of Environment Pollution(unit)			23
污染事故直接经济损失(万元)	Direct Economy Losing for Pollute Accident(10000 yuan)			13.40
火灾、交通事故	**Basic Statistics on Fires and Traffic Accidents**			
火灾发生数(起)	Number of Fires(case)	2501	1608	1919
直接财产损失(万元)	Losses Converted into Cash(10000 yuan)	1734.21	2814.70	1194.20
交通事故发生数(起)	Number of Traffic Accidents(case)	3104	2593	2734
损失折款(万元)	Losses Converted into Cash(10000 yuan)	236.07	1899.62	1869.39

注：1.年末总人口及分项指标1978、2000年为常住一年口径，2006–2009年数据已根据第六次人口普查数据进行修订。2.规模以上工业统计口径2000–2010年为年主营业务收入500万元及以上的工业企业，2011年起为年主营业务收入2000万元及以上工业企业(以下相关表同)。3.全社会固定资产投资统计口径2007–2010年为计划总投资50万元及以上固定资产项目投资、房地产开发投资及农村农户投资，2011年起为计划总投资500万元及以上固定资产项目投资、房地产开发投资及农村农户投资(以下相关表同)。4.本表速度指标中，生产总值、工业增加值和城乡居民收入及分项指标均按可比价格计算，全社会固定资产投资及分项指标平均增长速度按累计法计算。5.原煤产量1978–2007年为全社会口径。6.工业生产者出厂价格指数2010年及以前为全部工业品出厂价格指数，工业生产者购进价格指数2010年及以前为全部原材料、燃料、动力价格指数，统计口径不变。7.储蓄存款2010年及以前为城乡居民储蓄存款(以下相关表同)。8.“△”为1979年数据；“☆”为1981年数据；“※”为1985年数据；“●”为“标台”。

continued

Aggregate Indicators						速度指标 (%) Indices and Growth Rates (%)					
2007	2008	2009	2010	2011	2012	指数 (2012为以下各年) Index (2012 as Percentage of the Following Years)				平均增长速度 Average Annual Growth Rate	
						1978	2000	2007	2011	1979–2012	2001–2012
90.86	140.50	171.40	201.56	256.94	310.85		1359.4	342.1	121.0		24.3
80.57	98.24	122.73	151.41	181.74	229.08		978.4	284.3	126.0		20.9
1939	1934	1982	2005	2071	2210	49.0	117.7	114.0	106.7	-2.1	1.4
4.21	3.88	4.02	4.22	4.40	4.92	231.9	107.8	116.9	111.8	2.5	0.6
7.14	7.81	9.12	9.75	10.80	12.97	345.6	235.2	181.7	120.1	3.7	7.4
68297	64871	61971	63572	67766	71168	1320.6	155.8	104.2	105.0	7.9	3.8
4724	4796	5047	5507	5977	6148	2872.9	369.2	130.1	102.9	10.4	11.5
23491	26613	26886	26963	30515	34167			145.4	112.0		
13411	13768	14700	15087	17196	20600		280.2	153.6	119.8		9.0
5083	5140	4864	4984	5364	5429			106.8	101.2		
3772	3836	3933	4081	4487	4875	2649.5	290.4	129.2	108.6	10.1	9.3
41410	41841	43781	45500	48024	51081	4925.8	513.9	123.4	106.4	12.1	14.6
48.88	50.74	69.78	89.52	106.70	97.35		886.6	199.2	91.2		19.9
18	10	4	4	7	4			22.2	57.1		
673.20	14.70	10.00	107.30	450.00	677.27			100.6	150.5		
833	800	869	1630	1170	959	38.3	59.6	115.1	82.0	-2.8	-4.2
3075.20	3436.52	3435.55	4416.80	6625.40	5147.20	296.8	182.9	167.4	77.7	3.3	5.2
2292	2219	1816	1764	1566	1361	43.8	52.5	59.4	86.9	-2.4	-5.2
1848.85	1480.23	1214.50	1208.00	1611.39	1698.58	719.5	89.4	91.9	105.4	6.0	-0.9

Note:1.As to total population at the year-end and subitems in this table,the year 1978 and 2000 refer to permanent population in one year scope, additionly the year 2006 to 2009 had been amendmented on the base of the result of the Sixth National Population Census.2.The scale above industrial enterprises statistics was the industrial of main business income of 5 million yuan and above in 2000 to 2010. And from 2011, it is the industrial of main business income of 20 million yuan and above(The relative tables in this chapter are the same). 3.From 2007 to 2010, data in the table referred to those projects that planned to invest 5000,000 yuan at least in investment in fixed assets, real estate development and rural household investment.From 2011,the statistical coverage has referred to those projects that planned to invest 50000,000 yuan at least in investment in fixed assets, real estate development and rural household investment.(The relative tables in the chapter are the same) 4.As to growth rates,GDP, value-added of industry, per capita annual disposable income of urban households and per capita annual net income of rural residents and their sub items were calculated at constant price.The average annual growth rate of total inve stment in fixed assets in the whole province and its sub items were calculated by accumulation method .5.Output of raw coal in the year 1978 to 2007 refer to the scope of the whole province. 6.The year 2010 and before , Ex-Factory price index of industrial product refere to the ex-factory price index of the whole industrial products and purchasing price index of industrial producer refer to the price index of the whole raw materials,fuels and power.The statistics caliber isn't changed.7.The year 2010 and before,savings deposit refer to resident savings deposit of urban and rural(The relative tables in this chapter are the same).8.Data with "△" refer to the year 1979,with "☆" refer to the year 1981,with "※" refer to the year 1985,and with "●" refer to standard unit.

1-4 社会经济主要指标结构

Composition Indicators on National Economic and Social Development

单位：% (%)

指 标	Item	2007	2008	2009	2010	2011	2012
人口与就业	**Population and Employment**						
人口	**Population**						
城镇、乡村结构	Grouped by Urban and Rural Area						
城 镇	Urban Population	28.2	29.1	29.9	33.8	35.0	36.4
乡 村	Rural Population	71.8	70.9	70.1	66.2	65.0	63.6
性别结构	Grouped by Sex						
男	Male	51.8	52.0	51.7	51.7	51.9	52.2
女	Female	48.2	48.0	48.3	48.3	48.1	47.8
就业	**Employment**						
产业结构	Grouped by Three Industries						
第一产业	Primary Industry	74.1	72.3	70.5	68.3	66.6	65.1
第二产业	Secondary Industry	9.2	9.7	10.7	11.5	12.0	13.0
第三产业	Tertiary Industry	16.7	18.0	18.7	20.2	21.3	21.8
宏观经济	**Macro Economy**						
国民经济核算	**National Accounting**						
生产总值产业结构	In GDP						
第一产业	Primary Industry	15.5	15.1	14.1	13.6	12.7	13.0
第二产业	Secondary Industry	39.0	38.5	37.7	39.1	38.5	39.1
第三产业	Tertiary Industry	45.5	46.4	48.2	47.3	48.8	47.9
投资	**Investment in Fixed Assets**						
全社会固定资产投资结构	Structure of Total Investment in Fixed Assets in the Whole Province						
#中央	Central	16.1	16.5	14.2	10.2	8.2	6.8
地方	Local	83.9	83.5	85.8	89.8	91.8	93.2
#国有经济	State-owned Economic Unit	46.9	48.8	51.0	50.4	47.0	44.3
非国有经济	Non-State-owned Economic Unit	53.1	51.2	49.0	49.6	53.0	55.7
资金来源结构	Grouped by Source of Funds						
国家预算内资金	State Budgetary Appropriation	5.0	6.4	8.9	8.7	10.7	8.6
国内贷款	Domestic Loans	22.7	22.2	22.3	20.8	16.1	15.3
利用外资	Foreign Investment	0.9	0.7	0.3	0.3	0.3	0.2
自筹资金	Self-raising Funds	50.7	50.7	44.6	45.5	49.6	52.5
其他资金	Others	20.7	20.1	23.9	24.8	23.4	23.4
对外贸易	**Foreign Trade**						
出 口	Total Exports	64.5	56.4	58.9	61.0	61.1	74.7
进 口	Total Imports	35.5	43.6	41.1	39.0	38.9	25.3
财政	**Government Finance and Tax**						
公共财政收入结构	Structure of Local Financial Revenue						
省 级	Provincial Level	24.7	25.6	22.6	20.3	21.4	17.7
地 级	Prefectural Level	21.0	20.2	21.3	23.3	21.9	20.2
县 级	County level	39.7	39.8	43.3	44.0	45.7	51.2
乡 级	Township Level	14.5	14.4	12.8	12.4	11.0	10.9

1-4 续表1 continued

单位：% (%)

指 标	Item	2007	2008	2009	2010	2011	2012
能源	**Energy**						
一次能源生产总量结构	Structure of Total Energy Production						
原 煤	Coal	91.5	86.7	88.3	89.9	91.4	88.8
水 电	Hydro-power	8.5	13.3	11.7	10.1	8.6	11.2
能源终端消费总量结构	Structure of Total Energy Consumption						
#原 煤	Coal	45.6	45.4	47.6	48.0	48.8	48.0
天然气	Natural Gas	1.1	1.0	0.8	0.8	0.6	0.7
电 力	Electricity	33.1	32.0	32.4	33.3	33.2	33.1
产 业	**Industry**						
农业	**Agriculture**						
农林牧渔业增加值结构	Structure of Value-added of FFAFS						
农 业	Farming	58.3	57.1	60.1	61.7	59.3	62.9
林 业	Forestry	4.1	4.3	4.6	4.5	4.4	4.2
畜牧业	Animal Husbandry	32.6	33.9	30.5	28.7	30.7	27.5
渔 业	Fishery	1.3	1.3	1.3	1.4	1.8	2.0
农林牧渔服务业	FFAF Seryices	3.6	3.4	3.6	3.7	3.8	3.4
工业	**Industry**						
规模以上工业增加值	In the Industrial Enterprises above Designated Size						
#轻 工 业	Light Industry	30.1	28.8	30.1	33.7	32.7	37.6
重 工 业	Heavy Industry	69.9	71.2	69.9	66.3	67.3	62.4
#大型企业	Large Industry	46.0	40.9	37.0	38.0	37.2	44.0
中型企业	Medium-sized Industry	28.2	26.5	28.4	24.6	23.9	26.2
小型企业	Small Industry	25.8	32.7	34.6	37.4	36.6	29.2
建筑业	**Construction**						
建筑业总产值结构	Structure of Gross Output Value of Construction						
国有经济	State-owned	77.9	77.0	77.9	79.6	79.9	82.7
非国有经济	Non-state-owned	22.1	23.0	22.1	20.4	20.1	17.3
交通运输业	**Transportation**						
货运量结构	Structure of Freight Traffic						
铁 路	Railways	27.2	19.9	20.1	19.8	16.1	12.6
公 路	Highways	70.3	77.9	77.6	77.9	81.7	85.3
水 运	Waterways	2.5	2.2	2.3	2.3	2.2	2.1
客运量结构	Structure of Passenger Traffic						
铁 路	Railways	4.0	4.0	3.8	3.5	3.3	2.7
公 路	Highways	94.5	94.1	94.2	94.5	94.9	95.6
水 运	Waterways	1.5	1.9	2.0	2.0	1.8	1.7
旅游业	**Tourism**						
来黔涉外旅游人数结构	Structure of Tourists Visiting Guizhou						
外 国 人	Foreigners	36.0	46.1	40.8	37.2	40.4	43.1
港澳同胞	Compatriots from Hong Kong and Macao	30.3	27.3	27.1	27.3	28.9	29.6
台湾同胞	Compatriots from Taiwan	33.7	26.6	32.1	35.5	30.7	27.3
金融业	**Financial Intermediation**						
金融机构人民币存款结构	Structure of Total Savings Deposit Balance						
#财政存款	Treasury Deposit	3.8	4.7	5.1	4.9	5.1	3.9
储蓄存款	Savings Deposit	46.8	47.2	45.4	44.1	45.0	45.6

1-4 续表2 continued

单位：% (%)

指 标	Item	2007	2008	2009	2010	2011	2012
金融机构人民币贷款结构	Structure of Total Loan Balance						
#短期贷款	Short-Term Loan	27.5	25.0	23.4	17.7	18.9	21.1
中长期贷款	Middle-Term & Long-Term Loan	69.6	72.5	73.7	79.7	79.5	77.4
教育	**Education**						
教育(学历教育口径)	**Education**						
在校学生结构	Structure of Students Enrollment						
#高等教育阶段	Higher Education	3.2	3.5	4.0	4.4	4.7	5.4
高中阶段	Senior Secondary Schools	7.3	7.4	7.7	8.4	9.5	11.0
初中阶段	Junior Secondary Schools	27.0	27.1	27.9	28.8	29.5	29.8
小学阶段	Primary Schools	62.5	62.0	60.4	58.5	56.3	53.8
专任教师结构	Structure of Full-time Teachers						
#高等教育阶段	Higher Education	5.0	5.1	5.5	5.6	6.0	6.0
高中阶段	Senior Secondary Schools	8.6	8.6	8.8	9.2	9.9	11.0
初中阶段	Junior Secondary Schools	30.0	29.7	30.1	30.3	30.3	30.4
小学阶段	Primary Schools	56.5	56.6	55.6	54.9	53.8	52.5
生活、环境保护	**People's Living Conditions and Environment**						
人民生活	**People's Living Conditions**						
城市居民消费结构	Consumption Structure of Urban Residents						
#食品类	Food	40.2	43.1	41.5	39.9	40.2	39.7
衣着类	Clothing	11.7	10.2	11.2	11.0	10.7	11.1
居 住	Residence	9.3	10.0	8.3	8.9	9.7	8.0
家庭设备用品及服务	Household Facilities,Articles and Services	6.0	6.3	6.5	6.7	7.6	6.8
医疗保健	Medicines and Medical Services	4.6	5.6	5.9	5.4	5.1	5.2
交通和通信	Transport and Communications	11.5	10.4	10.9	12.6	12.3	15.0
教育文化娱乐服务	Education, Cultural and Recreation Services	13.4	11.2	12.7	12.5	11.7	11.1
农村居民消费结构	Consumption Structure of Rural Residents						
#食品类	Food	52.2	51.7	45.2	46.3	47.6	44.6
衣着类	Clothing	5.2	5.2	5.2	4.8	5.4	5.8
居 住	Residence	17.2	19.7	24.3	21.8	18.5	19.4
家庭设备、用品及服务	Household Facilities,Articles and Services	3.7	4.4	4.8	4.8	5.6	5.4
医疗保健	Medicines and Medical Services	4.1	4.5	5.5	6.2	7.1	7.2
交通和通信	Transport and Communications	8.1	7.4	7.2	8.1	8.8	9.5
文教、娱乐、用品及服务	Recreation,Education and Cultural Articles and Services	7.7	5.6	6.3	6.5	5.3	5.8
卫生	**Health Care**						
卫生机构床位结构	Structure of Beds of Health Care Institutions						
#医院、卫生院	Hospitals and Health Centers	94.2	94.0	93.5	92.6	91.9	95.0
卫生技术人员结构	Structure of Medical Technical Personnels						
#执业(助理)医师	Licensed(Assistant) Doctors	49.4	43.5	42.2	41.1	39.2	37.9
环境	**Environment**						
环境保护投入资金结构	Structure of Environment Protection Investment						
#老工业污染源治理资金	Old Industry Pollute Fountain Treatment	16.2	20.1	12.8	7.6	13.2	12.5
城市环境基础设施建设	Urban Environment Infrastructure Investment	27.5	30.4	38.2	32.3	35.6	38.4

1-5 社会经济主要指标比例、效益

Major Indicators on Proportions and Efficiency in Economic Social Development

指 标	Item	2007	2008	2009	2010	2011	2012
人口与就业	**Population and Employment**						
城镇人口比重	Proportion of Urban Population	28.2	29.1	29.9	33.8	35.0	36.4
人口出生率(‰)	Birth Rate(‰)	13.28	13.49	13.65	13.96	13.31	13.27
人口死亡率(‰)	Death Rate(‰)	6.60	6.77	6.69	6.55	6.93	6.96
人口自然增长率(‰)	Natural Growth Rate(‰)	6.68	6.72	6.96	7.41	6.38	6.31
城镇登记失业率(%)	Registered Unemployment Rate in Urban Areas(%)	3.97	3.98	3.81	3.63	3.63	3.29
国民经济核算	**National Accounting**						
县域经济增加值占GDP比重	Add Value in County Economy Share of GDP	64.8	65.3	65.9	66.5	65.8	66.4
民营经济增加值占GDP比重	Add Value in Non-public-owned Economic Share of GDP	31.3	32.4	33.1	35.0	36.9	40.3
人均生产总值(元)	Per Capita Gross Domestic Product(yuan)	7878	9855	10971	13119	16413	19710
固定资产投资	**Investment in Fixed Assets**						
全社会固定资产投资相当于生产总值比例(%)	Proportion of Investmetn in Fixed Assets to GDP(%)	51.6	52.3	62.6	69.2	74.3	83.4
全社会房屋建筑面积竣工率(%)	Rate of Total Floor Space of Buildings Completed in the Whole Province (%)	40.2	34.2	38.9	36.8	21.4	18.9
消费	**Consumption**						
社会消费品零售总额相当于生产总值比例(%)	Proportion of Retail Sales of Consumer Goods to GDP(%)	29.8	30.2	31.9	32.2	30.7	29.6
人均社会消费品零售额(元)	Per Capita Ratail Sales of Consumer Goods(yuan)	2344	2975	3497	4227	5042	5832
对外贸易	**Foreign Trade**						
进出口总额相当于生产总值比例(%)	Proportion of Total Value of Imports and Exports as Percentage to GDP(%)	5.4	6.6	4.0	4.6	5.6	6.1
财政	**Government Finance**						
财政总收入相当于生产总值比例(%)	Proportion of Total Financial Revenues to GDP(%)	19.3	18.9	19.9	21.1	23.3	24.0
公共财政支出相当于生产总值比例(%)	Proportion of General Budget Expenditure to GDP (%)	27.6	29.6	35.1	35.5	39.5	40.2
能源	**Energy**						
能源生产弹性系数	Elasticity Ratio of Energy Production	0.32	0.82	1.71	1.43		1.26
电力生产弹性系数	Elasticity Ratio of Electricity Production	1.35	1.27	1.39	0.03		1.27
能源消费弹性系数	Elasticity Ratio of Energy Consumption	0.69	0.37	0.60	0.63	0.73	0.65
电力消费弹性系数	Elasticity Ratio of Electricity Consumption	1.01	0.13	0.92	0.89	0.87	0.80
每万元生产总值能耗(吨标准煤/万元)(可比价)	Energy Consumption Per Unit of GDP (ton of SCE/10000 yuan) (equivalent value)	2.6173	2.4495	2.3480	2.2480	1.7140	1.6444
农业	**Agriculture**						
每亩播种面积农产品产量	Output of Farm Crops Per Mu of Sowning Area						
粮 食(公斤)	Grain(kg)	260	264	261	244	191	236
油 料(公斤)	Oil-bearing Crops(kg)	107	100	102	76	98	106

注：县域经济增加值占GDP比重，是除贵阳市南明区、云岩区、花溪区、乌当区、白云区、小河区，六盘水市钟山区，遵义市红花岗区、汇川区，安顺市西秀区、毕节市七星关区，铜仁市碧江区、万山区等13个区之外的75个县(市、特区)经济总量占88个县(市、区、特区)GDP合计数的比重。

Note:The add value in county economy share of GDP is the proportion of 75 counties economy besides the 13 districts such as Nanming,Yunyan, Huaxi,Wudang,Baiyun,Xiaohe,Zhongshan,Honghuagang,Huichuan,Xixiu,Qixingguan,Bijiang,Wanshan,etc to total GDP of 88 counties.

1–5 续表1 continued

指标	Item	2007	2008	2009	2010	2011	2012
工业(规模以上)	**Industry(above Designated Size)**						
总资产贡献率(%)	Ratio of Total Assets to Industrial Output Value(%)	12.89	12.96	10.69	12.84	14.13	15.97
资本保值增值率(%)	Capital Maintenance and Appreciation Rate (%)	114.86	124.99	106.87	125.32	127.96	125.65
流动资产周转次数(次/年)	Number of Times of Turnover of Circulating Fund (times/year)	2.04	1.92	1.88	1.75	1.92	1.89
成本费用利润率(%)	Ratio of Profits to Industrial Cost(%)	8.10	6.42	6.56	9.04	9.63	11.89
建筑业	**Construction**						
建筑业劳动生产率(元/人)(按增加值计算)	Overall Labour Productivity in Construction(yuan/person) (account by value-added)	25096	28116	70294	89177	98494	141459
技术装备率(元/人)	Value of Machinery Per Laborer (yuan/person)	7531	8248	7398	8232	9982	8148
产值利税率(%)	Ratio of Per-tax Profits to Gross Output Value(%)	4.7	5.8	5.1	5.9	5.9	5.5
交通运输业	**Transportation**						
铁路网密度(公里/万平方公里)	Railway Density(km/10000 sq.km)	114.21	111.37	112.57	113.64	117.50	116.82
公路网密度(公里/万平方公里)	Highway Density(km/10000 sq.km)	6996.15	7116.38	8092.52	8608.12	8958.70	9340.26
邮电通信业	**Postal and Telecommunication Services**						
电话普及率(包括移动电话)(部/百人)	Popularization Rate of Telephone (set/100 persons)	37.31	46.87	57.52	68.90	74.35	83.27
移动电话普及率(部/百人)	Popularization Rate of Mobile Telephone (set/100 persons)	22.96	32.97	44.76	56.46	62.71	72.34
旅游业	**Tourism**						
每一来黔境外旅游者消费支出(美元/人天)	Daily Expenditure of Per Tourists Visiting Guizhou(USD/preson and day)	171.54	169.30	169.12	171.76	168.68	167.13
金融	**Finance**						
金融机构人民币存款余额相当于生产总值比例(%)	Deposit of Financial Institutions as Percentage of GDP(%)	132.7	133.0	150.7	160.0	153.3	153.8
金融机构人民币贷款余额相当于生产总值比例(%)	Loans of Financial Institutions as Percentage of GDP(%)	108.5	100.2	119.0	124.9	120.0	120.8

1-5 续表2 continued

指 标	Item	2007	2008	2009	2010	2011	2012
教育	**Education**						
学龄儿童入学率(%)	Enrollment Rate of School-age Children(%)	98.6	97.2	98.4	97.9	98.6	99.3
初中阶段毛入学率(%)	Enrollment Rate of Primary School Graduates Entering into Junior Secondary Schools(%)	97.5	95.9	98.2	97.6	94.2	97.4
高中阶段毛入学率(%)	Enrollment Rate of Junior secondary School Graduates Entering into Senior secondary Schools(%)	42.2	47.9	53.4	55.0	58.9	62.2
高等教育毛入学率(%)	Enrollment Rate of Senior secondary School Graduates Entering into Institution of Higher Learning(%)	11.5	11.8	18.4	20.0	23.2	25.5
教师负担学生系数(学生/教师)	Student-Teacher Ratio (student/teacher)						
普通高校	Regular Institution of Higher Education	14.25	14.83	15.23	15.89	15.74	16.83
普通高中	Regular Senior Secondary Schools	18.68	18.56	18.51	18.75	19.02	18.59
普通初中	Regular Junior Secondary Schools	19.77	19.56	19.58	19.52	19.23	18.31
小 学	Primary Schools	24.29	23.49	22.94	21.90	20.74	19.20
城乡收入比例	**Urban-rural income ratio**						
城市与农村居民收入比例(以农民人均纯收入＝1)	Ratio of Annual Income of Urban Residents to Rural(rural resident=1)	4.50	4.20	4.28	4.07	3.98	3.93
卫生	**Health Care**						
每万人拥有执业(助理)医师数(人)	Number of Licensed(Assistant) Doctors Per 10000 Persons(person)	11.5	10.7	11.3	12.0	10.4	11.2
每万人拥有医院、卫生院床位数(张)	Number of Beds in Hospitals and Health Centers Per 10000 Persons(bed)	19.5	21.6	25.6	27.8	25.5	30.5
城市建设	**City Construction**						
人均公园绿地面积(平方米)	Per Capita Area of Parks and Green Land (sq.m)	4.23	4.44	4.65	5.33	5.50	6.68
用水普及率(%)	Percentage of Population with Access to Tap Water(%)	79.7	83.2	85.4	86.5	86.9	87.6
燃气普及率(%)	Percentage of Households with Access to Tap Gas(%)	51.1	54.1	54.2	54.5	55.0	55.2
环境、灾害	**Environment and Disaster**						
环保投入相当于生产总值比例(%)	Environment Protection Investment as Percentage to GDP(%)	1.7	1.4	1.8	1.9	1.9	1.5
平均每起环境污染事故直接经济损失(万元)	Average Loss Converted into Cash Per Pollution Accident(10000 yuan)	37.4	1.5	2.5	26.8	64.3	169.3
亿元生产总值生产安全事故死亡人数(人/亿元)	Deaths of Industrial Accidents per Unit of GDP(person/100 million yuan)	0.96	0.73	0.56	0.42	0.29	0.19
平均每起火灾损失(万元)	Average Loss of Per Fire(10000 yuan)	3.69	4.30	3.95	2.71	5.66	5.37
平均每起交通事故损失(万元)	Average Loss of Per Traffic Accident (10000 yuan)	0.81	0.67	0.67	0.68	1.03	1.25

1-6 贵州社会经济主要指标占全国比重

Proportion of Guizhou's Main Economic and Social Indicators to the Whole Country

指 标	Item	全 国 China		贵 州 Guizhou		贵州占全国比重(%) Proportion of Guizhou to China(%)	
		2007	2012	2007	2012	2007	2012
土地面积(万平方公里)	**Area of Territory(10000 sq.km)**	**960**	**960**	**17.62**	**17.62**	**1.8**	**1.8**
人口	**Population**						
年末总人口(万人)	Total Population at the Year-end (10000 persons)	132129	135404	3632	3484	2.7	2.6
就业	**Employment**						
就业人员(万人)	Employees(10000 persons)	75321	76704	1872.64	1825.82	2.5	2.4
非私营单位职工平均工资(元)	Average Wage of Staff and Workers(yuan)	24721	46769	20668	42733	83.6	91.4
国民经济核算	**National Accounting**						
生产总值(亿元)	Gross Domestic Product(100 million yuan)	265810	519322	2884.11	6852.20	1.1	1.3
第一产业	Primary Industry	28627	52377	446.38	891.91	1.6	1.7
第二产业	Secondary Industry	125831	235319	1124.79	2677.54	0.9	1.1
第三产业	Tertiary Industry	111352	231626	1312.94	3282.75	1.2	1.4
人均生产总值(元)	Per Capita Gross Domestic Product(yuan)	20169	38449	7878	19710	39.1	51.3
固定资产投资	**Investment in Fixed Assets**						
全社会固定资产投资(亿元)	Total Investment in Fixed Assets (100 million yuan)	137324	374676	1488.80	5717.80	1.1	1.5
消费	**Consumption**						
社会消费品零售总额(亿元)	Total Retail Sales of Consumer Goods (100 million yuan)	93572	210307	858.15	2027.64	0.9	1.0
对外贸易	**Foreign Trade**						
进出口总额(亿美元)	Total Value of Imports and Exports (USD 100 million)	21766	38668	22.73	66.32	0.1	0.2
#出口	Total Exports	12205	20489	14.65	49.52	0.1	0.2
财政	**Government Finance**						
公共财政收入(亿元)	Local Financial Revenue(100 million yuan)	23573	61077	285.14	1014.05	1.2	1.7
公共财政支出(亿元)	Financial Expenditure (100 million yuan)	38339	106947	795.40	2755.68	2.1	2.6
能源	**Energy**						
一次能源生产总量(万吨标准煤)	Total Production of Primary Energy(10000 tons of SCE)	247279	333300	8480.62	14932.17	3.4	4.5
能源终端消费总量(万吨标准煤)	Consumption of Energy(10000 tons of SCE)	280508	361700	6278.96	9156.04	2.2	2.5
农业	**Agriculture**						
粮食产量(万吨)	Output of Grain(10000 tons)	50160	58958	1101	1080	2.2	1.8
油料产量(万吨)	Output of Oil-bearing Crops (10000 tons)	2569	3437	69.66	87.38	2.7	2.5
工业	**Industry**						
原煤产量(亿吨)	Output of Coal(100 million tons)	26.9	36.5	1.09	1.50	4.0	4.1
发电量(亿千瓦小时)	Output of Electricity (100 million kwh)	32816	48187	1166	1548	3.6	3.2
卷 烟(亿支)	Output of Cigarettes(100 million pieces)	21439	25161	1104	1247	5.1	5.0

注：表中2012年工业产品产量为全部年主营业务收入2000万元及以上工业企业数据。

Note:Output of industrial products in 2012 in the table refer to the data of industrial enterprises that total main business income is 20 million yuan and above.

1-6 续表 continued

指 标	Item	全 国 China		贵 州 Guizhou		贵州占全国比重(%) Proportion of Guizhou to China(%)	
		2007	2012	2007	2012	2007	2012
交通运输业	**Transportation**						
铁路营业里程(万公里)	Length of Railways(10000 km)	7.8	9.8	0.20	0.21	2.6	2.1
公路里程(万公里)	Length of Highways(10000 km)	358	424	12.32	16.45	3.4	3.9
旅客周转量(亿人公里)	Passenger-Kilometers(100 million passenger-km)	21593	33383	369.20	718.22	1.7	2.2
货物周转量(亿吨公里)	Freight Ton-Kilometers(100 million ton-km)	101419	173771	721.26	1177.78	0.7	0.7
邮电通信业	**Post and Telecommunication**						
电信业务总量(亿元)	Business Revenue of Telecommunications (100 million yuan)	18591	12985	283.31	244.11	1.5	1.9
邮政业务总量(亿元)	Business Volume of Post (100 million yuan)	1214	2037	9.08	17.93	0.7	0.9
旅游业	**Tourism**						
入境旅游人数(万人次)	Number of Visitor Arrivals(10000 person-times)	13187	13241	43.00	70.50	0.3	0.5
国内旅游人数(亿人次)	Domestic Tourists(100 million person-times)	16.1	29.6	0.62	2.13	3.9	7.2
国际旅游外汇收入(亿美元)	International Earnings from Tourism (USD 100 million)	419	500	1.29	1.69	0.3	0.3
国内旅游收入(亿元)	Domestic Earnings from Tourism (100 million yuan)	7771	22706	504.04	1849.49	6.5	8.1
金融业	**Finance**						
金融机构人民币存款余额(亿元)	Total Savings Deposit Balance(100 million yuan)	389371	917555	3826.37	10540.06	1.0	1.1
金融机构人民币贷款余额(亿元)	Total Loan Balance(100 million yuan)	261691	629910	3128.63	8274.78	1.2	1.3
教育	**Education**						
普通高等学校(所)	Regular Institutions of Higher Education(unit)	1908	2442	37	49	1.9	2.0
普通高等学校专任教师(万人)	Full-time Teachers of Regular Institutions of Higher Education(10000 persons)	116.8	144.0	1.70	2.28	1.5	1.6
普通高校在校大学生(万人)	Students Enrollment of Regular Institutions of Higher Education(10000 persons)	1884.9	2391.3	24.17	38.38	1.3	1.6
文化	**Culture**						
广播人口覆盖率(%)	Radio Coverage Rate of the Population(%)	95.4	97.5	84.1	88.5	-11.3(百分点)	-9.0(百分点)
电视人口覆盖率(%)	TV Coverage Rate of the Population(%)	96.6	98.2	91.1	93.0	-5.5(百分点)	-5.2(百分点)
卫生	**Health Care**						
医院、卫生院(个)	Number of Hospitals and Health Centers(unit)	19852	23170	1939	2210	9.8	9.5
执业(助理)医师(万人)	Number of Licensed(Assistant) Doctors (10000 persons)	212.3	261.6	4.21	4.92	2.0	1.9
医院、卫生院床位(万张)	Number of Beds in Hospitals and Health Centers(10000 beds)	267.5	416.1	7.14	12.97	2.7	3.1
人民生活	**People's Livelihood**						
城镇居民人均可支配收入(元)	Per Capita Annual Disposable Income of Urban Households(yuan)	13786	24565	10678	18701	77.5	76.1
农村居民人均纯收入(元)	Annual Per Capita Net Income of Rural Residents(yuan)	4140	7917	2374	4753	57.3	60.0

主要统计指标解释

行政区划 指国家对行政区域的划分。根据有关法规规定，我国的行政区域划分如下：(1) 全国分为省、自治区、直辖市；(2) 省、自治区分为自治州、县、自治县、市；(3) 自治州分为县、自治县、市；(4) 县、自治县分为乡、民族乡、镇；(5) 直辖市和较大的市分为区、县；(6) 国家在必要时设立的特别行政区。

国民经济行业分类 自 2012 年定期报表开始使用新的《国民经济行业分类》（GB/T4754-2011）。该分类是由国家统计局组织修订，经国家质检总局和国家标准化委员会批准，于 2011 年 4 月 29 日发布实施。这次修订是在 2002 年分类标准的基础上，参照联合国《国际标准产业分类》修订第四版（ISIC/Rev.4）进行的。修订后的《国民经济行业分类》（GB/T4754-2011）共有门类 20 个，大类 96 个，中类 432 个，小类 1094 个。

企业（单位）登记注册类型 是以在工商行政管理机关登记注册的各类企业为划分对象，以工商行政管理部门对企业登记注册的类型为依据，将企业登记注册类型分为内资企业、港澳台商投资企业和外商投资企业三大类。内资企业包括国有企业、集体企业、股份合作企业、联营企业、有限责任公司、股份有限公司、私营公司和其他企业；港澳台商投资企业和外商投资企业分别包括合资经营企业、合作经营企业、独资经营企业和股份有限公司。对不在工商行政管理部门进行登记注册的行政机关、事业单位和社会团体，主要按其经费来源和管理方式进行划分。

国有企业 指企业全部资产归国家所有，并按《中华人民共和国企业法人登记管理条例》规定登记注册的非公司制的经济组织。不包括有限责任公司中的国有独资公司。

集体企业 指企业资产归集体所有，并按《中华人民共和国企业法人登记管理条例》规定登记注册的经济组织。

股份合作企业 指以合作制为基础，由企业职工共同出资入股，吸收一定比例的社会资产投资组建，实行自主经营，自负盈亏，共同劳动，民主管理，按劳分配与按股分红相结合的一种集体经济组织。

联营企业 指两个及两个以上相同或不同所有制性质的企业法人或事业单位法人，按自愿、平等、互利的原则，共同投资组成的经济组织。联营企业包括国有联营企业、集体联营企业、国有与集体联营企业和其他联营企业。

有限责任公司 指根据《中华人民共和国公司登记管理条例》规定登记注册，由两个以上、五十个以下的股东共同出资，每个股东以其所认缴的出资额对公司承担有限责任，公司以其全部资产对其债务承担责任的经济组织。有限责任公司包括国有独资公司以及其他有限责任公司。

股份有限公司 指根据《中华人民共和国公司登记管理条例》规定登记注册，其全部注册资本由等额股份构成并通过发行股票筹集资本，股东以其认购的股份对公司承担有限责任，公司以其全部资产对其债务承担责任的经济组织。

私营企业 指由自然人投资设立或由自然人控股，以雇佣劳动为基础的营利性经济组织。包括按照《公司法》、《合伙企业法》、《私营企业暂行条例》规定登记注册的私营有限责任公司、私营股份有限公司、私营合伙企业和私营独资企业。

其他内资企业 指上述企业之外的其他内资经济组织。

与港澳台商合资经营企业 指港澳台地区投资者与内地企业依照《中华人民共和国中外合资经营企业法》及有关法律的规定，按合同规定的比例投资设立、分享利润和分担风险的企业。

与港澳台商合作经营企业 指港澳台地区投资者与内地企业依照《中华人民共和国中外合作经营企业法》及有关法律的规定，依照合作合同的约定进行投资或提供条件设立、分配利润和分担风险的企业。

港澳台商独资经营企业 指依照《中华人民共和国外资企业法》及有关法律的规定，在内地由港澳台地区投资者全额投资设立的企业。

港澳台商投资股份有限公司 指根据国家有关规定，经原外经贸部依法批准设立，其中港、澳、台商的股本占公司注册资本的比例达 25% 以上的股份有限公司。凡其中港、澳、台商的股本占公司注册资本的比例小于 25% 的，属于内资企业中的股份有限公司。

中外合资经营企业 指外国企业或外国人与中国内地企业依照《中华人民共和国中外合资经营企业法》及有关法律的规定，按合同规定的比例投资设立、分享利润和分担风险的企业。

中外合作经营企业 指外国企业或外国人与中国内地企业依照《中华人民共和国中外合作经营企业法》及有关法律的规定，依照合作合同的约定进行投资或提供条件设立、分配利润和分担风险的企业。

外资企业 指依照《中华人民共和国外资企业法》及有关法律的规定，在中国内地由外国投资者全额投资设立的企业。

外商投资股份有限公司 指根据国家有关规定，经原外经贸部依法批准设立，其中外资的股本占公司注册资本的比例达 25% 以上的股份有限公司。凡其中外资股本占公司注册资本的比例小于 25% 的，属于内资企业中的股份有限公司。

行政机关、事业单位和社会团体 参照企业登记注册类型，主要按其经费来源和管理方式划分。具体规定如下:

(1) 行政机关：包括国家机关和政党机关，原则上均列为“国有”。但有特殊规定的，如供销社等，则列为“集体”

(2) 事业单位：包括经国家机构编制部门和有关业务主管部门批准成立的各类事业单位，不包括实行企业化管理的事业单位。事业单位的划分办法如下:

①由国家财政预算拨款或列入财政预算外资金管理以及经费主要来源于国有主管部门或国有上级单位的事业单位，列为“国有”。

②经费主要来源于集体单位的事业单位，列为“集体”。

③公民个人（或个人合伙）开办的事业单位，列为“私营”。

④上述以外的其他事业单位，如果其经费来源不明确，按管理方式进行归类。

(3) 社会团体：包括经民政部门批准成立以及未纳入社会团体管理条例范围的工会、妇联等各类社会团体。社会团体的划分办法如下:

①未纳入民政部社会团体管理条例范围的工会、妇联、共青团、青联、工商联、科协、侨联等社会团体，国家拨款设立的基金会或基金管理组织以及经费主要来源于国有业务主管部门或国有上级单位的社会团体，列为“国有”。

②经费主要来源于集体单位的社会团体，列为“集体”。

③公民个人（或个人合伙）开办的社会团体，划为“私营”。

④上述以外的其他社会团体，如果其经费来源不明确，改按管理方式进行归类。

Explanatory Notes on Main Statistical Indicators

Divisions of Administrative Areas refers to the division of administrative areas by the state. The relative laws stipulate that: 1) The whole country is divided into provinces, autonomous regions and municipalities directly under the central government; 2) Provinces and autonomous regions are divided into autonomous prefectures, counties, autonomous counties and cities; 3) Autonomous prefectures are divided into counties, autonomous counties and cities; 4) Counties and autonomous counties are divided into townships, nationality townships and towns; 5) Municipalities and large cities are divided into districts and counties, 6) The state shall, when necessary, establish special administrative regions.

Industrial Classification of the National Economy The new Industrial Classification of the National Economy (GB/T 4754-2011) is introduced starting from the compilation of 2012 annual statistics. The revision, based on the 2002 classification, was organized by the National Bureau of Statistics taking into consideration of the International Standards of the Industrial Classification of All Economic Activities (ISIC/Rev.4) of the United Nations. The new Classification was promulgated by the National Administration of Quality Supervision, Inspection and Quarantine and State Committee for Standardization on April 29, 2011. The revised version of the Industrial Classification of the National Economy (GB/T 4754-2002) is composed of 20 major divisions, 96 divisions, 432 major groups and 1094 groups.

Registration Status of Enterprises Enterprises are classified into 3 categories, namely domestic-funded enterprises, enterprises with investment from Hong Kong, Macau and Taiwan, and enterprises with foreign investment, in the light of the registration status of an enterprise in industrial and commercial administration agencies. Domestic-funded enterprises include state-owned enterprises, collective-owned enterprises, cooperative enterprises, joint ownership enterprises, limited liability corporations, share-holding corporations Ltd., private enterprises and other enterprises. Included in the enterprises with investment from Hong Kong, Macau and Taiwan and enterprises with foreign investment are joint-venture enterprises, cooperative enterprises, sole investment enterprises and share-holding corporations Ltd. For government agencies, institutions and social organizations which are not requested to be registered in industrial and commercial administration agencies, they are classified mainly by their sources of funds and way of management.

State-owned Enterprises refer to non-corporation economic units where the entire assets are owned by the state and which have registered in accordance with the Regulation of the Peoples Republic of China on the Management of Registration of Corporate Enterprises. Excluded from this category are sole state-funded corporations in the limited liability corporations.

Collective-owned Enterprises refer to economic units where the assets are owned collectively and which have registered in accordance with the Regulation of the Peoples Republic of China on the Management of Registration of Corporate Enterprises.

Cooperatve Enterprises refer to a form of collective economic units (enterprises) where capitals come mainly from employees as their shares, with certain proportion of capital from the outside, where production is organized on the basis of independent operation, independent accounting for profits and losses, joint work, democratic management, and a distribution system that integrates remuneration according to work with dividend according to capital share.

Joint Ownership Enterprises refer to economic units established by two or more corporate enterprises or corporate institutions of the same or different ownership, through joint investment on the basis of equality, voluntary participation and mutual benefits. They include state joint ownership enterprises, collective joint ownership enterprises, joint state-collective enterprises, other joint ownership enterprises.

Limited Liability Corporations refer to economic units established with investment from 2-50 investors and registered in accordance with the Regulation of the Peoples Republic of China on the Management of Registration of Corporations, each investor bearing limited liability to the corporation depending on its share of investment, and the corporation bearing liability to its debt to the maximum of its total assets. Limited liability corporations include exclusive state-funded limited liability corporations and other limited liability corporations.

Share-holding Corporations Ltd. refer to economic units registered in accordance with the Regulation of the Peoples Republic of China on the Management of Registration of Corporations, with total registered capitals divided into equal shares and raised through issuing stocks. Each investor bears limited liability to the corporation depending on the holding of shares, and the corporation bears liability to its debt to the maximum of its total assets.

Private Enterprises refer to profit-making economic units invested and established by natural persons, or controlled by natural persons using employed labour. Included in this category are private limited liability corporations, private share-holding corporations Ltd., private partnership enterprises and private-funded enterprises registered in accordance with the Corporation Law, Partnership Enterprises Law and Interim Regulations on Private Enterprises .

Other Domestic-funded Enterprises refer to domestic-funded economic units other than those mentioned above.

Joint-venture Enterprises with Funds from Hong Kong, Macau and Taiwan refer to enterprises jointly established by investors from Hong Kong, Macau and Taiwan with enterprises in the mainland of China in accordance with the Law of the Peoples Republic of China on Sino-foreign Joint Venture Enterprises and other relevant laws, where the share of investment, profits and risks is stipulated in the contract.

Cooperative Enterprises with Funds from Hong Kong Macau and Taiwan established by investors from Hong Kong, Macau and Taiwan with enterprises in the mainland of China in accordance with the Law of the Peoples Republic of China on Sino-foreign Cooperative Enterprises and other relevant laws, where the investment or provision of facilities, and the share of profits and risks is stipulated in the cooperative contract.

Enterprises with Sole (exclusive) Investment from Hong Kong, Macau and Taiwan refer to enterprises established in the mainland of China with exclusive investment from investors from Hong Kong, Macau and Taiwan in accordance with the Law of the Peoples Republic of China on Foreign-Funded Enterprises and other relevant laws.

Share-holding Corporations Ltd. with Investment from Hong Kong, Macau and Taiwan refer to share-holding corporations Ltd. established with the approval former Ministry of Foreign Trade and Economic Relations in line with relevant state regulations, where the share of investment from Hong Kong, Macau or Taiwan businessmen exceeds 25% of the total registered capital of the corporation. In case the share of investment from Hong Kong, Macau or Taiwan is less than 25% of the total registered capital, the enterprise is to be classified as domestic-funded share-holding corporation Ltd.

Joint-venture Enterprises with Foreign Investment refer to enterprises jointly established by foreign enterprises or foreigners with enterprises in the mainland of China in accordance with the Law of the Peoples Republic of China on Sino-foreign Joint Venture Enterprises and other relevant laws, where the share of investment, profits and risks is stipulated in the contract.

Cooperation Enterprises with Foreign Investment refer to enterprises jointly established by foreign enterprises or foreigners with enterprises in the mainland of China in accordance with the Law of the Peoples Republic of China on Sino-foreign Cooperative Enterprises and other relevant laws, where the investment or provision of facilities, and the share of profits and risks is stipulated in the cooperative contract.

Enterprises with Sole (exclusive) Foreign Investment refer to enterprises established in the mainland of China with exclusive investment from foreign investors in accordance with the Law of the Peoples Republic of China on Foreign-Funded Enterprises and other relevant laws.

Share-holding Corporations Ltd. with Foreign Investment refer to share-holding corporations Ltd. established with the approval former Ministry of Foreign Trade and Economic Relations in line with relevant state regulations, where the share of investment from foreign investors exceeds 25% of the total registered capital of the corporation. In case the share of foreign investment is less than 25% of the total registered capital, the enterprise is to be classified as domestic-funded share-holding corporation Ltd.

Government Agencies, Institutions and Social Organizations are classified into following categories by source of funds and way of management taking reference of the registration status of enterprises:

(1) Government agencies: include state and party agencies, classified in principle as "state-owned". There are exceptions, such as supply and marketing cooperatives which are classified as "collective".

(2) Institutions: include institutions of various types established with the approval by organization and staffing departments of the government, but exclude institutions where enterprise management system is introduced. Institutions are further classified as follows:

(a) Institutions whose main budget is listed in the government budget appropriations or extra-budget funds, or allocated from the budget of their competent government agencies. Such institutions are classified as "state-owned".

(b) Institutions whose budget mainly comes from collective units. Such institutions are classified as "collective".

(c) Social organizations established by individual or a group of citizens, which are classified as "private".

(d) Institutions other than those mentioned above whose source of budget is not clear. Such institutions are classified by way of management.

(3) Social organizations: include social organizations established with the approval from the Ministry of Civil Affairs, and organizations that are not covered by social organization management regulations such as trade unions, women's federations etc. Social organizations are further classified as follows:

(a) Social organizations that are not covered by social organization management regulations of the Ministry of Civil Affairs such as trade unions, women's federations, communist youth leagues, youth associations, industrial and commerce associations, scientists associations, overseas Chinese associations, etc., foundations and fund management organizations established with funds from the state, and social organizations whose funds mainly come from the budget of their competent government agencies. Such institutions are classified as "state-owned".

(b) Social organizations whose budget mainly comes from collective units. Such institutions are classified as "collective".

(c) Social organizations established by individual or a group of citizens, which are classified as "private".

(d) Social organizations other than those mentioned above whose source of budget is not clear. Such organizations are classified by way of management.

2 Two

国民经济核算

National Accounts

2-1 全省生产总值

Gross Domestic Product

单位：亿元 (100 million yuan)

指　标	Item	2007	2008	2009	2010	2011	2012	2012年比2011年增长(%) Increase Rate in 2012 over 2011(%)
地区生产总值	**Gross Domestic Product**	**2884.11**	**3561.56**	**3912.68**	**4602.16**	**5701.84**	**6852.20**	**13.6**
第一产业	Primary Industry	446.38	539.19	550.27	625.03	726.22	891.91	8.6
第二产业	Secondary Industry	1124.79	1370.03	1476.62	1800.06	2194.33	2677.54	16.8
工　业	Industry	978.86	1195.30	1252.67	1516.87	1829.20	2217.06	15.6
建筑业	Construction	145.93	174.73	223.95	283.19	365.13	460.48	23.3
第三产业	Tertiary Industry	1312.94	1652.34	1885.79	2177.07	2781.29	3282.75	12.1
交通运输、仓储和邮政业	Transport, Storage and Post	282.04	370.65	399.77	480.32	590.91	687.45	13.8
批发和零售业	Wholesale and Retail Trade	198.79	248.83	293.53	367.52	448.77	514.49	10.9
住宿和餐饮业	Hotel and Catering Services	90.09	130.41	153.41	180.73	224.40	266.58	7.8
金融业	Financial Intermediation	122.25	151.55	194.44	231.51	297.27	365.87	14.3
房地产业	Real Estate	93.19	104.81	136.15	139.64	160.30	176.75	8.4
其他服务业	Other Services	526.58	646.09	708.49	777.35	1059.64	1271.61	12.5
营利性服务业	For-profit Services	168.46	213.55	250.39	283.45	398.09	467.57	12.0
非营利性服务业	Non-profit Services	358.12	432.54	458.10	493.90	661.55	804.04	12.8
人均生产总值(元)	**Per Capita Gross Domestic Product(yuan)**	**7878**	**9855**	**10971**	**13119**	**16413**	**19710**	**13.5**

注：人均生产总值及增速按人口普查修订后常住半年人口计算(以下相关表同)。

Note: per capital GDP and its growth ratewere caculated based on permanent population in half a year scope which had been adjusted on the basis of the National PopulationCensus(the related tables in the chapter are the same).

2–2 全省生产总值构成

Composition of Gross Domestic Product

单位：% (%)

指　　标	Item	2007	2008	2009	2010	2011	2012
地区生产总值	**Gross Domestic Product**	**100.0**	**100.0**	**100.0**	**100.0**	**100.0**	**100.0**
第一产业	Primary Industry	15.5	15.1	14.1	13.6	12.7	13.0
第二产业	Secondary Industry	39.0	38.5	37.7	39.1	38.5	39.1
工　业	Industry	33.9	33.6	32.0	33.0	32.1	32.4
建筑业	Construction	5.1	4.9	5.7	6.1	6.4	6.7
第三产业	Tertiary Industry	45.5	46.4	48.2	47.3	48.8	47.9
交通运输、仓储和邮政业	Transport Storage and Post	9.8	10.4	10.2	10.4	10.4	10.0
批发和零售业	Wholesale and Retail Trade	6.9	7.0	7.5	8.0	7.9	7.5
住宿和餐饮业	Hotel and Catering Services	3.1	3.7	3.9	3.9	3.9	3.9
金融业	Financial Intermediation	4.2	4.3	5.0	5.0	5.2	5.3
房地产业	Real Estate	3.2	2.9	3.5	3.0	2.8	2.6
其他服务业	Other services	18.3	18.1	18.1	17.0	18.6	18.6
营利性服务业	For-profit Services	5.8	6.0	6.4	6.2	7.0	6.8
非营利性服务业	Non-profit Services	12.5	12.1	11.7	10.8	11.6	11.8

2–3 全省生产总值(按支出法计算)

Gross Domestic Product(Accounted by Expenditure Approach)

指　标	Item	2007	2008	2009	2010	2011	2012	2012年比2011年增长(%) Increase Rate in 2012 over 2011(%)
绝对数(亿元)	**Absolute Value(100 million yuan)**							
地区生产总值	**Gross Domestic Product**	**2884.11**	**3561.56**	**3912.68**	**4602.16**	**5701.84**	**6852.20**	**13.6**
最终消费	Final Consumption Expenditure	2087.54	2354.11	2603.31	2931.13	3438.71	3950.64	11.2
居民消费	Household Consumption	1560.80	1763.74	1945.99	2181.37	2566.78	2910.93	9.3
农村居民	Rural Households	553.35	623.42	689.41	770.06	908.51	994.67	8.8
城镇居民	Urban Households	1007.45	1140.32	1256.58	1411.31	1658.27	1916.26	9.5
政府消费	Government Consumption	526.74	590.37	657.32	749.76	871.93	1039.71	16.8
资本形成总额	Gross Capital Formation	1442.35	1782.31	2100.53	2575.27	3229.30	4164.37	20.9
固定资本形成总额	Gross Fixed Capital Formation	1363.42	1691.89	2046.84	2510.39	3147.46	4067.26	21.0
库存增加	Changes in Inventories	78.93	90.42	53.69	64.88	81.84	97.11	19.8
货物和服务净出口	Net Outflow of Goods and Services	-645.78	-574.86	-791.16	-904.24	-966.17	-1262.81	
构成(%)	**Composition(%)**							
以最终消费为100	Final Consumption Expenditure=100							
居民消费	Household Consumption	74.8	74.9	74.8	74.4	74.6	73.7	
政府消费	Government Consumption	25.2	25.1	25.2	25.6	25.4	26.3	
以居民消费为100	Household Consumption=100							
农村居民	Rural Households	35.5	35.3	35.4	35.3	35.4	34.2	
城镇居民	Urban Households	64.5	64.7	64.6	64.7	64.6	65.8	
最终消费率(%)	**Final Consumption Rate(%)**	**72.4**	**66.1**	**66.5**	**63.7**	**60.3**	**57.7**	
资本形成率(%)	**Capital Formation Rate(%)**	**50.0**	**50.0**	**53.7**	**56.0**	**56.6**	**60.8**	
城乡居民人均消费水平比(农村居民=1)	**Urban/Rural Consumption Ratio (rural households=1)**	**4.72**	**4.55**	**4.36**	**3.92**	**3.49**	**3.47**	

注：表中居民消费按常住半年人口计算城乡居民人均消费水平比根据第六次人口普查数据进行修订，2007–2010年居民消费数据根据新农合数据进行修订。

Note:The Data of Household Consumption in the table are calculated based on permanent population in half a year scope.Urban/Rural Consumption ratio is adjusted according to the result of the sixth National population census.The year 2007 to 2010,the data of household consumption were adjusted according to the data of New cooperatrie Medical.

2-4 三次产业对全省生产总值增长的拉动

Contribution of the Three Strata of Industry to GDP Growth

单位：百分点 (percentage points)

指　标	Item	2007	2008	2009	2010	2011	2012
地区生产总值	**Gross Domestic Product**	**14.8**	**11.3**	**11.4**	**12.8**	**15.0**	**13.6**
第一产业	Primary Industry	0.6	1.0	0.6	0.6	0.2	1.1
第二产业	Secondary Industry	5.4	3.3	4.8	6.6	7.0	6.7
#工　业	Industry	5.0	3.1	3.5	5.3	5.9	5.3
第三产业	Tertiary Industry	8.8	7.0	6.0	5.6	7.8	5.8

2-5 三次产业贡献率

Share of the Contributions of the Three Strata of Industry to the Increase of the GDP

单位：% (%)

指　标	Item	2007	2008	2009	2010	2011	2012
地区生产总值	**Gross Domestic Product**	**100.0**	**100.0**	**100.0**	**100.0**	**100.0**	**100.0**
第一产业	Primary Industry	3.8	9.2	5.5	5.0	1.1	7.6
第二产业	Secondary Industry	36.6	29.2	41.8	51.1	46.8	49.6
#工　业	Industry	33.7	27.0	30.8	41.6	39.2	38.7
第三产业	Tertiary Industry	59.6	61.6	52.7	43.9	52.1	42.8

主要统计指标解释

国内生产总值（GDP） 指一个国家所有常住单位在一定时期内生产的全部最终产品和服务的价值总和。国内生产总值有三种表现形态，即价值形态、收入形态和产品形态。从价值形态看，它是所有常住单位在一定时期内生产的全部产品和服务价值减去同期投入的全部产品和服务价值的差额，即所有常住单位的增加值之和；从收入形态看，它是所有常住单位在一定时期内的生产活动所形成的原始收入之和；从产品形态看，它是所有常住单位在一定时期内最终使用的产品和服务减去进口的产品和服务的价值总和。在实际核算中，国内生产总值有三种计算方法，即生产法、收入法和支出法。三种方法分别从不同的方面反映国内生产总值及其构成。

对于一个地区来说，称为地区生产总值。

三次产业 三次产业的划分是世界上较为常用的产业结构分类，但各国的划分不尽一致。我国的三次产业划分是:

第一产业是指农业、林业、畜牧业、渔业。

第二产业是指采矿业（不含开采辅助活动），制造业（不含金属制品、机械和设备修理业），电力、热力、燃气及水的生产和供应业，建筑业。

第三产业是指除第一、二产业以外的其他行业。

劳动者报酬 指劳动者因从事生产活动所获得的全部报酬。包括劳动者获得的各种形式的工资、奖金和津贴，既包括货币形式的，也包括实物形式的，还包括劳动者所享受的公费医疗和医药卫生费、上下班交通补贴、单位支付的社会保险费、住房公积金等。

生产税净额 指生产税减生产补贴后的余额。生产税指政府对生产单位从事生产、销售和经营活动以及因从事生产活动使用某些生产要素（如固定资产、土地、劳动力）所征收的各种税、附加费和规费。生产补贴与生产税相反，指政府对生产单位的单方面转移支出，因此视为负生产税，包括政策亏损补贴、价格补贴等。

固定资产折旧 指一定时期内为弥补固定资产损耗按照规定的固定资产折旧率提取的固定资产折旧，或按国民经济核算统一规定的折旧率虚拟计算的固定资产折旧。它反映了固定资产在当期生产中的转移价值。各类企业和企业化管理的事业单位的固定资产折旧是指实际计提的折旧费；不计提折旧的政府机关、非企业化管理的事业单位和居民住房的固定资产折旧是按照统一规定的折旧率和固定资产原值计算的虚拟折旧。原则上，固定资产折旧应按固定资产当期的重置价值计算，但是目前我国尚不具备对全社会固定资产进行重估价的基础，所以暂时只能采用上述办法。

营业盈余 指常住单位创造的增加值扣除劳动者报酬、生产税净额和固定资产折旧后的余额。

支出法国内（地区）生产总值 是从最终使用的角度反映一个国家（或地区）一定时期内生产活动最终成果的一种方法，包括最终消费支出、资本形成总额及货物和服务净出口三部分。计算公式为:

支出法国内（地区）生产总值 = 最终消费支出 + 资本形成总额 + 货物和服务净出口

最终消费支出 指常住单位为满足物质、文化和精神生活的需要，从本国经济领土和国外购买的货物和服务的价值。它不包括非常住单位在本国经济领土内的消费支出。最终消费支出分为居民消费支出和政府消费支出。

居民消费支出 指常住住户在一定时期内对于货物和服务的全部最终消费支出。居民消费支出除了直接以货币形式购买的货物和服务的消费支出外，还包括以其他方式获得的货物和服务的消费支出，即所谓的虚拟消费支出。居民虚拟消费支出包括如下几种类型：单位以实物报酬及实物转移的形式提供给居民的货物和服务；住户生产并由本住户消费了的货物和服务，其中的服务仅指住户的自有住房服务和付酬的家庭雇员提供的家庭和个人服务；金融机构提供的金融中介服务，保险结构提供的保险服务。

政府消费支出 指政府部门为全社会提供的公共服务的消费支出和免费或以较低的价格向居民住户提供的货物和服务的支出，主要包括行政管理、卫生文教、国防支出等。

资本形成总额 指常住单位在一定时期内新形成的固定资产和增加的库存存货的价值，包括固定资本形成总额和存货增加两部分。

固定资本形成总额 指生产者在一定时期内获得的固定资产减处置的固定资产的价值总额。固定资产是通过生产活动生产出来的，且其使用年限在一年以上、单位价值在规定标准以上的资产，不包括自然资产。可分为有形固定资本形成总额和无形固定资本形成总额。有形固定资本形成总额主要包括住宅、非住宅建筑物、机器设备的购置价值、土地改良支出、大牲畜和新增经济林价值。无形固定资本形成总额包括矿藏的勘探、计算机软件等获得减处置。

存货增加　指常住单位在一定时期内存货实物量变动的市场价值，即期末价值减期初价值的差额，再扣除当期由于价格变动而产生的持有收益。存货增加可以是正值，也可以是负值，正值表示存货比基期上升，负值表示存货比基期下降。存货包括生产单位购进的原材料、燃料和储备物资等存货，以及生产单位生产的产成品、在制品和半成品等存货。

货物和服务净出口　指货物和服务出口减货物和服务进口的差额。出口包括常住单位向非常住单位出售或无偿转让的各种货物和服务的价值；进口包括常住单位从非常住单位购买或无偿得到的各种货物和服务的价值。由于服务活动的提供与使用同时发生，一般把常住单位从非常住单位得到的服务作为进口，非常住单位从常住单位得到的服务作为出口。货物的出口和进口价值都按离岸价格计算，服务业出口和进口价值按交易发生时的市场价格计算。

Explanatory Notes on Main Statistical Indicators

Gross Domestic Product (GDP) refers to the final products and services produced by all resident units in a country (or a region) during a certain period of time. Gross domestic product is expressed in three different perspectives, namely value, income, and products respectively. GDP in its value perspective refers to the total value of all goods and services produced by all resident units during a certain period of time, minus the total value of input of goods and services of the nature of non-fixed assets; in other words, it is the sum of the value-added of all resident units. GDP from the perspective of income includes the primary income created by all resident units and distributed to resident and non-resident units. GDP from the perspective of products refers to the value of all goods and services for final demand by all resident units plus the net exports of goods and services during a given period of time. In the practice of national accounting, gross domestic product is calculated from three approaches, namely production approach, income approach and expenditure approach, which reflect gross domestic product and its composition from different angles.

For a region, it is called as Gross Regional Product.

Three Strata of Industry Classification of economic activities into three strata of industry is a common practice in the world, although the grouping varies to some extent from country to country. In China economic activities are categorized into the following three strata of industry:

Primary industry refers to agriculture, forestry, animal husbandry and fishery .

Secondary industry refers to mining and quarrying(excluding mining support activities), manufacturing(excluding metal products, machinery and equipment repair industry), production and supply of electricity, heat, gas and water, and construction.

Tertiary industry refers to all other economic activities not included in the primary or secondary industries.

Compensation of Employees refers to the total payment of various forms to employees for the productive activities they are engaged in. It includes wages, bonuses and allowances, which the employees earn in cash or in kind. It also includes the free medical services provided to the employees and the medicine expenses, transport subsidies and social insurance, and housing fund paid by the employers.

Net Taxes on Production refers to taxes on production less subsidies on production. The taxes on production refers to the various taxes, extra charges and fees levied on the production units on their production, sale and business activities as well as on the use of some factors of production, such as fixed assets, land and labour in the production activities they are engaged in. In contrast to taxes on production, subsidies on production refer to the unilateral government transfer to the production units and are therefore regarded as negative taxes on production. They include subsidies on the loss due to implementation of government policies, price subsidies, etc.

Depreciation of Fixed Assets refers to the depreciation of fixed assets in a given period, drawn in accordance with the stipulated depreciation rate for the purpose of compensating the wear-and-tear loss of the fixed assets or the depreciation of fixed assets imputed in accordance with the stipulated unified depreciation rate in the national economic accounting system. It reflects the value of transfer of the fixed assets in the production of the current period. The depreciation of fixed assets in various enterprises and institutions managed as enterprises refers to the depreciation expenses actually drawn. In government agencies and institutions not managed as enterprises which do not draw the depreciation expenses, as well as for the houses of residents, the depreciation of fixed assets is the imputed depreciation, which is calculated in accordance with the stipulated unified depreciation rate. In principle, the depreciation of fixed assets should be calculated on the basis of the re-purchased value of the fixed assets. However, currently the conditions in China do not facilitate the revaluation of all the fixed assets. Therefore, only the above-mentioned methods can be adopted at present.

Operating Surplus refers to the balance of the value added created by the resident units after deducting the labourers remuneration, net taxes on production and the depreciation of fixed assets.

GDP by Expenditure Approach refers to the method of measuring the final results of production activities of a country (region) during a given period from the perspective of final uses. It includes final consumption expenditure, gross capital formation and net export of goods and services. The formula for computation is.:

GDP by expenditure approach = final consumption expenditure + gross capital formation + net export of goods and services

Final Consumption Expenditure refers to the total expenditure of resident units for purchases of goods and services from both the domestic economic territory and abroad to meet the needs of material, cultural and spiritual life. It does not include the expenditure of non-resident units on consumption in the economic territory of the country. The final consumption expenditure is broken down into household consumption expenditure and government consumption expenditure.

Household Consumption Expenditure refers to the total expenditure of resident households on the final consumption of goods and services. In addition to the consumption of goods and services bought by the households directly with money, the household consumption expenditure also includes expenditure on goods and services obtained by the households in other ways, i.e. the so-called imputed consumption expenditure, which includes the following: (a) the goods and services provided to households by employers in the form of payment in kind and transfer in kind; (b) goods and services produced and consumed by the households themselves, in which the services refer to the owner-occupied housing and services offered by payed family employees; (c) financial intermediate services provided by financial institution;(d) insurance services provided by the insurance structure.

Government Consumption Expenditure refers to the consumption expenditure spent for the provision of public services provided by the government to the whole country and the net expenditure on the goods and services provided by the government to households free of charge or at reduced prices, including administration, health and educational, education, expenditure on national defense, etc.

Gross Capital Formation refers to the newly formed fixed assets and increased the net value of inventory during a given period, thus including gross fixed capital formation and changes in inventories.

Gross Fixed Capital Formation refers to the value of acquisitions less those disposals of fixed assets during a given period. Fixed assets are the assets produced through production activities with unit value above a specified amount and which could be used for over one year. Natural assets are not included.Gross fixed capital formation can be categorized into total tangible fixed capital formation and total intangible fixed capital formation. Total tangible fixed capital formation includes the value of the construction projects and installation projects completed and the equipment, apparatus and instruments purchased (less those disposed) as well as the value of land improved, the value of draught animals, breeding stock and animals for milk, for wool and for recreational purposes and the newly increased forest with economic value. Total intangible fixed capital formation includes the prospecting of minerals and the acquisition of computer software minus the disposal of them.

Changes in Inventories refers to the market value of the change in the physical volume of inventory of resident units during a given period, i.e. the difference between the values at the beginning and at the end of the period minus the gains due to the change in prices. The changes in inventories can have a positive or a negative value. A positive value indicates an increase in inventory while a negative value indicates a decrease in inventory. The inventory includes raw materials, fuels and reserve materials purchased by the production units as well as the inventory of finished products, semi-finished products and work-in-progress.

Net Export of Goods and Services refers to the exports of goods and services subtracting the imports of goods and services. Exports include the value of various goods and services sold or gratuitously transferred by resident units to non-resident units. Imports include the value of various goods and services purchased or gratuitously acquired resident units from non-resident units. Because the provision of services and the use of them happen simultaneously, the acquisition of services by resident units from abroad is usually treated as import while the acquisition of services by non-resident units in this country is usually treated as export. The exports and imports of goods are calculated at FOB.

3

Three

人 口

Population

3-1 历次人口普查主要指标

Main Indicators on National Population Census in 1953,1964,1982,1990,2000 and 2010

单位：万人　　(10000 persons)

指标名称	Item	第一次(1953年) The First	第二次(1964年) The Second	第三次(1982年) The Third	第四次(1990年) The Forth	第五次(2000年) The Fifth	第六次(2010年) The Sixth
总人口	**Total Population**	**1503.73**	**1714.05**	**2855.29**	**3239.11**	**3524.77**	**3474.65**
按城镇、乡村分	**Grouped by Residence**						
城镇人口	Urban population	109.91	203.55	540.22	623.17	844.51	1174.78
乡村人口	Rural population	1393.82	1510.51	2315.07	2615.94	2680.25	2299.87
城镇人口比重（%）	The proportion of urban population(%)	7.31	11.88	18.92	19.24	23.96	33.81
按男女分	**Grouped by Male and Female**						
男	Male	759.80	868.48	1464.08	1676.88	1846.45	1795.15
女	Female	743.93	845.57	1391.21	1562.22	1678.32	1679.50
性别比(以女性为100)	Sex Ratio(female=100)	102.13	102.71	105.24	107.34	110.02	106.89
人口年平均增长率（%）	The growth rate of Annual Average Population(%)		1.32	2.89	1.59	0.82	-0.14
家庭总户数（万户）	Total Number of Household (10000 households)	340.15	390.96	565.93	721.04	923.94	1038.96
户均规模（人/户）	Average Family Size(person/household)	4.42	4.38	4.93	4.41	3.74	3.24
人口自然变动（‰）	**Natural Change of Population(‰)**						
出生率	Birth Rate	38.43	52.62	24.81	23.09	20.59	13.96
死亡率	Death Rate	17.61	20.66	7.60	7.90	7.53	6.55
自然增长率	Natural Growth Rate	20.82	31.96	17.21	15.19	13.06	7.41
年龄结构（%）	**Age Composition (%)**						
0-14岁	Aged 0-14	37.88	38.82	40.88	32.68	30.17	25.22
15-64岁	Aged 15-64	58.52	58.42	54.45	62.71	63.87	66.21
65岁及以上	Aged 65 and Over	3.59	2.76	4.66	4.61	5.97	8.57
民族	**Population by Ethnicity**						
汉族	Han	1109.84	1312.89	2112.95	2114.88	2191.17	2219.85
占总人口比重（%）	% to Total Population(%)	73.81	76.61	74.00	65.29	62.16	63.89
年均增长率（%）	Annual average growth rate(%)		0.37	-0.35	-1.24	-0.49	0.27
少数民族	Minority	393.89	401.16	742.35	1124.23	1333.60	1254.80
占总人口比重（%）	% to Total Population(%)	26.19	23.39	26.00	34.71	37.84	36.11
年均增长率（%）	Annual average growth rate(%)		-1.12	1.06	2.93	0.87	-0.46
受教育程度	**Education Attainments**						
小　学	Primary School		352.71	822.65	1210.75	1535.30	1368.07
初　中	Junior Secondary School		53.80	325.86	475.78	727.48	1035.07
高　中	Senior Secondary School		13.38	84.72	127.50	199.67	253.02
大专以上	Junior College and Above		3.96	11.09	25.06	67.49	183.88
文盲人口	Illiterate Population			1202.24	969.11	598.58	303.85
文盲率（%）	Illiterate Rate(%)			42.11	29.92	16.98	8.74
每十万人口拥有的各种受教育程度人口（人）	**Population with Various Education Attainments Per 100000 Persons (person)**						
大专及以上	Junior College and Above				774	1915	5292
高中/中专	Senior Secondary School and Technical Secondary School				3973	5665	7282
初　中	Junior Secondary School				14688	20639	29789
小　学	Primary School				37379	43557	39373

注：表中数据来源于历次人口普查公报。

Note:Data in this table come from the communique of the six national population censuses.

3-2 第六次人口普查各民族人口数
Population of all ethnic groups on the Sixth National Population Census

单位：万人 (10000 persons)

指标名称	Item	第六次人口普查(2010年)
总人口	Total Population	3474.86
男	Male	1790.55
女	Female	1684.31
汉族	Han	2234.42
男	Male	1151.79
女	Female	1082.63
蒙古族	Mongolian	4.16
男	Male	2.32
女	Female	1.84
回族	Hui	18.48
男	Male	9.50
女	Female	8.98
苗族	Miao	396.84
男	Male	204.09
女	Female	192.75
彝族	Yi	83.45
男	Male	42.96
女	Female	40.49
壮族	Zhuang	5.26
男	Male	2.65
女	Female	2.61
布依族	Bouyei	251.06
男	Male	127.11
女	Female	123.95
满族	Manchu	2.31
男	Male	1.19
女	Female	1.12
侗族	Dong	143.19
男	Male	75.02
女	Female	68.17
瑶族	Yao	4.09
男	Male	2.14
女	Female	1.95
白族	Bai	17.95
男	Male	9.59
女	Female	8.36
土家族	Tujia	143.70
男	Male	73.65
女	Female	70.05
畲族	She	3.66
男	Male	1.91
女	Female	1.75
水族	Shui	34.87
男	Male	18.03
女	Female	16.84
仫佬族	Mulam	2.50
男	Male	1.33
女	Female	1.17
羌族	Qiang	0.16
男	Male	0.09
女	Female	0.07
毛南族	Maonan	2.73
男	Male	1.42
女	Female	1.31
仡佬族	Gelao	49.52
男	Male	25.89
女	Female	23.62
未定族称人们共同体	Undetermined called People Community	61.28
男	Male	32.01
女	Female	29.27

注：表中数据来源于第六次人口普查机器汇总数。
Note:Data in this table are obtained from the Sixth Population Census.

3-3 常住人口(半年口径)

Permanent Resident Population (at least half a year)

单位：万人 (10000 persons)

指 标	Item	2007	2008	2009	2010	2011	2012
年末总人口	**Total Population at the Year-end**	**3632**	**3596**	**3537**	**3479**	**3469**	**3484**
按城镇、乡村分	Grouped by Residence						
城 镇	Urban	1025.68	1046.79	1057.21	1176.25	1212.76	1268.52
乡 村	Rural	2606.32	2549.21	2479.79	2302.75	2256.24	2215.48
按性别分	Grouped by Sex						
男	Male	1879.70	1868.73	1827.56	1797.43	1801.21	1818.61
女	Female	1752.30	1727.27	1709.44	1681.57	1667.79	1665.39
性别比(以女性为100)	Sex Ratio(female=100)	107.27	108.19	106.91	106.89	108.00	109.20
年平均人口	Annual Average Population	3661	3614	3567	3508	3474	3477
家庭年末总户数(万户)	Total Number of Household (10000 households)	1056.84	1053.61	1046.28	1038.96	1066.13	1103.77
家庭户规模(人/户)	Average Family Size(person/household)	3.34	3.31	3.28	3.24	3.16	3.10
人口自然变动	**Natural Change of Population**						
出生人数	Number of Birth	48.62	48.75	48.68	48.52	46.24	46.13
出生率(‰)	Birth Rate(‰)	13.28	13.49	13.65	13.96	13.31	13.27
死亡人数	Number of Death	24.16	24.47	23.86	22.76	24.07	24.20
死亡率(‰)	Death Rate(‰)	6.60	6.77	6.69	6.55	6.93	6.96
自然增长人数	Natural Increase of Population	24.46	24.28	24.82	25.76	22.17	21.93
自然增长率(‰)	Natural Growth Rate(‰)	6.68	6.72	6.96	7.41	6.38	6.31

注：2007—2009年数据根据第六次人口普查数据进行修订。
Note:Data from 2007 to 2009 had been adjusted according to the result of the Sixth National Population Census.

3-4 户籍人口
Household Registered Population

单位：万人 (10000 persons)

指　　标	Item	2007	2008	2009	2010	2011	2012
年末总人口	**Total Population at the Year-end**	**3985.04**	**4036.75**	**4090.78**	**4189.00**	**4238.44**	**4249.48**
农　业	Agriculture	3346.09	3385.66	3429.36	3512.92	3551.18	3557.14
非农业	Non-agriculture	638.95	651.09	661.43	676.07	687.26	692.34
构成(以年末总人口=100)(%)	**Composition (total population at the year-end=100)(%)**						
农　业	Agriculture	84.0	83.9	83.8	83.9	83.8	83.7
非农业	Non-agriculture	16.0	16.1	16.2	16.1	16.2	16.3

注：资料来源于省公安厅。
Note:Data in the table above are obtained from the Public Security Department of Guizhou Province.

3-5 计划生育
Family Planning

单位：万人 (10000 persons)

指　　标	Item	2007	2008	2009	2010	2011	2012
生育政策符合率(%)	Family Planning Rates(%)	94.5	94.1	92.5	92.8	93.9	94.7
采取节育措施人数	Number of Contraception Users	649.53	596.74	621.67	563.07	572.94	611.10
避孕率(含复合使用药具)(%)	Contraception Rates(Including Using contraceptives)(%)	90.1	90.3	89.6	88.2	88.1	89.0

注：资料来源于省人口计生委。
Note:Data in the table are provided from the Committee of Population and Family Planning of Guizhou Provincial.

主要统计指标解释

人口数 指一定时点、一定地区范围内的有生命的个人的总和。年度统计的年末人口数指每年 12 月 31 日 24 时的人口数。

城镇人口和乡村人口 城镇人口是指居住在城镇范围内的全部常住人口；乡村人口是除上述人口以外的全部人口。

出生率（又称粗出生率） 指在一定时期内（通常为一年）一定地区的出生人数与同期内平均人数（或期中人数）之比，用千分率表示。本资料中的出生率指年出生率，其计算公式为:

$$出生率=\frac{年出生人数}{年平均人数}\times 1000‰$$

公式中: 出生人数指活产婴儿，即胎儿脱离母体时（不管怀孕月数），有过呼吸或其他生命现象。年平均人数指年初、年底人口数的平均数，也可用年中人口数代替。

死亡率（又称粗死亡率） 指在一定时期内（通常为一年）一定地区的死亡人数与同期内平均人数（或期中人数）之比，用千分率表示。本资料中的死亡率指年死亡率，其计算公式为:

$$死亡率=\frac{年死亡人数}{年平均人数}\times 1000‰$$

人口自然增长率 指在一定时期内（通常为一年）人口自然增加数（出生人数减死亡人数）与该时期内平均人数（或期中人数）之比，用千分率表示。计算公式为:

$$人口自然增长率=\frac{本年出生人数-本年死亡人数}{年平均人数}\times 1000‰$$

$$=人口出生率-人口死亡率$$

Explanatory Notes on Main Statistical Indicators

Total Population refers to the total number of people alive at a certain point of time within a given area. The annual statistics on total population is taken at midnight, the 3lst of December.

Urban Population and Rural Population Urban population refers to all people residing in cities and towns, while rural population refers to population other than urban population.

Birth Rate (or Crude Birth Rate) refers to the ratio of the number of births to the average population (or mid-period population) during a certain period of time (usually a year), expressed in ‰. Birth rate in the chapter refers to annual birth rate. The following formula is used:

$$\text{Birth Rate} = \frac{\text{Number of Births}}{\text{Annual Average Population}} \times 1000‰$$

Number of births in the formula refers to live births, i.e. when a baby has breathed or showed any vital phenomena regardless of the length of pregnancy.

Annual average population is the average of the number of population at the beginning of the year and that at the end of the year. Sometimes it is substituted by the mid-year population.

Death Rate(or Crude Death Rate) refers to the ratio of the number of deaths to the average population (or mid-period population) during a certain period of time (usually a year), expressed in ‰. Death rate in the chapter refers to annual death rate. The following formula is used:

$$\text{Death Rate} = \frac{\text{Number of Death}}{\text{Annual Average Population}} \times 1000‰$$

Natural Growth Rate of Population refers to the ratio of natural increase in population (number of births minus number of deaths) in a certain period of time (usually a year) to the average population (or mid-period population) of the same period, expressed in ‰. The following formula is applie:

$$\text{Natural Growth Rate of Population} = \frac{\text{Number of Births-Number of Deaths}}{\text{Annual Average Population}} \times 1000‰$$

Natural Growth Rate of Population = Birth Rate-Death Rate

就业人员和职工工资

4

Four

Employment and Wages

4-1 就业人员及劳动报酬

Number of Employed Personnels and Wages

指 标	Item	2007	2008	2009	2010	2011	2012	2012年比2011年增长(%) Increase Rate in 2012over 2011(%)
就业人员(万人)	**Number of Employed Persons (10000 persons)**	**1872.64**	**1867.20**	**1841.92**	**1770.90**	**1792.80**	**1825.82**	**1.8**
按产业分	**Grouped by Three Strata of Industry**							
第一产业	Primary Industry	1388.02	1350.32	1299.29	1209.55	1194.39	1189.04	-0.4
第二产业	Secondary Industry	172.31	180.73	197.60	203.52	215.86	238.10	10.3
第三产业	Tertiary Industry	312.31	336.15	345.03	357.82	382.55	398.68	4.2
按城乡分	**Grouped by Urban and Rural**							
城镇	Urban Area	489.96	501.33	512.95	525.76	554.14	596.06	7.6
乡村	Rural Area	1382.67	1365.87	1328.96	1245.14	1238.66	1229.76	-0.7
非私营单位在岗职工人数(万人)	**Total Number of Staff and Workers (10000 persons)**	**207.53**	**199.76**	**206.44**	**210.67**	**225.91**	**249.67**	**10.5**
国有单位	State-owned Unit	141.48	140.97	141.79	146.81	158.26	161.19	1.9
集体单位	Collective-owned Unit	8.10	7.42	6.69	6.41	7.17	6.16	-14.1
其他单位	Others	57.95	51.37	57.96	57.45	60.47	82.32	36.1
非私营单位在岗职工工资总额(亿元)	**Total Wages of Staff and Wokers (100 million yuan)**	**439.24**	**509.54**	**572.67**	**649.55**	**830.11**	**1050.68**	**26.6**
国有单位	State-owned Unit	320.64	377.51	416.87	470.49	606.80	729.04	20.1
集体单位	Collective-owned Unit	13.47	15.21	14.65	15.72	22.12	24.29	9.8
其他单位	Others	105.13	116.82	141.15	163.34	201.19	297.36	47.8
非私营单位在岗职工平均工资(元)	**Average Wage of Staff and Workers(yuan)**	**20668**	**24602**	**28245**	**31458**	**37331**	**42733**	**14.5**
国有单位	State-owned Unit	22106	25874	29956	32718	38914	45825	17.8
集体单位	Collective-owned Unit	16893	20914	22167	24703	31601	40420	27.9
其他单位	Others	17668	21659	24772	29006	33851	36816	8.8

注：2007–2009年就业人员总数及分产业、分城乡就业数据根据第六次人口普查结果修订。

Note:From 2007 to 2009，total number of employed persons and data of employment by three strata of industry and urban and rural have been adjusted according to the result of the Six National population census.

4-2 非私营单位就业人员年末人数(2012)

Number of Employed Persons in Non-private Units at Year-end

单位：人 (person)

指 标	Item	就业人员 Number of Employed	国有单位 State-owned Unit	集体单位 Collective-owned Unit	其他单位 Unit of Other Type of Ownership
总 计	**Total**	**2694970**	**1745657**	**68178**	**881135**
按企事业、机关分组	**By Enterprises,Institutions and Agencies**				
企 业	Enterprises	1574976	635686	65591	873699
事 业	Institutions	762399	753060	2486	6853
机 关	Agencies	357595	356911	101	583
按产业分	**By Three Strata of Industry**				
第一产业	Primary Industry	16169	13598	278	2293
第二产业	Secondary Industry	1090947	438228	41401	611318
第三产业	Tertiary Industry	1587854	1293831	26499	267524
按国民经济行业分组	**By Sector**				
农、林、牧、渔业	Farming,Forestry,Animal Husbandry and Fishing	16169	13598	278	2293
采矿业	Mining and Quarrying	181719	63368	3796	114555
制造业	Manufacturing	476220	121411	12448	342361
电力、热力、燃气及水生产和供应业	Production and Supply of Electricity,Heat , Gas and Water	84348	67282	608	16458
建筑业	Construction	348660	186167	24549	137944
批发和零售业	Wholesale and Retail Trade	131690	48404	4790	78496
批发业	Wholesale	73481	41367	2360	29754
零售业	Retail	58209	7037	2430	48742
交通运输、仓储和邮政业	Transportation,Storage and Post	91459	78169	1419	11871
住宿和餐饮业	Hotels and Catering Services	39394	8941	822	29631
信息传输、软件和信息技术服务业	Information Transmit,Computer Services and Software Trade	24640	13038	34	11568
金融业	Financial Intermediation	73829	21168	9876	42785
房地产业	Real Estate	54316	6171	1517	46628
租赁和商务服务业	Leasing and Commerce Services	29628	8452	3753	17423
租赁业	Leasing Services	1708	657	15	1036
商务服务业	Commerce Services	27920	7795	3738	16387
科学研究、技术服务业	Scientific Research,Technic Serviced and Geological Prospecting	54272	47699	167	6406
水利、环境和公共设施管理业	Water Conservancy,Environment and Public Facilities Services	41628	38629	1200	1799
居民服务、修理和其他服务业	Services to Households and Other Services	9668	4014	366	5288
教 育	Education	441638	431112	1319	9207
卫生和社会工作	Health Care and Social Work	146060	140655	1176	4229
卫 生	Health Care	142454	137322	1046	4086
社会工作	Social Work	3606	3333	130	143
文化、体育和娱乐业	Culture,Sports and Entertainment	16416	14349	55	2012
#新闻和出版业	News Publishing Company	3891	3705		186
广播、电视、电影和影视录音制作业	Broadcasting,Television,Film and Video Trade	4604	4202	14	388
体 育	Sports	1363	861		502
公共管理、社会保障和社会组织	Public Administration Social Security and Social Organization	433216	433030	5	181

4-3 非私营单位女性就业人员年末人数(2012)

Number of Employed Female in Non-private Units at the Year-end

单位：人 (person)

行 业	Sector	女性就业人员数 Number of Female Employed	国有单位 State-owned Unit	集体单位 Collective-owned Unit	其他单位 Unit of Other Type of Ownership
总 计	**Total**	**869049**	**592591**	**18675**	**257783**
农、林、牧、渔业	Farming,Forestry,Animal Husbandry and Fishing	4524	3665	65	794
采矿业	Mining and Quarrying	20920	9182	242	11496
制造业	Manufacturing	153380	39160	4052	110168
电力、热力、燃气及水生产和供应业	Production and Supply of Electricity,Heat, Gas and Water	24078	19714	142	4222
建筑业	Construction	38286	20986	3652	13648
批发和零售业	Wholesale and Retail Trade	54799	16109	1947	36743
批发业	Wholesale	25052	13104	983	10965
零售业	Retail	29747	3005	964	25778
交通运输、仓储和邮政业	Transportation,Storage and Post	26184	21857	563	3764
住宿和餐饮业	Hotels and Catering Services	22619	5062	467	17090
信息传输、软件和信息技术服务业	Information Transmit,Computer Services and Software Trade	9601	5184	13	4404
金融业	Financial Intermediation	35732	9934	4288	21510
房地产业	Real Estate	18642	2451	514	15677
租赁和商务服务业	Leasing and Commerce Services	7493	2487	502	4504
租赁业	Leasing Services	514	237	5	272
商务服务业	Commerce Services	6979	2250	497	4232
科学研究、技术服务业	Scientific Research,Technic Services and Geological Prospecting	14986	13175	55	1756
水利、环境和公共设施管理业	Water Conservancy,Environment and Public Facilities Services	20561	19079	620	862
居民服务、修理和其他服务业	Services to Households and Other Services	4370	1863	152	2355
教 育	Education	192455	186501	715	5239
卫生和社会工作	Health Care and Social Work	86067	82751	674	2642
卫 生	Health Care	84603	81480	577	2546
社会工作	Social Work	1464	1271	97	96
文化、体育和娱乐业	Culture,Sports and Entertainment	6011	5168	10	833
#新闻和出版业	News Publishing Company	1320	1277		43
广播、电视、电影和影视录音制作业	Broadcasting,Television,Film and Video Trade	1430	1245	5	180
体 育	Sports	334	138		196
公共管理、社会保障和社会组织	Public Administration Social Security and Social Organization	128341	128263	2	76

4-4 非私营单位各行业在岗职工年末人数(2012)

Working Staff and Workers in Non-private units at the Year-end by Sector

单位：人 (person)

行 业	Sector	职工人数 Number of Staff and Workers	国有单位 State-owned Unit	集体单位 Collective-owned Unit	其他单位 Unit of Other Type of Ownership
总 计	**Total**	**2496743**	**1611863**	**61637**	**823243**
按企事业、机关分组	**By Enterprises,Institutions and Agencies**				
企 业	Enterprises	1461879	586723	59084	816072
事 业	Institutions	713104	704064	2452	6588
机 关	Agencies	321760	321076	101	583
按产业分	**By Three Strata of Industry**				
第一产业	Primary Industry	14863	12397	278	2188
第二产业	Secondary Industry	997194	398600	35826	562768
第三产业	Tertiary Industry	1484686	1200866	25533	258287
按国民经济行业分组	**By Sector**				
农、林、牧、渔业	Farming,Forestry,Animal Husbandry and Fishing	14863	12397	278	2188
采矿业	Mining and Quarrying	178133	62610	3622	111901
制造业	Manufacturing	463909	115856	11985	336068
电力、热力、燃气及水生产和供应业	Production and Supply of Electricity,Heat, Gas and Water	82697	65895	602	16200
建筑业	Construction	272455	154239	19617	98599
批发和零售业	Wholesale and Retail Trade	127283	46442	4358	76483
批发业	Wholesale	70190	39779	2040	28371
零售业	Retail	57093	6663	2318	48112
交通运输、仓储和邮政业	Transportation,Storage and Post	87244	74226	1409	11609
住宿和餐饮业	Hotels and Catering Services	38586	8415	814	29357
信息传输、软件和信息技术服务业	Information Transmit,Computer Services and Software Trade	24442	12898	28	11516
金融业	Financial Intermediation	69188	20519	9615	39054
房地产业	Real Estate	52132	5735	1339	45058
租赁和商务服务业	Leasing and Commerce Services	29149	8230	3738	17181
租赁业	Leasing Services	1693	642	15	1036
商务服务业	Commerce Services	27456	7588	3723	16145
科学研究、技术服务业	Scientific Research,Technic Services and Geological Prospecting	52096	46036	161	5899
水利、环境和公共设施管理业	Water Conservancy,Environment and Public Facilities Services	34457	31475	1189	1793
居民服务、修理和其他服务业	Services to Households and Other Services	9100	3548	362	5190
教 育	Education	421285	411169	1312	8804
卫生和社会工作	Health Care and Social Work	133980	128652	1148	4180
卫 生	Health Care	130478	125421	1020	4037
社会工作	Social Work	3502	3231	128	143
文化、体育和娱乐业	Culture,Sports and Entertainment	15604	13567	55	1982
#新闻和出版业	News Publishing Company	3861	3676		185
广播、电视、电影和影视录音制作业	Broadcasting,Television,Film and Video Trade	4239	3857	14	368
体 育	Sports	1354	852		502
公共管理、社会保障和社会组织	Public Administration Social Security and Social Organization	390140	389954	5	181

注：在岗职工包含劳务派遣人员(以下相关表同)。

Note:The working staff and workers include labor dispatching personnel(the related tables in the chapter are the same).

4-5 非私营单位在岗职工工资总额(2012)

Total Wages Bill of Working Staff and Workers in Non-private units

单位：亿元 (100 million yuan)

指标	Item	工资总额 Total Wage Bill	国有单位 State-owned Unit	集体单位 Collective-owned Unit	其他单位 Unit of Other Type of Ownership
总计	**Total**	**1050.68**	**729.04**	**24.29**	**297.36**
按企事业、机关分	**By Enterprises,Institutions and Agencies**				
企业	Enterprises	608.09	290.14	23.17	294.78
事业	Institutions	301.41	298.02	1.10	2.29
机关	Agencies	141.18	140.89	0.01	0.28
按产业分	**By Three Strata of Industry**				
第一产业	Primary Industry	4.91	4.46	0.06	0.39
第二产业	Secondary Industry	396.42	189.60	9.53	197.29
第三产业	Tertiary Industry	649.35	534.97	14.70	99.68
按国民经济行业分	**By Sector**				
农、林、牧、渔业	Farming,Forestry,Animal Husbandry and Fishing	4.91	4.46	0.06	0.39
采矿业	Mining and Quarrying	75.61	26.96	1.25	47.39
制造业	Manufacturing	168.48	56.59	2.82	109.07
电力、热力、燃气及水生产和供应业	Production and Supply of Electricity,Heat, Gas and Water	49.36	41.75	0.15	7.47
建筑业	Construction	102.97	64.29	5.31	33.36
批发和零售业	Wholesale and Retail Trade	53.56	30.78	0.89	21.89
批发业	Wholesale	37.19	28.46	0.47	8.27
零售业	Retail	16.37	2.32	0.43	13.62
交通运输、仓储和邮政业	Transportation,Storage and Post	41.36	36.15	0.50	4.71
住宿和餐饮业	Hotels and Catering Services	9.52	2.43	0.17	6.91
信息传输、软件和信息技术服务业	Information Transmit,Computer Services and Software Trade	12.91	7.27	0.01	5.64
金融业	Financial Intermediation	57.55	13.76	10.92	32.87
房地产业	Real Estate	16.98	1.98	0.32	14.67
租赁和商务服务业	Leasing and Commerce Services	8.68	2.72	0.78	5.18
租赁业	Leasing Services	0.58	0.22	0.00	0.35
商务服务业	Commerce Services	8.10	2.50	0.78	4.83
科学研究、技术服务业	Scientific Research,Technic Services and Geological Prospecting	20.53	18.44	0.04	2.04
水利、环境和公共设施管理业	Water Conservancy,Environment and Public Facilities Services	10.34	9.84	0.19	0.31
居民服务、修理和其他服务业	Services to Households and Other Services	2.64	1.25	0.09	1.31
教育	Education	181.70	178.91	0.41	2.37
卫生和社会工作	Health Care and Social Work	60.00	58.38	0.36	1.26
卫生	Health Care	58.77	57.21	0.33	1.23
社会工作	Social Work	1.23	1.17	0.03	0.03
文化、体育和娱乐业	Culture,Sports and Entertainment	5.73	5.21	0.03	0.48
#新闻和出版业	News Publishing Company	1.38	1.34		0.05
广播、电视、电影和影视录音制作业	Broadcasting,Television,Film and Video Trade	1.51	1.38		0.13
体育	Sports	0.37	0.26		0.11
公共管理、社会保障和社会组织	Public Administration Social Security and Social Organization	167.88	167.84		0.04

4-6 非私营单位各行业在岗职工平均工资(2012)

Average Wages of Working Staff and Workers in Non-private units by Sector

单位：元 (yuan)

指　标	Item	平均工资 Average Wage	国有单位 State-owned Unit	集体单位 Collective-owned Unit	其他单位 Unit of Other Type of Ownership
总　计	**Total**	**42733**	**45825**	**40420**	**36816**
按企事业、机关分	**By Enterprises,Institutions and Agencies**				
企　业	Enterprises	42270	49986	42594	36821
事　业	Institutions	42957	43021	46190	35152
机　关	Agencies	44333	44335	13752	48510
按产业分	**By Three Industries**				
第一产业	Primary Industry	32995	35929	19860	17919
第二产业	Secondary Industry	40376	48082	27489	35687
第三产业	Tertiary Industry	44415	45177	58478	39448
按国民经济行业分	**By Sector**				
农、林、牧、渔业	Farming,Forestry,Animal Husbandry and Fishing	32995	35929	19860	17919
采矿业	Mining and Quarrying	43371	44011	34854	43293
制造业	Manufacturing	36655	48359	23412	32994
电力、热力、燃气及水生产和供应业	Production and Supply of Electricity,Heat, Gas and Water	60184	63927	24652	46330
建筑业	Construction	38733	42656	28807	34510
批发和零售业	Wholesale and Retail Trade	42413	66476	20573	28938
批发业	Wholesale	53177	71736	22942	29285
零售业	Retail	29050	35011	18490	28731
交通运输、仓储和邮政业	Transportation,Storage and Post	48118	49381	35358	41552
住宿和餐饮业	Hotels and Catering Services	25339	30630	21141	23996
信息传输、软件和信息技术服务业	Information Transmit,Computer Services and Software Trade	53634	57158	24214	49753
金融业	Financial Intermediation	84924	67424	116028	86623
房地产业	Real Estate	33950	34482	25187	34140
租赁和商务服务业	Leasing and Commerce Services	30249	34091	21464	30316
租赁业	Leasing Services	34310	35653	16923	33716
商务服务业	Commerce Services	29997	33958	21481	30097
科学研究、技术服务业	Scientific Research,Technic Services and Geological Prospecting	39834	40432	24969	35502
水利、环境和公共设施管理业	Water Conservancy,Environment and Public Facilities Services	30673	32021	15242	17740
居民服务、修理和其他服务业	Services to Households and Other Services	28758	34227	24419	25218
教　育	Education	43753	44145	31929	27257
卫生和社会工作	Health Care and Social Work	46138	46748	31232	31412
卫　生	Health Care	46424	47007	32158	31845
社会工作	Social Work	35647	36839	23891	19570
文化、体育和娱乐业	Culture,Sports and Entertainment	36800	38617	52855	24146
#新闻和出版业	News Publishing Company	35848	36428		24476
广播、电视、电影和影视录音制作业	Broadcasting,Television,Film and Video Trade	36071	36236	20071	34976
体　育	Sports	27201	31213		20625
公共管理、社会保障和社会组织	Public Administration Social Security and Social Organization	43448	43458	12000	21448

4-7 非私营单位各行业从业人员平均工资(2012)

Average Wages of Working Staff and Workers in Non-private units by Sector

单位：元 (yuan)

指标	Item	平均工资 Average Wage	国有单位 State-owned Unit	集体单位 Collective-owned Unit	其他单位 Unit of Other Type of Ownership
总计	**Total**	**41156**	**43702**	**38882**	**36223**
按企事业、机关分	**By Enterprises,Institutions and Agencies**				
企业	Enterprises	41061	47802	38666	36228
事业	Institutions	41276	41324	45510	34545
机关	Agencies	41321	41317	13752	48510
按产业分	**By Three Industries**				
第一产业	Primary Industry	30850	33254	19860	17705
第二产业	Secondary Industry	39266	46176	27097	35049
第三产业	Tertiary Industry	42554	42974	56934	39066
按国民经济行业分	**By Sector**				
农、林、牧、渔业	Farming,Forestry,Animal Husbandry and Fishing	30850	33254	19860	17705
采矿业	Mining and Quarrying	43113	43797	34356	43027
制造业	Manufacturing	36187	46811	23343	32807
电力、热力、燃气及水生产和供应业	Production and Supply of Electricity,Heat, Gas and Water	59344	62922	24504	46041
建筑业	Construction	36560	40449	28028	32638
批发和零售业	Wholesale and Retail Trade	40325	59106	19603	28727
批发业	Wholesale	48768	62907	21396	28920
零售业	Retail	28800	33931	17880	28607
交通运输、仓储和邮政业	Transportation,Storage and Post	47049	48169	35316	41022
住宿和餐饮业	Hotels and Catering Services	25372	30117	21235	24113
信息传输、软件和信息技术服务业	Information Transmit,Computer Services and Software Trade	53384	56815	22529	49609
金融业	Financial Intermediation	81630	66131	113793	82007
房地产业	Real Estate	33617	32999	23587	34035
租赁和商务服务业	Leasing and Commerce Services	30121	33778	21418	30214
租赁业	Leasing Services	34058	34955	16923	33716
商务服务业	Commerce Services	29877	33678	21434	29989
科学研究、技术服务业	Scientific Research,Technic Services and Geological Prospecting	39087	39559	25198	35893
水利、环境和公共设施管理业	Water Conservancy,Environment and Public Facilities Services	27779	28657	15204	17793
居民服务、修理和其他服务业	Services to Households and Other Services	28224	32590	24291	25165
教育	Education	42432	42795	31805	27014
卫生和社会工作	Health Care and Social Work	44289	44790	30769	31369
卫生	Health Care	44528	45003	31655	31796
社会工作	Social Work	34997	36114	23669	19570
文化、体育和娱乐业	Culture,Sports and Entertainment	35937	37594	52855	23875
#新闻和出版业	News Publishing Company	35677	36247		24457
广播、电视、电影和影视录音制作业	Broadcasting,Television,Film and Video Trade	34906	35114	20071	33230
体育	Sports	27116	31035		20625
公共管理、社会保障和社会组织	Public Administration Social Security and Social Organization	40549	40558	12000	20619

4-8 城乡私营企业户数和就业人员(2012)
Number of Private Enterprises and Employed Persons in Urban and Rural Areas by Sector

指标	Item	私营企业户数(户) Number of Private Enterprises (Household)	城镇 Urban Areas	乡村 Rural Areas	就业人员(人) Number of Employees (Person)	城镇 Urban Areas	乡村 Rural Areas
总计	**Total**	**143935**	**84874**	**59061**	**1235776**	**667448**	**568328**
农、林、牧、渔业	Farming,Forestry,Animal Husbandry and Fishing	14788	3354	11434	109457	29550	79907
采掘业	Mining and Quarrying	5869	1344	4525	66548	15552	50996
制造业	Manufacturing	16169	7621	8548	208142	101232	106910
电力、燃气及水的生产和供应业	Production and Supply of Electricity,Gas and Water	1115	507	608	14055	6783	7272
建筑业	Construction	6352	4782	1570	65846	52599	13247
交通运输、仓储和邮政业	Transportation,Storage and Post	2912	1738	1174	25475	15821	9654
信息传输、计算机服务和软件业	Information Transmit,Computer Services and Software Trade	4608	3109	1499	33574	23791	9783
批发和零售业	Wholesale and Retail Trade	52420	35105	17315	398116	203838	194278
住宿和餐饮业	Hotels and Catering Services	3292	2124	1168	32784	22101	10683
房地产业	Real Estate	6710	4524	2186	67084	49276	17808
租赁和商务服务业	Leasing and Commerce Services	14972	11410	3562	98442	73220	25222
居民服务和其他服务业	Services to Households and Other Services	7036	4483	2553	47882	32179	15703
卫生、社会保障和社会福利业	Health Care,Social Security and Social Welfare	461	281	180	7101	4298	2803
文化、体育和娱乐业	Culture,Sports and Entertainment	756	499	257	7019	4823	2196
其他行业	Others	6475	3993	2482	54251	32385	21866

注：资料来源于省工商局(下表同)。

Note:Data in the table are obtained from Guizhou Provincial Industrial and Commercial Bureau(the same applies to the next table).

4–9 城乡个体工商户数和就业人员(2012)

Number of Household and Self-Employed Individuals in Urban and Rural Areas

指标	Item	个体工商户户数(户) Number of individual industrial and commercial households(Household)	城镇 Urban Areas	乡村 Rural Areas	就业人员(人) Number of Employed (Person)	城镇 Urban Areas	乡村 Rural Areas
总计	**Total**	**899111**	**494410**	**404701**	**1541187**	**845171**	**696016**
农、林、牧、渔业	Farming,Forestry,Animal Husbandry and Fishing	13801	4704	9097	26999	9328	17671
采掘业	Mining and Quarrying	3852	978	2874	18145	8199	9946
制造业	Manufacturing	47901	24070	23831	95223	44516	50707
电力、燃气及水的生产和供应业	Production and Supply of Electricity,Gas and Water	428	187	241	1068	383	685
建筑业	Construction	4384	3017	1367	13668	7795	5873
交通运输、仓储和邮政业	Transportation,Storage and Post	24860	10969	13891	39435	16938	22497
信息传输、计算机服务和软件业	Information Transmit,Computer Services and Software Trade	4768	2164	2604	8027	3665	4362
批发和零售业	Wholesale and Retail Trade	597973	328153	269820	939142	519424	419718
住宿和餐饮业	Hotels and Catering Services	98689	61718	36971	208179	121529	86650
房地产业	Real Estate	83	71	12	227	193	34
租赁和商务服务业	Leasing and Commerce Services	9134	5816	3318	21509	13613	7896
居民服务和其他服务业	Services to Households and Other Services	70040	40909	29131	128779	76044	52735
卫生、社会保障和社会福利业	Health Care,Social Security and Social Welfare	3139	1931	1208	9628	6550	3078
文化、体育和娱乐业	Culture,Sports and Entertainment	3864	2581	1283	9804	6991	2813
其他行业	Others	16195	7142	9053	21354	10003	11351

4-10 城镇新就业人数和失业人数

Number of Newly Employed Persons and Unemployed Persons in Urban Areas

单位：万人 (10000 persons)

指 标	Item	2007	2008	2009	2010	2011	2012	2012年比2011年增长(%) Increase Rate in 2012 over 2011(%)
新就业人数总计	Total Incremental Employed Personnels	22.4	21.1	21.10	27.71	35.94	58.63	63.1
城镇登记失业人数	Number of Registered Unemployed Persons in Urban Areas	12.13	12.56	12.34	12.18	12.51	12.56	0.4
城镇登记失业率(%)	Registered Unemployment Rate in Urban Areas(%)	3.97	3.98	3.81	3.63	3.63	3.29	-0.3(百分点)

注：资料来源于省人力资源社会保障厅(以下相关表同)。
Note: Data in the table are obtained from Guizhou Department of Human Resources and Social Security(the related tables in the chapter are the same).

4-11 下岗失业人员享受再就业优惠政策情况

Statistics of Re-employment Preferential Policies for Laid-off Workers

单位：人 (person)

指 标	Item	2011	2012	2012年比2011年增长(%) Increase Rate in 2012 over 2011(%)
下岗失业人员实现再就业	Laid-off Workers	108060	132516	22.6
#就业困难对象实现就业	Residents Experiencing Employment Difficulty	49438	63812	29.1
消除零就业家庭(户)	Number of Households rased Zero-employment	683	767	12.3
促进零就业家庭成员就业	Promoting Zero-employment Families Employed	713	906	27.1
从事公益性岗位人数	Number of Persons Engaged in Public-service Jobs	103460	82636	-20.1
享受职业培训补贴人数	Number of Persons Receiving Professional Training Subsidies	154626	168433	8.9
享受职业介绍补贴人数	Number of Persons Receiving Job Services Subsidies	16952	4839	-71.5
享受技能鉴定补贴人数	Number of Persons Receiving Skill Identification Subsidies	42925	52403	22.1
享受社会保险补贴人数	Number of Persons Receiving Social Insurance Subsidies	119711	117017	-2.3
使用就业再就业资金(万元)	Using Employment and Re-employment Fund(10000 yuan)	175915	212864	21.0
#社会保险补贴	Social Insurance Subsidies	49470	63969	29.3
岗位补贴	Post Subsidies	87877	94311	7.3
职业培训补贴	Professional Training	25919	35623	37.4
职业介绍补贴	Job Services	917	202	-78.0
扶持公共就业服务	Supporting Public Employment Service	2300	1602	-30.3

4-12 职业技能鉴定

Occupation Skill Appraisal

单位:人 (person)

指标名称	Item	2007	2008	2009	2010	2011	2012
参加职业技能鉴定	Number of Persons Joining in Occupation Skill Appraisal	96145	87352	77735	82135	114691	135948
获取证书人数	Number of Persons With Qualification Certificates	86067	79352	69781	73717	105141	125959
#高级技工	Advanced Mechanic	5148	6274	6205	5989	11322	13454
#技 师	Technician	1315	1272	487	372	615	364
#高级技师	Advanced Technician	190	230	161	163	138	115

4-13 劳动力市场需求人员、求职人员及构成
Components of Persons Required by Labor Market and Applying for a Job

单位：人 (person)

行业分组	by Sector	2011 绝对数 Level	2011 构成(%) Composition	2012 绝对数 Level	2012 构成(%) Composition	2012年比2011年增长(%) Increase Rate in 2012 over 2011(%)
劳动力市场需求人员合计	**Number of Persons Required by Labor Market**	**278542**	**100.0**	**255570**	**100.0**	**-8.2**
农林牧渔业	Farming,Forestry,Animal Husbandry and Fishing	4264	1.5	4093	1.6	-4.0
采矿业	Mining and Quarrying	4391	1.6	4488	1.8	2.2
制造业	Manufacturing	55877	20.1	38190	14.9	-31.7
电力煤气和水的生产和供应业	Production and Supply of Electricity, Gas and Water	4937	1.8	2819	1.1	-42.9
建筑业	Construction	7405	2.7	7908	3.1	6.8
交通运输、仓储和邮政业	Transportation,Storage and Post	12409	4.5	9574	3.7	-22.8
信息传输、计算机服务和软件业	Information Transmit,Computer Services and Software Trade	10051	3.6	14443	5.7	43.7
批发和零售业	Wholesale and Retail Trade	63141	22.7	59433	23.3	-5.9
住宿和餐饮业	Hotels and Catering Services	45767	16.4	40682	15.9	-11.1
金融业	Financial Intermediation	1490	0.5	1879	0.7	26.1
房地产业	Real Estate	5215	1.9	4668	1.8	-10.5
租赁和商务服务业	Leasing and Commerce Services	5190	1.9	8241	3.2	58.8
科学研究、技术服务和地质勘查业	Scientific Research,Technic Services and Geological Prospecting	247	0.1	354	0.1	43.3
水利、环境和公共设施管理业	Water Conservancy,Environment and Public Facilities Services	294	0.1	678	0.3	130.6
居民服务和其他服务业	Services to Households and Other Services	37989	13.6	34584	13.5	-9.0
教　育	Education	1951	0.7	3010	1.2	54.3
卫生、社会保障和社会福利业	Health Care,Social Securities and Social Welfare	1303	0.5	2446	1.0	87.7
文化、体育和娱乐业	Culture,Sports and Entertainment	15583	5.6	16003	6.3	2.7
公共管理与社会组织	Public Administration and Social Organization	1038	0.4	2077	0.8	100.1
劳动力市场求职人员合计	**Number of Person Applying for A Job**	**223260**	**100.0**	**197453**	**100.0**	**-11.6**
新成长的失业青年	New grown Unemployed Youngth	41798	18.7	35389	17.9	-15.3
#应届高校毕业生	Graduating Students from higer School	22773	10.2	19937	10.1	-12.5
就业转失业人员	Working Staff Transmiting into Unemployed	65848	29.5	57909	29.3	-12.1
其他失业人员	Other Unempolyed	29088	13.0	27014	13.7	-7.1
在业人员	Working Staff	5751	2.6	6891	3.5	19.8
下岗职工	Laid-off Workers	12297	5.5	9284	4.7	-24.5
退休人员	Retired	529	0.2	680	0.3	28.5
在学人员	Enrollment	5552	2.5	5881	3.0	5.9
本市农村人员	Persons of Domesitc Country	38382	17.2	33778	17.1	-12.0
外埠人员	Outside	24015	10.8	20627	10.4	-14.1

主要统计指标解释

经济活动人口 指在 16 周岁及以上，有劳动能力，参加或要求参加社会经济活动的人口。包括就业人员和失业人员。

就业人员 指在 16 周岁及以上，从事一定社会劳动并取得劳动报酬或经营收入的人员。这一指标反映了一定时期内全部劳动力资源的实际利用情况，是研究我国基本国情国力的重要指标。

单位就业人员 指在各级国家机关、政党机关、社会团体及企业、事业单位中工作，取得工资或其他形式的劳动报酬的全部人员。包括在岗职工、再就业的离退休人员、民办教师以及在各单位中工作的外方人员和港澳台方人员、兼职人员、借用的外单位人员和第二职业者。不包括离开本单位仍保留劳动关系的职工。各单位的就业人员反映了各单位实际参加生产或工作的全部劳动力。

城镇私营和个体就业人员 城镇私营就业人员指在工商管理部门注册登记，其经营地址设在县城关镇（含县城关镇）以上的私营企业就业人员，包括私营企业投资者和雇工。城镇个体就业人员指在工商管理部门注册登记，并持有城镇户口或在城镇长期居住，经批准从事个体工商经营的就业人员，包括个体经营者和在个体工商户劳动的家庭帮工和雇工。

国有单位 指资产归国家所有的经济组织。包括按《中华人民共和国企业法人登记管理条例》规定登记注册的非公司制的经济组织，以及中央、地方各级国家机关、事业单位和社会团体。

集体单位 指生产资料归集体所有，并按《中华人民共和国企业法人登记管理条例》规定登记注册的经济组织。

其他单位 包括股份合作单位、联营单位、有限责任公司、股份有限公司、港澳台商投资单位以及外商投资单位等其他登记注册类型单位。

在岗职工 指在本单位工作并由单位支付工资的人员，以及有工作岗位，但由于学习、病伤产假等原因暂未工作，仍由单位支付工资的人员。

工资总额 指各单位在一定时期内直接支付给本单位全部就业人员的劳动报酬总额。工资总额的计算原则应以直接支付给就业人员的全部劳动报酬为根据。各单位支付给就业人员的劳动报酬以及其他根据有关规定支付的工资，不论是计入成本的还是不计入成本的，不论是按国家规定列入计征奖金税项目的，还是未列入计征奖金税项目的，不论是以货币形式支付的还是以实物形式支付的，均包括在工资总额内。

平均工资 指企业、事业、机关单位的就业人员在一定时期内平均每人所得的货币工资额。它表明一定时期职工工资收入的高低程度，是反映就业人员工资水平的主要指标。计算公式为：

$$\text{平均工资} = \frac{\text{报告期实际支付的全部就业人员工资总额}}{\text{报告期全部就业人员平均人数}}$$

平均工资指数 指报告期就业人员平均工资与基期就业人员平均工资的比率，是反映不同时期就业人员货币工资水平变动情况的相对数。计算公式为：

$$\text{平均工资指数} = \frac{\text{报告期就业人员平均工资}}{\text{基期就业人员平均工资}} \times 100\%$$

平均实际工资指数 就业人员平均实际工资指指扣除物价变动因素后的就业人员平均工资。就业人员平均实际工资指数是反映实际工资变动情况的相对数，表明就业人员实际工资水平提高或降低的程度。计算公式为:

$$\text{平均实际工资指数} = \frac{\text{报告期就业人员平均工资指数}}{\text{报告期城镇居民消费价格指数}} \times 100\%$$

城镇登记失业人员 指有非农业户口，在一定的劳动年龄内（16 周岁至退休年龄），有劳动能力，无业而要求就业，并在当地劳动保障部门进行失业登记的人员。

城镇登记失业率 城镇登记失业人员与城镇单位就业人员（扣除使用的农村劳动力、聘用的离退休人员、港澳台及外方人员）、城镇单位中的不在岗职工、城镇私营业主、个体户主、城镇私营企业和个体就业人员、城镇登记失业人员之和的比。计算公式为:

$$\text{城镇登记失业率} = \frac{\text{城镇登记失业人数}}{\begin{array}{l}\text{（城镇单位就业人员 − 使用的农村劳动力 − 聘用的离退休人员 − 聘用的港澳}\\ \text{台及外方人员）+ 不在岗职工 + 城镇私营业主 + 城镇个体户主 + 城镇私营企}\\ \text{业及个体就业人员 + 城镇登记失业人数}\end{array}} \times 100\%$$

Explanatory Notes on Main Statistical Indicators

Economically Active Population refers to the population aged 16 and over who are capable of working, are participating in or willing to participate in economic activities, including employed persons and unemployed persons.

Employed Persons refer to persons aged 16 and over who are engaged in gainful employment and thus receive remuneration payment or earn business income. This indicator reflects the actual utilization of total labour force during a certain period of time and is often used for the research on China's economic situation and national power.

Persons Employed in Various Units refer to all the persons working in government agencies of various levels, political and party organizations, social organizations, enterprises and institutions, and receiving wages or other forms of payment. They include fully-employed staff and workers, re-employed retirees, teachers in the schools run by the local people, foreigners and Chinese compatriots from Hong Kong, Macao, and Taiwan working in various units, part-time employees, employees of other units working temporarily at current posts, and employees holding the second job, but do not include persons who have left their working units while keeping their labour contract (employment relation) unchanged. This indicator reflects the total number of laborers actually engaged in production or other operations in various units.

Persons Employed in Private Enterprises and Self-Employed Individuals in Urban Areas Persons employed in private enterprises refer to the persons employed in the private enterprises which have been registered at the departments of industrial and commercial administration for which the business operation are situated at a county town (i.e. a town where the county government is located), or at urban areas with administrative hierarchy higher than a county town. The self-employed individuals in urban areas refer to persons who hold the certificates of residence in urban areas or have resided in the urban areas for a long time and have been registered at the departments of industrial and commercial administration and approved to be engaged in individual industrial or commercial business, including self-employed persons as well as helpers and hired labourers who work in individual households.

State-owned Units refer to economic units whose assets are owned by the state, including non-corporation units registered according to Regulation of the People's Republic of China on the Registration of Enterprises and Corporations, state organs, institutions and social organizations at the central-level and local levels.

Collective-owned Units refer to economic units registered according to Regulation of the People's Republic of China on the Registration of Enterprises and Corporations where the means of production are collectively owned.

Units of Other Types of Ownership refer to units registered with other types of ownership, including cooperative units, joint ownership units, limited liability corporations, share holding corporations, units funded by entrepreneurs from Hong Kong, Macao, and Taiwan, and foreign- funded units.

Employed Staff and Workers refer to persons who work in, and receive wages from their working units, including persons who have their work posts but are temporarily absent from work for reasons of study or on sick, injury or maternal leave and still receive wages from their working units.

Total Wage Bill refers to the total remuneration payment to employed persons in various units during a certain period of time. The calculation of total wage bill is based on the total remuneration payment to employed persons . Therefore, all the wages and salaries and other payments to employed persons are included in the total wage bill regardless of sources, reckoning the cost of production or not, category, listing as items of premium taxation or not, and forms, paying in cash or in kind.

Average Wage refers to the average wage in money terms per person during a certain period of time for employed persons in enterprises, institutions, and government agencies, which reflects the general level of wage income during a certain period of time and is calculated as follows:

$$\text{Average Wage}=\frac{\text{Total Wage Bill of Employed Persons at Reference Time}}{\text{Average Number of Persons Employed at Reference Time}}$$

Average Wage Indices refers to the ratio of average wage of employed persons the reference period to that at the base period, which reflects the change of wage of employed persons at the different period. It is calculated as follows:

$$\text{Average Wage Indices}=\frac{\text{Average Wage of Employed Persons at Reference Time}}{\text{Average Wage of Persons Employed at Base Period}}\times 100\%$$

Average Real Wage Indices average real wage of employed persons refers to the average wage of employed persons after removing the effects of the price changes and average real wage indices of employed persons refers to the change of real wage, which reflects the relative increasing or decreasing level of real wage of employed persons ,which is calculated as follows:

$$\text{Average Real Wage Indices}=\frac{\text{Average Wage Indices of Employed Persons at the Reference Time}}{\text{Urban Consumer Price Indices at Reference Time}}\times 100\%$$

Registered Unemployed Persons in Urban Areas refer to the persons with non-agricultural household registration at certain working ages (16 years old to retirement age), who are capable of working, unemployed and willing to work, and have been registered at the local employment service agencies to apply for a job.

Registered Unemployment Rate in Urban Areas refers to the ratio of the number of the registered unemployed persons to the sum of the number of persons employed in various units (minus the employed rural labour force, re-employed retirees, and Hong Kong, Macao, Taiwan or foreign employees), laid-off staff and workers in urban units, owners of private enterprises in urban areas, owners of self-employed individuals in urban areas, employees of private enterprises in urban areas, employee of self-employed individuals in urban areas, and the registered unemployed persons in urban areas. The formula is as follows:

$$\text{Registered unemployment rate in urban areas}=\frac{\text{unmber of registered urban unemployed persons}}{\begin{array}{c}\text{number of persons employed in urban units-employed}\\ \text{rural labour forcere-empioyed retirees-Hong Kong,Macao}\\ \text{Taiwan or foreign employees +laid-off staff and workers}\\ \text{of urban private enterprises+owners of urban self-employed}\\ \text{individuals +employees of urban self-employed individuals}\\ \text{+registered unemployed persons in urban areas}\end{array}}\times 100\%$$

5

Five

固定资产投资

Investment in Fixed Assets

5-1 全社会固定资产投资

Total Investment in Fixed Assets in the whole Province

单位：亿元 (100 million yuan)

指　标	Item	2007	2008	2009	2010	2011	2012	2012年比2011年增长(%) Increase Rate in 2012 over 2011(%)
全社会固定资产投资	**Total Investment in Fixed Assets in theWhole Province**	**1488.80**	**1864.45**	**2450.99**	**3186.28**	**4234.44**	**5717.80**	**35.0**
#房地产开发	Real Estate Development	249.67	311.26	371.25	556.69	873.48	1467.60	68.0
按隶属关系分	Grouped by Jurisdiction of Management							
中　央	Central	239.96	308.09	348.79	324.62	343.59	389.96	13.5
地　方	Local	1248.84	1556.36	2102.20	2861.66	3890.85	5327.85	36.9
按经济类型分	Grouped by Registration Status							
国有经济	State-owned Units	697.68	910.69	1250.42	1605.82	1989.06	2530.97	27.2
集体经济	Collective-owned Units	17.27	25.23	29.70	29.01	42.61	42.55	-0.1
个体经济	Self-employed Units	93.86	108.74	144.07	172.91	879.44	1141.36	29.8
联营经济	Joint Ownership Units	1.84	3.68	0.42	2.16	3.69	6.71	81.9
股份制经济	Share Holding Units	382.27	466.73	523.58	774.14	174.15	205.34	17.9
外商投资经济	Foreign Funded Units	18.57	31.31	54.21	35.85	29.78	29.45	-1.1
港澳台商投资经济	Units with Funds from Hong Kong,Macao and Taiwan	14.85	18.78	19.70	34.18	72.49	117.60	62.2
其他经济	Others	262.46	299.29	428.89	532.21	1043.22	1643.81	57.6
按构成分	Grouped by Structure							
建筑安装工程	Construction and Installation	874.47	1118.74	1607.26	2010.16	3047.70	4150.18	36.2
设备工具器具购置	Purchase of Equipment and Instruments	329.11	381.20	431.77	494.07	520.42	531.71	2.2
其他费用	Others	285.22	364.51	411.96	682.04	666.32	1035.91	55.5
按三次产业分	Grouped by Three Industries							
第一产业	Primary Industry	29.32	50.87	73.42	80.71	126.48	150.58	19.1
第二产业	Secondary Industry	647.85	794.79	911.72	1087.87	1357.21	1636.25	20.6
工　业	Industry	644.88	787.60	905.01	1074.55	1333.06	1614.00	21.1
建筑业	Construction	2.97	7.19	6.70	13.32	24.15	22.26	-7.8
第三产业	Tertiary Industry	811.63	1018.79	1465.85	2017.70	2750.75	3930.97	42.9
资金来源合计	**Total Sources of Funds**	**1725.63**	**2157.38**	**3192.06**	**4108.87**	**5150.89**	**6219.71**	**20.8**
国家预算内资金	State Budget	86.36	138.06	283.38	355.96	548.98	537.04	-2.2
国内贷款	Domestic Loans	391.62	479.25	710.79	852.62	827.08	950.02	14.9
利用外资	Foreign Investment	15.56	14.33	10.89	10.71	14.72	11.49	-22.0
自筹资金	Self-raising Funds	874.97	1092.78	1424.18	1869.01	2555.43	3263.76	27.7
其他资金	Others	357.12	432.96	762.82	1020.58	1204.69	1457.41	21.0
房屋建筑面积（万平方米）	**Floor Space of Buildings(10000 sq.m)**							
施工面积	Floor Space under Construction	8112	9383	12176	14456	13959	18510	32.6
#住　宅	Residential Buildings	5814	6791	8535	10123	8875	11045	24.5
竣工面积	Floor Space Completed	3259	3207	4734	5325	2988	3496	17.0
#住　宅	Residential Buildings	2527	2500	3782	4054	1671	1880	12.5

注：固定资产投资统计口径2007—2010年为计划总投资50万元及以上固定资产项目投资，房地产开发投资及农村农户投资；2011年起为计划总投资500万元及以上固定资产项目投资，房地产开发投资及农村农户投资(以下相关表同)。

Note：From 2007 to 2010, data in the table referred to those projects that planned to invest 500000 yuan at least in investment in fixed assets, real estate development and rural household investment. From 2011,the statistical coverage has referred to those projects that planned to invest 5000000 yuan at least in investment in fixed assets, real estate development and rural household investment(The relative tables in the chapter are the same).

5-2 全社会工业投资
Industry Investment in the Whole Province

单位：亿元 (100 million yuan)

指 标	Item	2009	2010	2011	2012	2012年比2011年增长(%) Increase Rate in 2012over 2011(%)
工业投资	**Industry Investment**	**905.01**	**1074.55**	**1333.06**	**1614.00**	**21.1**
按隶属关系分	**Grouped by Jurisdiction of Management**					
中 央	Central Investment	205.47	152.19	141.13	115.55	-18.1
地 方	Local Investment	699.54	922.36	1191.93	1498.45	25.7
按国民经济行业分	**By Sector**					
采矿业	Mining	272.87	374.61	404.25	408.35	1.0
#煤炭开采和洗选业	Mining and Washing of Coal	252.26	337.39	347.88	308.38	-11.4
黑色金属矿采选	Mining and Processing of Ferrous Metal Ores	1.04	1.68	4.25	12.44	192.7
有色金属矿采选	Mining and Processing of Non-Ferrous Metal Ores	7.12	9.92	17.84	26.64	49.3
制造业	Manufacturing	354.98	428.33	687.42	951.83	38.5
#化学原料及化学制品制造	Manufacture of Raw Chemical Materials and Chemical Products	72.07	65.09	64.58	75.76	17.3
黑色金属冶炼及压延加工	Smelting and Pressing of Ferrous Metals	20.32	32.89	60.27	85.21	41.4
有色金属冶炼及压延加工	Smelting and Pressing of Non-ferrous Metals	38.02	49.90	58.49	55.41	-5.3
电力、燃气及水的生产和供应业	Production and Supply of Electricity, Gas and Water	277.15	271.61	241.39	253.81	5.1
#电力、热力的生产和供应业	Production and Supply of Electric Power and Heat Power	252.19	254.12	215.20	219.16	1.8

注：行业划分2009—2010年按国民经济行业分类GB/T 4754—2002分，2011年起按国民经济行业分类GB/T 4754—2011分(以下相关表同)。

Note:From 2009 to 2010, industry was divided by industrial classification GB / T 4754-2002. Since 2011,it has been divided by Sector Classification GB / T 4754-2011(The relative tables in the chapter are the same).

5-3 固定资产投资新增主要生产能力(2012)

Newly Increased Production Capacity through Capital Construction and Innovation

生产能力名称	Production Capacity	数 量 Amount
原煤开采(万吨/年)	Coal Mining(10000 tons/year)	5772.60
洗煤(万吨/年)	Coal Washing(10000 tons/year)	3611.16
焦炭(万吨/年)	Coke(10000 tons/year)	281.80
生铁(万吨/年)	Pig Iron(10000 tons/year)	88.00
铁合金(折标万吨/年)	Iron Alloy(10000 tons/year)	697.23
水力发电(万千瓦)	Hydropower(10000 kw)	156.84
火力发电(万千瓦)	Thermal Power(10000 kw)	65.58
输电线路长度(11万伏及以上)(公里)	Transmit Electricity Line (110000 Volt-amper Level and above)(km)	3635.79
水泥(万吨/年)	Cement(10000 tons/year)	1749.50
电石(万吨/年)	Calcium Carbide(10000 tons/year)	0.57
氮肥(万吨/年)	Nitrogen Fertilizers(10000 tons/year)	25.32
磷肥(万吨/年)	Phosphate Fertilizers(10000 tons/year)	35.50
白酒(万吨/年)	Liquor(10000 tons/year)	13.97
新建公路(公里)	Length of New Highways(km)	4484.27
#高速公路(公里)	Freeway(km)	534.00
改建公路(公里)	Length of Reconstructed Highways(km)	7568.72
新建独立公路桥梁(延长米)	New Independent Highway Bridge(extending.m)	4154.50
(座)	New Independent Highway Bridge(bridge)	35.00
新(扩)建公路客、货运站(个)	Newly-built or Expanded Passenger Transport and Freight Station(unit)	9.00
新(扩)建公路客、货运站面积(平方米)	Newly-built or Expanded Passenger Transport and Freight Station(sq.m)	31380.00
城市自来水供水能力(万吨/日)	Volume of Tap Water Supply in Cities(10000 ton/day)	31.70
城市公共交通车辆购置(辆)	Vehicle Purchase of Public Transportation in Cities(unit)	
城市污水处理能力(万吨/日)	Disposal Capacity of Sewage in Cities(10000 tons/year)	11.81

注：本表统计口径为计划总投资500万元及以上固定资产项目投资，房地产开发投资。

Note:Date in the table refer to those projects planned to invest 5000,000 yuan at least in fixed assets and real estate development.

5-4 按行业、隶属关系和注册类型分固定资产投资(2012)

单位：亿元

指标	Item	固定资产投资 Investment in Fixed Assets
固定资产投资	**Investment in Fixed Assets**	**5504.95**
农、林、牧、渔业	Agriculture, Forestry, Animal Husbandry and Fishery	115.62
#农　业	Farming	50.69
畜牧业	Animal Husbandry	26.18
农、林、牧、渔服务业	Services in Support of Agriculture	20.20
采矿业	Mining	408.35
#煤炭开采和洗选业	Mining and Washing of Coal	308.38
制造业	Manufacturing	951.83
#饮料制造业	Manufacture of Beverages	13.66
烟草制品业	Manufacture of Tobacco	3.94
造纸及纸制品业	Manufacture of Paper and Paper Products	7.02
石油加工、炼焦及核燃料加工业	Processing of Petroleum, Coking, Processing of Nuclear Fuel	32.13
化学原料及化学制品制造业	Manufacture of Raw Chemical Materials and Chemical Products	75.76
医药制造业	Manufacture of Medicines	26.55
非金属矿物制品业	Manufacture of Non-metallic Mineral Products	157.40
黑色金属冶炼及压延加工业	Smelting and Pressing of Ferrous Metals	85.21
有色金属冶炼及压延加工业	Smelting and Pressing of Non-ferrous Metals	55.41
交通运输设备制造业	Manufacture of Transport Equipment	
电力、燃气及水的生产和供应业	Production and Supply of Electricity, Gas and Water	253.81
#电力、热力的生产和供应业	Production and Supply of Electric Power and Heat Power	219.16
建筑业	Construction	22.13
#房屋和土木工程建筑业	Construction of Buildings and Civil Engineering	
交通运输、仓储和邮政业	Transport, Storage and Post	1002.30
#铁路运输业	Railway Transport	263.45
道路运输业	Road Transport	695.76
仓储业	Storage	20.97
信息传输、计算机服务和软件业	Information Transmission, Computer Services and Software	19.74
#电信和其他信息传输服务业	Telecommunications and Other Information Transmission Services	16.34
批发和零售业	Wholesale and Retail Trades	56.66
住宿和餐饮业	Hotels and Catering Services	54.55
金融业	Financial Intermediation	3.05
#银行业	Bank	
房地产业	Real Estate	1682.85
租赁和商务服务业	Leasing and Business Services	17.60
租赁业	Leasing	0.62
商务服务业	Business Services	16.98
科学研究、技术服务和地质勘查业	Scientific Research, Technical Service and Geologic Prospecting	9.20
#研究与试验发展	Research and Experimental Development	1.35
水利、环境和公共设施管理业	Management of Water Conservancy, Environment and Public Facilities	696.96
#水利管理业	Management of Water Conservancy	50.07
居民服务和其他服务业	Services to Households and Other Services	12.44
教　育	Education	85.25
卫生、社会保障和社会福利业	Health, Social Security and Social Welfare	25.90
#卫　生	Health	21.15
文化、体育和娱乐业	Culture, Sports and Entertainment	32.69
#文化艺术业	Cultural and Art Activities	15.14
公共管理和社会组织	Public Management and Social Organization	54.00

注：本表统计口径为计划总投资500万元及以上的固定资产项目投资，房地产开发投资。

Investment in Fixed Assets by Sector, Jurisdiction of Management and Registration Status

(100 million yuan)

按隶属关系分 Grouped by Jurisdiction of Management		按注册类型分 Grouped by Registration Status			
中央 Central Investment	地方 Local Investment	内资企业 Domestic Funds	港、澳、台商投资企业 Hong Kong, Macao and Taiwan	外商投资企业 Foreign Funded	个体经营 Self-employed Individual
389.96	**5114.99**	**5314.86**	**117.60**	**29.45**	**43.03**
0.59	115.03	109.71	0.38	0.83	4.70
0.35	50.34	48.92	0.36		1.41
	26.18	23.21		0.74	2.23
0.09	20.10	19.92	0.02	0.05	0.21
1.72	406.63	385.96	9.68	3.21	9.50
0.21	308.17	293.83	9.68	0.11	4.76
29.65	922.18	915.55	18.31	8.72	9.25
	13.66	13.22		0.11	0.32
1.07	2.87	3.87	0.07		
	7.02	6.87			0.15
	32.13	25.36	6.53	0.24	
1.76	73.99	72.44	0.22	2.43	0.66
	26.55	26.28		0.27	
0.28	157.12	149.58	3.25	0.93	3.64
	85.21	83.98	0.19	1.00	0.04
4.29	51.13	54.75	0.35	0.31	
84.18	169.63	250.73	2.25	0.70	0.14
82.57	136.59	218.79		0.30	0.06
0.02	22.11	21.86			0.28
249.22	753.08	999.54	2.45	0.31	
236.30	27.15	263.45			
3.39	692.37	693.55	1.90	0.31	
0.33	20.65	20.43	0.55		
7.01	12.73	16.27	0.28	3.12	0.07
6.99	9.35	12.99	0.28	3.07	
0.57	56.09	56.23			0.43
	54.55	48.19		0.30	6.06
0.38	2.67	3.05			
2.69	1680.17	1581.36	79.87	11.31	10.31
	17.60	17.54			0.06
	0.62	0.60			0.02
	16.98	16.94			0.04
1.60	7.60	9.11	0.09		
0.74	0.61	1.35			
11.04	685.92	693.45	2.52	0.69	0.30
1.04	49.03	49.92		0.12	0.03
0.01	12.42	12.26			0.18
0.21	85.04	82.99	1.77	0.07	0.43
0.73	25.18	25.06	0.02		0.82
0.68	20.46	20.37	0.02		0.75
0.03	32.66	32.44			0.24
	15.14	15.14			
0.32	53.69	53.56		0.20	0.25

Note:Date in the table refer to those projects planned to invest 5 million yuan at least in fixed assets and real estate development.

5-5 按行业分500万元以上固定资产投资施工项目(2012)

Number of Construction Projects over 5 Million Yuan under Construction by Sector

行 业	Sector	本年施工项目(个) Number of Projects under Construction This Year (unit)	#本年新开工 Number of Projects Started This Year	本年投产项目(个) Number of Projects Put into Use (unit)	项目建成投产率(%) Percentage of Projects Completed and Putinto Use
总计	**Total**	**7593**	**5683**	**5030**	**66.2**
农、林、牧、渔业	Agriculture, Forestry, Animal Husbandry and Fishery	581	513	437	75.2
#农、林、牧、渔服务业	Service in Support of Agriculture	114	102	89	78.1
采矿业	Mining	950	664	716	75.4
#煤炭开采和洗选业	Mining and Washing of Coal	657	412	474	72.1
制造业	Manufacturing	1481	1095	976	65.9
#饮料制造业	Manufacture of Beverages	36	25	25	69.4
烟草制品业	Manufacture of Tobacco	18	15	14	77.8
造纸及纸制品业	Manufacture of Paper and Paper Products	18	14	12	66.7
石油加工、炼焦及核燃料加工业	Processing of Petroleum, Coking and Processing of Nuclear Fuel	16	7	8	50.0
化学原料及化学制品制造业	Manufacture of Raw Chemical Materials and Chemical Products	100	77	63	63.0
医药制造业	Manufacture of Medicines	50	39	32	64.0
非金属矿物制品业	Manufacture of Non-metallic Mineral Products	303	243	216	71.3
黑色金属冶炼及压延加工业	Smelting and Pressing of Ferrous Metals	60	38	39	65.0
有色金属冶炼及压延加工业	Smelting and Pressing of Non-ferrous Metals	39	25	27	69.2
电力、燃气及水的生产和供应业	Production and Supply of Electricity,Gas and Water	380	251	215	56.6
#电力、热力的生产和供应业	Production and Supply of Electric Power and Heat Power	262	162	147	56.1
建筑业	Construction	125	104	108	86.4
交通运输、仓储和邮政业	Transport, Storage and Post	978	704	597	61.0
#铁路运输业	Railway Transport	21	8	5	23.8
道路运输业	Road Transport	899	655	563	62.6
仓 储 业	Storage	36	25	17	47.2

5-5 续表 continued

行 业	Sector	本年施工项目(个) Number of Projects under Construction This Year (unit)	#本年新开工 Number of Projects Started This Year	本年投产项目(个) Number of Projects Put into Use (unit)	项目建成投产率(%) Percentage of Projects Completed and Put into Use
信息传输、计算机服务和软件业	Information Transmission, Computer Services and Software	98	89	77	78.6
#电信和其他信息传输服务业	Telecommunications and Other Information Transmission Services	90	82	72	80.0
批发和零售业	Wholesale and Retail Trades	154	121	91	59.1
住宿和餐饮业	Hotels and Catering Services	193	153	152	78.8
金 融 业	Financial Intermediation	17	11	11	64.7
房地产业	Real Estate	577	424	375	65.0
租赁和商务服务业	Leasing and Business Services	32	26	18	56.3
租 赁 业	Leasing	1	1	1	100.0
商务服务业	Business Services	31	25	17	54.8
科学研究、技术服务和地质勘查业	Scientific Research, Technical Service and Geologic Prospecting	32	27	20	62.5
#研究与试验发展	Research and Experimental Development	2	1	0	0
水利、环境和公共设施管理业	Management of Water Conservancy, Environment and Public Facilities	1227	947	785	64.0
#水利管理业	Management of Water Conservancy	218	176	147	67.4
居民服务和其他服务业	Services to Households and Other Services	52	36	32	61.5
教 育	Education	283	198	166	58.7
卫生、社会保障和社会福利业	Health, Social Security and Social Welfare	111	77	67	60.4
#卫 生	Health	81	53	49	60.5
文化、体育和娱乐业	Culture, Sports and Entertainment	71	50	46	64.8
#文化艺术业	Cultural and Art Activities	36	24	22	61.1
公共管理和社会组织	Public Management and Social Organization	251	193	142	56.6

5–6 房地产开发企业基本情况(2012)

单位：亿元

指　标	Item	总 计 Total
企业个数(个)	**Number of Enterprises(unit)**	**2133**
年末从业人员总计(人)	**Number of Employed Persons at the Year-end (person)**	**48003**
本年完成投资	**Investment Completed This Year**	**1467.60**
按工程用途分	By Use of Project	
#商品住宅	Residential Buildings	930.31
办公楼	Office Building	42.23
商业营业用房	House for Business Used	212.56
其　他	Others	282.49
按构成分	By Type of Construction	
建筑工程	Construction	1050.87
安装工程	Installation	70.72
设备工器具购置	Purchase of Equitment and Instruments	19.28
其他费用	Others	326.73
本年资金来源合计	**Total Source of Funds This Year**	**1696.00**
#国内贷款	Domestic Loans	230.61
利用外资	Foreign Investment	4.29
自筹资金	Fundraising	518.44
其他资金来源	Others	664.82
#个人按揭贷款	Personal Housing Mortgage Loans	246.62
土地购置费	Land Acquisition Costs	119.50
待开发土地面积(万平方米)	Land Space to Be Developed (10000 sq.m)	1005.18
本年购置土地面积(万平方米)	Land Space Purchased This Year(10000 sq.m)	707.51
主营业务收入	Revenue From Principal Business	5499.83
税金总额	Total Tax	566.55
资产总计	Total Assets	42288.48
负债合计	Total Liabilities	33795.07
所有者权益合计	Total Owners Equities	8493.40
资产负债率(%)	Assets-Liability Ratio(%)	79.9
施工房屋面积(万平方米)	Floor Space Under Construction(10000 sq.m)	13245.31
竣工房屋面积(万平方米)	Floor Space of Completed(10000 sq.m)	1416.77
房屋建筑面积竣工率(%)	Rate of Floor Space Completed(%)	0.11
本年新开工房屋面积(万平方米)	**Floor Space Started This Year(10000 sq.m)**	**3787.67**
住　宅	Residential Buildings	2578.41
办公楼	Office Building	176.24
商业营业用房	House for Business Used	567.91
其　他	Others	465.12

Basic Conditions of Real Estate Development Enterprises

(100 million yuan)

内资企业 Domestic Funded	#国有企业 State-owned Enterprises	#私营有限责任公司 Private Limited Liability Company	#私营股份有限公司 Private Share-holding Corporations Limited	港澳台商投资企业 Enterprises with Funds from HongKong, Macao and TaiWan	外商投资企业 Foreign Funded Enterprises
2091	**76**	**774**	**101**	**32**	**10**
46819	**1842**	**15039**	**1848**	**1023**	**161**
1377.32	**64.00**	**289.90**	**36.45**	**79.56**	**10.72**
875.68	45.78	186.97	24.45	51.84	2.79
39.17	1.59	6.64	0.44	0.91	2.15
202.12	5.95	44.56	3.87	9.07	1.37
260.36	10.68	51.73	7.70	17.73	4.41
970.14	52.15	224.74	32.07	70.02	10.71
70.39	1.07	15.12	1.31	0.33	
19.18	0.75	4.05	0.44	0.10	
317.62	10.03	45.98	2.63	9.11	0.01
1632.47	**73.23**	**371.91**	**61.67**	**56.02**	**7.50**
221.27	24.01	42.26	3.08	8.95	0.39
				4.29	
503.94	22.78	148.54	19.02	12.56	1.95
639.45	14.72	128.56	21.41	20.78	4.59
239.49	3.19	53.09	9.05	6.17	0.95
112.22	0.14	25.09	0.86	7.28	
882.78	18.43	254.07	15.05	121.80	0.60
670.99	2.49	226.96	18.41	36.52	
5383.44	473.04	1560.67	203.75	83.57	32.82
556.84	45.29	151.65	21.48	7.11	2.59
40786.71	3856.51	9547.97	1155.52	1162.47	339.29
32698.83	2661.97	7576.22	1003.71	765.69	330.56
8087.88	1194.54	1971.75	151.82	396.79	8.74
80.2	69.0	79.3	86.9	65.9	97.4
12951.62	574.81	3440.85	458.35	198.11	95.59
1382.54	158.87	391.50	63.05	34.23	
0.11	0.28	0.11	0.14	0.17	
3726.36	**162.35**	**975.02**	**109.44**	**50.27**	**11.04**
2539.44	118.50	646.11	78.75	38.97	
162.52	1.21	42.57		5.37	8.35
563.94	19.55	166.27	11.57	1.77	2.19
460.46	23.09	120.08	19.12	4.15	0.50

5-7 房地产开发投资主要指标

Main Indicator on Real Estate Development

指标	Item	2007	2008	2009	2010	2011	2012	2012年比2011年增长(%) Increase Rate in 2012 over 2011(%)
本年土地购置面积(万平方米)	**Land Space Purchased This Year (10000 sq.m)**	**661**	**590**	**373**	**1027**	**883**	**708**	**-19.9**
本年完成投资额(亿元)	**Investment Completed This Year (100 million yuan)**	**249.67**	**311.26**	**371.25**	**556.69**	**873.48**	**1467.60**	**68.0**
#住　宅	Residential Buildings	156.07	195.49	249.46	328.63	576.44	930.31	61.4
资金来源合计(亿元)	**Source of Funds(100 million yuan)**	**444.77**	**520.31**	**773.47**	**1135.61**	**1533.83**	**1696.00**	**10.6**
#国内贷款	Domestic Loans	95.81	79.98	133.11	160.10	172.78	230.61	33.5
利用外资	Foreign Investment	2.24	1.20	0.26	0.72	4.47	4.29	-4.0
自筹资金	Self-raising Funds	109.36	160.40	168.24	268.68	526.09	518.44	-1.5
房屋建筑面积(万平方米)	**Floor Space of Buildings(10000 sq.m)**							
施工面积	Floor Space under Construction	4277	5229	6101	7906	10261	13245	29.1
#本年新开工面积	Floor Space Started This Year	1575	1594	1755	2871	2885	3788	31.3
#住　宅	Residential Buildings	3369	4210	4715	5971	7689	9654	25.6
竣工面积	Floor Space Completed	695	721	1224	1048	1455	1417	-2.6
#住　宅	Residential Buildings	559	589	1041	826	1102	1120	1.6

5-8 商品房屋销售面积(2012)

Floor Space of Commercialized Buildings

单位：万平方米 (10000 sq.m)

指　标	Item	商品房屋销售面积 Floor Space of Commercialized Buildings Sold	#住 宅 Residential Buildings
总计	**Total**	**2186.95**	**2002.40**
#现房	Existing House	252.87	196.24
期房	Forward House	1934.07	1806.16
#内资企业	Domestic Funded Enterprises	2154.74	1974.71
#国有企业	State-owned Enterprises	91.74	84.79
集体企业	Collective-owned Enterprises	2.09	1.78
其他有限责任公司	Other Limited Liability Corporations	1355.84	1253.84
股份有限公司	Share-holding Corporations Ltd.	78.11	65.45
私营独资企业	Private-funded Enterprises	41.30	38.00
私营有限责任公司	Private Limited Liability Corporations	483.15	438.31
私营股份有限公司	Private Share-holding Corporations Ltd.	60.41	56.90
港澳台商投资企业	Enterprises with Funds from Hong Kong,Macao and Taiwan	21.33	19.64
#与港澳台商合资经营企业	Joint-venture Enterprises	7.32	5.96
港澳台商独资经营企业	Enterprises with Sole Fund	14.01	13.68
外商投资企业	Foreign Funded Enterprises	10.88	8.04
#中外合资经营企业	Joint-venture Enterprises	2.41	2.41
外资企业	Enterprises with Sole Fund	2.67	

5-9 商品房屋销售额(2012)

Total Sale of Commercialized Buildings

单位：万元 (10000 yuan)

指　标	Item	商品房屋销售额 Total Sale of Commercialized Buildings Sold	#住 宅 Residential Buildings
总计	**Total**	**900.08**	**739.96**
#现房	Existing House	106.31	58.37
期房	Forward House	793.76	681.59
#内资企业	Domestic Funded Enterprises	879.97	723.74
#国有企业	State-owned Enterprises	47.26	40.13
集体企业	Collective-owned Enterprises	0.79	0.60
其他有限责任公司	Other Limited Liability Corporations	570.05	482.16
股份有限公司	Share-holding Corporations Ltd.	30.70	22.09
私营独资企业	Private-funded Enterprises	13.04	11.63
私营有限责任公司	Private Limited Liability Corporations	182.99	140.40
私营股份有限公司	Private Share-holding Corporations Ltd.	21.82	18.05
港澳台商投资企业	Enterprises with Funds from Hong Kong,Macao and Taiwan	14.76	12.93
#与港澳台商合资经营企业	Joint-venture Enterprises	5.17	3.80
港澳台商独资经营企业	Enterprises with Sole Fund	9.58	9.12
外商投资企业	Foreign Funded Enterprises	5.35	3.29
#中外合资经营企业	Joint-venture Enterprises	0.69	0.69
外资企业	Enterprises with Sole Fund	1.90	

主要统计指标解释

全社会固定资产投资　是以货币形式表现的在一定时期内全社会建造和购置固定资产的工作量以及与此有关的费用的总称。该指标是反映固定资产投资规模、结构和发展速度的综合性指标，又是观察工程进度和考核投资效果的重要依据。全社会固定资产投资包括固定资产项目投资、房地产开发投资和农户投资。全社会固定资产投资按登记注册类型可分为国有、集体、个体、联营、股份制、外商、港澳台商、其他等。

房地产开发投资　指各种登记注册类型的房地产开发公司、商品房建设公司及其他房地产开发法人单位和附属于其他法人单位实际从事房地产开发或经营活动的单位统一开发的包括统代建、拆迁还建的住宅、厂房、仓库、饭店、宾馆、度假村、写字楼、办公楼等房屋建筑物和配套的服务设施，土地开发工程（如道路、给水、排水、供电、供热、通讯、平整场地等基础设施工程）的投资；不包括单纯的土地交易活动。

固定资产投资的资金来源　根据固定资产投资的资金来源不同，分为国家预算资金、国内贷款、债券、利用外资、自筹资金和其他资金。

(1) 国家预算资金　自 2011 年起，按照全国人大和国务院的要求，各级财政的所有资金，包括税收和非税收入，均必须纳入预算管理，我国已不存在预算外资金的概念，因此各级政府用于固定资产投资的财政资金均为预算资金。由于已经没有预算外资金，因此名称改为国家预算资金，包括中央预算资金和地方预算资金，旧的国家预算内资金的内容和现中央预算资金的内容基本一致。

国家预算包括一般预算、政府性基金预算、国有资本经营预算和社保基金预算。各类预算中用于固定资产投资的资金全部作为国家预算资金填报，其中一般预算中用于固定资产投资的部分包括基建投资、车购税、灾后恢复重建基金和其他财政投资。各级政府债券也应归入国家预算资金。

根据《2011 年政府收支分类科目》确定的收支范围，目前纳入政府性基金预算的资金主要包括：农网还贷资金、山西省煤炭可持续发展基金、铁路建设基金、民航基础设施建设基金、民航机场管理建设费、海南省高等级公路车辆通行附加费、转让政府还贷道路收费权、港口建设费、散装水泥专项资金、新型墙体材料专项基金、旅游发展基金、文化事业建设费、地方教育附加、江苏省地方教育基金、国家电影事业发展专项资金、新菜地开发建设基金、新增建设用地土地有偿使用费、育林基金、森林植被恢复费、中央水利建设基金、地方水利建设基金、南水北调工程基金、残疾人就业保障金、政府住房基金、城市公用事业附加、国有土地使用权出让金、国有土地收益基金、农业土地开发资金、大中型水库移民后期扶持基金、大中型水库库区基金、三峡水库库区基金、中央特别国债经营基金、中央特别国债经营基金财务收支、彩票公益金、城市基础设施配套费、小型水库移民扶助基金、国家重大水利工程建设基金、车辆通行费、船舶港务费、体育部门收费、司法部门的涉外涉港澳台公证书工本费、贸促会收费、长江口航道维护费、电力改革预留资产变现资金、铁路资产变现资金、其他政府性基金。

(2) 国内贷款　指报告期固定资产投资项目单位向银行及非银行金融机构借入用于固定资产投资的各种国内借款，包括银行利用自有资金及吸收存款发放的贷款、上级主管部门拨入的国内贷款、国家专项贷款（包括煤代油贷款、劳改煤矿专项贷款等），地方财政专项资金安排的贷款、国内储备贷款、周转贷款等。

(3) 利用外资　指报告期收到的境外（包括外国及港澳台地区）资金（包括设备、材料、技术在内）。包括对外借款（外国政府贷款、国际金融组织贷款、出口信贷、外国银行商业贷款、对外发行债券和股票）、外商直接投资、外商其他投资（包括利用外商投资收益在国内进行固定资产再投资活动的资金）。不包括我国自有外汇资金（国家外汇、地方外汇、留成外汇、调济外汇和国内银行自有资金发放的外汇贷款等）。各类外资按报告期末的外汇牌价（中间价）折成人民币计算。

(4) 自筹资金　指固定资产投资单位在报告期收到的，由各企事业单位筹集用于固定资产投资的资金，包括各类企事业单位的自有资金和从其他单位筹集的用于固定资产投资的资金，但不包括各类财政性资金、从各类金融机构借入资金和国外资金。与原有的自筹资金概念相比，最大的变化是地方财政资金全部归为国家预算资金，自筹资金中不再含有财政资金。

(5) 其他资金来源　指在报告期收到的除以上各种资金之外的用于固定资产投资的资金。包括社会集资、个人资金、无偿捐赠的资金及其他单位拨入的资金等。

固定资产投资按国民经济行业分　根据建设项目建成投产后的主要产品或主要用途及社会经济活动性质来确定国民经济行业。一般情况下，一个建设项目或一个企业、事业单位只能属于一种国民经济行业。

固定资产投资按隶属关系分　是按建设单位或企业、事业、行政单位的主管上级机关确定的。

(1) 中央 是由中共中央、人大常委会和国务院各部、委、局、总公司以及直属机构直接领导的建设项目和企业、事业、行政单位。这些单位的固定资产投资计划由国务院各部门直接编制和下达，统一组织或委托下级实施。

(2) 地方 是由省（自治区、直辖市）、地区（州、盟、省辖市）、县（旗、县级市）三级政府及业务主管部门直接领导和管理的建设项目、企业、事业、行政单位。地方项目还包括不隶属以上各级政府及主管部门的建设项目和企业、事业单位，如外商投资企业和无主管部门的企业等。

固定资产投资按建设性质分 根据整个建设项目情况来确定。建设项目的性质一般分为新建、扩建、改建和技术改造、迁建、恢复。房地产开发单位不划分建设性质。

(1) 新建 指从无到有“平地起家”开始建设的项目。现有企业、事业、行政单位投资的项目一般不属于新建。但如有的单位原有基础很小，经过建设后新增的固定资产价值超过该企业、事业、行政单位原有固定资产价值（原值）三倍以上的，也应作为新建。

(2) 扩建 指在厂内或其他地点，为扩大原有产品的生产能力（或效益）或增加新的产品生产能力，而增建的生产车间（或主要工程）、分厂、独立的生产线的企业、事业单位。行政、事业单位在原单位增建业务性用房（如学校增建教学用房、医院增建门诊部、病房等）也作为扩建。

现有企业、事业单位为扩大原有主要产品生产能力或增加新的产品生产能力，增建一个或几个主要生产车间（或主要工程）、分厂，同时进行一些更新改造工程的，也应作为扩建。

(3) 改建和技术改造 指现有企业、事业单位对原有设施进行技术改造或更新（包括相应配套的辅助性生产、生活福利设施）的建设项目。改建项目包括现有企业、事业单位为适应市场变化的需要，而改变企业的主要产品种类（如军工企业转民用产品等）的建设项目，原有产品生产作业线由于各工序（车间）之间能力不平衡，为填平补齐充分发挥原有生产能力而增建不增加本企业主要产品设计能力的车间的建设项目。技术改造是指企业、事业单位在现有基础上，用先进的技术代替落后的技术，用先进的工艺和装备代替落后的工艺和装备，以改变企业落后的技术经济面貌，实现以内涵为主的扩大再生产，达到提高产品质量、促进产品更新换代、节约能源、降低消耗、扩大生产规模、全面提高社会经济效益的目的。技术改造具体包括以下内容：机器设备和工具的更新改造；生产工艺改革、节约能源和原材料的改造；厂房建筑和公共设施的改造；保护环境进行的“三废”治理改造；劳动条件和生产环境的改造等。

固定资产投资按构成分 固定资产投资活动按其工作内容和实现方式分为建筑安装工程，设备、工具、器具购置，其他费用三个部分。

(1) 建筑安装工程(建筑安装工作量)：指各种房屋、建筑物的建造工程和各种设备、装置的安装工程。包括各种房屋建造工程；各种用途设备基础和各种工业窑炉的砌筑工程及金属结构工程；为施工而进行的各种准备工作和临时工程以及完工后的清理工作等；铁路、道路的铺设，矿井的开凿及石油管道的架设等；水利工程；防空地下建筑等特殊工程；列入房屋工程预算内的暖气、卫生、通风、照明、煤气等设备的价值及装设油饰工程；列入建筑工程预算内的各种管道(蒸汽、压缩空气、石油、给排水等管道)、电力、电讯、电缆、导线等的敷设工程；以及各种机械设备的安装工程；为测定安装工程质量，对设备进行的试运工作；房地产开发单位进行的商品房屋开发建设工程、土地开发工程。

在安装工程中，不包括被安装设备本身的价值。

(2) 设备、工具、器具购置：指建设单位或企、事业单位购置或自制的，达到固定资产标准的设备、工具、器具的价值。新建单位及扩建单位的新建车间，按照设计或计划要求购置或自制的全部设备、工具、器具，不论是否达到固定资产标准均计入〃设备、工具、器具购置〃中。

(3) 其他费用：指在固定资产建造和购置过程中发生的，除建筑安装工程和设备、工器具购置投资完成额以外的应当分摊计入固定资产投资的费用，不指经营中财务上的其他费用。

施工项目个数、本年投产项目个数和本年新开工项目个数：每一个建设项目只计算为一个项目个数。

施工项目个数 指本年正式进行过建筑或安装施工活动的建设项目个数。包括本年新开工项目，以前年度开工跨入本年继续施工项目，本年全部建成投产项目、以前年度全部停缓建在本年恢复施工的项目，本年进行过施工又在本年内全部停缓建的项目。

本年投产项目个数 指报告期内按设计文件规定建成主体工程和相应配套的辅助设施，形成生产能力或工程效益，经过验收合格，并且已正式投入生产或交付使用的建设项目。建成投产项目个数是反映报告期建设成果和考核投资效果的重要依据。

全部建成投入生产或交付使用的工业项目是指设计文件规定形成生产能力的主体工程及其相应配套的辅助设施全部建成，经负荷试运转，证明具备生产设计规定合格产品的条件，并经过验收鉴定合格或达到竣工验收标准，与生产性工程配套的生活福利设施可以满足近期正常生产的需要，正式移交生产的建设项目；非工业项目是指设计文件规定的主体工程和相应配套工程全部建成，能够发挥设计规定的工程效益，经验收鉴定合格或达到竣工验收标准，正式移交使用的建设项目。

凡对环境有污染的建设项目，要按照有关部门规定，在"三废"治理工程按设计规定建成，并经环保部门验收鉴定合格，交付使用后，整个项目才能作为全投项目。达不到要求的则不能作为全投项目统计。

本年新开工项目个数 指报告期内新开工的建设项目。包括新开工的新建项目、扩建项目、改建项目、单纯建造生活设施项目、迁建项目和恢复项目。新开工项目的确定以总体设计或计划文件中所规定的永久性工程正式开工为准。本年新开工项目个数是反映全年新开工的固定资产投资规模的指标。

新增生产能力（或工程效益） 指通过固定资产投资活动而增加的设计能力（或工程效益），该指标是以实物形态表现的反映固定资产投资成果的指标，也是考核投资经济效果的重要依据之一。

新增生产能力（或工程效益）一般有以下几种表现形式:

(1) 用产品数量表示，以工程在单位时间内（一般是一年）所能生产的产品数量（即年产量）表示。如原煤开采用万吨／年表示，化学农药用吨／年表示，拖拉机制造用台／年表示等。某些化工产品由于含量差别较大，按其设计含量计算折合量表示，如硫酸、纯碱、烧碱等。

(2) 用单位时间内所能处理的原料数量表示，以工程每天（或小时）所能处理原料的数量表示。如机制糖工程用日处理原料吨表示，食用植物油用日处理原料吨表示，城市污水处理能力用万吨／日表示等。

(3) 用新增加的主要设备的数量或容量表示，如新增棉布织机、丝织机等台数，毛纺锭等锭数，发电厂新增发电机组容量用千瓦表示等。

(4) 用建筑物容积、容量、面积、长度表示，是非工业项目或工程新增效益的一种表现形式。如铁路投产里程、新建公路、水库容量、粮食仓库、学校学生席位、医院病床、有效灌溉面积等。

根据工程的特点，有时需要用两种或两种以上的复合计量单位表示新增生产能力（或工程效益），如新增内燃机生产能力同时用年产台数、千瓦数表示等。

为了规范新增生产能力（或工程效益）的名称和计算单位，国家统计局制订了《新增生产能力（或工程效益）目录及代码》。各固定资产投资单位在统计新增生产能力（或工程效益）时，必须按目录中规定的名称、计量单位和代码填报。

房屋施工面积 指报告期内施工的全部房屋建筑面积。包括本期新开工的面积、上期跨入本期继续施工的房屋面积、上期停缓建在本期恢复施工的房屋面积、本期竣工的房屋面积以及本期施工后又停缓建的房屋面积。多层建筑应填各层建筑面积之和。

房屋竣工面积 指报告期内房屋建筑按照设计要求已全部完工，达到住人和使用条件，经验收鉴定合格或达到竣工验收标准，可正式移交使用的各栋房屋建筑面积的总和。

竣工面积以房屋单位工程（栋）为核算对象，在整栋房屋符合竣工条件后按其全部建筑面积一次性计算，而不是按各栋施工房屋中已完成的部分或层次分割计算。

计算本年房屋竣工面积，要求严格执行房屋竣工验收标准。民用建筑一般应按设计要求在土建工程和房屋本身附属的水、电、卫（包括设计中有的煤气、暖气）工程已经完工，通风、电梯等设备已经安装完毕，做到水通、灯亮，经验收鉴定合格，并正式交付给使用单位后，才能计算竣工面积。工业及科研等生产性房屋建筑一般应按设计要求在土建工程（包括水、暖、电、卫、通风）及属于房屋组成部分的生活间、操作间等已经完成（不包括安装设备的基础工程），可以进行工艺设备和管线安装时，方可计算本年房屋竣工面积。

房屋建筑面积竣工率 指一定时期内房屋竣工面积占同期房屋施工面积的比率。

新增固定资产 已经完成建造和购置过程，并已交付生产或使用单位的固定资产的价值，包括已经建成投入生产或交付使用的工程投资和达到固定资产标准的设备、工具、器具的投资及有关应摊入的费用。

属于增加固定资产价值的其他建设费用，应随同交付使用的工程一并计入新增固定资产。

项目建成投产率 指一定时期内全部建成投产项目个数与同期施工项目个数的比率。该指标是从建设单位建设速度的角度反映投资效果的指标。

商品房销售面积 指报告期内出售商品房屋的合同总面积（即双方签署的正式买卖合同中所确定的建筑面积）。由现房销售建筑面积和期房销售建筑面积两部分组成。

商品房销售额 指报告期内出售商品房屋的合同总价款（即双方签署的正式买卖合同中所确定的合同总价）。该指标与商品房销售面积同口径，由现房销售额和期房销售额两部分组成。

Explanatory Notes on Main Statistical Indicators

Total Investment in Fixed Assets in the Whole Country refers to the volume of activities in construction and purchases of fixed assets of the whole province and related fees, expressed in monetary terms during the reference period. It is a comprehensive indicator which shows the size, structure and growth of the investment in fixed assets, providing a basis for observing the progress of construction projects and evaluating results of investment. Total investment in fixed assets in the whole province includes investment in fixed assets , investment in real estate development and rural household investment. Total investment in fixed assets in the whole province includes, by type of ownership, the investment by State-owned units, collective-owned units, individuals, joint ownership units, share-holding units, as well as investments by entrepreneurs from foreign countries and from Hong Kong, Macao and Taiwan, and by other units.

Investment in Real Estate Development refers to investment by real estate development companies, commercialized buildings construction companies and other real estate development units of various types of ownership in the construction of buildings, such as residential buildings, factory buildings, warehouses, hotels, guesthouses, holiday villages, office buildings, and the complementary service facilities and land development projects, such as roads, water supply, water drainage, power supply, heating supply, telecommunications, land leveling and other infrastructural projects. It does not include activities in pure land transactions.

Sources of Funds for Investment in Fixed Assets are categorized as funds from the State budget, domestic loans, bonds , foreign investment, self-raised funds, and others, depending on the sources of investment.

(1) Fund from the State budget: From 2011, in accordance with the requirements of the NPC and the State Council, all levels of financial funds included tax and non-tax revenue that both of them must be included in the budget management. And our country has no concept of extra-budgetary funds. So the financial funds of all levels of government that is using for investment in fixed assets are budget funds. Because they have no extra-budgetary funds, the name was changed to state budget funds, including the central budget and local budget funds. The original contents of the state budget funds and the central budget funds are basically the same.

State budget includes the general budget, the government fund budget, the state capital budget and the social security fund budget. All kinds of budget funds for investment in fixed assets are as fill for state budget funds. Among them, the section of general budget which is for investment in fixed assets are including infrastructure investment portion, vehicle purchase, post-disaster restoration and reconstruction funds and other financial investments. All levels of government bonds should also be included in state budget funds.

According to "2011 Government revenue and expenditure classification of subjects" to determine the scope of revenue and expenditure, the current government funds into the capital budget include: rural loan funds, coal Sustainable Development Funds in Shanxi province, railway construction funds, CAAC Infrastructure Development funds, aviation airport management and construction fees, highway vehicle traffic surcharge in Hainan province, transfer government loan road pricing right,port construction fees, bulk cement special funds, new wall materials special funds, tourism development funds, culture construction fees, additional local education, local education funds in Jiangsu province, National Film career development funds, new vegetable field development and construction funds, new construction land use fees, silviculture funds, Forest vegetation restoration fees, central water conservancy construction funds, local water conservancy construction funds, North Water Transfer Project funds, disabled employment security funds, government housing funds, additional city utilities, State-owned land use right transfer fee, State-owned Land Income funds, agricultural land development funds, medium-sized reservoir resettlement support funds, medium-sized reservoir funds, Three Gorges Reservoir funds, central special treasury management funds, central special treasury fund financial revenue and expenditure operations, lottery, urban infrastructure fee, small reservoir resettlement support funds, major national water conservancy construction funds, vehicle tolls, harbor dues, sports department charges, the judiciary involving Hong Kong, Macao and Taiwan foreign notary fees, CCPIT charges, Yangtze Estuary Waterway maintenance fees, electricity reform realization of assets set aside funds, railway assets realized capital, other government funds.

(2) Domestic loans refer to loans of various forms borrowed by investing units from banks and non-bank financial institutions during the reference period for the purpose of investment in fixed assets, including loans issued by banks from their self-owned funds and deposit, loans appropriated by higher authorities, special loans by government(Including coal oil loans, special loans by correctional mine and so on), loans arranged by local government from special funds, domestic reserve loan, and working loan.

(3) Foreign investment refers to foreign funds received abroad (including foreign and Hong Kong, Macao and Taiwan regions) funds (covering equipment, materials and technology)during the reference period, including foreign borrowings (loans from foreign governments and international financial institutions, export credit, commercial loans from foreign banks, issue of bonds and stocks overseas), foreign direct investment and other foreign investments. Excluded from this category is capital in foreign exchanges owned by China (foreign exchanges owned by the central and local governments, foreign exchanges retained by enterprises, foreign exchanges by enterprises through the regulating mechanism, loans in foreign exchanges issued by the Bank of China with its own fund, etc.). Various types of foreign investment in accordance with the reporting period, the exchange rates (mid-point) converted into Renminbi.

(4) Self-raised funds refer to funds for investment in fixed assets received during the reference period by investing units, including investment in fixed assets using own funds of various enterprises and institutions or funds raised from other units other than financial funds, funds borrowed from financial institutions and overseas funds.Compared with the original concept of self-raised funds, the biggest change is all owned by funds for the state budget funds, self-raised funds in the longer contain financial funds .

(5) Others refer to funds for investment in fixed assets received from sources other than those listed above, including capital raised through issuing bonds by enterprises or financial institutions, funds raised from individuals and through donations, and funds transferred from other units.

Investment in Fixed Assets by Sector The classification of construction projects by sector is determined by the major products or the purpose of the projects when they are put into production or use, and by the nature of their social economic activities. In general, one project or one enterprise or institution can only be classified into one sector.

Investment in Fixed Assets by Jurisdiction of Management refers to the classification of investment by the competent authorities under which investment is made by construction units, enterprises, institutions or administrative units.

(1) Central investment refers to the investment in projects or by enterprises, institutions or administrative units which are under the direct leadership and management of the State Council and of the national commissions, ministries, agencies and State-owned large corporations. Various ministries and departments of the State Council prepare and implement plans for investment in fixed assets by those departments, and arrange and ensure the supply of materials and key equipment required for the projects.

(2) Local investment refers to the investment in projects or by enterprises, institutions or administrative units which are under the direct leadership and management of departments under the provincial, prefecture and county governments. Also included are projects by foreign-invested enterprises and enterprises without competent managing authorities.

Investment in Fixed Assets by Type of Construction Construction projects in general can be classified, by the type of construction, into new construction, expansion, reconstruction and technical transformation, moving and restoration. However, construction real Estate development unit is not divided nature.

(1)New construction in general refers to scratch "flat started" Start construction projects . Existing enterprises, institutions, administrative unit investment projects are generally not part of New. But in case the size of the existing unit is quite small, and the value of newly added fixed assets is more than three times of the the original value, the expansion will be considered as new construction.

(2) Expansion refers to construction of new major production workshop, branch factory or independent production

line within a factory or in other locations, for the purpose of increasing the production capacity (or improving efficiency) or adding new production capacity. Newly constructed accommodation for the operation of institutions and administrative organizations (such as newly constructed buildings for teaching in schools, buildings for clinics or wards in hospitals, etc.) are also classified as expansion.

Also included in expansion are investments by existing enterprises or institutions in building major production line(s) or branch factory(ies) along with some work on innovation, for the purpose of expanding the production capacity of original products or producing new products.

(3) Reconstruction and technical transformation refers to construction projects by existing enterprises or institutions in innovation or technical transformation of the old facilities (including auxiliary production equipment and welfare facilities). Also considered as reconstruction is the construction of new workshops by the existing enterprises or institutions to change the variety of products to meet the market demand (such as the production of civil products by defence industries), or to bring the designed production capacity into full play through a more balanced production process on production lines. Technical transformation refers to replacement of old technology or equipment by new technology or equipment, in order to expand the reproduction through improvement of technology contents in production, to improve product quality, to promote new products, to save energy, to reduce consumption, to expand the production scale and to improve overall social-economic efficiency. Contents of technical transformation include: updating of machinery, equipment and tools; reforming production process by using energy or materials saving technology; improvement of working conditions and environment, etc.

Investment in Fixed Assets by Structure By their contents and the mode of implementation, investment activities are classified into 3 categories, i.e. construction and installation, purchase of equipment and instrument, and other expenses.

(1) Construction and installation (work volume of construction and installation) refers to the construction of houses and buildings and the installation of various kinds of equipment and instruments. They include construction of houses; equipment foundations, industrial kilns and stoves, and metal structure work; preparation works and temporary works for project construction, and clearing up works post project construction; pavement of railways and roads, drilling of mines and putting up of oil pipes; construction of water conservancy; construction of underground air-raid shelters and construction of other special projects; value of equipment for heating, sanitation, ventilation, lighting, gas, painting, etc. that are covered by the budget of housing projects; laying out of various pipelines (for steam, compressed air, petroleum, tap water and sewage) and wiring and cabling for electric power and for communications; installation of various machinery and equipment; testing operation for pre-testing the quality of installation projects, and land and other development work conducted by real estate developers for commercialized housing. The value of equipment installed is itself not included in the value of installation projects.

(2) Purchase of equipment and instruments refers to the total value of equipment, tools, and instruments purchased or self-produced which come up to the cut-off point for fixed assets by the construction units or investing enterprises or institutions. Equipment, tools and instruments purchased or self-produced for new workshops by newly established or expanded units are categorized as "purchase of equipment and instruments" no matter whether they come up to the cut-off point for fixed assets.

(3) Other expenses refer to expenses arising during the construction or purchase of fixed assets other than those mentioned above.

Number of Projects under Construction, projects put into use and new projects : Every construction project is only counted as a number of projects.

Number of Projects under Construction refer to number of all projects with actual construction or installation activities in current year, including newly started projects, projects started previously and extended into the current year, projects completed and put into operation in current year, projects suspended previously and resumed in current year, and projects started this year but suspended or postponed in current year.

Number of Projects Put into Use refer to projects have completed the main construction and correspondent auxiliary facilities in accordance with the design documents, resulting in forming production capacity (efficiency) and have been checked and accepted after relevant tests, and have been formally delivered for use. Number of projects put into use is an important basis that reflects the results of the report and assessment phase of construction investment results.

All of the industrial projects which completed and put into production or delivery referred to the design document form a production capacity of the main project and its corresponding supporting ancillary facilities completed. After commissioning overloaded, prove that it has the conditions for production design which provide qualified products, And go through acceptance of accreditation or reach completion and acceptance criteria, and supporting productive projects and welfare facilities to meet the needs of normal production recently, formally handed over the production of construction projects; Non-industrial project is the main project design by documents and the corresponding ancillary works are completed, and be able to play the design requirements of the project benefits, go through acceptance of accreditation or reach completion and acceptance criteria, formally handed over to use for construction projects.

All of the construction projects which pollute the environment, in accordance with relevant regulations,in the "three wastes" treatment works built according to the design requirements, and accredited by the environmental protection department, after delivery and use, the entire project can be used as a all of investment projects. Below standard of projects can not be used as all of investment projects to count.

Number of new projects this year refers to newly started construction projects during the reporting period. It includes a newly started new projects and expansion projects, renovation projects, simple living facilities construction projects, relocation projects and restoration projects. New projects in order to determine the overall design or plan to file the required permanent project started prevail. The number of new projects this year is a reflection of newly started investment in fixed assets indicators.

Newly Increased Production Capacity (or Project Efficiency) refers to the increase in design capacity (or project efficiency) through investment in fixed assets. The indicator is based on the performance of the physical form reflects investment in fixed assets of achievement, but also the assessment of economic efficiency of investment is one important basis.

newly increased production capacity (project efficiency) are usually expressed in one of the following forms:

(1)Expressed with the number of products, in engineering in unit time (usually one year) can produce a number of products (ie, annual) representation. Such as coal expressed as 10,000 tons / year, chemical pesticides expressed as ton/ year, tractor manufacturing expressed as unit / year and so on. Because contents of some chemical products differ significantly, equivalent to the amount calculated in accordance with the design content expressed, such as sulfuric acid, soda ash, caustic soda and so on.

(2) Using a unit of time can handle the number of raw materials to represent, and using engineering which every day (or hour) can handle the amount of raw materials to represent. Such as Mechanisms Glycotechnology daily processing of raw materials tons, edible vegetable oil daily processing of raw materials tons, urban sewage treatment capacity using tons / day to represent and so on.

(3) Such as number of new cotton loom and silk, wool spindles and capacity of power generators is using kilowatts to represent.

(4) With the volume of buildings, capacity, area, length to represent is a form of expression which non-industrial projects for engineering new effective. Such as railway operation mileage, new highways, reservoirs capacity, grain warehouses, schools seats, hospital beds, the effective irrigation area, etc.

According to the characteristics of engineering, sometimes it is necessary to use two or more composite unit of measure new production capacity (or project efficiency). Such as new production capacity of the internal combustion engine, simultaneously using number of units with annual production and KW to represent.

In order to standardize the name and calculation of unit of new production capacity (or project efficiency), National Bureau developed "new production capacity (or project efficiency) catalogs and code." When investment in fixed assets units counted new production capacity (or project efficiency), it must fill in accordance with the provisions of the directory name, measurement units and code.

Floor Space under Construction refers to the total floor space of all the buildings in the reference period,, including floor space of newly started buildings during the reference period, floor space of construction extended form the previous period to the reference period, floor space of construction suspended or postponed in the previous period and resumed in the reference period, floor space of construction completed in the reference period, and floor space of construction started and then suspended or postponed in the reference period.

Floor Space Completed refers to the floor space of all buildings completed in the reference period, which have been appraised and accepted or come up to the designed standards and have been put into use.

The accounting object of the completion of the area is unit of housing project (building), the entire houses meet the completed conditions, in accordance with all construction area to disposable calculated, rather than divisional calculated in accordance with the construction of the building house which finished part or hierarchical.

In calculating the size of houses completed this year is demanded strictly enforced housing completion and acceptance criteria. Civil construction should generally be in accordance with the design requirements of civil works and the house itself attached water, electricity, health (including the design of some gas, heating) project has been completed, Ventilation, elevators and other equipment has been installed, to water and lights, through acceptance accreditation, and formally delivered to the use of the unit, in order to calculate the completion of the area. Industry and research and other production of housing construction general design requirements should be in the civil works (including water, heating, electricity, health, ventilation) and are an integral part of life, housing, the operating room, etc. have been completed (not including the installation of foundation engineering equipment), process equipment and piping can be installed, be counted this year housing area.

Housing construction area completion rate refers to the total gross floor area of completed housing area accounted for the same period the rate of housing construction area during the reference period.

Newly Increased Fixed Assets refer to the value of fixed assets that has completed the construction and purchase, and has been delivered to the production or owner units, including investment in projects that have been completed and put into operation in current year and the investment in equipment, tools and appliance that meet the standard of fixed assets and fees that should be apportioned.

Other construction costs that belong to Increase the value of fixed assets should be accompanied by delivery of the works included in new fixed assets.

Rate of Construction Projects Completed and Put into Use refers to the ratio of the number of construction projects completed and put into use in a certain period of time to the number of projects under construction in the same period. This reflects the investment efficiency from the perspective of the speed of projects construction.

Area of Commercialized Housing Sold refers to total contracted area of commercialized housing (i.e. area of floor space as designated in the formal contracts signed by both sides) during the reference time. It constitutes floor space of completed housing and floor space of future housing.

Value of Commercialized Housing Sold refers to the total contracted value (i.e. value of sales/purchase for selling/purchase of commercialized housing as designated in the contract signed by both sides) during the reference time. This indicator has the same coverage as the area of commercialized housing sold, which constitutes floor space of completed housing and floor space of housing yet to be completed.

6

Six

对外经济贸易

Foreign Trade and Economic Cooperation

6-1 进出口总额
Total Value of Imports and Exports

指　标	Item	2007	2008	2009	2010	2011	2012	2012年比2011年增长(%) Increase Rate in 2012 over 2011(%)
进出口总额(万元)	**Total Value of Imports and Exports(RMB 10000 yuan)**	**1558266**	**2350249**	**1576427**	**2132280**	**3172193**	**4189987**	**32.1**
出口总额	Total Exports	1004493	1324260	928258	1299881	1936946	3129409	61.6
进口总额	Total Imports	553773	1025989	648169	832399	1235246	1060578	-14.1
进出口差额	Balance	450720	298271	280089	467482	701700	2068791	194.8
进出口总额(万美元)	**Total Value of Imports and Exports(USD 10000)**	**227285**	**337037**	**230732**	**314680**	**488758**	**663156**	**35.7**
出口总额	Total Exports	146513	190084	135856	192018	298509	495223	65.9
进口总额	Total Imports	80772	146953	94876	122662	190249	167933	-11.7
进出口差额	Balance	65741	43131	40980	69356	108260	327290	202.3

注：资料来源于贵阳海关(以下相关表同)。
Note:Data in the table are obtained from Guiyang Customhouse(the same applies to the relative tables below) .

6-2 按地区分的出口商品总额
Foreign Export Trade with Related Countries(Territories)

单位：万美元 (USD 10000)

地区名	Country (Territory)	2007	2008	2009	2010	2011	2012
总　计	**Total**	**146513**	**190084**	**135856**	**192018**	**298509**	**495223**
亚　洲	Asia	84784	111949	88831	120024	186317	299176
非　洲	Africa	4306	5594	5514	5307	8296	33260
欧　洲	Europe	20061	23111	13711	18937	23746	57520
拉丁美洲	Latin America	12672	10551	3859	8998	29284	23704
北 美 洲	North America	18716	23009	13331	22826	35270	61443
大 洋 洲	Oceania	5974	15870	10610	15926	15596	20120

6-3 按地区分的进口商品总额
Foreign Import Trade with Related Countries(Territories)

单位：万美元 (USD 10000)

地区名	Country (Territory)	2007	2008	2009	2010	2011	2012
总　计	**Total**	**80772**	**146953**	**94876**	**122662**	**190249**	**167933**
亚　洲	Asia	44453	69268	32219	64064	79069	54464
非　洲	Africa	3053	8083	9538	8595	22188	16509
欧　洲	Europe	11844	13333	14004	7770	9946	8317
拉丁美洲	Latin America	3247	3203	12271	14950	22722	23920
北 美 洲	North America	11364	41685	9304	11670	18644	25409
大 洋 洲	Oceania	6811	11381	17540	15613	37680	39314

6-4 海关出口商品分类

单位：万美元

指　标	Item	2007
总　计	**Total**	**146513**
活动物；动物产品	Live Animals;Animal Products	83
植物产品	Vegetable Products	489
动、植物油、脂及其分解产品；精制的食用油脂；动、植物蜡	Animal or Vegetable Oils,Fats and Their Cleavage Products; Refined Edible Oils and Fats;Animal or Vegetable Wax	158
食品；饮料、酒及醋；烟草及烟草代用品的制品	Food;Beverages, Liquor and Vinegar;Tobacco and Manufactured Tobacco Substitutes	6516
矿产品	Mineral Products	10433
化学工业及其相关工业的产品	Products of Chemical Industries and Related Industies	68668
塑料及其产品；橡胶及其产品	Plastics and Related Products;Rubber and Related Products	11466
生皮、皮革、毛皮及其制品；鞍具及挽具；旅行用品、手提包及类似物品；动物肠线(蚕胶丝除外)制品	Raw Hides, Leather, Furs and Related Products; Saddle;Travel Articles, Handbags and Similar Containers;Containers;Articles of Animal Gut(Other Than Silk-Worm Gut)	92
木及木制品；木炭；软木及软木制品；稻草、秸秆、针茅或其他编结材料制品；篮筐及柳条编织品	Wood and Wooden Products;Charcoal;Corkand Related Products; Straws,Straws,Plaited Products;Baskets and Wickerwork	54
木浆及其他纤维状纤维素浆；回收(废碎)纸或纸板；纸、纸板及其制品	Paper Pulp and Cellulose Pulp;Paper and Waste Paper; Paperboard and Related Products	14
纺织原料及纺织制品	Textile Materials and Products	3973
鞋、帽、伞、杖、鞭及其零件；已加工的羽毛及其制品；人造花；人发制品	Footwear, Headgear,Umbrellas,Canes,Whips and Parts Thereof; Processed Feather, and Articles Made Therewith;Artificial Flowers;Wigs	15
石料、石膏、水泥、石棉、云母及类似材料的制品；陶瓷产品；玻璃及其制品	Gypsum, Cement, Asbestos,Mica or Similar Materials;Ceramic Products;Glass and Glassware	514
珠宝、贵金属及制品	Jewelry, Precious Metal and Rolled Precious Metal	1
贱金属及其制品	Base Metals and Related Products	24806
机器、机械器具、电气设备机器零件、录音机及放声机、电视图象、声音的录制和重放设备及其零件、附件	Machinery,Electric Equipment and Accessories,Recorders, Videorecorderand Accessories	15752
车辆、航空器、船舶及有关运输设备	Vehicles, Aircraft,Ship and Related Transportation Equipment	2696
光学、照相、电影、计量、检验、医疗或外科用仪器及设备、精密仪器及设备，钟表，乐器及其零附件	Optical,Photographic,Film,Measuring, Checking, PrecisionMedical or Surgical Instruments and Equipment; Clocks, Musical and Related Parts and Accessories	305
杂项制品	Miscellaneous Products	478
艺术品、收藏品及古物	Art,Collection and Antique	

Value of Expert Commodities by Category

(USD 10000)

2008	2009	2010	2011	2012	2012年比2011年增长(%) Increase Rate in 2012 over 2011(%)
190084	**135856**	**192018**	**298509**	**495223**	**65.9**
47	101	97	116	120	3.4
384	448	457	721	1620	124.7
342	215	413	335	295	-11.9
9797	13560	17476	20772	26934	29.7
31326	8133	12790	11185	13313	19.0
74712	53762	100049	171897	129288	-24.8
12457	12324	19117	28879	53324	84.6
92	46	44	419	17137	39.9倍
165	96	52	3	206	75.6倍
14	15	107	144	5403	36.6倍
1401	739	994	1635	45892	27.1倍
24	39	128	164	17649	106.7倍
890	1211	2201	5906	24899	3.2倍
2	3	4	5	44	7.2倍
28242	6678	6415	10858	38193	2.5倍
25643	34252	28060	37541	50648	34.9
3460	2664	2137	2451	8196	2.3倍
370	801	333	577	4872	7.5倍
716	769	1144	4796	56868	10.9倍
			105	322	2.1倍

6-5 海关进口商品分类

Value of Import Commodities by Category

单位：万美元 (USD 10000)

指　标	Item	2007	2008	2009	2010	2011	2012	2012年比2011年增长(%) Increase Rate in 2012 over 2011(%)
总　计	**Total**	**80772**	**146953**	**94876**	**122662**	**190249**	**167933**	**-11.7**
活动物；动物产品	Live Animals;Animal Products					0.36	282	793.6倍
植物产品	Vegetable Products	5	4	27	30	21	96	3.6倍
动、植物油、脂及分解品；精制的食用油脂动、植物蜡	Animal or Vegetable Oils,Fats and Their Cleavage Products;Refined Edible Oils and Fats;Animal or Vegetable Wax	0.06	0.95			0.01	1	79.6倍
食品；饮料、酒及醋；烟草及烟草代用品的制品	Food;Beverages, Liquor and Vinegar; Tobacco and Tobacco Substitutes	18	31	25	13	18	54	197.4
矿产品	Mineral Products	53697	108189	53620	73337	135384	118523	-12.5
化学工业及其相关工业的产品	Products of Chemical Industries and Related Industies	1616	2736	1763	1712	1471	1713	16.4
塑料及其产品；橡胶及其产品	Plastics and Related Products;Rubber and Related Products	11348	16005	11900	25366	28578	22983	-19.6
生皮、皮革、毛皮及其制品；旅行用品、手提包及类似品；动物肠线制品	Raw Hides, Leather, Furs and Related Products; Saddle;Travel Articles, Handbags and Similar Containers; Containers;Articles of Animal Gut (Other Than Silk-Worm Gut)					4	9	154.1
木及木制品木炭软木及软木制品；稻草、秸秆、针茅或其他缠结材料制品篮筐及柳条编结品	Wood and Wooden Products; Charcoal;Corkand Related Products;Straws,Straws,Plaited Products;Baskets and Wickerwork					15	5	-64.8
木浆及其他纤维状纤维素浆；回收(废碎) 纸或纸板；纸、纸板及其制品	Paper Pulp and Cellulose Pulp;Paper and Waste Paper;Paperboard and Related Products	333	376	387	382	849	412	-51.5
纺织原料及纺织制品	Textile Materials and Products	33	68	10	19	65	328	4.0倍
鞋、帽、伞、杖、鞭及其零件；已加工的羽毛及其制品人造花；人发制品	Footwear, Headgear,Umbrellas, Canes,Whips and Parts Thereof; Processed Feather, and Articles Made Therewith;Artificial Flowers; Wigs					8		-99.8

6-5 续表 continued

单位：万美元 (USD 10000)

指　标	Item	2007	2008	2009	2010	2011	2012	2012年比2011年增长(%) Increase Rate in 2012 over 2011(%)
石料、石膏、水泥、石棉、云母及类似材料的制品；陶瓷产品；玻璃及其制品	Gypsum, Cement, Asbestos,Mica or Similar Materials;Ceramic Products; Glass and Glassware	9	27	63	210	62	50	-20.3
天然或养殖珍珠、宝石或半宝石、贵金属、包贵金属及其制品;仿首饰;硬币	Natural or Cultured Pearls,Precious or Semi-Precious Stones,Precious Metals,Metals Clad With Precious Metal and Stones, Precious Metals,Metals Clad With Precious Metal and Articles Thereof;Imitation Jewellery;Coin					2	38	18.2倍
贱金属及其制品	Base Metals and Related Products	1471	2706	7649	6079	7308	2870	-60.7
机电、音像设备及其零件机及放声机、电视图象、声音的录制和重放设备及其零件、附件	Machinery, Electric Equipment and Accessories,Recorders,Videorecorder and Accessories	9918	9552	15654	10629	10552	15409	46.0
车辆、航空器、船舶及有关运输设备	Vehicles, Aircraft,Ship and Related Transportation Equipment	491	5691	603	2311	1769	642	-63.7
光学、照相、电影、计量、检验、医疗或外科用仪器及设备、精密仪品及设备，钟表，乐器及其零附件	Optical,Photographic,Film,Measuring, Checking, PrecisionMedical or Surgical Instruments and Equipment; Clocks, Musical and Related Parts and Accessories	1830	1503	3162	2550	3904	4496	15.2
杂项制品	Miscellaneous Products	2	65	13	24	239	22	-90.8
艺术品、收藏品及古物	Art,Collection and Antique	1						

6–6 利用外资
Foreign Capital Absorbed

指 标	Item	2007	2008	2009	2010	2011	2012
项目数(个)	**Number of Signed Contracts(unit)**	**51**	**50**	**39**	**42**	**70**	**53**
#直接利用外资	Direct Foreign Investment	50	40	37	37	66	53
合资企业	Joint Venture	18	13	19	4	26	22
合作经营企业	Cooperative Venture	7	11	2	7	6	
独资企业	Sole-foreign Enterprise	25	16	16	26	34	31
签订合同金额(万美元)	**Contracted Foreign Capital(USD 10000)**	**53610**	**59402**	**37397**	**45024**	**170785**	**57383**
#直接利用外资	Direct Foreign Investment	43610	59402	16397	45024	170785	57383
合资企业	Joint Venture	10643	4355	9738	8591	73566	37868
合作经营企业	Cooperative Venture	8901	6269	2380	5486	9922	240
独资企业	Sole-foreign Enterprise	24066	48778	4279	30947	87297	19275
实际利用外资额(万美元)	**Foreign Capital Actually Absorbed(USD 10000)**	**15333**	**17379**	**18027**	**34026**	**71674**	**109805**
#直接利用外资	Direct Foreign Investment	12651	14904	13364	29546	51541	49116
合资企业	Joint Venture	4288	4401	5230	8885	23856	17845
合作经营企业	Cooperative Venture	52	3783	228	73	657	320
独资企业	Sole-Foreign Enterprise	8311	6720	7906	20588	27028	30951
外商投资企业基本情况	**Registered Foreign-funded Enterprise**						
年末实有外商投资法人企业(户)	Number of Foreign-funded Enterprises at the year-end(unit)	603	601	622	603	644	686
#本年登记户数(户)	Number of Registered Enterprises at the year-end(unit)	50	30	32	31	46	46
投资总额(万美元)	Total Investment(USD 10000)	279741	321526	356542	413189	568345	766967
注册资本(万美元)	Registered Capital(USD 10000)	169718	193101	213730	250964	321179	419657
#外 方	Capital from Foreign Partners	119505	141801	158456	186005	255181	329321

注：1.资料来源于省发改委、省商务厅。2.2011年起实际利用外资统计口径变化，除直接利用外资外，还包括外商投资企业投注差外债实际到位资金和外商投资企业境内投资实际到位资金两部分(以下相关表同)。

Note:1.Data in the table are obtained from the Provincial Development and Reform Commission,the Provincial Department of Commerce. 2.From 2011, the statistical of actual utilization of foreign capital had changed, which in addition to the direct use of foreign capital,but also including FIEs bets poor external debt actual funds and foreign-invested enterprises in the territory of actual funds invested in two parts(the same applies to the relative tables below).

6–7 外商直接投资按行业分项目个数

Number of Projects for Contracted Foreign Direct Investment by Sector

单位：个 (unit)

行业	Sector	2007	2008	2009	2010	2011	2012
总计	**Total**	**50**	**40**	**37**	**37**	**66**	**53**
农、林、牧、渔业	Farming,Forestry,Animal Husbandry and Fishery	3	3	5	6	6	11
采矿业	Mining and Quarrying	10	3		2	2	3
制造业	Manufacturing	17	19	11	8	16	20
电力、燃气及水的生产和供应业	Electric Power,Gas and Water Production and Supply		3	2	1	7	3
建筑业	Construction	2	1		1	2	1
交通运输、仓储和邮政业	Transport, Storage and Post			1	3		1
信息传输、计算机服务和软件业	Information Transmission,Computer Services and Software	1			1	1	
批发和零售业	Wholesale and Retail Trade	3	2	8	7	7	3
住宿和餐饮业	Hotel and Catering Services	4		1	2		2
金融业	Financial Intermediation				1	2	
房地产业	Real Estate	6	2	1		5	1
租赁和商务服务业	Leasing and Business Services	2	5	7	3	10	6
科学研究、技术服务和地质勘查业	Scientific Research,Technic Services and Geological Prospecting	1			1	3	
水利、环境和公共设施管理业	Water Conservancy,Environment and Public Facilities Services	1	1		1	3	1
居民服务和其他服务业	Services to Households and Other Services			1		1	
文化、体育和娱乐业	Culture, Sports and Entertainment		1			1	
公共管理和社会组织	Public Management and Social Organization						1

6–8 按行业分外商直接投资协议金额

Agreement Value of Foreign Direct Investment by Sector

单位：万美元 (USD 10000)

行业	Sector	2007	2008	2009	2010	2011	2012
总计	**Total**	**43610**	**59402**	**16397**	**45024**	**170785**	**57383**
农、林、牧、渔业	Farming,Forestry,Animal Husbandry and Fishery	514	2973	3042	12736	8666	5783
采矿业	Mining and Quarrying	1657	1233	491	1235	1875	3677
制造业	Manufacturing	16911	27419	5948	16014	55293	23779
电力、燃气及水的生产和供应业	Electric Power,Gas and Water Production and Supply		6120	2210	500	15492	3068
建筑业	Construction	1838	3220		20	12083	142
交通运输、仓储及邮电通讯业	Transport, Storage and Post			368	3857		8053
信息传输、计算机服务和软件业	Information Transmission,Computer Services and Software	14		-50	100	500	
批发和零售业	Wholesale and Retail Trade	1754	1389	-616	1808	6512	-1160
住宿和餐饮业	Hotel and Catering Services	8036	-96	15	1720	-8	155
金融业	Financial Intermediation				1000	5142	510
房地产业	Real Estate	7514	12019	587	697	24520	483
租赁和商务服务业	Leasing and Business Services	905	3212	3593	2103	27913	12314
科学研究、技术服务和地质勘查业	Scientific Research,Technic Services and Geological Prospecting	1113		799	1951	7118	
水利、环境和公共设施管理业	Water Conservancy,Environment and Public Facilities Services	3354	410		500	3993	64
居民服务和其他服务业	Services to Households and Other Services			10		304	
文化、体育和娱乐业	Culture, Sports and Entertainment		1503		783	1382	
公共管理和社会组织	Public Management and Social Organization						515

6-9 按行业分外商实际直接投资额

Actually Used Amount of Foreign Direct Investment by Sector

单位：万美元 (USD 10000)

指　　标	Item	2007	2008	2009	2010	2011	2012
总　　计	**Total**	**12651**	**14904**	**13364**	**29546**	**51541**	**49116**
农、林、牧、渔业	Farming, Forestry,Animal Husbandry and Fishery	70			4300	8200	755
采矿业	Mining and Quarrying	434	469	372	905	737	450
制造业	Manufacturing	6111	7641	11370	14318	20078	5179
电力、燃气及水的生产和供应业	Electric Power,Gas and Water Production and Supply		750			7330	8188
建筑业	Construction					21	5328
交通运输、仓储和邮政业	Transport, Storage and Post					3006	
信息传输、计算机服务和软件业	Information Transmission,Computer Services and Software						500
批发和零售业	Wholesale & Retail Trade and Catering Services	400	1275	472	368	1172	2526
住宿和餐饮业	Quarter and Catering Services				15		103
金融业	Financial Intermediation				1000		
房地产业	Real Estate	4870	1339	617	3125	2272	22484
租赁和商务服务业	Leasing and Business Services	104	76	10	3385	6327	548
科学研究、技术服务和地质勘查业	Scientific Research,Technic Services and Geological Prospecting	662		523	2120	1985	2991
水利、环境和公共设施管理业	Water Conservancy,Environment and Public Facilities Services		3354				64
居民服务和其他服务业	Services to Households and Other Services				10	313	
文化、体育和娱乐业	Culture,Sports and Entertainment					100	

6-10 对外经济合作

Economic Cooperation with Foreign Countries or Territories

指　　标	Item	2007	2008	2009	2010	2011	2012
境外经济合作	**Economic Cooperation with Foreign Countries or Territories**						
签订合同项目(个)	Number of Contracts(unit)	4	3	10	24	25	22
#对外承包工程	Contracted Projects	4	3	10	24	25	22
签订合同金额(万美元)	Value of Contracts(USD 10000)	6774	20000	16461	32431	29649	21430
#对外承包工程	Contracted Projects	6774	20000	16461	32431	29649	21430
实际营业额(万美元)	Actual Turnover(USD 10000)	6065	12425	13700	22003	30015	40007
#对外承包工程	Contracted Projects	6065	12425	13700	22003	30015	40007
年末在外人员(人)	Persons in Abroad(year-end)(person)	620	897	1649	1789	1938	2442
#对外承包工程	Contracted Projects	620	897	1649	1789	1926	2442
省外经济合作	**Economic Cooperation with Other Provinces**						
引进省外项目(个)	Number of Contracted Projects(unit)	2056	2157		2640	4637	2368
引进省外资金(亿元)	Contracted Value(100 million yuan)	401	510		992	2580	3857

注：表中数据不含铝镁设计院及国内国际标项目。

Note: Data in the table don't contain bidding projects of the Magnesium and Design Institute and the domestic and international.

主要统计指标解释

进出口总额 指实际进出我国国境并引起我国物质资源存量增加或者减少的货物金额。包括我国国境内法人和其他组织、个人进出口的一般贸易、易货贸易、加工贸易、补偿贸易、保税区和保税仓库进出境货物、国际援助物资或捐赠品。我国规定出口货物按离岸价格统计，进口货物按到岸价格统计。

利用外资 指我国各级政府、部门、企业和其他经济组织通过对外借款、吸收外商直接投资以及用其他方式筹措的境外现汇、设备、技术等。

对外借款 指通过对外正式签订借款协议，从境外筹措资金的方式，包括外国政府贷款、国际金融组织贷款、外国银行商业贷款、出口信贷以及对外发行债券等。1996 年及以前还包括对外发行股票。

外商直接投资 指外国企业和经济组织或个人(包括华侨、港澳台胞以及我国在境外注册的企业)按我国有关政策、法规，用现汇、实物、技术等在我国境内开办外商独资企业、与我国境内的企业或经济组织共同举办中外合资经营企业、合作经营企业或合作开发资源的投资（包括外商投资收益的再投资），以及经政府有关部门批准的项目投资总额内企业从境外借入的资金。

外商其他投资 指除对外借款和外商直接投资以外的各种利用外资的形式。包括企业在境内外股票市场公开发行的以外币计价的股票（目前主要是在香港证券市场发行的 H 股和在境内证券市场发行的 B 股）发行价总额，国际租赁进口设备的应付款，补偿贸易中外商提供的进口设备、技术、物料的价款，加工装配贸易中外商提供的进口设备、物料的价款。

对外承包工程 指各对外承包公司以招标议标承包方式承揽的下列业务：(1) 承包国外工程建设项目，(2) 承包我国对外经援项目，(3) 承包我国驻外机构的工程建设项目，(4) 承包我国境内利用外资进行建设的工程项目，(5) 与外国承包公司合营或联合承包工程项目时我国公司分包部分，(6) 对外承包兼营的房屋开发业务。对外承包工程的营业额是以货币表现的本期内完成的对外承包工程的工作量，包括以前年度签订的合同和本年度新签订的合同在报告期内完成的工作量。

对外劳务合作 指以收取工资的形式向业主或承包商提供技术和劳动服务的活动。我国对外承包公司在境外开办的合营企业，中国公司同时又提供劳务的，其劳务部分也纳入劳务合作统计。劳务合作营业额按报告期内向雇主提交的结算数（包括工资、加班费和奖金等）统计。

Explanatory Notes on Main Statistical Indicators

Total Imports and Exports refer to the actual cause of out of our borders and the stock of material resources to increase or decrease the amount of goods, including my own country legal persons and other organizations, individuals, import and export of general trade, barter trade, processing trade, compensation trade, bonded and bonded warehouse entry and exit of goods, international aid or donations. China provides export goods at FOB, CIF value of imported goods according to statistics.

Utilization of Foreign Capitals refers to remittance, equipment and technology financed from abroad, by loans, foreign direct investment and other forms undertaken by the Chinese governments at all levels, by various departments, enterprises and other economic units.

Foreign Borrowings refer to funds borrowed from abroad through formal signing of borrowing agreements with foreign institutions, including loans of foreign governments, loans of international financial institutions, commercial loans of foreign banks, export credit, and funds raised by Chinese bonds (and shares before 1996) issued abroad.

Foreign Direct Investment refers to the investments inside China by foreign enterprises and economic organizations or individuals (including overseas Chinese, compatriots from Hong Kong, Macao and Taiwan, and Chinese enterprises registered abroad), following the relevant policies and laws of China, for the establishment of ventures exclusively with foreign own investment, Sino-foreign joint ventures and cooperative enterprises or for co-operative exploration of resources with enterprises or economic organizations in China. It includes the re- investment of the foreign entrepreneurs with the profits gained from the investment and the funds that enterprises borrow from abroad in the total investment of projects which are approved by the relevant department of the government.

Other Foreign Investment refers to all forms of utilization of foreign capitals other than foreign borrowings and foreign direct investment. It includes the total value of stock shares in foreign currencies issued by enterprises at domestic or foreign stock exchanges(now mainly consisting of H shares issued at Hong Kong Security Market and B shares issued at domestic security markets.), rent payable for the imported equipment through international leasing arrangement, cost of imported equipment, technology and materials provided by foreign counterparts in compensation trade and processing and assembly trade.

Overseas Contracted Project refers to projects undertaken by Chinese contractors (project contracting companies) through bidding process. They include: (1) overseas civil engineering construction projects financed by foreign investors; (2) overseas projects financed by the Chinese government through its foreign aid programs; (3) construction projects of Chinese diplomatic missions, trade offices and other institutions stationed abroad; (4) construction projects in China financed by foreign investment; (5) sub-contracted projects to be taken by Chinese contractors through a joint umbrella project with foreign contractor(s); (6) housing development projects. The business income from international contracted projects is the work volume of contracted projects completed during the reference period, expressed in monetary terms, including completed work on projects signed in previous years.

Overseas Labour Services refer to the activities of providing technology and labour services to employers or contractors in the forms of receiving salaries and wages. Labour services providing by contractual joint ventures of Chinese international contracting corporations should be included in the statistics of service co-operation with foreign countries. The business income of labour service cooperation is the income in the form of wages and salaries, overtime pay, bonuses and other remuneration received from the employers during the reference period.

7

Seven

能　源

Energy

7-1 能源生产、消费总量及构成

Total Production and Consumption of Energy and Its Composition

单位：万吨标准煤 (10000 tons of SCE)

指 标	Item	2007	2008	2009	2010	2011	2012
一、绝对数	**Absolute Figure**						
一次能源生产总量	Total Production of Primary Energy	8480.62	9262.34	11070.09	13100.00	12739.97	14932.17
原 煤	Coal	7760.28	8028.53	9779.48	11778.54	11642.93	13264.62
水 电	Hydro-power	720.34	1233.81	1290.61	1321.46	1097.04	1667.56
能源终端消费总量	Final Consumption of Energy	6278.96	6486.30	6918.98	7373.10	8359.80	9156.04
#原 煤	Coal	2861.98	2947.29	3295.82	3538.23	4079.55	4390.45
天然气	Natural Gas	68.36	63.04	55.59	55.71	53.05	62.08
电 力	Electricity	2075.79	2076.32	2241.06	2457.22	2777.89	3031.64
二、构成(%)	**Composition(%)**						
一次能源生产总量	Total Production of Primary Energy	100.0	100.0	100.0	100.0	100.0	100.0
原 煤	Coal	91.5	86.7	88.3	89.9	91.4	88.8
水 电	Hydro-power	8.5	13.3	11.7	10.1	8.6	11.2
能源终端消费总量	Final Consumption of Energy	100.0	100.0	100.0	100.0	100.0	100.0
#原 煤	Coal	45.6	45.4	47.6	48.0	48.8	48.0
天然气	Natural Gas	1.1	1.0	0.8	0.8	0.6	0.7
电 力	Electricity	33.1	32.0	32.4	33.3	33.2	33.1

注：电力、热力按等价热值折算(以下各表同)。

Note:Electric power and heat are converted on the basic of equal caloric value(The same as in the following tables).

7-2 综合能源平衡表

Overall Energy Balance

单位：万吨标准煤 (10000 tons of SCE)

指 标	Item	2007	2008	2009	2010	2011	2012
可供消费的能源总量	**Total Energy Available for Consumption**	**6632.05**	**6903.39**	**7529.73**	**8237.33**	**9551.40**	**10082.26**
一次能源生产量	Primary Energy Output	8480.62	9262.34	11070.09	13100.00	12739.97	14932.17
省外调入	Inflow from Other Provinces	599.49	695.73	789.95	769.65	1040.78	1000.35
调出省外(一)	Outflow from Guizhou Province(-)	2837.71	3292.89	4323.14	5827.75	4028.72	5729.88
年初年末库存差额	Stock Changes in the Year	239.74	87.52	-94.89	48.17	-200.62	-121.04
能源消费总量	**Total Energy Consumption**	**6799.72**	**7083.99**	**7566.33**	**8175.43**	**9067.85**	**9878.38**
在总量中：	Consumption by Sector						
农、林、牧、渔、水利业	Farming,Forestry,Animal Husbandry, Fishery and Water Conservancy	141.28	146.50	152.95	141.96	129.52	127.17
工 业	Industry	4472.19	4613.69	4945.37	5289.48	5895.88	6431.08
建筑业	Construction	62.55	63.54	75.65	82.51	76.13	85.00
交通运输、仓储和邮政业	Transport,Storage and Post	390.57	453.32	467.62	538.48	597.73	706.39
批发、零售业和住宿、餐饮业	Wholesale and Retail Trades, Hotels and Catering Services	356.50	415.31	488.22	513.29	554.60	662.18
其 他	Others	472.84	534.85	566.35	614.04	675.13	581.22
生活消费	Residential Consumption	903.78	856.78	870.17	995.67	1138.87	1285.34
在总量中：	Consumption by Usage						
终端消费	Final Consumption	6278.96	6486.30	6918.98	7373.10	8359.80	9156.04
#工 业	Industry	3951.43	4016.00	4298.02	4487.15	5187.82	5708.78
加工转换损失量	Losses in Processing and Transformation	347.55	422.10	452.28	577.64	484.95	465.90
#炼 焦	Coking	100.81	91.83	85.60	80.12	67.93	106.40
损失量	Other Losses	173.21	175.59	195.07	224.69	223.10	256.44
平衡差额	**Balance**	**-167.66**	**-180.59**	**-36.60**	**61.90**	**483.55**	**203.88**

注：2008年发电损失量分摊到电力工业消费量中。

Note:The data of Power Generation Losses have been distributed to electricity industry consumption in 2008.

7-3 煤炭平衡表
Coal Balance Sheet

单位：万吨 (10000 tons)

指 标	Item	2007	2008	2009	2010	2011	2012
可供量	**Total Energy Available for Consumption**	**9363.87**	**9513.90**	**10867.59**	**11230.30**	**12738.14**	**13568.87**
生产量	Output	10864.18	11239.72	13691.00	15954.02	15601.02	18107.05
调出省外(一)	Outflow from Guizhou Province(-)	1812.99	1844.95	2747.44	4993.21	2812.84	4221.14
年初年末库存差额	Stock Changes in the Year	318.60	125.13	-188.79	269.49	-217.46	-485.23
消费量	**Total Energy Consumption**	**9572.63**	**9732.18**	**10912.47**	**11177.47**	**12084.97**	**13327.63**
在消费量中：	Consumption by Sector						
农、林、牧、渔、水利业	Farming,Forestry,Animal Husbandry, Fishery and Water Conservancy	153.51	159.12	168.62	132.66	115.69	131.04
工 业	Industry	7774.81	7976.40	9054.38	9415.02	10145.51	11057.47
建筑业	Construction	24.04	20.08	25.49	24.67	20.26	20.00
交通运输、仓储和邮政业	Transport,Storage and Post	7.85	7.23	12.62	14.06	15.16	42.76
批发、零售业和住宿、餐饮业	Wholesale and Retail Trades, Hotels and Catering Services	368.86	425.81	507.10	463.13	510.90	695.00
其 他	Others	453.10	491.22	529.95	503.30	563.10	504.14
生活消费	Residential Consumption	790.46	652.32	614.31	624.63	714.36	877.22
在消费量中：	Consumption by Usage						
终端消费	Final Consumption	3688.47	3707.66	4182.50	3976.62	4779.70	5808.55
#工 业	Industry	1890.65	1951.88	2324.41	2214.17	2840.74	3538.39
中间消费(用于加工转换)	Intermediate Consumption (Consumed in Transformation)	5856.16	5999.52	6704.97	7165.85	7265.27	7464.08
#发 电	Power Generation	4179.22	4130.83	4936.90	4913.10	5557.29	5391.75
炼 焦	Coking	1149.07	1129.76	1078.70	1005.61	948.43	1034.10
损失量	Losses in Coal Washing and Dressing	28.00	25.00	25.00	35.00	40.00	55.00
平衡差额	**Balance**	**-208.76**	**-218.28**	**-44.88**	**52.83**	**653.17**	**241.24**

7-4 电力平衡表

Electricity Balance Sheet

单位：亿千瓦小时 (100 million kwh)

指　标	Item	2007	2008	2009	2010	2011	2012
可供量	**Total Energy Available for Consumption**	**669.09**	**679.18**	**750.30**	**835.52**	**944.13**	**1046.72**
生产量	Output	1042.27	1191.69	1380.03	1385.64	1372.87	1610.89
水　电	Hydropower	216.57	375.60	400.88	416.58	348.88	537.30
火　电	Thermal Power	825.70	816.09	979.15	969.06	1023.99	1073.59
调出省外(—)	Outflow from Guizhou Province(-)	373.28	515.84	630.63	550.40	428.74	564.17
消费量	**Total Energy Consumption**	**669.09**	**679.18**	**750.30**	**835.52**	**944.13**	**1046.72**
在消费量中：	Consumption by Sector						
农、林、牧、渔、水利业	Farming,Forestry,Animal Husbandry, Fishery and Water Conservancy	5.33	4.22	4.48	4.22	3.89	3.95
工　业	Industry	538.21	531.64	578.46	639.64	715.53	782.96
建筑业	Construction	6.87	8.04	10.03	11.10	10.33	13.33
交通运输、仓储和邮政业	Transport,Storage and Post	19.96	18.02	20.50	22.71	25.94	26.26
批发、零售业和住宿、餐饮业	Wholesale and Retail Trades, Hotels and Catering Services	8.16	9.67	10.43	12.42	14.80	18.72
其　他	Others	15.86	18.80	20.25	23.26	25.58	31.53
生活消费	Residential Consumption	74.70	88.79	106.15	122.17	145.06	169.98
在消费量中：	Consumption by Usage						
终端消费	Final Consumption	624.09	632.08	696.10	774.62	883.42	976.82
#工　业	Industry	493.21	484.54	524.26	578.74	654.82	713.06
输配损失量	Losses in Transmission	45.00	47.10	54.20	60.90	60.71	69.90

7–5 分行业能源消费总量

Basic Statistics on Energy Consumption by Sector

单位：万吨标准煤 (10000 tons of SCE)

行 业	Sector	2007	2008	2009	2010	2011
工业	Industry	4472.20	4613.69	4945.38	5289.48	5895.87
采掘业	Mining and Quarring	480.69	483.17	645.89	751.50	685.36
#煤炭采选业	Coal Mining and Dressing	444.62	430.61	546.11	682.81	606.00
黑色金属矿采选业	Ferrous Metals Mining and Dressing	2.38	6.22	10.32	9.58	9.85
有色金属矿采选业	Nonferrous Metals Mining and Dressing	13.23	15.40	14.90	14.08	16.91
非金属矿采选业	Nonmetal Minerals Mining and Dressing	11.78	21.70	22.50	22.03	27.37
制造业	Manufacturing	3606.00	3584.32	3844.63	4028.50	4733.39
农副食品加工业	Processing of Food from Agricultural Products	13.70	11.84	14.31	12.76	14.23
食品制造业	Food Production	9.06	7.35	8.95	9.41	13.13
饮料制造业	Beverage Production	34.62	46.70	54.51	50.43	73.72
烟草加工业	Tobacco Processing	30.38	29.85	30.87	22.07	20.51
纺织业	Textile Industry	5.62	4.18	3.06	2.60	2.73
服装及其他纤维制品制造业	Garments and Other Fiber Products	1.17	1.50	0.98	1.12	1.43
皮革、毛皮、羽绒及其制品业	Leather,Furs,Down and Related Products	0.01		0.13	0.16	0.21
木材加工及竹、藤、棕、草制品业	Timber Processing,Bamboo,Cane,Palm Fiber and Straw Products	7.39	6.50	6.49	6.43	7.50
家具制造业	Furniture Manufacturing	0.73	0.36	0.03	0.33	0.42
造纸及纸制品业	Papermaking and Paper Products	12.41	8.28	7.74	10.69	25.27
印刷业,记录媒介的复制	Printing and Record Medium Reproduction	2.10	2.07	2.00	1.75	1.66
文教体育用品制造业	Cultural,Educational and Sports Articles	0.20	0.13	0.10	0.31	0.49
石油加工及炼焦业	Petroleum Processing and Coking	128.25	122.42	91.07	127.21	207.44
化学原料及化学制品制造业	Raw Chemical Materials and Chemical Products	978.23	1055.77	1034.99	1000.00	1189.63
医药制造业	Medical and Pharmaceutical Products	14.13	16.45	16.24	13.94	18.56

注：表中数据按国民经济行业分类(GB/T4754—2002)分。

Note:Data in this table is classified by sector of the National Economy (GB/T4754-2002).

7-5 续表 continued

行业	Sector	2007	2008	2009	2010	2011
化学纤维制造业	Chemical Fibers	0.50	0.66	21.60	22.27	14.06
橡胶制品业	Rubber Products	44.92	49.41	50.02	51.82	54.92
塑料制品业	Plastic Products	1.30	4.15	6.77	9.87	9.17
非金属矿物制品业	Nonmetal Mineral Products	601.75	652.21	829.55	870.29	945.45
黑色金属冶炼及压延加工业	Smelting and Pressing of Ferrous Metals	897.34	835.45	851.89	955.29	1066.28
有色金属冶炼及压延加工业	Smelting and Pressing of Nonferrous Metals	739.99	612.57	678.60	759.11	943.84
金属制品业	Metal Products	18.91	53.57	61.08	28.22	36.74
普通机械制造业	Ordinary Machinery Manufacturing	13.91	18.93	12.72	17.00	17.34
专用设备制造业	Special Purposes Equipment Manufacturing	6.59	3.93	8.10	7.72	7.71
交通运输设备制造业	Transportation Equipment Manufacturing	22.79	20.37	19.70	16.74	17.54
电气机械及器材制造业	Electric Equipment and Machinery	3.61	3.35	2.64	2.35	3.75
电子及通信设备制造业	Electronic and Telecommunications Equipment	1.90	2.57	1.77	1.69	2.64
仪器仪表及文化、办公用机械制造业	Instruments,Meters,Cultural and Office Machinery	0.55	0.52	0.42	0.27	0.27
其他制造业	Others	13.94	13.22	28.31	26.65	36.74
电力、煤气及水的生产和供应业	Electric Power, Gas and Tap Water Production and Distribution	385.51	546.20	454.86	509.49	477.12
电力、蒸汽、热水的生产和供应业	Electric Power、Steam and Hot Water Production and Distribution	363.22	513.34	424.46	471.33	437.02
煤气生产和供应业	Gas Production and Distribution	10.87	21.76	19.32	26.14	26.59
自来水的生产和供应业	Tap Water Production and Distribution	11.42	11.09	11.08	12.02	13.51
建筑业	Construction	62.55	63.54	75.65	82.51	76.13
交通运输、仓储和邮政业	Transport,Storage and Post	390.57	453.32	467.62	538.48	597.73
批发、零售业和住宿、餐饮业	Wholesale and Retail Trades, Hotels and Catering Services	356.50	415.31	488.22	513.29	554.60
其他行业	Others	472.84	534.85	566.35	614.04	675.13
生活消费	Residential Consumption	903.78	856.78	870.17	995.67	1138.87

7–6 分行业能源消费总量(2012)
Basic Statistics on Energy Consumption by Sector

单位：万吨标准煤 (10000 tons of SCE)

指 标	Item	2012
工业	Industrial	6431.08
采矿业	Mining and Quarring	565.37
#煤炭开采和洗选业	Mining and Washing of Coal	536.75
黑色金属矿采选业	Mining and Dressing of Ferrous Metals	13.89
有色金属矿采选业	Mining and Dressing of Nonferrous Metals	5.85
非金属矿采选业	Mining and Dressing of Nonmetal Minerals	8.88
制造业	Manufacturing	5209.02
#农副食品加工业	Processing of Food from Agricultural Products	18.13
食品制造业	Manufacture of Foods	10.48
酒、饮料和精制茶制造业	Manufacture of Beverages	66.06
烟草制品业	Manufacture of Tobacco	18.18
纺织业	Manufacture of Textile	0.95
纺织服装、服饰业	Manufacture of Textile Wearing Apparel, Footware and Caps	0.67
皮革、毛皮、羽毛及其制品和制鞋业	Manufacture of Leather,Furs,Feather and Related Products	1.45
木材加工和木、竹、藤、棕、草制品业	Timber Processing,Manufacture of Wood, Bamboo, Rattan,Palm and Straw Products	5.98
家具制造业	Manufacture of Furniture	0.26
造纸和纸制品业	Manufacture of Paper and Paper Products	29.23
印刷业和记录媒介复制业	Printing,Reproduction of Recording Media	0.70
文教、工美、体育和娱乐用品制造业	Manufacture of Culture and Education,Industrial,Sports, and Entertainment Products	0.58

7-6 续表　continued

单位：万吨标准煤　(10000 tons of SCE)

指　标	Item	2012
石油加工、炼焦和核燃料加工业	Processing of Petroleum,Coking,Processing of Nuclear Fuel	335.63
化学原料和化学制品制造业	Manufacture of Raw Chemical Materials and Chemical Products	1349.97
医药制造业	Manufacture of Medicines	15.88
化学纤维制造业	Chemical fiber manufacturing industry	7.69
橡胶和塑料制品业	Manufacture of Rubber and Plastics	251.57
非金属矿物制品业	Manufacture of Non-metallic Mineral Products	1249.33
黑色金属冶炼和压延加工业	Smelting and Pressing of Ferrous Metals	1283.58
有色金属冶炼和压延加工业	Smelting and Pressing of Non-ferrous Metals	500.51
金属制品业	Manufacture of Metal Products	4.44
通用设备制造业	Manufacture of General Purpose Machinery	19.91
专用设备制造业	Manufacture of Special Purpose Machinery	5.18
汽车制造业	Manufacture of Automotive	11.87
铁路、船舶、航空航天和其他运输设备制造业	Manufacture of Railroad, Marine, Aerospace and Other Transportation Equipment	9.34
电气机械和器材制造业	Manufacture of Electrical Equipment and Machinery	3.74
计算机、通信和其他电子设备制造业	Manufacture of Communication Equipment, Computers and Other Electronic Equipment	0.90
仪器仪表制造业	Manufacture of Measuring Instruments and Machinery for Cultural Activity and Office Work	0.96
其他制造业	Others	1.15
废弃资源综合利用业	Recycling and Disposal of Waste	4.72
金属制品、机械和设备修理业	Metal products, Machinery and Equipment Repair Industry	
电力、燃气及水的生产和供应业	Production and Distribution of Electric Power,Gas and Water	656.69
电力、热力生产和供应业	Production and Distribution of Electric Power and Heat Power	630.71
燃气生产和供应业	Production and Distribution of Gas	19.62
水的生产和供应业	Production and Distribution of Water	6.35
建筑业	Construction	85.00
交通运输、仓储及邮电通信业	Transportation,Storage,Postal & Telecommunications Services	706.39
批发和零售贸易餐饮业	Wholesale,Retail Trade and Catering Services	662.18
其他行业	Others	581.22
生活消费	Residential Consumption	1285.34

注：表中数据按国民经济行业分类(GB/T4754—2011)分。
Note:Data in this table is classified by sector of the National Economy (GB/T4754-2011).

7-7 能源生产消费弹性系数

Elasticity Ratio of Energy Production and Consumption

指 标	Item	2007	2008	2009	2010	2011	2012
生产总值比上年增长(%)	Growth Rate of Gross Domestic Product (GDP) over Preceding Year	14.8	11.3	11.4	12.8	15.0	13.6
能源生产比上年增长(%)	Growth Rate of Energy Production over Preceding Year	4.8	9.2	19.5	18.3	-2.8	17.2
能源消费总量比上年增长(%)	Growth Rate of Energy Consumption over Preceding Year	10.2	4.2	6.8	8.1	10.9	8.9
电力生产比上年增长(%)	Growth Rate of Electricity Production over Preceding Year	20.0	14.3	15.8	0.4	-0.9	17.3
电力消费比上年增长(%)	Growth Rate of Electricity Consumption over Preceding Year	15.0	1.5	10.5	11.4	13.0	10.9
能源生产弹性系数	Elasticity Ratio of Energy Production	0.32	0.82	1.71	1.43		1.26
能源消费弹性系数	Elasticity Ratio of Energy Consumption	0.69	0.37	0.60	0.63	0.73	0.65
电力生产弹性系数	Elasticity Ratio of Electricity Production	1.35	1.27	1.39	0.03		1.27
电力消费弹性系数	Elasticity Ratio of Electricity Consumption	1.01	0.13	0.92	0.89	0.87	0.80

注：生产总值增长速度按可比价格计算。
Note:The growth rates of GDP are calculated at comparable prices.

7-8 生活能源消费量

Energy Consumption for Non-Production Purpose

能源品种	Item	2007	2008	2009	2010	2011	2012
生活能源消费量(万吨标准煤)	**Energy Consumption for Non-Production Purpose (10000 tons of SCE)**	**903.78**	**856.78**	**870.17**	**995.67**	**1138.87**	**1285.34**
煤炭(万吨)	Coal (10000 tons)	790.46	652.32	614.31	624.63	714.36	877.22
煤油(万吨)	Kerosene (10000 tons)	0.48	0.05	0.05	0.04	0.04	0.05
液化石油气(万吨)	Liquefied Petroleum Gas (10000 tons)	7.60	10.12	8.33	8.82	9.55	8.49
天然气(亿立方米)	Natural Gas(100 million cu.m)	0.10	0.10	0.11	0.12	0.13	0.99
煤气(亿立方米)	Gas (100 million cu.m)	0.94	0.94	1.09	1.14	1.28	1.43
电力(亿千瓦小时)	Electricity (100 million kwh)	74.70	88.79	106.15	122.17	145.06	169.98

7–9 人均生活能源消费量
Annual Average Per Capita Energy Consumption for Non-Production Purpose

指标	Item	2007	2008	2009	2010	2011	2012
平均每人生活消费能源（千克标准煤/人）	**Annual Average Non-Productive Consumption Per Capita(kg of SCE/person)**	**240.38**	**226.80**	**229.27**	**287.26**	**327.83**	**369.73**
煤炭(千克)	Coal(kg)	210.24	172.68	161.85	180.21	205.63	252.33
电力(千瓦小时)	Electricity(kwh)	198.68	235.04	279.67	352.48	417.56	488.94
液化石油气(千克)	Liquefied Petroleum Gas(kg)	2.02	2.68	2.19	2.54	2.75	2.44
煤气(立方米)	Gas(cu.m)	2.50	2.49	2.87	3.29	3.68	4.11

7–10 能源利用效率
Using Efficiency of Energy

指标	Item	2007	2008	2009	2010	2011	2012
每万元生产总值能源消费量(吨标准煤/万元)(可比价)	**Energy Consumption Per Unit of GDP (ton of SCE/10000 yuan) (at comparable prices)**	**2.6173**	**2.4495**	**2.3480**	**2.2480**	**1.7140**	**1.6444**
每万元生产总值电力消费量（千瓦小时/万元)	**Electricity Consumption Per Unit of GDP(kwh/10000 yuan)**	**2575.41**	**2348.47**	**2328.02**	**2297.45**	**1784.56**	**1742.36**
每万元生产总值煤炭消费量(吨/万元)	**Coal Consumption Per Unit of GDP (ton/10000 yuan)**	**3.68**	**3.37**	**3.39**	**3.07**	**2.28**	**2.22**
能源消费总量(万吨标准煤)	Total Energy Consumption (10000 tons of SCE)	6799.72	7083.99	7566.33	8175.43	9067.85	9878.38
每吨能源生产的生产总值(万元/吨)	GDP Produced by Per Unit of Energy (10000 yuan/ton)	0.38	0.41	0.43	0.44	0.58	0.61
规模以上工业能源消费量(万吨标准煤)	Energy Consumption of Industry above Designated Size(10000 tons of SCE)	3931.63	3827.03	4231.41	4373.38	4803.14	5142.00
规模以上工业万元增加值能源消费量(吨标准煤/万元)	Energy Consumption Per Unit of Value-added of Industry above Designated Size (ton of SCE/10000 yuan)	4.890	4.323	4.322	3.857	3.18	2.93

注：2011年起，生产总值和工业增加值按2010年可比价格计算，其余年份按2005年可比价格计算。

Note:From 2011,industry value-added and GDP are calculated at 2010 comparable prices and they in other years were calculated at 2005 comparable prices .

主要统计指标解释

能源生产总量 指一定时期内全省一次能源生产量的总和。一次能源生产量包括原煤、原油、天然气、水电、核能及其他动力能(如风能、地热能等)发电量,不包括低热值燃料生产量、生物质能、太阳能等的利用和由一次能源加工转换而成的二次能源产量。

能源消费总量 指一定时期内全省各行业和居民生活消费的各种能源的核算能源消费总量指标。能源消费总量分为终端能源消费量、能源加工转换损失量和损失量三部分。

(1) 终端能源消费量:指一定时期内全省各行业和居民生活消费的各种能源在扣除了用于加工转换二次能源消费量和损失量以后的数量。

(2) 能源加工转换损失量:指一定时期内全省投入加工转换的各种能源数量之和与产出各种能源产品之和的差额,是观察能源在加工转换过程中损失量变化的指标。

(3) 能源损失量:指一定时期内能源在输送、分配、储存过程中发生的损失和由客观原因造成的各种损失量,不包括各种气体能源放空、放散量。

能源生产弹性系数 是能源生产量的增长与国民经济增长速度之间的比值。计算公式为:

$$能源生产弹性系数 = \frac{能源生产总量年平均增长速度}{地区生产总值年平均增长速度}$$

电力生产弹性系数 是电力生产量的增长与国民经济增长速度之间的比值。计算公式为:

$$电力生产弹性系数 = \frac{电力生产量年平均增长速度}{地区生产总值年平均增长速度}$$

能源消费弹性系数 是能源消费增长速度与国民经济增长速度之间的比值。计算公式为:

$$能源消费弹性系数 = \frac{能源消费量年平均增长速度}{地区生产总值年平均增长速度}$$

电力消费弹性系数 是电力消费增长速度与国民经济增长速度之间的比值。计算公式为:

$$电力消费弹性系数 = \frac{电力消费量年平均增长速度}{地区生产总值年平均增长速度}$$

能源加工转换效率 指一定时期内能源经过加工、转换后,产出的各种能源产品的数量与投入加工转换的各种能源数量的比率。它是观察能源加工转换装置和生产工艺先进与落后、管理水平高低等的重要指标。计算公式为:

$$能源加工转换效率 = \frac{能源加工、转换产出量}{能源加工、转换投入量} \times 100\%$$

单位生产总值能耗 指一定时期内,每生产一个计量单位的生产总值所消耗的能源。计算公式为:

$$单位生产总值能耗 = \frac{能源消费总量}{地区生产总值}$$

单位生产总值电耗 指一定时期内,每生产一个计量单位的生产总值所消耗的电力。计算公式为:

$$单位生产总值电耗 = \frac{全社会用电量}{地区生产总值}$$

单位工业增加值能耗 指一定时期内,每生产一计量个单位的工业增加值所消耗的能源。计算公式为:

$$单位工业增加值能耗 = \frac{工业能源消费量}{工业增加值}$$

Explanatory Notes on Main Statistical Indicators

Total Energy Production refers to the total production of primary energy by all energy producing enterprises in the country in a given period of time. The production of primary energy includes that of coal, crude oil, natural gas, hydro-power and electricity generated by nuclear energy and other means such as wind power and geothermal power. However, it excludes the production of fuels of low calorific value, bio-energy, solar energy and the secondary energy converted from the primary energy.

Total Energy Consumption refers to the total consumption of energy of various kinds by the production sectors and the households in our province in a given period of time. Total energy consumption can be divided into three parts: end-use energy consumption; loss during the process of energy conversion; and energy loss.

(1)End-use Energy Consumption: It refers to the total energy consumption by material production sectors, non material production sectors and households in the country(region)in a given period of time, but excludes the consumption in conversion of the primary energy into the secondary energy and the loss in the process of energy conversion.

(2)Loss During the Process of Energy Conversion: It refers to the total input of various kinds of energy for conversion, minus the total output of various kinds of energy in the country in a given period of time. It is an indicator to show the loss that occurs during the process of energy conversion.

(3)Loss: It refers to the total of the loss of energy during the course of energy transport, distribution and storage and the loss caused by any objective reason in a given period of time. The loss of various kinds of gas due to gas discharges and stocktaking is excluded.

Elasticity Ratio of Energy Production is an indicator to show the relationship between the growth rate of energy production and the growth rate of the national economy. The formula is:

$$\text{Elasticity Ratio of Energy Production}=\frac{\text{Average Annual Growth Rate of Energy Production}}{\text{Average Annual Growth Rate of National(regional) Economy}}$$

Elasticity Ratio of Electricity Production is an indicator to show the relationship between the growth rate of electricity production and the growth rate of the national economy. Its formula is:

$$\text{Elasticity Ratio of Electricity Production}=\frac{\text{Average Annual Growth Rate of Electricity Production}}{\text{Average Annual Growth Rate of National(regional) Economy}}$$

Elasticity Ratio of Energy Consumption is an indicator to show the relationship between the growth rate of energy consumption and the growth rate of the national economy. The formula is:

$$\text{Elasticity Ratio of Energy Consumption}=\frac{\text{Average Annual Growth Rate of Energy Consumption}}{\text{Average Annual Growth Rate of National(regional) Economy}}$$

Elasticity Ratio of Electricity Consumption is an indicator to show the relationship between the growth rate of electricity consumption and the growth rate of the national economy. The formula is:

$$\text{Elasticity Ratio of Electricity Consumption}=\frac{\text{Average Annual Growth Rate of Electricity}}{\text{Average Annual Growth Rate of National(regional) Economy}}$$

Efficiency of Energy Processing and Conversion refers to the ratio of the total output of energy products of various kinds after processing and conversion to the total input of energy of various kinds for processing and conversion in the same reference period. It is an important indicator to show the current conditions of energy processing and conversion equipment, production technique and management. The formula is:

$$\text{Efficiency of Energy Processing \& Conversion}=\frac{\text{Output of Energy After Processing \& Conversion}}{\text{Input of Energy for Processing \& Conversion}}\times 100\%$$

Energy Consumption per Unit of GDP refers to the energy consumption per unit of Gross Domestic Product in a country or the Gross Regional Product in a region in the same reference period. The formula is:

$$\text{Energy Consumption per Unit of GDP}=\frac{\text{Total Energy Consumption}}{\text{Gross Domestic(regional) Product}}$$

Electricity Consumption per Unit of GDP refers to the electricity consumption per unit of Gross Domestic Product in a country or the Gross Regional Product in a region in the same reference period. The formula is:

$$\text{Electricity Consumption per Unit of GDP}=\frac{\text{Total Electricity Consumption}}{\text{Gross Domestic (regional)Product}}$$

Energy Consumption per Unit of Industrial Value-added refers to the energy consumption per unit of industrial value-added in a country or region in the same reference period. The formula is:

$$\text{Energy Consumption per Unit of Industrial Value-added}=\frac{\text{Total Energy Consumption}}{\text{Industrial Value-added}}$$

8

Eight

财政税收

Government Finance and Taxation

8-1 财政收入

Financial Revenue

单位：亿元 (100 million yuan)

指 标	Item	2007	2008	2009	2010	2011	2012	2012年比2011年增长(%) Increase Rate in 2012 over 2011(%)
财政总收入	**Total Government Revenue**	**556.98**	**674.58**	**779.59**	**969.57**	**1329.99**	**1644.48**	**23.6**
#公共财政收入	Public Financial Revenue	285.14	349.55	416.48	533.73	773.08	1014.05	31.2
#增值税	Value-added Tax	45.94	55.14	57.47	66.00	76.41	85.74	12.2
营业税	Business Tax	68.27	80.33	104.31	136.73	181.73	241.53	32.9
企业所得税	Company Income Tax	29.88	35.70	42.34	51.14	70.69	86.53	22.4
个人所得税	Personal Income Tax	14.72	18.41	21.32	27.42	33.24	32.29	-2.9
资源税	Resource Tax	4.32	5.33	8.49	11.01	11.95	12.72	6.4
城市维护建设税	Urban Maintenance and Development Tax	18.89	22.07	24.45	29.18	37.82	45.79	21.1
房产税	Tax on Real Estates	5.78	6.29	7.43	8.41	9.73	11.60	19.3
契 税	Contract Tax	6.34	7.85	8.69	13.98	23.91	33.00	38.0
土地增值税	Value-added Tax on Land	3.01	3.73	5.81	11.98	13.76	19.07	38.6
国有资本经营收入	State-owned Assets Profit	6.42	4.34	6.04	4.88	6.38	7.21	12.9
罚没收入	Penalty and Confiscatory Income	12.90	12.67	14.23	16.66	23.50	25.14	7.0
行政事业性收费收入	Income from Administrative Fees	18.48	19.76	19.08	30.06	45.98	65.71	42.9
专项收入	Special Project Income	24.85	40.65	46.56	59.07	85.91	84.85	-1.2

注：资料来源于省财政厅(以下相关表同)。
Note:Data in the table are provided by the Provincial Department of Finance(The relative tables in this chapter are the same).

8-2 财政支出

Financial Expenditure

单位：亿元 (100 million yuan)

指 标	Item	2008	2009	2010	2011	2012	2012年比2011年增长(%) Increase Rate in 2012 over 2011(%)
公共财政支出	**Public Financial Expenditure**	**1055.39**	**1372.27**	**1631.48**	**2249.40**	**2755.68**	**22.5**
#一般公共服务	Common Public Service	184.21	196.78	212.69	307.21	430.16	40.0
国 防	National Defence	1.58	2.81	3.66	4.15	4.58	10.4
公共安全	Public Security	68.07	82.95	101.46	117.31	146.21	24.6
教 育	Education	229.77	256.72	292.06	376.86	500.51	32.8
科学技术	Science and Technology	12.99	14.27	16.66	21.68	28.98	33.7
文化体育与传媒	Culture,Sports and Media	17.84	23.62	23.98	35.31	49.85	41.2
社会保障和就业	Social Security and Jobs	107.46	150.04	140.76	194.78	235.40	20.9
医疗卫生	Health Care	67.44	102.84	127.68	173.26	201.05	16.0
节能环保	Energy Saving	40.44	55.31	54.32	55.45	65.73	18.5
城乡社区事务	Urban and Country Community Affairs	46.51	43.74	53.00	65.52	100.65	53.6
农林水事务	Affairs of Agriculture,Forest and Water	121.71	204.13	246.76	278.47	361.87	29.9
交通运输	Transport	49.39	120.80	109.61	305.16	288.56	-5.4

注：节能环保2008-2011年为环境保护数据。
Note:Data of energy saving refer to the data of environmental protection in 2008 to 2011.

8-3 分级公共财政收入(2012)
Public Financial Revenue by Level

单位：亿元 (100 million yuan)

指 标	Item	总 计 Provincial Total	省 级 Province	地 级 Prefecture	县 级 County	乡镇级 Villages and Towns
公共财政收入	**Public Financial Revenue**	**1014.05**	**179.50**	**204.84**	**518.91**	**110.81**
税收收入	**Tax revenue**	**681.66**	**118.78**	**138.49**	**320.24**	**104.15**
#增值税	Value-added Tax	85.74	34.30	11.22	29.92	10.30
营业税	Business Tax	241.53	47.81	47.13	107.86	38.73
企业所得税	Company Income Tax	86.53	28.52	17.81	30.60	9.60
个人所得税	Personal Income Tax	32.29	0.02	6.81	17.87	7.59
资源税	Resource Tax	12.72	3.82	1.48	4.29	3.14
城市维护建设税	Urban Maintenance and Development Tax	45.79	0.00	19.78	21.71	4.30
房产税	Tax on Real Estates	11.60		4.25	6.00	1.35
契 税	Contract Tax	33.00		9.40	21.01	2.59
土地增值税	Value-added Tax on Land	19.07		4.83	11.81	2.43
非税收入	**Non-tax revenue**	**332.39**	**60.72**	**66.34**	**198.66**	**6.67**
#专项收入	Special Project Income	84.85	24.74	20.91	36.89	2.31
行政性收费收入	Income from Administrative Fees	65.71	13.90	11.41	38.53	1.87
罚没收入	Penalty and Confiscatory Income	25.14	4.11	5.00	15.46	0.57
国有资本经营收入	State-owned Assets Profit	7.21	0.01	0.81	6.29	0.10

8-4 分级公共财政支出(2012)
Public Financial Expenditure by Level

单位：亿元 (100 million yuan)

指 标	Item	总计 Total	省 级 Province	地 级 Prefecture	县 级 County	乡镇级 Villages and Towns
公共财政支出	**Public Financial Expenditure**	**2755.68**	**612.11**	**368.97**	**1601.45**	**173.16**
#一般公共服务	Common Public Service	430.16	50.01	61.20	236.78	82.17
国 防	National Defence	4.58	1.16	1.94	1.47	0.01
公共安全	Public Security	146.21	41.51	28.86	75.18	0.66
教 育	Education	500.51	50.67	43.62	392.37	13.84
科学技术	Science and Technology	28.98	12.13	5.44	11.32	0.09
文化体育与传媒	Culture,Sports and Media	49.85	23.90	10.09	14.20	1.67
社会保障和就业	Social Security and Jobs	235.40	44.68	40.81	141.46	8.45
医疗卫生	Health Care	201.05	13.08	26.00	159.54	2.44
节能环保	Energy saving	65.73	6.41	13.87	43.82	1.63
城乡社区事务	Urban and Country Community Affairs	100.65	0.94	23.37	70.03	6.31
农林水事务	Affairs of Agriculture,Forest and Water	361.87	78.78	20.56	222.64	39.90
交通运输	Transport	288.56	237.30	17.01	33.45	0.81

8-5 税收收入(按产业分)

Tax Revenue(by Industry)

单位：亿元 (100million yuan)

项 目	Item	2007	2008	2009	2010	2011	2012
税收收入合计	**Total**	**464.73**	**577.62**	**673.83**	**831.97**	**1072.87**	**1308.63**
第一产业	Primary Industry	0.02	0.18	0.57	1.26	1.20	1.63
第二产业	Secondary Industry	287.17	349.16	383.55	448.88	574.26	684.06
采矿业	Mining and Quarrying	42.40	67.05	87.91	118.05	142.59	152.21
制造业	Manufacturing	166.32	194.37	197.47	226.09	293.84	330.55
电力、燃气及水的生产和供应业	Production and Distribution of Electric Power,Gas and Water	55.36	61.80	66.34	60.65	59.42	70.72
建筑业	Construction	23.09	25.94	31.82	44.09	78.41	130.58
第三产业	Tertiary Industry	177.54	228.28	289.72	381.83	497.40	622.92
交通运输、仓储及邮政业	Transport,Storage and Post	13.95	15.04	13.96	16.10	19.04	19.13
信息传输、计算机服务和软件业	Information Transmission,Computer Services and Software	7.15	8.23	11.83	12.14	14.19	17.64
批发和零售业	Wholesale and Retail Trade	78.50	95.46	107.79	131.90	170.04	205.71
住宿和餐饮业	Hotel and Catering Services	4.76	5.65	6.20	7.21	9.05	10.45
金融业	Financial Intermediation	14.77	22.51	28.40	39.12	55.61	77.11
房地产业	Real Estates	26.10	29.24	55.90	94.64	138.36	137.09
租赁和商务服务业	Leasing and Business Services	15.67	17.59	13.99	17.59	24.01	37.52
科学研究和技术服务业							9.68
居民服务和其他服务业	Services to Households and Other Services	3.63	8.76	8.12	10.49	20.08	38.24
教 育	Education	0.44	0.74	0.89	1.14	1.45	1.54
卫生和社会工作	Health and Social Work	0.43	0.54	0.85	1.61	1.71	1.53
文化、体育和娱乐业	Culture,Sports and Entertainment	1.12	1.55	2.12	2.36	2.80	2.90
公共管理、社会保障和社会组织	Public Management and Social Organization		3.64	5.39	6.39	9.41	31.13
其他行业	Others	11.02	19.33	34.30	41.13	31.65	33.26

注：1.资料来源于省国税局、省地税局。2.2009年起地税包含耕地占用税、契税。3.2007—2011年按国民经济行业分类GB/T4754—2002分，2012年按国民经济行业分类GB/T4754—2011分。（以下相关表同）

Note:1.Data in the table are provided by Guizhou Provincial National Taxation Beaura and Local Taxation Beaura of Guizhou Province.2.Since 2009, local taxation has included contract tax and farm land occupation tax .3.From 2007 to 2011,date in this table is classified by sector of the National Economy(GB/T4754-2002).And in 2012,date in this table is classified by sector of the National Economy(GB/T4754-2011).(The relative tables in this chapter are the same)

8-6 税收收入(按企业类型分)

Taxation Revenue (by Business Entities)

单位：亿元 (100 million yuan)

项 目	Item	2007	2008	2009	2010	2011	2012
总 计	**Total**	**464.73**	**577.62**	**673.83**	**831.97**	**1072.87**	**1308.63**
内资企业	Domestic Enterprises	414.65	511.52	598.93	745.52	966.07	1188.71
国有企业	State-owned Enterprises	157.93	192.95	108.23	117.19	126.59	154.24
集体企业	Collective-owned Enterprises	8.01	8.59	10.19	12.57	15.17	19.31
股份合作企业	Cooperative Enterprises	2.95	4.41	4.95	7.67	11.52	14.61
联营企业	Joint Ownership Enterprises	0.58	0.72	0.95	0.78	0.87	0.88
#国有控股	State-owned and State-controlled Enterprises	0.07	0.03	0.03	0.10	0.48	0.32
股份公司	Share-holding Corporations Limited	197.14	238.68	381.45	474.28	636.01	824.87
#国有控股	State-owned and State-controlled Enterprises	69.59	63.69	143.76	177.53	274.39	316.77
私营企业	Private Enterprises	38.52	55.02	65.50	87.90	100.32	111.52
其它企业	Other Enterprises	9.52	11.15	27.65	45.14	75.57	63.28
港澳台投资企业	Enterprises with Funds from Hong Kong, Macao and Taiwan	3.12	3.91	4.44	5.01	5.30	7.47
#国有控股	State-owned and State-controlled Enterprises	0.14	0.24	0.18	0.12	0.46	0.26
外商投资企业	Foreign Funded Enterprises	10.75	12.07	18.24	21.03	24.70	19.42
#国有控股	State-owned and State-controlled Enterprises	0.28	0.24	0.30	0.27	2.71	1.49
个体经营	Individual Operators	36.21	50.12	52.22	60.41	76.79	93.03
附：乡(镇)企业	Township and Village Enterprises	20.04	22.14	26.07	35.23	48.93	82.53

8-7 国税税收收入(按产业分)

National Tax Revenue (by Industry)

单位：亿元 (100 million yuan)

项目	Item	2007	2008	2009	2010	2011	2012
税收收入合计	**Total**	**285.04**	**353.45**	**385.38**	**458.13**	**568.60**	**647.79**
第一产业	Primary Industry	0.01	0.15	0.51	1.16	1.03	1.35
第二产业	Secondary Industry	220.02	261.91	275.14	312.66	382.23	422.69
采矿业	Mining and Quarrying	28.23	42.64	51.31	70.37	82.10	85.08
制造业	Manufacturing	144.31	165.91	167.98	189.93	250.64	279.55
电力、燃气及水的生产和供应业	Production and Distribution of Electric Power,Gas and Water	47.03	52.41	54.63	50.66	47.18	54.28
建筑业	Construction	0.45	0.95	1.22	1.69	2.31	3.78
第三产业	Tertiary Industry	65.02	91.39	109.73	144.31	185.33	223.74
交通运输、仓储及邮政业	Transport,Storage and Post	0.24	0.70	1.45	2.48	3.05	2.33
信息传输、计算机服务和软件业	Information Transmission,Computer Services and Software	3.51	3.43	6.57	6.15	7.09	9.33
批发和零售业	Wholesale and Retail Trade	49.21	60.70	68.56	89.03	111.23	132.19
住宿和餐饮业	Hotel and Catering Services	0.03	0.07	0.08	0.12	0.17	0.23
金融业	Financial Intermediation	2.90	5.31	6.50	11.38	19.84	27.57
房地产业	Real Estates	2.03	3.09	7.26	10.73	13.99	15.30
租赁和商务服务业	Leasing and Business Services	0.20	0.43	1.16	1.87	2.25	1.29
科学研究和技术服务业	Scientific Research and Technical Services						2.62
居民服务和其他服务业	Services to Households and Other Services	0.12	0.55	0.72	0.78	0.89	1.54
教　育	Education	0.01	0.03	0.06	0.09	0.13	0.14
卫生、社会保险和社会福利业	Health,Social Security and Social Welfare	…	0.02	0.05	0.10	0.15	0.15
文化、体育和娱乐业	Culture,Sports and Entertainment	0.01	0.03	0.18	0.18	0.24	0.25
公共管理和社会组织	Public Management and Social Organization		1.65	1.58	2.14	3.91	4.44
其他行业	Others	6.77	15.39	15.55	19.24	22.38	26.36

8-8 地方系统税收收入(按产业分)

Local Tax Revenue(by Industry)

单位：亿元 (100 million yuan)

项目	Item	2007	2008	2009	2010	2011	2012
税收收入合计	**Total**	**179.69**	**224.17**	**288.45**	**373.83**	**504.27**	**660.84**
第一产业	Primary Industry	0.01	0.03	0.05	0.10	0.17	0.28
第二产业	Secondary Industry	67.16	87.25	108.41	136.22	192.03	261.37
采矿业	Mining and Quarrying	14.17	24.41	36.61	47.68	60.49	67.13
制造业	Manufacturing	22.01	28.45	29.49	36.16	43.20	51.00
电力、燃气及水的生产和供应业	Production and Distribution of Electric Power,Gas and Water	8.33	9.39	11.71	9.99	12.24	16.44
建筑业	Construction	22.65	25.00	30.60	42.39	76.10	126.80
第三产业	Tertiary Industry	112.52	136.89	179.99	237.52	312.07	399.18
交通运输、仓储及邮政业	Transport,Storage and Post	13.71	14.34	12.50	13.62	15.99	16.80
信息传输、计算机服务和软件业	Information Transmission,Computer Services and Software	3.64	4.81	5.26	5.99	7.10	8.31
批发和零售业	Wholesale and Retail Trade	29.29	34.76	39.23	42.87	58.81	73.53
住宿和餐饮业	Hotel and Catering Services	4.72	5.58	6.11	7.09	8.88	10.22
金融业	Financial Intermediation	11.87	17.20	21.91	27.73	35.77	49.54
房地产业	Real Estates	24.08	26.15	48.65	83.92	124.37	121.79
租赁和商务服务业	Leasing and Business Services	15.47	17.16	12.82	15.72	21.76	36.23
科学研究和技术服务业	Scientific Research and Technical Services						7.06
居民服务和其他服务业	Services to Households and Other Services	3.52	8.21	7.40	9.71	19.19	36.70
教　育	Education	0.44	0.71	0.83	1.05	1.32	1.40
卫生和社会工作	Health and Social Work	0.43	0.53	0.80	1.51	1.56	1.38
文化、体育和娱乐业	Culture,Sports and Entertainment	1.12	1.52	1.94	2.18	2.56	2.65
公共管理、社会保障和社会组织	Public Management Social Security and Social Organization		1.99	3.80	4.25	5.50	26.69
其他行业	Others	4.25	3.94	18.75	21.89	9.27	6.90

8-9 国税税收收入(按企业类型分)

National Taxation Revenue(by Business Entities)

单位：亿元 (100 million yuan)

项　目	Item	2007	2008	2009	2010	2011	2012
总　计	**Total**	**285.04**	**353.45**	**385.38**	**458.13**	**568.60**	**647.79**
内资企业	Domestic Enterprises	263.81	321.67	348.82	412.92	514.21	592.32
国有企业	State-owned Enterprises	117.98	141.34	51.97	59.33	62.20	72.89
集体企业	Collective-owned Enterprises	2.12	2.45	3.56	5.26	7.65	9.20
股份合作企业	Cooperative Enterprises	1.18	1.64	2.71	4.80	7.95	9.70
联营企业	Joint Ownership Enterprises	0.44	0.54	0.73	0.50	0.62	0.66
#国有控股	State-owned and State-controlled Enterprises	0.06	0.03	0.03	0.08	0.47	0.31
股份公司	Share-holding Corporations Limited	116.01	138.23	248.46	289.50	376.54	436.34
#国有控股	State-owned and State-controlled Enterprises	47.15	40.67	116.02	146.25	220.87	265.56
私营企业	Private Enterprises	25.14	36.02	39.68	50.92	55.19	59.54
其它企业	Other Enterprises	0.94	1.46	1.72	2.62	4.06	3.99
港澳台投资企业	Enterprises with Funds from Hong Kong, Macao and Taiwan	2.13	2.97	3.12	3.44	3.30	3.88
#国有控股	State-owned and State-controlled Enterprises	0.13	0.22	0.16	0.10	0.08	0.15
外商投资企业	Foreign Funded Enterprises	8.18	8.33	13.74	15.67	17.83	12.50
#国有控股	State-owned and State-controlled Enterprises	0.20	0.18	0.25	0.23	0.36	0.26
个体经营	Individual Operators	10.93	20.48	19.70	26.10	33.25	39.09
附：乡(镇)企业	Township and Village Enterprises	12.93	14.62	17.38	23.39	32.41	29.10

8-10 地方系统税收收入(按企业类型分)

Local Taxation Revenue (by Business Entities)

单位：亿元 (100 million yuan)

项　目	Item	2007	2008	2009	2010	2011	2012
总　计	**Total**	**179.69**	**224.17**	**288.45**	**373.83**	**504.27**	**660.84**
内资企业	Domestic Enterprises	150.84	189.84	250.11	332.60	451.86	596.39
国有企业	State-owned Enterprises	39.95	51.60	56.26	57.86	64.39	81.35
集体企业	Collective-owned Enterprises	5.89	6.15	6.64	7.31	7.52	10.11
股份合作企业	Cooperative Enterprises	1.77	2.77	2.24	2.87	3.57	4.91
联营企业	Joint Ownership Enterprises	0.14	0.18	0.22	0.27	0.25	0.22
#国有控股	State-owned and State-controlled Enterprises	0.01	0.00	0.01	0.02	0.01	0.01
股份公司	Share-holding Corporations Limited	81.13	100.46	132.99	184.78	259.47	388.53
#国有控股	State-owned and State-controlled Enterprises	22.44	23.02	27.74	31.29	53.52	51.21
私营企业	Private Enterprises	13.38	19.00	25.83	36.98	45.13	51.98
其它企业	Other Enterprises	8.58	9.69	25.94	42.53	71.51	59.29
港澳台投资企业	Enterprises with Funds from Hong Kong, Macao and Taiwan	1.00	0.94	1.32	1.57	2.00	3.59
#国有控股	State-owned and State-controlled Enterprises	0.01	0.02	0.02	0.02	0.38	0.11
外商投资企业	Foreign Funded Enterprises	2.56	3.74	4.49	5.36	6.87	6.92
#国有控股	State-owned and State-controlled Enterprises	0.08	0.06	0.05	0.03	2.35	1.23
个体经营	Individual Operators	25.29	29.65	32.52	34.31	43.54	53.94
附：乡(镇)企业	Township and Village Enterprises	7.11	7.52	8.69	11.84	16.52	53.43

8−11 国家税收收入(分行业、分税种)(2012)

单位：万元

项　目	Item	合　计 Total
合　计	**Total**	**6477874**
第一产业	Primary Industry	13511
第二产业	Secondary Industry	4226929
采矿业	Mining and Quarrying	850847
制造业	Manufacturing	2795436
电力、燃气及水的生产和供应业	Production and Distribution of Electric Power, Gas and Water	542840
建筑业	Construction	37806
第三产业	Tertiary Industry	2237435
批发和零售业	Wholesale and Retail Trade	1321984
交通运输、仓储及邮政业	Transport,Storage and Post	23263
住宿和餐饮业	Hotel and Catering Services	2301
信息传输、软件和信息技术服务业	Information Transmission, Software and IT services	93270
金融业	Financial Intermediation	275730
房地产业	Real Estates	153015
租赁和商务服务业	Leasing and Business Services	12873
科学研究和技术服务业	Scientific and Technical services	26192
居民服务、修理和其他服务业	Resident Services, Repairs and other services	15400
教　育	Education	1375
卫生和社会工作	Health and Social work	1540
文化、体育和娱乐业	Culture,Sports and Entertainment	2464
公共管理、社会保障和社会组织	Public Management, social Security and Social Organizations	44397
其他行业	Others	263631

Taxation Revenue of the Central Government
(By Industrial Sector and Taxation Category)

(10000 yuan)

国内增值税 Domestic Value-added Tax	#一般纳税人增值税 Value-added Tax from General Taxpayer	国内消费税 Domestic Consumption Tax	企业所得税 Corporate Income Tax	外商投资企业和外国企业所得税 Foreign-invested Enterprises and Foreign Enterprises Income Tax	个人所得税 Personal Income Tax	车辆购置税 Vehicle Purchase Tax
3435374	**3217539**	**1653159**	**988270**	**60722**	**527**	**339822**
1946	1366		385			11180
2387827	2290361	1521930	262543	42669		11960
820154	801068		14609	13251		2833
1054600	1040025	1521930	188606	25540		4760
509468	445989		30554	1312		1506
3605	3279		28774	2566		2861
1045601	925812	131229	725342	18053	527	316682
983340	906237	131229	175532	8084		23799
766	702		6316	1612		14569
177	158		1413	516		195
5675	4647		86600	14		981
1513	1484		270587	2010		1620
390	222		145661	5160		1804
2975	2671		6637	469		2792
2906	2510		22032	12		1242
7754	4228		5061	172		2413
2			397	1		975
150	44		73			1317
1309	1214		575			580
35607			3550	3		5237
3037	1695		908		527	259158

8-12 地方系统税收收入(分行业、分税种)(2012)

单位：万元

项 目	Item	合 计 Total	营业税 Business Tax	企业所得税 Enterprises Income Tax
合 计	**Total**	**6608352**	**2415279**	**1030609**
第一产业	Primary Industry	2784	1030	425
第二产业	Secondary Industry	2613719	891390	464665
采矿业	Mining and Quarrying	671328	48645	174999
制造业	Manufacturing	509992	15751	96355
电力、燃气及水的生产和供应业	Production and Distribution of Electric Power, Gas and Water	164409	9040	22251
建筑业	Construction	1267990	817954	171060
第三产业	Tertiary Industry	3991849	1522859	565519
交通运输、仓储及邮政业	Transport,Storage and Post	167954	101603	11947
信息传输、软件和信息技术服务业	Information Transmission,Computer Services and Software	83131	61063	3750
批发和零售业	Wholesale and Retail Trade	735294	25597	391380
住宿和餐饮业	Hotel and Catering Services	102171	66125	3965
金融业	Financial Intermediation	495439	324822	5854
房地产业	Real Estates	1217875	560778	83137
租赁和商务服务业	Leasing and Business Services	362336	152705	22273
科学研究和技术服务业	Scientific and Technical services	70582	39316	10811
居民服务、修理和其他服务业	Resident Services, Repairs and other services	366959	138159	20848
教 育	Education	13979	5902	1613
卫生和社会工作	Health and Social Work	13753	807	398
文化、体育和娱乐业	Culture,Sports and Entertainment	26492	15344	1396
公共管理、社会保障和社会组织	Public Management，Social Security and Social Organization	266875	26473	7331
其他行业	Others	69009	4165	816

Taxation Revenue of the Local Government
(By Industrial Sector and Taxation Category)

(10000 yuan)

个人所得税 Personal Income Tax	城市维护建设税 Tax on City Maintenance and Construction	房产税 Tax on Real Estates	印花税 Stamp Tax	城镇土地使用税 Tax on the Use of Urban Land	土地增值税 Value-added Tax on Land	其他各税 Other Taxes
806756	**457947**	**116040**	**68656**	**143762**	**190706**	**1378597**
223	112	119	104	99	33	639
439979	293813	34356	29970	73363	7334	378849
274554	45461	2248	4758	12849	1135	106679
70546	179874	21247	11908	38267	1371	74673
23050	27024	7564	5468	10307	239	59466
71829	41454	3297	7836	11940	4589	138031
366554	164022	81565	38582	70300	183339	999109
31007	6582	3335	1795	3123	117	8445
7747	3957	4308	510	1298	104	394
34651	63223	14460	11285	10033	2878	181787
21101	4253	4077	104	1493	30	1023
70971	22001	9720	3648	1725	1493	55205
29027	35900	19263	9678	44430	166460	269202
41352	10437	12506	8310	3374	7831	103548
11478	3017	1261	462	865	6	3366
74033	9702	8720	2098	2344	2405	108650
4035	376	973	26	425	91	538
11970	55	249	33	52	76	113
7105	933	1262	47	372	22	11
20640	3147	1236	413	149	1815	205671
1437	439	195	173	617	11	61156

主要统计指标解释

公共财政收入 指政府为履行职能，按国家法律法规规定收取的纳入预算内管理的各项税收及非税收入总和。1994 年我国实行分税制改革后，公共财政收入划分为中央固定收入、地方固定收入、中央与地方共享收入三部分。其中，地方公共财政收入（习惯上称地方财政收入）由地方固定收入和中央与地方共享收入地方分成部分组成，具体又可分为税收收入和非税收入两类。

公共财政支出 指地方政府为履行职能需要，通过预算内资金安排的用于维持政权运转及支持各项社会事业发展等方面的支出。主要包括:

(1) 一般公共服务: 指政府提供基本公共管理与服务的支出，包括人大事务、政协事务、政府办公厅（室）及相关机构事务、发展与改革事务、统计信息事务、财政事务、税收事务、审计事务、海关事务、人力资源事务、纪检监察事务、人口与计划生育事务、商贸事务、知识产权事务、工商行政管理事务、国土资源事务、海洋管理事务、测绘事务、地震事务、气象事务、民族事务、宗教事务、港澳台侨事务、档案事务、共产党事务、民主党派事务及工商联事务、群众团体事务、彩票事务等。

(2) 国防: 指政府用于国防方面的支出，包括用于现役部队、预备役部队、民兵、国防科研事业、专项工程、国防动员等方面的支出。

(3) 公共安全: 指政府维护社会公共安全方面的支出，包括武装警察、公安、国家安全、检察、法院、司法行政、监狱、劳教、国家保密、缉私警察等。

(4) 教育: 指政府教育事务支出，包括教育行政管理、学前教育、小学教育、初中教育、普通高中教育、普通高等教育、初等职业教育、中专教育、技校教育、职业高中教育、高等职业教育、广播电视教育、留学生教育、特殊教育、干部继续教育、教育机关服务等。

(5) 科学技术: 指用于科学技术方面的支出，包括科学技术管理事务、基础研究、应用研究、技术研究与开发、科技条件与服务、社会科学、科学技术普及、科技交流与合作等。

(6) 文化教育与传媒: 指政府在文化、文物、体育、广播影视、新闻出版等方面的支出。

(7) 社会保障和就业: 指政府在社会保障与就业方面的支出，包括社会保障和就业管理事务、民政管理事务、财政对社会保险基金的补助、补充全国社会保障基金、行政事业单位离退休、企业改革补助、就业补助、抚恤、退役安置、社会福利、残疾人事业、城市居民最低生活保障、其他城镇社会救济、农村社会救济、自然灾害生活救助、红十字事务等。

(8) 医疗卫生: 指政府医疗卫生方面的支出，包括医疗卫生管理事务支出、医疗服务支出、医疗保障支出、疾病预防控制支出、卫生监督支出、妇幼保健支出、农村卫生支出等。

(9) 城乡社区事务: 指政府城乡社区事务支出，包括城乡社区管理事务支出、城乡社区规划与管理支出、城乡社区公共设施支出、城乡社区住宅支出、城乡社区环境卫生支出、建设市场管理与监督支出等。

(10) 农林水事务: 指政府农林水事务支出，包括农业支出、林业支出、水利支出、扶贫支出、农业综合开发支出等。

(11) 交通运输: 指政府交通运输和邮政业方面的支出，包括公路运输支出、水路运输支出、铁路运输支出、民用航空运输支出、邮政业支出等。

Explanatory Notes on Main Statistical Indicators

Public Revenue that the government is functioning, according to national laws and regulations charged into the budget management of the various tax and non-tax revenue totals. After the implementation of the tax reform in our country in 1994, public revenue divided into the central fixed income, local fixed-income, central and local revenue sharing three parts. Among them, the local public revenue (customarily known as local revenues) consists of Local fixed income and revenue sharing between central and local areas into parts, Specifically, it can be divided into tax revenues and non-tax revenue categories.

Public expenditure refers to local governments in order to fulfill functional needs, through budgetary funding arrangements for the operation and maintenance of the regime to support the development of social undertakings and other spending.It includes the following main items:

(1) Expenditure for general public services: It refers to the spending on the basic public management and services which provided by governments, including the expense on affairs of People's Congress, affairs of People's Political Consultative Conference, affairs of government general office and relative institutions, affairs of development and reform, affairs of statistics, affairs of finance, affairs of taxation, affairs of audit, affairs of customs, affairs of human resources and social security, affairs of discipline inspection and supervision, affairs of population and family planning, affairs of commerce and trade, affairs of intellectual property, affairs of administration for industry and commerce, affairs of land and resources, affairs of oceanic administration, affairs of surveying and mapping, affairs of earthquake, ethnic affairs, religious affairs, affairs of Hong Kong, Macao, Taiwan, and Overseas Chinese, affairs of archives administration, affairs of Chinese Communist Party, affairs of democratic parties and federation of industry and commerce, affairs of mass organization, and affairs of lottery, etc.

(2) Expenditure for national defence: It refers to the spending of government on national defence, including the expense on active force, reserve force, militia, scientific research on national defence, special projects, mobilization of national defence, etc.

(3) Expenditure for public security: It refers to the spending of government on maintaining social and public security, including the expense on armed police force, public security, state security, prosecution, courts, justice, prison, labour education and rehabilitation, protection of state secrecy, anti-smuggling police, etc.

(4) Expenditure for education: It refers to the spending of government on education, including the expense on the administration of education, pre-primary education, primary education, secondary education, high school education, regular higher education, primary vocational education, secondary vocational education, technical school education, vocational high school education and higher vocational education, radio and television education, student abroad education, special education, on the job training of cadres, education authorities services, etc.

(5) Expenditure for science and technology: It refers to the spending of government on science and technology (S&T), including the expense on the administration of S&T, basic research, applied research, research and development, conditions and services of S&T, popularization of social science, science and technology, exchanges and cooperation of S&T, etc.

(6) Expenditure for culture, sport and media: It refers to the spending of government on culture, cultural heritage, sports, radio, film, television, press and publication, etc.

(7) Expenditure for social safety net and employment effort: It refers to the spending of government on social safety net and employment, including the expense on administration of social safety net and employment, civil affairs, budgetary subsidy on the social insurance funds, subsidy on National Social Security Fund, retirees of administrative units and institutions, subsidy on enterprise reform, subsidy on employment effort, pension, placement of ex-serviceman, social

welfare, the handicapped undertakings, the system of cost of living allowances for urban residents, other urban social relief, rural social relief, living relief of natural disasters, affairs of Red Cross Society, etc.

(8) Expenditure for medical and health care: It refers to the spending of government on medical and health care, including the expense on administration of medical and health care, medical services, health care, disease prevention and control, health inspection and supervision, women and children's health, rural health care, etc.

(9) Expenditure for urban and rural community affairs: It refers to the spending of government on urban and rural community affairs, including the expense on administration of urban and rural community, planning and management of urban and rural community, public facilities of urban and rural community, housing of urban and rural community, sanitation of urban and rural community, management and supervision on the construction market, etc.

(10) Expenditure for agriculture, forestry and water conservancy: It refers to the spending of government on agriculture, forestry and water conservancy, including the expense on agriculture, forestry, water conservancy, poverty alleviation, comprehensive agricultural development, etc.

(11) Expenditure for transportation: It refers to the spending of government on transportation and postal services, including the expense on road transportation, waterway transportation, railway transportation, civil aviation transportation, and postal services.

9

Nine

价格指数

Price Indices

9-1 居民消费价格分类指数
Consumer Price Indices by Category

(上年=100) (preceding year=100)

指 标	Item	2007	2008	2009	2010	2011	2012
居民消费价格总指数	**General Consumer Price Index**	**106.4**	**107.6**	**98.7**	**102.9**	**105.1**	**102.7**
#非食品价格指数	Non-Food Price Index	101.4	102.5	98.9	100.5	101.2	101.6
#服务项目价格指数	Services Price Index	102.5	102.6	99.9	101.4	101.3	101.8
消费品价格指数	Consumer Goods Price Index	107.6	109.0	98.4	103.4	106.6	103.0
#食品	**Food**	**116.7**	**117.3**	**98.5**	**107.7**	**113.5**	**104.7**
粮食	Grain	106.9	107.6	103.0	120.5	116.8	104.5
淀粉及薯类	Starches and Tubers	104.2	104.9	120.1	110.7	108.9	107.2
干豆类及豆制品	Beans and Its Products	107.2	137.4	102.1	109.7	107.9	100.6
油脂	Oil or Fat	147.5	128.3	78.4	100.4	116.5	104.4
肉禽及其制品	Meat, Poultry and Their Products	134.8	124.7	91.0	104.9	124.5	101.3
食用畜肉及副产品	Livestock for Slaughtering and Sideline Products	144.3	129.8	84.9	102.5	129.9	100.1
禽	Poultry	124.4	108.0	97.8	114.7	113.4	100.1
肉禽加工制品	Products of Processed Meat and Poultry	116.1	120.3	100.3	101.9	109.5	112.3
蛋	Eggs	114.2	100.1	98.0	107.3	114.7	95.7
水产品	Aquatic Products	110.5	112.2	95.3	109.7	111.1	107.6
鱼	Fish	110.4	113.0	94.8	111.4	110.7	108.0
其他水产品	Other Aquatic Products	110.2	110.1	95.7	104.5	112.0	106.7
菜	Vegetables	107.8	108.1	114.7	116.6	108.7	109.0
鲜菜	Fresh Vegetables	105.4	107.7	119.0	114.3	108.3	110.8
调味品	Flavoring	109.9	108.9	103.7	105.3	107.3	102.7
糖	Sugar	102.3	105.6	101.0	109.7	111.7	104.6
茶及饮料	Tea and Beverages	101.0	101.8	100.8	100.9	102.6	103.0
干鲜瓜果	Dried and Fresh Melons and Fruits	94.3	108.5	112.7	120.3	112.0	100.0
糕点饼干面包	Cake, Biscuit and Bread	106.6	112.8	101.2	102.3	110.5	105.6
奶及奶制品	Milk and Its Products	100.5	120.0	103.4	101.0	100.5	104.0

9-1 续表1 continued

(上年=100) (preceding year=100)

指 标	Item	2007	2008	2009	2010	2011	2012
在外用膳食品	Outward Dinner Food	114.3	120.7	101.5	101.3	109.5	109.6
其他食品及食品加工服务	Other Foods and Manufacturing Services	101.3	106.7	95.4	100.8	103.5	106.6
烟酒及用品	**Tobacco, Liquor and Articles**	**102.2**	**104.0**	**100.9**	**102.0**	**102.4**	**102.8**
烟草	Tobacco	100.0	99.8	100.1	100.8	99.7	102.3
酒	Liquor	109.5	113.2	102.3	103.8	107.2	103.5
白酒	Distilled Spirit	114.5	117.5	103.5	106.5	110.0	104.5
啤酒	Beer	99.3	107.6	99.4	95.9	103.3	100.9
衣着	**Clothing**	**97.8**	**97.8**	**95.6**	**97.4**	**100.3**	**103.8**
服装	Garments	97.8	98.3	96.7	99.3	100.9	103.5
衣着材料	Clothing Materials	99.6	100.3	101.9	103.1	113.2	107.1
鞋袜帽	Footgear and Hats	97.4	96.4	92.5	92.5	97.1	104.0
家庭设备用品及维修服务	**Household Facilities Articles and Repair Services**	**101.8**	**103.5**	**99.6**	**99.3**	**100.2**	**101.1**
耐用消费品	Durable Consumer Goods	101.3	102.8	98.4	98.6	98.7	99.1
家 具	Furniture	100.1	102.8	100.2	100.8	101.7	101.9
家庭设备	Household Facilities	102.2	102.3	98.0	97.6	97.3	97.7
室内装饰品	Interior Decorations	97.4	96.1	97.6	101.0	97.6	99.4
床上用品	Bed Articles	97.3	100.6	97.7	93.2	103.4	100.4
家庭日用杂品	Daily Use Household Articles	102.1	102.7	100.9	99.8	100.7	101.2
家庭服务及加工维修服务	Household Services and Manufacturing Upkeep	109.8	127.1	103.0	109.7	103.2	111.5
医疗保健和个人用品	**Health Care and Personal Articles**	**100.6**	**100.7**	**100.9**	**101.3**	**102.6**	**102.5**
医疗保健	Health Care	99.2	99.2	100.1	100.9	103.5	102.3
医疗器具及用品	Medical Instrument and Articles	99.6	100.3	100.5	101.0	100.8	101.8
中药材及中成药	Traditional Chinese Medicine	99.6	104.4	102.4	103.8	115.1	108.2
西 药	Western Medicine	98.2	98.3	100.1	101.1	101.9	100.9
保健器具及用品	Health Care Appliances and Articles	101.0	100.2	99.8	99.5	99.6	99.7
医疗保健服务	Health Care Services	99.6	98.9	99.6	100.3	100.0	100.6

9-1 续表2 continued

(上年=100) (preceding year=100)

指 标	Item	2007	2008	2009	2010	2011	2012
个人用品及服务	Personal Articles and Services	102.4	102.4	102.0	101.8	101.3	102.8
化妆美容用品	Cosmetics	99.8	98.6	100.5	101.7	100.4	100.2
卫生用品	Sanitation Articles	101.7	98.4	100.7	101.9	101.3	104.5
个人饰品	Personal Ornaments	102.1	103.8	98.2	100.1	103.7	100.1
个人服务	Personal Services	104.7	107.1	108.1	103.5	99.9	105.6
交通和通讯	**Transportation and Communication**	**100.3**	**100.7**	**98.2**	**100.8**	**100.1**	**99.6**
交 通	Transportation	102.5	103.4	99.8	102.6	102.9	101.4
交通工具	Transportation Facility	99.7	99.9	99.6	99.8	100.7	100.0
车用燃料及零配件	Fuels and Parts	103.7	110.9	91.0	111.3	109.7	103.3
车辆使用及维修	Using and Upkeep Fare	99.8	102.6	103.3	102.5	108.2	103.1
市区公共交通	Incity Traffic Fare	100.8	102.9	100.4	101.5	99.3	101.5
城市间交通	Intercity Traffic Fare	105.3	106.4	103.0	102.7	104.9	100.8
通 信	Communication	98.6	98.3	96.7	99.1	97.2	97.8
通信工具	Communication Facility	84.3	89.2	91.3	92.6	84.0	85.4
通信服务	Communication Service	101.3	100.4	97.8	100.4	100.6	100.5
娱乐教育文化用品及服务	**Recreation,Education and Culture Articles and Services**	**101.3**	**101.6**	**100.2**	**100.4**	**99.9**	**101.2**
文娱用耐用消费品及服务	Durable Consumer Goods and Services for Culture and Recreation	94.1	94.6	94.0	96.9	96.0	96.8
教 育	Education	101.8	102.3	100.5	101.0	101.4	102.7
文化娱乐用品	Cultural and Recreational Articles	107.6	108.2	102.8	100.3	99.7	101.5
文化娱乐	Recreation and Culture	100.8	99.5	98.2	99.1	99.7	100.3
书报杂志	Books,Newspapers and Magazines	101.2	101.7	102.2	101.1	100.3	102.2
文娱费	Recreation Fee	114.4	115.0	106.0	100.2	99.5	101.8
旅游	Touring	99.8	96.8	105.6	106.2	100.1	101.5
居住	**Residence**	**104.9**	**107.5**	**98.4**	**102.4**	**102.8**	**101.4**
建房及装修材料	Building and Building Decoration Materials	103.9	104.4	100.9	100.4	102.5	100.9
租 房	Rent	111.9	107.4	104.6	102.5	99.5	103.2
自有住房	Private Housing	101.4	99.6	85.6	100.6	102.3	100.9
水、电、燃料	Water, Electricity and Fuels	106.4	112.4	99.8	105.0	103.9	101.9

9–2 商品零售价格分类指数
Retail Price Indices by Category

(上年=100) (preceding year=100)

指　标	Item	2007	2008	2009	2010	2011	2012
商品零售价格总指数	**Retail Price Index**	**104.2**	**107.2**	**97.6**	**103.0**	**105.5**	**102.0**
食品类	Food	117.4	117.8	98.3	108.2	113.9	104.6
粮食	Grain	107.0	108.8	103.7	120.4	117.1	104.8
油脂	Oil or Fat	144.6	123.7	77.0	98.9	116.5	104.3
肉禽及其制品	Meat,Poultry and Their products	134.5	125.9	89.9	104.9	123.6	101.8
蛋	Eggs	114.5	101.7	98.2	107.2	115.7	97.9
水产品	Aquatic Products	110.5	115.5	96.2	108.2	112.3	107.3
鲜菜	Frash Vegetables	105.9	108.1	118.1	114.4	109.5	110.6
干菜及菜制品	Dried Vegetables and Its Products	119.0	107.7	96.0	125.8	110.8	99.1
鲜果	Fresh Fruits	96.2	108.2	117.0	122.1	112.3	98.8
干(坚)果及瓜果制品	Dried Fruits and Its Products	119.8	118.0	101.4	120.8	113.4	101.3
在外用膳食品	Outward Dinner Food	113.9	119.0	101.5	101.3	109.3	109.9
饮料、烟酒	Beverages,Tobacco and Liquor	101.0	102.3	100.6	101.1	101.6	102.5
服装、鞋帽类	Garments,Shoes and Hats	98.7	98.6	96.1	98.3	100.4	103.5
纺织品类	Textiles	97.4	101.0	98.4	99.5	103.8	102.1
家用电器及音像器材	Household Appliances, Music and Video Equipment	98.0	98.1	95.7	97.9	96.3	97.2
文化办公用品	Cultural and Office Appliances	97.1	98.5	99.3	100.1	98.1	98.4
日用品	Articles for Daily Use	102.2	103.8	100.8	100.8	100.8	100.2
体育娱乐用品	Sports and Recreation Articles	100.5	99.8	97.3	99.2	100.3	101.4
交通、通信用品	Traffic and Commanication Appliances	96.3	97.4	98.2	97.6	96.2	96.3
家具	Furniture	100.3	102.7	100.9	99.8	101.9	104.8
化妆品类	Cosmetics	100.2	98.3	98.6	99.7	100.6	101.9
金银珠宝类	Gold,Silver and Jewelry	108.3	113.3	89.7	108.9	111.7	101.5
中西药品及医疗保健用品类	Traditional Chinese and Western Medicines & Health Care Articles	101.4	102.4	101.0	102.6	106.2	104.2
书报杂志及电子出版物类	Books, Newspapers, Magazines and Electronic Publications	99.8	100.3	102.2	100.5	100.2	102.0
燃料类	Fuels	108.1	124.5	93.7	111.2	113.7	102.2
建筑材料及五金电料类	Building Materials and Hardware	105.2	112.7	96.6	102.5	102.7	99.0

9-3 工业生产者出厂价格分类指数

Ex-Factory Price Indices of Industrial Products by Gategory

(上年=100) (preceding year=100)

指 标	Item	2007	2008	2009	2010	2011	2012
工业生产者出厂价格指数	**Total Ex-Factory Price Index of Industrial Products**	**105.0**	**112.4**	**95.1**	**104.7**	**105.4**	**101.0**
按轻、重工业分	**Grouped by Light or Heavy Industries**						
轻工业	Light Industry	103.8	107.5	99.7	100.5	102.9	103.6
重工业	Heavy Industry	105.4	114.4	93.3	106.2	106.0	100.4
按用途分	**Grouped by Use**						
生产资料	Means of Production	105.4	114.2	93.8	105.5	106.2	100.3
采掘工业	Mining & Quarrying Industry	106.0	118.1	96.9	116.1	107.2	99.0
原材料工业	Raw Materials Industry	101.6	107.1	97.1	105.4	106.4	102.3
加工工业	Manufacturing Industry	109.3	120.8	89.3	102.1	105.6	97.5
生活资料	Consumer Goods	103.3	105.4	100.6	100.9	102.8	103.5
食品类	Food	104.2	106.1	101.5	101.7	102.8	103.3
衣着类	Clothing	104.0	105.2	106.1	102.4	114.2	105.5
一般日用品	Non-Durable Consumer Goods	100.6	102.8	99.0	100.3	101.6	103.1
耐用消费品	Durable Consumer Goods	97.6	100.2	91.7	92.2	101.5	105.4
按工业大类行业分	**Grouped by Sector**						
#煤炭开采和洗选业	Mining and Washing of Coal	109.1	120.9	100.0	117.0	111.9	94.5
有色金属矿采选业	Mining and Processing of Non-Ferrous Metal Ores	106.6	106.4	86.8	105.6	104.5	98.1
非金属矿采选业	Mining and Processing of Nonmetal Ores	94.9	110.4	90.4	106.2	123.6	122.3
农副食品加工业	Processing of Food from Agricultural Products	117.8	126.0	95.0	102.5	111.9	110.5
食品制造业	Manufacture of Foods	104.0	110.5	101.2	98.9	104.4	102.6
饮料制造业	Manufacture of Beverages	100.8	112.1	103.5	102.3	103.0	104.4
烟草制品业	Manufacture of Tobacco	100.5	100.4	101.0	100.6	99.7	101.7
纺织业	Manufacture of Textile	104.1	100.7	87.9	113.0	120.9	86.6
纺织服装、鞋、帽制造业	Manufacture of Textile Wearing Apparel, Footware and Caps	100.1	101.9	100.6	103.8	104.6	101.8
皮革、毛皮、羽毛（绒)及其制品业	Manufacture of Leather, Fur, Feather and Related Products	100.2	100.0	100.0	100.0	119.0	107.3

9-3 续表 Continued

(上年=100) (preceding year=100)

指 标	Item	2007	2008	2009	2010	2011	2012
木材加工及木、竹、藤、棕、草制品业	Processing of Timber,Manufacture of Wood, Bamboo,Rattan,Palm and Straw Products	101.2	102.7	98.1	100.9	103.2	108.9
家具制造业	Manufacture of Furniture	103.1	104.4	98.6	103.1	119.8	100.6
造纸及纸制品业	Manufacture of Paper and Paper Products	105.1	107.3	101.2	104.4	103.0	95.6
印刷业和记录媒介的复制	Printing,Reproduction of Recording Media	101.8	102.7	98.9	99.3	100.0	98.6
文教体育用品制造业	Manufacture of Articles For Culture,Education and Sport Activities	104.4	100.2	100.0	100.0	109.3	109.3
石油加工、炼焦及核燃料加工业	Processing of Petroleum, Coking, Processing of Nuclear Fuel	107.8	142.1	92.3	110.6	112.4	94.3
化学原料及化学制品制造业	Manufacture of Raw Chemical Materials and Chemical Products	107.1	138.8	83.3	105.8	114.1	104.8
医药制造业	Manufacture of Medicines	108.5	101.6	104.0	103.7	101.9	101.0
橡胶制品业	Manufacture of Rubber	108.0	106.0	100.2	102.0	114.0	95.6
非金属矿物制品业	Manufacture of Non-metallic Mineral Products	105.1	123.8	99.1	93.1	102.2	96.7
黑色金属冶炼及压延加工业	Smelting and Pressing of Ferrous Metals	118.8	124.9	81.2	104.2	105.5	90.8
有色金属冶炼及压延加工业	Smelting and Pressing of Non-ferrous Metals	92.6	95.8	81.3	111.9	108.4	98.2
金属制品业	Manufacture of Metal Products	101.7	114.9	91.8	102.6	101.4	96.7
通用设备制造业	Manufacture of General Purpose Machinery	100.7	104.3	99.4	100.9	100.0	99.1
专用设备制造业	Manufacture of Special Purpose Machinery	102.4	104.9	102.4	99.9	105.0	102.2
交通运输设备制造业	Manufacture of Transport Equipment	99.3	102.4	99.8	97.8	100.0	90.6
电气机械及器材制造业	Manufacture of Electrical Machinery and Equipment	105.3	103.1	94.3	99.2	99.6	98.6
通信设备、计算机及其他电子设备制造业	Manufacture of Communication Equipment, Computers and Other Electronic Equipment	92.6	92.1	85.4	99.0	99.3	102.5
仪器仪表及文化、办公用机械制造业	Manufacture of Measuring Instruments and Machinery for Cultural Activity and Office Work	99.5	97.0	96.9	98.8	101.5	99.2
电力、热力的生产和供应业	Production and Distribution of Electric Power and Heat Power	103.0	104.3	104.5	102.1	101.6	106.9
燃气生产和供应业	Production and Distribution of Gas	116.3	100.0	116.0	120.3	102.4	104.8
水的生产和供应业	Production and Distribution of Water	108.3	104.6	103.3	107.1	104.3	103.2

注：1.工业生产者出厂价格指数2010年及以前为全部工业品出厂价格指数，统计口径不变。2.工业大类行业2011年及以前按国民经济行业分类GB/T 4754-2002分，2012年按国民经济行业分类GB/T 4754-2011分。

Note:1.For the year 2010 and before,Ex-Factory Price Index of Industrial Producer referred to Total Ex-Factory Price Index of Industrial Products; statistical standards are unchanged. 2.For the year 2011 and before, industrial sectors are classified by Sector of the National Economy(GB/T4754-2002) and by Sector of the National Economy(GB/T4754-2011) in the year of 2012 .

9-4 工业生产者购进价格指数

Purchasing Price Index of Industrial Producer

(上年=100) (preceding year =100)

指　标	Item	2007	2008	2009	2010	2011	2012
工业生产者购进价格指数	**Purchasing Price Index of Industrial Producer**	**107.5**	**112.5**	**93.5**	**109.8**	**115.0**	**102.3**
燃料、动力类	Fuels and Power	105.0	115.6	101.2	110.1	121.6	107.2
黑色金属材料类	Ferrous Metals	106.5	123.9	86.9	104.0	109.9	93.2
#钢　材	Rolled-steel	106.0	120.7	88.2	103.3	108.0	96.2
有色金属材料和电线类	Nonferrous Metals and Wire	109.4	95.4	85.6	122.5	112.4	98.4
化工原料类	Raw Chemical Materials	106.3	109.8	86.0	110.2	116.4	94.6
木材及纸浆类	Timber and Paper Pulps	103.5	112.9	98.5	105.2	107.8	100.9
建筑材料及非金属矿类	Building Materials and Nonmetal Minerals Processing	105.2	131.2	94.2	96.7	117.8	116.1
其他工业原材料及半成品类	Other Industrial Raw Materials and Semi-products	107.4	108.4	93.3	108.8	106.4	103.9
农副产品类	Agricultural Products	115.2	115.0	90.7	115.1	109.2	106.1
纺织原料类	Textile Raw Materials	104.1	103.4	99.1	105.0	118.1	100.0

注：工业生产者购进价格指数2010年及以前为全部原材料、燃料、动力价格指数，统计口径不变。

Note:For the year 2010 and before,Purchasing Price Index of Industrial Producer referred to Total Indices of Purchasing Prices of Raw Materials,Fuels and Power;statistical standards are unchanged.

9-5 农业生产资料价格分类指数

Price Indices of Means of Agricultural Production by Category

(上年=100) (preceding year =100)

指　标	Item	2007	2008	2009	2010	2011	2012
农业生产资料价格总指数	**General Price Index of Means of Agricultural Production**	**105.1**	**113.4**	**96.2**	**101.1**	**111.1**	**100.7**
小农具	Small Farm Tools	101.4	107.3	107.9	107.5	105.5	114.1
饲　料	Forage	107.5	108.5	100.6	109.4	104.1	97.8
产品畜	Production Livestocks	129.8	114.9	105.0	97.1	153.9	93.7
半机械化农具	Semi-mechanized Farm Tools	101.2	116.1	106.1	99.3	115.7	97.0
机械化农具	Mechanized Farm Machinery	98.3	110.6	98.8	98.9	106.0	99.5
化学肥料	Chemical Fertilizer	103.5	121.3	91.5	92.7	101.4	105.6
农药及农药器械	Pesticide & Its Appliances	101.8	100.3	100.8	99.1	100.6	106.4
化学农药	Chemical Pesticide	102.5	101.0	103.3	97.6	101.5	104.8
农药器械	Appliances for Pesticide	100.7	99.1	96.7	101.6	96.1	114.6
农机用油	Oil for Farm Machinery	103.4	106.5	95.4	107.5	103.8	100.8
其他农业生产资料	Others Means of Agricultural Production	105.0	103.7	100.6	99.9	107.8	97.9

9–6 固定资产投资和房地产销售价格指数

Price Indices of Investment in Fixed Assets and Real Estate

(上年=100) (preceding year =100)

指　标	Item	2007	2008	2009	2010	2011	2012
固定资产投资价格指数	**Price Indices of Investment in Fixed Assets**	**103.5**	**108.9**	**100.5**	**102.7**	**105.4**	**101.5**
建筑安装工程	Price Indices of Construction and Installation	105.4	114.3	102.1	103.6	107.5	102.0
人工费	Manpower	108.0	115.6	115.1	114.0	111.0	108.4
材料费	Materials	105.6	116.3	98.4	101.2	109.3	99.7
钢　材	Steel Products	106.0	122.8	88.6	102.2	114.6	96.2
木　材	Timber	104.8	108.8	103.6	108.0	110.0	101.3
水　泥	Cement	105.4	117.3	106.8	97.5	102.1	99.1
电　料	Electrical Materials	101.7	109.5	98.7	103.2	106.4	102.8
化工材料	Chemical Raw Materials	105.8	112.5	109.8	106.8	108.6	107.3
地方建筑材料	Local Materials	111.2	110.9	106.2	100.8	106.7	101.9
其他材料	Others	104.1	105.0	105.6	103.4	102.7	102.9
机械使用费	Costs for Using Machine	101.9	104.2	103.0	102.7	101.8	102.7
设备、工器具购置	Purchase of Equipment,Tools and Instruments	100.2	100.6	97.5	100.1	101.0	99.1
其他费用	Others	100.9	101.1	99.3	102.5	102.6	101.5
新建住宅价格指数(贵阳市)	**Price Indices of New Residential Housings(Guiyang)**	**106.9**	**106.6**	**103.6**	**108.2**	**104.4**	**101.2**
新建商品住宅价格指数(贵阳市)	Price Indices of New Commodity Residential Housings(Guiyang)	107.7	106.7	103.6	108.3	104.5	101.3

注：新建住宅价格指数2010年及以前为房屋销售价格指数,新建商品住宅价格指数2010年及以前为住宅销售价格指数，统计口径不一致。

Note:For the year 2010 and before,Price Indices of New Residential Housings referred to the Sales Price Indices of Real Estate;Price Indices of New Commodity Residential Housings referred to the Sales Price Indices of Residence Housings;statistical standards are unchanged.

主要统计指标解释

商品零售价格指数 是反映城乡商品零售价格变动趋势和程度的相对数。零售物价的变动直接反映城乡居民的生活支出和国家的财政收入，影响居民购买力和市场供需平衡，影响消费与积累的比例关系。

居民消费价格指数 是反映一定时期内城乡居民所购买的生活消费品价格和服务项目价格变动趋势和程度的相对数。

工业生产者价格指数 工业生产者价格包括工业企业产品第一次出售时的出厂价格和企业作为中间投入的原材料、燃料、动力购进价格（下简称工业生产者购进价格）。工业生产者价格调查的目的在于及时、准确、科学地反映各工业行业产品价格水平及其变动趋势和幅度，为国民经济核算、计算工业发展速度、宏观经济分析和调控、理顺价格体系等提供科学、准确的依据。

固定资产投资价格指数 是反映固定资产投资额价格变动趋势和程度的相对数。固定资产投资额是由建筑安装工程投资完成额、设备、工器具购置投资完成额和其他费用投资完成额三部分组成的。编制固定资产投资价格指数应首先分别编制上述三部分投资的价格指数，然后采用加权算术平均法求出固定资产投资价格总指数。

农业生产资料价格指数 是反映一定时期内农业生产资料价格变动趋势和程度的相对数。农业生产资料价格指数分为小农具、饲料、产品畜、役畜、半机械化农具、机械化农具、化学肥料、农药及农具械、农机用油、其他农业生产资料十大类。

Explanatory Notes on Main Statistical Indicators

Retail Price Index reflects the general change in retail prices of commodities. The change and adjustment in retail prices directly affect the living expenditure of urban and rural residents, government revenue, purchasing power of residents and the equilibrium of market supply and demand, and the ratio of consumption to accumulation.

Consumer Price Index reflects the trend and degree of changes in prices of consumer goods and services purchased by urban and rural residents, and is a composite index derived from the urban consumer price index and the rural consumer price index.

Industrial producer prices the first sale of industrial enterprises and enterprises as the prices of intermediate inputs of raw materials, fuel and power purchase price (hereinafter referred to as industrial producer price). Industrial producer prices survey was designed to timely, accurate and scientifically reflect various industrial products industry trends and changes in the price level and the magnitude of national accounts to calculate the speed of industrial development, macroeconomic analysis and control, rationalize the price system to provide scientific and accurate basis.

Price Index of Investment in Fixed Assets reflects the trend and degree of changes in prices of investment in fixed assets. The investment in fixed assets consists of three components, namely the investment in construction and installation, the investment in purchases of equipment and instrument, and the investment in other items. Price index of investment in fixed assets is calculated as the weighted arithmetic mean of the price indices of the three components of investment in fixed assets.

Price Indices of Means of Agricultural Production reflect the trend and degree of changes in prices of means of agricultural production during a given period. Price indices of means of agricultural production are composed of 10 categories including small farm tools, feeds, domestic animals for meat, draught domestic animals, semi-mechanized farm machinery, mechanized farm machinery, chemical fertilizers, pesticides and spraying machinery, fuels for farm machinery and other means of agricultural production.

10

Ten

人民生活

People's Living Conditions

10-1 城乡人民生活水平
People's Livelihood in Urban and Rural Areas

指　标	Item	2007	2008	2009	2010	2011	2012
就业	**Employment**						
城镇居民家庭每户就业人口(人)	Average Number of Employed Persons per Urban Household(person)	1.52	1.37	1.43	1.43	1.43	1.45
城镇居民家庭每个就业者赡养人口(人)	Number of Dependents per Employee of Urban Household(person)	1.99	2.22	2.13	2.11	2.08	2.08
城镇平均每户就业面(%)	Proportion of Employment per Urban Household(%)	0.50	0.45	0.47	0.47	0.48	0.48
城镇登记失业人数(万人)	Registered Urban Unemployment Persons (10000 persons)	12.13	12.56	12.34	12.18	12.51	12.56
城镇登记失业率(%)	Registered Urban Unemployment Rate(%)	3.97	3.98	3.81	3.63	3.63	3.29
农村平均每户整、半劳动力(人)	Average Number of Full/Semi Laborer Force per Rural Household(person)	2.90	2.93	2.95	2.95	2.83	2.82
农村居民家庭每一劳动力赡养人口(人)	Number of Dependents per Laborer of Rural Household(person)	1.52	1.51	1.48	1.47	1.52	1.53
收入与支出	**Income and Expenditure**						
城镇居民人均可支配收入(元)	Annual Per Capita Disposable Income of Urban Households(yuan)	10678	11759	12863	14143	16495	18701
城镇居民人均消费性支出(元)	Annual Per Capita Consumption Expenditure of Urban Householdss(yuan)	7759	8349	9048	10058	11353	12586
在岗职工平均工资(元)	Average Wage of Staff and Workers in their Posts(yuan)	20668	24602	28245	31458	37331	42733
农村居民人均纯收入(元)	Annual Per Capita Net Income of Rural Households (yuan)	2374	2797	3005	3472	4145	4753
农村居民人均生活消费支出(元)	Annual Per Capita Living Expenditure of Rural Households (yuan)	1914	2166	2422	2852	3456	3902
生活质量	**Life Quality**						
居民家庭恩格尔系数(%)	**Household's Engle Coefficient(%)**						
城　镇	Urban	40.2	43.1	41.5	39.9	40.2	39.7
农　村	Rural	52.2	51.7	45.2	46.3	47.7	44.6
居住条件	**Residence Condition**						
城镇人均住宅建筑面积(平方米)	Per Capita Building Space in Urban Areas(sq.m)	27.52	26.95	27.57	27.42	27.83	27.86
农村居民人均住房面积(平方米)	Per Capita Living Space in Rural Areas(sq.m)	24.54	25.27	26.43	27.26	29.63	29.75
交通条件	**Traffic Condition**						
城市人均拥有道路面积(平方米)	Per Capita Area of Paved Roads in City(sq.m)	6.06	5.99	6.03	6.23	6.66	6.93
每百户城镇居民拥有家用汽车(辆)	Number of Family Vehicles Per 100 Urban Households(unit)	2.01	3.29	4.85	5.96	10.48	13.17
每百户农村居民拥有家用摩托车(辆)	Number of Motorcycles Per 100 Rural Households(unit)	17.20	19.60	26.80	30.76	35.98	39.02
通信条件	**Communication Condition**						
每百户拥有移动电话(部)	Mobile Telephone Per 100 Households(set)						
城　镇	Urban	160.87	163.27	177.27	183.54	204.75	214.73
农　村	Rural	34.20	53.80	82.50	102.10	156.96	173.26
城市公用设施普及占有率	City Public Utility Rate						
用水普及率(%)	Rate of Access to Tap Water(%)	79.7	83.2	85.4	86.5	86.9	87.6
燃气普及率(%)	Rate of Access to Gas(%)	51.1	54.1	54.2	54.5	55.0	55.2
人均公园绿地面积(平方米)	Per Capita Green Area(sq.m)	4.23	4.44	4.65	5.33	5.50	6.68

10-1 续表 continued

指 标	Item	2007	2008	2009	2010	2011	2012
文化、教育和卫生	**Culture, Education and Health Care**						
文化	**Culture**						
广播节目综合人口覆盖率(%)	Radio Coverage Rate of the Population (%)	84.1	86.1	86.6	87.5	88.0	88.5
电视节目综合人口覆盖率(%)	TV Coverage Rate of the Population(%)	91.1	91.3	91.3	92.5	92.8	93.0
每百户彩色电视机拥有量(部/百户)	Number of Color TV per 100 Households(set)						
城镇	Urban	122.02	118.85	122.03	121.93	115.78	115.67
农村	Rural	72.90	74.60	88.10	91.07	93.93	95.94
每百户家用电脑拥有量(部/百户)	Number of Computers per 100 Households(set)						
城镇	Urban	40.37	43.37	52.47	56.79	63.89	71.22
农村	Rural	1.07	1.07	0.98	1.65	4.11	4.87
居民家庭文教娱乐支出比重(%)	Percentage of Household Expenditure on Education,Culture and Entertainment(%)						
城镇	Urban	13.4	11.2	12.7	12.5	11.7	11.1
农村	Rural	7.7	5.6	6.3	6.5	5.3	5.8
教育	**Education**						
学龄儿童入学率(%)	Enrollment Rate of School-age Children(%)	98.6	97.2	98.4	97.9	98.6	99.3
初中阶段毛入学率(%)	Enrollment Rate of Primary School Graduates Entering into Junior Secondary Schools(%)	97.5	95.9	98.2	97.6	94.2	97.4
高中阶段毛入学率(%)	Enrollment Rate of Juniorsecondary School Graduates Entering into Senior secondary Schools(%)	42.2	47.9	53.4	55.0	58.9	62.2
高等教育毛入学率(%)	Enrollment Rate of Senior secondary School Graduates Entering into Institution of Higher Education(%)	11.5	11.8	18.4	20.0	23.2	25.5
卫生	**Health Care**						
居民家庭医疗保健支出比重(%)	Percentage of Resident Expenditure on Health Care(%)						
城镇	Urban	4.6	5.6	5.9	5.4	5.1	5.2
农村	Rural	4.1	4.5	5.5	6.2	7.1	7.2
社会保障	**Social Security**						
基本养老保险参保人数(万人)	Number of People Joining in Basic Pension Insurance(10 000 persons)	205.93	215.89	235.61	257.31	282.06	309.38
#参保职工	Number of Employees	149.39	156.57	172.14	190.29	210.71	231.67
城镇职工基本医疗保险参保人数(万人)	Number of Persons Joining in Urban Basic Medical Care System (10 000 persons)	228.22	257.35	279.53	293.52	314.06	329.27
失业保险参保人数(万人)	Number of Employees Joining in Unemployment Insurance (10 000 persons)	134.55	141.36	144.60	152.48	160.52	173.46
工伤保险参保人数(万人)	Number of Employees Joining in Injury Insurance (10 000 persons)	110.50	129.02	143.35	162.18	193.96	238.19
生育保险参保人数(万人)	Number of Persons Joining in Maternity Insurance(10 000 persons)	88.70	135.95	152.49	164.30	198.09	221.58
社会保险基金收入(亿元)	Revenue of Social Insurance Fund(100 million yuan)	90.86	140.50	171.40	201.56	256.94	310.85

10–2 城镇居民家庭生活基本情况

Basic Conditions of Urban Households Life

指　标	Item	2007	2008	2009	2010	2011	2012
调查户数(户)	Number of Households Surveyed(household)	1340	1490	1670	1670	1720	1720
平均每户常住家庭人口(人)	Average Household Size(person)	3.02	3.07	3.04	3.03	2.98	3.01
平均每户就业人员(人)	Number of Employed Persons Per Household(person)	1.52	1.37	1.43	1.43	1.43	1.45
平均每户就业面(%)	Proportion of Employment per Household(%)	0.50	0.45	0.47	0.47	0.48	0.48
平均每户国有经济单位职工人数(人)	Number of Staff and Workers in State-owned Units (person)	0.92	0.80	0.79	0.81	0.74	0.72
平均每户城镇集体经济单位职工人数(人)	Number of Staff and Workers in Urban Collective-ownedUnits (person)	0.05	0.04	0.04	0.03	0.04	0.03
平均每户其他各种经济类型单位职工(人)	Number of Staff and Workers in Other Types ofOwnership Units (person)	0.10	0.09	0.09	0.09	0.10	0.11
平均每个就业者赡养人口(人)	Number of Dependents per Employee(person)	1.99	2.22	2.13	2.11	2.08	2.08
平均每人年可支配收入(元)	**Per Capita Annual Disposable Income (yuan)**	**10678.40**	**11758.76**	**12862.53**	**14142.74**	**16495.01**	**18700.51**
平均每人年总收入(元)	**Per Capita Annual Income(yuan)**	**11066.43**	**12185.62**	**13793.38**	**15138.80**	**17598.87**	**20042.88**
工资性收入	Income of Wages and Salaries	7750.15	7811.16	9005.57	9627.99	10754.45	12309.17
工资及补贴收入	Income of Laborage and Allowance	7544.09	7503.85	8569.27	9190.47	10359.48	11951.96
其他劳动收入	Income of other Labor	206.06	307.32	436.30	437.52	394.97	357.21
经营者净收入	Net Business Income	764.63	770.86	1135.05	1174.02	1614.67	1982.45
财产性收入	Income from Property	161.30	110.90	134.34	213.83	356.41	355.70
转移性收入	Income from Transfer	2390.34	3492.70	3518.42	4122.96	4873.34	5395.56
#养老金或离退休金	Annuities or Pension	1969.84	3002.09	3026.06	3493.33	4229.54	4673.43
出售财物收入(元)	Income of Selling Property and Goods(yuan)	1.46	13.87	17.66	181.55	46.61	271.17
借贷收入(元)	Income on Loan(yuan)	1705.94	1802.29	2277.39	3651.74	4390.30	5976.40
平均每人消费性支出（元）	**Per Capita Annual Consumption Expenditure (yuan)**	**7758.69**	**8349.21**	**9048.29**	**10058.29**	**11352.88**	**12585.70**
食　品	Food	3122.46	3597.94	3755.61	4013.67	4565.85	4992.85
衣　着	Clothing	910.30	851.50	1012.14	1102.41	1209.88	1399.00
居　住	Residence	718.65	836.54	747.57	890.75	1102.99	1013.53
家庭设备用品及服务	Household Facilities, Articles and Services	463.56	525.70	589.35	673.33	857.55	849.94
医疗保健	Health Care and Medical Services	354.52	471.39	535.43	546.84	578.33	654.53
交通和通信	Transport and Communication	895.04	871.15	983.13	1270.49	1395.28	1891.03
教育文化娱乐服务	Education, Culture and Recreation Services	1035.96	934.73	1146.35	1254.56	1331.43	1396.00
其他商品与服务	Miscellaneous Goods and Services	258.21	260.27	278.71	306.24	311.57	388.82
平均每人消费性支出构成(%)(人均消费性支出=100)	**Composition of Per Capita Annual Consumption Expenditure (%)**						
食　品	Food	40.2	43.1	41.5	39.9	40.2	39.7
衣　着	Clothing	11.7	10.2	11.2	11.0	10.7	11.1
居　住	Residence	9.3	10.0	8.3	8.9	9.7	8.0
家庭设备用品及服务	Household Facilities, Articles and Services	6.0	6.3	6.5	6.7	7.6	6.8
医疗保健	Health Care and Medical Services	4.6	5.6	5.9	5.4	5.1	5.2
交通和通信	Transport and Communication	11.5	10.4	10.9	12.6	12.3	15.0
教育文化娱乐服务	Education, Culture and Recreation Services	13.4	11.2	12.7	12.5	11.7	11.1
其他商品与服务	Miscellaneous Goods and Services	3.3	3.1	3.1	3.0	2.7	3.1

10-3 城镇居民家庭人均现金收支

Per Capita Annual Cash Income and Expenditure of Urban Households

单位：元 (yuan)

指　标	Item	2007	2008	2009	2010	2011	2012
家庭总收入	**Total Households Income**	**11066.43**	**12185.62**	**13793.38**	**15138.80**	**17598.87**	**20042.88**
#可支配收入	Disposable Income	10678.40	11758.76	12862.53	14142.74	16495.01	18700.51
#工资性收入	Income of Wages and Salaries	7750.15	7811.16	9005.57	9627.99	10754.45	12309.17
工资及补贴收入	Income of Laborage and Allowance	7544.09	7503.85	8569.27	9190.47	10359.48	11951.96
其他劳动收入	Income of other Labor	206.06	307.32	436.30	437.52	394.97	357.21
经营净收入	Net Business Income	764.63	770.86	1135.05	1174.02	1614.67	1982.45
财产性收入	Income from Property	161.30	110.90	134.34	213.83	356.41	355.70
#利息收入	Interest Income	2.06	1.71	6.81	10.22	19.03	31.84
股息与红利收入	Dividends and Bonus Income	38.76	6.91	4.70	4.29	12.63	11.76
转移性收入	Income from Transfer	2390.34	3492.70	3518.42	4122.96	4873.34	5395.56
#养老金或离退休金	Annuities or Pension	1969.84	3002.09	3026.06	3493.33	4229.54	4673.43
出售财物收入	**Income of Selling Property and Goods**	**1.46**	**13.87**	**17.66**	**181.55**	**46.61**	**271.17**
借贷收入	**Income on Loan**	**1705.94**	**1802.29**	**2277.39**	**3651.74**	**4390.30**	**5976.40**
#提取储蓄存款	Drawing Money from Banks	1521.12	1689.76	1922.08	3082.85	3955.57	5491.68
其他借贷收入	Others	3.11	2.91	86.91	172.05	37.54	79.80
家庭总支出	**Total Households Expenditure**	**9735.19**	**10236.67**	**12085.93**	**13479.37**	**15558.27**	**17312.83**
消费支出	Consumption Expenditure	7758.69	8349.21	9048.29	10058.29	11352.88	12585.70
#服务性消费支出	Services	2019.82	2115.23	2350.91	2830.23	3014.21	3248.15
财产性支出	Property Expenditure	3.09	4.45	55.23	52.40	88.39	87.07
转移性支出	Transfer Expenditure	1414.12	1442.97	1857.66	1923.23	2364.36	2601.30
#交纳的个人收入税	Individual Income Tax	12.82	9.98	14.96	20.67	15.95	14.70
各种非储蓄性保险支出	Various Nonsaving Insurance Expenditure	10.16	18.80	30.22	32.84	39.87	38.43
其他转移性支出	Others	46.00	45.57	51.66	56.49	73.40	66.80
社会保障支出	Social Seurity Expenditure	347.73	357.08	820.86	859.17	996.60	1178.02
购房与建房支出	Expenditure of Purchasing or Building House	211.56	82.96	303.88	586.28	756.04	860.73
借贷支出	Expenditure on Loan	2265.82	2851.94	3284.53	4725.38	5277.74	7714.27
#存入储蓄款	Saving Deposits	1865.85	2526.66	2903.20	4316.79	4842.53	6842.64
购置有价证券	Purchasing Seurities	36.47	2.64	4.28	2.31	17.74	0.90
其他借贷支出	Others	9.66	23.67	39.32	5.51	39.58	29.42

10-4 城镇居民家庭人均消费性支出

Per Capita Annual Consumption Expenditure of Urban Household

单位：元 (yuan)

指　标	Item	2007	2008	2009	2010	2011	2012
消费性支出	**Consumption Expenditure**	**7758.69**	**8349.21**	**9048.29**	**10058.29**	**11352.88**	**12585.70**
食　品	**Food**	**3122.46**	**3597.94**	**3755.61**	**4013.67**	**4565.85**	**4992.85**
#粮　食	Grain	248.81	303.11	295.28	320.00	374.20	395.96
糖、烟、酒、饮料类	Sugar, Cigarette,Liquor and Beverage	388.28	432.85	470.42	494.98	508.79	592.09
在外饮食	Dining Out	593.27	642.09	741.81	818.58	918.02	1054.53
衣　着	**Clothing**	**910.30**	**851.50**	**1012.14**	**1102.41**	**1209.88**	**1399.00**
居　住	**Residence**	**718.65**	**836.54**	**747.57**	**890.75**	**1102.99**	**1013.53**
#房　租	Rent	14.05	28.11	19.16	24.19	50.08	80.11
水　费	Water	71.55	83.12	91.99	98.60	94.38	101.47
电　费	Electricity	293.11	332.22	354.97	385.54	412.22	462.74
燃料费	Fuels	150.87	205.27	139.27	147.89	158.01	162.20
家庭设备用品及服务	**Household Facilities,Articles and Services**	**463.56**	**525.70**	**589.35**	**673.33**	**857.55**	**849.94**
#耐用消费品	Durable Consumer Goods	162.60	186.10	212.21	199.59	366.57	270.72
医疗保健	**Health Care and Medical Services**	**354.52**	**471.39**	**535.43**	**546.84**	**578.33**	**654.53**
交通和通信	**Transport and Communications**	**895.04**	**871.15**	**983.13**	**1270.49**	**1395.28**	**1891.03**
交　通	Transport	386.34	400.19	436.24	606.34	698.37	1146.18
通　信	Communications	508.70	470.96	546.89	664.15	696.91	744.85
教育文化娱乐服务	**Education,Culture and Recreation Services**	**1035.96**	**934.73**	**1146.35**	**1254.56**	**1331.43**	**1396.00**
#文化娱乐用品	Recreation Articles	235.94	221.73	309.29	269.35	323.35	315.85
书报杂志	Books,Newspaper and Magazines	35.34	28.26	30.68	31.26	29.84	26.53
文化娱乐服务	Recreation Services	310.01	276.76	401.43	491.18	520.72	580.28
学杂费	Tuition Fee	248.29	226.11	184.92	209.62	191.07	189.54
托幼费	Child-care Fee	30.80	28.56	35.12	50.76	44.43	42.62
其他商品和服务	**Miscellaneous Goods and Services**	**258.21**	**260.27**	**278.71**	**306.24**	**311.57**	**388.82**
恩格尔系数(%)	**Engel Coefficient(%)**	**40.2**	**43.1**	**41.5**	**39.9**	**40.2**	**39.7**

10–5 城镇居民家庭人均购买主要商品数量

Per Capita Annual Purchases of Major Commodities of Urban Househoulds

单位：公斤 (kg)

指　标	Item	2007	2008	2009	2010	2011	2012
粮　食	Grain	52.02	59.33	51.92	70.69	78.88	68.13
食用植物油	Edible Vegetable Oil	9.84	9.96	9.16	8.70	9.91	8.40
猪　肉	Pork	24.80	24.80	26.41	25.66	27.89	24.93
牛、羊肉	Beef and Mutton	1.95	1.72	1.71	1.88	2.15	1.82
禽　类	Poultry	7.33	7.24	7.66	8.64	9.41	8.61
蛋　类	Eggs	5.14	5.21	5.09	5.70	6.68	5.70
水产品类(元)	Aquatic Products(yuan)	59.21	66.49	74.64	81.01	86.94	99.05
鲜 菜	Fresh Vegetables	94.62	102.58	98.69	93.57	106.12	92.88
糖类(元)	Sugar(yuan)	39.74	39.74	42.55	43.48	53.33	61.01
烟草类(元)	Cigarettes(yuan)	226.78	258.42	266.26	278.65	277.38	308.76
酒　类	Liquor	4.79	4.85	4.45	4.03	3.59	3.56
糕点类	Cake	2.96	2.65	3.20	3.08	3.34	2.90
干鲜瓜果类	Dried and Fresh Melons and Fruits	46.36	39.45	43.89	41.94	44.08	38.70
奶类及制品(元)	Milk and Its Products(yuan)	118.30	118.35	133.15	154.78	157.23	169.88

10–6 每百户城镇居民家庭耐用消费品拥有量

Number of Major Durable Consumer Goods Owned Per 100 Urban Households

单位：台 (set)

指　标	Item	2007	2008	2009	2010	2011	2012
摩托车(辆)	Motorcycle(unit)	4.92	5.13	6.15	5.79	5.46	5.42
家用汽车(辆)	Automobile(unit)	2.01	3.29	4.85	5.96	10.48	13.17
洗衣机	Washing Machine	98.32	96.73	99.03	99.23	99.15	99.87
电冰箱	Refrigerator	94.22	92.54	94.42	94.56	97.21	97.63
彩色电视机	Color TV Set	122.02	118.85	122.03	121.93	115.78	115.67
家用电脑	Household Computer	40.37	43.37	52.47	56.79	63.89	71.22
组合音响(套)	Hi-Fi Stereo Component System(unit)	38.94	35.41	36.84	37.06	31.22	28.02
照相机(架)	Camera(unit)	32.95	25.25	28.78	28.03	29.01	29.87
钢　琴	Piano	1.06	1.84	1.88	1.79	2.07	2.66
微波炉	Microwave Oven	43.70	43.77	45.28	45.71	45.76	47.59
空调器	Air Conditioner	14.69	16.25	17.49	17.00	20.46	21.71
淋浴热水器	Water Heater for Shower	68.61	69.36	72.24	72.42	75.11	78.51
健身器材(套)	Healthy Equipment(unit)	2.04	2.86	4.47	4.20	3.30	4.06
固定电话(部)	Telephone(unit)	80.40	70.87	71.38	71.51	64.94	62.15
移动电话(部)	Mobile Phone(unit)	160.87	163.27	177.27	183.54	204.75	214.73

10-7 按收入等级分城镇居民家庭收入、消费情况(2012)

指　标	Item	总平均 Average	最低收入户 (10%) Lowest Income Households (first decile group)
平均每人年总收入(元)	**Per Capita Annual Total Income(yuan)**	**20042.88**	**6613.79**
平均每人年可支配收入(元)	**Per Capita Annual Disposable Income(yuan)**	**18700.51**	**5949.96**
人均购买主要商品数量	**Per Capita Purchases of Major Commodities**		
粮食(千克)	Grain(kg)	68.13	68.65
食用植物油(千克)	Edible Vegetable Oil(kg)	8.40	8.35
猪肉(千克)	Pork(kg)	24.93	18.87
牛肉(千克)	Beef(kg)	1.66	0.77
鸡(千克)	Chicken(kg)	6.12	3.20
鸭(千克)	Duck(kg)	1.16	0.85
鲜蛋(千克)	Eggs(kg)	5.14	3.35
鱼(千克)	Fish(kg)	3.02	1.86
鲜菜(千克)	Fresh Vegetables(kg)	92.88	77.60
糖类(元)	Sugar(yuan)	61.01	26.94
烟草类(元)	Cigarettes(yuan)	308.76	110.95
白酒(千克)	Liquor(kg)	2.00	1.38
鲜果(千克)	Fresh Fruit(kg)	34.00	16.80
糕点(千克)	Cakes(kg)	2.90	1.28
鲜乳品(千克)	Fresh Milk Products(kg)	10.92	3.14
服装(件)	Clothing(unit)	6.30	2.66
每百户耐用消费品拥有量	**Ownership of Major Durable Consumer Goods Per 100 Urban Househoulds**		
摩托车(辆)	Motorcycle(unit)	5.42	3.96
家用汽车(辆)	Automobile(unit)	13.17	0.53
洗衣机(台)	Washing Machine(set)	99.87	93.71
电冰箱(台)	Refrigerator(set)	97.63	86.46
彩色电视机(台)	Color TV Set(set)	115.67	100.68
家用电脑(台)	Household Computer(set)	71.22	32.20
组合音响(套)	Hi-Fi Stereo Component System(unit)	28.02	9.94
照相机(架)	Camera(unit)	29.87	4.82
钢琴(架)	Piano(set)	2.66	
微波炉(台)	Microwave Oven(set)	47.59	23.40
空调器(台)	Air Conditioner(set)	21.71	4.03
淋浴热水器(台)	Water Heater for Shower(set)	78.51	56.02
健身器材(套)	Healthy Equipment(unit)	4.06	0.66
固定电话(部)	Telephone(unit)	62.15	51.17
移动电话(部)	Mobile Phone(unit)	214.73	163.44

Statistics of Income and Consumption of Urban Househoulds by Level of Income

低收入户 (10%) Low Income Households (second decile group)	较低收入户 (20%) Lower Middle Income Households (second quintile group)	中间收入户 (20%) Middle Income Households (third quintile group)	较高收入户 (20%) Upper Middle Income Households (fourth quintile group)	高收入户 (10%) High Income Households (ninth decile group)	最高收入户 (10%) Highest Income Households (tenth decile group)
10443.85	**14454.09**	**19275.33**	**25365.58**	**33477.64**	**48804.43**
9698.74	**13383.00**	**18031.35**	**23720.89**	**31388.71**	**45882.00**
69.49	67.40	69.90	70.29	67.40	58.93
7.66	8.62	9.04	8.37	8.32	7.58
21.90	24.51	26.14	27.93	27.82	27.80
1.08	1.67	1.85	2.26	2.15	1.65
5.34	5.74	6.74	7.67	7.79	6.41
0.91	1.14	1.23	1.30	1.58	1.15
4.28	4.82	5.91	5.81	5.96	6.04
2.33	2.47	3.35	3.56	4.36	4.18
96.74	87.69	97.49	99.94	99.87	93.58
34.37	57.94	60.53	78.70	85.45	100.77
175.91	222.94	277.81	390.48	544.60	729.87
1.60	2.33	2.57	1.72	1.77	2.16
24.33	31.19	37.44	42.58	42.12	48.69
2.04	2.59	3.23	3.48	3.82	4.72
5.69	8.60	11.32	15.28	18.09	20.00
4.27	5.91	6.47	7.74	9.17	9.77
5.75	7.37	7.89	4.51	2.43	2.76
3.71	7.64	10.96	16.64	21.24	38.35
95.38	98.97	102.38	100.61	101.26	105.88
93.44	94.95	101.07	100.34	103.96	102.04
105.38	110.07	114.94	120.26	126.69	136.43
43.18	67.96	72.20	82.57	92.19	105.37
12.98	28.78	26.94	36.92	40.27	33.83
7.73	20.71	28.74	40.58	44.22	67.20
0.91	1.36	2.82	2.14	3.70	10.07
26.36	42.49	46.27	57.99	60.03	76.97
9.18	8.46	19.70	28.84	33.28	61.45
65.95	77.44	84.34	80.94	85.20	96.53
0.31	1.14	3.21	6.69	7.82	10.63
48.61	55.80	65.09	71.94	69.11	70.21
203.03	222.21	227.84	222.47	221.39	220.97

10-8 农村居民家庭生活基本情况
Basic Conditions of Rural Households Life

指　标	Item	2007	2008	2009	2010	2011	2012
调查户数(户)	**Households Surveyed(household)**	**2240**	**2240**	**2240**	**2240**	**2240**	**2240**
平均每户常住人口(人)	Average Number of Persons Per Household (person)	4.43	4.40	4.38	4.34	4.32	4.31
平均每户整、半劳动力(人)	Average Number of Laborers Per Household (person)	2.90	2.93	2.95	2.95	2.83	2.82
平均每一劳动力赡养人口(人)	Average Number Persons Supported by a Laborer (person)	1.52	1.51	1.48	1.47	1.52	1.53
平均每百个劳动力中(人)	In Per 100 Laborers (person)						
文盲或半文盲	Illiterate or Semi-Illiterate	14.09	13.06	12.93	12.32	10.29	10.35
小学程度	Elementary School	36.23	35.78	35.86	35.70	38.63	38.16
初中程度	Junior High School	42.45	43.29	42.59	42.56	43.23	42.92
高中程度	Senior High School	5.24	5.32	5.98	6.59	3.78	4.12
中专程度	Technical Secondary School	1.74	1.83	1.82	1.91	1.69	1.93
大专以上	Junior College	0.66	0.72	0.83	0.92	1.31	1.42
劳动力平均受教育年限(年)	Average Fixed Number of Year of Receiving Education of the Laborers(year)	6.86	7.02	7.05	7.14	7.07	7.11
平均每人年收入(元)	**Per Capita Annual Income (yuan)**						
总收入	Total Income	3217.96	3889.69	4050.40	4560.52	5659.58	6443.90
工资性收入	Income from Wages and Salaries	846.85	1002.68	1074.32	1303.85	1713.52	1977.73
家庭经营收入	Income from Household Operations	2116.54	2541.26	2502.62	2674.22	3367.61	3809.21
财产性收入	Income from Properties	46.69	63.92	81.90	117.19	59.50	71.54
转移性收入	Income from Transfers	207.87	281.83	391.57	465.26	518.96	585.42
现金收入	Cash Income	2347.33	3013.00	3188.31	3448.33	4439.54	5078.31
工资性收入	Income from Wages and Salaries	846.72	1002.52	1072.54	1303.65	1712.31	1976.43
家庭经营收入	Income from Household Operations	1250.95	1670.77	1652.25	1571.86	2169.90	2460.43
财产性收入	Income from Properties	45.51	62.60	79.31	114.47	48.31	70.88
转移性收入	Income from Transfers	204.15	277.11	384.22	458.35	509.02	570.57
平均每人年纯收入(元)	**Annual Average Net Income Per Capita(yuan)**	**2373.99**	**2796.93**	**3005.41**	**3471.93**	**4145.35**	**4753.00**
工资性收入	Payment for Labour	846.85	1002.68	1074.32	1303.85	1713.52	1977.73
家庭经营纯收入	Income from Household Operations	1320.06	1512.47	1537.57	1706.33	1980.21	2249.21
转移性收入	Income from Transfers	160.39	217.86	311.63	344.56	392.13	454.53
财产性收入	Income from Properties	46.69	63.92	81.90	117.19	59.50	71.54
平均每人年总支出(元)	**Annual Average Expenditure Per Capita(yuan)**	**2960.37**	**3590.51**	**3862.77**	**4350.25**	**5722.46**	**6370.25**
#人均生活消费支出	Living Expenditure	1913.50	2165.70	2421.95	2852.48	3455.76	3901.71
人均年末使用房屋面积(平方米)	Average Per Capita Living Space at the Year-end(sq.m)	24.54	25.27	26.43	27.26	29.63	29.75

10–9 农村居民家庭人均年纯收入

Per Capita Annual Net Income of Rural Households

单位：元 (yuan)

指　标	Item	2007	2008	2009	2010	2011	2012
全年纯收入	**Annual Net Income**	**2373.99**	**2796.93**	**3005.41**	**3471.93**	**4145.35**	**4753.00**
工资性收入	Income from Wage	846.85	1002.68	1074.32	1303.85	1713.52	1977.73
家庭经营收入	Income from Household Operation	1320.06	1512.47	1537.57	1706.33	1980.21	2249.21
第一产业	Primary Industry	1116.45	1246.85	1233.79	1396.65	1500.94	1686.76
农业收入	Farming	789.52	864.19	899.31	1081.82	1065.10	1275.43
林业收入	Forestry	24.94	29.00	34.70	42.99	63.41	78.38
牧业收入	Animal Husbandry	301.20	349.84	296.58	268.61	368.01	328.76
渔业收入	Fishery	0.79	3.82	3.21	3.23	4.41	4.19
第二产业	Secondary Industry	44.94	51.33	60.20	49.97	58.49	72.71
工业收入	Industry	15.36	16.14	21.54	9.30	12.91	21.97
建筑业收入	Construction	29.58	35.19	38.65	40.66	45.57	50.74
第三产业	Tertiary Industry	158.67	214.27	243.58	259.72	420.78	489.74
交通运输邮电业收入	Transport, Post and Telecommunication Services	47.16	65.95	73.49	74.27	146.97	193.29
批发贸易餐饮业收入	Wholesale and Retail Trade & Catering Services	63.71	84.83	93.20	99.41	175.44	201.04
社会服务业收入	Social Services	16.71	24.28	32.52	29.92	39.27	43.93
其他家庭经营收入	Others	31.09	39.20	44.37	56.12	59.10	51.48
转移性收入	Income from Transfer	160.39	217.86	311.63	344.56	392.13	454.53
财产性收入	Income from Property	46.69	63.92	81.90	117.19	59.50	71.54

10-10 农村居民家庭人均年总支出

Per Capita Annual Gross Expenditures of Rural Households

单位：元 (yuan)

指　标	Item	2007	2008	2009	2010	2011	2012
全年总支出	**Gross Expenditure**	**2960.37**	**3590.51**	**3862.77**	**4350.25**	**5722.46**	**6370.25**
#生活消费支出	Living Expenditure for Consumption	1913.50	2165.70	2421.95	2852.48	3455.76	3901.71
食　品	Food	998.39	1119.64	1093.94	1319.43	1646.51	1740.58
衣　着	Clothing	99.44	112.46	125.35	137.49	186.22	226.81
居　住	Residence	329.44	427.40	588.42	621.80	639.32	758.37
家庭设备、用品及服务	Household Facilities,Articles and Services	70.93	94.36	115.39	135.64	192.78	211.36
医疗保健	Medicines and Medical Services	79.31	96.38	133.15	178.07	246.28	282.51
交通和通信	Transport and Telecommunications	154.52	159.61	175.08	229.66	304.51	371.35
文教娱乐用品及服务	Culture,Education and Recreation Articles and Services	147.31	122.10	151.59	186.19	183.03	226.44
其他商品和服务	Miscellaneous Goods and Services	34.16	33.75	39.03	44.21	57.10	84.30
家庭经营费用支出	Expenditure for Household Operation	722.95	944.61	872.54	871.62	1218.87	1367.00
#种植业生产支出	Farming Production Costs	240.83	288.09	298.33	312.74	374.98	467.74
牧业生产支出	Animal Husbandry Costs	429.48	580.29	497.29	484.31	628.23	644.05
购置生产用固定资产支出	Expenditure for Purchasing Productive Fixed Assets	76.66	167.99	166.61	102.89	209.95	183.17
税费支出	Taxes	2.18	1.43	1.64	2.06	2.14	8.04
转移性支出	Transfer Expenditures	235.59	308.48	393.75	508.59	809.31	900.84
#寄给和带给在外人口	Posting or Taking to Outside City	23.75	30.26	30.24	30.67	74.84	99.89
财产性支出	Property Expenditures	5.02	1.51	5.63	8.52	24.55	8.20
恩格尔系数(%)	**Engel Coefficient(%)**	**52.2**	**51.7**	**45.2**	**46.3**	**47.7**	**44.6**

10−11 农村居民家庭人均年现金收入
Per Capita Annual Cash Income of Rural Households

单位：元 (yuan)

指 标	Item	2007	2008	2009	2010	2011	2012
现金收入合计	**Total Annual Cash Income**	**2347.33**	**3013.00**	**3188.31**	**3448.33**	**4439.54**	**5078.31**
工资性收入	Income from Wage	846.72	1002.52	1072.54	1303.65	1712.31	1976.43
家庭经营现金收入	Income from Household Business Operation	1250.95	1670.77	1652.25	1571.86	2169.90	2460.43
#出售产品收入	Income from Selling Product	985.49	1327.84	1263.26	1162.33	1440.86	1611.76
工业服务性收入	Industry Processing Fee	11.00	10.62	13.33	8.80	7.72	10.40
建筑业收入	Construction	38.82	39.97	49.43	52.15	65.33	76.45
交通运输邮电业收入	Transport, Post and Telecommunication Services	73.04	105.95	116.47	118.38	271.86	317.64
批发和零售贸易餐饮业收入	Wholesale and Retail Trade & Catering Services	74.61	103.84	113.72	120.40	251.27	310.52
社会服务业收入	Social Service	18.57	25.80	34.60	31.66	45.10	49.65
文教卫生业收入	Culture, Education and Health Care	15.35	15.76	17.60	16.77	34.53	32.08
其他家庭经营现金收入	Others	21.03	29.84	34.23	45.35	35.11	32.99
转移性现金收入	Transfer Cash Income	204.15	277.11	384.22	458.35	509.02	570.57
#在外人口寄回和带回	Income from Outside City	12.87	16.87	31.02	24.65	5.35	2.03
亲友赠送	Income from Friends' and Relatives' Presents	59.47	70.03	84.26	125.70	141.13	134.91
抚恤金	Pension	1.98	1.60	2.03	3.63	3.11	3.30
财产性现金收入	Property Cash Income	45.51	62.60	79.31	114.47	48.31	70.88
#租金收入	Rental Income	22.18	36.42	34.47	26.45	18.26	22.67
非收入所得合计	**Reward From Other Way**	**436.75**	**579.71**	**944.54**	**1046.65**	**1690.01**	**1663.71**
#银行、信用社贷款	Loans of Bank and Credit Union	49.11	82.50	121.20	130.30	271.12	226.41
借入款	Borrowed Money	104.74	164.87	244.11	260.04	440.70	421.58
收回借出款	Drawing Back Loan	30.46	26.82	36.19	51.78	54.72	62.75
从银行、信用社取回存款	Drawing Money from Banks and Credit Union	50.16	60.91	114.19	165.05	200.05	241.46
收回投资款	Disinvestment	0.01		0.05		0.10	0.05

10-12 农村居民家庭人均年现金支出

Per Capita Annual Cash Expenditures of Rural Households

单位：元 (yuan)

指 标	Item	2007	2008	2009	2010	2011	2012
现金支出合计	**Total Cash Expenditure**	**2112.32**	**2701.82**	**3039.16**	**3339.45**	**4659.81**	**5390.31**
#生产费用支出	Expenditure for Operating Costs	532.50	806.49	756.46	666.48	1153.38	1316.52
缴纳税金	Taxes	2.18	1.43	1.64	2.06	2.14	8.04
生活消费支出	Living Expenditure for Consumption	1338.85	1585.40	1888.12	2159.14	2670.71	3157.39
转移性支出	Transfer Expenditures	233.77	307.00	387.31	503.26	809.03	900.15
#寄给在外人口	Posting to Outside City	23.46	30.26	30.12	30.65	74.84	99.89
赠送亲友	Present to Relatives and Friends	195.54	249.94	331.71	431.91	654.27	704.88
非消费性现金支出	Nonconsumptive Expenditure	333.18	345.89	462.73	599.03	668.28	613.96
#归还银行、信用社存款	Deposits of Bank and Credit Union Recession	51.43	35.07	45.87	64.56	90.04	109.85
借出款	Loan	12.91	12.90	12.06	18.14	25.86	17.88
归还借款	Loan Recession	63.36	78.16	108.81	99.02	150.47	159.16
存入银行、信用社	Deposit	157.26	152.16	186.84	286.23	187.3	129.65

注：现金支出合计不包括非消费性现金支出数据在内。

Note:Data of total expenditure in cash don't include the data of non-consumptive expenditure paid in cash.

10-13 农村居民家庭经营情况

Statistics of Household Operations in Rural Households

指 标	Item	2007	2008	2009	2010	2011	2012
经营耕地面积(亩/人)	Management Cultivated Area(mu/person)	1.07	1.09	1.11	1.10	1.10	1.18
年内出售肥猪头数(头/户)	Number of Selling Fattened Hogs in the Year (head/household)	1.26	1.01	1.11	1.19	0.98	0.99
年内自宰肥猪头数(头/户)	Number of Fattened Hogs Slaughtered by Peasants Themselves(head/household)	0.87	0.79	0.81	0.71	0.77	0.57
出售、自宰肥猪肉产量(公斤/户)	Output of Pork Slaughtered by Peasants Themselves and Sold(kg/household)	189.60	160.94	180.12	178.98	151.17	142.70
每头猪肉产量(公斤/头)	Output of Per Slaughtered Hog(kg/head)	89.16	89.63	93.53	93.85	86.05	91.80
年内出售菜羊只数(只/户)	Number of Sold Mutton Sheep and Goat in the Year (head/household)	0.04	0.05	0.05	0.09	0.13	0.11
出售、自宰羊的肉产量(公斤/户)	Output of Mutton Slaught ered by Peasants Themselves and Sold(kg/household)	0.85	1.02	1.51	2.06	2.68	2.65
年内出售肉牛数(头/百户)	Number of Sold Fattened Cattle in the Year (head/100 households)	3.04	2.86	2.88	2.95	4.15	5.45

10-14 农村居民家庭每人主要消费品消费量
Per Capita Annual Consumption of Major Consumer Goods in Rural Households

单位：公斤 (kg)

指　标	Item	2007	2008	2009	2010	2011	2012
粮　食	Grain	183.69	186.38	173.17	164.63	162.62	149.10
#大　米	Rice	136.05	143.02	136.32	130.26	135.55	121.17
食　油	Edible Oil	3.23	3.36	3.21	3.01	4.34	4.80
肉禽及其制品	Meat,Poultry and Related Product	28.37	27.63	28.46	27.77	25.73	23.67
#猪　肉	Pork	25.98	25.01	25.93	25.21	23.04	20.98
家　禽	Poultry	1.96	2.25	2.04	1.98	2.10	2.05
蛋类及蛋制品	Eggs and Their Products	1.25	1.72	1.66	1.81	1.93	2.35
水产品	Aquatic Products	0.48	0.36	0.41	0.38	0.43	0.53
#鱼　类	Fish	0.42	0.31	0.36	0.33	0.39	0.48
蔬　菜	Vegetables	130.60	133.36	126.10	116.74	110.42	97.43
瓜　果	Melon and Fruits	10.78	8.63	9.11	8.93	10.33	12.39
食　糖	Sugar	0.83	0.89	0.93	0.78	0.68	0.70
卷　烟(盒)	Cigarette(pack)	22.40	22.91	23.69	22.44	25.34	25.83
酒	Liquor	6.30	6.69	6.71	6.83	7.52	7.75

10-15 每百户农村居民家庭年末耐用消费品拥有量
Number of Durable Consumer Goods Owned By Per 100 Rural Households at the Year-end

单位：台 (set)

指　标	Item	2007	2008	2009	2010	2011	2012
黑白电视机	Black/White TV Set	7.0	4.0	2.3	2.1	0.4	0.3
彩色电视机	Color TV Set	72.9	74.6	88.1	91.1	93.9	95.9
电冰箱	Refrigerator	9.8	12.9	19.3	27.2	39.9	45.2
洗衣机	Washing Machine	33.6	36.4	48.7	55.2	62.5	69.8
影碟机	Video Disc Player	44.3	46.7	49.1	51.0	48.6	43.0
热水器	Water Heater for Shower	3.0	3.4	4.3	6.2	9.7	12.0
摩托车(辆)	Motorcycle(unit)	17.2	19.6	26.8	30.8	36.0	39.0
自行车(辆)	Bicycle(unit)	8.5	7.7	6.3	7.1	5.3	5.4
电话机(部)	Telephone(unit)	37.8	38.5	38.1	37.5	17.9	15.4
移动电话(部)	Mobile Telephone(unit)	34.2	53.8	82.5	102.1	157.0	173.3

10-16 按收入五等份分农村居民家庭收入、消费情况（2012）
Income and Consumption of Rural Househoulds by Income Quintile

项 目	Item	低收入户 Low Income Households	中低收入户 Lower Middle Income Households	中等收入户 Middle Income Households	中高收入户 Upper Middle Income Households	高收入户 High Income Households
平均每人总收入（元）	**Per Capita Annual Income(yuan)**	**3353.37**	**4726.24**	**5948.13**	**7717.84**	**12533.29**
#现金收入	Cash Income	2281.41	3461.02	4579.71	6185.97	10790.00
平均每人总支出（元）	**Per Capita Annual Expenditures(yuan)**	**4556.13**	**4986.62**	**6269.78**	**7016.87**	**10335.09**
#现金支出	Cash Expenditures	3719.45	4047.07	5271.60	5986.77	9168.61
平均每人纯收入（元）	**Per Capita Annual Net Income(yuan)**	**1949.22**	**3293.41**	**4422.75**	**5920.95**	**9977.18**
平均每人主要消费品消费量（公斤）	**Per Capita Consumption of Majar Consumor Goods(kg)**					
粮 食	Grain	135.16	147.34	145.66	153.42	171.48
#大 米	Rice	108.95	117.80	118.43	124.44	143.52
食 油	Edible Oil	3.67	4.46	4.49	5.28	6.79
肉禽及其制品	Meat,Poultry and Related Product	16.99	21.41	24.86	26.61	31.80
#猪 肉	Pork	14.95	19.19	22.25	23.58	27.75
家 禽	Poultry	1.65	1.81	2.04	2.25	2.76
蛋类及蛋制品	Eggs and Their Products	1.91	2.26	2.20	2.54	3.09
水产品	Aquatic Products	0.31	0.77	0.39	0.50	0.71
#鱼 类	Fish	0.28	0.71	0.35	0.45	0.64
蔬 菜	Vegetables	83.37	90.47	93.68	108.30	120.08
瓜 果	Melon and Fruits	9.83	9.47	12.39	14.60	17.66
食 糖	Sugar	0.70	0.66	0.67	0.73	0.73
卷 烟(盒)	Cigarette(pack)	20.77	21.12	23.88	31.21	36.12
酒	Liquor	6.40	7.74	7.34	8.43	9.52
每百户耐用消费品拥有量	**Number of Durable Consumer Goods Owned By Per 100 Rural Households**					
黑白电视机(台)	Black/White TV Set(set)	0.45	0.22	0.22	0.45	0.22
彩色电视机(台)	Color TV Set(set)	90.63	93.30	96.43	96.65	102.68
电冰箱(台)	Refrigerator(set)	33.71	41.74	41.52	47.54	61.38
洗衣机(台)	Washing Machine(set)	57.81	64.51	70.31	76.56	79.91
影碟机(台)	Video Disc Player(set)	34.15	43.08	40.40	45.09	52.23
热水器(台)	Water Heater(set)	6.03	10.71	10.04	11.38	21.88
摩托车(辆)	Motorcycles(set)	32.59	32.59	36.61	45.54	47.77
自行车(辆)	Bicycle(unit)	5.58	3.13	5.80	4.69	7.81
电话机(部)	Telephone(unit)	17.86	14.51	13.62	13.17	18.08
移动电话(部)	Mobile Telephone(unit)	151.34	159.15	173.88	177.90	204.02

10-17 农村居民家庭人均经营费用和生产性固定资产购置

Per Capita Expenditure for Household Operations and Expenditure for Purchasing Productive Fixed Assets of Rural Households

单位：元 (yuan)

指　标	Item	2007	2008	2009	2010	2011	2012
家庭经营费用支出	**Expenditure for Household Operations**	**722.95**	**944.61**	**872.54**	**871.62**	**1218.87**	**1367.00**
农业生产支出	Farming	240.83	288.09	298.33	312.74	374.98	467.74
林业生产支出	Forestry	1.80	2.69	2.13	2.65	8.64	12.35
牧业生产支出	Animal Husbandry	429.48	580.29	497.29	484.31	628.23	644.05
渔业生产支出	Fishery	1.88	2.29	3.34	2.51	1.03	2.33
工业生产支出	Industry	5.13	12.47	6.18	4.50	26.90	21.43
建筑业支出	Construction	7.51	3.78	10.08	10.51	17.15	22.45
交通运输邮电业支出	Transport, Post and Telecommunication	18.47	27.11	26.48	26.82	86.41	85.12
批发和零售贸易、餐饮业支出	Wholesale and Retail Trade & Catering Services	9.16	17.67	18.70	18.40	63.42	96.43
社会服务业支出	Social Services	1.47	1.13	1.42	1.07	4.78	4.91
文教卫生支出	Culture, Education and Health Care	5.10	5.39	4.83	3.62	4.06	3.33
其他经营支出	Others	2.13	3.69	3.78	4.49	3.27	6.85
购置生产用固定资产支出	**Expenditure for Purchasing Productive Fixed Assets**	**76.66**	**167.99**	**166.61**	**102.89**	**209.95**	**183.17**
#农林牧渔业机械	Machinery of Farming, Forestry, Animal Husbandry and Fishery	13.78	15.60	21.61	22.89	52.80	50.11
工业机械	Industrial Machinery	2.06	6.87	3.46	5.74	5.91	0.35
运输机械	Transportation Machinery	19.96	70.27	92.13	36.32	86.99	43.82
役畜、产品畜	Draught Animals and Commodity Animals	30.89	48.53	26.02	16.46	38.80	47.04

10-18 农村居民家庭主要产品商品率

Commodity Rate of Major Agricultural Products in Rural Households

单位：% (%)

指 标	Item	2007	2008	2009	2010	2011	2012
大农业	**Agriculture**	**53.3**	**60.2**	**59.6**	**51.5**	**54.3**	**54.2**
小农业	**Farming**	**38.9**	**43.8**	**46.6**	**39.9**	**39.5**	**38.8**
#粮 食	Grain	17.9	17.2	19.1	15.2	26.9	13.5
油 料	Oil-bearing Crops	53.9	32.2	36.0	46.3	36.5	38.3
糖 料	Sugar Crops	88.6	79.4	80.8	83.5	93.5	71.4
烟 叶	Tobacco	92.0	93.7	88.0	91.4	84.7	81.7
蔬 菜	Vagetable	27.7	29.0	27.7	31.6	33.0	38.9
果用瓜	Melon	72.3	94.8	96.3	98.0	92.2	87.9
水 果	Fruits	48.8	71.9	71.5	79.5	75.3	79.8
茶 叶	Tea	26.9	40.0	41.9	26.1	27.3	9.1
油桐籽	Tung-oil Seeds	69.6	89.9	100.0	100.0	100.0	100.0
油茶籽	Tea-oil Seeds	36.6	100.0	100.0		100.0	100.0
核 桃	Walnuts	60.3	81.3	82.9	85.4	72.9	96.3
出售自宰猪肉	Pork Slaughtered by Peasants Themselves & Sold	60.7	58.6	61.3	59.7	60.0	66.1
出售自宰羊肉	Mutton Slaughtered by Peasants Themselves & Sold	94.0	95.7	82.9	93.2	95.2	98.4
出售自宰家禽	Poultry Slaughtered by Peasants Themselves & Sold	53.4	57.1	57.3	50.8	70.2	72.1
禽 蛋	Poultry and Eggs	29.0	27.7	33.1	23.1	38.6	48.4

10-19 农村居民人均粮食收支存

Per Capita Grain Income,Expense and Stock of Rural Households

单位：公斤 (kg)

指 标	Item	2007	2008	2009	2010	2011	2012
年内粮食收入合计	**Grain Income within Current Year**	**451.54**	**485.84**	**478.34**	**448.93**	**392.63**	**471.75**
家庭经营生产	Household Operations	391.14	419.08	405.73	376.48	312.08	382.35
购 入	Bought Grain	56.16	63.45	69.95	70.40	80.00	85.77
借 入	Borrowed Grain	1.55	0.10	0.19	0.10		
收回借出粮	Recall of Loaned Grain	1.61	2.01	1.27	0.93	0.24	0.56
其它粮食收入	Other Grain Income	1.08	1.20	1.20	1.02	0.32	3.06
年内粮食支出合计	**Grain Expense within Current Year**	**423.05**	**446.88**	**434.86**	**381.53**	**400.77**	**340.20**
#主食用粮	Staple Food Grain	183.69	186.38	173.17	164.63	162.62	149.10
出 售	Sold Grain	70.00	72.12	77.67	57.35	83.90	69.30
种 籽	Seed	12.96	5.51	4.56	3.93	8.30	6.45
饲 料	Forage	153.30	181.01	170.46	153.39	145.78	114.94
借 出	Loaned Grain	1.48	0.33	4.58	0.51		0.04
其它粮食支出	Other Grain Expenses	1.44	1.04	3.85	1.67	0.04	0.19
年末结存	**Stock of Grain at the Year-end**	**392.60**	**409.11**	**389.24**	**386.35**	**302.41**	**362.41**

主要统计指标解释

一、城镇住户

城镇家庭人口 指居住在一起，经济上合在一起共同生活的家庭成员。凡计算为家庭人口的成员其全部收支都包括在本家庭中。

城镇就业面 指就业人口占家庭人口的百分比。

城镇就业者负担人数 指家庭人口与就业人口之比。

城镇家庭总收入 指家庭成员得到的工薪收入、经营净收入、财产性收入、转移性收入之和，不包括出售财物收入和借贷收入。

城镇家庭可支配收入 指家庭成员得到可用于最终消费支出和其它非义务性支出以及储蓄的总和，即居民家庭可以用来自由支配的收入。它是家庭总收入扣除交纳的所得税、个人交纳的社会保障支出以及记账补贴后的收入。计算公式为:

可支配收入 = 家庭总收入 - 交纳所得税 - 个人交纳的社会保障支出 - 记帐补贴

城镇家庭总支出 指除借贷支出以外的全部家庭支出。包括消费性支出、购房建房支出、转移性支出、财产性支出、社会保障支出。

城镇家庭消费性支出 指家庭用于日常生活的支出，包括食品、衣着、家庭设备用品及服务、医疗保健、交通和通信、娱乐教育文化服务、居住、杂项商品和服务等八大类支出。

城镇家庭服务性消费支出 指家庭用于支付社会提供的各种非商品性服务费用。

城镇家庭收入分组方法 将所有调查户依户人均可支配收入由低到高排队，按 10%，10%，20%，20%，20%，10%，10% 的比例依次分成：最低收入户、低收入户、中等偏下收入户、中等收入户、中等偏上收入户、高收入户、最高收入户等七组。总体中最低 5% 的户为困难户。

恩格尔系数 指食物支出金额在生活消费总支出金额中所占的比例。计算公式为:

$$恩格尔系数 = \frac{食品支出金额}{生活消费总支出金额} \times 100\%$$

二、农村住户

农村住户 指农村常住户。农村常住户指长期（一年以上）居住在乡镇（不包括城关镇）行政管理区域内的住户，以及长期居住在城关镇所辖行政村范围内的农村住户。户口不在本地而在本地居住一年及以上的住户也包括在本地农村常住户范围内；有本地户口，但举家外出谋生一年以上的住户，无论是否保留承包耕地都不包括在本地农村住户范围内。

常住人口 指全年经常在家或在家居住 6 个月以上，而且经济和生活与本户连成一体的人口。外出从业人员在外居住时间虽然在 6 个月以上，但收入主要带回家中，经济与本户连为一体，仍视为家庭常住人口；在家居住，生活和本户连成一体的国家职工、退休人员也为家庭常住人口。但是现役军人、中专及以上（走读生除外）的在校学生、以及常年在外（不包括探亲、看病等）且已有稳定的职业与居住场所的外出从业人员，不算家庭常住人口。家庭常住人口主要作为计算农村住户平均每人收入、消费和积累水平及分析家庭人口状况的依据。

整、半劳动力 整劳动力指男子 18 周岁到 50 周岁，女子 18 周岁到 45 周岁；半劳动力指男子 16 周岁到 17 周岁，51 周岁到 60 周岁；女子 16 周岁到 17 周岁，46 周岁到 55 周岁，同时具有劳动能力的人。虽然在劳动年龄之内，但已丧失劳动能力的人，不应算为劳动力；超过劳动年龄，但能经常参加劳动，计入半劳动力数内。常住人口中的职工，若这些职工为劳动力，就包括在本户的整半劳动力中。

总收入 指调查期内农村住户和住户成员从各种来源渠道得到的收入总和。按收入的性质划分为工资性收入、家庭经营收入、财产性收入和转移性收入。

工资性收入 指农村住户成员受雇于单位或个人，靠出卖劳动而获得的收入。

家庭经营收入 指农村住户以家庭为生产经营单位进行生产筹划和管理而获得的收入。农村住户家庭经营活动按行业划分为农业、林业、牧业、渔业、工业、建筑业、交通运输业邮电业、批发和零售贸易餐饮业、社会服务业、文教卫生业和其他家庭经营。

财产性收入 指金融资产或有形非生产性资产的所有者向其他机构单位提供资金或将有形非生产性资产供其支配，作为回报而从中获得的收入。

转移性收入 指农村住户和住户成员无须付出任何对应物而获得的货物、服务、资金或资产所有权等，不包括无偿提供的用于固定资本形成的资金。一般情况下，是指农村住户在二次分配中的所有收入。

现金收入 指农村住户和住户成员在调查期内得到以现金形态表现的收入。按来源分成工资性收入、家庭经营现金收入、财产性收入、转移性收入。

纯收入 指农村住户当年从各个来源得到的总收入相应地扣除所发生的费用后的收入总和。计算方法:

纯收入 = 总收入 - 家庭经营费用支出 - 税费支出 - 生产性固定资产折旧 - 赠送农村外部亲友支出

纯收入主要用于再生产投入和当年生活消费支出，也可用于储蓄和各种非义务性支出。“农民人均纯收入”按人口平均的纯收入水平，反映的是一个地区或一个农户农村居民的平均收入水平。

总支出 指农村住户用于生产、生活和再分配的全部支出。家庭经营费用支出、购置生产性固定资产支出、生产性固定资产折旧、税费支出、生活消费支出、财产性支出和转移性支出。

Explanatory Notes on Main Statistical Indicators

I. Urban Households

Population of Urban Households refer to members of the household living and sharing economically together. All income and expenditure of the population of the household are included in the income and expenditure of the household.

Proportion of Urban Employment refer to the proportion of employed population to the population of urban households.

Number of Dependents Per Urban Employee refers to the ratio between number of persons in urban households and the number of dependents.

Total Income of Urban Households refers to the sum of wage and salary, net business income, income from properties, and income from transfers of members of the households, excluding income from selling of properties and income from borrowings.

Disposable Income of Urban Households refers to the actual income at the disposal of members of the households which can be used for final consumption, other non-compulsory expenditure and savings. This equals to total income minus income tax, personal contribution to social security and sample household subsidy for keeping diaries. Following formula is used:

Disposable income = total household income - income tax - personal contribution to social security - sample household subsidy for keeping diaries

Total expenditure of Urban Households refer to all expenditure of the households except expenditure on leading. It includes expenditure on consumption, on purchasing or building houses, on transfers, on properties and on social security.

Consumption Expenditure of Urban Households refers to total expenditure of the sample households for consumption in daily life, including expenditure on eight categories such as food, clothing, household appliances and services, health care and medical services, transport and communications, recreation, education and cultural services, housing, miscellaneous goods and services.

Expenditure of Urban Households on Consumption of Services refers to expenditure of households on services of various kinds provided by the society.

Urban Households by Income Group All households in the sample are grouped, by per capita disposable income of the household, into groups of lowest income, low income, lower middle income, middle income, upper middle income, high income and highest income, each group consisting of 10%, 10%, 20%, 20%, 20%, 10% and 10% of all households respectively. The lowest 5% of households are also referred to as poor households.

Engel Coefficient refers to the percentage of expenditure on food in the total consumption expenditure, using the following formula:

$$\text{Engel Coefficient} = \frac{\text{expenditure on food}}{\text{total consumption expenditure}} \times 100\%$$

II. Rural Households

Rural Households refer to resident households in rural areas. Resident households in rural areas are the households residing for more than one year in the areas under the jurisdiction of administration of township governments(excluding county towns), and in the areas under the jurisdiction of administration of villages in county towns. Migrated households residing in the current addresses for over one year with their household registration in other places are included in the resident households of their current addresses. For households with their household registration in one place but all members of the households moving away for living in another place for over one year, they will not be included in the rural households of the area where they are registered, irrespective of whether they still keep their contracted land.

Resident Population refers to population staying at home permanently or for over 6 months during a year and sharing life economically with the household. Members of the household staying away from the household for over 6 months but keeping a close economic relation with the household by sending the majority of income to the household are regarded as resident population of the household. Government staff and workers or retirees living as close members of the household are also considered as resident population. However, servicemen, students of secondary technical schools or schools of higher education and persons with stable jobs and residence outside the household (excluding those visiting relatives or seeking medical service) are not included as resident population of the household. Resident population is used in calculating income, consumption, accumulation on per capita basis of rural households and in analyzing composition of rural households.

Full/Semi Labour Force Full labour force refers to persons capable of work, aged 18-50 for males and 18-45 for females. Semi labour force refers to persons capable of work, aged 16-17 and 51-60 for males and 16-17 and 46-55 for females. Persons at their working ages but not capable of work are not to be included as labour force. Persons not at working ages but participating regularly in work are included in semi labour force. For staff and workers as resident population of the household, they are included as full or semi labour force of the household if they are in the labour force.

Total Income refers to the sum of income earned from various sources by the rural households and their members during the reference period, and is classified as income from wages and salaries, income from household operations, income from properties and income from transfers.

Income from Wages and Salaries refers to income from labour earned by the members of rural households employed by other units or individuals.

Income from Household Operations refers to income by the rural households as units of production and operations. Operations by rural households are classified by economic activities as agriculture, forestry, animal husbandry, fishery, manufacturing, construction, transportation, post and telecommunications, wholesale, retail and catering, social service, culture, education, health, and other household operations.

Income from Properties refers to the income received as returns by owners of financial assets or tangible non-productive assets by providing capitals or tangible non-productive assets to other institutional units.

Income from Transfers refers to the receipt by rural households and their members of goods, services, capitals or rights of assets without giving or repaying accordingly, excluding capitals provided to them for the formation of fixed assets. In general, it refers to all income received by rural households through redistribution.

Cash Income refers to income received by rural households and their members in the form of cash during the reference period. It is classified, by source of income, into income from wages and salaries, cash income from household operations, income from properties and income from transfers.

Net Income refers to the total income of rural households from all sources minus all corresponding expenses. The formula for calculation is as follows:

Net income = total income - household operation expenses - taxes and fees - depreciation of fixed assets for production - gifts to non-rural relatives

Net income is mainly used as input for reproduction and as consumption expenditure of the year, and also used for savings and non-compulsory expenses of various forms. ?°Per capita net income of farmers?±is the level of net income averaged by population which reflects the average income level of rural households in a given area.

Total Expenditure refers to total expenses of rural households on production, consumption and redistribution, including expenditure on household operations, on purchase of productive fixed assets, depreciation of productive fixed assets, taxes and fees, expenses on household consumption, expenses on properties and expenses on transfer

11

Eleven

城市概况

General Survey of Cities

11—1 城市公用事业

Basic Statistics on City Public Utilities

项　　目	Item	2007	2008	2009	2010	2011	2012
城市建设	**City Areas and Floor Space of Buildings**						
城区面积(平方公里)	Urban Area(sq.km)	4044.45	4042.57	4057.98	4103.09	4108.16	4543.68
建成区面积(平方公里)	Area of Built Districts(sq.km)	812.30	821.60	883.56	972.99	986.50	1121.68
城市建设用地面积(平方公里)	Area of Land Used for Urban Construction (sq.km)	932.05	952.04	999.81	1002.15	1005.73	1026.84
征用土地面积(人/平方公里)	Area of Land Put in Requisition for State Construction Projects(persons/sq.km)	17.45	13.97	16.97	26.03	36.20	57.19
城市人口密度(人/平方公里)	Population Density of City Districts (persons/sq.km)	2331	2379	2440	2481	2579	2410
城市供水、燃气	**Supply Water and Gas**						
年末供水综合生产能力(万立方米/日)	Production Capacity of Tap Water Supply at Year-end (10000 cu.m)	367.70	357.05	348.56	352.11	364.56	376.94
全年供水管道长度(公里)	Annual Length of Water Pipelines(km)	7401.30	7719.80	8706.10	9376.00	11107.57	11629.67
建城区城市供水管道密度(公里/平方公里)	Water Pipelines Pensity of Built Districts of city(km/sq.km)	9.1	9.4	9.85	9.64	11.26	10.37
供水总量(万立方米)	Volume of Tap Water Supply (10000 cu.m)	68297	64871	61971	63572	67766	71168
#生活用水	Water Consumption for Residential Use	32278	31560	32584	33064	36091	38367
生产用水	Water Consumption for Productive Use	16555	13850	10517	12109	11335	10728
用水人口(万人)	Number of Residents with Access to Tap Water (10000 persons)	751.80	800.32	845.78	880.83	920.40	959.30
人均日生活用水(升)	Per Capita Daily Consumption of Tap Water for Residential Use (liter)	141.57	127.72	124.32	116.88	127.82	128.92
用水普及率 (%)	Coverage Rate of Urban Population with Access to Tap Water (%)	79.7	83.2	85.4	86.5	86.9	87.6
人工煤气生产能力(万立方米)	Production Capacity of Gaswork Gas (10 000 cu.m)	190.80	191.80	191.80	191.80	187.00	187.00
管道长度(公里)	Length of Gas Pipelines (km)	2850.10	2925.10	3051.20	3207.50	3264.27	3597.19
人工煤气	Coal Gas	2639.30	2693.90	2784.40	2829.70	2741.53	2902.89
液化石油气	Liquefied Petroleum Gas	136.00	146.16	154.82	182.72	182.72	184.95
天然气	Natural Gas	74.77	85.05	111.93	195.07	340.02	509.35
全年供气总量	Annual Volume of Gas Supply						
人工煤气(万立方米)	Coal Gas (10 000 cu.m)	23491	26613	26886	26963	30515	34167
#家庭用量	Consumption of Gaswork Gas for Residential Use	9439	10493	10921	11436	13118	14259
天然气(万立方米)	Natural Gas Supply(10 000 cu.m)	1449	1378	2336	3546	5496	9879
#家庭用量	Consumption of Natural Gas for Residential Use	1005	1017	1070	1160	674	1096
液化石油气 (吨)	Liquefied Petroleum Gas(ton)	81565	86863	89770	94481	99396	101606
#家庭用量	Consumption of Liquefied Gas for Residential Use	74171	79149	82645	86703	91742	93089
用气人口(万人)	Population with Access to Gas (10 000 persons)	481.67	520.28	536.53	554.35	582.54	603.88
人工煤气	Coal Gas	145.11	156.15	161.33	166.76	207.69	176.05
液化石油气	Liquefied Petroleum Gas	327.91	355.35	364.88	375.94	350.98	372.81
天 然 气	Natural Gas	8.65	8.78	10.32	11.65	23.87	55.02
燃气普及率(%)	Coverage Rate of Urban Population with Access to Gas (%)	51.1	54.1	54.2	54.5	55.0	55.2
城市市政设施	**Municipal Infrastructure**						
年末实有道路长度(公里)	Length of Paved Roads at Year-end(km)	3772	3836	3933	4081	4487	4875

11-1 续表 continued

项　　目	Item	2007	2008	2009	2010	2011	2012
年末实有道路面积(万平方米)	Area of Paved Roads at Year-end(10 000sq.m)	5711	5759	5972	6342	7054	7585
人均拥有道路面积(平方米)	Per Capita Area of Paved Roads(sq.m)	6.06	5.99	6.03	6.23	6.66	6.93
城市排水管道长度(公里)	Length of City Sewage Pipes(km)	4724	4796	5047	5507	5977	6148
城市污水日处理能力(万立方米)	Daily Disposal Capacity of City Sewage (10 000 cu.m)	57.0	66.0	93.5	170.5	170.5	173.0
建城区城市排水管道密度（公里/平方公里)	Density of City Sewage Pipes(km/sq.km)	5.82	5.84	5.71.	5.66	6.06	5.48
城市桥梁(座)	Number of City Bridges (unit)	714	715	727	735	776	783
城市道路照明灯(千盏)	Number of Street Lights (1 000 units)	232	260	299	302	391	428
城市公共交通	**Public Traffic**						
年末公共交通运营数(辆)	Number of Public Vehicles under Operation at Year-end (Buses and Trolley Buses, etc.) (unit)	5083	5140	4864	4984	5364	5429
运营线路网长度(公里)	Network Length (km)	1456	1527	3523	6056	6212	6518
公共交通客运总量(万人次)	Passengers Transported by Public Vehicles (10 000person-times)	98999	103383	109586	120220	130976	143499
出租汽车(辆)	Number of Taxi(unit)	13411	13768	14700	15087	17196	20600
城市绿化和园林	**City Greening**						
城市园林绿地面积(公顷)	Area of Parks and Green Land (hectare)	41410	41841	43781	45500	48024	51081
公园绿地面积	Park Green Areas	3984	4271	4602	5422	5830	7311
人均公园绿地面积(平方米)	Per Capita Area of Parks and Green Land(sq.m)	4.23	4.44	4.65	5.33	5.50	6.68
公园个数(个)	Number of Parks and Zoos(unit)	117	121	128	130	146	147
公园面积(万公顷)	Area of Parks (10 000 hectares)	3914	3773	3965	4622	4941	5074
建成区绿化覆盖率(%)	Green Covered Area as % of Completed Area (%)	21.48	21.55	22.12	21.83	24.57	25.06
城市环境卫生	**Environmental Sanitation**						
清扫保洁面积(万平方米)	Area under Cleaning Program (10 000 sq.m)	4900	4916	5374	5948	6982	7831
生活垃圾清运量(万吨)	Volume of Garbage Disposal (10 000 tons)	402.90	413.80	426.60	428.51	431.46	449.41
市容环卫专用车辆设备总数(台)	Number of Special Vehicles for Environmental Sanitation (unit)	1160	1216	1315	1588	2320	2696
公共厕所(座)	Number of Public Lavatories (unit)	1924	2055	2116	2147	2121	2110
#三类以上	Third Grade and Above	1207	1284	1358	1463	1445	1461

注：1.资料来源于省住房城乡建设厅、省交通厅(以下相关表同)。2.运营线路长度2009年及以前为运营线路网长度。

Note:1.Data are provided by provincial department of transport and department of housing and urban and rural development(The relative tables in the chapter are the same). 2.For the year 2009 and before,Operating line length referred to network Length.

11-2 城市气象(2012)

Climate of Major Cities

城市名称	City	年平均气温(℃) Annual Average Temperature(℃)	年降水量(毫米) Annual Precipitation(mm)	年日照时数(小时) Annual Sunshine Hours(hour)	年平均相对湿度(%) Annual Average Relative Humidity(%)
贵阳市	Guiyang	13.7	1226.4	681.6	85
六盘水市	Liupanshui	12.6	1168.7	1117.3	81
遵义市	Zunyi	15.1	899.6	830.6	77
安顺市	Anshun	13.7	1075.2	971.2	81
毕节市	Bijie	12.4	828.5	873.2	85
铜仁市	Tongren	16.8	1490.6	801.8	77
兴义市	Xingyi	16.3	1325.8	1409.0	81
凯里市	Kaili	15.1	1115.7	1057.1	82
都匀市	Duyun	14.3	1298.7	802.6	86
清镇市	Qingzhen	14.0	1264.7	982.9	84
赤水市	Chishui	17.7	1021.2	934.9	83
仁怀市	Renhuai	15.0	1037.5	732.8	87
福泉市	Fuquan	14.2	1208.2	773.1	79

注：资料来源于省气象局(下表同)。
Note:Data in the table are provided by the provincial bureau of meteorology(The same applies to the next table).

11-3 主要城市平均气温（2012）

Monthly Average Temperature of Major Cities

单位：℃ ℃

城市名称	City	1月 Jan.	2月 Feb.	3月 Mar.	4月 Apr.	5月 May	6月 June	7月 July	8月 Aug.	9月 Sept.	10月 Oct.	11月 Nov.	12月 Dec.
贵阳市	Guiyang	0.7	2.5	9.6	17.1	19.2	19.8	22.8	23.0	18.2	15.6	10.2	5.1
六盘水市	Liupanshui	1.2	3.4	9.7	15.4	17.9	17.6	20.2	20.3	16.0	14.3	9.8	5.0
遵义市	Zunyi	2.7	3.9	9.6	17.9	20.5	21.8	25.6	25.3	20.8	16.5	11.0	5.8
安顺市	Anshun	1.4	3.1	10.2	16.9	18.8	19.4	21.8	22.3	17.7	15.7	10.7	5.9
毕节市	Bijie	0.8	2.2	8.7	15.2	18.5	18.3	21.6	21.4	17.1	13.8	8.1	3.6
铜仁市	Tongren	4.3	5.3	10.6	19.0	21.8	25.0	28.8	28.0	22.9	18.1	11.9	6.0
兴义市	Xingyi	4.8	7.1	13.4	21.0	21.4	21.1	22.6	23.1	19.1	18.1	14.3	9.3
凯里市	Kaili	2.2	3.4	9.6	18.4	20.6	22.4	26.1	24.8	20.4	17.0	10.8	5.9
都匀市	Duyun	1.1	2.8	9.8	17.7	19.8	21.1	24.0	23.6	19.1	16.3	10.5	5.4
清镇市	Qingzhen	1.5	3.2	10.0	16.8	19.3	19.9	22.9	23.0	18.5	16.0	10.6	5.7
赤水市	Chishui	6.9	8.6	14.0	19.7	22.4	23.1	27.1	28.3	22.5	18.1	12.7	9.4
仁怀市	Renhuai	2.9	4.1	10.2	17.9	20.5	21.1	24.9	25.2	20.6	16.2	10.4	6.0
福泉市	Fuquan	1.3	2.7	9.0	17.3	19.7	21.0	24.5	23.8	19.3	16.1	10.4	5.3

11–4 城市建设(2012)

Basic Statistics on City Construction

城市名称	City	城区面积 (平方公里) Urban Area (sq.km)	建成区面积 (平方公里) Area of Built Districts (sq.km)	城市建设用地面积 (平方公里) Area of Land Used for Urban Construction (sq.km)
贵阳市	Guiyang	414.77	211.34	211.34
六盘水市	Liupanshui	129.00	38.50	36.67
遵义市	Zunyi	220.00	62.00	61.88
安顺市	Anshun	109.48	38.60	34.36
铜仁市	Tongren	40.10	33.90	29.32
兴义市	Xingyi	73.40	35.00	34.02
毕节市	Bijie	166.09	36.51	36.51
凯里市	Kaili	111.50	67.00	50.93
都匀市	Duyun	301.50	16.71	16.71
清镇市	Qingzhen	51.60	15.30	15.08
赤水市	Chishui	91.00	9.00	8.85
仁怀市	Renhuai	89.00	12.00	9.94
福泉市	Fuquan	19.20	10.20	9.92

11–5 城市设施水平(2012)

Basic Statistics on Level of Public Facilities in Cities

城市名称	City	城市用水普及率 (%) Coverage Rate of Urban Population with Access to Tap Water (%)	城市燃气普及率 (%) Coverage Rate of Urban Population with Access to Gas (%)	每万人拥有公共交通车辆 (标台) Number of Public Transportation Vehicles Per 10 000 Population (unit)	人均城市道路面积 (平方米) Per Capita Area of Paved Roads (sq.m)	人均公园绿地面积 (平方米) Per Capita Park Green Areas (sq.m)
贵阳市	Guiyang	94.49	93.08	12.8	5.30	12.81
六盘水市	Liupanshui	91.86	89.26	7.9	10.77	2.53
遵义市	Zunyi	99.07	62.20	6.7	5.18	8.08
安顺市	Anshun	91.24	44.11	6.2	6.28	1.75
铜仁市	Tongren	78.83	26.28	4.0	6.32	2.66
兴义市	Xingyi	92.48	30.44	3.6	16.28	7.59
毕节市	Bijie	91.73	47.83	2.9	10.90	14.99
凯里市	Kaili	72.67	71.08	9.0	8.15	14.97
都匀市	Duyun	99.13	79.83	10.5	7.66	8.22
清镇市	Qingzhen	86.44	62.54	2.6	5.62	6.11
赤水市	Chishui	79.57	46.96	5.4	4.96	5.57
仁怀市	Renhuai	93.58	44.00	3.3	5.21	1.58
福泉市	Fuquan	97.73	59.49	2.0	7.75	9.89

11-6 城市供水（2012）
Basic Statistics on Tap Water Supply in Cities

城市名称	City	年末供水综合生产能力（万立方米/日）Production Capacity of Tap Water Supply (year-end) (10 000 cu.m/day)	年末供水管道长度（公里）Length of Water Supply Pipelines (year-end) (km)	全年供水总量（万立方米）Total Annual Volume of Water Supply (10 000 cu.m)	#生活用水 For Residential Use	#生产用水 For Productive Use	用水人口（万人）Number of Residents with Access to Tap Water (10 000 persons)	人均日生活用水量（升）Per Capita Daily Consumption of Tap Water for Residential Use(liter)
贵阳市	Guiyang	125.40	3535.88	25886.62	11334.22	3998.61	240.29	166.33
六盘水市	Liupanshui	10.00	950.00	3388.00	1410.00	1108.00	29.00	190.08
遵义市	Zunyi	23.40	305.00	4893.00	3370.00	522.00	73.59	137.30
安顺市	Anshun	9.30	152.80	2157.80	1290.00	450.20	46.95	87.01
铜仁市	Tongren	17.26	148.18	1778.55	1040.51	377.14	25.50	117.29
兴义市	Xingyi	13.76	380.00	1980.00	1130.00	345.00	29.50	113.77
毕节市	Bijie	19.25	597.70	2530.94	1174.55	237.16	22.40	168.21
凯里市	Kaili	8.38	698.77	1967.50	1056.00	202.00	24.75	118.94
都匀市	Duyun	12.71	259.72	1807.76	798.43	356.12	22.80	143.70
清镇市	Qingzhen	3.50	151.00	472.00	314.00	101.00	12.30	71.95
赤水市	Chishui	2.00	64.80	382.00	257.00	33.00	9.15	86.53
仁怀市	Renhuai	3.00	78.00	767.00	520.00	118.00	12.40	125.28
福泉市	Fuquan	2.39	144.60	875.14	466.97	257.30	7.31	179.51

11-7 城市燃气(2012)

Basic Statistics on Supply of Gas in Cities

城市名称	City	人工煤气生产能力(万立方米/日) Production Capacity of Gaswork Gas (10 000 cu.m/day)	管道长度(公里) Length of GasPipelines(km)			全年供气总量 Volume of Gas Supply			用气人口(万人) Population with Accessto Gas (10 000 persons)		
			人工煤气 Coal Gas	液化石油气 Liquefied Petroleum Gas	天然气 Natural Gas	人工煤气(万立方米) Coal Gas (10 000 cu.m)	液化石油气(吨) Liquefied Petroleum Gas (ton)	天然气(万立方米) Natural Gas (10 000 cu.m)	人工煤气 Coal Gas	液化石油气 Liquefied Petroleum Gas	天然气 Natural Gas
贵阳市	Guiyang	180	1992		150.43	26909	36000.00	5830.44	140.45	72.00	24.25
六盘水市	Liupanshui	6	770			6680	485.00		26.70	1.48	
遵义市	Zunyi			9.56	20.00		10090.00	2400.00		41.00	5.20
安顺市	Anshun				90.68		3883.00	170.00		11.20	11.50
铜仁市	Tongren			91.26			1905.00			8.50	
兴义市	Xingyi				49.50		2401.80	28.29		9.50	0.21
毕节市	Bijie				74.07		1581.70	270.00		7.68	4.00
凯里市	Kaili				70.00		6640.60	163.08		19.81	4.40
都匀市	Duyun			30.13			1817.62			18.36	
清镇市	Qingzhen	1	140			578			8.90		
赤水市	Chishui			4.00	24.00		271.00	843.00		0.85	4.55
仁怀市	Renhuai				6.87		516.00	148.12		5.13	0.70
福泉市	Fuquan						508.98			4.45	

11-8 城市市政设施(2012)

Statistics on Municipal Infrastructure in Cities

城市名称	City	年末实有道路长度(公里) Length of Paved Roads (year-end) (km)	年末实有道路面积(万平方米) Area of Paved Roads (year-end) (10 000 sq.m)	城市桥梁(座) Number of City Bridges (unit)	城市排水管道长度(公里) Length of City Sewage Pipes (km)	城市污水日处理能力(万立方米) Daily Disposal Capacity of City Sewage (10 000 cu.m)	城市道路照明灯(千盏) Number of Street Lights (1 000 units)
贵阳市	Guiyang	872.00	1347.60	203	1910.00	58.0	145.42
六盘水市	Liupanshui	170.00	340.00	25	70.00	6.5	22.00
遵义市	Zunyi	276.00	385.00	28	222.00	11.0	21.07
安顺市	Anshun	192.00	323.23	20	314.90	5.0	13.10
铜仁市	Tongren	199.30	204.40	26	148.75	5.3	8.11
兴义市	Xingyi	242.00	519.20	25	261.00	5.5	13.36
毕节市	Bijie	133.76	266.10	38	139.22	8.0	4.66
凯里市	Kaili	164.63	277.56	24	218.72	8.0	24.06
都匀市	Duyun	96.60	176.17	30	158.00	6.0	5.98
清镇市	Qingzhen	39.80	80.00	4	55.38	5.0	3.37
赤水市	Chishui	42.00	57.00	2	72.00	2.0	4.23
仁怀市	Renhuai	26.00	69.00	5	40.00	3.0	4.10
福泉市	Fuquan	67.00	58.00	6	37.80	1.5	1.56

11–9 城市绿地和园林(2012)

Basic Statistics on Parks and Green Areas in Cities

城市名称	City	城市园林绿地面积(公顷) Area of Parks and Green Land(hectare)	公园绿地 Park Green Areas	公园(个) Number of Parks (unit)	公园面积(公顷) Area of Parks (hectare)	建成区绿化覆盖率(%) Green Covered Area as % of Completed Area (%)
贵阳市	Guiyang	21451	3257	13	2359	40.47
六盘水市	Liupanshui	230	80	5	73	25.04
遵义市	Zunyi	2384	600	4	337	40.24
安顺市	Anshun	2630	90	2	90	21.76
铜仁市	Tongren	786	86	6	73	24.25
兴义市	Xingyi	746	242	7	58	21.37
毕节市	Bijie	1092	366	4	213	32.35
凯里市	Kaili	1759	510	7	684	25.55
都匀市	Duyun	577	189	6	129	34.71
清镇市	Qingzhen	533	87	1	6	37.32
赤水市	Chishui	362	64	2	15	30.22
仁怀市	Renhuai	134	21	1	1	15.67
福泉市	Fuquan	264	74	3	74	29.02

11–10 城市市容环境卫生(2012)

Basic Statistics on Urban Sanitation in Cities

城市名称	City	清扫保洁面积(万平方米) Area under Cleaning Program (10 000 sq.m)	生活垃圾清运量(万吨) Volume of Garbage Disposal (10 000 tons)	市容环卫专用车辆设备总数(台) Number of Special Vehicles for Environmental Sanitation (unit)	公共厕所(座) Number of Public Lavatories (unit)	#三类以上 Third Grade and Above	生活垃圾无害化处理率(%) Garbage harmless treatment rate
贵阳市	Guiyang	2237	89.41	875	542	542	95.68
六盘水市	Liupanshui	265	16.00	84	38	11	100.00
遵义市	Zunyi	510	34.42	283	310	310	95.21
安顺市	Anshun	254	15.30	90	24	18	64.71
铜仁市	Tongren	485	11.30	38	124	30	86.73
兴义市	Xingyi	158	9.60	27	50		100.00
毕节市	Bijie	350	16.00	142	40	29	100.00
凯里市	Kaili	308	13.14	31	33	33	100.00
都匀市	Duyun	118	11.16	18	39	39	98.57
清镇市	Qingzhen	63	4.16	34	19	19	100.00
赤水市	Chishui	44	3.60	16	14	14	100.00
仁怀市	Renhuai	60	5.60	30	21	19	91.43
福泉市	Fuquan	58	6.00	13	8		-

主要统计指标解释

供水综合生产能力　指按供水设施取水、净化、送水、出厂输水干管等环节设计能力计算的综合生产能力。包括在原设计能力的基础上，经挖、革、改增加的生产能力。计算时，以四个环节中最薄弱的环节为主确定能力。原则上按设计能力填报，对于经过更新改造后，实际生产能力与设计能力相差很大的，按实际能力填报。

供水管道长度　指从送水泵至用户水表之间所有管道的长度。不包括新安装尚未使用、水厂内以及用户建筑物内的管道。在同一条街道埋设两条或两条以上管道时，应按每条管道的长度计算。

供水总量　指报告期供水企业（单位）供出的全部水量。包括有效供水量和漏损水量。

有效供水量指水厂将水供出厂外后，各类用户实际使用到的水量。包括售水量和免费供水量。

生活用水量　包括公共服务用水和居民家庭用水。公共服务用水指为城市社会公共生活服务的用水。包括行政事业单位、部队营区和公共设施服务、社会服务业、批发零售贸易业、旅馆饮食业以及其他公共服务业等单位的用水。居民家庭用水指城市范围内所有居民家庭的日常生活用水。包括城市居民、农民家庭、公共供水站用水。

用水普及率　指报告期末城区用水人口数与总人口的比率。计算公式:

$$用水普及率=\frac{城区用水人口（含暂住人口）}{城区人口+城区暂住人口}\times 100\%$$

人工煤气生产能力　指报告期末人工煤气生产厂制气、净化、输送等环节的综合生产能力，不包括备用设备能力。一般按设计能力计算，如果实际生产能力大于设计能力时，应按实际测定的生产能力计算。测定时应以制气、净化、输送三个环节中最薄弱的环节为主。

供气管道长度　指报告期末从气源厂压缩机的出口或门站出口至各类用户引入管之间的全部已经通气投入使用的管道长度。不包括煤气生产厂、输配站、液化气储存站、灌瓶站、储配站、气化站、混气站、供应站等厂（站）内的管道。按不同的材质、管径分别统计。

供气总量　指报告期燃气企业（单位）向用户供应的燃气数量。包括销售量和损失量。

燃气普及率　指报告期末使用燃气的人口与总人口的比率。计算公式为:

$$燃气普及率=\frac{城区用气人口（含暂住人口）}{城区人口+城区暂住人口}\times 100\%$$

供热能力　指供热企业（单位）向城市热用户输送热能的设计能力。不是热电厂的生产能力。

供热总量　指在报告期供热企业（单位）向城市热用户输送全部蒸汽和热水的总热量。

供热管道长度　指从各类热源到热用户建筑物接入口之间的全部蒸汽和热水的管道长度。不包括各类热源厂内部的管道长度。可按管道敷设方式（管沟、直埋、架空等）分类统计。

道路长度　指道路长度和与道路相通的桥梁、隧道的长度，按车行道中心线计算。

桥梁　指为跨越天然或人工障碍物而修建的构筑物。包括跨河桥、立交桥、人行天桥以及人行地下通道等。

排水管道长度　指所有排水总管、干管、支管、检查井及连接井进出口等长度之和。计算时应按单管计算，即在同一条街道上如有两条或两条以上并排的排水管道时，应按每条排水管道的长度相加计算。

污水处理能力　指污水处理厂（或处理装置）每昼夜处理污水量的设计能力。

年末运营车数　指年末公交企业（单位）用于运营业务的全部车辆数。以企业（单位）固定资产台帐中已投入运营的车辆数为准。

绿地面积　指报告期末用作园林和绿化的各种绿地面积。包括公园绿地、生产绿地、防护绿地、附属绿地和其他绿地的面积。其中:

公园绿地　城市中向公众开放的、以游憩为主要功能，有一定的游憩设施和服务设施，同时兼有健全生态、美化景观、防灾减灾等综合作用的绿化用地。它是城市建设用地、城市绿地系统和城市市政公用设施的重要组成部分。

生产绿地　指为城市绿化提供苗木、花草、种子的苗圃、花圃、草圃等圃地。

防护绿地　指城市中具有卫生、隔离和安全防护功能的绿地。包括卫生隔离带、道路防护绿地、城市高压走廊绿带、防风林、城市组团隔离带等。

附属绿地　指城市建设用地中绿地之外各类用地中的附属绿化用地。包括居住用地、公共设施用地、工业用地、仓储用地、对外交通用地、道路广场用地、市政设施用地和特殊用地中的绿地。

其他绿地　指对城市生态环境质量、居民休闲生活、城市景观和生物多样性保护有直接影响的绿地。包括风景名胜区、水源保护区、郊野公园、森林公园、自然保护区、风景林地、城市绿化隔离带、野生动植物园、湿地、垃圾填埋场恢复绿地等。

公共绿地　指向公众开放的市级、区级、居住区级各类公园、街旁游园，包括其范围内的水域。其中居住区级公园应不小于 1 万平方米，街旁游园的宽度不小于 8 米，面积不小于 400 平方米。

Explanatory Notes on Main Statistical Indicators

Production Capacity of Water Supply refers to the designed overall production capacity of water facilities, covering the four segments of water collection, purification, conveyance, and outflow through trunk pipelines. Increased capacity through transformation and innovation projects is included as well. The capacity is determined mainly on the weakest of the above-mentioned four segments. In principle, according to the design capacity reporting, for after renovation, the actual production capacity and design capabilities are vary greatly. It is according to the actual ability reported.

Length of Water Supply Pipelines at Year-end refers to the total length of all the pipelines between the water pumps and the user water meters, excluding pipelines newly installed but not used yet, pipeline in the water factory,and pipeline in the user's buildings. Buried in the same street two or more pipes, each pipe length shall be calculated. Effective water supply refers to water for the water outside the factory, the various users of water are actually used, including the sale of water and free water supply.

Annual Volume of Water Supply refers to the total volume of water supplied by water-works (units) during the reference period, including both the effective water supply and loss during the water supply.

Consumption of Water for Residential Use refers to water consumption of households for daily life and water consumption of public service facilities. The latter refers to water consumption for urban public services, including the consumption of government agencies and public institutions, military barracks, public facilities, wholesale and retail outlets, restaurants, hotels, and other units providing public services. Household water consumption refers to consumption of water for daily life of all households within the boundary of cities, including households of urban residents and farmers, and public water supply stations.

Coverage Rate of Urban Population with Access to Tap Water refers to the ratio of the urban population with access to tap water to the total urban population. The formula is:

$$\text{Coverage of urban population with access to tap water} = \frac{\text{Urban population with access to tap water}}{\text{Urban population}} \times 100\%$$

Production Capacity of Gaswork Gas refers to the overall production capacity of the urban gasworks in gas generation, purification and delivery at the end of the reference period, excluding capacity of the reserved facilities. In general, it is determined by the designed capacity, and when actual production capacity is larger than the designed capacity, the capacity is determined by the actual measurement on the weakest segment in the production, purification and delivery.

Length of Gas Pipelines refers to the total length of pipelines in use between the outlet of the compressor of gas-work or outlet of gas stations and the leading pipe of users, excluding pipelines within gasworks, delivery stations, LPG storage stations, refilling stations, gas-mixing stations and supply stations. It is according to different material, diameter, respectively statistics.

Volume of Gas Supply refers to the total volume of gas provided to users by gas-producing enterprises (units) in a year, including the volume sold and the volume lost.

Coverage Rate of Urban Population with Access to Gas refers to the ratio of the urban population with access to tap water to the total urban population. The formula is:

$$\text{Coverage rate of urban population with access to gas} = \frac{\text{Urban population with access to gas}}{\text{Urban population}} \times 100\%$$

Heating Capacity in Urban Areas refers to the designed capacity of heating enterprises (units) in supplying heating energy to urban users during the reference period. It is not the production capacity of thermal power plants.

Quantity of Heat Supplied in Urban Areas refers to the total quantity of heat from steam and hot water supplied to urban users by heating enterprises (units) during the reference period.

Length of Urban Heating Pipelines refers to the total length of steam or hot water pipelines for sources of heat to the leading pipelines of the buildings of the users, excluding internal pipelines in heat generating enterprises. It can be counted by laying pipe trench (trench, buried, overhead, etc.) classification.

Length of Paved Roads at Year-end refers to the length of roads with paved surface including bridges and tunnels connected with roads by the end of the year.

Bridges refer to bridges built to cross over natural or man-made barriers, including bridges over rivers, overpasses for traffic and for pedestrians, underpasses for pedestrians, etc.

Length of Sewage Pipes refers to the total length of general drainage, trunks, branch and inspection wells, connection wells, inlets and outlets, etc. In the calculation, calculation shall be single-tube that is on the same street if two or more side by side drains, they should be added to the length of each drainage calculations.

Disposal Capacity of Urban Sewage refers to the designed 24-hour capacity of sewage disposal by the sewage treatment works or facilities.

Number of Vehicles under Operation at Year-end refers to the total number of vehicles under operation by public transport enterprises (units) at the end of the year, based on the records of operational vehicles by the enterprises (units).

Area of Parks and Green Land refers to the total area occupied for green projects at the end of the reference period, including park green land, production green land, protection green land, green land attached to institutions, and other green areas.

Park Green Area refers to green areas open to the public for amusement and rest with the facilities of amusement, rest and services. Its function includes perfecting ecology, beautifying landscape, and preventing and reducing disaster. It is important part of the urban construction land, urban green space systems and urban municipal utilities.

Production green land refers to the production of green seedlings greening provide, flowers, seeds, nursery, garden, grass and other nursery nursery

Protective green land refers to the city has health, isolation and security features of the green, including health isolation belt, road protection green, urban high green belt corridor, windbreaks, buffer zone and other urban groups.

Attached green land refers to green urban construction land in various sites in addition to a subsidiary of green space, including residential land, public facilities, industrial sites, warehouse space, transportation land, land for roads and squares, municipal facilities, land and special sites in the green field.

Other green refers to the urban ecological environment quality, residents' leisure life, urban landscape and biodiversity conservation has a direct impact on the green, including scenic spots, water source protection areas, country parks, forest parks, nature reserves, scenic woodland, urban greenbelt, wildlife parks, wetlands, landfills restore green space.

Public Green Area refers to green areas open to the public such as municipal, community and neighborhood parks and roadside parks, including waters within parks. Neighborhood parks should occupy an area larger than 10,000 square meters, and the width of roadside parks should occupy an area larger than 400 square meters, with a width of more that 8 meters.

12

Twelve

资源和环境

Resources and Environment

12-1 主要河流(省内部分)主要特征值(2012)

Major Feature of Some Part of The Main River

水　系	Water System	流域面积(平方公里) Drainage Area(sq.km)	河长(千米) Length of River (1000 m)	平均坡降(‰) Average Slope Falling(‰)
长江流域	**Changjiang River Drainage**			
#赤水河	Chishuihe	11412	299	1.52
乌　江	Wujiang	66807	889	1.02
清水江	Qingshuijiang	17145	459	3.04
洪州河	Hongzhouhe	975	81	2.55
㵲阳河	Wuyanghe	6474	258	0.99
锦　江	Jinjiang	4017	168	1.16
松桃河	Songtaohe	1536	88	1.55
宋坎河	Songkanhe	2321	56	1.37
牛栏河	Niulanhe	2014	79	4.35
横江(洛泽河)	Hengjiang(Luozehe)	2874	120	4.18
珠江流域	**Zhujiang River Drainage**			
#南盘江	Nanpanjiang	7651	263	0.51
北盘江	Beipanjiang	20982	352	2.61
红水河	Hongshuihe	15978	106	0.51
都柳江	Duliujiang	11586	330	0.43
打狗河	Dagouhe	4184	139	1.40

注：资料来源于省水利厅。
Note:Data in the table are provided by the Provincial Hydrographic Regulatory Burea.

12-2　主要矿产资源(2012)

Major Mineral Resources

名　称	Item	资源储量 Reserves	居全国位次 Order in Whole Country
矿产资源	**Mineral Resources(Ensured Reserves)**		
煤炭(亿吨)	Coal(100 million tons)	475.51	5
锰矿(万吨)	Manganese(10000 tons)	15246.99	2
钒矿(万吨)	Vanadium(10000 tons)	268.75	7
铅矿(万吨)	Plumbum(10000 tons)	72.88	19
锌矿(万吨)	Zincum(10000 tons)	269.48	15
铝土矿(亿吨)	Bauxite Ore(100 million tons)	6.09	4
镁(炼镁白云岩)(万吨)	Magnesium(10000 tons)	11729.33	8
汞矿(万吨)	Hydrargyrum(10000 tons)	3.10	1
锑矿(万吨)	Antimony(10000 tons)	29.93	4
金矿(岩金)(吨)	Gold mine(ton)	279.66	5
冶金用砂岩(万吨)	Gritstone for Metallurgy(10000 tons)	8512.80	2
硫铁矿(亿吨)	Pyrites Ore(100 million tons)	7.83	3
重晶石(万吨)	Barite Ore(10000 tons)	9236.17	1
磷矿(亿吨)	Phosphorus Ore(100 million tons)	31.4	3
稀土矿(万吨)	Rare Earth Mine(10000 tons)	86.01	8
水泥用灰岩(亿吨)	Limestone for Cement(100 million tons)	18.32	21

注：资料来源于省国土资源厅。
Note:Data in this table are obtained from the Provisional Department of Land and Resoures.

12-3　森林资源

Forest Resources

指　　标	Item	2007	2008	2009	2010	2011	2012	2012年比2011年增长(%) Increase Rate in 2012 over 2011(%)
森林面积(万公顷)	**Areas of Forest(10000 Ha.)**	**703.39**	**703.39**	**703.39**	**713.80**	**732.00**	**828**	
森林覆盖率(%)	Rate of Forest Covered (%)	39.93	39.93	39.93	40.52	41.53	47	
活立木总蓄积量(亿立方米)	Total Standing Fovest Stock (100 million stere)	3.10	3.10	3.10	3.33	3.89	3.97	2.1
完成造林面积(万公顷)	Area of Fulfilled Foyestation(10000 Ha.)	8.20	6.60	9.05	7.27	13.13	19.93	51.8
封山育林面积(万公顷)	Area of Seal Mountain Pass for Forestation(10000 Ha.)	9.19	13.07	17.36	13.39	14.48	8.10	-44.1
实施退耕还林工程中：	**In Implement Cancel Infield for Forest Project**							
宜林荒山造林(万公顷)	Forestation for Feasible deserted Mountain(10000 Ha.)	5.30	2.00	1.33	1.33	1.20	1.00	**-16.7**
天然林保护工程中：	**In Savageness Forest Protect Project**							
封山育林(万公顷)	Seal Mountain Pass for Forestation (10000 Ha.)	3.40	3.50	7.28	4.66	0.60	0.67	11.7
森林保护	**Forest Protection**							
森林火灾(起)	Forest Fire (unit)	1254	2612	1626	2537	430	275	-36.0
森林火灾受害率(‰)	Rate of Fall Victim for Forest Fire (‰)	0.27	0.63	0.53	1.29	0.13	0.07	-0.06(百分点)
森林病虫鼠害面积(万公顷)	Area of Fall Victim for Insect Pest(10000 ha.)	26.90	22.94	28.97	26.85	27.18	20.60	-24.2
森林病虫鼠害防治面积(万公顷)	Prevention Area of Forest Insect Pest(10000 ha.)	22.60	16.04	25.65	19.63	18.91	16.63	-12.1
森林病虫鼠害防治率(%)	Prevention Rate of Forest Insect Pest (%)	84.0	70.0	88.5	73.1	69.6	80.7	16.0

注：1.资料来源于省林业厅(以下相关表同)。2.森林面积、森林覆盖率2012年数据是以县为单位，以2006年底结束的全省第三次森林资源二类调查小班数据为基础，结合2011年度林地保护利用规划年度变更数据，以及2012年的森林资源增长和消耗的监测、抽样调查、核实而得出。

Note:1.The data in this table are obtained from Forest Department of Guizhou Province(The relative tables in the chapter are the same).2.The data in this table of forest area and forest coverage rate for 2012,which is based on the town as a unit,with the basis of the Guizhou province's third inventory date of two kinds of forest resources at the end of 2006,combined with the annal change date of 2011Annual Forest Protection and utilization planning and the date of forest growth and consuption for 2012,is obtained by the following steps:detection,sampling investigation, and verification.

12-4 自然保护区
Natural Reserves

指　标	Item	2007	2008	2009	2010	2011	2012
自然保护区个数(个)	**Number of Nature Reserves (unit)**	**130**	**130**	**130**	**130**	**130**	**130**
#国家级自然保护区	Nature Reserves of National-level	9	9	9	9	9	9
省级自然保护区	Nature Reserves of Guizhou Province	4	4	4	4	4	4
地市级自然保护区	Nature Reserves of Region	21	21	21	21	21	21
县级自然保护区	Nature Reserves of County	96	96	96	96	96	96
自然保护区面积(万公顷)	Area of Nature Reserves (10000 hectares)	96.02	96.02	96.02	96.02	96.02	96.02
自然保护区面积占全省国土面积(%)	Percentage of Nature Reserves in Guizhou Province Land(%)	5.5	5.5	5.5	5.5	5.5	5.5
自然保护区中：	**In Nature Reserves**						
森林生态系统、野生动、植物类型(个)	Forest Biogeocenose,Wildness Animal and Plant(unit)	120	120	120	120	120	120
内陆湿地类型(个)	Wetlands inside Land(unit)	8	8	8	8	8	8
古生物遗迹类型(个)	Ancient Biology Relic(unit)	1	1	1	1	1	1
地质地貌类型(个)	Geological features(unit)	1	1	1	1	1	1

12-5 森林公园
Forest Parks

指　标	Item	2007	2008	2009	2010	2011	2012	2012年比2011年增长(%) Increase Rate in 2012 over 2011(%)
森林公园(个)	Number of Forest Park (unit)	61	65	66	70	72	74	2.8
#国家级森林公园	Forest Park of National-level	21	21	21	21	21	22	4.8
省级森林公园	Forest Park of Guizhou Province-level	25	26	26	31	32	31	-3.1
森林公园面积(万公顷)	Area of Forest Park (10000 hectares)	24.0	24.7	24.7	25.4	26.1	26.2	0.5
森林公园面积约占全省国土面积(%)	Percentage of Forest Park Area to the Guizhou Total Land Areas(%)	1.4	1.4	1.4	1.5	1.5	1.5	持平

12–6　水资源和水质监测

Basic Statistics on Water Resource and Monitoring of Water Quality

指　标	Item	2007	2008	2009	2010	2011	2012	2012年比2011年增长(%) Increase Rate in 2012 over 2011(%)
水资源总量(亿立方米)	**Total Water Resources (100 million cu.m)**	**1054.62**	**1140.67**	**910.46**	**956.54**	**626.02**	**974.02**	**55.6**
#地表水	Surface Water Resources	1054.62	1140.67	910.46	956.54	626.02	974.02	55.6
人均水资源量(立方米)	Per Capita Water Resources (cu.m)	2649	2824	2226	2284	1805	2796	54.9
供水总量(亿立方米)	Water Supply(100 million cu.m)	98.03	101.89	100.38	101.45	99.19	100.82	1.6
#地表水	Surface Water Supply	91.33	93.51	93.18	93.75	98.89	98.05	-0.8
用水总量(亿立方米)	Water Use(100 million cu.m)	98.03	101.89	100.38	101.45	99.19	100.82	1.6
河流水质	**Water Quality of River**							
监测河流(条)	Monitored River (unit)	33	33	33	44	44	44	持平
监测河段断面(个)	Monitored Section of River (unit)	74	74	74	85	85	82	-3.5
满足规定水质类别的断面占总监测断面百分比(%)	the Sections Meeting the Standard of Water Quality I-III Genus As Percentage of total Monitored Sections(%)	64.9	67.6	66.2	71.8	72.9	69.5	-4.7
水质良好的出境断面(个)	Number of Favorable Water Quality Section(unit)	11	10	10	11	12	10	-16.7
湖泊水质	**Water Quality of Lake**							
监测湖库(个)	Monitored Lake (unit)	8	8	8	8	8	15	87.5
监测点(个)	Monitored Point (unit)	25	25	25	25	25	16	-36.0
满足规定水质类别的监测点(个)	Ratio of the Points Meeting Water Quality I-III Genus(unit)	4	8	5	14	11	14	27.3
占总监测点百分比(%)	As Percentage of total Monitored Points (%)	16.0	32.0	20.0	56.0	44.0	87.5	98.9

注：资料来源于省水利厅、省环保厅。

Note:Data in the table are provided by the Provincial Department of Water Resources and Provincial Department of Environmental Protection.

12-7 环保系统机构、人员数

Enviornmental Protection Agencies and Persons Engaged

指　标	Item	2007	2008	2009	2010	2011	2012
机构总数(个)	**Number of Agencies(unit)**	**295**	**311**	**359**	**404**	**400**	**370**
#省	Province	12	13	13	13	14	14
地	Prefecture	38	45	47	48	53	57
县	County	241	249	258	306	296	292
年末人员总数(人)	**Number of Staff and Workers at the Year-end(person)**	**2454**	**2644**	**2650**	**3220**	**3168**	**3633**
#省	Province	336	372	368	360	380	375
地	Prefecture	579	594	609	649	730	895
县	County	1526	1665	1661	2137	1984	2363
#科研人员	Scientific and Technical Personnel	108	111	109	101	93	93
监测人员	Monitoring Personal	618	693	665	720	838	857
监察人员	Supervising and Administrative Personnel	727	752	727	786	900	886

注：资料来源于省环保厅(以下相关表同)。
Note: The data in the table are provided by the provinvial Department of Environmental Protection(The relative tables in the chapter are the same).

12-8 环境保护资金投入

Investment in Environmental Protection

单位：亿元 (100 million yuan)

指　标	Item	2007	2008	2009	2010	2011	2012	2012年比2011年增长(%) Increase Rate in 2012 over 2011(%)
环保资金投入	**Investment in Environmental Protection**	**48.88**	**50.74**	**69.78**	**89.52**	**106.70**	**97.35**	**-8.8**
环保资金投入占生产总值比重(%)	Investment in Environmental Protection as Percent of GDP(%)	1.7	1.4	1.8	1.9	1.9	1.4	-0.5(百分点)
环保资金投入中：	**In Investment of Environmental Protection**							
#老工业污染源治理	Old Industry Pollution Source Treatment	7.91	10.20	8.95	6.81	14.05	12.47	-11.2
建设项目“三同时”污染防治	"Three Simultaneities" Environmental Investment for New Project	9.73	5.07	7.11	16.47	13.74	5.37	-60.9
城市环境基础设施建设	Investment in Urban Environmental Infrastructure	13.42	15.42	26.63	28.91	37.95	35.73	1.4
环境管理能力建设	Construction of Environment Management Capacity	0.77	1.52	1.92	1.81	1.21	1.83	51.2
工业污染治理设施运行费用	Operating Expense of Industry Pollution Treatment Facilities	17.05	18.53	25.17	35.52	39.75	41.95	5.5
征收排污费总额	**Pollutant Discharge Fees**	**4.43**	**4.48**	**4.51**	**4.47**	**4.58**	**4.73**	**3.3**

注：表中“城市环境基础设施建设”数据2006—2010年由省环保厅提供，2011年由省住房城乡建设厅提供。
Note:The data of investment in urban environmental infrastructure were provided by Provincial Department of Environmental Protection from 2006 to 2010,but they were provided by provincial Department of urban and Rural development in 2011.

12–9 废水治理
Waste Water Treatment

指 标	Item	2007	2008	2009	2010	2011	2012	2012年比2011年增长(%) Increase Rate in 2012 over 2011(%)
废水排放总量(亿吨)	**Total Volume of Waste Water Discharged(100 million tons)**	**5.51**	**5.59**	**5.92**	**8.45**	**7.80**	**9.14**	**17.2**
工业废水	Volume of Industrial Waste Water Discharged	1.21	1.17	1.35	2.55	2.07	2.34	13.0
生活废水	Volume of Residential Waste Water Discharged	4.30	4.42	4.57	5.89	5.73	6.80	18.7
废水中化学需氧排放量(万吨)	**COD Discharged from Industrial Waste Water(10000 tons)**	**22.70**	**22.18**	**21.60**	**34.83**	**34.22**	**33.30**	**-2.7**
工业废水	Industrial Sector	1.84	1.37	1.30	6.07	6.55	6.47	-1.2
生活污水	Residential Sector	20.86	20.81	20.30	22.05	21.49	19.97	-7.1
当年完成工业废水治理项目(个)	Item of Industry Waste Water Treatment Completed in This Year(unit)	76	76	63	45	82	122	48.8
新增废水治理能力(万吨/日)	Newly Desinged Treatment and Utilization Capacity of Waste Water(10000 tons/day)	43.70	47.96	97.00	1.61	29.91	16.62	-44.4
城市污水处理率(%)	Treatment Rate of City Waste Water (%)	29.0	31.2	42.0	74.8	82.0	83.9	1.9个百分点

注：2010年数据采用污染源普查动态更新数据(以下相关表同)。

Note:The data of 2010 were updated by the methods of survey of pollution sources dynamic(The relative tables in the chapter are the same).

12-10 空气质量及污染治理

Air Quality and Treatment of Industrial Waste Gas

指　　标	Item	2007	2008	2009	2010	2011	2012	2012年比2011年增长(%) Increase Rate in 2012 over 2011(%)
城市空气质量	**Atmosphere Quality of City**							
达到国家环境空气质量二级标准城市(个)	Number of Cities Reaching the National Grade Ⅱ Standard of Atmosphere Quality of City (unit)	8	7	7	7	11	12	9.1
占统计城市数(%)	Percentage in Total (%)	66.7	58.3	58.3	58.3	91.7	92.3	0.6
城市空气污染物	**Contamination in City Atmosphere**							
二氧化硫年均浓度值(毫克/立方米)	Annud Average SO2 Concentration in Downtown(mg/cu.m)	0.056	0.052	0.051	0.048	0.044	0.038	-13.6
达到国家空气质量二级标准城市(个)	Number of Cities Reaching the National Grade Ⅱ Standard of Atmosphere Quality of City (unit)	9	7	8	9	12	12	持平
二氧化氮年均浓度值(毫克/立方米)	Annual Average NO2 Concentration in Downtown(mg/cu.m)	0.019	0.017	0.017	0.018	0.021	0.021	持平
达到国家空气质量一级标准城市(个)	Number of Cities Reaching the National Grade I Standard of Atmosphere Quality of City (unit)	12	12	12	12	12	13	8.3
城市可吸入颗粒物年均浓度值(毫克/立方米)	Average Chroma of City Suspend Grain (mg/cu.m)	0.078	0.073	0.073	0.077	0.078	0.069	-11.5
达到国家空气质量二级标准城市(个)	Number of Cities Reaching the National Grade Ⅱ Standard of Atmosphere Quality of City (unit)	11	12	11	10	11	13	18.2
废气中污染物排放	**Contamination Discharged of Exhaust Gas**							
二氧化硫排放总量(万吨)	Volume of SO2 Emission(10000 tons)	137.51	123.59	117.55	116.17	110.42	104.11	-5.7
#工业	Industry	92.06	74.13	62.37	96.05	90.3	83.71	-7.3
生活及其它废气中二氧化硫排放量	Volume of SO2 from Living and Other Exhaust Gas Emission	45.45	49.46	55.18	20.13	20.12	20.40	1.4
烟(粉)尘排放总量(万吨)	Total Volume of soot(Dust) Emission (10000 tons)	29.52	32.62	43.98	29.08	28.97	29.45	1.7
#工业	Industry	19.11	14.57	11.78	24.88	24.34	25.65	5.4
生活及其它废气中烟(粉)尘排放量	Discharged Volume of soot(Dusts) from Living and Other Exhaust Gas Emission	10.41	18.05	32.20	3.32	3.69	2.82	-23.6
空气污染治理	**Air Pollution Treatment**							
工业废气中：	In Industrial Exhaust Gas							
二氧化硫去除率(%)	Rate of SO2 Removed (%)	41.2	52.0	67.9	59.9	66.3	69.0	2.7
烟(粉)尘去除率(%)	Rate of Soot(Dust) Removed (%)	97.5	98.6	99.2	98.2	98.9	98.7	-0.2
当年完成废气治理项目(个)	Item of Exhaust Gas Treatment Fulfilled in This Year (unit)	81	154	90	34	29	45	55.2
新增废气治理能力(万标立方米/小时)	New Exhaust Gas Treatment Capacity inThis Year (10000 stere/hour)	3484.70	466.39	562.09	268.31	725.51	2777.86	282.9
城市燃气普及率(%)	Popularization Rate of City Coal Gas (%)	57.3	54.1	54.2	54.5	55.0	55.2	2个百分点

注："烟(粉)尘排放总量"为原"烟尘排放总量"，"烟(粉)尘去除率"为原"烟尘去除率"。

Note:"Total volume of soot(dust)emission"refers to the original"total volume of dust emission"."Rate of soot(dust) removed"refers to the original"Rate of soot removed".

12−11 固体废物生产及处理
Production and Treatment of Industrial Solid Wastes

指　　标	Item	2007	2008	2009	2010	2011	2012	2012年比2011年增长(%) Increase Rate in 2012 over 2011(%)
工业固体废物产生量(万吨)	**Volume of Industrial Solid Wastes Produced (10000 tons)**	**5988.58**	**5843.56**	**7317.37**	**8187.68**	**7660.70**	**7835.25**	**2.3**
工业固体废物倾倒丢弃量	Dumping Volume of Industrial Solid Waste Discarded	81.88	55.59	94.49	59.76	28.88	14.05	-51.4
工业固体废物治理	**Industrial Solid Wastes Treatment**							
当年完成工业固体废物治理项目(个)	Item of Industrial Solid Wastes Fulfilled in This Year (unit)	14	6	11	8	4	5	25.0
工业固体废物综合利用量(万吨)	Volume of Industrial Solid Wastes Utilized(10000 tons)	2251.83	2339.22	3350.67	4174.13	4089.09	4838.75	18.3
工业固体废物处置量(万吨)	Volume of Industrial Solid Wastes Treated (10000 tons)	2559.34	2126.11	2109.39	2497.55	2102.95	2067.44	-1.7
工业固体废物综合利用率(%)	Ratio of Industrial Solid Wastes Utilized(%)	37.5	39.9	45.6	50.9	52.7	60.9	8.2(百分点)
生活垃圾处理	**Consumption Wastes Treatment**							
生活垃圾清运总量(万吨)	Consumption Wastes Collected and Transported (10000 tons)	402.85	413.83	426.61	428.51	431.46	449.41	4.2
生活垃圾处理总量(万吨)	Consumption Wastes Treated (10000 tons)	214.74	242.55	284.02	294.92	296.15	324.07	9.4
#无害化处理量	Volume of Wastes Disposed	130.85	147.23	169.59	194.62	205.11	231.80	13.0
城市生活垃圾无害化处理率(%)	Treatment Rate of Consumption Wastes in Cities(%)	32.5	35.6	39.8	45.4	47.5	51.6	4.1(百分点)

注："工业固体废物倾倒丢弃量"为原"工业固体废物排放量"。
Note:"Dumping volume of industrial solid waste discarded" refers to original "volume of industrial solid wastes discharged".

12-12 环境污染事故

Accident of Environment Pollution

指 标	Item	2007	2008	2009	2010	2011	2012	2012年比2011年增 长(%) Increase Rate in 2012 over 2011(%)
环境污染事故(起)	**Number of Environmental Pollution Accidents(unit)**	**18**	**10**	**4**	**4**	**7**	**4**	**-42.9**
#重大事故	Fatal Accident	5				1	1	持平
较大事故	Major Accident					1		
一般事故	Commonly Accident	13	10	4	4	5	3	-40.0
#水污染事故	Water Pollution Accident	15	4	4	2	5	4	-20.0
空气污染事故	Air Pollution Accident	3	1		2	2		
污染事故直接经济损失(万元)	**Direct Economy Loss on Pollution Accident(10000 yuan)**	**673.20**	**14.70**	**10.00**	**107.30**	**450.00**	**677.27**	**50.5**

12-13 自然灾害

Natural Disasters

指 标	Item	2007	2008	2009	2010	2011	2012	2012年比2011年增长(%) Increase Rate in 2012 over 2011(%)
遭受自然灾害县个数(个)	Number of Counties Suffering from Natural Disasters(unit)	84	88	84	86	88	86	-2.3
受灾人口(万人次)	The Population Affected by Natural Disasters (10000 person-times)	1345.39	2935.00	1687.12	2633.40	2883.44	1227.66	-57.4
农作物受灾面积(万公顷)	Area of Crop Affected by Natural Disasters (10000 ha)	52.47	211.90	89.16	195.64	253.75	55.27	-78.2
#绝收面积	The Gainless Area of Crop for Natural Disasters	7.19	52.20	12.85	55.72	51.51	6.74	-86.9
因自然灾害造成直接经济损失(亿元)	The Direct Economy Loss for Natural Disasters (100 million yuan)	38.27	487.22	35.60	179.77	250.67	66.21	-73.6

注：资料来源于省民政厅。

Note: The data in the table are provided by the provinvial Department of Civil Affairs.

主要统计指标解释

国土 指中华人民共和国国家管辖下的领土、领海和领空。

气候 指地球与大气之间长期能量交换与质量交换所形成的一种自然环境状态，它是多种因素综合作用的结果。气候既是人类生活和生产的环境要素之一，又是供给人类生活和生产的重要资源。气温、降水、湿度等气象要素的多年平均值是用来描述一个地区气候状况的主要参数，而各种气象要素某年、某月的平均值（或总量）则可以反映出该时期天气气候状况的重要特征。

自然资源 指人类可以直接从自然界获得，并用于生产和生活的物质资源。自然资源一般可以分成可再生资源和非再生资源两大类。可再生资源指在较短时间内可以再生、可以循环利用的资源，包括土地资源、水资源、气候资源、生物资源和海洋资源等。非再生资源指在使用后不能再生的资源，包括矿产资源和地热能源。

土地资源 土地指陆地的表层部分，它主要由岩石、岩石的风化物和土壤构成。土地资源按利用类型可以分为农用地、建筑用地和未利用地。农用地包括耕地、园地、林地、牧草地和水面。建筑用地包括居民点及工矿用地、交通用地和水利设施用地。未利用地指农用地和建筑用地以外的土地，包括滩涂、荒漠、戈壁、冰川和石山等。

耕地面积 指经过开垦用以种植农作物并经常进行耕耘的土地面积。包括种有作物的土地面积、休闲地、新开荒地和抛荒未满三年的土地面积。

森林资源 指森林、林木、林地以及依托森林、林木、林地生存的野生动物、植物和微生物。林木指树木和竹子。森林指以乔木为主体的植物群落，是集生的乔木及与共同作用的植物、动物、微生物和土壤、气候等的总体。

活立木总蓄积量 指一定范围内土地上全部树木蓄积的总量，包括森林蓄积、疏林蓄积、散生木蓄积和四旁树蓄积。

森林面积 指由乔木树种构成，郁闭度 0.2 以上（含 0.2）的林地或冠幅宽度 10 米以上的林带的面积，即有林地面积。森林面积包括天然起源和人工起源的针叶林面积、阔叶林面积、针阔混交林面积和竹林面积，不包括灌木林地面积和疏林地面积。

森林蓄积量 指一定森林面积上存在着的林木树干部分的总材积。它是反映一个国家或地区森林资源总规模和水平的基本指标之一，也是反映森林资源的丰富程度、衡量森林生态环境优劣的重要依据。

森林覆盖率 指一个国家或地区森林面积占土地总面积的百分比。森林覆盖率是反映森林资源的丰富程度和生态平衡状况的重要指标。在计算森林覆盖率时，森林面积包括郁闭度 0.2 以上的乔木林地面积和竹林地面积，国家特别规定的灌木林地面积、农田林网以及四旁（村旁、路旁、水旁、宅旁）林木的覆盖面积。计算公式为:

$$森林覆盖率 = \frac{森林面积}{土地总面积} \times 100\%$$

水资源 水在自然界中以固体、液体和气态三种聚集状态存在，分布于海洋、陆地（包括土壤）以及大气之中，通过水循环形成水资源。水资源包括经人类控制并直接可供灌溉、发电、给水、航运、养殖等用途的地表水和地下水，以及江河、湖泊、井、泉、潮汐、港湾和养殖水域等。水资源是发展国民经济不可缺少的重要自然资源。

地表水和地下水 陆地上的水因空间分布不同，分为地表水和地下水。地表水指分别存在于河流、湖泊、沼泽、冰川和冰盖等水体中水分的总称，又称陆地水。地下水指储存在地面以下饱和岩土孔隙、裂隙及溶洞中的水。

矿产资源 矿产指由地质作用形成，富集于地壳中或出露于地表达到工农业利用要求的有用矿物。矿产是一种重要的自然资源，是社会发展的重要物质基础。

流域 每条河流都有自己的干流和支流，干支流共同组成这条河流的水系。每条河流都有自己的集水区域，这个集水区域就称为该河流的流域。

气温 指空气的温度，我国一般以摄氏度（℃）为单位表示。气象观测的温度表是放在离地面约 1.5 米处通风良好的百叶箱里测量的，因此，通常说的气温指的是离地面 1.5 米处百叶箱中的温度。其统计计算方法为：月平均气温是将全月各日的平均气温相加，除以该月的天数而得。年平均气温是将 12 个月的月平均气温累加后除以 12 而得。

相对湿度 指空气中实际所含水蒸气密度和同温度下饱和水蒸气密度的百分比值。其统计方法与气温相同。

降水量 指从天空降落到地面的液态或固态（经融化后）水，未经蒸发、渗透、流失而在地面上积聚的深度。其统计计算方法为：月降水量是将全月各日的降水量累加而得。年降水量是将 12 个月的月降水量累加而得。

日照时数 指太阳实际照射地面的时间。其统计方法与降水量相同。

水资源总量 一定区域内的水资源总量指当地降水形成的地表和地下产水量，即地表径流量与降水入渗补给量之和，不包括过境水量。

用水总量 指分配给用户的包括输水损失在内的毛用水量。按用户特性分为农业、工业、生活和生态用水四大类。

农业用水 包括农田灌溉和林牧渔业用水。林牧渔业用水指林果地灌溉、草地灌溉和鱼塘补水。

工业用水 按新水取用量计，不包括企业内部的重复利用水量。

生活用水 包括城镇生活用水和农村生活用水。城镇生活用水由居民用水和公共用水（含服务业、商饮业、货运邮电业及建筑业等用水）组成；农村生活用水除居民生活用水外，还包括畜用水在内。

工业废水排放量 指经过企业厂区所有排放口排到企业外部的工业废水量。包括生产废水、外排的直接冷却水、超标排放的矿井地下水和与工业废水混排的厂区生活污水，不包括外排的间接冷却水（清污不分流的间接冷却水应计算在内）。

工业废水排放达标量 指报告期内废水中各项污染物指标都达到国家或地方排放标准的外排工业废水量，包括未经处理外排达标的，经废水处理设施处理后达标排放的，以及经污水处理厂处理后达标排放的。

工业废水排放达标率 指工业废水排放达标量占工业废水排放量的百分率，计算公式为:

$$\text{工业废水排放达标率}=\frac{\text{工业废水排放达标量}}{\text{工业废水排放量}}\times 100\%$$

城镇生活污水排放量 指城镇居民每年排放的生活污水中的COD的量。用人均系数法测算。测算公式为:

城镇生活污水排放量 = 城镇生活污水排放系数 × 市镇非农业人口 × 365

生活污水中化学需氧量（COD）排放量 指城镇居民每年排放的生活污水中的COD的量。用人均系数法测算。测算公式为:

城镇生活污水中COD排放量 = 城镇生活污水中COD产生系数 × 市镇非农业人口 × 365

工业废气排放量 指报告期内企业厂区内燃料燃烧和生产工艺过程中产生的各种排入大气的含有污染物的气体的总量，以标准状态（273K，101325Pa）计算。测算公式为:

工业废气排放量 = 燃料燃烧过程中废气排放量 + 生产工艺过程中废气排放量

生活及其他SO2排放量 以生活及其他煤炭消费量和其含硫量为基础，根据以下公式计算:

生活及其他SO2排放量 = 生活及其他煤炭消费量 × 含硫量 × 0.8 × 2

工业SO_2排放量 指报告期内企业在燃料燃烧和生产工艺过程中排入大气的SO_2总量，计算公式为:

工业SO_2排放量 = 燃料燃烧过程中SO_2排放量 + 生产工艺过程中SO_2排放量

工业烟尘排放量 指企业厂区内燃料燃烧过程中产生的烟气中夹带的颗粒物排放量。

生活及其他烟尘排放量 指除工业生产活动以外的所有社会、经济活动及公共设施的经营活动中燃烧所排放的烟尘纯重量。以生活及其他煤炭消费量为基础进行测算。

工业粉尘排放量 指企业在生产工艺过程中排放的能在空气中悬浮一定时间的固体颗粒物排放量。如钢铁企业的耐火材料粉尘、焦化企业的筛焦系统粉尘、烧结机的粉尘、石灰窑的粉尘、建材企业的水泥粉尘等。不包括电厂排入大气的烟尘。

工业固体废物产生量 指报告期内企业在生产过程中产生的固体状、半固体状和高浓度液体状废弃物的总量，包括危险废物、冶炼废渣、粉煤灰、炉渣、煤矸石、尾矿、放射性废物和其他废物等；不包括矿山开采的剥离废石和掘进废石（煤矸石和呈酸性或碱性的废石除外）。酸性或碱性废石指采掘的废石其流经水、雨淋水的pH值小于4或pH值大于10.5者。

危险废物 指列入国家危险废物名录或根据国家规定的危险废物鉴别标准和鉴别方法认定的，具有爆炸性、易燃性、易氧化性、毒性、腐蚀性、易传染疾病等危险特性之一的废物。

工业固体废物综合利用量 指报告期内企业通过回收、加工、循环、交换等方式，从固体废物中提取或者使其转化为可以利用的资源、能源和其他原材料的固体废物量（包括当年利用往年的工业固体废物贮存量），如用作农业肥料、生产建筑材料、筑路等。综合利用量由原产生固体废物的单位统计。

工业固体废物综合利用率 指工业固体废物综合利用量占工业固体废物产生量（包括综合利用往年贮存量）的百分率。计算公式为:

$$\text{工业固体废物综合利用率}=\frac{\text{工业固体废物综合利用量}}{\text{工业固体废物产生量}+\text{综合利用往年贮存量}}\times 100\%$$

工业固体废物贮存量 指报告期内企业以综合利用或处置为目的，将固体废物暂时贮存或堆存在专设的贮存设施或专设的集中堆存场所内的数量。专设的固体废物贮存场所或贮存设施必须有防扩散、防流失、防渗漏、防止污染大气、水体的措施。

工业固体废物处置量 指报告期内企业将固体废物焚烧或者最终置于符合环境保护规定要求的场所，并不再回取的工业固体废物量（包括当年处置往年的工业固体废物贮存量）。处置方式有填埋（其中危险废物应安全填埋）、焚烧、专业贮存场（库）封场处理、深层灌注、回填矿井及海洋处置（经海洋管理部门同意投海处置）等。

工业固体废物排放量　指报告期内企业将所产生的固体废物排到固体废物污染防治设施、场所以外的数量，不包括矿山开采的剥离废石和掘进废石（煤矸石和呈酸性或碱性的废石除外）。

“三废”综合利用产品产值　指报告期内利用“三废”作为主要原料生产的产品价值（现行价）；已经销售或准备销售的应计算产品价值，留作生产自用的不应计算产品价值。

生活垃圾清运量　指报告期收集和运送到各生活垃圾处理场（厂）和生活垃圾最终消纳点的生活垃圾的数量。统计时仅计算从生活垃圾源头和从生活垃圾转运站直接送到处理场和最终消纳点的清运量，对于二次中转的清运量不要重复计算。

生活垃圾无害化处理率　指报告期内生活垃圾无害化处理量与生活垃圾产生量的比率。计算公式为:

$$生活垃圾无害化处理率=\frac{生活垃圾无害化处理量}{生活垃圾产生量}\times 100\%$$

在统计时，由于生活垃圾产生量不易取得，可用清运量代替。“垃圾清运量”在审核时要与总人口（包括暂住人口）对应，一般城市人均日产生垃圾为1kg左右。

造林总面积　指报告期内在荒山、荒地、沙丘、退耕地等一切可以造林的土地上，采用人工播种、飞机播种、植苗造林、分植造林等方法新植成片乔木林和灌木林，经过检查验收符合《造林技术规程》要求的单位面积株数，并按《中华人民共和国森林法实施条例》规定，成活率达85%以上（含85%，年降雨量在400毫米以下且无浇灌条件的地区造林成活率达70%以上）的总面积。四旁植树如一侧在四行以上，连片面积0.066公顷（一亩）以上，应统计在造林面积内。造林面积，通常按所有制（国有、国有集体合作、集体和个人）、造林方式（人工、飞机播种）、主要林种用途（用材林、经济林、防护林、薪炭林、特种用途林）分组进行统计。

退耕还林还草工程　是我国林业建设上涉及面最广、政策性最强、工序最复杂、群众参与度最高的生态建设工程。主要解决重点地区的水土流失问题。

自然保护区　指对有代表性的自然生态系统、珍稀濒危野生动植物物种的天然分布区、水源涵养区、有特殊意义的自然历史遗迹等保护对象所在的陆地、陆地水体或海域，依法划出一定面积进行特殊保护和管理的区域。以县及县以上各级人民政府正式批准建立的自然保护区为准（包括“六五”以前由部门或“革委会”批准且现仍存在的自然保护区）。风景名胜区、文物保护区不计在内。

生态示范区　指省级以上环境保护行政主管部门批准，以省、地、县政府为主按批准的生态示范区建设规划实施的行政区域。包括已经过国家或省级环境保护行政主管部门验收的和正在开展试点工作的。

环境污染与破坏事故　指由于违反环境保护法规的经济、社会活动与行为，以及意外因素的影响或不可抗拒的自然灾害等原因，致使环境受到污染，国家重点保护的野生动植物、自然保护区受到破坏，人体健康受到危害，社会经济和人民财产受到损失，造成不良社会影响的突发性事件。

环境污染治理投资　指在工业污染源治理和城市环境基础设施建设的资金投入中，用于形成固定资产的资金。包括工业新老污染源治理工程投资、建设项目“三同时”环保投资，以及城市环境基础设施建设所投入的资金。

Explanatory Notes on Main Statistical Indicators

Territory refers to territorial land, sea and air space under the administration of the People's Republic of China.

Climate refers to the natural environmental status formed by the long-term exchange of energy and mass between the earth and the air, and is the results of interaction of many factors. Climate is both one of the environment factors and the important resources for the living and production activities of the human being. The average values across several years of meteorological factors such as temperature, rainfall and humidity are used as important parameters to describe the climate of a region, while the average values (or total values) of a given year or month of meteorological factors reflect the key characteristics of climate for that period of time.

Natural Resources refer to material resources that could be obtained from the nature by human being and used for production and living. Natural resources in general can be classified as renewable resources and non-renewable resources. Renewable resources refer to resources that could be renewed and recycled during a relatively short period of time, including land resource, water resource, climate resource, biology resource and marine resource. Non-renewable resources include resources that could not be renewed, such as minerals and geothermal resource.

Land Resource Land refers to the surface of the earth, consisting of mainly rocks and its weathering and earth. Land resource can be classified, by its utilization, as land for agriculture, land for construction and unused land. Land for agriculture includes cultivated land, plantation land, forestland, grassland and waters. Land for construction includes land for residential purpose, for manufacturing and mining, for transportation and for water-conservancy projects. Unused land refers to land other than land for agriculture and construction, including beaches, deserts, Gobi, glaciers and rock mountains.

Area of Cultivated Land refers to area of land reclaimed for the regular cultivation of various farm crops, including crop-cover land, fallow, newly reclaimed land and land laid idle for less than 3 years.

Forest Resource refers to forests, trees, forestland and wild animals, plants and microorganism that live on forest and trees. Trees include trees and bamboo. Forest refers to the population of clusters of trees and other plants, animals and microorganism as well as the earth and climate that have interactions with the trees.

Forest Area refers to the area of forest where trees and bamboo grow with canopy density above 0.2, including land of natural woods and planted woods, but excluding bush land and thin forest land. It reflects the total areas of afforestation.

Stock Volume of Forest refers to total stock volume of wood growing in forest area, which shows the total size and level of forest resources of a country or a region. It is also an important indicator illustrating the richness of forest resource and the status of forest ecological environment.

Forest Coverage Rate refers to the ratio of area of afforested land to total land area. It is a very important indicator that reflects the status of abundance of forest resource and ecosystem balance. Forest area includes the area of trees and bamboo grow with canopy density above 0.2, the area of shrubby tree according to regulations of the government, the area of forest land inside farm land and the area of trees planted by the side of villages, farm houses and along roads and rivers. The formula for calculating forest coverage rate is as follows:

$$\text{Forestry coverage rate (\%)} = \frac{\text{Area of Afforested Land}}{\text{Area of Total Land}} \times 100\%$$

Water Resource Water exists in the nature in solid, liquid and gaseous states, is distributed in the ocean, land (including earth) and air, and constitutes the water resource through the circulation of water. Water resource includes the surface water and underground water that is controlled by the human being for irrigation, power-generation, water supply, navigation and cultivation. It also includes rivers, lakes, wells, springs, tides, gulf and water area for cultivation.

Water resource as an important natural resource is indispensable for the development of the national economy.

Surface Water and Underground Water Water on earth can be divided into surface water and underground water according to its distribution. Surface water refers to moisture exists in rivers, lakes, swamps, glaciers, icecaps and so on. It is also called land water. The underground water refers to water deposited underground in the cranny and the hole of saturated rock soil and in the water-eroded cave.

Mineral Resources refer to useful minerals that can be used for industrial or agricultural purposes enriched in lithosphere or on earth due to the geological process. Minerals are important natural resources, and important material base for social development.

Drainage Area Each river has its own main stream and branches to form the water system of the river. Each river has its own catchment's area, which is also called as the drainage area of the river.

Temperature refers to the air temperature. China uses centigrade as the unit. The thermometry used for weather observation is put in a breezy shutter, which is 1.5 meters high from the ground. Therefore, the commonly used temperature refers to the temperature in the breezy shutter 1.5 meters away from the ground. The calculation method is as follows:Monthly average temperature is the summation of average daily temperature of one month divided by the actual days of that particular month.Annual average temperature is the summation of monthly average of a year divided by 12 months.

Relative Humidity refers to the ratio of actual water vapor pressure to the saturation water vapor density under the current temperature. The statistical method is the same as that of temperature.

Volume of Precipitation refers to the deepness of liquid state or solid state (thawed) water falling from the sky to the ground that has not been evaporated, infiltrated or run off. The calculation method is as follows:Monthly precipitation is the summation of daily precipitation of a month.Annual precipitation is the summation of 12 months precipitation of a year.

Sunshine Hours refer to the actual hours of sun irradiating the earth. The calculation method is the same as that of the precipitation.

Total Water Resources refers to total volume of water resources measured as run-off for surface water from rainfall and recharge for groundwater in a given area, excluding transit water.

Water Use refers to gross water use distributed to users, including loss during transportation, broken down with use by agriculture, industry, living consumption and biological protection.

Water Use by Agriculture includes uses of water by irrigation of farming fields and by forestry, animal husbandry and fishing. Water use by forestry, animal husbandry and fishing includes irrigation of forestry and orchards, irrigation of grassland and replenishment of fishing pools.

Water Use by Industry refers to new withdrawals of water, excluding reuse of water within enterprises.

Water Use by Living Consumption includes use of water for living consumption in both urban and rural areas. Urban water use by living consumption is composed of household use and public use (including services, commerce, restaurants, cargo transportation, posts, telecommunication and construction). Rural water use by living consumption includes both households and animals.

Waste Water Discharged by Industry refers to the volume of waste water discharged by industrial enterprises through all their outlets, including waste water from production process, directly cooled water, groundwater from mining wells which does not meet discharge standards and sewage from households mixed with waste water produced by industrial activities, but excluding indirectly cooled water discharged (It should be included if the discharge is not separated with waste water).

Industrial Waste Water Meeting Discharge Standards refers to volume of industrial waste water discharge which, with or without treatment, reaches national or local standards with regard to all pollutants.

Ratio of Industrial Waste Water Meeting Discharge Standards refers to percentage of industrial waste water meeting discharge standards over total industrial waste water discharge. It is calculated as:

$$\text{Ratio of industrial waste water meeting discharge standards}=\frac{\text{industrial waste water meeting discharge standards}}{\text{total industrial waste water discharge}}\times 100\%$$

Urban Non-industrial Waste Water Discharge refers to annual discharge of the amount of COD in non-industrial waste water by urban households. It is estimated by per capita coefficient using the formula:

Urban non-industrial waste water discharge = urban non-industrial waste water discharge coefficient urban non-agricultural population × 365

Volume of Chemical Oxygen Demand(COD) Generated by Urban Non-industrial Waster Water refers to chemical oxygen demand generated through the annual discharge of non-industrial waste water by urban households. It is estimated as:

Volume of chemical oxygen demand(cod) generated by urban non-industrial waster water = Coefficient of COD generated through urban non-industrial waste water urban non-agricultural population × 365

Industrial Waste Air Emission refers to discharge into atmosphere of waste air containing pollutants generated from fuel burning and production process in enterprises within a given period of time. It is calculated at standard status (273K, 101325Pa) as:

Industrial waste air emission = emission through fuel burning + emission through production process

SO_2 Emission through Non-industrial and Other Activities is calculated on the basis of consumption of coal by households and other activities and the sulphur content of coal with the following formula:

SO_2 emission through non-industrial and other activities = consumption of coal by households and other activities × sulphur content × 0.8 × 2

SO_2 Emission through Industrial Activities refers to volume of sulphur dioxide emission from fuel burning and production process by enterprises during a given period of time. It is calculated as:

SO_2 emission through industrial activities = SO_2 emission from fuel burning + SO_2 emission from production process

Industrial Soot Emission refers to volume of soot in smoke emitted in process of fuel burning in premises of enterprises.

Soot Emission by Consumption and Others refers to net volume of soot emitted by fuel burning from all social and economic activities and operation of public facilities other than industrial activities. It is calculated on the basis of coal consumption by households and others.

Industrial Dust Emission refers to volume of dust emitted by production process of enterprises and suspended in the air for a given period of time, including dust from refractory material of iron and steel works, dust from coke-screening systems and sintering machines of coke plants, dust from lime kilns and dust from cement production in building material enterprises, but excluding soot and dust emitted from power plants.

Industrial Solid Wastes Produced refers to total volume of solid, semi-solid and high concentration liquid residues produced by industrial enterprises from production process in a given period of time, including hazardous wastes, slag, coal ash, gangue, tailings, radioactive residues and other wastes, but excluding stones stripped or dug out in mining (gangue and acid or alkaline stones not included). A stone is acid or alkaline depending on the pH value of the water below 4 or above 10.5 when the stone is in, or soaked by, the water.

Hazardous Wastes refers to those included in the national hazardous wastes catalogue or specified as any one of the following properties in the national hazardous wastes identification standards: explosive, ignitable, oxidizable, toxic, corrosive or liable to cause infectious diseases or lead to other dangers.

Industrial Solid Wastes Utilized refers to volume of solid wastes from which useful materials can be extracted or which can be converted into usable resources, energy or other materials by means of reclamation, processing, recycling and exchange (including utilizing in the year the stocks of industrial solid wastes of the previous year). Examples of such utilizations include fertilizers, building materials and road materials. The information shall be collected by the producing units of the wastes.

Rate of Utilization of Industrial Solid Wastes refers to the percentage of industrial solid wastes utilized over industrial solid wastes produced (including stocks of the previous years). It is calculated as:

$$\text{Rate of Utilization of Industrial Solid Wastes}=\frac{\text{volume of industrial solid wastes utilized}}{\text{industrial solid wastes produced + stock of previous years}}\times 100\%$$

Stocks of Industrial Solid Wastes refers to volume of solid wastes placed in special facilities or special sites for purposes of utilization or disposal. The sites or facilities should take measures against dispersion, loss, seepage, and air and water contamination.

Industrial Solid Wastes Disposed refers to quantity of industrial solid wastes which are burnt or placed ultimately in the sites meeting the requirements for environmental protection and not salvaged or recycled (including disposition in the year of those wastes of previous years). The disposition includes landfill (Safe landfills should be conducted for hazardous wastes), incineration, containment spaces, deep underground disposal, backfill in mining pits and disposal at sea.

Industrial Solid Wastes Discharged refers to volume of industrial solid wastes discharged by producing enterprises to disposal facilities or to other sites. The wastes exclude stones stripped or dug from mining (gangue and acid or alkaline waste stones not included).

Output Value of Products Made from Waste Gas, Waste Water and Solid Wastes refers current value of products with waste gas, waste water and solid wastes as main materials of production. Products sold and ready to sell shall be included while those produced for own use shall not be included.

Consumption Wastes Transported refers to volume of consumption wastes collected and transported to disposal factories or sites. Statistical calculations only when the source from garbage and garbage transfer station directly to the treatment plant and the final consumer satisfaction point clearance volume, for the secondary transit clearance volume can not be duplicated.

Ratio of Consumption Wastes Treated refers to consumption wastes treated over that produced. It is calculated as:

$$\text{Ratio of consumption wastes treated}=\frac{\text{consumption wastes treated}}{\text{consumption wastes produced}}\times 100\%$$

In practical statistics, as it is difficult to estimate, the volume of consumption wastes produced is replaced with that transported. During the audit, "Garbage clearance volume" and the total population to be (including temporary residents) corresponds, generally, urban waste generated per capita is about 1kg.

Total Area of Afforestation refers to the total area of land suitable for afforestation, including barren hills, idle land, sand dunes, rain for green land, on which acres of arbores or bushes are planted through manual planting, airplane planting, plant seedlings, etc. in accordance with the required density standards of the Technical Procedures of Afforestation, and with a survival rate of over 85% in line with the Implementing Rules of the Forest Law of the People's Republic of China (or a survival rate of 75% in areas with less that 400 mm of annual rainfall and without irrigation facilities). Included in the this category are trees planted alone the roadsides, riversides, or next to houses that occupy an area over 0.066 hectares, or where more than 4 lines of trees are planted. Total area of afforestation is further classified by ownership (state-owned, state-collective, collective or private), by approach of planting (manual, airplane), and by type of forests (timber, by-products, protection, fuel, special use, etc.).

Projects on Converting Cultivated Land to Forests and Grassland(Grain for Green Projects) aiming at preventing soil erosion in key regions, these projects are ecological construction projects in the development of forest industry that have the widest coverage and most sophisticated procedures, with strong policy implications and most active participation of the people.

Nature Reserves refer to certain areas of land, waters or sea that are representative in natural ecological systems, or are natural habitats for rare or endangered wild animals or plants, or water conservation zones, or the location of important natural or historic relics, which are demarked by law and put under special protection and management. Nature reserves are designated by the formal approval of governments at and above county level (including those approved by relevant departments or "revolutionary committees" before 1980). Scenic spots and cultural preservationzones are not included.

Ecological Demonstration Zones refer to administrative areas approved by the environment protection agencies of central and provincial governments and established by provincial, prefecture or county governments in line with the approved programme for ecological demonstration zones. They include those evaluated and accepted by the environment protection agencies of central and provincial governments and those under pilot development stage.

Environment Pollution and Destruction Accidents refer to sudden accidents, due to economic or social activities that are in contrast to environment protection laws or due to unforeseen factors or natural disasters, that lead to the environment pollution, the destruction of protected wild animals, plants or nature reserves, the damage to human health, the economic and property losses, and the negative impact on the society.

Investment in Environment Pollution Harnessing Projects refers to the proportion of investment in fixed assets in the total investment in harnessing industrial pollution and in the construction of urban environment infrastructure facilities. It includes investment in harnessing sources of industrial pollution, investment in environment protection facilities designed concurrently with construction projects, and investment in urban environment infrastructure facilities.

13 Thirteen

农　业

Agriculture

13-1 农村基本情况及农业生产条件

Basic Conditions of Rural Areas and Agricultural Production

指 标	Item	2007	2008	2009	2010	2011	2012
农村基层组织	**Rural Grassroots Units**						
乡镇个数(个)	Number of Township and Town Governments(unit)	1449	1449	1446	1446	1445	1439
村委会个数(个)	Number of Villagers' Committees(unit)	18091	17332	17568	17672	17583	18099
农村社会基础设施	**Basic Facilities in Rural Areas**						
自来水受益村数(个)	Number of Villages with Access to Tap Water(unit)	13269	13113	13639	13636	13922	14443
通汽车的村数(个)	Villages with Automobile(unit)	15980	15930	17334	17388	17336	17717
通电话的村数(个)	Villages with Telephone Communication(unit)	15354	15612	16725	16772	16823	17066
通有线广播的村数(个)	Villages with Wire Broadcast(unit)	5655	5913	5912	6332	6690	7713
农业机械化	**Agricultural Mechanization**						
农用机械总动力(万千瓦)	Total Power of Agricultural Machinery(10000 kw)	1411.74	1537.50	1606.42	1730.31	1851.40	2106.65
柴油机	Diesel Engine	980.69	1055.54	1122.17	1192.24	1308.11	1489.89
汽油机	Gas Engine	30.69	45.56	49.39	53.42	60.50	74.68
电动机	Electromotor	393.68	423.94	421.34	472.21	473.46	535.01
其他机械	Others	6.68	12.46	13.52	12.44	9.33	7.08
农村主要物资消耗	**Main Materials Consumption for Agricultural Use**						
农用化肥施用量(折纯法)(万吨)	Consumption of Chemical Fertilizer(pure)(10000 tons)	82.05	83.09	86.54	86.53	94.06	98.17
农药使用量(吨)	Consumption of Chemical Pesticides(ton)	10722	12920	12464	12938	14469	14450
农用塑料薄膜使用量(吨)	Consumption of Farm Plastic Membrane(ton)	33710	47765	46470	36174	40857	44062
农田水利建设	**Farmland and Water Conservancy**						
有效灌溉面积(千公顷)	Effective Irrigated Area(1000 hectares)	894.28	987.41	1087.41	1195.33	1266.80	1317.59
旱涝保收面积(千公顷)	Area that Ensure Stable Yields Despite Droughtor Excessive Rain(1000 hectares)	570.21	586.55	633.73	646.02	659.31	656.50
机电排灌面积(千公顷)	Area with Motorized Drainage and Irrigation Facilities (1000 hectares)	72.04	74.11	75.14	77.86	80.14	81.04

注：表中“农业机械化”资料来源于省农委，“农田水利建设”资料来源于省水利厅(以下相关表同)。

Note:The data of "agricultural mechanization" are provided by the provincial agricultural commission; and the data of "farmland and water conservancy" are provided by the provincial department of water resources(The relative tables in the chapter are the same).

13-2 年末主要农业机械拥有量

Major Agricultural Machinery at the Year-end

指　标	Item	2007	2008	2009	2010	2011	2012	2012年比2011年增长(%) Increase Rate in 2012 over 2011(%)
大中型拖拉机(万台)	Large and Medium Agricultural Tractors(10000 sets)	1.92	2.36	2.50	2.53	3.12	3.92	25.6
大中型拖拉机配套农具(万套)	Suited Farm Tools by Large and Medium Agricultural Tractors(10000 sets)	0.61	1.20	1.29	1.36	1.38	1.43	3.4
小型拖拉机(万台)	Mini Agricultural Tractors(10000 sets)	5.12	4.82	5.34	5.66	6.64	7.31	10.1
小型拖拉机配套农具(万套)	Suited Farm Tools by Mini Agricultural Tractors(10000 sets)	1.55	1.64	2.14	2.47	2.61	2.88	10.0
农用排灌电动机(万台)	Number of Drainage and Irrigation Electromotor Engines(10000 units)	17.56	17.11	18.13	19.03	19.06	21.09	10.7
农用排灌柴油机(万台)	Number of Drainage and Irrigation Diesel Engines(10000 units)	15.42	17.42	18.28	18.72	18.45	19.95	8.1
联合收割机(台)	Combine Harvesters(unit)	440	507	602	642	695	1057	52.1

注：资料来源于省农委。

Note:The data in this table are provided by the provincial agricultural commission.

13-3 灌溉、除涝治水

Irrigation, Flood Prevention, Water and Soil Conservation

项　目	Item	2007	2008	2009	2010	2011	2012
水利投入(亿元)	Input of Water Conservancy(100 million yuan)	24.25	40.40	49.18	102.01	151.78	175.18
有效灌溉面积(千公顷)	Effective Irrigation Area(1000 hectares)	894.28	987.41	1087.41	1195.33	1266.80	1317.59
节水灌溉面积(千公顷)	Water-saving Irrigated Area (1000 hectares)		380.00	386.31	391.74	396.00	403.28
除涝面积(千公顷)	Areas with Flood Prevention Measures(1000 hectares)		50.47	52.38	54.00	54.81	55.70
水土流失治理面积(千公顷)	Area of Soil Erosion under Control(1000 hectares)	2490.80	2567.60	2701.50	2811.50	2956.00	3225.99
堤防长度(公里)	Total Length of Dikes(km)		1534.83	1557.60	1598.40	1634.60	2256.55
堤防保护面积(千公顷)	Area of Land Protected by Dikes (1000 hectares)		164.45	165.21	167.68	169.12	215.79

13-4 农林牧渔业总产值、增加值
Gross Output Value and Value-Added of Farming,Forestry, Animal Husbandry, Fishery and Their Services

单位：亿元 (100 million yuan)

指 标	Item	2007	2008	2009	2010	2011	2012	2012年比2011年增长(%) Increase Rate in 2012over 2011(%)
农林牧渔业总产值	**Gross Output Value of Farming,Forestry, Animal Husbandry and Fishery**	**697.01**	**843.80**	**875.20**	**997.82**	**1165.46**	**1436.61**	**9.3**
农 业	Farming	392.20	464.80	501.52	587.31	655.30	864.86	12.0
林 业	Forestry	27.77	35.63	36.92	41.01	46.66	54.19	7.1
畜牧业	Animal Husbandry	231.60	291.65	281.53	304.16	381.95	421.55	5.3
渔 业	Fishery	9.04	10.49	11.06	13.82	19.90	28.21	23.2
农、林、牧、渔服务业	FFAF Services	36.40	41.23	44.17	51.52	61.65	67.80	3.5
农林牧渔业增加值	**Added Value of FFAFS**	**446.38**	**540.27**	**550.27**	**625.04**	**726.21**	**891.91**	**8.6**
农 业	Farming	260.30	308.48	330.50	385.61	430.84	561.32	110.6
林 业	Forestry	18.27	23.44	25.11	28.07	31.99	37.03	106.8
畜牧业	Animal Husbandry	145.68	183.16	167.79	179.51	223.22	245.70	105.0
渔 业	Fishery	5.89	6.84	7.21	8.98	12.78	17.83	121.2
农、林、牧、渔服务业	FFAF Services	16.24	18.35	19.66	22.86	27.38	30.03	103.2

13-5 农林牧渔业总产值
Gross Output Value of Farming,Forestry,Animal Husbandry, Fishery and Their Services

单位：亿元 (100 million yuan)

指 标	Item	2007	2008	2009	2010	2011	2012	2012年比2011年增长(%) Increase Rate in 2012over 2011(%)
农林牧渔业总产值	**Gross Output Value of Farming,Forestry, AnimalHusbandry and Fishery**	**697.01**	**843.80**	**875.20**	**997.82**	**1165.46**	**1436.61**	**9.3**
农业产值	**Farming**	**392.20**	**464.80**	**501.52**	**587.31**	**655.30**	**864.86**	**12.0**
谷物及其他作物的种植	Planting of Cereal and other Crops	240.51	289.75	307.19	340.56	340.36	389.45	11.9
蔬菜、园艺作物的种植	Planting of Vegetable and Gardening Crops	120.40	140.60	155.83	194.69	249.10	387.95	9.4
水果、坚果、饮料和香料作物的种植	Planting of Fruits, nuts, Beverages and Spice Crops	18.94	20.73	23.61	35.64	46.12	54.69	11.6
中药材的种植	Planting of Chinese Traditional Medicine	12.35	13.71	14.89	16.42	19.72	32.77	48.0
林业产值	**Forestry**	**27.77**	**35.63**	**36.92**	**41.01**	**46.66**	**54.19**	**7.1**
林木的培育和种植	Cultivating and planting of forest	4.15	4.91	5.17	5.49	5.90	6.90	6.6
木材和竹材的采运	Logging and Transporting of Timber & bamboo	5.43	8.88	9.46	11.47	12.51	14.46	6.8
林产品的采集	Collecting of Forest Products	18.19	21.84	22.29	24.04	28.25	32.83	7.3
畜牧业产值	**Animal Husbandry**	**231.60**	**291.65**	**281.53**	**304.16**	**381.95**	**421.55**	**5.3**
牲畜的饲养	Animal Raising	30.60	37.16	39.82	56.13	70.05	85.31	8.7
猪的饲养	Hogs Raising	165.62	212.99	195.52	196.23	253.35	273.87	4.7
家禽的饲养	Poultry Raising	33.96	39.84	44.43	50.00	56.69	60.43	3.7
狩猎和捕捉动物	Hunting and Catching Animales	0.09	0.09	0.10	0.09	0.09	0.10	6.5
其他畜牧业	Others	1.33	1.57	1.66	1.71	1.76	1.84	0.6
渔业产值	**Fishery**	**9.04**	**10.49**	**11.06**	**13.82**	**19.90**	**28.21**	**23.2**
农林牧渔服务业产值	**Gross Output Value of FFAF Services**	**36.40**	**41.23**	**44.17**	**51.52**	**61.65**	**67.80**	**3.5**

13-6 主要农作物播种面积
Sown Areas of Major Farm Crops

单位：千公顷 (1000 hectares)

指　标	Item	2007	2008	2009	2010	2011	2012	2012年比2011年增长(%) Increase Rate in 2012 over 2011(%)
农作物总播种面积	**Total Sown Areas of Farm Crops**	**4464.53**	**4619.43**	**4780.69**	**4889.30**	**5021.22**	**5182.86**	**3.2**
#粮食作物	Grain Crops	2821.84	2919.57	2984.73	3039.50	3055.56	3054.28	…
#稻　谷	Rice	676.22	691.15	698.24	695.81	681.53	682.95	0.2
小　麦	Wheat	242.71	262.44	262.93	260.77	257.62	259.76	0.8
玉　米	Corn	731.20	734.64	751.49	781.14	787.80	775.15	-1.6
大　豆	Soybeans	121.26	125.74	126.63	128.95	132.78	133.82	1.9
薯　类	Tubers	788.14	842.53	876.23	894.83	912.94	919.41	0.8
#马铃薯	Irish Potato	604.90	605.76	634.96	645.84	668.01	676.27	1.4
油　料	Oil-bearing Crops	433.13	455.15	513.13	529.14	536.14	547.50	2.1
#油菜籽	Rapeseeds	400.12	412.77	466.88	479.19	488.98	496.96	1.6
花　生	Peanuts	25.40	33.50	38.76	40.81	38.90	41.02	5.4
糖　料	Sugar Crops	17.15	17.67	16.47	13.74	12.02	21.83	81.6
#甘　蔗	Sugarcane	17.07	17.63	16.43	13.70	11.98	21.71	81.2
烟　叶	Tobacco	192.79	207.74	197.82	195.37	212.24	249.17	17.4
#烤　烟	Flue-cured Tobacco	177.39	194.77	184.94	182.74	200.01	237.01	18.5
药材类	Crude Drugs	24.72	24.86	25.60	28.12	44.35	74.68	68.4
蔬　菜	Vegetable	527.85	558.29	599.58	647.92	708.52	774.32	9.3

13-7 主要农作物产品产量

Yields of Major Farm Crops

单位：万吨 (10000 tons)

指　　标	Item	2007	2008	2009	2010	2011	2012	2012年比2011年增长(%) Increase Rate in 2012 over 2011(%)
粮食作物	**Grain Crops**	**1100.86**	**1158.00**	**1168.27**	**1112.30**	**876.90**	**1079.50**	**23.1**
#稻　谷	Rice	449.84	461.10	453.17	445.65	303.93	402.43	32.4
小　麦	Wheat	47.86	42.81	44.52	24.83	50.38	52.39	4.0
玉　米	Corn	357.10	391.19	405.20	415.43	243.71	342.25	40.4
大　豆	Soybeans	14.93	16.57	15.87	15.99	7.11	7.84	10.3
薯　类	Tubers	199.00	214.81	208.84	174.13	239.31	235.83	-1.5
#马铃薯	Irish Potato	152.73	150.30	153.50	141.43	189.38	179.74	-5.1
油料作物	**Oil-bearing Crops**	**69.66**	**68.39**	**78.68**	**60.34**	**78.85**	**87.38**	**10.8**
#油菜籽	Rapeseeds	64.59	60.38	70.40	51.62	71.81	78.18	**8.9**
花　生	Peanuts	4.93	6.44	7.31	7.68	6.07	7.86	**29.5**
甘　蔗	**Sugarcane**	**66.97**	**71.76**	**64.27**	**52.24**	**43.60**	**127.96**	**193.4**
烤　烟	**Flue-cured Tobacco**	**31.22**	**37.71**	**36.92**	**37.02**	**32.50**	**37.31**	**14.8**
蔬　菜	**Vegetable**	**877.34**	**991.15**	**1077.81**	**1202.04**	**1250.05**	**1375.63**	**10.0**

13-8 主要农作物单产

Yields of Major Farm Crops Per Mu

单位：公斤/亩 (kg/mu)

指　　标	Item	2007	2008	2009	2010	2011	2012	2012年比2011年增长(%) Increase Rate in 2012 over 2011(%)
粮食作物	**Grain Crops**	**260**	**264**	**261**	**244**	**191**	**236**	**23.2**
#稻　谷	Rice	443	445	433	427	297	393	32.1
小　麦	Wheat	131	109	113	63	130	134	3.1
玉　米	Corn	326	355	359	355	206	294	42.7
大　豆	Soybeans	82	88	84	83	36	39	8.2
薯　类	Tubers	168	170	159	130	175	171	-2.2
#马铃薯	Irish Potato	168	165	161	146	189	177	-6.4
油料作物	**Oil-bearing Crops**	**107**	**100**	**102**	**76**	**98**	**106**	**8.5**
#油菜籽	Rapeseed	108	98	101	72	98	105	7.1
花　生	Peanuts	129	128	126	125	104	128	22.8
甘　蔗	**Sugarcane**	**2615**	**2714**	**2608**	**2542**	**2427**	**3930**	**61.9**
烤　烟	**Flue-cured Tobacco**	**117**	**129**	**133**	**135**	**108**	**105**	**-3.1**

13-9 茶叶、水果面积及产量

Total Sown Areas and Yields of Tea,Fruit

指 标	Item	2007	2008	2009	2010	2011	2012	2012年比2011年增长(%) Increase Rate in 2012 over 2011(%)
面 积(千公顷)	**Area(1000 hectares)**							
茶园面积	Tea Field Area	71.81	105.17	132.19	167.19	196.37	251.52	28.1
桑园面积	Mulberry Field Area	5.35	5.50	5.01	4.63	4.47	3.92	-12.4
柞坡面积	Breed Tussah Field Area	4.11	3.14	3.10	2.79	5.46	3.72	-31.9
果园面积	Orchards Filed Area	124.55	133.28	140.83	151.83	169.02	192.96	14.2
产 量(万吨)	**Yield(10000 tons)**							
茶 叶	Tea	2.84	3.49	4.19	5.23	5.84	7.44	27.4
水 果	Fruit	112.86	114.28	119.74	123.47	128.03	147.72	15.4
#园林水果	Garden Fruit	60.32	61.68	64.22	69.61	79.52	90.06	13.2
#苹 果	Apples	1.10	1.22	1.62	1.55	2.17	2.49	14.7
梨	Pears	14.80	16.29	16.77	18.21	19.54	21.72	11.2
柑 桔	Citrus	19.07	19.11	19.42	20.37	20.81	22.74	9.2
香 蕉	Bananas	0.88	0.80	0.79	0.61	0.59	0.61	2.9
杨 梅	Red Bayberry	2.94	2.33	3.05	2.90	3.19	3.19	0.2
猕猴桃	Chinese Gooseberrys	1.15	1.24	1.18	1.30	1.70	1.76	4.0
柿 子	Persimmons	1.45	1.27	1.28	1.36	1.25	1.46	17.2

13-10 造林及林产品产量

Areas of Forestation and Output of Forest Products

单位：吨 (ton)

指 标	Item	2007	2008	2009	2010	2011	2012	2012年比2011年增长(%) Increase Rate in 2012 over 2011(%)
当年造林面积(千公顷)	**Areas of Forestation in this year(1000 hectares)**	**81.80**	**65.96**	**90.49**	**72.70**	**131.30**	**199.3**	**51.8**
林产品产量	**Output of Forest Products**							
生 漆	Lacquer	1426	1641	1526	1614	2001	1698	-15.1
油桐籽	Tung-oil Seed	78147	73395	61796	63815	75769	81638	7.7
油茶籽	Tea-oil Seed	12177	16233	19057	20368	23166	26657	15.1
乌桕籽	Tallow-seed	2839	2874	2396	2468	2487	2370	-4.7
五倍籽	Nutgall	1698	1739	1581	2216	1624	1922	18.3
棕 片	Palm-flake	4615	4510	4396	4365	4530	4387	-3.2
松 脂	Pine Resin	11799	9382	7734	8215	12001	13014	8.4
竹笋片	Bamboo Shoot	10934	11719	13780	20382	19897	20495	3.0
核 桃	Walnuts	12187	12316	13125	15356	17364	23680	36.4
板 栗	Chestnut	17336	16707	17278	19316	22653	26076	15.1

注：表中"造林面积"资料来源于省林业厅。

Note:The areas of forestation in this table are obtained from the Provincial Department of Forest.

13−11　畜牧业生产及水产品
Basic Statistics on Livestock and Aquatic Products

指　　标	Item	2007	2008	2009	2010	2011	2012	2012年比2011年增长(%) Increase Rate in 2012 over 2011(%)
当年出栏数	**Number of Slaughtered Fattened Hogs, Ox,Goats and Sheep**							
猪(万头)	Slaughtered Fattened Hogs(10000 heads)	1445.40	1561.10	1596.10	1688.67	1689.66	1734.76	2.7
牛(万头)	Ox by Sold and Killed(10000 heads)	75.20	84.20	92.14	96.56	97.21	105.99	9.0
羊(万头)	Goats by Sold and Killed(10000 heads)	162.20	178.50	190.10	198.70	197.31	206.78	4.8
肉类总产量(万吨)	**Total Yield of Meat(10000 tons)**	**150.60**	**161.46**	**169.60**	**179.09**	**179.97**	**190.27**	**5.7**
#猪　肉	Pork	125.60	134.60	140.10	148.09	148.29	156.13	5.3
牛　肉	Beef	9.50	10.20	11.40	11.99	12.00	13.04	8.7
羊　肉	Mutton	2.80	3.00	3.23	3.40	3.37	3.53	4.7
禽　肉	Poultry	11.70	12.60	13.50	14.12	14.35	15.41	7.4
其他畜产品产量	**Others**							
牛　奶(万吨)	Cow Milk(10000 tons)	4.06	4.30	4.49	4.59	4.85	5.10	5.2
禽　蛋(万吨)	Poultry Eggs(10000 tons)	10.30	10.80	12.20	12.51	13.65	14.65	7.3
蜂　蜜(吨)	Honey(ton)	1988	3093	2017	1894	2029	2052	1.1
大牲畜年末存栏数(万头)	**Large Livestock(year-end)(10000 heads)**	**612.10**	**611.51**	**626.21**	**627.64**	**550.82**	**541.03**	**-1.8**
#牛	Cattle and Buffaloes	513.10	523.40	539.10	541.80	467.11	461.04	-1.3
猪年末存栏数(万头)	**Hogs(year-end)(10000 heads)**	**1548.70**	**1587.50**	**1617.96**	**1616.34**	**1521.60**	**1604.09**	**5.4**
羊年末存栏数(万只)	**Sheep and Goats(year-end)(10000 heads)**	**222.30**	**231.20**	**252.98**	**261.10**	**256.49**	**290.09**	**13.1**
水产品(万吨)	**Aquatic Products(10000 tons)**	**7.68**	**7.80**	**8.03**	**8.79**	**10.88**	**13.47**	**23.8**

注：表中“水产品”资料来源于省农委。

Note:Data of aquatic products in this table are obtained from the Provincial Agricultural Commission.

主要统计指标解释

农林牧渔业总产值　指以货币表现的农、林、牧、渔业全部产品和对农林牧渔业生产活动进行的各种支持性服务活动的价值总量，它反映一定时期内农业生产总规模和总成果。农业总产值的计算方法通常是按农林牧渔业产品及其副产品的产量分别乘以各自单位产品价格求得；然后将四业产品产值及农林牧渔服务业产值相加即为农业总产值。

粮食产量　指全社会的产量。包括国有经济经营的、集体统一经营的和农民家庭经营的粮食产量，还包括工矿企业办的农场和其他生产单位的产量。粮食除包括稻谷、小麦、玉米、高粱、谷子及其他杂粮外，还包括薯类和豆类。其产量计算方法，豆类按去豆荚后的干豆计算；薯类（包括甘薯和马铃薯，不包括芋头和木薯）1963 年以前按每 4 公斤鲜薯折 1 公斤粮食计算，从 1964 年开始改为按 5 公斤鲜薯折 1 公斤粮食计算。城市郊区作为蔬菜的薯类（如马铃薯等）按鲜品计算，并且不作粮食统计。其他粮食一律按脱粒后的原粮计算。

油料产量　指全部油料作物的生产量。包括花生、油菜籽、芝麻、向日葵籽、胡麻籽（亚麻籽）和其他油料。不包括大豆、木本油料和野生油料。花生以带壳干花生计算。

水产品产量　指人工养殖的水产品和天然生长的水产品的捕捞量。包括海水的鱼类、虾蟹类、贝类和藻类以及内陆水域的鱼类、虾蟹类和贝类，不包括淡水生植物。

猪、牛、羊肉产量　指当年出栏并已屠宰、除去头蹄下水后带骨肉（即胴体重）的重量。

期初（末）畜禽存栏头（只）数　指报告期初（末）农村各种合作经济组织和国营农场、农民个人、机关、团体、学校、工矿企业、部队等单位以及城镇居民饲养的大牲畜、猪、羊、家禽等畜禽的存栏数。

耕地面积　指可以用来种植农作物、经常进行耕锄的田地，包括熟地、当年新开荒地、连续撂荒未满三年的耕地和当年的休闲地（轮歇地），还包括以种植农作物为主并附带种植桑树、茶树、果树和其他林木的土地，以及沿海、沿湖地区已围垦利用的“海涂”、“湖田”等面积。不包括属于专业性的桑园、茶园、果园、果木苗圃、林地、芦苇地、天然或人工草地面积。

农作物播种面积　指实际播种或移植有农作物的面积。凡是实际种植有农作物的面积，不论种植在耕地上还是种植在非耕地上，均包括在农作物播种面积中。在播种季节基本结束后，因遭灾而重新改种和补种的农作物面积，也包括在内。

有效灌溉面积　指具有一定的水源，地块比较平整，灌溉工程或设备已经配套，在一般年景下当年能够进行正常灌溉的耕地面积。

农用化肥施用量　指本年内实际用于农业生产的化肥数量，包括氮肥、磷肥、钾肥和复合肥。化肥施用量要求按折纯量计算数量。折纯量是指把氮肥、磷肥、钾肥分别按含氮、含五氧化二磷、含氧化钾的百分之一百成份进行折算后的数量。复合肥按其所含主要成分折算。

农业机械总动力　指主要用于农、林、牧、渔业的各种动力机械的动力总和。包括耕作机械、排灌机械、收获机械、农用运输机械、植物保护机械、牧业机械、林业机械、渔业机械和其他农业机械〔内燃机按引擎马力折成瓦（特）计算、电动机按功率折成瓦（特）计算〕。不包括专门用于乡、镇、村、组办工业、基本建设、非农业运输、科学试验和教学等非农业生产方面用的动力机械与作业机械。

农林牧渔业劳动力　指全社会直接参加农林牧渔业生产活动的劳动力。

Explanatory Notes on Main Statistical Indicators

Gross Output Value of Agriculture, Forestry, Animal Husbandry and Fishery refers to the total value of products of agriculture, forestry, animal husbandry and fishery, and total value of services in support of agriculture, forestry, animal husbandry and fishery activities. It reflects the total scale and results of agricultural production during a given period.

Gross output value of agriculture is obtained by multiplying the output of each product or by-product by its price, resulting in the output value of each single item. The sum of output values of all products of agriculture, forestry, animal husbandry and fishery and services in support to those industries is then equal to the gross output value of agriculture.

Grain Output refers to the total output in the whole country including grains produced by State farms, collective units, rural households, as well as by farms affiliated to industrial and mining enterprises and other production units. Grain includes rice, wheat, corn, sorghum, millet and other miscellaneous grains as well as tubers and beans. Output of beans refers to dry beans without pods. The output of tubers (sweet potatoes and potatoes, not including taros and cassava) are converted into that of grain at the ratio 4:1, i.e. 4 kilograms of fresh tubers were equivalent to 1 kilogram of grain up to 1963. Since 1964 the ratio for conversion has been 5:1. Tubers supplied as vegetables (such as potatoes) in cities and suburbs are calculated as fresh vegetables and their output is not included in the output of grain. Output of all other grains refers to husked grain.

Output of Oil-bearing Crops refers to the total production of oil-bearing crops of various kinds, including peanuts (dry, in shell), rapeseeds, sesame, sunflower seeds, flax seeds, and other oil-bearing crops. Soybeans, oil-bearing woody plants, and wild oil-bearing crops are not included.

Output of Aquatic Products refers to catches of both artificially cultured and naturally grown aquatic products, including fish, shrimps, crabs and shellfish in sea and inland water as well as seaweed. Freshwater plants are not included.

Output of Pork, Beef, and Mutton refers to the meat of slaughtered hogs, cattle, sheep and goats with head, feet, and offal taken away.

Number of Livestock or Poultry in Stock at Beginning (or End) of Period refers to the total number of large animals, pigs, sheep, fowls, etc. raised by rural cooperative organizations, State farms, rural individuals, government agencies, schools, industrial and mining enterprises, army, and urban residents at the beginning (or end) of the reference period.

Sown Area of Crops refers to area of land sown or transplanted with crops regardless of being in cultivated area or non-cultivated area. Area of land re-sown due to natural disasters is also included.

Irrigated Area refers to area of land that are effectively irrigated, i.e. relatively level land, where there are water sources or complete sets of irrigation facilities to lift and move adequate water for irrigation purpose under normal conditions. Under normal situations, irrigated area is the sum of watered fields and irrigated fields where irrigation systems or equipment have been installed for regular irrigation purpose.

Consumption of Chemical Fertilizers in Agriculture refers to the quantity of chemical fertilizers applied in agriculture in the year, including nitrogenous fertilizer, phosphate fertilizer, potash fertilizer, and compound fertilizer. The consumption of chemical fertilizers is calculated in terms of volume of effective components by means of converting the gross weight of the respective fertilizers into weight containing effective component. Compound fertilizer is converted in regard to its major components.

Total Power of Agricultural Machinery refers to total mechanical power of machinery used in agriculture, forestry, animal husbandry and fishery, including machinery for ploughing, irrigation and drainage, harvesting, transport, plant protection, animal husbandry, forestry and fishery and other agricultural machineries. (For the power of internal combustion engines, it is converted from its horsepower into watts while for electric motors the output power is converted into watts.) Machinery employed for non-agricultural purposes, such as the machines used in township-run and village-run industry, construction, non-agricultural transport, scientific experiments and teaching, are not included. Data are mainly from agricultural machinery agencies.

Labour Force Engaged in Agricultural,Forestry,Animal Husbandry and Fishery refers to the total laborers who are directly engaged in production of agricultural, forestry, animal husbandry and fishery.

14 Fourteen

工　业

Industry

14-1 规模以上工业企业单位数

Number of Industrial Enterprises above Designated Size

单位：个 (unit)

指 标	Item	2007	2008	2009	2010	2011	2012
规模以上工业企业单位数	**Number of Industrial Enterprises above Designated Size**	**2296**	**2676**	**2791**	**2963**	**3687**	**2752**
#国有控股企业	State-holding Industry Enterprises	541	530	523	516	576	470
按轻重工业分	**Grouped by Type of Light and Heavy Industry**						
轻工业	Light Industry	536	578	600	634	842	571
重工业	Heavy Industry	1760	2098	2191	2329	2845	2181
按企业规模分	**Grouped by Scale of Enterprise**						
大型企业	Large Enterprises	25	31	31	30	70	80
中型企业	Medium-sized Enterprises	286	325	340	415	509	633
小型企业	Small Enterprises	1985	2320	2420	2518	2646	1966
微型企业	Micro-enterprises					462	73
按登记注册类型分	**By Status of Registration**						
内资企业	Domestic Funded	2200	2570	2686	2861	3590	2684
国有企业	State-owned Enterprises	362	331	315	309	349	267
集体企业	Collective-owned Enterprises	92	70	64	59	68	29
股份合作企业	Cooperative Enterprises	59	53	49	41	50	25
联营企业	Joint Ownership Enterprises	17	15	13	12	28	18
有限责任公司	Limited Liability Corporations	598	725	820	844	1100	886
股份有限公司	Share-holding Corporations Limited	101	100	100	113	140	111
私营企业	Private Enterprises	965	1267	1308	1469	1793	1313
其他企业	Other Enterprises	6	9	17	14	62	35
港、澳、台商投资企业	Enterprises with Funds from Hong Kong,Macao and Taiwan	46	49	48	51	47	32
外商投资企业	Foreign Funded Enterprises	50	57	57	51	50	36

注：1.规模以上工业统计口径2007—2011年为年主营业务收入500万元及以上的工业企业，2012年为年主营业务收入2000万元及以上工业企业(以下相关表除特殊标注外，均同)。2.企业规模从2011年开始，按国家统计局新制定的《统计上大中小微企业划分办法》执行。

Note:1.The scale above industrial enterprises statistics was the industrial of main business income of 5 million yuan and above in 2007 to 2011. And in 2012 it is the industrial of main business income of 20 million yuan. 2.From 2011,the designated size of industry is executed according to "Statistics issued by the division of the large, medium, small and micro-enterprises" which is the newly established by National Bureau of Statistics.

14-2 按行业分规模以上工业企业单位数

Number of Industrial Enterprises above Designated Size by Sector

单位：个 (unit)

指 标	Item	2007	2008	2009	2010	2011
规模以上工业企业单位数	**Number of Industrial Enterprises above Designated Size**	**2296**	**2676**	**2791**	**2963**	**3687**
采矿业	Mining and Quarring	476	745	760	929	1165
#煤炭开采和洗选业	Mining and Washing of Coal	372	617	652	827	999
黑色金属矿采选业	Mining and Dressing of Ferrous Metals	19	38	29	28	45
有色金属矿采选业	Mining and Dressing of Nonferrous Metals	50	47	30	30	44
非金属矿采选业	Mining and Dressing of Nonmetal Minerals	34	43	49	44	77
制造业	Manufacturing	1615	1706	1798	1814	2267
#农副食品加工业	Processing of Food from Agricultural Products	127	138	150	153	208
食品制造业	Manufacture of Foods	40	50	49	56	78
酒、饮料和精制茶制造业	Manufacture of Beverages	77	92	101	133	182
烟草制品业	Manufacture of Tobacco	7	8	8	3	6
纺织业	Manufacture of Textile	10	11	11	12	16
纺织服装、服饰业	Manufacture of Textile Wearing Apparel, Footware and Caps	6	5	6	7	13
皮革、毛皮、羽毛及其制品和制鞋业	Manufacture of Leather,Furs,Feather and Related Products	1	1	1	2	3
木材加工和木、竹、藤、棕、草制品业	Timber Processing,Manufacture of Wood, Bamboo, Rattan,Palm and Straw Products	52	64	69	69	85
家具制造业	Manufacture of Furniture	2	2	2	5	8
造纸和纸制品业	Manufacture of Paper and Paper Products	34	41	44	41	54
印刷业和记录媒介复制业	Printing,Reproduction of Recording Media	30	28	26	21	28
文教、工美、体育和娱乐用品制造业	Manufacture of Articles For Culture,Education and Sport Activity	3	3	3	3	3
石油加工、炼焦和核燃料加工业	Processing of Petroleum,Coking,Processing of Nuclear Fuel	44	49	45	27	35
化学原料和化学制品制造业	Manufacture of Raw Chemical Materials and Chemical Products	186	173	188	182	220
医药制造业	Manufacture of Medicines	101	98	97	96	107
橡胶制品业	Manufacture of Rubber	9	9	9	12	16
塑料制品业	Manufacture of Plastics	42	49	55	54	67
非金属矿物制品业	Manufacture of Non-metallic Mineral Products	276	299	327	345	457
黑色金属冶炼和压延加工业	Smelting and Pressing of Ferrous Metals	212	210	205	185	182
有色金属冶炼和压延加工业	Smelting and Pressing of Non-ferrous Metals	117	103	101	97	103
金属制品业	Manufacture of Metal Products	25	29	36	38	51
通用设备制造业	Manufacture of General Purpose Machinery	47	54	59	63	96
专用设备制造业	Manufacture of Special Purpose Machinery	34	33	43	39	49
交通运输设备制造业	Manufacture of Transport Equipment	63	67	70	67	82
电气机械和器材制造业	Manufacture of Electrical Equipment and Machinery	33	45	47	58	65
计算机、通信和其他电子设备制造业	Manufacture of Communication Equipment, Computers and Other Electronic Equipment	19	23	25	21	23
仪器仪表制造业	Manufacture of Measuring Instruments and Machinery for Cultural Activity and Office Work	8	11	11	12	14
工艺品及其他制造业	Manufacture of Artwork and Other Manufacturing	9	9	9	11	12
废弃资源综合利用业	Recycling and Disposal of Waste		1	1	2	4
电力、燃气及水的生产和供应业	Production and Distribution of Electric Power, Gas and Water	205	225	233	220	255
电力、热力生产和供应业	Production and Distribution of Electric Power and Heat Power	160	180	188	177	190
燃气生产和供应业	Production and Distribution of Gas	5	6	6	8	8
水的生产和供应业	Production and Distribution of Water	40	39	39	35	57

注：表中数据按国民经济行业分类(GB/T4754—2002)分。

Note:Data in this table is classified by sector of the National Economy (GB/T4754-2002).

14-3 按行业分规模以上工业企业单位数(2012)

Number of Industrial Enterprises above Designated Size by Sector

单位：个 (unit)

指 标	Item	2012
规模以上工业企业单位数	**Number of Industrial Enterprises above Designated Size**	**2752**
采矿业	Mining and Quarring	937
#煤炭开采和洗选业	Mining and Washing of Coal	843
黑色金属矿采选业	Mining and Dressing of Ferrous Metals	33
有色金属矿采选业	Mining and Dressing of Nonferrous Metals	17
非金属矿采选业	Mining and Dressing of Nonmetal Minerals	44
制造业	Manufacturing	1640
#农副食品加工业	Processing of Food from Agricultural Products	139
食品制造业	Manufacture of Foods	49
酒、饮料和精制茶制造业	Manufacture of Beverages	146
烟草制品业	Manufacture of Tobacco	6
纺织业	Manufacture of Textile	10
纺织服装、服饰业	Manufacture of Textile Wearing Apparel, Footware and Caps	7
皮革、毛皮、羽毛及其制品和制鞋业	Manufacture of Leather,Furs,Feather and Related Products	4
木材加工和木、竹、藤、棕、草制品业	Timber Processing,Manufacture of Wood, Bamboo, Rattan,Palm and Straw Products	63
家具制造业	Manufacture of Furniture	7
造纸和纸制品业	Manufacture of Paper and Paper Products	29
印刷业和记录媒介复制业	Printing,Reproduction of Recording Media	11
文教、工美、体育和娱乐用品制造业	Manufacture of Articles For Culture,Education and Sport Activity	5
石油加工、炼焦和核燃料加工业	Processing of Petroleum,Coking,Processing of Nuclear Fuel	31
化学原料和化学制品制造业	Manufacture of Raw Chemical Materials and Chemical Products	156
医药制造业	Manufacture of Medicines	79
橡胶和塑料制品业	Manufacture of Rubber and Plastics	44
非金属矿物制品业	Manufacture of Non-metallic Mineral Products	328
黑色金属冶炼和压延加工业	Smelting and Pressing of Ferrous Metals	193
有色金属冶炼和压延加工业	Smelting and Pressing of Non-ferrous Metals	66
金属制品业	Manufacture of Metal Products	38
通用设备制造业	Manufacture of General Purpose Machinery	35
专用设备制造业	Manufacture of Special Purpose Machinery	35
汽车制造业	Manufacture of Automotive	26
铁路、船舶、航空航天和其他运输设备制造业	Manufacture of Railroad, Marine, Aerospace and Other Transportation Equipment	31
电气机械和器材制造业	Manufacture of Electrical Equipment and Machinery	55
计算机、通信和其他电子设备制造业	Manufacture of Communication Equipment, Computers and Other Electronic Equipment	22
仪器仪表制造业	Manufacture of Measuring Instruments and Machinery for Cultural Activity and Office Work	9
其他制造业	Others	10
废弃资源综合利用业	Recycling and Disposal of Waste	5
金属制品、机械和设备修理业	Metal products, Machinery and Equipment Repair Industry	1
电力、燃气及水的生产和供应业	Production and Distribution of Electric Power,Gas and Water	175
电力、热力生产和供应业	Production and Distribution of Electric Power and Heat Power	153
燃气生产和供应业	Production and Distribution of Gas	8
水的生产和供应业	Production and Distribution of Water	14

注：表中数据按国民经济行业分类(GB/T4754—2011)分。
Note:Data in this table is classified by sector of the National Economy (GB/T4754-2011).

14-4 规模以上工业增加值

Value added of Industry above Designated Size

单位：亿元 (100 million yuan)

指　标	Item	2007	2008	2009	2010	2011	2012	2012年比2011年增长(%) Increase Rate in 2012 over 2011(%)
规模以上工业增加值	**Value added of Industry above Designated Size**	**890.48**	**1051.26**	**1170.29**	**1227.17**	**1723.58**	**2055.46**	**16.2**
#国有控股企业	State-holding Industry	602.51	685.93	732.65	749.55	924.79	1194.83	13.4
#私营企业	Private Enterprises	128.40	177.82	196.08	277.96	465.32	477.19	20.9
按轻重工业分	**Grouped by Type of Light and Heavy Industry**							
轻工业	Light Industry	267.87	302.25	352.38	413.99	563.48	773.04	17.6
重工业	Heavy Industry	622.61	749.01	817.91	813.18	1160.10	1282.42	15.5
按企业规模分	**Grouped by Scale of Enterprise**							
大型企业	Large Enterprises	409.99	429.49	433.21	465.95	640.70	904.47	12.9
中型企业	Medium-sized Enterprises	250.94	278.14	332.02	302.19	412.05	537.78	14.4
小型企业	Small Enterprises	229.55	343.64	405.06	459.03	631.37	600.11	23.5
微型企业	Micro-enterprises					39.46	13.10	12.1
按登记注册类型分	**By Status of Registration**							
国有企业	State-owned Enterprises	375.11	459.98	503.69	356.22	485.22	707.85	13.1
集体企业	Collective-owned Enterprises	6.53	7.75	6.00	6.81	3.09	9.91	42.7
股份合作企业	Cooperative Enterprises	7.56	12.29	5.75	8.35	4.73	10.01	18.8
股份制企业	Share-holding Enterprises	369.48	449.40	516.72	612.56	854.72	889.82	16.1
外商及港澳台商投资企业	Enterprises with Funds from Foreign,Hong Kong, Macao and Taiwan	20.69	26.26	25.47	40.44	41.39	60.42	8.5
其他企业	Other Enterprises	111.11	95.58	112.65	202.80	334.43	377.45	23.2

注：2010年以后工业增加值按收入法计算，增长速度按可比价计算(以下相关表同)。

Note:Value-added of industry above designated size is calculated by income approach and the increase rate is calculated at the comparable scope in 2010(the relative tables in the chapter are the same).

14-5 按行业分规模以上工业增加值

Value added of Industry above Designated Size by Sector

单位：亿元 (100 million yuan)

指 标	Item	2007	2008	2009	2010	2011
规模以上工业增加值	**Value added of Industry above Designated Size**	**890.48**	**1051.26**	**1170.29**	**1227.17**	**1723.58**
采矿业	Mining and Quarring	103.46	153.61	181.10	297.43	486.34
#煤炭开采和洗选业	Mining and Washing of Coal	90.85	129.66	158.48	276.68	441.75
黑色金属矿采选业	Mining and Dressing of Ferrous Metals	2.46	3.57	5.28	5.58	7.71
有色金属矿采选业	Mining and Dressing of Nonferrous Metals	4.00	7.18	2.07	3.28	5.83
非金属矿采选业	Mining and Dressing of Nonmetal Minerals	6.07	13.08	15.05	11.89	31.04
制造业	Manufacturing	576.93	665.32	712.64	721.35	995.21
#农副食品加工业	Processing of Food from Agricultural Products	9.47	11.47	14.22	11.50	23.08
食品制造业	Manufacture of Foods	8.07	10.24	9.42	15.41	14.99
饮料制造业	Manufacture of Beverages	75.21	94.86	112.29	162.79	243.65
烟草制品业	Manufacture of Tobacco	101.59	106.27	116.99	152.62	176.21
纺织业	Manufacture of Textile	1.10	1.07	0.97	1.12	3.11
纺织服装、鞋、帽制造业	Manufacture of Textile Wearing Apparel, Footware,and Caps	0.81	1.06	0.87	0.65	1.99
皮革、毛皮、羽毛(绒)及其制造业	Manufacture of Leather,Furs,Feather and Related Products	0.24	0.18	0.43	0.05	0.02
木材加工及木、竹、藤、棕、草制品业	Timber Processing,Manufacture of Wood, Bamboo, Rattan,Palm, and Straw Products	2.45	4.55	6.73	5.55	13.49
家具制造业	Manufacture of Furniture	0.01	0.01	0.02	1.30	1.45
造纸及纸制品业	Manufacture of Paper and Paper Products	1.66	2.10	4.30	3.81	5.14
印刷业和记录媒介的复制	Printing,Reproduction of Recording Media	3.45	3.20	4.11	6.60	6.62
文教体育用品制造业	Manufacture of Articles For Culture, Education and Sport Activity	0.23	0.21	0.29	0.32	0.40
石油加工、炼焦及核燃料加工业	Processing of Petroleum,Coking,Processing of Nuclear Fuel	10.97	25.68	24.32	13.46	12.34
化学原料及化学制品制造业	Manufacture of Raw Chemical Materials and Chemical Products	68.43	79.07	71.49	58.47	100.62
医药制造业	Manufacture of Medicines	46.04	48.31	59.98	40.50	54.31
橡胶制品业	Manufacture of Rubber	9.67	12.58	14.18	19.12	15.98
塑料制品业	Manufacture of Plastics	3.39	5.20	5.94	4.51	7.39
非金属矿物制品业	Manufacture of Non-metallic Mineral Products	21.08	29.41	37.64	47.86	70.29
黑色金属冶炼及压延加工业	Smelting and Pressing of Ferrous Metals	72.52	87.86	75.94	54.42	67.42
有色金属冶炼及压延加工业	Smelting and Pressing of Non-ferrous Metals	61.70	55.95	58.05	32.92	58.64
金属制品业	Manufacture of Metal Products	8.23	9.72	6.49	7.56	10.41
通用设备制造业	Manufacture of General Purpose Machinery	5.97	11.98	12.75	14.92	23.54
专用设备制造业	Manufacture of Special Purpose Machinery	7.65	7.02	10.66	5.77	7.88
交通运输设备制造业	Manufacture of Transport Equipment	29.87	26.30	29.16	31.50	33.58
电气机械及器材制造业	Manufacture of Electrical Equipment and Machinery	11.29	12.90	14.48	8.66	8.60
通信设备、计算机及其他电子设备制造业	Manufacture of Communication Equipment, Computers and Other Electronic Equipment	8.24	10.46	12.00	8.94	10.87
仪器仪表及文化、办公用机械制造业	Manufacture of Measuring Instruments and Machinery for Cultural Activity and Office Work	3.53	3.22	2.66	1.91	3.05
工艺品及其他制造业	Manufacture of Artwork and Other Manufacturing	4.04	4.43	6.24	9.05	19.46
废弃资源和废旧材料回收加工业	Recycling and Disposal of Waste		…	…	0.07	0.68
电力、燃气及水的生产和供应业	Production and Distribution of Electric Power,Gas and Water	210.08	232.33	276.55	208.40	242.03
#电力、热力的生产和供应业	Production and Distribution of Electric Power and Heat Power	205.06	228.40	272.24	203.60	236.91
燃气生产和供应业	Production and Distribution of Gas	2.16	0.79	0.81	0.67	1.24
水的生产和供应业	Production and Distribution of Water	2.86	3.14	3.49	4.13	3.88

注：表中数据按国民经济行业分类(GB/T4754—2002)分。

Note:Data in this table is classified by sector of the National Economy (GB/T4754-2002).

14–6 按行业分规模以上工业增加值(2012)

Value added of Industry above Designated Size by Sector

单位：亿元 (100 million yuan)

指　标	Item	2012	2012年比2011年增长(%) Increase Rate in 2012 over 2011(%)
规模以上工业增加值	**Value added of Industry above Designated Size**	**2055.46**	**16.2**
采矿业	Mining and Quarring	523.80	18.4
#煤炭开采和洗选业	Mining and Washing of Coal	472.21	18.2
石油和天然气开采业	Extraction of Petroleum and Natural Gas		
黑色金属矿采选业	Mining and Dressing of Ferrous Metals	9.54	43.6
有色金属矿采选业	Mining and Dressing of Nonferrous Metals	3.69	18.1
非金属矿采选业	Mining and Dressing of Nonmetal Minerals	37.77	15.0
开采辅助活动	Support activities for mining	0.58	2.0
制造业	Manufacturing	1230.24	16.8
#农副食品加工业	Processing of Food from Agricultural Products	20.56	10.4
食品制造业	Manufacture of Foods	21.35	10.2
饮料制造业	Manufacture of Beverages	378.82	21.1
烟草制品业	Manufacture of Tobacco	246.89	15.6
纺织业	Manufacture of Textile	0.78	1.1
纺织服装、鞋、帽制造业	Manufacture of Textile Wearing Apparel, Footware,and Caps	1.82	13.6
皮革、毛皮、羽毛(绒)及其制造业	Manufacture of Leather,Furs,Feather and Related Products	1.84	-11.9
木材加工及木、竹、藤、棕、草制品业	Timber Processing,Manufacture of Wood, Bamboo, Rattan,Palm, and Straw Products	15.49	33.1
家具制造业	Manufacture of Furniture	4.27	29.7
造纸及纸制品业	Manufacture of Paper and Paper Products	9.91	17.5
印刷业和记录媒介的复制	Printing,Reproduction of Recording Media	4.60	-5.9
文教体育用品制造业	Manufacture of Articles For Culture,Education and Sport Activity	0.64	12.2
石油加工、炼焦及核燃料加工业	Processing of Petroleum,Coking,Processing of Nuclear Fuel	20.68	14.4
化学原料及化学制品制造业	Manufacture of Raw Chemical Materials and Chemical Products	109.43	7.8
医药制造业	Manufacture of Medicines	52.70	19.2
橡胶和塑料制品业	Manufacture of Rubber and Plastics	16.84	10.0
非金属矿物制品业	Manufacture of Non-metallic Mineral Products	66.34	22.8
黑色金属冶炼及压延加工业	Smelting and Pressing of Ferrous Metals	58.92	15.1
有色金属冶炼及压延加工业	Smelting and Pressing of Non-ferrous Metals	75.20	18.1
金属制品业	Manufacture of Metal Products	17.31	20.0
通用设备制造业	Manufacture of General Purpose Machinery	12.47	10.1
专用设备制造业	Manufacture of Special Purpose Machinery	9.57	30.3
汽车制造业	Manufacture of Automotive	14.81	12.8
铁路、船舶、航空航天和其他运输设备制造业	Manufacture of Railroad, Marine, Aerospace and Other Transportation Equipment	23.92	17.5
电气机械及器材制造业	Manufacture of Electrical Equipment and Machinery	10.75	7.4
通信设备、计算机及其他电子设备制造业	Manufacture of Communication Equipment, Computers and Other Electronic Equipment	14.52	29.6
仪器仪表及文化、办公用机械制造业	Manufacture of Measuring Instruments and Machinery for Cultural Activity and Office Work	3.75	-1.5
其他制造业	Others	14.33	6.4
废弃资源和废旧材料回收加工业	Recycling and Disposal of Waste	0.57	116.2
金属制品、机械和设备修理业	Metal products, Machinery and Equipment Repair Industry	1.17	57.0
电力、燃气及水的生产和供应业	Production and Distribution of Electric Power,Gas and Water	301.42	11.6
#电力、热力的生产和供应业	Production and Distribution of Electric Power and Heat Power	295.39	9.8
燃气生产和供应业	Production and Distribution of Gas	1.57	23.7
水的生产和供应业	Production and Distribution of Water	4.46	4.9

注：表中数据按国民经济行业分类(GB/T4754-2011)分。
Note:Data in this table is classified by sector of the National Economy (GB/T4754-2011).

14-7 规模以上工业总产值

Gross Output Value of Industry above Designated Size

单位：亿元 (100 million yuan)

指 标	Item	2007	2008	2009	2010	2011	2012
规模以上工业总产值	**Gross Output Value of Industry above Designated Size**	**2520.36**	**3111.13**	**3426.69**	**4206.37**	**5794.83**	**6544.02**
#国有控股企业	State-holding Enterprises	1607.15	1878.69	2094.77	2429.41	2987.30	3284.31
按轻重工业分	**Grouped by Type of Light and Heavy Industry**						
轻工业	Light Industry	527.16	641.78	758.14	914.19	1253.14	1389.71
重工业	Heavy Industry	1993.20	2469.34	2668.55	3292.18	4541.70	5154.31
按企业规模分	**Grouped by Scale of Enterprise**						
大型企业	Large Enterprises	1065.56	1236.25	1318.12	1523.30	2213.39	2769.32
中型企业	Medium-sized Enterprises	764.93	982.98	1122.55	1349.06	1585.19	2013.99
小型企业	Small Enterprises	689.87	891.90	986.02	1334.01	1894.07	1760.10
微型企业	Micro-enterprises					102.18	0.61
按登记注册类型分	**By Status of Registration**						
内资企业	Domestic Funded	2440.98	2995.35	3300.03	4048.82	5591.28	6375.58
国有企业	State-owned Enterprises	1055.98	1068.74	1026.67	1212.22	1504.98	1812.38
集体企业	Collective-owned Enterprises	18.21	17.43	14.62	23.28	30.39	32.78
股份合作企业	Cooperative Enterprises	22.68	28.00	22.56	17.22	45.45	49.79
联营企业	Joint Ownership Enterprises	8.69	6.99	6.95	6.18	19.35	19.71
有限责任公司	Limited Liability Corporations	685.00	1003.27	1287.94	1501.31	2012.22	2389.65
股份有限公司	Share-holding Corporations Limited	260.52	331.62	378.35	440.28	620.75	470.07
私营企业	Private Enterprises	388.90	536.98	555.24	839.58	1334.71	1555.54
其他企业	Other Enterprises	1.00	2.34	7.69	8.74	23.42	45.66
港、澳、台商投资企业	Enterprises with Funds from Hong Kong, Macco and Taiwan	28.07	39.38	44.42	57.93	74.70	58.51
外商投资企业	Foreign Funded Enterprises	51.32	76.39	82.25	99.62	128.86	109.93

14-8 按行业分规模以上工业总产值

Gross Output Value of Industry above Designated Size by Sector

单位：亿元 (100 million yuan)

指 标	Item	2007	2008	2009	2010	2011
规模以上工业总产值	**Gross Output Value of Industry above Designated Size**	**2520.36**	**3111.13**	**3426.69**	**4206.37**	**5794.83**
采矿业	Mining and Quarring	212.54	399.32	436.46	704.13	1169.11
#煤炭开采和洗选业	Mining and Washing of Coal	183.82	353.76	403.15	655.72	1062.53
黑色金属矿采选业	Mining and Dressing of Ferrous Metals	4.09	6.66	6.09	7.52	15.69
有色金属矿采选业	Mining and Dressing of Nonferrous Metals	11.62	22.10	5.82	12.00	23.06
非金属矿采选业	Mining and Dressing of Nonmetal Minerals	12.74	16.82	21.39	28.89	67.83
制造业	Manufacturing	1666.04	1998.82	2135.40	2554.94	3597.34
#农副食品加工业	Processing of Food from Agricultural Products	46.10	54.54	69.20	83.13	146.66
食品制造业	Manufacture of Foods	26.95	41.59	40.19	56.53	81.91
酒、饮料和精制茶制造业	Manufacture of Beverages	103.64	150.79	179.04	227.04	333.38
烟草制品业	Manufacture of Tobacco	139.99	164.23	183.12	208.65	253.47
纺织业	Manufacture of Textile	4.72	4.38	3.69	5.08	8.86
纺织服装、服饰业	Manufacture of Textile Wearing Apparel,Footware and Caps	2.83	3.44	3.48	3.63	5.29
皮革、毛皮、羽毛及其制造业和制鞋业	Manufacture of Leather,Furs,Feather and Related Products	0.69	0.94	1.35	1.17	1.95
木材加工和木、竹、藤、棕、草制品业	Timber Processing,Manufacture of Wood, Bamboo, Rattan,Palm and Straw Products	8.81	16.56	23.80	26.51	53.06
家具制造业	Manufacture of Furniture	0.08	0.13	0.19	1.63	8.44
造纸和纸制品业	Manufacture of Paper and Paper Products	6.10	11.05	17.16	24.36	42.61
印刷和记录媒介复制业	Printing,Reproduction of Recording Media	10.70	10.09	12.60	13.13	14.96
文教、工美、体育和娱乐用品制造业	Manufacture of Articles For Culture, Education and Sport Activity	0.64	0.71	0.88	1.09	1.31
石油加工、炼焦和核燃料加工业	Processing of Petroleum,Coking,Processing of Nuclear Fuel	31.90	62.11	63.83	67.18	78.48
化学原料和化学制品制造业	Manufacture of Raw Chemical Materials and Chemical Products	244.15	313.02	283.34	336.03	495.93
医药制造业	Manufacture of Medicines	109.60	119.46	150.87	180.61	238.29
橡胶制品业	Manufacture of Rubber	48.96	58.76	67.03	85.09	113.97
塑料制品业	Manufacture of Plastics	13.42	18.18	22.73	23.43	40.15
非金属矿物制品业	Manufacture of Non-metallic Mineral Products	76.37	104.71	134.71	182.22	314.43
黑色金属冶炼和压延加工业	Smelting and Pressing of Ferrous Metals	288.80	364.09	330.16	408.41	542.78
有色金属冶炼和压延加工业	Smelting and Pressing of Non-ferrous Metals	218.44	177.54	171.13	219.70	303.56
金属制品业	Manufacture of Metal Products	35.10	59.37	47.86	42.33	51.20
通用设备制造业	Manufacture of General Purpose Machinery	22.42	25.22	25.86	32.62	63.39
专用设备制造业	Manufacture of Special Purpose Machinery	28.31	23.91	31.99	36.00	40.98
交通运输设备制造业	Manufacture of Transport Equipment	95.12	109.00	143.13	144.21	183.32
电气机械和器材制造业	Manufacture of Electrical Equipment and Machinery	50.82	57.70	65.54	75.45	97.52
计算机、通信和其他电子设备制造业	Manufacture of Communication Equipment, Computers and Other Electronic Equipment	25.98	30.18	38.44	43.00	48.72
仪器仪表制造业	Manufacture of Measuring Instruments and Machinery for Cultural Activity and Office Work	6.68	6.12	8.49	9.24	11.17
工艺品及其他制造业	Manufacture of Artwork and Other Manufacturing	18.43	10.86	15.51	17.35	17.41
废弃资源综合利用业	Recycling and Disposal of Waste		0.09	0.09	0.12	4.11
电力、燃气及水的生产和供应业	Production and Distribution of Electric Power,Gas and Water	641.78	712.99	854.84	947.31	1028.39
#电力、热力的生产和供应业	Production and Distribution of Electric Power and Heat Power	623.35	687.92	832.87	913.38	987.63
燃气生产和供应业	Production and Distribution of Gas	11.98	17.41	13.69	24.19	27.79
水的生产和供应业	Production and Distribution of Water	6.46	7.65	8.27	9.74	12.97

注：表中数据按国民经济行业分类(GB/T4754-2002)分。

Note:Data in this table is classified by sector of the National Economy (GB/T4754-2002).

14–9 按行业分规模以上工业总产值(2012)

Gross Output Value of Industry above Designated Size by Sector

单位：亿元 (100 million yuan)

指 标	Item	2012
规模以上工业总产值	**Gross Output Value of Industry above Designated Size**	**6544.02**
采矿业	Mining and Quarring	1352.90
#煤炭开采和洗选业	Mining and Washing of Coal	1244.16
黑色金属矿采选业	Mining and Dressing of Ferrous Metals	20.22
有色金属矿采选业	Mining and Dressing of Nonferrous Metals	16.52
非金属矿采选业	Mining and Dressing of Nonmetal Minerals	72.00
制造业	Manufacturing	4017.15
#农副食品加工业	Processing of Food from Agricultural Products	146.22
食品制造业	Manufacture of Foods	69.48
酒、饮料和精制茶制造业	Manufacture of Beverages	438.60
烟草制品业	Manufacture of Tobacco	316.71
纺织业	Manufacture of Textile	5.04
纺织服装、服饰业	Manufacture of Textile Wearing Apparel, Footware and Caps	4.88
皮革、毛皮、羽毛及其制造业和制鞋业	Manufacture of Leather,Furs,Feather and Related Products	15.66
木材加工和木、竹、藤、棕、草制品业	Timber Processing,Manufacture of Wood, Bamboo, Rattan,Palm and Straw Products	71.01
家具制造业	Manufacture of Furniture	11.20
造纸和纸制品业	Manufacture of Paper and Paper Products	30.79
印刷和记录媒介复制业	Printing,Reproduction of Recording Media	12.15
文教、工美、体育和娱乐用品制造业	Manufacture of Articles For Culture,Education and Sport Activity	2.84
石油加工、炼焦和核燃料加工业	Processing of Petroleum,Coking,Processing of Nuclear Fuel	105.81
化学原料和化学制品制造业	Manufacture of Raw Chemical Materials and Chemical Products	555.67
医药制造业	Manufacture of Medicines	227.33
橡胶和塑料制品业	Manufacture of Rubber and Plastics	141.23
非金属矿物制品业	Manufacture of Non-metallic Mineral Products	362.09
黑色金属冶炼和压延加工业	Smelting and Pressing of Ferrous Metals	576.05
有色金属冶炼和压延加工业	Smelting and Pressing of Non-ferrous Metals	371.57
金属制品业	Manufacture of Metal Products	67.76
通用设备制造业	Manufacture of General Purpose Machinery	47.32
专用设备制造业	Manufacture of Special Purpose Machinery	39.20
汽车制造业	Manufacture of Automotive	89.57
铁路、船舶、航空航天和其他运输设备制造业	Manufacture of Transport Equipment	126.67
电气机械和器材制造业	Manufacture of Electrical Equipment and Machinery	86.95
计算机、通信和其他电子设备制造业	Manufacture of Communication Equipment, Computers and Other Electronic Equipment	63.89
仪器仪表制造业	Manufacture of Measuring Instruments and Machinery for Cultural Activity and Office Work	9.91
其他制造业	Manufacture of Artwork and Other Manufacturing	17.77
废弃资源综合利用业	Recycling and Disposal of Waste	3.30
金属制品、机械和设备修理业	Metal products, Machinery and Equipment Repair Industry	0.49
电力、燃气及水的生产和供应业	Production and Distribution of Electric Power,Gas and Water	1173.97
#电力、热力的生产和供应业	Production and Distribution of Electric Power and Heat Power	1134.82
燃气生产和供应业	Production and Distribution of Gas	29.41
水的生产和供应业	Production and Distribution of Water	9.74

注：表中数据按国民经济行业分类(GB/T4754–2011)分。
Note:Data in this table is classified by sector of the National Economy (GB/T4754-2011).

14-10 规模以上工业企业主要经济指标

Major Economic Indicators of Industrial Enterprises above Designated Size

指　　标	Item	2007	2008	2009	2010	2011	2012
固定资产净值年平均余额(亿元)	Average Balance of Net Value of Fixed Assets (100 million yuan)	1476.49	1645.22	2535.38	2653.16	2721.62	2953.25
流动资产年平均余额(亿元)	Average Balance of Circulating Funds (100 million yuan)	1188.62	1485.62	1716.85	2015.98	2480.37	2932.98
主营业务收入(亿元)	Revenue from Principal Business (100 million yuan)	2430.62	2922.35	3234.59	3926.01	5290.90	5966.52
利税总额(亿元)	Total Profits and Taxes (100 million yuan)	403.49	453.53	470.60	671.39	924.04	1172.15
#利润	Total Profits	174.41	181.83	191.73	317.63	464.89	627.02
产值利税率(%)	Ratio of Pre-Tax Profit to Output Value(%)	16.01	14.58	13.73	15.96	16.78	17.91
资金利税率(%)	Ratio of Pre-Tax Profit to Assets(%)	15.14	14.49	10.31	12.62	17.76	19.91
销售利税率(%)	Ratio of Pre-Tax Profit to Sales(%)	16.60	15.52	14.55	17.10	16.99	19.29
资本保值增值率(%)	Increment Ratio of Capital(%)	114.86	124.99	106.87	125.32	127.96	125.65
总资产贡献率(%)	Ratio of Total Assets to Industrial Output Value(%)	12.89	12.96	10.69	12.84	14.13	15.97
资产负债率(%)	Asset-Liability Ratio(%)	64.46	66.28	67.00	64.85	64.45	64.90
流动资产周转次数(次/年)	Number of Times of Turnover of Circulating Fund(times/year)	2.04	1.92	1.88	1.75	1.92	1.89
成本费用利润率(%)	Ratio of After-tax Profits to Cost and Expenses(%)	8.10	6.42	6.56	9.04	9.63	11.89
产销率(%)	Proportion of Industrial Products Sold(%)	96.68	95.36	94.8	95.44	95.01	94.30

14-11 大中型工业企业主要经济指标

Major Economic Indicators of Large and Medium-sized Industrial Enterprises

指　　标	Item	2007	2008	2009	2010	2011	2012
固定资产净值年平均余额(亿元)	Average Balance of Net Value of Fixed Assets (100 million yuan)	1179.16	1310.40	1643.79	2009.61	2084.76	2481.32
流动资产年平均余额(亿元)	Average Balance of Circulating Funds (100 million yuan)	939.37	1148.78	1317.62	1526.28	1636.84	2297.86
主营业务收入(亿元)	Revenue from Principal Business (100 million yuan)	1779.30	2123.08	2366.97	2752.96	3583.56	4484.76
利税总额(亿元)	Total Profits and Taxes(100 million yuan)	343.17	361.47	390.73	516.99	746.51	981.36
#利润	Total Profits	154.16	146.13	166.30	240.89	376.07	520.55
资本保值增值率(%)	Increment Ratio of Capital(%)	115.99	120.58	104.78	122.88	129.90	119.19
总资产贡献率(%)	Ratio of Total Assets to Industrial Output Value(%)	13.36	17.21	11.00	12.72	14.84	16.33
资产负债率(%)	Asset-Liability Ratio(%)	63.99	65.81	67.80	65.46	64.91	65.40
流动资产周转次数(次/年)	Number of Times of Turnover of Circulating Fund(times/year)	1.89	1.85	1.80	1.63	1.76	1.81
成本费用利润率(%)	Ratio of After-tax Profits to Cost and Expenses(%)	9.90	7.76	7.92	9.88	11.56	13.29
产销率(%)	Proportion of Products Sold(%)	97.20	95.67	95.65	96.01	95.22	94.42

14-12 规模以上工业主要产品产量

Output of Major Industrial Products above Designated Size

单位：万吨 (10000 tons)

产品名称	Item	2007	2008	2009	2010	2011	2012
原煤	Coal	10864.18	11798.46	10001.00	12656.00	14014.80	15030.94
粗钢	Steel	349.36	345.64	343.10	360.48	434.01	531.27
成品钢材	Steel Products	328.14	337.52	337.62	391.04	462.77	560.22
铁合金	Iron Alloy	178.87	156.62	220.87	208.18	263.90	309.68
铝	Aluminium	75.07	58.15	80.27	88.79	90.36	104.35
氧化铝	Aluminum Oxide	128.27	144.28	136.91	134.84	211.03	270.04
铝材	Aluminium Material	1.19	1.33	1.42	1.49	13.16	11.70
磷矿石	Phosphorite Mineral	1198.83	1317.18	1360.66	1579.21	2084.18	2281.95
生铁	Pig Iron	342.61	331.01	374.82	366.65	482.35	552.93
农用化肥	Chemical Fertilizer	321.84	262.21	347.28	384.92	364.66	503.82
轮胎外胎(万条)	Tires(10000 units)	443.90	457.29	517.21	558.59	536.77	622.78
水泥	Cement	1943.10	2048.94	2664.78	3694.84	5250.89	6100.45
发电量(亿千瓦小时)	Electricity(100 million kwh)	1166.32	1192.08	1363.09	1358.69	1359.01	1548.44
#水电	Hydropower	340.62	380.86	400.88	389.65	334.66	511.65
煤气生产量(亿立方米)	Gas Production (100 million cu.m)	59.64	64.19	65.18	67.81	84.15	98.63
卷烟(万箱)	Cigarettes(10000 cases)	220.71	226.74	232.24	239.24	245.23	249.35
饮料酒(万千升)	Alcohol Beverages(10000 kiloliters)	35.87	41.65	41.35	48.72	61.80	67.14
#白酒	White Spirit	14.57	18.35	13.79	16.04	25.49	26.83
食用植物油	Edible Vegetable Oil	8.79	5.50	11.20	10.22	12.23	23.09
中成药	Traditional Chinese Medicine	4.65	4.72	4.58	5.00	4.92	5.74
家用电冰箱(万台)	Household Refrigerators (10000 units)	132.24	143.81	168.16	196.35	169.54	159.04
彩色电视机(万部)	Color TV Sets(10000 units)	76.21	79.25	72.56	66.93	77.87	90.61

注：2008年及以前原煤产量为全社会口径。

Note:Before 2008,output of Coal refered to the statistical coverage of the whole province.

14-13 规模以上工业企业主要经济指标(2012)

单位：亿元

指 标	Item	企业单位数(个) Number of Enterprises (unit)	工业总产值 Total Output Value of Industry
总 计	**Total**	**2752**	**6544.02**
#国有控股企业	State-holding Enterprises	470	3284.31
#农村工业	Rural Industry	88	141.98
按登记注册类型分	**Goroupеd by Status of Registration**		
内资企业	Domestic-funded Enterprises	2684	6375.58
国有企业	State-owned Industry	267	1812.38
中央企业	Central Industry	47	815.61
地方企业	Local Industry	220	996.77
集体企业	Collective-owned Industry	29	32.78
股份合作企业	Cooperative Enterprises	25	49.79
联营企业	Joint Ownership Enterprises	18	19.71
有限责任公司	Limited Liability Corporations	886	2389.65
股份有限公司	Share-holding Enterprises	111	470.07
私营企业	Private Enterprises	1313	1555.54
其他企业	Others Enterprises	35	45.66
港、澳、台商投资企业	Enterprises with Funds from Hong kong, Macao and Taiwan	32	58.51
外商投资企业	Foreign Funded Enterprises	36	109.93
按轻重工业分	**Grouped by Light and Heavy Industry**		
轻工业	Light Industry	571	1389.71
重工业	Heavy Industry	2181	5154.31
按企业规模分	**Grouped by Scale of Enterprise**		
大型企业	Large Enterprises	80	2769.32
中型企业	Medium-sized Enterprises	633	2013.99
小型企业	Small Enterprises	1966	1760.10
微型企业	Micro-enterprises	73	0.61

Main Economic Indicators of Industrial Enterprises above Designated Size

(100 million yuan)

工业增加值 Value-Added of Industry	资产合计 Total Assets	主营业务收入 Revenue from Principal Business	利税总额 Total Profits and Taxes	#利润总额 Total Profits
2055.46	**8302.29**	**5966.52**	**1172.15**	**627.02**
1194.83	5320.52	3172.91	729.50	359.59
24.99	139.14	119.12	35.91	19.63
1995.04	8048.10	5822.97	1155.50	617.06
707.85	3256.36	1735.42	384.64	241.05
318.55	1467.90	818.05	52.22	17.80
389.30	1788.47	917.37	332.42	223.25
9.91	12.14	28.68	2.64	1.47
10.01	42.65	30.28	6.22	3.30
5.64	36.89	19.54	2.95	2.51
585.73	2563.88	2238.56	436.18	178.11
184.42	775.24	412.44	74.55	44.83
477.19	1321.87	1318.93	241.16	141.98
14.29	39.07	39.12	7.15	3.82
19.76	99.71	53.75	7.28	4.51
40.66	154.48	89.80	9.37	5.46
773.04	1458.24	1299.99	608.19	307.74
1282.42	6844.05	4666.53	563.96	319.28
904.47	4119.06	2716.32	684.21	336.85
537.78	2726.05	1768.44	297.15	183.70
600.11	1446.75	1481.72	190.95	106.64
13.10	10.43	0.04	-0.16	-0.16

14-14 规模以上工业企业分行业主要经济指标(2012)

单位：亿元

指 标	Item	企业单位数(个) Number of Enterprises (unit)
总 计	**Total**	**2752**
采矿业	Mining and Quarrying	937
#煤炭开采和洗选业	Mining and Washing of Coal	843
黑色金属矿采选业	Mining and Dressing of Ferrous Metals	33
有色金属矿采选业	Mining and Dressing of Nonferrous Metals	17
非金属矿采选业	Mining and Dressing of Nonmetal Minerals	44
制造业	Manufacturing	1640
农副食品加工业	Processing of Food from Agricultural Products	139
食品制造业	Manufacture of Foods	49
酒、饮料和精制茶制造业	Manufacture of Beverages	146
#白酒制造	Manufacture of Liquors	77
烟草制品业	Manufacture of Tobacco	6
纺织业	Manufacture of Textile	10
纺织服装、服饰业	Manufacture of Textile Wearing Apparel,Footware and Caps	7
皮革、毛皮、羽毛及其制品和制鞋业	Manufacture of Leather,Furs,Feather and Related Products	4
木材加工和木、竹、藤、棕、草制品业	Timber Processing, Manufacture of Wood, Bamboo, Rattan,Palm and Straw Products	63
家具制造业	Manufacture of Furniture	7
造纸和纸制品业	Manufacture of Paper and Paper Products	29
印刷和记录媒介复制业	Printing,Reproduction of Recording Media	11
文教、工美、体育和娱乐用品制造业	Manufacture of Articles For Culture,Education and Sport Activity	5
石油加工、炼焦和核燃料加工业	Processing of Petroleum, Coking,Processing of Nuclear Fuel	31
化学原料和化学制品制造业	Manufacture of Raw Chemical Materials and Chemical Products	156
医药制造业	Manufacture of Medicines	79
橡胶和塑料制品业	Manufacture of Rubber and Plastics	44
非金属矿物制品业	Manufacture of Non-metallic Mineral Products	328
黑色金属冶炼和压延加工业	Smelting and Pressing of Ferrous Metals	193
有色金属冶炼和压延加工业	Smelting and Pressing of Non-ferrous Metals	66
金属制品业	Manufacture of Metal Products	38
通用设备制造业	Manufacture of General Purpose Machinery	35
专用设备制造业	Manufacture of Special Purpose Machinery	35
汽车制造业	Manufacture of Automotive	26
铁路、船舶、航空航天和其他运输设备制造业	Manufacture of Railroad, Marine, Aerospace and Other Transportation Equipment	31
电气机械和器材制造业	Manufacture of Electrical Equipment and Machinery	55
计算机、通信和其他电子设备制造业	Manufacture of Communication Equipment, Computers and Other Electronic Equipment	22
仪器仪表制造业	Manufacture of Measuring Instruments and Machinery for Cultural Activity and Office Work	9
其他制造业	Others	10
废弃资源综合利用业	Recycling and Disposal of Waste	5
金属制品、机械和设备修理业	Metal products, Machinery and Equipment Repair Industry	1
电力、燃气及水的生产和供应业	Production and Distribution of Electric Power,Gas and Water	175
电力、热力生产和供应业	Production and Distribution of Electric Power and Heat Power	153
#电力生产	Production of Electric Power	70
电力供应	Distribution of Electric Power	83
燃气生产和供应业	Production and Distribution of Gas	8
水的生产和供应业	Production and Distribution of Water	14

Main Economic Indicators of Industrial Enterprises above Designated Size by Sector

(100 million yuan)

工业总产值 Total Output Value of Industry	工业增加值 Value-Added of Industry	资产合计 Total Assets	主营业务收入 Revenue from Principal Business	利税总额 Total Profits and Taxes	#利润总额 Total Profits
6544.02	**2055.46**	**8302.29**	**5966.52**	**1172.15**	**627.02**
1352.90	523.80	1597.89	1093.05	277.93	161.35
1244.16	472.21	1525.47	994.69	248.43	141.28
20.22	9.54	13.74	18.81	3.73	1.68
16.52	3.69	12.63	14.34	3.93	2.73
72.00	37.77	46.05	65.21	21.83	15.66
4017.15	1230.24	4403.13	3733.53	793.82	420.04
146.22	20.56	56.01	137.14	8.62	6.26
69.48	21.35	39.30	66.73	15.79	12.03
438.60	378.82	724.10	436.89	302.39	211.83
379.63	354.31	682.74	378.69	291.00	203.96
316.71	246.89	234.68	305.07	225.58	42.21
5.04	0.78	7.17	4.23	-0.08	-0.20
4.88	1.82	2.84	4.44	0.19	0.14
15.66	1.84	8.65	30.26	1.11	0.62
71.01	15.49	25.33	67.18	6.36	2.21
11.20	4.27	4.91	9.99	2.14	1.69
30.79	9.91	42.25	30.85	3.03	1.82
12.15	4.60	15.40	10.20	3.02	2.35
2.84	0.64	1.08	2.01	0.14	0.06
105.80	20.68	104.03	85.72	8.37	4.82
555.67	109.43	867.03	575.97	55.99	42.10
227.33	52.70	194.51	170.81	40.28	25.55
141.23	16.84	100.68	106.04	7.19	4.19
362.09	66.34	440.17	310.69	25.44	11.41
576.05	58.92	370.06	534.84	12.21	1.32
371.57	75.20	468.91	316.93	40.05	26.37
67.76	17.31	78.47	65.15	3.98	1.50
47.32	12.47	54.35	36.09	5.71	4.46
39.20	9.57	52.83	35.36	3.08	2.33
89.57	14.81	87.61	110.65	6.94	2.95
126.67	23.92	250.08	122.54	5.13	3.58
86.95	10.75	54.23	71.18	4.44	3.08
63.89	14.52	63.24	58.28	3.96	3.33
9.91	3.75	14.14	8.00	1.52	1.03
17.77	14.33	39.95	16.83	1.15	0.94
3.30	0.57	1.07	2.97	0.09	0.01
0.49	1.17	0.06	0.49	0.00	0.00
1173.97	301.42	2301.27	1139.94	100.40	45.64
1134.82	295.39	2210.89	1102.41	98.82	44.83
438.24	169.75	1569.39	410.66	71.06	40.61
696.58	124.11	641.50	691.75	27.76	4.22
29.41	1.57	41.98	29.49	0.99	0.74
9.74	4.46	48.40	8.03	0.59	0.07

14-15 规模以上国有控股工业企业主要经济指标(2012)

单位：亿元

指标	Item	企业单位数(个) Number of Enterprises (unit)
总计	**Total**	**470**
按轻重工业分	**Grouped by Type of Light and Heavy Industry**	
轻工业	Light Industry	75
重工业	Heavy Industry	395
按企业规模分	**Grouped by Scale of Enterprise**	
大型企业	Large Enterprises	55
中型企业	Medium-sized Enterprises	193
小型企业	Small Enterprises	211
微型企业	Micro-enterprises	11
按工业行业分	**Grouped by Industrial Sector**	
采矿业	Mining and Quarrying	73
#煤炭开采和洗选业	Mining and Washing of Coal	64
有色金属矿采选业	Mining and Processing of Nonferrous Metal Ores	3
非金属矿采选业	Mining and Processing of Nonmetal Ores	6
制造业	Manufacturing	258
#农副食品加工业	Processing of Food from Agricultural Products	11
食品制造业	Manufacture of Foods	6
酒、饮料和精制茶制造业	Manufacture of Wine,Soft drinks and Refined tea	11
烟草制品业	Manufacture of Tobacco	4
纺织业	Manufacture of Textile	1
纺织服装、服饰业	Manufacture of Textile Wearing Apparel,Footware and Caps	2
皮革、毛皮、羽毛及其制品和制鞋业	Manufacture of Leather, Fur, Feathers and other Products and Footwear	1
木材加工和木、竹、藤、棕、草制品业	Timber Processing , Bamboo , Cane , Palm Fiber and Straw Products	6
造纸和纸制品业	Manufacture of Paper and Paper Products	2
印刷和记录媒介复制业	Printing,Reproduction of Recording Media	3
文教、工美、体育和娱乐用品制造业	Manufacture of Articles For Culture, Education and Sport Activity	1
石油加工、炼焦和核燃料加工业	Processing of Petroleum,Coking,Processing of Nuclear Fuel	1
化学原料和化学制品制造业	Manufacture of Raw Chemical Materials and Chemical Products	41
医药制造业	Manufacture of Medicines	11
橡胶和塑料制品业	Manufacture of Rubber and Plastics	5
非金属矿物制品业	Manufacture of Non-metallic Mineral Products	37
黑色金属冶炼和压延加工业	Smelting and Pressing of Ferrous Metals	16
有色金属冶炼和压延加工业	Smelting and Pressing of Non-ferrous Metals	11
金属制品业	Manufacture of Metal Products	7
通用设备制造业	Manufacture of General Purpose Machinery	12
专用设备制造业	Manufacture of Special Purpose Machinery	8
汽车制造业	Manufacture of Automotive	9
铁路、船舶、航空航天和其他运输设备制造业	Manufacture of Railroad, Marine, Aerospace and Other Transportation Equipment	26
电气机械和器材制造业	Manufacture of Electrical Equipment and Machinery	5
计算机、通信和其他电子设备制造业	Manufacture of Communication Equipment, Computers and Other Electronic Equipment	15
仪器仪表制造业	Manufacture of Measuring Instruments and Machinery for Cultural Activity and Office.Work	1
其他制造业	Others	5
电力、燃气及水的生产和供应业	Production and Distribution of Electric Power,Gas and Water	139
#电力、热力的生产和供应业	Production and Distribution of Electric Power and Heat Power	126
燃气生产和供应业	Production and Distribution of Gas	3
水的生产和供应业	Production and Distribution of Water	10

Major Economic Indicators of State-controlled Industrial Enterprises above Designated Size

(100 million yuan)

工业总产值 Total Output Value of Industry	资产合计 Total Assets	主营业务收入 Revenue from Principal Business	利税总额 Total Profits and Taxes	#利润总额 Total Profits
3284.31	**5320.52**	**3172.91**	**729.50**	**359.59**
710.15	908.55	714.19	497.20	236.39
2574.16	4411.98	2458.72	232.30	123.20
2334.42	3666.77	2332.80	629.71	304.59
734.00	1368.36	657.07	78.55	44.20
215.88	285.25	183.04	21.24	10.80
	0.14			
353.49	692.13	282.22	72.03	38.27
332.27	674.84	262.71	67.19	35.02
5.81	4.56	5.75	2.11	1.61
15.41	12.72	13.76	2.74	1.64
1852.46	2559.41	1840.69	564.21	278.82
10.57	5.82	9.62	0.74	0.54
6.41	8.86	5.43	0.66	0.44
278.80	569.45	304.76	264.09	189.60
307.64	199.23	295.94	222.79	40.44
0.88	0.45	0.57	0.05	0.00
3.78	2.38	3.42	0.15	0.11
11.10	6.99	26.09	0.82	0.51
7.36	2.59	6.72	0.42	0.10
	27.91	6.12	-0.40	-0.77
	7.53	4.34	1.40	1.09
	0.16	0.25	0.02	0.01
	24.90	20.55	1.79	1.15
	715.95	413.40	40.42	31.20
	15.74	17.65	4.93	3.41
	68.48	68.28	4.15	2.14
	79.27	49.74	3.27	1.78
	227.52	239.44	-2.86	-5.37
	138.28	90.37	4.48	1.06
	40.75	40.29	1.40	-0.03
	22.70	17.23	2.53	2.12
	24.24	8.44	1.37	0.98
	40.88	32.98	1.90	0.63
	230.67	105.72	4.09	2.89
	10.39	21.78	1.20	0.70
	51.78	34.92	3.46	3.07
	3.50	1.96	0.47	0.29
	32.97	14.68	0.85	0.73
	2068.99	1050.00	93.26	42.50
	2043.77	1043.99	92.98	42.55
	4.33	1.63	-0.20	-0.25
	20.89	4.38	0.48	0.20

14-16 规模以上集体工业企业主要经济指标(2012)

单位：万元

指 标	Item	企业单位数 (个) Number of Enterprises (unit)
总 计	**Total**	**29**
#亏损企业	Loss Making Enterprise	6
按轻重工业分	**Grouped by Type of Light and Heavy Industry**	
轻工业	Light Industry	3
重工业	Heavy Industry	26
按企业规模分	**Grouped by Size of Enterprise**	
中型企业	Medium-sized Enterprises	9
小型企业	Small Enterprises	19
微型企业	Micro-enterprises	1
按工业行业分	**Grouped by Industrial Sector**	
采矿业	Mining and Quarrying	11
#煤炭开采和洗选业	Mining and Washing of Coal	7
黑色金属矿采选业	Mining and Processing of Ferrous Metal Ores	4
制造业	Manufacturing	16
#食品制造业	Manufacture of Foods	1
皮革、毛皮、羽毛及其制品和制鞋业	Manufacture of Leather, Fur, Feathers and other Products and Footwear	1
造纸和纸制品业	Manufacture of Paper and Paper Products	1
非金属矿物制品业	Manufacture of Non-metallic Mineral Products	5
黑色金属冶炼和压延加工业	Smelting and Pressing of Ferrous Metals	4
有色金属冶炼和压延加工业	Smelting and Pressing of Non-ferrous Metals	1
金属制品业	Manufacture of Metal Products	2
汽车制造业	Manufacture of Automotive	1
电力、燃气及水的生产和供应业	Production and Distribution of ElectricPower,Gas and Water	2
#电力、热力的生产和供应业	Production and Distribution of Electric Power and Heat Power	2

Main Economic Indicators of All Collective-owned Industrial Enterprises above Designated Size

(10000 yuan)

工业总产值 Total Output Value of Industry	资产合计 Total Assets	主营业务收入 Revenue from Principal Business	利税总额 Total Profits and Taxes	#利润总额 Total Profits
327773	**121363**	**286850**	**26396**	**14702**
38335	34561	17524	-3123	-4099
45514	13247	41489	9307	6734
282259	108116	245361	17090	7968
167431	47030	161050	14465	8949
160342	73991	125800	11931	5753
	343			
95706	31347	94333	10069	6240
76472	24444	76446	10116	6643
19233	6903	17887	-47	-403
150476	63368	111401	12720	6806
24803	7446	24803	8915	6878
18488	4011	14477	501	3
2224	1791	2209	-109	-147
33553	17727	14507	-1959	-2996
40167	18690	39055	4150	2838
5072	8791	3187	145	12
9237	2706	9580	812	125
16933	2208	3584	267	94
81592	26649	81116	3607	1656
81592	26649	81116	3607	1656

14-17 规模以上外商投资和港澳台投资工业企业主要经济指标(2012)

单位：万元

指 标	Item	企业单位数(个) Number of Enterprises (unit)	工业总产值 Total Output Value of Industry
总 计	**Total**	**68**	**1684361**
#亏损企业	Loss Making Enterprises	17	215743
#港、澳、台商投资企业	Enterprises with Funds from Hong kong, Macao and Taiwan	32	585098
合资经营企业(港或澳、台资)	Joint Venture Enterprises(with Funds from Hong Kong, Macao and Taiwan)	14	314866
港澳台商独资企业	Enterprises with Sole Funds from Hong Kong,Macao and Taiwan	17	260229
港澳台商投资股份有限公司	Share Holding Enterprises with Funds from Hong kong, Macao and Taiwan	1	10003
外商投资企业	Foreign Funded Enterprises	36	1099263
中外合资经营企业	Joint-venture Enterprises	16	384236
中外合作经营企业	Cooperation Enterprises	1	113712
外资企业	Enterprises Funds with Sole Foreigner	16	224607
外商投资股份有限公司	Share Holding Enterprises with Funds from Foreigner	2	367215
其他外商投资企业	Other Foreign-invested Enterprises	1	9493
按轻重工业分	**Grouped by Type of Light and Heavy Industry**		
轻工业	Light Industry	15	466194
重工业	Heavy Industry	53	1218167
按企业规模分	**Grouped by Size of Enterprise**		
大型企业	Large Enterprises	2	181368
中型企业	Medium-sized Enterprises	18	1108101
小型企业	Small Enterprises	48	394892
按工业行业分	**Grouped by Industrial Sector**		
采矿业	Mining and Quarrying	7	86904
#煤炭开采和洗选业	Mining and Washing of Coal	2	25991
黑色金属矿采选业	Mining and Dressing of Ferrous Metals	2	18894
有色金属矿采选业	Mining and Dressing of Nonferrous Metals	2	23682
非金属矿采选业	Mining and Dressing of Nonmetal Minerals	1	18337

Major Economic Indicators of all above Designated Size Industrial Enterprises Funded by Foreigners and Hong kong,Macao and Taiwan

(10000 yuan)

资产合计 Total Assets	主营业务收入 Revenue from Principal Business	利税总额 Total Profits and Taxes	#利润总额 Total Profits
2541914	**1435515**	**166528**	**99649**
320863	189901	-7200	-15183
997120	537511	72832	45065
671890	287554	35791	20998
320304	240224	36588	24027
4926	9732	453	40
1544794	898004	93696	54585
499835	323007	38110	18725
232473	113715	21191	21167
309946	158458	19255	11264
499707	293332	13031	3119
2834	9493	2109	311
209436	367197	26680	16828
2332478	1068318	139848	82822
468041	136221	24098	9933
1612995	976926	94154	62292
460878	322367	48276	27425
52665	42466	23187	16074
9004	11333	2811	1873
4512	5999	2379	1177
23127	6798	1281	139
16022	18337	16716	12886

14−17 续表

单位：万元

指　标	Item	企业单位数（个） Number of Enterprises (unit)
制造业	Manufacturing	59
#农副食品加工业	Processing of Food from Agricultural Products	2
食品制造业	Manufacture of Foods	1
酒、饮料和精制茶制造业	Manufacture of Beverages	1
木材加工和木、竹、藤、棕、草制品业	Timber Processing , Bamboo , Cane , Palm Fiber and Straw Products	1
印刷和记录媒介复制业	Printing,Reproduction of Recording Media	1
文教、工美、体育和娱乐用品制造业	Manufacture of Articles For Culture, Education and Sport Activity	1
石油加工、炼焦和核燃料加工业	Processing of Petroleum,Coking,Processing of Nuclear Fuel	2
化学原料和化学制品制造业	Manufacture of Raw Chemical Materials and Chemical Products	4
医药制造业	Manufacture of Medicines	5
橡胶和塑料制品业	Manufacture of Rubber and Plastics	4
非金属矿物制品业	Manufacture of Non-metallic Mineral Products	22
黑色金属冶炼和压延加工业	Smelting and Pressing of Ferrous Metals	4
有色金属冶炼和压延加工业	Smelting and Pressing of Non-ferrous Metals	4
专用设备制造业	Manufacture of Special Purpose Machinery	1
电气机械和器材制造业	Manufacture of Electrical Equipment and Machinery	2
计算机、通信和其他电子设备制造业	Manufacture of Communication Equipment,Computers and Other Electronic Equipment	2
仪器仪表制造业	Manufacture of Measuring Instruments and Machinery for Cultural Activity and Office Work	2
电力、燃气及水的生产和供应业	Production and Distribution of Electric Power,Gas and Water	2
电力、热力生产和供应业	Production and Distribution of Electric Power and Heat Power	1
燃气生产和供应业	Production and Distribution of Water	1

continued

(10000 yuan)

工业总产值 Total Output Value of Industry	资产合计 Total Assets	主营业务收入 Revenue from Principal Business	利税总额 Total Profits and Taxes	#利润总额 Total Profits
1407987	1826343	1203588	116479	64370
18157	5245	15250	817	561
20972	4465	16771	2864	2050
6453	3109	6203	498	316
1673	30513	755	-332	-340
21673	17934	17340	5765	4740
6136	3756	4651	136	127
138575	430068	110760	9028	-609
77321	146046	70161	19390	12826
141719	74042	86363	13259	6715
32840	26537	18085	407	214
294643	499119	270396	28277	12011
128931	77634	118818	3768	1265
175256	334422	162205	27158	21485
14082	8892	13922	2072	1372
78199	65182	74719	1066	355
246228	95315	212801	2089	1435
5130	4064	4389	218	-154
189471	662907	189460	26862	19205
143537	470389	143537	17687	11432
45934	192518	45924	9175	7773

14−18　规模以上工业企业主要经济效益指标(2012)
Main Indicators on Economic Efficiency of all Industrial Enterprises above Designated Size

单位：%　　(%)

指　标	Item	产值利税率 Ratio of Pre-Tax Profit to Output Value	资金利税率 Ratio of Pre-Tax Profit to Asset	销售利税率 Ratio of Pre-Tax Profit to Sales
总　计	**Total**	**17.9**	**19.9**	**19.3**
内资企业	Domestic Enterprises	18.1	20.3	19.5
国有企业	State-owned	21.2	17.4	21.7
中央企业	Central	6.4	5.3	6.3
地方企业	Local	33.3	27.2	35.5
集体企业	Collective-owned	8.1	27.7	9.1
股份合作企业	Cooperation Enterprises	12.5	22.5	20.5
联营企业	Joint-owned Enterprises	15.0	12.2	15.1
有限责任公司	Limited Liability Corporations	18.3	22.8	19.1
股份有限公司	Share Holding Enterprises	15.9	11.7	17.8
私营企业	Private Enterprises	15.5	28.7	18.2
其他企业	Others	15.7	33.9	17.7
港、澳、台商投资企业	Enterprises with Funds from Hong kong,Macao and Taiwan	12.4	7.5	13.1
外商投资企业	Foreign Funded Enterprises	8.5	9.1	10.1
在总计中：	of the Total:			
#国有控股企业	State-controlled Enterprises	22.2	18.5	22.6
在总计中：	of the Total:			
#农村工业	Rural Industry	25.3	39.9	30.1
按轻重工业分	**Grouped by Type of Light and Heavy Industry**			
轻工业	Light Industry	43.8	55.1	46.5
重工业	Heavy Industry	10.9	11.8	11.8
按企业规模分	**Grouped by Size of Enterprise**			
大型企业	Large Enterprises	24.7	23.5	24.6
中型企业	Medium-sized Enterprises	14.8	17.0	16.5
小型企业	Small Enterprises	10.8	25.4	12.8
微型企业	Micro-enterprises	-26.5	-1.1	-84.5
按工业行业分	**Grouped by Industrial Sector**			
采矿业	Mining and Quarrying	20.5	28.4	25.1
#煤炭开采和洗选业	Mining and Washing of Coal	20.0	26.5	24.7
黑色金属矿采选业	Mining and Processing of Ferrous Metal Ores	18.5	35.6	19.8
有色金属矿采选业	Mining and Processing of Nonferrous Metal Ores	23.8	53.0	27.2
非金属矿采选业	Mining and Processing of Nonmetal Ores	30.3	91.7	32.7
制造业	Manufacturing	19.8	26.0	20.9
#农副食品加工业	Processing of Food from Agricultural Products	5.9	21.6	6.3
食品制造业	Manufacture of Foods	22.7	51.7	23.5
酒、饮料和精制茶制造业	Manufacture of Beverages	68.9	57.1	68.7
烟草制品业	Manufacture of Tobacco	71.2	117.1	73.9
纺织业	Manufacture of Textile	-1.6	-2.2	-1.9
纺织服装、服饰业	Manufacture of Textile Wearing Apparel,Footware and Caps	4.0	8.7	4.2
皮革、毛皮、羽毛及其制品和制鞋业	Manufacture of Leather,Furs,Feather and Related Products	7.1	28.6	3.7

14-18 续表 continued

单位：% (%)

指 标	Item	产值利税率 Ratio of Pre-Tax Profit to Output Value	资金利税率 Ratio of Pre-Tax Profit to Assets	销售利税率 Ratio of Pre-Tax Profit to Sales
木材加工和木、竹、藤、棕、草制品业	Processing of Timber,Manufacture of Wood,Bamboo,Rattan, Palm and Straw Products	9.0	31.6	9.5
家具制造业	Manufacture of Furniture	19.1	96.9	20.7
造纸和纸制品业	Manufacture of Paper and Paper Products	9.8	7.9	9.8
印刷和记录媒介复制业	Printing,Reproduction of Recording Media	24.9	21.3	29.2
文教、工美、体育和娱乐用品制造业	Manufacture of Articles For Culture,Education and Sport Activity	4.9	20.5	7.0
石油加工、炼焦和核燃料加工业	Processing of Petroleum,Coking, Processing of Nuclear Fuel	7.9	17.0	9.6
化学原料和化学制品制造业	Manufacture of Raw Chemical Materials and Chemical Products	10.1	10.1	9.6
医药制造业	Maufacture of Medicines	17.7	26.7	23.6
橡胶和塑料制品业	Manufacture of Rubber and Plastics	5.1	8.3	6.7
非金属矿物制品业	Manufacture of Non-metallic Mineral Products	7.0	8.4	8.1
黑色金属冶炼和压延加工业	Smelting and Pressing of Ferrous Metals	2.1	4.1	2.2
有色金属冶炼和压延加工业	Smelting and Pressing of Non-ferrous Metals	10.8	11.8	11.5
金属制品业	Manufacture of Metal Products	5.9	7.2	5.9
通用设备制造业	Manufacture of General Purpose Machinery	12.1	12.7	15.4
专用设备制造业	Manufacture of Special Purpose Machinery	7.9	6.9	8.4
汽车制造业	Manufacture of Automotive	7.8	18.9	6.2
铁路、船舶、航空航天和其他运输设备制造业	Manufacture of Transport Equipment	4.1	5.1	4.0
电气机械和器材制造业	Manufacture of Electrical Equipment and Machinery	5.1	8.9	6.2
计算机、通信和其他电子设备制造业	Manufacture of Communication Equipment Computers and Other Electronic Equipment	6.2	9.3	6.6
仪器仪表制造业	Manufacture of Measuring Instruments and Machinery for Cultural Activity and Office Work	15.3	14.4	18.2
其他制造业	Others	6.5	7.4	6.5
废弃资源综合利用业	Recycling and Disposal of Waste	2.6	7.9	2.9
金属制品、机械和设备修理业	Metal products, Machinery and Equipment Repair Industry	0.6	10.6	0.6
电力、燃气及水的生产和供应业	Production and Distribution of Electric Power,Gas and Water	8.6	5.8	8.6
#电力、热力的生产和供应业	Production and Distribution of Electric Power and Heat Power	8.7	6.0	8.8
燃气生产和供应业	Production and Distribution of Gas	3.4	3.7	3.1
水的生产和供应业	Production and Distribution of Water	6.0	1.6	6.8

14-19 规模以上国有控股工业企业主要经济效益指标(2012)
Major Indicators on Economic Efficiency of State-controlled Industrial Enterprises above Designated Size

单位：%　　(%)

指　标	Item	产值利税率 Ratio of Pre-Tax Profit to Output Value	资金利税率 Ratio of Pre-Tax Profit to Assets	销售利税率 Ratio of Pre-Tax Profit to Sales
总　计	**Total**	**22.2**	**18.5**	**22.6**
按轻重工业分	**Grouped by Type of Light and Heavy Industry**			
轻工业	Light Industry	63.5	50.6	62.2
重工业	Heavy Industry	7.9	5.8	7.8
按企业规模分	**Grouped by Size of Enterprise**			
大型企业	Large Enterprises	24.5	18.2	23.0
中型企业	Medium-sized Enterprises	7.6	5.3	8.2
小型企业	Small Enterprises	6.0	5.6	6.3
微型企业	Micro-enterprises	7.0	9.5	70.9
按工业行业分	**Grouped by Industrial Sector**			
采矿业	Mining and Quarrying	20.4	17.5	24.8
#煤炭开采和洗选业	Mining and Washing of Coal	20.2	16.7	24.8
有色金属矿采选业	Mining and Processing of Nonferrous Metal Ores	36.3	74.7	36.1
非金属矿采选业	Mining and Processing of Nonmetal Ores	17.8	43.0	19.9
制造业	Manufacturing	30.5	30.8	30.2
#农副食品加工业	Processing of Food from Agricultural Products	7.0	25.1	7.7
食品制造业	Manufacture of Foods	10.3	14.9	12.1
酒、饮料和精制茶制造业	Manufacture of Beverages	94.7	61.7	86.5
烟草制品业	Manufacture of Tobacco	72.4	125.9	75.2
纺织业	Manufacture of Textile	5.8	8.1	9.0
纺织服装、服饰业	Manufacture of Textile Wearing Apparel, Footware and Cap	4.0	7.9	4.3
皮革、毛皮、羽毛及其制品和制鞋业	Manufacture of Leather, Fur, Feathers and other Products and Footwear	7.4	26.6	3.1
木材加工和木、竹、藤、棕、草制品业	Processing of Timber,Manufacture of Wood, Bamboo,Rattan,Palm and Straw Products	5.8	20.6	6.3
造纸和纸制品业	Manufacture of Paper and Paper Products	-6.4	-1.6	-6.6

14-19 续表 continued

单位：% (%)

指 标	Item	产值利税率 Ratio of Pre-Tax Profit to OutputValue	资金利税率 Ratio of Pre-Tax Profit to Assets	销售利税率 Ratio of Pre-Tax Profit to Sales
印刷和记录媒介复制业	Printing,Reproduction of Recording Media	32.6	35.0	31.6
文教、工美、体育和娱乐用品制造业	Manufacture of Articles For Culture, Education and Sport Activity	9.1	29.0	9.1
石油加工、炼焦和核燃料加工业	Processing of Petroleum,Coking, Processing of Nuclear Fuel	8.8	15.7	8.7
化学原料和化学制品制造业	Manufacture of Raw Chemical Materials and Chemical Products	10.9	9.3	9.7
医药制造业	Manufacture of Medicines	16.3	68.3	27.8
橡胶和塑料制品业	Manufacture of Rubber and Plastics	4.3	6.4	6.0
非金属矿物制品业	Manufacture of Rubber	5.0	5.5	6.5
黑色金属冶炼和压延加工业	Smelting and Pressing of Ferrous Metals	-1.2	-1.6	-1.2
有色金属冶炼和压延加工业	Smelting and Pressing of Non-ferrous Metals	4.9	2.9	4.7
金属制品业	Manufacture of Metal Products	3.5	3.7	3.3
通用设备制造业	Manufacture of General Purpose Machinery	14.0	9.8	14.4
专用设备制造业	Manufacture of Special Purpose Machinery	15.7	6.0	14.4
汽车制造业	Manufacture of Automotive	6.0	10.7	5.6
铁路、船舶、航空航天和其他运输设备制造业	Manufacture of Railroad, Marine, Aerospace and Other Transportation Equipment	3.8	4.3	3.8
电气机械和器材制造业	Manufacture of Electrical Equipment and Machinery	3.9	7.4	5.5
计算机、通信和其他电子设备制造业	Manufacture of Communication Equipment,Computers and Other Electronic Equipment	9.3	9.4	9.7
仪器仪表制造业	Manufacture of Measuring Instruments and Machinery for Cultural Activity and Office Work	19.3	8.5	23.2
其他制造业	Others	5.7	7.0	5.5
电力、燃气及水的生产和供应业	Production and Distribution of Electric Power, Gas and Water	8.6	5.9	8.7
电力、热力生产和供应业	Production and Distribution of Electric Power and Heat Power	8.7	6.0	8.7
燃气生产和供应业	Production and Distribution of Gas	-19.9	-1.4	-11.9
水的生产和供应业	Production and Distribution of Water	10.2	1.9	10.0

14-20 规模以上集体工业企业主要经济效益指标(2012)
Main Indicators on Economic Benefit of Collective-owned Industrial Enterprises above Designated Size

单位：% (%)

指 标	Item	产值利税率 Ratio of Pre-Tax Profit to Output Value	资金利税率 Ratio of Pre-Tax Profit to Assets	销售利税率 Ratio of Pre-Tax Profit to Sales
总 计	**Total**	**8.1**	**27.7**	**9.1**
#亏损企业	Loss Making Enterprises	-8.1	-12.0	-17.8
按轻重工业分	**Grouped by Type of Light and Heavy Industry**			
轻工业	Light Industry	20.4	140.1	22.2
重工业	Heavy Industry	6.1	19.3	6.9
按企业规模分	**Grouped by Size of Enterprise**			
中型企业	Medium-sized Enterprises	8.6	46.8	8.9
小型企业	Small Enterprises	7.4	18.9	9.5
按工业行业分	**Grouped by Industrial Sector**			
采矿业	Mining and Quarrying	10.5	83.6	10.7
#煤炭开采和洗选业	Mining and Quarrying	13.2	84.6	13.2
黑色金属矿采选业	Mining and Processing of Ferrous Metal Ores	-0.2	-0.7	-0.3
制造业	Manufacturing	8.5	49.6	11.2
#食品制造业	Manufacture of Foods	35.9	413.8	35.9
皮革、毛皮、羽毛及其制品和制鞋业	Manufacture of Leather, Fur, Feathers and other Products and Footwear	2.7	104.5	3.4
造纸和纸制品业	Manufacture of Paper and Paper Products	-4.9	-6.2	-4.9
非金属矿物制品业	Manufacture of Non-metallic Mineral Products	-5.8	-9.4	-13.5
黑色金属冶炼和压延加工业	Smelting and Pressing of Ferrous Metals	10.3	25.1	10.5
有色金属冶炼和压延加工业	Smelting and Pressing of Non-ferrous Metals	2.8	2.7	4.4
金属制品业	Manufacture of Metal Products	8.8	17.7	8.0
汽车制造业	Manufacture of Automotive	1.6	24.2	7.4
电力、燃气及水的生产和供应业	Production and Distribution of Electric Power, Gas and Wate	4.4	24.6	4.4
#电力、热力的生产和供应业	Production and Distribution of Electric Power and Heat Power	4.4	24.6	4.4

14-21 大中型工业企业主要经济指标占全省规模以上工业比重(2012)

Percentages of Main Indicators of Large and Medium Industrial Enterprises as the whole Industrial Enterprises above Designated Size

单位：亿元 (100 million yuan)

指 标	Item	规模以上工业 Industrial Enterprises above Designated Size	#大中型工业企业 Large and Medium industrial Enterprises		#国有大中型 State-owned Large and Medium Industrial Enterprises	
			绝对数 Absolute Figure	占规模以上工业比重(%) Percentage Taken to Industrial Enterprises above Designated Size(%)	绝对数 Absolute Figure	占规模以上工业比重(%) Percentage Taken to Industrial Enterprises above Designated Size(%)
企业单位数(个)	Number of Industrial Enterprises(unit)	2752	713	25.9	134	4.9
#亏损企业个数(个)	Number of Loss Making Industrial Enterprises(unit)	684	141	20.6	28	4.1
工业总产值	Gross Output Value of Industry	6544.02	4783.31	73.1	1685.08	25.7
工业增加值	Value-added of Industry	2055.46	1442.25	70.2	830.42	40.4
资产总计	Total Assets	8302.29	6845.11	82.4	3106.60	37.4
#流动资产年平均余额	Average Balance of Circulating Funds	2932.98	2297.86	78.3	851.60	29.0
固定资产净值年平均余额	Annual Average Balance Net Value of Fixed Assets	2953.25	2481.32	84.0	1197.68	40.6
负债总计	Total Liabilities	5388.12	4476.49	83.1	1537.57	28.5
主营业务收入	Revenue from Principal Business	5966.52	4484.76	75.2	1625.51	27.2
#产品销售成本	Cost of Sales	4486.91	3303.61	73.6	1201.00	26.8
产品销售税金及附加	Sales Tax and Extra Charges	213.83	190.21	89.0	11.95	5.6
亏损企业亏损额	Total Deficit of Loss Making Industrial Enterprises	-71.77	-45.68	63.6	-18.29	25.5
利税总额	Total Profits and Taxes	1172.15	981.36	83.7	372.92	31.8
资金利税率(%)	Ratio of Pre-Tax Profit and Assets(%)	19.91	20.53	103.1	18.20	91.4

14-22 规模以上大中型工业企业分行业主要经济指标(2012)

单位：亿元

指 标	Item	企业单位数(个) Number of Enterprises (unit)
总 计	**Total**	**713**
采矿业	Mining and Quarrying	279
#煤炭开采和洗选业	Mining and Washing of Coal	270
黑色金属矿采选业	Mining and Processing of Ferrous Metal Ores	2
有色金属矿采选业	Mining and Processing of Nonferrous Metal Ores	3
非金属矿采选业	Mining and Processing of Nonmetal Ores	4
制造业	Manufacturing	345
#农副食品加工业	Processing of Food from Agricultural Products	7
食品制造业	Manufacture of Foods	7
酒、饮料和精制茶制造业	Manufacture of Beverages	27
烟草制品业	Manufacture of Tobacco	2
纺织业	Manufacture of Textile	3
纺织服装、服饰业	Manufacture of Textile Wearing Apparel, Footware and Caps	2
皮革、毛皮、羽毛及其制品和制鞋业	Manufacture of Leather, Fur, Feathers and other Products and Footwear	3
木材加工和木、竹、藤、棕、草制品业	Timber Processing, Manufacture of Wood, Bamboo, Rattan,Palm and Straw Products	14
家具制造业	Manufacturing of Furniture	2
造纸和纸制品业	Manufacture of Paper and Paper Products	4
印刷和记录媒介复制业	Printing, Reproduction of Recording Media	2
文教、工美、体育和娱乐用品制造业	Manufacture of Articles For Culture, Education and Sport Activity	1
石油加工、炼焦和核燃料加工业	Processing of Petroleum, Coking, Processing of Nuclear Fuel	6
化学原料和化学制品制造业	Manufacture of Raw Chemical Materials and Chemical Products	37
医药制造业	Manufacture of Medicines	23
橡胶和塑料制品业	Manufacture of Plastics	7
非金属矿物制品业	Manufacture of Non-metallic Mineral Products	47
黑色金属冶炼和压延加工业	Smelting and Pressing of Ferrous Metals	43
有色金属冶炼和压延加工业	Smelting and Pressing of Non-ferrous Metals	18
金属制品业	Manufacture of Metal Products	7
通用设备制造业	Manufacture of General Purpose Machinery	12
专用设备制造业	Manufacture of Special Purpose Machinery	6
汽车制造业	Manufacture of Automotive	12
铁路、船舶、航空航天和其他运输设备制造业	Manufacture of Transport Equipment	23
电气机械和器材制造业	Manufacture of Electrical Equipment and Machinery	13
计算机、通信和其他电子设备制造业	Manufacture of Communication Equipment, Computers and Other Electronic Equipment	11
仪器仪表制造业	Manufacture of Measuring Instruments and Machinery for Cultural Activity and Office Work	3
其他制造业	Others	3
电力、燃气及水的生产和供应业	Production and Distribution of Electric Power,Gas and Water	89
#电力、热力的生产和供应业	Production and Distribution of Electric Power and Heat Power	80
燃气生产和供应业	Production and Distribution of Gas	2
水的生产和供应业	Production and Distribution of Water	7

Main Indicators on Economic of Large and Medium Industrial Enterprises by Sector

(100 million yuan)

工业总产值 Total Output Value of Industry	资产合计 Total Assets	主营业务收入 Revenue from Principal Business	利税总额 Total Profits and Taxes	#利润总额 Total Profits
4783.31	**6845.11**	**4484.76**	**981.36**	**520.55**
801.86	1124.36	663.90	184.45	108.29
761.58	1099.03	624.58	172.42	100.21
3.65	**1.70**	**3.65**	**0.46**	**0.00**
7.15	4.28	6.88	2.28	1.56
29.49	19.35	28.79	9.28	6.52
2902.45	3613.07	2770.61	710.66	374.85
20.12	9.02	18.71	1.54	1.06
39.44	25.23	37.99	9.97	7.65
346.06	649.36	355.65	284.62	202.03
312.47	233.98	303.88	225.55	42.20
2.19	2.61	1.73	-0.01	-0.07
3.78	2.38	3.42	0.15	0.11
15.59	7.54	30.25	1.13	0.65
25.81	6.12	24.78	2.48	1.00
8.89	3.25	8.09	1.99	1.59
17.60	36.10	19.05	2.21	1.44
4.16	6.93	4.22	1.44	1.12
0.61	0.38	0.47	0.01	0.01
58.86	82.23	47.25	5.71	3.49
447.29	792.52	479.31	46.41	36.21
168.61	146.58	123.75	31.97	20.74
114.89	79.01	82.63	5.99	3.54
165.77	239.39	138.60	12.17	5.92
408.23	296.93	390.60	11.24	2.87
318.20	431.94	279.57	38.19	25.67
41.62	54.46	43.87	1.91	-0.25
28.97	38.91	22.55	4.02	3.23
19.69	29.28	18.89	1.99	1.59
77.32	79.39	100.49	6.70	2.96
121.47	244.57	119.58	4.87	3.36
57.61	29.22	45.15	3.26	2.30
57.27	57.23	52.80	3.68	3.26
5.18	5.78	3.39	0.62	0.39
14.76	22.72	13.94	0.86	0.77
1078.99	2107.68	1050.25	86.26	37.41
1047.14	2031.41	1020.34	84.86	36.55
24.59	34.69	24.16	0.93	0.78
7.26	41.58	5.75	0.47	0.08

14-23 规模以上工业销售产值(2012)
Industrial Sales Output Value

单位：亿元 (100 million yuan)

类 别	Item	销售产值 Sales Value	#出口交货值 Delivery Value of Industry
总 计	**Total**	**6170.82**	**109.74**
#国有控股企业	State-controlled Enterprises	3136.20	96.77
按登记注册类型分	**Grouped by Registration**		
内资企业	Domestic Enterprises	6020.91	106.97
国有企业	State-owned Enterprises	1725.15	30.98
中央企业	Central	807.17	
地方企业	Local	917.99	30.98
集体企业	Collective-owned Enterprises	30.57	0.01
股份合作企业	Cooperation Enterprises	46.08	
联营企业	Joint-owned Enterprises	19.07	
有限责任公司	Limited Liability Corporations	2279.53	48.72
股份有限公司	Share Holding Enterprises	402.32	22.27
私营企业	Private Enterprises	1476.23	5.00
其他企业	Others	41.95	
港、澳、台商投资企业	Enterprises with Funds from Hong kong,Macao and Taiwan	52.87	2.20
外商投资企业	Foreign Funded Enterprises	97.05	0.56
按轻重工业分	**Grouped by Type of Light and Heavy Industry**		
轻工业	Light Industry	1267.39	15.42
重工业	Heavy Industry	4903.43	94.32
按企业规模分	**Grouped by Scale of Enterprise**		
大型企业	Large Enterprises	2624.05	93.62
中型企业	Medium-sized Enterprises	1892.56	6.04
小型企业	Small Enterprises	1653.70	10.08
微型企业	Micro-enterprises	0.51	

14-24 规模以上工业主要产品产量、销售量和产销率(2012)

Sales Volume of Major Industrial Products and Proportion of Products Sold

产品名称	Item	产 量 Output	销售量 Sales Volume	产销率 (%) Ratio of Products Sold(%)	2012年比2011年增长(%) Increase Rate in 2012 over 2011(%)	
					产 量 Output	销售量 Sales Volume
原煤(万吨)	Raw Coal(10000 tons)	15030.94	12578.24	83.7	16.4	16.8
洗煤(万吨)	Washed Coall(10000 tons)	4757.10	4486.42	94.3	25.4	25.2
煤气生产量(亿立方米)	Volume of Coal Gas Production(100 million cu.m)	98.63			22.4	
发电量(亿千瓦小时)	Electricity(100 million kwh)	1548.44			14.8	
#水电	Hydropower	511.65			59.1	
磷矿石(生产量含P2O530%)(万吨)	Phosphorite Mineral(10000 tons)	2281.95	1442.15	63.2	18.7	26.2
配混合饲料(万吨)	Forage(10000 tons)	69.56	66.02	94.9	-11.0	-14.4
成品糖(万吨)	Sugar(10000 tons)	1.58	0.30	18.8	1336.4	176.8
乳制品(吨)	Dairy Products(ton)	58830.00	58850.00	100.0	7.1	6.8
罐头(吨)	Canned Food(ton)	14313.30	14388.76	100.5	165.0	173.5
饮料酒(万千升)	Alcohol Beverages(10000 kiloliter)	67.14	64.14	95.5	9.7	14.1
#白酒	White Spirit	26.83	23.47	87.5	18.6	22.6
啤酒	Beer	40.20	40.67	101.2	4.2	9.7
软饮料(万吨)	Soft Drink(10000 tons)	137.81	122.59	89.0	26.7	38.9
卷烟(万箱)	Cigarettes(10000 cases)	249.35	243.42	97.6	1.7	-1.5
纱(万吨)	Yarn(10000 tons)	1.29	1.20	93.2	-21.8	-15.7
布(万米)	Cloth(10000 m)	548.11	478.90	87.4	-30.6	-40.2
丝(吨)	Silk(ton)	127.50	125.50	98.4	-29.9	-28.7
服装(万件)	Garment(10000 pieces)	465.53	471.42	101.3	-4.0	-1.8
人造板(万立方米)	Artificial Board(10000cu.m)	171.14	163.09	95.3	41.7	39.0
机制纸(万吨)	Machine-made Paper(10000 tons)	13.45	13.35	99.2	24.0	25.0
焦炭(万吨)	Coke(10000 tons)	754.54	608.19	80.6	22.8	21.0
硫酸(折100%)(万吨)	Sulfuric Acid(10000 tons)	657.87	25.77	3.9	2.6	91.0
氢氧化钠(烧碱折100%)(万吨)	Caustic Soda(10000 tons)	18.64	17.28	92.7	-14.5	-15.4
碳化钙(电石折300升/千克)(万吨)	Calcium Carbide(10000 tons)	37.29	37.44	100.4	-18.7	-18.2
合成氨(万吨)	Synthetic Ammonia(10000 tons)	155.91	51.26	32.9	15.7	31.5
农用化学肥料总计(折纯)(万吨)	Chemical Fertilizer(10000 tons)	503.82	510.42	101.3	20.7	31.8
#氮肥(折含N100%)	Nitrogen Fertilizer	235.61	236.61	100.4	22.6	28.3
#尿素	Carbamide	94.23	93.77	99.5	9.9	11.1
磷肥(折合P2O5100%)	Phosphate Fertilizer	263.88	270.08	102.3	18.9	35.3

14-24 续表 continued

产品名称	Item	产 量 Output	销售量 Sales Volume	产销率(%) Proportion of Products Sold(%)	2012年比2011年增长(%) Increase Rate in 2012 over 2011(%) 产 量 Output	销售量 Sales Volume
纯苯(吨)	Pure Benzene(ton)	13310	13332	100.2	7.7	8.3
合成洗涤剂(万吨)	Synthetic Detergents(10000 tons)	2.83	2.83	100.0	-3.7	-4.9
轮胎外胎(万条)	Tires(10000 tires)	622.78	543.69	87.3	16.0	2.1
塑料制品(万吨)	Plastic Products(10000 tons)	34.15	31.15	91.2	18.9	18.3
#农用薄膜(吨)	Rural Use Membrane(ton)	2569.68	2569.68	100.0	-19.0	-19.0
水泥(万吨)	Cement(10000 tons)	6100.45	6063.12	99.4	28.8	33.2
生铁(万吨)	Pig Iron(10000 tons)	552.93	83.59	15.1	20.6	-2.3
粗钢(万吨)	Steel(10000 tons)	531.27	9.84	1.9	23.1	106.8
成品钢材(万吨)	Steel Products(10000 tons)	560.22	559.91	99.9	23.1	24.9
#盘条(线材)	Wire Rod	152.00	152.52	100.3	35.2	36.5
无缝钢管	Seamless Steel Pipe	23.30	23.05	98.9	52.7	54.6
铁合金(万吨)	Iron Alloy(10000 tons)	309.68	293.95	94.9	20.6	18.7
十种有色金属(万吨)	Ten kinds of Nonferrous Metals(10000 tons)	110.61	111.27	100.6	19.8	21.2
#铅(吨)	Lead(ton)	6546.00	6546.00	100.0	-17.4	-17.4
锌(万吨)	Zinc(10000 tons)	2.78	2.69	96.6	23.0	22.4
铝(万吨)	Aluminium(10000 tons)	104.35	105.22	100.8	19.3	20.8
氧化铝(万吨)	Alumina(10000 tons)	270.04	184.22	68.2	32.7	50.0
铝材(万吨)	Aluminium Material(10000 tons)	11.70	11.39	97.3	-3.3	-6.1
金属切削机床(台)	Metal-cutting Machine Tools(set)	1075	990	92.1	-23.7	-29.6
小型拖拉机(辆)	Mini-tractors(set)	3439	2221	64.6	95.3	282.9
交流电动机(万千瓦)	Alternating Current Motor(10000 kw)	41.40	28.20	68.1	-21.5	-18.0
家用电冰箱(万台)	Household Refrigerators(10000 sets)	159.04	150.16	94.4	-6.2	-10.2
集成电路(万块)	Semiconductor Integrated Circui(10000 pcs)	1558.83	1651.06	105.9	31.0	63.5
彩色电视机(万部)	Color TV Sets(10000 sets)	90.61	87.78	96.9	29.5	27.7

14–25 高技术产业基本情况

Basic Statistics on High-tech Industry

行 业	Item	2007	2008	2009	2010	2011	2012
规模以上工业企业数(个)	Number of Enterprises (unit)	155	154	149	155	157	187
从业人员年平均人数(万人)	Annual Average Number of Employees (10 000 persons)	6.69	6.66	6.78	6.77	6.82	7.43
工业总产值(亿元)	Gross Output Value(100 million yuan)	204.83	231.56	273.92	320.96	392.87	423.57
主营业务收入(亿元)	Revenue from Principal Business (100 million yuan)	168.03	190.57	225.65	260.26	316.59	345.80
利税总额(亿元)	Pre-Tax Profits(100 million yuan)	21.73	25.67	29.32	33.21	35.18	45.17
利润总额(亿元)	Profits (100 million yuan)	14.07	16.16	18.89	21.38	22.38	28.07

注：高技术产业统计口径为全部年主营业务收入500万元及以上工业企业。

Note:High-tech Industry statistics was the industrial of main business income of 5 million yuan and above.

主要统计指标解释

工业 指从事自然资源的开采，对采掘品和农产品进行加工和再加工的物质生产部门。具体包括：(1)对自然资源的开采，如采矿、晒盐等(但不包括禽兽捕猎和水产捕捞)；(2)对农副产品的加工、再加工，如粮油加工、食品加工、缫丝、纺织、制革等；(3)对采掘品的加工、再加工，如炼铁、炼钢、化工生产、石油加工、机器制造、木材加工等，以及电力、自来水、煤气的生产和供应等；(4)对工业品的修理、翻新，如机器设备的修理、交通运输工具的修理等。

1984年以前农村的村及村以下办工业归属农业，1984年以后划归工业。

工业统计调查单位为独立核算法人工业企业。

独立核算法人工业企业指从事工业生产经营活动的单位。独立核算法人工业企业应同时具备以下条件：①依法成立，有自己的名称、组织机构和场所，能够承担民事责任；②独立拥有和使用资产，承担负债，有权与其他单位签订合同；③独立核算盈亏，并能够编制资产负债表。

本年鉴中涉及的企业登记注册类型：

国有企业 国有企业(即原全民所有制工业或国营工业)指企业全部资产归国家所有，并按《中华人民共和国企业法人登记管理条例》规定登记注册的非公司制的经济组织。包括国有企业、国有独资公司和国有联营企业。1957年以前的公私合营和私营工业，后均改造为国营工业，1992年改为国有工业，这部分工业的资料不单独分列时，均包括在国有企业内。

集体企业 指企业资产归集体所有，并按《中华人民共和国企业法人登记管理条例》规定登记注册的经济组织。是社会主义公有制经济的组成部分。包括城乡所有使用集体投资举办的企业，以及部分个人通过集资自愿放弃所有权并依法经工商行政管理机关认定为集体所有制的企业。

股份合作企业 指以合作制为基础，由企业职工共同出资入股，吸收一定比例的社会资产投资组建，实行自主经营，自负盈亏，共同劳动，民主管理，按劳分配与按股分红相结合的一种集体经济组织。

联营企业 指两个及两个以上相同或不同所有制性质的企业法人或事业单位法人，按自愿、平等、互利的原则，共同投资组成的经济组织。联营企业包括：

国有联营企业指国有企业与国有企业间的联营；

集体联营企业指集体企业与集体企业间的联营；

国有与集体联营企业指国有企业与集体企业间的联营。

有限责任公司 指根据《中华人民共和国公司登记管理条例》规定登记注册，由两个以上，五十个以下的股东共同出资，每个股东以其所认缴的出资额对公司承担有限责任，公司以其全部资产对其债务承担责任的经济组织。

有限责任公司包括国有独资公司以及其他有限责任公司。

股份有限公司 指根据《中华人民共和国企业法人登记管理条例》规定登记注册，其全部注册资本由等额股份构成并通过发行股票筹集资本，股东以其认购的股份对公司承担有限责任，公司以其全部资产对其债务承担责任的经济组织。

私营企业 指由自然人投资设立或由自然人控股，以雇佣劳动为基础的营利性经济组织。包括按照《公司法》、《合伙企业法》、《私营企业暂行条例》规定登记注册的私营有限责任公司、私营股份有限公司、私营合伙企业和私营独资企业。

港、澳、台商投资企业 指企业注册登记类型中的港、澳、台资合资、合作、独资经营企业和股份有限公司之和。

外商投资企业 指企业注册登记类型中的中外合资、合作经营企业、外资企业和外商投资股份有限公司之和。

国有控股 国有控股企业是对混合所有制经济的企业进行的"国有控股"分类。它是指这些企业的全部资产中国有资产(股份)相对其他所有者中的任何一个所有者占资(股)最多的企业。该分组反映了国有经济控股情况。

轻工业 指主要提供生活消费品和制作手工工具的工业。按其所使用的原料不同，可分为两大类：(1)以农产品为原料的轻工业，是指直接或间接以农产品为基本原料的轻工业。主要包括食品制造、饮料制造、烟草加工、纺织、缝纫、皮革和毛皮制作、造纸以及印刷等工业；(2)以非农产品为原料的轻工业，是指以工业品为原料的轻工业。主要包括文教体育用品、化学药品制造、合成纤维制造、日用化学制品、日用玻璃制品、日用金属制品、手工工具制造、医疗器械制造、文化和办公用机械制造等工业。

重工业 指为国民经济各部门提供物质技术基础的主要生产资料的工业。按其生产性质和产品用途，可以分为下列三类：(1)采掘(伐)工业，是指对自然资源的开采，包括石油开采、煤炭开采、金属矿开采、非金属矿开采等工业；(2)原材料工业，指向国民经济各部门提供基本材料、动力和燃料的工业。包括金属冶炼及加工、炼焦及焦炭、化学、化工原料、水泥、人造板以及电力、石油和煤炭加工等工业；(3) 加工工业，是指对工业原材料进行再加工制造的工业。包括装备国民经济各部门的机械设备制造工业、金属结构、水泥制品等工业，以及为农业提供的生产资料如化肥、农药等工业。

根据上述划分原则，修理业中以重工业产品为修理作业对象的划为重工业，反之划为轻工业。

工业总产值

(1) 定义：工业总产值是以货币形式表现的，工业企业在一定时期内生产的工业最终产品或提供工业性劳务活动的总价值量。它反映一定时间内工业生产的总规模和总水平。

(2) 计算原则：

工业生产的原则，即凡是企业在报告期生产的经检验合格的产品，不管是否在报告期销售，均包括在内。

最终产品的原则，即凡是计入工业总产值的产品，必须是本企业生产的经检验合格的，不需要再进行任何加工的最终产品。如果企业有中间产品（半成品）对外销售，则对外销售的中间产品应视为企业的最终产品。

工厂法原则，即工业总产值是以工业企业作为基本计算（核算）单位，即按企业的最终产品计算工业总产值。按这种方法计算的工业总产值，不允许同一产品价值在企业内部重复计算，不能把企业内部各个车间（分厂）生产的成果相加，但允许企业间的重复计算。

(3) 内容及计算方法：1995 年全国工业普查对工业总产值（原规定）的内容及计算原则和方法做了某些修订，修订后的工业总产值（新规定）包括三项内容：即本期生产成品价值、对外加工费收入、在制品半成品期末期初差额价值三部分。

本期生产成品价值：指企业本期生产，并在报告期内不再进行加工，经检验、包装入库的全部工业成品（半产品）价值合计，包括企业生产的自制设备及提供给本企业在建工程、其他非工业部门和福利部门等单位使用的成品价值。本期生产成品价值为按自备原材料生产的产品的数量乘以本期不含增值税（销项税额）的产品实际销售平均单价计算；会计核算中按成本价格转帐的自制设备和自产自用的成品，按成本价格计算生产成品价值。生产成品价值中不包括用定货者来料加工的成品（半产品）价值。

对外加工费收入：指企业在报告期内完成的对外承接的工业品加工（包括用定货者来料加工产品）的加工费收入和对外工业修理作业所取得的加工费收入。对外加工费收入按不含增值税（销项税额）的价格计算，可根据会计“产品销售收入”科目的有关资料取得。

对于本企业对内非工业部门提供的加工修理、设备安装的劳务收入，如果企业会计核算基础较好，能取得这部分资料，而且这部分价值所占比重较大，应包括在对外加工费收入中。

自制半成品在制品期末期初差额价值：指企业报告期在制品期末减期初的差额价值，本指标一般可以从会计核算资料中取得。如果会计产品成本核算中不计算半成品、在制品的成本，则总产值中也不包括这部分价值，反之则包括。

(4) 工业总产值统计范围变化和计算方法修订情况：

1984 年以前工业总产值不包括村办工业，村办工业总产值划归农业。1984 年以后工业总产值包括村办工业。

1995 年工业普查对工业总产值计算方法做了修订，即从 1995 年始按新修订（新规定）方法计算工业总产值。新规定与原规定的区别如下：

全价与加工费的计算原则不同：新规定为凡自备原材料，不论其生产繁简程度如何，一律按全价计算工业总产值；凡来料加工，允许按加工费计算工业总产值。原规定则视生产加工的繁简程度不同，规定哪些行业按全价，哪些行业按加工费计算工业总产值。

自制半成品、在产品期末期初差额价值的计算原则不同：新规定要求，凡会计产品成本核算时计算了成本的差额价值，总产值中就应包括，否则可不包括；原规定则按生产周期六个月的界限区分，凡生产周期六个月以上的企业，总产值计算中应包括这部分差额价值，否则可不包括。

计算价格不同：新规定按不含增值税（销项税额）的价格计算；原规定则按含增值税（销项税额）的价格计算。

工业增加值 指工业企业在报告期内以货币表现的工业生产活动的最终成果。

工业增加值有两种计算方法：一是生产法，即工业总产出减去工业中间投入加上应交增值税；二是收入法，是从工业生产过程中创造的原始收入初次分配角度入手，对工业生产活动最终成功进行核算的一种方法。本年鉴中的工业增加值是以收入法计算的。

收入法工业增加值的计算方法为：

工业增加值 = 固定资产折旧 + 劳动者报酬 + 生产税净额 + 营业盈余

固定资产折旧是一定时期内工业企业为弥补固定资产损耗，按照核定的固定资产折旧率提取的折旧额，反映固定资产在当期生产中的转移价值。

劳动者报酬是指工业企业的劳动者因从事生产活动所获得的全部报酬。包括劳动者获得的各种形式的工资、奖金和津贴，既包括货币形式的，也包括实物形式的，还包括劳动者所享受的公费医疗和医药卫生费、上下班交通补贴、单位支付的社会保障费、住房公积金等。对于个体经济来说，其所有者所获得的劳动报酬和经营利润不易区分，这两部分统一作为劳动者报酬处理。

生产税净额是指工业企业的生产税减生产补贴后的余额。生产税指政府对生产单位从事生产、销售和经营活动以及因从事生产活动使用某些生产要素（如固定资产、土地、劳动力）所征收的各种税、附加费和规费。生产补贴与生产税相反，指政府对生产单位的单方面转移支出，因此视为负生产税，包括政策亏损补贴、价格补贴等。

营业盈余是指工业企业创造的增加值扣除劳动者报酬、生产税净额和固定资产折旧后的余额。它相当于企业的营业利润加上生产补贴，但要扣除从利润中开支的工资和福利等。

资产总计　指企业拥有或控制的能以货币计量的经济资源，包括各种财产、债权和其他权利。资产按流动性分为流动资产、长期投资、固定资产、无形资产、递延资产和其他资产。该指标根据企业会计“资产负债表”中“资产总计”项目的期末数增列。

流动资产平均余额　指企业在报告期内全部流动资产的平均余额。

固定资产净值年平均余额　指固定资产净值在报告期内余额的平均数。计算公式为:

$$固定资产净值年平均余额 = \frac{1至12月各月月初 + 月末固定资产净值}{24}$$

该指标根据“资产负债表”中“固定资产原价”、“累计折旧”指标的期初、期末数计算填列。

固定资产净值指固定资产原价减去历年已提折旧额后的净额。计算公式为:

固定资产净值 = 固定资产原价 - 累计折旧

产品销售收入　指企业在报告期内生产的成品、自制半成品和工业性劳务取得的收入。

产品销售成本　指企业在报告期内销售本企业生产的成品、自制半成品和工业性劳务等的实际成本。

产品销售税金及附加　指企业在报告期内销售产品、提供的劳务等主要经营业务应负担的城市维护建设税、消费税、资源税和教育费附加等。

利润总额　指企业生产经营活动的最终成果，是企业在一定时期内实现的盈亏相抵后的利润总额（亏损以“-”号表示），它等于营业利润加上补贴收入加上投资收益加上营业外净收入再加上以前年度损益调整。

本年应交增值税　指企业在报告期内应交纳的增值税额。它等于本年销项税额加上出口退税加上进项税额转出数减去本年进项税额。小规模纳税企业直接按全年计税销售额乘以征收率计算取得。

总资产贡献率　反映企业全部资产的获利能力，是企业经营业绩和管理水平的集中体现，是评价和考核企业盈利能力的核心指标。计算公式为:

$$总资产贡献率 = \frac{利润总额 + 税金总额 + 利息支出}{平均资金总额} \times 100\%$$

公式中：税金总额为产品销售税金及附加与应交增值税之和；平均资产总额为期初期末资产之和的算术平均值。

资产负债率　该指标既反映企业经营风险的大小，也反映企业利用债权人提供的资金从事经营活动的能力。计算公式为:

$$资产负债率 = \frac{负债总额}{资产总额} \times 100\%$$

资产与负债均为报告期期末数。

流动资产周转次数　指一定时期内流动资产完成的周转次数，反映投入工业企业流动资金的周转速度。计算公式为:

$$流动资产周转次数 = \frac{产品销售收入}{全部流动资产平均余额}$$

公式中：全部流动资产平均余额为期初和期末的流动资产之和的算术平均值。

成本费用利润率　反映企业投入的生产成本及费用的经济效益，同时也反映企业降低成本所取得的经济效益。计算公式为:

$$成本费用利润率 = \frac{利润总额}{成本费用总额} \times 100\%$$

公式中：成本费用总额为产品销售成本、销售费用、管理费用、财务费用之和。

Explanatory Notes on Main Statistical Indicators

Industry refers to the material production sector which is engaged in the extraction of natural resources and processing and reprocessing of minerals and agricultural products, including (1) extraction of natural resources, such as mining, salt production (but not including hunting and fishing); (2) processing and reprocessing of farm and sideline produces, such as rice husking, flour milling, wine making, oil pressing, silk reeling, spinning and weaving, and leather making; (3) manufacture of industrial products, such as steel making, iron smelting, chemicals manufacturing, petroleum processing, machine building, timber processing; water and gas production and electricity generation and supply; (4)repairing of industrial products such as the repairing of machinery and means of transport (including cars).

Before 1984, the rural village and home office industrial were placed under the agriculture, but after 1984 were placed under the industry.

In industrial statistics surveys, the units of enquiry are corporate industrial enterprises with independent accounting systems.

Corporate industrial enterprises with independent accounting systems refer to enterprises engaging in industrial production activities, which meet the following requirements: (1) They are established legally, having their own names, organizations, location and able to take civil liability; (2) They possess and use their assets independently, assume liabilities and are entitled to sign contracts with other units; (3) They are financially independent and compile their own balance sheets.

Enterprises covered in the industrial statistics in the Yearbook include the following categories by their registration:

State-owned Enterprises refer to state-owned enterprises plus State-holding enterprises. State-owned enterprises (originally known as State-run enterprises with ownership by the whole society) are non-corporate economic entities registered in accordance with the Regulation of the People's Republic of China on the Management of Registration of Legal Enterprises, where all assets are owned by the State. Included in this category are State-owned enterprises, State-funded corporations and State-owned joint-operation enterprises. Joint State-private industries and private industries, which existed before 1957, were transformed into state-run industries since 1957, and into State-owned industries after 1992. Statistics on those enterprises are included in the State-owned industries instead of being grouped them separately.

Collective-owned Enterprises refer to economic entities registered in accordance with the Regulation of the People's Republic of China on the Management of Registration of Legal Enterprises, where assets are owned collectively. Collective enterprises constitute an integral part of the socialist economy with public ownership. They include urban and rural enterprises invested collectively, and some enterprises registered in industrial and commercial administration agency as collective units where funds are pooled together by individuals who voluntarily give up their right of ownership.

State-controlled State-holding enterprises are a mixed ownership economy enterprises of the "state-controlled" category. It refers to all of the assets of these enterprises China Assets (share) compared to other owners in the share capital of any one owner (shares) of the largest enterprises. The grouping reflects the state-owned economy holding situation.

Cooperative Enterprises refer to economic units set up on a cooperative basis, with funding partly from employees of the enterprise and partly from outside investment, where the operation and management is decided by all the members who also participate in the production, and the distribution of income is based both on work (labour input) and on shares (capital input).

Joint Ownership Enterprises refer to economic units that are established by joint investment by two or more corporate enterprises or institutions of the same or different types of ownership on voluntary, equal and mutual-beneficial basis. They include:

a) State-owned joint-operation enterprises (joint operation between State-owned enterprises);

b) Collective joint-operation enterprises (joint operation between collective enterprises; and

c) State-collective joint-operation enterprises (joint operation between state and collective enterprises).

Limited Liability Corporations refer to economic units registered in accordance with the Regulation of the People's Republic of China on the Management of Registration of Corporations, with capital from 2 to 49 investors, each investor bears limited liability to the corporation depending on his/her holding of shares, and the corporation bears liability to its debt to the maximum of its total assets.

Limited liability corporations include state sole funded corporations and other limited liability corporations.

Share-holding Corporations Ltd. refer to economic units registered in accordance with the Regulation of the People's Republic of China on the Management of Registration of Corporate Enterprises, with total registered capital divided into equal shares and raised through issuing stocks. Each investor bears limited liability to the corporation depending on the holding of shares, and the corporation bears liability to its debt to the maximum of its total assets.

Private Enterprises refer to economic units invested or controlled (by holding the majority of the shares) by natural persons who hire labours for profit-making activities. Included in this category are private limited liability corporations, private share-holding corporations Ltd., private partnership enterprises and private sole investment enterprises registered in accordance with the Corporation Law, Partnership Enterprise Law and Tentative Regulation on Private Enterprises.

Enterprises with Funds from Hong Kong, Macao and Taiwan refers to all industrial enterprises registered as the joint-venture, cooperative, sole (exclusive) investment industrial enterprises and limited liability corporations with funds from Hong Kong, Macao and Taiwan.

Foreign Funded Enterprises refer to all industrial enterprises registered as the joint-venture, cooperative, sole (exclusive) investment industrial enterprises and limited liability corporations with foreign funds.

Light Industry refers to the industry that produces consumer goods and hand tools. It consists of two categories, depending on the materials used:

(1) Industries using farm products as raw materials. These are the branches of light industry which directly or indirectly use farm products as basic raw materials, including the manufacture of food and beverages, tobacco processing, textile, clothing, fur and leather manufacturing, paper making, printing, etc.

(2) Industries using non-farm products as raw materials. These are the branches of light industry which use manufactured goods as raw materials, including the manufacture of cultural, educational articles and sports goods, chemicals, synthetic fibre, chemical products for daily use, glass products for daily use, metal products for daily use, hand tools, medical apparatus and instruments, and the manufacture of cultural and office machinery.

Heavy Industry refers to the industry which produces capital goods, and provides various sectors of the national economy with necessary material and technical basis for production. It consists of the following three branches according to the purpose of production or the use of products:

(1) Mining, quarrying and logging industry, which refers to the industry that extracts natural resources, including extraction of petroleum, coal, metal and non-metal ores.

(2) Raw materials industry refers to the industry that provides various sectors of the national economy with raw materials, fuels and power. It includes smelting and processing of metals, coking and coke chemistry, chemical materials and building materials such as cement, plywood, and power, petroleum refining and coal dressing.

(3) Manufacturing industry which refers to the industry that processes raw materials. It includes machine-building industries which equip sectors of the national economy; industries producing metal structure and cement products; and industries producing means of agricultural production, such as chemical fertilizers and pesticides.

In accordance with the above principles of classification, the repairing trades, which are engaged primarily in repairing products of heavy industry, are classified as heavy industry while those which are engaged in repairing products of light industry are classified as light industry.

Gross Industrial Output Value

(1) Definition: Gross industrial output value is the total volume of final industrial products produced and industrial services provided during a given period. It reflects the total achievements and overall scale of industrial production during a given period.

(2) Principles for calculation:

Statistics on industrial production follow the principle that all products produced by the enterprises and accepted through quality check during the reference period are to be included no matter whether they are sold or not during the reference period.

Determination of final products follows the principle that all products that are included in the calculation of gross industrial output value are the final products of the enterprise which have been accepted through quality check and require no further processing. If an enterprise has intermediate (semi-finished) products to sell, these intermediate products are considered as the final products of the enterprise.

Gross industrial output value is calculated following the principle of factory approach, i.e. industrial enterprise is used as the basic accounting unit in calculating the gross industrial output value. By this approach, value of the same product is not to be double-counted, and the output value of different workshops (branch factories) within the enterprise should not be added. However, this approach allows the possibility of double counting between enterprises.

(3) Content and method of calculation: The old definition of gross industrial output value was modified during the 1995 National Industrial Census. The revised (new) definition of gross industrial output value consists of 3 components: value of the finished products during the reference period, income from processing for external parties, and value of change in semi-finished products between the end and the beginning of the reference period.

Value of finished products during the reference period: refers to the value of all finished (semi-finished) industrial products that are produced during the reference period without the need for further processing, checked for acceptance, packed and put into the warehouse of the enterprise, including the value of own-produced equipment and the value of products provided to the projects under construction of the enterprise, and to other non-industrial or welfare units. Value of finished products during the reference period is calculated by the quantity of products produced using own materials multiplied by the average unit prices at which products are sold (excluding value-added tax). Own-produced equipment and products produced for own use are valued at cost prices as in the case of enterprise accounting. Value of finished products does not include the value of finished products (semi-finished products) that are produced using the materials from the clients who place the orders.

Income from external processing: refers to income from contracted external processing of industrial products (including processing of industrial products using materials from the clients), and the income from industrial repairing work provided to other parties. Income from external processing is calculated using information from the item "products sales income" in the enterprise accounting at the prices with value-added tax excluded.

For income from services such as processing, repairing and installation of equipment provided to non-industrial units within the enterprise, if the accounting work of the enterprise is good enough to separate it from other records, and the share of such services is significant, it should also be included in the income from external processing.

Value of change in semi-finished products between the end and the beginning of the reference period: refers to the value of change in semi-finished products between the end and the beginning of the reference period, which generally can be obtained from accounting records of enterprises. If the enterprise accounting excludes the cost of semi-finished products, then it should not be included in the gross industrial output value, and the reverse if otherwise.

(4) Changes in the scope and method of calculation of the gross industrial output value

Prior to 1984, the value of rural industry run by villages was classified into agriculture instead of industry. Since 1984, it has been included in the gross industrial output value. Method of calculation for the gross industrial output value was modified in the industrial census in 1995. The difference in the new method as compared with the old one is outlined below:

Principle in using full value vs. processing fee: The new method stipulates that all products produced using own materials are to be calculated with full value in reporting the gross industrial output value irrespective of the complexity of production, and for external processing, it allows calculation using processing fee. In the old method, however, the use of full value or processing fee was determined by the degree of complexity of production in different branches of industries.

Principle in determining the value of change in semi-finished products: The new method requires that value of change in semi-finished products should be included in the gross industrial output value if it is included in the accounting record of the enterprise, otherwise it should not be included. In the old method, it is determined by the type of enterprises in terms of production cycle. If the production cycle is over 6 months, the value of change in semi-finished products is included in the gross industrial output value, otherwise it is not.

Difference in prices: The new method uses prices excluding value-added tax in the calculation of gross industrial output value, while the old method used prices including value-added tax.

Value-added of Industry refers to the final results of industrial production of industrial enterprises in money terms during the reference period.

Industrial value-added can be calculated by two approaches: the production approach, i.e. gross industrial output value minus intermediate input plus value-added tax, and the income approach, i.e. income for various factors used in the course of production, including depreciation of fixed assets, remuneration of labourers, net of production tax, and operating surplus. Value-added of industry in the Yearbook is calculated by the income approach as follows.

Revenue Act of industrial added value is calculated as:

Value-added of industry = depreciation of fixed assets + remuneration of labourers + net of production tax + operating surplus

Depreciation of fixed assets of industrial enterprises is a period of time to compensate for losses of fixed assets, depreciation of fixed assets in accordance with the approved rate of extraction amount of depreciation of fixed assets in the current period reflects the transfer of the production value.

Workers compensation refers to the workers of industrial enterprises engaged in production activities due to get all the rewards. Including various forms of laborers earned wages, bonuses and allowances, including both monetary forms, including physical form, but also workers enjoyed free medical and pharmaceutical health costs, commuting subsidies paid to units of social security charges, housing fund. For the individual economy, its owners have obtained labor remuneration and operating profit is not easy to distinguish, both are treated as workers compensation processing.

Net taxes on production refers to the production of industrial enterprises after taxes less subsidies on production balance. Production tax refers to the government of the production units engaged in production, sales and business activities as a result of engaging in production activities using certain factors of production (such as fixed assets, land, labor) from the collection of various taxes, surcharges and fees. Production subsidies and production taxes contrary, refers to the government's unilateral transfer of the production units and expenditure, so as negative taxes on production, including the loss subsidy policy, price subsidies.

Operating Surplus is the added value of industrial enterprises to create deducted workers compensation, net taxes on production and fixed asset depreciation balance. It is equivalent to the business profits plus subsidies on production, but should be deducted from the profits of expenses such as wages and benefits.

Total Assets refer to all economic resources, in monetary term, these are owned or controlled by enterprises, including properties, creditor's equity and other economic rights of all forms. Classified by the degree of liquidity, total assets include working capitals, long-term investment, fixed assets, intangible assets, deferred assets and other assets. Data on this indicator can be obtained by the year-end figures of total assets in the Assets and Liability Table of accounting records of enterprises.

Annual Average Value of Working Capital refers to the average value of all working capital of the enterprise during the reference period.

Annual Average of Net Value of Fixed Assets refers to the average of the net value of fixed assets during the reference period, calculated with the following formula:

$$\text{Annual Average of Net Value of Fixed Assets} = \frac{\text{sum of net value of fixed assets at the beginning and at the end of each month from January to December}}{24} \times 100\%$$

Information on this indicator can be obtained from the beginning and ending figures of the original value of fixed assets and cumulative depreciation from the Assets and Liability Table of enterprises.

Net value of fixed assets refers to the original value of fixed assets minus depreciation over the years, i.e.:

Net value of fixed assets = original value of fixed assets - cumulative depreciation

Product sales revenue refers to the production of finished products, semi-finished goods and industrial services of the revenue during the reporting period.

Cost of goods sold refers to the sale of the production of finished products, semi-finished goods and industrial services of the actual cost during the reporting period.

Sales taxes and surcharges refers to selling products, providing services, and other main business should be borne by the city maintenance and construction tax, consumption tax, resources tax and education surtax, etc during the reporting period.

Total Profits refer to the final achievement of production and operation activities of the enterprises, represented by total profits after deducting losses (loss is expressed by the negative figure). It is the sum of profits from operation, income from subsidies, investment earnings, net income from activities other than operation, and adjustment of profits and losses of previous years.

Value-added Tax Payable in the Current Year refers to the amount of the value-added tax which should be paid by the enterprises during the reference period. It is the sum of tax on sales, export rebate, and transferred tax on purchases of the current year, minus the tax on purchases of the current year. Value-added tax payable of small-size enterprises is determined by the taxable sales of the year multiplied by the tax rate.

Ratio of Profits, Taxes and Interests to Average Assets reflects the profit-making capability of all assets of the enterprise and is a key indicator manifesting the performance and management and evaluating the profit-making potential of the enterprise. It is calculated as follows:

$$\text{Ratio of Profits, Taxes and Interests to Average Asset(\%)} = \frac{\text{total profits + total taxes + interest payment}}{\text{average assets}} \times 100\%$$

In the above formula, total taxes is the sum of tax and extra charges on the sales of products and value-added tax payable; and average assets is the arithmetic mean of the sum of beginning assets and ending assets.

Ratio of Debts to Assets reflects both the operation risk and the capability of the enterprise in making use of the capital from the creditors. It is calculated as follows:

$$\text{Ratio of Debts to Assets (\%)} = \frac{\text{total debts}}{\text{total assets}} \times 100\%$$

Both assets and debts are figures at the end of the reference period.

Turnover of Working Capital refers to the number of times of turnover of working capital in a given period of time, which reflects the speed of the turnover of working capital of industrial enterprises, and is calculated as follows:

$$\text{Turnover of Working Capital} = \frac{\text{sales revenue of products}}{\text{average balance of total working capital}}$$

In the above formula, average balance of total working capital refers to the arithmetic mean of the sum of working capital at the beginning and at the end of the reference period.

Ratio of Profits to Total Industrial Costs refers to the ratio of profits realized in a given period to the total costs in the same period, which reflects the economic efficiency of input cost and is calculated as follows:

$$\text{Ratio of Profits to Total Industrial Cost(\%)} = \frac{\text{total profits}}{\text{total costs}} \times 100\%$$

Total costs in the above formula are the sum of cost of products sold, marketing cost, management cost and financial cost.

建筑业

15

Fifteen

Construction

15-1 建筑业主要指标

Main Economic Indicators on Construction Enterprises

指　标	Item	2007	2008	2009	2010	2011	2012
建筑业企业个数(个)	**Number of Enterprises (unit)**	**614**	**609**	**611**	**605**	**581**	**628**
年末从业人员(万人)	Number of Emplyed Persons at the Year-end(10000 persons)	29.12	30.16	33.05	33.83	33.14	35.57
自有固定资产原价(亿元)	Fixed Assets Owned(original value)(100 million yuan)	77.08	77.77	86.38	87.43	92.00	101.17
自有固定资产净价(亿元)	Fixed Assets Owned(net value)(100 million yuan)	51.72	50.78	59.12	57.16	57.33	61.62
自有机械设备台数(万台)	Number of Machinery and Equipment Owned(10000 sets)	6.84	6.22	6.21	7.97	7.26	6.74
自有机械设备净值(亿元)	Net Value of Machinery and Equipment Owned (100 million yuan)	21.93	23.54	24.45	27.85	33.08	24.45
自有机械设备总功率(万千瓦)	Total Power of Machinery and Equipment Owned (10000 kw)	116.79	128.90	113.22	142.88	153.03	143.00
建筑业总产值(亿元)	**Gross Output Value of Construction (100 million yuan)**	**348.79**	**393.88**	**523.91**	**622.96**	**824.72**	**1039.95**
建筑业增加值(亿元)	**Value Added of Construction(100 million yuan)**	**69.18**	**80.29**	**223.95**	**283.19**	**365.13**	**460.48**
#本年固定资产折旧	Depreciation of Fixed Assets	3.85	3.38	4.44	5.44	5.56	6.75
应付职工薪酬	Wages Payable	43.87	49.94	55.51	75.25	90.07	121.89
工程结算税金及附加	Taxes and Extra Charges on Project Settle Accounts	11.60	13.69	18.00	22.67	29.86	34.65
管理费用中的税金	Taxes in Management Expenses	0.54	0.90	0.60	0.8	0.83	1.34
营业利润	Operating Profits	3.58	6.05	6.84	9.78	14.31	12.51
房屋建筑施工面积(万平方米)	**Floor Space of Buildings under Construction (10000 sq.m)**	**3813**	**4230**	**4953**	**5756**	**6779**	**8254**
房屋建筑竣工面积(万平方米)	**Floor Space of Buildings Completed(10000 sq.m)**	**1204**	**1216**	**1244**	**1350**	**1530**	**1863**
利润总额(亿元)	Total Profits(100 million yuan)	4.08	6.46	6.63	10.48	14.4	16.30
税金总额(亿元)	Total Taxes(100 million yuan)	12.14	16.23	20.24	26.24	34.08	40.69
劳动生产率(元/人)	Overall Labor Productivity(yuan/person)						
按总产值计算	In Terms of Gross Output Value	126528	138070	159654	196170	222471	319469
按增加值计算	In Terms of Value-added	25096	28116	70294	89177	98494	141459
技术装备率(元/人)	Value of Machines Per Laborer(yuan/person)	7531	8248	7398	8232	9982	8148
动力装备率(千瓦/人)	Power of Machines Per Laborer(kw/person)	4.01	4.52	3.43	4.22	4.52	4.76
房屋建筑面积竣工率(%)	Ratio of Floor Space of Buildings Completed(%)	31.6	28.7	25.1	23.5	22.6	22.6
产值利润率(%)	Ratio of Profit to Gross Output Value(%)	1.2	1.6	1.3	1.7	1.7	1.6
产值利税率(%)	Ratio of Pre-tax Profit to Gross Output Value(%)	4.7	5.8	5.1	5.9	5.9	5.5

注：应付职工薪酬2007-2011年为应付工资数据。

Note:From 2007 to 2011, data of accrued payroll refers to the wages payable.

15-2 建筑业企业主要生产指标(2012)

指　　标	Item	企业个数(个) Number of Construstion Enterprises (unit)	年末从业人员(万人) Number of Persons Engaged (10000 persons)	签订合同额(亿元) Value of Signed Contract (100 million yuan)	#本年新签合同额 New Value of Signed Contract in this year
总　　计	**Total**	**628**	**35.57**	**2331.67**	**1311.85**
#国有及国有控股	State-owned and state-controlled Construction Enterprises	129	24.44	2003.50	1123.93
#施工总承包企业	General Contractors	470	34.32	2280.38	1284.23
专业承包企业	Special Contractors	158	1.25	51.29	27.63
按登记注册类型分组	**By Registration Status**				
#内资企业	Domestic Funded	627	35.57	2331.67	1311.85
#国有企业	State-owned	97	16.79	1388.12	807.78
集体企业	Collective-owned	98	2.22	46.77	29.97
股份有限公司	Company Limited with Share Holding	2	0.81	1.00	0.70
私营企业	Private Enterprises	171	2.80	117.29	68.73
按国民经济行业分组	**By Sector**				
房屋和土木工程建筑业	Building and Civil Engineering Construction	469	33.59	2099.22	1149.62
房屋工程建筑	Building Engineering Construction	385	21.86	1244.62	732.66
土木工程建筑	Civil Engineering Construction	84	11.73	854.60	416.96
建筑安装业	Construction Installation	66	1.47	181.95	131.63
建筑装饰业	Construction Decoration	60	0.20	23.41	19.21
其他建筑业	Others	33	0.31	27.09	11.39

Main Production Indicators on Construction Enterprises

建筑业总产值(亿元) Total Output Value of Construction (100 million yuan)	#在省外完成的产值 Value of Construction Which Fulfilled outside of Guizhou Province	#建筑工程 Output Value of Construction	#安装工程 Output Value of Installation	房屋建筑施工面积(万平方米) Floor Space of Buildings under Construction (10000 sq.m)	#本年新开工面积 Started This Year	#实行投标承包面积 Verified Eligible Area of the First Time	自有机械设备年末净值(万元) Net Value of Machinery and Equipment Owned (10000 yuan)	自有机械设备年末总台数(台) Number of Machinery and Equipment Owned (year-end) (unit)	自有机械设备年末总功率(万千瓦) Total Power of Machinery and Equipment Owned (year-end) (10000 kw)
1039.95	**200.00**	**911.06**	**90.64**	**8254**	**3099**	**6608**	**244530**	**67440**	**143.00**
859.68	193.36	755.23	73.42	6412	2116	5521	173565	41945	90.94
999.00	199.71	883.28	80.73	8250	3095	6607	239050	65841	137.96
40.95	0.30	27.78	9.92	4	4	1	5480	1599	5.03
1039.95	200.00	911.06	90.64	8254	3099	6608	244530	67440	143.00
589.68	166.66	520.02	49.47	5950	1838	5089	93821	27230	41.84
30.55		28.44	1.47	293	183	200	12411	5408	11.65
0.41		0.41		7	4				
63.77	4.75	55.74	5.82	784	400	409	27619	11091	23.52
886.32	165.20	826.68	37.20	7715	2799	6108	224380	61260	131.25
584.83	129.47	549.57	14.70	7480	2697	6020	107227	36596	66.52
301.48	35.73	277.11	22.50	235	102	87	117153	24664	64.73
118.73	34.80	54.50	51.58	410	209	409	15316	5141	8.29
13.08		11.02	0.62	99	90	90	267	228	0.18
21.82		18.86	1.24	30	1	1	4567	811	3.28

15-3 建筑业企业主要财务指标(2012)

单位：万元

指标	Item	年末资产负债 Assets 资产合计 Total Assets	#流动资产小计 Liquid Assets	#固定资产小计 Fixed Assets
总计	**Total**	**10310387**	**8212243**	**754605**
#国有及国有控股	Construction Enterprises of State-owned and state-controlled	8190066	6515281	497150
#施工总承包企业	General Contractors	9393599	7681518	693686
专业承包企业	Special Contractors	916788	530725	60920
按登记注册类型分组	**By Registration Status**			
#内资企业	Domestic Funded	10308680	8210559	754583
#国有企业	State-owned	4964379	4117009	301679
集体企业	Collective-owned	295186	223071	50784
股份有限公司	Company Limited with Share Holding	2532	2026	176
私营企业	Private Enterprises	681612	556947	87779
按国民经济行业分组	**By Sector**			
房屋和土木工程建筑业	Building and Civil Engineering Construction	8876592	7035939	681742
房屋工程建筑	Building Engineering Construction	4637345	3995274	337163
土木工程建筑	Civil Engineering Construction	4239247	3040666	344579
建筑安装业	Construction Installation	927264	818664	53229
建筑装饰业	Construction Decoration	133867	126994	3413
其他建筑业	Others	372665	230646	16222

Main Financial Indicators of Construction Enterprises

(10000 yuan)

and Liabilities(year-end)		所有者权益合计 Creditors' Equity	损益及分配 Loss-profit and Allocation			
负债合计 Total Liabilities	#流动负债小计 Liquid Liabilities		主营业务收入 Revenue of Project Settlement Accounts	其他业务收入 Revenue From Other Business	营业利润 Operating Profits	利润总额 Total Profits
8036279	**7306725**	**2274108**	**10042764**		**159823**	**162973**
6691199	6128094	1498867	8271209		125059	127213
7494245	6937693	1899354	9616209		135476	138344
542034	369032	374754	426555		24348	24629
8035739	7306185	2272941	10042764		159873	163023
4062873	3838757	901507	5692318		104901	107396
182923	162488	112263	305103		4603	3769
472	172	2061	4078		632	662
432344	386877	249268	607154		11770	11673
6966600	6386808	1909992	8565757		110852	113241
3688667	3499993	948677	5543925		98271	99950
3277933	2886815	961315	3021833		12581	13291
736273	699121	190991	1143028		32735	32991
92909	64976	40958	133814		1544	1828
240497	155821	132168	200165		14692	14913

15-4 建筑业企业房屋建筑(2012)

指　标	Item	竣工面积(平方米) Floor Space of Buildings Completed (sq.m)	#厂房、仓库 Workshop Storehouse	#住宅 Residential Buildings	#教育用房 Educational Buildings
总　计	**Total**	**18632538**	**1071077**	**11302479**	**1659731**
#国有及国有控股	Construction Enterprises of State-owned and state-controlled	11043058	774005	7248033	654330
#施工总承包企业	General Contractors	18608164	1071077	11288060	1659731
专业承包企业	Special Contractors	24374		14419	
按登记注册类型分组	**By Registration Status**				
#内资企业	Domestic Funded	18632538	1071077	11302479	1659731
#国有企业	State-owned	9951004	563758	6436318	644445
集体企业	Collective-owned	1679451	66589	931043	176541
股份有限公司	Company Limited with Share Holding	42160		17560	
私营企业	Private Enterprises	2357395	144683	1206639	329645
按国民经济行业分组	**By Sector**				
房屋和土木工程建筑业	Building and Civil Engineering Construction	17497674	1039513	10533092	1659731
房屋工程建筑	Building Engineering Construction	16914949	921398	10103818	1659731
土木工程建筑	Civil Engineering Construction	582725	118115	429274	
建筑安装业	Construction and Installation	805854	10864	754277	

Basic Statistics on House Buildings by Construction Enterprises

		总造价 (元/平方米) Total cost of Buildings Completed (yuan/sq.m)					
#卫生医疗用房 Medical Buildings	#科研用房 Scientific Research Buildings		#厂房、仓库 Workshop Storehouse	#住宅 Residential Buildings	#教育用房 Educational Buildings	#卫生医疗用房 Medical Buildings	#科研用房 Scientific Research Buildings
397673	**144549**	**1280**	**1584**	**1168**	**1761**	**1228**	**2645**
216591	109322	1410	1725	1192	2723	1235	3109
397673	144549	1280	1584	1169	1761	1228	2645
		926		766			
397673	144549	1280	1584	1169	1761	1228	2645
196917	109322	1423	1870	1183	2745	1214	3109
39761	3964	1012	1007	994	1004	1168	1018
8650	13500	874		735		1138	900
30167	11621	1232	1417	1212	1201	1349	1468
397673	144549	1304	1599	1169	1761	1228	2645
397673	144549	1301	1713	1151	1761	1228	2645
		1393	703	1580			
		1198	679	1164			

主要统计指标解释

建筑业统计单位 指从事房屋、构筑物建造和设备安装活动的法人企业。建筑业法人企业应同时具备的条件是：①依法成立，有自己的名称、组织机构和场所，能够承担民事责任；②独立拥有和使用资产，承担负债，有权与其他单位签订合同；③独立核算盈亏，能够编制资产负债表。

建筑业总产值（即自行完成施工产值） 是以货币形式表现的建筑业企业在一定时期内生产的建筑业产品和提供的服务的总和。建筑业总产值包括:

(1) 建筑工程产值：指列入建筑工程预算内的各种工程价值。

(2) 安装工程产值：指设备安装工程价值，不包括被安装设备本身价值。

(3) 其他产值：建筑业总产值中除建筑工程、安装工程以外的产值。包括房屋构筑物修理产值、非标准设备制造产值、总包企业向分包企业收取的管理费以及不能明确划分的施工活动所完成的产值。

a. 房屋构筑物修理产值：指房屋和构筑物修理所完成的产值，但不包括被修理房屋、构筑物本身价值和生产设备的修理价值。

b. 非标准设备制造产值：指加工制造没有定型的非标准生产设备的加工费和原材料价值（如化工厂、炼油厂用的各种罐、槽，矿井生产统一使用的各种漏斗、三角槽、阀门等）以及附属加工厂为本企业承建工程制作的非标准设备的价值。

建筑业增加值 指建筑业企业在报告期内以货币表现的建筑业生产经营活动的最终成果。建筑业现价增加值按生产法和分配法（收入法）两种方法计算，以收入法的计算结果为准，即从收入的角度出发，根据生产要素在生产过程中应得的收入份额计算。

房屋建筑施工面积 指在报告期内施过工的全部房屋建筑面积，包括本期新开工的房屋面积、上期施工跨入本期继续施工的房屋面积、上期停缓建在本期恢复施工的房屋面积、本期竣工的房屋面积及本期施工后又停缓建的房屋面积。

房屋建筑竣工面积 指在报告期内房屋建筑按照设计要求全部完工，达到了住人和使用条件，经验收鉴定合格，正式移交使用单位的房屋建筑面积。

企业总收入 指与企业生产经营直接有关的各项收入，包括工程结算收入和其他业务收入。计算公式为:

企业总收入＝工程结算收入＋其他业务收入

主营业务收入 指企业确认的销售商品、提供劳务等主营业务的收入。根据会计“主营业务收入”科目的期末贷方余额(结转前）填报。执行 2006 年《企业会计准则》的企业，如未设置该科目，以“营业收入”代替填报。

Explanatory Notes on Main Statistical Indicators

Statistical Unit in Construction refers to corporate enterprise engaged in the construction of buildings and structures and in the installation of equipment.A corporate construction enterprise should meet the following 3 requirements: ① being set up in line with relevant legal basis,having its full name,organization and location,and capable of taking civil liabilities; ② independently possessing and using its assets and assuming its liabilities,and entitled to sign contracts with other institutions; ③ and making independent accounts of its profits and losses,and capable of compiling its own balance sheet.

Gross Output Value of Construction refers to total of construction products and services, expressed in money terms, produced or rendered by construction and installation enterprises during a given period of time. It includes:

(1) Output value of construction projects: the value of projects covered by the project budgets;

(2) Output value of installation projects: the value of the installation of equipment, (excluding the value of the equipment to be installed);

(3) Other output values: the output value of construction industry apart from that of construction projects and installation projects. It includes: output value of repair of buildings and structures; output value of non-standard equipment manufacturing; overhead expenses received by contracted enterprises from the sub-contracted enterprises and the completed output value of construction activities for which there is no clear definition.

a. Output value of repair of buildings and structures: the value created through the repairs of buildings or structures. It does not include the value of buildings or structures being repaired and the value of the repair of production equipment;

b. Output value of manufactured non-standard equipment: the value of non-standard production equipment, including raw materials and manufacturing cost, made for the construction project (i.e., chemical plant; kettles or tanks used by refineries; various fillers, triangle tanks, valves used by mines). It also includes the output value of equipment manufactured by subsidiary workshops.

Value-added of Construction refers to the final result of the activities of production and operation of enterprises of the construction industry in monetary terms during the reference period. Value-added of construction is calculated by both production approach and income approach, with the figures from the income approach as the final figures., Under the income approach,, calculation starts from the perspective of income and is based on the share of income derived from the production process by the relevant factors of production.

Floor Space of Buildings Under Construction refers to floor space of buildings under construction during the reference period,including newly started buildings,buildings started earlier and continued during the reference period,and buildings suspended earlier but restarted during the reference period, buildings completed during the reference period, and buildings under construction and then suspended during the reference period.

Floor Space of Buildings Completed refers to the floor space of buildings that are completed in the reference period in accordance with the requirements of the design, up to the standard for putting them into use, and have been checked and accepted by concerned departments as qualified ones.

Total Revenue of Enterprises refers to the sum of income from production and operation of enterprises, including income from settlement of projects and other operational income, namely:

Total Revenue of Enterprises=Income from Settlement of Projects+Other Operational Income.

Income from Settlement of Projects refers to the income received by the construction enterprise from the contracted project through settlement procedures, and other charges to the contractoree as operational costs in addition to the value of the project,such as temporary facility fee,labour insurance premium,moving cost of construction equipment,as well as various types of claims to the contractee.

Profit from Settlement of Projects refers to profit realized through settled projects. It is calculated with the following formula:

Profit from Settlement of Projects=Income from Settlement of Projects-Settled Cost-Settled Taxes and Other Cost

16

Sixteen

运输和邮电

Transport, Postal and Telecommunication Services

16-1 境内运输线路长度
Length of Transport Routes

单位：公里 (km)

指　标	Item	2007	2008	2009	2010	2011	2012	2012年比2011年增长(%) Increase Rate in 2012 over 2011(%)
铁路营业里程	**Length of Railways in Operation**	**2012**	**1962**	**1983**	**2002**	**2070**	**2058**	**-0.6**
#复线里程	Double-tracking Length	560	560	604	643	643	678	5.4
公路线路里程	**Total Length of Highways**	**123247**	**125365**	**142561**	**151644**	**157820**	**164542**	**4.3**
按行政等级分	**Classified by Administrative Level**							
国　道	State Road	3658	3658	3717	3924	4132	4436	7.4
#国家高速公路	State Highway	986	868	1050	1259	1467	1772	20.8
省　道	Provincial Road	7217	7210	7346	7463	7769	8071	3.9
县　道	County Road	15534	17324	17272	17311	17350	17572	1.3
乡　道	Township Road	21079	18432	18459	18465	18447	18455	…
村　道	Village Road	75013	78051	95072	103785	109384	115267	5.4
专用公路	Accommodation Highway	746	690	697	697	737	741	0.6
按技术等级分	**Classified by Technical Grade**							
等级公路	Standard Highway	55517	64044	68046	72557	79643	86577	8.7
高速公路	Expressway	924	924	1189	1507	2022	2630	30.1
#四车道	Four-lane	920	920	1189	1507	1979	2587	30.7
一　级	First Class	120	139	151	153	164	179	9.2
二　级	Second Class	2658	2706	3171	3578	3831	4060	6.0
三　级	Third Class	8650	8412	8309	8222	8367	8453	1.0
四　级	Fourth Class	43165	51864	55226	59096	65258	71255	9.2
等外公路	Substandard Highway	67730	61321	74516	79087	78177	77965	-0.3
按路面类型分	**Classified by Pavement**							
有铺装路面(高级)	Paved Road (advanced)	6841	8045	9245	10474	14859	21610	45.4
沥青混凝土	Asphalt Concrete	2002	1919	2867	3663	4512	5781	28.1
水泥混凝土	Cement Concrete	4839	6126	6378	6810	10347	15830	53.0
简易铺装路面	Simple Paved Road	19272	20995	23748	26589	29167	31988	9.7
未铺装路面	Not-paved Road	97135	96325	109569	114581	113794	110944	-2.5
晴雨通车里程	Can be open to traffic in rainy or sunny days	100121	93845	112237	151644	157820	164542	4.3
可绿化里程	Can be green	89026	114213	132813	141768	147643	153072	3.7
养护里程	Maintained Road	109562	125032	142483	151644	157820	164542	4.3
内河航道里程	**Length of Navigable Inland Waterways**	**3322**	**3563**	**3563**	**3563**	**3563**	**3563**	**持平**

注：1.资料来源于省交通运输厅、成都铁路分局(以下相关表同)。2.2007年及以后公路线路里程包括村道里程。

Note:1.Data in the table are obtained from the Provincial Department of Transports and Chengdu Railway Branch(The relative tables in the chapter are the same). 2.Since 2007, the total length of highways has included the length of village road.

16–2 民用航空运输
Civil Aviation

指　标	Item	2007	2008	2009	2010	2011	2012	2012年比2011年增长(%) Increase Rate in 2012 over 2011(%)
机场个数(个)	**Numbei of Civil Airports(unit)**	**5**	**6**	**6**	**6**	**6**	**6**	**持平**
通航城市(个)	Cities Reachable (unit)	53	51	59	59	62	59	-4.8
#国际及地区城市	International and Regional Cities	4	4	5	6	6	5	-16.7
起降航班(架次)	Flight Movements (unit)	47829	48990	60680	64835	72009	81928	13.8
进出港旅客(万人次)	**Passengers Get in and Get out of the Airports(10000 person-times)**	**437.27**	**442.93**	**578.24**	**637.59**	**747.02**	**890.99**	**19.3**
#进港旅客	Passengers Get in the Airports	203.53	213.97	278.86	302.82	353.01	421.25	19.3
货物吞吐量(万吨)	**Volume of Freight Handled in Civil Aviation(10000 tons)**	**4.00**	**4.20**	**5.16**	**6.17**	**6.93**	**7.97**	**15.0**

注：资料来源于贵州省机场集团有限公司。
Note:Data in the table are provided by Airports Group Corporation Ltd. of Guizhou Province.

16–3 民用汽车拥有量
Possession of Civil Vehicles

单位：万辆 (10000 units)

指　标	Item	2007	2008	2009	2010	2011	2012	2012年比2011年增长(%) Increase Rate in 2012 over 2011(%)
民用汽车合计	**Total**	**65.05**	**77.15**	**96.83**	**121.30**	**140.12**	**166.72**	**19.0**
#载客汽车	Passenger Vehicles	40.36	48.95	63.40	82.19	101.14	126.47	25.0
载货汽车	Trucks	19.10	22.26	27.29	32.73	34.23	36.72	7.3
#私人汽车	Private Vehicles	44.74	54.27	71.28	92.77	109.54	134.19	22.5

注：资料来源于省交警总队车辆管理所。
Note:Data in the table are obtained from the vehicle management office of the provincial traffic police corps.

16-4 旅客运量及周转量

Passenger Traffic and Passenger-Kilometers

指　标	Item	2007	2008	2009	2010	2011	2012	2012年比2011年增长(%) Increase Rate in 2012 over 2011(%)
旅客运量(万人)	**Total Passenger Traffic(10000 persons)**	**74440**	**80056**	**84981**	**97793**	**120554**	**142809**	**18.5**
铁　路	Railways	2979	3199	3204	3437	3939	3902	-0.9
公　路	Highways	70377	75350	80044	92426	114429	136454	19.2
水　运	Waterways	1084	1507	1733	1930	2186	2453	12.2
旅客周转量(亿人公里)	**Passenger-Kilometers(100 million passenger-km)**	**369.20**	**407.59**	**430.56**	**514.41**	**631.74**	**718.22**	**13.7**
铁　路	Railways	160.51	163.00	162.41	189.38	204.58	199.20	-2.6
公　路	Highways	206.40	241.15	264.06	320.46	422.01	513.07	21.6
水　运	Waterways	2.29	3.44	4.09	4.57	5.15	5.95	15.5

注：2008年以后公路、水路运输量采用全国公路水路运输量专项调查数据(下表同)。

Note:Since 2008 the data of highways and waterways freight traffic have adopted the data of the special investigation on highways and waterways freight traffic(the same applies to the next table).

16-5 货物运输量及周转量

Freight Traffic and Ton-Kilometers

指　标	Item	2007	2008	2009	2010	2011	2012	2012年比2011年增长(%) Increase Rate in 2012over 2011(%)
货物运输量(万吨)	**Total Freight Traffic (10000 tons)**	**26788**	**33576**	**34844**	**40310**	**44890**	**52765**	**17.5**
铁　路	Railways	7289	6683	6997	7991	7219	6665	-7.7
公　路	Highways	18834	26156	27031	31409	36684	45000	22.7
水　运	Waterways	665	737	816	910	987	1100	11.4
货物周转量(亿吨公里)	**Total Freight Ton-Kilometers (100 million ton-km)**	**721.26**	**809.93**	**897.38**	**1012.20**	**1060.69**	**1177.78**	**11.0**
铁　路	Railways	583.85	564.31	644.41	706.45	696.36	693.68	-0.4
公　路	Highways	127.99	234.96	241.60	293.00	350.10	467.60	33.6
水　运	Waterways	9.42	10.66	11.37	12.75	14.23	16.50	16.0

16–6 电信主要指标

Major Indicators of Telecommunications

指　　标	Item	2007	2008	2009	2010	2011	2012	2012年比2011年增长 (%) Increase Rate in 2012 over 2011(%)
电信业务收入(亿元)	Business Revenue of Telecommunications (100 million yuan)	104.02	123.90	138.11	147.38	164.56	187.47	13.9
电信业务总量(亿元)	Business Revenue of Telecommunications (100 million yuan)	283.31	361.37	453.33	566.40	204.35	244.11	19.5
交换机总容量(万门)	Capacity of Telephone Exchanges (10000 line)	2334.67	2858.70	3182.88	3673.01	4838.00	5026.53	3.9
移动电话交换机容量(万户)	Capacity ofMobileTelephoneExchanges (10000 subscribers)	1442.50	1960.04	2332.20	2724.50	4433.00	4106.76	-7.4
长途光缆线路长度(万公里)	Length of LongDistance OpticalCable Lines(km)	3.01	2.98	2.86	3.02	3.45	3.32	-3.8
年末固定电话用户数(万户)	Number of Telephone Subscribers at Year-end (10000 subscribers)	521.19	499.61	451.13	432.61	403.96	380.00	-5.9
#农话用户数	Number of Rural Telephone Subscribers	209.99	217.60	196.64	184.37	149.07	115.55	-22.5
城市电话用户	Number of Local(urban)Telephone Subscribers	311.20	282.01	254.49	248.24	254.90	264.45	3.7
#公　用	Number of Public Telephone Subscribers	40.97	35.97	34.76	39.29	34.63	33.43	-3.5
移动电话用户(万户)	Number of Mobile Telephone Subscribers (10000 subscribers)	834.05	1185.84	1583.28	1964.40	2175.22	2515.00	15.6
移动短信业务量(亿条)	Mobile SMS Business Volume (100 million messages)	45.46	66.63	111.85	120.84	129.26	124.49	-3.7
互联网宽带接入端口(万个)	Number of Subscribers of Internet Service (10000 subscribers)	96.65	119.89	163.63	231.69	437.87	435.79	-0.5
电话普及率(包括移动电话)(部/百人)	Popularization Rate of Telephone (set/100 persons)	37.31	46.87	57.52	68.90	74.35	83.27	12.0
#移动电话普及率	Popularization Rate of Mobile Telephone	22.96	32.97	44.76	56.46	62.71	72.34	15.4
已通电话的行政村比重(%)	Percentage of Administrative Village with Phone Sets(%)	100	100	100	100	100	100	持平
国内长途电话(万分钟)	Number of Long Distance Telephone Calls Inside Country(10000 minutes)	103754	114322	91235	138922	111354	88786	-20.3
国际及港澳长途电话(万分钟)	Number of Long Distance Telephone Calls outside Country or to Macao、Hong Kong(10000 minutes)	252.32	313.66	65.00	121.83	111.00	79.22	-28.6

注：1.资料来源于省通信管理局。2.国内长途电话、国际及港澳长途电话2008年及以前单位为万次。3.电信业务总量增长速度按可比价计算。

Note:1.Data in the table are obtained from the provincial communications authority bureau. 2.Before 2008,Unit of measuring long- distance-telephone -calls inside and outside the country is 10000 person-time.3.The increase rate of business volume of telecommunication services is calculated at comparable prices.

16−7 邮政主要指标

Major Indicators of Post

指　标	Item	2007	2008	2009	2010	2011	2012	2012年比2011年增长(%) Increase Rate in 2012 over 2011(%)
邮电局所总数(处)	**Number of Post and Telecommunication Offices(unit)**	**8143**	**10995**	**29262**	**19372**	**21496**	**19482**	**-9.4**
邮政	Post	2082	2194	2259	1795	1425	1307	-8.3
电信	Telecommunication	6061	8801	27003	17577	20071	18175	-9.4
邮路总长度(公里)	Number of Postal Routes(km)	60747	65236	61854	96174	99155	136429	37.6
#汽车邮路	Number of Highway Postal Routes	25222	24733	28799	55901	58062	76734	32.2
铁路邮路	Number of Railways Postal Routes	6379	6876	6413	6413	6413	5880	-8.3
邮政业务总量(亿元)	Business Volume of Post (100 million yuan)	9.08	10.42	11.69	15.50	14.97	17.93	19.8
函件(万件)	Number of Letters(10000 pcs)	5735	6566	6768	5939	5041	6036	19.7
报刊、杂志累计订销数(万份)	Issue of Newspapers and Magazines(10000 copies)	28291	31899	32007	32084	35056	38027	8.5
国内特快专递(万件)	Pieces of Express Mail Services inside Nation (10000 pcs)	459	524	926	1115	1529	1796	17.4
国际特快专递(万件)	Pieces of Express Mail Services outside Nation (10000 pcs)	0.79	0.79	4.20	5.60	4.90	5.33	8.8
邮政储蓄期末余额(亿元)	Post Deposits at the Year-end(100 million yuan)	195.30	229.20	270.13	336.90	431.56	458.00	6.1
集邮业务(万枚)	Stamps for Collection(10000 pcs)	901	945	749	1226	1907	1918	0.6
长话业务电路(2M)	Long Distance Cable Lines(2M)	68658	97773	114805	127660	118618	178267	

注：1.资料来源于省邮政公司。2.2009年起邮电局所总数含电信部门特约代理点。3.2009年起国内、国际特快专递含快递企业数据。4.邮政业务总量增长速度按可比价计算。5.长话业务电路统计口径2011年及以前为固定长话电路业务(2M)、移动长话电路业务(2M)指标；2012年包含固定长话电路业务(2M)、移动长话电路业务(2M)、数据及互联网电路业务等，与以往年份数据不可比。

Notes:1.Data in the table are obtained from the provincial post company.2.Since 2009，the number of post and telecommunication offices include the special agent point,but not for the year 2008 and before. 3.Since 2009,pieces of express mail services inside and outside the country cover the courier companies. 4.The growth rates of the business volume of postal are calculated at comparable prices. 5.For the year 2011 and before ,the coverage of the long distance cable lines(2M) statistics referred fixed long distance circuit service (2M), mobile long distance circuit services (2M). It contained a fixed long-distance circuit service (2M), mobile long distance circuit services (2M), data and internet services, etc. circuits, and the data are not comparable with previous years.

主要统计指标解释

铁路营业里程 又称营业长度，指投入客货运输营业或临时营业的线路长度。

公路里程 指报告期末公路的实际长度。统计范围：包括城间、城乡间、乡（村）间能行驶汽车的公共道路，公路通过城镇街道的里程，公路桥梁长度、隧道长度、渡口宽度。不包括城市街道里程，断头路里程，农（林）业生产用道路里程，工（矿）企业等内部道路里程。统计原则：按已竣工验收或交付使用的实际里程计算；两条或多条公路共同经由同一路段的重复里程，只计算一次。

内河航道里程 指在一定时期内，能通航运输船舶及排筏的天然河流、湖泊水库、运河及通航渠道的长度。包括全年季节性通航累计三个月以上的航道，不包括仅供零散流放竹、木排的河道。两省以河为界的航道里程，双方均按一半计算，以免重复。该指标可以反映内河水运网的规模、水平和发展情况。

民用航空航线里程 指民航运输定期班机飞行的航线长度的总和。航线长度按机场之间的距离计算，通常有两种计算方法：一是将每条航线长度相加称为重复计算航线里程；一是将两线或两条以上航线经过同一区段里程，只计算一次航线长度称为不重复计算航线里程，一般常用的是后者。

货（客）运量 指在一定时期内，各种运输工具实际运送的货物（旅客）数量。货运按吨计算，客运按人计算。货物不论运输距离长短、货物类别，均按实际重量统计。旅客不论行程远近或票价多少，均按一人一次客运量统计；半价票、小孩票也按一人统计。

货物（旅客）周转量 指在一定时期内，由各种运输工具运送的货物（旅客）数量与其相应运输距离的乘积之总和。计算货物周转量通常按发出站与到达站之间的最短距离，也就是计费距离计算。计算公式为：

货物（旅客）周转量＝Σ货物（旅客）运输量 × 运输距离

邮电业务总量 指以价值量形式表现的邮电通信企业为社会提供各类邮电通信服务的总数量。邮电业务量按专业分类包括函件、包件、汇票、报刊发行、邮政快件、特快专递、邮政储蓄、集邮、传真、长途电话、出租电路、移动电话、分组交换数据通信、出租代维等。计算方法为各类产品乘以相应的平均单价（不变价）之和，再加上出租电路和设备、代用户维护电话交换机和线路等的服务收入。该指标综合反映了一定时期邮电业务发展的总成果，是研究邮电业务量构成和发展趋势的重要指标。计算公式为：

邮电业务总量＝Σ（各类邮电业务量 × 不变单价）+ 出租代维及其他业务收入
＝邮政业务总量＋电信业务总量

移动电话用户 指通过移动电话交换机进入移动电话网、占用移动电话号码的电话用户。用户数量以报告期末在移动电话营业部门实际办理登记手续进入移动电话网的户数进行计算，一部移动电话统计为一户。

固定电话用户 指在电信运营企业营业网点办理开户登记手续并已接入固定电话网上的全部电话用户。包括普通电话用户、公用电话用户、窄带综合业务数字网（N—ISDN）用户、智能网专用接入终端用户等。按行政区划分为城市电话用户和农村电话用户。1997年以前，“市内电话用户”是指接入县城及县以上城市的电话网上的电话用户；“农村电话用户”是指接入县邮电局农话台及县以下农村电话交换点，以县城为中心（除市话用户外）联通县、乡（镇）、行政村、村民小组的用户。从1997年起，电话用户数分组调整为以用户所在区域划分为“城市电话用户”和“乡村电话用户”，与过去的按市内电话和农村电话划分方法不同。而电话用户总数、电话机总部数统计范围不变。

城市电话用户 指直辖市、省辖市、地级市、县级市的市区、市郊区及县城（包括县人民政府所在地的县城关区或行政建制相当于县人民政府所在地的镇）范围内接入局用交换机的电话用户数，包括分布在农村地区的独立工矿区、林区、驻军等接入局用交换机的电话用户数。

农村电话用户 指县城关区以下的集镇和农村接入局用交换机的电话用户数。

Explanatory Notes on Main Statistical Indicators

Length of Railways in Operation also is known as operating length and refers to the investment business or temporary operating passenger and freight transport line length.

Length of Highways refers to the actual length of road during the reporting period. Statistical range: The length of highways includes that the car can travel on public roads in intercity, urban and rural areas, township (village). Road through the town streets mileage, length of roads and bridges, tunnel length, crossing width.It does not include the length of streets in big and medium-sized cities and highways built for the production purpose at factories, mines, forest areas and agricultural areas. Statistical principles: It is on the basis of final acceptance or delivery of the actual mileage calculation. If two or more highways go the same section of the way,the length of the section is only calculated for once and no duplication is allowed.

Length of Navigable Inland Waterways is an indicator reflecting the size and development of inland water network. It refers to the length of the natural rivers, lakes, reservoirs, canals, and ditches open to navigation during a given period, which enables transportation by ships and rafts. It includes the channels open to navigation for over an accumulated period of 3 months in a year, yet this does not include the river courses which are only used to float odd logs and bamboo rafts. For fear of repeating calculation, the length of waterways of boundary rivers between two provinces is reckon in a half for each province. This indicator can reflect the scale, level and development situation of the inland waterway network.

Length of Civil Aviation Routes refers to the length of all routes for regular civil aviation flights.There are usually two ways to calculate the distance between airports connected by the route length: One is to put the length of all air routes together, called duplicated calculation of the length of the routes;the other is not to allow the duplication in calculation when two or more routes passing the same section of aviation routes. The latter is usually used,as it can precisely show the size of the civil aviation network and indicate the extent of civil aviation serving the national economy and the people.

Freight(Passenger)Traffic refers to the volume of freight(passenger)transported with various means. Freight transport is calculated in tons and passenger traffic is calculated in the number of persons. Despite the type of freight and travelling distance,the freight transport is calculated in the actual weight of the goods:and despite the travelling distance and ticket price,the passenger traffic is calculated by the principle that one person can be counted only once in one travel. The passenger who travel with a half price ticket or a child ticket is also calculated as one person.

Freight Ton-kilometers(Passenger-kilometers) refer to the sum of the products of the volume of transported cargo (passengers) multiplying by the transport distance,usually using ton-kilometer and passenger-kilometer as units for measurement.Normally, the shortest distance between the departure station and the destination station (i.e., the payable distance) is the basis to calculate the freight ton-kilometers. The formula is as follows:

Freight Ton-kilometers (Passenger-kilometers) =∑{Freight (Passenger) Traffic × Distance of Transportation}

Measuring unit: ton-kilometer (person-kilometer)

Business Volume of Post and Telecommunications refers to the total amount of postal and telecommunication services, expressed in value terms, provided by the post and telecommunications departments for society. It can be classified as: letters, parcels, drafts, circulating presses, postal expresses, EMS, postal savings, stamp collecting, faxes, long distance telephones, rent circuitries, mobile phones, packet switching digital communication and lease and maintenance etc. This indicator reflects the overall results of development of postal and telecommunication services in a certain period, and it is an important indicator for researching construction and development of business volume of post and telecommunications. The calculating formula is:

Business Volume of Post and Telecommunications = ∑(various Business Volume of Post and Telecommunications × fixed unit prices) + lease and maintenance and other business incomes

= Business Volume of Post + Business Volume of Telecommunications

Mobile Telephone Subscribers are connected with the mobile telephone communication network through the mobile telephone switchboards and occupy mobile phone numbers. In the reporting period the number of users in the mobile phone operating divisions actual registration number of households into the mobile phone network to calculate a statistic as a mobile phone.

Local Telephone Subscribers refers to all subscribers who have gone through registration procedures in the operation points of enterprises engaged in telecommunications and are hence connected to the local telecommunications service provider through fixed line network. Included are general subscribers, public telephones subscribers, N-ISDN subscribers and intelligent network terminal subscribers. They are also classified in terms of administrative districts as urban telephone subscribers and rural telephone subscribers according to location. Before 1997, the "local phone users" refers to access cities above county and county telephone line telephone subscribers; "Rural Telephone User" refers to access the post office, if farmers Taiwan county and below county rural telephone exchange points, to the county as the center (except local subscriber outside) Unicom county and township (town), administrative villages, village groups of users. From 1997 onwards, the number of telephone users adjust to the user group area classified as "urban telephone subscribers" and "rural telephone subscribers," with the past by local and rural telephone divided in different ways. But the number of telephone users and telephone statistical range are unchanged.

Urban Telephone Subscribers refers to number of telephone subscribers, located at municipalities, cities under the jurisdiction of province, cities at prefecture level, downtown and suburb of city at county level town and county towns (including country towns where county government located, and towns of county level according to the administrative organizational system), that are connected to the public line telephone network, including rural mineral area, forest area, military area.

Rural Telephone Subscribers refers to telephone subscribers, located at the towns below the level of county town and villages, that are connected to the public line telephone network.

17

Seventeen

批发和零售业

Wholesale and Retail Trades

17−1 社会消费品零售总额

Total Retail Sales of Consumer Goods

单位：亿元 (100 million yuan)

指 标	Item	2007	2008	2009	2010	2011	2012
社会消费品零售总额	**Total Retail Sales of Consumer Goods**	**858.15**	**1075.24**	**1247.25**	**1482.68**	**1751.62**	**2027.64**
按地域分	**By Area**						
城镇	Urban	667.83	838.81	971.37	1213.66	1439.22	1667.36
乡村	Rural	190.32	236.43	275.88	269.02	312.40	360.28
按行业分	**By Sector**						
批发和零售业	Wholesale and Retail Trade	720.80	952.04	1114.40	1329.51	1576.66	1829.28
住宿和餐饮业	Hotel and Catering Services	121.43	106.90	132.85	153.17	174.96	198.36

注：表中2009年及以前的“城镇”数据为市、县消费品零售总额合计数，“乡村”数据为县以下消费品零售额。

Note:The urban data in the table were the total number of cities and counties in total retail sales of consumer goods before 2009.The rural data were under County level in total retail sales of consumer goods.

17−2 限额以上批发业和零售业

Basic Conditions of Enterprises above Designated Size in Wholesale and Retail Trade Services

指 标	Item	2007	2008	2009	2010	2011	2012
批发业	**Wholesale Trade**						
法人企业(个)	Number of Corporations(unit)	143	248	283	306	332	487
年末从业人数(人)	Employees at Year-end(person)	38040	66821	38332	41066	45691	51372
商品购进额(亿元)	Total Purchases(100 million yuan)	316.06	579.92	575.07	776.73	1124.58	1419.29
商品销售额(亿元)	Total Sales(100 million yuan)	534.56	815.21	825.77	1095.34	1309.90	1907.99
期末商品库存额(亿元)	Inventory at year-end(100 million yuan)	47.02	83.85	80.45	93.47	127.38	175.80
零售业	**Retail Trade**						
法人企业(个)	Number of Corporations(unit)	108	303	371	494	555	793
年末从业人数(人)	Employees at Year-end(person)	18085	24998	30806	38154	44045	54865
商品购进额(亿元)	Total Purchases(100 million yuan)	107.72	200.02	278.82	423.39	588.27	764.09
商品销售额(亿元)	Total Sales(100 million yuan)	127.22	260.20	358.02	487.38	690.58	898.82
期末商品库存额(亿元)	Inventory at Year-end(100 million yuan)	10.75	32.77	28.67	42.11	59.71	76.89
年末零售营业面积(万平方米)	Retail Operating Area at year-end(10000 sq.m)	116.00	142.28	195.96	212.03	230.85	203.48

17-3 限额以上批发业企业(2012)

单位：万元

指标	Item	法人企业(个) Number of Corporation (Unit)	从业人数(人) Employees (person)
合计	**Total**	**487**	**51372**
按登记注册类型分组	**by Types of Registration Status**		
内资企业	**Domestic Funded Enterprises**	**486**	**51213**
国有企业	State-owned Enterprises	72	31517
集体企业	Collective-owned Enterprises	18	953
股份合作企业	Cooperation Enterprises	6	263
联营企业	Joint Ownership Enterprises		
有限责任公司	Limited Liability Corporations	249	13030
股份有限公司	Share-holding Corporations Ltd.	12	1498
私营企业	Private Enterprises	117	3505
其他	Other Enterprises	12	447
港、澳、台商投资企业	**Enterprises with Funds From HongKong, Macao and Taiwan**		
合资经营企业(港或澳、台资)	Joint-venture Enterprises		
合作经营企业(港或澳、台资)	Cooperative Enterprises		
港、澳、台商独资经营企业	Enterpises with Sole Investment		
港、澳、台商投资股份有限公司	Share-holding Corporations Ltd.		
外商投资企业	**Foreign Funded Enterprises**	**1**	**159**
中外合资经营企业	Joint-venture Enterprises	1	159
中外合作经营企业	Cooperation Enterprises		
外资企业	Enterprises with Sole Fund		
外商投资股份有限公司	Share-holding Corporations Ltd.		
按国民经济行业分组	**by Sector**		
农畜产品批发	**Wholesale of Farm Produce and Livestock Products**	**2**	**95**
谷物、豆及薯类批发	Wholesale of Grain, Beans and Potatoes		
种子、饲料批发	Wholesale of Seeds and Feed	2	95
棉、麻批发	Wholesale of Cotton and hemp		
牲畜批发	Wholesale of Livestock		
其他农畜产品批发	Others		
食品、饮料及烟草制品批发	**Wholesale of Food,Beverages and Tobaccos**	**67**	**25243**
米、面制品及食用油批发	Wholesale of Rice,Flour and Edible oil	12	1056
糕点、糖果及糖批发	Wholesale of Pastries, Candy and Sugar	1	39
果品、蔬菜批发	Wholesale of Fruit and Vegetables	3	330
肉、禽、蛋及水产品批发	Wholesale of Meat, Poultry, Eggs and Aquatic Products	4	258
盐及调味品批发	Wholesale of Salt and Condiment	12	723
酒、饮料及茶叶批发	Wholesale of Wine,Beverages and Tea	25	3986
烟草制品批发	Wholesale of Tobaccos and Related Products	10	18851
其他食品批发	Wholesale of Other Food		
纺织、服装及家庭用品批发	**Wholesale of Textiles,Garments and Daily Consumer Goods**	**17**	**1320**
纺织品、针织品及原料批发	Wholesale of Textiles ,Knitwear and Raw Materials		

注：表中行业分类按国民经济行业分类GB/T4754-2011分(以下相关表同)。

Basic Conditions of Enterprises above Designated Size in Wholesale Trade

(10000 yuan)

购进总额 Total Purchases	销售总额 Total Sales	批发 Wholesale Trade	零售 Retail Trade	年末库存额 Inventory (year-end)
14192923	**19079910**	**17379306**	**1700604**	**1758048**
14175795	**19064253**	**17366781**	**1697473**	**1749177**
7736304	11960595	10773730	1186865	1226445
78816	78748	70747	8001	11059
17337	16473	16079	394	2200
4286261	4414471	4229180	185292	288937
996129	1507086	1212588	294498	133066
976084	1001070	979605	21465	80822
84865	85811	84852	959	6648
17128	**15657**	**12526**	**3131**	**8872**
17128	15657	12526	3131	8872
10222	**10622**	**10622**		**310**
10222	10622	10622		310
4475126	**8027251**	**7478179**	**549072**	**1103481**
146537	141605	131613	9992	68425
4039	3792	3792		248
40661	40747	23694	17053	598
15146	16936	16590	346	1506
59790	81154	77900	3254	6715
998330	3487317	2971147	516170	144560
3210623	4255700	4253444	2256	881429
262484	**258349**	**245633**	**12716**	**35854**

Note:Date in this table is classified by sector of the National Economy(GB/T4754-2011)(The relative tables in the chapter are the same).

17-3 续表

单位：万元

指 标	Item	法人企业(个) Number of Corporation (Unit)
服装批发	Wholesale of Garments	4
鞋帽批发	Wholesale of Shoes and Hats	
厨房、卫生间用具及日用杂货批发	Wholesale of Kitchen and Lavatory Appliance and Daily Consumer Groceries	1
化妆品及卫生用品批发	Wholesale of Cosmetics and Hygiene Products	1
家用电器批发	Wholesale of Household Electrical Appliances	10
其他家庭用品批发	Wholesale of Other Daily Consumer Goods	1
文化、体育用品及器材批发	**Wholesale of Culture,Sports Goods and Equipments**	**11**
文具用品批发	Wholesale of Stationery	3
体育用品批发	Wholesale of Sports Goods	
图书批发	Wholesale of Books	6
报刊批发	Wholesale of Newspapers and Periodicals	
音像制品及电子出版物批发	Wholesale of Audio and Visual Products and Electronic Publications	
首饰、工艺品及收藏品批发	Wholesale of Jewelry,Arts and Crafts and Collections	
其他文化用品批发	Wholesale of Other Cultural Articles	2
医药及医疗器材批发	**Wholesale of Medicines and Medical Appliances**	**52**
西药批发	Wholesale of Western Medicines	40
中药批发	Wholesale of Traditional Chinese Medicines	12
医疗用品及器材批发	Wholesale of Medical Articles and Appliances	
矿产品、建材及化工产品批发	**Wholesale of Mininery Products,Building Materials and Chemical Materials**	**267**
煤炭及制品批发	Wholesale of Coal and Related Products	122
石油及制品批发	Wholesale of Petroleum and Related Products	11
非金属矿及制品批发	Wholesale of Non-metallic Minerals and Related Products	3
金属及金属矿批发	Wholesale of Metal Materials	35
建材批发	Wholesale of Building Materials	17
化肥批发	Wholesale of Chemical Fertilizers	43
农药批发	Wholesale of Pesticide	
农用薄膜批发	Wholesale of Agricultural Film	
其他化工产品批发	Wholesale of Other Chemical Materials	36
机械设备、五金交电及电子产品批发	**Wholesale of Machinery,Hardware,Transport, Electric and Electronic Products**	**57**
农业机械批发	Wholesale of Agricultural Machinery	1
汽车批发	Wholesale of Automotive	14
汽车零配件批发	Wholesale of Auto Parts	8
摩托车及零配件批发	Wholesale of Motorcycle Parts & Accessories	4
五金产品批发	Wholesale of Hardware Products	3
电气设备批发	Wholesale of Electrical Equipment	
计算机、软件及辅助设备批发	Wholesale of Computer,Software and Assistance Appliances	4
通讯及广播电视设备批发	Wholesale of Communication , Radio and Television Equipments	4
其他机械设备及电子产品批发	Wholesale of Other Machinery Equipments and Electric Products	19
贸易经纪与代理	**Trade Broker and Agent**	
其他批发	**Others**	**14**
再生物资回收与批发	Wholesale and Reclaim of Regeneration Materials	6
其他未列明的批发	Other Wholesale Unlisted	8

continued

(10000 yuan)

从业人数（人） Employees (person)	购进总额 Total Purchases	销售总额 Total Sales	批发 Wholesale Trade	零售 Retail Trade	年末库存额 Inventory (year-end)
265	35486	37500	37037	463	6734
40	558	609	609		255
20	1096	1482	1482		314
973	221933	215127	202875	12253	28217
22	3411	3630	3630		335
509	**164609**	**156195**	**154293**	**1902**	**39062**
87	20781	21026	20552	474	7329
364	134615	125951	125792	159	30380
58	9213	9218	7949	1269	1353
3995	**676179**	**706443**	**680273**	**26170**	**53988**
3436	571177	585291	565396	19896	45248
559	105002	121152	114878	6275	8740
16763	**7551956**	**8841508**	**7772456**	**1069053**	**445106**
4094	2233323	2259802	2199232	60571	70415
8668	1069225	1700670	742257	958413	80389
30	16349	18215	18215		19
833	1198857	1217840	1212599	5241	41164
217	134721	133579	124631	8948	9418
1583	2044879	2118651	2104203	14448	130213
1338	854601	1392750	1371319	21432	113487
2908	**981590**	**1005056**	**963416**	**41640**	**74491**
32	8520	8438		8438	1536
633	111188	111529	96679	14850	12193
477	495358	496292	487780	8512	5127
115	53278	58900	58685	215	5872
103	23708	25108	24849	258	3215
171	35093	35997	30353	5643	1933
132	24746	26384	24003	2382	2573
1245	229699	242407	241067	1340	42043
539	**70758**	**74487**	**74435**	**52**	**5757**
296	34029	34072	34072		3962
243	36730	40415	40363	52	1795

17–4 限额以上批发业企业主要财务指标(2012)
Main Financial Indicators of Enterprises above Designated Size in Wholesale Trade

单位：万元 (10000 yuan)

指标	Item	主营业务收入 Revenue from Principal Business	主营业务成本 Cost of Principal Business	主营业务税金及附加 Tax and Extra Charges on Principal Business	销售费用 Selling Expenses	营业利润 Operating Profits
总计	**Total**	**17540145**	**13499914**	**301270**	**720228**	**2258320**
#国有控股	State-Controlled	2451780	2512548	4662	99270	113757
按登记注册类型分组	**Grouped by Registration Status**					
内资企业	**Domestic-funded Enterprise**	**17526763**	**13489556**	**301219**	**716515**	**2259079**
国有企业	State-owned Enterprise	730310	602313	2256	39117	98544
集体企业	Collective-owned Enterprise	33043	22920	165	820	8195
股份合作企业	Copperative Enterprise	383942	355560	474	6720	17711
联营企业	Joint Ownership Enterprises	15445	13590	3	672	318
有限责任公司	Limited Liability Corporations	2955364	2569732	11828	193313	45497
股份有限公司	Share Holding Co.Ltd	1200287	1443105	1447	46002	-8826
私营企业	Private Enterprise	1152373	1050456	3680	46110	15239
其他	Other Enterprises	160074	141195	537	9287	3320
港、澳、台商投资企业	**Enterprises with Funds From HongKong, Macao and Taiwan**					
合资经营企业(港或澳、台资)	Joint-venture Enterprises					
合作经营企业(港或澳、台资)	Cooperative Enterprises					
港、澳、台商独资经营企业	Enterpises with Sole Investment					
港、澳、台商投资股份有限公司	Share-holding Corporations Ltd.					
外商投资企业	**Foreign Funded Enterprises**	**13382**	**10358**	**51**	**3712**	**-759**
中外合资经营企业	Joint-venture Enterprises	13382	10358	51	3712	-759
中外合作经营企业	Cooperation Enterprises					
外资企业	Enterprises with Sole Fund					
外商投资股份有限公司	Share-holding Corporations Ltd.					
按国民经济行业分组	**by Sector**					
农畜产品批发	**Wholesale of Farm Produce and Livestock Products**	**9779**	**9034**	**18**	**14**	**56**
谷物、豆及薯类批发	Wholesale of Grain, Beans and Potatoes					
种子、饲料批发	Wholesale of Seeds and Feed	9779	9034	18	14	56
棉、麻批发	Wholesale of Cotton and hemp					
牲畜批发	Wholesale of Livestock					
其他农畜产品批发	Others					
食品、饮料及烟草制品批发	**Wholesale of Food,Beverages and Tobaccos**	**7233851**	**4031934**	**245150**	**437544**	**2032363**
米、面制品及食用油批发	Wholesale of Rice,Flour and Edible oil	141161	118698	116	6142	2893
糕点、糖果及糖批发	Wholesale of Pastries, Candy and Sugar	3496	3206		250	3
果品、蔬菜批发	Wholesale of Fruit and Vegetables	40727	39474	50	438	515
肉、禽、蛋及水产品批发	Wholesale of Meat, Poultry, Eggs and Aquatic Products	16427	14677	28	1466	4
盐及调味品批发	Wholesale of Salt and Condiment	78118	58912	348	4977	3049
酒、饮料及茶叶批发	Wholesale of Wine，Beverages and Tea	3113068	824316	85350	234848	1776911
烟草制品批发	Wholesale of Tobaccos and Related Products	3840854	2972651	159258	189423	248988
其他食品批发	Wholesale of Other Food					
纺织、服装及家庭用品批发	**Wholesale of Textiles,Garments and Daily Consumer Goods**	**225043**	**204980**	**513**	**13796**	**401**
纺织品、针织品及原料批发	Wholesale of Textiles ,Knitwear and Raw Materials					

17-4 续表 continued

单位：万元 (10000 yuan)

指 标	Item	主营业务收入 Revenue from Principal Business	主营业务成本 Cost of Principal Business	主营业务税金及附加 Tax and Extra Charges on Principal Business	销售费用 Selling Expenses	营业利润 Operating Profits
服装批发	Wholesale of Garments	33233	30624	38	1002	424
鞋帽批发	Wholesale of Shoes and Hats					
厨房、卫生间用具及日用杂货批发	Wholesale of Kitchen and Lavatory Appliance and Daily Consumer Groceries	609	579	25	144	-284
化妆品及卫生用品批发	Wholesale of Cosmetics and Hygiene Products	1482	1304	0	8	75
家用电器批发	Wholesale of Household Electrical Appliances	186089	169038	429	12511	188
其他家庭用品批发	Wholesale of Other Daily Consumer Goods	3630	3435	21	131	-3
文化、体育用品及器材批发	**Wholesale of Culture,Sports Goods and Equipments**	**136170**	**126742**	**248**	**4731**	**1145**
文具用品批发	Wholesale of Stationery	18707	17218	28	519	254
体育用品批发	Wholesale of Sporting Goods					
图书批发	Wholesale of Books	109550	101864	201	3965	858
报刊批发	Wholesale of Newspapers and Periodicals					
音像制品及电子出版物批发	Wholesale of Audio and Visual Products and Electronic Publications					
首饰、工艺品及收藏品批发	Wholesale of Jewelry,Arts and Crafts and Collectibles					
其他文化用品批发	Wholesale of Other Cultural Articles	7914	7660	20	247	33
医药及医疗器材批发	**Wholesale of Medicines and Medical Appliances**	**629861**	**577263**	**1710**	**23330**	**10270**
西药批发	Wholesale of Western Medicine	521630	484122	1325	12206	10116
中药批发	Wholesale of Chinese Traditional Medicines	108231	93141	385	11124	153
医疗用品及器材批发	Wholesale of Medical Articles and Appliances					
矿产品、建材及化工产品批发	**Wholesale of Mininery Products,Building Materials and Chemical Materials**	**8331965**	**7642608**	**52019**	**199988**	**209354**
煤炭及制品批发	Wholesale of Coal and Related Products	2144247	1912343	3839	99390	-15763
石油及制品批发	Wholesale of Petroleum and products	1476144	1210451	1357	31695	205265
非金属矿及制品批发	Wholesale of Non-metallic Minerals and Products	17642	16435	181	178	501
金属及金属矿批发	Wholesale of Metal Materials	1109785	1079104	1319	11164	11261
建材批发	Wholesale of Building Materials	105681	103242	101	1262	-1617
化肥批发	Wholesale of Chemical Fertilizer	2112232	2054136	21526	22661	-4203
农药批发	Wholesale of Pesticide					
农用薄膜批发	Wholesale of Agricultural Film					
其他化工产品批发	Wholesale of Other Chemical Materials	1366233	1266898	23694	33637	13909
机械设备、五金交电及电子产品批发	**Wholesale of Machinery,Hardware, Transport, Electric and Electronic Products**	**901918**	**842375**	**1038**	**38559**	**3648**
农业机械批发	Wholesale of Agricultural Machinery	8438	6685	1	800	654
汽车批发	Wholesale of Automotive	83819	80347	165	5391	-3093
汽车零配件批发	Wholesale of Auto Parts	444720	423649	103	14340	3173
摩托车及零配件批发	Wholesale of Motorcycle Parts & Accessories	57793	54983	73	826	682
五金产品批发	Wholesale of Hardware Products	21285	20048	12	679	-8
电气设备批发	Wholesale of Electrical Equipment					
计算机、软件及辅助设备批发	Wholesale of Computer,Software and Assistance Appliances	33933	32612	35	534	172
通讯及广播电视设备批发	Wholesale of Communications and Broadcasting Equipment	23217	19365	71	339	65
其他机械设备及电子产品批发	Others	228712	204686	578	15649	2002
贸易经纪与代理	**Trade Broker and Agent**					
其他批发	**Others**	**71558**	**64979**	**575**	**2267**	**1084**
再生物资回收与批发	Wholesale and Reclaim of Regeneration Materials	32565	31072	371	1012	-463
其他未列明的批发	Other Wholesale Unlisted	38993	33907	204	1255	1546

17-5 限额以上零售业企业(2012)

单位：万元

指 标	Item	法人企业(个) Number of Corporations (Unit)
合 计	**Total**	**793**
按登记注册类型分组	**by Types of Registration Status**	
内资企业	**Domestic Funded Enterprises**	**774**
国有企业	State-owned Enterprises	72
集体企业	Collective-owned Enterprises	7
股份合作企业	Cooperation Enterprises	7
联营企业	Joint Ownership Enterprises	2
有限责任公司	Limited Liability Corporations	360
股份有限公司	Share-holding Corporations Ltd.	17
私营企业	Private Enterprises	281
其他	Other Enterprises	28
港、澳、台商投资企业	**Enterprises with Funds From Hongkong, Macao and Taiwan**	**8**
#合资经营企业(港或澳、台资)	Joint-venture Enterprises	5
合作经营企业(港或澳、台资)	Cooperative Enterprises	
港、澳、台商独资经营企业	Enterpises with Sole Investment	2
港、澳、台商投资股份有限公司	Share-holding Corporations Ltd.	
其他港、澳、台商投资企业	Others	1
外商投资企业	**Foreign Funded Enterprises**	**11**
中外合资经营企业	Joint-venture Enterprises	3
中外合作经营企业	Cooperation Enterprises	
外资企业	Enterprises with Sole Fund	8
外商投资股份有限公司	Share-holding Corporations Ltd.	
按国民经济行业分组	**by Sector**	
综合零售	**Integrated Retail**	**109**
#百货零售	Retail of General Merchandise	40
超级市场零售	Retail of Supermarkets	62
其他综合零售	Other Integrated Retail	7
食品、饮料及烟草制品专门零售	**Retail of Food,Beverages and Tobaccos**	**58**
粮油零售	Retail of Grain and Oil	12
糕点、面包零售	Retail of Pastries and Bread	
果品、蔬菜零售	Retail of Fruits and Vegetables	1
肉、禽、蛋及水产品零售	Retail of Meat, Poultry, Eggs and Aquatic Products	2
酒、饮料及茶叶零售	Retail of Wine,Beverages and Tea	42
烟草制品零售	Retail of Tobaccos and Related Products	
其他食品零售	Other Food Retail	1
纺织品、服装及日用品专门零售	**Retail of Textiles,Garments and Daily Consumer Goods**	**18**
纺织品及针织品零售	Retail of Textiles and Knitwear	
服装零售	Retail of Garments	15
鞋帽零售	Retail of Shoes and Hats	

Basic Conditions of Enterprises above Designated Size in Retail Sales

(10000 yuan)

从业人数(人) Employees (person)	购进总额 Total Purchases	销售总额 Total Sales			年末库存额 Inventory at year-end
			批发 Wholesale Trade	零售 Retail Trade	
54865	**7640896**	**8988187**	**888347**	**8099840**	**768891**
51020	**7169031**	**8472241**	**879983**	**7592258**	**723652**
4348	874640	1429806	212351	1217456	61835
81	39709	36282	7141	29141	4814
1021	328267	460795	129300	331496	21385
58	26506	15675		15675	11810
26537	3325487	3416654	194010	3222644	417477
3457	1200535	1696297	222034	1474262	41979
12609	1200671	1250812	108175	1142637	142850
2909	173215	165920	6972	158948	21501
1271	**237821**	**260939**	**8364**	**252575**	**16968**
817	209363	225612	5703	219909	12607
340	9528	12469	2662	9808	4361
114	18930	22858		22858	
2574	**234044**	**255007**		**255007**	**28272**
1318	139286	151299		151299	14892
1256	94759	103708		103708	13380
17527	**1107726**	**1117746**	**4666**	**1113080**	**107268**
5793	651625	656993	2237	654756	32883
10743	397523	413448	1390	412058	57620
991	58578	47305	1039	46266	16766
1731	**249930**	**323721**	**87147**	**236573**	**36848**
651	47970	45786	23166	22620	11548
20	580	579		579	2
47	52554	74841	37991	36850	223
982	148218	201442	24917	176525	24819
31	608	1073	1073		257
1469	**88894**	**103588**	**27462**	**76125**	**20837**
1387	86034	100017	26691	73326	19626

17-5 续表

单位：万元

指　标	Item	法人企业(个) Number of Corporations (Unit)	从业人数(人) Employees (person)
钟表、眼镜零售	Retail of Horologe and Spectacles	2	41
化妆品及卫生用品零售	Retail of Cosmetics and Hygiene Products		
厨房用具及日用杂品零售	Retail of Kitchen utensils and household goods	1	41
其他日用品零售	Retail of Other Daily Consumer Use		
文化、体育用品及器材专门零售	**Retail of Culture,Sports Apliances and Equipments**	**57**	**1724**
文具用品零售	Retail of Stationery	1	12
体育用品及器材零售	Retail of Sports Goods	2	45
图书零售、报刊零售	Retail of Books, newspapers and periodicals	48	1325
音像制品及电子出版物零售	Retail of Audio and Visual Products and Electronic Publications	1	44
珠宝首饰零售	Retail of Jewelry	3	236
工艺美术品及收藏品零售	Retail of Arts and Crafts and Collections	1	39
照相器材零售	Retail of Photographic Equipment	1	23
其他文化用品零售	Retail of Other Cultural Articles		
医药及医疗器材专门零售	**Retail of Medicines and Medical Appliances**	**42**	**5644**
#药品零售	Retail of Medicines	40	5607
医疗用品及器材零售	Retail of Medical Articles and Appliances	2	37
汽车、摩托车、燃料及零配件专门零售	**Retail of Motor Vehicles, Motorcycles, Fuel and Parts**	**352**	**19808**
#汽车零售	Retail of Motor Vehicles	290	12753
汽车零配件零售	Retail of Auto Parts and Accessories	4	63
摩托车及零配件零售	Retail of Motorcycles,Parts and Accessories	20	346
机动车燃料零售	Retail of Fuel of Motor Vehicles	38	6646
家用电器及电子产品专门零售	**Retail of Household Electric Appliances and Electronic Products**	**127**	**4751**
家用试听设备零售	Retail of Listen household equipment	19	519
日用家电设备零售	Retail of Household appliances	63	2740
计算机、软件及辅助设备零售	Retail of Computer,Software and Assistant Appliances	34	607
通讯设备零售	Retail of Communication Equipments	10	665
其他电子产品零售	Retail of Other Electronic Products	1	220
五金、家具及室内装修材料专门零售	**Retail of Hardware, Furniture and Interior Decoration Materials**	**9**	**104**
五金零售	Retail of Hardware	3	23
家具零售	Retail of Furniture	3	29
涂料零售	Retail of Paint	1	18
木制装饰材料零售	Retail of Wooden decorative materials	1	23
其他室内装修材料零售	Retail of Other Interior Decoration Materials	1	11
货摊、无店铺及其他零售	**Stalls,Non-shop and Other Retails**	**21**	**2107**
流动货摊零售	Retail of Flow Stalls		
互联网零售	Retail of Internet	1	8
邮购及电视、电话零售	Retail of Mail order, TV and telephone	2	1327
生活用燃料零售	Retail of life Fuel	9	495
花卉零售	Retail of Flowers		
旧货零售	Retail of Second-hand Goods		
其他未列明的零售	Other Retails Unlisted	9	277

continued

(10000 yuan)

购进总额 Total Purchases	销售总额 Total Sales	批发 Wholesale Trade	零售 Retail Trade	年末库存额 Inventory at Year-end
2149	2417	772	1645	937
711	1154		1154	274
125341	**122704**	**14864**	**107840**	**18628**
1208	1285	365	920	559
3452	3891		3891	681
108859	105811	11944	93867	13686
2977	2656	2555	102	438
4781	5023		5023	2717
1355	1188		1188	167
2709	2849		2849	380
283047	**313656**	**81056**	**232601**	**44745**
276421	306406	81056	225351	41787
6627	7250		7250	2958
5130306	**6305144**	**601929**	**5703215**	**488615**
2948587	2989413	81306	2908106	371897
15974	17081	566	16515	15787
17627	18393	640	17754	3984
2148119	3280257	519417	2760840	96947
435143	**468640**	**52680**	**415960**	**43981**
40168	42619	3161	39458	7712
301840	319597	18656	300941	27185
56162	59068	6635	52433	5632
32474	41645	21952	19693	3253
4500	5712	2277	3435	200
8306	**8905**	**936**	**7969**	**1685**
2712	3569	575	2995	53
1287	1263		1263	174
924	972	361	610	441
2758	2589		2589	904
624	512		512	113
212203	**224085**	**17608**	**206477**	**6284**
5499	5499		5499	
151106	151280		151280	2243
28217	34961	11250	23711	2155
27381	32345	6358	25987	1886

17–6 限额以上零售业企业主要财务指标(2012)
Main Financial Indicators of Enterprises above Designated Size in Retail Trade

单位：万元 (10000 yuan)

指　　标	Item	主营业务收入 Revenue from Principal Business	主营业务成本 Cost of Principal Business	主营业务税金及附加 Tax and Extra Charges on Principal Business	销售费用 Selling Expenses	营业利润 Operating Profits
总　计	**Total**	**7096029**	**6587069**	**23094**	**386116**	**209799**
#国有控股	State-Controlled	2451780	2512548	4662	99270	113757
按登记注册类型分组	**by Types of Registration**					
内资企业	**Domestic Funded Enterprises**	**6630838**	**6198871**	**20389**	**342040**	**179997**
国有企业	State-owned Enterprises	730310	602313	2256	39117	98544
集体企业	Collective-owned Enterprises	33043	22920	165	820	8195
股份合作企业	Cooperation Enterprises	383942	355560	474	6720	17711
联营企业	Joint Ownership Enterprises	15445	13590	3	672	318
有限责任公司	Limited Liability Corporations	2955364	2569732	11828	193313	45497
股份有限公司	Share-holding Corporations Ltd.	1200287	1443105	1447	46002	-8826
私营企业	Private Enterprises	1152373	1050456	3680	46110	15239
其他	Other Enterprises	160074	141195	537	9287	3320
港、澳、台商投资企业	**Enterprises with Funds From HongKong, Macao and Taiwan**	**238104**	**205079**	**1251**	**18340**	**15164**
#合资经营企业(港或澳、台资)	Joint-venture Enterprises	207660	180380	971	14544	13141
合作经营企业(港或澳、台资)	Cooperative Enterprises					
港、澳、台商独资经营企业	Enterpises with Sole Investment	10907	8520	33	1425	359
港、澳、台商投资股份有限公司	Share-holding Corporations Ltd.					
其他港、澳、台商投资企业	Others	19537	16180	247	2372	1664
外商投资企业	**Foreign Funded Enterprises**	**227087**	**183119**	**1453**	**25736**	**14638**
中外合资经营企业	Joint-venture Enterprises	128773	103175	1012	12799	11748
中外合作经营企业	Cooperation Enterprises					
外资企业	Enterprises with Sole Fund	98315	79945	441	12937	2890
外商投资股份有限公司	Share-holding Corporations Ltd.					
按国民经济行业分组	**by Sector**					
综合零售	**Integrated Retail**	**1022098**	**845993**	**8325**	**109051**	**38542**
#百货零售	Retail of General Merchandise	579627	473780	5969	56578	30305
超级市场零售	Retail of Supermarkets	399087	334228	2291	49119	8263
其他综合零售	Other Integrated Retail	43385	37986	65	3355	-27
食品、饮料及烟草制品专门零售	**Retail of Food,Beverages and Tobaccos**	**299036**	**221721**	**2235**	**10379**	**56172**
粮油零售	Retail of Grain and Oil	45603	42816	45	2485	-2278
糕点、面包零售	Retail of Pastries and Bread	579	457	23	29	28
果品、蔬菜零售	Retail of Fruits and Vegetables	74841	73795	659	323	-102
肉、禽、蛋及水产品零售	Retail of Meat, Poultry, Eggs and Aquatic Products					
酒、饮料及茶叶零售	Retail of Wine,Beverages and Tea	176940	103905	1504	7408	58521
烟草制品零售	Retail of Tobaccos and Related Products					
其他食品零售	Other Food Retail	1073	748	4	134	3
纺织品、服装及日用品专门零售	**Retail of Textiles,Garments and Daily Consumer Goods**	**91619**	**73729**	**577**	**13605**	**-70**
纺织品及针织品零售	Retail of Textiles and Knitwear					
服装零售	Retail of Garments	88495	71205	562	13325	-121
鞋帽零售	Retail of Shoes and Hats					

17-6 续表 continued

单位：万元 (10000 yuan)

指 标	Item	主营业务收入 Revenue from Principal Business	主营业务成本 Cost of Principal Business	主营业务税金及附加 Tax and Extra Charges on Principal Business	销售费用 Selling Expenses	营业利润 Operating Profits
钟表、眼镜零售	Retail of Horologe and Spectacles	2138	1863	7	89	12
化妆品及卫生用品零售	Retail of Cosmetics and Hygiene Products					
厨房用具及日用杂品零售	Retail of Kitchen utensils and household goods	986	661	8	191	39
其他日用品零售	Retail of Other Daily Consumer Use					
文化、体育用品及器材专门零售	**Retail of Culture,Sports Apliances and Equipments**	**104014**	**81466**	**572**	**8467**	**3878**
文具用品零售	Retail of Stationery	1098	945	2	112	6
体育用品及器材零售	Retail of Sports Goods	3326	2914	7	201	13
图书、报刊零售	Retail of Books, newspapers and periodicals	88609	69495	292	6912	3951
音像制品及电子出版物零售	Retail of Audio and Visual Products and Electronic Publications	2318	1792	19	205	16
珠宝首饰零售	Retail of Jewelry	5074	3312	245	628	-126
工艺美术品及收藏品零售	Retail of Arts and Crafts and Collections	1153	718	5	276	14
照相器材零售	Retail of Photographic Equipment	2435	2291	2	133	4
其他文化用品零售	Retail of Other Cultural Articles					
医药及医疗器材专门零售	**Retail of Medicines and Medical Appliances**	**280678**	**239987**	**834**	**19515**	**6232**
#药品零售	Retail of Medicines	274481	234800	820	19451	6089
医疗用品及器材零售	Retail of Medical Articles and Appliances	6197	5188	14	64	143
汽车、摩托车、燃料及零配件专门零售	**Retail of Motor Vehicles, Motorcycles, Fuel and Parts**	**4734813**	**4664972**	**7478**	**153310**	**87739**
#汽车零售	Retail of Motor Vehicles	2654853	2432157	4294	71731	25154
汽车零配件零售	Retail of Auto Parts and Accessories	14745	13979	31	225	221
摩托车及零配件零售	Retail of Motorcycles,Parts and Accessories	17799	15356	70	639	490
机动车燃料零售	Retail of Fuel of Motor Vehicles	2047416	2203480	3083	80715	61875
家用电器及电子产品专门零售	**Retail of Household Electric Appliances and Electronic Products**	**364367**	**323447**	**1433**	**29752**	**5555**
家用试听设备零售	Retail of Listen household equipment	39222	34438	104	3121	-60
日用家电设备零售	Retail of Household appliances	226923	200560	896	21632	4849
计算机、软件及辅助设备零售	Retail of Computer,Software and Assistant Appliances	53605	49455	126	1940	-59
通讯设备零售	Retail of Communication Equipments	37426	33357	190	3033	-79
其他电子产品零售	Retail of Other Electronic Products	7192	5638	118	26	904
五金、家具及室内装修材料专门零售	**Retail of Hardware, Furniture and Interior Decoration Materials**	**8219**	**6648**	**35**	**353**	**150**
五金零售	Retail of Hardware	3401	2542	5	79	-1
家具零售	Retail of Furniture	1263	1039	20	37	103
涂料零售	Retail of Paint	830	726	2	33	13
木制装饰材料零售	Retail of Wooden decorative materials	2213	1910	8	157	23
其他室内装修材料零售	Retail of Other Interior Decoration Materials	512	431	1	46	12
货摊、无店铺及其他零售	**Stalls,Non-shop and Other Retails**	**191186**	**129106**	**1603**	**41685**	**11602**
流动货摊零售	Retail of Flow Stalls					
互联网零售	Retail of Internet	4787	4642		38	-37
邮购及电视、电话零售	Retail of Mail order,TV and Telephone	122498	74878	1356	37085	7650
生活用燃料零售	Retail of life Fuel	33013	27293	149	2304	2794
花卉零售	Retail of Flowers					
旧货零售	Retail of Second-hand Goods					
其他未列明的零售	Other Retails Unlisted	30888	22293	98	2258	1194

17-7 商品交易市场
Commodity Exchange Markets

单位：个 (unit)

指 标	Item	2007	2008	2009	2010	2011	2012
商品交易市场	**Number of Commodity trading markets**	**1940**	**2135**	**2215**	**2216**	**2211**	**1658**
消费品市场数	**Number of Consumable Markets**	**1818**	**2057**	**2173**	**2175**	**2170**	**1614**
消费品综合市场	Consumable Goods Integrative Market	1178	1252	1195	1190	1176	705
农副产品市场	Agricultural Subproduct Market	543	724	881	890	894	811
农副产品综合市场	Agricultural Subproduct Integrative Market	507	675	836	844	846	786
农副产品专业市场	Agricultural Subproduct Special Market	36	49	45	46	48	25
工业消费品市场	Industrial Consumable Goods Market	43	54	61	59	58	58
工业消费品综合市场	Industrial Consumable Goods Integrative Market	32	45	53	51	50	32
工业消费品专业市场	Industrial Consumer Goods Special Market	11	9	8	8	8	26
其他消费品市场	Other Consumable Goods Market	54	27	36	36	42	40
生产资料市场数	**Number of Production Market**	**112**	**78**	**42**	**41**	**41**	**44**
生产资料综合市场	Production Integrative Market	30	29	5	4	4	3
工业生产资料市场	Industrial Production Market	33	28	27	27	27	31
机动车交易市场	Motor vehicle market	14	11	9	9	11	12
钢材交易市场	Steel market	9	6	6	6	5	7
煤炭交易市场	Coal market	3	1	2	2	2	1
木材交易市场	Timber market	6	6	6	6	5	6
其他工业生产资料市场	Other Means of Industrial Production Market	1	4	4	4	4	5
农业生产资料市场	Agricultural Production Market	46	19	5	5	5	7
农业生产资料综合市场	Agricultural Production Integrative Market	25	15	3	3	3	4
农业生产资料专业市场	Agricultural Production Special Market	21	4	2	2	2	3
其他生产资料市场	Others	3	2	5	5	5	3

注：资料来源于省工商局。

Note:Data in the table are provided by the provincial administration for industry and commerce.

主要统计指标解释

社会消费品零售总额 指国民经济各行业直接售给城乡居民和社会集团的消费品总额。它是反映各行业通过多种商品流通渠道向居民和社会集团供应的生活消费品总量，是研究国内零售市场变动情况、反映经济景气程度的重要指标。

社会消费品零售总额包括：⑴售给城乡居民作为生活用的商品和修建房屋用的建筑材料；⑵售给社会集团的各种办公用品和公用消费品；⑶售给机关、团体、学校、部队、企业、事业单位的职工食堂和旅店（招待所）附设专门供本店旅客食用，不对外营业的食堂的各种食品、燃料；企业、单位和国营农场直接售给本单位职工和职工食堂的自己生产的产品；⑷售给部队干部、战士生活用的粮食、副食品、衣着品、日用品、燃料；⑸售给来华的外国人、华侨、港澳台同胞的消费品；⑹居民自费购买的中、西药品、中药材及医疗用品；⑺报社、出版社直接售给居民和社会集团的报纸、图书、杂志，集邮公司出售的新、旧纪念邮票、特种邮票、首日封、集邮册、集邮工具等；⑻旧货寄售商店自购、自销部分的商品；⑼煤气公司、液化石油气站售给居民和社会集团的煤气灶具和罐装液化石油气；⑽农民售给非农业居民和社会集团的商品。不包括售给国民经济各部门企业、事业单位（包括国有经济的农场）生产经营用的各种原材料、燃料、设备、工具等和售给批发和零售贸易业、住宿和餐饮业作为转卖用的商品，旧货寄售商店受托寄售卖出的商品，服务业的营业收入，邮局出售邮票的收入，自来水、电力、煤气生产（供应）单位的产品供应收入，也不包括农民之间的商品销售。

批发和零售业商品购进、销售、库存额 指各种登记注册类型的批发和零售业企业（单位）以本企业（单位）为总体的，从国内、国外市场购进的商品总量，销售和出口的商品总量、库存的商品总量等情况。该指标可以反映商品流转过程中商品的购进、销售、库存之间的比例关系和存在的问题。

商品购进总额 指从本企业以外的单位和个人购进（包括从国外直接进口）作为转卖或加工后转卖的商品金额（含增值税）。商品包括：（1）从工农业生产者、批发和零售业企业、住宿和餐饮业企业、出版社或报社的出版发行部门和其他服务业企业购进的商品；（2）从机关团体、事业单位购进的商品；（3）从海关、市场管理部门购进的缉私和没收的商品；（4）从居民收购的废旧商品等，不包括：（1）企业为本单位自身经营用，不是作为转卖而购进的商品，如材料物资、包装物、低值易耗品、办公用品等；（2）未通过买卖行为而收入的商品，如接受其他部门移交的商品、借入的商品、收入代其他单位保管的商品、其他单位赠送的样品、加工回收的成品等；（3）经本单位介绍，由买卖双方直接结算，本单位只收取手续费的业务；（4）销售退回和买方拒付货款的商品；（5）商品溢余。

商品销售总额 指对本单位以外的单位和个人出售的商品金额(包括售给本单位消费用的商品,含增值税)。商品包括(1)售给城乡居民和社会集团消费用的商品；（2）售给农业、工业、建筑业、运输邮电业、服务业、公用事业等国民经济各行业用于生产、经营用的商品，包括售予批发和零售业作为转卖或加工后转卖的商品；（3）对国（境）外直接出口的商品，不包括：（1）未通过买卖行为付出的商品，如随机构变动移交给其他企业单位的商品、借出的商品、归还受其他单位委托代保管的商品、付出的加工原料和赠送给其他单位的样品等；（2）经本单位介绍，由买卖双方直接结算，本单位只收取手续费的业务；（3）购货退回的商品；（4）商品损耗和损失；（5）出售本单位自用的废旧物资。

商品库存额 指报告期末各种登记注册类型的批发和零售业企业（单位）已取得所有权的商品。它反映批发和零售业企业（单位）的商品库存情况和对市场商品供应的保证程度。商品库存包括：(1)存放在批发和零售业经营单位（如门市部、批发站、经营处）仓库、货场、货柜和货架中的商品；(2)挑选、整理、包装中的商品；(3)已记入购进而尚未运到本单位的商品，即发货单或银行承兑凭证已到而货未到的商品；(4)寄放他处的商品，如因购货方拒绝承付而暂时存放在购货方的商品和已办完加工成品收回手续而未提回的商品；(5)委托其他单位代销（未作销售或调出）尚未售出的商品；(6)代其他单位购进尚未交付的商品。不包括所有权不属于本单位的商品、委托外单位加工生产尚未收回成品的商品、外贸企业代理其他单位从国外进口尚未付给订货单位的商品、代国家物资储备部门保管的商品等。

消费品市场成交额 指从事消费品交易的商品市场的全部商品成交金额。消费品市场包括农副产品市场和工业消费品市场。

Explanatory Notes on Main Statistical Indicators

Total Retail Sales of Consumer Goods refer to the sum of retail sales of consumer goods sold by all sectors of the national economy to urban and rural residents and social groups. This indicator is used to show the supply of consumers goods through various channels to households and institutions, and is very important for the study on changes at the domestic retail market, and on economic cycles.

The retail sales of consumer goods include: (1) commodities sold to urban and rural residents for their daily use and building materials sold to them for the construction or repair of houses; (2) office appliances and supplies sold to institutions; (3) food and fuels sold to canteens of institutions, enterprises ,schools ,military units and to canteens of hotels and hostels that only serve their guests ,and commodities produced by enterprises ,institutions or state farms and sold directly to their employees or their canteens; (4) grain and non-staple food, clothing ,daily articles and fuels sold to military personnel; (5)consumer goods sold to foreigners, overseas Chinese, and Chinese compatriots from Taiwan, Hong Kong and Macao during their stay in the mainland of China; (6) Chinese and western medicines, herbs and medical facilities purchased by residents; (7) newspapers, books and magazines directly sold to residents and social groups by publishers, new and old commemorative stamps, special stamps, first-day covers, stamp albums and other stamp-collection articles sold by stamp companies; (8) consumer goods purchased and then sold by second-hand shops; (9) stoves and other heating facilities and liquefied gas sold by gas companies to households and institutions; and (10) commodities sold by farmers to non-agricultural residents and social groups. Excluded under this heading are:raw materials, fuels, equipment, tools sold to enterprises, institutions and state farms for production purpose; commodities sold to trade establishments for re-selling; commissioned sales at second-hand shops; operational income of urban public utilities; stamps sold at post offices; income of water, power, gas production and supply establishments from the supply of their products; and sales of commodities among farmers.

Purchase, Sales and Stock of Commodities by Wholesale and Retail Trades refer to the total volume of commodities purchased, total volume of sales and exports, and the stock of commodities by wholesale and retail enterprises (establishments) of different status of registration from domestic and overseas markets. This indicator reflects the relationship among purchase, sales and stock of commodities in the circulation of goods and reveals the existing problems.

Total Purchases of Commodities refer to the total value of purchases of commodities by enterprises (establishments) from other establishments or individuals (including direct import from abroad) for the purpose of re-selling, either with or without further processing of the commodities purchased. The commodities include: (1) commodities purchased from agricultural and industrial producer, wholesaler, retailer, publishing hourse and other service business; (2) commodities purchased from institutions and government departments; (3) confiscated goods purchased from the custums authorities or market management agencies; (4) second-hand goods and wastes purchased from residents; The commodities exclude 1 commodities purchased by enterprises (establishments) for use in their own business operation, commodities obtained without buying or selling procedures such as materials, consumable goods of low value, office appliances,etc. 2 received goods without trading, such as goods handed over from others, borrowed goods, preserved goods for others, donated goods from others, processed and retrieved goods, etc. 3. goods of direct settlement between buyer and seller with handling fees introduced by others, 4. goods returned or refused to pay by the buyer, 5. excessive goods.

Total Sales of Commodities refer to value of commodities sold by the establishments to other establishments and individuals (including goods sold for self consumption, including the value-added tax). The commodities include: (1) commodities sold to urban and rural residents and social groups for their consumption; (2) commodities sold to establishments in all industries for their production and operation, including agriculture, industry, construction, transportation, post and telecommunications, catering services, and public utility including commodities sold to wholesale and retail establishments for re-selling, with or without further processing; and (3) commodities for direct export to abroad. Excluded are (1) extended commodities without trading, such as goods handed over to other enterprises and institutions becase of the change of organizations, lent goods, returned goods preserved for others, extended processing materials and samples donated to others, (2) goods of direct settlement between buyer and seller with handling fees introduced by others, 3. goods returned after purchase, (4) damaged and spoiled goods, (5) waste and used goods of self use.

Total Stock of Commodities refers to total commodities possessed by wholesaler and retailer of various types of registration status at the end of the reference period, reflecting the commodity stock level of various wholesaler and retailer and the potential for market supply. It includes: (1) commodities located in storage, garages, counters, and shelves of operating places (such as sale stores, wholesale centres, and operating offices); (2) commodities in the process of being selected, sorted, and packed; (3) commodities not arrived but recorded as purchase in the account, i.e. commodities not arrived but payment receipts for the commodities from the sellers or the banks arrived; (4) commodities deposited in other places rather than places mentioned above, for instance: commodities in the hold of purchasers temporarily due to the refusal of payment and commodities not taken back after going through the formalities; (5) commodities entrusted to other units to sell but not sold yet; (6) commodities purchased for other units but not delivered yet. Commodities not included as stock are those not owned by the enterprises (units), commodities on commission for processing but not yet delivered, imported commodities of agency of foreign trade enterprise but not yet delivered to ordering units and finally those put in stock on behalf of the state material reserves units.

Volume of Transaction at Free Markets for Consumer Goods refers to the value of transaction of all goods at the free trade markets for consumer goods, where markets include both free markets for farm and sideline products and for manufactured consumer goods.

18

Eighteen

住宿、餐饮业和旅游业

Hotel, Catering Services and Tourism

18-1 限额以上住宿业和餐饮业

Basic Conditions of Enterprises above Designated Size in Hotels and Catering Services

指 标	Item	2007	2008	2009	2010	2011	2012
住宿业	**Hotels**						
法人企业(个)	Number of Corporations(unit)	164	180	181	234	260	318
年末从业人数(人)	Employed Persons(person)	17179	20367	20064	23289	26236	31793
营业额(亿元)	Business Revenue (100 million yuan)	11.78	15.69	16.91	20.53	27.07	35.88
#客房收入	Reveneu From Hotel Rooms	6.92	9.32	9.65	11.71	15.58	20.31
餐费收入	Reveneu from Meals	3.77	5.16	5.96	7.35	9.30	12.25
客房数(万间)	Number of Hotel Rooms(10000 rooms)		2.04	2.11	2.79	3.05	3.76
床位数(万位)	Number of Beds(10000 beds)	2.90	3.59	3.73	5.07	5.20	6.32
年末餐饮营业面积(万平方米)	Catering Services Operating Area at year-end(10000 sq.m)	18.60	19.02	18.65	23.03	49.19	64.65
餐饮业	**Catering Services**						
法人企业(个)	Number of corporation Unit (unit)	73	111	110	134	153	183
年末从业人数(人)	Employed Persons(person)	7880	10338	10108	12088	15234	17593
营业额(亿元)	Business Revenue (100 million yuan)	6.46	9.01	9.45	11.65	15.88	19.02
#餐费收入	Reveneu from Meals	6.00	8.42	8.60	10.45	13.63	16.42
年末餐饮营业面积(万平方米)	Catering Services Operational Area at Year-end(10000 sq.m)	14.90	28.83	20.59	23.51	36.24	40.44

18–2 限额以上住宿业企业(2012)

单位：万元

项 目	Item	法人企业(个) Number of Corporations (unit)	年末从业人数(人) Employed Persons (person)	营业额 Business Revenue	#客房收入 Revenue from Hotel Rooms	#餐费收入 Reveneu from Meals
合计	**Total**	**318**	**31793**	**358836**	**203057**	**122511**
按登记注册类型分	**by Types of Registration**					
内资企业	**Domestic Funded Enterprises**	**312**	**30520**	**342178**	**194748**	**114556**
国有企业	State-owned Enterprises	49	4851	58598	29929	23450
集体企业	Collective-owned Enterprises	12	427	8291	4655	2158
股份合作企业	Cooperation Enterprises	3	140	1343	1269	72
联营企业	Joint Ownership Enterprises					
有限责任公司	Limited Liability Corporations	115	14477	175724	98736	58024
股份有限公司	Share-holding Corporations Ltd.	3	190	2186	1024	1144
私营企业	Private Enterprises	115	9137	84839	52643	26321
其他企业	Other Enterprises	15	1298	11197	6492	3387
港、澳、台商投资企业	**Enterprises with Funds From Honkong, Macao and Taiwan**	**5**	**1014**	**13605**	**6838**	**6466**
合资经营企业	Joint-venture Enterprises	2	527	7869	3540	4188
合作经营企业	Cooperative Enterprises					
独资经营企业	Enterpises with Sole Funds	3	487	5736	3299	2278
投资股份有限公司	Share-holding Corporations Ltd.					
外商投资企业	**Foreign Funded Enterprises**	**1**	**259**	**3054**	**1472**	**1489**
中外合资经营企业	Joint-venture Enterprises	1	259	3054	1472	1489
中外合作经营企业	Cooperation Enterprises					
外资企业	Enterprises with Sole Fund					
外商投资股份有限公司	Share-holding Corporations Ltd.					
按国民经济行业分	**by Sector**					
旅游饭店	Tourist Hotels	230	26033	298104	165300	104651
一般旅馆	General Hotels	81	5150	53989	34857	15035
其他住宿服务	Other Hotel Services	7	610	6742	2901	2824

Basic Conditions of Enterprises above Designated Size in Hotel Services

(10000yuan)

主营业务收入 Revenue from Principal Business	主营业务成本 Cost of Principal Business	主营业务税金及附加 Tax and Extra Charges on Principal Business	利润总额 Total profit	资产总计 Total Assets	#流动资产合计 Total Current Assets	#固定资产合计 Total Fixed Assets	负债合计 Total Liabilities	所有者权益合计 Total Owners' Equity
354823	**135078**	**19602**	**-11721**	**973089**	**340585**	**469730**	**656473**	**316616**
338164	**132171**	**18658**	**-10966**	**932520**	**334647**	**444622**	**632154**	**300366**
57516	21576	3379	-1130	100565	29054	53977	43587	56978
8139	4660	406	2127	21700	3657	17847	3629	18072
1269	225	63	71	2380	1131	1250	496	1884
173618	61041	9287	-12689	496728	176994	236313	399510	97218
2177	652	111	130	3266	1014	2105	2633	633
84549	38957	4791	-57	269563	109819	109377	166371	103192
10897	5061	622	582	38318	12978	23753	15928	22390
13605	**2381**	**762**	**-112**	**23110**	**5393**	**16102**	**16930**	**6180**
7869	1404	446	-8	9375	3328	4556	6952	2423
5736	978	316	-104	13735	2065	11546	9978	3757
3054	**525**	**182**	**-643**	**17459**	**545**	**9006**	**7389**	**10070**
3054	525	182	-643	17459	545	9006	7389	10070
294967	113301	16098	-12327	843621	294700	404315	593506	250116
53133	19579	3148	1407	125701	43273	64572	61213	64488
6722	2198	356	-801	3766	2613	844	1754	2013

18-3 限额以上餐饮业企业(2012)

单位：万元

项 目	Item	法人企业(个) Number of corporation (unit)	年末从业人数(人) Employees (person)	营业额 Business Revenue	#餐费收入 From Meals
合计	**Total**	**183**	**17593**	**190209**	**164163**
按登记注册类型分	**by Types of Registration**				
内资企业	**Domestic funded Enterprises**	**182**	**17290**	**185414**	**159367**
国有企业	State-owned Enterprises	12	2200	16037	12432
集体企业	Collective-owned Enterprises				
股份合作企业	Copperative Enterprises	2	66	1021	1021
联营企业	Joint Ownership Enterprises				
有限责任公司	Limited Liability Corporations	57	7281	80577	72523
股份有限公司	Share Holding Corporations Ltd.	2	311	4510	2698
私营企业	Private Enterprises	94	6225	69575	60466
其他企业	Other Enterprises	15	1207	13693	10228
港、澳、台商投资企业	**Enterprises with Funds from Hong Kong,Macao and Taiwan**				
合资经营企业	Joint-venture Enterprises				
合作经营企业	Cooperative Enterprises				
独资经营企业	Corporations with Sole Fund				
投资股份有限公司	Share-holding Corporations Ltd.				
外商投资企业	**Foreign Funded Enterprises**	**1**	**303**	**4795**	**4795**
中外合资经营企业	Joint-venture Enterprises				
中外合作经营企业	Cooperation Enterprises				
外资企业	Enterprises with Sole Fund				
外商投资股份有限公司	Share-holding Corporations Ltd.	1	303	4795	4795
按国民经济行业分	**by Sector**				
正餐服务业	Restaurant Services	181	17386	186020	159973
快餐服务业	Snack Counter Services	2	207	4189	4189
饮料及冷饮服务业	Beverages and Cold Drinks				
其他餐饮服务业	Others				

Basic Conditions of Enterprises above Designated Size in Catering Services

(10000yuan)

主营业务收入 Revenue from Principal Business	主营业务成本 Cost of Principal Business	主营业务税金及附加 Tax and Extra Charges on Principal Business	利润总额 Total profit	资产总计 Total Assets	#流动资产合计 Current Assets	#固定资产合计 Total Fixed Assets	负债合计 Total Liabilities	所有者权益合计 Total Owners' Equities
178844	**88923**	**10536**	**-1638**	**227139**	**114274**	**71118**	**162112**	**65026**
174049	**87196**	**10262**	**-1788**	**223587**	**111551**	**71002**	**158676**	**64912**
11019	6594	617	-920	23626	9312	7660	22070	1556
1035	373	40	142	1436	407	93	697	740
78424	38117	4469	-2868	88439	54449	19902	67371	21068
4510	1712	257	194	5034	4877	158	4373	662
65659	34818	4050	3178	79858	30511	32765	44339	35519
13403	5582	829	-1513	25194	11996	10424	19826	5368
4795	**1727**	**273**	**150**	**3551**	**2722**	**116**	**3437**	**115**
4795	1727	273	150	3551	2722	116	3437	115
174654	86536	10297	-1779	225981	113277	70995	161864	64118
4190	2387	239	141	1157	996	123	249	909

18–4 旅游业主要指标
Basic Statistics on Development of Tourism

指　标	Item	2007	2008	2009	2010	2011	2012
旅行社总数(个)	**Total Number of Travel Agencies(unit)**	**177**	**218**	**201**	**260**	**270**	**302**
出境游组团旅行社	International Travel Agencies	17	18	18	11	11	13
国内及入境旅游旅行社	Domestic Travel Agencies	160	200	183	249	259	289
旅行社职工人数(人)	**Number of Staff and Workers of Travel Agencies(person)**	**2215**	**3071**	**2979**	**3132**	**3240**	**3624**
出境游组团旅行社	International Travel Agencies	910	365	370	225	226	260
国内及入境旅游旅行社	Domestic Travel Agencies	1305	2706	2609	2907	3014	3364
旅游总人数(万人次)	**Total Number of Tourists(10000 person-times)**	**6262.89**	**8190.23**	**10439.95**	**12913.02**	**17019.36**	**21401.18**
入境旅游人数	Total Number of International Tourists Inbound	43.00	39.54	39.95	50.01	58.51	70.50
外国人	Foreigners	15.48	18.22	16.28	18.61	23.62	30.42
港澳同胞	Compatriots from Hong Kong and Macao	13.05	10.79	10.84	13.64	16.91	20.85
台湾同胞	Compatriots from Taiwan	14.47	10.52	12.83	17.76	17.98	19.23
国内旅游人数	Total Number of Domestic Tourists	6219.89	8150.69	10400.00	12863.01	16960.85	21330.68
旅游总收入(亿元)	**Tourism Earnings(100 million yuan)**	**512.28**	**653.13**	**805.23**	**1061.23**	**1429.48**	**1860.16**
国际旅游外汇收入(万美元)	Earnings from International Tourism (USD 10000)	12917.55	11697.37	11044.40	12957.88	13507.18	16893.60
国内旅游收入(亿元)	Earnings from Domestic Tourism (100 million yuan)	504.04	643.82	797.69	1052.64	1420.70	1849.49
三大旅行社接待入境旅游人数(万人次)	**Number of International Tourists Received by Three Major Travel Service (10000 person-times)**	**3.30**	**3.87**	**5.25**	**1.76**	**1.51**	**1.27**
中国国际旅行社	China International Travel Service	0.41	1.67	1.31	0.23	0.39	0.77
贵州海外旅游总公司	Guizhou Overseas Tourism Corporation	2.48	2.06	3.83	1.47	0.69	0.14
中国青年旅行社	China Youth Travel Service	0.41	0.14	0.11	0.06	0.43	0.36

注：资料来源于省旅游局(以下相关表同)。
Note:Data in the table are obtained from the provincial tourism administration(The relative tables are the same).

18−5 来黔境外旅游人数及人均消费支出

Number of Overseas Tourists Visiting Guizhou and Average Per Capita Spending

类 别	Item	2007	2008	2009	2010	2011	2012	2012年比2011年增长(%) Increase Rate in 2012 over 2011(%)
来黔境外旅游人数(万人次)	**Number of Foreign Tourists Visiting Guizhou(10000 person-times)**	**43.00**	**39.54**	**39.95**	**50.01**	**58.51**	**70.50**	**20.5**
外国人	Foreigner	15.48	18.22	16.28	18.61	23.62	30.42	28.8
港澳同胞	Compatriots from Hong Kong and Macao	13.05	10.79	10.84	13.64	16.91	20.85	23.3
台湾同胞	Compatriots from Taiwan	14.47	10.52	12.83	17.76	17.98	19.23	7.0
平均每人逗留天数(天/人)	Average Days Tourists Stay in Guizhou Per Capita (day/person)	1.86	1.75	1.63	1.43	1.39	1.43	2.9
平均每人每天消费支出(美元/人、天)	Average Per Capita Daily Spending (USD/person-day)	171.54	169.30	169.12	171.76	168.68	167.13	-0.9

18−6 接待外国旅游人数(按地区分)

Number of Overseas Tourists Visiting Guizhou(by Country/Territory)

单位：人次 (person-time)

地区名	Country (Territory)	2007	2008	2009	2010	2011	2012	2012年比2011年增长(%) Increase Rate in 2012 over 2011(%)
接待外国旅游人数	**Number of Overseas Tourists Visiting Guizhou**	**154762**	**182231**	**162792**	**186054**	**236244**	**304168**	**28.8**
亚 洲	Asia	69077	81560	75042	85383	104624	122958	17.5
非 洲	Africa	752	1120	980	1110	1536	2165	41.0
欧 洲	Europe	36234	43325	39094	44799	57619	81799	42.0
拉丁美洲	Latin America	30355	35076	30493	35239	45379	61853	36.3
大洋洲	Oceania	15456	17564	14814	16861	23518	30354	29.1
其 他	Others	2888	3586	2369	2662	3568	5039	41.2

18-7 旅游外汇收入
Tourism Foreign Exchange Earnings

单位：万美元 (USD 10000)

类　别	Item	2007	2008	2009	2010	2011	2012	2012年比2011年增长(%) Increase Rate in 2012 over 2011(%)
旅游外汇收入	**Tourism foreign exchange earnings**	**12917.56**	**11697.37**	**11044.40**	**12957.88**	**13507.18**	**16893.60**	**25.1**
长途交通	Long Distance Transportation	3100.22	3661.28	3224.96	5001.74	5200.26	5084.97	-2.2
游　览	Visiting	490.86	432.80	441.78	596.06	540.29	658.85	21.9
住　宿	Accommodation	1459.68	1368.59	1336.37	1399.45	1701.9	1756.93	3.2
餐　饮	Food and Beverage	1072.16	959.18	949.82	997.76	729.39	1114.98	52.9
商品销售	Shopping	3733.18	3193.38	3379.59	2410.17	3241.72	4983.61	53.7
娱　乐	Entertainment	477.95	514.68	452.82	583.10	634.84	929.15	46.4
邮电通讯	Postal and Communication Services	426.28	514.68	353.42	362.83	324.17	439.23	35.5
市内交通	Local Transportation	232.51	362.64	77.31	220.28	108.06	388.55	259.6
其他服务	Other Services	1924.72	690.14	828.33	1386.49	1026.55	1537.33	49.8

18-8 旅馆业接待经营

Operation of Hotels

类 别	Item	2007	2008	2009	2010	2011	2012	2012年比2011年增长(%) Increase Rate in 2012 over 2011(%)
接待能力	**Capacity**							
年末客房数(间)	Guest Rooms (Year-end) (unit)	18625	21278	23578	25191	26120	29358	12.4
年末客房床位数(张)	Guest Beds (Year-end) (bed)	34974	39142	42885	45683	46204	51687	11.9
客房开房率(%)	Room Occupancy Rate(%)	65.5	63.0	63.5	63.6	64.2	64.3	0.1(百分点)
#星级宾馆	Star-rated Hotels	66.0	64.0	64.5	65.1	64.6	64.1	-0.5(百分点)
实际住宿人次数(万人次)	Actual Number of Guests (10000 person-times)	435.65	510.89	540.32	625.63	740.49	775.15	4.7
#海外来黔	Overseas Visitors	43.00	39.53	39.95	50.01	58.51	70.50	20.5
实际住宿人天数(万人天)	Actual Number of Guests and Days of Stay (10000 person-days)	689.21	748.61	801.35	866.84	997.23	1092.97	9.6
#海外来黔	Overseas Visitors	80.01	69.09	65.30	71.39	81.22	101.18	24.6
经营和财务	**Management and Financial**							
营业收入(万元)	Operational Revenue(10000 yuan)	171256	180254	187002	195639	228252	245265	7.5

18-9 星级饭店

Star-rated Hotels

单位：个　　(unit)

指 标	Item	2007	2008	2009	2010	2011	2012
星级饭店个数	**The number of Star-rated Hotels**	**243**	**279**	**323**	**344**	**340**	**368**
按经济类型分	**Grouped by Ownership**						
国有经济	State-owned	111	97	111	103	90	80
集体经济	Collective-owned	130	175	210	241	250	287
外商投资经济	Foreign Funded	2	7	2			1
按规模分	**Grouped by Capacity**						
客房总数300间以上	With Above than 300 Rooms	2	2	4	3	3	5
客房总数200-299间	With 200-299 Rooms	8	10	13	14	16	16
客房总数100-199间	With 100-199 Rooms	45	45	65	54	63	76
客房总数99间以下	With Less than 100 Rooms	188	222	241	273	258	271

18–10 风景名胜区
Scenic Spots

名　称	Name	级 别	地　址
红枫湖风景名胜区	Hongfeng Lake Scenic Spot	国家级	贵州省贵阳市清镇市
黄果树风景名胜区	Huangguoshu Waterfalls Scenic Spot	国家级	贵州省安顺市镇宁县
龙宫风景名胜区	The Dragon Palace Scenic Spot	国家级	贵州省安顺市
织金洞风景名胜区	Zhijin Cave Scenic Spot	国家级	贵州省毕节市织金县
九洞天风景名胜区	Jiudongtian Scenic Spot	国家级	贵州省毕节市
马岭河峡谷风景名胜区	Malinghe Canyon Scenic Spot	国家级	贵州省黔西南州兴义市
㵲阳河风景名胜区	Wuyang River Scenic Spot	国家级	贵州省黔东南州镇远县
黎平侗乡风景名胜区	Liping Dong-Village Scenic Spot	国家级	贵州省黔东南州黎平县
荔波樟江风景名胜区	Libo Zhangjiang Scenic Spot	国家级	贵州省黔南州荔波县
都匀斗篷山——剑江风景名胜区	Duyun Doupeng Mountain----Jianjiang Scenic Spot	国家级	贵州省黔南州
赤水风景名胜区	Chishui Scenic Spot	国家级	贵州省遵义市赤水市
九龙洞风景名胜区	Jiulong Cave Scenic Spot	国家级	贵州省铜仁市
紫云格凸河风景名胜区	Ziyun Getu River Scenic Spot	国家级	贵州省安顺市紫云县
平塘风景名胜区	Pingtang Scenic Spot	国家级	贵州省黔南州平塘县
瓮安江界河风景名胜区	Wengan Jiangjie River Scenic Spot	国家级	贵州省黔南州瓮安县
榕江古榕风景名胜区	Rongjiang Gurong Scenic Spot	国家级	贵州省黔东南州榕江县
石阡温泉群风景名胜区	Shiqian Hot Well Flock Scenic Spot	国家级	贵州省铜仁市石阡县
沿河乌江山峡风景名胜区	Yanhe Wujiang River Sanxia Scenic Spot	国家级	贵州省铜仁市沿河县
百花湖风景名胜区	Baihua Lake Scenic Spot	省级	贵州省贵阳市
花溪风景名胜区	Huaxi Scenic Spot	省级	贵州省贵阳市花溪区
息烽风景名胜区	Xifeng Scenic Spot	省级	贵州省贵阳市息烽县
修文阳明风景名胜区	Xiuwen Yangming Scenic Spot	省级	贵州省贵阳市修文县
香纸沟风景名胜区	Xiangzhigou Scenic Spot	省级	贵州省贵阳市
开阳风景名胜区	Kaiyang Scenic Spot	省级	贵州省贵阳市开阳县
相思河风景名胜区	Xiangsi River Scenic Spot	省级	贵州省贵阳市
清镇暗流河风景名胜区	Qingzhen Undercurrent River Scenic Spot	省级	贵州省贵阳市清镇市
普定梭筛风景名胜区	Puding Suoshai Scenic Spot	省级	贵州省安顺市普定县
关岭花江大峡谷风景名胜区	Guanling Huajiang Canyon Scenic Spot	省级	贵州省安顺市关岭县花江镇
平坝天台山——斯拉河风景名胜区	Pingba Tiantai Mountain ----Sila River Scenic Spot	省级	贵州省安顺市平坝县
百里杜鹃风景名胜区	One-Hundred-Li Azalea Belt Scenic Spot	省级	毕节市大方、黔西县
贵州屋脊赫章韭菜坪风景名胜区	Guizhou Fastigium Hezhang Jiucaiping Scenic Spot	省级	贵州省毕节市赫章县
鲁布革风景名胜区	Lubuge Scenic Spot	省级	贵州省黔西南州兴义市
泥凼石林风景名胜区	Nidang shilin Scenic Spot	省级	贵州省黔西南州兴义市泥凼镇
安龙招堤风景名胜区	Anlong Zhaodi Scenic Spot	省级	贵州省黔西南州安龙县
贞丰三岔河风景名胜区	Zhenfeng Sancha River Scenic Spot	省级	贵州省黔西南州贞丰县

18-10 续表 continued

名　称	Name	级别	地　址
晴隆三望坪风景名胜区	Qinglong Sanwangping Scenic Spot	省级	贵州省黔西南州晴隆县
兴仁放马坪风景名胜区	Xingren Fangmaping Scenic Spot	省级	贵州省黔西南州兴仁县
岑巩龙鳌河风景名胜区	Cengong Longao River Scenic Spot	省级	贵州省黔东南州岑巩县
剑河风景名胜区	Jianhe Scenic Spot	省级	贵州省黔东南州剑河县
麻江下司风景名胜区	Majiang Xiasi Scenic Spot	省级	贵州省黔东南州麻江县
镇远高过河风景名胜区	Zhenyuan Gaoguo River Scenic Spot	省级	贵州省黔东南州镇远县
雷山风景名胜区	Leishan Scenic Spot	省级	贵州省黔东南州雷山县
锦屏三板溪——隆里古城风景名胜区	Jinping Sanbanxi----Longli Scenic Spot	省级	贵州省黔东南州锦屏县
丹寨龙泉山——岔河风景名胜区	Danzhai Longquanshan----Chahe Scenic Spot	省级	贵州省黔东南州丹寨县
从江风景名胜区	Congjiang Scenic Spot	省级	贵州省黔东南州从江县
龙里猴子沟风景名胜区	Longli Monkey Fossa Scenic Spot	省级	贵州省黔南州龙里县
福泉洒金谷风景名胜区	Fuquan Sajingu Scenic Spot	省级	贵州省黔南州福泉市
惠水涟江——燕子洞风景名胜区	Huishui Lianjiang--Yanzi Cave Scenic Spot	省级	贵州省黔南州惠水县
长顺杜鹃湖——白云山风景名胜区	Changshun Dujuan Lake--Baiyun Mountain Scenic Spot	省级	贵州省黔南州长顺县
三都都柳江风景名胜区	Sandu Duliu River Scenic Spot	省级	贵州省黔南州三都县
贵定洛北河风景名胜区	Guiding Luobei River Scenic Spot	省级	贵州省黔南州贵定县
独山深河桥风景名胜区	Dushan Shenhe Bridge Scenic Spot	省级	贵州省黔南州独山县
遵义娄山风景名胜区	Zunyi Loushan Mountain Scenic Spot	省级	贵州省遵义市遵义县板桥镇
绥阳宽阔水风景名胜区	Suiyang Kuankuoshui Scenic Spot	省级	贵州省遵义市绥阳县
仁怀茅台风景名胜区	Renhuai Moutai Scenic Spot	省级	贵州省遵义仁怀市茅台镇
习水风景名胜区	Xishui Scenic Spot	省级	贵州省遵义市习水县东皇镇
余庆大乌江风景名胜区	Yuqing Wujiang River Scenic Spot	省级	贵州省遵义市余庆县白泥镇
湄潭湄江风景名胜区	Meitan Scenic Spot	省级	贵州省遵义市湄潭县
梵净山——太平河风景名胜区	Fanjing Mountain----Taiping River Scenic Spot	省级	贵州省铜仁市江口县
印江木黄风景名胜区	Yinjiang Muhuang Scenic Spot	省级	贵州省铜仁市印江县
思南乌江白鹭洲风景名胜区	Sinan Wujiang River Bailuzhou Scenic Spo	省级	贵州省铜仁市思南县
松桃豹子岭——寨英风景名胜区	Songtao Baozi Mountain----Zhaiying Scenic Spot	省级	贵州省铜仁市松桃县
万山夜郎谷风景名胜区	Wanshan Yelang Canyon Scenic Spot	省级	贵州省铜仁市万山区
玉屏北洞萧笛之乡风景名胜区	Yuping Beidong Xiaodi-Village Scenic Spot	省级	贵州省铜仁市玉屏县
六枝牂牁江风景名胜区	Liuzhi Zangke River Scenic Spot	省级	贵州省六盘水市六枝特区
盘县古银杏风景名胜区	Panxian Ancientry Gingko Scenic Spot	省级	贵州省六盘水市盘县石桥镇
盘县大洞竹海风景名胜区	PanXian Dadong Banboo Sea Scenic Spot	省级	贵州省六盘水市盘县珠东乡、老厂镇
盘县坡上草原风景名胜区	PanXian Grassland on Mountain Scenic Spot	省级	贵州省六盘水市盘县四格乡、坪地乡
南开风景名胜区	Nankai Scenic Spot	省级	贵州省六盘水市水城县
务川洪渡河风景名胜区	Wuchuan hongduhe Scenic Spot	省级	贵州省遵义市务川县
罗甸大小井风景名胜区	Luodian daxiaojin Scenic Spot	省级	贵州省黔南州罗甸县
德江乌江傩文化风景名胜区	Dejiang Wjiang Riverside Scenic Spot	省级	贵州省铜仁市德江县

18-11 全国重点文物保护单位

Historical and Cultrual Relics under Key Protection

文物单位名称	Name	地址
平坝天台山伍龙寺	Pingba Tiantai Wulong Temple	贵州省安顺市平坝县
云山屯古建筑群(含本寨)	The Ancientry Construction of Yunshantun(Including the Village)	贵州省安顺市西秀区
安顺文庙	Anshun Temple	贵州省安顺市西秀区
穿洞遗址	The Ruins of Chuandong	贵州省安顺市普定县
宁谷遗址	The Ruins of Ninggu	贵州省安顺市西秀区
黔西观音洞遗址	The Site of Kwan-yin Cave Qianxi	贵州省毕节市黔西县
赫章可乐遗址	The Ruins of Kele in Hezhang	贵州省毕节市赫章县
织金古建筑群	The Ancientry Construction Zhijin	贵州省毕节市织金县
川滇黔省革命委员会旧址	Finish the committee old address of Chuan Dian Qian province revolution	贵州省毕节市大方县
奢香墓	The Mausoleum of Lady She Xiang	贵州省毕节市大方县
大屯土司庄园	Datun Headman's Castle	贵州省毕节市毕节市
马头寨古建筑群	The Ancientry Construction of Matouzhai	贵州省贵阳市开阳县
阳明洞和阳明祠	Yangming Cave and Yangming Ancestral Temple	贵州省贵阳市修文县、云岩区
文昌阁和甲秀楼	Wenchang Pavilion and Jiaxiu Floor	贵州省贵阳市贵阳市
息烽集中营旧址(含玄天洞)	The Site of Concentration Camp Xifeng(including Tien-dong)	贵州省贵阳市息烽县
大洞遗址	The Site of Dadong Cave	贵州省六盘水市盘县
郎德上寨古建筑群	The Ancientry Construction Langdeshangzhai	贵州省黔东南州雷山县
地坪风雨桥	Diping Pavilion Bridge	贵州省黔东南州黎平县
飞云崖古建筑群	The Ancientry Construction of Feishanya	贵州省黔东南州黄平县
旧州古建筑群	The Ancientry Construction of Jiuzhou	贵州省黔东南州黄平县
黎平会议会址	The Site of Liping Conference	贵州省黔东南州黎平县
和平村旧址	The former site of Peace village	贵州省黔东南州镇远县
青龙洞	Qinglong Cave	贵州省黔东南州镇远县
增冲鼓楼	Zengchong Drum-tower	贵州省黔东南州从江县
福泉城墙	Ming Dynasty Wall in Fuquan	贵州省黔南州福泉市
葛镜桥	Gejing Bridge	贵州省黔南州福泉市
交乐墓群	Jiaole Tombs	贵州省黔西南州兴仁县
“二十四道拐”抗战公路	"twenty-four Shui" road war	贵州省黔西南州晴隆县
石阡万寿宫	Shiqian Wanshou Palace	贵州省铜仁市石阡县
万山汞矿遗址	The Site of Wanshan Hydrargyrum	贵州省铜仁市万山区
东山古建筑群	The Ancient Building Complex of Dongshan	贵州省铜仁市铜仁市
寨英古建筑群	The Ancient Building Complex of Zhaiying	贵州省铜仁市松桃县
思唐古建筑群	The Ancientry Construction Sitang	贵州省铜仁市思南县
黔东特区革命委员会旧址	The site of Qiandong SAR revolution committee	贵州省铜仁市沿河县、德江县、印江县
遵义会议会址	The Site of Zunyi Conference	贵州省遵义市红花岗区
遵义海龙屯	Zunyi Hailongtun	贵州省遵义市汇川区
杨粲墓	Yangcan Tomb	贵州省遵义市汇川区
红军四渡赤水战役旧址	The former site of Battle of the Red Army Siduchishui	贵州省遵义市习水县、仁怀市、汇川区
湄潭浙江大学旧址	The former site of Zhejiang University in Meitan	贵州省遵义市湄潭县

注：资料来源于省文化厅，表中文物单位为第六批全国重点文物保护单位。

Note:Data in this table come from the Provinvial Department of Culture.The units in this table are the sixth batch of national key cultural relics protection units.

18-11 续表 continued

文物单位名称	Name	地址
龙广观音洞遗址	The Ruins of Guanglong Cave	贵州省黔西南州安龙县
普安铜鼓山遗址	The Ruins of Puan Timbal Hill	贵州省黔西南州普安县
茶马古道	Tea-Horse Road	贵州省四川、云南、贵州
务川大坪墓群	Wuchuan Daping Tombs	贵州省遵义市务川县
兴义万屯墓群	Xingyi Wan Tuen Tombs	贵州省黔西南州兴义市
平坝棺材洞	Pingba coffin hole	贵州省安顺市平坝县
惠水仙人桥洞葬	Huishui Fairy bridge Burial cave	贵州省黔南州惠水县
黔南水族墓群	Qiannan Aquarium Tombs	贵州省黔南州三都县、荔波县
小冲墓群	Small punch Tombs	贵州省六盘水市盘县
明十八先生墓	Eighteen persons' Tomb of Ming Dynasty	贵州省黔西南州安龙县
鲍家屯水利工程	Baojiatun Hydraulic	贵州省安顺市西秀区
镇远城墙	Zhenyuan walls	贵州省黔东南州镇远县
安顺武庙	Anshun Wumiao	贵州省安顺市西秀区
隆里古建筑群	The Ancient Building Complex of Longli	贵州省黔东南州锦屏县
石阡府文庙	Shiqian Temple	贵州省铜仁市石阡县
榕江大利村古建筑群	The Ancient Building Complex in the village Rongjiang Dali	贵州省黔东南州榕江县
楼上村古建筑群	The Ancient Building Complex in the village Loushang	贵州省铜仁市石阡县
岩门长官司城	Yanmen Long lawsuit City	贵州省黔东南州黄平县
锦屏飞山庙	Jinping Feishan Temple	贵州省黔东南州锦屏县
高阡鼓楼	Gaoqian Drum-tower	贵州省黔东南州从江县
宰俄鼓楼	Zaie Drum-tower	贵州省黔东南州从江县
金勾风雨桥	Jingou Pavilion Boasting	贵州省黔东南州从江县
鲁屯牌坊群	Lu Tun archway	贵州省黔西南州兴义市
复兴江西会馆	Jiangxi Hall in the town of Fuxing	贵州省遵义市赤水市
三门塘古建筑群	The Ancient buildings Complex in the Village of Sanmentang	贵州省黔东南州天柱县
敖氏和罗氏墓群石刻	Ao and Roche' Tombs of Carved stone	贵州省毕节市金沙县
尚稽陈玉壂祠	Chenyu Temple in the town of Shangji	贵州省遵义市遵义县
兴义刘氏庄园	The Liu manor in Xingyi	贵州省黔西南州兴义市
茅台酒酿酒工业遗产群	Maotai wine industry heritage group	贵州省遵义市仁怀市
王若飞故居	Wang Ruofei's former residence	贵州省安顺市西秀区
述洞独柱鼓楼	Duzhu Drum-tower in the Village of Shudong	贵州省黔东南州黎平县
重安江水碾群	Chongan River Shuinian group	贵州省黔东南州黄平县

注：表中文物单位为第七批全国重点文物保护单位。

Note:Data in this table come from the Provinvial Department of Culture.The units in this table are the seventh batch of national key cultural relics protection units.

18-12 星级饭店
Star-rated Hotels

名 称	Name	星级 Level	评定日期 Date of Assess	客房数 Rooms	床位数 Beds	地 址 Address	电 话 Telephone
贵州天怡豪生大酒店	Guizhou Howard Johnson Plaza Hotel	5	2005.03	310	439	贵阳市枣山路29号	0851-6518888
喜来登贵航大酒店	Sheraton Guiyang Hotel	5	2010.08	346	629	贵阳市中华南路49号	0851-5888888
黔西南州金州翠湖宾馆	Jinzhoucuihu Hotel in Qianxinanzhou	5	2010.12	203	294	兴义市瑞金南路60号	0859-3619999
贵阳世纪金源大饭店	Empark Grand Hotel - Guiyang	5	2012.03	520	755	贵阳市金阳新区金阳南路6号	0851-3928888
贵州饭店	Guizhou Park Hotel	4	1998.07	382	660	贵阳市北京路66号	0851-6823888
贵州鲜花酒店	Guizhou Flower Hotel	4	2001.12	260	403	贵阳市中华南路1号	0851-5867888
贵州柏顿酒店	Trade-Point Hotel Guizhou	4	2001.05	254	343	贵阳市延安东路18号	0851-5827888
贵州丽豪大饭店	Gui Zhou Regal Hotel	4	2005.07	220	355	贵阳市瑞金北路115号	0851-6521888
贵龙饭店	Gui Long Hotel - Guiyang	4	2001.06	168	316	贵阳市神奇路52号	0851-5593888
能辉酒店	Neng Hui Hotel	4	2003.12	125	205	贵阳市瑞金南路38号	0851-5898888
贵州武岳酒店	Guizhou Wuyue Hotel	4	2007.09	192	306	贵阳市南厂路1号	0851-8651777
贵州雅迪尔国际大酒店	Gui Zhou Yonder International Hotel	4	2010.04	218	342	贵阳市中华南路7号	0851-5578888
凯里嘉瑞禾腾龙酒店	Jiaruihe Tenglong Hotel - Kaili	4	2004.05	166	311	凯里市宁波东路	0855-8066666
凯里金冠酒店	Kaili Jin Guan Hotel	4	2006.11	168	316	凯里市支庄路18号	0855-8068888
安顺凯旋大酒店	Triumphal Hotel - Anshun	4	2006.12	246	403	安顺市开发区南马广场	0853-3461999
毕节腾龙凯悦酒店	Tenglong Kaiyue Hotel - Bijie	4	2006.12	254	343	毕节市桂花路2号	0857-8291111
铜仁宝鑫大酒店	Baoxin Hotel - Tongren	4	2006.07	151	280	铜仁市东太大道88号	0856-5937888
荔波县三力酒店	San Li Hotel in Libo county	4	2007.09	152	293	荔波县玉屏镇思铭大道	0854-3615888
贵侯苑商务大酒店	Guihouyuan Business Hotel	4	2009.03	85	138	都匀市开发区龙山大道	0854-7121111
金鹏国际酒店	Vantage International Hotel	4	2009.08	88	126	都匀市剑江中路67号	0854-7127777
伯爵花园酒店	Earl Garden Hotel	4	2009.01	149	204	都匀市开发区	0854-8759999
毕节大酒店	Bijie Hotel	4	2008.09	151	269	毕节市砂石路	0857-8689999
金凯帝豪酒店	Jin Kai Di Hao Hotel	4	2008.09	109	187	凯里市北京西路	0855-8276688
遵义大世界酒店	Zuyi Grand World Hotel	4	2008.12	167	238	遵义市汇川区珠海路一号	0852-8666666
遵义东方酒店	Zunyi Oriental Hotel	4	2008.12	204	327	遵义市中华南路2号	0852-8867777
赤水中悦大酒店	Zhong Yue Hotel	4	2008.12	140	250	赤水市南正街22号	0852-2823888
六盘水时代假日酒店	Liupanshui Times Holiday Hotel	4	2009.08	265	381	六盘水钟山区钟山中路66号	0858-8108888
六盘水凤凰祥林大酒店	Liupanshui Fenghuang Xianglin Hotel	4	2010.12	130	224	六盘水市凤凰新区青峰路18号	0858-8296789
贵州峰润喀斯特酒店	Guizhou Casite Hotel	4	2011.01	197	309	南明区神奇路1号	0851-8196888
金芦笙小镇精品特色酒店	Jinlusheng town boutique Featured Hotels	4	2011.04	138	245	宝山南路88号	0851-5623999
贵州民族大酒店	Guizhou Ethnic Hotel	4	2011.08	121	209	南明区箭道街23号	0851-5571888
贵阳蓝天宾馆	Guiyang Blue Sky Hotel	4	2011.08	112	191	南明区解放路158号	0851-5795988
西苑锦润酒店	Xiyuan Jinrun Hotel	4	2011.08	134	214	小河区锦江路5号	0851-5975555
西湖花园大酒店	West Lake Garden Hotel	4	2011.08	252	451	宝山北路133号	0851-5292802
宏洲国际大酒店	Hongzhou International Hotel	4	2011.10	203	298	织金县城关镇金北路151号	0857-7758888
都市怡景酒店	City Scene Hotel	4	2011.10	117	202	贵阳市都司路122号	0851-5848888
贵州铝厂宾馆	Guizhou Aluminum Hotel	4	2011.11	78	134	贵阳市白云区刚玉街57号	0851-4896111
贵阳夏日康桥酒店	Guiyang Summer Cambridge Hotel	4	2011.11	89	141	贵阳市白云区白云南路299号	0851-4439655
六盘水红果大酒店	Liupanshui Hongguo Hotel	4	2011.12	189	353	盘县红果经济开发区凤鸣路	0858-3631888
遵义森林大酒店	Zunyi Woods Hotel	4	2011.12	121	212	遵义市汇川区深圳路新客运大楼	0852-8988888
三都福丰假日酒店	Sandu Fufeng Holiday Hotel	4	2011.12	165	236	三都县三合镇龙嘴角移民新村	0854-3029999
松桃松闽大酒店	Songtao Song Min Hotel	4	2012.01	142	220	贵州省松桃县麻阳街24号	0856-6966666
毕节大众国际酒店	Bijie Dazhong International Hotel	4	2012.05	179	321	毕节市翠屏路12号	0857-8933333
福泉大酒店	Fuquan Hotel	4	2012.08	148	257	福泉市金山办事处洒金北路174号	0854-2212888
天柱大酒店	Tianzhu Hotel	4	2012.08	80	144	天柱县凤城镇北部新区1号	0855-7821888
泰翔柏丽酒店	Taixiang Boutique Hotel	4	2012.08	116	183	安顺市开发区西航路	0853-8186666
关岭坝陵酒店	Guanling Baling Hotel	4	2012.08	232	432	关岭县关索镇大龙滩高速公路出口	0853-7116888
贵阳诺富特酒店	Guiyang Novotel Hotel	4	2012.08	242	314	贵阳市中华南路8号	0851-5881888
铜仁温州大酒店	Tongren Wenzhou Hotel	4	2012.10	115	177	铜仁市大庆北路85号	0856-6968888
铜仁江华国际大酒店	Tongren Jin Hua International Hotel	4	2012.10	158	238	铜仁市火车站转盘	0856-5266091
遵义金城大酒店	Zunyi Jincheng Hotel	4	2012.10	131	215	遵义市香港路中段	0852-8621666

18-12 续表1 continued

名称	Name	星级 Level	评定日期 Date of Assess	客房数 Rooms	床位数 Beds	地址 Address	电话 Telephone
国酒门温泉酒店	GJM Hotspring Hotel	4	2012.12	50	116	仁怀市盐津河风景区国酒门旁	0852-2316666
金黔嘉华大酒店	Jinqianjiahua Hotel	4	2012.12	169	281	桐梓县娄山关镇河滨大道南段888号	0852-6666666
遵义市丽都酒店	Zunyi Lidu Hotel	4	2012.12	111	166	遵义市香港路638号	0852-8959999
牂牁江假日酒店	Zangkejiang Holiday Hotel	4	2012.12	114	178	六枝特区人民路22号	0858-8101666
贵阳林城万宜酒店	Guiyang Linchengwanyi Hotel	4	2012.12	388	639	贵阳市遵义路326号	0851-6878888
贵州华联酒店	Guizhou Hualian Hotel	3	1999.09	141	261	贵阳市中华中路137号	0851-5810999
黔灵大酒店	Qianling Hotel	3	2000.04	152	273	贵阳市北京路225号	0851-8271521
贵阳神奇星岛酒店	Guiyang Shenqixingdao Hotel	3	2002.09	101	180	贵阳市贵开路1号	0851-6751888
贵州立云酒店	Guizhou Liyun Hotel	3	2002.12	254	468	贵阳市浣沙路5号	0851-8126666
紫林宾馆	Zilin Hotel	3	2004.02	195	365	贵阳市延安中路110号	0851-5283000
久远饭店	Jiuyuan Hotel	3	2004.08	169	300	贵阳市瑞金南路36号	0851-5849999
修文珍珠岛度假中心	Xiuwen Pearl Island Resort	3	2004.11	89	220	贵阳修文酒长镇	0851-2436002
贵阳市金品大酒店	Guiyang Jinpin Hotel	3	2004.12	112	196	贵阳朝阳洞路建材巷1号	0851-8216666
贵阳南翔酒店	Guiyang Nanxiang Hotel	3	2004.12	63	108	贵阳市延安西路185号	0851-6522888
贵州宏业宾馆	Guizhou Hongye Hotel	3	2005.02	75	143	贵阳市解放路87号	0851-5566755
贵阳久泰大酒店	Guiyang Jiutai Hotel	3	2005.01	120	191	贵阳市瑞金北路116号	0851-6685998
花溪溪山酒店	Huaxi Xishan Hotel	3	2006.01	49	96	贵阳市花溪区迎宾路	0851-3630166
贵阳山水大酒店	Guiyang Shanshui Hotel	3	2006.11	38	41	贵阳市沙冲路198号	0851-3831838
新联大厦	New Union Building	3	1997.12	120	200	贵阳市外环东路227号	0851-6765555
红阳宾馆	Hongyang Hotel	3	2005.01	73	140	贵阳花溪区150号信箱	0851-3853306
金泉酒店	Jinquan Hotel	3	2007.01	91	172	贵阳花溪区花谷路6号	0851-3851484
贵阳方源酒店	Guiyang Fangyuan Hotel	3	2007.08	95	152	贵阳市小河区香江路6号	0851-8316655
贵阳机场宾馆	Guiyang Airport Hotel	3	2007.11	168	315	贵阳市	0851-5498585
黔景宾馆	Qianjing Hotel	3	2007.12	117	246	贵阳市	0851-3990188
京瑞宾馆	Jingrui Hotel	3	2005.06	134	300	贵阳市北京路194号	0851-6891602
贵阳瑞金酒店	Ruijin Hotel	3	2008.06	168	312	贵阳市瑞金南路62号	0851-5209999
贵州铁路通达饭店	Guizhou Railway Tongda Hotel	3	2008.11	234	468	贵阳市遵义路86号	0851-8213888
贵阳益宏酒店有限公司	Guiyang Yihong Hotels Ltd.	3	2009.12	99	157	贵阳市油榨街2号	0851-3818888
云岩浣溪假日大酒店	Yunyan Huanxi Holiday Hotel	3	2010.05	138	230	贵阳市浣沙路104号	0851-8598888
燕安大酒店	Yan'an Hotel	3	1997.12	81	167	安顺市贵黄路5公里处	0853-3228988
安顺西秀山宾馆	Anshun Xixiushan Hotel	3	2002.04	92	153	安顺市南华路48号	0853-3223900
神奇福运大酒店	Shenqifuyun Hotel	3	2002.09	90	160	安顺市外环西南路3号	0853-3290000
黔中大厦	Qianzhong Building	3	2005.07	66	113	安顺市南华路68好	0853-3292019
白马湖山庄	Baima Lake Villa	3	2005.07	33	59	安顺市镇宁县白马哨	0853-6791111
安顺若飞宾馆	Anshun Ruofei Hotel	3	2001.04	41	73	安顺市南华路48号	0853-3225325
龙宫酒店	Dragon Palace Hotel	3	2006.01	41	79	安顺市龙宫风景名胜区	0853-3661388
关岭黔岭宾馆	Guanling Qianling Hotel	3	2006.11	50	92	关岭县外环路128号	0853-7228888
安顺纽曼宾馆	Anshun Newman Hotel	3	2008.03	36	70	安顺市	0853-3467777
龙宫水电宾馆	Longgong Shuidian Hotel	3	2009.11	31	60	安顺市龙宫风景名胜区	0853-3661166
廊桥华油酒店	Langqiao Huayou Hotel	3	2010.07	82	152	安顺市塔山西路15号	13308530111
平坝白云大酒店	Pingba Baiyun Hotel	3	2010.07	47	52	平坝县城关镇高新区	
遵义港澳大酒店	Zunyi Gang'ao Hotel	3	2005.11	81	148	遵义市澳门路8号	0852-8716655
遵义宾馆	Zunyi Hotel	3	2000.01	181	329	遵义市石龙路3号	0852-8224902
遵义京腾丽湾酒店	Zunyi Jingtengliwan Hotel	3	2006.11	140	252	遵义市北京路	0852-8649898
茅园宾馆	Maoyuan Hotel	3	2004.01	56	110	遵义仁怀市茅台镇	0852-2386290
习水绿洲酒店	Xishui Lvzhou Hotel	3	2006.11	83	150	遵义习水县经济开发区	0852-2732100
遵义县顺天酒店	Shuntian Hotel in Zunyi county	3	2007.09	44	80	遵义县南白镇万寿广场	0852-7232188
广电酒店	Guangdian Hotel	3	2007.09	109	192	遵义市中华北路广电大厦	0852-8700888
仁怀市名酒宾馆	Renhuai Mingjiu Hotel	3	2007.09	60	100	仁怀市国酒大道	0852-3226999
嘉联宾馆	Jialian Hotel	3	2008.12	64	110	赤水市人民南路运管大厦	0852-2820222
鹏程大酒店	Pengcheng Hotel	3	2010.01	51	92	余庆县城内	0852-4625868
赤天化宾馆	Chitianhua hotel	3	2010.01	95	170	赤水市	0852-2887081
都匀港龙大酒店	Duyun Ganglong Hotel	3	2002.08	126	210	都匀市河滨路134号	0854-8222895

18-12 续表2 continued

名　称	Name	星级 Level	评定日期 Date of Assess	客房数 Rooms	床位数 Beds	地　址 Address	电　话 Telephone
金利源大酒店	Jinliyuan Hotel	3	2010.01	89	182	都匀市	0854-3619188
五月花景山酒店	Wuyuehua Jingshan Hotel	3	2005.01	89	121	都匀市剑江中路112号	0854-8756999
西苑假日酒店	Xiyuan Holiday Hotel	3	2007.09	54	96	都匀市开发区	0854-8758888
锦绣园	Jinxiuyuan Park	3	2005.09	48	101	龙里县城郊	0854-5669508
顺庆大酒店	Shunqing Hotel	3	2005.03	98	218	荔波樟江北街	0854-3610388
荔波吉妮丽吉大酒店	Libo Jeanne Liji Hotel	3	2006.11	86	170	荔波县教师新村	0854-3619666
神泉大酒店	Shenquan Hotel	3	2005.03	46	96	罗甸县政府路	0854-7620758
都匀市桥城宾馆	Duyun Qiaocheng Hotel	3	2007.09	92	166	都匀市文明路50号	0854-8222189
独山县南方大酒店	Dushan Southern Hotel	3	2007.09	61	91	独山县四通路十八号	0854-3238525
荔波县金谷宾馆	Libo Jingu Hotel	3	2007.09	53	120	荔波县樟江北路	0854-3613888
纪龙大酒店	Jilong Hotel	3	2005.09	44	80	龙里县	0854-5620333
贵定县环岛大酒店	Guiding Huandao Hotel	3	2009.01	38	78	贵定县城关镇八一村	0854-5221000
瓮安县金福大酒店	Weng'an Jinfu Hotel	3	2009.03	49	83	瓮安县文峰中路	0854-2635100
荔波县大鹏商务酒店	Libo Dapeng Business Hotel	3	2008.03	95	178	荔波县漳江中路12号	0854-3615499
独山县翠泉宾馆	Dushan Cuiquan hotel	3	2009.04	62	116	独山县	0854-3239018
凯里凯莱酒店	Kaili Gloria Plaza Hotel	3	2006.12	96	182	凯里市韶山南路21号	0855-8277888
凯里鸿祺宾馆	Kaili Hongqi Hotel	3	2006.08	84	140	凯里市韶山南路3号	0855-8275555
黎平大酒店	Liping Hotel	3	2006.11	80	148	黎平德风镇富民北路	0855-6210666
贵州清酒醉翁宾馆	Guizhou Qingjiuzuiweng Hotel	3	2004.05	46	92	镇远县	0855-5823238
施秉县三丰迎宾馆	Shibing Sanfeng Guest House	3	2004.05	89	190	施秉县平宁桥	0855-4227188
凯铁大酒店	Kaitie Hotel	3	2008.09	63	121	凯里市清江路	0855-3811999
凯里大酒店	Kaili Hotel	3	2008.09	156	275	凯里市韶山北路	0855-8277778
忠德园假日酒店	Zhongdeyuan Holiday Hotel	3	2008.09	70	160	凯里市环城东路	0855-8538888
港赛大酒店	Gangsai Hotel	3	2008.09	63	114	黎平县城内	0855-6230888
久格里吉温泉度假酒店	Jiugeliji Spa Resort	3	2008.09	60	115	剑河县温泉风景区内	0855-5158288
清源酒店	Qingyuan Hotel	3	2008.12	30	56	下司镇皮划艇激流回旋训练基地	0855-2685666
营盘坡民族宾馆	Yingpanpo National Hotel	3	2009.07	92	163	凯里市	0855-3837779
凯里市天华宾馆	Kaili Tianhua Hotel	3	2009.07	82	153	凯里市	0855-8276411
镇远县铁溪度假酒店	Zhenyuan Tiexi Resort	3	2009.07	33	57	镇远县	0855-5721888
剑河县馨泉山庄	Jianhe Xinquan Villa	3	2009.11	38	74	剑河县	0855-5158168
凯里宾馆	Kaili Hotel	3	2010.04	57	130	凯里市	0855-8066100
从江县奥悦酒店	Congjiang Aoyue Hotel	3	2009.11	33	66	从江县	0855-6411808
金正酒店	Jinzheng Hotel	3	2010.06	67	107	凯里市经济开发区	0855-8558988
麻江县怡景湾酒店	Majiang Yijing Hotel	3	2010.08	34	48	麻江县下司镇	0855-2684777
城城大厦	Chengcheng Building	3	2005.07	68	128	兴义市神奇路159号	0859-3112222
龙宇大酒店	Longyu Hotel	3	2007.11	56	112	兴义市神奇西路26号	0859-3126888
盘江宾馆	Panjiang Hotel	3	2005.07	123	231	兴义市盘江西路4号	0859-3223456
兴义神禧大酒店	Xingyi Shenxi Hotel	3	2008.05	80	158	兴义市坪东路	0859-3818188
贞丰县贞丰宾馆	Zhenfeng Hotel	3	2009.09	120	214	贞丰县金丰大道29号	0859-6777777
贞丰县怡景酒店	Zhenfeng Yijing Hotel	3	2009.09	36	60	贞丰县	0859-6613777
兴义市三生酒店	Xingyi Sansheng Hotel	3	2009.09	111	200	兴义市瑞金北路中段	0859-3244888
六盘水金三角大酒店	Liupanshui Jinsanjiao Hotel	3	2006.12	44	79	六盘水市明湖路3号	0858-8233888
雨田酒店	Yutian Hotel	3	2005.07	75	126	六盘水钟山西路48号	0858-8261888
源丰商务酒店	Yuanfeng Business Hotel	3	2005.07	62	99	铜仁市锦江南路1号	0856-5222222
思南远航大酒店	Sinan Yuanhang Hotel	3	2009.06	62	110	思南县城北街29号	0856-7220777
江口县索菲特大酒店	Jiangkou Sofite Hotel	3	2009.12	57	112	江口县三星西路17号	0856-6622288
德江县金平大酒店	Dejiang Jinping Hotel	3	2009.12	44	83	德江县清龙镇	0856-8527555
铜仁市金顶酒店	Tongren Jinding Hotel	3	2009.12	41	73	铜仁市清水大道80号	0856-5211168
毕节天工大酒店	Bijie Tiangong Hotel	3	1999.06	66	150	毕节市洪山路60号	0857-2136188
威宁县黑颈鹤大酒店	Weining Heijinghe Hotel	3	2008.07	78	162	威宁建设东路79号	0857-6224426
金沙县黄金大酒店	Jinsha Huangjin Hotel	3	2008.07	95	179	金沙县长安街138号	0857-7258888
洪南大酒店	Hongnan Hotel	3	2008.09	81	117	毕节市迎宾大道	0857-8292888
赫章夜郎大酒店	Hezhang Yelang Hotel	3	2008.12	145	255	赫章县城南路	0857-3238998
煌都帝豪酒店	Huangdudihao Hotel	3	2008.09	78	120	黔西县城内	0857-4888888

18-12 续表3 continued

名 称	Name	星级 Level	评定日期 Date of Assess	客房数 Rooms	床位数 Beds	地 址 Address	电 话 Telephone
铜仁市梵天索菲特酒店	Tongren Brahma Sofitel Hotel	3	2010.12	57	97	铜仁锦江大道8号	0856-5218888
沿河沙洲大酒店	Yanhe Shazhou Hotel	3	2010.11	55	87	铜仁市沿河县沙坨电站	0856-6998666
玉屏宾馆	Yuping Hotel	3	2010.12	66	114	玉屏县平溪镇人民路333号	0856-3227888
三江宏晟度假酒店	Sanjiang Hongsheng Holiday Hotel	3	2010.08	30	40	福泉市金山办事处双桥村金鸡山	0854-2210999
怡景苑宾馆	Yijingyuan hotel	3	2010.08	54	108	荔波县漳江北街42号	0854-3618300
华通大酒店	Huatong Hotel	3	2010.11	45	70	独山县五星花园二期	0854-3222399
夜郎大酒店	Yelang Hotel	3	2010.12	70	126	惠水县和平镇建设路	0854-6234567
沿河金红大酒店	Yanhe Jinhong Hotel	3	2010.12	57	130	铜仁市沿河县城南路	0856-8228055
华侨大酒店	Huaqiao Hotel	3	2010.11	70	110	三穗城关	0855-3855555
柏悦酒店	Boyue Hotel	3	2010.11	56	101	凯里市	0855-8270000
万豪酒店	Wanhao Hotel	3	2010.11	72	128	凯里市	0855-8603999
湄潭大酒店	Meitan Hotel	3	2010.12	82	136	湄潭县兴湄北路35号	0852-4366595
花溪玉龙宾馆	Huaxi Yulong Hotel	3	2011.03	35	70	花溪区大吉路1号	0851-3863865
聚鑫酒店	Juxin Hotel	3	2011.04	114	189	贵阳市环城北路228号	0851-6851999
黔西化屋度假酒店	Qianxi Huawu Holiday Hotel	3	2011.08	36	66	黔西县新仁乡化屋村	0857-4634166
纳雍华熙酒店	Nayong Huaxi Hotel	3	2010.01	114	173	纳雍县城南大道	0857-3685777
龙都大酒店	Longdu Hotel	3	2011.06	139	216	铜仁市清水大道128号	0856-4133333
贵武花园大酒店	Guiwu Garden Hotel	3	2011.09	91	151	贵阳市金阳新区云潭南路	0851-5625678
大正酒店	Dazheng Hotel	3	2011.09	60	126	贵阳市南明区翠微巷60号	0851-5515666
桂花园度假酒店	Guihuayuan Holiday Hotel	3	2011.09	80	150	都匀市大河村村卫生院对面	0854-8190559
南江度假酒店	Nanjiang Holiday Hotel	3	2011.07	146	257	开阳南江大峡谷景区内	0851-7524089
金海大酒店	Jinhai Hotel	3	2011.09	67	120	毕节市洪南路	0857-8615555
草海大酒店	Caohai Hotel	3	2011.09	108	188	威宁威双大道	0857-7115388
红楼酒店	Honglou Hotel	3	2004.06	48	90	大方县奢香大道南段	0857-5233712
和泰大酒店	Hetai Hotel	3	2010.06	101	175	大方县城利民路中段	0857-5250998
红枫湖旅游度假村	Hongfeng Lake Tourist Resort	3	2011.07	126	207	清镇市望城坡	0851-8575042
清镇皇朝大酒店	Qingzhen Dynasty Hotel	3	2011.07	90	144	清镇市云岭东路	0851-2581888
金竹大酒店	Jinzhu Hotel	3	2011.12	100	189	赤水市文化办财神涂	0852-2853555
镇远府城宾馆	Zhenyuan Fucheng Hotel	3	2011.11	69	130	镇远县兴隆街	0855-5711888
安顺凤凰山大酒店	Anshun Fenghuangshan Hotel	3	2011.12	121	240	安顺市塔山东路58号	0853-3225998
贵州林都酒店	Guizhou Lindu Hotel	3	2011.12	105	189	云岩区延安西路2号	0851-5360367
安龙泰安宾馆	Anlong Tai'an Hotel	3	2012.02	75	132	贵州省安龙县西区开发大道	0859-5555222
台江金红阳生态酒店	Taijiang Jinhongyang Eco-hotel	3	2012.01	63	120	台江国家级南宫森林公园景区18号	
海钰酒店	Haiyu Hotel	3	2012.02	152	266	兴义市瑞金北路10号	0859-8711111
九九大酒店	Jiujiu Hotel	3	2011.12	51	94	贵州省长顺县和平西路	0854-6898888
杉木河酒店	Shanmuhe Hotel	3	2011.03	57	115	施秉县舞阳河路	0855-4221177
黔锦假日酒店	Qianjin Holiday Hotel	3	2012.03	137	208	盘县红果经济开发区	0858-3668995
兴凯花园酒店	Xingkai Garden Hotel	3	2012.03	76	122	盘县红果镇杜鹃西路1号	0858-3635059
松桃世纪华园大酒店	Songtao Shijiyuan Hotel	3	2012.04	50	87	松桃县大十字	0856-2681555
贵阳腾晖酒店	Guiyang Tenghui Hotel	3	2012.05	76	131	贵阳市修文县翠屏路	0851-2327777
君临大酒店	Junlin Hotel	3	2012.05	123	202	安顺市新大十字塔山西路1号	0853-3350777
瓮安灵江大酒店	Weng'an Lingjiang Hotel	3	2012.06	30	47	瓮安县新区武装部	0854-2776666
铜仁盛世佳华酒店	Tongren Shengshijiahua Hotel	3	2012.06	64	125	铜仁市清水路火车站旁	0856-6903888
铜仁世纪大酒店	Tongren Century Hotel	3	2012.06	149	272	铜仁市清水南路公园道1号	0856-5629999
铜仁亨达酒店	Tongren Hengda Hotel	3	2012.06	55	92	铜仁市火车站旁	0856-5230999
西江黔森大酒店	Xijiang Qian Sen Hotel	3	2012.05	72	140	西江千户苗寨黔森路1号	0855-3347909
紫鑫酒店	Zixin Hotel	3	2012.06	102	184	西秀区黄果树大街消防支队内	0853-3332777
新华宾馆	Xinhua Hotel	3	2012.06	108	189	开发区西航路138号	0853-3459888
福源酒店	Fuyuan Hotel	3	2012.06	36	72	开发区北航路广电大楼旁	0853-3320666
鑫焰酒店	Xinyan Hotel	3	2012.06	52	87	平坝县南客运站大楼	0853-4616789
汇景酒店	Huijing Hotel	3	2012.06	51	93	普定县龙潭加油站对面	0853-8718888
紫云宾馆	Ziyun Hotel	3	2012.06	139	271	紫云县商业街格凸大道中断	0853-5238888

18-12 续表4 continued

名 称	Name	星级 Level	评定日期 Date of Assess	客房数 Rooms	床位数 Beds	地 址 Address	电 话 Telephone
金龙酒店	Jinlong Hotel	3	2012.07	79	142	织金县金北路	0857-7755777
金鑫酒店	Jinxin Hotel	3	2012.07	78	138	大方县奢香大道北段	0857-2198888
奢香大酒店	Shexiang Hotel	3	2012.11	79	136	七星关区清毕路长弘花苑内	0857-8631888
余庆广电酒店	Yuqing Guangdian Hotel	3	2012.11	56	91	余庆县香港路	0852-4626888
佳乐家酒店	Jialejia Hotel	3	2012.11	106	171	遵义市大连路	0852-3195555
枫叶山庄	Fengye Villa	2	2000.01	66	129	贵阳市红枫发电总厂内	0851-2554168
天洋楼大酒店	Tianyanglou Hotel	2	2004.09	42	100	贵阳市民权路5号	0851-5832088
贵州民族宾馆	Guizhou National Hotel	2	2004.12	86	170	贵阳市市北路68号	0851-8633666
开阳金都宾馆	Kaiyang Jindu Hotel	2	2004.01	41	87	贵阳市开阳县环城北路	0851-5832088
仁达饭店	Renda Hotel	2	2004.09	112	300	贵阳市中华北路319号	0851-6825301
开阳尚怡宾馆	Kaiyang Shangyi Hotel	2	2009.04	22	41	开阳	
开阳江南宾馆	Kaiyang Jiangnan Hotel	2	2010.05	35	65	开阳县城关镇环城北路	
腾达酒店	Tenda Hotel	2	2005.06	27	54	安顺市	0853-7228886
安顺情源宾馆	Anshun Qingyuan Hotel	2	1994.11	86	151	安顺普定县城内	0853-8221999
长城宾馆	Great Wall Hotel	2	2009.07	29	48	安顺平坝县武装部	0853-4227333
钟山宾馆	Zhongshan Hotel	2	1994.11	138	330	六盘水钟山中路52号	0858-8223285
六枝工矿迎宾馆	Liuzhi Gongkuang Guest House	2	2002.05	57	114	六枝特区团结路13号	0858-5713548
凯豪大酒店	Kaihao Hotel	2	2007.01	40	72	六枝特区交通西路	0858-5319999
六枝宾馆	Liuzhi Hotel	2	2005.01	65	160	六枝平寨镇友谊路	0858-5322660
印江腾龙大酒店	Yinjiang Tenglong Hotel	2	2003.08	55	100	印江县城西环开发区	0856-6228888
石阡宾馆	Shiqian hotel	2	2005.06	61	115	石阡县汤山镇	0856-7652777
石阡临江宾馆	Shiqian Linjiang Hotel	2	2005.09	41	82	石阡县汤山镇河西街	0856-8957399
沿河天龙大酒店	Yanhe Tianlong Hotel	2	2005.09	96	350	沿河县城南路23号	0856-8228054
思南县明星宾馆	Sinan Mingxing Hotel	2	2009.12	26	54	思南县民政局内	0856-7225085
玉屏贵阳大酒店	Yuping Guiyang Hotel	2	2010.08	30	60	玉屏火车站附近	0856-3228886
洪山宾馆	Hongshan Hotel	2	2004.08	208	388	毕节市洪山路1号	0857-8251829
黔西雍和酒店	Qianxi Yonghe Hotel	2	2008.01	38	71	黔西县城内	0857-4220888
金辉酒店	Jinhui Hotel	2	2006.07	60	102	金沙县城内	0857-7251999
毕节迎宾馆	Bijie Guest House	2	2009.07	49	90	毕节市环东路1号	0857-8312222
织金平远酒店	Zhijin Pingyuan Hotel	2	2009.07	43	83	织金县沿河路	0857-7636999
威宁明珠酒店	Weining Mingzhu Hotel	2	2009.07	27	51	威宁县开发区	0857-6233088
威宁穗苑宾馆	Weining Suiyuan Hotel	2	2009.07	30	66	威宁县星光路	0857-6282222
赫章维尔乐宾馆	Hezhang wei'erle Hotel	2	2009.07	20	33	赫章县南环路	0857-3239898
瑞海酒店	Ruihai Hotel	2	2001.12	74	108	遵义市外环路沙坝	0852-8866333
名族酒店	Mingzu Hotel	2	2004.06	46	86	遵义市红花岗武装部	0852-8433888
蓝天宾馆	Blue Sky Hotel	2	2005.12	138	248	遵义市北京路99号	0852-8622916
通达酒店	Tongda Hotel	2	2001.06	148	276	遵义市北京路134号	0852-8822925
正华大酒店	Zhenghua Hotel	2	2002.05	46	105	桐梓县娄山关镇	0852-6657869
利永宾馆	Liyong Hotel	2	2004.05	83	136	仁怀市国酒中路	0852-2250882
聚贤楼宾馆	Juxianlou Hotel	2	2005.12	33	50	绥阳县博雅苑陈列馆内	0852-6233848
娄山关生态乐园酒店	Loushanguan Eco Paradise Hotel	2	2009.01	27	49	桐梓县娄山关镇娄山村	0852-6825333
彩阳酒店	Caiyang Hotel	2	2008.12	35	49	桐梓县城	0852-3208788
金马大酒店	Jinma Hotel	2	2008.12	45	90	桐梓县河滨大道南大门	0852-6661118
博雅宾馆	Boya Hotel	2	2008.12	40	76	绥阳县北大街	0852-6223855
香山宾馆	Xiangshan Hotel	2	2008.12	67	129	遵义市红花岗区大兴路狮子桥头	0852-8234444
赤水大酒店	Chishui Hotel	2	2008.12	36	74	赤水市西内环路106号	0852-2821334
云门囤宾馆	Yunmentun Hotel	2	2009.01	38	71	遵义县三渡镇花桥村	0852-6581555
枫香温泉	Fengxiang Spa	2	2009.01	38	82	遵义县枫香镇	0852-7572608
凤岗宾馆	Fenggang hotel	2	2009.01	57	105	凤岗县县府路	0852-5224567
恒源酒店	Hengyuan Hotel	2	2009.01	37	66	凤岗县政通路	0852-5222768
明星宾馆	Mingxing hotel	2	2009.01	24	43	凤岗县商贸街	0852-5220088
安龙县麗月鸿钰酒店	Anlong Liyuehongyu Hotel	2	2010.01	36	63	安龙县	0859-5216111
凯里市西湖大酒店	Kaili Westlake Hotel	2	2002.12	44	83	凯里市北京西路74号	0855-3826888

18-12 续表5 continued

名称	Name	星级 Level	评定日期 Date of Assess	客房数 Rooms	床位数 Beds	地址 Address	电话 Telephone
国穗大酒店	Guosui Hotel	2	2003.01	28	52	凯里市国税务局大院内	0855-8276888
岑巩县凯华大酒店	Cengong Kaihua Hotel	2	2007.01	65	128	岑巩县	0855-3895988
从江宾馆	Congjiang hotel	2	2008.12	34	67	从江县	0855-6418669
仁和大酒店	Renhe Hotel	2	2008.12	29	43	从江县	0855-6412900
雷山县圣城嘉源酒店	Leishan Shengchengjiayuan Hotel	2	2008.12	27	51	雷山县	0855-3336718
麻江县下司第一楼	Majiang Xiasi Diyilou	2	2008.12	32	65	麻江县	0855-2684000
金鼎龙大酒店	Jindinglong Hotel	2	2009.04	22	41	雷山县城关镇	0855-5158168
剑河温泉剑泉山庄	Jianhe Spa and Jianquan Villa	2	2008.05	33	61	剑河县	0855-5158088
马家岩大酒店	Majiayan Hotel	2	2010.05	36	70	黄平县	0855-2431199
凯里香山大酒店	Kaili Xiangshan Hotel	2	2010.07	40	68	凯里市北京西路39号	0855-8601099
西苑酒店	Xiyuan Hotel	2	2006.04	50	104	都匀市剑江中路	0854-8682132
都匀丽都酒店	Duyun Lidu Hotel	2	2005.09	63	97	都匀州地税局培训中心	0854-8318869
樟江大厦	Zhangjiang Building	2	2003.04	34	66	荔波县城内	0854-3618888
荔波宾馆	Libo Hotel	2	2003.04	46	93	荔波县政府大院内	0854-3612169
鲁黔宾馆	Luqian Hotel	2	2003.04	20	52	荔波县樟江中路	0854-3617098
政协宾馆	CPPCC Hotel	2	2003.04	24	48	荔波县城内	0854-3615573
锦源宾馆	Jinyuan Hotel	2	2004.01	21	47	荔波县广场东路	0854-3618818
水上人间	Water world	2	2003.12	15	27	荔波县内	0854-8939979
松源宾馆	Songyuan Hotel	2	2003.12	31	56	荔波县内	0854-8967651
东方宾馆	Dongfang Hotel	2	2003.04	20	40	荔波县内	0854-3618968
青旅大酒店	CYTS Hotel	2	2006.05	35	70	荔波县广场东路	0854-3613158
再富酒店	Zaifu Hotel	2	2006.05	38	76	荔波县城樟江北街	0854-3618118
晟圆酒店	Shengyuan Hotel	2	2006.05	20	40	荔波县广场东路	0854-8971162
蓝天宾馆	Blue Sky Hotel	2	2003.04	32	63	荔波县城	0854-3619831
荔伊宾馆	Liyi Hotel	2	2006.05	27	52	荔波县城樟江北街	0854-8808668
荔波南江宾馆	Libo Nanjiang Hotel	2	2006.09	21	48	荔波	13985787238
荔波前锦宾馆	Libo Qianjin Hotel	2	2006.09	45	57	荔波	13595418295
怡心宾馆	Yixin Hotel	2	2005.09	15	24	三都三启镇县府路	0854-3927818
望月宾馆	Wangyue Hotel	2	2006.04	48	87	罗甸县委	0854-7611554
沙梨园宾馆	Shaliyuan Hotel	2	2007.05	18	48	荔波县城	0854-3618258
腾龙宾馆	Tenglong Hotel	2	2006.09	27	46	平塘县	0854-7222888
银河大酒店	Yinhe Hotel	2	2008.12	23	41	平塘县	0854-7230988
金胜宾馆	Jinsheng Hotel	2	2008.12	25	44	平塘县	0854-7223688
富源宾馆	Fuyuan Hotel	2	2008.12	20	44	荔波县	0854-3619298
金容宾馆	Jinrong Hotel	2	2008.12	30	60	荔波县	0854-3613818
祥和宾馆	Xianghe Hotel	2	2008.12	30	62	荔波县	0854-3616177
金林宾馆	Jinlin Hotel	2	2008.12	30	57	荔波县	0854-3619780
玉屏镇信合宾馆	Xinhe Hotel in the town of Yuping	2	2008.12	36	69	荔波县	0854-3615828
东篱宾馆	Dongli Hotel	2	2008.12	30	60	荔波县	0854-3619758
名豪大酒店	Minghao Hotel	2	2008.12	41	69	瓮安县	0854-2625555
东利酒店	Dongli Hotel	2	2008.12	30	50	瓮安县	0854-2621889
水电宾馆	Shuidian Hotel	2	2008.12	26	47	瓮安县	0854-2624584
杜鹃苑宾馆	Dujuanyuan Hotel	2	2008.12	48	87	长顺县	0854-6936222
凤凰宾馆	Fenghuang Hotel	2	2008.12	40	90	三都县	0854-3927898
都柳江宾馆	Duliujiang Hotel	2	2008.12	38	72	三都县	0854-3928888
三林时尚酒店	Sanlinshishang Hotel	2	2008.12	52	88	都匀市	0854-8239828
惠水县百联商务酒店	Huishui Bailian Business Hotel	2	2009.12	32	58	惠水县涟江中路中段	0854-6283989
荔波县溪桥宾馆	Libo Xiqiao Hotel	2	2009.12	55	103	荔波县樟江东路17号	0854-3618666
荔波县齐鲁宾馆	Libo Qilu Hotel	2	2009.12	26	51	荔波县玉屏镇文明路24号	0854-3617118
贵储酒店	Guichu Hotel	2	2010.06	35	50	贵定县	0854-5236666
贵定飞龙大酒店	Guiding Feilong Hotel	2	2010.06	28	54	贵定县	0854-5233298
三都地中海宾馆	Sandu Dizhonghai Hotel	2	2010.07	22	35	三都县城中心	0854-3028777
三都润丰宾馆	Sandu Runfeng Hotel	2	2010.07	23	27	三都县三合镇团结路	0854-3929123

18-12 续表6 continued

名称	Name	星级 Level	评定日期 Date of Assess	客房数 Rooms	床位数 Beds	地址 Address	电话 Telephone
南昆宾馆	Nankun Hotel	2	2004.11	44	69	兴义市顶效开发区	0859-2282188
兴义市心意酒店	Xingyi Xinyi Hotel	2	2007.05	61	118	兴义市	0859-3811658
盘江紫薇园宾馆	Panjiang Ziweiyuan Hotel	2	2006.09	42	87	安龙县	0859-5211888
安龙招堤宾馆	Anlong Zhaodi hotel	2	2007.02	20	40	安龙县	0859-5210721
黔西南州隆泰酒店	Qianxinanzhou Longtai Hotel	2	2007.07	27	53	兴义市	0859-3290555
沿河壹佳怡假日酒店	Yanhe Yijiayi Holiday Hotel	2	2010.12	39	59	沿河县开发区团结大道东段	0856-8230000
祥华酒店	Xianghua Hotel	2	2010.08	26	55	龙里县龙山镇青龙路	0854-5636088
馨豪酒店	Xinhao Hotel	2	2010.08	40	78	龙里县龙山镇兴龙路	0854-5635789
育才宾馆	Yucai Hotel	2	2010.11	32	64	荔波县建设西路41号	0854-3619852
虹泰宾馆	Hongtai Hotel	2	2010.09	15	27	平塘县平湖镇环城路	0854-7225888
聚丰园宾馆	Jufengyuan Hotel	2	2010.09	20	30	平塘县新区大道	0854-7230568
银都宾馆	Yindu Hotel	2	2010.11	38	63	贵定县红旗大道1号	0854-5231878
纳雍良源大酒店	Nayong Liangyuan Hotel	2	2009.12	40	100	纳雍县农贸街1号(法院旁)	0857-3536116
金沙富豪大酒店	Jinsha Fuhao Hotel	2	2010.08	17	27	新武装部旁	0857-7235555
万乐商务酒店	Wanle Business Hotel	2	2011.11	65	87	贵阳市白云区同心路1号	0851-6617999
一家快捷酒店	Yijia Inn	2	2011.11	43	48	贵阳市白云区白云南路402号	0851-4485308
君安宾馆	Jun'an Hotel	2	2011.10	92	148	贵阳黔灵西路62号	0851-6816999
七天连锁酒店花溪行政中心店	7 Days Inn in the Administrative center of Huaxi	2	2011.12	93	99	贵阳市花溪区清溪路493号	0851-8516677
新怡龙湾酒店	Xinyilongwan Hotel	2	2011.11	21	42	清镇市云岭西路	0851-2600678
平达快捷酒店	Pinda Inn	2	2011.11	38	47	开阳县城关镇环城北路68号	0851-7228369
温馨宾馆	Wenxin Hotel	2	2011.11	20	35	开阳县城关镇三中小区	0851-7250839
南江农庄	Nanjiang Farm	2	2011.12	21	30	开阳县南江乡杉木冲	13595005415
开阳舜熙酒店	Kaiyang Xishun Hotel	2	2011.12	21	32	开阳县城关镇吉祥路	0851-7315399
名望宾馆	Mingwang Hotel	2	2011.12	15	23	赫章县城关镇环城路	0857-3221513
贵阳金关大酒店	Guiyang Jinguan Hotel	2	2011.12	70	120	贵阳市云岩区金关村	0851-4766665
龙潭酒店	Longtan Hotel	2	2012.01	20	30	关岭县关索镇大龙潭	13985302309
天生桥假日酒店	Tianshengqiao Holiday Hotel	2	2011.12	16	29	铜仁市碧江区川东镇云盘村32号	13668562598
丰鑫假日酒店	Fengxin Holiday Hotel	2	2012.05	75	120	六枝特区团结路5号	0858-5898888
惠馨时尚酒店	Huixin Fashion Hotel	2	2011.12	23	29	贵州省惠水县和平镇涟江北路	0854-6225333
施秉县王府酒店	Shibing Wangfu Hotel	2	2011.06	33	62	施秉县城关镇中沙大道	0855-4326999
滨江假日酒店	Binjiang Holiday Hotel	2	2012.09	56	110	松桃县滨江花园D区6号	0856-2835899
黔闽商务酒店	Qianmin Business Hotel	2	2012.11	31	58	松桃县滨江花园A区2号	0856-2323888
乐喜商务酒店	Lexi Business Hotel	2	2012.09	46	64	都匀市开发区沙坝供销社综合楼	0854-8518688
尚客优酒店	Shangkeyou Hotel	2	2012.05	63	96	独山县城关镇四通路秀山商城	0854-3233666
鸿雁宾馆	Hongyan Hotel	1	2004.06	39	97	黔西县东路	0857-4225666
亲情宾馆	Qingqin Hotel	1	2006.09	19	34	平塘县	13985085075
玖玖宾馆	Jiujiu Hotel	1	2006.09	15	34	平塘县	13385185973
紫金大酒店	Zijin Hotel	1	2006.09	29	51	平塘县	13885455082
思南县电力宾馆	Sinan Dianli Hotel	1	2003.07	25	53	思南县中山街55号	0856-7229948
从江文广宾馆	Congjiang Wenguang Hotel	1	2007.03	28	47	从江县	0855-6418316
从江观音阁山庄	Congjiang Guanyinge Villa	1	2007.03	30	52	从江县	0855-6418488
黄平谦和大酒店	Huangping Qianhe Hotel	1	2006.12	27	54	黄平	0855-2436366
黄平丰丰宾馆	Huangping Feng Feng Hotel	1	2006.12	43	86	黄平	0855-2438298
岑巩兴岑大酒店	Cengong Xingcen Hotel	1	2007.09	15	25	岑巩县	0855-3575333
岑巩万向宾馆	Cengong Wanxiang Hotel	1	2007.09	17	30	岑巩县	0855-3573086
瑞权宾馆	Ruiquan Hotel	1	2010.06	70	110	黔西南州	0859-3815588
青松宾馆	Qingsong Hotel	1	2010.12	78	143	罗甸县	0854-7620518
天竹名人酒店	Tianzhumingren Hotel	1	2011.10	32	108	贵阳市乌当区航天大道1号	0851-6402020
港湾快捷酒店	Gangwan Inn	1	2011.08	42	65	贵阳市白云区建设路4号	0851-4611112
赛菲尔商务宾馆	Saifeier Business Hotel	1	2011.11	38	45	贵阳市白云区金塘北街四合院	0851-4480899
博纳快捷酒店	Bona Inn	1	2011.11	43	62	贵阳市白云区大山洞尖山路	0851-5619999
三江商务宾馆	Sanjiang Business Hotel	1	2011.11	13	20	小河区清水江路71号	0851-3845709

主要统计指标解释

住宿业　指有偿为顾客提供临时住宿的服务活动。不包括：提供长期住宿场所的活动，如出租房屋、公寓等，列入房地产开发经营。

餐饮业　指在一定场所，对食物进行现场烹饪、调制，并出售给顾客主要供现场消费的服务活动。

营业额　指住宿和餐饮业法人企业（单位）在经营活动中因提供服务或销售商品等取得的收入。包括：客房收入、餐费收入、商品销售额和其他收入。其中，客房收入指住宿和餐饮业法人企业（单位）在经营活动中因提供住宿服务取得的收入。餐费收入指住宿和餐饮业法人企业（单位）因为顾客提供就餐服务取得的收入，包括经烹饪、调制加工后出售的各种食品，如主食、炒菜、凉拌菜等的收入。

游客人数

(1) 入境游客人数　指报告期内来中国（大陆）观光、度假、探亲访友、就医疗养、购物、参加会议或从事经济、文化、体育、宗教活动的外国人、港澳台同胞等游客（即入境旅游人数）。统计时，入境游客按每入境 1 次统计 1 人次。

入境游客包括入境过夜游客和入境一日游游客。

(2) 国内游客人数　指报告期内在中国（大陆）观光游览、度假、探亲访友、就医疗养、购物、参加会议或从事经济、文化、体育、宗教活动的中国（大陆）居民，其出游的目的不是通过所从事的活动谋取报酬。统计时，国内游客按每出游 1 次统计 1 人次。

国内游客包括国内过夜游客和国内一日游游客。

国际旅游（外汇）收入　入境游客在中国（大陆）境内旅行、游览过程中用于交通、参观游览、住宿、餐饮、购物、娱乐等全部花费。

出境游组团旅行社　指从事招徕、组织、接待中国内地居民出国旅游，赴香港特别行政区、澳门特别行政区和台湾地区旅游，以及招徕、组织、接待在中国内地的外国人、在内地的香港特别行政区、澳门特别行政区居民和在大陆的台湾地区居民出境旅游的业务的旅行社。

国内及入境旅游旅行社　指从事招徕、组织和接待中国内地居民在境内旅游的业务和从事招徕、组织、接待外国旅游者来我国旅游，香港特别行政区、澳门特别行政区旅游者来内地旅游，台湾地区居民来大陆旅游，以及招徕、组织、接待在中国内地的外国人，在内地的香港特别行政区、澳门特别行政区居民和在大陆的台湾地区居民在境内旅游的业务的旅行社。

国内旅游收入　国内游客在旅游过程中（由游客或游客的代表为游客）支付的一切旅游支出就是国家（省、区、市）的国内旅游收入。旅游支出应包括过夜游客和一日游游客在整个游程中行、游、住、食、购、娱，以及为亲友、家人购买纪念品、礼品等方面的旅游支出，不包括为商业目的购物、购买房、地、车、船等资本性或交易性的投资、馈赠亲友的现金及给公共机构的捐赠。

星级饭店　指设备、设施、服务符合《旅游饭店星级的划分与评定》(GB/T14308-2003)，通过相关旅游管理部门评定，并取得星级饭店称号的饭店（含预备星级饭店）。

Explanatory Notes on Main Statistical Indicators

Hotel Services refer to the activities of enterprises providing paid services of lodging to the customer, excluding the activities of providing long period of services of lodging, such as leased house and apartments, which are shown in development and operation of real estate.

Catering Services refer to the activities of enterprises prvideing on-the-spot services of selling food cooked and prepared to the customer in certain sites

Business Revenue refers to revenue received from providing services or selling commodities by enterprises and establishments engaged in hotels and catering services, including income from hotels, from catering services, from selling of commodities and from other services. Income from hotels refers to income of enterprises and establishments engaged in hotels and catering services by providing lodging services. Income from catering services refers to income of enterprises and establishments engaged in hotels and catering services by providing catering services, including selling of cooked or prepared foods, such as staple food, cooked dishes, or cold dishes.

Number of Visitor

(1) Visitor arrivals refer to the number of foreigners, Chinese compatriots from Hong Kong, Macao and Taiwan Chinese who come to China for sight-seeing, vacation, visiting relatives, medical treatment, shopping, attending conference, or to engage in economic, cultural, sports and religious activities(That tourist arrivals). In compiling statistics, each time of entering China is counted as one person-time.

Inbound tourists are including inbound overnight tourists and inbound tour tourists.

(2) Number of domestic tourists refers to the number of Chinese (mainland) residents who travel within China (mainland) for sight-seeing, vacation, visiting relatives, medical treatment, shopping, attending conference, or to engage in economic, cultural, sports and religious activities. In compiling statistics, each time of travelling is counted as one person-time.

Domestic tourists are including domestic overnight visitors and domestic day trip visitors.

Foreign Exchange Earnings from International Tourism refer to the total expenditure of foreigners, overseas Chinese, Chinese compatriots from Hong Kong, Macao and Taiwan during their stay in the mainland of China on transportation of sighting, accommodation, food, shopping and entertainment.

Outbound travel agencies is engaged in the solicitation, organization, hospitality Chinese mainland residents to travel abroad, to visit Hong Kong SAR, Macao SAR and Taiwan tourism and attract, organize the reception of foreigners in the Chinese mainland, the mainland Hong Kong SAR, Macao SAR residents and residents of Taiwan on the mainland outbound travel business travel.

Domestic and inbound tourism travel is engaged in soliciting travel, organization and hospitality Chinese mainland residents to travel in the territory and engaged in soliciting business, organization, reception of foreign tourists to China's tourism, Hong Kong SAR, Macao SAR mainland tourists to travel to the mainland for Taiwan residents tourism and attract, organization, reception of foreigners in China Mainland, the Mainland Hong Kong SAR, Macao SAR residents and residents of Taiwan on the mainland tourism business in the territory of the travel agency.

Domestic tourism revenue domestic tourists in the tourism process (by the representatives of visitors or tourists for tourists) payment of all tourism expenditure is the national (provincial, autonomous regions and municipalities) of domestic tourism tourism revenue. Travel expenses shall include overnight visitors and day visitors in the entire run Bank of China, travel, housing, food, shopping and entertainment, as well as friends, family, buy souvenirs, gifts and other aspects of tourism expenditure, not including for commercial purposes, shopping, purchase house , ground, cars, boats and other capital investment or trading, cash and gift donations to public institutions.

Star-rated Hotels refer to hotels rated with stars as assessed by the relevant tourism authorities according to GB/T14308-2003 standard with reference to their infrastructure, facilities and service levels.

中国人民银行贵阳中心支行

The People's Bank of China Guiyang Central Sub-branch

2012年9月4日，人民银行周小川行长到人行贵阳中心支行调研时观看营业部廉政文化建设板报

September 4, 2012, the People's Bank Governor Zhou Xiaochuan to the People's Bank of China Guiyang Central Sub-branch watch business department of culture of clean government poster during the survey

2012年，中国人民银行贵阳中心支行在贵州省委、省政府和上级行的正确领导下，积极履行央行分支机构职责，为促进贵州经济社会“又好又快”发展提供了强有力的金融支持。

认真贯彻落实稳健的货币政策，截至2012年末，全省金融机构人民币存款余额10540.1亿元，同比增长20.56%，人民币贷款余额8274.8亿元，同比增长20.94%，有力支持了地区经济平稳较快发展。

积极拓宽企业融资渠道，2012年全年省内企业在银行间债券市场融资总量达294亿元，同比增长394.1%。稳妥推进地方金融机构改革，切实维护地方金融稳定。改进外汇管理和服务。进一步提升金融服务水平。

In 2012, the People's Bank of China Guiyang Central Sub-branch,under the correct leadership of the Guizhou Provincial Party Committee and Provincial Government and the higher bank, and actively fulfill central bank branches duties, provide strong financial support to promote the sound and rapid of Guizhou's economic and social development.

Conscientiously implement the prudent monetary policy, by the end of 2012, the province's financial institutions RMB deposit balance of 1.05401 trillion yuan, an increase of 20.56%, RMB loan balance of 827.48 billion yuan, an increase of 20.94%, a strong support of the region stable and rapid economic development. And actively expand the financing channels for enterprises, 2012 enterprises in the province throughout the year in the inter-bank bond market financing total of 29.4 billion yuan, an increase of 394.1%. And steadily push forward the reform of local financial institutions, and earnestly safeguard the stability of the local financial. Improve foreign exchange management and service. Further enhance the level of financial services.

2012年8月8日，签订《借助银行间市场助推贵州省经济发展合作备忘录》，全年企业在银行间债券市场融资总量达294亿元

August 8, 2012, signed “With the cooperation of the inter-bank market and boost economic development in Guizhou Province Memorandum”, throughout the year in the inter-bank bond market financing a total of 29.4 billion yuan

截止2012年9月底，江口县71个行政村建立了89个助农取款点，人行贵阳中心支行召开了改善农村支付服务环境现场推进会

By the end of September 2012, 71 administrative villages in Jiangkou County established 89 the help farmers withdrawals point, the People's Bank of China Guiyang Central Sub-branch held a site promote will to improve rural payment service environment

国家开发银行贵州省分行

China Development Bank Guizhou Province Branch

2013年3月，姚中民监事长与贵州省委书记赵克志座谈
March 2013, Yao Zhongmin Supervisors and Guizhou Provincial Party Secretary Zhao Zhi had discussion

2012年，国家开发银行贵州省分行（以下简称分行）管理资产余额1517.23亿元，比上年增加335.34亿元。本外币表内贷款余额达到1062.49亿元，增加192.62亿元；其中，表内人民币贷款余额1037.06亿元；表内人民币余额新增180.04亿元。发放表内人民币贷款260亿元，外汇贷款2.96亿美元；完成社会融资总量573.24亿元。当期和累计本息回收率均为99.99%，不良贷款率0.27%，比上年降低0.09个百分点。2012年末，分行表内人民币贷款余额全省同业占12.53%，排名第二。非个人中长期人民币贷款余额同业占21.90%，比上年提高1.05个百分点，排名第一。外汇贷款余额同业占33.73%，排名第二。

统筹资源，支持贵州省重大项目建设。2012年，在国家宏观调控背景下，分行统筹平衡支持重大项目融资，在交通、能源、水利和城镇基础设施等“两基一

在国家开发银行王用生副行长、贵州省委常委、常务副省长谌贻琴、副省长禄智明的见证下，贵州省分行与省水投公司就“三位一体”规划首批水利项目签署《借款合同》
In the China Development Bank president Wang Yongsheng, deputy governor of Guizhou Provincial Committee and Vice Governor Chen Yiqin, deputy governor Lu Zhiming witness, Guizhou Province Branch and the provincial branch of Water Investment Company “Trinity planning” signed by the first water projects “loan Contract”

国家开发银行贵州省分行王永进行长向石阡茶农现场发放首批农业产业化开发扶贫小额贷款
China Development Bank Guizhou Branch president Wang Yongjin to hand over the first industrialization of agriculture development Microfinance Poverty to the Shiqian tea farmers

19

Nineteen

金融业

Financial Intermediation

19-1 金融机构人民币存贷款余额(含外资)

Total Deposits and Total Loans of Financial Institutions (Including Foreign Investment)

单位：亿元 (100 million yuan)

指 标	Item	2007	2008	2009	2010	2011	2012	2012年比2011年增长(%) Increase Rate in 2012 over 2011(%)
资金来源合计	**Funds Sources**	**3524.42**	**4290.47**	**5280.86**	**7029.92**	**8300.17**	**9891.66**	**19.2**
各项存款	Total Deposits	3826.37	4736.93	5898.26	7363.92	8742.79	10540.06	20.6
#财政存款	Fiscal Deposits	146.05	223.69	301.77	361.52	447.67	412.56	-7.8
储蓄存款	Savings Deposit	1790.14	2237.05	2676.09	3244.99	3934.48	4806.09	22.2
资金运用合计	**Funds Uses**	**3524.42**	**4290.47**	**5280.86**	**7029.92**	**8300.17**	**9891.66**	**19.2**
各项贷款	Total Loans	3128.63	3569.27	4656.50	5747.53	6841.92	8274.78	20.9
#短期贷款	Short-term Loans	860.81	890.77	1090.72	1015.30	1293.00	1744.63	34.9
中长期贷款	Medium-term & Long-term Loans	2177.66	2586.49	3433.03	4582.34	5439.64	6405.81	17.8

注：1.资料来源于中国人民银行贵阳中心支行。2.储蓄存款2010年及以前为城乡居民储蓄存款。
Note:1.Data in the table are obtained from Guiyang Central Branch of PBC.2.The year 2010 and brfore, savings deposit refer to resident savings deposit of urban and rural.

19-2 保险系统基本情况

Basic Conditions of Insurance System

单位：个 (unit)

项 目	Item	2007	2008	2009	2010	2011	2012	2012年比2011年增长(%) Increase Rate in 2012 over 2011(%)
机构数	**Total**	**652**	**774**	**854**	**883**	**930**	**949**	**2.0**
省级分公司	Provincial Branches	15	18	19	20	22	23	4.5
地市级分公司	Branches at Prefecture Level	70	91	102	110	117	123	5.1
县级支公司	Branches at County Level	207	220	268	328	384	416	8.3
办事处或营业部	Business Offices and Departments	42	40	39	38	38	38	持平
营销服务部	Marketing Deparements	318	405	426	387	369	349	-5.4
职工人数	**Total**	**6615**	**7331**	**9421**	**10472**	**11283**	**11390**	**0.9**
省级分公司	Provincial Branches	1803	1926	2296	2552	2666	2732	2.5
地市级分公司	Branches at Prefecture Level	2635	3068	3914	4650	5444	5335	7.2
县级支公司	Branches at County Level	1638	1729	2421	2546	2597	2504	-3.6
办事处或营业部	Business Offices and Departments	47	23	39	60	33	218	560.6
营销服务部	Marketing Departments	492	585	751	664	543	601	10.7

注：资料来源于中国保险监督管理委员会贵州监管局(以下相关表同)。
Note:Data in the table are obtained from the provincial insurance regulatory bureau(the relative tables in the chapter are the same).

19–3 财产保险公司业务

Major Business Indicators of Property Insurance Companies

单位：万元 (10000 yuan)

指　标	Item	2007	2008	2009	2010	2011	2012	2012年比2011年增长(%) Increase Rate in 2012 over 2011(%)
保费收入	**Premium**	**239669**	**300413**	**377293**	**489187**	**617886**	**738037**	**19.4**
企业财产保险	Enterprise Property Insurance	16012	21091	22231	28222	38138	35794	-6.1
机动车辆保险	Motor Vehicle Insurance	186426	226527	301561	392399	480928	593675	23.4
货物运输保险	Freight Transport Insurance	5521	6696	5824	7289	7290	6713	-7.9
责任保险	Liability Insurance	9926	13428	16396	20552	29781	34106	14.5
信用保证保险	Credit Guarantee Insurance	286	544	494	1346	7624	12478	63.7
农业保险	Agriculture Insurance	7058	7150	5516	920	2119	6876	224.5
其他保险	Other Insurance	14440	24978	25271	38459	52006	48396	-6.9
储金	**Deposits**	**7386**	**6996**	**6446**	**4362**	**5822**	**7225**	**24.1**
赔案件数(万件)	**Cases of Claims(10000 cases)**	**38**	**57**	**53**	**42**	**50**	**66**	**33.1**
赔款支出	**Claim and Payment**	**107672**	**188553**	**253010**	**192351**	**262491**	**395728**	**50.8**
企业财产保险	Enterprise Property Insuance	7370	32791	80899	6159	10467	28811	175.3
机动车辆保险	Motor Vehicle Insurance	91040	133453	145450	163175	225500	324388	43.9
货物运输保险	Freight Transport Insurance	593	679	805	408	517	412	-20.3
责任保险	Liability Insurance	3179	5503	7064	8013	10904	17514	60.6
信用保证保险	Credit Guarantee Insurance	79	95	73	68	193	558	188.5
农业保险	Agriculture Insurance	162	7836	8531	1686	1311	2316	76.7
其他保险	Other Insurance	5249	8196	10187	12842	13598	21728	59.8
未决赔款	**Unsettled Claim**	**43893**	**147554**	**85005**	**117217**	**189131**	**196770**	**4.0**

注：本表包括人保、太保产险、平安产险、天安保险、安邦保险、阳光产险、大地产险、国寿产险、都邦产险、太平保险、华安产险、鼎和产险、华泰产险、安诚产险14家财产保险分公司数据(下表同)。

Note:.Data in this table include figures of the Guizhou Branches of PICC,Pacific Property Insurance Company, Ping'an Property Insurance Company, Tianan Insurance Company,Anbang Insurance Company,Yangguang Property Insurance Company, Dadi Property Insurance Company, China Life Property & Casualty Insurance Company, DuBang Insurance,Dinghe Insurance Company，Huatai Insuurance company and An-cheng Insurance Company (the same applies to the next table) .

19–4 财产保险主要指标(2012)

Major Indicators on Property Insurance

指 标	Item	合 计 Total	企业财产保险 Enterprise Property Insurance	家庭财产保险 Family Property Insurance	机动车辆保险 Transportation Equipment Insurance	工 程 保 险 Engineering Insurance	责 任 保 险 Responsibility Insurance	保 证 保 险 Pledge Insurance	信 用 保 险 Credit Insurance
承保件数(万件)	Amount Insured (10000 cases)	499	2	2	329	…	9	1	…
保险金额或责任限额(亿元)	Insurance Value or Liability Limit (100 million yuan)	30250.63	3146.81	139.55	8239.36	381.00	12080.56	9.10	2.40
签单保费(万元)	Premium of Sign Bill (10000 yuan)	737923	35794	2521	593772	10898	34123	12256	89
赔付件数(万件)	Amount Claim and Payment (10000 cases)	66	…	…	62	…	…	…	…
已决赔款(万元)	Indemnity Expenditure (10000 yuan)	377012	28659	2546	307455	4618	17100	526	…
未决赔款(万元)	Indefinite Expenditure (10000 yuan)	196770	13352	282	146696	8136	17253	163	…

19–4 续表 continued

指 标	Item	船 舶 保 险 Boats and Ships Insurance	货物运输保险 Freight Transport Insurance	特殊风险保险 Special Risk Insurance	农 业 保 险 Agricultural Insurance	健康险 Health Insurance	意外伤害保险 Unforeseen Injury Insurance	其他险 Others
承保件数(万件)	Amount Insured(10000 cases)	…	8		…	4	144	…
保险金额或责任限额（亿元）	Insurance Value or Liability Limit (100 million yuan)	1.31	748.75	2.73	31.06	1395.47	3957.39	115.14
签单保费(万元)	Premium of Sign Bill(10000 yuan)	164	6591	37	6876	10562	23570	671
赔付件数(万件)	Amount Claim and Payment (10000 cases)		…		1	2	…	…
已决赔款(万元)	Indemnity Expenditure(10000 yuan)	85	331	44	2116	5228	8071	235
未决赔款(万元)	Indefinite Expenditure(10000 yuan)	60	383	345	2045	2162	5714	177

注：赔付件数指已决赔付件数。

Note:Amount Claim and Payment refers to indemnity Expenditure.

19-5 人寿保险公司业务

Major Business Indicators of Life Insurance Companies

单位：万元 (10000 yuan)

指 标	Item	2007	2008	2009	2010	2011	2012	2012年比2011年增长(%) Increase Rate in 2012 over 2011(%)
保费收入	**Premium**	**349758**	**498647**	**574137**	**735914**	**700228**	**764119**	**9.1**
#新单保费	Premium of New Guarantee Slip	178006	309841	341664	423733	368371	310106	-15.8
#个人业务	Personal Business	319447	475109	543109	702187	670327	733130	9.4
人寿保险	Life Insurance	293387	445525	513918	662714	624908	676263	8.2
意外伤害险	Accident Injury Insurance	9663	10965	9846	11983	13608	16385	20.4
健康险	Health Insurance	16397	18619	19345	27490	31811	40482	27.3
团体业务	Group Business	30311	23538	31028	33727	29901	30988	3.6
人寿保险	Life Insurance	15903	8817	10798	14277	7051	7285	3.3
意外伤害险	Accident Injury Insurance	7485	6002	9030	11396	15121	14618	-3.3
健康险	Health Insurance	6923	8719	11199	8054	7730	9085	17.5
有效保单件数(万件)	**Cases of Virtual Guarantee Slip(10000 cases)**	**238**	**289**	**354**	**416**	**459**	**491**	**7.0**
赔款及给付支出	**Claim and Payment**	**91702**	**97339**	**102861**	**113982**	**132696**	**157626**	**18.8**
个人业务	Personal Business	76691	84798	87775	74656	93250	110036	18.0
赔款支出	Benefit Paid	8978	8041	5131	7753	9495	7967	-16.1
年金给付	Payment for Annuity	4177	5350	8878	11862	14179	22935	61.8
满期给付	Payment for Expiration	56461	63116	64447	43237	54158	60679	12.0
死伤医疗给付	Payment for Death and Injured person	7075	8291	9320	11804	15418	18454	19.7
团体业务	Group Business	15011	12541	15086	39326	39446	47591	20.6
赔款支出	Benefit Paid	11625	9621	12719	13253	10766	13123	21.9
年金给付	Payment for Annuity	2253	1874	1311	3283	2465	3130	27.0
满期给付	Payment for Expiration	1025	875	700	21412	25039	30248	20.8
死伤医疗给付	Payment for Death and Injured Person	108	171	357	1378	1177	1090	-7.4

注：本表数据包含国寿、太保寿险、平安寿险、新华人寿、泰康人寿、平安养老、太平人寿、人保寿险、生命人寿9家人寿保险分公司数据(下表同)。

Note:data in this table include figures of the Guizhou Branches of China Life Insurance Company,Pacific Life Insurance Company, Ping'an Life Insurance Company, Xinhua Life Insurance Company, Taikang Life Insurance Company , Ping'an pension Insurance and Life Insurance Company (the same applies to the next table) .

19–6 人寿保险主要指标(2012)

Major Indicators on Life Insurance

单位：万元 (10000 yuan)

指标项目	Item	合 计 Total	寿险业务 Life Insurance Business	普通寿险 Normal Life Insurance	个人业务 Personal	团体业务 Group	分红寿险 Share out Bonus	个人业务 Personal	团体业务 Group
保费收入	Premium	764119	683547	89183	81902	7282	585185	585182	3
期末有效保险金额(亿元)	Virtual Insurance Value at the year-end(100 million yuan)	7246.77	1763.92	1105.10	996.31	108.79	446.48	442.80	3.68
期末有效承保人次(万人)	Virtual Insurance Person-time at the year-end (10000 persons)	3388	744	595	579	17	123	114	9
期末有效承保保单件数(万件)	Cases of Virtual Guarantee Slip at the year-end (10000 cases)	491	302	169	165	4	109	108	1
赔款和给付支出	Expenditure for Claim and Payment	157626	132563	63442	28978	34464	67285	67281	4
#赔款支出	Settled Claim	21091							
死伤医疗给付	Payment for Death,Injury or Medical Treatmnet	19544	15631	9250	8160	1089	5049	5049	
满期给付	Mature Payment	90927	90867	37113	6866	30248	53250	53250	
年金给付	Payment for Annuity	26065	26065	17079	13952	3127	8986	8983	4
退保金	Insurance withdrawed	90927	89692	6913	6335	579	82769	82769	
在售产品数量（个）	Amount of Products under Selling(unit)	1212	471	179	142	37	237	230	7

19–6 续表 continued

单位：万元 (10000 yuan)

指标项目	Item	投资连结产品 Life Insurance Product in inve-stment	万能寿险 Omnip-otence Life Insu-rance	健康险业务 Health Insu-rance	个人业务 Personal	团体业务 Group	意外伤害保险业务 Unforeseen Injury Insurance
保费收入	Premium	219	8959	49568	40482	9085	31004
期末有效保险金额(亿元)	Virtual Insurance Value at the year-end(100 million yuan)	4.68	207.66	1819.63	868.77	950.86	3663.22
期末有效承保人次(万人)	Virtual Insurance Person-time at the year-end(10000 persons)	1	25	1099	820	279	1545
期末有效承保保单件数(万件)	Cases of Virtual Guarantee Slip at the year-end(10000 cases)	1	23	84	74	9	105
赔款和给付支出	Expenditure for Claim and Payment	129	1707	16643	9179	7463	8421
#赔款支出	Settled Claim			12670	5206	7463	8421
死伤医疗给付	Payment for Death,Injury or Medical Treatmnet	8	1324	3913	3913	…	
满期给付	Mature Payment	121	383	60	60		
年金给付	Payment for Annuity						
退保金	Insurance withdrawed	2	9	1235	1235		
在售产品数量（个）	Amount of Products under Selling (unit)	15	40	475	317	158	266

19-7 贵州上市公司股票发行情况(A股)(2012)
Summary List of Stocks Publicly Issued by Guizhou Enterprises(A Shares)

单位：亿股 (100 million shares)

上市公司名称	Listed Companies	上市时间 Listed Time	板块类别 Setor of Listed Companies	总股本 Total Capital Stock	流通股 Gover-nment Share	募集资金总额(亿元) Total Amount Issued (100 million yuan)
中天城投	CENTURY ZHONGTIAN INVESTMENT JIONT STOCK CO.,LTD.	1994.02.02	主板	12.79	12.78	
黔轮胎	GUI ZHOU TYRE CO., LTD.	1996.03.08	主板	4.89	4.89	
中航重机	GUIZHOU LIYUAN HYDRAULIC COMPONENTS CO.,LTD.	1996.11.06	主板	7.78	7.78	10.00
振华科技	CHINA ZHENHUA(GROUP) SCIENCE & TECHNOLOGY CO.,LTD.	1997.07.03	主板	3.58	3.58	
长征电气	GUIZHOU CHANGZHENG ELECTRICAL APPARATUS CO.,LTD.	1997.11.27	主板	5.09	5.09	
高鸿股份	GOHIGH DATA NETWORKS TECHNOLOGY CO.,LTD.	1998.06.09	主板	5.16	3.21	11.20
南方汇通	SOUTH HUITON CO.,LTD.	1999.06.06	主板	4.22	4.22	
ST国创	ST GUIZHOU GUOCHUANG ENERGY HOLDING(GROUP)CO.,LTD.	1999.09.23	主板	3.78	3.78	
赤天化	GUIZHOU CHITIANHUA CORP.	2000.02.21	主板	9.5	9.31	
红星发展	GUIZHOU REDSTAR DEVELOPING CO.,LTD.	2001.03.20	主板	2.91	2.91	
盘江股份	GUIZHOU PANJIANG REFINED COAL CO.,LTD.	2001.05.31	主板	16.55	16.55	
贵州茅台	KWEICHOW MOUTAI CO.,LTD.	2001.08.27	主板	10.38	10.38	
贵航股份	GUIZHOU GUIHANG AUTOMOTIVE COMPONENTS CO.,LTD.	2001.12.27	主板	2.89	1.96	
益佰制药	GUIZHOU YIBAI PHAMACY CO.,LTD.	2004.03.23	主板	3.61	3.53	
贵绳股份	GUIZHOU GUISHENG CO.,LTD.	2004.05.14	主板	1.64	1.64	
航天电器	GUIZHOU SPACEFLIGHT DIANQI CO.,LTD	2004.07.26	中小板	3.3	3.3	
久联发展	GUIZHOU JIULIAN DEVELOPMENT CO.,LTD.	2004.09.08	中小板	2.05	1.73	6.00
黔源电力	GUIZHOU QIANYUAN ELECTRIC POWER CO.,LTD.	2005.03.03	中小板	2.04	1.7	
信邦制药	GUIZHOU XINBANG PHARMACEUTICAL CO.,LTD.	2010.04.16	中小板	1.74	0.93	
贵州百灵	GUIZHOU BAILING GROUP PHARMACEUTICAL CO.,LTD.	2010.06.03	中小板	4.7	1.18	
朗玛信息	LONGMASTRR INFORATION & TECHNOLOGY CO., LTD.	2012.02.16	创业版	0.53	0.13	3.00

注：1.资料来源于中国证监会贵州监管局。2.ST国创于2011年3月9日迁入贵州。3.募集资金总额包括首发、增发、配股、可转债等募集的资金。盘江股份的募集资金总额含资产注入。

Note:1.Data in the table are provided by the Guizhou Securities Regulatory Bureau of the CSRC. 2.ST GUIZHOU GUOCHUANG ENERGY HOLDING(GROUP)CO.,LTD. Removed to Guizhou on March3,2011. 3.Total Raised Capitals, including money raised by the first, issuing, convertible bonds of listed companies.The total amount of funds raised of Guizhou Panjiang Refined coalco.,LTD.indude infusion of funds.

主要统计指标解释

信贷资金 指金融机构以信用方式积聚和分配的货币资金。金融机构信贷资金的来源有各项存款、对国际金融机构负债、流通中货币、银行自有资金及当年结益等；信贷资金的运用有各项贷款、黄金占款、外汇占款、财政借款及在国际金融机构中的资产等。

存款 指企业、机关、团体或居民根据资金必须收回的原则，把货币资金存入银行或其他信用机构保管并取得一定利息的一种信用活动形式。根据存款对象的不同可划分为企业存款、财政存款、机关团体存款、基本建设存款、城镇储蓄存款、农村存款等科目。它是银行信贷资金的主要来源。

贷款 指银行或其他信用机构根据资金必须归还的原则，按一定利率，为企业、个人等提供资金的一种信用活动形式。我国银行贷款分为流动资金贷款、固定资产贷款、城乡个体工商户贷款以及农业贷款等科目。

保险金额 指保险人承担赔偿或者给付保险金责任的最高限额。

保费 指投保人为取得保险保障，按保险合同约定向保险人支付的费用。

赔款 指保险人对保险事故造成的损失，根据合同约定向被保险人或受益人给予的经济补偿。

给付 人身保险合同中，保险人向被保险人或受益人给付保险金的行为。

股票市值 指统计期末根据上市公司股票价格和对应股票数量计算的股权价值合计。

上市公司市值 指统计期末根据上市公司股票价格和对应股本计算的股权价值合计。

股票成交量 在统计期内全部股票成交数量合计。

股票成交金额 指在统计期内全部股票成交金额合计。

Explanatory Notes on Main Statistical Indicators

Credit Funds refer to the funds issued as loans by banking institutions. The sources of credit funds of the banking institutions included deposits, liabilities to international financial institutions, currency in circulation, self-owned funds and current retained profits, etc. The credit funds can be used in forms of loans, gold, foreign exchange, government debt and assets in the international financial institutions.

Deposit is a form of credit by which enterprises, institutions, organizations or households can put money into banks and other credit institutions for safekeeping and interest earning under the principle of free withdrawal. According to different depositors, deposits are divided into enterprise deposits,treasury deposits, deposits of government agencies and organizations,capital construction deposits, urban savings deposits, rural deposits and other deposits. Deposits are major sources of the credit funds of banks.

Loan is a form of credit by which banks and other credit institutions provide funds at certain interest rate to enterprises and individuals in the light of the principle of unconditional repayment. Loans from Chinese banks include circulating capital loans, fixed assets loans, loans to urban and rural individuals engaged in industrial and commercial business and agricultural loans.

Amount Insured refers to the maximum that the insurant will get for the claim of the case insured.

Premium refers to the fee that in order to obtain insurance coverage and in accordance with the insurance contract, the insured paid to the insurer.

Settled Claim is the economic compensation that for the insurance losses caused by the accident and according to the contract, the insurer paid to the insured or the beneficiary.

Payment is the Insurance payments behavior that in the life insurance contract, the insurer paid for the insured or the beneficiary.

Stock market value refers to the total equity value that calculated by listed companies stock price and number of shares at the end of statistical period.

Market capitalization of listed companies refers to total equity value that based on stock prices of listed companies and the corresponding value of the total equity capital calculations at the end of statistical period.

Trading Volume refers to trade volume of shares during the statistical period.

Total Turnover refers to all of stock turnover during the statistical period.

20 Twenty

教育和科技

Education, Science and Technology

20-1 各级各类学校数

Number of Schools by Level and Type

单位：所 (unit)

指　　标	Item	2007	2008	2009	2010	2011	2012
研究生培养机构	Institutions Providing Postgraduate Programs	8	8	8	8	8	9
普通高等学校	Regular Institutions of Higher Education	37	37	47	47	48	49
#成人高等学校	Adult Institutions of Higher Education	5	5	4	4	4	4
中等职业教育	Vocational Secondary Education	244	259	255	249	227	229
调整后中等职业教育	Adjusted Vocational Secondary Schools	36	36	36	35	32	34
普通中等专业教育	Regular Specialized Secondary Schools	60	61	61	63	54	54
职业高中	Vocational Senior Secondary Schools	129	141	136	130	126	125
#成人中等专业学校	Adult Specialized Secondary Schools	19	21	22	21	15	16
普通中学	Regular Secondary Schools	2674	2626	2614	2592	2641	2661
高　中	Senior Secondary Schools	485	456	451	444	447	446
初　中	Junior Secondary Schools	1652	1635	1622	1617	1635	1621
九年一贯制学校	Schools of Nine-year Consistent System	537	535	541	531	559	594
小　学	Primary Schools	13645	13107	12862	12422	12008	11529
幼儿园	Kindergartens	1838	1960	2063	2196	2677	3159
特殊教育	Special Education	40	49	49	53	52	56
工读学校	Schools for Juvenile Delinquents	4	4	4	4	4	5
成人中学	Adult Secondary Schools	5	45	22	33	13	51
成人技术培训学校	Adult Technical Training Schools	11747	12999	11852	7711	8202	7863
成人小学	Adult Primary Schools	8972	9433	9377	5405	5059	4935

注：资料来源于省教育厅(以下相关表同)。

Note:Data in the table are Provided by the Provinvial Department of Education(The relative tables in the chapter are the same).

20–2 各级各类学校专任教师数

Number of Full-time Teachers by Level and Type of School

单位：人 (person)

指　标	Item	2007	2008	2009	2010	2011	2012
专任教师	**Number of Full-time Teachers**						
培养研究生的单位	Institutions Providing Postgraduate Programs	2196	2236	2398	2760	2971	3133
普通高等学校	Regular Institutions of Higher Education	16964	18037	19634	20351	21855	22803
#成人高等学校	Adult Institutions of Higher Education	1131	555	282	296	314	361
中等职业教育	Vocational Secondary Education	9954	10237	10889	11291	11635	12585
调整后中等职业教育	Adjusted Vocational Secondary Schools	1015	863	1015	1211	1339	1712
普通中等专业教育	Regular Specialized Secondary Schools	3763	3647	3708	3857	3677	3841
职业高中	Vocational Senior Secondary Schools	3662	4396	4698	4883	5354	5784
#成人中等专业学校	Adult Specialized Secondary Schools	1064	1148	1201	1190	1233	1216
其它机构	Other Institutions	450	183	267	150	32	32
普通中学	Regular Secondary Schools	131087	135360	139302	142508	147396	156325
高　中	Senior Secondary Schools	29226	30284	31413	33072	36223	41572
初　中	Junior Secondary Schools	101861	105076	107889	109436	111173	114753
小　学	Primary Schools	191991	200024	199189	197913	197094	197983
幼儿园	Kindergartens	11293	12095	13105	14623	18120	23846
特殊教育	Special Education	627	695	740	796	901	996
工读学校	Schools for Juvenile Delinquents	75	73	75	76	65	82
成人中学	Adult Secondary Schools	60	125	30	169	33	35
成人技术培训学校	Adult Technical Training Schools	5902	6277	5201	3983	5515	5339
成人小学	Adult Primary Schools	7972	6324	5781	4463	3403	3155

20-3 各级各类学校招生数

Number of New Students Enrollment by Level and Type of School

单位：人 (person)

指 标	Item	2007	2008	2009	2010	2011	2012
研究生	Institutions Providing Postgraduate Programs	3017	3327	3908	4246	4417	4769
普通高等教育	Regular Institutions of Higher Education	84208	94530	99026	101548	107841	127963
成人高等教育	Adult Higher Education	29795	32254	26966	26580	26054	32661
#成人高等学校	Adult Institutions of Higher Education	7299	8483	2431	2345	3041	4004
中等职业教育	Vocational Secondary Education	166093	161156	162831	155527	148242	150784
调整后中等职业教育	Adjusted Vocational Secondary Schools	20361	10000	14556	13675	16283	20395
普通中等专业教育	Regular Specialized Secondary Schools	64706	66640	65367	62260	61181	58945
职业高中	Vocational Senior Secondary Schools	74722	75470	72514	62199	64443	68119
成人中等专业教育	Adult Specialized Secondary Education	6304	9046	10394	17393	4042	3325
#成人中等专业学校	Adult Specialized Secondary Schools	6288	7757	8302	14584	1788	986
普通中学	Regular Secondary Schools	910979	960665	981374	1004948	1022950	1050119
高 中	Senior Secondary Schools	201185	212253	219062	240208	277290	318188
初 中	Junior Secondary Schools	709794	748412	762312	764740	745660	731931
小 学	Primary Schools	735245	722009	698976	656919	626379	591024
幼儿园	Kindergartens	616014	623254	623660	627154	632789	668389
特殊教育	Special Education	2331	2265	2616	2755	2858	2904
工读学校	Schools for Juvenile Delinquents	630	571	253	432	660	609

20-4 各级各类学校在校生数

Number of Students Enrollment by Level and Type of School

单位：人 (person)

指　标	Item	2007	2008	2009	2010	2011	2012
在校生数	**Students Enrollment**						
研究生	Institutions Providing Postgraduate Programs	8366	9083	10169	11406	12436	13344
普通高等教育	Regular Institutions of Higher Education	241692	267526	299072	323293	344100	383815
成人高等教育	Adult Higher Education	89554	87963	86209	86630	79615	85575
#成人高等学校	Adult Institutions of Higher Education	19133	17617	5612	5827	6064	6488
中等职业教育	Vocational Secondary Education	333383	356725	386865	375740	379908	383367
调整后中等职业教育	Adjusted Vocational Secondary Schools	34766	23873	29514	32084	39497	47532
普通中等专业教育	Regular Specialized Secondary Schools	163002	171559	177178	169033	170659	165583
职业高中	Vocational Senior Secondary Schools	122322	144393	159943	145853	151786	158059
成人中等专业教育	Adult Specialized Secondary Education	13293	16900	20230	28770	17966	12193
#成人中等专业学校	Adult Specialized Secondary Schools	12151	14752	18028	24855	14057	8008
普通中学	Regular Secondary Schools	2559983	2617812	2694521	2756820	2827096	2873822
高　中	Senior Secondary Schools	545873	562138	581604	620221	689042	772972
初　中	Junior Secondary Schools	2014110	2055674	2112917	2136599	2138054	2100850
小　学	Primary Schools	4663136	4697910	4568716	4334971	4087382	3800803
幼儿园	Kindergartens	732590	737988	747351	769144	877824	982511
特殊教育	Special Education	15867	15186	16507	16231	14474	13657
工读学校	Schools for Juvenile Delinquents	579	727	271	233	400	549
成人中学	Adult Secondary Schools	2127	4779	5637	16869	1203	7500
成人技术培训学校	Adult Technical Training Schools	2727306	2750734	2627205	2058138	2180591	2014520
成人小学	Adult Primary Schools	323074	303429	302286	239936	128006	135401

20–5 各级各类学校毕业生数

Number of Graduates by Level and Type of School

单位：人 (person)

指　标	Item	2007	2008	2009	2010	2011	2012
毕业生数	**Graduates**						
研究生	Institutions Providing Postgraduate Programs	2080	2458	2706	2910	3335	3820
普通高等教育	Regular Institutions of Higher Education	61743	66050	64212	74777	83016	85285
成人高等教育	Adult Higher Education	44795	28919	28147	24365	29953	23343
#成人高等学校	Adult Institutions of Higher Education	6930	7199	1547	2015	2166	1742
中等职业教育	Vocational Secondary Education	62027	75594	82599	100997	90966	100340
调整后中等职业教育	Adjusted Vocational Secondary Schools	4168	6012	3548	7101	6933	10647
普通中等专业教育	Regular Specialized Secondary Schools	32756	42624	45361	50118	46622	47080
职业高中	Vocational Senior Secondary Schools	21637	24230	30096	39099	35230	39931
成人中等专业教育	Adult Specialized Secondary Education	3466	2728	3594	4679	2181	2682
#成人中等专业学校	Adult Specialized Secondary Schools	3033	2560	3077	4643	1913	1560
普通中学	Regular Secondary Schools	794744	785763	780888	807515	830799	859136
高　中	Senior Secondary Schools	149254	161279	165392	171704	180203	195861
初　中	Junior Secondary Schools	645490	624484	615496	635811	650596	663275
小　学	Primary Schools	751878	763062	784574	798173	773003	760174
幼儿园	Kindergartens	366027	349472	334120	328152	365936	477201
特殊教育	Special Education	1212	1116	1799	1350	1244	1389
工读学校	Schools for Juvenile Delinquents	458	544	930	393	652	268
成人中学	Adult Secondary Schools	1500	3541	4453	7701	3243	10005
成人技术培训学校	Adult Technical Training Schools	2562038	2643529	2517318	2065482	2195836	1984866
成人小学	Adult Primary Schools	272343	236418	243022	214867	129893	125809

20–6 教师职称

Technical Rank of Teachers

单位：人 (person)

类　别	Item	2007	2008	2009	2010	2011	2012
高等学校教师数	**Regular Institutions of Higher Education**	**18095**	**18592**	**19916**	**20647**	**22169**	**23164**
正高级	Senior	1285	1467	1615	1801	2038	2166
副高级	Sub-senior	4871	5410	5673	5913	6544	7129
中　级	Middle	6887	7226	7757	8403	8863	8726
初　级	Junior	3908	3326	3302	3288	3383	3387
无职称	No Rank	1144	1163	1569	1242	1341	1756
中等职业学校教师数	**Vocational Secondary Schools**	**9954**	**10237**	**10889**	**11291**	**11635**	**12585**
正高级	Senior	87	69	70	60	68	89
副高级	Sub-senior	1731	1771	1954	2065	2101	2302
中　级	Middle	3960	4106	4375	4583	4605	4708
初　级	Junior	3347	3366	3547	3457	3492	3698
无职称	No Rank	829	925	943	1126	1369	1788
普通中学教师数	**Regular Secondary Schools**	**131087**	**135360**	**139302**	**142508**	**147396**	**156325**
中学高级	Senior-rank of Secondary Teacher	11460	12531	13568	14825	16522	18031
中学一级	First-rank of Secondary Teacher	35573	38573	40760	43329	46402	49150
中学二级	Second-rank of Secondary Teacher	56549	59778	62704	64060	63548	63585
中学三级	Third-rank of Secondary Teacher	16355	13837	10311	8491	6640	5030
未评职称	No Rank of Secondary Teacher	11150	10641	11959	11803	14284	20529
小学教师数	**Regular Primary Schools**	**191991**	**200024**	**199189**	**197913**	**197094**	**197983**
中学高级	Senior-rank of Secondary Teacher	177	120	173	205	763	326
小学高级	Senior-rank of Primary Teacher	56460	66357	71854	77589	82258	81489
小学一级	First-rank of Primary Teacher	92422	89232	86256	80881	76802	75320
小学二级	Second-rank of Primary Teacher	26918	24348	22228	21409	18572	15801
小学三级	Third-rank of Primary Teacher	3005	2943	1996	1141	971	840
未评职称	No rank of Primary Teacher	13009	17024	16682	16688	17728	24207

20−7 各级各类学校女学生和女教师数

Female Students and Teachers by Level and Type of School

单位：人 (person)

指 标	Item	2007	2008	2009	2010	2011	2012
在校女生数	**Number of Female Students Entrollment**						
普通高等教育	Regular Institutions of Higher Education	116680	130225	151165	163824	178663	201277
成人高等教育	Adult Higher Education	42803	40792	40018	39923	40274	43189
中等职业教育	Vocational Secondary Education	162419	174100	186657	184525	193289	199383
普通中学	Regular Secondary Schools	1175084	1218257	1269927	1310999	1356343	1387546
#高 中	Senior Secondary Schools	238471	250847	267571	290983	330129	377426
初 中	Junior Secondary Schools	936613	967410	1002356	1020016	1026214	1010120
小 学	Primary Schools	2221262	2232813	2160956	2038362	1913008	1775234
女教师数	**Number of Female Teachers**						
普通高等学校	Regular Institutions of Higher Education	7865	8428	9261	9712	10690	11131
成人高等学校	Adult Higher Education	526	280	153	157	167	191
中等职业学校	Vocational Secondary Education	4133	4254	4527	4746	5053	5534
普通中学	Regular Secondary Schools	44948	47339	49549	51868	55196	60701
#高 中	Senior Secondary Schools	10737	11282	11805	12618	14186	16829
初 中	Junior Secondary Schools	34211	36057	37744	39250	41010	43872
小 学	Primary Schools	82535	86520	88954	90208	91253	94049

20-8 各级各类学校师生比

Student-Teacher Ratio by Level of School

单位：学生/教师 (Student/Teacher)

类　别	Item	2007	2008	2009	2010	2011	2012
普通高等学校	Regular Institutions Of Higher Education	14.25	14.83	15.23	15.89	15.74	16.83
普通高中	Regular Senior Secondary School	18.68	18.56	18.51	18.75	19.02	18.59
初中	Regular Junior Secondary School	19.77	19.56	19.58	19.52	19.23	18.31
小　学	Primary School	24.29	23.49	22.94	21.90	20.74	19.20

20-9 各级各类学校学生入学率

Enrollment Rate by Level and Type of School

单位：% (%)

指　标	Item	2007	2008	2009	2010	2011	2012
小学学龄儿童入学率	Enrollment Rate of Primary Schools	98.6	97.2	98.4	97.9	98.6	99.3
小学毕业生升学率	Percentage of Graduates of Primary Schools Entering into Junior Secondary Schools	95.6	98.7	97.7	96.3	96.5	96.3
初中阶段毛入学率	Rate of Primary School Graduates Entering into Junior Secondary Schools	97.5	95.9	98.2	97.6	94.2	97.4
高中阶段毛入学率	Rate of Junior Secondary School Graduates Entering into Senior Secondary Schools	42.2	47.9	53.4	55.0	58.9	62.2
高等教育毛入学率	Rate of Senior Secondary School Graduates Entering into Institution of Higher Learning	11.5	11.8	18.4	20.0	23.2	25.5

20-10 普通高等学校(2012)

Basic Statistics on Regular Institutions of Higher Education

单位：人 (person)

类别	Sort	学校数(所) Number of Schools (unit)	毕业生数 Graduates with Degrees or Diplomas	招生数 New Enrollment	在校学生人数 Enro-llment	教职员工 Teachers, Staff & Workers	#专任教师 Full-time Teachers	#正、副教授 Senior and Sub-senior Professors
总　计	**Total**	**49**	**85285**	**127963**	**383815**	**32153**	**22803**	**9188**
#综合大学	Comprehensive Universities	19	30741	46128	130145	11884	8108	3029
理工院校	Science & Engineering	6	10670	15190	37509	2545	2030	448
医药院校	Medicine & Pharmacy	9	11358	17117	56897	5570	3858	1894
师范院校	Teacher Training	9	21531	30274	99541	7804	5811	2322
财经院校	Finance & Economics	3	6553	12348	34081	2144	1572	748
政法院校	Politics and Law	1	1022	1758	5314	462	297	126
民族院校	Ethnic Minortities	2	3410	5148	20328	1744	1127	621
#高等职业技术学院	Vocational and Technical Colleges	21	27134	44333	103743	8208	5923	1521

20-11 普通高等学校分科专任教师数(2012)

Number of Full-time Teachers in Institutions of Higher Education by Field of Study

单位：人 (person)

类别	Sort	专任教师数 Full-time Teachers	正高级 Senior	副高级 Subsenior	中级 Middle	初级 Junior	无职称 No Rank
总　计	**Total**	**22803**	**2148**	**7040**	**8595**	**3266**	**1754**
哲　学	Philosophy	883	80	315	341	77	70
经济学	Economics	1175	114	342	444	171	104
法　学	Law	1224	115	421	462	142	84
教育学	Education	1969	146	599	754	298	172
文　学	Literature	4378	330	1278	1796	577	397
历史学	History	594	67	223	207	60	37
理　学	Science	3142	248	1005	1193	386	310
工　学	Engineering	3785	289	1033	1517	733	213
农　学	Agriculture	802	130	281	295	63	33
医　学	Medicine	3402	492	1160	1049	461	240
管理学	Management	1449	137	383	537	298	94

20-12 研究生数

Number of Postgraduates

单位：人 (person)

指标	Item	2007	2008	2009	2010	2011	2012
招研究生数	Number of New Postgraduates Enrollment	3017	3327	3908	4246	4417	4769
#女 性	Female	1278	1544	1885	2206	2248	2362
在校研究生数	Number of Postgraduates Enrollment	8366	9083	10169	11406	12436	13344
#女 性	Female	3626	4103	4726	5622	6211	6673
毕业研究生数	Number of Postgraduates Graduate	2080	2458	2706	2910	3335	3820
#女 性	Female	846	1090	1153	1269	1570	1837

20-13 技工学校

Statistics on Technical Schools

单位：人 (person)

指标	Item	2011	2012	2012年比2011年增 长(%) Increase Rate in 2012 over 2011(%)
学校数（所）	Number of Schools (unit)	30	33	10.0
招生数	Number of Enrollment	16939	16647	-1.7
在校学生数	Number of Students	36719	38001	3.5
毕业生数	Number of Graduates	9580	8240	-14.0
教职工数	Teachers and Staff	2911	2977	2.3
专任教师数	Full-time Teachers	2170	2523	16.3
文化技术理论课教师	Classroom Teachers	1210	1255	3.7
生产实习课指导教师	Practical Training Teachers	562	711	26.5
理论实习一体化教师	Classroom cum Practical Training Teachers	398	557	39.9

注：资料来源于省人力资源社会保障厅。

Note: Date in the table are obtained from Provincial Department of Human Resources and Social Security.

20−14　中等职业学校(机构)数（2012）

Number of Secondary Vocational Schools

单位：个　　(unit)

项　　目	Item	总　计 Total	地 方 部 门 Local Depart-ments	教 育 部 门 Depart-ments of Education	非教育 部　门 Departments of Non-Education	民 办 Private
中等职业学校	Secondary Vocational Schools	229	165	118	47	64
调整后中等职业学校	Adjusted Secondary Vocational Schools	34	22	21	1	12
普通中等专业学校	Regular Specialized Secondary Schools	54	54	21	33	0
成人中等专业学校	Adult Specialized Secondary Schools	16	13	4	9	3
职业高中学校	Vocational Junior Secondary Schools	125	76	72	4	49
其他机构(教学点)(不计入学校数)	Other Institutions	3	2	1	1	1

20−15　中等职业学校(2012)

Basic Statistics on Vocational Secondary Education

单位：人　　(person)

类　　别	Item	学校数(所) Schools (unit)	毕 业 生 数 Grad-uates	招生数 New Students Enrollment	在　校 学生数 Students Enrolment	教职员工 Teachers, Staff & Workers	#专任教师 Full-time Teachers
中等职业学校	Secondary Vocational Schools	232	100340	150784	383367	16473	12585
调整后中等职业学校	Adjusted Vocational Secondary Schools	34	10647	20395	47532	2023	1712
普通中等专业学校	Regular Specialized Secondary Schools	54	47080	58945	165583	5423	3841
成人中等专业学校	Adult Specialized Secondary Educaiton	16	2682	3325	12193	1699	1216
职业高中	Vocational Senior Secondary Schools	125	39931	68119	158059	7277	5784
其他机构(教学点)	Others Institutions	3				51	32

20-16 中等职业学校（机构)学生分科类情况（2012）

Students in Secondary Vocational Schools by Field of Study

单位：人 (person)

项目	Item	招生数 New Enrollment	#初中毕业生 Junior Secondary School Graduates	#应届毕业生 Current Year Graduates	在校学生数 Total Enrollment	毕业生数 Graduates	#获得职业资格证书 With Certificate On Professional Competence
总计	**Total**	**150784**	**134330**	**127779**	**383367**	**100340**	**68419**
农林牧渔类	Agriculture,Forestry,Animal Husbandry and Fishery	18041	12261	10654	44198	13190	7911
资源环境类	Resources and Environment	4326	3676	2789	8436	1487	322
能源与新能源类	Energy and New Energy	842	842	698	2337	604	473
土木水利类	Civil and Hydraulic Engineering	8777	8205	7543	20908	4251	3103
加工制造类	Manufacturing	15762	14660	14314	42588	13465	11465
石油化工类	Petroleum and Chemical	560	438	438	1334	272	268
轻纺食品类	Textile and Foods	1322	1238	1238	3609	844	652
交通运输类	Communication & Transportation	11717	10425	10074	26787	4651	3422
信息技术类	Information Technologies	25412	23966	23602	72155	23232	17698
医药卫生类	Medicine and Health	16007	12766	12347	47330	14473	5706
休闲保健类	Leisure and Health-care	321	316	286	1020	326	284
财经商贸类	Finance and Trade	8583	8336	7907	22616	6111	2556
旅游服务类	Tourism and services	7568	6955	6620	19327	4851	4193
文化艺术类	Culture and Art	2666	2332	2324	7926	1967	1427
体育与健身	Physical Education	392	389	389	1127	448	414
教育类	Education	24983	24073	23271	54199	7721	6696
司法服务类	Justice Service	694	669	651	1941	497	278
公共管理与服务类	Public Management and Service	740	731	724	2137	996	685
其他	Other	2071	2052	1910	3392	954	866

20-17 民族教育
Minority Nationality Education

类　别	Item	2007	2008	2009	2010	2011	2012
学校数(所)	**Number of Schools(unit)**						
普通高校	Regular Institutions of Higher Education	1	1	2	2	2	2
普通中学	Regular Secondary Schools	98	117	119	121	194	205
小　学	Primary Schools	129	151	146	161	637	614
专任教师数(人)	**Full-time Teachers(person)**						
普通高校	Regular Institutions of Higher Education	3756	3960	4293	4407	5189	5872
成人高校	Adult Institutions of Higher Education	126	102	50	42	40	49
普通中学	Regular Secondary Schools	52834	54958	57007	58519	60519	64441
#高　中	Senior Secondary Schools	11114	11655	12444	13044	14041	16552
中等职业学校	Vocational Secondary Schools	2282	2451	3723	2778	3501	3351
小　学	Primary Schools	79151	82614	83173	82892	80267	84680
在校生数(人)	**Number of Students Enrollment(person)**						
普通高等教育	Regular Institutions of Higher Education	71896	87733	105693	110549	117205	141345
成人高等教育	Adult Institutions of Higher Education	17251	16986	20108	17428	22601	27640
普通中学	Regular Secondary Schools	1008786	1029863	1067179	1092467	1127199	1148755
#高　中	Senior Secondary Schools	216937	220728	228599	243987	275147	313056
中等职业学校	Vocational Secondary Schools	99795	111662	115309	125407	135113	138442
小　学	Primary Schools	1887449	1901478	1585233	1775808	1697558	1596713
毕业生数(人)	**Number of Graduates(person)**						
普通中学	Regular Secondary Schools	315141	312418	306943	315968	325984	343094
#高　中	Senior Secondary Schools	59990	64322	65177	66977	70296	77553
小　学	Primary Schools	294004	299419	315294	316272	304096	303243

20-18 民办教育
Private Education

类　别	Item	2007	2008	2009	2010	2011	2012
学校数(所)	**Number of Schools(unit)**						
普通高等学校	Regular Institutions of Higher Education	1	1	9	9	10	11
中等职业教育学校	Vocational Secondary Schools	56	70	66	70	62	64
普通中学	Regular Secondary Schools	376	320	310	319	346	372
#高　中	Senior Secondary Schools	123	99	88	89	94	92
小　学	Primary Schools	384	305	297	259	269	273
在校学生数(人)	**Number of Students Enrollment(person)**						
普通高等学校	Regular Institutions of Higher Education	37364	44758	50636	54552	58030	64527
中等职业教育学校	Vocational Secondary Schools	34625	50276	63404	49919	41267	40114
普通中学	Regular Secondary Schools	120631	124767	130776	155165	169007	183239
#高　中	Senior Secondary Schools	35890	36082	38134	44672	55248	58441
小　学	Primary Schools	185477	164894	167078	162362	173050	173542
教职员工数(人)	**Teachers, Staff and Workers(person)**						
普通高等学校	Regular Institutions of Higher Education	2392	2674	3062	3251	3818	4111
中等职业教育学校	Vocational Secondary Schools	1873	2259	2440	2610	2226	2175
普通中学	Regular Secondary Schools	8321	7978	8710	9719	13771	15814
小　学	Primary Schools	7548	6817	7161	7456	4770	5094
专任教师数(人)	**Full-time Teachers(person)**						
普通高等学校	Regular Institutions of Higher Education	1977	2217	2528	2653	2993	3037
中等职业教育学校	Vocational Secondary Schools	1096	1371	1447	1448	1264	1302
普通中学	Regular Secondary Schools	5594	5543	5999	6811	10138	11766
小　学	Primary Schools	6300	5825	5922	6146	3928	4181

20-19 成人教育
Adult Education

类　别	Item	2007	2008	2009	2010	2011	2012
学校数(所)	**Number of Schools(unit)**						
成人高等教育学校	Adult Institutions of Higher Education	5	5	4	4	4	4
成人中等专业教育学校	Adult Specialized Secondary Schools	19	21	22	21	15	16
成人中学	Adult Secondary Schools	5	45	22	33	13	51
成人技术培训学校	Adult Technical Training Schools	11747	12999	11852	7711	8202	7863
成人小学	Adult Primary Schools	8972	9433	9377	5405	5059	4935
在校生数(万人)	**Number of Students Enrollment(10000 persons)**						
成人高等教育	Adult Institutions of Higher Education	8.96	8.80	8.62	8.66	7.96	8.56
成人中等专业教育	Adult Specialized Secondary Schools	1.33	1.69	2.02	2.88	1.80	1.22
成人中学	Adult Secondary Schools	0.21	0.48	0.56	1.69	0.12	0.75
成人技术培训学校	Adult Technical Training Schools	272.73	275.07	262.72	205.81	218.06	201.45
成人小学	Adult Primary Schools	32.31	30.34	30.23	23.99	12.80	13.54
毕业生数(万人)	**Number of Graduates(10000 persons)**						
成人高等教育	Adult Institutions of Higher Education	4.48	2.89	2.81	2.43	3.00	2.33
成人中等专业教育	Adult Specialized Secondary Schools	0.35	0.27	0.36	0.47	0.22	0.27
成人中学	Adult Secondary Schools	0.15	0.35	0.45	0.77	0.32	1
成人技术培训学校	Adult Technical Training Schools	256.20	264.35	251.73	206.55	219.58	198.49
成人小学	Adult Primary Schools	27.23	23.64	24.30	21.49	12.99	12.58

20-20 科技活动

Basic Statistics on Scientific and Technological Activities

指 标	Item	2011	2012	2012年比2011年增长(%) Increase Rate in 2012 over 2011(%)
科技活动人员(人)	**Persons Engaged in Scientific and Technological Activities (person)**	**60366**	**64016**	**6.0**
科研机构	**Scientific Research Institutions**			
科研机构数(个)	Number of Institutions(unit)	331	332	0.3
科研用仪器设备原价(万元)	Original Cost of Instrument and Equipment for Scientific Research(10000yuan)	435225	415824.8	-4.5
#进 口	Import	91212	105000.9	15.1
研究与实验发展(R&D)	**Research and Development**			
研究与试验发展(R&D)人员(人)	R&D Personnel(person)	24875	29967	20.5
#博士毕业	Doctor	1492	1733	16.2
硕士毕业	Master	4220	4873	15.5
研究与试验发展(R&D)经费支出(万元)	Expenditure on R&D(10000yuan)	363089	417261	14.9
科技产出	**S&T Output**			
专利申请数(件)	Number of Patents Application(unit)	2485	3408	37.1
#发明专利	Inventions	1075	1690	57.2
专利授权数(件)	Number of Patents Granted(unit)	208	303	45.7
#发明专利	Inventions	91	119	30.8
有效发明专利数(件)	Number of Valid Patents for Invention(unit)	1560	1939	24.3
专利所有权转让及许可数(件)	Number of Patents Ownership Assigned and Granted (unit)	37	24	-35.1
专利所有权转让及许可收入(万元)	Revenue from Patents Ownership Assigned and Granted(10000yuan)	31644	241	-99.2
集成电路布图设计登记数(件)	Number of IC Layout Design Registrations(unit)	1		
植物新品种权授予数(项)	Number of New Plant Breed Rights Granted(unit)	17	8	-52.9
形成国家或行业标准数(项)	Number of Standards Adopted by State or Industry(unit)	286	184	-35.7
发表科技论文(篇)	Scientific Papers Issued(piece)	16514	17641	6.8
出版科技著作(种)	Publication on Science an Technology(kind)	400	478	19.5

20–21　研究与试验发展(R&D)活动

Basic Statistics on Scientific Research and Development

指　　标	Item	2011	2012	2012年比2011年增长(%) Increase Rate in 2012 over 2011(%)
有研究与试验发展(R&D)活动单位(个)	**Number of Institutions Having R&D Activities(unit)**	**316**	**339**	**7.3**
R&D人员	**Bisic Statistics on R&D Personnel**			
R&D人员(人)	R&D Personnel(person)	24875	29967	20.5
#女性	Female	8130	9629	18.4
#研究人员	Research Personnel	14746	16801	13.9
#全时人员	Full-time Personnel	12641	14905	17.9
非全时人员	Part-time Personnel	12234	15062	23.1
#博士毕业	Doctor	1492	1733	16.2
硕士毕业	Master	4220	4873	15.5
本科毕业	Bachelor	9526	11008	15.6
其他学历	Others	9637	12353	28.2
R&D人员折合全时当量(人年)	Full-time Equivalent of R&D Personnel(person-year)	15886	18732	17.9
#研究人员	Research Personnel	8861	9687	9.3
#基础研究	Basic Research	2436	2713	11.4
应用研究	Applied Research	2337	2241	-4.1
试验发展	Experimental Development	11114	13778	24.0
R&D经费	**R&D Expenditure**			
R&D经费内部支出(万元)	Intramural Expenditure on R&D (10000yuan)	363089	417260.8	14.9
#基础研究	Basic Research	29228	38298	31.0
应用研究	Applied Research	38962	35624	-8.6
试验发展	Experimental Development	294900	343337.7	16.4
#日常性支出	Daily Expenditure	326471	368419.7	12.8
#人员劳务费	Personnel Service Fees	71751	91860	28.0
资产性支出	Expenditure on Assets	36620	48841	33.4
#仪器和设备	Insrument and Equipment	32315	34974	8.2
#政府资金	Government Appropration Funds	75230	88969	18.3
企业资金	Self-raised Funds by Enterprises	268920	288498.6	7.3
境外资金	Overseas Funds	238	250	5.0
其他资金	Other Funds	18705	39543	111.4
经费投入强度(%)	**Intensity of Funds Input(%)**	**0.64**	**0.61**	**-0.03(百分点)**
R&D项目(课题)	**R&D Topics**			
R&D项目(课题)数(项)	Projects of R&D(unit)	10975	12185	11.0
R&D项目(课题)参加人员折合全时当量(人年)	Participants(person-year)	13747	16969	23.4
#研究人员	Research Personnel	8375		
R&D项目(课题)经费内部支出(万元)	Intramural Expenditure (10000yuan)	295405	351276	18.9

20–22 大中型工业企业科技活动

Basic Statistics on Science and Technology Activities of Large and Medium-sized Industrial Enterprises

指　标	Item	2007	2008	2009	2010	2011	2012
企业基本情况	**Statistics on Industrial Enterprises**						
有R&D活动企业数(个)	Number of Enterprises Having R&D Activities(unit)	68	77	90	69	94	79
有R&D活动企业所占比重(%)	Percentage of Enterprises Having R&D Activities to Total Number of Enterprises(%)	26.1	21.6	24.1	26.5	16.7	13.7
R&D活动情况	**Statitstics on R&D Activities**						
R&D人员全时当量(万人年)	Full-time Equivalent of R&D Personnel (10 000 man-years)	0.59	0.57	0.67	0.86	0.89	0.58
R&D经费内部支出(亿元)	Intramural Expenditure on R&D(100 million yuan)	10.13	14.10	17.77	21.78	26.01	18.92
R&D经费内部支出与主营业务	Percentage of Intramural Expenditure on R&D to						
收入之比(%)	Sales Revenue(%)	0.67	0.66	0.75	1.01	0.75	0.48
R&D项目数(项)	Projects of R&D(item)	1112	740	1120	995	1158	787
R&D项目经费内部支出（亿元)	Intramural Expenditure on R&D Projects(100 million yuan)	9.38	13.80	14.70	16.71	21.94	16.76
企业办R&D机构情况	**Statistics on R&D Institutions**						
机构数(个)	Number of R&D Institutions(unit)	104	116	131	109	124	77
机构人员数(万人)	R&D Personnel(10 000 persons)	0.91	1.01	1.01	1.14	0.92	0.71
机构经费支出(亿元)	Expenditure on R&D(100 million yuan)	13.41	18.74	19.30	18.88	12.26	21.68
新产品开发及生产情况	**Statitstics on New Products Development and Production**						
新产品开发项目数(个)	Number of New Products(unit)	642	1278	1698	1344	1527	858
新产品开经费支出(亿元)	Expenditure on New Products Development(100 million yuan)	12.38	17.10	23.60	26.43	34.07	23.50
新产品销售收入(亿元)	Sales Revenue of New Products(100 million yuan)	184.88	177.62	177.48	310.65	424.59	294.11
#新产品出口	Export	16.04	11.71	9.01	21.19	29.88	31.20
专利情况	**Statistics on Patent**						
专利申请数(件)	Patent Applications(piece)	580	906	1222	1302	1675	1661
#发明专利	Inventions	254	405	567	648	654	746
有效发明专利数(件)	Number of Patents In Force (piece)	300	583	629	757	835	803
技术获取和技术改造情况	**Statistics on Technology Acquisition and Technology Reconstruction**						
引进国外技术经费支出(亿元)	Expenditure for Acquisition of Foreign Technology (100 million yuan)	0.62	1.34	0.24	1.35	0.45	0.23
引进技术消化吸收经费支出(亿元)	Expenditure for Assimilation of Technology(100 million yuan)	0.54	0.13	0.20	0.29	0.53	2.15
购买国内技术经费支出(亿元)	Expenditure for Purchase of Domestic Technology (100 million yuan)	0.33	0.52	1.03	1.97	0.60	1.02
技术改造经费支出(亿元)	Expenditure for Technical Renovation(100 million yuan)	55.91	71.30	78.40	54.37	66.79	109.14

注：2012年划分企业规模的标识指标变化。

Note:The division identifies indicators of firm size changes in 2012.

20–23 政府属独立研究与开发机构科技活动
Scientific and Technological Activities of Government-affiliated Independent Research Institutions

指标	Item	2007	2008	2009	2010	2011	2012	2012年比2011年增长(%) Increase Rate in 2012 over 2011(%)
科技机构数(个)	**Number of S&T Institutions(unit)**	**111**	**111**	**106**	**107**	**105**	**106**	**1.0**
县级以上研究与开发机构	Scientific Research and Development Institution at County and Higher Levels	70	66	62	62	60	63	5.0
社会、人文科学研究机构	Research Institutions of Social and Human Studies	3	3	3	4	4	4	持平
县级以上研究与开发转制机构	Conversed Scientific Research and Development Institution at County and Higher Levels	21	25	24	24	25	24	-4.0
县级以上部门属科技情报与文献机构	Department of S&T Informations and Literature Institutions at County and Higher Levels	6	6	6	6	6	6	持平
县级政府部门属研究与开发机构	Scientific Research and Development Institutions at County Level	11	11	11	11	10	9	-10.0
科技活动人员数(人)	**Personnel Engaged in S&T Activities(person)**	**5523**	**5547**	**4336**	**4594**	**5019**	**4626**	**-7.8**
县级以上研究与开发机构	Scientific Research and Development Institution at County and Higher Levels	3879	3484	2656	2847	3218	3032	-5.8
社会、人文科学研究机构	Research Institutions of Social and Human Studies	179	203	204	226	223	224	0.4
县级以上研究与开发转制机构	Conversed Scientific Research and Development Institution at County and Higher Levels	1256	1675	1280	1300	1348	1138	-15.6
县级以上部门属科技情报与文献机构	Department of S&T Informations and Literature Institutions at County and Higher Levels	109	92	100	120	128	130	1.6
县级政府部门属研究与开发机构	Scientific Research and Development Institutions at County Level	100	93	96	101	102	102	持平
大学本科及以上学历(人)	**University,College and Above(person)**	**3938**	**4066**	**2873**	**3103**	**3612**	**3431**	**-5.0**
县级以上研究与开发机构	Scientific Research and Development Institution at County and Higher Levels	2785	2497	1660	1848	2273	2182	-4.0
社会、人文科学研究机构	Research Institutions of Social and Human Studies	145	158	168	205	200	200	持平
县级以上研究与开发转制机构	Conversed Scientific Research and Development Institution at County and Higher Levels	909	1324	913	950	1027	924	-10.0
县级以上部门属科技情报与文献机构	Department of S&T Informations and Literature Institutions at County and Higher Levels	79	68	64	74	84	97	15.5
县级政府部门属研究与开发机构	Scientific Research and Development Institutions at County Level	20	19	68	26	28	28	持平

20-23 续表 continued

指　标	Item	2007	2008	2009	2010	2011	2012	2012年比2011年增长(%) Increase Ratein 2012 over 2011(%)
经费收入总额(万元)	**Funding for S&T Activities(10000 yuan)**	**104375**	**123392**	**115296**	**140870**	**175937**	**198686**	**12.9**
县级以上研究与开发机构	Scientific Research and Development Institution at County and Higher Levels	71422	73498	65448	84360	96246	112779	17.2
社会、人文科学研究机构	Research Institutions of Social and Human Studies	2641	2962	3302	3266	3469	4575	31.9
县级以上研究与开发转制机构	Conversed Scientific Research and Development Institution at County and Higher Levels	28732	44407	43860	50253	72992	77151	5.7
县级以上部门属科技情报与文献机构	Department of S&T Informations and Literature Institutions at County and Higher Levels	1068	2039	2033	1851	1972	2846	44.3
县级政府部门属研究与开发机构	Scientific Research and Development Institutions at County Level	513	487	653	1140	1259	1335	6.0
经费支出总额(万元)	**Expenditures on S&T Activities(10000 yuan)**	**95949**	**118029**	**125340**	**139117**	**171663**	**182105**	**6.1**
县级以上研究与开发机构	Scientific Research and Development Institution at County and Higher Levels	67612	64397	70890	73690	87132	105899	21.5
社会、人文科学研究机构	Research Institutions of Social and Human Studies	2549	2623	2869	2724	3262	4585	40.6
县级以上研究与开发转制机构	Conversed Scientific Research and Development Institution at County and Higher Levels	24119	48842	48828	59396	77872	67423	-13.4
县级以上部门属科技情报与文献机构	Department of S&T Informations and Literature Institutions at County and Higher Levels	1062	1536	2021	1957	2003	2780	38.8
县级政府部门属研究与开发机构	Scientific Research and Development Institutions at County Level	607	631	732	1350	1394	1418	1.7
研究与试验发展经费支出(R&D经费支出)(万元)	**Expenditure on R&D(10000 yuan)**	**22806**	**27013**	**30666**	**24771**	**30422**	**40566**	**33.3**
县级以上研究与开发机构	Scientific Research and Development Institution at County and Higher Levels	18380	20443	26448	19682	20024	25693	28.3
社会、人文科学研究机构	Research Institutions of Social and Human Studies	1103	431	584	839	1001	1690	68.8
县级以上研究与开发转制机构	Conversed Scientific Research and Development Institution at County and Higher Levels	3288	5796	3464	3963	9398	13154	40.0
县级以上部门属科技情报与文献机构	Department of S&T Informations and Literature Institutions at County and Higher Levels		257	104	257			
县级政府部门属研究与开发机构	Scientific Research and Development Institutions at County Level	35	86	66	30		29	

注：1.资料来源于省科技厅(以下相关表同)。2."大学本科及以上学历"2006-2008年为"科学家和工程师"。3.2006-2008年"科技机构数"与2009年及以后的统计口径不一致。

Note:1.Data in the table are obtained from the Department of Science and Technology(The relative tables in the chapter are the same).2.The indicator of university,college and above for the year 2006 to 2008 refer to scientists and engineers.3.The statistical coverage of number of S&T institutions from 2006 to 2008 had been changed from the year 2009.

20–24 国家级科技计划项目人员
Personnel of National S&T Program Projects

指标	Item	2007	2008	2009	2010	2011	2012
项目参加人员(人)	**Personnel in Project (person)**	**1034**	**2948**	**3011**	**3191**	**2533**	**2166**
按计划类别分	by Typt of Progarm						
973计划	973 Program	196	223	216	282	230	108
863计划	863 Program	60	171	190	180	189	148
支撑计划	Key Technologies R&D Program	171	1609	1759	1598	794	755
火炬计划	Torch Program	275	408	354	386	492	649
星火计划	Spark Program	332	537	489	745	828	506
按职称类别分	by Type of Professional Title						
#高级职称	Senior Title	452	984	1045	979	803	714
中级职称	Middle Title	382	1196	1160	1131	733	730
初级职称	Primary Title	16	204	189	132	84	97
其他人员	Other	43	284	361	422	300	258
按学历分	by Education Background						
#博士	Doctor	144	256	295	295	208	199
硕士	Master	163	386	347	406	257	223
工作投入量(人月)	**Personnel Input (man-month)**	**2997**	**15665**	**14906**	**13043**	**6694**	**6166**
973计划	973 Program	1618	2419	1475	2127	1458	995
863计划	863 Program	342	1140	1617	1129	1134	572
支撑计划	Key Technologies R&D Program	1037	12106	11814	9787	4102	4599

注：1.初级职称和其他人员在火炬计划及星火计划统计中无该两项指标。 2.973计划为国家重点基础研究计划，863计划为国家高技术研究发展计划(以下相关表同)。

Note:1.The statistics of Torch Program and Spark Program exclude primary title and other title personel. 2.973 program is the national program on key basic research, and 863 program is the national high technology research and development program (The relative tables in the chapter are the same).

20–25 国家级科技计划项目资金及支出

Funds and Expenditure of National S&T Program

指标	Item	2007	2008	2009	2010	2011	2012
按计划类别分(项)	**by Type of Program (item)**	**61**	**120**	**124**	**138**	**135**	**131**
973计划	National Basic Research Program of China (973 Program)	2	2	10	13	10	6
863计划	High Technology Research and Development Program of China(863 Program)	4	8	10	11	11	8
支撑计划	Key Technologies R&D Program	6	29	34	39	26	18
火炬计划	Torch Program	20	37	34	37	42	51
星火计划	Spark Program	29	44	36	38	46	48
当年到位资金(万元)	**Funds Arranged (10000 yuan)**	**13477**	**119361**	**68180**	**131469**	**83426**	**99722**
973计划	973 Program	2190	1383	701	1119	376	700
863计划	863 Program	221	3519	1757	798	737	5022
支撑计划	Key Technologies R&D Program	2967	85685	37238	47561	5382	5200
火炬计划	Torch Program	3070	20386	19298	73513	64010	76706
星火计划	Spark Program	5029	8388	9186	8478	12921	12094
项目支出(万元)	**Project Expenditure (10000 yuan)**	**8024**	**96684**	**59839**	**97775**	**62601**	**89109**
973计划	973 Program	888	1814	625	1040	498	337
863计划	863 Program	401	3511	7737	674	900	2733
支撑计划	Key Technologies R&D Program	1842	72362	34052	49580	10958	7119
火炬计划	Torch Program	3070	12132	9165	38940	39917	67689
星火计划	Spark Program	1823	6865	8260	7541	10328	11231

20–26 国家级科技计划项目培养和引进人才

Cultivated and Introduced Talents of National S&T Program

指标	Item	2007	2008	2009	2010	2011	2012
培养博士和硕士(人)	**Cultivated Master and Doctor (person)**	**48**	**191**	**299**	**249**	**152**	**83**
973计划	973 Program	31	82	45	84	47	27
863计划	863 Program	14	22	35	31	23	9
支撑计划	Key Technologies R&D Program	3	87	219	134	82	47
引进人才(人)	**Introduction of Talents (person)**	**3**	**24**	**23**	**27**	**23**	**16**
973计划	973 Program			6	9	10	7
863计划	863 Program		2	3	4	3	1
支撑计划	Key Technologies R&D Program	3	22	14	14	10	8

20–27 国家级科技计划实施项目效益

Benefit of National S&T Program

单位：万元 (10000 yuan)

指标	Item	2007	2008	2009	2010	2011	2012
新增产值	**Added Value of Output**	**80929**	**207698**	**230480**	**236270**	**307027**	**303254**
支撑计划	Key Technologies R&D Program	1856	57896	82840	71388	93092	78362
火炬计划	Torch Program	74070	119762	122867	130213	183817	199083
星火计划	Spark Program	5003	30040	24773	34669	30118	25809
净利润	**After-Tax Profit**	**5976**	**14877**	**15629**	**23024**	**25958**	**40295**
支撑计划	Key Technologies R&D Program		3196	3121	1484	5455	9219
火炬计划	Torch Program	4693	8251	9032	12006	15981	23433
星火计划	Spark Program	1283	3430	3476	9534	4522	7643
实交税金	**Tax**	**3587**	**15392**	**8513**	**10760**	**13119**	**12767**
支撑计划	Key Technologies R&D Program	7	8190	1801	796	3893	1824
火炬计划	Torch Program	3354	6000	5744	8799	8176	10410
星火计划	Spark Program	226	1202	968	1165	1050	533

20−28 省部级以上成果登记(完成人员)

Staffs Personnel of Provincial or Ministerial Level and above

单位：人次 (person-time)

指标	Item	2007	2008	2009	2010	2011	2012
合 计	**Total**	**1244**	**1279**	**1293**	**1306**	**979**	**1479**
按学历分	**by Type of Diploma**						
博 士	Doctor	147	143	134	143	133	215
硕 士	Master	253	288	269	279	255	365
大 本	Undergraduate Student	700	699	717	720	515	751
大 专	Junior College Student	96	111	135	139	68	114
中 专	Senoir Middle School	38	31	37	20	8	27
其 他	Below Senoir Middle School	10	7	1	5		7
按年龄结构分	**by Type of Age**						
35岁以下(含35岁)	thirty-five and below	284	366	379	388	328	380
36−45岁	thirty-six to forty-five	434	486	476	500	353	568
46−55岁	forty-six to fifty-five	384	321	338	341	238	393
56−65岁	fifty-six to sixty-five	100	78	69	55	45	106
65岁以上	above sixty-five	42	28	31	22	15	32
按技术职称分	**by Type of Title**						
院 士	Academicians	1		2			1
正 高	Senior Title	281	266	272	277	198	345
副 高	Sub-senior Title	406	378	377	380	302	468
中 级	Middle Title	413	451	452	486	345	464
初 级	Primary Title	98	133	142	134	91	120
其 他	No Rank	45	51	48	29	43	81

20-29 省部级以上成果登记(数量及投资额)

Number of Achievements and Investment of Projects at Provincial or Ministerial Level and above(number & investment)

指 标	Item	2007	2008	2009	2010	2011	2012
成果登记(项)	**Achievement Registration(item)**	**144**	**130**	**137**	**125**	**90**	**132**
发明专利授权数(件)	Invention of Patent Authorigations Granted (piece)	21	34	46	67	240	120
制订标准数(个)	Number of Standards for Formulation (unit)	19	19	27	12	8	21
按成果类别分(项)	by Typt of Achievement Sort (item)						
基础研究	Basic Research	30	23	14	16	19	28
应用研究	Applied Research	114	107	123	109	71	104
按成果应用属性分(项)	by Typt of Achievement Application Property (item)						
#原始性创新	Original Invention	63	65	68	63	22	11
国外引进消化 吸收创新	Absorb and Digest Invention of Foreign Indraught	21	20	22	15	11	18
国内技术二次开发	Twice Development of Inner Technology	30	22	33	31	38	75
项目投资额(万元)	**Project Investment (10000 yuan)**	**119313**	**104868**	**108623**	**95331**	**212819**	**109689**
国家资金	Government Funds	3757	4418	2847	12317	6127	11886
部门资金	Department Funds	34253	4635	5396	18234	947	10798
地方资金	Local Funds	34538	21585	26710	31433	6223	37697
基金投入	Fund Input	152	69	862	158	135	1176
自有资金	Self-raised Funds	37418	16082	53927	23420	195620	35323
银行贷款	Loans from Bank	720	1000	15646		200	200
国外资金	Foreign Funds.	117	3			12	6
其他资金	Other Funds	8358	57076	3235	9769	3555	12603
净利润(万元)	**After-Tax Profit (10000 yuan)**	**29188**	**60115**	**201281**	**78889**	**354367**	**120310**
实交税金(万元)	**Tax (10000 yuan)**	**21520**	**19269**	**17970**	**17699**	**104371**	**41289**

20–30 事业、企业单位各类专业技术人员

Specialized Technical Personnel in Enterprises and institutions

单位：万人 (10000 persons)

指　标	Item	2007	2008	2009	2010	2011	2012	2012年比2011年增长(%) Increase Rate in 2012 over 2011(%)
总　计	**Total**	**58.54**	**58.63**	**58.82**	**56.43**	**57.72**	**59.15**	**2.5**
#女　性	Female	23.30	23.48	23.85	23.19	24.16	25.55	5.8
按专业分	**By Specialized Subject**							
#工程技术人员	Engineering Technical Personnel	5.82	6.24	6.23	5.86	5.73	5.74	0.2
农业技术人员	Agricultural Technical Personnel	2.67	2.60	2.60	2.41	2.49	2.47	-0.7
卫生技术人员	Medical Technical Persomnel	7.47	7.38	7.45	7.27	7.84	8.12	3.5
科学研究人员	Scientific Research Personnel	0.14	0.14	0.15	0.15	0.16	0.20	21.1
教学人员	Teaching Personnel	36.48	36.87	37.11	36.12	37.09	38.20	3.0
按专业技术职务分	**By Professional Titles**							
#高　级	Senior	2.98	3.12	3.37	3.24	3.76	4.08	8.4
中　级	Medium	15.83	16.53	17.29	17.38	18.59	18.86	1.4
初　级	Junior	35.82	34.81	34.00	33.61	32.54	32.90	1.1
按学历分	**By Education Background**							
#大学本科以上	University,College and above	13.61	14.91	14.95	18.86	21.32	24.00	12.6
大学专科	Specialized Institutions of Higher Educat	26.97	27.36	27.37	26.16	26.35	26.35	0.0
中专以下	Senior Middle School and the Level belo	18.14	16.33	16.32	11.41	10.05	8.80	-12.4

注：1.资料来源于省人力资源社会保障厅。 2.本表数据按岗位统计，不含非公经济单位和中央驻黔单位数据。3.2010年开始，由于统计口径调整，事业单位部分专业技术人员划到管理人员统计，我省专业技术人员统计数据出现波动。

Note: 1.Data in the table are obtained from the Provinvial Department of Human Resources and Social Security.2.Data in this table count by post, and don't include non-public economic units and the central unit of data in Guizhou.3.Since 2010, due to adjustment of statistical ,part of the professional and technical personnel of institution have designated to manage personnel and statistics,and statistics of professional and technical personnel in our province have fluctuated

20-31 专利申请受理及授权

Patent Application Accepted and Granted

单位：件 (item)

指 标	Item	2007	2008	2009	2010	2011	2012	2012年比2011年增长(%) Increase Rate in 2012 over 2011(%)
受理专利总计	**Total Patent Applications Accepted**	**2759**	**2943**	**3709**	**4414**	**8351**	**11296**	**35.3**
按种类分	**Grouped by Sort**							
发 明	Inventions	874	873	1336	1322	2358	3103	31.6
实用新型	Utility Models	1287	1403	1659	2441	3170	4111	29.7
外观设计	Designs	598	667	714	651	2823	4082	44.6
按对象分	**Grouped by Applicant**							
非职务发明创造	Non-service Creations and Inventions	1223	1160	1114	1631	2072	2192	5.8
职务发明创造	Service Creations and Inventions	1536	1783	2595	2783	6297	9104	44.6
#大专院校	Universities and Colleges	70	133	139	172	312	366	17.3
科研单位	Research Institutions	437	446	388	633	357	530	48.5
工矿企业	Industrial and Mineral Enterprises	992	1192	2047	1937	5507	7949	44.3
机关团体	Government Agencies and Organizations	37	12	21	41	103	259	151.5
授权专利总计	**Total Patent Authorigations Granted**	**1727**	**1728**	**2084**	**3034**	**3386**	**6054**	**78.8**
按种类分	**Grouped by Sort**							
发 明	Inventions	233	270	322	434	596	635	6.5
实用新型	Utility Models	1120	1183	1234	1904	1885	3149	67.1
外观设计	Designs	374	275	528	696	905	2270	150.8
按对象分	**Grouped by Applicant**							
非职务发明创造	Non-service Creations and Inventions	834	704	712	961	992	1283	29.3
职务发明创造	Service Creations and Inventions	893	1024	1372	2073	2394	4771	99.3
#大专院校	Universities and Colleges	40	31	50	116	141	182	29.1
科研单位	Research Institutions	299	322	337	366	378	269	-28.8
工矿企业	Industrial and Mineral Enterprises	539	660	972	1569	1841	4214	128.9
机关团体	Government Agencies and Organizations	15	11	13	22	34	106	211.8

注：资料来源于省知识产权局。

Note: Data in the table are obtained from the Provincial Intellectual Property Right Bureau.

主要统计指标解释

普通高等学校　指通过国家普通高等教育招生考试，招收高中毕业生为主要培养对象，实施高等学历教育的全日制大学、独立设置的学院，独立学院和高等专科学校、高等职业学校及其他普通高教机构。

成人高等学校　指通过国家成人高等教育招生考试，招收具有高中毕业或同等学历的人员为主要培养对象，利用函授、业余、脱产等多种形式，对其实施高等学历教育的学校。包括：职工高等学校、农民高等学校、管理干部学院、教育学院、独立函授学院、广播电视大学、其他成人高教机构。

小学学龄儿童入学率　指调查范围内已入小学学习的学龄儿童占校内外学龄儿童总数（包括弱智儿童，不包括盲聋哑儿童）的比重。计算公式为:

$$\text{小学学龄儿童入学率}=\frac{\text{已入学的小学学龄儿童数}}{\text{校内外小学学龄儿童总数}}\times 100\%$$

科技活动　指在自然科学、农业科学、医药科学、工程与技术科学、人文与社会科学领域（简称科学技术领域）中，与科技知识的产生、发展、传播和应用密切相关的有组织的活动。可分为研究与试验发展(R&D)、研究与试验发展成果应用及相关的科技服务三类活动。

科技活动人员　指直接从事科技活动、以及专门从事科技活动管理和为科技活动提供直接服务，累计的实际工作时间占全年制度工作时间10%及以上的人员。(1)直接从事科技活动的人员包括：在独立核算的科学研究与技术开发机构、高等学校、各类企业及其他事业单位内设的研究室、实验室、技术开发中心及中试车间（基地）等机构中从事科技活动的研究人员、工程技术人员、技术工人及其它人员；虽不在上述机构工作，但编入科技活动项目（课题）组的人员；科技信息与文献机构中的专业技术人员；从事论文设计的研究生等。(2)专门从事科技活动管理和为科技活动提供直接服务的人员，包括：独立核算的科学研究与技术开发机构、科技信息与文献机构、高等学校、各类企业及其他事业单位主管科技工作的负责人，专门从事科技活动的计划、行政、人事、财务、物资供应、设备维护、图书资料管理等工作的各类人员，但不包括保卫、医疗保健人员、司机、食堂人员、茶炉工、水暖工、清洁工等为科技活动提供间接服务的人员。该指标用来反映投入科技活动人力的规模。

科学家与工程师　指科技活动人员中具有高、中级技术职称（职务）的人员和不具有高、中级技术职称（职务）的大学本科及以上学历人员。该指标用来反映投入科技活动人力的素质。

研究与试验发展(R&D)　指在科学技术领域，为增加知识总量、以及运用这些知识去创造新的应用进行的系统的创造性的活动，包括基础研究、应用研究、试验发展三类活动。国际上通常采用R&D活动的规模和强度指标反映一国的科技实力和核心竞争力。

基础研究　指为了获得关于现象和可观察事实的基本原理的新知识（揭示客观事物的本质、运动规律，获得新发现、新学说）而进行的实验性或理论性研究，它不以任何专门或特定的应用或使用为目的。其成果以科学论文和科学著作为主要形式。用来反映知识的原始创新能力。

应用研究　指为获得新知识而进行的创造性研究，主要针对某一特定的目的或目标。应用研究是为了确定基础研究成果可能的用途，或是为达到预定的目标探索应采取的新方法（原理性）或新途径。其成果形式以科学论文、专著、原理性模型或发明专利为主。用来反映对基础研究成果应用途径的探索。

试验发展　指利用从基础研究、应用研究和实际经验所获得的现有知识，为产生新的产品、材料和装置，建立新的工艺、系统和服务，以及对已产生和建立的上述各项作实质性的改进而进行的系统性工作。其成果形式主要是专利、专有技术、具有新产品基本特征的产品原型或具有新装置基本特征的原始样机等。在社会科学领域，试验发展是指把通过基础研究、应用研究获得的知识转变成可以实施的计划（包括为进行检验和评估实施示范项目）的过程。人文科学领域没有对应的试验发展活动。主要反映将科研成果转化为技术和产品的能力，是科技推动经济社会发展的物化成果。

研究与试验发展人员　指参与研究与试验发展项目研究、管理和辅助工作的人员，　包括项目组（课题）人员，企业科技行政管理人员和直接为项目（课题）活动提供服务的辅助人员。不包括全年从事研究与试验发展活动工作量不到0.1年的人员。反映投入从事拥有自主知识产权的研究开发活动的人力规模。

研究与试验发展人员全时当量　指全时人员折合成全时工作量与所有非全时人员折合成全时工作量的总计。一个全时人员的折合全时工作量计为1，非全时人员按实际投入工作量进行累加。例如：有两个全时人员和三个非全时人员（工作量分别为20%、30%和70%），则全时当量为1+1+0.2+0.3+0.7=3.2人年。为国际上比较科技人力投入而制定的可比指标。

专业技术人员 指从事专业技术工作和专业技术管理工作的人员，即企事业单位中已经聘任专业技术职务从事专业技术工作和专业技术管理工作的人员，以及未聘任专业技术职务，现在专业技术岗位上工作的人员。包括工程技术人员，农业技术人员，科学研究人员，卫生技术人员，教学人员，经济人员，会计人员，统计人员，翻译人员，图书资料、档案、文博人员，新闻出版人员，律师、公证人员，广播电视播音人员，工艺美术人员，体育人员，艺术人员及企业政治思想工作人员，共十七个专业技术职务类别。用来反映科技人力资源情况。

科技活动经费筹集 指从各种渠道筹集到的计划用于科技活动的经费，包括政府资金、企业资金、事业单位资金、金融机构贷款、国外资金和其他资金等。反映各社会经济主体对促进科技进步所做的努力。

政府资金 指从各级政府部门获得的计划用于科技活动的经费，包括科学事业费、科技三项费、科研基建费、科学基金、教育等部门事业费中计划用于科技活动的经费以及政府部门预算外资金中计划用于科技活动的经费等。

企业资金 指从自有资金中提取或接受其他企业委托的、科研院所和高校等事业单位接受企业委托获得的，计划用于科研和技术开发的经费。不包括来自政府、金融机构及国外的计划用于科技活动的资金。

金融机构贷款 指从各类金融机构获得的用于科技活动的贷款。

科技活动经费内部支出 指报告年内用于科技活动的实际支出，包括劳务费、科研业务费、科研管理费，非基建投资购建的固定资产、科研基建支出以及其他用于科技活动的支出。不包括生产性活动支出、归还贷款支出及转拨外单位支出。反映科技投入实际完成情况。

劳务费 指以现金或实物形式支付给科技活动人员的工资、薪金，以及所有其它的劳务费用，如奖金、奖金税、社会保障支出等。反映改善科技人员待遇情况。

固定资产购建费 指报告年内使用非基建投资购建的固定资产和用于科研基建投资的实际支出额，即固定资产实际支出和科研基建投资实际完成额之和。固定资产是指长期使用而不改变原有实物形态的主要物资设备、图书资料、实验材料和标本以及其他设备和家具、房屋、建筑物。反映用于改善科研条件和科研手段方面的投入情况。

新产品 指采用新技术原理、新设计构思研制、生产的全新产品，或在结构、材质、工艺等某一方面比原有产品有明显改进，从而显著提高了产品性能或扩大了使用功能的产品。既包括政府有关部门认定并在有效期内的新产品，也包括企业自行研制开发，未经政府有关部门认定，从投产之日起一年之内的新产品。用来反映科技产出及对经济增长的直接贡献。

专利 一般是专利权的简称，指专利权人对发明创造享有的专利权。即国家依法在一定时期内授予发明创造或者其权利继受者独占使用其发明创造的权利。

专利同时也指具体专利技术，即受国家认可并在公开的基础上进行法律保护的技术或者方案。

专利还可指具体的物质文件，即国家颁发的确认申请人对其发明创造享有的专利证书或记载发明创造内容的专利文献。

发明 对产品、方法或其改进所提出的新的技术方案。

实用新型 对产品的形状、构造或者其结合所提出的适于实用的新的技术方案。

外观设计 对产品的形状、图案、色彩或者其结合以及色彩与形状、图案的结合所作出的富有美感并适于工业上应用的新设计。

Explanatory Notes on Main Statistical Indicators

Regular Institutions of Higher Education refer to recruiting graduates from senior secondary schools as the main target by National Matriculation TEST. They include full-time universities, colleges, institutions of higher professional education, institutions of higher vocational education, institutions of higher vocational education and others.

Institutions of Higher Education for Adults refer to educational establishments, enrolling staff and workers with senior secondary school or equivalent education, and providing higher education courses in many forms of correspondence, spare time, or full time for adults. Professionals thus trained receive a qualification equivalent to graduates studying regular courses at regular universities, colleges and professional colleges. Institutions of higher learning for adults include schools of higher education for staff and workers, schools of higher education for peasants, colleges for management cadres, pedagogical colleges, independent correspondence colleges, Radio and TV universities and other educational establishments.

Enrollment Ratio of Primary Schools refers to the proportion of school age children enrolled at schools to the total number of school age children both in and outside schools (including retarded children, but excluding blind, deaf and mute children). The formula is:

$$\text{Net Enrollment Rate of Primary Schools} = \frac{\text{Total Primary School-age Children at Schools}}{\text{Total Primary School-age Children Whether or Not Attending Schools}} \times 100\%$$

Scientific and Technological Activities(S&T Activities) refer to organized activities which are closely related with the creation, development, dissemination and application of the scientific and technical knowledge in the fields of natural sciences, agricultural science, medical science, engineering and technological science, humanities and social sciences (referred to as scientific and technological fields). S&T activities can be classified in to 3 categories: research and development (R&D) activities, application of R&D results, and related S&T services.

Personnel Engaged in S&T Activities refer to personnel directly engaged in S&T activities, in the management of S&T activities, and in providing direct service to S&T activities, who spend over 10% of the total working hours in a year in S&T activities. (1) Personnel directly engaged in S&T activities include researchers, engineers, technicians and other related personnel engaged in S&T activities in independent-accounting R&D institutions, institutions of higher learning, and in research institutes, laboratories, technology development centers and central experiment workshops under enterprises and institutions. Also included are people working in S&T research project teams, professional and technical personnel working in S&T information archiving institutes, and graduate students working on the design of their thesis. (2) Personnel engaged in the management of S&T activities and in providing direct service to S&T activities include senior management people responsible for S&T activities in independent-accounting R&D institutions, S&T information archiving institutes, institutions of higher learning, and in enterprises and institutions where S&T activities are undertaken. Also included are people responsible for the planning, administration, personnel management, financial management, logistics supply, equipment maintenance, information and library management that are related with S&T activities. People providing indirect services are excluded, such as security, medical service, drivers, plumbers, cleaners and those providing catering and related service. This indicator reflects the size of personnel engaged in S&T activities.

Scientists and Engineers refer to persons engaged in S&T activities who have obtained titles of senior and middle level professional positions, and those without such position but having completed university or higher education. This indicator reflects the quality of personnel engaged in S&T activities.

Research and Development (R&D) refers to systematic and creative activities in the field of science and technology aiming at increasing the knowledge and using the knowledge for new application. R&D includes 3 categories of activities: basic research, applied research and experimentation for development. The scale and intensity of R&D are widely used internationally to reflect the strength of S&T and the core competitiveness of a country in the world.

Basic Research refers to empirical or theoretical research aiming at obtaining new knowledge on the fundamental principles regarding phenomena or observable facts to reveal the intrinsic nature and underlying laws and to acquire new discoveries or new theories. Basic research takes no specific or designated application as the aim of the research. Results of basic research are mainly released or disseminated in the form of scientific papers or monographs. This indicator reflects the innovation capacity for original knowledge.

Applied Research refers to creative research aiming at obtaining new knowledge on a specific objective or target. Purpose of the applied research is to identify the possible uses of results from basic research, or to explore new (fundamental) methods or new approaches. Results of applied research are expressed in the form of scientific papers, monographs, fundamental models or invention patents. This indicator reflects the exploration of ways to apply the results of basic research.

Experiments and Development refer to systematic activities aiming at using the knowledge from basic and applied researches or from practical experience to develop new products, materials and equipment, to establish new production process, systems and services, or to make substantial improvement on the existing products, process or services. Results of experiment and development activities are embodied in patents, exclusive technology, and monotype of new products or equipment. In social sciences, experiment and development activities refer to the process of converting the knowledge from basic or applied researches into feasible programmes (including conduct of demonstration projects for assessment and evaluation). There are no experiment and development activities in the science of humanities. This indicator reflects the capability of transferring the results of S&T into technique and products, and measures the realization of S&T in spearheading the economic and social development.

R & D Personnel refer to persons engaged in research, management and supporting activities of R & D, including persons in the project teams, persons engaged in the management of S&T activities of enterprises and supporting staff providing direct service to the research projects, and not including annual research and experimental development activities in less than 0.1 years of staff workload. This indicator reflects the size of personnel engaged in R&D activities with independent intellectual property.

Full-time Equivalent of R&D Personnel refers to the sum of the full-time persons and the full-time equivalent of part-time persons converted by workload. A full-time staff equivalent to full-time work is counted as a part-time personnel according to actual efforts to accumulate.For instance, if there are 2 full-time persons and 3 part-time workers (20%, 30% and 70% of working hours respectively on R&D activities), the full-time equivalent are 2+0.2+0.3+0.7=3.2 person-years. This is an internationally comparable indicator of S&T manpower input.

Professional and Technical Personnel refer to persons engaged in professional and technical work or in the management of professional and technical activities, i.e., people with professional or technical positions who are engaged in professional and technical work or in the management of professional and technical activities, and people without professional or technical positions but are working on professional or technical posts. They include professionals and technicians working in 17 categories of technical occupations including engineering, agriculture, scientific researches, medical service, teaching, economic research and application, accounting, statistics, translation, libraries, archives, cultural and museum service, journalism and publication, lawyers, notarization service, radio and television broadcasting, handicraft and fine arts, sports, performing art, and political workers in enterprises. This indicator reflects the condition of human resources in S&T.

Government Funds refer to funds obtained from government agencies at all levels to be used for S&T activities, including fund for scientific undertakings, 3 kinds of fund for S&T activities, fund for capital construction for scientific researches, science fund, funds from education expenditures by education departments for S&T activities, and extra-budget fund from government agencies for S&T activities.

Self-raised Funds by Enterprises refers to self-raised funds by enterprises from their own expenditure or from other enterprises and funds received by universities or research institutions from enterprises for scientific research or technical development projects. Excluded in this category are funds from government agencies, financial institutions or from foreign institutions.

Loans from Financial Institutions refer to loans from various financial institutions for S&T activities.

Internal Expenditures on S&T activities refer to the actual expenditures on S&T activities during the reference year, including service fees, expenditure on research activities, expenditure on research management, purchase or construction of fixed assets not included in the investment for capital construction, expenditure on capital construction for scientific researches, and other expenditures on S&T activities. Not included are expenditure on production activities, repayment of loans and transfer expenditure. This indicator reflects the real accomplishment of input in S&T.

Service Fees refer to direct or indirect payment, in cash or in kind, made to personnel engaged in S&T activities as remuneration and other fees. They include, in various forms, salaries, subsidies, bonus, benefits, retirement pension, stipend, etc. This indicator reflects the improvement of treatment toward S&T personnel.

Purchase or Construction of Fixed Assets refers to the fixed assets purchased or constructed using funds other than the investment in capital construction, and the actual expenditure on capital construction for scientific researches. In other words, it is the sum of the actual expenditure on fixed assets and the accomplished investment in capital construction for scientific researches. Fixed assets refer to main materials and equipment, literatures and documents in libraries, materials for experiments, specimen, instruments, furniture, buildings and constructions that can be used for a long time without changing the form and shape of those articles or constructions. This indictor reflects the input in improving the condition of S&T and the means of scientific research.

New Products refer to new products produced with new technology and new design, or products that represent noticeable improvement in terms of structure, material, or production process so as to improve significantly the character or function of the older versions. They include new products certified by relevant government agencies within the period of certification, as well as new products designed and produced by enterprises within a year without certification by government agencies. This indictor reflects the direct contribution of S&T output to economic growth.

Patent is an abbreviation for the patent right and refers to the exclusive right of ownership by the inventors or designers for the creation or inventions, given from the patent offices after due process of assessment and approval in accordance with the Patent Law.

Patent also refers to a specific patented technology that recognized by the State and public legal protection on the basis of technical or program.

Patent document also refers to a specific substance, which confirm that the applicant issued by the state enjoyed their inventions patented inventions certificate or record the content of patent documents.

Inventions refer to new technical proposals to the products or methods or their modifications.

Patented Utility Models refer to the practical and new technical proposals on the shape and structure of the product or the combination of both.

Designs refer to the aesthetics and industrially applicable new designs for the shape, pattern and colour of the product, or their combinations.

21

Twenty-one

文化、体育和卫生

Culture, Sports and Public Health

21-1 文化事业机构和人员

Number of Institutions and Personnel in Cultural Industry

指 标	Item	2007	2008	2009	2010	2011	2012	2012年比2011年增长(%) Increase Rate in 2012 over 2011(%)
机构总计(个)	**Total Number of Institutions(unit)**	**1838**	**1869**	**1966**	**2041**	**2075**	**2213**	**6.7**
#艺术事业	Art Institutions	61	59	76	65	56	90	60.7
文物事业	Cultural Relics	111	113	153	145	130	151	16.2
图书馆事业	Libraries	92	92	93	93	94	93	-1.1
群众文化事业	Mass Culture	1443	1470	1514	1524	1579	1661	5.2
文艺科研	Cultural and Art Research Institutions	4	4	5	4	4	2	-50.0
其他文化事业	Other Culture Units	129	137	125	210	212	216	1.9
人员总计(人)	**Total Number of Persons Engaged(person)**	**10013**	**10714**	**12520**	**12949**	**14945**	**16380**	**9.6**
#艺术事业	Art Institntions	2147	2184	2965	2421	2259	2531	12.0
文物事业	Cultural Relics	979	1133	1466	1665	1691	2166	28.1
图书馆事业	Libraries	895	913	946	937	950	976	2.7
群众文化事业	Mass Culture	4106	4400	4808	4790	5223	5320	1.9
文艺科研	Cultural and Art Research Institutions	27	27	36	31	33	21	-36.4
其他文化事业	Other Culture Units	1577	1955	2299	3105	4789	5366	12.0

注：1.资料来源于省文化厅(以下相关表同)。2.2008年及以后数据含电影机构和人员。3.2008年及以后其他文化事业数据含其他艺术和执法机构。4.机构和人员数不含文化市场新分的机构和人员数。

Note:1.Data in the table are provided by the Provinvial Department of Culture(The relative tables in the chapter are the same).2.Data in the table include the cinema institution and staff from 2008. 3.The data of Other Culture Units in the table include the Other Culture institution and market executing the law institution from 2008. 4.Number of Institutions and Personnel in the table exclude newly increased Institutions and Personnel.

21–2 文化事业单位数

Basic Statistics on Culture Establishment

单位：个 (unit)

类　别	Item	2007	2008	2009	2010	2011	2012
艺术表演场所	Arts Centers	11	11	9	7	11	10
公共图书馆	Public Libraries	92	92	93	93	94	93
博物馆、纪念馆	Museums and Memorials	18	23	53	59	53	66
群众艺术馆、文化馆	Mass Art Centers and Cultural Centers	95	95	95	95	97	97
档案馆	Archives	98	107	107	107	107	107

注：2012年博物馆、纪念馆个数包含没有纳入免费开放的机构。

Note:The number of museums and monuments include the agency that is free and open in 2012.

21–3 文化娱乐业(2012)

Culture and Entertainment Industry

类　别	Sort	机构数(个) Institutions (unit)	从业人员(人) Number of Employed Persons(person)	营业收入(万元) Operating Revenue (10000 yuan)	主营业务利润(万元) Primary Business Profit (10000 yuan)
总　计	**Total**	**4959**	**32671**	**263435**	**97385**
文艺表演团体	Performing Arts Groups	39	970	5189	772
演出场所经营单位	Venues Operating Units	2	48	34	-4
演出经纪机构	Performance Broker Institution	41	787	10832	-1430
娱乐场所	Entertainment Centers	2554	17980	122968	46626
经营性互联网文化单位	Commercial Internet Cultural Units	3	1160	17696	8195
互联网上网服务营业场所(网吧)	Internet access service establishments (cafes)	2231	9991	96468	39568
艺术品经营机构	Artwork Operators	56	626	2979	912
文化市场连锁经营机构	Cultural Market Chain Operators	33	1109	7269	2745

21–4 艺术表演场所(2012)

Art Preformances Places

类　别	Sort	机构数(个) Number of Institutions (unit)	从业人员(人) Number of Staff and Workers (person)	座席数(个) Seats (unit)	演(映)出场次(场) Number of Performances (show)	#艺术演出场次 Art Performance	观众人次(万人次) Number of Spectators (10000 person -times)
总　计	**Toatl**	**10**	**159**	**8326**	**620**	**410**	**29.5**
#省　级	Province Level	4	63				
地　级	Prefectural Level	2	39	1826	370	370	26.7
县　级	County Level	4	57	6500	250	40	2.8
#文化系统	Cultural Organizations and Institutions	8	111	2026	390	380	26.9

21-5 文化部门艺术剧团(2012)
Art Troupes of Culture Sector

指　标	Item	剧团数(个) Number of Troupes (unit)	从业人员(人) Number of Employed Persons (person)	国内演出(场) Number of Domestic Performances (show)	#在农村演出 Shows in Rural Areas	国内观众人数(万人次) Number of Domestic Spectators (10000 person-times)
总　计	**Total**	**40**	**1399**	**3210**	**1220**	**426**
按隶属关系分	Grouped by Ownership					
#国有剧团	State-owned Troupes	34	1171	2590	1070	204
按剧种分	Grouped by Art Troupes					
话剧、儿童剧、滑稽剧团	Drama, Children's Plays and Comedy Troupes	1	54	240		12
乐团、歌舞团、轻音乐团	Philharmonic, Song and Dance Troupe, Light Music Troupes	23	714	1830	780	280
戏曲剧团	Local Opera Troupes	3	243	370	140	44
曲艺、杂技、木偶、皮影团	Recitation and Ballad Troupes,Acrobatics and Circus Troupes,Puppet Show Troupes and ShadowPlay Troupes	2	141	170	50	18
文工团	Cultural and Performance Troupes	10	217	600	250	72
综合性艺术表演团体	General Art Performing Troupes	1	30			

21-6 文化馆(站)(2012)
Culture Centers(Stations)

指　标	Item	合计 Total	文化馆 Culture Centers	文化站 Culture Stations
馆(站)个数(个)	**Number of Centers(unit)**	**1661**	**97**	**1564**
组织各类讲座次数(次)	Organizing Lectures(time)	448	448	
组织文艺活动次数(次)	Organizing Art Performances(time)	12731	3694	9037
举办业余文艺训练班(班次)	Conducting Amateur Art Training Courses(class)	6059	2245	3814
#结业人数(万人次)	Number of Persons Completed(10000 person-times)	40.50	17.07	23.43
举办展览次数(次)	Number of Exhibitions(unit)	1610	482	1128

21-7 广播、电视
Radio and Television Industry

指　　标	Item	2007	2008	2009	2010	2011	2012
广播电视台(座)	Broadcasting and Television Stations(unit)	77	77	78	79	79	84
广播节目综合人口覆盖率(%)	Radio Coverage Rate of the Population(%)	84.1	86.1	86.6	87.5	88.0	88.5
#农村	Rural	81.9	84.2	84.4	85.6	86.1	86.6
广播节目自办套数(套)	Number of Radio Programs with Ownership(set)	23	23	24	27	31	39
#公共广播	Public Radio	23	23	24	27	31	39
广播节目制作时间(万小时)	Length of Radio Programs Produced(10 000 hours)	6.73	6.69	7.37	6.23	10.58	12.94
公共广播节目播出时间(万小时)	Length of Public Radio Programs Broadcasted (10 000 hours)	11.37	13.58	14.34	15.78	18.92	20.87
电视节目综合人口覆盖率(%)	TV Coverage Rate of Population(%)	91.1	91.3	91.3	92.5	92.8	93.0
#农村	Rural	90.0	90.0	90.0	91.4	91.7	91.9
有线广播电视用户数(万户)	Number of Users of Cable Radio and TV (10 000 households)	335.35	338.23	340.61	335.23	396.57	396.61
#农村	Rural	166.20	113.92	93.07	91.26	210.53	218.20
数字电视用户数(万户)	Number of Users of Digital TV(10 000 households)	69.01	130.05	208.19	234.51	349.67	357.69
有线广播电视入户率(%)	Popularization Rate of Cable Radio and TV(%)	29.3	31.1	31.4	29.9	34.3	32.9
#农村	Rural	20.1	14.4	10.5	9.9	22.0	22.2
电视节目自办套数(套)	Number of TV Programs with Ownership(set)	99	99	100	101	101	101
#公共电视	Public TV	99	99	100	101	101	101
电视节目制作时间(万小时)	Length of TV Programs Produced(10 000 hours)	3.71	3.98	3.74	4.35	3.10	4.61
公共电视节目播出时间(万小时)	Length of Public TV Programs Broadcasted (10 000 hours)	29.94	24.78	23.49	24.69	22.71	24.00
电视剧播出数(万部)	Number of TV Plays Broadcasted(10 000 sets)	0.30	0.27	0.26	0.30	0.26	0.26
#进口电视剧播出数(部)	Imported TV Plays(set)	355	153	84	140	127	115
电视剧播出数(万集)	Number of TV Plays Broadcasted(10 000 parts)	6.22	5.59	6.28	7.24	6.45	6.29
#进口电视剧播出数	Imported TV Plays	0.97	0.50	0.32	0.38	0.26	0.23

注：资料来源于省广电局(下表同)，广播电视台2011年及以前未含县级，2012年含县级。

Note:Data in the table are provided by the provinvial Radio and TV Administration(The relative tables in the chapter are the same).In 2011 and before, radio and television were excluding county, but they are including county in 2012.

21−8 广播、电视节目播出时间(2012)

Broadcasting Hours of Radio and Television Programs

单位：小时 (hour)

指 标	Item	全年 公共节目播出时间 Broadcasting Hours	#新闻咨询类节目 News	#专题服务类节目 Special Subject	#综合益智类节目 General Entertainment
广播电台	**All Radio Broadcasting Stations**	**208683**	**37862**	**50770**	**56684**
省 级	Province Level	60225	4429	17307	17105
地 级	Prefectural Level	116943	20075	27749	34911
县 级	County Level	31515	13358	4614	4668
电视台	**All Television Stations**	**240032**	**64758**	**25836**	**18376**
省 级	Province Level	59860	7587	10574	3135
地 级	Prefectural Level	121510	18391	11769	9985
县 级	County Level	58662	38780	3483	3256

21−9 图书出版

Number of Books Published

类 别	Sort	2007	2008	2009	2010	2011	2012
出版图书(种)	**Number of Publications(kind)**	**861**	**1549**	**943**	**830**	**856**	**966**
#新出版	New Publications	502	602	500	647	545	575
总印数(万册)	Printed Copies(10000 copies)	8626	10457	9263	8069	8492	7304
总印张数(万印张)	Printed Sheets(10000 sheets)	47107	39635	57032	55778	57278	48304

注：资料来源于省新闻出版局(以下相关表同)。
Note: The data in the table are provided by the provinvial Press and Publication Administration(The relative tables in the chapter are the same).

21-10 杂志出版

Number of Magazines Published

类　别	Sort	2007	2008	2009	2010	2011	2012
出版杂志(种)	**Number of Publications(kind)**	**87**	**88**	**89**	**88**	**88**	**88**
每期平均印数(万册)	Average Printed Copies Per Issue(10000 copies)	91	98	93	85	78	86
总印数(万册)	Printed Copies(10000 copies)	1376	1420	1358	1300	1413	1485
总印张数(万印张)	Printed Sheets(10000 sheets)	7784	8145	9243	7117	7257	7062

21-11 报纸出版

Number of Newspaper Published

类　别	Sort	2007	2008	2009	2010	2011	2012
出版报纸(种)	**Number of Publications(kind)**	**45**	**44**	**44**	**44**	**44**	**44**
每期平均印数(万份)	Average Printed Copies Per Issue(10000 copies)	135	138	149	162	175	174
总印数(万份)	Printed Copies(10000 copies)	34676	35110	36286	37004	44931	45032
总印张数(万印张)	Printed Sheets(10000 sheets)	129069	139002	142079	145831	200712	248813

21-12 报纸分类出版数量(2012)

Number of Newspaper Published by Category

类　别	Sort	出版报纸(种) Number of Public-ations (kind)	每期平均印数(万份) Average Publication Per Issue (10000 copies)	总印数(万份) Total Printed (10000 copies)	总印张数(万印张) Total Printed Sheets (10000 sheets)
总　计	**Total**	**44**	**174**	**45032**	**248813**
#贵州日报	Guizhou Daily	1	14.83	5427.96	14415.25
贵州都市报	Guizhou Urban Newspaper	1	18.47	6630.59	44548.68
贵阳晚报	Guiyang Evening Newspaper	1	27.79	9947.71	77636.60
文　摘	Tabloid	1	4.20	428.40	856.80
每周广播电视报	Broadcasting and Television Weekly Newspaper	1	1.68	87.36	393.12

21-13 体育运动员
Athletes

单位：人 (person)

指 标	Item	2007	2008	2009	2010	2011	2012
优秀运动员	**Excellent Athletes**	**244**	**136**	**145**	**145**	**189**	**173**
#女运动员	Female	66	49	50	50	67	66
专职教练员	**Full-time Coaches**	**200**	**207**	**215**	**215**	**219**	**167**
#女专职教练员	Female	52	52	56	56	61	46
等级运动员发展人数	**Number of Certified Athletes**	**213**	**256**	**332**	**450**	**488**	**511**
等级裁判员发展人数	**Number of Certified Referees**	**242**	**29**	**24**	**153**	**5130**	**939**

注：1.资料来源于省体育局(以下相关表同)。2.表中等级裁判员数据，2006和2007年为当年一级以上裁判员登记数，2008年后为当年发展数。

Note: 1.The data in the table are provided by the provinvial Sport Administration(The relative tables in the chapter are the same).2.The data of Referee in the table refers to data of current newly increase referee after 2008,it refers to data of current registrated Referees in the year 2006 and 2007.

21-14 体育运动获奖
Medals Won by Guizhou Athletes in Domestic and International Competitions

单位：项 (unit)

指 标	Item	2007	2008	2009	2010	2011	2012
国内外大赛第一名	Number of the First-Order	30	31	19	16	12	9
国内外大赛第二名	Number of the Second-Order	18	26	19	19	21	2
国内外大赛第三名	Number of the Third-Order	21	27	22	12	28	5

21-15 公共体育场地
Number of Public Stadiums and Gymnasiums

单位：个 (unit)

指　标	Item	2007	2008	2009	2010	2011	2012
总　计	**Total**	**21547**	**21547**	**21550**	**21588**	**21596**	**21601**
#体育场	Stadiums	49	49	52	56	61	61
体育馆	Gymnasiums	21	21	21	24	27	32
游泳池	Swimming Pools	89	89	89	90	90	90
有固定看台的灯光球场	Illuminated Fields with Fixed Seating	173	174	174	202	202	202

注：本表数据含全民健身场地数。
Note:The data in the table includes national fit-keeping fields in rural area.

21-16 群众体育活动
Activities of Mass Sports

指　标	Item	2007	2008	2009	2010	2011	2012
举办县级以上运动会(万次)	Number of Sports Meeting at County level and above(10000 times)	0.14	0.19	0.21	0.29	0.21	0.20
参加运动会的运动员(万人次)	Number of Athletes Attending Sports Meeting (10000 person-times)	203.12	283.14	210.86	323.13	410.12	298.52
青少年体育俱乐部(个)	Athletic Club for Youngsters(unit)	56	70	81	86	94	98
全民健身工程(条)	Body-building Activities of The Whole Nation(unit)	75	75	84	180	640	750

21-17 卫生事业
Health Care

指　标	Item	2007	2008	2009	2010	2011	2012
卫生机构(个)	**Number of Health Institutions(unit)**	**5907**	**5848**	**5736**	**5637**	**5683**	**27379**
#医院、卫生院	Hospitals and Township Hospitals	1939	1934	1982	2005	2071	2210
床位数(万张)	**Number of Beds(10000 beds)**	**7.58**	**8.31**	**9.75**	**10.53**	**11.75**	**13.65**
#医院、卫生院床位	Number of Hospital and Township Hospitals Beds	7.14	7.81	9.12	9.75	10.80	12.97
卫生人员合计(万人)	**Number of Employed Personnel in Health Care Institutions (10000 persons)**	**10.11**	**10.60**	**11.34**	**12.13**	**13.29**	**19.21**
#卫生技术人员	Medical Technical Personnels	8.53	8.93	9.53	10.25	11.22	12.98
#执业(助理)医师	Certified Doctors	4.21	3.88	4.02	4.22	4.40	4.92
#注册护士	Registered Nurse	2.65	2.86	3.18	3.60	4.16	4.87
医疗机构病床使用率(%)	**Utilization Rate in Medical Institutions(%)**	**75.9**	**79.3**	**79.8**	**79.7**	**79.6**	**83.2**
人均卫生费(元)	**Expenditure for Health of each Person(yuan)**			**729**	**947**	**1221**	**1580**
平均每千人拥有：	**Per 1000 Person：**						
床位数(张)	Beds(set)	2.07	2.30	2.73	3.00	2.77	3.21
#医院、卫生院床位	Number of Hospital Beds	1.95	2.16	2.56	2.78	2.55	3.05
卫生人员(人)	Number of Employed Personnel in Health Care Institutions(person)	2.76	2.93	3.18	3.46	3.14	4.52
#卫生技术人员	Medical Technical Personnels	2.33	2.47	2.67	2.92	2.65	3.06
#执业(助理)医师	Certified Doctors	1.15	1.07	1.13	1.20	1.04	1.12
医院服务情况	**Hospital Services**						
诊疗人次(万人次)	Visits (10000 person-times)	5012.44	2054.31	2413.97	2536.82	2910.53	3464.00
入院人数(万人)	Inpatients (10000 persons)	244.30	148.12	194.43	211.91	243.34	325.04
出院人数(万人)	Patients Discharged from Hospital (10000 persons)	244.77	147.29	193.14	208.93	240.59	320.49
每百门诊急诊入院人数（人）	Numer of Inpatients Per 100Outpatients and Emergency Cases (person)	6.70	7.40	8.40	8.50	8.70	9.75
病床使用率(%)	Utilization Rate of Beds (%)	75.9	79.3	84.0	86.4	87.1	89.11
出院者平均住院日(天)	Average Stay Days in Hospital(day)	10.10	9.80	9.40	9.70	9.20	8.90

注：1.资料来源于省卫生厅,表中数据2011年及以前的数据不含村卫生室,2012年起含村卫生室(以下相关表同)。2.医院服务情况2005年至2007年包括全部医疗机构，从2008年起指医院类别的医疗服务情况。3.每千人口指标2010年及以前以常住人口数为基数计算，2011年起以户籍人口数为基数计算。人均卫生费2009—2011年为测算数，2012年为推算数。

Note:1.Data in the table are provided from the Department of Health.In the year of 2011 and before data in this table exclude health clinics of village, but including health clinics of village in 2012(the same applies to the next table).2.The Hospital Services include all medical institutions from 2005 to 2007, but since 2008 only refer to hospitals' services.3.Indicators of per thousand population and expenditure for health of each Person were calculated by the permanent resident population before 2011,but that were calculated by the household registered population in 2011. Per capita health costs were estimated number in 2009 to 2011,but they are projections data in 2012.

21−18 卫生机构、床位、人员数(2012)

Number of Health Institutions,Beds and Personnels

类 别	Item	机构数(个) Institutions (unit)	床位数(张) Hospital Beds (Bed)	人员数(人) Number of Personels (person)	#卫生技术人员数 Medical Technical Personels
合 计	**Total Number of Institutions**	**27379**	**136542**	**192142**	**129823**
医 院	Hospitals	772	96502	99862	82113
市	City	351	50030	60495	49562
县	County	421	46472	39367	32551
综合医院	Genaral Hospital	600	75927	80297	66274
#县医院	Hospitals at County Level	70	20211	18645	16217
中医医院	Hospital Specialized in TCM	70	12205	11361	9636
中西医结合医院	Combine Hospitals of Chinese and Western Medicine	8	743	422	365
其他专科医院	Other Specialized Hospitals	89	7221	7447	5562
民族医院	Nationality Medicine Hospital	4	346	302	255
疗养院(所)	Sanitariums	2	268	226	190
社区卫生服务中心(站)	Total Health Service Centers for Community	468	4262	5429	4606
#社区卫生服务中心	Health Service Centers for Community	139	2379	2747	2314
社区卫生服务站	Health Service Stations for Community	329	1883	2682	2292
卫生院	Health Centers	1438	33168	26147	23180
#农村乡镇卫生院	Health Centers of Villages and Towns in Country	1436	33148	26113	23156
中心卫生院	Health Centers Focus Villages and Towns	557	18315	13440	11881
乡卫生院	Health Centers of Commonly Villages and Towns	879	14833	12673	11275
门诊部、诊所、医务室	Outpatient Department Clinic and Infirmary	2888		8236	7943
#私人办诊所	Private Clinique	2498		6836	6623
专科防治所(站)	Specialized Disease Prevention and Treatment Centers	7	440	202	162
疾控中心(卫生防疫站)	CDC(Epidemic Prevention Station)	101		4737	3627
#县疾控中心	CDC at County Level	71		2661	2225
卫生监督机构	Sanitation Supervise Centers	101		2141	1589
#县卫生监督机构	Sanitation Supervise Centers at County Level	68		1215	937
妇幼保健院(所、站)	MCH Center	96	3785	4216	3601
#县妇幼保健院(所、站)	MCH Centers at County level	58	1939	1936	1676
医学科学研究机构	Research Institution of Medicine Science	2		192	191
其他卫生机构	Other Health Project Institution	13		123	42
卫生部门	Health Department	2061	98100	105081	89479
工业及其他部门	Industrial and Other Department	22070	10453	59579	17940
集体所有制	Collective-owned	128	451	807	691
私人办	Private	3120	27538	26675	21713

21−19　卫生防疫防治和妇幼卫生事业
Sanitation and Epidemic Prevention,Maternity and Child Care

类　　别	Sort	2007	2008	2009	2010	2011	2012
防治所、站机构数(个)	**Prevention and Treatment Centers or Stations(unit)**	**8**	**8**	**8**	**8**	**9**	**7**
人员总数(人)	Number of Personnels(person)	155	158	182	186	243	202
#卫生技术人员数	Medical Technical Personnels	125	126	140	144	191	162
床位数(张)	Hospital Beds(bed)	136	144	213	199	280	440
卫生防疫机构数(个)	**Institutions of Sanitation and Antiepidemic Agencies(unit)**	**105**	**105**	**103**	**103**	**103**	**101**
人员总数(人)	Number of Personnels(person)	4674	4637	4643	4561	4542	4737
#卫生技术人员数(人)	Medical Technical Personnels(person)	3811	3787	3795	3689	3629	3627
妇幼保健机构合计(个)	**Institutions of Maternity and Child Care(unit)**	**90**	**90**	**88**	**89**	**94**	**96**
人员总数(人)	Number of Personnels(person)	3269	3322	3595	3692	3888	4216
#卫生技术人员数(人)	Medical Technical Personnels(person)	2742	2802	3060	3151	3341	3601
床位数(张)	**Hospital Beds(bed)**	**2176**	**2442**	**2928**	**3049**	**4398**	**3785**

21−20 县及县以上医院、卫生院(2012)

Basic Statistics on Hospitals and Health Centers at County Level and above

类 别	Sort	机构合计(个) Insti-tutions (unit)	诊疗人次数(万人次) Number of Visits and Inpatients (10000 person-times)	#门 诊(万人次) Number of Visits in Clinics (10000 person-times)	入院人数(万人次) Inpatients (10000 person -times)	出院人数(万人次) Outpatients (10000 person -times)
县及县以上医院合计	**Hospitals at County Level and above**	**772**	**3464.00**	**3334.77**	**325.04**	**320.49**
#综合医院	Comprehensive Hospitals	600	2805.69	2711.64	267.85	263.06
中医医院	Hospital of Chinese Medicine	70	468.25	447.47	37.81	38.12
妇幼保健院(所、站)	**Maternity and Child Care Hospital(Centers orStations)**	**96**	**251.18**	**235.17**	**17.80**	**16.91**
#妇幼保健院	Maternity and Child Care Hospital	30	195.15	183.56	13.60	12.80
卫生院合计	**Township Hospitals**	**1438**	**2060.73**	**1930.57**	**196.55**	**200.56**
#农村乡镇卫生院	Rural Township Hospitals	1436	2060.62	1930.46	196.55	200.56
中心卫生院	Central Township Hospitals	557	1060.63	994.71	107.64	109.88
乡卫生院	Ecumenic Township Hospitals	879	999.98	935.75	88.91	90.68

21−20 续表 continued

类 别	Sort	平均开放病床数(张) Average Sickbeds Setup (bed)	病床周转次数(次/年) Turnover of Beds (time/year)	病床工作日(日) Number of Days Per Bed in Use (day)	病床使用率(%) Utili-zation Rate of Beds(%)	出院者平均住院日(天) Average Stay Days in Hospital (day)	每100次门(急)诊入院人数(人) Hospital Admissions Per 100 Out-Patient Times and Emergency Patient-Times (person)
县及县以上医院合计	**Hospitals at and above County Level**	**91406.0**	**35.1**	**326.1**	**89.11**	**8.9**	**9.75**
#综合医院	Comprehensive Hospitals	72158.5	36.5	329.5	90.02	8.5	9.88
#中医医院	Hospital of Chinese Medicine	11369.0	33.5	328.4	89.74	9.6	8.45
妇幼保健院(所、站)	**Maternity and Child Care Hospital(Centers orstations)**	**3582.9**	**47.2**	**270.3**	**73.86**	**5.6**	**7.57**
#妇幼保健院	Maternity and Child Care Hospital	2398.8	53.4	318.5	87.01	6.0	7.41
卫生院合计	**Township Hospitals**	**31572.6**	**63.5**	**257.2**	**70.27**	**3.8**	**10.18**
#农村乡镇卫生院	Rural Township Hospitals	31552.6	63.6	257.3	70.31	3.8	10.18
中心卫生院	Central Township Hospitals	17521.2	62.7	260.3	71.13	3.9	10.82
乡卫生院	Ecumenic Township Hospitals	14031.4	64.6	253.6	69.30	3.7	9.50

21-21 县、乡、村三级医疗、预防、保健

Health Organization at County,Town and Village Level

指标	Item	2007	2008	2009	2010	2011	2012	2012年比2011年增长(%) Increase Rate in 2012 over 2011(%)
县医院个数(个)	**Number of Hospitals at County Level(unit)**	**69**	**72**	**70**	**70**	**70**	**77**	**10.0**
平均每院病床数(张)	Average Number of Beds Per Hospital(bed)	159.32	173.69	211.40	230.01	242.36	278.74	**15.0**
平均每院人员数(人)	Average Personnels Per Hospital(person)	173.60	171.20	180.11	193.10	233.37	258.26	**10.7**
#平均每院卫生技术人员数	Average Medical Technical Personnels Per Hospital	146.49	146.17	155.79	167.53	203.16	224.81	**10.7**
县妇幼保健院(所、站)机构数(个)	**Maternity and Child Care Centers at County Level (unit)**	**67**	**62**	**61**	**58**	**57**	**58**	**1.8**
平均每院(所、站)床位数(张)	Average Number of Beds Per Station (bed)	17.85	20.60	23.72	26.91	28.54	33.43	**17.1**
平均每院(所、站)人员数 (人)	Average Personnels Per Station (person)	26.95	26.40	27.39	28.98	30.49	33.38	**9.5**
#每院(所、站)卫生技术人员数	Medical Technical Personnels Per Stati on	23.32	22.73	23.98	25.47	26.91	33.38	**24.0**
县卫生防疫站机构数(个)	**Institutions of Epidemic Prevention Station at County Level(unit)**	**77**	**70**	**69**	**69**	**69**	**71**	**2.9**
平均每所站人员数(人)	Personnels Per Station(person)	36.74	34.40	35.06	35.01	35.14	37.48	**6.6**
#平均每站卫生技术人员数	Average Medical Technical Personnels Per Station	31.26	29.20	29.94	29.83	29.45	31.34	**6.4**
农村乡镇卫生院机构数(个)	**Institutions of Rural Township Hospitals(unit)**	**1451**	**1448**	**1439**	**1437**	**1436**	**1438**	**0.1**
农村乡镇卫生院床位数 (张)	Number of Beds of Rural Township Hospitals(bed)	19136	21201	25841	28123	29541	33148	**12.2**
平均每院床位数(张)	Average Number of Beds Per Hospital(bed)	13.19	14.64	17.96	19.57	20.57	23.05	**12.1**
平均每千农业人口乡镇卫生院床位数(张)	Average Number of Beds of Rural Township Hospitals Per 1000 Rural Personnels(bed)	0.57	0.65	0.75	0.80	0.83	0.93	12.3
农村乡镇卫生院人员数(人)	Personnels of Rural Township Hospitals (person)	19257	19531	20317	20893	23047	26113	13.3
平均每院人员数(人)	Average Personnels Per Hospital(person)	13.27	13.49	14.12	14.54	16.05	18.16	13.1
平均每千农业人口乡镇卫生院人员数(人)	Average Medical Technical Personnels of Rural Township Hospitals Per 1000 Rural Personnels(person)	0.58	0.60	0.59	0.59	0.65	0.73	13.1
村卫生室个数(个)	**Number of Villages with Medical Treatment Sations(unit)**	**19057**	**19031**	**18971**	**19783**	**20260**	**21445**	**5.8**
村卫生室覆盖率(%)	Coverage Rate of Township Hospitals(%)	96.9	96.1	88.3	90.1	93.8	100.0	6.2
开展合作医疗的村数(个)	Number of Villages of Carrying out Rural Cooperative Medical Treatment(unit)	19669	19803	17568	17672	17583	18099	2.9
开展合作医疗的村覆盖率(%)	Coverage Rate of Villages of Carrying out Rural Cooperative Medical Treatment(%)	100.0	100.0	100.0	100.0	100.0	100.0	持平
平均每村设置医疗点数(个)	Average Number of Medical Treatment Stations Per Village(unit)	0.97	0.96	1.08	1.12	1.15	1.18	2.4
乡村医生和卫生员数(人)	Doctors and Health Workers(person)	27073	25469	32450	31517	34587	37760	9.2
#乡村医生所占比例(%)	Proportion of Rural Doctors(%)	82.1	83.0	71.6	78.0	76.7	73.4	-3.3
平均每村乡村医生和卫生员数(人)	Average Number of Doctors and Health Workers Per Village(person)	1.37	1.29	1.85	1.78	1.97	2.09	6.1
平均每千农业人口乡村医生和卫生员数(人)	Average Number of Doctors and Health Workers Per 1000 Rural Personnels (person)	0.81	0.78	0.95	0.90	0.97	1.06	9.0

注：2008年及以前的"村卫生室覆盖率"=村卫生室个数/行政村数，2009年后"村卫生室覆盖率"=设置村卫生室的村数/行政村总数。

Note:Before 2008,"the coverage rate of township hospitals"=number of village medical treatment sations/the number of administrative villages, While after 2009,"the coverage rate of township hospitals"=number of villages with medical treatment sations/the number of administrative villages.

21-22　28种传染病报告发病及死亡人数(2012)
List of 28 Infectious Diseases Reported and Number of Death

单位：人　(person)

顺位 No.	发病 Diseases 疾病名称 Diseases	发病人数 Persons	死亡 Death 疾病名称 Diseases	死亡人数 Persons
1	肺结核 Pulmonary Tuberculosis	45546	艾滋病 AIDS	333
2	病毒性肝炎 Viral Hepatitis	25348	肺结核 Pulmonary Tuberculosis	247
3	梅毒 Syphilis	7761	狂犬病 Hydrophobia	101
4	细菌性和阿米巴性痢疾 Dysentery	6025	乙脑 Encephalitis B	8
5	淋病 Gonorrhea	1224	新生儿破伤风 Newborn Tetanus	7
6	伤寒副伤寒 Typhoid and Paratyphoid Fever	853	病毒性肝炎 Viral Hepatitis	6
7	艾滋病 AIDS	757	梅毒 Syphilis	3
8	猩红热 Scarlet Fever	606	细菌性和阿米巴　性痢疾 Dysentery	2
9	流行性乙型脑炎 Encephalitis B	156	钩端螺旋体病 Leptospirosis	2
10	狂犬病 Hydrophobia	113	流行性脑脊髓膜炎 Epidemic Encephalitis	1
11	流行性出血热 Hemorrhage Fever	94	流行性出血热 Hemorrhage Fever	1
12	百日咳 Pertussis	59	人感染高致病性　禽流感 Highly Pathogenic Bird Flu	1
13	麻疹 Measles	31	淋病 Gonorrhea	1
14	钩端螺旋体病 Leptospirosis	30	伤寒副伤寒 Typhoid and Paratyphoid Fever	
15	新生儿破伤风 Newborn Tetanus	29	疟疾 Malaria	
16	疟疾 Malaria	15	麻疹 Measles	
17	甲型H1N1流感 A(H1N1)Flu	12	甲型H1N1流感 A(H1N1)Flu	
18	布鲁氏菌病 Brucellosis	11	炭疽 Anthrax	
19	流行性脑脊髓膜炎 Epidemic Encephalitis	9	鼠疫 The Plague	
20	炭疽 Anthrax	2	血吸虫病 Schistosomiasis	
21	人感染高致病性禽流感 Highly Pathogenic Bird Flu	1	百日咳 Pertussis	
22	血吸虫病 Schistosomiasis		布鲁氏菌病 Brucellosis	
23	霍乱 Cholera		猩红热 Scarlet Fever	
24	鼠疫 The Plague		登革热 Dengue Fever	
25	登革热 Dengue Fever		霍乱 Cholera	
26	传染性非典型肺炎 SARS		传染性非典型肺炎 SARS	
27	脊髓灰质炎 Poliomyelitis		脊髓灰质炎 Poliomyelitis	
28	白喉 Diphtheria		白喉 Diphtheria	

21-23 28种传染病报告发病率、死亡率及病死率(2012)
List of Incidence,Death and Mortality Rates of 28 Infectious Disease Reported

顺位 No.	发病 Disease Incidence		死亡 Death		病死 Mortality Rate	
	疾病名称 Diseases	发病率 (1/10万) Incidence (1/100 000)	疾病名称 Diseases	死亡率 (1/10万) Death Rate (1/100 000)	疾病名称 Diseases	病死率 (%) Mortality Rate(%)
1	肺结核 Pulmonary Tuberculosis	131.2944	狂犬病 Hydrophobia	0.3027	人禽流感 Highly Pathogenic Bird Flu	100.0000
2	病毒性肝炎 Viral Hepatitis	73.0701	艾滋病 AIDS	0.9599	狂犬病 Hydrophobia	92.9204
3	梅毒 Syphilis	22.3725	肺结核 Pulmonary Tuberculosis	0.7120	艾滋病 AIDS	43.6400
4	细菌性和阿米巴性痢疾 Dysentery	17.3681	流行性乙型脑炎 Encephalitis B	0.0231	新生儿破伤风 Newborn Tetanus	24.1379
5	淋病 Gonorrhea	3.5284	肝 炎 Viral Hepatitis	0.0173	流脑 Epidemic Encephalitis	11.1111
6	伤寒+副伤寒 Typhoid and Paratyphoid Fever	2.4589	新生儿破伤风 Newborn Tetanus	0.0142	钩体病 Leptospirosis	6.6667
7	艾滋病 AIDS	2.1995	梅毒 Syphilis	0.0086	乙脑 Encephalitis B	5.1282
8	猩红热 Scarlet Fever	1.7469	细菌性和阿米巴性痢疾 Dysentery	0.0058	出血热 Hemorrhage Fever	1.0638
9	流行性乙型脑炎 Encephalitis B	0.4497	流脑 Epidemic Encephalitis	0.0029	肺结核 Pulmonary Tuberculosis	0.5423
10	狂犬病 Hydrophobia	0.3257	流行性出血热 Hemorrhage Fever	0.0029	淋病 Gonorrhea	0.0817
11	流行性出血热 Hemorrhage Fever	0.2710	人禽流感 Highly Pathogenic Bird Flu	0.0029	梅毒 Syphilis	0.0387
12	百日咳 Pertussis	0.1701	淋病 Gonorrhea	0.0029	痢疾 Dysentery	0.0332
13	麻疹 Measles	0.0894	伤寒+副伤寒 Typhoid and Paratyphoid Fever		病毒性肝炎 Viral Hepatitis	0.0237
14	钩端螺旋体病 Leptospirosis	0.0865	疟疾 Malaria		炭疽 Anthrax	
15	新生儿破伤风 Newborn Tetanus	0.0590	甲型H1N1流感 A(H1N1)Flu		甲型H1N1流感 A(H1N1)Flu	
16	疟疾 Malaria	0.0432	炭疽 Anthrax		鼠疫 The Plague	
17	甲型H1N1流感 A(H1N1)Flu	0.0346	麻疹 Measles		麻疹 Measles	
18	布鲁氏菌病 Brucellosis	0.0317	血吸虫病 Schistosomiasis		疟疾 Malaria	
19	流脑 Epidemic Encephalitis	0.0259	鼠疫 The Plague		百日咳 Pertussis	
20	炭疽 Anthrax	0.0058	百日咳 Pertussis		血吸虫病 Schistosomiasis	
21	人禽流感 Highly Pathogenic Bird Flu	0.0029	淋病 Gonorrhea		伤寒+副伤寒 Typhoid and Paratyphoid Fever	
22	登革热 Dengue Fever		布鲁氏菌病 Brucellosis		布病 Brucellosis	
23	血吸虫病 Schistosomiasis		猩红热 Scarlet Fever		猩 红 热 Scarlet Fever	
24	鼠疫 The Plague		登革热 Dengue Fever		登革热 Dengue Fever	
25	霍乱 Cholera		霍乱 Cholera		霍 乱 Cholera	
26	传染性非典型肺炎 SARS		传染性非典型肺炎 SARS		传染性非典型肺炎 SARS	
27	脊灰 Poliomyelitis		脊灰 Poliomyelitis		脊 灰 Poliomyelitis	
28	白喉 Diphtheria		白喉 Diphtheria		白 喉 Diphtheria	

21–24 5岁以下儿童和孕产妇死亡率

Mortality Rate of the Maternal and Children Aged under 5

指标	Item	2007	2008	2009	2010	2011	2012
新生儿死亡率(‰)	**Newborn Mortality Rate(‰)**	**13.2**	**12.7**	**12.2**	**7.1**	**5.1**	**5.9**
城 市	Urban	7.2	5.6	6.6	6.3	4.7	4.9
农 村	Rural	15.8	14.9	13.9	7.3	5.1	6.8
婴儿死亡率(‰)	**Infant Mortality Rate(‰)**	**21.2**	**21.1**	**17.7**	**11.9**	**8.6**	**11.4**
城 市	Urban	10.4	11.0	9.4	10.9	8.4	6.8
农 村	Rural	25.4	24.3	20.3	12.2	8.9	13.8
5岁以下儿童死亡率(‰)	**Mortality Rate of Children under 5(‰)**	**27.3**	**27.1**	**22.3**	**15.0**	**11.2**	**15.1**
城 市	Urban	12.7	13.0	11.8	14.0	10.8	8.1
农 村	Rural	31.9	31.5	25.6	15.3	11.3	18.7
孕产妇死亡率(1/10万)	**Maternal Mortality Rate(1/100 000)**	**62.6**	**67.3**	**49.8**	**35.4**	**24.5**	**32.0**
城 市	Urban	56.6	51.6	42.8	35.7	30.2	32.0
农 村	Rural	62.3	70.6	51.0	35.3	22.5	34.2

注：2010–2011年的数据取自妇幼卫生年报表，其余数据源自妇幼卫生监测数据。

Note:Data were obtained from the Annual Report of Maternal and Child Health in 2010 to 2011.The remaining data are from maternal and child health surveillance data

21–25 新型农村合作医疗

Conditions of New Cooperative Medical System

指标	Indicator	2007	2008	2009	2010	2011	2012
开展新农合县（市、区、特区)数(个)	Number of Counties Implementing of NCMS (unit)	88	88	88	88	88	88
参加新农合人数(万人)	Number of Enrollees(100 million persons)	2608.93	2831.87	2912.38	3029.17	3074.80	3112.21
参合率(%)	Enrollment Rate(%)	84.9	92.1	94.3	96.3	97.1	98.0
当年筹资总额(亿元)	Total Fund Raised at Current Year (100 million yuan)	12.63	25.15	30.13	44.35	68.73	90.25
人均筹资(元)	Per Capita Premiums(yuan)	50	90	100	140	230	290
当年基金支出(亿元)	Payout at Current Year(100 million yuan)	8.11	16.21	30.78	37.12	52.25	85.75
补偿受益人次(万人次)	Number of Beneficiaries from Reimbursement (100 million person-times)	1314.90	1874.61	3573.96	3949.88	4408.91	4890.82

主要统计指标解释

文化事业机构 指由文化部门主办或实行行业管理的文化及相关产业机构以及由文化部门主办的非文化及相关产业机构等。

艺术表演团体 指由文化部门主办或实行行业管理（经文化行政部门审批并领取营业性演出许可证），专门从事表演艺术等活动的各类专业艺术表演团体，含民间职业剧团（不包括群众业余文艺表演团队）。

电影放映单位 指具有放映机器设备、固定或不固定的放映场所与专职或兼职的放映技术人员，经有关部门登记批准，经常为一定的观众对象放映电影的机构。包括经批准对外开放进行营业，并与电影发行放映管理机构分帐的专用放映单位和军委系统租片单位。

艺术表演观众人数（人次） 指在国内和国外的艺术表演的观众人数。包括售票、包场等有演出收入的场次人数和政府采购的公益性演出场次人数及参加汇演、调演等无演出收入的公开演出场次人数，包括流动舞台车演出场次人数，不包括彩排和内部观摩等无演出收入的场次人数。

广播节目综合人口覆盖率 指根据国家广电总局制定的《广播电视人口覆盖率统计技术标准和方法》进行统计调查的，在对象区内采用无线、有线、卫星等技术手段能够收听到包括中央、省、地市、县广播节目其中任意一套的人口数占全国总人口数的百分比。

电视节目综合人口覆盖率 指根据国家广电总局制定的《广播电视人口覆盖率统计技术标准和方法》进行统计调查的，在对象区内采用无线、有线、卫星等技术手段能够收看到包括中央、省、地市、县级电视节目中任意一套的人口数占全国总人口数的百分比。

等级运动员人数 指经考核正式批准授予等级运动员称号的人数。运动员等级分为国际级运动健将、运动健将、一级运动员、二级运动员。

等级裁判员人数 指经考核正式批准授予等级裁判员称号的人数。裁判员等级分为国际级裁判员、国家级裁判员、一级裁判员、二级裁判员。

体育场 指有400米跑道（中心含足球场），有固定道牙，跑道6条以上，并有固定看台的室外田径场地。体育场按看台容纳观众人数分为：甲级25000人以上，乙级15000-25000人，丙级5000-15000人，丁级5000人以下。

体育馆 指有固定看台，可供篮球、排球、羽毛球、乒乓球、体操等项目训练比赛活动用的室内运动场地。体育馆按看台容纳观众人数分为：甲级6000人以上，乙级4000-6000人，丙级2000-4000人，丁级2000人以下。

医疗卫生机构 指从卫生行政部门取得《医疗机构执业许可证》或从民政、工商行政、机构编制管理部门取得法人单位登记证书，为社会提供医疗服务、公共卫生服务或从事医学科研和在职培训等工作的单位。医疗卫生机构包括医院、基层医疗卫生机构（卫生服务中心（站）、乡镇（街道）卫生院、村卫生室、门诊部、诊所（卫生所、医务室））、专业公共卫生机构（疾病预防控制中心、专科疾病防治机构、妇幼保健机构、健康教育机构、急救中心（站）、采供血机构、卫生监督机构、取得医疗机构执业许可证的计划生育技术服务中心）、其他医疗卫生机构（疗养院、临床检验中心（所、站）、医学科研机构、医学在职教育机构、卫生监督（监测、检测）机构、医学考试中心、农村改水中心、人才交流中心、统计信息中心等卫生事业单位）。

医疗机构 指从卫生行政部门取得《医疗机构执业许可证》或从民政、工商行政、机构编制管理部门取得法人单位登记证书，为社会提供医疗服务的单位。包括医院、疗养院、社区卫生服务中心（站）、乡镇（街道）卫生院、村卫生室、门诊部、诊所（卫生所、医务室）、急救中心（站）、妇幼保健院（所、站）、专科疾病防治院（所、站）、临床检验中心（所、站）。

医院 包括综合医院、中医医院、中西医结合医院、民族医院、各类专科医院和护理院。包括医学院校附属医院，不包括专科疾病防治院、妇幼保健院和疗养院。

社区卫生服务中心（站） 指为本社区居民提供预防、医疗、保健、康复、健康教育、计划生育技术服务等的基层卫生机构。包括社区卫生服务中心和社区卫生服务站。

执业医师 指具有《医师执业证》及其“级别”为“执业医师”且实际从事临床工作的人员，不包括取得执业证书但从事管理工作的人员（如院长、书记等）。执业医师类别分为临床、中医、口腔和公共卫生。

执业助理医师 指具有《医师执业证》及其“级别”为“执业助理医师”且实际从事临床工作的人员，不包括取得执业证书但从事管理工作的人员。执业助理医师类别分为临床、中医、口腔和公共卫生。

甲乙类法定报告传染病发病率　指某年某地区每10万人口中甲、乙类法定报告传染病发病情况。即：

$$甲乙类法定报告传染病发病率=\frac{甲、乙类法定报告传染病发病数\times 10万}{人口数\times 10万}。$$

孕产妇死亡率　$孕产妇死亡率=\frac{该年该地区孕产妇死亡人数\times 10万}{某年某地区活产数\times 10万}。$

5岁以下儿童死亡率　$5岁以下儿童死亡率=\frac{该年该地区5岁以下儿童死亡人数}{某年某地活产数}\times 1000‰。$

新生儿死亡率　指某地区一年内出生未满28天（0—27天）的新生儿死亡人数与该地区当年全部活产数的比率。

$$新生儿死亡率=\frac{该年该地新生儿死亡人数}{某年某地活产数}\times 1000‰。$$

参加新农合人数　指根据本地新农合的实施方案，到本年度新农合筹资截止时，已缴纳参加新农合资金的人口数。

卫生技术人员　包括执业医师、执业助理医师、注册护士、药师（士）、检验及影像技师（士）、卫生监督员和见习医（药、护、技）师（士）等卫生专业人员（不包括药剂员、检验员、护理员等），不包括从事管理工作的卫生技术人员（如院长、副院长、党委书记等）。其中见习医师（士）指毕业于高中等院校医学专业但尚未取得医师执业证书的医师和医士。

Explanatory Notes on Main Statistical Indicators

Cultural Institutions defined by the cultural industry management department sponsored or cultural institutions and related industries as well as non-organized by the cultural sector and related industries and cultural institutions.

Art Troupe defined by the cultural industry management department sponsored or carried (by the cultural administrative departments for approval and obtain business performance license), specializing in the performing arts and other activities of the various professional performing arts groups, including the professional troupes (Excluding the masses of amateur theatrical performance team).

Film Projection Units refer to units with film projection equipment, full or part time projectionists, permanent or non permanent places, approved by related administrative departments to show films regularly for certain groups of audience, including those film projection units which have been approved to give commercial shows and run business with independent accounting system as well as those film renting units of the military system.

Number of Spectators at Art Performance refers to the domestic and foreign performing arts attendance. Including ticketing, private use, which are the number of performances and screenings of revenue for government procurement and participation in the number of public performances show and other non-public performances show the number of performances, including the number of mobile stage vehicle, not including rehearsals and internal observation and other the number of non-performing income screenings.

Radio Coverage of Population refers to the percentage of population, which can listen to one of central, provincial, city, prefecture, and county radio programs by wireless, cable, satellite and other technical means, in the surveying area, to national total population, according to Statistical Standard and Method on Television and Radio Coverage of Population established by the State Administration of Broadcasting, Film and Television.

Television Coverage of Population refers to the percentage of population, which can watch one of central, provincial, city, prefecture, and county television programs by wireless, cable, satellite and other technical means, in the surveying area, to national total population, according to Statistical Standard and Method on Television and Radio Coverage of Population established by the State Administration of Broadcasting, Film and Television.

Number of Athletes in Grades refers to the number of athletes who have been given titles through examination. The titles of athletes include international masters of sports, masters of sports, first-grade and second-grade.

Number of Referees in Grades refers to the number of referees who have been given titles after examination. They are classified as international referees, national referees and referees of the first and second grades.

Stadiums refer to stadiums for track and field events with six lane 400-meter tracks around soccer fields, permanent track marks and permanent bleachers. Stadiums are classified according to seating capacity. They include: Class A stadiums seating 25000 people each. Class B stadiums seating 15000 to 25000 people each. Class C stadiums seating 5000 to 15000 people each, and Class D stadiums seating fewer than 5000 people.

Gymnasiums refer to indoor sports grounds with permanent seats in which basketball, volleyball. badminton, table tennis and gymnastics competitions can be held. Gymnasiums are classified according to seating capacity. They include Class A gymnasiums seating over 6000 people. Class B gymnasiums seating 4000 to 6000 people. Class C gymnasiums seating 2000 to 4000 people, and Class D gymnasiums seating fewer than 2000 people.

Health Care Institutions refer to the units which have been qualified the Certification of Health Care Institution by the administration of public health, or qualified the Certification of Corporate Unit by the civil affairs, administration for industry and commerce, commission office for public sector reform, and engaging in medical care, disease prevention and control, health supervision and inspection, medicine research and health education, etc., including: hospitals, sanatoriums, community health service centers (stations), health centers, clinics (health stations and infirmaries), first-aid centers (stations), blood gathering and supplying institutions, women and children care agencies (centers and stations), special disease prevention and curing agencies (centers and stations), disease prevention and control centers (epidemic prevention stations), health supervision and inspection agencies, sanitary inspection institutions, medicinal scientific research and on-job training institutions, health education centers and so on.

Medical Organizations refer to the institutions which have been qualified the Certification of Health Care Institution by the administration of public health, or qualified the Certification of Corporate Unit by the civil affairs, administration for industry and commerce, commission office for public sector reform and engaging in medical care, including: hospitals, sanatoriums, community health service centers (stations), health centers, clinics (health stations and infirmaries), women and children care agencies (centers and stations), special disease prevention and curing agencies (centers and stations), first-aid centers (stations) and clinic inspection centers.

Hospitals include: polyclinics, traditional Chinese medical hospitals, hospitals integrated with traditional Chinese therapeutics and western therapeutics, ethical hospitals, various specialties hospitals and nursing hospitals, including medical colleges affiliated hospitals, but excluding specialized prevention and treatment hospital and health centers and nursing homes.

Community Health Service Centers (stations) refer to the primary units that provide the health care for community residents, such as disease prevention and control, medical treatment, health care, rehabilitation, health education, family planning technical services, including community health service centers and community health service stations.

Licensed Doctors refer to the medical workers who have obtained the licenses of qualified doctors and are employed in medical treatment, disease prevention or healthcare institutions, excluding the licensed doctors engaged in management job. The classification of licensed doctors is clinician, Chinese medicine, dentist and public health.

Licensed Assistant Doctors refer to the medical workers who have obtained the licenses of qualified assistant doctors and are employed in medical treatment, disease prevention or healthcare institutions, excluding the licensed assistant doctors engaged in management job. The classification of licensed assistant doctors is clinician, Chinese medicine, dentist and public health.

Incidence Rate of Notifiable Infectious Diseases refer to the incidence cases notifiable class A and class B infectious diseases per 100 thousand population in the reference region in the reference year. The formula is:

$$\text{Incidence Rate of Notifiable Infectious Diseases}=\frac{\text{Incidence Cases Notifiable Class A and Class B Infectious Diseases} \times 100{,}000}{\text{Population} \times 100{,}000}.$$

Maternal Mortality Rate $\text{Maternal Mortality Rate}=\frac{\text{number of maternal deaths} \times 100{,}000}{\text{live births} \times 100{,}000}.$

Mortality Rate of Children under 5 $\text{Mortality Rate of Children under 5}=\frac{\text{death number of children under 5}}{\text{live birth}} \times 1000‰.$

Newborn Mortality Rate refers to the ratio of neonatal deaths of new birth under the age of 28 days (0-27 days) in a year of the region to the total number of live births of this region.

$$\text{Newborn Mortality Rate}=\frac{\text{death number of newborn}}{\text{live birth}} \times 1000‰.$$

Number of Persons Participated in the New Rural Cooperative Medical System refers to the number of persons who have given payment to the new cooperative medical system by the deadline of fundraising during the year according to the implementation plan of the new system.

Medical Technical Personnel refers to practicing physicians, practicing physician assistant, registered nurses, pharmacists (who), inspection and imaging technician (who), health supervisors and trainee doctors (medicine, nursing, technology) division (disabilities) and other health professionals (not including pharmacy staff , inspectors, care workers, etc.), not including those engaged in the management of health and technical personnel (such as president, vice president, party secretary, etc.). The trainee doctors (who) refers graduated from high school and other institutions but has not yet obtained physician medical specialty physicians and healers practicing certificate.

22

Twenty-two

社会服务及其他

Social Services and Others

22-1 律师、公证、调解工作

Basic Statistics on Lawyers,Notarization and Mediation

指　标	Item	2007	2008	2009	2010	2011	2012
律师工作	**Lawyers**						
法律律师事务所(个)	Number of Law Offices(unit)	196	206	222	244	267	286
专职律师(人)	Full-time Lawyers(person)	1421	1371	1562	1809	2030	2359
辅助工作人员(人)	Assistant(person)	386	693	829	952	879	468
聘请常年法律顾问(个)	Number of Permanent Legal Advisors(person)	2052	2366	5726	7392	8973	4708
全年办理(件)	Number of Cases in Whole Year(case)	82019	59379	79533	81398	84788	78097
刑事案件诉讼代理	Agent of Criminal Cases	6271	6301	7011	6532	5698	5882
民事诉讼代理	Agent of Civil Cases	11672	12397	12966	13437	14156	16969
行政诉讼代理	Agent of Administrative Action	588	438	429	572	431	627
经济案件诉讼代理	Agent of Economic Cases	5828	4180	4463	5300	5783	6049
非诉讼法律事务	Agent of Non-litigious Legal Affairs	1484	1445	1062	1367	1860	1569
解答法律询问	Agent of Legal Advisory Services	52009	33637	52070	52623	55172	53228
代写法律事务文书	Agent of Legal Document Written on Behalf of Clients	9264	4632	5518	6076	6620	8650
调解成功	Successful Mediation	731	529	477	791	851	3792
公证工作	**Notarization**						
公证处(个)	Number of Notarial Offices(unit)	97	97	97	97	97	97
公证员(人)	Notaries(person)	173	164	189	226	256	230
公证辅助人员(人)	Notarial Assistant(person)	58	106	56	92	63	77
办理公证文书(件)	Number of Notarized Documents(case)	79498	76217	156768	79398	75353	77937
#经济合同公证	Notarized Documents on Economic Affairs	27326	25431	22323	17630	15335	20924
#涉外公证	Foreign-related Notarization	10544	10237	35823	10189	10023	11046
国内公证	Domestic Notarization	67471	52988	93941	67451	63482	45967
公证费收入(万元)	Income of Notarization(10000 yuan)	2072	1027	1596	935	1280	1263
人民调解工作	**People's Mediation**						
人民调解委员会(个)	Number of People's Mediation Committees(unit)	23762	23762	23762	22275	22976	22498
人民调解人员(人)	Number of Mediators(person)	111707	105060	111068	109270	115699	115315
调解民间纠纷(件)	Number of Civil Disputes Mediated(case)	113531	98515	113568	134667	198778	184749
调解成功率(%)	The Rate of Success of Mediation(%)	96.0	95.9	95.2	97.1	96.7	95.7
基层法律服务工作	**Law Service at Basic Level**						
法律服务所(个)	Offices for Law Service(unit)	567	501	485	484	451	477
法律工作者(人)	Law Staffs(person)	2372	2241	2103	2138	1431	1774
代理案件(件)	Cases Deputed(case)	11128	11699	13817	9914	12654	12691
避免经济损失(万元)	Number of Avoided Economical Loss(10000 yuan)	15931	15448	14010	12472	24869	21853
刑释解教人员安置帮教工作	**Settling and Assisting and Teaching Work for People That Has Been Released After Serving a Sentence**						
设立工作机构(个)	Institutions Established(unit)	99	96	98	99	99	102
工作人员(人)	Staffs(person)	1498	313	457	279	194	197
安置人数(人)	Number of Persons Settled Down(person)	15945	14701	15029	16973	24209	14764
帮教人数(人)	Number of Persons Assisted and Teached(person)	14547	15715	15150	15794	27642	33598

注：资料来源于省司法厅(下表同)。
Note:Data in the table are obtained from provinvial department of justice(the same applies to the next table).

22-2 国内公证文书分类

Domestic Notarial Documents by Type

单位：件 (piece)

指 标	Item	2012
总 计	**Total**	**46248**
经济合同(协议)合计	**Total Economic contracts (agreements)**	**19387**
买卖合同(购销、房屋买卖)	Contract of sale (purchase and sales, house sale)	2513
企业经营合同(联营合同、企业租赁、资产经营责任制)	Business Contracts (joint venture contract, corporate leasing, asset management responsibility)	167
借款合同(贷款)	Loan Agreement (Loan)	13197
劳务(劳动)合同	Labor (labor) Contract	41
建筑工程合同(建筑工程承包)	Construction Contracts (Construction Contract)	22
承包合同(农林牧副渔承包、工商服务承包、乡镇企业承包)	Contract (agriculture, forestry, animal husbandry and fisherycontracting, business services contracting, township enterprises contracting)	
租赁合同(财产租赁、房屋租赁)	Lease Contract (property lease, rental)	101
扶养协议(遗赠扶养协议、赡养协议)	Support Agreement(Legacy support agreement, maintenance agreement)	181
出国留学协议(留学协议)	Study abroad agreement(Study protocol)	37
其他(其他民事协议、计划生育)	Other (Other Civil Agreements,Planned Parenthood)	3128
民事法律关系公证合计	**Total civil legal relations Notary**	**9080**
收养关系(收养、解除收养)	Adoptive Relationship (adoption, termination of adoptive)	36
继承(继承权)	Inherit(Inheritance)	7957
财产权(产权、宅基地使用权)	Property rights (property， land use rights)	412
亲属关系	Kinship	671
组织资格(法人(代表)资格)	Organization Qualifications(Legal (Representative) Qualification)	4
单方法律行为	**Unilateral legal acts(By the end of 2012 after the Justice Department modified statistical reports,the notarial matters were classified)**	
委托(委托书、法人委托书)	Delegate (power of attorney, power of attorney)	10355
声明(声明书)	Statement	7326
赠与(赠与书)	handsel(Gift book)	3549
遗嘱	testament	17731
现场监督类	**Site supervision class**	
招标投标	Bidding	50

22-3 消费者协会受理投诉

Cases Accepted and Heard by Consumer Association

单位：件 (piece)

指　　标	Item	2007	2008	2009	2010	2011	2012
总　　计	**Total**	**9333**	**7900**	**8099**	**5981**	**4986**	**3931**
#家用电器类	Household Appliances	2021	2192	1935	1517	1228	876
#视听产品	Televison	373	375	303	253	218	58
电冰箱	Refrigerators	106	118	94	110	77	10
洗衣机	Washing Machines	152	21	95	93	86	20
空调器	Air-Conditioner	77	68	91	58	77	24
#摩托车	Motorcycles	72	52	85	47	53	6
#医疗器械	Assistant Things of Medical Treatment	9	2	5	7	13	3
服装鞋帽	Garment,Shoes and Caps	1254	674	799	712	550	588
家　具	Furniture	126	66	83	75	58	38
食　品	Foods	592	548	463	325	368	361
#房屋及装修建材	Houses and Fitment Material	483	821	667	469	364	283
#房　屋	Houses	204	530	283	151	87	47
装饰材料	Fitment Material	194	149	228	191	170	141
#电信服务	Telecome	972	629	663	589	641	283
邮政业服务	Mail	10	316	230	46	35	42
#农用生产资料类	Agricultural Production Materials	186	195	257	168	93	115
#其他类	Others	1077	653	557	492	407	265

注：资料来源于省消费者协会。

Note: Data in the table are obtained from provinvial consumers association.

22-4 检察院主要业务

Cases of Procuratorate

年 份 year	职务犯罪(件) Crime by Taking Advantage of Duty(case)			批捕、决定批捕 Total of Arrests		决定起诉 Total of Public Prosecutions	
	受 案 Cases Accepted	立 案 Cases Registered	结 案 Cases Settled	(万件) (10000 cases)	(万人) (10000 persons)	(万件) (10000 cases)	(万人) (10000 persons)
2001	2284	1130	1089	1.98	3.09	1.94	2.88
2002	2288	1163	1106	1.85	2.79	1.98	2.85
2003	2110	1138	1073	1.72	2.63	1.71	2.51
2004	2356	1160	1133	1.69	2.60	1.79	2.64
2005	2155	1122	1118	1.67	2.58	1.83	2.71
2006	1920	1104	1068	1.63	2.54	1.79	2.67
2007	1709	1060	1071	1.67	2.71	1.80	2.78
2008	1457	981	1020	1.84	2.99	1.96	3.00
2009	1469	1002	967	2.06	3.30	2.18	3.45
2010	1223	983	978	1.94	3.07	2.28	3.59
2011	1003	929	908	1.88	2.89	2.24	3.42
2012	1019	977	1013	2.16	3.22	2.62	3.93

注：资料来源于省人民检察院。
Note:Data in the table are obtained from the provincial people's procuratorate.

22-5 人民法院刑事一审案件收案

First Trail Criminal Cases Accepted by Courts

单位：件 (case)

类 别	Sort	2007	2008	2009	2010	2011	2012	2012年比2011年增长(%) Increase Rate in 2012over 2011(%)
总 计	**Total**	**19098**	**20154**	**22480**	**23294**	**22570**	**26448**	**17.2**
危害国家安全罪	Offences Against State Security	1	1		2	2	3	50.0
危害公共安全罪	Offences Against Public Security	1969	2269	1974	2368	2334	3115	33.5
破坏社会主义市场经济秩序罪	Offences Against Socialist Economic Order	281	294	332	399	360	433	20.3
侵犯公民人身权利民主权利罪	Offences Against Citizens' Personal and Democratic Rights	4469	4490	5338	5327	4944	5382	8.9
侵犯财产罪	Offences Against Properties	8401	8565	9819	9854	9320	10730	15.1
妨害社会管理秩序罪	Offences Against Social Management of Order	2958	3497	4121	4250	4688	5622	19.9
危害国防利益罪	Offences Against National Defense	4		2			2	
贪污贿赂罪	Offences on Corruption and Bribery	854	877	769	938	801	1016	26.8
渎职罪	Offences on Abuse and Dereliction of Duty	148	153	119	143	116	137	18.1
其 他	Other	13	8	6	13	5	8	60.0

注：资料来源于省高级人民法院(以下相关表同)。
Note:Date in the table are obtained from provincial higher people's court(The relative tables in the chapter are the same).

22-6 人民法院刑事一审案件结案

First Trail Criminal Cases Settled by Courts

单位：件 (case)

类 别	Sort	2007	2008	2009	2010	2011	2012	2012年比2011年增长(%) Increase Rate in 2012 over 2011(%)
总 计	**Total**	**18803**	**19934**	**22201**	**23143**	**22412**	**26260**	**17.2**
危害国家安全罪	Offences Against State Security	1	1		2	1	3	200.0
危害公共安全罪	Offences Against Public Security	1955	2259	1964	2362	2326	3096	33.1
破坏社会主义市场经济秩序罪	Offences Against Socialist Economic Order	275	288	323	393	352	418	18.8
侵犯公民人身权利民主权利罪	Offences Against Citizens' Personal and Democratic Rights	4310	4409	5200	5275	4898	5344	9.1
侵犯财产罪	Offences Against Properties	8362	8527	9781	9839	9295	10694	15.1
妨害社会管理秩序罪	Offences Against Social Management of Order	2929	3463	4084	4232	4655	5577	19.8
危害国防利益罪	Offences Against National Defense	4		2			2	
贪污贿赂罪	Offences on Corruption and Bribery	815	829	727	894	776	983	26.7
渎职罪	Offences on Abuse and Dereliction of Duty	139	150	114	133	104	135	29.8
其 他	Other	13	8	6	13	5	8	60.0

22-7 人民法院刑事案件中青少年犯罪

Juvenile Delinquency Among Criminal Cases

单位：人 (person)

指 标	Item	2007	2008	2009	2010	2011	2012	2012年比2011年增长(%) Increase Rate in 2012 over 2011(%)
刑事罪犯总数	**Number of Criminals**	**23987**	**24979**	**26834**	**28735**	**28171**	**30239**	**7.3**
#青少年罪犯	Juvenile Criminals	9330	9207	9594	10106	9266	9503	2.6
#不满18岁	Less Than 18	3294	3492	3155	3516	3014	2993	-0.7
18-25岁	Aged 18-25	6036	5715	6439	6590	6252	6510	4.1
青少年罪犯占刑事罪犯(%)	Proportion of Juvenile Criminals to Total Criminals(%)	38.9	36.9	35.8	35.2	32.9	31.4	-1.5 (百分点)

22-8 生产安全
Production Safety

项　目	Item	2007	2008	2009	2010	2011	2012
各类事故死亡人数合计(人)	**Number of Deaths for Production Security Accidents(person)**	**2588**	**2427**	**2183**	**1936**	**1655**	**1301**
工矿商贸企业	Enterprises of Industry,Mining,Commerce and Trade	985	863	776	659	523	296
煤　矿	Coal Mine	554	453	434	388	256	117
金属与非金属矿	Metallic and Non-metallic Mine	147	136	84	47	69	34
建筑业	Construction	102	100	90	105	81	74
其　他	Others	182	174	168	119	117	71
火　灾	Fire Accidents	81	77	77	64	54	31
道路交通	Roadway Traffic Accidents	1356	1348	1210	1136	1020	931
铁路交通	Railway Traffic Accidents	150	120	95	75	49	38
其　他	Others	16	19	25	2	9	5
亿元生产总值生产安全事故死亡人数(人/亿元)	Number of Deaths of Production Security Accidents Per of GDP (person/100 million yuan)	0.96	0.73	0.56	0.42	0.29	0.19
工矿商贸企业从业人员10万人死亡率(人/10万人)	Number of Deaths Per 100000 Persons of Employed Personels of Enterprises of Industry,Mining, Commerceand Trade(person/100000 persons)	9.77	8.56	7.65	6.45	5.08	2.88
煤矿百万吨死亡人数(人/百万吨)	Number of Deaths Per Unit of Yields of Coal Mine (person/per million tons)	4.99	3.84	3.17	2.43	1.64	0.65
道路交通万车死亡人数(人/万车)	Number of Deaths of Roadway Traffic Accidents Per Unit of Vehicles(person/10000 sets)	9.33	7.30	5.36	4.01	3.32	2.62

注：资料来源于省安全生产监督管理局。

Note: Data in the table are obtained from provincial production safety supervision management administration.

22–9 火灾
Fire Accidents

指标	Item	2011	2012
实际发生数(起)	**Number of Fire Accidents(case)**	**1170**	**959**
按火灾原因分	Grouped by Cause		
生产作业	Operation	67	54
电气	Electric	503	424
吸烟	Smoking	35	20
生活用火不慎	Not Careful with Cooking Fire	217	167
玩火	Playing with Fire	69	33
自燃	Natural Fire	21	17
不明	Uncertain	61	56
其他	Others	137	188
死亡人数(人)	Number of Deaths(person)	55	31
受伤人数(人)	Number of Injuries(person)	10	15
直接财产损失(万元)	Losses Converted into Cash(10000 yuan)	6625	5147
平均每起事故损失(万元)	Average Loss Per Fire(10000 yuan)	5.66	5.37

注：资料来源于省公安厅(下表同)。
Note: Data in the table are obtained from provincial department of public security(the same applies to the next table).

22–10 交通事故(2012)
Traffic Accidents

指标	Item	发生数(起) Number of Traffic Accidents(case)	死亡人数（人） Number of Deaths (person)	受伤人数(人) Number of Injuries (person)	损失折款(万元) Losses Converted into Cash(10000 yuan)
总计	**Total**	**1361**	**931**	**1984**	**1698.58**
#重大事故	Extraordinarily Serious	2	31	29	7.00
较大事故	Serious	51	223	196	271.25
机动车	Motor Vehicles	1299	894	1955	1657.30
#汽车	Automobiles	925	671	1499	1495.78
摩托车	Motorcycles	325	187	402	131.39
拖拉机	Tractors	31	18	35	11.01
非机动车	Non-motor-driven Vehicles	3	1	3	1.15
#自行车	Bicycles				
行人乘车人	Pedestrians and Passengers	56	35	22	39.23

注：重大事故为一次死亡10–29人，较大事故为一次死亡3–9人。
Note: A major accident refers to 10-29 people died at a time , and a larger accident refers to 3-9 people died at a time.

22−11 社会保险
Social Insurance

指　标	Item	2007	2008	2009	2010	2011	2012
社会保险基金	**Social Security Fund**						
社会保险基金收入(亿元)	Reveneu(100 million yuan)	90.86	140.50	171.40	201.56	256.94	310.85
社会保险基金支出(亿元)	Expenses(100 million yuan)	80.57	98.24	122.73	151.41	181.74	229.08
社会保险基金累计结余(亿元)	Balance at year-end(100 million yuan)	128.87	147.88	218.51	267.93	343.13	366.79
基本养老保险	**Basic Pension Insurance**						
基本养老保险参保人数(万人)	Number of Persons Joining Basic Pension Insurance(10 000 persons)	205.93	215.89	235.61	257.31	282.06	309.38
#参保职工	Number of Employees	149.39	156.57	172.14	190.29	210.71	231.67
基本养老保险基金收入(亿元)	Reveneu(100 million yuan)	80.21	101.08	125.47	144.85	179.25	216.94
基本养老保险基金支出(亿元)	Expenses(100 million yuan)	61.80	75.98	90.56	107.74	127.57	153.07
离退休人员社区管理服务率(%)	Rate of Community Management and Services for Retirees(%)	40.7	47.2	50.0	57.0	61.1	70.2
新型农村社会养老保险	**The New Rural Social Pension Insurance**						
新型农村社会养老保险参保人数(万人)	The number of insured (10 000 persons)				223.72	849.74	1226.78
新型农村社会养老保险基金收入(亿元)	Reveneu(100 million yuan)				6.94	24.84	36.51
新型农村社会养老保险基金支出(亿元)	Expenses(100 million yuan)				3.53	14.35	27.63
基本医疗保险	**Urban Employees Basic Medical Care Insurance**						
基本医疗保险参保人数(万人)	Number of Persons Joining Basic Medical Care Insurance(10 000 persons)	228.22	404.26	561.39	602.48	629.00	648.30
城镇职工	Number of Persons Joining Basic Medical Care Insurance	228.22	257.35	279.53	293.52	314.06	329.27
#农民工	Tagelöhners	8.79	20.20	17.70	14.01	14.76	13.79
城镇居民	Urban Residents		146.91	281.86	308.96	314.94	319.03
基本医疗保险基金收入(亿元)	Reveneu(100 million yuan)	19.04	28.08	36.93	45.23	61.26	72.93
城镇职工	Number of Persons Joining Basic Medical Care Insurance	19.04	28.08	34.51	41.64	54.31	65.75
城镇居民	Urban Residents			2.42	3.59	6.95	7.18
基本医疗保险支出(亿元)	Expenses(100 million yuan)	13.62	18.09	26.95	35.89	46.22	65.41
城镇职工	Number of Persons Joining Basic Medical Care Insurance	13.62	18.09	25.31	33.08	42.44	60.50
城镇居民	Urban Residents			1.64	2.82	3.78	4.91
失业保险	**Unemployment Insurance**						
失业保险参保人数(万人)	Number of Persons Joining Unemployment Insurance(10 000 persons)	134.55	141.36	144.60	152.48	160.52	173.46
领取失业金人数(万人)	Beneficiaries of Unemployment Insurance Fund(10 000 persons)	1.42	1.26	1.07	1.21	1.08	1.02
失业保险基金收入(亿元)	Reveneu(100 million yuan)	5.84	7.03	6.33	7.58	11.64	14.91
失业保险基金支出(亿元)	Expenses(100 million yuan)	3.46	2.08	5.83	5.29	2.34	6.49
#失业金	Jobless Claims	0.72	0.72	0.67	0.71	0.82	0.78
职业培训补贴支出(亿元)	Expenses of Professional Training(100 million yuan)	0.18	0.11	0.07	0.14	0.14	0.38
工伤保险	**Work Injury Insurance**						
工伤保险参保人数(万人)	Number of Persons Joining Injury Insurance (10 000 persons)	110.50	129.02	143.35	162.18	193.96	238.19
#农民工	Tagelöhners	28.87	38.37	49.19	59.65	69.78	81.13
工伤保险基金收入(亿元)	Reveneu(100 million yuan)	2.34	3.37	4.04	6.26	9.12	11.02
工伤保险支出(亿元)	Expenses(100 million yuan)	1.05	1.82	2.89	4.84	6.55	7.97
生育保险	**Maternity Insurance**						
生育保险参保人数(万人)	Number of PersonsJoining in Basic Maternity Insurance(10 000 persons)	88.70	135.95	152.49	164.30	198.09	221.58
生育保险基金收入(亿元)	Reveneu(100 million yuan)	0.53	0.95	1.05	1.23	1.47	2.22
生育保险支出(亿元)	Expenses(100 million yuan)	0.17	0.27	0.37	0.47	0.61	1.05

注：资料来源于省人力资源社会保障厅。
Note: Date in the table are obtained from Provincial Department of Human Resources and Social Security.

22-12 社会福利机构

Social Welfare Institutions and Enterprises

单位：个 (unit)

项　目	Item	2007	2008	2009	2010	2011	2012	2012年比2011年增长(%) Increase Rate in 2012over 2011(%)
总　计	**Total**	**1417**	**1434**	**1432**	**1454**	**1722**	**7020**	**307.7**
收养性福利单位	Adopting Social Welfare Institutions	900	919	948	974	1185	1240	4.6
社会福利企业	Social Welfare Enterprises	143	128	90	84	81	59	-27.2
优抚事业单位	Administration Agencies for Martyrs	52	54	56	59	62	63	1.6
救助类单位	Collecting and Repatriation Units	55	56	58	61	64	71	10.9
殡仪服务单位	Funeral and Interment Institutions	102	105	111	116	119	128	7.6
彩票发行单位	Lottery Issue Units	10	11	11	13	15	15	持平
社区服务单位	Community Service Institutions	155	161	158	147	196	5444	26.78倍

22-13 社会福利机构工作人员

Staff Employed by Social welfare Institutions and Enterprises

单位：人 (person)

项　目	Item	2007	2008	2009	2010	2011	2012	2012年比2011年增长(%) Increase Rate in 2012over 2011(%)
总　计	**Total**	**15638**	**15675**	**13800**	**13433**	**14679**	**35677**	**143.0**
收养性福利单位	Adopting Social Welfare Institutions	2873	3118	3124	3522	4274	4658	9.0
社会福利企业	Social Welfare Enterprises	8478	8211	6268	5512	5216	3343	-35.9
优抚安置事业单位	Administration Agencies for Martyrs	375	342	299	293	466	314	-32.6
救助类单位	Collecting and Repatriation Units	333	337	329	339	347	371	6.9
殡仪服务单位	Funeral and Interment Institutions	2652	2691	2589	2669	2925	2985	2.1
彩票发行单位	Lottery Issue Units	101	115	119	147	160	181	13.1
社区服务单位	Community Service Institutions	826	861	1072	951	1291	23825	17.45倍

22-14 社会服务及设施和民政事业发展主要指标

Main Indicators of Social Services & Facilities and Civil Administration Career Development

指标	Item	2007	2008	2009	2010	2011	2012	2012年比2011年增长(%) Increase Rate in 2012 over 2011(%)
城镇社区服务设施数(个)	**Number of Urban Community Service Facilities(unit)**	**4936**	**5102**	**5176**	**5920**	**6593**	**11587**	**75.7**
#社区服务单位数	Number of Community Service Institutions	155	161	158	147	196	5444	26.77倍
城镇便民利民服务网点(个)	Number of Urban Service Points for Civilian(unit)	17698	22340	22661	25715	26587	27699	4.2
乡镇敬老院覆盖率(%)	Coverage Rate of Villages and Town Elderly Welfare Homes(%)	55.0	55.8	56.4	56.5	68.3	72.3	4.0(百分点)
收养性福利单位床位数(张)	Number of Beds of Welfare Home (unit)	19121	21343	23396	28358	44025	52996	20.4
收养性福利单位床位利用率(%)	Using Rate of Bed(%)	64.9	64.0	65.0	60.2	61.8	53.4	-8.4(百分点)
享受城镇低保人数(万人)	Number of Persons Receiving Lowest Cost of living in Urban Area (10000 persons)	53.28	54.52	55.50	53.98	54.34	53	-2.5
城镇低保生活保障支出(万元)	Expenditure of Lowest Cost of living in Urban Area(10000 yuan)	63749	87999	104354	101685	143028	155819	8.9

注：资料来源于省民政厅(以下相关表同)。
Note:The data in the table are provided by the provinvial department of civil affairs(The relative tables in the chapter are the same).

22-15 社会福利救济主要支出

Major Expenditures of Welfare Relief Funds

单位：万元 (10000 yuan)

指标	Item	2007	2008	2009	2010	2011	2012	2012年比2011年增长(%) Increase Rate in 2012 over 2011(%)
总计	**Total**	**231788**	**319061**	**433055**	**522166**	**830472**	**891463**	**7.3**
优抚对象补助金额	Funds for Family Members of Martyrs and Disabled Veterans	39157	56748	66113	81660	95162	110456	16.1
#国家支出	Government Funds	39157	56748	66113	81660	95162	110456	16.1
传统救济对象的国家救济金额	Funds for Family Members of Traditional Relief	69833	11873	12575	14628	29995	33180	10.6
最低生活保障支出	Expenditure for Persons Receiving Lowest Cost-of-living	115493	243291	346696	419143	692908	731412	5.6
城镇	For Urban Areas	63749	87999	104354	101685	143028	155819	8.9
农村	For Rural Areas	51744	155292	242342	317458	549880	575593	4.7
收养性社会福利单位支出	Funds for Adopting Social Welfare Institution	7305	7149	7671	6735	12407	16415	32.3
#国家支出	Government Funds	7305	7149	7671	6735	12407	16415	32.3

注：2007年传统救济对象的国家救济金额含农村低保支出。
Note: Funds for family members of traditional relief include the expenditure for rural lowest cost-of-living areas in the year 2007.

22–16 享受补助、救济人员

Persons Receiving Subsidies and Relief Funds

单位：万人 (10000 persons)

指 标	Item	2007	2008	2009	2010	2011	2012	2012年比2011年增长(%) Increase Rate in 2012 over 2011(%)
城乡居民最低生活保障人数	**Number of Persons Receiving Lowest Cost-of-living in Urban Area and Rural Area**	**309.72**	**377.86**	**379.48**	**588.72**	**585.23**	**566.00**	**-3.3**
城 镇	Urban Area	53.28	54.52	55.50	53.98	54.34	53.00	-2.5
农 村	Rural Area	256.44	323.34	323.98	534.74	530.89	513.00	-3.4
传统救济人数	Number of Persons Receiving Traditional Relief Funds	1.89	1.81	1.72	1.70	1.71	1.74	1.8
收养性福利单位收养三无对象人数	Number of Persons Adopted by Adopting Social Welfare Institutions	1.05	1.12	1.14	1.35	2.25	2.34	4.0

注：2007年全省全面建立实施农村居民最低生活保障制度，原传统救济对象符合条件的均转为农村低保人数。

Note:Rural lowest cost-of living system was set up in Guizhou in 2007. The persons receiving traditional relief funds who meet the standard of rural lowest cost-of-living are counted in the nuber of persons receiving rural lowest cost-of-living allowance.

22–17 享受国家定期抚恤、补助、救济人员数

Persons Receiving Regular Subsidy and Commiseration of Country

单位：人 (person)

指 标	Item	2007	2008	2009	2010	2011	2012	2012年比2011年增长(%) Increase Rate in 2012over 2011(%)
合 计	**Total**	**187395**	**192744**	**195265**	**191988**	**223071**	**263107**	**17.9**
#伤残抚恤人数	Number of Persons Receiving Disability Commiseration	14982	15153	15830	15844	15809	16057	1.6
# “三属”抚恤人数	Number of Persons Comfort and Compensated Bereaved Family	5183	5069	5307	5121	4931	4810	-2.5
烈士家属	Family Numbers of Martyr	3023	2936	3129	3019	2911	2781	-4.5
牺牲、病故军人家属	Family Numbers of Immolate & Die of Illness Armyman	2160	2133	2178	2102	2020	2029	0.4
定期补助人数	Number of Persons Receiving Regular Subsidies	167230	172522	174128	171023	202331	242240	19.7
复退军人定补人数	Number of Ex-servicemen	88090	86965	87102	83506	80397	76315	-5.1
战、参试定补人数	Number of Persons Receiving Regular Subsidies for War and Test	78909	85178	86626	87034	88530	90147	1.8

注：参战、参试定补人数指参加对越自卫反击战及核试验等人员，2007年开始核查并接受定期补助。

Note:Persons receiving regular subsidies for sar and sest refer to these persons taking part in acting in self-defence war and nuclear test, who have obtained regular subsidies from the government since 2007.

22-18 残疾人事业基本情况

Basic Information of Person with Disablility

单位：人 (person)

项目	Item	2012
康复	**Rehabilitation**	
视力残疾康复	Rehabilitation of Persons with Sight Disability	
贫困白内障患者免费手术(例)	Free Surgeries for Poor Cataract Patients(case)	8451
低视力者配用助视器	Vision-aids Provided for Persons of Low-vision	2891
盲人定向行走训练	Blindman Trained with Direction Walking	2788
聋儿康复	Rehabilitation of Children with Hearing Disability	
年收训聋儿	Hearing and Speech Training	542
培训家长	Parents Trained	719
精神病防治康复	Prevention and Treatment of Psychiatric Diseases	
开展精神病防治康复工作市县数(个)	Counties Carried on the Works of Prevention and Treatment of Psychiatric Diseases(unit)	76
接受治疗的精神病患者	Treatment Provided for Patients with Sever Psychiatric Diseases	14523
孤独症儿童训练	Trained Persons with Infantile Autism	205
肢体残疾康复	Rehabilitation of Persons with Physical Disability	
肢体残疾人社区康复训练	Persons Rehabilitated at Community	871
脑瘫儿童机构康复训练	Rehabilitation of Children with Cerebral Palsy at Community	303
贫困肢体残疾儿童矫治手术	Rehabilitation of Children with Physical Disability in Poverty	239
智力残疾康复	Rehabilitation of Persons with Intellectual Disability	
智残儿童社区康复训练	Children Rehabilitated at Community	287
智残儿童机构康复训练	Children Rehabilitated at Institutions	253
辅助器具供应服务数(件)	Sabsidiary Implement Provided for the Disabled (unit)	11501
贫困残疾人假肢装配例数(例)	Artificial limb Assembled (case)	791
#大　腿	for Ham	344
小　腿	for Shank	406
特殊假肢	Special Artificial limb	41
社区康复协调员培训	Workers Trained for Disabled porsn at Community	1994

22-18 续表 Continued

单位：人 (person)

项目	Item	2012
教育	**Education**	
未入学适龄残疾儿童少年	School-age Disabled Children without Schooling	6912
职业教育与培训	Vocational Education and Training	
机构数(个)	Facilities (unit)	115
教育与培训人数(人次)	Number or Educated and Trained (person-time)	4163
就业	**Employment**	
城镇残疾人就业状况	Employment of Urban Handicapped	
当年安排就业	Persons Employed in the Year	4449
#按比列就业	Employed by Quote Scheme	1049
公益性岗位安置	Employed at Public Institution	95
集中就业	Employed at Welfare Enterprises	1135
个体及其他形式就业	Self-employed and Others	2143
农村残疾人就业状况	Employment of Rural Handicapped	
就　业	Employed	772910
残疾人就业服务机构(个)	Employment Service Institutions for Handicapped (unit)	
省	Provinces	1
市、州	Prefectures	9
县、市、区	County、Cities	61
盲人按摩	**Massage by Persons with Visual Disability**	
保健按摩人员培训	Massage Therapists Training	368
医疗按摩人员培训	Keep-fit Massage Training	17
扶贫	**Poverty Alleviation**	
本年度脱贫人数	Disabled Persons Overcoming Poverty	75232
农村贫困残疾	Rural Disabled persons in Poverty	825675
当地低收入残疾	Disabled Persons at the Local Low-income Level	592344
残联组织建设	**Organization of the Disabled Persons' Federation**	
残疾人工作者	Workers Working for the Disabled	3393

注：资料来源于省残联。
Note :Data in the table are provided by Disabled Federation of Gui zhou Province.

22-19 婚姻

Marriages and Divorces

指　标	Item	2007	2008	2009	2010	2011	2012
准予登记结婚(对)	**Registered Marriages(couple)**	**234938**	**263238**	**307940**	**375051**	**373423**	**417840**
#初婚(人)	First Marriages(person)	432161	486029	567633	692590	679348	780707
再婚(人)	Remarriages(person)	37715	40447	48247	57512	67498	54973
#女性	Female	18794	19223	22707	27696	34236	29838
涉外婚姻(对)	Registered Marriages with Foreigner and the Citizen of Hong Kong,Macao,Taiwan(couple)	586	491	467	369	500	440
#国内公民(人)	Domestic Citizen(person)	586	491	467	369	500	439
#女性	Female	559	458	440	330	457	367
离婚人数(人)	Divorces(person)	91674	102440	115914	127938	144420	162460
#民政部门批准	Permitted by Civil Administration Department	56772	65140	76146	89384	104032	118810

主要统计指标解释

公证人员　指按照《公证法》规定，在公证机构从事公证业务的执业公证员、公证助理员、行政人员、其他人员。

办理公证文书　指公证处在一定时期内办结的公证文书件数。公证文书按司法部规定或批准的格式制作，包括国内公证和涉外公证两部分。国内公证分为经济合同公证和民事法律关系公证两大类。

调解人员　指人民调解委员会委员和人民调解委员会聘任的，负责对《人民调解法》规定人民调解委员会可以受理的民间纠纷进行调解的人员。

调解民间纠纷　是指人民调解委员会通过说服、疏导等方法，促成当事人在平等协商基础上自愿达成调解协议，解决民间纠纷的活动。

特大火灾　指造成30人以上死亡，或者100人以上重伤，或者1亿元以上直接财产损失的火灾。

重大火灾　指造成10人以上30人以下死亡，或者50人以上100人以下重伤，或者5000万元以上1亿元以下直接财产损失的火灾。

较大火灾　指造成3人以上10人以下死亡，或者10人以上50人以下重伤，或者1000万元以上5000万元以下直接财产损失的火灾。

一般火灾　指造成3人以下死亡，或者10人以下重伤，或者1000万元以下直接财产损失的火灾。

人民检察院直接立案侦查案件　指按照管辖的规定，由人民检察院直接立案侦查的贪污贿赂犯罪、渎职犯罪、国家机关工作人员利用职权实施的侵犯公民人身权利和民主权利的犯罪以及经省级人民检察院决定立案侦查的国家机关工作人员利用职权实施的其他重大犯罪案件。

要案　指县、处级以上干部的犯罪案件。该指标主要反映职务犯罪案件中县、处级以上干部被人民检察院依法立案侦查的情况。

批准逮捕　指人民检察院对公安机关、国家安全机关、监狱管理机关提出逮捕的犯罪嫌疑人进行审查，根据事实，依法做出逮捕决定。该指标主要反映人民检察院对提请逮捕犯罪嫌疑人进行审查后依法做出批准逮捕决定的情况。

青少年罪犯　指人民法院在报告期内判决发生法律效力的有罪判决中14周岁以上不满25周岁的罪犯。其中14周岁以上不满18周岁的罪犯为未成年罪犯。

行政案件　指公民、法人和其他组织认为行政机关和行政机关的工作人员的具体行政行为侵犯其合法权益时，依照《行政诉讼法》规定的程序提出起诉，由人民法院立案处理的行政争议案件。

城市居民最低生活保障人数　指在报告期末家庭平均收入在当地规定的最低生活保障线以下的家庭人员及国家规定有民政部门救济的特殊人员和60年代精减退职老职工救济人员等。

农村居民最低生活保障人数　指报告期末在建立农村最低生活保障制度的地区，得到当地政府或集体给予最低生活保障的农业人口家庭人数。

五保户　指无法定抚养义务人，或者虽有法定抚养义务人，但是抚养人无抚养能力的；无劳动能力的；无生活来源的老年人、残疾人和未成年人。

农村传统定期救济人数　指国家规定由民政部门救济的特殊人员和60年代精减退职老职工救济人员，特殊人员包括麻风病人、原国民党企业、投诚人员、归侨、台胞、台属、宽大释放人员、摘掉右派帽子人员、因公负伤的下乡知青、因计划生育手术事故造成的死亡和丧失劳动能力人员、解除劳务人员、刑事犯罪家属及60年代精减退职职工等。登记这类人员时登入其他人员类，登记这种户数时登入其他户类。

社会福利企业　指以集中安置有一定劳动能力的残疾人就业为目的（残疾职工占生产人员10%以上）、带有社会福利性质的企业总称。社会福利企业分类为：社会福利工厂、假肢厂、其他福利企业。按性质分为：国有、集体和其他性质分别填列。

社区服务实施　是指社区服务站、社区服务中心、其他社区服务设施的总和。是面向老年人及家庭的商品递送、医疗保健、家庭保洁、日间照料、陪伴服务等为社区居家老服务的设施和突出综合服务功能，将党员活动室、就业保障网络、社区卫生服务站、文化活动室、图书馆、“爱心超市”社区捐款接收站点、警务站（室）、老年活动室、未成年人文化活动场所等具有综合服务功能的设施。原则上，每个社区服务站设施的最低标准时能满足社区居委会办公所需，并配置多功能社区活动场所，建筑面积不低于200平方米。在此基础上可根据社区居民的实际需求，重点强化若干类服务功能。

城镇职工基本养老保险

1、（参保）职工人数 指报告期末按照国家法律、法规和有关政策规定参加基本养老保险并在社保经办机构已建立缴费记录档案的职工人数，包括中断缴费但未终止养老保险关系的职工人数，不包括只登记未建立缴费记录档案的人数。

2、（参保）离退休人员人数 指报告期末参加基本养老保险的离休、退休和退职人员的人数。

3、基本养老保险基金收入 指根据国家有关规定，由纳入基本养老保险范围的缴费单位和个人按国家规定的缴费基数和缴费比例缴纳的养老保险基金，以及通过其他方式取得的形成基金来源的收入。包括单位和职工个人缴纳的基本养老保险费、基本养老保险基金利息收入、上级补助收入、下级上解收入、转移收入、财政补贴和其他收入。

4、基本养老保险基金支出 指按照国家政策规定的开支范围和开支标准从养老保险基金中支付给参加基本养老保险的个人的养老金、丧葬抚恤补助，以及由于保险关系转移、上下级之间调剂资金等原因而发生的支出。包括离休金、退休金、退职金、各种补贴、医疗费、死亡丧葬补助费、抚恤救济费、社会保险经办机构管理费、补助下级支出、上解上级支出、转移支出、其他支出等。

5、基本养老保险基金累计结余 指截止报告期末基本养老保险基金收支相抵后的累计余额。

城镇职工基本医疗保险

1、参保人数 指报告期末按国家有关规定参加基本医疗保险的人数。包括参加保险的职工人数和退休人员人数。

2、基金收入 指根据国家有关规定，由纳入城镇职工基本医疗保险范围的缴费单位和个人，按国家规定的缴费基数和缴费比例缴纳的基金，以及通过其他方式取得的形成基金来源的款项，包括：单位缴纳的社会统筹基金收入、个人缴纳的个人账户基金收入、财政补贴收入、利息收入、其他收入。

3、基金支出 指按照国家政策规定的开支范围和开支标准从社会统筹基金中支付给参加城镇职工基本医疗保险的职工和退休人员的医疗保险待遇支出，和从个人帐户基金中支付给参加基本医疗保险的职工和退休人员的医疗费用支出，以及其他支出。包括：住院医疗费用支出、门急诊医疗费用支出、个人账户基金支出、其他支出。

4、基金累计结余 指截止报告期末城镇职工基本医疗保险的社会统筹和个人帐户基金累计结余金额。

失业保险

1、参保人数 指报告期末按照国家法律、法规和有关政策规定参加了失业保险的城镇企业事业单位的职工及地方政府规定参加失业保险的其他人员的人数。

2、失业保险基金收入 指按照规定从企业、事业及其他单位筹集的失业保险费及其他并入失业保险基金收入的总额。包括单位和个人缴纳的失业保险费、失业保险基金利息收入、上级补助收入、下级上解收入、转移收入、财政补贴和其他收入。

3、失业保险基金支出 指报告期内为保障失业人员基本生活、促进其再就业等支出的基金总额。包括失业救济金、医疗费、死亡丧葬补助费、抚恤救济费、转业训练费支出、失业保险经办机构管理费、补助下级支出、上解上级支出、转移支出和其他支出。

4、基金累计结余 指截止报告期末失业保险基金收支相抵后的累计余额。

工伤保险

1、参加保险人数 指报告期末依据国家有关规定参加工伤保险的职工人数和有雇工的个体工商户的雇工数。

2、享受保险待遇人数 指劳动者因工负伤致残、死亡或因患职业病致残，根据有关规定享受工伤保险待遇职工或供养直系亲属人数。包括伤残人数、职业病人数、因工死亡人数、供养直系亲属人数。

3、基金收入 指根据国家有关规定，由参加工伤保险的单位按国家规定的缴费基数和缴费比例缴纳的工伤保险基金，以及通过其他形式取得的形成基金来源的款项。包括：单位缴纳的社会统筹基金收入、财政补贴收入、利息收入、其他收入。

4、基金支出 指按照国家政策规定的开支范围和开支标准从工伤保险基金中支付给参加工伤保险的人员及供养直系亲属工伤保险待遇支出及其他支出。包括工伤医疗费、伤残补助金、工亡补助金、护理费、丧葬补助费、工伤预防费用、职业康复费用和其他支出。

5、基金累计结余 指截止报告期末工伤保险基金累计结余金额。

生育保险

1、参保人数 指报告期末依据有关规定参加生育保险的职工人数。

2、基金收入 指根据国家有关规定，由参加生育保险的单位按照国家规定的缴费基数和缴费比例缴纳的生育保险基金，以及通过其他方式取得的形成基金来源的款项，包括：单位缴纳的基金收入、利息收入和其他收入。

3、基金支出 指按照国家政策规定的开支范围和开支标准，从生育保险基金中支付给参加生育保险的职工，因妊娠、分娩和计划生育手术而享受的待遇及其他支出。包括：生育津贴、医疗费用支出及其他支出。

4、基金累计结余 指截止报告期末生育保险基金累计结余金额。

Explanatory Notes on Main Statistical Indicators

Notary Personnel refers to judicial workers of the state notary offices handling notarization work according to law. They include notaries, assistant notaries, and other people working for notary offices.

Notarized Documents refer to the documents settled by notary offices in a year. The notary documents are drawn up in accordance with the regulations of the Ministry of Justice, including domestic documents and foreign-related documents. Domestic documents are divided into two major categories, documents on economic contracts and documents on civil legal relations.

Mediators refer to workers on peoples mediation committees responsible for mediating in civil disputes and cases of slight infraction of the law. They include members of the mediation committees and mediators of mediation groups.

Serious Fire Case refers to a case which has caused over 10 to 30 deaths; or over 50 to 100 serious injuries; or a direct property loss over 50 million to 100 million yuan.

Comparatively Serious Fire Case refers to a case which has caused over three to ten deaths; or over 10 to 50 serious injuries; or a direct property loss over 10 million to 50 million yuan.

Ordinary Fire Case refers to a case which has caused less than three deaths; or less than 10 serious injuries; or a direct property loss less than 10 million yuan.

Cases Registered and Handled Directly by People's Procuratorate Offices refer to those serious criminal cases that, according to the functional jurisdiction, are registered and handled by the People's Procuratorate Offices, including the ones on bribery and corruption, the ones on abuse and dereliction of duty, offences against citizens' personal and democratic rights by government officials abusing their powers; and that are registered and handled by the provincial Procuratorate offices in relation to other major crimes committed by government officials by abusing their powers.

Key Cases refer to crimes committed by county and director-level officials. This indicator reflects the situation of those county and director-level officials involved in criminal cases registered and handled by People's Procuratorate offices.

Approval for Arrest refers to the decision made by people's procuratorate office, in accordance with the law and relevant facts, to approve the arrest of the suspect(s) as proposed by the public security departments, state security departments or prisons authority. This indicator reflects approved arrests made by people's procuratorate offices that are proposed by related departments.

Juvenile Criminals refers to the offenders within the age range of 14 to 25 convicted guilty by the court during the reporting period while those between 14 and 18 are defined as minor offenders.

Administrative Cases refers to the cases filed by citizens, corporations and other organizations suggest that the executive and the executive staff of a specific administrative act infringe upon their legitimate interests, accordance with the "Administrative Procedure Law" provides the procedures to prosecute, filed and handled of administrative disputes by the people's court .

Number of Urban Residents Entitled to Minimum Living Allowances refers to the number of those whose average family income is below a minimum local standard by the end of the reporting period and special staff who were relieved by states provide State regulations and the District Department and 1960s streamline relief workers older workers retire,etc.

Number of Rural Residents Entitled to Minimum Living Allowances refers to the number of those receiving the minimum living allowances from the local government or community in the rural areas where this allowances system is in place as of the end of the reporting period.

Households Enjoying Five Guarantees refers to those senior citizens, handicapped or under-aged who, without labour ability, can’t make a living by themselves and whose statutory providers are unable to support them or who have no statutory providers at all.

Number of Rural Recipients　Refers to the national regulations by the civil affairs department of special relief personnel and streamline the retirement of older workers 1960s relief personnel, special personnel, including lepers, former KMT enterprises, surrendered personnel, returned overseas Chinese and Taiwan compatriots and Taiwan belong, large release of personnel, remove right hat personnel who are wounded in the countryside youth, family planning surgery because of deaths caused by accidents and loss of ability to work personnel, lift service personnel, their families and the criminal streamline the 1960s retired workers and so on. Registration Log when such persons other personnel, register other users logged on when this class households.

Social Welfare Enterprises　refers to those welfare-oriented enterprises employing a significant number of handicapped people with certain labour ability (handicapped employees shall exceed 10% of the production staff), including welfare factories, artificial limb plants as well as other welfare enterprises. Divided by nature: state, collective and other properties is listed separately.

Number of Service Facilities in Urban Communities　refers to community service centers, community service centers, other community service facilities combined. Is for the elderly and home delivery of goods, health care, household cleaning, day care, companionship services, home care services for community facilities and outstanding comprehensive service functions, will party room, employment security networks, community health service stations, cultural activities room, library, "love supermarket" community donations receiving stations, police stations (room), old activity room, minors and other cultural activities with comprehensive service functions of the facility. In principle, each community service station facilities to meet the minimum standards required for community neighborhood committee office, and configure the multi-purpose community activities, building area of not less than 200 square meters. On this basis, according to the actual needs of community residents, focusing on enhancing certain types of services.

Basic Pension Insurance

1.Number of staff and workers covered　refer to staff and workers participating in the basic pension insurance programme according to national laws, regulations and related policies at the end of the reference period, who have already had payment records in social security management agencies, including those who have interrupt payment without terminating the insurance programme. Those who have registered in the programme but with no payment records are not included.

2. Number of retirees participating in the basic pension insurance programme　refer to the number of retirees participating in basic pension insurance programmes by the end of the reference period.

3. Revenue of the basic pension insurance programme　refers to payments made by employers and individuals participating in the pension insurance programme in accordance with the basis and proportion stipulated in State regulations, and income from other sources that become source of pension insurance fund, including the premium paid by employers and staff and workers, interest income, subsidies from higher level agencies, income as transfer from subordinate agencies, transferred income, government financial subsidies and other income.

4. Expenditure of basic pension insurance programme　refers to payment made on pensions and funeral subsidies to those retired and resigned people covered in pension insurance programmes according to related national policies on scopeand standard of expenditure. Also included are expenditure which arises due to shift of the insurance relationship or adjustment of funds among agencies. More specifically, included are pensions for resigned people, pensions for retired people, pension for people quitting jobs, various subsidies, medical fees, funeral subsidies, compensation payments, management fees for social security agencies, expenses on subsidies to lower subordinates, expenses as transfer to agencies at higher level, transferred expenditure and other expenditure.

5. Balance of basic pension insurance programme　refers to the balance of basic pension insurance funds at the end of the reference period after deducting expenses from revenue.

Urban Basic Medical Care Insurance

1. Number of people participating in the insurance programme　refers to people participating in the basic medical care

insurance programme according to related regulations as at the end of reference period, including number of staff and workers and retirees participating in this insurance programme.

2. Revenue of the insurance programme refers to payments made by employers and individuals participating in the medical care insurance programme in accordance with the basis and proportion stipulated in State regulations, and income from other sources that become source of medical insurance fund, including income of social comprehensive funds paid by employers, income from individual accounts, government financial subsidies, interest income and other income.

3. Expenditure of the insurance programme refers to payment made from social comprehensive funds to those retired and resigned people covered in basic medical care insurance within the scope and standards of expenditure according to related national policies, and medical care payment made from individual accounts to staff and workers and retirees, and other expenses, including medical expenses of hospital inpatients, medical expenses for outpatients and emergency patients, payment from individual accounts and other expenditure.

4. Balance of the basic medical care insurance programme refer to the balance of medical care insurance of social comprehensive funds and individual accounts at the end of the reference period.

Unemployment Insurance

1. Number of people covered refers to staff and workers in urban enterprises or institutions who have participated in the unemployment insurance programme according to relevant policies and regulations, and other people who have participated according to local government regulations, as at the end of reference period.

2. Revenue of the unemployment insurance programme refers to payments made by employers and individuals participating in unemployment insurance programme in accordance with relevant regulations and other income contributed to this programme, including unemployment insurance premium made by employers and individuals, interest income, subsidies from higher level agencies, income as transfer from subordinate agencies, transferred income, government financial subsidies and other income.

3. Expenditure of the unemployment insurance programme refers to total expenses during the reference period to guarantee the basic livelihood of unemployed people and laid-off staff and workers and to encourage their re-employment. Included are unemployment relief, medical fees, funeral subsidies, compensation payments, training expenses, management fees for unemployment insurance agencies, subsidies to lower level agencies, expenses as transfer to higher level agencies, transferred expenditure and other expenditure.

4. Balance of the unemployment insurance programme refers to the balance of revenue of the programme after deducting expenses at the end of the reference period.

Work Injury Insurance

1. Number of people covered refers to staff and workers who have participated in the work injury insurance programme according to relevant national regulations and hirelings who were hired by individual industrial and commercial households.

2. Number of beneficiaries refers to staff and workers and their direct dependents who can, in accordance with relevant regulations, benefit from work injury insurance, as a result of work injury leading to disability or death of the staff/worker, or occupational disease leading to disability. Included in this category are number of injured and disabled people, number of people with occupational diseases, number of deaths at work places, and number of direct dependents.

3. Revenue of the work injury insurance programme refers to payments made by employers participating in the work injury insurance programme in accordance with the basis and proportion stipulated in State regulations, and income from other sources that become source of work injury insurance fund, including income of social comprehensive funds paid by employers, government financial subsidies, interest income and other income.

4. Expenditure of the work injury insurance programme refers to payments made from work injury insurance funds to those who participated in the work injury insurance programme and their direct dependents within the scope and standards of expenditure according to related national policies, and other expenditure, including medical fees for work injury, injury and disability subsidies, death subsidies, nursing fees, funeral subsidies, injury prevention fees, occupational rehabilitation

fees and other expenditure.

5. Balance of the work injury insurance programme refers to the balance of the work injury funds at the end of the reference period.

Maternity Insurance

1. Number of people covered refers to staff and workers who have participated in the maternity insurance programme according to relevant regulation at the end of the reporting period.

2. Revenue of maternity insurance refers to payments made by employers participating in the maternity insurance programme in accordance with the basis and proportion stipulated in State regulations, and income from other sources that become source of maternity insurance fund, including income of funds paid by employers, interest income and other income.

3. Expenditure of the maternity insurance programme refers to payments made from maternity insurance funds to staff and workers who participate in the maternity insurance programme within the scope and standards of expenditure in accordance with related national policies, expenses paid for pregnancy, child delivery or surgeries related to family planning, and other expenditure, including allowance for child bearing, medical fees and other expenditure.

4. Balance of the maternity programme refers to the balance of the maternity insurance funds at the end of reference period.

23 Twenty-three

民营经济

Private Economy

23-1 民营经济增加值

Value-added of Private Economy

单位：亿元 (100 million yuan)

指 标	Item	2007	2008	2009	2010	2011	2012
民营经济增加值	**Value—added of Private Economy**	**904.03**	**1152.42**	**1295.10**	**1610.76**	**2103.98**	**2759.40**
第一产业	Primary Industry	101.77	134.80	139.77	165.63	197.77	378.24
第二产业	Secondary Industry	380.81	472.35	525.39	674.31	856.50	1128.85
工 业	Industry	339.66	418.36	455.97	579.44	728.81	1042.88
建筑业	Construction	41.15	53.99	69.42	94.87	127.69	85.97
第三产业	Tertiary Industry	421.45	545.27	629.94	770.82	1049.71	1252.31
#交通运输、仓储和邮政业	Transport,Storage and Post	124.94	170.50	183.89	234.88	320.63	388.18
批发和零售业	Wholesale and Retail Trade	90.05	114.46	135.02	178.61	234.14	248.36
住宿和餐饮业	Hotel and Catering Services	70.72	103.55	121.96	148.74	193.28	240.62
房地产业	Real Estate	80.14	91.39	118.72	124.70	146.60	56.13

注：2012年民营经济增加值核算口径调整(以下相关表同)。
Note: The accounting caliber of the value—added of private economy was adjusted in 2012(the related tables in the chapter are the same) .

23-2 民营经济分产业增加值占该产业增加值比重

Value-added of Private Economy Unit as Percentage to GDP

单位：% (%)

指 标	Item	2007	2008	2009	2010	2011	2012
民营经济增加值占比	**Gross Domestic Product**	**31.3**	**32.4**	**33.1**	**35.0**	**36.9**	**40.3**
第一产业	Primary Industry	22.8	25.0	25.4	26.5	27.2	42.4
第二产业	Secondary Industry	33.9	34.5	35.6	37.5	39.0	42.1
工 业	Industry	34.7	35.0	36.4	38.2	39.8	47.0
建筑业	Construction	28.2	30.9	31.0	33.5	35.0	18.7
第三产业	Tertiary Industry	32.1	33.0	33.4	35.4	37.7	38.2
#交通运输、仓储和邮政业	Transport,Storage and Post	44.3	46.0	46.0	48.9	54.3	56.5
批发和零售业	Wholesale and Retail Trade	45.3	46.0	46.0	48.6	52.2	48.3
住宿和餐饮业	Hotel and Catering Services	78.5	79.4	79.5	82.3	86.1	90.3
房地产业	Real Estate	86.0	87.2	87.2	89.3	91.5	31.8

23-3 民营经济固定资产投资(2012)

Private Economic Investment in Fixed Assets

单位：亿元　　100 million yuan

指标名称	Item	2012	2012年比2011年增长(%) Increase Rate in 2012 over 2011(%)
民营经济固定资产投资	**Private economic investment in fixed assets**	**2585.45**	**48.6**
按登记注册类型分	By Status of Registration		
私　营	Private Enterprises	885.47	41.3
集　体	Collective-owned Enterprises	19.58	24.2
股份合作	Cooperative Enterprises	21.56	-14.1
集体联营	Collective Joint Ownership Enterprises	1.42	38.9
其他联营	Other Collective Ownership Enterprises	0.50	-44.4
其他有限责任公司	Other Limited Liability Corporations	1325.40	55.4
股份有限公司	Share Holding Enterprises	180.41	24.6
其他内资	Other domestic enterprises	108.08	129.4
个体经营	Self-employed	43.03	69.1
按行业分	By Industry		
第一产业	Primary Industry	63.36	101.3
第二产业	Secondary Industry	1041.81	27.7
工　业	Industry	1034.50	27.4
建筑业	Construction	7.31	102.2
第三产业	Tertiary Industry	1480.27	65.9
交通运输、仓储和邮政业	Transportation,Storage,Postal,& Telecommunication Services	30.97	60.3
批发和零售业	Wholesale & Retail Trade	41.56	74.4
住宿和餐饮业	Hotel & Catering Trade	43.51	54.0
金融业	Finance	1.39	-28.8
房地产业	Real Estate	1240.45	67.5
其他服务业	Other service industries	122.39	56.2

注：本表统计口径为计划总投资500万元及以上固定资产项目投资和房地产开发投资。

Note:1.Data of 2012 in the table refer to those projects that planned to invest 5 million yuan at least in urban areas, projects funded by rural non-farm households and real estate development.

23-4 规模以上民营经济工业企业主要经济指标(2012)

单位：万元

指　标	Item	企业单位数（个） Number of Enterprises (unit)
总　计	**Total**	**3794**
#亏损企业	Loss Making Enterprises	1000
按轻重工业分	**Grouped by Type of Light and Heavy Industry**	
轻工业	Light Industry	958
重工业	Heavy Industry	2836
按企业规模分	**Grouped by Size of Enterprise**	
#大型企业	Large	20
中型企业	Medium	373
小型企业	Small	3213
按登记注册类型分	**Grouped by Registration Categories**	
#股份合作企业	Share-holding Cooperative Enterprises	44
联营企业	Joint Owned Enterprises	21
有限责任公司	Companies with Limited Liabilities	1202
股份有限公司	Share-holding Companies with Limited Liabilities	107
私营企业	Private Enterprises	2263
其他企业	Others	90

注：民营经济工业统计口径为全部年主营业务收入500万元及以上工业企业。

Main Economic Indicators of Industrial Enterprises above Designated Size of Private Economy

(10000 yuan)

工业总产值 (当年价) Gross Industial OutputValue (current price)	固定资产 原　价 Original Value of Fixed Assets	主营业务 收　入 Revenue from Principal Business	利 润 总 额 Total Profits	从业人员平均 人数(万人) Annual Average Number of Employed Persons (10000 persons)
35729091	**13685194**	**30351235**	**2797283**	**52.66**
7969237	5751010	6032147	-455898	14.10
7416817	1989961	6413891	758867	10.89
28312274	11695233	23937344	2038416	41.77
3997610	2555053	3529001	261255	4.92
9487782	4397223	7707158	1043898	18.19
21928723	6478584	18910490	1502707	28.80
457116	786538	263957	28356	0.84
146239	28961	140854	20914	0.22
13592689	6151582	11612024	936600	16.64
1743777	654151	1678483	155633	2.47
18408594	5715927	15408752	1547231	30.54
917675	265832	835038	85049	1.13

Note:Private economic industrial statistical was the industrial of main business income of 5 million yuan and above.

23-4 续表

单位：万元

指　标	Item	单位数(个) Number of Enterprises (unit)
按工业行业分	**Grouped by Industrial Sector**	
煤炭开采和洗选业	Mining and Washing of Coal	1113
石油和天然气开采业	Mining and Processing of Ferrous Metal Ores	
黑色金属矿采选业	Mining and Processing of Non-Ferrous Metal Ores	54
有色金属矿采选业	Mining and Processing of Nonmetal Ores	37
非金属矿采选业	Processing of Food from Agricultural Products	122
开采辅助活动	Manufacture of Foods	1
其他采矿业	Manufacture of Beverages	1
农副食品加工业	Manufacture of Tobacco	240
食品制造业	Manufacture of Textile	87
酒、饮料和精制茶制造业	Manufacture of Textile Wearing Apparel,Footware and Caps	266
烟草制品业	Manufacture of Leather, Fur, Feather and Related Products	2
纺织业	Processing of Timber, Manufacture of Wood,Bamboo, Rattan, Palm and Straw Products	15
纺织服装、服饰业	Manufacture of Furniture	14
皮革、毛皮、羽毛及其制品和制鞋业	Manufacture of Paper and Paper Products	10
木材加工和木、竹、藤、棕、草制品业	Printing, Reproduction of Recording Media	106
家具制造业	Manufacture of Articles For Culture, Education and Sport Activities	14
造纸和纸制品业	Processing of Petroleum, Coking, Processing of Nuclear Fuel	51
印刷和记录媒介复制业	Manufacture of Raw Chemical Materials and Chemical Products	31
文教、工美、体育和娱乐用品制造业	Manufacture of Medicines	20
石油加工、炼焦和核燃料加工业	Manufacture of Rubber	37
化学原料和化学制品制造业	Manufacture of Plastics	198
医药制造业	Manufacture of Non-metallic Mineral Products	93
化学纤维制造业	Smelting and Pressing of Ferrous Metals	
橡胶和塑料制品业	Smelting and Pressing of Non-ferrous Metals	79
非金属矿物制品业	Manufacture of Metal Products	509
黑色金属冶炼和压延加工业	Manufacture of General Purpose Machinery	189
有色金属冶炼和压延加工业	Manufacture of Special Purpose Machinery	72
金属制品业	Manufacture of Transport Equipment	65
通用设备制造业	Manufacture of Electrical Machinery and Equipment	66
专用设备制造业	Manufacture of Communication Equipment, Computers and Other Electronic Equipment	65
汽车制造业	Manufacture of Measuring Instruments and Machinery for Cultural Activity and Office Work	34
铁路、船舶、航空航天和其他运输设备制造业	Manufacture of Artwork and Other Manufacturing	9
电气机械和器材制造业	Recycling and Disposal of Waste	69
计算机、通信和其他电子设备制造业	Production and Supply of Electric Power and Heat Power	20
仪器仪表制造业	Production and Supply of Gas	11
其他制造业	Production and Supply of Water	10
废弃资源综合利用业	Recycling and Disposal of Waste	6
金属制品、机械和设备修理业	Metal products, Machinery and Equipment Repair Industry	2
电力、热力生产和供应业	Production and Distribution of Electric Power and Heat Power	62
燃气生产和供应业	Production and Distribution of Gas	6
水的生产和供应业	Production and Distribution of Water	8

注：工业行业按国民经济行业分类(GB/T4754—2011)分。

Continued

(10000 yuan)

工业总产值 (当年价) Gross Industial OutputValue (current price)	固定资产 原价 Original Value of Fixed Assets	主营业务 收入 Revenue from Principal Business	利润 总额 Total Profits	从业人员数 (万人) Annual Average Number of Employed Persons (10000 persons)
10752235	2969801	8355462	1104584	20.56
235719	61869	227246	15625	0.46
192893	47643	173397	27473	0.38
1085825	121978	1038017	184528	0.86
1053	211	1041	-85	0.01
899	395	708	-44	0.00
1613478	202787	1504934	64496	1.54
702620	94126	673856	120095	0.95
1891337	550979	1589160	259136	3.08
90721	206128	91348	17714	0.04
61427	12214	56018	-2004	0.31
23330	8219	23465	977	0.10
65503	4467	48919	1484	0.24
767005	88553	726937	27483	1.54
120488	16657	108665	17064	0.14
306601	71093	292592	27654	0.37
81716	51749	66368	9355	0.17
53342	4930	46903	1301	0.13
757994	167181	566313	37376	0.60
1935131	1318938	1712628	100465	2.18
1919154	431069	1493755	214690	2.52
484845	117299	420760	22163	0.76
3212545	1925669	2820755	101059	5.05
3206905	478592	2879184	65582	2.80
2687050	2396676	2161936	235099	2.47
360620	157659	323071	18551	0.62
376307	81875	257007	24639	0.78
369223	89516	315325	14003	0.62
620376	156467	796305	23064	0.67
192454	90882	173040	6816	0.50
523231	74280	454036	23831	0.71
72805	19031	60447	598	0.29
80324	11704	62529	7789	0.23
31705	50643	28187	2070	0.08
35474	3738	32163	383	0.03
6997	1193	5577	35	0.01
516728	1279374	488763	21159	0.50
239355	114852	233835	1947	0.23
53680	204760	40585	-869	0.17

Note:Data in this table is classified by sector of the National Economy (GB/T4754-2011).

23-5 资质以上民营经济建筑企业主要经济指标(2012)

单位：万元

指 标	Item	有工作量企业数(个) Number of Workload Enterprises(unit)
总 计	**Total**	**442**
按登记注册类型分组	**Grouped by Registration Categories**	
内资企业	Domestic Funded Enterprises	442
#联营企业	Joint Owned Enterprises	2
其他联营企业	Others	2
有限责任公司	Companies with Limited Liabilities	180
其他有限责任公司	Others	180
股份有限公司	Share-holding Companies with Limited Liabilities	19
私营企业	Private Enterprises	142
私营独资企业	Private-funded Enterprises	2
私营合伙企业	Private Partnership Enterprise	1
私营有限责任公司	Private Limited Liabilities Companies	129
私营股份有限公司	Private Share-holding Companies Ltd.	10
按建筑业行业中类分组	**By Sector**	
房屋和土木工程建筑业	Housing Construction and Civil Engineering Industry	324
建筑安装业	Construction and Installation Industry	55
建筑装饰业	Construction and Descoration Industry	40
其他建筑业	Other Construction Industries	23
按企业资质等级分组	**By Qualification Standard**	
施工总承包	Chief Construction Contract	320
一级	First Grade	9
二级	Second Grade	93
三级及以下	Third and Lower Grade	218
专业承包	Professional Contract	122
一级	First Grade	6
二级	Second Grade	58
三级及以下	Third and Lower Grade	58

Main Economic Indicators of Construction Enterprises above Qualification of Private Economy

(10000 yuan)

建筑业总产值 Gross Output Value of Construction	固定资产原价 Original Value of Fixed Assets	工程结算收入 Prime Operating Revenue	利润总额 Total Profits	平均人数(人) Annual Average Number of Employed Persons(person)
1921592	**312559**	**1835728**	**37197**	**95259**
1921592	312559	1835728	37197	95259
3808	2534	3778	-41	218
3808	2534	3778	-41	218
724597	126986	730468	17199	46196
724597	126986	730468	17199	46196
114416	24748	109628	2264	5224
637740	92268	607154	11673	24867
1489	647	3552	21	52
3732	1351	2853	24	167
499394	82694	464456	10819	18643
133125	7576	136294	809	6005
1770295	273714	1668330	35475	87755
76940	20770	80434	1379	4194
35363	4156	44831	1042	1626
38994	13919	42133	-700	1684
1750031	271612	1627387	32672	86468
424492	28645	305375	5330	9765
685445	125440	699008	14568	38123
640094	117526	623004	12774	38580
171561	40947	208341	4525	8184
12938	1299	14972	39	633
100812	18580	112364	4125	4381
57810	21068	81006	362	3170

23-6 限额以上民营经济批发零售企业主要经济指标(2012)

单位：万元

指　标	Item	企业个数(个) Number of Enterprises(unit)
批发业	**Wholesale Trade**	**375**
按登记注册类型分组	**by Types of Registration**	
内资企业	Domestic Funded Enterprises	375
#集体企业	Collective-owned Enterprises	18
股份合作企业	Share-holding Cooperative Enterprises	4
有限责任公司	Limited Liabilities Companies	216
其他有限责任公司	Other Limited Liabilities Companies	216
股份有限公司	Share-holding Companies Ltd.	8
私营企业	Private Enterprises	117
私营独资企业	Private-funded Enterprises	12
私营合伙企业	Private Partnership Enterprise	5
私营有限责任公司	Private Limited Liabilities Companies	93
私营股份有限公司	Private Share-holding Companies Ltd.	7
其他企业	Other Enterprises	12
按批发行业分组	**by Wholesale Trade Sector**	
农畜产品批发业	Wholesale of Farm Produce and Livestack Products	1
食品、饮料及烟草制品批发	Food, Beverages, Tobacco	36
纺织、服装及日用品批发	Textiles Products,Clothing and Commodity	17
文化、体育用品及器材批发	Culture&Sports Articles and Equipments	4
医药及医疗器材批发	Medicines and Special Appliances of Medicines	44
矿产品、建材及化工产品批发	Mineral Products,Materials of Construction and Chemical Products	212
机械设备、五金交电及电子产品批发	Mechinery Equipments,Hardwares,Electric Appliances and Eletronic Products	51
其他批发	Others	10

Main Economic Indicators of Wholesale and Retail Trade Enterprises above Designated Size of Private Economy

(10000 yuan)

固定资产原价 Original Value of Fixed Assets	主营业务收入 Prime Operating Revenue	主营业务税金及附加 Tax and associate charge	利润总额 Total Profits
123094	**4287917**	**7928**	**16158**
123094	4287917	7928	16158
14010	74605	249	240
1274	8519	31	84
73105	3089533	5789	5606
73105	3089533	5789	5606
6217	126971	440	6657
24620	906173	1278	3181
1744	90047	50	7462
219	29434	7	-1309
21737	760294	1200	-2672
920	26398	21	-298
3867	82116	141	388
28	6659	2	44
16819	309643	1149	22432
3257	225043	513	1037
1086	12425	30	-13
25520	572016	1594	9683
57705	2675681	3381	-17942
15114	447699	886	1424
3565	38751	373	-507

23-6 续表

单位：万元

指　　标	Item	企业个数(个) Number of Enterprises(unit)
零售业	**Retail Trade**	**674**
按登记注册类型分组	**By Types of Registration**	
内资企业	Domestic Funded Enterprises	674
#集体企业	Collective-owned Enterprises	7
股份合作企业	Share-holding Cooperative Enterprises	6
联营企业	Associated Enterprises	2
有限责任公司	Limited Liabilities Companies	341
国有独资公司	State-owned Companies	1
其他有限责任公司	Other Limited Liabilities Companies	340
股份有限公司	Share-holding Companies Ltd.	9
私营企业	Private Enterprises	281
私营独资企业	Private-funded Enterprises	37
私营合伙企业	Private Partnership Enterprise	12
私营有限责任公司	Private Limited Liabilities Companies	215
私营股份有限公司	Private Share-holding Companies Ltd.	17
其他企业	Other Enterprises	28
按零售行业小类分组	**By Retail Trade Sector**	
综合零售	Comprehensive Retail Sale	97
食品、饮料及烟草制品专门零售	Food, Beverages, Tobacco	44
纺织、服装及日用品专门零售	Textiles Products,Gaments and Commodity	14
文化、体育用品及器材专门零售	Medicines and Special Appliances of Medicines	10
医药及医疗器材专门零售	Automobiles,Motocycles,Fuels and Their Parts	36
汽车、摩托车、燃料及零配件专门零售	Household Electrical Appliances and Electronic Products	327
家用电器及电子产品专门零售	Hardwares,Furnitures and Materials of Decoration	125
五金、家具及室内装修材料专门零售	Hardware,Furniture and Interior Decoration Materials	8
无店铺及其他零售	Non-shop and Other Retails	13

continued

(10000 yuan)

固定资产原价 Original Value of Fixed Assets	主营业务收入 Prime Operating Revenue	主营业务税金及附加 Tax and associate charge	利润总额 Total Profits
318011	**4179058**	**15728**	**77737**
318011	4179058	15728	77737
2163	33043	165	8661
2979	36792	81	245
2364	15445	3	326
233671	2714388	11207	48556
5034	1077	1	6
228636	2713312	11206	48549
1901	67008	56	328
66503	1152309	3680	16386
3534	44841	367	687
2704	19243	128	260
57319	1061419	3054	15311
2946	26806	131	129
8430	160074	537	3236
131872	731953	6308	20427
13172	182212	1277	13232
21504	62588	396	-266
1509	26923	271	29
6166	133775	478	2359
123274	2529662	4266	27411
9053	350745	1302	4852
1854	7018	32	209
9608	154182	1398	9485

23-7 限额以上民营经济住宿餐饮企业主要经济指标(2012)

单位：万元

指 标	Item	企业个数(个) Number of Enterprises(unit)
住宿业	**Quartering Services**	**256**
按登记注册类型分组	**by Types of Registration**	
内资企业	Domestic Funded Enterprises	256
#集体企业	Collective-owned Enterprises	12
股份合作企业	Share-holding Cooperative Enterprises	3
有限责任公司	Limited Liabilities Companies	108
其他有限责任公司	Other Limited Liabilities Companies	108
股份有限公司	Share-holding Companies Ltd.	3
私营企业	Private Enterprises	115
私营独资企业	Private-funded Enterprises	34
私营合伙企业	Private Partnership Enterprise	19
私营有限责任公司	Private Limited Liabilities Companies	53
私营股份有限公司	Private Share-holding Companies Ltd.	9
其他企业	Other Enterprises	15
按住宿行业分组	**by Quartering Services Sector**	
旅游饭店	Tourism Hotels	188
一般旅馆	General Hotels	63
其他住宿服务	Other Hotel Services	5
餐饮业	**Catering Services**	**169**
按登记注册类型分组	**by Registration Categories**	
内资企业	Domestic Funded Enterprises	169
#股份合作企业	Share-holding Cooperative Enterprises	2
有限责任公司	Companies with Limited Liabilities	56
其他有限责任公司	Others	56
股份有限公司	Share-holding Companies with Limited Liabilities	2
私营企业	Private Enterprises	94
私营独资企业	Private-funded Enterprises	38
私营合伙企业	Private Partnership Enterprise	9
私营有限责任公司	Private Limited Liabilities Companies	40
私营股份有限公司	Private Share-holding Companies Ltd.	7
其他企业	Others	15
按餐饮行业分组	**by Catering Services Sector**	
正餐服务	Restaurant	167
快餐服务	Snack Counter	2
饮料及冷饮服务	Beverages and Cold Drinks	
其他餐饮服务业	Others	

Main Economic Indicators of Accommodation and Catering Enterprises above Designated Size of Private Economy

(10000 yuan)

固定资产原价 Original Value of Fixed Assets	主营业务收入 Prime Operating Revenue	主营业务税金及附加 Taxes and Other charges on Principal Business	利润总额 Total Profits
385554	**253723**	**13809**	**171**
385554	253723	13809	171
18326	8139	406	2127
1662	1269	63	71
206313	146693	7817	-2682
206313	146693	7817	-2682
2442	2177	111	130
135213	84549	4791	-57
51025	30037	1733	2075
9210	11818	410	97
62717	33214	2043	-1038
12261	9480	605	-1190
21598	10897	622	582
323102	210335	11279	-883
62410	40440	2387	1190
43	2947	143	-136
84153	**162790**	**9633**	**-1840**
84153	162790	9633	-1840
848	1035	40	142
29868	78183	4457	-2868
29868	78183	4457	-2868
222	4510	257	194
41185	65659	4049	2205
13929	22005	1440	1498
3981	8717	416	458
21524	30003	1870	-192
1752	4935	325	441
12031	13403	829	-1513
83833	158599	9395	-1981
320	4190	239	141

24

Twenty-four

民族自治地方

Minority Nationality Autonomous Areas

24-1 民族自治地方行政区划(2012)
Administrative Division of Minority Nationality Autonomous Areas

单位：个 (unit)

民族自治州(县)名称	Autonomous State(County)	地级 Prefectural Level	县级 County Level	#县级市 City at County Level	成立时间 Time of Comeinto Existence	土地面积(平方公里) Total Land Area(sq.km)
黔西南布依族苗族自治州	Qianxinan(Bouyei & Miao)Autonomous State	1	8	1	1982年5月1日	16804
黔东南苗族侗族自治州	Qiandongnan(Miao & Dong)Autonomous State	1	16	1	1956年7月23日	30337
黔南布依族苗族自治州	Qiannan(Bouyei & Miao)Autonomous State	1	12	2	1956年8月8日	26197
道真仡佬族苗族自治县	Daozhen(Gelao & Miao)Autonomous County		1		1987年11月29日	2156
务川仡佬族苗族自治县	Wuchuan(Gelao & Miao)Autonomous County		1		1987年11月26日	2773
镇宁布依族苗族自治县	Zhenning(Bouyei & Miao)Autonomous County		1		1963年9月11日	1703
关岭布依族苗族自治县	Guanling(Bouyei & Miao)Autonomous County		1		1981年12月31日	1468
紫云苗族布依族自治县	Ziyun(Miao & Bouyei)Autonomous County		1		1966年2月11日	2284
威宁彝族回族苗族自治县	Weining(Yi,Hui & Miao)Autonomous County		1		1954年11月11日	6296
玉屏侗族自治县	Yuping(Dong)Autonomous County		1		1984年11月7日	516
印江土家族苗族自治县	Yinjiang(Tujia & Miao)Autonomous County		1		1987年11月20日	1961
沿河土家族自治县	Yanhe(Tujia)Autonomous County		1		1987年11月23日	2469
松桃苗族自治县	Songtao(Miao)Autonomous County		1		1956年12月31日	2861
三都水族自治县	Sandu(Shui)Autonomous County		1		1957年1月2日	2384

注：资料来源于省民政厅。
Note: Data in the table are provided by the provinvial department of civil affairs.

24-2 少数民族分布
Geographic Distribution of Minority Nationalities

民族	Nationality	分布的主要地区	Main Geographic Distribution
苗族	Miao	黔东南州、黔南州、黔西南州、松桃县、紫云县、务川县、水城县	Qiandongnan,Qiannan,Qianxinan,Songtao, Ziyun Wuchuan,Shuicheng
布依族	Bouyei	黔南州、黔西南州、镇宁县、紫云县	Qiannan,Qianxinan,Zhenning,Ziyun
侗族	Dong	黔东南州、玉屏县、碧江区、石阡县	Qiandongnan,Yuping,Bijiang,Shiqian
土家族	Tujia	铜仁市	Tongren
彝族	Yi	毕节市、六盘水市	Bijie,Liupanshui
仡佬族	Gelao	遵义市、关岭县、石阡县	Zunyi,Guanling,Shiqian
水族	Shui	三都县	Sandu
回族	Hui	威宁县、兴仁县、平坝县、兴义市	Weining,Xingren,Pingba,Xingyi
白族	Bai	毕节市、盘县	Bijie,panxian
瑶族	Yao	黔东南州、荔波县	Qiandongnan,Libo
壮族	Zhuang	从江县、独山县、荔波县、都匀市	Congjiang,Dushan,Libo,Duyun
畲族	She	凯里市、麻江县、都匀市、福泉市	Kaili,Majiang,Duyun,Fuquan
毛南族	Maonan	平塘县、独山县、惠水县	Pingtang,Dushan,Huishui
蒙古族	Mongoloid	毕节市、石阡县、思南县	Bijie,Shiqian,Sinan
仫佬族	Mulam	凯里市、麻江县、黄平县	Kaili,Majiang,Huangping
满族	Man	黔西县、大方县、金沙县、云岩区	Qianxi,Dafang,Jinsha,Yunyan
羌族	Qiang	石阡县、江口县	Shiqian,Jiangkou

24-3 民族自治地方经济社会主要指标

Major Social and Economic Indicators of Minority Nationality Autonomous Areas

指　标	Item	2011	2012	2012年比2011年增长(%) Increase Rate in 2012 over 2011(%)
人口	**Population**			
年末常住人口(万人)	Number of Resident Population at Year-end(10000 persons)	1347.16	1352.34	0.4
#少数民族人口	Minority Population	866.89	870.20	0.4
生产总值	**Gross Domestic Product**			
生产总值(亿元)	Gross Domestic Product(100 million yuan)	1560.50	1982.78	16.1
固定资产投资	**Investment in Fixed Assets**			
固定资产投资总额(亿元)	Total Investment in Fixed Assets(100 million yuan)	1311.02	2110.36	61.0
财政、金融	**Government Finance and Banking**			
公共财政收入(亿元)	Local Financial Revenue(100 million yuan)	155.85	227.65	46.1
公共财政支出(亿元)	Financial Expenditure(100 million yuan)	653.56	830.43	27.1
金融机构人民币存款余额(亿元)	Total Savins Deposit Balance at Year-end(100 million yuan)	1941.49	2321.55	19.6
金融机构人民币贷款余额(亿元)	Total Loan Balance at Year-end(100 million yuan)	1130.50	1426.37	26.2
城乡居民储蓄余额(亿元)	Urban and Rural Resident Savings Deposit Balance(100 million yuan)	1098.81	1344.64	22.4
农业	**Agriculture**			
农林牧渔业总产值(亿元)	Gross Agricultural Output Value(100 million yuan)	534.26	644.21	20.6
粮食产量(万吨)	Output of Grain(10000 tons)	385.85	475.96	23.4
油菜籽产量(万吨)	Output of Rapeseeds(10000 tons)	23.42	25.55	9.1
牛年底存栏数(万头)	Large Animals(year-end)(10000 heads)	257.06	256.77	-0.1
猪年底存栏数(万头)	Hogs(year-end)(10000 heads)	679.96	709.61	4.4
羊年底存栏数(万只)	Sheep and Goats(year-end)(10000 heads)	151.31	162.42	7.3
工业	**Industry**			
原煤产量(万吨)	Output of Coal(10000 tons)	2968.78	3348.28	12.8
发电量(亿千瓦小时)	Output of Electricity(100 million kwh)	263.01	385.17	46.5
生铁产量(万吨)	Pig Iron(10000 tons)	33.18	4.32	-87.0
运输邮电	**Transportation and Post**			
公路里程(公里)	Length of Highways(km)	61528	83454	35.6
邮路总长度(公里)	Length of Postal Routes(km)	18442	18719	1.5
商业	**Trade**			
社会消费品零售总额(亿元)	Total Retail Sales of Consumer Goods(100 million yuan)	456.92	530.63	16.1
教育	**Education**			
在校学生数(万人)	Students Enrollment(10000 persons)			
高等学校	Institutions of Higher Education	5.85	6.33	8.3
中等学校	Secondary Schools	110.52	111.36	0.8
小　学	Primary Schools	169.23	158.18	-6.5
专任教师(万人)	Full-time Teachers(10000 persons)			
高等学校	Institutions of Higher Education	0.34	0.37	8.2
中等学校	Secondary Schools	5.91	6.22	5.2
小　学	Primary Schools	8.40	8.53	1.5
人均水平	**Per Capita Standard of Living**			
人均生产总值(元)	Per Capita Gross Domestic Product(yuan)	11546	14690	15.6
人均公共财政收入(元)	Per Capita Local Financial Revenue(yuan)	1153	1687	46.3
城乡居民人均储蓄(元)	Per Capita Urban and Rural Resident Savings(yuan)	8130	9962	22.5

注：表中人均水平数据按常住半年人口计算。

Note:Data of Per Capita Standard of Living are calculated according to resident population staying at home for 6 months.

24-4 民族自治地方经济发展主要指标(2012)
Major Economic Indicators of Minority Nationality Autonomous Areas

指 标	Item	民族自治地方 Minority Nationality Autonomous Areas	民族自治州 Minority Nationality Autonomous State	民族自治县 Minority Nationality Autonomous County
生产总值(亿元)	**Gross Domestic Product(100 million yuan)**	**1982.78**	**1523.52**	**487.17**
第一产业	Primary Industry	395.64	265.62	136.71
第二产业	Secondary Industry	667.33	541.79	130.13
第三产业	Tertiary Industry	919.81	716.11	220.33
农业	**Agriculture**			
乡村从业人口(万人)	Rural Employment(10000 persons)	940.96	646.71	313.85
农用机械总动力(万千瓦)	Total Agricultural Machinery Power(10000 kw)	952.24	737.96	228.33
化肥使用量(折纯量)(万吨)	Consumption of Chemical Fertilizers(10000 tons)	42.46	25.81	17.01
有效灌溉面积(千公顷)	Irrigated Areas(1000 hectares)	501.49	448.75	78.41
农作物播种面积(千公顷)	Total Sown Areas (1000 hectares)	2213.12	1483.81	773.50
#粮 食	Grain Crops	1289.06	859.24	454.11
油菜籽	Rapeseeds	207.76	144.03	64.34
粮食总产量(万吨)	Total Grain Yield(10000 tons)	475.96	321.57	163.37
油菜籽产量(万吨)	Output of Rapeseeds(10000 tons)	25.55	18.18	8.19
烤烟产量(万吨)	Output of Flue -cured Tobacco (10000 tons)	17.79	9.76	8.03
茶叶产量(万吨)	Output of Tea (10000 tons)	2.98	1.92	1.12
当年造林面积(千公顷)	Afforested Areas in 2004(1000 hectares)	141.33	104.46	39.00
牲畜当年存栏数	Animals in Hand			
猪(万头)	Hogs(10000 heads)	709.61	440.63	282.15
牛(万头)	Large Animals(10000 heads)	256.77	176.99	85.82
羊(万只)	Sheep and Goats(10000 heads)	162.42	89.46	73.38
牲畜当年出栏数	Number of Slaughtered Animals			
猪(万头)	Hogs(10000 heads)	772.30	524.34	263.33
牛(万头)	Large Animals(10000 heads)	55.74	37.13	19.97
羊(万只)	Sheep and Goats(10000 heads)	110.76	51.53	59.70
肉类总产量(万吨)	Output of Meat(10000 tons)	80.83	52.88	29.47
水产品产量(万吨)	Total Aquatic Products(10000 tons)	8.82	6.30	2.75
农林牧渔业总产值(亿元)	Gross Output Value of Farming,Forestry,Animal Husbandry and Fishery(100 million yuan)	644.21	438.86	215.55
#农 业	Farming	346.23	231.47	120.43

24−4 续表 continued

指 标	Item	民族自治地方 Minority Nationality Autonomous Areas	民族自治州 Minority Nationality Autonomous State	民族自治县 Minority Nationality Autonomous County
林 业	Forestry	45.67	39.91	6.62
牧 业	Animal Husbandry	222.33	144.64	80.77
渔 业	Fishery	17.84	14.68	3.51
工业(规模以上)	**Industry(above designated size)**			
企业单位数(个)	Number of Industrial Enterprises(unit)	1007	777	233
工业总产值(亿元)	Total Gross Industrial Output Value(100 million yuan)	1489.62	1258.12	234.16
工业销售产值(亿元)	Sales Output Value of Industry(100 million yuan)	1396.23	1185.85	213.04
工业增加值(亿元)	Value-added of Industry(100 million yuan)	437.19	384.27	53.41
利润总额(亿元)	Total Profits and Taxes(100 million yuan)	88.14	79.46	8.63
主要工业产品产量	Output of Major Industrial Products			
原 煤(万吨)	Coal(10000 tons)	3348.28	3098.33	249.95
生 铁(万吨)	Pig Iron(10000 tons)	4.32	4.32	
水 泥(万吨)	Cement(10000 tons)	2372.59	1892.98	537.49
发电量(亿千瓦小时)	Electricity(100 million kwh)	385.17	328.16	57.01
固定资产投资	**Investment in Fixed Assets**			
固定资产投资完成额(亿元)	All Investment in Fixed Assets in the Whole Province (100 million yuan)	2110.36	1642.91	495.07
商业	**Trade**			
社会消费品零售总额(亿元)	Total Retail Sales of Consumer Goods(100 million yuan)	530.63	426.75	111.67
财政、金融	**Government Finance and Banking**			
公共财政收入(亿元)	Local Financial Revenue (100 million yuan)	227.66	192.37	37.01
公共财政支出(亿元)	Financial Expenditure(100 million yuan)	830.44	629.56	215.22
金融机构人民币存款余额(亿元)	Deposits Balance(100 million yuan)	2321.55	1866.55	484.67
#储蓄余额	Urban and Rural Resident Savings Deposit Balance	1344.64	1059.38	303.78
金融机构人民币贷款余额(亿元)	Loans Balance(100 million yuan)	1426.37	1144.23	301.40

24–5 民族自治地方公共财政收入(2012)
Public Financial Revenue of Minority Nationality Autonomous Areas

单位：万元 (10000 yuan)

指　标	Item	民族自治地方 Miniority Nationality Autonomous Area	民族自治州 Nationality Minority Autonomous State	民族自治县 Minority Nationality Autonomous County
公共财政收入	**Public Financial Revenue**	**2276519**	**1923655**	**370114**
税收收入	**Tax Income**	**1446456**	**1202548**	**255326**
#增值税	Value-added Tax	105586	87751	18229
营业税	Business Tax	474878	393562	85560
企业所得税	Enterprises' Income Tax	125240	105821	20465
个人所得税	Personal Income Tax	83503	74707	9301
资源税	Resource Tax	26868	22769	4224
城市维护建设税	Urban Maintenance and Development Tax	80128	69296	11202
耕地占用税	Cultivated Land Usage Tax	274176	234165	43328
契　税	Deed Tax	72692	61792	11417
烟叶税	Tobacco Tax	77835	41844	35991
非税收入	**Income from Non -tax**	**830063**	**721107**	**114788**
#专项收入	Expert Project Income	86711	70585	16516
行政事业性收费收入	Penalty and Confiscatory Income	147449	122798	25666
罚没收入	Expert Project Income	63809	52581	11769
国有资本经营收入	State-owned Assets Profit	12283	3446	8837
国有资源(资产)有偿使用收入	Planning Subsidies to Loss-suffering Stated-owned Enterprises Income from Administrative Fees	342084	303169	42155

注：资料来源于省财政厅(下表同)。

Note:Data in the table are obtained from Guizhou Provincial Finance Department(the same applies to the next table).

24-6 民族自治地方公共财政支出(2012)

Pnblic Financial Expenditure of Minority Nationality Autonomous Areas

单位：万元 (10000 yuan)

指 标	Item	民族自治地方 Miniority Nationality Autonomous Area	民族自治州 Minority Nationality Autonomous State	民族自治县 Minority Nationality Autonomous County
公共财政支出	**Public Financial Expenditure**	**8304313**	**6295506**	**2152229**
一般公共服务	General Public Service	1617138	1329007	322521
国 防	National Defense	10479	8709	1916
公共安全	Public Security	340640	265141	80670
教 育	Education	1797352	1291973	542123
科学技术	Science and Technology	39054	36039	3393
文化体育与传媒	Culture,Sports and Media	94984	77194	19219
社会保障和就业	Social Security and Jobs	800975	620081	193829
医疗卫生	Health Care	773302	563793	224467
节能环保	Energy Conservation and Environmental Protection	210051	150341	62690
城乡社区事务	Urban and Country Community Affairs	251799	195002	59327
农林水事务	Affairs of Agriculture,Forest and Water	1309708	965380	364671
交通运输	Transport	159039	127588	32516
其他支出	Other Expenditures	899792	665258	244887

24-7 少数民族教育(2012)

Education of Minority Nationality

单位：人 (person)

类 别	Sort	毕业生 Grad-uates	招 生 New Students Enro-llment	在校生 Total Students Enrollment	专任教师 Full-time Teachers	独立设置的少数民族学校 Minority Nationality Schools	
						学校数 Number of Schools	在校学生 Students Enrollment
普通中学	Regular Secondary Schools	343094	422504	1148755	64441	205	305334
#高 中	Senior	77553	128238	313056	16552		105516
初 中	Junior	265541	294266	835699	47889		199818
小 学	Primary Schools	303243	253674	1596713	84680	614	309669
特殊教育学校	Special Education Schools	361	789	3787	399		
幼儿园	Kindergartens	182790	250349	372274	8381	34	

注：资料来源于省教育厅。
Note:Data in the table are provided by the provinvial Department of Education.

24-8 民族自治地方社会发展主要指标(2012)
Major Indicators on Social Development of Minority Nationality Autonomous Areas

指　标	Item	民族自治地方 Minority Nationality Autonomous Areas	民族自治州 Minority Nationality Autonomous State	民族自治县 Minority Nationality Autonomous County
人口	**Population**			
年末常住半年人口(万人)	Number of Population at The Year-end (10000 persons)	1352.34	951.11	430.08
#少数民族人口	Minority Population	870.20	644.44	261.56
人口密度(人/平方公里)	Population Density(person/sq.km)	138.24	129.69	160.03
交通运输	**Traffic**			
公路里程(公里)	Length of Highways(km)	83454	58627	26167
邮电、通讯	**Post and Telecommunications**			
邮政所总数(处)	Number of Post Offices(unit)	492	405	101
邮路总长度(公里)	Length of Postal Routes(km)	18719	12446	6472
农村投递线路总长度(公里)	Length of Rural Delivery Routes(km)	24127	13539	10778
固定电话年末用户(万户)	Number of Telephone Sets at the Year-end (10000 units)	119.88	92.16	28.43
教育	**Education**			
普通高等学校	Regular Institutions of Higher Education			
学校数(所)	Number of Schools(unit)	9	9	
在校学生数(人)	Total Students Enrollment(person)	63335	63335	
招生数(人)	New Students Enrollment(person)	20817	20817	
毕业生数(人)	Graduates(person)	16358	16358	
专任教师数(人)	Full-time Teachers(person)	3680	3680	
高中学校	Specialized Secondary Schools			
学校数(所)	Number of Schools(unit)	155	118	39
在校学生数(人)	Total Students Enrollment(person)	287146	211036	81288
招生数(人)	New Students Enrollment(person)	120640	87009	35781
毕业生数(人)	Graduates(person)	72235	54871	18136
专任教师数(人)	Full-time Teachers(person)	15826	11988	4169
初中学校	Regular Secondary Schools			
学校数(所)	Number of Schools(unit)	897	647	269
在校学生数(万人)	Total Students Enrollment(10000 persons)	82.65	54.68	29.62
招生数(万人)	New Students Enrollment(10000 persons)	29.03	18.87	10.78
毕业生数(万人)	Graduates(10000 persons)	26.89	18.29	9.08
专任教师数(万人)	Full-time Teachers(10000 persons)	4.64	3.23	1.50
小　学	Primary Schools			
学校数(所)	Number of Schools(unit)	5132	3427	1816
在校学生数(万人)	Total Students Enrollment(10000 persons)	158.18	101.05	60.66
招生数(万人)	New Students Enrollment(10000 persons)	24.19	15.85	8.88
毕业生数(万人)	Graduates(10000 persons)	30.49	19.45	11.69
专任教师数(万人)	Full-time Teachers(10000 persons)	8.53	5.62	3.08

24-9 民族自治州经济发展主要指标(2012)
Major Indicators on Economic Development of Minority Nationality Autonomous States

指标名称	Item	黔西南州 Qianxinan	黔东南州 Qiandongnan	黔南州 Qiannan
生产总值(亿元)	**Gross Domestic Product(100 million yuan)**	**477.43**	**495.75**	**550.34**
第一产业	Primary Industry	75.43	101.39	88.80
第二产业	Secondary Industry	178.07	153.17	210.55
第三产业	Tertiary Industry	223.93	241.19	250.99
农业	**Agriculture**			
乡村从业人员(万人)	Rural Employment(10000 persons)	184.62	242.73	219.36
农用机械总动力(万千瓦)	Total Agricultural Machinery Power (10000 kw)	214.49	259.67	263.80
化肥使用量(折纯量)(万吨)	Consumption of Chemical Fertilizers(10000 tons)	7.89	7.72	10.20
有效灌溉面积(千公顷)	Effective Irrigated Areas(1000 hectares)	120.13	152.90	175.72
农作物播种面积(千公顷)	Sown Areas of Farm Crops(1000 hectares)	397.39	552.22	534.20
#粮　食	Grain Crops	239.66	303.24	316.35
油菜籽	Rapeseeds	24.50	51.53	68.00
粮食总产量(万吨)	Total Grain Yield(10000 tons)	87.84	112.62	121.10
油菜籽产量(万吨)	Output of Rapeseeds(10000 tons)	3.01	6.35	8.83
烤烟产量(万吨)	Output of Flue -cured Tobacco (10000 tons)	4.63	2.32	2.80
茶叶产量(万吨)	Output of Tea (10000 tons)	0.39	0.69	0.84
当年造林面积(千公顷)	Afforested Areas in 2004(1000 hectares)	33.85	39.05	31.56
牲畜当年存栏数	Animals in Hand			
猪(万头)	Hogs(10000 heads)	135.26	136.86	168.51
牛(万头)	Large Animals(10000 heads)	53.26	63.39	60.33
羊(万只)	Sheep and Goats(10000 heads)	41.53	25.60	22.33
牲畜当年出栏数	Number of Slaughtered Animals			
猪(万头)	Hogs(10000 heads)	142.09	180.05	202.21
牛(万头)	Large Animals(10000 heads)	11.85	12.42	12.86
羊(万只)	Sheep and Goats(10000 heads)	20.53	15.33	15.68
肉类总产量(万吨)	Output of Meat(10000 tons)	15.64	17.76	19.48
水产品产量(万吨)	Aquatic Products(10000 tons)	3.08	1.79	1.43
农林牧渔业总产值(亿元)	Gross Output Value of Farming,Forestry,Animal Husb andry and Fishery(100 million yuan)	119.03	161.97	157.86
#农　业	Farming	64.95	82.04	84.48

24-9 续表 continued

指标名称	Item	黔西南州 Qianxinan	黔东南州 Qiandongnan	黔南州 Qiannan
林 业	Forestry	7.01	26.66	6.24
牧 业	Animal Husbandry	39.80	43.49	61.35
渔 业	Fishery	5.76	6.04	2.88
工业(规模以上)	**Industry(above designated size)**			
企业单位数(个)	Number of Industrial Enterprises(unit)	271	222	284
工业总产值(亿元)	Total Gross Industrial Output Value(100 million yuan)	411.24	337.83	509.06
工业销售产值(亿元)	Sales Output Value of Industry(100 million yuan)	390.34	318.66	476.85
工业增加值(亿元)	Value-added of Industry(100 million yuan)	163.76	81.97	138.54
利润总额(亿元)	Total Profits(100 million yuan)	41.42	15.23	22.81
主要工业产品产量	Output of Major Industrial Products			
原煤(万吨)	Coal(10000 tons)	2579.64	125.58	393.11
生铁(万吨)	Pig Iron(10000 tons)	3.89	0.42	
水泥(万吨)	Cement(10000 tons)	387.38	400.65	1104.95
发电量(亿千瓦小时)	Electricity(100 million kwh)	243.80	61.46	22.90
固定资产投资	**Investment in Fixed Assets**			
固定资产投资完成额(亿元)	All Investment in Fixed Assets in the Whole Province (100 million yuan)	445.14	610.49	587.28
商业	**Trade**			
社会消费品零售总额(亿元)	Total Retail Sales of Consumer Goods(100 million yuan)	121.79	168.87	136.09
财政、金融	**Treasury and Finance**			
公共财政收入(亿元)	Local Government Financial Revenue(100 million yuan)	64.42	70.08	57.87
公共财政支出(亿元)	Local Government Financial Expenditure(100 million yuan)	181.17	248.53	199.86
金融机构人民币存款余额(亿元)	Deposits Balance(100 million yuan)	557.03	682.45	627.07
#储蓄存款	Urban and Rural Resident Savings Deposit Balance	266.07	432.76	360.56
金融机构人民币贷款余额(亿元)	Loans Balance(100 million yuan)	336.45	427.47	380.31

24-10 民族自治州社会发展主要指标(2012)
Major Indicators on Social Development of Minority Nationality Autonomous State

指标名称	Item	黔西南州 Qianxinan	黔东南州 Qiandongnan	黔南州 Qiannan
人口	**Population**			
年末常住半年人口(万人)	Number of Population at The Year-end (10000 persons)	281.2	347.27	322.64
#少数民族人口	Minority Population	137.45	271.81	235.18
人口密度(人/平方公里)	Population Density(person/sq.km)	167.34	114.47	123.16
交通运输	**Traffic**			
公路里程(公里)	Length of Highways(km)	15373	27324	15929
邮电、通讯	**Post and Telecommunications**			
邮政所总数(处)	Number of Post Offices(unit)	124	128	153
邮路总长度(公里)	Length of Postal Routes(km)	3381	6713	2352
农村投递线路总长度(公里)	Length of Rural Delivery Routes(km)	4111	4135	5293
固定电话年末用户(万户)	Number of Telephone Sets at the Year-end(10000 units)	19.50	39.61	33.05
教育	**Education**			
普通高等学校	Regular Institutions of Higher Education			
学校数(所)	Number of Schools(unit)	2	3	4
在校学生数(人)	Students Enrollment(person)	11406	28869	23060
招生数(人)	New Student Enrollment(person)	4045	9097	7675
毕业生数(人)	Graduates(person)	3875	6941	5542
专任教师数(人)	Full-time Teachers(person)	739	1686	1255
高中学校	Specialized Secondary Schools			
学校数(所)	Number of Schools(unit)	41	45	32
在校学生数(人)	Students Enrollment(person)	58194	81835	71007
招生数(人)	New Student Enrollment(person)	24766	34052	28191
毕业生数(人)	Graduates(person)	16671	20738	17462
专任教师数(人)	Full-time Teachers(person)	3425	4681	3882
初中学校	Regular Secondary Schools			
学校数(所)	Number of Schools(unit)	208	229	210
在校学生数(人)	Students Enrollment(person)	170845	197364	178551
招生数(人)	New Student Enrollment(person)	60233	69140	59358
毕业生数(人)	Graduates(person)	55967	62643	64306
专任教师数(人)	Full-time Teachers(person)	9782	11832	10657
小　学	Primary Schools			
学校数(所)	Number of Schools(unit)	1076	1231	1120
在校学生数(万人)	Students Enrollment(10000 persons)	35.14	36.05	29.87
招生数(万人)	New Student Enrollment(10000 persons)	5.72	5.58	4.55
毕业生数(万人)	Graduates(10000 persons)	6.38	6.96	6.10
专任教师数(万人)	Full-time Teachers(10000 persons)	1.79	2.05	1.78

24-11 民族自治县经济发展主要指标(2012)

指　标	Item	道真县 Daozhen	务川县 Wuchuan
生产总值(亿元)	**Gross Domestic Product(10000 yuan)**	**24.68**	**28.29**
第一产业	Primary Industry	7.98	9.80
第二产业	Secondary Industry	4.26	4.64
第三产业	Tertiary Industry	12.44	13.85
农业	**Agriculture**		
乡村从业人员(万人)	Rural Employment(10000 persons)	18.66	26.47
年末常用耕地面积(千公顷)	Cultivated Areas(year-end)(1000 hectares)		
农用机械总动力(万千瓦)	Total Agricultural Machinery Power (10000 kw)	16.70	
化肥使用量(折纯量)(万吨)	Consumption of Chemical Fertilizers(10000 tons)	3.00	0.46
有效灌溉面积(千公顷)	Effective Irrigated Areas(1000 hectares)	7.30	6.53
农作物播种面积(千公顷)	Sown Areas of Farm Crops(1000 hectares)	78.35	94.56
#粮　食	Grain Crops	38.90	57.25
油菜籽	Rapeseeds	4.78	10.26
粮食总产量(吨)	Total Grain Yield(ton)	133093	163758
油菜籽产量(吨)	Output of Rapeseeds(ton)	7179	8532
烤烟产量(吨)	Output of Flue -cured Tobacco (ton)	13665	15315
茶叶产量(吨)	Output of Tea (ton)	2301	241
当年造林面积(千公顷)	Afforested Areas in this Year(1000 hectares)	1.80	7.20
牲畜当年存栏数	Animals in Hand		
猪(万头)	Hogs(10000 heads)	17.63	19.40
牛(万头)	Large Animals(10000 heads)	3.64	8.68
羊(万只)	Sheep and Goats(10000 heads)	3.39	8.25
牲畜当年出栏数	Number of Slaughtered Animals		
猪(万头)	Hogs(10000 heads)	20.32	20.42
牛(万头)	Large Animals(10000 heads)	0.68	2.02
羊(万只)	Sheep and Goats(10000 heads)	1.51	5.59
肉类总产量(吨)	Output of Meat(ton)	19295	23117
水产品产量(吨)	Aquatic Products(ton)		1004
农林牧渔业总产值(万元)	Gross Output Value of Farming,Forestry,Animal Husb andry and Fishery(10000 yuan)	156444	166000
#农　业	Farming	95642	110096

Major Indicators on Economic Development of Minority Nationality Autonomous Counties

镇宁县 Zhenning	关岭县 Guanling	紫云县 Ziyun	威宁县 Weining	玉屏县 Yuping	印江县 Yinjiang	沿河县 Yanhe	松桃县 Songtao	三都县 Sandu
43.85	**42.30**	**28.85**	**100.66**	**39.06**	**40.41**	**49.60**	**61.56**	**27.91**
6.04	8.07	9.22	33.70	4.88	15.50	16.47	18.36	6.69
13.89	11.11	5.19	27.38	21.67	8.30	8.87	20.23	4.59
23.92	23.12	14.44	39.58	12.51	16.61	24.26	22.97	16.63
20.24	19.50	22.79	79.07	8.49	24.50	32.55	41.97	19.60
19.18	17.20	16.40	39.10	11.10	27.00	29.60	38.00	14.05
0.80	1.80	0.60	5.80	0.54	0.70	1.50	1.45	0.37
5.77	5.50	5.84	1.47	2.13	13.50	4.70	15.30	10.37
36.12	33.00	45.06	223.00	1.69	58.60	86.90	72.03	44.19
20.03	21.80	25.19	125.00	0.89	36.40	56.50	47.86	24.29
6.61	3.70	9.85	0.30	0.38	9.30	8.60	9.95	0.61
94700	98521	97052	396321	36012	127602	170614	226243	89742
9038	4183	6549	93	3537	13372	8548	12610	8232
59	96	2251	33811		5934	6245	2898	
158	56	90	64	24	4036	541	3100	560
3.37	3.80	0.42	4.90	0.02	2.90	7.80	4.66	2.03
10.65	14.27	27.46	81.97	5.88	18.95	36.27	36.50	13.17
6.14	7.93	10.85	17.74	1.72	4.23	12.11	6.74	6.04
0.62	2.32	2.86	24.28	0.94	3.40	21.62	5.28	0.42
10.11	13.78	27.94	62.16	8.97	25.37	26.59	32.30	15.37
1.22	1.97	2.36	4.11	0.65	1.62	2.16	1.82	1.36
0.28	1.52	1.81	15.09	1.10	5.98	18.02	8.33	0.47
11830	17194	31220	73728	9430	27805	30856	35038	15210
2380	891	1012	280	6925	3510	4827	4460	2190
90170	120981	137823	500842	82897	233459	272631	292249	102000
49873	68015	45523	303332	41056	118076	159659	156283	56752

24-11 续表

指 标	Item	道真县 Daozhen	务川县 Wuchuan
林 业	Forestry	7422	5264
牧 业	Animal Husbandry	51804	46995
渔 业	Fishery	956	1731
规模以上工业	**Industry above designated size**		
企业单位数(个)	Number of Industrial Enterprises(unit)	12	8
工业总产值(万元)	Total Gross Industrial Output Value(10000 yuan)	66441	58326
工业销售产值(万元)	Sales Output Value of Industry(10000 yuan)	65564	55965
工业增加值(万元)	Value-added of Industry(10000 yuan)	20463	18706
利润总额(万元)	Total Profits(10000 yuan)	-1015	6058
主要工业产品产量	Output of Major Industrial Products		
原煤(万吨)	Coal(10000 tons)	22.45	
生铁(万吨)	Pig Iron(10000 tons)		
水泥(万吨)	Cement(10000 tons)	44.06	
发电量(亿千瓦小时)	Electricity(100 million kwh)	4.28	5.53
固定资产投资	**Investment in Fixed Assets**		
固定资产投资额(万元)	All Investment in Fixed Assets in the Whole Province(10000 yuan)	260845	340369
商业	**Trade**		
社会消费品零售总额(万元)	Total Retail Sales of Consumer Goods(10000 yuan)	78847	79023
财政、金融	**Treasiury and Finance**		
公共财政收入(万元)	Local Government Financial Revenue(10000 yuan)	23804	29304
公共财政一支出(万元)	Local Government Financial Expenditure(10000 yuan)	140890	151938
金融机构人民币存款余额(亿元)	Deposits Balance(100 million yuan)	47.52	48.82
#储蓄存款	Urban and Rural Resident Savings Deposit Balance	35.39	30.65
金融机构人民币贷款余额(亿元)	Loans Balance(100 million yuan)	18.04	22.59

continued

镇宁县 Zhenning	关岭县 Guanling	紫云县 Ziyun	威宁县 Weining	玉屏县 Yuping	印江县 Yinjiang	沿河县 Yanhe	松桃县 Songtao	三都县 Sandu
2862	5082	8508	3692	4112	8200	4588	7865	8639
33538	46439	79948	185059	31791	95396	93091	112867	30788
3504	1219	1697	556	2576	6223	6762	6436	3471
18	13	13	37	36	32	28	33	3
159055	123722	71463	476035	679435	200335	108446	371699	26650
150306	79532	67739	428076	612683	195813	105466	342605	26634
26099	20212	16728	121300	132390	41778	31433	100079	4939
13296	1277	3688	44827	58	-2273	7749	13182	-581
	24.90	22.08	147.08		1.50	31.96		
	68.47	1.34	25.98	124.81	109.08	25.77	80.09	57.88
1.85	2.88		2.20	39.13	0.69	0.11	0.34	
306007	214963	188566	1165626	353225	469179	695786	679953	276188
116649	129488	90716	170487	56741	75183	105597	136023	77946
39009	26853	21200	77628	23183	21692	45768	44423	17250
163666	156344	155842	449437	106808	181289	236936	265657	143422
43.61	37.11	32.08	60.36	25.42	47.11	49.39	63.59	29.67
19.28	21.05	15.85	37.72	18.54	31.99	34.12	40.65	18.52
36.85	23.80	18.06	33.29	32.90	31.78	25.31	39.51	19.27

24-12 民族自治县社会发展主要指标(2012)

指　标	Item	道真县 Daozhen	务川县 Wuchuan	镇宁县 Zhenning
人口	**Population**			
年末常住人口(万人)	Number of Populations at The Year-end(10000 persons)	24.26	31.70	28.20
#少数民族人口	Minority Populations	18.02	29.10	16.32
人口密度(人/平方公里)	Population Density(person/sq.km)	112.51	114.32	165.63
交通运输	**Traffic**			
公路里程(公里)	Length of Highways(km)	2373	2111	1505
邮电、通讯	**Post and Telecommunications**			
邮政所总数(处)	Number of Post Offices(unit)	11	13	7
邮路总长度(公里)	Length of Postal Routes(km)	285	1372	336
农村投递线路总长度(公里)	Length of Rural Delivery Routes(km)	454	968	281
固定电话年末用户(万户)	Number of Telephone Sets(10000 units)	2.08	2.30	1.71
教育	**Education**			
普通高中	Regular Senior Secondary Schools			
学校数(所)	Number of Schools(unit)	2	3	1
在校学生数(人)	Students Enrollment(person)	6555	9052	2626
招生数(人)	New Student Enrollment(person)	2449	4293	1218
毕业生数(人)	Graduates(person)	1598	1446	626
专任教师数(人)	Full-time Teachers(person)	345	461	118
普通初中	Regular Junior Secondary Schools			
学校数(所)	Number of Schools(unit)	20	27	19
在校学生数(人)	Students Enrollment(person)	15712	26102	12084
招生数(人)	New Student Enrollment(person)	5622	8380	4797
毕业生数(人)	Graduates(person)	4094	8541	5233
专任教师数(人)	Full-time Teachers(person)	845	1467	869
小　学	Primary Schools			
学校数(所)	Number of Schools(unit)	82	136	107
在校学生数(人)	Students Enrollment(person)	26406	37949	31564
招生数(人)	New Student Enrollment(person)	4138	4932	5572
毕业生数(人)	Graduates(person)	5313	7994	6718
专任教师数(人)	Full-time Teachers(person)	1489	2076	1794

Major Indicators on Social Development of Minority Nationality Autonomous Counties

关岭县 Guanling	紫云县 Ziyun	威宁县 Weining	玉屏县 Yuping	印江县 Yinjiang	沿河县 Yanhe	松桃县 Songtao	三都县 Sandu
29.99	26.87	126.48	11.83	28.35	44.96	48.59	28.85
19.11	17.57	29.25	9.33	23.22	40.37	23.47	35.80
204.29	117.66	200.88	229.31	144.56	182.11	169.82	121.01
1469.87	1955	5184	1535	2709	2400	3586	1340
9	11	15	7	13	21	1	14
890	336	897	746.55	800		611	198
1050	532	5560	746.55	500		497	189
1.50	3.40	8.70	1.44	0.62	3.51	2.47	0.71
3	1	8	3	6	4	6	2
4109	3223	20505	3108	8690	7643	10599	5178
2001	1502	10101	1198	3538	3220	4111	2150
1123	920	3744	760	2320	1953	2874	772
246	156	864	213	470	364	601	331
19	18	56	8	18	30	35	19
14392	19563	99462	5857	19822	34903	31840	16495
5082	5257	41643	2026	6690	10963	11068	6268
5424	7544	23329	1769	6009	11764	12309	4805
854	894	3491	420	1134	1923	2189	962
119	136	428	44	126	224	303	111
31250	32109	221311	11384	38132	80842	60327	35358
4896	5116	30092	2006	5693	11452	9477	5459
5699	5724	44261	1990	6929	13298	12488	6532
1612	1839	9352	716	2239	3772	4161	1783

25

Twenty-five

经济强县

Economically Strong Counties

25-1 经济强县主要指标(一)(2012)

Major Indicators of Economically Strong County (1)

单位：亿元 (10000 yuan)

县(市、区) 名 称	County (City,Section)	生产总值 Gross Domestic Product	第一产业 Primary Industry	第二产业 Secondary Industry	第三产业 Tertiary Industry	2012年比2011年增长(%) Increase Rate in 2012 over 2011(%)	人均生产总值(元) Per Capita Gross Domestic Product(yuan)	2012年比2011年增长(%) Increase Rate in 2012 over 2011(%)
云岩区	Yunyan	441.29	0.43	157.87	282.99	15.7	45030	14.1
南明区	Nanming	375.50	2.09	84.85	288.56	17.5	44301	16.1
花溪区	Huaxi	119.53	9.19	46.99	63.35	17.0	32702	15.9
乌当区	Wudang	156.57	9.19	74.97	72.41	18.0	38707	12.2
白云区	Baiyun	101.86	3.22	57.13	41.51	18.1	37724	16.7
小河区	Xiaohe	110.74	1.00	73.34	36.40	17.6	43024	15.2
清镇市	Qingzhen	144.16	12.91	70.16	61.09	16.8	30561	16.1
修文县	Xiuwen	71.24	10.27	31.79	29.18	17.2	28134	16.0
息烽县	Xifeng	84.34	8.25	49.71	26.38	18.0	39357	17.4
开阳县	Kaiyang	102.88	15.74	59.82	27.32	17.2	28713	17.1
红花岗区	Honghuagang	221.49	9.46	66.08	145.95	17.4	33058	16.2
汇川区	Huicuan	164.01	6.02	84.24	73.75	17.3	36523	15.8
仁怀市	Renhuai	329.56	13.98	222.85	92.73	17.8	60177	17.7
赤水市	Chishui	49.45	8.34	22.46	18.65	16.9	20716	16.4
遵义县	Zunyi	192.28	33.56	92.06	66.66	17.5	20623	18.3
桐梓县	Tongzi	74.89	15.03	28.95	30.91	17.0	14455	17.3
钟山区	Zhongshan	258.76	2.28	142.83	113.65	15.9	41682	15.4
盘　县	Panxian	306.72	19.32	221.03	66.37	17.4	29606	17.3
西秀区	Xixiu	145.55	14.85	56.06	74.64	15.3	19148	15.8
平坝县	Pingba	62.20	7.35	35.80	19.05	17.4	21014	17.9
都匀市	Duyun	110.16	7.97	44.66	57.53	15.4	24946	15.6
福泉市	Fuquan	79.63	7.58	39.61	32.44	18.1	28387	19.1
凯里市	Kaili	123.93	8.56	42.81	72.56	18.9	25606	18.1
兴义市	Xingyi	203.96	20.59	84.40	98.97	16.6	26032	16.6
七星关区	Qixingguan	184.42	29.70	72.75	81.97	17.7	16306	18.0
金沙县	Jinsha	130.15	13.01	77.93	39.21	17.6	23352	18.4
碧江区	Bijiang	78.76	7.54	28.66	42.56	17.2	26359	15.8

25-2 经济强县主要指标(二)(2012)

Major Indicators of Economically Strong County (2)

县(市、区)名　称	County (City,Section)	社会消费品零售总额(亿元) Total Retail Sales of Consumer Goods(100 million yuan)	2012年比2011年增长(%) Increase Rate in 2012 over 2011(%)	固定资产投　资(亿元) Investment in Fixed Assets	2012年比2011年增长(%) Increase Rate in 2012 over 2011(%)	城镇居民人均可支配收入(元) Per Capita Annual Disposable Income of Urban Households (yuan)	2012年比2011年增长(%) Increase Rate in 2012 over 2011(%)	农村居民人均纯收入(元) Per Capita Net Income of Rural Residents (yuan)	2012年比2011年增长(%) Increase Rate in 2012 over 2011(%)
云岩区	Yunyan	255.25	16.7	232.67	32.9			10356	13.5
南明区	Nanming	227.67	18.3	301.45	104.1			10259	13.6
花溪区	Huaxi	26.63	18.0	177.08	56.8			8665	15.4
乌当区	Wudang	66.41	18.1	136.15	51.0			9607	15.3
白云区	Baiyun	27.00	18.2	224.12	68.3			10256	15.4
小河区	Xiaohe	62.71	18.2	210.02	55.8			10128	13.2
清镇市	Qingzhen	25.59	17.3	180.06	46.1			7953	15.3
修文县	Xiuwen	14.25	17.2	127.45	50.2			7460	15.3
息烽县	Xifeng	12.21	17.5	132.88	56.8			7456	15.9
开阳县	Kaiyang	23.31	17.5	175.49	57.0			7860	15.9
红花岗区	Honghuagang	126.32	18.1	193.31	68.1			8134	16.7
汇川区	Huicuan	69.06	16.5	98.58	64.9			8340	16.0
仁怀市	Renhuai	46.50	15.8	112.37	82.1			6753	16.9
赤水市	Chishui	15.31	16.6	69.70	71.9			6537	16.8
遵义县	Zunyi	42.49	16.6	204.46	83.0			7621	17.0
桐梓县	Tongzi	16.38	16.7	114.98	49.2			5981	16.8
钟山区	Zhongshan	101.36	16.0	186.93	66.8			6792	17.3
盘　县	Panxian	48.15	16.2	296.26	79.2			5060	17.5
西秀区	Xixiu	38.40	16.2	141.91	92.0			6420	16.1
平坝县	Pingba	14.45	16.0	45.57	146.3			5391	16.3
都匀市	Duyun	43.66	15.9	118.44	46.1	19338	13.9	6543	16.6
福泉市	Fuquan	14.34	16.1	69.00	47.1			5678	17.5
凯里市	Kaili	67.42	16.8	210.10	79.0	18831	14.8	6081	17.5
兴义市	Xingyi	84.57	15.6	181.00	63.0	19472	14.5	6389	18.4
七星关区	Qixingguan	64.58	18.1	177.48	70.6			5131	16.3
金沙县	Jinsha	18.35	15.0	173.67	92.3			5720	16.5
碧江区	Bijiang	28.19	15.6	100.38	74.3			6310	18.2

注：固定资产投资口径为50万元及以上固定资产投资项目和房地产开发投资项目。

Note:The caliber of fixed asset investment refers to those projects planned to invest 500 thousand yuan at least in fixed assets investment projects and real estate development investment projects.

26

Twenty-six

扶贫与开发

Anti-poverty and Development

26-1 扶贫开发重点县主要指标占全省比重(2012)
Major Indicators of Basilic County of Anti-poverty and Development and Its Percentage to Provincial Total

单位：亿元 (100 million yuan)

指 标	Item	全 省 合 计 Provincial Total	扶贫开发重点县合计 Poverty Counties Total	扶贫开发重点县占全省比重(%) As Percentage to Provincial Total(%)
国土面积(万平方公里)	Area of Territory(10000 sq.km)	17.61	11.63	66.0
年末常住人口(万人)	Permanent Resident Population at the Year-end (10000 persons)	3484	1780.09	51.1
生产总值	Gross Domestic Product	6852.20	2408.19	35.1
公共财政收入	Local Financial Revenue	1014.05	238.55	23.5
公共财政支出	Financial Expenditure	2755.68	957.15	34.7
农林牧渔业总产值	Gross Output Value of Farming,Forestry, Animal Husban dry and Fishery	1436.61	794.88	55.3
粮食产量(万吨)	Output of Grain(10000 tons)	1079.50	649.09	60.1
规模以上工业增加值	Value-added of Industry above Designated Size	2055.46	574.15	27.9
社会消费品零售总额	Total Retail Sales of Consumer Goods	2027.65	483.94	23.9
储蓄存款	Savings Deposit	4806.09	1318.79	27.4

26–2 贫困人口及发生率(2012)
Number of Poverty Population and It's Arisen Rate

县(市、区、特区)名称	County (City,Section, Special Region)	农村贫困人口(万人) Poverty Population (10 000 persons)	农村贫困发生率(%) Arisen Rate of Poverty (%)
全省合计	**Provincial Total**	**923**	**26.80**
扶贫开发重点县小计	**Basilic Counties of Antipoverty and Development**	**718.35**	**33.8**
贵阳市	**Guiyang**	**5.49**	**2.9**
南明区	Nanming		
云岩区	Yunyan		
花溪区	Huaxi	0.40	2.0
乌当区	Wudang	1.10	4.2
白云区	Baiyun	0.11	1.5
小河区	Xiaohe	0.05	1.8
开阳县	Kaiyang	1.00	3.0
息烽县	Xifeng	0.80	4.0
修文县	Xiuwen	0.73	2.7
清镇市	Qingzhen	1.30	3.2
六盘水市	**Liupanshui**	**76.23**	**29.9**
钟山区	Zhongshan	3.20	18.6
△六枝特区	Liuzhi	14.85	25.9
△水城县	Shuicheng	27.43	36.7
△盘　县	Panxian	30.75	29.1
遵义市	**Zunyi**	**115.61**	**17.4**
红花岗区	Honghuagang	1.93	8.9
汇川区	huichuan	2.26	10.8
遵义县	Zunyi	16.01	13.7
桐梓县	Tongzi	8.22	12.6
绥阳县	Suiyang	5.79	11.5
△正安县	Zhengan	15.74	26.6
△道真县	Daozhen	8.34	26.5
△务川县	Wuchuan	12.42	29.8
凤冈县	Fenggang	5.78	14.4
湄潭县	Meitan	6.21	13.8
余庆县	Yuqing	3.83	13.7
△习水县	Xishui	18.24	27.9
赤水市	Chishui	3.38	14.3
仁怀市	Renhuai	7.46	13.1
安顺市	**Anshun**	**63.08**	**25.7**
西秀区	Xixiu	7.38	11.1
平坝县	Pingba	5.59	18.4
△普定县	Puding	13.22	30.8
△镇宁县	Zhenning	11.29	31.7
△关岭县	Guanling	12.30	35.6
△紫云县	Ziyun	13.30	36.9
毕节市	**Bijie**	**207.04**	**30.0**
七星关区	Qixingguan	26.18	22.8
△大方县	Dafang	29.16	34.2
黔西县	Qianxi	17.13	23.0
金沙县	Jinsha	10.24	21.6
△织金县	Zhijin	34.49	39.6
△纳雍县	Nayong	28.04	34.5
△威宁县	Weining	38.34	29.7
△赫章县	Hezhang	23.46	32.8

26-2 续表 continued

县(市、区、特区)名称	County (City,Section, Special Region)	农村贫困人口(万人) Poverty Population (10 000 persons)	农村贫困发生率(%) Arisen Rate of Poverty (%)	县(市、区、特区)名称	County (City,Section, Special Region)	农村贫困人口(万人) Poverty Population (10 000 persons)	农村贫困发生率(%) Arisen Rate of Poverty (%)
铜仁市	**Tongren**	**115.10**	**30.5**	镇远县	Zhenyuan	5.85	32.6
碧江区	Bijiang	3.33	19.6	△岑巩县	Cengong	7.49	35.4
万山区	Wanshan	3.40	26.3	△天柱县	Tianzhu	13.79	38.5
△江口县	Jiangkou	6.44	30.4	△锦屏县	Jinping	8.70	41.2
玉屏县	Yuping	3.10	24.4	△剑河县	Jianhe	9.61	40.3
△石阡县	Shiqian	13.00	33.4	△台江县	Taijiang	6.33	41.0
△思南县	Sinan	19.09	29.7	△黎平县	Liping	16.34	35.1
△印江县	Yinjiang	12.59	30.8	△榕江县	Rongjiang	13.94	41.6
△德江县	Dejiang	14.18	33.9	△从江县	Congjiang	13.03	40.7
△沿河县	Yanhe	19.75	32.4	△雷山县	Leishan	5.39	35.7
△松桃县	Songtao	20.22	30.1	△麻江县	Majiang	9.43	46.8
黔西南州	**Qianxinan**	**86.35**	**28.1**	△丹寨县	Danzhai	6.44	42.3
兴义市	Xingyi	8.31	12.0	**黔南州**	**Qiannan**	**106.36**	**29.5**
△兴仁县	Xingren	11.64	26.6	都匀市	Duyun	6.13	18.9
△普安县	Puan	8.27	25.6	福泉市	Fuquan	6.16	24.1
△晴隆县	Qinglong	14.49	49.4	△荔波县	Libo	6.32	39.2
△贞丰县	Zhenfeng	12.47	32.7	贵定县	Guiding	6.11	23.0
△望谟县	Wangmo	11.75	38.5	瓮安县	Wengan	7.22	15.7
△册亨县	Ceheng	9.47	41.5	△独山县	Dushan	10.41	32.3
△安龙县	Anlong	9.95	24.0	△平塘县	Pingtang	12.19	39.5
黔东南州	**Qiandongnan**	**147.74**	**37.8**	△罗甸县	Luodian	13.61	43.3
凯里市	Kaili	6.15	19.6	△长顺县	Changshun	9.96	40.6
△黄平县	Huangping	13.58	41.7	龙里县	Longli	4.02	21.1
△施秉县	Shibing	3.32	37.9	惠水县	Huishui	8.79	21.2
△三穗县	Sansui	8.35	42.2	△三都县	Sandu	15.44	44.7

注：△为新阶段扶贫开发工作重点县。
Note: These counties with '△' refer to basilic counties of antipoverty and development.

26–3 扶贫开发重点县主要指标(2012)

单位：万元

扶贫开发重点县名称	County	年末总人口(万人) Population (year-end) (10000 persons)	生产总值(亿元) Gross Domestic Product (100 millon yuan)	公共财政收入 Local Financial Revenue	公共财政支出 Financial Expenditure	农林牧渔业总产值 Gross Output Value of Farming, Forestry, Animal Husbandry and Fishery
扶贫开发重点县合计	**Total**	**1780.09**	**2408.19**	**2385512**	**9571492**	**7948800**
六盘水市	**Liupanshui**					
六枝特区	Liuzhi	49.46	84.30	76227	273822	128189
水城县	Shuicheng	70.43	113.51	162768	351423	216835
盘　县	Panxian	103.73	306.72	410554	647041	296477
遵义市	**Zunyi**					
正安县	Zhengan	38.14	35.63	30412	190514	233966
※道真县	Daozhen	24.26	24.68	23804	140890	156444
※务川县	Wuchuan	31.70	28.29	29304	151938	166000
习水县	Xishui	51.77	74.53	60215	236724	221390
安顺市	**Anshun**					
普定县	Puding	37.59	50.49	42428	168961	122069
※镇宁县	Zhenning	28.20	43.85	39009	163666	90170
※关岭县	Guanling	29.99	42.30	26853	156344	120981
※紫云县	Ziyun	26.87	28.85	21200	155842	137823
毕节市	**Bijie**					
大方县	Dafang	77.73	109.24	116051	371026	274916
织金县	Zhijin	78.36	90.30	128366	372901	236911
纳雍县	Nayong	67.14	103.07	115676	273444	209182
※威宁县	Weining	126.48	100.66	77628	449437	500842
赫章县	Hezhang	65.19	54.59	33925	262808	232668
铜仁市	**Tongren**					
江口县	Jiangkou	17.29	23.26	15931	122005	113392
石阡县	Shiqian	30.35	32.21	23618	174736	201675
思南县	Sinan	49.79	62.40	31802	237526	326603
※印江县	Yinjiang	28.35	40.41	21692	181289	233459
德江县	Dejiang	36.71	50.52	33667	205816	271072
※沿河县	Yanhe	44.96	49.60	45768	236936	272631
※松桃县	Songtao	48.59	61.56	44423	265657	292249

Major Indicators on Basilic County of Anti-poverty and Development

(10000 yuan)

粮食产量(万吨) Output of Grain (10000 tons)	人均粮食(公斤) Per Capita Output of Grain (kg)	农村居民人均纯收入(元) Per Capita Annual Net Income of Rural Households	规模以上工业增加值 Value-added of Industry above Designated Size	储蓄存款 Savings Deposit	固定资产投资 Investment in Fixed Assets	社会消费品零售总额 Total Retail Sales of Consumer Goods
649.09	**365**		**5741462**	**13187911**	**26409493**	**4839370**
20.14	352	4728	153387		1109581	226671
21.62	281	4725	740493		1719371	106476
31.28	295	5060	1371064	1120469	2962593	481536
21.22	377	4333	29861	411013	388369	124996
13.31	423	4137	20463	353926	260845	78847
16.38	383	4052	18706	306541	340369	79023
24.64	377	4572	350123	495519	1076736	155265
10.44	243	4771	160477	200424	397170	109948
9.47	266	4667	26099	192795	306007	116649
9.85	285	4682	20212	210538	214963	129488
9.71	269	4633	16728	158537	188566	90716
25.71	302	4943	234112	516443	1057756	154865
30.22	347	4714	114859	475768	1383600	170626
22.87	281	4561	313535	351014	1258228	137940
39.63	307	4862	121300	377202	1165626	170487
19.18	268	4577	37531	331033	655212	101492
7.10	335	4662	21281	197122	386349	51932
11.54	296	4521	13769	257113	267311	60204
20.05	312	4335	70693	457716	805093	140057
12.76	312	4396	41778	319930	469179	75183
13.95	334	4138	40165	284810	436443	97523
17.06	280	4370	31433	341215	695786	105597
22.62	336	4346	100079	406467	679953	136023

26-3 续表

单位：万元

扶贫开发重点县名称	County	年末总人口(万人) Population (year-end) (10000 persons)	生产总值(亿元) Gross Domestic Product (100 millon yuan)	公共财政收入 Local Financial Revenue	公共财政支出 Financial Expenditure	农林牧渔业总产值 Gross Output Value of Farming, Forestry, Animal Husbandry and Fishery	粮食产量(万吨) Output of Grain (10000 tons)
黔西南州	**Qianxinan**						
兴仁县	Xingren	41.90	64.47	106180	246783	156201	15.29
普安县	Puan	25.50	36.73	47802	137941	93536	6.47
晴隆县	Qinglong	24.70	31.06	31426	148887	95657	7.32
贞丰县	Zhenfeng	30.40	53.40	74250	186755	138846	10.39
望谟县	Wangmo	25.20	21.37	15523	187597	120372	7.41
册亨县	Ceheng	19.10	18.97	16495	121519	94500	4.88
安龙县	Anlong	35.90	54.10	44119	165648	177310	15.32
黔东南州	**Qiandongnan**						
黄平县	Huangping	26.21	25.66	23131	135637	128152	8.99
施秉县	Shibing	13.03	19.75	24757	95547	79977	5.47
三穗县	Sansui	15.53	20.69	19009	102788	69624	4.98
岑巩县	Cengong	16.10	22.39	20151	111253	78338	5.89
天柱县	Tianzhu	26.00	41.37	39959	170959	134499	10.87
锦屏县	Jinping	15.34	21.12	19336	115486	58423	5.36
剑河县	Jianhe	18.04	21.83	21179	120158	92340	6.06
台江县	Taijiang	11.09	15.40	14234	90172	53171	4.05
黎平县	Liping	38.85	39.27	27449	187209	150032	12.25
榕江县	Rongjiang	28.63	29.75	26810	145753	151109	7.66
从江县	Congjiang	29.09	29.06	24470	162083	144218	10.10
雷山县	Leishan	11.67	14.59	15135	96251	54877	4.44
麻江县	Majiang	16.60	21.85	18563	108761	86705	6.13
丹寨县	Danzhai	12.20	15.22	17645	132212	58748	4.18
黔南州	**Qiannan**						
荔波县	Libo	14.50	27.47	18882	103810	70785	4.54
独山县	Dushan	25.93	36.62	27033	148861	133785	10.82
平塘县	Pingtang	23.02	26.64	21813	140552	121611	10.60
罗甸县	Luodian	25.00	33.99	19135	153681	132026	10.16
长顺县	Changshun	18.64	26.54	22455	121021	116016	9.75
※三都县	Sandu	28.85	27.91	17250	143422	102000	8.97

continued

(10000 yuan)

人均粮食 (公斤) Per Capita Output of Grain (kg)	农民人均 纯收入(元) Per Capita Annual Net Income of Rural Households	规模以上 工业增加值 Value-added of Industry above Designated Size	储蓄 存款 Savings Deposit	固定 资产 投资 Investment in Fixed Assets	社会消费品 零售总额 Total Retail Sales of Consumer Goods
361	4964	217608	278291	699956	110465
200	4287	162565	197532	337001	49089
249	4088	80572	165890	364317	40444
272	4732	333209	261254	459048	56255
243	3771	6552	114178	209607	27272
214	3970	11483	111324	160927	15697
369	4590	134496	327965	410588	73004
240	4349	15725	249022	255653	65711
525	4954	13553	139937	200329	48948
252	4642	32152	181117	241356	85916
278	4629	57888	175122	235075	66764
303	4841	81162	384278	450743	119487
254	4255	61704	218198	158310	64463
254	4413	14793	188097	205313	52498
262	4234	15824	121393	210800	36610
263	4484	46702	365014	412386	123511
228	4348	40604	237309	310514	78503
315	4628	19981	169531	348081	71302
295	4560	12634	118881	131283	39965
305	4422	52524	170612	259124	45183
275	4359	31778	134234	288637	35496
282	5124	62728	175896	308138	67850
336	5195	86313	291609	286258	98582
344	4955	7667	163193	281874	53221
323	5371	38789	163429	373080	68185
398	5115	49372	133795	309802	65458
260	4962	4939	185214	276188	77946

市（州）概貌

General Pictures of the municipalities

绿色林城　生态贵阳

Green Forest City　Ecological Guiyang

筑城广场全貌
Zhucheng Square Panorama

2012年，贵阳市抢抓国发【2012】2号文件历史性政策机遇，紧扣“主基调”、实施“主战略”，在“坚持走科学发展路，加快建生态文明市”的进程中，经济社会呈现出发展加速、质量提升、环境优化、民生改善、社会稳定、创新突破的良好局面，为实现“一二一”奋斗目标奠定了更加扎实的基础。

2012年，是经济稳中快进之年。全

贵阳国际展览中心
Guiyang International Exhibition Center

环城高速牛郎关立交全景
High-speed Niu Lang Guan overpass panorama

2012年7月27日，2012生态文明贵阳会议在贵阳国际生态会议中心隆重开幕
In July 27, 2012, 2012 ecological civilization Guiyang Conference opened in Guiyang international ecological Conference Center

2012年7月28日，2012生态文明贵阳会议电视高峰论坛举行，与会嘉宾围绕“建言‘新贵阳’”主题展开对话
In July 28, 2012, 2012 ecological civilization Guiyang conference TV Forum held, the guests dialogue around the “advice ‘new Guiyang’” theme

In 2012, Guiyang City, seize the State [2012] document No. 2 historic opportunities, focus on “the main tone”, the implementation of “main strategy”, “adhere to the scientific development of the road, to speed up the construction of ecological civilization city” the process, the economic society showing a good situation to accelerate the development, improve the quality, qualify the environment, optimization the improvement of people’s livelihood, social stability, innovation and breakthroughs, to lay a more solid foundation for achieving the goal of “one two one”.

In 2012, is fast economic growth in stability year . The city's various economic indicators continued to keep ahead in the capital city. To realize an annual production value of 170.03 billion yuan, the actual growth of 17%, contribution to the economic growth rate of 28.8%;

观山湖区新貌
Guanshanhu district new image

鸟瞰贵阳
A bird's eye view of Guiyang

市多项经济指标增速继续保持在全国省会城市前列。全年实现生产总值1700.3亿元，实际增长17%，对全省经济增长贡献率达28.8%；完成全社会固定资产投资2483亿元、增长55%；规模以上工业增加值480亿元、增长22%；社会消费品零售总额683亿元、增长16.9%；财政总收入488亿元、增长21.6%，公共财政预算收入241.2亿元、增长28.9%，分别比上年净增加87亿元和54亿元。金融机构存、贷款余额分别达4394.4亿元、3479.5亿元，增长21.9%、15.4%；银行表外融资规模达1160亿元，占全省的60%。

2012年，是结构优化调整之年。着力做特一产、做强二产、做优三产，三次产业结构优化为

青岩古镇
Qingyan Ancient Town

贵阳百花湖
Baihua Lake in Guiyang

completed investment in fixed assets 248.3 billion yuan, an increase of 55%; scale industrial added value of 48 billion yuan, an increase of 22%; total retail sales of social consumer goods 68.3 billion yuan, an increase of 16.9%; total fiscal revenue 48.8 billion yuan, up 21.6%, the public financial budget income 24.12 billion yuan, grow 28.9% respectively over the previous year, a net increase of 8.7 billion yuan and 5.4 billion yuan. Financial institutions, the loan balance reached 439.44 billion yuan, 347.95 billion yuan, up 21.9%, 15.4%, respectively; bank off-balance-sheet financing scale up to 116 billion yuan, accounting for 60% of the province.

In 2012, is the structure optimization and adjustment year. To do a special property of the first industry, strong the second industry, doing excellent the tertiary industry, three industrial structure optimization for 4.2:42.2:53.6. From the internal structure of industrial production, in the first industry, the grain and economic grain by ratio adjusted for 3:7, animal husbandry output value of total agricultural output value reached more than 30%; in the second industry,stage of light and heavy industry from 45:55 to 47:53, high-tech industrial

"两湖一库"执法人员在红枫湖水上巡逻
"Two lakes a bank" law enforcement officers patrolled the Hongfeng Lake

老干妈生产车间
The Laoganma production workshop

4.2:42.2:53.6。从产业内部结构看，一产中粮经比调整为3:7，畜牧业产值占农业总产值比重达30%以上；二产中轻重工业比从45:55调整为47:53，高新技术工业增加值98.4亿元、占规模以上工业增加值的20.5%；三产中现代服务业实现增加值428亿元，占服务业增加值的47%。从投资结构看，全社会固定资产投资中，产业投资占比37.7%、基础投资占比19.4%、民生及公共投资占比42.9%。从税收结构看，三次产业税收贡献比为0.2:45.9:53.9。从所有制经济结构看，民营经济实现增加值810亿元，占全市生产总值的47.6%，提高了3.6个百分点。

2012年，是改革创新突破之年。深入推进城市基层管理体制改革，撤销街道办事处，建立社区服务中心，把政府公共服务送到群众身边，被列为全国从整体上加强和创新社会

贵州皓天光电科技有限公司LED蓝宝石生产车间
Guizhou Hao Tian Photoelectric Technology Co., Ltd. LED sapphire production workshop

小河孟关先进装备制造业带
The Xiaohe Mengguan advanced equipment manufacturing industry belt

连接主城区和金阳新区的小关特大桥

Connecting the city and Jinyang district Xiaoguante bridge

added value of 9.84 billion yuan, accounting for above-scale industrial added value of 20.5%; realize the added value of 42.8 billion yuan of modern service industry in the tertiary industry production, accounting for 47% of the added value of the service industry. From the investment structure, the total social investment in fixed assets, investment accounted for more than 37.7%, infrastructure investment accounted for more than 19.4%, people's livelihood and public investment accounted for 42.9%. From the tax structure, the three industry tax contribution ratio is 0.2:45.9:53.9. From the ownership structure, the realization of the private economy added value of 81 billion yuan, accounting for the city's GDP 47.6%, an increase of 3.6 percentage points.

In 2012, is the reform and innovation breakthrough year. Deepening the reform of the city basic-level management system, cancel the subdistrict office, the establishment of community service center, send the government public services to the masses around, was listed as one of the three big city pilot to strengthen social management and innovation as a whole in the country. With the approval of the State Council, the establishment of Guanshanhu district and new Huaxi district. The frist national establishment of City Ecological Civilization Construction Committee, district (city, county) Ecological Civilization Construction Bureau, the state approved the implementation of “national ecological civilization construction of Guiyang demonstration city planning”. Education, culture, medical and health system

贵州开磷40万吨硫磺制酸

Guizhou Kailin 400,000 tons of sulfuric acid

贵阳贵御温泉
Guiyang Guiyu Spring

管理三个大城市试点之一。经国务院批准，设立观山湖区和新花溪区。在全国首家组建市生态文明建设委员会、区（市、县）生态文明建设局，国家批准实施《贵阳建设全国生态文明示范城市规划》。教育、文化、医药卫生体制改革深入推进。高新区被列为国家级新型工业化产业示范基地、科技兴贸创新基地，经开区被列为全国电子商务示范基地。

2012年，是开放水平提高之年。生态文明贵阳会议、酒博会等重要对外交流活动成功举办，规模及成效再创新高；完成贵阳综合保税区规划编制并上报国家审批，启动无水港建设；朗玛公司成功上市，实现了贵州创业板上市公司零的突破；新开通国际国内直航航线17条，贵阳机场获落地签证权；开放型经济迈上新台阶，获批国家外贸转型升级示范基地，被评为中国十大最具潜力会展城市、福

位于贵阳市环城林带上的长坡岭林场
In Guiyang city green belt the Changpoling Forest Farm

清镇市茶园
Qingzhen city tea garden

南江大峡谷
Nanjiang Grand Canyon

reform deeply pushed. High-tech Zone was listed as national new industrialization demonstration base, innovation base rejuvenating trade through science and technology, economic development zone was listed as the national e-commerce demonstration base.

In 2012, is open to raise the level of the year. Ecological civilization Guiyang conference, wine expo and other important foreign exchange activities held successfully, the scale and effectiveness of a new high; completed Guiyang comprehensive bonded area planning and reported to the state approval, start port construction; Lang Ma company successfully listed, the Guizhou GEM Listing Corporation zero breakthrough; the opening of the new international and domestic Flights 17, got Landing Visa right in Guiyang Airport; open economy to a new level, approved upgrade demonstration base transformation of national foreign trade, was named China's top ten most potential Exhibition City, Forbes, the best commercial city in mainland China.

In 2012, is the urban and rural development year. The State Council approved a new round of "Guiyang city land to use overall planning", urban construction land size from 155.3 square kilometers increased to 341.3 square kilometers; the completion of the "Three Zone five City five Belt" planning, implementation of the coverage of urban and rural planning.

红枫湖生态浮床
Hongfeng Lake Ecological Floating Bed

2012年，清镇职教城加快建设并有序入驻，截至2012年12月入驻的院校已达16所。图为清镇职教城局部效果图
In 2012, Qingzhen City to speed up the construction of vocational education and ordered to enter, as of 2012 December, the entered school already amounted to 16. For vocational education, local effects map

布斯•中国大陆最佳商业城市。

2012年，是城乡发展提升之年。国务院批准新一轮《贵阳市土地利用总体规划》，中心城区建设用地规模从155.3平方公里调增至341.3平方公里；完成“三区五城五带”总体规划，实现城乡规划全覆盖。富源南路、桐荫路、东站路、盐沙路建成通车，“三环十六射”骨干路网形成闭合“内循环”；龙洞堡机场扩建（二期）、市域快铁、轨道交通、跨区域高速公路建设加快推进，金清线建成通车，“外循环”城市交通体系逐步完善。农村生产生活条件不断改善，实施村庄整治50个，完成农房整治2200户，建成农村公路220公里，投资5.6亿元实施农村电网改造升级和县级电网工程建设。新增耕地300公顷；完成营造林23.7万亩，石漠化治理132.8平方公

2012年9月28日，贵阳孔学堂落成，并于2013年1月1日正式向市民开放。图为孔学堂全貌
In September 28, 2012, Guiyang Confucius School completed, and in January 1, 2013 officially open to the public. Confucius School picture

永乐桃园
Yongle Peach Garden

风景如画的花溪是前来贵阳游玩的游客必去的旅游胜地
The picturesque Huaxi is Guiyang tourists have to resort

花溪十里河滩城市湿地公园
Huaxi Shilihe Beach City Wetland Park

Fuyuan south Road, Tongyin Road, Dongzhan Road, Yansha Road was opened to traffic, "three-ring sixteen -radiation" backbone network to form a closed "interior circle"; Longdongbao airport expansion (phase II), city fast subway, rail transportation, regional highway construction accelerating, Jin Qing line was opened to traffic, "exterior cycle" city traffic system gradually improved. Rural production and living conditions continue to improve, the implementation of village - 50, completed 2,200 households housing renovation, completed the rural highway 220 kilometers, 560 million yuan investment in the implementation of the rural power grid upgrading and county power grid construction. Add 300 hectares of arable land; completed afforestation 237,000 acres, 132.8 square kilometers of governance desertification, forest coverage

阿哈水库
The Aha Reservoir

南明河畔的甲秀楼
The Nanming River
Jiaxiu Tower

里，森林覆盖率达43.2%。荣获CCTV2012年度中国城市品牌奖，“爽爽的贵阳”对外形象大幅提升。

2012年，是民生持续改善之年。民生支出占公共财政预算支出的60%；社会保障体系不断完善；新开工保障性住房27.6万平方米；实现整市脱贫，全市人均生产总值达6090美元，城市居民人均可支配收入、农民人均纯收入分别为22525元、8710元，分别增长16%、18%。

2012年，是社会全面进步之年。社会治安综合治理力度加大；安全生产事故起数、死亡人数明显下降；物价保持总体稳定；扎实推进医药卫生改革；各项工作全面发展。

2012年，是政府建设提质之年。坚持建设“创新型、服务型、法治型、廉洁型”政府，推动政府工作提速提质提效。

天河潭风景区
Tianhetan scenic area

2012年9月29日，贵阳市小车河城市湿地公园正式免费对外开放，贵阳城市中心再添生态游览休闲健身好去处
In September 29, 2012, Guiyang City Xiaochehe city wetland park officially open to the public for free, Guiyang city center add ecological tour leisure good place

rate reached 43.2%. Awarded the CCTV2012 China City Brand Award, greatly enhance the "wonderful Guiyang" external image.

In 2012, is the livelihood of the people continued to improve year. The people's livelihood expenditure accounted for 60% of public finance budget expenditure; constantly improve the social security system; new construction of affordable housing 276,000 square meters; the entire city out of poverty, the per capita GDP of $6,090, city residents per capita disposable income, per capita net income of farmers was 22,525 yuan, 8,710 yuan, respectively, grow 16%, 18%, respectively.

In 2012, is the overall progress of society year. The intensity of the comprehensive management of social security to increase; production safety accidents, the death toll decreased significantly; prices remain stable on the whole; to promote medical and health reform and overall development of the work.

In 2012, is the government construction and upgrading years. Adhere to the construction of "innovation, service-oriented, rule of law, clean government", promote the improvement of government work quality and efficiency.

遵义市

Zunyi City

今日遵义
Today's Zunyi

2012年，遵义市人民政府在省委、省政府和市委正确领导下，在市人大、市政协的监督支持下，深入贯彻落实党的十八大和国发【2012】2号文件精神，奋力拼搏、攻坚克难，实现了新一届政府工作良好开局。

2012年，预计完成地区生产总值1343.9亿元，同比增长（下同）15.9%；三次产业结构为13.5：45.1：41.4；全社会固定资产投资1306.5亿元，增长60.6%；规模工业增加值554.7亿元，增长22.1%；社会消费品零售总额409.9亿元，增长16.9%；财政总收入288.3亿元，增长42.6%；公共财政预算收入113亿元，增长33.5%；城镇居民人均可支配收入19748元，增长13.3%；农民人均纯收入6061元，增长16.2%。金融机构存、贷款余额分别达1712.2亿元、927.6亿元，比年初增长22.1%、30.3%。“四大

遵义会议会址正门
Site of the Zunyi meeting front gate

遵义机场全貌
Zunyi airport panorama

遵义会议会址
Site of the Zunyi meeting

In 2012, Zunyi City People's Government under the correct leadership of the provincial party committee, provincial government and municipal party committee, supervision of the Municipal People's Congress, the CPPCC's support, thoroughly implement the spirit of eighteenth National Congress of the CPC and the State Issued [2012] No. 2 document, work hard, overcome difficulties, to achieve a good start of a new session of the government work.

赤水河黄金水道
Chishui river golden waterway

In 2012, is expected to complete the region's GDP 134.39 billion yuan, an increase of 15.9% (the same below); the three industrial structure is 13.5: 45.1: 41.4; the total social investment in fixed assets 130.65 billion yuan, an increase of 60.6%; scale industrial added value of 55.47 billion yuan, an increase of 22.1%; total retail sales of social consumer goods 40.99 billion yuan, an increase of 16.9%; total fiscal revenue 28.83 billion yuan, an increase of 42.6%; the public finance budget revenue 11.3 billion yuan, an increase of 33.5%; per capita disposable income of urban residents 19,748 yuan, an increase of 13.3%; per capita net income of farmers 6,061 yuan, an increase of 16.2%. Financial institutions deposits, the loan balance reached 171.22 billion yuan, 92.76 billion yuan, respectively, an increase of 22.1%, 30.3% more than the beginning of the year. “Four big regions” developing with competition, county economy realize growth than binary, the city was granted the province’s first comprehensive evaluation.

Promoting “three simultaneous” strategy, the development of quality and efficiency improved significantly. The first is the accelerated pace of new-type industrialization. Built park standard plant 600,000 square meters, construction of 643,000 square meters, the new production projects 103.

The seven parks were listed in “511 demonstration park”in the province. Changzheng wind power, Panjiang Hailuo cement,

新茅台全景
New Maotai panorama

遵义新貌
Zunyi new image

马家湾立交桥
Majiawan overpass

区域”竞相发展，县域经济实现增比进位，我市获全省综合测评第一位。

强力推进“三化同步”战略，发展质量和效益明显提升。一是新型工业化步伐加快。建成园区标准厂房60万平方米、在建64.3万平方米，新投产项目103个。七个园区列入全省“511示范园区”。长征风电、盘江海螺水泥、裕能科尔微电子等新建项目和茅台酒厂、天蕴纺织等技改项目建成投产，务川氧化铝、绥阳煤电化、九鼎车辆等项目开工，桐梓电厂、二郎电厂等项目扎实推进。降低煤调基金征收标准和停征二次煤调基金，争取和发放原材料企业电价补贴近2亿元。二是城镇化进程加速推进。出台支持遵义国家级经济技术开发区、南部新城加快发展的政策措施。建投大厦、湿地公园、遵义四中及遵义医学院新蒲校区等项目加快推进，东南大道、高新快线、汇川大道延长线等骨干路网加快形成。县城“倍增计划”全面实施。茅台等示范镇建设全面启动。城镇化率达38.9%。三是农业现代化迈出坚实步伐。粮食、油菜籽总产量分别完成

美丽湘江河
The beautiful Xiangjiang river

乌江日出
Wujiang sunrise

土城渡口
Tucheng ferry

Yuneng Ke'er microelectronics and other new projects and Maotai distillery, Tianyun textile technical renovation project completed and put into production, Wuchuan aluminum, Suiyang coal power, Jiuding vehicle and other projects got started, project of Tongzi power plant, and Erlang power plant pushed forward. To reduce coal fund levy standard and suspension of two times coal adjustment fund, strive for and issuance of raw materials enterprises price subsidy of nearly 200 million yuan. The second is to accelerate the process of urbanization. Support the introduction of Zunyi national economic and technological development zone, policies and measures to speed up the development of South Metro. Jiantou Building, wetland park, the Zunyi fourth middle school and Zunyi Medical College Xinpu campus projects to accelerate, South East Avenue, new express, Huichuan Road extension line and speed up the formation of backbone network. The county "doubling growth plan" comprehensive implementation.

276.2万吨、24.2万吨，种植蔬菜224万亩、辣椒176.1万亩，新增茶园18万亩，收购烟叶202万担。思达、以晴集团在遵项目加快推进，新增市级以上龙头企业50家。实现一产增加值181.2亿元，增长8.9%。

着力建设“三宜”城市，遵义知名度和影响力不断提升。一是宜居城市建设迈出新步伐。投入5.7亿元实施“双创一巩固”工程。出台公共场所禁止吸烟管理办法、中心城区不文明行为管理试行办法。“国家卫生城市”通过复检。“全国文明城市”测评排名提升7位。编制中心城区综合交通规划。棚户区改造有序推进。启动100平方公里山体公园建设。全市森林覆盖率达48.6%。中心城区空气质量优良率达98.9%。中心城区、县城集中式饮用水源地水质达标率分别为100%、99.5%。二是宜业城市建设实现新突破。获“全国创业先进城市”称号。扶持创办微型企业3900户，带动就业2.1万人。城镇新增就业8.2万人，城镇登记失业率控制在4.2%以内。新增转移农业富余劳动力11.2万人。“国家商标战略实施示范城市”通过复查验收。新增驰名商标4个、地理标志保护产品4个、贵州名牌产品18个。三是宜游城市建设取得新成效。与省旅游局建立战略合作关系。成功举办全市首届旅游产业发展大会、第四届国际山地户外运动挑战赛。重点推出“红色遵义·醉美丹霞”旅游精品线。新开工旅游项目29个。新增三星级以上酒店6家，评定申报3A级以上景区10个。接待游客3354万人次，实现综合收入312亿元。

贵州海尔冰箱厂
Guizhou Haier refrigerator factory

航天成功汽车调研
Aerospace Chenggong Auto Research

核桃坝村农民多功能信息服务站
Walnut Village farmers multifunctional information service station

全力改善发展条件，基础设施建设持续加强。

一是交通建设实现突破。遵义机场建成通航，仁怀机场开工。高速公路新增90公里、在建631公里、通车里程达

桐梓重庆工业园鸟瞰
Bird's view of the Tongzi Chongqing industrial park

Maotai demonstration town construction started. The urbanization rate reached 38.9%. The third is the agricultural modernization has taken firm steps. The total output of grain, rapeseed completed 2,762,000 tons, 242,000 tons, respectively, planting 2,240,000 mu of vegetables, pepper 1,761,000 mu, 180,000 mu of new tea garden, to buy tobacco 2,020,000 tam. Sida, Yiqing group projects to accelerate in Zunyi, the new added municipal leading enterprises 50. To achieve a production value increase of 18.12 billion yuan, up 8.9%.

Focusing on the construction of "three suitable" city, Zunyi visibility and influence increasing. Firstly, a new step forward in building livable city. Invested 570 million yuan to implement the "double creative a consolidated" project. Introduction of the ban on smoking in public places, the measures for the administration of urban centres of uncivilized behavior management pilot scheme. "National health city" pass through the review. "National civilized city" evaluation rankings 7. Comprehensive transportation planning of the center city. Shanty towns transformation pushed in an orderly way. To start the 100 square kilometers of Mountain Park construction. The forest coverage rate reached 48.6%. Air quality and excellent rate city center reached 98.9%. Center city, the county centralized drinking water source to water quality compliance rate was 100%, 99.5% respectively. Secondly, is the industry city construction to achieve new breakthroughs. Won the "national advanced entrepreneurship city" title. Support the founder of miniature enterprise 3,900, driven 21,000 people in employment. 82,000 new urban jobs were created, the registered urban unemployment rate at 4.2%. The new added transfer of agricultural surplus labor force 112,000 people. "Model city of the national trademark strategy" pass through the review, approval. Add 4 well-known trademarks, geographical indications protection products 4, 18 brand-name products in Guizhou. Thirdly, is the leisure city construction has made new achievements. To establish a strategic cooperative relationship with the provincial tourism bureau. The success of the first tourist industry development conference, the fourth session of the international mountain outdoor sports challenge. Focus on the introduction of the "red Zunyi•drunk beautiful Danxia" tourism products line. New construction of tourism project 29. The new three star or above hotel 6, assessment of declaration of area of scene of 3A class above 10. Welcome visitors of 33,540,000 person-time, implementation of integrated income 31.2 billion yuan.

桐梓重庆工业园天祥科技有限公司生产车间
Tongzi Chongqing industrial park Tianxiang Science and Technology Co.,ltd. workshop

To improve the conditions for development, infrastructure construction continued to strengthen.

The first is to achieve a breakthrough in traffic construction. The opening of Zunyi airport, Renhuai Airport construction. New highways 90 kilometers, the construction of 631 km, the traffic mileage of 303 kilometers, county expressway project started. Built the

娄山关
Loushan Pass

沙滩博物馆
Beach Museum

303公里，县县通高速公路项目全部开工。建成通村公路553公里、通村油路1303公里。楠木渡、沿江渡、河闪渡码头投入运行。城市公共客运运力增加，智能化监管系统投入运行。二是水利建设持续推进。正安石峰、仁怀石板塘水库下闸蓄水，遵义中桥、桐梓新桥、凤冈河头水库实现截流，遵义灌区（一期）、道真大沙河、绥阳后水河等工程顺利推进，汇川麻沟、余庆魁龙、仁怀大沙坝等骨干水源工程开工建设。解决农村57万人饮水安全问题。实施54座病险水库除险加固，治理中小河流22条、水土流失面积240平方公里，完成10个小型农田水利重点县年度建设任务，新增、恢复、改善灌溉面积35万亩。遵义县绿竹坝、凤冈响滩子等重点烟水工程开工建设。完成烟水配套工程10万亩。水利水电工程移民工作有序推进。三是市场基础设施不断完善。黔北汽车国际博览城（一期）、富邦家装商城、星力百货城正式营业。遵义国际商贸城、中国茶城、绥阳农产品综合商贸城、凤冈有机食品城等项目有序推进。改造中心城区农贸市场32个。“新网工程”实现行政村全覆盖。新建粮食仓容31.5万吨。四是电力、信息基础设施建设加强。完成电力投资22.4亿元，500千伏诗乡输变电等工程加快实施。“天网工程”顺利推进；完成63个空白乡镇邮政局

余庆县龙家镇光明村
Yuqing county Longjia town Guangming village

苍茫海龙囤
The vast Hailongtun

village roads 553 kilometers, 1,303 kilometers village oil road. Nanmudu,Yanjiangdu, Heshandu wharf is put into operation. City public passenger transport capacity increased, the intelligent monitoring system put into operation. The second is to continue to promote the construction of water conservancy. Zhengan Shifeng, Renhuai stone pond reservoir impoundment, Zunyi bridge, Tongzi bridge, Fenggang river reservoir to achieve closure, Zunyi irrigation area (I phase), Daozhen Dashahe, Suiyanghou river project is progressing smoothly, Huichuan Ma Gou, Yuqing Kuilong, Renhuai large dam such as the backbone of water source engineering construction. Solve 570,000 rural people drinking water safety problem. Implementation of strengthening 54 dangerous reservoirs, governance of 22 rivers, soil erosion area of 240 square kilometers, the completion of 10 small key county water conservancy annual construction tasks, add, recovery, the improvement of the irrigation area of 350,000 mu. Zunyi County Lvzhu Dam, Fenggang Xiangtanzi and other key water project construction started. Completed 100,000 mu of smoking water project. Water conservancy and hydropower project resettlement work orderly. The third is the market improving infrastructure construction. North Guizhou International Auto Expo City (I phase), Fubon home mall, Xingli City Department Store officially opened. Zunyi International Trade City, China Tea Town, Suiyang comprehensive agricultural products trade city, Fenggang Organic Food City Project pushed in an orderly way. Transformation of central urban farmers market 32. "New network project" to achieve full coverage of administrative village. The new grain storage capacity of 315,000 tons. The fourth is to strengthen the power, information infrastructure construction. Complete power investment 2.24 billion yuan, 500 kilovolt Shixiang power transmission project to accelerate the implementation. "Skynet project" completed smoothly; 63 blank Township Post Office (station) for

甘沟瀑布
Gangou falls

美酒河
Miejiu river

（所）补建工作；乡乡通宽带、行政村通电话目标基本实现。

大力推进改革创新，开放开发战略深入实施。一是重点改革稳步推进。农村产权制度、中小企业融资、事业单位、矿产资源配置等改革取得突破。启动6个县级公立医院综合改革试点。“国家公共文化服务体系示范区”创建取得成效，文化体制改革获文化部表彰。邮政体制改革深入实施，遵义市邮政管理局挂牌成立。二是开放合作全面推进。与重庆綦江、北京海淀结为友好城市。遵渝合作取得积极进展，桐梓重庆工业园建设取得实效。与北大信息科技学院、浙江大学、西南大学、河海大学等签订市校合作协议。与农行、农发行、交行、农信社省级机构签订银政合作协议，浦发、招商、重庆等银行分（支）行挂牌营业，贵州茅台集团财务公司成立，中信银行遵义分行加快筹建，市投资集团公司等发行企业债券48亿元。与茅台、保利、中电投、中建等企业（集团）合作更加紧密。遵义国家级经济技术开发区正式挂牌，省级经济开发区达到11个。

湄潭天下第一壶
Meitan the best pot in the land

倾力办好民生实事，和谐遵义建设迈出新步伐。一是社会事业全面发展。实施各类教育工程1696项，其中新（改、扩）建乡镇公办幼儿园92所。乡村卫生服务一体化全面推行。连续6次荣获“全国无偿献血先进城市”称号。

茶乡魂
The soul of the Tea village

湄潭茶海
Meitan tea sea

the construction work; townships broadband, administrative village phone to achieve the basic objectives.

Vigorously promote the reform and innovation, thoroughly implement the open strategy of developing. The first is the key of reform steadily. The reform breakthrough of rural property rights system, the financing of small and medium-sized enterprises, institutions, the allocation of mineral resources. Start the 6 county public hospital comprehensive reform pilots. “national system of public cultural services demonstration zone” to create success, the reform of the cultural system by the Ministry of culture recognition. The postal system reform implementation, Zunyi postal administration was set up. The second is to promote openness and cooperation. With the Chongqing Qijiang, Beijing Haidian friendly city. Zunyi and Chongqing cooperation has achieved positive progress, Tongzi Chongqing industrial park construction to obtain actual effect. The signing of the agreement of cooperation of school and University City College with Peking University Information Science and Technology Collgege, Zhejiang University, Southwestern University, Hohai University, etc.. The Agricultural Bank of China, Agricultural Development Bank, Communication Bank, rural credit cooperatives provincial agencies signed bank-enterprise cooperation agreement, Shanghai Pudong Development Bank, China Merchants Bank, Chongqing branch (Branch) line of business listing, Moutai group finance company established, Zunyi branch of China CITIC Bank to speed up, city investment group company issued corporate bonds of 4.8 billion yuan. Closer cooperation with enterprise Moutai, poly, CPI, China construction (Group). Zunyi national economic and Technological Development Zone was formally established, the provincial Economic Development Zone reached 11.

To make well the people's livelihood, new steps were taken to the construction of a harmonious Zunyi. The first is the all-round development of social undertakings. The implementation of all kinds of education project 1,696,

唱出心底的颂歌——湄潭田家沟村民自编自演花灯戏《十谢共产党》
Sing the heart mantra -- Meitan Tianjiagou village self-composed self-played lantern show “ten thanks to the China communist party”

水上舞龙、独竹飘表演
The water dragon, single bamboo drift performance

人口出生率、自增率分别控制在10.5‰、5.1‰以内。获省级以上科技及知识产权立项276项，专利申请量、授权量分别突破2000件、1000件。《遵义百科全书》出版发行。遵义籍运动员卫冕奥运会冠军，成功举办全省第二届农运会，遵义代表团获金牌、奖牌数第一。改造农村危房4.3万户。新农保和城镇居民社会养老保险实现全覆盖。习水县及全市20个重点乡镇“减贫摘帽”，20 万人脱贫。“十八件民生实事”完成投资55亿元。二是社会管理创新持续加强。安全生产事故起数、死亡人数分别下降29.1%、36.2%，连续12年实现“双降”。政法基础设施、城市报警监控及智能交通指挥平台等项目全面启动。社会治安打防控体系逐步完善，群众安全感达92.4%。连续七次荣获“全国双拥模范城”称号。

赤水瀑布
Chishui falls

遵义杨粲墓
Zunyi Yangcan tomb

赤水桫椤
The Chishui Alsophila spinulosa

the new (change, extend) built villages and towns public kindergarten 92. Integration of health service of rural comprehensive fully pushed. Continuous 6 times won the "national advanced city for blood donation" title. The population birth rate, rate of natural increase was controlled within 10.5 ‰ and 5.1 ‰. By the provincial-level technology and intellectual property rights project 276, the amount of patent application, authorization amount exceeded 2000, 1000. "The Zunyi encyclopedia" published. Zunyi nationality athlete defending Olympic champion, successfully held the second session of the farmers' sports games, Zunyi delegation won the gold medal, the first medal in count. Transformation of 43,000 dilapidated rural houses. Cover the new agricultural insurance and old-age insurance for urban residents. Xishui County and other 20 townships "poverty reduction ST", 200,000 people out of poverty. "Eighteen people's livelihood matters" completed investment of 5.5 billion yuan. The second is to continue to strengthen social management innovation. Production safety accidents, deaths decreased by 29.1%, 36.2%, respectively, for 12 consecutive years to achieve the "double down". Political and legal infrastructure construction, city alarm monitoring and intelligent traffic commanding platform project started. Social security the fight control system gradually perfect, the safety of the masses up to 92.4%. Seven times consecutively won the title of "national double-support model city".

地久天长——鸳鸯桫椤
Forever -- Mandarin Alsophila spinulosa

立足新起点 抢抓新机遇 努力建设富裕和谐美丽新毕节

Based on the new starting point To seize new opportunities Strive to build a prosperous, harmonious beautiful new Bijie

市委书记张吉勇（右三）陪同时任贵州省委书记栗战书（右二）在黔西县城关镇乌螺坝调研
Party secretary Zhang Jiyong (third from right), accompanied when he was the provincial party secretary Li Zhanshu (second from right) to have research in Qianxi county Chengguan towns Wuluo dam

市委书记张吉勇陪同省委书记赵克志、时任省委副书记陈敏尔实地调研夹岩水利枢纽工程
Municipal Party committee secretary Zhang Jiyong accompanied provincial party committee secretary Zhao Kezh, the provincial deputy secretary Chen Miner to have investigationof the Jiayan water conservancy project

陈昌旭市长（左二）陪同时任副省长谢庆生（左一）在七星关区调研
Mayor Chen Changcu (second from left), accompanied by the former vice governor Xie Qingsheng (first from left) to have research in the Qixingguang district

2012年，全市上下积极抢抓国发2号文件颁布实施的机遇，认真贯彻落实党的十八大精神，牢牢把握试验区“三大主题”，坚持“两加一推”主基调，以“投资拉动、项目带动、招商推动”为总抓手，大力实施“工业强市、城镇化带动、旅游兴市、生态立市”四大战略，全市呈现“经济增长、政治稳定、民族团结、文化繁荣、生态良好、社会和谐”的喜人局面。全年完成生产总值872.4亿元、增长15.3%；完成财政总收入247.7亿元、增长36.36%；社会消费品零售总额177.5亿元，增长18%；全社会固定资产投资1300亿元、增长56%；城镇居民人均可支配收入19243元、农民人均纯收入4929元，分别增长19.3%和17.1%。

坚持把项目建设作为第一抓手，发展后劲持续增强。共储备项目10036个，总投资3.3万亿元，其中谋划国发2号文件项目5405个，总投资2.4万亿元。总投资1000万元以上的重大工程和重点项目1933个，计划总投资6601.54亿元，完成投资1233.53亿元。重大工程和重点项目建成578个、新开工589个，进一步扩大了有效投资，带动了经济快速发展。

坚持把结构调整作为主攻方向，发展质量稳步提高。三次产业结构调整到16.7:47.7:35.6。完成工业固定资产投

毕节飞雄机场航站楼
The Bijie Feixiong Airport Terminal

In 2012, the city actively seize opportunities of the State Issued document NO.2 promulgated and implemented conscientiously implement the spirit of 18th CPC National Congress, firmly grasp the "three themes" of the test area, to adhere to the "two-plus-one push" the main tone, to "investment-led, project-driven, investment promoting" total handle, vigorously implement the"strong city, driven by urbanization, tourism propers city, ecology buils city"four main strategies, the city presents "economic growth, political stability, national unity, cultural prosperity, ecological, social harmony" gratifying situation. Last year's GDP of 87.24 billion yuan, an increase of 15.3%; complete the total fiscal revenue of 24.77 billion yuan, an increase of 36.36%; total retail sales of social consumer goods was 17.75 billion yuan, an increase of 18%; total fixed asset investment of 130 billion yuan, an increase of 56%; the per capita disposable income of urban residents was 19,243 yuan, rural per capita net income of 4,929 yuan, an increase of 19.3% and 17.1%, respectively.

织金县火车站
Zhijin County RailwayStation

Adhere to the project construction as the first starting point, the potential for further development has continued to improve. The 10,036 total reserve project with a total investment of 3.3 trillion yuan, which the planning State Issued document NO.2 project 5,405, a total investment of 2.4 trillion yuan. 1,933 major projects and key projects with a total investment of more than 10 million yuan, plans a total investment of 660.154 billion yuan, completed an investment of 123.353 billion yuan. 578 major projects and key projects completed, 589 new construction projects, to further expand the effective investment, driven by rapid economic development.

纳雍县花园式公租房、廉租房小区
Nayong County garden-public rental, low-cost housing area

Adhere to structural adjustment as the main direction, development quality has improved steadily. The three industrial restructuring was 16.7:47.7:35.6. Industrial fixed assets investment of 42.01 billion yuan, an increase of 32.7%; above-scale industrial added value of 25.9 billion yuan, an increase of 21.3%. The proportion of grains, economic crops and crop adjustment from 63:37 to 55:45. Successful contractor province's Seventh Tourism Congress, total tourism income of 18.461 billion yuan, an increase of 50%. The

毕威高速田坝特大桥
Biwei Express Tianbate Bridge

资420.1亿元，增长32.7%；规模以上工业增加值达259亿元，增长21.3%。粮经作物种植比例从63:37调整到55:45。成功承办全省第七届旅发大会，完成旅游总收入184.61亿元，增长50%。第三产业增加值占生产总值比重达35.6%。森林覆盖率提高到43.1%。

坚持把城乡统筹作为重中之重，城乡面貌明显改善。启动建设特色小城镇87个、幸福小镇25个，新建和改造“黔西北民居”35万户。新增城市新区22平方公里，城镇化率提高到30.67%。新开工城市道路项目96个372.49公里、完成投资76.12亿元，改扩建城市道路项目22个53.3公里，完成投资8.39亿元。完成重点区域绿化2.25万亩、城镇绿化美化1179亩。

坚持把基础设施作为保障条件，发展瓶颈逐步突破。六沾铁路复线威宁段建成通车，林织铁路建设快速推进。黔织高速、杭瑞高速遵毕段、开发大道、机场高速全线贯通，毕威高速除部分线段外基本贯通，开工建设厦蓉高速

已建成的织金大新桥水库
The Zhijin Newbridge reservoir built

织金县桂果镇猫场村新貌
Zhijin County Guiguo town Maocahgn village new look

碧阳湖畔（毕节倒天河二期防洪工程）
Bi Yang Lakeside (Bijie Dao Tianhe flood control engineering project II)

proportion of tertiary industry accounted for 35.6% of the GDP. The forest coverage rate to 43.1%.

Adhere to the urban and rural areas as the most important, significant improvement in urban and rural areas. Start building characteristics, small towns 87, and the happiness of the town 25, built and upgraded the "northwest Guizhou residential houses" 350,000. Add the new urban area of 22 square kilometers, the urbanization rate increased to 30.67%. Urban road projects newly started 96 of 372.49 km, completed an investment of 7.612 billion yuan, the renovation and expansion of urban road project 22 of 53.3 km, completed an investment of 839 million yuan. Completion of key regional green 22,500 mu, urban greening and beautification of 1,179 mu.

Adhere to the infrastructure as security conditions, develop gradually break through the bottleneck. The Liuzhan railway double-track Weining section was opened to traffic, the rapid advance of Linzhi railway construction. Qianzhi high-speed, Hangtui high-speed Zuibi segment, Development Avenue, Airport Expressway all got through, Biwei high-speed basic through addition to the part of the line segment, started construction of the Xiamen-Chengdu Expressway Bijie segments, Hangrui high-speed Bijie to Duge segment, Qianxi to Dafang highway. The Bijie Airport is basically

已建成投产的赫章县韭菜坪风能发电
Hezhang County Jiucaiping wind power has been put into operation

毕节金河化工
The Bijie Jinhe Chemical

毕节小坝经济开发区在建的标准厂房
The Bijie Xiaoba Economic Development Zone in the construction of standard factory

毕节境内各段、杭瑞高速毕节至都格段、黔西至大方高速公路。毕节机场基本建成。夹岩水利枢纽工程前期工作进展顺利，农村饮水安全、骨干水源、病险水库除险加固、中小河流治理等水利工程建设成效明显。电力、信息等基础设施进一步加强。

坚持把改革开放作为强大动力，发展活力不断增强。不断深化行政审批、矿产资源管理、公共资源交易、文化体制、县域经济发展等改革，科学发展的内生动力和活力得到增强。新成立交通银行毕节分行和3家村镇银行、51家小额贷款公司、4家担保公司、9个小微企业金融服务中心。招商引资实际到位资金939.36亿元，增长54.48%。完成进出口3.2亿美元，利用外资8517万美元。

坚持把改善民生作为根本取向，群众幸福指数得到提升。减少农村贫困人口48.73万人，20个贫困乡镇达到“减贫摘帽”标准。城镇新增就业近14万人，城镇登记失业率3.79%。“营养改善计划”覆盖学生116万人。常驻人口符合政策生育率97.06%。群众安全感达92.97%。威宁、赫章地震灾后重建工作有序推进。各项社会事业全面进步。

当前，毕节正处在突破瓶颈、夯实基础、积蓄能量、调整结构的关键节点。站在新的起点上，毕节市将坚持“加速发展、加快转型、推动跨越”主基调，大力实施“工业强市、城镇化带

大方县食品药品工业园区——篮雁集团建设全景图
Dafang County Food and Drug Industrial Park -Lanyan Group building panorama

力帆时骏振兴车辆有限公司生产车间
Lifan Shijun Zhenxing Vehicles Limited production workshop

completed. Jiayan Water Control Project preparatory work is progressing smoothly, and the safety of drinking water in rural areas, the backbone of the water, the dam reinforcement, medium and small rivers and other water conservancy construction achieved remarkable success. Electricity, information and other infrastructure will be further strengthened.

Adhere to reform and opening up as a strong driving force, development vitality is growing. Continue to deepen the administrative examination and approval, the reform of the management of mineral resources, the transaction of public resources, the cultural system, county economic development, scientific development of endogenous motivation and vitality is enhanced. The newly established Bank of Communication Bijie Branch, 3 rural banks, 51 small loan companies, 4 security companies, 9 small micro-enterprise financial services center. Investment actual funds 93.936 billion yuan, an increase of 54.48%. $ 320 million of import and export, the use of foreign capital of $ 85,170,000.

Adhere to improve people's livelihood as a fundamental orientation, the masses happiness index would be enhanced. Reduce rural poverty population of 487,300 people, the 20 poor township reach "Poverty Reduction Name"standard. Nearly 140,000 new urban jobs, the registered urban unemployment rate of 3.79%."The Nutrition Improvement Plan" covering 1.16 million students. The permanent population policy-fertility 97.06%. The safety of the masses of 92.97%. Weining, the Hezhang earthquake reconstruction work in an orderly fashion. Various social undertakings get progress.

赫章县阿西里西大草原上的生态畜牧养殖（一）
Hezhang County Axilixi prairie ecological animal husbandry (one)

At present, Bijie is in a break through the bottleneck, lay a solid foundation for energy savings, adjust the structure of key nodes. Standing on a new starting point, Bijie City will adhere to "accelerate the development, accelerate the transformation, to promote across" the main tone, vigorously implement the two main strategies of the "industry strong city, driven by urbanization", "development and poverty alleviation, ecological construction,population control"three themes continue to deepen, and strive to improve the industrial economy, the urbanization rate, the private economy, the county economy "four proportions", to build industrial parks, efficient agriculture demonstration zone, the demonstration of small towns, urban complexes, tourist attractions "five platform", focus on building a specialized industry, infrastructure, urbanization and urban and rural development, the social undertakings and public services, the driving force for development, ecological environment "six systems", and building a moderately prosperous society in the province and the national synchronized. Focus on doing the following work:

赫章县阿西里西大草原上的生态畜牧养殖（二）
Hezhang County Axilixi prairie ecological animal husbandry (two)

The first is to accelerate the development of the industrial economy as an important engine. Accelerate the construction of energy, resources deep processing, equipment manufacturing,

威宁泰丰园花卉基地
The Weining Taifeng Garden Flower Base

金沙县台金现代农业产业产业园花卉基地
The Jinsha County Taijin modern agricultural industrial industrial park flower base

黔西乐义百家现代农业科技示范基地大棚——黄瓜种植
Qianxi Leyi Baijia modern agricultural demonstration base in greenhouses - cucumber planting

动”两大主战略，继续深化“开发扶贫、生态建设、人口控制”三大主题，努力提高工业经济、城镇化率、民营经济、县域经济等“四个比重”，全力打造产业园区、高效农业示范园区、示范小城镇、城市综合体、旅游景区等“五个平台”，着力构建特色产业、基础设施、城镇化和城乡统筹发展、社会事业和公共服务、发展动力、生态环境等“六大体系”，与全国全省同步全面建成小康社会。重点要做好以下几方面的工作：

一是把加快工业经济发展作为重要引擎。加快建设能源、资源深加工、装备制造业、特色轻工业、承接产业转移“五大基地”，加快发展“十大工业产业”，积极推进“四个一体化”建设，努力把工业经济做大做强。

二是把加快建设城乡一体化作为重要载体。积极稳妥推进大中小城市、特色小城镇和新农村建设。加快毕节、大方同城化进程，大力推进城镇基础设施、城市综合体和示范小城镇建设，抓好特色小城镇和“四在农家、美丽乡村”建设，缩小城乡差距，促进城乡繁荣。

三是把加快基础设施建设作为重要保障。坚持不懈地围绕加快立体交通枢纽建设的目标，进一步加大跑省、跑部力度，“铁、公、机”一起上、齐发展。切实加强水利基础设施建设，争取夹岩水利枢纽工程早日开工建设。大力推进毕节—大兴电力通道建设，提高跨越发展电力保障能力。

四是把加快发展现代农业作为重要基础。坚持以“三化”兴“三农”，用工业理念谋划农业，用现代管理手段经营农业，用龙头企业带动农业，用品牌战略打造农业，积极发展农业龙头企业和农民专业合作组织，加快转变农业发展方式，努力提高农业产业化水平。

五是把加快发展现代服务业作为重要支撑。大力打造“洞天湖地、花海鹤乡、避暑天堂”旅游品牌，迅速做大做好做强旅游产业；立足交通区位优势，做好省际商贸城市规划，把毕节市建设成为川滇黔渝结合部重要的商贸物流中心。积极引进金融机构在毕节设立分支机构，积极发展新型服务业态。

六是把加快打造生态文明建设先行区作为重要条件。大力推进退耕还林、石漠化治理、水土保持、天

夜郎国家森林公园平山景区生态建设成果
Yelang country Forest Park Pingshan area ecological construction

specialty light industry, industries to relocate "five bases", accelerate the development of "top 10 industrial" and actively promote the construction of "four integration", efforts for bigger and stronger industrial economy.

The second is to accelerate the construction of urban-rural integration as an important carrier. Actively and steadily push forward to cities and towns, the characteristics of small towns and new rural construction. Accelerate the Bijie, Dafang city of process, and vigorously promote the urban infrastructure construction of small towns, urban complexes and demonstration construction, grasp the characteristics of small towns and "four in the farm, beautiful countryside" construction, narrowing the gap between urban and rural areas, to promote urban and rural prosperity.

The third is to speed up the construction of infrastructure as an important safeguard. Adhere tirelessly around the goal of speeding up the construction of three-dimensional transportation hub, and further intensify efforts to run the province, running, "railway, highway, machine"get together and develop together. Effectively strengthen the construction of water infrastructure, the fight for the Jiayan water conservancy project start the construction as soon as possible. Vigorously promote Bijie - Daxing power channel construction, power protection capabilities increase by leaps and bounds.

苦荞花开——纳雍县沙包乡天星村新农村建设
Tartary buckwheat flowers -- Nayong Count Shabao Township Tianxng Village of new rural construction

The fourth is to accelerate the development of modern agriculture as an important foundation. Adhere to the "informationization, industrialization and localization" prosper "agriculture, rural and farmers ", use industrial concept planning in agriculture, farming with modern management tools, with the leading enterprises in agriculture, agricultural brand strategy to build positive development leading agricultural enterprises and farmers' specialized cooperative organizations, to accelerate transition agricultural development, efforts to raise the level of agricultural industrialization.

The fifth is to accelerate the development of modern service industry as an important support. Vigorously to create "the cave heaven lake area, flowers sea crane township, a summer paradise" tourism brand, rapidly enlarge and make stronger tourism industry; based traffic advantages, good inter-provincial commerce urban planning, made Bijie City become the Sichuan-Yunnan-Guizhou Chongqing combined with the Ministry of important trade and logistics center. Actively introduce financial institutions to set up branches in Bijie, actively develop new service format.

黔西县绿化乡大海子“同心新村”新貌
The Qianxi County Lvhua Township Dahaizi “Tongxin New Village”new look

纳雍县王家寨镇华阳广场全景
Nayong county Wangjia Zhai Town Huayang Plaza panorama

然林保护、生态产业等生态工程建设，构筑起“两江”上游的生态屏障。大力发展循环经济和生态产业，鼓励发展节能、降耗、减排的高新技术产业，在生态文明建设上作示范、走前列。

七是把加快保障和改善民生作为重要内容。坚持民生优先、民利至上、民需为要，大力发展教育事业，深化医疗卫生体制改革，积极推进科技创新，实施就业和创业工程，统筹推进社会保障体系建设，抓好城市保障性住房、农村危房改造，加强和创新社会管理。

八是把深化改革、扩大开放作为重要动力。充分发挥试验区“先行先试”的优势，大力推进体制机制创新，加快重点领域和关键环节改革，加快发展开放型经济，充分发挥深圳对口帮扶和东部十省市统一战线帮扶的优势，加大招商引资力度，借助外力推动发展。

新建AAA级景区米底河
New AAA level scenic Midi River

The sixth is to speed up creating an ecological civilization as an important condition for first area. Vigorously promote ecological projects in returning farmland to forests, rocky desertification control, water and soil conservation, protection of natural forests, ecological industry, to build ecological barrier "Two Rivers" upstream. Vigorously develop the circular economy and ecological industry, to encourage the development of energy conservation, energy saving high-tech industry, as a model, walking in the forefront in the construction of ecological civilization.

新建AAA级景区大方县慕俄格古城
The New AAA level scenic Dafang County Mu Ege ancient city

The seventh is to accelerate the protection and improvement of people's livelihood as an important content. Adhere to the people's livelihood priorities, people's interest as first, people's need as importance, to vigorously develop education, deepening medical and health system reform, and actively promote scientific and technological innovation, the implementation of employment and entrepreneurial projects, will coordinate development of the social security system, grasp the cities of affordable housing, renovation of dilapidated buildings in rural areas, strengthen and innovate the public administration.

The eighth is to make deepening of reform, opening wider to the outside world as an important impetus. Give full play to the advantages of the test area of "pilot", and vigorously promote institutional innovation, accelerate the reform of key areas and key links, speed up the development of an open economy, give full play to the advantage of helping their counterparts in Shenzhen and the ten provinces and cities of the eastern united front helping, increase investment, and promote the development of outside help.

六盘水市

Liupanshui City

市领导参加全市“三化同步”现场观摩会
City leaders to participate in the city's "three synchronization" on-site demonstrations

市领导了解本地特色产品
City leaders understand the local specialty products

2012年，六盘水市坚持“两加一推”主基调，大力实施“三化同步”主战略，着力保增长、调结构、增活力、惠民生、促和谐，全市呈现出“发展提速、投资增加、民生改善、后劲增强、社会和谐、人心思进”的良好局面。

全市生产总值完成753.67亿元，增长16%，增速高于全国、高于西部、高于全省。财政总收入完成156.35亿元，增长21.71%；公共财政预算收入完成103.49亿元，增长46.11%。社会消费品零售总额完成182.82亿元，增长16%。城镇居民人均可支配收入达到18764元，增长14.6%；农民人均纯收入达到5182元，增长16.8%。金融机构人民币存、贷款余额分别为676.21亿元、508.38亿元，分别增长17.19%、21.92%。全市综合排位实现前移进位，上升至全省第5名。

强力推进项目建设，固定资产投资大幅增加。通过建立“三化”现场观摩会、项目集中开工和固定资产投资“旬调度、月督查、季考核”等项目推进机制，项目建设掀起新高潮。全社会固定资产投资突破千亿元大关，达到1088.9

六盘水市“四在农家”建设成果
Liupanshui City "four in the farm" building results

盘县妥乐银杏村
Panxian county Tuole Yinxing village

In 2012, Liupanshui City, adhere to the "two plus one push" the main tone, vigorously implement the "three synchronization" main strategy, efforts to maintain growth, structural adjustment, increase vitality, benefit people's livelihood and promote harmony, the city presents a "speed development, investment increases, improved living conditions, increased stamina, social harmony, people make progress together" a good situation.

The city's GDP reached 75.367 billion yuan, an increase of 16%, higher than the national growth rate, higher than the west, higher than the province. Total fiscal revenue of 15.635 billion yuan, an increase of 21.71%; public budget revenue of 10.349 billion yuan, an increase of 46.11%. Total retail sales of social consumer goods completed 18.282 billion yuan, an increase of 16%. Per capita disposable income of urban residents reached 18,764 yuan, an increase of 14.6%; rural per capita net income reached 5,182 yuan, an increase of 16.8%. Financial institutions RMB deposit and loan balances were 67.621 billion yuan, 50.838 billion yuan, an increase of 17.19%, 21.92%, respectively. The city's overall ranking to achieve progress forward position, rose to the province No. 5.

Strongly promote the project construction, investment in fixed assets increased significantly. Through the establishment of the "three" on-site demonstrations, the project began to focus on and investment in fixed assets "late scheduling, supervision month, quarterly assessment" and other projects to promote mechanisms for projects set off a new upsurge. Total fixed asset investment exceeded 100 billion yuan mark, reaching 108.89 billion yuan, an increase of 97.8%, of which 500,000 yuan investment in fixed assets 76.639 billion yuan, an increase of 74.2%. 81 provincial key projects completed investment 14.77 billion yuan, 329 municipal key projects completed an investment of 42.8 billion yuan. New projects focus on quarterly cumulative 940, a total investment of 119.33 billion yuan, completed an investment of 33.4 billion yuan.

明湖湿地公园一景
Minghu Wetland Park one corner

Efforts to overcome the impact of the economic downturn, while the industrial economy into reverse traceability. By taking the adjustment of product structure, the drop in price supplement, high energy consuming industries supporting the price subsidies and other response measures, under the strong grasp of support, promote production, expand the market, the industrial economy to achieve stable and rapid development. The city's above-scale industrial

玉舍森林公园雪景
Yushe Forest Park Snow

玉舍森林公园
Yushe Forest Park

亿元，增长97.8%，其中50万元以上固定资产投资完成766.39亿元，增长74.2%。81个省级重点项目完成投资147.7亿元，329个市级重点项目完成投资428亿元。分季度集中新开工项目累计940个、总投资1193.3亿元，完成投资334亿元。

努力克服经济下行影响，工业经济溯逆而进。通过采取调整产品结构、价跌量补、高载能行业配套电价补贴等应对措施，下大力抓扶持、促生产、拓市场，工业经济实现平稳较快发展。全市规模以上工业增加值364.42亿元，增长21.6%。着力打造煤电钢、煤电铝、煤电化、煤电材“四个一体化”品牌。产业园区建设取得新进展，基础设施建设投入完成60.8亿元。

以交通为重点的基础设施建设得到进一步加强。六盘水月照机场飞行区土石方主体工程基本完成；长昆铁路客运专线建设进展顺利，六沾铁路复线建成通车，六盘水火车站站房改造主体工程基本建成；建成乡村公路756.7公里。

高度重视民生问题，发展成果更多惠及人民群众。扎实办好“十二件民生实事”，完成投资41.9亿元。全面实施积极的就业政策，基本医疗、基本养老、失业、工伤、生育等保险制度体系进一步完善。完成14284套保障性安居工程和33090户农村危房改造任务，被国家列为公积金支持保障性住房建设试点城市。全力打造“扶贫攻坚示范区”，12个乡镇实现“减贫摘帽”。

水城杜鹃
Shui Rhododendron

十里杜鹃
Shili Rhododendron

北盘江大峡谷
Beipanjiang Grand Canyon

added value of 36.442 billion yuan, an increase of 21.6%. Efforts to build coal-fired steel, coal, aluminum coal technology, coal timber "four integration" brand. Industrial park construction has made new progress, the infrastructure investment completed 6.08 billion yuan.

To focus on transport infrastructure has been further strengthened. Liupanshui Yue Zhao airfield earthwork main project basically completed; Chang-Kun Railway Passenger Dedicated Line construction progressing smoothly, Liuzhan double-track railway opened to traffic, Liupanshui main train station house renovation project was basically completed; build rural roads 756.7 kilometers.Attaches great importance to people's livelihood, the fruits of development to benefit more people. Solid run "twelve practical livelihood", completed an investment 4.19 billion yuan. Full implementation of the active employment policy, basic health care, basic pension, unemployment, work injury, maternity insurance system was further improved. Completed 14,284 units of affordable housing projects and 33,090 rural reconstruction task, was listed as fund to support construction of affordable housing pilot cities. To create "anti-poverty demonstration zone", 12 villages and towns to achieve "put off the poverty hats".

安 顺 市

Anshun City

发展中的安顺城
The developing Anshun city

安顺一角
One corner in Anshun

安顺市位于贵州省中西部，素有“黔之腹、滇之喉、粤蜀之唇齿”之称。全市面积9267平方公里，人口300万人，其中少数民族人口占39%。安顺市现辖一区、两县、三个自治县、三个管委会，分别是西秀区，平坝县、普定县，镇宁布依族苗族自治县、关岭布依族苗族自治县、紫云苗族布依族自治县，安顺经济技术开发区管理委员会、黄果树风景名胜区管理委员会和龙宫风景名胜区管理委员会。

安顺历史悠久、文化底蕴深厚，是贵州省历史文化名城，拥有穿洞文化、夜郎文化、牂牁文化、屯堡文化等独特的历史文化遗存。有国家级重点文物保护单位5处，省级文物保护单位27处。普定穿洞古人类文化遗址被誉为“亚洲文明之灯”，关岭“红崖天书”世称“千古之谜”，明代军事遗存屯堡村落和关岭古生物化石群堪称“世界唯一”，安顺蜡染被誉为“东方第一染”，安顺地戏被称为“中国戏剧活化石”。安顺是中国共产党老一辈无产阶级革命家王若飞同志的故乡，也是中国国民党中央常委 “谷氏三兄弟”谷正伦、谷正刚、谷正鼎的故地。

安顺夜景
The night view of Anshun

《"春笋"》
"Bamboo shoots in spring"

Anshun City is located in the Midwest of Guizhou Province, known as "the belly of Guizhou, Yunnan's throat, Guangdong Sichuan's lips and teeth" The city area of 9,267 square kilometers, population 3 million, of which 39% minority population. Anshun City has jurisdiction over an area, two counties, three autonomous counties, three CMC, namely Xixiu district, Pingba County, Puding County, Zhenning Buyi and Miao Autonomous County, Guanling Buyi and Miao Autonomous County, Ziyun Miao and Buyi Autonomous County, Anshun economic and Technological Development Zone Management Committee, Huangguoshu scenic Area Management Committee and the Dragon Palace scenic Area management Committee.

Anshun owns long history, profound culture, is a historical and cultural city in Guizhou Province, has a unique cultural advantages of the Chuandong culture, Yelang culture, the culture of Yangke, the Tunbao cultur and so on. There are five national key cultural relics protection units, the provincial cultural relics protection units 27. Puding Chuandong Paleolithic known as the "Asian Civilizations light", Guanling "Redcliffe bible" is said "Mystery", the Ming Dynasty military remains Tunbao villages and Guanling fossils group called "The world's only", Anshun batik as the "Oriental first dyeing", Anshun local play is called "living fossil of Chinese drama". Anshun is our party's older generation of proletarian revolutionaries, Wang Ruofei comrade's homeland, China the Kuomintang in the Standing Committee of the "Gu three brothers" Gu Zhenglun, Gu Zhenggang, Gu Zhengding's old haunt.

城市在延伸
The city is extending

城市中的宁静
Quiet city

开发区标准化厂房效果图
Development Zone standardized plant renderings

光照电站大坝
Illumination power station dam

关岭水泥厂
Guanling cement factory

安顺境内环境优美、气候宜人，是中国避暑胜地。境内生态环境良好，是最适宜人居的生态旅游城市。安顺是国家最早确定的甲类旅游开放城市之一，是“中国优秀旅游城市”和贵州省优先发展重点旅游区及西线旅游中心，2009年被评为“中国十大特色休闲城市”。

安顺素有“中国瀑乡”、“屯堡文化之乡”、“蜡染之乡”、“西部之秀”的美誉。全市风景区面积占幅员面积的12%以上。境内有黄果树、龙宫、格凸河3个国家级风景名胜区，有关岭古生物化石群国家地质公园、九龙山国家森林公园、国家4A级旅游区夜郎洞，有花江大峡谷、夜郎湖、斯拉河等省级风景名胜区，还有亚洲跨度第一、世界第六的坝陵河大桥。

安顺交通便捷。境内高速、高等级公路纵横交错，形成二横一纵二连线一环线的基本构架；株六铁路横贯全境，长昆快速铁路将在境内设置三个站点；军民两用的黄果树机场距市区仅6公里；距省会贵阳最近出海码头镇宁坝草码头正在扩建。公路、铁路、航空、水运协调发展的立体交通运输网络初步形成。

安顺金星啤酒厂
Anshun Jinxing Brewery

安顺电厂全景
Anshun power plant panorama

黄果树酒业公司
Huangguoshu Wine Company

平坝宝鑫公司
Pingba Baoxin Company

Anshun within a beautiful environment and pleasant weather, is China's summer resort. Territory of a good ecological environment, is the most suitable for living eco-tourism city. Anshun is the country's CPI to determine the earliest open cities tourism is one of "China Excellent Tourism City" and Guizhou Province tourism development priorities and West tourist center, in 2009 was named "China's top ten characteristics of leisure city".

Anshun is known as the "waterfall Township in China", the "Tunbao cultural village", and "batik village", "Westward beauty". The city's scenic area covers an area of 12%.The territory had Huangguoshu, Longgong, Getu river three national scenic area, Guanling paleontology fossils Ridge National Geo-park, Jiulongshan National Forest Park, a national 4A grade tourism area Yelang hole, there are Huajiang River Grand Canyon, Yelang Lake, Silal River provincial scenic area, as well as Asian span, the world's sixth Baling River Bridge.

Anshun has convenient transportation. Domestic high-speed, high-grade highways criss-cross to form two horizontal and one vertical two connections a basic framework of loop; strains of six railway running through the whole territory, Changkun express railway will set up three sites in the territory; military and civilian airport from thehuangguoshu area to the city is just 6 km; away from the provincial capital Guiyang recently Zhenning Bacao wharf pier dam expanded. Road, rail, aviation, water and coordinated development of three-dimensional transportation network initially formed.

普定明达水泥立窑厂厂区
Puding Mingda cement kiln plant factory

夏云工业园新貌
Xianyun Industrial Park new look

半边街观瀑
Watching the waterfall from the Babian street

林中观瀑
Watching the waterfall from the forest

安顺是“定产到组”联产承包责任制“顶云经验”的发源地，是中国民用航空产业国家高技术产业基地，也是省委、省政府确定的“贵州加快发展的经济特区”。

2012年，全市上下深入贯彻落实科学发展观，认真贯彻落实中央和省经济工作会议精神，紧紧围绕“加速发展、加快转型、推动跨越”的主基调和“抓机遇、提速度、上台阶”的总要求，加快推进工业化、城镇化、农业现代化和旅游产业化发展步伐，抢抓国发〔2012〕2号和黔党发〔2012〕15号文件出台的重大历史机遇，经济社会保持平稳较快的发展态势。

2012年，实现生产总值352.62亿元，增长15.4%，完成全社会固定资产投资400.06亿元，增长64.4%；财政总收入完成87.40亿元，增长32.9%，公共财政预算收入完成37.50亿元，增长41.5%；金融机构人民币存贷款余额分别达到483.14亿元和350.23亿元，分别比年初增长12.9%和30.4%；实现社会消费品零售总额97.53亿元，增长16.2%；城镇居民人均可支配收入18617元，增长14.2%；农民人均纯收入5088元，增长16.5%；居民消费价格总指数比上年上涨2.5%。全市生产总值增速在全省排位由2011年的第9位上升到第6位，固定资产投资增速和金融机构人民币贷款余额增速全省排名第一。

天星湖
Tianxing lake

龍宫景区天池之一
One of the Tianchi scenic in Longgong

过石桥
Guoshi bridge

洗蜡染
Wash batik

漩塘景区全景
Xuan Tong scenic panorama

Anshun is "quotas to the group" contract responsibility system "Top Cloud Experience" birthplace, is China's civil aviation industry national high-tech industrial base, but also the provincial government to determine the "Guizhou accelerate the development of special economic zones".

2012, the city's up and down thoroughly implement the scientific concept of development, conscientiously implement the spirit of the central and provincial economic work conference, closely around the "accelerated development, speed up transformation and promote across" main tone and "Seizing an opportunity, to mention speed, on the stage" general requirements and accelerating industrialization, urbanization, agricultural modernization and the pace of development of the tourism industry, seize State Issued [2012] No. 2 and Guizhou Party Issued [2012] No. 15 document a major historical opportunity, remained stable compared to the economic and social rapid development trend.

In 2012, the GDP of 35.262 billion yuan, an increase of 15.4% in fixed asset investment 40.006 billion yuan, an increase of 64.4%; fiscal revenue of 8.74 billion yuan, an increase of 32.9%, the public budget revenue of 3.75 billion yuan, an increase of 41.5%; financial institutions RMB deposit and loan balance reached 48.314 billion yuan and 35.023 billion yuan, respectively, an increase of 12.9% and 30.4%compared to the beginning of the year; total retail sales of social consumer goods, 9.753 billion yuan, an increase of 16.2%; urban residents per capita disposable income of 18,617 yuan, an increase of 14.2%; rural per capita net income of 5,088 yuan, an increase of 16.5%; consumer price index rose 2.5% over the previous year. The city's GDP growth rate in the province ranked by ninth in 2011 up to the sixth, fixed asset investment growth and the growth of RMB loans of financial institutions across the province ranked first.

黔东南州城乡规划局

Qiandongnan Urban and Rural Planning Bureau

吴春局长陪同规划西部行专家参观凯麻同城规划馆

The director Wu Chun, accompanied by the western planning experts visited Ma Kai city planning hall

完成年度城乡规划编制任务。县（市）城市总体规划（修编）完成，丹寨等7县已经批复实施，镇远等3县分别通过省州审查；控制性详细规划全州各县市共完成57个；编制完成了《凯里-麻江城市规划管理技术规定》；完成了60个规划方案和52个规划设计报建项目审查。启动并积极推进州域城镇体系规划编制工作；完成了《推动凯里麻江同城化发展综合研究报告》初步成果；委托完成了《黔东新城空间发展战略研究》、《镇远、岑巩、三穗区域综合发展专题研究》、《镇远、岑巩、三穗协调发展规划》。完成了《下司古镇总体城市设计、建筑和景观方案设计》、《凯里-麻江城市规划区综合交通方案设计和城市防洪、排水方案设计》。

中国城市规划设计研究院赴黔东南州考察座谈

China Academy of Urban Planning and Design went to inspect discussion in Qiandongnan state

凯麻城市路网规划图（初步成果）

Kai Ma urban road network plans (preliminary results)

Urban and rural planning to complete the annual task. County (city) City Master Plan (revision) completed, Danzhai and other seven counties have approved the implementation, Zhenyuan County and other three counties, respectively, through the provinces and states examined; controlling detailed planning statewide total of 57 counties and cities; compile "Kaili- Majiang urban Planning and Management technical requirements"; completed 60 planning programs and 52 reported that construction project planning and design review. Initiate and actively promote the state urban system planning work; completion of the "Majiang Kaili city of promoting the development of a comprehensive research report" Preliminary results; commissioned to complete the "Qiandong Metro spatial development strategy research", "Zhenyuan, Cengong, Sansui regional integrated development thematic studies", "Zhenyuan, Cengong, Sansui coordinated development planning". Completion of the "Xiasi ancient town general urban design, architecture and landscape design", "Kaili- Majiang Urban Planning Area Comprehensive Transportation design and urban flood control, drainage design".

黔东南州交通局

Qiandongnan Transportation Bureau

三凯高速公路
Sankai high speedway

2012年，全州交通系统抢抓发展机遇，围绕交通发展主题，圆满完成了各项工作任务。2012年度全州交通固定资产投资累计完成97亿元，同比增长22%。在《贵州省高速公路网规划》中，黔东南州境内列入省规划的高速公路有13条1040公里。截至2012年底，全州公路总里程27000公里，其中：高速393公里、国道405公里、省道1156公里、县道2786公里、乡道1298公里、村道20892公里、专用公路70公里；按照公路技术等级划分，全州公路通车里程为27000公里，其中高速公路393公里、一级公路18公里、二级公路406公里、三级公路1050公里、四级公路6360公里、等外级公路18773公里。

In 2012, the statewide transportation system seize opportunities for development around the transport development theme, the successful completion of various tasks. 2012 annual statewide transportation investment in fixed assets totaled 9.7 billion yuan, an increase of 22%. In the "Guizhou Provincial Expressway Network Plan", the Qiandongnan states included in the provincial territory planning motorway 13 with 1,040 km. By the end of 2012, the statewide total mileage 27,000 km, of which: high speed 393 km, state road 405 km, provincial highway 1,156 kilometers, county road 2,786 km, township road 1,298 km, village road 20,892 km, special highway 70 km; follow Highway Technology grading, statewide highway mileage of 27,000 km, of which 393 km highway, first class roads 18 km, secondary class roads 406 km, third class roads 1,050 kilometers, fourth class roads 63,60 kilometers, substandard grade highways 18,773 km.

从江腊娥至宰便通乡油路
Congjiang La'e to Zaibian rural oil road

黔东南州首条重点旅游公路——朗利至西江旅游公路
Qiandongnan's first major tourist highway - Langli to Xijiang Tourism Highway

黔东南州农业委员会

Qiandongnan State Agricultural Committee

省长陈敏尔（右三）、省委副书记李军（左一）、阿里巴巴集团董事局主席马云（左三）、原副省长禄智明（右二）到2012中国•贵阳国际特色农产品交易会黔东南馆参观

Governor Chen Miner (third from right), Provincial Committee Deputy Secretary Li Jun (first from left), Alibaba Group Chairman Ma Yun (third from left), former vice governor Lu Zhiming (second from right) visited to the 2012 China • Guiyang International Specialties Agricultural Products Fair Qiandongnan Pavilion

2012年7月29日，黔东南州农委举行挂牌仪式

July 29, 2012, Qiandongnan State Agricultural Committee held listing ceremony

2012年，全州农业部门按照“三化”兴“三农”的要求，推进农业产业园区建设和农业产业化的发展，完成了各项任务目标。全州实现第一产业增加值96.9亿元，比上年（下同）增长8.6%；其中农业增加值51.27亿元，增长11.5%；林业增加值18.45亿元，增长5.2%；牧业增加值20.24亿元，增长5.3%；渔业增加值4.56亿元，增长6.4%；农林牧渔服务业增加值2.28亿元，增长6%。全年农民人均纯收入4679元，增长18.5%。全年粮食产量112.62万吨；油菜籽产量7.6万吨；蔬菜种植面积188.87万亩；茶园面积40.03万亩；烤烟种植20.02万亩。肉类总产量20.89万吨；禽蛋产量1.25万吨；水产品产量3.6万吨。

烤烟育苗大棚

Tobacco nursery greenhouses

茶产业蓬勃发展

Tea industry is flourishing

In 2012, the state's agricultural sector in accordance with the “three changes” prosper “three rural” requirements, promote agricultural industrial park construction and development of agricultural industrialization, accomplished all mission objectives. Statewide achieve first industry added value 9.69 billion yuan, compared with last year (the same below) increased by 8.6%; among the agricultural added value 5.127 billion yuan, up 11.5%; forest industry added value of 1.845 billion yuan, an increase of 5.2%; animal husbandry added value 2.024 billion yuan, an increase of 5.3%; fisheries added value 456 million yuan, an increase of 6.4%; animal husbandry and fishery value added services to 228 million yuan, an increase of 6%. Annual per capita net income of farmers 4,679 yuan, an increase of 18.5%. Annual grain output 1,126,200 tons; rapeseed production 76,000 tons; vegetable cultivation area ,1888,700 acres; tea garden area of 400,300 mu; flue-cured tobacco planted 200,200 mu. Meat output 208,900 tons; egg output 12,500 tons; aquatic products 36,000 tons.

黔东南州投资促进局

Qiandongnan Investment Promotion Bureau

2012年第五届中国•凯里原生态民族文化旅游节暨2012中国•凯里银饰刺绣博览会投资贸易洽谈项目集中签约仪式开幕式现场

2012 Fifth China • Kaili original ecological culture tourism festival 2012 China • Kaili silver embroidery projects focused on Investment and Trade Expo signing ceremony opening ceremony

黔东南州投资促进局积极开展招商引资推介活动，2012年全州共签约项目1321个，签约资金5782.25亿元，同比增长41.67%，完成全年签约资金目标任务4500亿元的128.49%；到位资金701.38亿元，同比增长69.9%，完成全年确保目标任务540亿元的129.89%、工作目标任务590亿元的118.88%。实现了招商总量、强势企业引进、单次集中签约项目“三个新突破”。全州履约项目959个，履约率72.6%；累计开工898个，开工率93.64%；资金到位率39.51%；累计投产369个，投产率38.48%。开工率、资金到位率、投产率居全省第一位。

2012年7月21日，中国黔东南首届蓝莓节招商引资项目推介会暨签约仪式现场

July 21, 2012, China's first Qiandongnan Blueberry Festival to promote investment projects and the signing ceremony

第五届中国•凯里原生态民族文化旅游节暨2012中国•凯里银饰刺绣博览会投资贸易洽谈项目集中签约仪式上，62个项目的签约现场

Fifth China • Kaili original ecological culture tourism festival 2012 China • Kaili silver embroidery projects focused on Investment and Trade Expo signing ceremony, 62 projects signing site

Qiandongnan Investment Promotion Bureau actively carry out investment promotion activities, in 2012 the state signed a total of 1,321 projects, contract funds 578.225 billion yuan, an increase of 41.67%, the completion 128.49%of annual objectives and tasks of 450 billion yuan of funds contracted; funds in place 70.138 billion yuan, an increase of 69.9%, to ensure that 129.89% of the objectives and tasks of the annual 54 billion yuan , 118.88% of objectives and tasks of 59 billion yuan. To achieve a total investment, the introduction of a strong business, a single centralized contracted projects “three breakthroughs”. Statewide implementation project 959, 72.6% compliance rate; cumulative start 898, the operating rate 93.64%; funds rate 39.51%; cumulative production 369, production rate of 38.48%. Operating rates, funds rate, production rate in the province first.

黔东南州卫生局

Qiandongnan State Health Bureau

2012年7月29日，国家卫生部部长陈竺到麻江县下司镇调研时在花桥村卫生室查看村卫生员操作新农合信息机情况

July 29, 2012, the State Health Minister Chen Zhu to Majiang county Xiasi town had investigation of health in the Huaqiao Village and viewed village hygienist information machine operating conditions NCMS

2012年9月28日卫生部副部长、国家中医药管理局局长王国强在贵州省苗侗瑶民族医院揭牌仪式上讲话

September 28, 2012 Deputy Minister of Health, the State Administration of Traditional Secretary Wang Guoqiang made speech at the Guizhou Miao and Dong Yao National Hospital inaugurated ceremony

黔东南州卫生局紧紧围绕深化医药卫生体制改革这一主线，加大对公共卫生和基本医疗保障的投入，全面落实医改各项工作任务，不断提高医疗卫生服务质量和水平。2012年全州参合农民360.82万人，与上年度相比新增14.31万人，参合率达98.3%。进一步科学合理调整完善新农合补偿方案，各县市住院补偿比例总体上调了10-15个百分点，县外住院补偿比例调整到50-80%。2012年实施“家庭帐户+门诊统筹+住院统筹”三位一体的补偿模式，参合农民补偿受益面持续扩大，全州共有649.61万人次享受合作医疗补偿。医疗卫生服务工程取得新突破。

2012年4月7日，时任省委副书记、省长赵克志到丹寨县排调镇卫生院调研指导工作

April 7, 2012, when he was Provincial Committee Deputy Secretary, Governor Zhao Kezhi to research to guide the work of Danzhai County Paidiao town hospitals

Qiandongnan Health Bureau tightly around the main line to deepen the medical and health system, and increase public health and basic medical security investment, the full implementation of health reform various tasks, and continuously improve the quality and level of health services. In 2012, statewide participating farmers 3,608,200, compared with last year added 143,100, the participation rate was 98.3%. Further adjustment and improvement of scientific and reasonable compensation package NCMS, county and city general hospital compensation ratio increased by 10-15 percentage points, outside the county hospital compensation ratio adjusted to 50-80%. In 2012 implementation of the “family accounts + Hospital outpatient co-ordinate + inpatient co-ordination” of the Trinity compensation mode, farmer participation compensation benefit coverage continues to expand, the statewide total of 6,496,100 passengers enjoy cooperative medical compensation. Health services engineering made new breakthroughs.

2012年4月26日，时任贵州省省委常委、副省长刘晓凯带领参加全省新型农村合作医疗工作现场会的各地州县代表们到黔东南州民族医药研究院参观

April 26, 2012, when he was Guizhou Provincial Committee and Vice Governor Liu Xiaokai to lead the province to participate in the new rural cooperative medical work-site meetings of representatives around the county to visit Qiandongnan National Medical Academy

2012年1月13日，省卫生厅领导一行到贵阳龙洞堡机场迎接被评选为2011年“全国我最喜爱的健康卫士”的黔东南州中医医院护士潘满芝载誉归来

January 13, 2012, the provincial health department leaderships to Guiyang airport to greet been selected as 2011 “My Favorite National Health Guard” the Qiandongnan states Medicine Hospital care Shipan was full with victorious and returned back

黔东南州住房和城乡建设局

Qiandongnan Housing and Urban-Rural Construction Bureau

凯里城市建设蓬勃发展
Kaili urban construction booming development

黔东南州住房和城乡建设局围绕主基调主战略，全面推进全州住房城乡建设工作深入开展。圆满完成固定资产投资任务，城镇基础设施投资完成177.7亿元，同比增长101.9%。保障性安居工程稳步推进，续建项目方面年底基本建成保障性住房、棚户区改造住房基本建成26198套。2012年农村危房改造完成投资17.58亿元。积极推进小城镇建设。积极推动《黔东南州城镇建设三年行动计划》、《黔东南州村庄专项整治三年行动计划》落实，初步形成以凯里-麻江为中心的多层次城镇体系。村庄整治完成较好，抓好16个“风情小镇”和32个“特色村寨”的建设。建筑业监督管理得到进一步加强。勘查设计与“两金”征收工作成效显著。

魅力黎平翘街
Charming Liping Qiao Street

Qiandongnan Housing and Urban-Rural Construction Bureau around the main tone of the main strategies to comprehensively promote statewide housing and urban-rural construction work in depth. Successful completion of the task of investment in fixed assets, investment in urban infrastructure completed 17.77 billion yuan, an increase of 101.9%. Affordable housing projects pushed steadily, continued construction projects basically completed, by the end of the year, affordable housing in shantytowns, basically built 26,198 housing units. In 2012, rural reconstruction completed an investment of 1.758 billion yuan. Actively promote the construction of small towns. Actively promote the “three-year action Qiandongnan urban construction plan”, “special rectification Qiandongnan village three-year action plan” to implement, initially formed to Kaili- Majiang as the center of a multi-level urban system. Village renovation completed better grasp 16 “style town” and 32 “featured villages” of the building. Construction supervision and management has been further strengthened. Survey design and “two gold” collection work with remarkable results.

镇远县城全景
Zhenyuan County panorama

在城镇化建设中奋进的黔南

Endeavor in urbanization in the Qiannan

都匀城市建设新貌
The new image of Duyun city construction

近年来，在黔南州委、州政府的领导下，通过实施城镇化带动战略，力图把黔南打造成宜居、宜业、宜商、宜游的"生态之州、幸福黔南"。城镇化进程加快推进，城乡建设突飞猛进，城乡面貌日新月异，人居环境极大改善。2012年，全州城镇化率达38.7%，城市建成区面积135.91平方公里，比2008年增加了27%。村镇建设加快推进，实施农村危房改造12万户，近60万农村住房困难群众入住新居。加大村庄整治，公路沿线385个村庄整治一新，贵定音寨、平塘掌布、荔波梅园、瓮安猴场等一批乡村旅游品牌效应显现，实现

都匀市全景
Duyun city panorama

瓮安县城中心城区全景
Weng'an county central city panorama

长顺县城南新区新貌

The new image of Changshun county Nanxin district

长顺县城南新区鸟瞰

The bird's view of Changshun county Nanxin district

In recent years, under the leadership of Qiannan committee, the state government, through the implementation of urbanization led strategy, try to turn the Qiannan playing livable, desirable industry, desirable business, desirable visit the "ecological state, happiness Qiannan". Accelerating process of urbanization, urban and rural construction advances, changing urban and rural areas, greatly improved the living environment. In 2012, the urbanization rate reached 38.7% statewide, urban built area of 135.91 square kilometers, compared with 2008 increased by 27%. Towns and villages to accelerate the construction, the implementation of rural reconstruction 120,000, nearly 600,000 rural housing difficulties of the masses moved into new homes. Increase the village renovation,

长顺县东朝城市综合体建设

Changshun County Dongchao City complex construction

黔中地区新长顺（城南新区全景图）

New Changshun in central Guizhou (south city new district panorama)

福泉市城市一角
Fuquan city corner

玉带惠水
Yudai Huishui

平塘县城
Pingtang county

了新农村建设与旅游产业的有效结合。小城镇建设加快发展，全州20个示范小城镇实施建设项目106个，成为推动县域经济和城镇化率新的增长点。住房保障体系日趋完善，商品房建设如雨后春笋般迅猛发展，人均居住面积大幅提高，居住环境不断提升。廉租房、公租房、棚户区改造、经济适用房等保障性住房建设全面提速，已建成保障性住房16522套、82.6万平方米，“安得广厦千万间”已不再是遥不可及的梦想。建

2012年福泉市竣工投入使用的文峰广场
2012 completed and put into use Fuquan Wenfeng Square

贵定县京都广场一角
Guiding county Jingdu square corner

贵定县迎宾大道广场
Guiding county Yingbin Avenue Plaza

a new renovation of villages along the highway 385, Guding Yinzhai, Pingtagn Zhangbu, Libo Plum, Weng'an monkey farm and a number of rural tourism brand effects appear to achieve the new rural construction and tourism industry the effective combination. Accelerate the development of small towns, statewide implementation of 20 demonstration projects of small towns 106, becoming the county's economic and urbanization promote new growth point. Housing security system maturing, housing construction mushroomed rapid development of a substantial increase in per capita living space, and improve the living environment. Low-rent housing, public rental housing in shantytowns, affordable housing and

生态贵定——贵定师范一角
Eco Guiding - Guiding Normal University corner

贵定县城一角
Guiding county corner

三都县城全景
Sandu County panoramic

三都县凤凰小区
Sandu County Phoenix area

三都县建设路街景
Sandu County Jianshe Road streetscape

筑业较快发展，各类建设工程大兴土木，每年限额以上开工建设项目200个以上。世界自然遗产地和风景名胜区长足发展，全州拥有世界自然遗产地1个，国家级风景名胜区4个，省级风景名胜区8个，风景名胜区面积近2000平方公里。

三都县金谷帝都小区
Sandu County Jingu Didu district

三都县民族风情街
Sandu County National Customs Street

风景如画的较少民族乡、全省示范小城镇——平塘县卡浦乡建设新貌
The picturesque small townships, the province's model of small towns - Pingtang County Kapu Township building new look

旧貌变新颜——整治一新的新农村
Fundamentally change new face - a new regulation of the new rural

other affordable housing construction in full speed, has built 16,522 affordable housing units, 826,000 square meters, "ten million mansions in peace" is not a remote non-and dreams. Construction and rapid development of various types of construction of projects and construction projects annually above 200 or more. World Natural Heritage and the rapid development of scenic spots, all states have a world natural heritage, national scenic area 4, 8 provincial-level scenic spots, scenic area of nearly 2,000 square kilometers.

瓮安：村庄整治工程
Weng'an: village renovation project

福泉黄丝镇江边寨村庄整治
Fuquan Huangsi town Zhenjiang Baizhai village renovation

廉租房城镇化建设中的一道风景——惠水县南苑花城廉租房
Low-rent housing construction in an urban landscape - Huishui County Nanyuan Flower City low-rent housing

廉租房城镇化建设中的一道风景——龙里县廉租房
Low-rent housing construction in an urban landscape - Longli county low-rent housing

目前，黔南州按照“一圈两翼”发展格局，再次掀起新一轮城镇建设新高潮，力争通过两至三年的时间，全州城镇建设迅速上台阶、出形象、快发展，为与全省、全国实现同步小康而不懈努力、奋勇前进。

环境优美的廉租住房小区
Beautiful environment of low-rent housing complex

三都县沙井湾廉租房区
Sandu County Shajing Bay low-rent housing area

三都县城夜景
Sandu County Night

瓮安县中心城区亮化效果
Weng'an County Center City lighting effects

Currently, Qiannan state in accordance with the "one lap two wings" development pattern, once again set off a new upsurge of a new round of urban construction, and strive through two to three years, the rapid urban construction on a statewide level, the image of fast development, with full provincial, national well-off and make unremitting efforts to achieve synchronization, forge ahead.

都匀城市夜景
Duyun City Night

贵阳国家高新技术产业开发区

Guiyang National High-tech Industrial Development Zone

2012年7月28日 时任高新区党工委书记宗文在生态文明贵阳会议闭幕式上发表绿色倡议
July 28, 2012 when he was the Party Work Committees secretary of High-tech Zone, Zong Wen published Green Initiatives at the ecological civilization Guiyang closing meeting

2013年3月28日，高新区党工委书记、白云区委书记丁雄军在人才博览会上做主旨演讲
March 28, 2013, High-tech Zone Party Work Committee secretary, Baiyun District secretary Ding Xiongjun made keynote speech in the talent Expo

2012年12月6日，高新区党工委副书记、管委会主任徐昊调研项目建设情况
December 6, 2012, High-tech Zone Party Working Committee secretary, the CMC director Xu Hao had the research in project construction

贵州省产业技术发展研究院
Industrial Technology Development Institute of Guizhou Province

贵阳国家高新区是贵州省唯一的国家级高新区和人才特区。1992年，贵州省、贵阳市依托振华集团，以“三线企业”调迁为契机，大力开发建设新天高新技术工业园区，同年，贵阳国家高新区获国务院批准设立。2000年，贵州省、贵阳市全力开发建设金阳新区，并提出规划建设金阳科技园，以高新技术产业引领和带动城市新区发展，同年获国务院批准。2008年，为拓展贵阳国家高新区的发展空间，规划建设沙文生态科技产业园。2009年11月，沙文生态科技产业园获国务院批准设立。目前，已形成金阳园区、沙文园区、新天园区、罗格园区、环保生态园区、综合保税区、铝及铝加工园区“一区七园”的发展布局，全区规划面积89.94平方公里。

贵阳国家高新区结合自身实际，提出“筑梦‘北纬26度’，建设创新•生态城”的品牌，围绕“一区七园”（金

2012年12月12日中航工业贵阳基地投产暨综合办公大楼奠基仪式

December 12, 2012 Japan-China Aviation Industry Guiyang Base production and comprehensive office building the foundation stone laying ceremony

全省第二轮第一次重点项目建设现场观摩会代表在科学院现场

The representative of the province's second round of the first key projects to observe the academy scene

贵阳留学归国人才创业园

Guiyang talent returning from abroad Pioneer Park

高新区大学生创业园

High-tech Zone Students Pioneering Park

Guiyang National High-tech Zoneis the only national high-tech zones and the talent zone in Guizhou Province . In 1992, Guizhou Province, Guiyang City, relying Zhenhua Group, with "three-line enterprise" transfer as an opportunity to vigorously develop new Tiangao high-tech industrial park construction, the same year, Guiyang National High-tech Zone was approved the establishment by the State Council. In 2000, Guizhou, Guiyang city made efforts to construct Jinyang new development zone, and made plans to build Jinyang Science and Technology Park, the high-tech industry leading and driving the development of new urban areas, the same year by the State Council for approval. In 2008, Guiyang National High-tech Zone to expand space for development, planning and construction Shawen eco-technology industrial park. On November 2009, Shawen eco-technology industrial park was approved the establishment by the State Council. At present, the park has formed Jinyang park, Shawen park, Xintian parks, Luoge park, eco parks, comprehensive Free Trade Zone, aluminum and aluminum production park, "one zone seven parks" development layout, the whole planning area of 89.94 square kilometers.

Guiyang National High-tech Zone of its own reality, put "Dream 'north latitude 26 degrees', building an innovative & eco-city" brand, focusing on"one zone seven parks" (Jinyang park, Shawen park, Xintian park, Luoge park, environmental and ecological parks, comprehensive Free Trade Zone, aluminum and aluminum production park) the strategic layout, highlighting the "one integration four districts" (technological innovation drive area, high-tech industrial agglomeration area, modern business services area, the talent

贵阳高峰机械有限公司
Guiyang Gaofeng Machinery Co. Ltd.

贵阳国家高新区科技企业孵化器
Guiyang National High-tech Zone Science and technology business incubator

金苏大道
Jinsu Avenue

阳园区、沙文园区、新天园区、罗格园区、环保生态园区、综合保税区、铝及铝加工园区）的战略布局，突出“一体四区”（科技创新驱动区、高新产业集聚区、现代商务服务区、人才特区）的战略定位，大力实施“五五四三”（科技研发、技术交易、科技金融、孵化加速、云数据“五大中心”；新能源新材料产业，高端装备制造业、生物医药产业、软件与信息服务业、光电产业“五大基地”；产城互动、文化创意与数字内容、现代商贸、第2.5产业“四大板块”；人才优选教育、人才多样性、人才栖息环境“三大工程”）的战略任务，全力建设未来科技城、未来产业城、未来文教城、未来人才城。

高新区金阳科技产业园白鹭湖畔
High-tech Zone of Jinyang science and Technology Industrial Park Egret Lake

国家数字内容产业园
National Digital Content Industry Park

贵州航宇科技发展股份有限公司生产车间
Guizhou Aerospace Science and Technology Development Co., Ltd. production workshop

zone) strategic positioning, vigorously implement the "five five four three" (Research and development of science and technology, technical trading, technology finance, hatching acceleration, cloud data "five centers"; New energy and new materials industries, high-end equipment manufacturing, bio-pharmaceutical industry, software and information services, optoelectronics industry "five bases"; produce city interaction, cultural creativity and digital content, modern commerce, 2.5 Industry "four plates"; talent preferred education, talent diversity, talent habitat "three major projects") strategic task, make efforts build the future science and technology city, industrial city of the future, the future city of culture and education, future talent city.

贵州雅光电子科技股份有限公司
Guizhou Yaguang Electronic Science and Technology Co., Ltd.,

做信息生活的创新服务领导者

——贵州联通全面加快创新发展、后发赶超步伐

Innovative information services to make life leader

– Guizhou Unicom accelerate the innovation development, catch up with the pace

“创新，改变世界”。2012年是贵州联通推进增长速度、经营规模及市场份额实现跨式发展的关键一年。一年来，公司以集团公司“四新”工作要求为引领，始终坚持将“引领创新、加快发展、推动跨越”作为推进企业持续快速发展、构筑差异化竞争优势的主基调，突出聚焦规模、突出加速增长、突出创新驱动，顺利达成年度“一二三工程”目标，取得全面超额完成集团公司下达年度经营预算指标、全年主营业务收入同比增幅达45.7%并位列全集团和省内同行业首位、用户规模和市场份额实现整体突破并基本实现增量收入市场份额“三分天下有其一”的优异成绩，成功开创了“高于历史、高于西部、高于全国”的“贵州速度”，推动经营发展取得了前所未有的良好成效。

中国联通集团公司党组书记、董事长常小兵（右三）在贵州联通总经理张哲（右二）陪同下深入贵阳市中华南路联通旗舰营业厅现场调研

China Unicom Corporation party secretary and chairman Chang Xiaobing (third from right) accompanied by Guizhou Unicom general manager Zhang Zhe (second from right), had in-depth investigation of Guiyang City Zhonghua south Road China Unicom business hall flagship site

“Innovation, change the world”. 2012 is Guizhou Unicom to promote growth, business scale and market share across type development crucial year. Over the past year, the company group took the “four news” job requirements for the lead, always adhere to the “leading innovation, accelerate development and promote across” as promoting sustained and rapid business development, and build competitive differentiation of the main tone, highlighting the focus scale, highlighting accelerated growth, highlighting the innovation-driven, successfully achieved the annual “123 project” goal, to achieve a comprehensive group company issued over the completion of the annual operating budget targets, annual main business income increased by 45.7% year on year and ranked the whole group and the province with the industry first, the user scale and market share to achieve the overall breakthrough and basically achieve incremental revenue market share, “there is one-third of the world” the excellent results, successfully created a “higher than the historical, than the west, higher than the national” of “Guizhou speed”, to promote business development achieved unprecedented good results.

27

Twenty-seven

市（州）、县（市、区、特区）资料

Main Statistics of City(State,Prefecture) and County(City,District,Special Region)

27−1　各市(州)生产总值及构成(2012)

Gross Domestic Product and Its Composition by Region

市（州）名称	City (State, Prefecture)	生产总值 Gross Domestic Product	第一产业 Primary Industry	第二产业 Secondary Industry	#工业 Industry	第三产业 Tertiary Industry	人均生产总值(元) Per Capita Gross Domestic Product (yuan)
绝对数（亿元）	**Absolute Figure (100 million yuan)**						
贵阳市	Guiyang	1710.30	72.28	717.32	534.73	920.70	38673
六盘水市	Liupanshui	753.65	43.27	441.57	402.52	268.81	26402
遵义市	Zunyi	1361.93	181.24	626.23	541.84	554.46	22296
安顺市	Anshun	367.62	53.19	137.02	114.46	177.41	16112
毕节市	Bijie	884.96	160.07	390.97	333.06	333.92	13569
铜仁市	Tongren	457.91	123.93	131.79	99.63	202.19	14833
黔西南州	Qianxinan	477.43	75.43	178.07	153.86	223.93	17015
黔东南州	Qiandongnan	495.75	101.39	153.17	110.61	241.19	14302
黔南州	Qiannan	550.34	88.80	210.55	170.35	250.99	17101
比上年增长（%）	**Composition(%)**						
贵阳市	Guiyang	15.9	8.5	18.8	16.2	14.1	14.3
六盘水市	Liupanshui	16.0	8.8	15.9	15.5	17.3	15.9
遵义市	Zunyi	15.9	8.9	19.3	17.4	14.4	16.0
安顺市	Anshun	15.4	9.0	16.6	15.7	16.5	15.9
毕节市	Bijie	15.3	8.6	17.1	16.4	16.0	15.5
铜仁市	Tongren	15.3	8.8	15.3	15.6	19.5	15.4
黔西南州	Qianxinan	15.4	8.9	17.0	16.3	16.1	15.3
黔东南州	Qiandongnan	16.5	8.6	19.6	16.3	17.6	16.7
黔南州	Qiannan	15.5	9.2	15.9	16.4	17.4	15.6

注：表中绝对数按当年价格计算，增长速度按可比价格计算。

Note:Data of absolute Figure in the table are calculated at current prices,and increase rate is calculated at comparable prices.

27–2 各市(州)年末常住人口

Permanent Population at the year-end by Region

单位：万人　　(10000 persons)

市(州)名称	City (State, Prefecture)	2007	2008	2009	2010	2011	2012
贵阳市	Guiyang	405.26	413.44	423.12	432.93	439	445.17
六盘水市	Liupanshui	290.59	290.45	287.96	285.43	285	285.90
遵义市	Zunyi	653.98	641.63	627.37	613.29	610	611.70
安顺市	Anshun	243.68	240.28	235.14	230.04	228	228.34
毕节市	Bijie	676.71	673.58	664.09	654.57	652	652.41
铜仁市	Tongren	341.73	333.78	321.55	309.63	308	309.44
黔西南州	Qianxinan	291.74	290.38	285.70	281.02	280	281.20
黔东南州	Qiandongnan	377.18	369.17	358.76	348.52	346	347.27
黔南州	Qiannan	351.12	343.28	333.30	323.51	321	322.64

注：2007年—2009年数据根据第六次人口普查结果进行修订。

Note:Data from the year 2007 to 2009 had been adjusted according to the result of the Sixth National Population Census.

27-3 各市(州)户籍人口
Household Registered Population by Region

市(州)名称	City (State, Prefecture)	总户数(万户) Total Number of Household (10000 households) 2011	2012	平均每户人数(人) Population of Per Household(person) 2011	2012	年末人口数(万人) Total Population at The Year-end(10000 persons) 2011	2012
贵阳市	Guiyang	112.13	114.15	3.46	3.34	376.12	374.53
六盘水市	Liupanshui	96.55	99.02	3.48	3.34	321.41	322.53
遵义市	Zunyi	221.60	227.82	3.64	3.48	771.94	771.43
安顺市	Anshun	80.78	83.47	3.54	3.52	282.26	284.36
毕节市	Bijie	225.95	230.61	4.00	3.80	851.73	857.97
铜仁市	Tongren	121.85	124.90	3.68	3.50	427.20	426.46
黔西南州	Qianxinan	98.90	97.55	3.74	3.52	344.74	347.92
黔东南州	Qiandongnan	127.18	130.02	3.75	3.61	458.18	459.22
黔南州	Qiannan	119.43	122.09	3.46	3.39	404.87	405.06

注：资料来源于省公安厅(下表同)。
Note:Data in the table are obtained from Guizhou Provincial Department of Public Security.

27-3 续表 Continued

单位：万人 (10000 persons)

市(州)名称	City (state, Prefecture)	按农业与非农业分 By Agricultural and Non-Agricultural: 农业 Agricultural 2011	2012	非农业 Non-Agricultural 2011	2012	按性别分 Grouped by sex: 男 Male 2011	2012	女 Female 2011	2012
贵阳市	Guiyang	189.83	189.09	186.29	185.43	192.05	190.69	184.07	183.83
六盘水市	Liupanshui	248.84	249.54	72.57	72.99	168.95	170.82	152.46	151.72
遵义市	Zunyi	644.51	642.36	127.43	129.07	400.34	401.53	371.60	369.90
安顺市	Anshun	240.74	242.70	41.52	41.66	145.74	147.19	136.52	137.17
毕节市	Bijie	788.93	794.30	62.80	63.67	444.68	449.08	407.05	408.89
铜仁市	Tongren	376.16	374.49	51.04	51.97	223.81	224.18	203.39	202.28
黔西南州	Qianxinan	310.16	312.66	34.58	35.26	177.53	179.65	167.21	168.27
黔东南州	Qiandongnan	402.96	403.13	55.22	56.08	242.56	244.22	215.62	214.99
黔南州	Qiannan	349.08	348.85	55.79	56.21	210.10	210.62	194.77	194.44

27-4 各市(州)第六次人口普查各民族人口数

Population of all Ethnic group on the Sixth National Population Census by Region

单位：人 (person)

市(州)名称	City (State, Prefecture)	合计 Total	男 Male	女 Female	汉族 Han	男 Male	女 Female	蒙古族 Mongolian	男 Male	女 Female
贵阳市	Guiyang	4322611	2221896	2100715	3610233	1856295	1753938	4368	2291	2077
六盘水市	Liupanshui	2851332	1493973	1357359	2125906	1114273	1011633	3262	1871	1391
遵义市	Zunyi	6127082	3116640	3010442	5450132	2767218	2682914	515	278	237
安顺市	Anshun	2297612	1186013	1111599	1478796	768409	710387	1093	597	496
毕节市	Bijie	6537498	3387605	3149893	4845699	2515970	2329729	21899	12404	9495
铜仁市	Tongren	3093204	1577421	1515783	927216	460657	466559	7682	4228	3454
黔西南州	Qianxinan	2804612	1439828	1364784	1700052	880556	819496	1182	677	505
黔东南州	Qiandongnan	3481891	1817730	1664161	756587	396364	360223	318	182	136
黔南州	Qiannan	3232714	1664365	1568349	1449535	758131	691404	1242	675	567

27-4 续表1 continued

单位：人 (person)

市(州)名称	City (State, Prefecture)	回族 Hui	男 Male	女 Female	苗族 Miao	男 Male	女 Female	彝族 Yi	男 Male	女 Female
贵阳市	Guiyang	10052	5093	4959	247100	126525	120575	43314	21803	21511
六盘水市	Liupanshui	17682	9390	8292	198330	103640	94690	251629	129842	121787
遵义市	Zunyi	1766	950	816	261673	133186	128487	3432	1692	1740
安顺市	Anshun	13968	7136	6832	306551	154207	152344	8450	4454	3996
毕节市	Bijie	106601	54569	52032	447975	226554	221421	469925	241028	228897
铜仁市	Tongren	2655	1427	1228	450786	236545	214241	765	386	379
黔西南州	Qianxinan	27269	14047	13222	198491	100704	97787	44024	23382	20642
黔东南州	Qiandongnan	2448	1203	1245	1447257	751306	695951	5749	3125	2624
黔南州	Qiannan	2347	1194	1153	410237	208265	201972	7173	3841	3332

27-4 续表2 continued

单位：人 (person)

市(州)名称	City (State, Prefecture)	壮族 Zhuang	男 Male	女 Female	布依族 Bouyei	男 Male	女 Female	满族 Man	男 Male	女 Female
贵阳市	Guiyang	6086	3220	2866	202751	101969	100782	6708	3355	3353
六盘水市	Liupanshui	1265	648	617	82401	42935	39466	1752	872	880
遵义市	Zunyi	1599	713	886	4959	2342	2617	945	477	468
安顺市	Anshun	1443	718	725	346739	176769	169970	1400	748	652
毕节市	Bijie	2336	1157	1179	55123	28413	26710	9327	4942	4385
铜仁市	Tongren	875	418	457	1745	861	884	435	229	206
黔西南州	Qianxinan	4416	2200	2216	773004	388771	384233	775	449	326
黔东南州	Qiandongnan	24618	12838	11780	34599	17849	16750	637	335	302
黔南州	Qiannan	9939	4588	5351	1009244	511142	498102	1107	525	582

27-4 续表3 continued

单位：人 (person)

市(州)名称	City (State, Prefecture)	侗族 Dong	男 Male	女 Female	瑶族 Yao	男 Male	女 Female	白族 Bai	男 Male	女 Female
贵阳市	Guiyang	32645	17471	15174	1236	665	571	16048	8218	7830
六盘水市	Liupanshui	3511	1875	1636	210	112	98	46274	25189	21085
遵义市	Zunyi	5895	2982	2913	315	139	176	725	363	362
安顺市	Anshun	2560	1368	1192	623	333	290	9082	5045	4037
毕节市	Bijie	1491	785	706	316	176	140	103422	55052	48370
铜仁市	Tongren	361132	189551	171581	4058	2324	1734	414	208	206
黔西南州	Qianxinan	2172	1158	1014	2813	1402	1411	1994	1035	959
黔东南州	Qiandongnan	1010352	528230	482122	21732	11263	10469	495	250	245
黔南州	Qiannan	12170	6788	5382	9576	5014	4562	1056	563	493

27-4 续表4 continued

单位：人 (person)

市(州)名称	City (State, Prefecture)	土家族 Tujia	男 Male	女 Female	畲族 She	男 Male	女 Female	水族 Shui	男 Male	女 Female	仫佬族 Mulam	男 Male	女 Female
贵阳市	Guiyang	60076	31812	28264	511	262	249	4768	2464	2304	758	394	364
六盘水市	Liupanshui	4076	2257	1819	40	26	14	11064	5965	5099	180	93	87
遵义市	Zunyi	94154	50668	43486	99	45	54	469	218	251	161	75	86
安顺市	Anshun	3116	1758	1358	58	31	27	365	206	159	79	42	37
毕节市	Bijie	2265	1218	1047	107	64	43	5460	2851	2609	142	75	67
铜仁市	Tongren	1229710	624967	604743	168	115	53	251	145	106	26	7	19
黔西南州	Qianxinan	2737	1475	1262	49	31	18	1147	530	617	88	39	49
黔东南州	Qiandongnan	33676	18498	15178	31397	16477	14920	55357	29827	25530	21395	11600	9795
黔南州	Qiannan	7167	3873	3294	4129	2045	2084	269865	138111	131754	2127	968	1159

27-4 续表5 continued

单位：人 (person)

市(州)名称	City (State, Prefecture)	羌族 Qiang	男 Male	女 Female	毛南族 Maonan	男 Male	女 Female	仡佬族 Gelao	男 Male	女 Female	其他未识别的民族 Undetermined called People Community	男 Male	女 Female
贵阳市	Guiyang	177	94	83	412	209	203	25457	13639	11818	42839	22524	20315
六盘水市	Liupanshui	20	9	11	21	6	15	11693	6380	5313	82135	43483	38652
遵义市	Zunyi	41	23	18	35	12	23	297964	154186	143778	603	304	299
安顺市	Anshun	25	16	9	14	8	6	24718	13311	11407	16281	8641	7640
毕节市	Bijie	36	25	11	55	27	28	20585	10945	9640	440578	229271	211307
铜仁市	Tongren	1179	673	506	12	6	6	102849	54147	48702	464	201	263
黔西南州	Qianxinan	23	14	9	23	11	12	4705	2543	2162	693	381	312
黔东南州	Qiandongnan	61	22	39	56	27	29	3201	1590	1611	28189	14771	13418
黔南州	Qiannan	43	23	20	26704	13937	12767	4010	2194	1816	998	549	449

注：表中数据来源于第六次人口普查机器汇总数。

Note:Data in this table are obtained from the Sixth Population Census.

27-5 各市(州)非私营单位在岗职工年平均人数、年平均工资(2012)

Number of Staff and Workers and Their Annual Average Wages in Non-private units by Region

市(州)名称	City (State, Prefecture)	合计 Total	国有经济 State -owned units	城镇集体经济 Urban Collective-owned Units	其他经济类型 Units of Other Types of Ownership	2012年比2011年增长(%) Increase Rate in 2012 over 2011(%)
在岗职工年平均人数(万人)	**Number of Staff and Workers(10000 persons)**	**245.87**	**159.09**	**6.01**	**80.77**	**10.6**
贵阳市	Guiyang	75.31	37.73	1.62	35.96	6.2
六盘水市	Liupanshui	22.79	13.53	0.28	8.98	10.5
遵义市	Zunyi	34.21	24.13	0.81	9.27	14.8
安顺市	Anshun	14.30	9.59	0.68	4.03	4.0
毕节市	Bijie	26.20	19.53	0.71	5.96	12.9
铜仁市	Tongren	14.71	11.70	0.72	2.29	15.9
黔西南州	Qianxinan	13.78	9.31	0.23	4.24	10.9
黔东南州	Qiandongnan	19.70	14.79	0.38	4.53	14.2
黔南州	Qiannan	17.64	12.90	0.52	4.22	12.5
年平均工资(元)	**Annual Average Wages (yuan)**	**42733**	**45825**	**40420**	**36816**	**14.5**
贵阳市	Guiyang	42974	47668	31848	38552	11.1
六盘水市	Liupanshui	43323	43916	63301	41799	9.8
遵义市	Zunyi	45301	48227	39405	38201	14.1
安顺市	Anshun	39430	43429	46494	28716	11.6
毕节市	Bijie	41035	43335	47392	32733	24.0
铜仁市	Tongren	41657	44240	35013	30672	22.7
黔西南州	Qianxinan	41071	44563	44933	33186	27.2
黔东南州	Qiandongnan	39796	42242	44125	31439	16.0
黔南州	Qiannan	39409	42052	41921	31013	10.8

27–6 各市(州)固定资产投资(2012)

Investment in Fixed Assets by Region

单位：亿元 (100 million yuan)

市(州)名称	City (State, Prefecture)	固定资产投资 Investment in Fixed Assets	2012年比2011年增长(%) Increase Rate in 2012 over 2011(%)
贵阳市	Guiyang	1897.35	33.9
六盘水市	Liupanshui	766.39	74.2
遵义市	Zunyi	1176.48	71.7
安顺市	Anshun	298.16	80.1
毕节市	Bijie	1052.81	66.9
铜仁市	Tongren	540.07	80.0
黔西南州	Qianxinan	445.14	47.8
黔东南州	Qiandongnan	610.49	74.2
黔南州	Qiannan	587.28	46.8

注：本表统计口径为计划总投资50万元及以上固定资产项目投资和房地产开发投资，不含跨区域项目固定资产完成投资。

Note:Data in the table refer to those projects planned to invest 500,000 yuan at least in investment in fixed assets and real estate development. but it doesn't include investment in cross-regional projects.

27–7 各市(州)社会消费品零售总额(2012)

Total Retail Sales of Social Consumer Goods by Region

单位：亿元 (100 million yuan)

市(州)名称	City (State, Prefecture)	社会消费品零售总额 Total retail sales of social consumer goods	按销售地区分 Grouped by Distribution Area	
			城镇 Urban	乡村 Rural
贵阳市	Guiyang	683.19	680.34	2.85
六盘水市	Liupanshui	182.82	158.60	24.22
遵义市	Zunyi	409.87	334.69	75.18
安顺市	Anshun	97.53	76.25	21.28
毕节市	Bijie	174.42	123.11	51.31
铜仁市	Tongren	103.90	81.25	22.65
黔西南州	Qianxinan	121.79	101.52	20.27
黔东南州	Qiandongnan	168.87	135.19	33.68
黔南州	Qiannan	136.09	117.50	18.59

27–8 各市(州)能源利用效率(2012)

Basic Statistics on Energy Consumption by Region

市(州)名称	City (State, Prefecture)	单位生产总值能耗(吨标准煤/万元) Energy Consumption Per Unit of GDP(ton of SEC/10000 yuan)	单位生产总值能耗比上年增长(%) Growth Rate of Energy Consumption Per Unit of GDP over Preceding Year(%)	单位工业增加值能耗(吨标准煤/万元) Energy Consumption Per Unit of Industrial Value-added (ton of SEC/10000 yuan)
贵 阳 市	Guiyang	1.3531	-4.42	1.963
六盘水市	Liupanshui	2.7245	-3.84	5.195
遵 义 市	Zunyi	1.2908	-3.45	1.281
安 顺 市	Anshun	2.0648	-3.24	4.110
毕 节 市	Bijie	1.7980	-4.13	5.256
铜 仁 市	Tongren	1.5820	-3.35	3.744
黔西南州	Qianxinan	1.6521	-3.33	2.654
黔东南州	Qiandongnan	1.8668	-2.99	4.652
黔 南 州	Qiannan	1.7113	-3.59	2.300

27–8 续表 continued

市(州)名称	City (State, Prefecture)	单位工业增加值能耗比上年增长(%) Growth Rate of Energy Consumption of Industrial Value-added over Preceding Year(%)	单位生产总值电耗(千瓦小时/万元) Electricity Consumption Per Unit of GDP(ton of SEC/10000 yuan)	单位生产总值电耗比上年增长(%) Growth Rate of Electricity Consumption Per Unit of GDP over Preceding Year(%)
贵 阳 市	Guiyang	-12.84	1631	-5.52
六盘水市	Liupanshui	-10.59	1953	-2.67
遵 义 市	Zunyi	-10.37	1408	-2.16
安 顺 市	Anshun	-4.70	2180	-1.56
毕 节 市	Bijie	-14.13	1309	-1.73
铜 仁 市	Tongren	-10.28	1847	-6.85
黔西南州	Qianxinan	1.96	1825	-9.20
黔东南州	Qiandongnan	10.50	2248	-3.61
黔 南 州	Qiannan	-3.32	1808	-4.59

注：1.单位生产总值能耗与单位工业增加值能耗均按2010年可比价计算。2.单位工业增加值能耗增长幅度是用工业增加值增幅和工业能耗增幅计算，不用两年的单位工业增加值能耗计算。3.单位生产总值电耗增长幅度是用生产总值增幅和全社会用电量增幅计算，不用两年的单位生产总值电耗计算。

Note:1.Both energy consumption per unit of GDP and Energy consumption per unit of industrial value-added are calculated at 2010 comparable prices. 2.Growth rate of energy consumption per unit of industrial value-added is caculated based on growth rate of industrial value-added and energy consumption,but it isn't caculated based on two years of Energy consumption per unit of industrial added value. 3.Growth rate of power consumptionper unit of GDP is caculated based on growth rate of GDP and social electricity consumption,but it is not caculated based on two years of power consumption per unit of GDP.

27–9 各市(州)公共财政收入(2012)

Public Financial Revenue by Region

市(州)名称	City (State, Prefecture)	公共财政收入(亿元) Total (100 million yuan)	税收收入 Tax revenue	#增值税 Value-added Tax	#营业税 Operation Tax	#企业所得税 Enterprises' Income Tax	#个人所得税 Personal Income Tax	非税收入 Non-tax revenue	#专项收入 Special Project Income	2012年比2011年增长(%) Increase Rate in 2012 over 2011(%)	人均公共财政收入(元) Per Capita Local Financial Revenue(yuan)
贵阳市	Guiyang	241.19	193.65	13.83	75.87	26.86	8.46	47.54	20.60	28.9	5456
六盘水市	Liupanshui	103.50	56.44	6.52	15.89	3.87	3.97	47.06	5.06	47.0	3626
遵义市	Zunyi	113.00	84.68	11.60	28.08	6.92	4.81	28.31	6.54	33.5	1850
安顺市	Anshun	37.50	26.86	2.39	11.74	3.15	1.07	10.64	1.52	41.5	1644
毕节市	Bijie	110.43	56.39	6.37	14.23	4.67	5.64	54.04	18.16	36.7	1693
铜仁市	Tongren	36.57	24.60	1.97	8.56	1.96	0.85	11.97	1.16	28.8	1185
黔西南州	Qianxinan	64.42	37.46	3.70	10.78	3.85	3.73	26.96	3.08	41.5	2296
黔东南州	Qiandongnan	70.08	45.46	2.14	16.27	3.40	2.02	24.62	1.48	54.8	2022
黔南州	Qiannan	57.87	37.34	2.93	12.31	3.33	1.72	20.53	2.50	47.6	1798

注：资料来源于省财政厅(下表同)。

Note:Data in the table were obtained from Guizhou Provincial Financial Department(the same applies to the next table).

27–10 各市(州)公共财政支出(2012)

Public Financial Expenditure by Region

市(州)名称	City (State, Prefecture)	公共财政支出(亿元) Total (100 million yuan)	#一般公共服务 Common Public Service	#教育 Edu-cation	#科学技术 Science and Techn-ology	#文化体育与传媒 Culture, Sports and Commun-ication	#社会保障和就业 Social Security and Jobs	#医疗卫生 Health Care	#节能环保 Enviro-nmental Prote-ction	#农林水事务 Affairs of Agriculture, Forest and Water	2012年比2011年增长(%) Increase Rate in 2012 over 2011(%)	人均财政支出(元) Per Capita Financial Expend-iture(yuan)
贵阳市	Guiyang	349.33	66.63	62.61	6.59	4.78	25.06	20.88	12.78	24.18	25.9	7902
六盘水市	Liupanshui	187.84	32.96	34.97	0.99	1.72	14.07	12.44	4.23	21.89	28.3	6580
遵义市	Zunyi	320.20	50.39	73.97	2.99	4.38	26.24	33.46	9.70	46.21	24.9	5242
安顺市	Anshun	130.79	22.20	26.40	0.88	1.53	13.99	14.36	4.13	18.87	29.5	5732
毕节市	Bijie	318.96	44.63	76.01	1.29	3.06	28.83	31.02	6.19	40.22	28.0	4891
铜仁市	Tongren	206.91	30.42	46.68	0.53	2.77	20.52	19.45	7.26	35.19	26.9	6702
黔西南州	Qianxinan	181.17	32.46	39.69	1.01	2.24	19.13	14.52	4.29	29.77	31.7	6456
黔东南州	Qiandongnan	248.53	55.81	49.60	1.30	3.20	24.12	23.89	5.52	37.79	27.7	7170
黔南州	Qiannan	199.86	44.63	39.90	1.30	2.27	18.76	17.96	5.22	28.97	23.1	6210

27-11 各市(州)金融机构人民币存贷款余额(2012)

Saving Deposits and Loans Balance of Financial Institutions by Region

单位：亿元 (100 million yuan)

市(州)名称	City (State, Prefecture)	金融机构人民币存款余额 Total Deposits	#储蓄存款 Savings Deposit	金融机构人民币贷款余额 Total Loans
贵阳市	Guiyang	4394.37	1498.20	3479.47
六盘水市	Liupanshui	676.21	321.46	508.38
遵义市	Zunyi	1712.22	931.95	927.63
安顺市	Anshun	483.14	246.39	350.23
毕节市	Bijie	736.03	415.85	433.45
铜仁市	Tongren	536.21	332.46	381.35
黔西南州	Qianxinan	557.03	266.07	336.45
黔东南州	Qiandongnan	682.45	432.76	427.47
黔南州	Qiannan	627.07	360.56	380.31

注：资料来源于中国人民银行贵阳中心支行。

Note:Data in the table are obtained from the People's bank of China Guiyang Branch.

27-12 各市(州)税收收入(2012)

Taxation Revenue by region

单位：万元 (10000 yuan)

市(州)名称	City (Stat, Prefecture)	税收总计 Total	国税 National Taxation	地税 Local Taxation	2012年比2011年增长(%) Increase Rate in 2012 over 2011(%)	国税 National Taxation	地税 Local Taxation
贵阳市	Guiyang	4397182	2336135	2061047	18.5	14.3	23.7
六盘水市	Liupanshui	1207992	534632	673360	9.2	-7.2	27.1
遵义市	Zunyi	2671699	1423789	1247910	27.0	25.6	28.6
安顺市	Anshun	547123	247522	299601	31.7	23.1	39.7
毕节市	Bijie	1361335	710869	650466	22.5	10.8	38.4
铜仁市	Tongren	514801	227975	286826	27.2	17.3	36.4
黔西南州	Qianxinan	816199	374527	441672	20.7	5.3	37.8
黔东南州	Qiandongnan	753775	230380	523395	39.7	17.4	52.4
黔南州	Qiannan	816120	392045	424075	23.3	14.0	33.3

注：1.资料来源于省国税局、省地税局。2.地税税收收入含契税、耕地占用税。

Note:1.Data in the table are provided by Guizhou Provincial National Taxation Bureau and Local Taxation Bureau of Guizhou Province.2.The Local Taxation doesn't include deed tax and farm land occupation tax.

27-13 各市(州)所在城市城镇居民家庭人均年收支(2012)

Per Capital Annual Disposable Income and Expenditure of Urban Households of Major Cities

单位：元 (yuan)

城市名称	City	城镇居民家庭人均可支配收入 Per Capita Annual Disposable Income of Urban Households	位次 Order	2012年比2011年增长(%) Increase Rate in 2012 over 2011(%)	城镇居民家庭人均消费性支出 Per Capita Annual Consumption Expenditnre of Urban Households	位次 Order	2012年比2011年增长(%) Increase Rate in 2012 over 2011(%)
贵阳市	Guiyang	21796.26	1	12.2	15718.30	1	9.9
六盘水市	Liupanshui	18764.05	7	14.6	10216.48	9	7.8
遵义市	Zunyi	19747.58	2	13.3	13288.17	2	11.2
安顺市	Anshun	18617.45	8	14.2	12852.86	4	8.0
毕节市	Bijie	19554.64	3	14.1	13267.19	3	7.9
铜仁市	Tongren	15910.52	9	14.9	11242.23	8	19.8
兴义市	Xingyi	19471.56	4	14.5	11887.74	6	12.7
凯里市	Kaili	18831.41	6	14.8	11791.32	7	12.1
都匀市	Duyun	19338.40	5	13.9	12480.52	5	8.1

注：表中增长速度未扣除同期价格因素。
Note:The Increase Rate in the table doesn't deducting price factors over the same period.

27-14 各市(州)农村居民家庭人均年收支(2012)

Per Capita Net Income and Living Expenditure of Rural Households by Region

单位：元 (yuan)

市(州)名称	City (State, Prefecture)	农村居民人均纯收入 Per Capita Net Income of Rural Households	位次 Order	农村居民人均期内现金收入 Annual Per Capita Cash Income of Rural Households	位次 Order	农村居民人均生活消费支出 Annual Per Capita Living Expenditures of Rural Households	位次 Order
贵阳市	Guiyang	8488	1	9211	1	6161	1
六盘水市	Liupanshui	5182	4	5258	5	4001	4
遵义市	Zunyi	6061	2	6377	2	4226	3
安顺市	Anshun	5088	5	5545	4	3489	9
毕节市	Bijie	4926	6	5050	6	3972	5
铜仁市	Tongren	4673	7	4861	8	4250	2
黔西南州	Qianxinan	4625	8	4945	7	3953	7
黔东南州	Qiandongnan	4625	8	4340	9	3969	6
黔南州	Qiannan	5445	3	5803	3	3847	8

27–15 各市(州)所在城市分类价格指数

Urban Residents Consumer Price Indices of Major Cities by Region

(上年=100) (preceding year=100)

城市名称	City	居民消费价格指数 Residents Consumer Price Index		商品零售价格指数 Retail Price Index of Commodities	
		2011	2012	2011	2012
贵阳市	Guiyang	105.5	102.6	105.0	102.0
六盘水市	Liupanshui	105.4	102.7	104.7	102.4
遵义市	Zunyi	105.4	102.2	105.4	102.0
安顺市	Anshun	105.0	102.5	104.4	101.4
毕节市	Bijie	105.0	102.8	106.9	102.3
铜仁市	Tongren	104.6	102.3	104.4	102.1
兴义市	Xingyi	105.5	102.7	105.4	102.1
凯里市	Kaili	105.6	102.5	105.9	101.1
都匀市	Duyun	104.8	102.6	106.0	101.8

27–16 各市(州)乡村从业人员数(2012)

Rural Employment by Region

单位：万人 (10000 persons)

市(州)名称	City (State, Prefecture)	合计 Total	农业 Agriculture	工业 Industry	建筑业 Construction	交通运输仓储和邮政业 Transport, Storage and Post	信息传输、计算机服务和软件业 Information Transmission, Computer Services and Software	批发与零售业 Wholesale and Retail Trade	住宿和餐饮业 Hotel and Restaurants	其他行业 Other Sectors
贵阳市	Guiyang	117.48	59.80	9.80	7.57	3.95	0.80	4.94	4.56	26.06
六盘水市	Liupanshui	142.46	83.54	10.33	5.66	3.57	0.15	4.03	1.47	33.71
遵义市	Zunyi	406.98	190.05	27.70	22.69	7.70	1.43	15.39	6.58	135.43
安顺市	Anshun	147.27	82.02	7.94	8.66	3.40	0.48	3.69	2.48	38.60
毕节市	Bijie	454.48	227.17	29.98	20.53	8.23	1.72	12.63	6.42	147.80
铜仁市	Tongren	229.34	118.94	11.34	12.41	3.54	0.61	5.35	2.95	74.20
黔西南州	Qianxinan	184.62	113.43	8.85	8.02	3.97	0.49	4.86	2.13	42.87
黔东南州	Qiandongnan	242.73	132.13	10.45	10.07	3.28	0.37	5.35	3.48	77.62
黔南州	Qiannan	219.36	125.63	10.27	8.11	3.31	0.23	5.19	2.95	63.66

27-17 各市(州)农业机械总动力及拥有量(2012)

Total Power and Possession of Agricultural Machinery by Region

市(州)名称	City (State, Profecture)	农业机械总动力(万千瓦) Total Power of Agricultural Machinery (10000 kw)	大中型拖拉机(台) Large and Medium Agricultural Tractors(unit)	小型拖拉机(台) Mini Agricultural Tractors(unit)	农用水泵(台) Agricultural Water Pump(unit)
贵阳市	Guiyang	153.12	3058	3557	21556
六盘水市	Liupanshui	172.49	1600	4754	16119
遵义市	Zunyi	335.38	7212	8119	87697
安顺市	Anshun	162.12	2749	3786	49791
毕节市	Bijie	267.99	4961	25431	26464
铜仁市	Tongren	277.61	3901	11563	65500
黔西南州	Qianxinan	214.49	3235	4892	41900
黔东南州	Qiandongnan	259.67	3681	3924	51039
黔南州	Qiannan	263.80	8815	7037	71705

注：资料来源于省农委。

Note:Data in this table are obtained from the Agricultural Committee of Guizhou Province.

27-18 各市(州)农林牧渔业总产值(2012)

Gross Output Value of Farming,Forestry, Animal Husbandary, Fishery and Their Services by Region

单位：亿元 (100 million yuan)

市(州)名称	City (State, Prefecture)	合计 Total	农业 Farming	林业 Forestry	牧业 Animal Husbandary	渔业 Fishery	农林牧渔服务业 Services of FFAF	2012年比2011年增长(%) Increase Rate in 2012 over 2011 (%)
贵阳市	Guiyang	111.49	73.24	0.76	35.21	1.48	0.81	8.8
六盘水市	Liupanshui	69.25	34.85	3.13	29.26	0.16	1.85	9.1
遵义市	Zunyi	304.43	186.15	14.80	93.59	5.90	3.99	9.2
安顺市	Anshun	81.97	40.72	2.19	36.82	1.69	0.54	9.3
毕节市	Bijie	236.34	143.82	3.46	83.70	1.07	4.29	9.1
铜仁市	Tongren	200.46	110.20	5.05	74.53	4.77	5.90	9.2
黔西南州	Qianxinan	119.03	64.95	7.01	39.80	5.76	1.51	8.9
黔东南州	Qiandongnan	161.97	82.04	26.66	43.49	6.04	3.75	8.9
黔南州	Qiannan	157.86	84.48	6.24	61.35	2.88	2.91	9.5

27-19　各市(州)农用化肥施用量(2012)

Consumption of Chemical Fertilizers for Agricultural Use by Region

单位：吨　　(ton)

市(州)名称	City (State, Profecture)	合计 Total	氮肥 Nitrogenous Fertilizer	磷肥 Phosphate Fertilizer	钾肥 Potash Fertilizer	复合肥 Compound Fertilizer	2012年比2011年增长(%) Increase Rate in 2012 over 2011(%)
贵阳市	Guiyang	66514	32293	6107	8726	19388	1.5
六盘水市	Liupanshui	68823	43706	6998	5644	12475	3.6
遵义市	Zunyi	219195	122115	23927	22166	50987	6.4
安顺市	Anshun	61090	27916	11323	3809	18042	1.2
毕节市	Bijie	213099	111370	20611	18486	62632	3.1
铜仁市	Tongren	94887	46546	11719	8600	28022	9.5
黔西南州	Qianxinan	78866	50668	10200	7779	10219	9.5
黔东南州	Qiandongnan	77243	30488	9939	5493	31323	0.7
黔南州	Qiannan	102009	58261	11918	10603	21227	1.8

注:本表按折纯法计算。

Note:Consumption of chemical fertilizers is required in calculation to convert the gross weight into weight containing 100% effective component.

27-20　各市(州)主要农作物播种面积(2012)

Sown Areas of Major Farm Crops by Region

单位：千公顷　　(1000 hectares)

市(州)名称	City (State, Profecture)	总计 Total	粮食作物 Sown Areas of Grain Arops	#夏粮 Summer Grain Crops	按品种分 #稻谷 Rice	#小麦 Wheat	#玉米 Corn	#大豆 Soja	油菜籽 Rapeseeds	烤烟 Flue-cured Tobacco
贵阳市	Guiyang	272.18	110.93	28.00	34.05	5.17	38.06	7.04	39.82	12.30
六盘水市	Liupanshui	243.95	180.15	77.99	16.05	28.47	67.86	7.34	6.79	6.62
遵义市	Zunyi	1235.86	755.61	242.55	157.76	32.20	151.81	31.70	130.82	65.47
安顺市	Anshun	263.55	142.82	32.47	52.95	10.23	44.09	4.59	55.23	8.28
毕节市	Bijie	1109.05	652.93	270.09	41.70	67.30	172.16	34.70	57.38	62.85
铜仁市	Tongren	573.67	351.81	101.98	94.30	22.82	72.09	16.86	62.89	21.57
黔西南州	Qianxinan	397.39	239.66	66.04	49.74	49.81	89.11	7.38	24.50	28.44
黔东南州	Qiandongnan	552.22	303.24	78.89	127.09	4.74	45.17	9.62	51.53	13.35
黔南州	Qiannan	534.20	316.35	88.55	108.83	36.46	84.91	10.41	68.00	18.12

27–21 各市(州)主要农产品产量(2012)

Output of Major Farm Crops by Region

单位：万吨 (10000 tons)

市(州)名称	City (State, Prefecture)	粮食 Grain	#夏粮 Summer Grain Crops	2012年比2011年增长(%) Increase Rate in 2012 over 2011	油菜籽 Rapeseeds	烤烟 Fluecured Tobacco	茶叶 Tea	水果 Fruits
贵 阳 市	Guiyang	44.50	8.22	10.6	6.57	1.83	0.30	15.17
六盘水市	Liupanshui	75.29	18.71	33.4	0.85	1.52	0.04	3.67
遵 义 市	Zunyi	276.22	63.21	21.6	24.19	11.29	3.39	28.72
安 顺 市	Anshun	65.15	6.79	22.3	7.35	1.23	0.19	7.72
毕 节 市	Bijie	229.35	56.64	19.5	11.41	8.19	0.11	13.50
铜 仁 市	Tongren	121.41	27.73	24.6	9.63	3.49	1.49	16.88
黔西南州	Qianxinan	87.84	13.37	38.8	3.01	4.63	0.39	10.41
黔东南州	Qiandongnan	112.62	16.71	24.0	6.35	2.32	0.69	29.01
黔 南 州	Qiannan	121.10	17.73	21.0	8.83	2.80	0.84	22.64

27–22 各市(州)牲畜出、存栏量(2012)

Amount of Livestocks in Hand and Slaughtered by Region

单位：头、只 (head)

市(州)名称	City (State, Prefecture)	出栏 Amount of Slaughtered Livestocks			存栏 Amount of Livestock in Hand		
		猪 Hogs	牛 Cattle and Buffalo	羊 Sheep and Goats	猪 Hogs	牛 Cattle and Buffalo	羊 Sheep and Goats
贵 阳 市	Guiyang	1262873	46586	20008	939823	234890	34848
六盘水市	Liupanshui	1050441	67862	110915	1127761	312656	188529
遵 义 市	Zunyi	4536099	184006	513561	3422012	849098	624922
安 顺 市	Anshun	1174556	107501	44141	1203149	455544	67911
毕 节 市	Bijie	2799386	179237	291401	3065470	794993	538157
铜 仁 市	Tongren	2150712	126888	657985	2200089	528801	600500
黔西南州	Qianxinan	1420853	118532	205292	1352625	532644	415342
黔东南州	Qiandongnan	1800466	124230	153277	1368642	633883	255985
黔 南 州	Qiannan	2022081	128582	156755	1685053	603349	223297

27-23　各市(州)主要畜产品、水产品产量(2012)

Output of Major Livestock Products and Aquatic Products by Region

市(州)名称	City (State, Profecture)	肉类总产量(万吨) Total Output of Meat (10000 tons)	2012年比2011年增长(%) Increase Rate in 2012 over 2011	禽蛋(万吨) Poulty and Eggs (10000 tons)	水产品(吨) Aquatic Products(ton)
贵阳市	Guiyang	14.46	3.7	2.31	10647
六盘水市	Liupanshui	11.33	3.9	0.59	1060
遵义市	Zunyi	45.82	4.8	3.91	31446
安顺市	Anshun	13.83	6.0	1.33	5552
毕节市	Bijie	33.45	4.6	2.58	5029
铜仁市	Tongren	23.19	4.5	2.08	17986
黔西南州	Qianxinan	15.64	5.6	1.90	30783
黔东南州	Qiandongnan	17.76	5.4	1.07	17884
黔南州	Qiannan	19.48	5.1	1.00	14288

注：表中“水产品产量”数据由省农委提供。

Note:Output of aquatic products in this table are obtained from the Agricultural Commission of Guizhou province.

27-24　各市(州)主要林产品产量(2012)

Output of Major Forestry Products by Region

单位：吨　　(ton)

市(州)名称	City (State, Profecture)	生漆 Lacquer	油桐籽 Tung-Oil Seed	油茶籽 Tea-Oil Seed	乌桕籽 Tallow-seeds	五倍籽 Nutgall	棕片 Palm-flake	核桃 Walnuts	板栗 Chestnut
贵阳市	Guiyang	12	24	130	2	18	54	173	145
六盘水市	Liupanshui	145	52	98			169	2989	540
遵义市	Zunyi	658	4551	8795	1041	859	1424	1354	2160
安顺市	Anshun	14	4997	324	108	12	119	237	322
毕节市	Bijie	386	82	95	14	50	60	14212	1218
铜仁市	Tongren	144	5351	2078	850	413	456	1095	2326
黔西南州	Qianxinan	137	46618	5951	82	120	1375	1612	9603
黔东南州	Qiandongnan	78	8680	8681	268	257	363	1048	2149
黔南州	Qiannan	124	11283	505	5	193	367	960	7613

27–25 各市(州)规模以上工业增加值(2012)

Total Gross Industrial Value-added above Designated Size by Region

单位：亿元 (100 million yuan)

市(州)名称	City (State, Profecture)	工业增加值 Industrial Value-added	轻工业 Light Industry	重工业 Heavy Industry
贵 阳 市	Guiyang	453.71	220.36	233.35
六盘水市	Liupanshui	310.95	10.38	300.58
遵 义 市	Zunyi	549.37	411.97	137.41
安 顺 市	Anshun	83.95	12.06	71.90
毕 节 市	Bijie	206.69	49.75	156.94
铜 仁 市	Tongren	67.08	17.18	49.90
黔西南州	Qianxinan	163.76	7.85	155.92
黔东南州	Qiandongnan	81.97	10.04	71.93
黔 南 州	Qiannan	138.54	40.94	97.60

注：本表统计口径为全部年主营业务收入2000万元及以上的工业企业。(下表同)

Note:Data in the table refer to the revenue from principal business of 20 million yuan and above of industry enterprises(The same applies to the next table).

27–26 各市(州)规模以上工业企业主要工业产品产量(2012)

Ouput of Major Industrial Products above Designated Size by Region

市(州)名称	City (State, Profecture)	原 煤 (万吨) Coal (10000 tons)	发电量 (亿千瓦小时) Electricity (100 million kwh)	化 肥 (吨) Chemical Fertilizer(ton)	水 泥 (万吨) Cement (10000 tons)
贵 阳 市	Guiyang	385.82	89.55	297.94	996.88
六盘水市	Liupanshui	5657.86	347.15		514.28
遵 义 市	Zunyi	804.09	222.31	26.67	956.33
安 顺 市	Anshun	1215.61	86.92	14.56	534.26
毕 节 市	Bijie	3825.36	393.55	28.46	611.08
铜 仁 市	Tongren	43.86	81.27	0.74	594.64
黔西南州	Qianxinan	2579.64	243.80	39.39	387.38
黔东南州	Qiandongnan	125.58	61.46		400.65
黔 南 州	Qiannan	393.11	22.90	96.07	1104.95

27–27 各市(州)公路里程(2012)
Length of Highways by Region

单位：公里 (km)

市(州)名称	City (State, Profecture)	公路里程 Total Length of Highways	#等级公路 Standard Highway	#高速公路 Expressway	#有铺装路面(高级) Paved Road (advanced)	#沥青混凝土 Asphalt concrete
贵 阳 市	Guiyang	9386.15	8461.01	289.64	5059.91	597.45
六盘水市	Liupanshui	12061.62	8825.47	149.20	1709.29	889.56
遵 义 市	Zunyi	24714.33	12024.46	417.12	3251.78	975.42
安 顺 市	Anshun	9668.37	3928.71	245.87	1226.90	467.20
毕 节 市	Bijie	27908.03	15053.10	274.87	1736.35	623.01
铜 仁 市	Tongren	22176.59	8649.98	169.91	2519.49	438.69
黔西南州	Qianxinan	15373.40	10394.30	259.41	1726.95	465.38
黔东南州	Qiandongnan	27324.21	9733.95	363.52	2681.48	751.92
黔 南 州	Qiannan	15929.02	9505.78	460.54	1698.33	572.21

注：资料来源于省交通厅。
Note:Data in the table are obtained from Guizhou Provincial Department of Transportation.

27–28 各市(州)电信、邮政主要指标(2012)
Major Indicators of Telecommunications and Post by Region

市(州)名称	City (State, Profecture)	年末固定电话用户数(万户) Number of Telephone Subscribers at Year-end (10000 subscribers)	移动电话用户(万户) Number of Mobile Telephone Subscribers (10000 subscribers)	互联网宽带接入用户(万户) Number of Subscribers of Internet Service (10000 subscribers)	交换机总容量(万门) Capacity of Telephone Exchanges (10000 line)	报刊、杂志累计订销数(万份) Issue of Newspapers and Magazines (10000 copies)	邮政储蓄期末余额(亿元) Post Deposits at the Year-end(100 million yuan)
贵 阳 市	Guiyang	101.97	640.85	80.77	1024	10454	68.32
六盘水市	Liupanshui	28.11	211.13	15.13	327	2721	31.45
遵 义 市	Zunyi	75.91	449.28	44.94	1043	7079	144.90
安 顺 市	Anshun	21.13	142.58	11.38	337	2008	21.18
毕 节 市	Bijie	35.39	295.59	20.58	639	3211	53.18
铜 仁 市	Tongren	25.33	171.04	14.28	386	2897	70.29
黔西南州	Qianxinan	19.50	179.47	13.58	430	2449	34.83
黔东南州	Qiandongnan	39.61	223.74	24.45	485	4105	68.18
黔 南 州	Qiannan	33.05	201.31	18.82	355	3103	68.91

注：资料来源于省通信管理局、省邮政管理局、省邮政储蓄银行。
Note:Data in the table are obtained from the Provincial Communications Authority Bureau,the Provincial Postal Service and Postal Savings bank of China Guizhou Branch.

27–29 各市(州)教育事业主要指标(2012)

Major Indicators of Education by Region

市(州)名称	City (State, Prefecture)	高等教育 Higher Education 学校数(所) Number of schools (unit)	高等教育 Higher Education 在校学生(人) Students Enrollment (person)	普通中学 Secondary Schools 学校数(所) Number of schools (unit)	普通中学 Secondary Schools 在校学生(人) Students Enrollment (person)	小学 Primary Schools 学校数(所) Number of schools (unit)	小学 Primary Schools 在校学生(人) Students Enrollment (person)
贵阳市	Guiyang	29	307173	315	262927	671	322319
六盘水市	Liupanshui	2	9262	221	258229	753	287894
遵义市	Zunyi	6	53155	471	528194	1868	575768
安顺市	Anshun	4	15505	148	159798	904	243484
毕节市	Bijie	2	17230	485	603361	2453	958741
铜仁市	Tongren	2	17074	256	303517	1453	402048
黔西南州	Qianxinan	2	11406	249	229039	1076	351363
黔东南州	Qiandongnan	3	28869	274	279199	1231	360469
黔南州	Qiannan	4	23060	242	249558	1120	298717

注：1.资料来源于省教育厅。2.高等教育学校数包括：中科院地化所、普通高等学校、成人高等学校，高等教育在校学生包括：研究生、普通高等教育、成人高等教育。

Note:1.Data in the table are obtained from Guizhou Provincial Department of Education.2.Institutions of higher education include Localization of Chinese Academy of Sciences,regular schools of higher education,and adult institutions of higher education.Students enrollment include those students enrolling in postgradu-ates education,ragular institutions of higher education and adult institution of higher education.

27–30 各市(州)卫生人员数(2012)

Number of Employed Persons in Health Care Institutions by Region

单位：人 (person)

市(州)名称	City (State, Prefecture)	总计 Total	卫生技术人员 Medical Technical Personnel	#执业(助理)医师 Licensed (Assistant) Doctors	执业医师 Licensed Doctor	#注册护士 Registered Nurse	#药师(士) Pharmacist	#技师(士) Laboratory Technician	乡村医生和卫生员 Village Doctors and Assistants	其他技术人员 Other Technical Personnel	管理人员 Admini-strative Personnel	工勤技能人员 Logistics Technical Workers
贵阳市	Guiyang	39029	30383	11820	10922	13079	1428	1674	2059	2169	2028	2368
六盘水市	Liupanshui	15285	10246	3954	3147	3978	392	542	2904	433	770	931
遵义市	Zunyi	33647	23188	8507	6841	8844	1034	1256	6286	1246	1226	1687
安顺市	Anshun	10762	7119	2686	2092	2683	292	430	2259	309	632	443
毕节市	Bijie	26614	15480	5561	3956	5362	579	791	8140	983	909	1100
铜仁市	Tongren	17391	10243	3912	2970	3164	439	705	5135	592	788	633
黔西南州	Qianxinan	12955	8513	3094	2485	3067	287	429	2924	375	438	704
黔东南州	Qiandongnan	20467	13249	4894	3494	4611	485	804	5162	629	848	577
黔南州	Qiannan	15992	11402	4800	3684	3863	511	632	2891	286	664	749

注：资料来源于省卫生厅，含村卫生室。(以下相关表同)

Note:Data in the table are obtained from Guizhou Provincial Department of Health(the same applies to relative tables below).

27−31 各市(州)每千人口拥有卫生技术人员数(2012)

Medical Technical Personnel in Health Care Institutions Per 1000 Persons by Region

单位：人 (person)

市(州)名称	City (State, Prefecture)	卫生技术人员 Medical Technical Personnel 合计 Total	每千人口拥有 Per 1000 Person	执业(助理)医师 Lecensed(Assistant) Doctors 合计 Total	每千人口拥有 Per 1000 Person	注册护士 Registered Nurses 合计 Total	每千人口拥有 Per 1000 Person
贵阳市	Guiyang	30383	8.11	11820	3.16	13079	3.49
六盘水市	Liupanshui	10246	3.18	3954	1.23	3978	1.23
遵义市	Zunyi	23188	3.01	8507	1.10	8844	1.15
安顺市	Anshun	7119	2.50	2686	0.94	2683	0.94
毕节市	Bijie	15480	1.80	5561	0.65	5362	0.62
铜仁市	Tongren	10243	2.40	3912	0.92	3164	0.74
黔西南州	Qianxinan	8513	2.45	3094	0.89	3067	0.88
黔东南州	Qiandongnan	13249	2.89	4894	1.07	4611	1.00
黔南州	Qiannan	11402	2.81	4800	1.19	3863	0.95

注：每千人口数以2012年户籍人口数为基数。

Note:Number per thousand population are based on household population of 2012.

27−32 各市(州)医院服务情况(2012)

Services in Hospitals by Region

市(州)名称	City (State, Prefecture)	诊疗人次(万人次) Visits (10 000 person-times)	#农村乡镇卫生院 Rural Township Hospitals	入院人数(万人) Inpatients (10 000 persons)	出院人数(万人) Patients Discharged from Hosptials (10 000 persons)	每百门诊急诊入院人数（人） Number of Inpatients Per 100 Outpatients and Emergency Cases (person)	病床使用率(%) Utilization Rate of Beds (%)	#农村乡镇卫生院 Rural Township Hospitals	出院者平均住院日(天) Average Stay Days in Hospital (day)	#农村乡镇卫生院 Rural Township Hospitals
贵阳市	Guiyang	942.69	185.07	51.02	50.76	5.53	88.64	45.62	12.8	4.8
六盘水市	Liupanshui	204.10	131.04	22.88	22.12	11.77	82.38	69.98	9.5	5.6
遵义市	Zunyi	620.58	378.09	58.14	57.96	9.64	101.73	81.45	9.3	4.4
安顺市	Anshun	195.37	72.82	18.73	18.49	9.86	85.30	65.25	8.6	2.3
毕节市	Bijie	383.39	312.08	50.81	50.35	14.49	77.88	73.98	6.6	4.2
铜仁市	Tongren	267.27	239.24	35.70	34.70	13.97	86.33	69.24	7.6	4.1
黔西南州	Qianxinan	247.86	217.31	24.72	23.53	10.40	83.95	71.82	6.5	2.5
黔东南州	Qiandongnan	303.61	238.37	36.68	36.41	12.78	96.31	65.72	8.2	3.5
黔南州	Qiannan	299.15	286.58	26.34	26.16	8.99	93.10	52.01	9.0	3.8

27-33 各市(州) 社区卫生服务中心(站)医疗服务情况(2012)

Medical Services of Community Health Service Centers(Stations) by Region

市(州)名称	City (State, Prefecture)	社区卫生服务中心 Community Health Service Centers						社区卫生服务站 mmunity Health Service Stati	
		诊疗人次(万人次) Visits (10 000 person-times)	入院人数(人) Inpatients (person)	病床使用率(%) Utilization Rate (%)	出院者平均住院日(日) Average Stay Days in Hospital (day)	医师日均担负诊疗人次(人次) Daily Visits Each Doctor (person-time)	医师日均担负住院床日(日) Daily Inpatients Each Doctor (day)	诊疗人次(万人次) Visits (10 000 person-times)	医师日均担负诊疗人次(人次) Daily Visits Each Doctor (person-time)
贵阳市	Guiyang	59.83	7165	56.59	10.7	7.65	1.07	56.77	9.30
六盘水市	Liupanshui	1.82	1374	45.52	8.3	2.60	1.26	38.51	9.00
遵义市	Zunyi	37.44	49191	74.95	2.1	10.05	2.07	62.69	9.40
安顺市	Anshun	4.32	5059	85.30	4.7	6.40	2.46	17.02	6.10
毕节市	Bijie	18.20	27664	71.12	3.8	4.89	2.13	2.19	5.50
铜仁市	Tongren	7.18	3400	38.59	4.6	7.37	1.10	6.68	5.20
黔西南州	Qianxinan							26.19	11.40
黔东南州	Qiandongnan	6.85	2765	73.82	2.9	4.49	0.75	0.15	1.50
黔南州	Qiannan	7.11	4435	41.40	3.6	3.65	0.58	4.78	12.80

27-34 各市(州)火灾(2012)

Fires by Region

市(州)名称	City (State, Prefecture)	火灾(起) Number (case)	死亡(人) Deaths (person)	受伤(人) Injuries (person)	直接财产损失(万元) Direct Property Losses(10000 yuan)
贵阳市	Guiyang	530	8	3	2076
六盘水市	Liupanshui	32			74
遵义市	Zunyi	71	3	2	1079
安顺市	Qiandongnan	66		3	219
毕节市	Bijie	47	3		298
铜仁市	Tongren	58	4	2	270
黔西南州	Qianxinan	19	1		100
黔东南州	Qiannan	57	8	5	650
黔南州	Anshun	79	4		379

注：资料来源于省公安厅。

Note:Data in the table are obtained from Guizhou Provincial Department of Public Security.

27−35 各县(市、区、特区)生产总值(2012)

Gross Domestic Product by County(City,District,Special region)

单位：亿元 (100 million)

县(市、区、特区)名称	County (City, District, Special region)	生产总值 Gross Domestic Product	第一产业 Primary Industry	第二产业 Secondary Industry	#工业 Industry	第三产业 Tertiary Industry	按生产总值排位 Order by Gross Domestic Product	2012年比2011年增长(%) Increase Rate in 2012 over 2011(%)
南明区	Nanming	375.50	2.09	84.85	43.86	288.56	2	17.5
云岩区	Yunyan	441.29	0.43	157.87	129.42	282.99	1	15.7
花溪区	Huaxi	119.53	9.19	46.99	28.17	63.35	16	17.0
乌当区	Wudang	156.57	9.19	74.97	44.83	72.41	11	18.0
白云区	Baiyun	101.86	3.22	57.13	50.21	41.51	24	18.1
小河区	Xiaohe	110.74	1.00	73.34	65.22	36.40	19	17.6
开阳县	Kaiyang	102.88	15.74	59.82	44.69	27.32	23	17.2
息烽县	Xifeng	84.34	8.25	49.71	46.26	26.38	27	18.0
修文县	Xiuwen	71.24	10.27	31.79	24.56	29.18	33	17.2
清镇市	Qingzhen	144.16	12.91	70.16	36.35	61.09	13	16.8
钟山区	Zhongshan	258.76	2.28	142.83	130.83	113.65	5	15.9
六枝特区	Liuzhi	84.30	9.09	39.68	35.08	35.53	28	17.7
水城县	Shuicheng	113.51	12.58	70.42	61.59	30.51	17	18.8
盘　县	Panxian	306.72	19.32	221.03	198.83	66.37	4	17.4
红花岗区	Honghuagang	221.49	9.46	66.08	53.47	145.95	6	17.4
汇川区	Huicuan	164.01	6.02	84.24	76.70	73.75	10	17.3
遵义县	Zunyi	192.28	33.56	92.06	75.97	66.66	8	17.5
桐梓县	Tongzi	74.89	15.03	28.95	21.38	30.91	31	17.0
绥阳县	Suiyang	49.15	16.79	12.80	9.25	19.56	46	16.8
正安县	Zhengan	35.63	13.16	6.60	3.59	15.87	61	17.1
※道真县	Daozhen	24.68	7.98	4.26	2.46	12.44	75	15.8
※务川县	Wuchuan	28.29	9.80	4.64	2.39	13.85	69	16.5
凤冈县	Fenggang	32.29	11.03	6.44	3.85	14.82	63	17.2
湄潭县	Meitan	44.11	12.07	11.25	8.46	20.79	48	17.6
余庆县	Yuqing	36.58	9.78	10.00	6.29	16.80	60	16.2
习水县	Xishui	74.53	13.33	31.88	24.01	29.32	32	18.1
赤水市	Chishui	49.45	8.34	22.46	18.60	18.65	45	16.9
仁怀市	Renhuai	329.56	13.98	222.85	216.47	92.73	3	17.8
西秀区	Xixiu	145.55	14.85	56.06	51.07	74.64	12	15.3
平坝县	Pingba	62.20	7.35	35.80	30.49	19.05	36	17.4
普定县	Puding	50.49	7.66	23.79	21.18	19.04	43	18.2
※镇宁县	Zhenning	43.85	6.04	13.89	8.09	23.92	50	18.0
※关岭县	Guanling	42.30	8.07	11.11	5.03	23.12	52	18.0
※紫云县	Ziyun	28.85	9.22	5.19	3.20	14.44	68	18.1
七星关区	Qixingguan	184.42	29.70	72.75	62.45	81.97	9	17.7
大方县	Dafang	109.24	18.11	51.29	42.74	39.84	21	17.0
黔西县	Qianxi	111.81	18.15	50.84	40.74	42.82	18	16.0
金沙县	Jinsha	130.15	13.01	77.93	68.23	39.21	14	17.6
织金县	Zhijin	90.30	15.93	37.12	29.04	37.25	26	16.9
纳雍县	Nayong	103.07	12.15	59.41	54.44	31.51	22	15.2
※威宁县	Weining	100.66	33.70	27.38	23.04	39.58	25	17.1
赫章县	Hezhang	54.59	15.74	14.66	11.46	24.19	39	16.5
碧江区	Bijiang	78.76	7.54	28.66	21.55	42.56	30	17.2
万山区	Wanshan	21.31	5.45	9.41	7.62	6.45	81	17.5

注：2012年贵阳市部分行政区划调整，表中统计数据为行政区划调整前数据。(以下相关表同)

Note:The data in the table indicates the data of the previous administrative districts which of Guiyang city were adjusted in 2012.(the same as the related tables)

27-35 续表 continued

单位：亿元 (100 million)

县(市、区、特区)名 称	County (City, District, Special region)	生产总值 Gross Domestic Product	第一产业 Primary Industry	第二产业 Secondary Industry	#工 业 Industry	第三产业 Tertiary Industry	按生产总值排 位 Order by Gross Domestic Product	2012年比2011年增长(%) Increase Rate in 2012 over 2011(%)
江口县	Jiangkou	23.26	6.91	6.64	3.47	9.71	76	16.8
※玉屏县	Yuping	39.06	4.88	21.67	19.64	12.51	56	17.1
石阡县	Shiqian	32.21	11.95	4.83	2.87	15.43	64	16.6
思南县	Sinan	62.40	19.47	14.53	9.86	28.40	35	17.0
※印江县	Yinjiang	40.41	15.50	8.30	6.33	16.61	54	17.3
德江县	Dejiang	50.52	17.39	9.80	6.50	23.33	42	16.8
※沿河县	Yanhe	49.60	16.47	8.87	5.11	24.26	44	16.6
※松桃县	Songtao	61.56	18.36	20.23	17.21	22.97	37	15.1
兴义市	Xingyi	203.96	20.59	84.40	75.92	98.97	7	16.6
兴仁县	Xingren	64.47	10.11	26.86	21.88	27.50	34	17.0
普安县	Puan	36.73	6.01	18.39	15.65	12.33	58	16.8
晴隆县	Qinglong	31.06	5.75	12.60	10.22	12.71	65	17.2
贞丰县	Zhenfeng	53.40	8.95	30.22	26.91	14.23	41	17.0
望谟县	Wangmo	21.37	6.82	2.50	1.56	12.05	80	16.2
册亨县	Ceheng	18.97	5.86	2.73	2.11	10.38	85	15.3
安龙县	Anlong	54.10	11.33	20.48	18.08	22.29	40	16.6
凯里市	Kaili	123.93	8.56	42.81	30.34	72.56	15	18.9
黄平县	Huangping	25.66	8.01	3.05	1.85	14.60	74	17.6
施秉县	Shibing	19.75	4.96	5.24	4.32	9.55	84	17.2
三穗县	Sansui	20.69	3.99	6.23	4.07	10.47	83	18.0
镇远县	Zhenyuan	38.60	8.49	17.75	15.33	12.36	57	18.3
岑巩县	Cengong	22.39	4.99	7.87	7.23	9.53	77	17.0
天柱县	Tianzhu	41.37	8.94	16.58	13.92	15.85	53	16.6
锦屏县	Jinping	21.12	3.69	7.62	7.03	9.81	82	15.5
剑河县	Jianhe	21.83	5.91	4.00	2.79	11.92	79	17.7
台江县	Taijiang	15.40	3.62	3.64	2.53	8.14	86	18.0
黎平县	Liping	39.27	8.66	11.66	6.12	18.95	55	17.3
榕江县	Rongjiang	29.75	10.12	7.83	4.24	11.80	66	17.2
从江县	Congjiang	29.06	8.82	8.61	3.27	11.63	67	17.0
雷山县	Leishan	14.59	3.60	3.36	2.29	7.63	88	16.9
麻江县	Majiang	21.85	5.19	7.90	6.87	8.76	78	16.5
丹寨县	Danzhai	15.22	3.84	4.26	2.82	7.12	87	18.4
都匀市	Duyun	110.16	7.97	44.66	28.30	57.53	20	15.4
福泉市	Fuquan	79.63	7.58	39.61	32.99	32.44	29	18.1
荔波县	Libo	27.47	4.15	9.10	7.83	14.22	71	16.9
贵定县	Guiding	44.11	6.08	21.60	17.47	16.43	48	17.1
瓮安县	Wengan	60.57	11.21	25.77	24.76	23.59	38	17.5
独山县	Dushan	36.62	8.38	13.40	12.91	14.84	59	17.0
平塘县	Pingtang	26.64	7.62	5.79	4.05	13.23	72	17.2
罗甸县	Luodian	33.99	7.85	13.26	11.22	12.88	62	16.9
长顺县	Changshun	26.54	5.69	7.93	7.09	12.92	73	18.4
龙里县	Longli	46.64	5.13	31.94	27.91	9.57	47	17.9
惠水县	Huishui	43.12	10.46	16.28	14.50	16.38	51	17.3
※三都县	Sandu	27.91	6.69	4.59	2.23	16.63	70	16.8

注：1.※为少数民族自治县(以下相关表同)。2.表中绝对数按当年价格计算，增长速度按可比价格计算。
Note:1.Counties with ※ are autonomous counties(The relative tables in this chapter are the same).2.Absolute Figures in the table are calculated at prices,and increase rates are calculated at comparable prices.

27-36　各县(市、区、特区)人均生产总值(2012)

Per Capita Gross Domestic Product by County(City，District，Special region)

单位：元　　(yuan)

县(市、区、特区)名　称	County (City，District，Special region)	人　均生产总值 Per Capita Gross Domestic Product(yuan)	位次 Order	县(市、区、特区)名　称	County (City，District，Special region)	人　均生产总值 Per Capita Gross Domestic Product(yuan)	位次 Order
南明区	Nanming	44301	3	万山区	Wanshan	18875	31
云岩区	Yunyan	45030	2	江口县	Jiangkou	13484	57
花溪区	Huaxi	32702	12	※玉屏县	Yuping	33130	10
乌当区	Wudang	38707	7	石阡县	Shiqian	10627	75
白云区	Baiyun	37724	8	思南县	Sinan	12541	65
小河区	Xiaohe	43024	4	※印江县	Yinjiang	14269	48
开阳县	Kaiyang	28713	15	德江县	Dejiang	13779	56
息烽县	Xifeng	39357	6	※沿河县	Yanhe	11042	73
修文县	Xiuwen	28134	17	※松桃县	Songtao	12682	63
清镇市	Qingzhen	30561	13				
				兴义市	Xingyi	26032	19
钟山区	Zhongshan	41682	5	兴仁县	Xingren	15423	41
六枝特区	Liuzhi	17061	33	普安县	Puan	14432	46
水城县	Shuicheng	16133	36	晴隆县	Qinglong	12600	64
盘　县	Panxian	29606	14	贞丰县	Zhenfeng	17595	32
				望谟县	Wangmo	8501	86
红花岗区	Honghuagang	33058	11	册亨县	Ceheng	9958	81
汇川区	Huichuan	36523	9	安龙县	Anlong	15112	44
遵义县	Zunyi	20623	26				
桐梓县	Tongzi	14455	45	凯里市	Kaili	25606	21
绥阳县	Suiyang	12946	62	黄平县	Huangping	9802	82
正安县	Zhengan	9342	84	施秉县	Shibing	15157	43
※道真县	Daozhen	10159	78	三穗县	Sansui	13333	60
※务川县	Wuchuan	8924	85	镇远县	Zhenyuan	19015	29
凤冈县	Fenggang	10501	76	岑巩县	Cengong	13932	54
湄潭县	Meitan	11805	70	天柱县	Tianzhu	15974	37
余庆县	Yuqing	15636	39	锦屏县	Jinping	13804	55
习水县	Xishui	14396	47	剑河县	Jianhe	12106	69
赤水市	Chishui	20716	25	台江县	Taijiang	13934	53
仁怀市	Renhuai	60177	1	黎平县	Liping	10129	79
				榕江县	Rongjiang	10397	77
西秀区	Xixiu	19148	28	从江县	Congjiang	9991	80
平坝县	Pingba	21014	24	雷山县	Leishan	12527	66
普定县	Puding	13442	59	麻江县	Majiang	13197	61
※镇宁县	Zhenning	15562	40	丹寨县	Danzhai	12499	67
※关岭县	Guanling	14117	49				
※紫云县	Ziyun	10749	74	都匀市	Duyun	24946	22
				福泉市	Fuquan	28387	16
七星关区	Qixingguan	16306	34	荔波县	Libo	19014	30
大方县	Dafang	14030	51	贵定县	Guiding	19156	27
黔西县	Qianxi	16223	35	瓮安县	Wengan	15905	38
金沙县	Jinsha	23352	23	独山县	Dushan	14011	52
织金县	Zhijin	11551	72	平塘县	Pingtang	11653	71
纳雍县	Nayong	15367	42	罗甸县	Luodian	13449	58
※威宁县	Weining	7974	88	长顺县	Changshun	14111	50
赫章县	Hezhang	8385	87	龙里县	Longli	25970	20
				惠水县	Huishui	12493	68
碧江区	Bijiang	26359	18	※三都县	Sandu	9795	83

27-37 各县(市、区、特区)年末常住人口

Permanent Population at Year-end by County(City,District,Special region)

单位：万人 (10000 persons)

县(市、区、特区)名称	County (City, District, Special region)	2007	2008	2009	2010	2011	2012
南明区	Nanming	74.39	76.28	80.79	83.07	84.47	85.06
云岩区	Yunyan	84.93	88.38	92.04	95.83	97.60	98.39
花溪区	Huaxi	36.97	37.69	35.80	36.05	36.39	36.72
乌当区	Wudang	32.97	34.57	36.18	37.75	39.22	41.68
白云区	Baiyun	22.21	23.57	25.00	26.49	26.87	27.13
小河区	Xiaohe	17.64	19.19	21.93	24.85	25.60	25.89
开阳县	Kaiyang	38.82	37.82	36.84	35.85	35.74	35.92
息烽县	Xifeng	22.47	22.10	21.71	21.31	21.33	21.53
修文县	Xiuwen	26.48	25.98	25.47	24.93	25.17	25.48
清镇市	Qingzhen	48.39	47.84	47.35	46.80	46.96	47.39
钟山区	Zhongshan	53.73	56.75	59.22	61.76	61.88	62.28
六枝特区	Liuzhi	55.76	54.03	51.78	49.56	49.36	49.46
水城县	Shuicheng	71.60	71.69	71.14	70.52	70.29	70.43
盘　县	Panxian	109.50	107.98	105.82	103.59	103.47	103.73
红花岗区	Honghuagang	62.48	63.79	64.78	65.74	66.83	67.17
汇川区	Huichuan	40.23	41.56	42.73	43.90	44.78	45.01
遵义县	Zunyi	101.71	99.53	97.04	94.52	93.24	93.23
桐梓县	Tongzi	56.60	55.26	53.75	52.23	51.68	51.94
绥阳县	Suiyang	43.38	41.65	39.82	38.04	37.87	38.06
正安县	Zhengan	46.60	44.02	41.43	38.97	38.14	38.14
※道真县	Daozhen	27.56	26.52	25.46	24.42	24.13	24.26
※务川县	Wuchuan	36.86	35.34	33.74	32.19	31.70	31.70
凤冈县	Fenggang	35.56	34.17	32.73	31.32	30.67	30.83
湄潭县	Meitan	40.71	39.83	38.80	37.77	37.27	37.46
余庆县	Yuqing	25.10	24.62	24.06	23.49	23.34	23.45
习水县	Xishui	57.73	56.01	54.15	52.32	51.77	51.77
赤水市	Chishui	25.07	24.68	24.20	23.72	23.82	23.92
仁怀市	Renhuai	54.39	54.65	54.68	54.66	54.77	54.76
西秀区	Xixiu	79.51	78.97	77.81	76.63	75.95	76.07
平坝县	Pingba	32.36	31.68	30.76	29.85	29.58	29.62
普定县	Puding	38.68	38.55	38.22	37.88	37.54	37.59
※镇宁县	Zhenning	31.89	30.86	29.62	28.41	28.15	28.20
※关岭县	Guanling	31.33	31.12	30.66	30.20	29.95	29.99
※紫云县	Ziyun	29.91	29.10	28.07	27.07	26.82	26.87
七星关区	Qixingguan	120.02	118.76	116.33	113.86	113.00	113.20
大方县	Dafang	87.28	84.61	81.15	77.74	78.00	77.73
黔西县	Qianxi	76.03	74.39	72.02	69.68	69.00	68.84
金沙县	Jinsha	56.91	57.04	56.61	56.15	56.00	55.47
织金县	Zhijin	84.91	83.31	80.89	78.48	78.00	78.36
纳雍县	Nayong	71.62	70.59	68.84	67.09	67.00	67.14
※威宁县	Weining	116.77	120.68	123.61	126.56	126.00	126.48
赫章县	Hezhang	63.17	64.19	64.63	65.01	65.00	65.19
碧江区	Bijiang	33.99	34.95	35.59	36.23	29.52	30.24
万山区	Wanshan	4.64	4.97	4.88	4.79	11.25	11.33

27-37 续表 continued

单位：万人 (10000 persons)

县(市、区、特区)名称	County (City, District, Special region)	2007	2008	2009	2010	2011	2012
江口县	Jiangkou	19.48	18.88	18.08	17.30	17.21	17.29
※玉屏县	Yuping	12.70	12.50	12.18	11.86	11.75	11.83
石阡县	Shiqian	32.87	32.31	31.38	30.45	30.27	30.35
思南县	Sinan	57.29	54.96	52.44	49.99	49.72	49.79
※印江县	Yinjiang	34.45	32.63	30.48	28.44	28.29	28.35
德江县	Dejiang	40.81	39.79	38.30	36.84	36.62	36.71
※沿河县	Yanhe	49.72	48.56	46.78	45.01	44.88	44.96
※松桃县	Songtao	55.78	54.24	51.45	48.72	48.49	48.59
兴义市	Xingyi	74.79	76.60	77.57	78.53	78.20	78.50
兴仁县	Xingren	43.78	43.49	42.67	41.85	41.70	41.90
普安县	Puan	26.94	26.66	26.07	25.47	25.40	25.50
晴隆县	Qinglong	26.89	26.36	25.53	24.70	24.60	24.70
贞丰县	Zhenfeng	32.65	32.15	31.29	30.42	30.30	30.40
望谟县	Wangmo	26.70	26.40	25.80	25.20	25.10	25.20
册亨县	Ceheng	20.53	20.19	19.63	19.07	19.00	19.10
安龙县	Anlong	39.46	38.52	37.14	35.79	35.70	35.90
凯里市	Kaili	46.27	47.03	47.49	47.92	48.22	48.57
黄平县	Huangping	30.06	28.93	27.61	26.34	26.14	26.21
施秉县	Shibing	13.07	13.13	13.10	13.06	13.02	13.03
三穗县	Sansui	16.23	16.10	15.85	15.60	15.50	15.53
镇远县	Zhenyuan	22.08	21.62	21.01	20.40	20.28	20.32
岑巩县	Cengong	18.77	17.98	17.09	16.22	16.04	16.10
天柱县	Tianzhu	31.97	30.18	28.25	26.42	25.80	26.00
锦屏县	Jinping	17.44	16.86	16.18	15.51	15.26	15.34
剑河县	Jianhe	19.94	19.40	18.73	18.08	18.02	18.04
台江县	Taijiang	12.12	11.88	11.56	11.24	11.02	11.09
黎平县	Liping	44.40	42.82	40.97	39.16	38.70	38.85
榕江县	Rongjiang	30.31	29.91	29.30	28.68	28.60	28.63
从江县	Congjiang	30.39	30.12	29.63	29.13	29.07	29.09
雷山县	Leishan	12.19	12.10	11.92	11.73	11.63	11.67
麻江县	Majiang	18.62	18.08	17.42	16.78	16.52	16.60
丹寨县	Danzhai	13.32	13.02	12.64	12.26	12.17	12.20
都匀市	Duyun	45.86	45.50	45.03	44.43	44.04	44.29
福泉市	Fuquan	29.07	29.12	28.81	28.44	28.17	27.93
荔波县	Libo	15.62	15.30	14.90	14.50	14.39	14.50
贵定县	Guiding	25.49	24.92	24.02	23.13	22.95	23.10
瓮安县	Wengan	42.08	40.80	39.49	38.10	37.74	38.43
独山县	Dushan	30.48	29.31	27.89	26.53	26.34	25.93
平塘县	Pingtang	26.00	25.02	23.93	22.86	22.71	23.02
罗甸县	Luodian	29.26	28.21	26.93	25.68	25.55	25.00
长顺县	Changshun	21.09	20.53	19.81	19.12	18.98	18.64
龙里县	Longli	18.84	18.67	18.39	18.09	17.95	17.96
惠水县	Huishui	38.08	36.77	35.35	34.27	34.04	34.99
※三都县	Sandu	29.24	29.14	28.77	28.36	28.14	28.85

注：表中数据为常住半年及以上人口数，其中2007年–2009年数据根据第六次人口普查结果修订。

Note:Poulations in the table refer to permanent population in the scope at least half a year;Data from the year 2007 to 2009 had been adjusted according to the result of the Sixth National Population Census.

27−38 各县(市、区、特区)户籍人口(2012)

Household Registered Population by County (City，District，Special region)

单位：万人 (10000 persons)

县(市、区、特区)名 称	County (City，District，Special region)	户籍人口 Permanent Population at the year-end
南明区	Nanming	55.36
云岩区	Yunyan	63.50
花溪区	Huaxi	31.20
乌当区	Wudang	35.56
白云区	Baiyun	19.48
小河区	Xiaohe	17.35
开阳县	Kaiyang	43.86
息烽县	Xifeng	25.73
修文县	Xiuwen	30.58
清镇市	Qingzhen	51.90
钟山区	Zhongshan	49.94
六枝特区	Liuzhi	69.69
水城县	Shuicheng	83.96
盘　县	Panxian	118.94
红花岗区	Honghuagang	51.40
汇川区	Huichuan	35.52
遵义县	Zunyi	121.14
桐梓县	Tongzi	72.53
绥阳县	Suiyang	54.64
正安县	Zhengan	63.94
※道真县	Daozhen	34.10
※务川县	Wuchuan	45.02
凤冈县	Fenggang	43.18
湄潭县	Meitan	49.32
余庆县	Yuqing	29.90
习水县	Xishui	71.79
赤水市	Chishui	30.99
仁怀市	Renhuai	67.96
西秀区	Xixiu	87.65
平坝县	Pingba	35.59
普定县	Puding	47.68
※镇宁县	Zhenning	38.74
※关岭县	Guanling	37.57
※紫云县	Ziyun	37.12
七星关区	Qixingguan	152.90
大方县	Dafang	110.43
黔西县	Qianxi	94.78
金沙县	Jinsha	65.74
织金县	Zhijin	113.26
纳雍县	Nayong	97.91
※威宁县	Weining	143.79
赫章县	Hezhang	79.15
碧江区	Bijiang	30.16
万山区	Wanshan	15.31
江口县	Jiangkou	24.15
※玉屏县	Yuping	15.26
石阡县	Shiqian	41.29
思南县	Sinan	67.08
※印江县	Yinjiang	43.76
德江县	Dejiang	52.56
※沿河县	Yanhe	66.24
※松桃县	Songtao	70.65
兴义市	Xingyi	83.05
兴仁县	Xingren	53.62
普安县	Puan	33.68
晴隆县	Qinglong	33.66
贞丰县	Zhenfeng	41.38
望谟县	Wangmo	32.11
册亨县	Ceheng	23.76
安龙县	Anlong	46.66
凯里市	Kaili	50.04
黄平县	Huangping	38.18
施秉县	Shibing	16.87
三穗县	Sansui	22.19
镇远县	Zhenyuan	26.85
岑巩县	Cengong	22.79
天柱县	Tianzhu	40.51
锦屏县	Jinping	22.72
剑河县	Jianhe	25.57
台江县	Taijiang	16.14
黎平县	Liping	53.13
榕江县	Rongjiang	35.58
从江县	Congjiang	34.73
雷山县	Leishan	15.30
麻江县	Majiang	21.74
丹寨县	Danzhai	16.88
都匀市	Duyun	48.05
福泉市	Fuquan	32.92
荔波县	Libo	17.58
贵定县	Guiding	29.18
瓮安县	Wengan	46.62
独山县	Dushan	34.81
平塘县	Pingtang	32.29
罗甸县	Luodian	34.22
长顺县	Changshun	25.86
龙里县	Longli	22.43
惠水县	Huishui	45.11
※三都县	Sandu	36.01

注：资料来源于省公安厅。

Note:Data in the table above are obtained from the Public Security Department of Guizhou Province.

27-39 各县(市、区、特区)第六次人口普查主要指标

Basic Statistics on the Sixth National Population Census by County

单位：人 (person)

县(市、区、特区)名 称	County (City, District, Special region)	普查时点常住人口 Permanent Population	出生率(‰) Birth Rate (‰)	死亡率(‰) Death Rate (‰)	自然增长率(‰) Natural Growth Rate (‰)	城镇人口占比(%) Urbanization Rate (%)
南明区	Nanming	829706	9.11	3.72	5.39	95.66
云岩区	Yunyan	957343	8.16	3.25	4.91	97.31
花溪区	Huaxi	359141	11.87	4.91	6.95	43.71
乌当区	Wudang	377146	13.60	4.18	9.42	55.80
白云区	Baiyun	264621	11.80	3.99	7.80	76.05
小河区	Xiaohe	248185	11.88	3.11	8.78	96.07
开阳县	Kaiyang	358403	11.83	6.41	5.42	30.93
息烽县	Xifeng	212992	13.57	6.64	6.93	28.90
修文县	Xiuwen	249034	15.67	6.35	9.32	29.35
清镇市	Qingzhen	467992	13.16	5.77	7.38	35.93
钟山区	Zhongshan	616178	10.71	2.72	7.99	79.74
六枝特区	Liuzhi	495135	14.40	7.69	6.71	26.16
水城县	Shuicheng	704579	12.88	7.08	5.80	2.41
盘　县	Panxian	1035288	12.96	6.76	6.20	17.25
红花岗区	Honghuagang	656584	10.29	3.92	6.37	64.59
汇川区	Huichuan	438274	11.13	3.68	7.45	66.21
遵义县	Zunyi	942893	12.26	7.06	5.20	29.71
桐梓县	Tongzi	521834	14.97	6.60	8.37	28.31
绥阳县	Suiyang	380078	15.39	7.73	7.66	27.38
正安县	Zhengan	389629	13.29	9.69	3.60	24.99
※道真县	Daozhen	244156	11.62	8.86	2.76	26.62
※务川县	Wuchuan	321653	12.66	7.45	5.21	26.55
凤冈县	Fenggang	313124	11.78	8.12	3.66	26.21
湄潭县	Meitan	377353	11.85	6.79	5.06	27.82
余庆县	Yuqing	234736	13.72	7.56	6.16	33.01
习水县	Xishui	523174	13.71	6.53	7.18	25.74
赤水市	Chishui	237049	13.77	8.56	5.21	34.00
仁怀市	Renhuai	546471	10.91	6.56	4.35	31.45
西秀区	Xixiu	765309	13.68	5.79	7.89	48.97
平坝县	Pingba	297954	16.49	6.79	9.70	33.62
普定县	Puding	378406	13.87	6.23	7.64	19.66
※镇宁县	Zhenning	284029	12.37	7.66	4.71	25.70
※关岭县	Guanling	301327	15.91	7.45	8.46	19.31
※紫云县	Ziyun	270312	17.82	8.20	9.62	15.42
七星关区	Qianxiguan	1137189	15.12	6.39	8.73	37.14
大方县	Dafang	776191	15.55	6.70	8.86	25.58
黔西县	Qianxi	695827	17.15	7.62	9.52	32.57
金沙县	Jinsha	560482	15.68	6.83	8.85	30.04
织金县	Zhijin	783984	13.10	6.61	6.49	25.82
纳雍县	Nayong	670156	15.65	6.00	9.65	24.95
※威宁县	Weining	1263299	15.02	6.32	8.70	18.93
赫章县	Hezhang	649242	14.31	6.31	8.00	16.83
碧江区	Bijiang	361579	12.47	4.74	7.73	57.01
万山区	Wanshan	47804	16.81	9.24	7.57	26.21

27-39 续表 continued

单位：人 (person)

县(市、区、特区)名 称	County (City, District, Special region)	普查时点常住人口 Permanent Population	出生率(‰) Birth Rate (‰)	死亡率(‰) Death Rate (‰)	自然增长率(‰) Natural Growth Rate (‰)	城镇人口占比(%) Urbanization Rate (%)
江口县	Jiangkou	172716	14.75	6.08	8.66	23.45
※玉屏县	Yuping	118491	17.29	8.35	8.94	39.52
石阡县	Shiqian	304305	12.95	8.15	4.80	24.04
思南县	Sinan	499192	12.51	7.48	5.04	23.12
※印江县	Yinjiang	284142	12.83	8.07	4.76	23.23
德江县	Dejiang	367819	15.11	6.73	8.38	21.89
※沿河县	Yanhe	449690	17.08	6.65	10.43	17.19
※松桃县	Songtao	486626	16.04	6.74	9.29	17.46
兴义市	Xingyi	783467	16.83	5.79	11.04	43.01
兴仁县	Xingren	418106	15.50	6.79	8.71	26.57
普安县	Puan	254361	11.72	6.23	5.49	20.29
晴隆县	Qinglong	246918	17.56	7.66	9.90	19.59
贞丰县	Zhenfeng	304020	14.91	7.45	7.46	22.52
望谟县	Wangmo	252074	13.11	8.20	4.91	18.25
册亨县	Ceheng	190498	16.30	8.26	8.04	17.77
安龙县	Anlong	356414	17.35	6.54	10.80	26.18
凯里市	Kaili	478835	11.91	5.39	6.53	59.34
黄平县	Huangping	263272	13.36	7.83	5.53	18.57
施秉县	Shibing	130416	13.52	7.43	6.09	29.80
三穗县	Sansui	155679	20.55	8.84	11.71	27.97
镇远县	Zhenyuan	203548	16.78	8.36	8.42	33.84
岑巩县	Cengong	162385	15.49	8.82	6.67	20.05
天柱县	Tianzhu	263753	16.99	8.57	8.42	22.94
锦屏县	Jinping	154812	18.22	8.99	9.22	26.99
剑河县	Jianhe	180557	15.61	8.46	7.15	19.65
台江县	Taijiang	112281	15.19	7.79	7.40	21.83
黎平县	Liping	390905	16.64	8.60	8.04	18.76
榕江县	Rongjiang	286216	16.99	6.52	10.47	16.34
从江县	Congjiang	290851	18.30	8.77	9.53	13.55
雷山县	Leishan	117147	17.04	9.89	7.15	23.44
麻江县	Majiang	167578	14.37	8.67	5.70	20.07
丹寨县	Danzhai	122390	15.50	8.37	7.13	20.16
都匀市	Duyun	443511	11.85	6.39	5.46	50.85
福泉市	Fuquan	283768	15.67	6.79	8.88	33.77
荔波县	Libo	144793	14.91	7.68	7.22	23.80
贵定县	Guiding	231009	14.27	7.40	6.87	34.89
瓮安县	Wengan	380135	14.62	6.29	8.33	33.04
独山县	Dushan	265086	14.20	7.88	6.32	23.14
平塘县	Pingtang	228447	14.58	8.97	5.62	21.19
罗甸县	Luodian	257111	14.94	8.57	6.38	17.70
长顺县	Changshun	191038	14.16	6.90	7.26	25.30
龙里县	Longli	180780	16.57	7.89	8.69	31.09
惠水县	Huishui	342480	14.47	7.26	7.21	22.43
※三都县	Sandu	283001	17.82	7.57	10.24	14.08

27–40 各县(市、区、特区)固定资产投资

Investment in Fixed Assets by County(City,District,Special region)

单位：万元 (10000 yuan)

县(市、区、特区)名称	County (City,District, Special region)	2011	2012	2012年比2011年增长(%) Increase Ratein 2012 over 2011(%)
南明区	Nanming	1476787	3014515	104.1
云岩区	Yunyan	1750400	2326675	32.9
花溪区	Huaxi	1129330	1770789	56.8
乌当区	Wudang	901946	1361507	51.0
白云区	Baiyun	1331860	2241154	68.3
小河区	Xiaohe	1347574	2100164	55.8
开阳县	Kaiyang	1117756	1754877	57.0
息烽县	Xifeng	847425	1328762	56.8
修文县	Xiuwen	848509	1274460	50.2
清镇市	Qingzhen	1232584	1800597	46.1
钟山区	Zhongshan	1120785	1869330	66.8
六枝特区	Liuzhi	502019	1109581	121.0
水城县	Shuicheng	956755	1719371	79.7
盘　县	Panxian	1653224	2962593	79.2
红花岗区	Honghuagang	1149859	1933119	68.1
汇川区	Huicuan	597783	985792	64.9
遵义县	Zunyi	1117542	2044554	83.0
桐梓县	Tongzi	770636	1149843	49.2
绥阳县	Suiyang	284204	490432	72.6
正安县	Zhengan	207426	388369	87.2
※道真县	Daozhen	137550	260845	89.6
※务川县	Wuchuan	193791	340369	75.6
凤冈县	Fenggang	121952	260182	113.3
湄潭县	Meitan	325354	599832	84.4
余庆县	Yuqing	254658	414016	62.6
习水县	Xishui	669857	1076736	60.7
赤水市	Chishui	405533	697023	71.9
仁怀市	Renhuai	616958	1123689	82.1
西秀区	Xixiu	739191	1419108	92.0
平坝县	Pingba	185027	455736	146.3
普定县	Puding	140534	397170	182.6
※镇宁县	Zhenning	176309	306007	73.6
※关岭县	Guanling	119732	214963	79.5
※紫云县	Ziyun	95044	188566	98.4
七星关区	Qixingguan	1040316	1774795	70.6
大方县	Dafang	628992	1057756	68.2
黔西县	Qianxi	744568	1268254	70.3
金沙县	Jinsha	902956	1736741	92.3
织金县	Zhijin	781439	1383600	77.1
纳雍县	Nayong	755690	1258228	66.5
※威宁县	Weining	679512	1165626	71.5
赫章县	Hezhang	386711	655212	69.4
碧江区	Bijiang	671034	1003757	74.3
万山区	Wanshan	106498	303555	50.6

27–40 续表 continued

单位：万元 (10000 yuan)

县(市、区、特区)名 称	County (City,District, Special region)	2011	2012	2012年比2011年增长(%) Increase Ratein 2012 over 2011(%)
江口县	Jiangkou	211309	386349	82.8
※玉屏县	Yuping	195936	353225	80.3
石阡县	Shiqian	154393	267311	73.1
思南县	Sinan	437584	805093	84.0
※印江县	Yinjiang	246979	469179	90.0
德江县	Dejiang	228455	436443	91.0
※沿河县	Yanhe	355210	695786	95.9
※松桃县	Songtao	392719	679953	73.1
兴义市	Xingyi	1110136	1810002	63.0
兴仁县	Xingren	430156	699956	62.7
普安县	Puan	210436	337001	60.1
晴隆县	Qinglong	230647	364317	58.0
贞丰县	Zhenfeng	279217	459048	64.4
望谟县	Wangmo	115612	209607	81.3
册亨县	Ceheng	88851	160927	81.1
安龙县	Anlong	222956	410588	84.2
凯里市	Kaili	1173673	2101049	79.0
黄平县	Huangping	138064	255653	85.2
施秉县	Shibing	120556	200329	66.2
三穗县	Sansui	135095	241356	78.7
镇远县	Zhenyuan	143210	287247	100.6
岑巩县	Cengong	134701	235075	74.5
天柱县	Tianzhu	275448	450743	63.6
锦屏县	Jinping	97094	158310	63.0
剑河县	Jianhe	122414	205313	67.7
台江县	Taijiang	114225	210800	84.5
黎平县	Liping	236297	412386	74.5
榕江县	Rongjiang	182544	310514	70.1
从江县	Congjiang	185532	348081	87.6
雷山县	Leishan	80590	131283	62.9
麻江县	Majiang	154494	259124	67.7
丹寨县	Danzhai	145727	288637	98.1
都匀市	Duyun	810488	1184385	46.1
福泉市	Fuquan	469075	689977	47.1
荔波县	Libo	210089	308138	46.7
贵定县	Guiding	262186	384706	46.7
瓮安县	Wengan	474100	698210	47.3
独山县	Dushan	194932	286258	46.9
平塘县	Pingtang	191803	281874	47.0
罗甸县	Luodian	254958	373080	46.3
长顺县	Changshun	210621	309802	47.1
龙里县	Longli	365100	539090	47.7
惠水县	Huishui	368056	541042	47.0
※三都县	Sandu	188808	276188	46.3

注：1.本表统计口径为50万元及以上的固定资产项目投资，房地产开发投资。2.本表不包括跨县(市、区)域项目，也不包括220KV及以上输电线路投资。

Note:1.Data in the table refer to those projects that planned to invest 500,000 yuan at least in investment in fixed assets and real estate development
2.Data in the table do not include investment in cross-regional projects,nor investment in power transmission and distribution projects as the voltage reach 220KV and above.

27-41 各县(市、区、特区)公共财政收入(2012)

Public Financial Revenue by County (City,District,Special region)

县（市、区、特区）名称	County (City,District, Special region)	公共财政收入(万元) Public Financial Revenue (10000 yuan)	#增值税 Value Added Tax	位次 Order	2012年比2011年增长(%) Increase Rate in 2012 over 2011(%)	人均公共财政收入(元) Per Public Financial Revenue(yuan)
南明区	Nanming	267309	13541	2	43.6	3154
云岩区	Yunyan	259813	17291	3	26.7	2651
花溪区	Huaxi	89520	4537	26	37.3	2449
乌当区	Wudang	114560	6359	19	30.7	2832
白云区	Baiyun	135683	11935	12	42.8	5026
小河区	Xiaohe	108152	6254	20	30.1	4202
开阳县	Kaiyang	128024	8019	15	80.0	3573
息烽县	Xifeng	60009	2466	34	36.6	2801
修文县	Xiuwen	54229	3972	36	40.2	2142
清镇市	Qingzhen	99495	5104	24	26.9	2109
钟山区	Zhongshan	153746	7260	9	39.4	2477
六枝特区	Liuzhi	76227	2724	29	52.9	1543
水城县	Shuicheng	162768	8525	8	64.5	2313
盘　县	Panxian	410554	32292	1	58.7	3963
红花岗区	Honghuagang	140274	5138	10	40.9	2094
汇川区	Huichuan	87793	4115	27	30.5	1956
遵义县	Zunyi	136197	7783	11	30.1	1461
桐梓县	Tongzi	57105	3406	35	44.9	1102
绥阳县	Suiyang	36657	1064	47	50.4	966
正安县	Zhengan	30412	862	56	46.1	797
※道真县	Daozhen	23804	990	65	56.7	984
※务川县	Wuchuan	29304	1150	57	20.8	924
凤冈县	Fenggang	22746	750	69	43.6	740
湄潭县	Meitan	37641	1112	46	40.0	1007
余庆县	Yuqing	27648	1805	58	30.1	1182
习水县	Xishui	60215	6906	33	42.1	1163
赤水市	Chishui	35967	1762	49	32.4	1507
仁怀市	Renhuai	231827	67434	6	43.7	4233
西秀区	Xixiu	127364	10221	16	41.7	1676
平坝县	Pingba	51292	3315	37	42.3	1733
普定县	Puding	42428	2961	43	41.5	1129
※镇宁县	Zhenning	39009	1506	45	40.8	1385
※关岭县	Guanling	26853	1249	61	37.9	896
※紫云县	Ziyun	21200	521	73	98.3	790
七星关区	Qixingguan	100017	3595	23	29.1	884
大方县	Dafang	116051	6385	17	45.5	1490
黔西县	Qianxi	100247	4930	22	41.4	1455
金沙县	Jinsha	219553	19132	7	38.8	3939
织金县	Zhijin	128366	6718	14	32.2	1642
纳雍县	Nayong	115676	5852	18	38.6	1725
※威宁县	Weining	77628	3444	28	37.9	615
赫章县	Hezhang	33925	2661	50	49.1	521
碧江区	Bijiang	61289	1570	32	30.7	2051
万山区	Wanshan	12730	1135	88	54.2	1128

27-41 续表 continued

县（市、区、特区）名称	County (City,District, Special region)	公共财政收入(万元) Public Financial Revenue (10000 yuan)	#增值税 Value Added Tax	位次 Order	2012年比2011年增长(%) Increase Rate in 2012over 2011(%)	人均公共财政收入(元) Per Public Financial Revenue(yuan)
江口县	Jiangkou	15931	509	84	32.7	924
※玉屏县	Yuping	23183	2253	67	8.5	1966
石阡县	Shiqian	23618	512	66	49.4	779
思南县	Sinan	31802	1925	54	37.6	639
※印江县	Yinjiang	21692	763	72	40.2	766
德江县	Dejiang	33667	820	51	44.8	918
※沿河县	Yanhe	45768	3004	39	25.4	1019
※松桃县	Songtao	44423	2955	40	40.4	915
兴义市	Xingyi	245700	10739	4	53.5	3136
兴仁县	Xingren	106180	6374	21	39.8	2540
普安县	Puan	47802	4614	38	35.6	1878
晴隆县	Qinglong	31426	1748	55	22.8	1275
贞丰县	Zhenfeng	74250	5258	30	35.0	2446
望谟县	Wangmo	15523	1390	85	73.9	617
册亨县	Ceheng	16495	974	83	96.1	866
安龙县	Anlong	44119	4084	41	37.8	1232
凯里市	Kaili	244842	3868	5	70.6	5059
黄平县	Huangping	23131	689	68	60.9	884
施秉县	Shibing	24757	736	63	36.6	1901
三穗县	Sansui	19009	480	78	50.9	1225
镇远县	Zhenyuan	32359	2969	53	37.0	1594
岑巩县	Cengong	20151	1233	75	87.6	1254
天柱县	Tianzhu	39959	1006	44	64.2	1543
锦屏县	Jinping	19336	1110	76	38.7	1264
剑河县	Jianhe	21179	899	74	69.9	1175
台江县	Taijiang	14234	1007	87	32.7	1288
黎平县	Liping	27449	1026	59	48.3	708
榕江县	Rongjiang	26810	853	62	63.8	937
从江县	Congjiang	24470	890	64	55.7	841
雷山县	Leishan	15135	521	86	47.3	1299
麻江县	Majiang	18563	1529	80	57.1	1121
丹寨县	Danzhai	17645	689	81	75.0	1448
都匀市	Duyun	130391	3319	13	45.6	2953
福泉市	Fuquan	92370	3269	25	62.3	3293
荔波县	Libo	18882	1133	79	12.6	1307
贵定县	Guiding	33200	1886	52	61.8	1442
瓮安县	Wengan	73512	4948	31	55.9	1930
独山县	Dushan	27033	1331	60	51.3	1034
平塘县	Pingtang	21813	410	71	57.8	954
罗甸县	Luodian	19135	2314	77	3.6	757
长顺县	Changshun	22455	969	70	71.9	1194
龙里县	Longli	42792	2640	42	57.4	2383
惠水县	Huishui	36444	2438	48	56.2	1056
※三都县	Sandu	17250	394	82	35.1	605

注：资料来源于省财政厅(下表同)。
Note:Data in the table are obtained from Guizhou Provincial Financial Department(the same applies to the next table).

27-42 各县(市、区、特区)公共财政支出(2012)

Public Financial Expenditure by County(City,District,Special region)

县（市、区、特区）名称	County (City,District, Special region)	公共财政支出(万元) Public Financial Expenditures (10000 yuan)	#教育支出 Operating Expenses for Education	位次 Order	2012年比2011年增长(%) Increase Rate in 2012 over 2011	人均公共财政支出(元) Per Public Financial Expenditure(yuan)
南明区	Nanming	303836	83753	14	46.4	3585
云岩区	Yunyan	361421	80950	9	61.4	3688
花溪区	Huaxi	166426	43304	45	21.2	4553
乌当区	Wudang	177796	27419	40	22.6	4395
白云区	Baiyun	182267	43851	37	34.4	6752
小河区	Xiaohe	140120	26291	66	36.1	5444
开阳县	Kaiyang	233821	47350	27	42.1	6526
息烽县	Xifeng	155576	33527	53	34.6	7261
修文县	Xiuwen	138327	26149	67	25.3	5463
清镇市	Qingzhen	202634	59995	30	17.2	4296
钟山区	Zhongshan	243384	48074	23	28.8	3920
六枝特区	Liuzhi	273822	65501	16	27.0	5542
水城县	Shuicheng	351423	71293	10	34.5	4995
盘　县	Panxian	647041	122606	1	32.6	6246
红花岗区	Honghuagang	244372	49541	22	37.8	3647
汇川区	Huichuan	158072	32337	50	12.8	3521
遵义县	Zunyi	366142	102940	7	21.1	3927
桐梓县	Tongzi	205826	51386	28	24.2	3973
绥阳县	Suiyang	153826	38907	54	21.2	4052
正安县	Zhengan	190514	51998	31	26.5	4995
※道真县	Daozhen	140890	36833	64	25.4	5823
※务川县	Wuchuan	151938	42247	56	20.4	4793
凤冈县	Fenggang	145961	34251	61	30.6	4747
湄潭县	Meitan	180141	46498	39	28.4	4821
余庆县	Yuqing	121544	32525	74	25.0	5195
习水县	Xishui	236724	67873	26	26.9	4573
赤水市	Chishui	149401	26215	57	22.9	6259
仁怀市	Renhuai	327603	81616	12	35.3	5982
西秀区	Xixiu	316195	72372	13	26.2	4160
平坝县	Pingba	149171	33150	58	10.0	5040
普定县	Puding	168961	36134	44	41.5	4498
※镇宁县	Zhenning	163666	30532	47	30.0	5809
※关岭县	Guanling	156344	36222	51	32.9	5217
※紫云县	Ziyun	155842	30069	52	39.9	5805
七星关区	Qixingguan	422390	113759	3	29.0	3735
大方县	Dafang	371026	92754	6	35.4	4765
黔西县	Qianxi	289115	64449	15	34.6	4195
金沙县	Jinsha	364160	80988	8	35.7	6534
织金县	Zhijin	372901	70462	5	38.0	4770
纳雍县	Nayong	273444	77434	17	21.6	4077
※威宁县	Weining	449437	129228	2	14.7	3560
赫章县	Hezhang	262808	71869	19	27.5	4037
碧江区	Bijiang	185538	35501	36	32.4	6209
万山区	Wanshan	101237	17047	85	36.5	8967

27-42 续表 continued

县（市、区、特区）名称	County (City,District, Special region)	公共财政支出(万元) Public Financial Expenditures (10000 yuan)	#教育支出 Operating Expenses for Education	位次 Order	2012年比2011年增长(%) Increase Rate in 2012 over 2011	人均公共财政支出(元) Per Public Financial Expenditure(yuan)
江口县	Jiangkou	122005	27685	73	28.5	7073
※玉屏县	Yuping	106808	17527	82	20.8	9059
石阡县	Shiqian	174736	36650	42	10.4	5765
思南县	Sinan	237526	61458	24	21.2	4774
※印江县	Yinjiang	181289	48700	38	29.2	6401
德江县	Dejiang	205816	55764	29	27.6	5613
※沿河县	Yanhe	236936	64366	25	31.6	5275
※松桃县	Songtao	265657	69655	18	36.1	5473
兴义市	Xingyi	407970	76855	4	38.0	5207
兴仁县	Xingren	246783	56218	20	33.9	5904
普安县	Puan	137941	34557	68	21.4	5420
晴隆县	Qinglong	148887	30412	59	27.6	6040
贞丰县	Zhenfeng	186755	44857	35	26.6	6153
望谟县	Wangmo	187597	46046	33	38.4	7459
册亨县	Ceheng	121519	26272	76	27.5	6379
安龙县	Anlong	165648	54579	46	26.7	4627
凯里市	Kaili	333300	68742	11	44.7	6887
黄平县	Huangping	135637	27652	69	15.4	5181
施秉县	Shibing	95547	20867	87	21.9	7335
三穗县	Sansui	102788	23485	84	24.0	6624
镇远县	Zhenyuan	121531	26660	75	27.3	5987
岑巩县	Cengong	111253	21995	80	33.5	6922
天柱县	Tianzhu	170959	43377	43	28.9	6601
锦屏县	Jinping	115486	24686	79	20.7	7549
剑河县	Jianhe	120158	21135	78	27.7	6664
台江县	Taijiang	90172	16026	88	17.0	8157
黎平县	Liping	187209	38423	34	16.6	4828
榕江县	Rongjiang	145753	34376	62	26.4	5094
从江县	Congjiang	162083	31217	48	32.1	5574
雷山县	Leishan	96251	20283	86	13.3	8260
麻江县	Majiang	108761	23682	81	16.6	6567
丹寨县	Danzhai	132212	26404	70	49.8	10850
都匀市	Duyun	245492	34037	21	23.0	5559
福泉市	Fuquan	175483	37363	41	42.9	6256
荔波县	Libo	103810	20753	83	16.1	7186
贵定县	Guiding	124043	27034	72	15.1	5387
瓮安县	Wengan	188085	30403	32	24.5	4939
独山县	Dushan	148861	41115	60	36.7	5696
平塘县	Pingtang	140552	26734	65	23.7	6147
罗甸县	Luodian	153681	34283	55	20.1	6080
长顺县	Changshun	121021	25366	77	7.9	6434
龙里县	Longli	125458	22507	71	43.7	6986
惠水县	Huishui	160109	37969	49	19.2	4639
※三都县	Sandu	143422	36744	63	23.8	5033

27-43 各县(市、区、特区)农民人均纯收入(2012)

Per Capita Net Income of Rural Households by County(City,District,Special region)

单位：元 (yuan)

县(市、区、特区)名称	County (City,District, Special region)	农民人均纯收入 Per Capita Annual Net Income of Rural Households	位次 Order
南明区	Nanming	10259	2
云岩区	Yunyan	10356	1
花溪区	Huaxi	8665	6
乌当区	Wudang	9607	5
白云区	Baiyun	10256	3
小河区	Xiaohe	10128	4
开阳县	Kaiyang	7860	10
息烽县	Xifeng	7456	13
修文县	Xiuwen	7460	12
清镇市	Qingzhen	7953	9
钟山区	Zhongshan	6792	15
六枝特区	Liuzhi	4728	52
水城县	Shuicheng	4725	53
盘　县	Panxian	5060	40
红花岗区	Honghuagang	8134	8
汇川区	Huichuan	8340	7
遵义县	Zunyi	7621	11
桐梓县	Tongzi	5981	26
绥阳县	Suiyang	6768	16
正安县	Zhengan	4333	78
※道真县	※Daozhen	4137	84
※务川县	※Wuchuan	4052	86
凤冈县	Fenggang	5211	35
湄潭县	Meitan	6816	14
余庆县	Yuqing	6147	23
习水县	Xishui	4572	64
赤水市	Chishui	6537	19
仁怀市	Renhuai	6753	17
西秀区	Xixiu	6420	20
平坝县	Pingba	5391	33
普定县	Puding	4771	50
※镇宁县	※Zhenning	4667	56
※关岭县	※Guanling	4682	55
※紫云县	※Ziyun	4633	59
七星关区	Qixingguan	5131	37
大方县	Dafang	4943	46
黔西县	Qianxi	4986	41
金沙县	Jinsha	5720	28
织金县	Zhijin	4714	54
纳雍县	Nayong	4561	65
※威宁县	※Weining	4862	48
赫章县	Hezhang	4577	63
碧江区	Bijiang	6310	22
万山区	Wanshan	4229	82
江口县	Jiangkou	4662	57
※玉屏县	※Yuping	6092	24
石阡县	Shiqian	4521	67
思南县	Sinan	4335	77
※印江县	※Yinjiang	4396	71
德江县	Dejiang	4138	83
※沿河县	※Yanhe	4370	72
※松桃县	※Songtao	4346	76
兴义市	Xingyi	6389	21
兴仁县	Xingren	4964	42
普安县	Puan	4287	79
晴隆县	Qinglong	4088	85
贞丰县	Zhenfeng	4732	51
望谟县	Wangmo	3771	88
册亨县	Ceheng	3970	87
安龙县	Anlong	4590	62
凯里市	Kaili	6081	25
黄平县	Huangping	4349	74
施秉县	Shibing	4954	45
三穗县	Sansui	4642	58
镇远县	Zhenyuan	4884	47
岑巩县	Cengong	4629	60
天柱县	Tianzhu	4841	49
锦屏县	Jinping	4255	80
剑河县	Jianhe	4413	70
台江县	Taijiang	4234	81
黎平县	Liping	4484	68
榕江县	Rongjiang	4348	75
从江县	Congjiang	4628	61
雷山县	Leishan	4560	66
麻江县	Majiang	4422	69
丹寨县	Danzhai	4359	73
都匀市	Duyun	6543	18
福泉市	Fuquan	5678	29
荔波县	Libo	5124	38
贵定县	Guiding	5425	32
瓮安县	Wengan	5791	27
独山县	Dushan	5195	36
平塘县	Pingtang	4955	44
罗甸县	Luodian	5371	34
长顺县	Changshun	5115	39
龙里县	Longli	5631	30
惠水县	Huishui	5488	31
※三都县	※Sandu	4962	43

27-44 各县（市、区、特区）乡村从业人员(2012)

Number of Rural Employment by County (City,District,Special region)

单位：人 (person)

县(市、区、特区)名称	County (City,District, Special region)	合计 Total	第一产业 Primary Industry	第二产业 Secondary Industry	第三产业 Tertiary Industry	2012年比2011年增长(%) Increase Rate in 2012 over 2011(%)
南明区	Nanming	37932	22010	5319	10603	-1.5
云岩区	Yunyan	59741	5651	21366	32724	-4.7
花溪区	Huaxi	118571	59444	17032	42095	-11.0
乌当区	Wudang	150527	56482	26290	67755	6.4
白云区	Baiyun	48180	25010	10022	13148	1.1
小河区	Xiaohe	18941	8837	1709	8395	-8.7
开阳县	Kaiyang	191947	95685	26114	70148	2.2
息烽县	Xifeng	128584	62428	16750	49406	5.2
修文县	Xiuwen	162884	91014	18357	53513	-3.1
清镇市	Qingzhen	257485	171472	30650	55363	-1.6
钟山区	Zhongshan	92407	54583	17969	19855	11.4
六枝特区	Liuzhi	330480	151251	41702	137527	2.9
水城县	Shuicheng	395417	226016	37958	131443	-1.8
盘　县	Panxian	606260	403521	62213	140526	2.3
红花岗区	Honghuagang	124360	56712	19419	48229	-1.6
汇川区	Huicuan	119610	52416	29011	38183	2.6
遵义县	Zunyi	737654	307514	104883	325257	2.9
桐梓县	Tongzi	386784	170405	52352	164027	4.8
绥阳县	Suiyang	316605	168516	22425	125664	0.6
正安县	Zhengan	387138	132312	52026	202800	1.4
※道真县	Daozhen	186633	85772	12687	88174	1.6
※务川县	Wuchuan	264740	147207	11677	105856	-0.7
凤冈县	Fenggang	257456	141830	22027	93599	0.9
湄潭县	Meitan	263496	152844	22593	88059	-0.3
余庆县	Yuqing	175376	85671	17330	72375	1.0
习水县	Xishui	366889	153230	53915	159744	1.5
赤水市	Chishui	145558	75380	13759	56419	4.7
仁怀市	Renhuai	337545	170727	69840	96978	0.7
西秀区	Xixiu	394530	187234	67854	139442	3.7
平坝县	Pingba	201069	133074	18942	49053	3.4
普定县	Puding	251852	125830	29912	96110	1.6
※镇宁县	Zhenning	202367	113612	17221	71534	1.9
※关岭县	Guanling	195029	122857	13730	58442	3.1
※紫云县	Ziyun	227863	137605	18306	71952	1.5
七星关区	Qixingguan	832313	369199	112421	350693	5.5
大方县	Dafang	677721	368323	69133	240265	2.3
黔西县	Qianxi	522489	217196	74273	231020	3.4
金沙县	Jinsha	295489	129762	34162	131565	-17.1
织金县	Zhijin	536881	286740	63742	186399	-1.1
纳雍县	Nayong	504150	222847	63265	218038	0.0
※威宁县	Weining	790664	495541	58898	236225	5.1
赫章县	Hezhang	385072	182047	29204	173821	0.3
碧江区	Bijiang	112187	57096	12339	42752	
万山区	Wanshan	69562	32408	8577	28577	

注：因行政区划调整，碧江区、万山区无增长速度。

Note: Due to adjustment of administrative divisions, Bijiang and Wanshan are without growth rate.

27-44 续表 continued

单位：人 (person)

县(市、区、特区)名称	County (City,District, Special region)	合计 Total	第一产业 Primary Industry	第二产业 Secondary Industry	第三产业 Tertiary Industry	2012年比2011年增长(%) Increase Rate in 2012 over 2011(%)
江口县	Jiangkou	127536	72316	8826	46394	7.4
※玉屏县	Yuping	84902	37315	14838	32749	3.1
石阡县	Shiqian	260756	137568	16918	106270	9.5
思南县	Sinan	397373	194709	72501	130163	3.5
※印江县	Yinjiang	245035	107441	32308	105286	2.7
德江县	Dejiang	250786	137033	22531	91222	-3.2
※沿河县	Yanhe	325526	186026	20440	119060	1.6
※松桃县	Songtao	419742	227525	28203	164014	1.4
兴义市	Xingyi	412795	263785	50168	98842	1.1
兴仁县	Xingren	247638	161167	18035	68436	-2.1
普安县	Puan	172006	101995	16919	53092	-1.0
晴隆县	Qinglong	175713	110999	10453	54261	1.9
贞丰县	Zhenfeng	228121	133963	21147	73011	0.1
望谟县	Wangmo	166168	97319	10680	58169	-0.9
册亨县	Ceheng	135081	75843	10788	48450	0.0
安龙县	Anlong	308643	189196	30561	88886	3.8
凯里市	Kaili	178441	88219	23035	67187	2.0
黄平县	Huangping	223922	150434	25815	47673	7.7
施秉县	Shibing	61636	44942	4161	12533	0.6
三穗县	Sansui	125140	45839	11053	68248	0.4
镇远县	Zhenyuan	121632	67806	16839	36987	0.3
岑巩县	Cengong	126492	71920	6040	48532	0.7
天柱县	Tianzhu	223550	102122	7486	113942	-0.4
锦屏县	Jinping	124469	58776	13923	51770	0.6
剑河县	Jianhe	144866	77205	9401	58260	2.7
台江县	Taijiang	94840	44873	12636	37331	-4.2
黎平县	Liping	291201	153654	21258	116289	-4.0
榕江县	Rongjiang	209223	120326	16412	72485	7.9
从江县	Congjiang	185149	124927	12665	47557	-0.2
雷山县	Leishan	94738	51927	7222	35589	1.3
麻江县	Majiang	125910	77494	9991	38425	-0.1
丹寨县	Danzhai	96090	40800	7253	48037	1.8
都匀市	Duyun	197254	104689	17024	75541	3.0
福泉市	Fuquan	147624	90047	23546	34031	0.5
荔波县	Libo	100471	57200	7628	35643	1.3
贵定县	Guiding	167995	81474	13399	73122	3.1
瓮安县	Wengan	288349	130972	28188	129189	2.6
独山县	Dushan	205058	114751	17947	72360	3.5
平塘县	Pingtang	195843	136191	8608	51044	0.8
罗甸县	Luodian	175236	98743	12113	64380	-0.1
长顺县	Changshun	136330	86438	8413	41479	1.7
龙里县	Longli	115585	86549	6980	22056	1.7
惠水县	Huishui	267890	155593	28749	83548	1.3
※三都县	Sandu	195987	113675	11211	71101	2.3

27–45 各县(市、区、特区)农林牧渔业总产值(2012)

Gross Output Value of Farming,Forestry,Animal Husbandry and Fishery and Its Order by County(City,District,Special region)

单位：万元 (10000 yuan)

县(市、区、特区)名称	County (City,District, Special region)	合计 Total	农业 Farming	林业 Forestry	牧业 Animal Husbandry	渔业 Fishery	农林牧渔服务业 Services	位次 Order	2012年比2011年增长(%) Increase Rate in 2012 over 2011(%)
南明区	Nanming	32938	24644		8162	12	120	86	8.5
云岩区	Yunyan	6026	4614		1392		20	88	2.0
花溪区	Huaxi	142087	100143	507	39483	163	1791	42	9.5
乌当区	Wudang	142076	84400	1566	28367	1093	1660	43	9.5
白云区	Baiyun	51767	37066	392	13773	73	463	84	9.7
小河区	Xiaohe	14586	12243		2098	150	95	87	8.2
开阳县	Kaiyang	236581	132484	1666	99697	1047	1687	15	9.7
息烽县	Xifeng	127377	77369	729	41279	7088	912	54	9.8
修文县	Xiuwen	167826	119210	912	46641	652	411	32	9.6
清镇市	Qingzhen	193647	117519	1198	67431	4134	715	29	9.7
钟山区	Zhongshan	51041	18885	350	30071	42	1692	85	8.8
六枝特区	Liuzhi	128189	71876	4384	44783	789	6357	52	7.8
水城县	Shuicheng	216835	123679	5385	84854	123	2794	23	9.0
盘　县	Panxian	296477	134017	21141	132941	687	7691	6	9.1
红花岗区	Honghuagang	152211	74886	650	70025	1668	4982	37	10.3
汇川区	Huicuan	105452	54010	602	43611	695	6534	66	9.3
遵义县	Zunyi	567056	385983	5612	141743	27130	6588	1	10.1
桐梓县	Tongzi	245969	153714	14598	73893	3081	683	13	11.3
绥阳县	Suiyang	275489	207377	3952	57020	4730	2410	8	12.0
正安县	Zhengan	233966	146738	26619	57463	1421	1725	16	12.0
※道真县	Daozhen	156444	95642	7422	51804	956	620	35	11.7
※务川县	Wuchuan	166000	110096	5264	46995	1731	1914	33	11.7
凤冈县	Fenggang	189943	111640	18780	56464	1009	2050	30	12.3
湄潭县	Meitan	199903	138581	5474	48294	3662	3892	27	11.6
余庆县	Yuqing	164055	99864	5655	51755	5416	1365	34	12.1
习水县	Xishui	221390	112383	5404	99391	1933	2279	21	11.7
赤水市	Chishui	139164	58695	41597	33567	3241	2064	45	10.2
仁怀市	Renhuai	227298	111937	6351	103893	2317	2800	20	9.4
西秀区	Xixiu	232981	121703	2131	104344	3850	953	18	12.4
平坝县	Pingba	115635	65044	1981	44588	3273	749	62	15.7
普定县	Puding	122069	57084	1362	59301	3403	919	56	12.2
※镇宁县	Zhenning	90170	49873	2862	33538	3504	393	72	12.7
※关岭县	Guanling	120981	68015	5082	46439	1219	226	59	11.1
※紫云县	Ziyun	137823	45523	8508	79948	1697	2147	47	11.9
七星关区	Qixingguan	429549	264403	8438	145957	833	9918	3	6.7
大方县	Dafang	274916	167347	3502	97840	1485	4742	9	5.3
黔西县	Qianxi	267374	172025	2060	87113	1699	4477	12	26.4
金沙县	Jinsha	212003	128999	5531	68354	4110	5009	24	15.4
织金县	Zhijin	236911	135967	2888	92290	430	5336	14	11.6
纳雍县	Nayong	209182	121638	4964	79289	1206	2085	25	5.5
※威宁县	Weining	500842	303332	3692	185059	556	8203	2	6.2
赫章县	Hezhang	232668	144524	3513	81077	402	3152	19	3.3
碧江区	Bijiang	122338	70901	3346	39087	5062	3942	55	9.0
万山区	Wanshan	88264	49396	2202	31641	2545	2480	73	8.7

27-45 续表 continued

单位：万元 (10000 yuan)

县(市、区、特区)名 称	County (City,District, Special region)	合 计 Total	农 业 Farming	林 业 Forestry	牧 业 Animal Husbandry	渔 业 Fishery	农林牧渔服务业 Services	位次 Order	2012年比2011年增长(%) Increase Rate in 2012 over 2011(%)
江口县	Jiangkou	113392	60191	5636	39759	3790	4016	64	9.3
※玉屏县	Yuping	82897	41056	4112	31791	2576	3362	75	8.8
石阡县	Shiqian	201675	106363	6494	80409	3154	5255	26	9.0
思南县	Sinan	326603	178685	3860	127047	7504	9507	4	9.0
※印江县	Yinjiang	233459	118076	8200	95396	6223	5564	17	9.1
德江县	Dejiang	271072	161405	4190	94242	3686	7549	11	8.9
※沿河县	Yanhe	272631	159659	4588	93091	6762	8531	10	8.8
※松桃县	Songtao	292249	156283	7865	112867	6436	8798	7	9.2
兴义市	Xingyi	313922	168514	5279	111419	23110	5600	5	9.5
兴仁县	Xingren	156201	99115	4553	51717	210	605	36	9.2
普安县	Puan	93536	48960	9429	33837	481	830	70	9.8
晴隆县	Qinglong	95657	47562	3480	38300	5095	1220	68	9.2
贞丰县	Zhenfeng	138846	72877	2745	61576	472	1176	46	8.8
望谟县	Wangmo	120372	62352	13728	36545	6137	1609	60	8.8
册亨县	Ceheng	94500	47583	15563	25872	3862	1621	69	9.0
安龙县	Anlong	177310	102577	15284	38757	18242	2450	31	9.0
凯里市	Kaili	151086	86348	7838	51404	3904	1592	39	7.0
黄平县	Huangping	128152	78801	13037	30810	2051	3453	53	9.3
施秉县	Shibing	79977	59458	4774	13939	649	1157	76	9.3
三穗县	Sansui	69624	30786	8218	28042	993	1584	79	9.0
镇远县	Zhenyuan	128425	74303	23663	27005	2697	756	51	9.5
岑巩县	Cengong	78338	40818	5291	23701	853	7675	77	8.6
天柱县	Tianzhu	134499	72167	18323	41850	1435	725	48	8.2
锦屏县	Jinping	58423	19887	14600	16430	5610	1896	81	9.7
剑河县	Jianhe	92340	33251	18176	31535	8499	878	71	9.1
台江县	Taijiang	53171	22481	13312	12360	3993	1025	83	8.5
黎平县	Liping	150032	52858	42325	41070	11395	2384	40	9.1
榕江县	Rongjiang	151109	72495	47448	25214	5179	773	38	8.8
从江县	Congjiang	144218	67812	31744	32834	9928	1900	41	9.9
雷山县	Leishan	54877	33998	4606	13369	1118	1786	82	10.1
麻江县	Majiang	86705	46114	4356	27083	1027	8125	74	8.5
丹寨县	Danzhai	58748	28858	8902	18210	1033	1745	80	8.0
都匀市	Duyun	140014	57286	4698	74030	2350	1650	44	9.5
福泉市	Fuquan	121470	66055	3372	50416	1271	356	58	9.6
荔波县	Libo	70785	34132	7016	25197	2543	1896	78	9.4
贵定县	Guiding	108273	68451	3420	31008	2084	3309	65	9.5
瓮安县	Wengan	198687	95289	3329	94380	3389	2300	28	9.4
独山县	Dushan	133785	82685	3865	45128	1303	804	49	9.4
平塘县	Pingtang	121611	81489	4910	33457	594	1161	57	9.4
罗甸县	Luodian	132026	79957	6466	34896	9012	1695	50	9.7
长顺县	Changshun	116016	55019	2978	53053	646	4320	61	9.7
龙里县	Longli	114332	58402	1240	52680	560	1450	63	9.6
惠水县	Huishui	219574	109240	12447	88477	1578	7832	22	9.5
※三都县	Sandu	102000	56752	8639	30788	3471	2350	67	9.2

27–46 各县(市、区、特区)粮食、肉类产量(2012)

Output of Grain, Meat and Its Order by County(City,Section,Special region)

县(市、区、特区)名称	County (City,Section, Special region)	粮食产量(吨) Output of Grain (ton)	位次 Order	2012年比2011年增长(%) Increase Rate in 2012 over 2011(%)	人均粮食产量(公斤) Per Capita Output of Grain (kg)	位次 Order	肉类产量(吨) Output of Meat (ton)	位次 Order	2012年比2011年增长(%) Increase Rate in 2012 over 2011(%)
南明区	Nanming	4471	86	8.0	75	86	3270	86	6.1
云岩区	Yunyan	32	88	-96.2	…	88	488	88	-27.8
花溪区	Huaxi	53922	74	9.4	264	67	15900	51	4.6
乌当区	Wudang	40273	82	8.3	154	83	10786	70	-7.2
白云区	Baiyun	11147	85	8.6	149	84	5071	84	5.5
小河区	Xiaohe	1719	87	5.0	61	87	934	87	-5.4
开阳县	Kaiyang	99580	47	13.4	295	50	42284	8	5.5
息烽县	Xifeng	67034	67	10.3	338	29	15722	52	11.0
修文县	Xiuwen	78685	56	10.1	291	53	18578	44	5.6
清镇市	Qingzhen	88167	54	11.6	220	80	31570	18	1.1
钟山区	Zhongshan	22571	84	15.9	131	85	16109	50	32.5
六枝特区	Liuzhi	201434	18	31.6	352	25	20369	38	5.9
水城县	Shuicheng	216166	14	30.3	281	57	28921	23	2.0
盘　县	Panxian	312751	4	38.3	295	49	47905	5	-2.9
红花岗区	Honghuagang	70482	65	12.0	327	37	16773	46	4.3
汇川区	Huicuan	69486	66	15.6	332	35	20310	39	5.3
遵义县	Zunyi	563557	1	10.5	481	5	90399	1	4.2
桐梓县	Tongzi	231606	10	18.1	356	24	38749	11	4.7
绥阳县	Suiyang	234457	9	13.1	466	6	26090	29	5.2
正安县	Zhengan	212219	16	32.1	377	17	22546	34	4.3
※道真县	Daozhen	133093	32	20.0	423	10	19295	42	6.0
※务川县	Wuchuan	163758	24	27.2	383	15	23117	32	4.8
凤冈县	Fenggang	157974	25	58.8	395	14	27010	27	3.6
湄潭县	Meitan	194264	20	13.9	431	8	27579	26	7.6
余庆县	Yuqing	149859	29	56.7	535	1	27962	24	3.7
习水县	Xishui	246402	8	48.4	377	18	59735	3	5.3
赤水市	Chishui	120814	35	8.5	512	3	13962	57	7.1
仁怀市	Renhuai	214229	15	11.9	365	20	44638	7	3.9
西秀区	Xixiu	155007	26	29.8	234	78	40526	10	6.6
平坝县	Pingba	101826	43	19.0	335	32	16247	49	5.1
普定县	Puding	104394	41	20.2	243	75	21323	37	6.7
※镇宁县	Zhenning	94700	51	23.0	266	66	11830	66	7.9
※关岭县	Guanling	98521	48	19.0	285	54	17194	45	5.7
※紫云县	Ziyun	97052	50	19.5	269	64	31220	20	4.8
七星关区	Qixingguan	414101	2	22.9	360	23	59019	4	5.2
大方县	Dafang	257111	7	5.0	302	46	36698	13	4.4
黔西县	Qianxi	273389	6	70.5	342	28	34225	16	3.4
金沙县	Jinsha	229875	11	32.0	484	4	31371	19	3.4
织金县	Zhijin	302248	5	19.7	347	26	36068	14	3.8
纳雍县	Nayong	228725	12	21.2	281	58	30493	22	3.9
※威宁县	Weining	396321	3	4.8	307	43	73728	2	5.6
赫章县	Hezhang	191766	21	4.5	268	65	32874	17	5.3
碧江区	Bijiang	73342	61		433	7	12459	61	
万山区	Wanshan	53954	73		417	12	11176	69	

27-46 续表 continued

县(市、区、特区)名称	County (City,District, Special region)	粮食产量(吨) Output of Grain (ton)	位次 Order	2012年比2011年增长(%) Increase Rate in 2012 over 2011(%)	人均粮食产量(公斤) Per Capita Output of Grain (kg)	位次 Order	肉类产量(吨) Output of Meat (ton)	位次 Order	2012年比2011年增长(%) Increase Rate in 2012 over 2011(%)
江口县	Jiangkou	71023	64	6.6	335	33	14245	56	4.5
※玉屏县	Yuping	36012	83	18.8	284	55	9430	75	4.4
石阡县	Shiqian	115356	36	53.5	296	48	22575	33	4.5
思南县	Sinan	200468	19	22.5	312	40	41885	9	4.5
※印江县	Yinjiang	127602	33	23.0	312	41	27805	25	4.5
德江县	Dejiang	139486	30	40.1	334	34	26429	28	4.4
※沿河县	Yanhe	170614	22	25.6	280	59	30856	21	4.4
※松桃县	Songtao	226243	13	19.9	336	30	35038	15	4.4
兴义市	Xingyi	207744	17	47.0	301	47	44851	6	5.3
兴仁县	Xingren	152929	28	34.4	361	22	21555	35	4.4
普安县	Puan	64684	68	55.1	200	82	11954	64	4.6
晴隆县	Qinglong	73169	62	49.5	249	74	11686	67	8.6
贞丰县	Zhenfeng	103850	42	35.5	272	63	14420	55	5.1
望谟县	Wangmo	74079	60	13.6	243	76	16518	47	6.7
册亨县	Ceheng	48800	77	41.5	214	81	10026	73	6.6
安龙县	Anlong	153173	27	38.5	369	19	25355	30	5.5
凯里市	Kaili	85643	55	24.1	272	62	21378	36	3.8
黄平县	Huangping	89850	52	24.4	240	77	11410	68	7.3
施秉县	Shibing	54651	72	24.4	525	2	6607	82	6.5
三穗县	Sansui	49805	76	24.3	252	73	11856	65	7.3
镇远县	Zhenyuan	76315	59	25.1	425	9	9719	74	6.1
岑巩县	Cengong	58917	71	23.2	278	60	9036	77	5.2
天柱县	Tianzhu	108737	37	25.1	303	45	19838	40	5.5
锦屏县	Jinping	53579	75	23.2	254	72	8368	79	6.6
剑河县	Jianhe	60601	70	24.4	254	71	12413	62	3.9
台江县	Taijiang	40534	81	25.6	262	69	4519	85	5.6
黎平县	Liping	122466	34	20.7	263	68	15388	53	4.5
榕江县	Rongjiang	76567	58	24.8	228	79	10726	71	5.3
从江县	Congjiang	100969	45	24.7	315	39	12690	60	5.0
雷山县	Leishan	44444	79	23.2	295	51	5542	83	6.3
麻江县	Majiang	61342	69	24.2	305	44	10663	72	5.5
丹寨县	Danzhai	41780	80	25.7	275	61	7476	81	5.3
都匀市	Duyun	99635	46	22.6	307	42	23519	31	6.1
福泉市	Fuquan	107451	39	21.2	420	11	13014	59	5.3
荔波县	Libo	45412	78	17.2	282	56	8719	78	2.9
贵定县	Guiding	78106	57	24.2	295	52	9324	76	5.4
瓮安县	Wengan	167800	23	17.7	364	21	37408	12	3.7
独山县	Dushan	108194	38	22.8	336	31	16428	48	3.3
平塘县	Pingtang	105981	40	25.0	344	27	13015	58	7.4
罗甸县	Luodian	101642	44	18.8	323	38	19626	41	6.0
长顺县	Changshun	97524	49	19.6	398	13	12000	63	6.2
龙里县	Longli	72007	63	21.3	378	16	7819	80	5.0
惠水县	Huishui	137549	31	24.4	331	36	18734	43	4.8
※三都县	Sandu	89742	53	17.4	260	70	15210	54	6.9

注：因行政区划调整，碧江区、万山区无增长速度。
Note:Due to adjustment of administrative divisions, Bijiang and Wanshan are without growth rate.

27–47 各县(市、区、特区)油菜籽、烤烟产量(2012)

Output of Rapeseed and Fluecured Tobacco and Its Order by County(City,District,Special region)

县(市、区、特区)名称	County (City,District, Special region)	油菜籽产量(吨) Output of Rapeseed (ton)	位次 Order	2012年比2011年增长(%) Increase Rate in 2012 over 2011(%)	烤烟产量(吨) Output of Fluecured Tobacco (ton)	位次 Order	2012年比2011年增长(%) Increase Rate in 2012 over 2011(%)
南明区	Nanming	70	86	-54.8			
云岩区	Yunyan						
花溪区	Huaxi	4496	57	24.6	53	67	341.7
乌当区	Wudang	5281	46	23.3	42	69	
白云区	Baiyun	833	77	-9.8			
小河区	Xiaohe	205	81	57.7			
开阳县	Kaiyang	19376	7	-0.7	9022	14	-5.9
息烽县	Xifeng	11366	21	3.3	1810	53	-2.1
修文县	Xiuwen	14088	15	86.4	2403	46	3.4
清镇市	Qingzhen	9950	23	31.8	5013	29	12.8
钟山区	Zhongshan						
六枝特区	Liuzhi	6545	43	19.5	323	61	53.1
水城县	Shuicheng	203	82	163.6	5285	27	7.1
盘　县	Panxian	1733	74	43.0	9549	11	102.8
红花岗区	Honghuagang	6609	41	0.1	49	68	8.9
汇川区	Huicuan	6617	40	-7.3	2511	44	20.6
遵义县	Zunyi	73594	1	5.1	20333	2	15.4
桐梓县	Tongzi	17048	11	7.9	8986	15	4.8
绥阳县	Suiyang	28916	4	8.8	9503	12	3.5
正安县	Zhengan	19188	8	8.4	10290	9	1.9
※道真县	Daozhen	7179	36	13.5	13665	6	16.7
※务川县	Wuchuan	8532	29	3.4	15315	3	3.9
凤冈县	Fenggang	15523	13	2.9	7500	17	20.0
湄潭县	Meitan	20723	6	3.0	9441	13	16.3
余庆县	Yuqing	16463	12	0.2	10693	7	15.2
习水县	Xishui	7854	33	9.9	1799	54	98.9倍
赤水市	Chishui	285	80	6.3			
仁怀市	Renhuai	13343	17	2.7	2805	42	20.9
西秀区	Xixiu	33113	3	30.2	4785	31	-11.0
平坝县	Pingba	10870	22	9.5	4237	35	92.6
普定县	Puding	9760	25	38.4	871	57	31.0
※镇宁县	Zhenning	9038	27	17.1	59	66	
※关岭县	Guanling	4183	61	6.2	96	65	
※紫云县	Ziyun	6549	42	44.1	2251	48	28.3
七星关区	Qixingguan	4878	49	3.4	10301	8	-2.7
大方县	Dafang	7396	34	0.5	13805	5	-22.0
黔西县	Qianxi	62694	2	7.3	6648	21	13.7
金沙县	Jinsha	25703	5	2.7	4178	37	-27.3
织金县	Zhijin	12927	19	14.9	3835	38	-10.9
纳雍县	Nayong	199	83	-27.1	4237	36	-7.5
※威宁县	Weining	93	85	-34.0	33811	1	24.2
赫章县	Hezhang	198	84	5.3	5101	28	-36.6
碧江区	Bijiang	4390	58		123	64	
万山区	Wanshan	2330	68				

27-47 续表 continued

县(市、区、特区)名称	County (City,District, Special region)	油菜籽产量(吨) Output of Rapeseed (ton)	位次 Order	2012年比2011年增长(%) Increase Rate in 2012 over 2011(%)	烤烟产量(吨) Output of Fluecured Tobacco (ton)	位次 Order	2012年比2011年增长(%) Increase Rate in 2012 over 2011(%)
江口县	Jiangkou	4071	62	-2.0	2169	49	12.2
※玉屏县	Yuping	3537	65	15.4			
石阡县	Shiqian	15397	14	7.8	5834	25	10.8
思南县	Sinan	19118	9	8.3	4693	32	0.9
※印江县	Yinjiang	13372	16	2.0	5934	23	4.0
德江县	Dejiang	12956	18	-0.7	7000	19	3.8
※沿河县	Yanhe	8548	28	9.5	6245	22	3.8
※松桃县	Songtao	12610	20	8.3	2898	41	25.3
兴义市	Xingyi	9388	26	8.5	14543	4	91.9
兴仁县	Xingren	5540	45	9.2	8715	16	77.1
普安县	Puan	1186	76	49.6	9555	10	72.0
晴隆县	Qinglong	1391	75	40.6	2316	47	155.3
贞丰县	Zhenfeng	4318	59	3.8	3775	39	86.8
望谟县	Wangmo	1888	73	9.5			
册亨县	Ceheng	2305	69	34.5			
安龙县	Anlong	4037	64	1.7	7413	18	47.8
凯里市	Kaili	2854	66	12.9	961	56	6.1
黄平县	Huangping	4801	51	9.0	2510	45	77.0
施秉县	Shibing	4561	56	18.6	5887	24	19.1
三穗县	Sansui	2296	70	5.7	244	63	-4.7
镇远县	Zhenyuan	7069	37	4.7	5006	30	70.0
岑巩县	Cengong	5138	48	28.8	4250	34	88.9
天柱县	Tianzhu	4767	54	2.0	851	58	-29.4
锦屏县	Jinping	4217	60	8.4	281	62	325.8
剑河县	Jianhe	1920	72	11.8			
台江县	Taijiang	2090	71	16.4			
黎平县	Liping	7325	35	3.5	10	71	-52.4
榕江县	Rongjiang	5792	44	3.1			
从江县	Congjiang	4800	52	3.2			
雷山县	Leishan	445	79	22.3			
麻江县	Majiang	4618	55	11.0	2737	43	73.1
丹寨县	Danzhai	799	78	21.2	491	60	126.3
都匀市	Duyun	7991	32	1.8	743	59	-66.4
福泉市	Fuquan	9936	24	4.7	4521	33	11.5
荔波县	Libo	4050	63	0.4	16	70	-57.9
贵定县	Guiding	6862	39	3.6	1964	50	10.7
瓮安县	Wengan	18403	10	11.7	6896	20	1.1
独山县	Dushan	7013	38	9.5	1962	51	11.6
平塘县	Pingtang	8259	30	11.0	3179	40	8.9
罗甸县	Luodian	2621	67	7.0			
长顺县	Changshun	5259	47	6.4	5306	26	0.9
龙里县	Longli	4780	53	13.5	1840	52	21.9
惠水县	Huishui	4863	50	10.6	1608	55	-13.3
※三都县	Sandu	8232	31	3.7			

注：因行政区划调整，碧江区、万山区无增长速度。

Note: Due to adjustment of administrative divisions, Bijiang and Wanshan are without growth rate.

27–48 各县(市、区、特区)规模以上工业增加值(2012)

Value-added of Industry above Designated Size and Its Order by County(City,District,Special region)

单位：万元 (10000 yuan)

县(市、区、特区)名称	County (City,District, Special region)	工业增加值 Value-added of Industry	轻工业 Light Industry	重工业 Heavy Industry	位次 Order
南明区	Nanming	307886	155528	152359	19
云岩区	Yunyan	1352153	1160079	192075	3
花溪区	Huaxi	138763	56058	82705	40
乌当区	Wudang	340607	162803	177804	16
白云区	Baiyun	469640	81245	388395	13
小河区	Xiaohe	680358	390954	289404	8
开阳县	Kaiyang	273461	1189	272272	21
息烽县	Xifeng	474254	36160	438094	12
修文县	Xiuwen	262820	135527	127293	23
清镇市	Qingzhen	237189	24105	213084	25
钟山区	Zhongshan	844589	101653	742936	4
六枝特区	Liuzhi	153387	1320	152067	38
水城县	Shuicheng	740493		740493	6
盘　县	Panxian	1371064	795	130269	2
红花岗区	Honghuagang	288285	107704	180581	20
汇川区	Huicuan	818160	616655	201505	5
遵义县	Zunyi	594786	101324	493462	9
桐梓县	Tongzi	189231	22076	167155	30
绥阳县	Suiyang	77873	41080	36793	51
正安县	Zhengan	29861	19264	10597	71
※道真县	Daozhen	20463	3261	17202	74
※务川县	Wuchuan	18706	2521	16185	77
凤冈县	Fenggang	38875	25253	13622	65
湄潭县	Meitan	76800	68713	8087	52
余庆县	Yuqing	74381	1192	73189	53
习水县	Xishui	350123	253854	96269	15
赤水市	Chishui	157621	115114	42507	37
仁怀市	Renhuai	2758551	2741650	16901	1
西秀区	Xixiu	442562	86691	355872	14
平坝县	Pingba	173468	12732	160735	34
普定县	Puding	160477	10741	149736	36
※镇宁县	Zhenning	26099	8531	17568	72
※关岭县	Guanling	20212		20212	75
※紫云县	Ziyun	16728	1887	14842	78
七星关区	Qixingguan	550130	415798	134333	10
大方县	Dafang	234112		234112	26
黔西县	Qianxi	203492	6281	197211	29
金沙县	Jinsha	491990	74619	417371	11
织金县	Zhijin	114859		114859	44
纳雍县	Nayong	313535		313535	18
※威宁县	Weining	121300	801	120500	43
赫章县	Hezhang	37531		37531	67
碧江区	Bijiang	177052	91136	85915	33
万山区	Wanshan	42168	4500	37668	61

27–48 续表　continued

单位：万元　(10000 yuan)

县(市、区、特区)名称	County (City,District, Special region)	工业增加值 Value-added of Industry	轻工业 Light Industry	重工业 Heavy Industry	位次 Order
江口县	Jiangkou	21281	9333	11949	73
※玉屏县	Yuping	132390	3213	129176	42
石阡县	Shiqian	13769	4474	9295	82
思南县	Sinan	70693	1767	68926	54
※印江县	Yinjiang	41778	19356	22422	62
德江县	Dejiang	40165	23259	16906	64
※沿河县	Yanhe	31433	7999	23434	70
※松桃县	Songtao	100079	6781	93297	47
兴义市	Xingyi	691152	58698	632454	7
兴仁县	Xingren	217608	4733	212875	27
普安县	Puan	162565		162565	35
晴隆县	Qinglong	80572		80572	50
贞丰县	Zhenfeng	333209		333209	17
望谟县	Wangmo	6552	4179	2373	87
册亨县	Ceheng	11483	6876	4607	85
安龙县	Anlong	134496	4000	130496	41
凯里市	Kaili	182545	10724	171821	32
黄平县	Huangping	15725		15725	80
施秉县	Shibing	13553		13553	83
三穗县	Sansui	32152	15679	16473	68
镇远县	Zhenyuan	140090	50485	89605	39
岑巩县	Cengong	57888	3827	54061	57
天柱县	Tianzhu	81162		81162	49
锦屏县	Jinping	61704	2720	58984	56
剑河县	Jianhe	14793		14793	81
台江县	Taijiang	15824		15824	79
黎平县	Liping	46702	5270	41432	60
榕江县	Rongjiang	40604		40604	63
从江县	Congjiang	19981		19981	76
雷山县	Leishan	12634		12634	84
麻江县	Majiang	52524		52524	58
丹寨县	Danzhai	31778	10687	20091	69
都匀市	Duyun	184441	62826	124165	31
福泉市	Fuquan	273405	971	274983	22
荔波县	Libo	62728		62728	55
贵定县	Guiding	213955	201947	14556	28
瓮安县	Wengan	246782	1758	247574	24
独山县	Dushan	86313	5678	80635	48
平塘县	Pingtang	7667	2614	5053	86
罗甸县	Luodian	38789	26849	11940	66
长顺县	Changshun	49372	14887	34486	59
龙里县	Longli	105734	61774	46509	46
惠水县	Huishui	111296	34751	79094	45
※三都县	Sandu	4939		4939	88

27-49 各县(市、区、特区)社会消费品零售总额(2012)

Total Retail Sales of Social Consumer Goods by County (City,District,Special Region)

单位：万元 (10000 yuan)

县(市、区、特区)名称	County (City,District, Special Region)	社会消费品零售总额 Total retail sales of social consumer goods	城镇 Urban	乡村 Rural
南明区	Nanming	2276701	2276701	
云岩区	Yunyan	2552452	2552452	
花溪区	Huaxi	266305	266305	
乌当区	Wudang	664080	664080	
白云区	Baiyun	269958	268003	1955
小河区	Xiaohe	627076	627076	
开阳县	Kaiyang	233090	91281	141809
息烽县	Xifeng	122138	69491	52647
修文县	Xiuwen	142468	59412	83056
清镇市	Qingzhen	255878	189367	66511
钟山区	Zhongshan	1013563	1013563	
六枝特区	Liuzhi	226671	181337	45334
水城县	Shuicheng	106476	53000	53476
盘　县	Panxian	481536	337076	144461
红花岗区	Honghuagang	1263247	1110929	152318
汇川区	Huicuan	690648	627406	63242
遵义县	Zunyi	424949	379273	45676
桐梓县	Tongzi	163778	101902	61876
绥阳县	Suiyang	123998	87846	36152
正安县	Zhengan	124996	68094	56902
※道真县	Daozhen	78847	33696	45151
※务川县	Wuchuan	79023	44104	34919
凤冈县	Fenggang	107950	66648	41302
湄潭县	Meitan	164487	106110	58377
余庆县	Yuqing	103409	69949	33460
习水县	Xishui	155265	129323	25942
赤水市	Chishui	153111	108652	44459
仁怀市	Renhuai	465021	412948	52073
西秀区	Xixiu	383963	318362	65601
平坝县	Pingba	144491	117555	26936
普定县	Puding	109948	79354	30594
※镇宁县	Zhenning	116649	83596	33053
※关岭县	Guanling	129488	97250	32238
※紫云县	Ziyun	90716	66352	24365
七星关区	Qixingguan	645814	455947	189868
大方县	Dafang	154865	112176	42690
黔西县	Qianxi	179518	129735	49783
金沙县	Jinsha	183496	131923	51573
织金县	Zhijin	170626	114844	55782
纳雍县	Nayong	137940	91867	46073
※威宁县	Weining	170487	122768	47719
赫章县	Hezhang	101492	71821	29672
碧江区	Bijiang	281858	233894	47964
万山区	Wanshan	33914	27288	6626

27-49 续表 continued

单位：万元 (10000 yuan)

县(市、区、特区)名 称	County (City,District, Special Region)	社会消费品零售总额 Total retail sales of social consumer goods	城镇 Urban	乡村 Rural
江口县	Jiangkou	51932	40993	10940
※玉屏县	Yuping	56741	44716	12025
石阡县	Shiqian	60204	48346	11859
思南县	Sinan	140057	106122	33935
※印江县	Yinjiang	75183	58340	16843
德江县	Dejiang	97523	73135	24388
※沿河县	Yanhe	105597	78529	27068
※松桃县	Songtao	136023	101175	34848
兴义市	Xingyi	845653	701098	144555
兴仁县	Xingren	110465	100022	10443
普安县	Puan	49089	38644	10445
晴隆县	Qinglong	40444	29714	10730
贞丰县	Zhenfeng	56255	47959	8296
望谟县	Wangmo	27272	20187	7085
册亨县	Ceheng	15697	11841	3856
安龙县	Anlong	73004	65707	7297
凯里市	Kaili	674222	546592	127630
黄平县	Huangping	65711	52691	13020
施秉县	Shibing	48948	39682	9266
三穗县	Sansui	85916	60230	25685
镇远县	Zhenyuan	80161	64723	15438
岑巩县	Cengong	66764	53541	13224
天柱县	Tianzhu	119487	64287	55200
锦屏县	Jinping	64463	51505	12958
剑河县	Jianhe	52498	38224	14274
台江县	Taijiang	36610	29357	7253
黎平县	Liping	123511	99231	24281
榕江县	Rongjiang	78503	52636	25867
从江县	Congjiang	71302	48456	22845
雷山县	Leishan	39965	26302	13663
麻江县	Majiang	45183	36631	8552
丹寨县	Danzhai	35496	28448	7048
都匀市	Duyun	436554	417376	19178
福泉市	Fuquan	143361	117797	25564
荔波县	Libo	67850	55352	12499
贵定县	Guiding	85054	69298	15757
瓮安县	Wengan	104612	85819	18793
独山县	Dushan	98582	80699	17884
平塘县	Pingtang	53221	43548	9673
罗甸县	Luodian	68185	56274	11910
长顺县	Changshun	65458	53423	12035
龙里县	Longli	63747	52298	11448
惠水县	Huishui	96325	79061	17265
※三都县	Sandu	77946	64054	13893

27-50 各县(市、区、特区)金融机构人民币存贷款余额(2012)

Urban and Rural Resident Savings Deposit Balance and Its Order by County(City,District,Special region)

单位：亿元 (100 million yuan)

县(市、区、特区)名称	County (City,District, Special region)	金融机构人民币存款余额 Total Deposits	#储蓄存款 Saving Deposit	金融机构人民币贷款余额 Total Loans
开阳县	Kaiyang	68.74	38.27	62.29
息烽县	Xifeng	47.28	25.93	42.94
修文县	Xiuwen	41.26	25.33	27.22
清镇市	Qingzhen	87.74	54.66	53.82
六枝特区	Liuzhi	83.59	44.18	56.46
盘　县	Panxian	206.06	112.05	132.17
遵义县	Zunyi	159.00	108.69	124.93
桐梓县	Tongzi	73.23	52.07	42.28
绥阳县	Suiyang	55.87	42.00	24.13
正安县	Zhengan	58.71	41.10	20.20
※道真县	Daozhen	47.52	35.39	18.04
※务川县	Wuchuan	48.82	30.65	22.59
凤冈县	Fenggang	47.62	31.30	20.35
湄潭县	Meitan	68.93	50.66	35.67
余庆县	Yuqing	42.83	30.77	27.37
习水县	Xishui	86.28	49.55	27.54
赤水市	Chishui	68.77	48.04	41.37
仁怀市	Renhuai	277.65	95.56	80.20
平坝县	Pingba	71.36	40.26	59.09
普定县	Puding	37.19	20.04	52.96
※镇宁县	Zhenning	43.61	19.28	36.85
※关岭县	Guanling	37.11	21.05	23.80
※紫云县	Ziyun	32.08	15.85	18.06
七星关区	Qixingguan	254.67	116.50	145.32
大方县	Dafang	78.93	51.64	43.07
黔西县	Qianxi	64.46	41.06	62.82
金沙县	Jinsha	80.01	53.15	48.45
织金县	Zhijin	86.71	47.58	46.91
纳雍县	Nayong	61.23	35.10	34.88
※威宁县	Weining	60.36	37.72	33.29
赫章县	Hezhang	49.66	33.10	18.71
碧江区	Bijiang	158.84	80.31	114.75
万山区	Wanshan	15.82	7.17	4.73

27-50 续表 continued

单位：亿元 (100 million yuan)

县(市、区、特区)名称	County (City,District, Special region)	金融机构人民币存款余额 Total Deposits	#储蓄存款 Saving Deposit	金融机构人民币贷款余额 Total Loans
江口县	Jiangkou	33.04	19.71	22.14
※玉屏县	Yuping	25.42	18.54	32.90
石阡县	Shiqian	37.94	25.71	25.11
思南县	Sinan	66.10	45.77	58.01
※印江县	Yinjiang	47.11	31.99	31.78
德江县	Dejiang	38.96	28.48	27.11
※沿河县	Yanhe	49.39	34.12	25.31
※松桃县	Songtao	63.59	40.65	39.51
兴义市	Xingyi	269.18	120.42	192.84
兴仁县	Xingren	51.40	27.83	36.87
普安县	Puan	34.16	19.75	21.34
晴隆县	Qinglong	29.39	16.59	14.35
贞丰县	Zhenfeng	54.47	26.13	23.00
望谟县	Wangmo	35.21	11.42	12.17
册亨县	Ceheng	28.20	11.13	16.80
安龙县	Anlong	55.01	32.80	19.07
凯里市	Kaili	233.72	125.13	175.79
黄平县	Huangping	36.42	24.90	14.18
施秉县	Shibing	19.65	13.99	13.07
三穗县	Sansui	23.88	18.11	12.50
镇远县	Zhenyuan	29.90	22.36	18.19
岑巩县	Cengong	25.83	17.51	15.50
天柱县	Tianzhu	53.29	38.43	19.30
锦屏县	Jinping	34.07	21.82	11.78
剑河县	Jianhe	26.11	18.81	12.58
台江县	Taijiang	17.87	12.14	25.16
黎平县	Liping	52.93	36.50	29.92
榕江县	Rongjiang	34.87	23.73	28.67
从江县	Congjiang	25.14	16.95	15.31
雷山县	Leishan	16.50	11.89	11.66
麻江县	Majiang	25.53	17.06	15.26
丹寨县	Danzhai	26.74	13.42	8.61
都匀市	Duyun	197.43	98.80	114.40
福泉市	Fuquan	56.79	34.32	58.73
荔波县	Libo	28.67	17.59	15.27
贵定县	Guiding	35.78	25.36	16.80
瓮安县	Wengan	63.35	43.28	34.32
独山县	Dushan	44.81	29.16	26.62
平塘县	Pingtang	25.28	16.32	14.54
罗甸县	Luodian	34.68	16.34	20.88
长顺县	Changshun	25.53	13.38	13.95
龙里县	Longli	45.33	24.12	23.95
惠水县	Huishui	39.77	23.36	21.60
※三都县	Sandu	29.67	18.52	19.27

注：资料来源于中国人民银行贵阳中心支行。
Notes:Data in the table are obtained from Guiyang Central Branch of PBC.

27−51　各县(市、区、特区)普通中学(2012)

县(市、区、特区)名　称	County (City,Distric, SpecialRegion)	学校数(所) Total Schools (unit)	#初中 Junior Secondary Shools	毕业生数(人) Graduates(person) 初中 Junior Secondary Shools	高中 Junior Secondary Shools
南明区	Nanming	72	59	8174	2458
云岩区	Yunyan	54	39	10017	4863
花溪区	Huaxi	38	30	4652	1822
乌当区	Wudang	39	30	4785	2357
白云区	Baiyun	12	9	4036	1715
小河区	Xiaohe	16	11	2736	987
开阳县	Kaiyang	23	15	7273	2735
息烽县	Xifeng	14	11	3864	1155
修文县	Xiuwen	17	12	4503	1298
清镇市	Qingzhen	30	23	8874	2409
钟山区	Zhongshan	49	38	11593	6279
六枝特区	Liuzhi	44	39	9638	2331
水城县	Shuicheng	54	51	12692	2032
盘　县	Panxian	74	65	26844	5557
红花岗区	Honghuagang	40	28	9558	4905
汇川区	Huicuan	31	23	6862	2739
遵义县	Zunyi	67	58	21194	7450
桐梓县	Tongzi	47	39	9009	2355
绥阳县	Suiyang	31	25	8304	1676
正安县	Zhengan	40	37	9002	2073
※道真县	Daozhen	22	20	4094	1598
※务川县	Wuchuan	30	27	8541	1446
凤冈县	Fenggang	23	20	8172	2387
湄潭县	Meitan	25	22	7955	2019
余庆县	Yuqing	16	13	4360	2254
习水县	Xishui	42	35	8030	2854
赤水市	Chishui	19	16	3633	1246
仁怀市	Renhuai	38	31	11560	3124
西秀区	Xixiu	49	38	12164	4554
平坝县	Pingba	23	16	4990	1621
普定县	Puding	15	13	5488	1073
※镇宁县	Zhenning	20	19	5233	626
※关岭县	Guanling	22	19	5424	1123
※紫云县	Ziyun	19	18	7544	920
七星关区	Qixingguan	131	114	24054	7759
大方县	Dafang	55	41	15128	4470
黔西县	Qianxi	59	48	11691	4487
金沙县	Jinsha	39	32	7701	3153
织金县	Zhijin	47	40	14687	3939
纳雍县	Nayong	37	31	13267	2163
※威宁县	Weining	64	56	23329	3744
赫章县	Hezhang	53	44	18066	3026
碧江区	Bijiang	23	16	5357	4006
万山区	Wanshan	9	8	2450	253

Statistics on Regular Secondary Schools by County(City,District,Special region)

招生数(人) New Enrollment(person)		在校学生数(人) Students Enrollment(person)		专任教师(人) Full-time Teachers(person)	
初中 Junior Secondary Shools	高中 Junior Secondary Shools	初中 Junior Secondary Shools	高中 Junior Secondary Shools	初中 Junior Secondary Shools	高中 Junior Secondary Shools
8427	2970	25105	8455	1657	553
11709	5136	32769	15142	2152	1111
5198	2871	15109	7654	1011	449
6575	3126	18152	8479	1305	622
4669	2614	13551	7192	746	513
3503	1531	9834	4614	516	287
5852	4189	19461	10097	1073	488
3419	1998	10597	4617	578	256
3570	1833	11548	4908	682	319
8212	4001	25537	10106	1401	654
14495	9027	38938	24215	1641	1098
10379	3903	33974	9555	1520	378
14134	3995	42910	9234	2073	268
23315	10547	74553	24850	3785	1111
9670	6008	29311	16238	1762	879
7357	4094	21761	10084	1248	615
18940	12406	60191	30588	3357	1295
10125	4638	30854	10893	1883	386
8239	3008	24898	6683	1513	398
9049	3094	27365	8046	1684	483
5622	2449	15712	6555	845	345
8380	4293	26102	9052	1467	461
8020	3948	24669	9606	1302	500
8850	3641	26365	8686	1377	445
4773	2657	14925	7032	717	360
9649	3619	27159	10275	1811	660
3250	1795	10181	4476	669	266
12961	5477	38067	12420	2049	740
14058	7606	41775	18402	2274	997
5398	2438	15972	5529	877	323
6760	2004	17723	4400	1086	237
4797	1218	12084	2626	869	118
5082	2001	14392	4109	854	246
5257	1502	19563	3223	894	156
33441	12421	92166	29489	3777	1393
19264	7857	52501	18055	2922	867
16111	6046	44130	14923	2509	738
11216	4005	29724	10109	1430	632
21086	7244	53652	16522	2588	1044
18459	5983	45480	13242	2256	747
41643	10101	99462	20505	3491	864
17825	7221	49109	14292	2399	540
6444	6436	17617	16692	908	852
2300	413	6737	878	371	80

27−51 续表

县(市、区、特区)名 称	County (City,Distric, SpecialRegion)	学校数(所) Total Schools (unit)	#初中 Junior Secondary Shools	毕业生数(人) Graduates(person) 初中 Junior Secondary Shools	高中 Junior Secondary Shools
江口县	Jiangkou	17	14	3378	1413
※玉屏县	Yuping	11	8	1769	760
石阡县	Shiqian	26	23	6367	2356
思南县	Sinan	41	35	12938	4232
※印江县	Yinjiang	24	18	6009	2320
德江县	Dejiang	30	26	9297	2041
※沿河县	Yanhe	34	30	11764	1953
※松桃县	Songtao	41	35	12309	2874
兴义市	Xingyi	79	57	13736	8691
兴仁县	Xingren	33	28	9128	1672
普安县	Puan	27	25	5468	1124
晴隆县	Qinglong	24	22	4703	1402
贞丰县	Zhenfeng	20	18	7036	1080
望谟县	Wangmo	19	17	4226	761
册亨县	Ceheng	18	16	4547	369
安龙县	Anlong	29	25	7123	1572
凯里市	Kaili	37	25	7375	4204
黄平县	Huangping	15	13	4315	1397
施秉县	Shibing	11	9	2073	616
三穗县	Sansui	13	10	2498	738
镇远县	Zhenyuan	19	17	3104	1108
岑巩县	Cengong	15	12	3519	886
天柱县	Tianzhu	23	20	4466	2322
锦屏县	Jinping	18	16	3478	1516
剑河县	Jianhe	14	12	2992	1137
台江县	Taijiang	9	8	2251	650
黎平县	Liping	28	24	7569	2212
榕江县	Rongjiang	23	20	5709	912
从江县	Congjiang	21	20	6937	822
雷山县	Leishan	8	7	2208	559
麻江县	Majiang	11	8	2429	1032
丹寨县	Danzhai	9	8	1720	627
都匀市	Duyun	31	21	6312	3613
福泉市	Fuquan	19	16	5385	1498
荔波县	Libo	9	8	3084	921
贵定县	Guiding	16	14	4447	828
瓮安县	Wengan	28	23	6980	2982
独山县	Dushan	16	14	6220	1341
平塘县	Pingtang	18	17	5489	987
罗甸县	Luodian	22	20	5588	1289
长顺县	Changshun	20	19	4729	762
龙里县	Longli	15	14	3055	739
惠水县	Huishui	27	25	8212	1730
※三都县	Sandu	21	19	4805	772

continued

招生数(人) New Enrollment(person)		在校学生数(人) Students Enrollment(person)		专任教师(人) Full-time Teachers(person)	
初中 Junior Secondary Shools	高中 Junior Secondary Shools	初中 Junior Secondary Shools	高中 Junior Secondary Shools	初中 Junior Secondary Shools	高中 Junior Secondary Shools
3523	1945	10073	4694	713	291
2026	1198	5857	3108	420	213
7335	2835	20257	7717	1195	443
13575	6916	40446	17312	1827	874
6690	3538	19822	8690	1134	470
10537	4052	29207	9425	1752	554
10963	3220	34903	7643	1923	364
11068	4111	31840	10599	2189	601
15764	9382	45630	25210	2748	1531
9651	2749	25044	5936	1524	422
6296	2104	16589	4182	985	219
4925	2094	14614	4798	764	233
5897	1942	18984	4027	938	237
5514	1779	14456	4127	863	203
4309	1044	12421	2559	745	131
7877	3672	23107	7355	1215	449
9391	5824	25921	16018	1441	922
5619	2616	16422	6247	811	330
2786	1092	7711	2615	459	164
2891	1625	7785	3439	532	214
3854	1771	10523	4127	605	234
3916	1919	11128	3911	585	245
4767	3089	14078	8113	1075	443
2997	2111	9926	5500	658	318
3861	1607	10255	3500	620	175
2428	1363	6779	2877	424	164
8191	3487	22565	8213	1265	439
5301	2337	14862	4905	927	302
4958	1462	15318	3037	904	152
2489	1239	7308	2901	434	179
3145	1470	9773	3842	675	244
2546	1040	7010	2590	417	156
6271	4173	18734	11584	1125	585
4251	2145	14190	5603	971	264
2748	1829	8670	4420	487	238
4259	1276	11802	3216	758	224
6206	3920	20055	10937	1083	519
4633	2742	16166	6702	988	443
4703	1342	14024	3742	909	182
4513	2862	14211	5880	946	373
4186	1903	12300	4225	647	221
3294	1580	9156	3393	581	167
8026	2269	22748	6127	1200	335
6268	2150	16495	5178	962	331

27-52 各县(市、区、特区)小学(2012)

Statistics on Primary Schools by County(City,District,Special region)

县(市、区、特区)名称	County (City,Distric, Special Region)	学校数(个) Schools (unit)	毕业生数(人) Gruaduates (person)	招生数(人) New Enrollment (person)	在校学生数(人) Students Enrollment (person)	专任教师(人) Full-time Teachers (person)	学龄儿童入学率(%) Enrollment Ratio of Primary Schools(%)	学龄女童入学率(%) Enrollment Ratio of School Girls(%)
南明区	Nanming	82	11237	10151	59643	2782	175.5	175.6
云岩区	Yunyan	80	11938	12062	65703	3158	206.0	193.7
花溪区	Huaxi	81	4934	4195	24580	1552	127.3	127.2
乌当区	Wudang	76	5464	6803	35823	1972	139.9	139.3
白云区	Baiyun	53	4207	3850	24384	1242	196.1	194.4
小河区	Xiaohe	28	3701	3884	22081	891	164.6	157.4
开阳县	Kaiyang	70	5904	3561	23061	1482	99.9	99.8
息烽县	Xifeng	46	3394	2786	15992	1077	99.1	99.4
修文县	Xiuwen	42	3361	2933	16222	1127	97.3	99.2
清镇市	Qingzhen	113	7748	6140	34830	2008	114.4	117.4
钟山区	Zhongshan	94	13628	11234	73870	2838	115.4	114.6
六枝特区	Liuzhi	160	14924	8019	59474	2825	99.2	99.5
水城县	Shuicheng	212	19645	10662	74662	3798	95.9	100.1
盘　县	Panxian	287	23243	10621	79888	4488	99.3	98.3
红花岗区	Honghuagang	76	9959	8702	52188	2189	133.6	130.9
汇川区	Huicuan	78	6712	5928	35138	1658	132.9	135.6
遵义县	Zunyi	316	18297	12355	75133	5382	88.4	91.4
桐梓县	Tongzi	186	9773	8346	51870	2678	81.8	81.6
绥阳县	Suiyang	154	8446	5224	37133	2163	80.8	83.2
正安县	Zhengan	149	8465	6232	38594	2585	72.2	73.0
※道真县	Daozhen	82	5313	4138	26406	1489	83.8	85.4
※务川县	Wuchuan	136	7994	4932	37949	2076	76.8	79.2
凤冈县	Fenggang	108	7650	4401	31938	1731	94.7	96.0
湄潭县	Meitan	102	8383	5051	34959	2088	88.2	90.0
余庆县	Yuqing	102	4439	3874	23873	1188	83.3	84.5
习水县	Xishui	217	9491	8802	53751	2722	86.1	88.3
赤水市	Chishui	57	3223	3269	18698	1372	76.3	77.5
仁怀市	Renhuai	105	13333	7911	58138	3167	99.3	99.3
西秀区	Xixiu	231	14636	12157	75845	4298	114.8	115.4
平坝县	Pingba	147	6009	5532	32728	1743	102.4	106.2
普定县	Puding	164	7927	6712	39988	2198	98.2	97.9
※镇宁县	Zhenning	107	6718	5572	31564	1794	92.3	95.1
※关岭县	Guanling	119	5699	4896	31250	1612	97.4	97.5
※紫云县	Ziyun	136	5724	5116	32109	1839	95.1	90.3
七星关区	Qixingguan	370	31030	28470	170711	6889	101.8	100.5
大方县	Dafang	342	19751	16107	105731	5065	93.5	93.4
黔西县	Qianxi	269	16167	10178	74642	4306	105.5	108.3
金沙县	Jinsha	189	11377	10694	61727	2872	88.5	87.0
织金县	Zhijin	321	22024	16948	112393	4578	89.8	92.4
纳雍县	Nayong	241	20325	17572	110587	4092	99.1	99.0
※威宁县	Weining	428	44261	30092	221311	9352	102.0	103.0
赫章县	Hezhang	293	20027	14566	101639	4764	95.9	95.8
碧江区	Bijiang	89	5548	4878	28837	1573	117.4	118.0
万山区	Wanshan	66	2263	1854	10788	706	93.8	94.8

27-52 续表 continued

县(市、区、特区)名 称	County (City,Distric, Special Region)	学校数(个) Schools (unit)	毕业生数(人) Gruaduates (person)	招生数(人) New Enrollment (person)	在校学生数(人) Students Enrollment (person)	专任教师(人) Full-time Teachers (person)	学龄儿童入学率(%) Enrollment Ratio of Primary Schools(%)	学龄女童入学率(%) Enrollment Ratio of School Girls(%)
江口县	Jiangkou	97	3597	3181	17519	1023	86.2	87.7
※玉屏县	Yuping	44	1990	2006	11384	716	86.2	88.2
石阡县	Shiqian	105	7356	5503	36330	2236	97.9	100.1
思南县	Sinan	201	13881	9124	61239	3427	93.8	94.6
※印江县	Yinjiang	126	6929	5693	38132	2239	98.8	98.2
德江县	Dejiang	198	11867	8660	56650	2795	95.1	96.3
※沿河县	Yanhe	224	13298	11452	80842	3772	98.4	103.0
※松桃县	Songtao	303	12488	9477	60327	4161	98.0	97.4
兴义市	Xingyi	240	13811	13385	76871	4138	103.7	102.3
兴仁县	Xingren	164	9885	9842	58522	2777	99.6	99.7
普安县	Puan	105	6291	6843	35611	1798	85.1	86.9
晴隆县	Qinglong	94	5782	5767	35104	1553	99.1	98.9
贞丰县	Zhenfeng	139	9284	6606	48284	2307	99.3	99.3
望谟县	Wangmo	121	6104	5019	37965	2119	98.6	98.4
册亨县	Ceheng	66	4459	3207	21950	1142	92.0	92.2
安龙县	Anlong	147	8231	6510	37056	2096	89.8	92.0
凯里市	Kaili	71	8852	7729	49472	2110	111.6	112.1
黄平县	Huangping	78	5629	4393	31889	1506	99.8	99.6
施秉县	Shibing	58	2801	2277	14563	893	103.8	103.3
三穗县	Sansui	39	2898	2555	15996	864	89.5	91.6
镇远县	Zhenyuan	48	3883	3056	21092	1200	98.5	96.9
岑巩县	Cengong	80	3858	2763	19243	1128	80.9	80.0
天柱县	Tianzhu	62	4680	4097	22114	1642	91.4	96.8
锦屏县	Jinping	112	2983	2356	14244	897	92.2	93.3
剑河县	Jianhe	71	3988	3273	20719	1135	99.1	99.0
台江县	Taijiang	36	2447	2274	14243	896	99.1	99.2
黎平县	Liping	204	8292	5569	34617	2235	99.8	99.5
榕江县	Rongjiang	101	5652	4645	30402	1573	94.3	94.1
从江县	Congjiang	117	5407	4250	29646	1609	97.6	96.9
雷山县	Leishan	58	2451	1856	12157	842	84.3	84.0
麻江县	Majiang	59	3281	2400	15695	1097	98.4	96.1
丹寨县	Danzhai	37	2539	2298	14377	893	89.5	90.8
都匀市	Duyun	94	6224	4297	29467	1993	99.6	100.4
福泉市	Fuquan	94	4453	3248	19368	1426	96.0	94.8
荔波县	Libo	67	2719	1889	13190	829	95.7	97.6
贵定县	Guiding	88	4754	3408	20939	1431	99.5	99.5
瓮安县	Wengan	106	6122	5091	30451	1807	91.3	92.3
独山县	Dushan	72	4559	3213	18475	1525	96.3	100.4
平塘县	Pingtang	112	4639	3848	25814	1268	89.4	91.6
罗甸县	Luodian	89	4755	4433	31417	1487	96.1	97.3
长顺县	Changshun	80	4179	2638	19786	1163	86.9	79.9
龙里县	Longli	75	3391	2624	16078	1085	99.7	98.0
惠水县	Huishui	132	8661	5400	38374	1958	97.5	92.9
※三都县	Sandu	111	6532	5459	35358	1783	99.4	94.9

28

Twenty-eight

全国各省（区、市）资料

Main Statistics of Provinces (autonomous regions, municipalities) in the Whole Country

28-1 全国及各省(区、市)人口、生产总值(2012)

单位：亿元

地区	Region	年末总人口(万人) Total Population (year-end) (10000 persons)	位次 Order	地区生产总值 Gross Domestic Product	位次 Order	第一产业 Primary Industry	位次 Order
全　国	**National Total**	**135404**		**519322**		**52377**	
北　京	Beijing	2069	26	17879.40	13	150.20	29
天　津	Tianjin	1413	27	12893.88	20	171.60	28
河　北	Hebei	7288	6	26575.01	6	3186.66	5
山　西	Shanxi	3611	18	12112.83	21	698.32	25
内蒙古	Inner Mongolia	2490	23	15880.58	15	1448.58	17
辽　宁	Liaoning	4389	14	24846.43	7	2155.82	11
吉　林	Jilin	2750	21	11939.24	22	1412.11	18
黑龙江	Heilongjiang	3834	15	13691.58	17	2113.66	12
上　海	Shanghai	2380	24	20181.72	11	127.80	30
江　苏	Jiangsu	7920	5	54058.22	2	3418.29	3
浙　江	Zhejiang	5477	10	34665.33	4	1667.88	14
安　徽	Anhui	5988	8	17212.05	14	2178.73	9
福　建	Fujian	3748	17	19701.78	12	1776.71	13
江　西	Jiangxi	4504	13	12948.88	19	1520.23	16
山　东	Shandong	9685	2	50013.24	3	4281.70	1
河　南	Henan	9406	3	29599.31	5	3769.54	2
湖　北	Hubei	5779	9	22250.45	9	2848.77	7
湖　南	Hunan	6639	7	22154.23	10	3004.21	6
广　东	Guangdong	10594	1	57067.92	1	2847.26	8
广　西	Guangxi	4682	11	13035.10	18	2172.37	10
海　南	Hainan	887	28	2855.54	28	711.54	24
重　庆	Chongqing	2945	20	11409.60	23	940.01	21
四　川	Sichuan	8076	4	23872.80	8	3297.21	4
贵　州	**Guizhou**	**3484**	**19**	**6852.20**	**26**	**891.91**	**22**
云　南	Yunnan	4659	12	10309.47	24	1654.55	15
西　藏	Tibet	308	31	701.03	31	80.38	31
陕　西	Shanxi	3753	16	14453.68	16	1370.16	19
甘　肃	Gansu	2578	22	5650.20	27	780.50	23
青　海	Qinghai	573	30	1893.54	30	176.91	27
宁　夏	Ningxia	647	29	2341.29	29	199.40	26
新　疆	Xinjiang	2233	25	7505.31	25	1320.57	20

注：本表数据为最终核实数。

The Population and GDP of the Whole Country and All Provinces

(100 million yuan)

第二产业 Secondary Industry	位次 Order	第三产业 Tertiary Industry	位次 Order	地区生产总值比上年增长(%) Increase Rate of GDP in 2012 over 2011(%)	位次 Order	人均生产总值(元) Per Capita Gross Domestic Product(yuan)	位次 Order
235319		**231626**		**7.8**		**38449**	
4059.27	24	13669.93	5	7.7	30	87475	2
6663.82	18	6058.46	14	13.8	1	93173	1
14003.57	6	9384.78	8	9.6	25	36584	15
6731.56	17	4682.95	19	10.1	20	33628	19
8801.50	13	5630.50	15	11.5	13	63886	5
13230.49	7	9460.12	7	9.5	26	56649	7
6376.77	19	4150.36	24	12.0	10	43415	11
6037.61	21	5540.31	17	10.0	23	35711	17
7854.77	15	12199.15	6	7.5	31	85373	3
27121.95	2	23517.98	2	10.1	20	68347	4
17316.32	4	15681.13	4	8.0	29	63374	6
9404.84	12	5628.48	16	12.1	9	28792	26
10187.94	11	7737.13	13	11.4	15	52763	9
6942.59	16	4486.06	22	11.0	19	28800	25
25735.73	3	19995.81	3	9.8	24	51768	10
16672.20	5	9157.57	9	10.1	20	31499	23
11193.10	9	8208.58	12	11.3	16	38572	13
10506.42	10	8643.60	10	11.3	16	33480	20
27700.97	1	26519.69	1	8.2	28	54095	8
6247.43	20	4615.30	20	11.3	16	27952	27
804.47	30	1339.53	28	9.1	27	32377	22
5975.18	22	4494.41	21	13.6	2	38914	12
12333.28	8	8242.31	11	12.6	6	29608	24
2677.54	**26**	**3282.75**	**25**	**13.6**	**2**	**19710**	**31**
4419.20	23	4235.72	23	13.0	4	22195	29
242.85	31	377.80	31	11.8	12	22936	28
8073.87	14	5009.65	18	12.9	5	38564	14
2600.09	27	2269.61	27	12.6	6	21978	30
1092.34	29	624.29	30	12.3	8	33181	21
1159.37	28	982.52	29	11.5	13	36394	16
3481.56	25	2703.18	26	12.0	10	33796	18

Note:Data in this table is the final verification number.

28–2 全国及各省(区、市)固定资产投资(不含农户)、房地产开发情况(2012)

地 区	Region	固定资产投资额(亿元) Investment in Fixed Assets(100 million yuan)	位 次 Order	房地产投资(亿元) Real Estate Investment (100 million yuan)	位 次 Order
全国总计	**National Total**	**364835.07**		**71803.79**	
北 京	Beijing	6064.15	23	3153.44	7
天 津	Tianjin	7913.26	21	1260.00	23
河 北	Hebei	19104.63	5	3086.52	9
山 西	Shanxi	8584.85	20	1010.45	24
内蒙古	Inner Mongolia	11732.22	13	1291.44	22
辽 宁	Liaoning	21535.37	3	5455.82	2
吉 林	Jilin	9462.09	16	1310.03	21
黑龙江	Heilongjiang	9376.10	17	1535.84	19
上 海	Shanghai	5114.64	26	2381.36	14
江 苏	Jiangsu	30427.25	1	6206.10	1
浙 江	Zhejiang	17000.96	7	5226.27	4
安 徽	Anhui	14902.31	10	3151.61	8
福 建	Fujian	12165.64	12	2824.12	11
江 西	Jiangxi	11388.92	15	969.62	25
山 东	Shandong	30319.76	2	4708.31	5
河 南	Henan	20870.16	4	3035.29	10
湖 北	Hubei	15162.21	9	2539.46	12
湖 南	Hunan	13966.26	11	2210.52	15
广 东	Guangdong	18248.04	6	5352.79	3
广 西	Guangxi	9345.18	18	1554.94	18
海 南	Hainan	2045.38	28	886.64	26
重 庆	Chongqing	8606.46	19	2508.35	13
四 川	Sichuan	16526.89	8	3266.40	6
贵 州	**Guizhou**	**5304.93**	**25**	**1467.60**	**20**
云 南	Yunnan	7553.51	22	1782.14	17
西 藏	Tibet	670.52	31	6.87	31
陕 西	Shanxi	11705.83	14	1835.93	16
甘 肃	Gansu	5040.53	27	561.02	28
青 海	Qinghai	1773.67	30	189.68	30
宁 夏	Ningxia	2033.03	29	429.15	29
新 疆	Xinjiang	5857.58	24	606.09	27

注：本表统计口径为计划总投资500万元及以上固定资产项目投资，房地产开发投资，分省数据不含跨省项目。

The Investment in Fixed Assets(Excluding Farmer) and Real Estate Development of the Whole Country and All Province

房屋施工面积 (万平方米) Floor Space under Construction(10000 aq.m)	位 次 Order	房屋竣工面积 (万平方米) Floor Space Completed (10000 aq.m)	位 次 Order	商品房销售面积 (万平方米) Floor Space of Commercial Houses(10000 aq.m)	位 次 Order
573417.52		**99424.96**		**111303.65**	
13122.49	21	2390.86	16	1943.74	22
9864.22	24	2542.75	14	1661.69	24
27577.83	8	4894.56	7	5144.92	8
11714.28	22	1732.99	24	1497.88	25
16507.40	14	2449.13	15	2523.52	18
38502.02	4	6438.15	3	8827.95	2
10935.80	23	1927.87	20	2452.42	19
13484.97	18	3245.73	13	3806.82	13
13249.97	19	2305.06	18	1898.46	23
45097.54	1	9848.40	1	9019.18	1
33422.97	5	4292.94	9	4005.29	12
24836.06	9	3965.39	11	4828.81	9
21121.50	12	2232.78	19	3258.94	14
9465.63	25	1747.48	22	2397.10	20
42958.91	2	7324.97	2	8632.76	3
29559.36	7	5870.54	5	5968.49	6
16819.71	13	3273.71	12	4037.85	11
21356.89	11	4457.97	8	5150.48	7
39296.27	3	6356.12	4	7898.99	4
15018.46	16	2333.58	17	2759.26	16
5109.49	28	856.41	28	931.84	28
22009.03	10	3990.63	10	4522.40	10
29865.50	6	5866.58	6	6455.93	5
13245.31	**20**	**1416.77**	**26**	**2186.95**	**21**
14362.00	17	1851.57	21	3237.75	15
47.33	31	9.23	31	22.50	31
15410.57	15	1653.94	25	2755.59	17
5634.95	27	844.50	29	978.44	27
1891.23	30	416.20	30	262.96	30
5033.26	29	1151.97	27	804.43	29
6896.55	26	1736.17	23	1430.31	26

Note:Data in the table refer to those projects planned to invest 500,0000 yuan at least in investment in fixed assets and real estate development, but provincial data don't include inter-provincial project.

28–3 全国及各省(区、市)进出口总额(2012)

Imports and Exports of the Whole Country and All Provinces

单位：亿美元 (USD 100 million)

地 区	Region	进出口总额 Total Exports and Imports	位 次 Order	#出口额 Exports	位 次 Order	#进口额 Imports	位 次 Order
全国总计	**National Total**	**38667.60**		**20489.35**		**18178.26**	
北 京	Beijing	4079.16	4	596.50	7	3482.66	2
天 津	Tianjin	1156.23	8	483.14	9	673.09	7
河 北	Hebei	505.48	13	296.04	13	209.44	12
山 西	Shanxi	150.43	23	70.16	23	80.27	23
内蒙古	Inner Mongolia	112.60	26	39.70	26	72.90	24
辽 宁	Liaoning	1039.91	9	579.50	8	460.41	9
吉 林	Jilin	245.72	20	59.83	24	185.89	14
黑龙江	Heilongjiang	378.21	15	144.36	19	233.85	10
上 海	Shanghai	4365.40	3	2067.44	4	2297.96	3
江 苏	Jiangsu	5480.93	2	3285.38	2	2195.55	4
浙 江	Zhejiang	3122.35	5	2245.69	3	876.66	6
安 徽	Anhui	393.25	14	267.52	14	125.73	17
福 建	Fujian	1559.27	7	978.36	6	580.91	8
江 西	Jiangxi	334.09	16	251.11	15	82.98	22
山 东	Shandong	2455.45	6	1287.32	5	1168.13	5
河 南	Henan	517.50	12	296.78	12	220.72	11
湖 北	Hubei	319.59	17	194.01	16	125.58	18
湖 南	Hunan	219.41	21	126.00	20	93.41	21
广 东	Guangdong	9838.15	1	5741.36	1	4096.79	1
广 西	Guangxi	294.74	18	154.69	18	140.05	16
海 南	Hainan	143.30	25	31.43	29	111.87	19
重 庆	Chongqing	532.04	11	385.71	10	146.33	15
四 川	Sichuan	591.28	10	384.64	11	206.64	13
贵 州	**Guizhou**	**66.32**	**28**	**49.52**	**25**	**16.79**	**28**
云 南	Yunnan	210.05	22	100.18	21	109.87	20
西 藏	Tibet	34.24	29	33.55	28	0.69	31
陕 西	Shanxi	147.99	24	86.52	22	61.47	25
甘 肃	Gansu	89.04	27	35.73	27	53.31	27
青 海	Qinghai	11.60	31	7.30	31	4.30	30
宁 夏	Ningxia	22.17	30	16.41	30	5.76	29
新 疆	Xinjiang	251.71	19	193.47	17	58.24	26

注：表中数据按经营单位所在地分。

Note:Data in the table are estimated according to the enterprise's location of business activitity.

28-4　全国及各省(区、市)主要农产品产量(2012)

The Output of Main Agricultural Products of the Whole Country and All Provinces

单位：万吨　　(10000 tons)

地　区	Region	粮食产量 Output of Grain	位 次 Order	油料产量 Oil-bearing Crops	位 次 Order	肉类产量 Output of Pork, Beef and Mutton	位 次 Order	蔬菜产量 Vegetables Products	位 次 Order
全国	**National**	**58957.97**		**3436.77**		**8387.24**		**70883.06**	
北　京	Beijing	113.77	29	1.34	30	43.19	27	279.90	29
天　津	Tianjin	161.76	27	0.56	31	45.80	26	447.70	27
河　北	Hebei	3246.60	8	142.83	9	442.91	6	7695.13	2
山　西	Shanxi	1274.10	17	19.57	25	77.40	25	1073.34	22
内蒙古	Inner Mongolia	2528.50	10	145.08	8	245.75	15	1476.29	17
辽　宁	Liaoning	2070.50	13	120.87	10	418.70	7	2977.60	9
吉　林	Jilin	3343.00	5	80.72	14	259.96	14	957.54	23
黑龙江	Heilongjiang	5761.49	1	22.52	24	216.20	16	866.41	24
上　海	Shanghai	122.39	28	1.73	29	25.80	30	406.93	28
江　苏	Jiangsu	3372.48	4	146.95	7	396.52	11	4984.60	4
浙　江	Zhejiang	769.80	23	38.30	21	180.79	20	1819.81	12
安　徽	Anhui	3289.10	7	227.69	5	397.74	10	2327.50	11
福　建	Fujian	659.30	24	28.07	23	200.85	18	1673.93	13
江　西	Jiangxi	2084.80	12	117.08	11	311.10	13	1213.11	21
山　东	Shandong	4511.40	3	350.95	2	764.16	1	9386.01	1
河　南	Henan	5638.60	2	569.51	1	677.35	2	7011.68	3
湖　北	Hubei	2441.81	11	319.66	3	412.27	8	3506.38	6
湖　南	Hunan	3006.50	9	207.82	6	515.27	4	3480.91	7
广　东	Guangdong	1396.33	16	96.61	12	443.21	5	2982.71	8
广　西	Guangxi	1484.90	15	54.49	19	411.03	9	2356.72	10
海　南	Hainan	199.50	26	10.36	27	79.53	24	499.00	25
重　庆	Chongqing	1138.54	20	50.11	20	201.21	17	1509.34	16
四　川	Sichuan	3315.00	6	287.76	4	670.23	3	3764.72	5
贵　州	**Guizhou**	**1079.50**	**22**	**87.38**	**13**	**190.27**	**19**	**1375.63**	**20**
云　南	Yunnan	1749.10	14	62.84	16	348.68	12	1472.66	18
西　藏	Tibet	94.89	31	6.33	28	25.19	31	65.59	31
陕　西	Shanxi	1245.10	19	60.33	17	107.09	22	1525.62	15
甘　肃	Gansu	1109.70	21	67.00	15	87.81	23	1460.42	19
青　海	Qinghai	101.50	30	35.22	22	30.47	28	158.75	30
宁　夏	Ningxia	375.00	25	18.03	26	26.53	29	471.11	26
新　疆	Xinjiang	1273.00	18	59.04	18	134.23	21	1656.02	14

28-5 全国及各省(区、市)主要工业产品产量(2012)
The Output of Main Industrial Products of the Whole Country and All Provinces

地 区	Region	发电量 (亿千瓦时) Electricity (100 million kwh)	成品钢材 (万吨) Products Steel (10000 tons)	水 泥 (万吨) Cement (10000 tons)	农用化肥 (万吨) Chemical Fertilizers (10000 tons)	家用电冰箱 (万台) Refrigerator (10000 sets)	十种有色金属 (万吨) Ten Kinds of Nonferrous Metals (10000 tons)	电解铝 (万吨) Electrolyzed Aluminum (ton)	铁合金 (吨) Ferroalloy (ton)
全国总计	**National Total**	**48187.5**	**95186.1**	**218405.3**	**7432.4**	**8427.0**	**3691.2**	**1988.3**	**3129.3**
北 京	Beijing	290.8	253.8	874.5		80.4			1.1
天 津	Tianjin	589.7	5708.6	784.3	11.8	51.4	1.0		0.5
河 北	Hebei	2370.9	20995.2	12809.8	186.6		17.1	1.9	24.5
山 西	Shanxi	2454.8	3797.6	4720.4	389.1		138.7	105.6	187.3
内蒙古	Inner Mongolia	3116.9	1661.8	5872.1	123.0		243.9	179.4	358.7
辽 宁	Liaoning	1414.7	5916.1	5709.9	82.2	101.5	71.3	26.3	92.1
吉 林	Jilin	684.4	1229.5	4158.0	64.7		3.5	2.6	49.5
黑龙江	Heilongjiang	843.1	610.2	3872.9	71.6				
上 海	Shanghai	886.2	2340.8	794.7	2.6	151.6	9.2		
江 苏	Jiangsu	3928.4	10989.2	16775.5	270.6	1103.2	57.7	11.3	110.6
浙 江	Zhejiang	2710.0	3361.3	11539.6	27.8	887.2	48.2	15.3	17.7
安 徽	Anhui	1767.5	2765.4	10869.8	309.8	2589.1	140.5		6.3
福 建	Fujian	1622.6	2034.4	7197.6	48.1		33.3	15.0	39.7
江 西	Jiangxi	664.7	2368.9	7420.9	93.7	107.0	145.3		1.3
山 东	Shandong	3195.2	7817.9	15386.0	1304.6	575.0	281.1	196.9	105.3
河 南	Henan	2626.9	3481.4	14805.1	435.5	455.9	568.7	368.8	119.5
湖 北	Hubei	2174.1	3558.4	10255.5	1164.3	202.4	96.9	28.6	37.6
湖 南	Hunan	1260.1	1847.5	10445.4	211.2	17.2	276.2	33.6	305.4
广 东	Guangdong	3593.2	2993.0	11384.3	48.6	1655.0	26.0		0.1
广 西	Guangxi	1133.0	2142.4	9864.1	127.8		121.9	65.6	384.6
海 南	Hainan	192.0	20.9	1672.4	60.0				
重 庆	Chongqing	536.5	1150.2	5499.6	206.6	191.2	30.6	26.8	43.1
四 川	Sichuan	2002.4	2281.6	13342.1	425.3	68.8	81.3	62.1	206.9
贵 州	**Guizhou**	**1548.4**	**560.2**	**6100.5**	**503.8**	**159.0**	**110.6**	**104.3**	**309.7**
云 南	Yunnan	1533.9	1600.0	7793.7	345.4		286.5	89.5	163.1
西 藏	Tibet	19.6		286.7					
陕 西	Shanxi	1330.5	1283.6	7552.7	97.9	31.1	124.3	29.9	51.4
甘 肃	Gansu	1083.2	883.0	3615.1	79.2		294.1	176.0	127.8
青 海	Qinghai	556.3	139.5	1371.0	357.0		215.8	203.2	171.8
宁 夏	Ningxia	1005.9	109.1	1605.3	88.0		164.3	152.4	198.1
新 疆	Xinjiang	1051.6	1284.6	4025.8	295.6		103.2	93.2	15.6

28-5 续表　continued

地　区	Region	轮胎外胎（万条） Tires (10000 tires)	磷肥（万吨） Phosphate Fertilizers (10000 tons)	磷矿石（万吨） Phosphorite Mineral (10000 tons)	卷　烟（亿支） Cigarettes (100 million pieces)	白　酒（万千升） Liquor (10000 kiloliter)	中成药（万吨） Traditional Chinese Medicine (10000 tons)
全 国	**National Total**	**89166.8**	**1955.7**	**9529.6**	**25160.9**	**1153.1**	**293.8**
北　京	Beijing	427.6			198.6	24.1	3.7
天　津	Tianjin	3790.7			239.0	2.8	0.4
河　北	Hebei	54.2	5.9	32.9	827.5	29.1	4.9
山　西	Shanxi	170.3	9.8		156.0	13.1	1.4
内蒙古	Inner Mongolia		18.9		315.0	54.0	1.0
辽　宁	Liaoning	1767.1	0.1		276.4	80.6	3.1
吉　林	Jilin	387.9	11.9		465.0	53.5	48.9
黑龙江	Heilongjiang	424.1			437.0	38.0	14.0
上　海	Shanghai	1004.4	0.6		916.9	0.6	0.7
江　苏	Jiangsu	10725.8	20.3	10.7	1006.2	91.4	1.6
浙　江	Zhejiang	10207.5	0.8		901.1	2.2	2.0
安　徽	Anhui	2517.4	63.8	46.1	1286.1	40.8	3.3
福　建	Fujian	3479.3	1.4	3.9	921.2	3.5	2.0
江　西	Jiangxi	385.5	28.6		599.0	15.7	10.6
山　东	Shandong	38123.6	361.8		1383.1	124.4	15.1
河　南	Henan	2419.1	21.2	0.2	1691.0	99.9	16.5
湖　北	Hubei	710.4	600.2	3515.9	1367.4	72.1	55.0
湖　南	Hunan	75.9	29.8	8.4	1837.7	19.9	14.7
广　东	Guangdong	5676.0	39.6		1370.9	11.0	19.1
广　西	Guangxi	54.6	30.8		753.5	6.8	19.6
海　南	Hainan				105.0		0.1
重　庆	Chongqing	3880.9	65.6	32.7	551.0	18.2	7.7
四　川	Sichuan	1922.9	92.4	1185.3	978.9	295.2	34.8
贵　州	**Guizhou**	**622.8**	**263.9**	**2282.0**	**1246.7**	**26.8**	**5.7**
云　南	Yunnan		229.2	2410.1	3841.2	6.5	3.2
西　藏	Tibet						0.1
陕　西	Shanxi	70.3	23.9	1.4	879.5	9.3	3.2
甘　肃	Gansu		21.4		440.0	3.7	0.9
青　海	Qinghai					1.9	0.2
宁　夏	Ningxia	141.9	11.3			1.7	
新　疆	Xinjiang	126.6	2.5		170.0	6.3	0.3

注：本表统计口径为年主营业务收入2000万元及以上工业企业。
Note:Data in the table refer to the revenue from principal business of 20 million yuan and above of industry enterprises.

28–6 全国及各省(区、市)贸易和旅游(2012)

The Trade and Tourism of the Whole Country and All Provinces

地　区	Region	社会消费品零售总额(亿元) Total Retail Sales of Consumer Goods (100 million yuan)	位 次 Order	国际旅游外汇收入(亿美元) Foreign Exchange Earnings (USD 100 million)	位 次 Order	入境旅游人数(万人次) Number of International Tourists Received (10000 person-times)	位 次 Order	#接 待外国人 Foreigners	位 次 Order
全国总计	**National Total**	**210306.98**		**500.30**		**13240.50**		**2719.20**	
北　京	Beijing	7702.82	11	51.49	5	500.86	5	434.40	5
天　津	Tianjin	3921.43	23	22.26	9	73.75	25	63.71	23
河　北	Hebei	9254.03	9	5.45	23	129.32	22	106.71	20
山　西	Shanxi	4506.81	19	7.20	20	189.18	19	120.42	18
内蒙古	Inner Mongolia	4572.55	17	7.72	19	159.17	20	151.46	16
辽　宁	Liaoning	9346.57	7	32.64	7	473.13	7	388.59	6
吉　林	Jilin	4772.94	16	4.95	24	118.27	23	100.90	21
黑龙江	Heilongjiang	5491.02	15	8.35	17	207.62	17	194.73	10
上　海	Shanghai	7412.32	12	54.93	3	651.23	4	539.64	4
江　苏	Jiangsu	18331.33	3	63.00	2	791.54	3	575.21	2
浙　江	Zhejiang	13588.34	4	51.52	4	865.93	2	570.51	3
安　徽	Anhui	5736.56	14	15.63	12	331.47	12	190.41	13
福　建	Fujian	7256.54	13	42.26	6	493.67	6	167.01	14
江　西	Jiangxi	4027.25	22	4.85	25	156.18	21	50.39	25
山　东	Shandong	19651.94	2	29.24	8	469.91	8	342.23	7
河　南	Henan	10915.62	5	6.11	21	190.77	18	118.74	19
湖　北	Hubei	9562.50	6	12.03	14	264.72	13	192.96	11
湖　南	Hunan	7921.89	10	9.28	16	224.55	15	90.64	22
广　东	Guangdong	22677.11	1	156.11	1	3489.43	1	773.05	1
广　西	Guangxi	4516.59	18	12.79	13	350.27	10	192.70	12
海　南	Hainan	870.84	28	3.48	26	81.58	24	51.97	24
重　庆	Chongqing	4033.69	21	11.68	15	224.28	16	152.63	15
四　川	Sichuan	9268.61	8	7.98	18	227.34	14	151.29	17
贵　州	**Guizhou**	**2027.64**	**25**	**1.69**	**27**	**70.50**	**26**	**30.42**	**27**
云　南	Yunnan	3511.65	24	19.47	10	457.84	9	329.77	8
西　藏	Tibet	254.64	31	1.06	28	19.49	28	17.46	28
陕　西	Shanxi	4383.75	20	15.97	11	335.24	11	233.66	9
甘　肃	Gansu	1906.54	26	0.22	30	10.20	29	6.69	29
青　海	Qinghai	476.04	30	0.24	29	4.73	30	3.84	30
宁　夏	Ningxia	548.83	29	0.05	31	1.90	31	1.43	31
新　疆	Xinjiang	1858.59	27	5.51	22	62.49	27	49.02	26

29

Twenty-nine

历年资料

Historical Statistics

29-1 全省生产总值

Gross Domestic Product

单位：亿元 (100 million yuan)

年份 Year	地区生产总值 Gross Domestic Product	第一产业 Primary Industry	第二产业 Secondary Industry	工业 Industry	建筑业 Construction	第三产业 Tertiary Industry	#交通运输、仓储、邮政业 Transportation, Storage, Post and Telecommunications	人均生产总值(元) Per Capita Gross Domestic Product(yuan)
1978	46.62	19.42	18.73	15.24	3.49	8.47	1.68	175
1979	55.28	23.29	22.41	18.33	4.08	9.58	1.86	204
1980	60.26	24.86	24.00	19.37	4.63	11.40	2.01	219
1981	67.89	29.90	24.95	20.36	4.59	13.04	2.56	242
1982	79.39	37.37	27.44	22.58	4.86	14.58	2.74	278
1983	87.38	37.76	33.14	28.16	4.98	16.48	3.76	302
1984	108.27	45.73	43.51	36.85	6.66	19.03	4.66	371
1985	123.92	50.45	49.88	41.96	7.92	23.59	5.86	420
1986	139.57	56.46	50.96	43.57	7.39	32.15	7.34	467
1987	165.50	66.46	60.11	49.93	10.18	38.93	7.74	546
1988	211.79	85.20	78.63	68.32	10.31	47.96	9.78	683
1989	235.84	92.88	86.74	77.26	9.48	56.22	12.36	750
1990	260.14	100.10	92.83	82.15	10.68	67.21	11.69	810
1991	295.90	115.71	101.54	88.96	12.58	78.65	13.98	896
1992	339.91	121.18	122.08	106.41	15.67	96.65	19.00	1034
1993	417.69	133.41	155.03	135.40	19.63	129.25	25.45	1234
1994	524.46	183.56	194.80	173.03	21.77	146.10	18.02	1527
1995	636.21	227.13	232.52	208.75	23.77	176.56	22.77	1826
1996	723.18	254.53	255.09	225.36	29.73	213.56	26.79	2048
1997	805.79	271.96	288.99	251.10	37.89	244.84	23.51	2250
1998	858.39	265.04	319.40	273.82	45.58	273.95	29.14	2364
1999	937.50	267.75	350.41	294.42	55.99	319.34	59.17	2545
2000	1029.92	271.20	391.20	328.73	62.47	367.52	75.86	2759
2001	1133.27	274.41	433.52	360.73	72.79	425.34	88.47	3000
2002	1243.43	281.10	481.96	395.45	86.51	480.37	102.48	3257
2003	1426.34	298.69	569.37	473.38	95.99	558.28	119.26	3701
2004	1677.80	334.50	681.50	577.40	104.10	661.80	134.90	4317
2005	2005.42	368.94	821.16	707.35	113.81	815.32	138.65	5394
2006	2338.98	382.06	967.54	839.13	128.41	989.38	192.95	6305
2007	2884.11	446.38	1124.79	978.86	145.93	1312.94	282.04	7878
2008	3561.56	539.19	1370.03	1195.30	174.73	1652.34	370.65	9855
2009	3912.68	550.27	1476.62	1252.67	223.95	1885.79	399.77	10971
2010	4602.16	625.03	1800.06	1516.87	283.19	2177.07	480.32	13119
2011	5701.84	726.22	2194.33	1829.20	365.13	2781.29	590.91	16413
2012	6852.20	891.91	2677.54	2217.06	460.48	3282.75	687.45	19710

注：1.1978–2004年按老行业分类标准计算，2005–2009年按新行业分类标准计算，第三产业中"交通运输、仓储、邮电通信业"从2005年起按新标准分类为"交通运输、仓储和邮政业"。2.2005–2011年人均生产总值按人口普查修订数修订。3.2005年以来人均生产总值按常住半年人口计算，以往年份按常住一年人口计算(以下相关表同)。

Note:1.From 1978 to 2004,data in the table were calculated by the Old Industry Classification Standard;from 2005 to 2009, data in the table were calculated by the New Industry Classification Standard;from 2005,acording to the New the Industry Classification Standard，the data of Transportation, Storage,Post and telecommunications refers to data of Transportation，Storage and Post.2.From 2005 to 2011,the data of per capital GDP have been adjusted according to the result of national population census.3.Data from 2005 to 2011 were calculated by permanent population in half a year scope,while they were calculated by permanent population in a year scope in the past(the relative tables in the chapte are the same).

29-2 全省生产总值指数(上年=100)

Indices of Gross Domestic Product(Preceding year=100)

单位：% (%)

年份 Year	地区生产总值 Gross Domestic Product	第一产业 Primary Industry	第二产业 Secondary Industry	工业 Industry	建筑业 Construction	第三产业 Tertiary Industry	#交通运输、仓储、邮电通信业 Transportation, Storage, Post and Telecommunications	人均生产总值 Per Capita Gross Domestic Product
1978	123.7	106.6	137.3	139.7	123.7	132.7	133.6	121.4
1979	111.0	102.8	117.3	119.1	105.2	111.4	107.2	109.1
1980	104.4	100.4	104.3	106.9	85.6	111.7	106.5	102.7
1981	106.5	109.9	101.7	99.1	112.7	109.5	109.8	104.7
1982	115.8	123.0	109.3	111.4	101.3	112.6	103.6	113.8
1983	112.6	104.6	122.9	126.4	108.8	112.3	134.6	111.2
1984	119.8	118.2	123.8	123.8	123.5	114.9	137.6	118.6
1985	107.9	98.8	112.8	112.0	116.6	117.8	124.3	106.7
1986	105.6	106.1	98.0	99.7	90.5	120.9	108.7	104.3
1987	110.8	102.9	116.2	113.8	128.6	114.8	113.9	109.3
1988	108.6	99.0	113.2	115.5	103.1	115.0	108.3	106.2
1989	104.5	106.3	103.9	106.8	89.4	103.3	113.0	103.1
1990	104.3	101.7	106.1	105.6	108.8	104.6	84.9	102.1
1991	109.2	113.2	103.5	103.5	103.8	111.2	106.8	106.2
1992	108.1	99.3	115.0	116.0	108.0	112.6	121.2	108.6
1993	110.4	103.9	113.5	115.8	95.2	114.8	115.1	108.8
1994	108.4	103.7	111.8	112.4	105.8	109.8	111.9	106.9
1995	107.5	102.4	110.5	111.1	104.0	109.3	107.8	105.9
1996	108.9	103.8	112.6	112.1	117.8	109.2	111.1	107.4
1997	109.0	104.2	112.3	111.8	118.0	109.3	112.5	107.5
1998	108.5	101.5	111.8	110.4	126.4	110.5	117.5	106.9
1999	108.8	103.4	113.2	111.8	125.1	107.3	114.5	107.3
2000	108.4	103.6	107.6	107.5	108.3	113.7	117.5	107.0
2001	108.8	101.1	109.4	109.2	110.7	113.6	112.0	107.5
2002	109.1	102.2	113.2	111.0	124.5	109.4	105.4	107.9
2003	110.1	104.6	113.3	113.3	113.5	110.1	110.9	109.1
2004	111.4	105.3	114.2	115.9	106.5	112.0	116.0	110.4
2005	112.7	105.2	112.0	113.0	107.4	117.6	126.5	117.9
2006	112.8	104.6	113.4	113.8	111.2	116.0	129.6	113.1
2007	114.8	103.3	113.2	114.0	107.8	121.1	129.4	116.4
2008	111.3	106.8	108.1	108.6	104.7	115.8	119.4	112.8
2009	111.4	104.3	112.1	110.2	125.6	113.1	105.3	112.9
2010	112.8	104.7	116.6	115.7	122.1	112.1	115.2	114.7
2011	115.0	101.2	117.9	117.8	118.3	116.5	115.3	116.1
2012	113.6	108.6	116.8	115.6	123.3	112.1	113.8	113.5

29-3 全省生产总值指数(1978=100)

Indices of Gross Domestic Product(year of 1978=100)

单位：% (%)

年份 Year	地区生产总值 Gross Domestic Product	第一产业 Primary Industry	第二产业 Secondary Industry	工 业 Industry	建筑业 Construction	第三产业 Tertiary Industry	人均生产总值 Per Capita Gross Domestic Product
1978	100.0	100.0	100.0	100.0	100.0	100.0	100.0
1979	111.0	102.8	117.3	119.1	105.2	111.4	109.1
1980	115.9	103.2	122.3	127.3	90.1	124.4	112.0
1981	123.4	113.4	124.4	126.2	101.5	136.3	117.3
1982	142.9	139.5	135.9	140.5	102.9	153.4	133.5
1983	160.9	145.9	167.1	177.6	111.9	172.3	148.4
1984	192.8	172.5	206.8	219.9	138.2	198.0	176.0
1985	208.0	170.4	233.4	246.3	161.1	233.2	187.9
1986	219.6	180.8	228.7	245.6	145.8	281.9	195.9
1987	243.4	186.0	265.8	279.4	187.5	323.7	214.1
1988	264.3	184.2	300.9	322.8	193.3	372.2	227.5
1989	276.2	195.8	312.6	344.7	172.8	384.5	234.4
1990	288.1	199.1	331.7	364.1	188.0	402.2	239.4
1991	314.6	225.4	343.3	376.8	195.1	447.2	254.2
1992	340.1	223.8	394.8	437.1	210.8	503.6	276.1
1993	375.3	232.5	448.3	506.1	200.6	578.3	300.5
1994	407.0	241.2	501.1	568.7	212.2	635.2	321.2
1995	437.4	246.8	553.7	632.0	220.6	693.9	340.3
1996	476.1	256.3	623.4	708.7	259.8	757.9	365.3
1997	519.0	267.1	700.3	792.3	306.6	828.6	392.8
1998	562.9	271.0	783.1	874.8	387.6	915.3	420.0
1999	612.4	280.0	886.4	978.4	485.0	982.5	450.5
2000	663.7	290.2	953.4	1051.5	525.1	1117.4	481.8
2001	721.8	293.4	1043.5	1148.3	581.5	1269.5	517.9
2002	787.2	300.0	1181.3	1274.5	724.2	1388.3	558.7
2003	866.6	313.8	1338.4	1443.5	821.8	1528.6	609.4
2004	965.4	330.4	1528.4	1673.0	874.9	1711.4	673.1
2005	1088.0	347.6	1711.8	1890.5	939.6	2012.6	793.6
2006	1227.3	363.6	1941.2	2151.4	1044.8	2334.6	897.6
2007	1408.9	375.6	2197.4	2452.6	1126.3	2827.2	1044.8
2008	1568.1	401.1	2375.4	2663.5	1179.2	3273.9	1178.5
2009	1746.9	418.3	2662.8	2935.2	1481.1	3702.8	1330.5
2010	1970.5	438.0	3104.8	3396.0	1808.4	4150.8	1526.1
2011	2266.1	443.3	3660.6	4000.5	2139.3	4835.7	1771.8
2012	2574.3	481.4	4275.6	4624.6	2637.8	5420.8	2011.0

29-4 年末常住人口

Permanent Population at the Year-end

单位：万人 (10000 persons)

年 份 Year	合 计 Total	按城镇、乡村分 Grouped by Urban and Rural		按性别分 Grouped by Sex		性别比 Sex Ratio	年平均人口 Annual
		城 镇 Urban	乡 村 Rural	男 Male	女 Female	(女=100) (female=100)	Average Population
1978	2686.40	323.97	2362.43	1364.82	1321.58	103.27	2663.27
1979	2730.99	520.82	2210.17	1386.93	1344.06	103.19	2708.70
1980	2776.67	543.18	2233.49	1409.61	1367.06	103.11	2753.83
1981	2826.78	528.41	2298.37	1439.89	1386.89	103.82	2801.73
1982	2875.21	542.13	2333.08	1470.43	1404.78	104.67	2851.00
1983	2901.46	550.96	2350.50	1484.73	1416.73	104.80	2888.33
1984	2931.85	854.14	2077.71	1501.55	1430.30	104.98	2916.65
1985	2972.18	883.18	2089.00	1522.93	1449.25	105.08	2952.02
1986	3025.86	909.55	2116.31	1550.90	1474.96	105.15	2999.02
1987	3072.58	1002.93	2069.65	1576.23	1496.35	105.34	3049.22
1988	3127.27	951.23	2176.04	1599.01	1528.26	104.63	3099.93
1989	3171.00	1000.26	2170.74	1628.85	1542.15	105.62	3149.14
1990	3267.53	1083.67	2183.86	1684.53	1583.00	106.41	3219.27
1991	3314.63	1238.48	2076.15	1709.31	1605.32	106.48	3291.08
1992	3360.96	2256.05	1104.91	1735.46	1625.50	106.76	3337.8
1993	3408.69	2324.92	1083.77	1761.65	1647.04	106.96	3384.83
1994	3458.41	2371.06	1087.35	1789.32	1669.09	107.20	3433.55
1995	3508.08	2408.78	1099.30	1815.63	1692.45	107.28	3483.25
1996	3555.41	2457.33	1098.08	1840.38	1715.03	107.31	3531.75
1997	3605.81	2503.75	1102.06	1866.48	1739.33	107.31	3580.61
1998	3657.60	2539.76	1117.84	1893.29	1764.31	107.31	3631.70
1999	3710.06	2539.80	1170.26	1920.40	1789.66	107.30	3683.83
2000	3755.72	896.49	2859.23	1968.00	1787.72	110.08	3732.89
2001	3798.51	910.12	2888.39	1973.41	1825.10	108.13	3777.12
2002	3837.28	932.11	2905.17	1993.15	1844.13	108.08	3817.90
2003	3869.66	958.52	2911.14	2010.22	1859.44	108.11	3853.47
2004	3903.70	1025.89	2877.81	2022.22	1881.48	107.48	3886.68
2005	3730	1002.25	2727.75	1920.55	1809.45	106.14	3717.61
2006	3690	1013.27	2676.73	1908.85	1781.15	107.17	3710.0
2007	3632	1025.68	2606.32	1879.70	1752.30	107.27	3661.0
2008	3596	1046.79	2549.21	1868.73	1727.27	108.19	3614.0
2009	3537	1057.21	2479.79	1827.56	1709.44	106.91	3566.5
2010	3479	1176.25	2302.75	1797.43	1681.57	106.89	3508.0
2011	3469	1212.76	2256.24	1801.21	1667.79	108.00	3474.0
2012	3484	1268.52	2215.48	1818.61	1665.39	109.20	3476.5

注：1.2000年以后的城镇、乡村人口的划分标准按国家统计局1999年发布的《关于统计上划分城乡的规定》计算，以前年份数据不可比。
2.2005年及以后为常住半年口径(下表同)。3.2006年～2009年常住总人口数据已根据第六次人口普查数据进行修订(下表同)。

Note:1.Data on grouped by residence from 2000 was calculated on the basis of Statistical Partition Ordain about Urban or Rural that had been issued by National Bureau of Statistial of China, So the date are not comparable with the preceding years. 2.Population since 2005 have refer to permanent population in half a year scope(the same applies to the next table).3.Data from 2006 to 2009 had been verified according to the Six National Population Census(the same applies to the next table).

29-5 人口自然变动

Natural Change of Population

单位：万人 (10000 persons)

年 份 Year	出 生 Birth		死 亡 Death		自然增长 Natural Increase	
	人 数 Number of Persons	率(‰) Rate	人 数 Number of Persons	率(‰) Rate	人 数 Number of Persons	率(‰) Rate
1978	76.22	28.62	19.65	7.38	56.57	21.24
1979	72.84	26.89	19.23	7.10	53.61	19.79
1980	68.02	24.70	19.39	7.04	48.63	17.66
1981	66.46	23.72	21.07	7.52	45.39	16.20
1982	70.73	24.81	21.67	7.60	49.06	17.21
1983	60.11	20.81	26.46	9.16	33.65	11.65
1984	54.98	18.85	21.29	7.30	33.69	11.55
1985	59.97	20.33	17.43	5.91	42.54	14.42
1986	72.04	24.11	18.08	6.05	53.96	18.06
1987	71.77	23.69	25.87	8.54	45.90	15.15
1988	73.76	23.81	18.62	6.01	55.14	17.80
1989	67.08	21.23	21.58	6.83	45.50	14.40
1990	74.13	23.09	25.36	7.90	48.77	15.19
1991	72.96	22.42	26.39	8.11	46.57	14.31
1992	73.61	22.40	28.00	8.52	45.61	13.88
1993	74.96	22.60	28.19	8.50	46.77	14.10
1994	76.93	22.92	27.32	8.14	49.61	14.78
1995	76.14	21.86	26.47	7.60	49.67	14.26
1996	77.88	22.05	27.16	7.69	50.72	14.36
1997	79.31	22.15	27.46	7.67	51.85	14.48
1998	79.97	22.02	28.18	7.76	51.79	14.26
1999	80.75	21.92	28.29	7.68	52.46	14.24
2000	76.86	20.59	28.11	7.53	48.75	13.06
2001	70.10	18.56	27.31	7.23	42.79	11.33
2002	68.57	17.96	27.53	7.21	41.04	10.75
2003	61.31	15.91	26.47	6.87	34.84	9.04
2004	58.61	15.08	24.68	6.35	33.93	8.73
2005	54.00	14.59	25.00	7.21	29.00	7.38
2006	51.83	13.97	24.89	6.71	26.94	7.26
2007	48.62	13.28	24.16	6.60	24.46	6.68
2008	48.75	13.49	24.47	6.77	24.28	6.72
2009	48.68	13.65	23.86	6.69	24.82	6.96
2010	48.52	13.96	22.76	6.55	25.76	7.41
2011	46.24	13.31	24.07	6.93	22.17	6.38
2012	46.13	13.27	24.20	6.96	21.93	6.31

29–6 户籍人口

Household Registered Population

单位：万人 (10000 persons)

年 份 Year	年末总人口 Total Population at the Year-end	按农业非农业分 Grouped by Agriculture and Non-agriculture		占总人口比重(%) Proportion	
		农 业 Agriculture	非农业 Non-agriculture	农 业 Agriculture	非农业 Non-agriculture
1978	2686.40	2380.52	305.88	88.6	11.4
1979	2730.99	2416.67	314.32	88.5	11.5
1980	2776.67	2456.37	320.30	88.5	11.5
1981	2826.78	2500.74	326.04	88.5	11.5
1982	2875.21	2544.10	331.11	88.5	11.5
1983	2901.46	2564.92	336.54	88.4	11.6
1984	2931.85	2588.11	343.74	88.3	11.7
1985	2967.91	2609.04	358.87	87.9	12.1
1986	3007.99	2643.57	364.42	87.9	12.1
1987	3051.39	2678.60	372.79	87.8	12.2
1988	3143.94	2760.47	383.47	87.8	12.2
1989	3184.05	2793.35	390.70	87.7	12.3
1990	3236.97	2840.21	396.76	87.7	12.3
1991	3271.40	2868.27	403.13	87.7	12.3
1992	3300.97	2887.95	413.02	87.5	12.5
1993	3332.30	2910.71	421.59	87.3	12.7
1994	3380.58	2927.54	453.04	86.6	13.4
1995	3419.54	2957.32	462.22	86.5	13.5
1996	3459.54	2979.85	479.69	86.1	13.9
1997	3495.50	3004.76	490.74	86.0	14.0
1998	3536.54	3032.50	504.04	85.7	14.3
1999	3582.05	3063.23	518.82	85.5	14.5
2000	3676.63	3144.98	531.65	85.5	14.5
2001	3710.20	3156.33	553.87	85.1	14.9
2002	3747.68	3175.17	572.51	84.7	15.3
2003	3786.84	3196.70	590.14	84.4	15.6
2004	3831.19	3224.62	606.57	84.2	15.8
2005	3867.73	3258.05	609.68	84.2	15.8
2006	3921.91	3295.08	626.83	84.0	16.0
2007	3985.04	3346.09	638.95	84.0	16.0
2008	4036.75	3385.66	651.09	83.9	16.1
2009	4090.78	3429.36	661.43	83.8	16.2
2010	4189.00	3512.92	676.07	83.9	16.1
2011	4238.44	3551.18	687.26	83.8	16.2
2012	4249.48	3557.14	692.34	83.7	16.3

注：1984年前为公安、统计共同使用的数据，1984年后为公安户籍人口统计口径。

Note: Data after 1984 in the table are obtained from the Public Security Department of Guizhou Province,while data before 1984 are used by Statistics Beaura and Public Security Department of Guizhou Province.

29-7 就业人员
Employed Persons

单位：万人 (10000 persons)

年份 Year	就业人员 Employed Persons	第一产业 Primary Industry	第二产业 Secondary Industry	第三产业 Tertiary Industry
1978	1053.67	872.89	108.26	72.52
1979	1060.62	873.88	105.63	81.11
1980	1109.63	919.69	102.01	87.93
1981	1152.95	954.55	102.64	95.76
1982	1207.06	989.78	109.53	107.75
1983	1234.18	1014.15	109.99	110.04
1984	1285.32	1037.71	122.12	125.49
1985	1335.17	1018.38	185.98	130.81
1986	1383.17	1053.26	197.09	132.82
1987	1435.85	1115.35	180.53	139.97
1988	1501.32	1172.51	185.80	143.01
1989	1570.84	1228.64	163.19	179.01
1990	1651.75	1292.30	169.10	190.35
1991	1701.47	1329.56	177.72	194.19
1992	1739.03	1359.00	173.35	206.68
1993	1779.01	1374.00	171.00	234.01
1994	1828.30	1365.00	181.90	281.40
1995	1812.20	1312.80	268.80	230.60
1996	1783.20	1235.60	278.50	269.10
1997	1796.70	1251.10	256.60	289.00
1998	1844.43	1284.72	251.57	308.14
1999	1832.50	1299.90	201.40	331.20
2000	1866.28	1305.28	221.80	339.20
2001	2068.01	1692.33	133.88	241.80
2002	2106.14	1698.39	108.89	298.86
2003	2145.00	1671.20	120.49	353.31
2004	2186.00	1672.29	124.60	389.11
2005	1944.29	1497.26	164.00	283.04
2006	1953.24	1487.40	174.17	291.67
2007	1872.64	1388.02	172.31	312.31
2008	1867.20	1350.32	180.73	336.15
2009	1841.92	1299.29	197.60	345.03
2010	1770.90	1209.55	203.52	357.82
2011	1792.80	1194.39	215.86	382.55
2012	1825.82	1189.04	238.10	398.68

注：就业人员数2010年根据第六次人口普查长表数据推算，2005–2009年根据人口普查结果，采用趋势离差法修订，2011年及以后按同口径进行推算。

Note:Date of employed persons were estimated according to the 6th National Population Census in 2010,From 2005 to 2009,according to the result of National Population Census,the total number of employed persons were revised by the trend deviation method,and the same to 2011.

29–8 非私营单位在岗职工人数

Number of Staff and Workers in Non-private Units

单位：万人 (10000 persons)

年份 Year	合 计 Total	国有单位 State-owned Unit	集体单位 Collective-owned Unit	其他单位 Other Ownership Unit
1978	171.19	137.66	33.53	
1979	175.56	142.32	33.24	
1980	178.18	146.14	32.04	
1981	185.73	153.50	32.23	
1982	191.03	158.08	32.95	
1983	193.33	160.54	32.79	
1984	197.13	159.53	37.60	
1985	202.33	162.11	40.03	0.19
1986	206.69	167.81	38.78	0.10
1987	211.92	172.58	38.88	0.46
1988	214.43	176.32	37.56	0.55
1989	216.70	180.10	35.90	0.70
1990	225.48	185.35	39.19	0.94
1991	231.88	190.45	40.49	0.94
1992	235.80	193.61	40.94	1.25
1993	233.11	192.83	38.35	1.93
1994	230.88	194.47	34.87	1.54
1995	226.55	193.36	29.63	3.56
1996	231.64	196.60	30.45	4.59
1997	232.80	196.08	31.33	5.39
1998	207.01	167.14	23.98	15.89
1999	197.80	156.86	21.03	19.91
2000	193.96	153.55	19.00	21.41
2001	189.18	148.87	15.73	24.58
2002	188.47	146.96	14.39	27.12
2003	188.70	141.75	13.71	33.24
2004	192.67	139.57	12.77	40.33
2005	202.02	140.50	9.81	51.71
2006	201.87	137.86	8.86	55.15
2007	207.53	141.48	8.10	57.95
2008	199.76	140.97	7.42	51.37
2009	206.44	141.79	6.69	57.96
2010	210.67	146.81	6.41	57.45
2011	225.91	158.26	7.17	60.47
2012	249.67	161.19	6.16	82.32

29–9 非私营单位在岗职工平均工资

Average Wages of Staff and Workers in Non-private Units

单位：元 (yuan)

年 份 Year	在岗职工平均工资 Average Wages of Staff and Workers	国有单位 State-owned Unit	集体单位 Collective-owned Unit	其他单位 Other Ownership Unit
1978	616	642	450	
1979	654	692	448	
1980	755	797	502	
1981	774	804	535	
1982	783	815	562	
1983	801	830	608	
1984	913	949	708	
1985	1066	1132	787	
1986	1216	1297	859	1236
1987	1319	1395	961	1204
1988	1531	1627	1072	1389
1989	1676	1777	1158	1647
1990	1947	2070	1347	2281
1991	2090	2214	1489	2527
1992	2406	2543	1717	3286
1993	2823	2958	2104	3375
1994	3870	4085	2618	4475
1995	4475	4672	3061	5369
1996	4917	5125	3456	5613
1997	5206	5434	3556	6461
1998	5775	5819	4426	7289
1999	6595	6695	5008	7456
2000	7453	7594	5444	8325
2001	8991	9308	6218	8831
2002	9810	10150	6566	9680
2003	11037	11390	7504	10975
2004	12431	12870	8630	12103
2005	14344	14681	10506	14161
2006	16815	17638	12873	15365
2007	20668	22106	16893	17668
2008	24602	25874	20914	21659
2009	28245	29956	22167	24772
2010	31458	32718	24703	29006
2011	37331	38914	31601	33851
2012	42733	45825	40420	36816

29—10 全社会固定资产投资

Total Investment in Fixed Assets in the Whole Province

单位：亿元 (100 million yuan)

年 份 Year	全社会固定资产投资 Total Investment in Fixed Assets in the Whole Province	增长速度(%) Growth Rate(%)	按经济类型分 (Grouped by Ownership)		
			国有经济 State-owned Units	集体经济 Collective-Owned Units	其 他 Others
1978	10.93		9.73	0.56	0.64
1979	11.94	9.2	10.20	0.61	1.13
1980	13.97	17.0	11.59	0.83	1.55
1981	15.16	8.5	12.06	0.99	2.11
1982	15.52	2.4	11.56	1.08	2.88
1983	17.07	10.0	11.88	1.23	3.96
1984	23.02	34.9	15.02	0.98	7.02
1985	33.14	44.0	21.24	1.76	10.14
1986	35.99	8.6	24.09	1.71	10.19
1987	42.97	19.4	27.10	3.61	12.26
1988	45.42	5.7	33.05	2.74	9.63
1989	44.08	-3.0	32.29	2.73	9.06
1990	51.51	16.9	36.95	2.14	12.42
1991	58.44	13.5	42.97	3.67	11.80
1992	78.82	34.9		3.59	16.41
1993	106.30	34.9	77.84	6.81	21.65
1994	140.95	32.6	93.74	9.77	37.44
1995	173.66	23.2	108.85	12.94	51.87
1996	207.10	19.3	133.19	14.75	59.16
1997	247.23	19.4	149.75	15.09	82.39
1998	304.91	23.3	188.93	19.34	96.64
1999	333.90	9.5	210.80	22.19	100.91
2000	402.50	20.5	259.95	28.45	114.10
2001	533.74	32.6	357.69	22.45	153.60
2002	632.44	18.5	423.88	18.86	189.70
2003	754.13	19.2	457.10	39.26	257.77
2004	869.25	15.3	507.74	38.41	323.10
2005	1018.25	17.1	545.37	12.61	460.27
2006	1197.68	17.6	602.50	12.93	582.25
2007	1488.80	24.3	697.68	17.27	773.85
2008	1864.45	25.2	910.69	25.23	928.53
2009	2450.99	31.5	1250.42	29.70	1170.87
2010	3186.28	30.0	1605.82	29.01	1551.45
2011	5101.55	60.1	2412.97	57.23	2631.36
2012	5717.80	35.0	2530.97	42.55	3144.28

注：表中2011年及以前数据为计划总投资50万元及以上固定资产项目投资，房地产开发投资及农户投资；2012年数据为计划总投资500万元及以上的固定资产项目投资，房地产开发投资及农村农户投资，增长速度为可比口径速度。

Note:Date in the table refer to those projedts planned to invest 500000 yuan at least in investment in fixed assets,real estate development and rural household investment be from 2011.And date to 2012 in the table refer to those projects that planned to invest 5000,000 yuan at least in investment in fixed assets, real estate development and rural household investment and the growth rate is the speed of comparable caliber.

29−11 财政收支

Financial Revenue and Expenditure

单位：亿元 (100 million yuan)

年份 Year	财政总收入 Total Government Financial Revenue		公共财政收入 Public Financial Revenue		公共财政支出 Public Financial Expenditure	
	绝对数 Absolute Numbers	增长速度(%) Growth Rates(%)	绝对数 Absolute Numbers	增长速度(%) Growth Rates(%)	绝对数 Absolute Numbers	增长速度(%) Growth Rates(%)
1978	14.20	48.2	6.26	157.6	12.30	39.9
1979	14.26	0.4	6.54	4.5	13.30	8.1
1980	13.23	-7.2	6.69	2.3	12.66	-4.8
1981	13.74	3.9	6.32	-5.5	13.28	4.9
1982	16.00	16.4	7.70	21.8	15.11	13.8
1983	18.26	14.1	9.56	24.2	16.38	8.4
1984	21.81	19.4	11.81	23.5	22.28	36.0
1985	26.71	22.5	15.17	28.5	24.55	10.2
1986	31.38	17.5	17.01	12.1	30.43	24.0
1987	36.80	17.3	21.37	25.6	31.43	3.3
1988	39.55	7.5	25.96	21.5	36.14	15.0
1989	45.37	14.7	32.14	23.8	45.89	27.0
1990	49.36	8.8	35.37	10.0	47.87	4.3
1991	55.71	12.9	42.80	21.0	53.42	11.6
1992	60.98	9.5	47.28	10.5	60.63	13.5
1993	68.43	12.2	56.50	19.5	67.39	11.1
1994	77.30	13.0	31.24	-44.7	74.23	10.1
1995	87.40	13.1	38.80	24.2	85.33	15.0
1996	103.92	18.9	49.46	27.5	99.58	16.7
1997	116.19	11.8	57.90	17.1	113.79	14.3
1998	136.31	17.3	65.34	12.8	133.09	17.0
1999	133.75	-1.9	74.26	13.7	170.72	28.3
2000	153.04	14.4	85.23	14.8	201.57	18.1
2001	177.04	15.7	99.75	17.0	275.20	36.5
2002	203.03	14.7	108.28	8.6	316.67	15.1
2003	236.64	16.6	124.56	15.0	332.35	5.0
2004	296.48	25.3	149.29	19.9	418.42	25.9
2005	366.16	23.5	182.50	22.2	520.73	24.5
2006	448.88	22.6	226.82	24.3	610.64	17.3
2007	556.98	24.1	285.14	25.7	795.40	30.3
2008	674.58	21.1	349.55	22.6	1055.39	32.7
2009	779.59	15.6	416.48	19.1	1372.27	30.0
2010	969.57	24.4	533.73	28.2	1631.48	18.9
2011	1329.99	37.2	773.08	44.8	2249.40	37.9
2012	1644.48	23.6	1014.05	31.2	2755.68	22.5

注：资料来源于省财政厅。
Note:Data in the table are obtained from provincial financial department.

29-12 人民生活

单位：元

年 份 Year	城镇居民人均可支配收入 Urban Households Per Capita Disposable Income	指 数 (上年=100) Index (preceding year=100)	指 数 (1978=100) Index (year of 1978=100	城镇居民人均消费性支出 Urban Households Per Capita Living Expenditures	#食 品 #Food
1978	261.26	101.2	100.0	246.53	150.15
1979	279.66	105.2	105.2	273.60	176.64
1980	343.83	111.9	117.7	334.32	202.32
1981	434.10	122.5	144.1	393.24	237.60
1982	459.73	103.8	149.6	403.92	243.96
1983	483.33	103.5	154.8	426.36	258.72
1984	558.00	112.3	173.8	480.36	279.48
1985	682.27	110.9	192.7	617.52	324.24
1986	824.40	113.6	218.8	722.28	381.84
1987	912.26	100.9	220.7	788.76	431.40
1988	1101.84	99.4	219.4	1050.24	554.52
1989	1275.45	98.2	215.4	1102.56	640.20
1990	1399.36	108.5	233.8	1163.25	658.19
1991	1593.54	109.6	256.2	1338.86	750.79
1992	1887.51	109.7	281.0	1564.34	886.89
1993	2300.38	105.1	295.4	1876.24	1021.42
1994	3196.06	114.1	337.2	2531.78	1353.13
1995	3916.25	102.2	344.5	3250.55	1752.41
1996	4210.74	97.1	334.4	3572.78	1923.49
1997	4438.05	101.8	340.4	3555.69	1819.90
1998	4566.17	102.3	348.3	3799.38	1839.64
1999	4935.47	109.0	379.6	3964.35	1683.38
2000	5121.22	105.1	399.0	4278.28	1847.63
2001	5451.91	103.9	414.5	4492.25	1832.26
2002	5944.02	109.8	455.1	4598.30	1788.61
2003	6568.91	109.5	498.4	4947.62	1967.67
2004	7322.04	107.7	536.8	5494.43	2260.46
2005	8147.13	110.6	593.7	6156.27	2457.09
2006	9116.61	110.1	653.7	6848.39	2649.02
2007	10678.40	110.6	723.0	7758.69	3122.46
2008	11758.76	102.9	744.0	8349.21	3597.94
2009	12862.53	110.9	825.1	9048.29	3755.61
2010	14142.74	107.0	882.9	10058.29	4013.67
2011	16495.01	110.8	978.3	11352.88	4565.85
2012	18700.51	110.4	1080.0	12585.70	4992.85

注:表中指数已扣除价格因素。

People's Living Conditions

(yuan)

农村居民人均纯收入 Rural Households Per Capita Net Income	指数(上年=100) Index (preceding year=100)	指数(1978=100) Index (year of 1978=100)	农村居民人均生活消费支出 Rural Households Per Capita Living Expenditures	#食品 #Food
109.30	103.5	100.0	104.52	72.20
131.09	115.4	115.4	116.23	82.44
161.50	116.6	134.5	139.24	96.45
208.87	127.3	171.2	162.51	105.16
223.13	105.3	180.3	187.02	121.67
224.87	100.5	181.1	185.20	126.01
262.81	115.5	209.1	208.87	144.00
302.14	108.8	227.5	254.58	177.83
303.57	96.1	218.6	271.60	190.60
341.84	106.4	232.5	304.22	212.90
397.74	99.2	230.7	359.73	254.32
430.34	92.7	213.9	407.28	282.92
435.14	98.7	211.0	403.28	281.92
465.53	103.5	218.4	420.44	286.60
506.13	102.0	222.9	454.47	309.77
579.67	98.6	219.8	550.11	390.45
786.84	106.6	234.2	684.27	484.41
1086.62	106.6	249.6	930.59	661.85
1276.67	105.5	263.3	1068.09	774.62
1298.54	104.2	274.4	1065.70	742.16
1334.46	104.4	286.5	1094.39	757.55
1363.07	104.7	299.9	1069.81	722.16
1374.16	103.6	310.7	1096.59	687.32
1411.73	103.7	322.2	1098.39	659.37
1489.91	104.3	336.1	1137.56	661.35
1564.66	104.7	353.2	1185.17	674.71
1721.55	105.6	373.0	1296.34	754.39
1876.96	105.2	392.4	1552.39	819.87
1984.62	104.7	410.8	1627.07	838.42
2373.99	111.6	458.5	1913.50	998.39
2796.93	108.9	499.3	2165.70	1119.64
3005.41	109.2	545.2	2421.95	1093.94
3471.93	112.6	613.9	2852.48	1319.43
4145.35	114.0	699.8	3455.76	1646.51
4753.00	111.5	780.3	3901.71	1740.58

Note:The Indices in the table have been deducting price factors.

29–13 农林牧渔业总产值

Gross Output Value of Farming, Forestry, Animal Husbandry and Fishery

单位：亿元 (100 million yuan)

年 份 Year	合 计 Total	农 业 Farming	林 业 Forestry	畜牧业 Animal Husbandry	渔 业 Fishery	农林牧渔服务业 Services of Farming, Forestry,Animal Husbandry and Fishery
1978	27.46	21.72	1.07	4.64	0.03	
1979	31.74	24.54	1.27	5.90	0.03	
1980	36.44	28.05	1.46	6.89	0.04	
1981	41.93	32.07	2.08	7.69	0.09	
1982	51.49	38.93	2.49	9.95	0.12	
1983	52.66	38.17	3.48	10.84	0.17	
1984	63.09	45.43	4.44	12.94	0.28	
1985	70.24	47.42	5.37	17.05	0.40	
1986	79.34	53.54	5.27	20.05	0.48	
1987	92.25	61.95	5.50	24.23	0.57	
1988	123.39	78.90	6.13	37.55	0.81	
1989	133.69	85.64	5.90	41.30	0.85	
1990	145.53	95.23	7.95	41.38	0.97	
1991	165.34	112.08	9.44	42.68	1.14	
1992	176.73	116.03	12.22	47.18	1.30	
1993	201.40	126.20	11.85	62.33	1.02	
1994	277.13	180.26	13.61	81.18	2.08	
1995	344.85	224.16	15.29	102.54	2.86	
1996	388.29	265.57	14.99	104.57	3.16	
1997	417.54	289.20	15.39	109.37	3.58	
1998	402.32	274.55	15.48	108.12	4.17	
1999	407.12	278.67	16.02	108.07	4.36	
2000	412.97	279.61	18.04	110.67	4.65	
2001	418.61	279.95	15.08	118.46	5.13	
2002	431.39	278.88	18.17	128.80	5.54	
2003	466.72	275.46	25.87	139.48	6.08	19.83
2004	524.64	317.69	23.25	168.79	7.02	7.89
2005	571.84	335.53	23.91	194.20	9.41	8.79
2006	601.54	347.97	25.85	189.79	7.44	30.49
2007	697.01	392.20	27.77	231.60	9.04	36.40
2008	843.80	464.80	35.63	291.65	10.49	41.23
2009	875.20	501.52	36.92	281.53	11.06	44.17
2010	997.82	587.31	41.01	304.16	13.82	51.52
2011	1165.46	655.30	46.66	381.95	19.90	61.65
2012	1436.61	864.86	54.19	421.55	28.21	67.80

注：1.2006年数据为第二次农业普查修订数(以下相关表同)。2.农林牧渔服务业2004、2005年计算口径有变化(以下相关表同)。

Note:1.Data were adjusted according to the Second National Agricultural Census in 2006.2.Calculate the caliber of Farming,Forestry,Animal Husbandry and Fishery have changed in the year of 2004 and 2005(The same applies to the relative tables below).

29−14 农林牧渔业总产值指数(上年=100)

Indices of Gross Output Value of Farming, Forestry, Animal Husbandry and Fishery (preceding year=100)

单位：% (%)

年 份 Year	合 计 Total	农 业 Farming	林 业 Forestry	畜牧业 Animal Husbandry	渔 业 Fishery	农林牧渔服务业 Services of Farming, Forestry,Animal Husbandry and Fishery
1978	102.9	100.7	107.7	113.2	99.5	
1979	101.0	98.9	102.4	111.0	101.4	
1980	104.3	103.7	106.2	106.1	159.3	
1981	106.9	107.3	86.6	109.9	96.3	
1982	119.8	120.9	113.8	116.9	104.4	
1983	102.6	98.6	139.8	108.2	136.9	
1984	111.4	109.0	123.1	115.6	148.9	
1985	100.4	96.9	100.9	112.6	112.5	
1986	108.4	109.4	88.4	112.3	102.6	
1987	104.0	103.3	101.1	107.0	102.6	
1988	102.3	101.2	94.4	107.4	105.2	
1989	104.8	105.9	97.6	103.5	97.1	
1990	102.4	102.9	106.4	100.2	106.6	
1991	113.1	116.5	109.2	106.3	109.9	
1992	100.8	98.4	114.0	103.6	102.4	
1993	104.2	105.9	90.1	103.9	120.2	
1994	103.7	104.0	100.7	103.6	109.7	
1995	103.0	100.8	100.3	108.9	116.6	
1996	104.5	105.6	94.5	103.9	107.2	
1997	104.9	105.0	101.4	104.8	120.2	
1998	100.3	97.3	102.2	107.1	119.2	
1999	103.6	103.6	99.5	104.0	109.6	
2000	103.8	103.1	111.0	103.7	113.4	
2001	101.2	99.9	84.1	106.9	110.2	
2002	102.5	98.6	116.7	108.5	108.1	
2003	105.4	104.9	101.0	108.8	106.4	
2004	105.5	105.4	85.6	109.2	108.7	105.2
2005	105.9	104.3	99.9	109.8	106.7	107.3
2006	104.8	102.4	104.4	108.2	119.8	109.2
2007	103.3	103.4	102.3	102.1	106.5	106.4
2008	106.8	106.1	115.5	107.1	101.5	106.9
2009	104.6	102.8	100.7	108.5	102.6	104.7
2010	105.2	102.7	109.7	108.2	111.6	109.2
2011	101.4	99.8	107.4	101.2	125.1	110.3
2012	109.3	112.0	107.1	105.3	123.2	103.5

29-15 农林牧渔业总产值指数(1978=100)

Indices of Gross Output Value of Farming, Forestry, Animal Husbandry and Fishery(year of 1978=100)

单位：%　　(%)

年份 Year	合计 Total	农业 Farming	林业 Forestry	畜牧业 Animal Husbandry	渔业 Fishery	农林牧渔服务业 Services of Farming, Forestry,Animal Husbandry and Fishery
1978	100.0	100.0	100.0	100.0	100.0	
1979	101.0	98.9	102.4	111.0	101.4	
1980	105.3	102.6	108.7	117.8	161.5	
1981	112.6	110.0	94.2	129.4	155.6	
1982	134.9	133.0	107.2	151.3	162.4	
1983	138.4	131.2	149.8	163.7	222.3	
1984	154.2	143.0	184.4	189.2	331.0	
1985	154.8	138.6	186.1	213.1	372.4	
1986	167.8	151.6	164.5	239.3	382.1	
1987	174.5	156.6	166.3	256.1	392.0	
1988	178.5	158.5	157.0	275.0	412.4	
1989	187.1	167.8	153.2	284.6	400.5	
1990	191.6	172.7	163.0	285.2	426.9	
1991	216.7	201.2	178.0	303.2	469.2	
1992	218.4	198.0	203.0	314.1	480.4	
1993	227.6	209.6	182.9	326.3	577.5	
1994	236.0	218.0	184.2	338.1	633.5	
1995	243.1	219.8	184.7	368.2	738.6	
1996	254.1	232.1	174.6	382.5	791.8	
1997	266.5	243.7	177.0	400.9	951.8	
1998	267.3	237.1	180.9	429.4	1134.5	
1999	276.9	245.6	180.0	446.5	1243.4	
2000	287.5	253.2	199.8	463.0	1410.0	
2001	290.9	253.0	168.0	495.0	1553.8	
2002	298.2	249.4	196.1	537.1	1679.7	
2003	314.3	261.6	198.1	584.4	1787.2	100.0
2004	331.6	275.7	169.5	638.1	1942.7	105.2
2005	351.1	287.6	169.4	700.7	2072.8	112.9
2006	368.0	294.5	176.8	758.1	2483.3	123.3
2007	380.1	305.1	180.9	774.8	2647.2	131.2
2008	406.0	323.7	207.0	829.8	2686.9	140.3
2009	424.6	332.8	208.4	900.3	2756.8	146.9
2010	446.7	341.8	228.6	974.1	3076.6	160.4
2011	453.0	341.1	245.5	985.8	3848.8	176.9
2012	495.1	382.0	262.9	1038.0	4741.7	183.1

29-16 主要农产品产量

Output of Major Farm Crops

单位：万吨 (10000 tons)

年 份 Year	粮 食 Grain	油 料 Oil-Bearing Crops	烤 烟 Flue-cured Tobacco	水 果 Fruits	肉类总产量 Total Yield of Meat	水产品 Aquatic Products
1978	643.36	9.89	8.11	4.82	12.80	0.37
1979	623.05	10.90	9.54	4.68	22.84	0.38
1980	648.35	15.59	5.56	4.97	26.67	0.55
1981	567.36	34.04	11.93	6.23	31.61	0.58
1982	654.00	48.10	16.41	6.58	35.26	0.60
1983	703.00	28.50	13.62	7.19	38.58	0.81
1984	757.80	30.59	21.48	9.23	44.76	1.22
1985	594.96	31.97	26.55	10.14	50.46	1.35
1986	672.34	41.90	19.24	13.88	57.09	1.40
1987	673.17	46.34	21.19	15.19	62.26	1.80
1988	635.68	39.87	29.15	15.63	68.73	1.86
1989	708.25	32.93	31.58	16.80	71.82	2.01
1990	721.00	43.87	28.66	16.68	74.47	2.24
1991	885.50	61.79	38.53	17.17	81.65	2.29
1992	788.90	53.38	44.90	14.18	85.59	2.36
1993	869.50	43.28	49.66	16.53	88.91	2.55
1994	938.70	47.32	33.04	16.47	95.02	2.80
1995	948.85	58.83	33.53	20.97	105.69	3.27
1996	1002.60	55.62	52.27	19.46	103.65	3.50
1997	1025.90	58.97	68.66	25.14	106.77	4.21
1998	1100.00	62.24	29.19	27.50	113.33	5.02
1999	1125.21	67.31	32.32	32.57	117.09	5.50
2000	1161.30	74.34	31.09	58.33	124.06	6.24
2001	1100.30	71.32	26.38	62.93	131.70	6.89
2002	1034.20	72.48	30.65	71.57	145.02	7.46
2003	1104.30	72.31	28.72	78.75	156.99	7.96
2004	1149.58	82.71	29.98	87.17	171.06	8.85
2005	1152.06	84.89	34.45	95.96	187.01	9.46
2006	1038.00	68.24	30.71	109.19	163.70	6.71
2007	1100.86	69.66	31.22	112.86	150.60	7.68
2008	1158.00	68.39	37.71	114.28	161.46	7.80
2009	1168.27	78.68	36.92	119.74	169.60	8.03
2010	1112.30	60.34	37.02	123.47	179.09	8.79
2011	876.90	78.85	32.50	128.03	179.97	10.88
2012	1079.50	87.38	37.31	147.72	190.27	13.47

注：1.肉类总产量1978—1984年为猪牛羊肉产量,1985—1988年为猪牛羊禽肉产量,1989年以后为猪牛羊禽肉产量和其他肉(如：马肉、狗肉、兔肉等)产量。2.2000年以后的水果包含果用瓜。

Note:1.The Data of Total Yield of Meat included output of pock,beef and mutton from 1978 to 1984;it included Output of Pock,Beef,Mutton and Meat of Poultry from 1985 to 1988;after 1989,it includes output of pock,beef,mutton,meat of poultry and other meat(e.g.horse,dog,rabbit meat and so on). 2.After 2000,the data of yield of fruits included output of melon used as fruits.

29-17 工业总产值

Gross Output Value of Industry

单位：亿元 (100 million yuan)

年份 Year	规模以上工业总产值 Gross Output Value of Industry above Designated Size	轻工业 Light Industry	重工业 Heavy Industry
1996	514.10	191.40	322.70
1997	575.49	211.58	363.91
1998	507.91	185.66	322.25
1999	551.93	187.05	364.88
2000	631.60	206.30	425.30
2001	696.63	220.11	476.52
2002	797.90	253.00	544.90
2003	977.64	279.50	698.14
2004	1394.91	307.81	1087.10
2005	1690.40	380.85	1309.55
2006	2066.77	449.67	1617.10
2007	2520.36	527.16	1993.20
2008	3111.13	641.78	2469.34
2009	3426.69	758.14	2668.55
2010	4206.37	914.19	3292.18
2011	5527.11	1199.35	4327.76
2012	6544.02	1389.71	5154.31

注：1.1998年以前为乡及乡以上数据，1998—2010年为年主营业务收入500万元及以上企业数据，2011—2012年为年主营业务收入2000万元及以上企业数据(以下各表同)。2.2004年数据为经济普查数据(以下各表同)。

Notes:1.Before 1998,Industrial Statistics were based on type of industrial enterprises above county level.In 1998 to 2010,industrial statistics referred to the revenue from principal business of 5 million yuan and above of industry enterprises.In 2011 to 2012,industrial statistics referred to the revenue from principal business of 20 million yuan and above of industry enterprises(The relative tables in the chapter are the same).

2.Data in the table refer to the data of the First Economic Census in 2004(The relative tables in the chapter are the same).

29−18 工业增加值

Value-added of Industry

单位：亿元 (100 million yuan)

年 份 Year	全部工业增加值 Value-added of Industry	#规模以上工业增加值 Value-added of Industry above Designated Size	轻工业 Light Industry	重工业 Heavy Industry
1996	225.36	188.43	74.71	113.72
1997	251.10	204.72	75.27	129.45
1998	273.82	181.80	76.48	105.32
1999	294.42	196.04	77.46	118.58
2000	328.73	216.99	82.16	134.83
2001	360.73	236.57	87.66	148.91
2002	395.45	271.09	88.20	182.89
2003	473.38	346.49	116.72	229.77
2004	577.40	476.75	147.79	328.96
2005	707.35	585.85	177.19	408.66
2006	839.13	747.38	218.52	528.86
2007	978.86	890.48	267.87	622.61
2008	1195.30	1051.26	302.25	749.01
2009	1252.67	1170.29	352.38	817.91
2010	1516.87	1227.17	413.99	813.18
2011	1829.20	1715.06	571.20	1143.86
2012	2217.06	2055.46	773.04	1282.42

注：本表数据自2011年起口径改为年主营业务收入2000万元及以上的工业企业（下表同）。

Note: The statistical of data in this table were changed to the industrial of main business income of 20 million yuan and above(The same applies to the next table).

29-19 工业增加值指数(上年=100)

Indices of Value-added of Industry (preceding year=100)

单位：%　　　　(%)

年 份 Year	全部工业增加值 Value-added of Industry	#规模以上工业增加值 Value-added of Industry above Designated Size	轻工业 Light Industry	重工业 Heavy Industry
1996	112.1	110.3	111.0	109.8
1997	111.8	109.0	106.0	111.1
1998	110.4	110.2	108.1	111.5
1999	111.8	106.2	100.8	109.3
2000	107.5	113.8	112.2	114.7
2001	109.2	112.6	106.4	113.6
2002	111.0	116.2	113.4	117.6
2003	113.3	116.9	109.8	120.3
2004	115.9	120.1	122.1	119.2
2005	113.0	117.0	125.3	113.3
2006	113.8	117.5	113.1	119.7
2007	114.0	116.8	113.9	118.1
2008	108.6	110.1	114.0	108.4
2009	110.2	110.6	111.6	110.2
2010	115.7	115.8	115.9	115.7
2011	117.8	121.0	122.7	120.1
2012	115.6	116.2	117.6	115.5

29–20 规模以上工业主要经济指标

Major Economic Indicators of Industrial Enterprises above Designated Size

单位：亿元 (100 million yuan)

年 份 Year	主营业务收入 Revenue from Principal Business	轻工业 Light Industry	重工业 Heavy Industry	利税总额 Total Profits and Taxes	轻工业 Light Industry	重工业 Heavy Industry
1996	434.00	129.12	304.88	50.61	29.73	20.88
1997	419.82	128.07	291.75	60.82	38.42	22.40
1998	463.24	149.81	313.43	62.25	37.38	24.87
1999	507.55	162.34	345.21	65.81	40.47	25.34
2000	593.80	178.54	415.26	87.44	45.66	41.78
2001	646.01	193.35	452.66	94.30	51.27	43.03
2002	752.97	213.50	539.47	104.43	57.76	46.67
2003	974.30	248.48	725.82	135.87	72.15	63.72
2004	1325.95	274.04	1051.91	201.21	85.43	115.78
2005	1577.16	338.02	1239.14	232.49	113.50	118.99
2006	1948.57	389.38	1559.19	299.09	137.05	162.04
2007	2430.62	486.28	1944.34	403.49	187.27	216.22
2008	2922.35	567.80	2354.55	453.53	233.66	219.87
2009	3234.59	674.36	2560.23	470.60	252.25	218.35
2010	3926.01	807.13	3118.88	671.39	326.72	344.67
2011	5022.11	1091.79	3930.32	901.36	463.03	438.33
2012	5966.52	1299.99	4666.53	1172.15	608.19	563.96

29-20 续表 continued

年 份 Year	利润总额 Total Profits	轻工业 Light Industry	重工业 Heavy Industry	资产合计 Total Assets	轻工业 Light Industry	重工业 Heavy Industry
1996	-3.57	-2.47	-1.10	960.79	257.78	703.01
1997	0.76	0.65	0.11	1076.72	294.65	782.07
1998	1.64	-0.65	2.29	1166.76	312.79	853.97
1999	0.65	1.14	-0.49	1328.55	357.12	971.43
2000	12.56	4.48	8.08	1517.13	371.83	1145.30
2001	18.59	6.98	11.61	1698.58	412.57	1286.01
2002	21.41	10.82	10.59	1797.46	404.54	1392.92
2003	37.52	19.00	18.52	1958.57	409.35	1549.22
2004	61.99	18.03	43.96	2441.52	430.64	2010.88
2005	70.79	34.31	36.48	2734.05	458.41	2275.64
2006	110.91	48.52	62.39	3214.39	514.26	2700.13
2007	174.41	81.29	93.12	3521.19	541.49	2979.70
2008	181.83	108.56	73.27	4566.10	700.92	3865.18
2009	191.73	109.42	82.31	5066.17	819.69	4246.48
2010	317.63	149.62	168.01	5960.13	1007.10	4953.03
2011	456.20	220.40	235.80	6990.58	1200.82	5789.76
2012	627.02	307.74	319.28	8302.29	1458.24	6844.05

29–21 主要工业产品产量
Output of Major Industrial Products

年 份 Year	卷 烟 (万箱) Cigarettes (10000 cases)	茅台酒 (吨) Mao-Tai Chiew (ton)	原煤 (万吨) Coal (10000 tons)	发电量 (亿千瓦小时) Electricity (100 million kwh)	粗钢 (万吨) Steel (10000 tons)	成品钢材 (万吨) Steel Products (10000 tons)	水泥 (万吨) Cement (10000 tons)	农用化肥 (万吨) Chemical Fertilizer (10000 tons)	磷矿石 (万吨) Phosphorite Material (10000 tons)
1978	31.60	1067	1669	41.43	8.73	4.95	130.93	11.57	169.02
1979	34.30	1143	1636	44.90	9.11	6.48	148.38	21.8	124.61
1980	44.00	1200	1398	45.17	8.66	7.75	144.47	30.34	188.02
1981	48.70	1055	1416	43.55	8.60	5.17	145.82	30.22	170.03
1982	56.10	1181	1695	57.86	10.62	9.43	161.07	30.98	207.98
1983	64.40	1189	1847	69.51	11.63	13.73	182.26	32.37	216.72
1984	85.70	1320	2027	76.46	13.87	18.93	206.94	36.85	214.34
1985	106.10	1266	2344	78.07	19.28	20.47	231.26	30.31	92.77
1986	102.10	1267	2554	82.52	26.34	21.45	247.31	34.99	162.58
1987	146.40	1331	3170	84.90	32.67	25.30	258.10	39.32	248.39
1988	188.40	1300	3210	90.12	33.17	23.13	293.38	39.23	281.82
1989	205.10	1727	3496	96.53	37.78	22.96	295.51	43.49	285.46
1990	208.00	1879	3695	103.87	47.11	25.36	278.29	46.73	323.86
1991	194.00	1959	3723	116.03	52.71	31.87	308.13	51.65	342.96
1992	202.90	2089	4162	129.35	64.19	48.83	370.44	51.54	348.42
1993	193.60	2281	4529	146.56	70.67	53.03	406.68	60.06	307.00
1994	204.90	3390	5128	197.21	69.89	56.14	463.10	53.60	341.43
1995	202.90	3978	5472	231.55	65.94	51.69	468.34	61.02	390.81
1996	197.70	4365	6143	248.80	59.47	51.60	522.00	57.50	446.40
1997	205.30	4468	6597	255.75	78.77	57.65	632.00	69.17	509.91
1998	195.80	5072	6561	291.77	100.28	77.28	559.42	72.82	436.51
1999	187.60	5074	4025	334.46	140.09	118.77	710.29	73.12	493.92
2000	187.40	5397	3677	404.70	166.90	150.93	783.88	84.05	588.70
2001	180.80	7317	3731	480.25	146.99	138.61	920.01	86.75	669.91
2002	177.80	9625	5001	547.12	194.65	177.79	1121.11	158.49	729.20
2003	183.19	10869	7816	636.60	206.10	192.97	1324.66	186.89	783.68
2004	194.74	12836	9757	713.04	208.07	203.22	1428.80	213.78	801.98
2005	208.21	8885	10615	786.78	237.83	214.85	1557.97	268.28	878.79
2006	211.73	9719	11817	974.66	332.51	256.57	1799.40	338.76	1034.60
2007	220.71	10789	10864	1166.32	349.36	328.14	1943.10	321.84	1198.83
2008	226.74	11308	11798	1192.08	345.64	337.52	2048.94	262.21	1317.18
2009	232.24	12161	10001	1363.09	343.10	337.62	2664.78	347.28	1360.66
2010	239.24	12911	12656	1358.69	360.48	391.04	3694.84	384.92	1579.21
2011	245.23	15523	13033	1344.14	434.01	462.36	5000.19	360.37	2052.82
2012	249.35	15806	15031	1548.44	531.27	560.22	6100.45	503.82	2281.95

注：1.表中工业产品产量1998年前为全社会口径，1998年及以后为规模以上工业企业数据，其中原煤产量2008年以后为规模以上工业企业数据。2.茅台酒产量从2001年后计量单位为千升，2005年开始按包装量统计。

Note:1.Before 1998, output of industrial products refer to the caliber of total society,but from 1998,it refer to the output of industrial enterprises above designated size.And output of coal refer to the output .of industrial enterprises above designated size after 2008. 2.Measurement units of Mao-Tai chiew since 2001 has been changed into kiloliter,Output of Mao-Tai was counted by packing quantity from the year 2005 and later.

29-22 建筑业总产值和房屋建筑面积

Gross Output Value of Construction and Floor Space of Building

年份 Year	建筑业总产值(亿元) Gross Output Value of Construction Enterprises (100 million yuan)	#国有及国有控股 State-owned and State-controlled	施工面积(万平方米) Floor Space of Building Under Construction (10000 sq.m)	竣工面积(万平方米) Floor Space of Building Completed (10000 sq.m)
1978	4.40	3.55	313	164
1979	4.44	3.40	371	185
1980	4.55	3.37	380	198
1981	4.76	3.27	392	213
1982	5.34	3.46	450	236
1983	6.22	3.85	501	258
1984	7.54	4.79	551	293
1985	9.81	6.34	662	342
1986	11.27	7.21	720	368
1987	12.93	8.62	725	378
1988	15.30	10.43	823	326
1989	15.57	11.07	765	305
1990	16.98	11.85	699	328
1991	20.32	14.09	739	335
1992	26.20	18.13	906	393
1993	37.65	26.63	1250	597
1994	48.69	36.65	1119	467
1995	55.40	44.58	1191	477
1996	66.49	52.45	1216	510
1997	76.70	59.78	1278	585
1998	83.20	62.42	1457	592
1999	96.65	70.91	1671	694
2000	109.06	77.04	1792	824
2001	150.20	110.40	1946	892
2002	181.12	133.62	2309	1054
2003	212.29	164.02	2520	980
2004	255.45	191.63	2820	1251
2005	271.23	207.88	3153	1150
2006	312.34	247.90	3369	1108
2007	348.79	271.69	3813	1204
2008	393.88	303.28	4230	1216
2009	523.91	408.00	4953	1244
2010	622.96	496.00	5756	1350
2011	824.72	659.29	6779	1530
2012	1039.95	859.68	8254	1863

29–23 交通运输
Transportation

年 份 Year	铁路营业里程(公里) Length of Railways(km)	公路线路里程(公里) Length of Highways(km)	客运量(万人) Passenger Traffic (10000 persons)	铁 路 Railway	公 路 Highway	水 运 Waterway	货运量(万吨) Freight Traffic (10000 tons)	铁 路 Railway	公 路 Highway	水 运 Waterway
1978	1365	25954	3294	977	2260	57	3467	1320	2083	64
1979	1373	26166	4608	1083	3462	63	3599	1314	2209	76
1980	1374	27367	5950	1164	4700	86	3424	1395	1953	76
1981	1373	27422	7175	1224	5873	78	3541	1481	1991	69
1982	1396	27499	8026	1288	6648	90	3825	1581	2164	80
1983	1396	27675	8259	1456	6707	96	4233	1665	2488	80
1984	1411	27872	9915	1620	8184	111	4600	1777	2735	88
1985	1419	27999	10874	1638	9102	134	5717	1874	3758	85
1986	1419	28383	11033	1458	9387	188	6551	1949	4510	92
1987	1420	29823	13512	1461	11854	197	7613	2043	5479	91
1988	1420	30445	14361	1633	12564	164	8570	2074	6413	83
1989	1420	30716	14923	1530	13125	268	9459	2178	7170	111
1990	1420	31157	17048	1256	15682	110	9840	2315	7414	111
1991	1419	31588	19081	1255	17718	108	10008	2365	7551	92
1992	1423	31889	21641	1251	20262	128	11349	2498	8752	99
1993	1423	32092	23494	1366	22010	118	11495	2537	8851	107
1994	1423	32398	27076	1515	25313	248	12189	2599	9453	137
1995	1423	32487	36151	1572	34304	275	12586	2657	9806	123
1996	1423	32700	42429	1843	40245	341	12182	2770	9192	220
1997	1640	33211	46644	1957	44416	271	13077	2739	10117	221
1998	1648	33604	48468	2048	45987	433	13577	3044	10219	314
1999	1654	33973	49457	2194	46807	456	14065	3272	10449	344
2000	1641	34643	53032	2251	50313	468	15615	3577	11684	354
2001	1644	34618	54665	2017	52154	494	16344	3875	12114	355
2002	1893	44220	55980	1947	53478	555	17399	4356	12685	358
2003	1900	45304	55074	1796	52695	583	18224	4971	12886	367
2004	1891	46128	58707	1855	56077	775	19439	5504	13541	394
2005	1986	46893	64450	2191	61414	845	21771	6169	15082	520
2006	2014	113278	69270	2536	65786	948	24709	6826	17284	599
2007	2012	123247	74440	2979	70377	1084	26788	7289	18834	665
2008	1962	125365	80056	3199	75350	1507	33576	6683	26156	737
2009	1983	142561	84981	3204	80044	1733	34844	6997	27031	816
2010	2002	151644	97793	3437	92426	1930	40310	7991	31409	910
2011	2070	157820	120554	3939	114429	2186	44890	7219	36684	987
2012	2058	164542	142809	3902	136454	2453	52765	6665	45000	1100

注：1.资料来源于省交通厅、成都铁路分局(下表同)。2.2006年起，公路线路里程包括村道里程；2008年公路、水路运输量采用全国公路水路运输量专项调查数据(下表同)。

Notes:1.Data in the table are obtained from provincial transports department and Chengdu Railway Branch(the same applies to the next table).2.Since 2006,the data of total length of highways have been included the length of village road;the data of highways and waterways freight traffic refers to data of highways and waterways freight traffic special investigation in 2008 (the same applies to the next table).

29–24 旅客周转量和货物周转量
Passenger-kilometers and Freight Ton-kilometers

年 份 Year	旅客周转量 (亿人公里) Passenger-kilometers (100 million passenger-km)	铁 路 Railway	公 路 Highway	水 运 Waterway	货物周转量 (亿吨公里) Freight Ton-kilometers (100 million ton.km)	铁 路 Railway	公 路 Highway	水 运 Waterway
1978	25.50	16.04	9.26	0.20	79.60	72.30	6.57	0.73
1979	31.54	19.66	11.68	0.20	93.99	86.49	6.59	0.91
1980	37.69	22.77	14.67	0.25	96.03	88.99	5.91	1.13
1981	43.28	25.32	17.73	0.23	100.43	93.19	6.23	1.01
1982	46.93	26.70	19.99	0.24	109.69	98.99	9.50	1.20
1983	52.35	30.69	21.40	0.26	117.22	104.86	10.97	1.39
1984	61.04	36.21	24.55	0.28	132.72	119.19	11.61	1.92
1985	74.07	45.11	28.64	0.32	151.42	133.22	16.32	1.88
1986	76.45	47.39	28.70	0.36	171.03	148.13	20.44	2.46
1987	93.19	53.22	39.60	0.37	186.09	156.33	26.87	2.89
1988	105.67	61.20	44.14	0.33	196.04	159.75	33.50	2.79
1989	105.73	58.08	47.16	0.49	216.45	174.59	38.96	2.90
1990	102.90	49.20	53.34	0.36	224.31	179.72	41.84	2.75
1991	117.61	54.84	62.52	0.25	232.91	186.96	42.51	3.44
1992	136.77	66.62	69.84	0.31	268.80	214.88	49.84	4.08
1993	156.26	80.86	75.12	0.28	292.96	239.40	49.12	4.44
1994	173.71	88.72	84.53	0.46	298.44	243.87	50.06	4.51
1995	180.09	91.23	88.32	0.54	301.28	245.76	51.34	4.18
1996	185.94	88.32	96.84	0.78	317.70	261.99	51.07	4.64
1997	191.02	97.97	92.52	0.53	336.08	277.95	54.06	4.07
1998	201.77	101.13	99.97	0.67	330.30	270.40	54.84	5.06
1999	229.20	118.37	109.95	0.88	370.03	305.68	60.28	4.07
2000	238.36	120.79	116.54	1.03	404.07	334.11	65.86	4.10
2001	251.06	124.22	125.76	1.08	439.30	364.71	70.36	4.23
2002	250.79	116.10	133.60	1.09	486.03	407.26	74.25	4.52
2003	248.55	112.08	135.31	1.16	547.01	465.92	76.63	4.46
2004	278.21	125.87	150.79	1.55	610.88	520.70	84.27	5.91
2005	312.40	145.71	164.91	1.78	646.55	544.31	94.15	8.09
2006	349.82	160.98	186.91	1.93	680.96	557.70	114.48	8.78
2007	369.20	160.51	206.40	2.29	721.26	583.85	127.99	9.42
2008	407.59	163.00	241.15	3.44	809.93	564.31	234.96	10.66
2009	430.56	162.41	264.06	4.09	897.38	644.41	241.60	11.37
2010	514.41	189.38	320.46	4.57	1012.20	706.45	293.00	12.75
2011	631.74	204.58	422.01	5.15	1060.69	696.36	350.10	14.23
2012	718.22	199.20	513.07	5.95	1177.78	693.68	467.60	16.50

29-25 内外贸易

Domestic Trade,Foreign Trade and Economic Cooperation

年 份 Year	社会消费品零售总额(亿元) Total Retail Sales of Consumer Goods (100 million yuan)	进出口总 额(万美元) Total Imports and Exports (USD 10000)	#出口额 Exports	实际利用外资额(万美元) Foreign Capital Actually Utilized (USD 10000)	#国 外 贷 款 Foreign Loans	#外商直接投资 Direct Foreign Investments
1978	21.23	1645	285			
1979	23.57	2111	703			
1980	26.73	2797	1641			
1981	30.48	4782	3617			
1982	34.55	5455	4522			
1983	38.43	5238	4186			
1984	43.64	6997	4548	61	61	
1985	52.25	8720	4010	286	12	148
1986	57.25	8605	6361	1276	38	74
1987	66.39	12488	9296	376	127	101
1988	83.40	15527	11586	1408	425	440
1989	83.84	18681	13322	2102	826	747
1990	85.90	21802	15358	2983	1925	463
1991	92.92	24614	18958	2845	1436	1034
1992	106.75	33907	22424	3574	1595	1979
1993	143.09	36470	24491	4922	628	4294
1994	165.01	53595	37346	8363	2000	6363
1995	204.45	68144	43023	9637	3934	5703
1996	241.57	64240	43554	10628	7490	3138
1997	274.68	67660	48239	13834	8857	4977
1998	299.97	62243	38794	18100	13565	4535
1999	324.67	54763	35780	19532	15442	4090
2000	355.58	66002	42060	19545	17044	2501
2001	391.14	64978	42170	14010	11181	2829
2002	430.64	69141	44181	9383	5684	3700
2003	474.57	98477	58834	13191	7565	5626
2004	535.31	151442	86709	13932	7399	6533
2005	615.75	140425	85925	19568	8800	10768
2006	710.00	161745	103874	18413	9029	9384
2007	858.15	227285	146513	15333	2682	12651
2008	1075.24	337037	190084	17379	2475	14904
2009	1247.25	230732	135856	18027	4663	13364
2010	1482.68	314680	192018	34026	4480	29546
2011	1751.62	488758	298509	71674	4353	51541
2012	2027.64	663156	495223	109805	5223	49116

注：1.进出口总额1997年及以前数据来源于原省对外贸易经济合作厅，1998年及以后数据来源于贵阳海关。2.实际利用外资额数据来源于省发改委、省商务厅。

Note:1.The yrar 1997and before,total imports and exports were obtained from the former provincial department of foreign trade and economic cooperation.After 1998 they obtained from Guiyang Customs.2.Data of foreign capital actually utilized are obtained from Provincial Development and Reform Commission and Department of Commerce.

29–26 旅 游
Tourism

年 份 Year	国内旅游人数 (万人次) Total Number of Domestic Tourists (10000 person-times)	国内旅游收入 (亿元) Earnings from Domestic Tourism (100 million yuan)	入境旅游人数 (万人次) Total Number of International Tourists Inbound (10000 person-times)	#外国人 Foreigners	国际旅游外汇收入(万美元) Foreign Exchange Income from Tourism(USD 10000)
1980			0.17	0.07	0.70
1981			0.23	0.06	2.49
1982			0.51	0.18	5.73
1983			0.71	0.19	8.03
1984	204	0.07	1.02	0.27	15.86
1985	244	0.07	1.13	0.29	61.95
1986	248	0.05	1.40	0.46	100.19
1987	261	0.07	1.88	0.77	137.22
1988	296	0.18	2.36	0.75	162.54
1989	397	0.18	1.37	0.47	136.75
1990	399	0.19	2.41	0.74	180.90
1991	630	0.66	3.75	1.04	307.35
1992	1426	2.21	7.63	1.87	686.13
1993	1647	4.29	10.25	4.26	1049.45
1994	1700	4.28	12.08	7.61	2109.63
1995	1750	7.18	13.65	7.78	2897.73
1996	1800	8.53	12.53	6.67	3811.95
1997	1850	30.81	15.02	7.81	4429.10
1998	1880	35.14	15.13	6.77	4831.18
1999	1910	43.75	16.70	6.57	5501.54
2000	1980	57.95	18.39	7.12	6092.23
2001	2100	75.81	20.55	7.85	6873.23
2002	2200	99.86	22.81	8.45	7950.63
2003	1835	114.36	7.70	2.40	2893.91
2004	2480	161.02	23.10	7.63	8020.27
2005	3099	242.83	27.62	9.26	10141.36
2006	4716	377.79	32.14	10.70	11515.66
2007	6220	504.04	43.00	15.48	12917.55
2008	8151	643.82	39.54	18.22	11697.37
2009	10400	797.69	39.95	16.28	11044.40
2010	12863	1052.64	50.01	18.61	12957.88
2011	16961	1420.70	58.51	23.62	13507.18
2012	21331	1849.49	70.50	30.42	16893.60

注：资料来源于省旅游局。
Note:Data in the table are obtained from Provincial Tourism Bureau.

29–27 金融机构存贷款余额

Saving Deposits and Loans Balance of Financial Institutions

单位：亿元 (100 million yuan)

年 份 Year	各项存款 合 计 Total Deposits	#储蓄存款 Saving Deposit	人均储蓄余额 (元) Per Captia Savings Deposit (yuan)	各项贷款 合 计 Total Loans
1978	18.05	1.84	6.91	21.62
1979	19.82	2.42	8.93	23.31
1980	24.43	3.73	13.54	24.94
1981	25.75	5.28	18.85	30.10
1982	30.75	7.26	25.46	33.99
1983	35.25	8.86	30.68	36.07
1984	45.33	12.33	42.27	46.22
1985	52.27	16.61	56.27	63.41
1986	69.76	22.21	74.06	89.67
1987	83.79	30.37	99.60	107.76
1988	91.92	34.99	112.87	125.17
1989	107.35	44.54	141.44	142.73
1990	144.39	61.27	190.32	183.91
1991	187.06	80.30	243.99	234.56
1992	232.80	102.07	305.80	290.01
1993	291.22	141.88	419.16	357.00
1994	364.84	181.05	527.30	421.07
1995	478.21	247.62	710.89	513.41
1996	586.26	311.19	881.12	610.51
1997	712.80	362.87	1013.43	761.88
1998	815.43	423.08	1164.96	840.63
1999	945.80	484.51	1315.23	899.83
2000	1106.64	539.49	1445.23	1064.82
2001	1341.11	641.67	1698.83	1212.23
2002	1553.00	759.05	1988.13	1403.92
2003	1898.62	912.84	2368.88	1714.04
2004	2322.27	1094.55	2816.16	2020.04
2005	2777.54	1350.90	3633.79	2303.93
2006	3300.08	1596.86	4304.20	2696.11
2007	3826.37	1790.14	4889.76	3128.63
2008	4736.93	2237.05	6189.96	3569.27
2009	5898.26	2676.09	7503.41	4656.50
2010	7363.92	3244.99	9250.26	5747.53
2011	8742.79	3934.48	11325.50	6841.92
2012	10540.06	4806.09	13824.51	8274.78

注：1.资料来源于中国人民银行贵阳中心支行。2.2005年及以后各年人均储蓄余额采用按人口普查修订后常住半年的年平均人口计算，以前年份按常住一年口径计算。3.表中储蓄存款及人均储蓄2010年及以前为城乡居民储蓄存款和城乡居民人均储蓄。

Note:1.Data in the table are obtained from Guiyang Central Branch of PBC. 2.Per captia savings deposit are calculated by permanent population in half a year scope since 2005,and by permanent population in one year scope before 2005.3.The year 2010 and before,savings deposit refer to resident savings deposit of urban and rural.

29-28 教 育

年份 Year	在校学生数(万人) Students Enrollment(1 0000 persons)			小学毕业生 升学率(%) Percentage of Graduates of Primary Schools Entering into Junior Secondary Schools(%)
	普通高等学校 Regular Institutions of Higher Education	普通中学 Regular Secondary Schools	小学 Primary Schools	
1978	1.33	137.17	423.60	76.1
1979	1.78	126.07	413.71	70.0
1980	1.71	110.24	404.22	62.6
1981	1.81	96.58	403.49	56.7
1982	1.67	89.53	412.30	53.8
1983	1.68	82.39	415.79	51.5
1984	2.03	85.13	436.56	53.1
1985	2.30	91.59	447.68	54.2
1986	2.52	99.00	461.99	53.8
1987	2.60	102.35	458.27	47.7
1988	2.73	98.63	449.70	56.6
1989	2.76	93.31	440.36	67.1
1990	2.70	96.54	435.05	60.8
1991	2.57	100.23	433.85	59.6
1992	2.67	103.99	435.94	59.9
1993	2.93	100.55	439.81	63.9
1994	3.23	103.08	455.30	70.5
1995	3.47	108.43	475.34	72.7
1996	3.57	113.47	489.32	71.5
1997	3.85	121.54	503.82	75.8
1998	4.26	127.10	505.36	75.1
1999	5.65	138.63	500.96	77.8
2000	7.55	157.20	500.21	78.7
2001	10.82	184.60	490.17	84.4
2002	12.27	212.81	484.28	88.2
2003	14.94	235.30	476.87	92.4
2004	17.99	249.34	479.41	96.0
2005	20.68	254.96	473.76	97.4
2006	22.15	256.31	474.38	97.8
2007	24.17	256.00	466.31	95.6
2008	26.75	261.78	469.79	98.7
2009	29.91	269.45	456.87	97.7
2010	32.33	275.68	433.50	96.3
2011	34.41	282.71	408.74	96.5
2012	38.38	287.38	380.08	96.3

注：资料来源于省教育厅。

Education

学龄儿童入学率(%) Percentage of School-Aged Children Enrolled(%)	专任教师数(人) Number of Full-time Teachers(person)		
	普通高等学校 Regular Institutions of Higher Education	普通中学 Regular Secondary Schools	小学 Primary Schools
89.5	2753	54227	155930
86.1	3357	55532	151860
80.8	3638	51950	155708
78.5	3606	46892	159494
78.3	3986	44646	152176
81.2	4183	43821	152338
83.6	4555	41879	155715
84.9	4830	45159	157622
86.9	5177	47119	162105
89.2	5559	50216	161689
89.9	5588	51618	163514
88.8	5530	53279	164298
91.3	5469	55528	166662
90.3	5371	57074	168364
92.4	5542	59006	166769
93.8	5550	60453	165276
95.1	5540	63059	168842
96.0	5599	64292	168358
96.7	5600	66842	166526
97.4	5699	69355	168493
97.7	5929	72865	167823
98.2	6050	76654	170680
98.5	7240	81156	174822
98.2	9007	88079	173238
98.2	11079	97641	177920
98.2	11775	107312	179367
97.8	13792	115616	180793
98.3	14353	122721	183679
98.6	15398	128274	188762
98.6	16964	131087	191991
97.2	18037	135360	200024
98.4	19634	139302	199189
97.9	20351	142508	197913
98.6	21855	147396	197094
99.3	22803	156325	197983

Note:Data in the table are obtained from Provincial Education Department.

29–29 卫生
Health Care

年 份 Year	卫 生 机构数 (个) Number of Health Institutions (unit)	#医 院、卫生院 Hospitals	卫生机构 床位数 (张) Number of Beds in Health Institution (bed)	#医院、卫生院 Hospitals	卫生技术 人员数 (人) Medical Technical Personnels (person)	#执业(助理) 医 师 Doctors	每万人口拥有 Per 10000 person 床位数 (张) Number of Beds(bed)	执业(助理) 医师数(人) Number of Doctors (person)
1978	6274	4510	40274	37533	58190	21228	14.0	7.9
1979	6267	4516	42812	40001	60635	21868	14.6	8.0
1980	6246	4529	43627	40835	63766	26491	14.7	9.5
1981	6634	4588	44752	41314	68918	26798	14.6	9.5
1982	6595	4605	46226	42301	70671	27097	14.7	9.4
1983	6605	4602	47555	43292	72988	28433	14.9	9.8
1984	6673	4643	49271	44123	75808	29309	15.0	10.0
1985	6480	3295	49805	45226	76722	29153	15.2	9.8
1986	6760	3358	50893	46259	79776	30475	15.3	10.1
1987	6716	3349	52595	48059	81599	31305	15.6	10.2
1988	7021	3896	54193	49543	84904	35249	15.8	11.3
1989	6926	3620	57428	52063	84891	35646	16.4	11.2
1990	6949	3721	59013	53074	86120	37185	16.2	11.4
1991	6908	3630	59168	53978	87774	37978	16.3	11.5
1992	4734	1624	57767	52405	87927	38537	15.6	11.5
1993	3908	1623	57720	51888	84409	38060	15.2	11.2
1994	3930	1660	59648	53766	88053	40358	15.5	11.7
1995	3934	1692	60295	54475	87005	40260	15.5	11.5
1996	10932	1870	58205	54051	84273	43548	15.2	12.2
1997	8955	1870	57560	53627	84348	43236	14.9	12.0
1998	9113	1877	57844	54492	84400	44138	14.9	12.1
1999	9703	1874	58624	55138	85613	45473	14.9	12.3
2000	8992	1878	58380	55148	85397	45673	14.8	12.2
2001	8791	1872	59120	55876	86103	46412	14.8	12.3
2002	7027	1857	59850	57742	79727	36964	15.1	11.3
2003	6499	1866	59281	56273	77557	36911	14.9	11.2
2004	6664	1850	61313	58113	76699	36911	14.9	12.2
2005	6571	1843	61784	58398	77805	35521	16.6	9.5
2006	6147	1855	66452	62586	82324	41147	17.9	11.1
2007	5907	1939	75806	71400	85298	42100	20.7	11.5
2008	5848	1934	83132	78129	89313	38830	23.0	10.7
2009	5736	1982	97527	91164	95270	40171	27.3	11.3
2010	5637	2005	105277	97490	102527	42158	30.0	12.0
2011	5683	2071	117534	108029	112210	44037	27.7	10.4
2012	27379	2210	136542	129670	152608	47745	32.1	11.2

注：1.资料来源于省卫生厅,表中数据2011年及以前的数据不含村卫生室,2012年起含村卫生室。2.每万人口指标2011年以前以常驻人口数为基数计算，2011年起以户籍人口数为基数计算。

Note:1.Data in the table are provided from the Department of Health.2.In the year of 2011 and before data in this table exclude health clinics of village, but including health clinics of village in 2012. 3.Before 2011, per ten thousand population indicators were calculated on the number of resident population , but since 2011 they have calculated on the number of household population.

中国统计出版社最新图书简目

（仅供参考，以最后出书为准）

统计资料

中国统计年鉴 -2013
中国统计摘要 -2013
国际统计年鉴 -2013
2013 中国发展报告
中国第三产业统计年鉴 -2013
中国区域经济统计年鉴 -2013
中国劳动统计年鉴 -2013
中国社会统计年鉴 -2013
中国城市统计年鉴 -2013
中国建筑业统计年鉴 -2013
中国人口和就业统计年鉴 -2013
中国工业经济统计年鉴 -2013
中国商品交易市场统计年鉴 -2013
中国房地产统计年鉴 -2013
中国能源统计年鉴 -2013
中国民政统计年鉴 -2013
中国贸易外经统计年鉴 -2013
2013 中国地区经济监测报告
中国科技统计年鉴 -2013
中国农村统计年鉴 -2013
中国农产品价格调查年鉴 -2013
中国高技术产业统计年鉴 -2013
中国教育经费统计年鉴 -2013
中国农村贫困监测报告 -2013
全国农产品成本收益资料汇编 -2013
中国科学技术协会统计年鉴 -2013
工业企业科技活动资料 -2013
大中型批发零售和住宿餐饮企业统计年鉴 -2013
中国价格统计年鉴 -2013
第二次全国 R&D 资源清查资料汇编 - 工业企业卷
中国住户调查年鉴 -2013
中国农村全面建设小康监测报告 -2013
中国县域统计年鉴 -2013
第二次全国 R&D 资源清查资料汇编 - 综合卷
中国人才资源统计报告 -2011
中国零售和餐饮连锁企业统计年鉴 -2013
中国民族统计年鉴 -2013
2010 年中国第六次人口普查公报

2013 年省级综合统计年鉴系列

北京 天津 河北 山西 内蒙古 辽宁 吉林 黑龙江 上海 江苏 浙江 安徽 福建 江西 山东
河南 湖北 湖南 广东 广西 海南 重庆 四川 贵州 云南 西藏 陕西 甘肃 青海 宁夏
新疆 新疆生产建设兵团

2013 年市（县）级综合统计年鉴系列

天津滨海新区 石家庄 唐山 邯郸 太原 大同 长治 阳泉 晋城 朔州 晋中
运城 忻州 临汾 呼和浩特 包头 沈阳 大连 长春 吉林市 四平 哈尔滨 黑龙江垦区
上海浦东新区 南京 苏州 无锡 常州 徐州 南通 盐城 镇江 江阴 丹阳
杭州 宁波 绍兴 台州 温州 金华 嘉兴 衢州 福州 福州经济技术开发区
厦门经济特区 南昌 上饶 济南 青岛 潍坊 郑州 洛阳 三门峡 南阳 武汉 宜昌
十堰 荆州 咸宁 长沙 广州 东莞 惠州 深圳 桂林 南宁 柳州 来宾 河池 海口 成都 绵阳
贵阳 昆明 庆阳 西安 兰州 银川 乌鲁木齐

2010 年人口普查资料系列

中国 2010 年人口普查资料
北京 天津 河北 山西 内蒙古 辽宁 吉林 黑龙江 上海 江苏
浙江 安徽 福建 江西 山东 河南 湖北 湖南 广东 广西 海南 重庆 四川 贵州 云南
西藏 陕西 甘肃 青海 宁夏 新疆 新疆生产建设兵团
河南省各市 2010 年人口普查资料丛书
中国分县 2010 年人口普查资料
中国分乡镇、街道 2010 年人口普查资料
中国分民族 2010 年人口普查资料

“十一五”规划教材

统计学（“十二五”规划，黄良文）
抽样调查理论与实践（“十二五”规划，冯士雍）
统计学（“十二五”规划，单微）
试验设计（“十二五”规划，茆诗松）
贝叶斯统计（“十二五”规划，茆诗松）
统计学：从数据到结论（十二五规划，吴喜之）
医学统计学（陆守曾）
非参数统计（吴喜之）
概率论与数理统计（茆诗松）
现代金融投资统计分析（李腊生）
多元统计分析（任雪松）
应用时间序列分析（王振龙）
统计指数理论及应用（徐国祥）
经济计量学教程（贺铿）
质量管理统计方法（茆诗松）
统计实验系列教材（许涤龙）
社会统计学（蒋萍）
市场调查与预测（蒋志华）
统计学原理（非统计专业使用，朱胜）
国民经济核算教程（杨灿）
概率论与数理统计（经济、管理类专业使用，朱胜）

重点图书

挑大学选专业 2013—高考志愿填报指南
挑大学选专业 2013—考研择校指南

增比进位 后发赶超
——奋进中的县(市、区、特区)

Incrementary ratio and ranking, Catching-up and surpassing
—Counties (cities, districts and special regions) in advance

仁怀市

Renhuai City

中国酒都仁怀城区一角
One corner of Renhuai city--the China liquor capital

茅台酒包装车间
Maotai wine packaging workshop

仁怀市行政区域面积1788平方公里，2012年全市耕地保有量83.4万亩，基本农田保有量62.9万亩。辖6个乡（其中1个民族乡）、12个镇、3个街道，146个村民委员会、27个居民委员会。年末总人口68万。2012年，仁怀市经济社会发展取得良好成效。

综合实力大幅增强。完成生产总值341亿元，增长22%；三次产业比重由4.6：65.4：30调整为3.1：69.6：27.3；实现财政总收入114亿元，增长72.5%，其中公共财政预算收入23.18亿元，增长43.7%；完成全社会固定资产投资170亿元，增长154%；城镇居民人均可支配收入20656元，增长21.5%；农民人均纯收入6752元，增长16.9%；社会消费品

中国酒都，与时俱进
Chinese wine capital, advancing with the times

城乡教育协调发展，义务教育水平不断提高。图为发展中的仁怀一中全景图

Coordinated development of urban and rural education, and constantly improve the level of compulsory education. The picture shows the development of Renhuai first middle school panorama

Renhuai city owns administrative area of 1,788 square kilometers,in 2012, 834,000 mu of cultivated land quantity in the city, 629,000 mu of basic farmland ownership. Jurisdiction over 6 townships (of which 1 minority townships), 12 towns, 3 streets, 146 village committees, 27 residents committees. At the end of the year, the total population of 680,000. In 2012, the economic and social development of Renhuai city has achieved good results.

Greatly enhance the comprehensive strength. The GDP of 34.1 billion yuan, an increase of 22%; the proportion of three industries by 4.6: 65.4: 30 to 3.1: 69.6: 27.3; total financial revenue 11.4 billion yuan, up 72.5%, of which the public budget income was 2.318 billion yuan, up 43.7%; completed investment in fixed assets 17 billion yuan, an increase of 154%; urban residents per capita disposable income of 20,656 yuan, an increase of 21.5%; per capita net income of farmers 6,752 yuan, an increase of 16.9%; total retail sales of social consumer goods is expected to 5.17 billion yuan, an increase of 28.7%; the balance of deposits in the financial institutions reached 27.76 billion yuan, an increase of 31.4%, the loan balance of 8.02 billion yuan, an increase of 66.5%. The comprehensive economic strength of preprogrammed each column ranked the second in the whole province.

The rapid development of industrial economy. Throughout the year above-scale industrial output value of 31.7 billion yuan, an increase of 31.6%; expected above-scale industrial added value of 28 billion yuan, an increase of

农民在农民运动会上展现风采

The farmers shows the charming in the farmer's sport game

红军四渡赤水纪念园

The Red Army of the Chishui Memorial Park

茅台镇全景
Maotai town panorama

美丽新农村
The beautiful new rural

零售总额预计51.7亿元，增长28.7%；全市金融机构各项存款余额达到277.6亿元，同比增长31.4%，各项贷款余额80.2亿元，同比增长66.5%。经济综合实力预排名位列全省第二位。

工业经济高速发展。全年实现规模以上工业总产值317亿元，同比增长31.6%；预计规模以上工业增加值280亿元，同比增长27.4%。白酒产量完成30万千升，同比增长26%。茅台集团实现利税245亿元，增长62%。工业园区建设快速推进，入园开工建设项目57个，投产企业41家，实现产能5.1万千升。品牌效应不断彰显，新增中国驰名商标1件、贵州省著名商标20件、贵州名牌产品3个。

高粱基地一角
One corner of sorghum base

27.4%. Liquor production 300,000 kiloliters, an increase of 26%. Maotai group to achieve profits and taxes 24.5 billion yuan, an increase of 62%. Fast promote the construction of Industrial Park, the park construction project 57, 41 production enterprises, implementation capacity of 51,000 kiloliters. Brand effect has been demonstrated, add 1 well-known trademark in China, 20 famous trademarks of Guizhou Province, 3 famous brand products in Guizhou.

To speed up the pace of urban construction. Constantly optimize the layout, two years ahead of schedule in the province to achieve full coverage of urban and rural planning; environmental remediation rapid advance of Maotai, national liquor metro resettlement area north 1 groups of completion settlement, 3 groups of subjects completed; Zunren high-speed across the board through the comprehensive road, the ring east road extend to north, Erhebin Avenue, central city road white to black and other projects completed; urbanization rate reached 45%; to promote urban and rural power grid renovation and upgrading, power grid construction investment reached 214 million yuan, city power supply basically guaranteed.

"Three rural" work to strengthen. Food production to maintain stable, production reached

建设中的仁赤高速公路五岔河特大桥
The construction of Wuchahe bridge Renchi highway

茅台高速路边夕阳红
Maotai high speed roadside red sunset

仁怀市污水处理厂
Renhuai city sewage treatment plant

城镇建设步伐加快。不断优化规划布局，提前两年在全省率先实现城乡规划全覆盖；茅台环境整治快速推进，国酒新城安置区北区1组团完工安置，3组团主体基本完工；遵仁高速全线贯通，环城东路北段延伸、二合河滨大道、中枢城区道路白改黑等工程全面完成；城镇化率达到45%；推进城乡电网改造和升级扩容，电网建设投资达2.14亿元，城市电力供应基本得到保障。

“三农”工作得到加强。粮食生产保持稳定，产量达23.5万吨；有机农业加速发展；生态畜牧业健康发展；农业产业化加速发展；实施项目整合；切实抓好项目扶贫和产业扶贫，减少贫困人口1.5万人；创建新农村建设示范点65个。

项目带动成效明显。狠抓项目谋划和项目争取，调整充实“十二五”项目库，使项目储备总量达1200多个，估算投资达4200多亿元；争取到2013年中央投资项目76个、中央资金27亿元，创历史新高。

环保工作扎实有效。加强环保基础设施建设；深化环境综合治理；扎实开展以打击“四非”为重点的白酒企业环境整治专项行动；新增营造林6.3万亩，森林面积和蓄积稳步增长。

改革开放不断深化。文化旅游长足进步。人民生活持续改善。

高标准农田一角
One corner of the high standard farmland

整合项目资金建成3.2万亩高标准农田。图为高标准农田核心示范区
The integrated project capital to build up 32,000 mu high standard farmland. The picture is the central demonstration area of the high standard farmland

建设中的名酒工业园区

Construction of the famous liquor industrial park

235,000 tons; to accelerate the development of organic agriculture; the healthy development of ecological animal husbandry; accelerate the development of agricultural industrialization; project integration; earnestly carry out the project of poverty alleviation and poor industry, 15,000 people reduction in poverty; create new rural construction demonstration point 65.

Project driven got results. Pay close attention to the project plan and project ,to adjust and fulfill the "Twelfth Five-Year Plan" project library, the project total reserves reached more than 1,200, estimated investment of about 420 billion yuan; strive get to the central investment project 76 in 2013, the capital of 2.7 billion yuan, make a record high.

Environmental protection got solid and effective work. Strengthen the construction of environmental protection infrastructure; to deepen the comprehensive management of the environment; carry out to combat the "four non" as focus of the liquor business environmental remediation special action; new afforestation 63,000 mu, forest area and volume of steady growth.

Deepening reform and opening up constantly. Cultural tourism make progress. Continued to improve people's lives.

盘 县

Panxian

英武大桥
Yingwu bridge

红果夜景
Hongguo night

盘县地处滇黔桂三省区结合部，隶属六盘水市。面积4056平方公里，辖37个乡镇、450个行政村、49个社区（居委会），人口118万，其中农业人口96万。境内聚居着汉、彝、苗、白、回等28个民族。有“滇黔锁钥”、“川黔要塞”、“金三角下的一颗明珠”之美誉。

自然气候宜人。年平均气温为13.5°C，森林覆盖率达42.07%。境内有世界古银杏之乡、乌蒙大草原、大洞竹海三个省级旅游风景名胜区，特别是有“活化石”之称的千年古银杏树群，因此被誉为“世界古银杏之乡”。

物产资源丰富。境内现已探明的矿产资源有煤、铁、铜、黄金等20多种，其中煤炭资源以储量大、品种全、质量优等特点著称，是贵州省乃至全国的重点产煤县和“黔电送粤”重要电源点，被誉为“煤电之都”。

交通快捷便利。320国道、国家高速公路G60镇胜段横穿东西，212省道和在建的水盘高速公路纵贯南北，长昆快速铁路客运专线、毕水兴高速公路正加快建设，为盘县东进贵阳、西出昆明、北上川渝、南下两广提供了便捷的交通条件。

文化底蕴深厚。古人类文化遗址“盘县大洞”扬名中外，佛教八小名山“丹霞山”孤峰耸立，“碧云洞”喀斯特

红果新城
Hongguo new city

镇胜高速红果北
Zhensheng highwei north Hongguo

Panxian is located in the junction of Yunnan, Guizhou and Guangxi three Provinces, and is belonged to Liupanshui City. Area of 4,056 square kilometers, jurisdiction over 37 townships, 450 administrative villages, 49 communities (neighborhood), population of 1.18 million, of which agricultural population of 960,000. Territory inhabited by the Han, Yi, Miao, Bai, Hui and other 28 ethnic groups. It owns the "Yunnan-Guizhou key", "Sichuan-Guizhou fortress", "a Pearl under golden triangle " reputation.

盘县石桥妥乐古银杏
Panxian Shiqiao Tuole old Gingko

Natural climate is moderate. The annual average temperature is 13.5°C, the forest coverage rate reached 42.07%. The territory of the ancient world, the hometown of ginkgo, Wumeng prairie, Dadong Bamboo sea three provincial tourism scenic spots, especially those with a "living fossil" said the Gingko tree base, so as the "world Gingko town".

Rich in resources. Domestic had been proven mineral resources of coal, iron, copper, gold and other 20 kinds, including large reserves of coal known for abundant resources, variety, excellent quality and other features, Guizhou Province and the country's key coal-producing counties and the "Guizhou Power send to Guangdong" important power point, known as the "coal capital".Convenient transportation. 320 State Road, National Highway G60 Zhensheng segments across the east and west, Highway 212 and the construction of Shuipan highway north to south, Changkun fast passenger rail lines, Bishuixing highway is speeding up construction, provides a convenient traffic conditions for Panxian into Guiyang from east, west of Kunming, Chongqing north, south Guangdong and Guangxi .

Deep cultural heritage. Paleolithic "Panxian Dadong" is famous Chinese and foreign, Buddhist eight small mountain "Danxia Mountain" Koho stands, "Biyun hole" karst landscape strange, "Shuangfeng ancient city" charming, Yi Torch Festival and other national holidays and the "Seahorse Dance" and other folk dances welcome by by domestic and foreign tourists.

红果东湖
Hongguo east lake

盛宇洗煤
Shengyu coal washing

盘北煤矸石电厂
Panbei gangue power plant

盘县普田乡雁子小流域治理
Panxian Putian village Yanzi sub watershed management

溶洞景观千奇百怪，“双凤古城”独具魅力，彝族火把节等民族节日和“海马舞”等民间舞蹈深受国内外游客青睐。

2012年，县域经济发展综合排名全省第2位，综合经济实力迈上新台阶，地区生产总值达300.72亿元，同比增长17.4%，人均生产总值达29027元，同比增长17.28%。农村经济稳步发展，农业生产形势总体稳定，全县农民人均纯收入达5060元，同比增长17.54%，农林牧渔业总产值29.65亿元，同比增长9.1%，粮食总产量达31.28万吨，同比增长38.29%。工业经济快速发展，完成工业总产值506.14亿元，同比增长16.31%，实现工业增加值198.83亿元，同比增长16.7%。固定资产投资高速增长，全社会固定资产投资完成423.81亿元，同比增长111.6%，50万元以上固定资产投资（不含跨区项目）完成296.26亿元，同比增长79.2%。财政收支持续增长，财政总收入完成65.46亿元，同比增长19.86%，公共财政预算收入完成41.06亿元，同比增长58.69%，公共财政预算支出完成64.7亿元，同比增长32.6%。金融业稳健发展，2012年末，金融机构存款余额206.06亿元，其中：个人存款113.14亿元，金融机构贷款余额132.17亿元。消费品市场保持繁荣的良好态势，全年实现社会消费品零售总额48.15亿元，同比增长16.2%。旅游业保持良好的发展势头，全年实现旅游总收入7.42亿元，同比增长38.62%。

天能焦化
Tianneng coking

乌蒙大草原景区木栈道
Wumeng prairie scenic boardwalk

清底河水库
Qingdihe reservoir

In 2012, the county's economic development ranking second in the province, comprehensive economic strength to a new level, GDP reached 30.072 billion yuan, an increase of 17.4%, per capita GDP reached 29,027 yuan, an increase of 17.28%. The steady development of the rural economy, agricultural production situation is generally stable, the county's per capita net income of farmers reached 5,060 yuan, an increase of 17.54%, agriculture, forestry, animal husbandry and fishery output value 2.965 billion yuan, an increase of 9.1%, total grain output reached 312,800 tons, up growth of 38.29%. The rapid development of industrial economy, industrial output value of 50.614 billion yuan, an increase of 16.31%, industrial added value of 19.883 billion yuan, an increase of 16.7%. Rapid growth of investment in fixed assets, total fixed asset investment of 42.381 billion yuan, an increase of 111.6%, more than 500,000 yuan investment in fixed assets (excluding cross-project) completed 29.626 billion yuan, an increase of 79.2%. Continued growth in financial revenue and expenditure, total fiscal revenue 6.546 billion yuan, an increase of 19.86%, the public budget revenue of 4.106 billion yuan, an increase of 58.69%, public finance budget expenditure was 6.47 billion yuan, an increase of 32.6%. Healthy development of the financial industry, by the end of 2012, financial institutions deposits 20.606 billion yuan, of which: personal deposits 11.314 billion yuan, 13.217 billion yuan loans of financial institutions. Consumer goods market to maintain a good momentum of prosperity, the annual total retail sales of social consumer goods 4.815 billion yuan, an increase of 16.2%. Maintain a good momentum of development of tourism, the annual 742 million yuan of tourism revenue, an increase of 38.62%.

龙滩口水库
Longtankou reservoir

许家屯水库
Xujiatun reservoir

以苦干实干实现凯里市增比进位

Carry hard work and practical work to make Kaili growth

2012年6月21日，州委书记廖少华（右二），州委常委、市委书记黄远良（左二）陪同现任省委书记赵克志（左一）和中央军委首长（右一）到凯里市舟溪镇农业产业园视察

On June 21, 2012, State committee secretary Liao Shaohua (second from right), the state commission committee and Party Secretary the Huang Yuanliang (second from left) accompanied by the incumbent Provincial Party Secretary Zhao Kezhi (first from left) and the Heads of the Central Military Commission (first from right) to have inspections of Kaili Zhouxi Town agricultural industrial park

2012年3月23日，黔东南州委常委、州委秘书长耿生茂（左二），黔东南州人民政府副州长、凯里市人民政府市长洪金洲（右二）陪同原贵州省委书记栗战书（左一）到凯里经济开发区对项目建设情况和产业发展情况进行调研

March 23, 2012, Qiandongnan Standing Committee, the Secretary-General of the State Committee of Geng Shengmao (second from left), Qiandongnan State Government Vice Governor, the Kaili Municipal People's Government Mayor Hong Jinzhou (second from right), accompanied by former secretary of the Guizhou Provincial Li Zhanshu (first from left) to have research of the Kaili Economic Development Zone project construction and industrial development

率先在全国实施老龄补贴制度，累计发放1.46亿元，惠及64867人

Take the lead in the implementation of the subsidy system on aging, issued a total of 146 million yuan, benefiting 64,867 people

凯里市作为黔东南苗族侗族自治州首府所在地，是全州政治、经济、文化、交通中心，辖9个乡镇、7个街道，面积1306平方公里，人口63万人，少数民族占总人口的75.36%，其中苗族人口占66.98%，是一个以苗族为主体、多民族聚居的城市。

凯里市委、市人民政府认真贯彻落实省委、省政府“两加一推”主基调和工业强省、城镇化带动两大战略，同步推进农业现代化。团结带领全市各族干部群众发扬“敢闯敢干”的创新精神和“敢试敢拼”的创业精神，推动凯里市经济社会实现跨越发展。一是敢于闯出工业发展新天地。炉碧工业园区已初具规模，落户企业95户，建成投产35户，被评为省级新型工业化产业示范基地。二是敢于干出凯麻同城新气象。2012年共投资100亿元以上，建设200公里路网，推动了凯麻同城化的进

鑫明星瓷业有限责任公司生产一线

Xinmingxing Porcelain Co., Ltd. production line

特色凯里
Featured Kaili

打造全国首个大型苗侗风情舞台秀《银秀》
To build the country's first large-scale Miao and Dong style stage show "Silver Show"

Kaili city as the capital of Miao and Dong Autonomous Prefecture, is the statewide political, economic, cultural and transportation center, the jurisdiction of 9 townships 7 streets, an area of 1,306 square kilometers, a population of 630,000 people, a minority people accounted for 75.36% of the total population, of which the Miao population accounted for 66.98%, is a Miao as the main, multi-ethnic city.

The Kaili Municipal Committee, Municipal People's Government to seriously implement the provincial committee, provincial government, "two plus one push" the main tone and industrial strong the province and urbanization driven two strategic, to proceed with the modernization of agriculture. Unite and lead the cadres and masses of all ethnic groups in the city to carry forward the "daring to do" spirit of innovation and the "dare to try" entrepreneurship, the Kaili economic and social achieve leapfrog development. First, dare to break a new world of industrial development. Lubi Industrial Park has begun to take shape, 95 enterprises settled, put into operation 35, was named provincial new industrialization demonstration base. Second, dare to dry out the new atmosphere of Kai Ma city. In 2012, a total investment of 10 billion yuan, the construction of 200 km road network, and promote the process of the Kai Ma city. At present, 4 towns hosting management, Kaili, Ma Jiang integration of the development is also

凯里"斑马线"文明
Kaili "zebra line" civilization

凯里新貌
Kaili new look

炉山工业园区企业建设如火如荼（一）
The Lushan industrial enterprises in the park construction is in full swing (one)

炉山工业园区企业建设如火如荼（二）
The Lushan industrial enterprises in the park construction is in full swing (two)

程。目前，4个乡镇已实现托管管理，凯里、麻江融合发展也即将实现。三是敢于试出农业发展新模式。凯里市集中力量办大事，充分发挥农业示范园区效应。打造了舟溪镇都市型蔬菜种植示范园区、大风洞乡晚熟葡萄种植示范园区和13个特色农业示范园。四是敢于拼出文明城市新形象。凯里市先后获得中国优秀旅游城市、省级文明城市、省级卫生城市、中国100个最具幸福感城市等称号。

2012年，在全省88个县市区经济发展增比进位综合测评预排位中，凯里市名列第4位，为全省9个州、市首府所在地之首。其中：全市生产总值完成119.23亿元，同比增长18.9%；50万元以上固定资产投资完成210亿元，同比增长79%；规模以上工业总产值完成82.7亿元，同比增长18.1%；财政总收入完成31.13亿元，同比增长55%，公共财政预算收入完成24.48亿元，同比增长70.6%；社会消费品零售总额完成67.42亿元，同比增长16.8%；农民人均纯收入达6081元，同比增长17.48%；城镇居民家庭人均可支配收入达18831元，同比增长14.75%。

炉山工业园区景观
Lushan Industrial Park Landscape

大力推进凯麻同城路网建设
Vigorously promote the city road network construction of Kai Ma

宏大生猪原种场——省级农业产业化龙头企业
Hongda Pig Breeding Farm - provincial agricultural industrialization leading enterprises

coming true. Third, dare to try out the new model of agricultural development. Kaili is concentrating power, give full play to the effect of agricultural demonstration zone. Build Zhouxi town urban vegetable demonstration garden area, the Dafengdong township late-maturing grape growing demonstration garden area and 13 specialty agriculture demonstration garden. Fourth, dare to show out the new image of the civilized city. Kaili has won the title of China excellent tourism city, the provincial civilized city, the provincial health city, 100 happiest cities and other titles.

蔬菜基地——平茶蔬菜产业园区
Vegetable base - Pingcha vegetable industrial park

In 2012, the province's 88 county and municipal economic development growth than comprehensive evaluation of the pre-qualifying, Kaili City, ranked No. 4, the municipal seat of the first 9 states across the province. Among which: the city's GDP completed 11.923 billion yuan, an increase of 18.9%; above 500,000 yuan investment in fixed assets of 21 billion yuan, an increase of 79%; completion of the above-scale industrial output value of 8.27 billion yuan, an increase of 18.1%; total fiscal revenue of 3.113 billion yuan, an increase of 55%, the public budget revenue of 2.448 billion yuan, an increase of 70.6%; total retail sales of social consumer goods completed 6.742 billion yuan, an increase of 16.8%; rural per capita net income reached 6,081 yuan, an increase of 17.48%; urban residents per capita disposable income reached 18,831 yuan, an increase of 14.75%.

凯里全景
Kaili panoramic

遵义县

Zunyi County

遵南大道县城段
Zunnan Avenuew Daoxian paragraph

乐山大坝美如画
Leshan dam picturesque view

南白镇民主农民文化家园
Nanbai town Minzhu cultural home of farmers

遵义县是黔北综合经济区和黔中城市带核心区域，是彪炳史册的红色圣地、千年古县。面积4093.77平方公里，辖29个镇、2个民族乡、222个村民委员会、12个居民委员会和32个社区居民委员会。人口121.14万人，其中少数民族1.91万人。

近年来，按照省委加速发展、加快转型、推动跨越主基调和工业强省、城镇化带动主战略，围绕提高工业经济、城镇人口、民营经济、县域经济“四个比重”，推进新型工业化、新型城镇化、农业现代化和信息化“四化同步”，县域综合实力明显提升，城乡面貌日新月异，社会事业全面进步，民生福祉持续改善。2012年，实现地区生产总值192.28亿元，同比增长17.5%，工业增加值75.97亿元，增长16.9% ，规模工业增加值66.71亿元，增长19.9%，全社会固定资产投资228.99亿元，增长44.7%；招商引资到位资金237.54亿元，增长70.9%；财政总收入22.60亿元，增长18.6%；社会消费品零售总额42.49亿元，增长16.6%；城镇居民人均可支配收入19546元，农民人均纯收入7621元，分别增长14.6%和17.0%；金融机构存款余额159.00亿元、贷款余额124.93亿元，分别增长17.8%和23.4%。

县城全景图
County panorama

Zunyi County is a comprehensive economic zones in the north of Guizhou and cities with a core area in the middle of Guizhou, is annals red army sacred place, the Millennium ancient county. Area of 4,093.77 square kilometers, jurisdiction over 29 towns and 2 townships, 222 village committees, 12 neighborhood committees and 32 community residents' committees. Population of 1,211, 400, of which 19,100 minority.

In recent years, according to the provincial committee accelerated development, speed up transformation and promote across the main tone and industrial province and urbanization drive the main strategy, focusing on improving the industrial economy of the urban population, the private economy, the county economy "four proportions", promoting new industrialization, new urbanization, agricultural modernization and information technology "four modernizations sync", the county comprehensive strength has improved significantly, changing urban and rural areas, social progress got full progress, continued to improve people's livelihood and well-being. In 2012, to achieve GDP 19.228 billion yuan, an increase of 17.5%, industrial added value of 7.597 billion yuan, an increase of 16.9%, the scale of industrial added value of 6.671 billion yuan, an increase of 19.9%, total fixed asset investment 22.899 billion yuan, an increase of 44.7%; investment funds 23.754 billion yuan, an increase of 70.9%; fiscal revenue 2.26 billion yuan, an increase of 18.6%; retail sales of consumer goods of 4.249 billion yuan, an increase of 16.6%; urban residents per capita disposable income of 19,546 yuan, rural per capita net income of 7,621 yuan, respectively, an increase of 14.6% and 17.0%; financial institutions to deposits 15.9 billion yuan, loans 12.493 billion yuan, were up 17.8% and 23.4%, respectively.

尚嵇氧化铝厂全貌

Shang Ji alumina plant picture

贵州九鼎车辆公司车间一角

Guizhou Jiuding Vehicle Company Workshop

贵州九鼎汽车有限公司厂区

GuizhouJ iuding Automobile Co., Ltd. factory

枫香镇苟坝村新农村建设
Fengxiang town Gouba village new rural construction

枫香镇柿花田煤矿利用瓦斯发电
Fengxiang town Shihuatian coal power generation using gas

2012年，全县上下抢抓国发2号文件历史性机遇，紧紧围绕加速发展、加快转型、推动跨越主基调，以全力打造“三宜”城市示范区为核心，以深入实施强县战略、全力推进小康行动、加快建设幸福工程为统揽，着力兴产业、保增长，强基础、增后劲，惠民生、促和谐，解放思想，真抓实干，奋力赶超，使全县经济总量快速增长，综合实力大幅提升；工业经济蓄势待发，项目建设加快推进；城镇建设提质增速，基础设施建设如火如荼；现代农业蓬勃发展，经济结构不断优化；财政税收稳定增长，金融业健康运行；民生事业成效显著，社会管理全面加强；政府职能加快转变，自身建设不断加强。先后荣获“中国西部百强县”、“中国产业百强县”、“全国县域经济科学发展范例县”、“中国最具投资潜力特色示范县”、“全国创先争优先进县”、“全国文化先进县”、“全国粮食生产先进县”、“中国辣椒之都”等称号。

枫香苟坝村
Fengxiang Gouba village

In 2012, the county up and down to seize the historic opportunity to the country send the 2nd file, closely around the accelerated development, speed up transformation and promote across the main tone, in order to create "three good" urban demonstration area as the core, in-depth implementation of the county strategy, to promote the well-off action to speed up construction projects to take on the overall well-being, focus on emerging industries, to maintain growth, strong foundation, increase stamina, benefit people's livelihood and promote harmony, emancipate the mind, do solid work, struggling to catch up, so that the county total economic got rapid growth, the overall strength significantly improved; Industrial economy poised to accelerate the project construction; urban construction and quality and growth, infrastructure construction in full swing; modern agriculture flourish, optimize the economic structure; steady growth of fiscal revenue, the healthy operation of the financial sector; livelihood career achievement is remarkable, social management comprehensively strengthen; accelerate the transformation of government functions, continue to strengthen self-construction. Has won the "hundred counties in western China", "China hundred industry county", "national scientific development paradigm county", "Chinese most investment potential characteristics demonstration counties", "National Advanced County", "National culturally advanced counties", "national food production advanced counties", "Chinese pepper capital" title.

县烟草公司立体育苗基地

County tobacco companies stereoscopic breeding base

茅栗养鸡场

Maoli chicken breeding farm

南白镇民主蔬菜示范区育种

Nanbai town Minzhu vegetable breeding demonstration area

云 岩 区
Yunyan District

2013年5月23日，中国科协申维辰书记、省委常委、省委宣传部长喻红秋一行到云岩区中天社区调研考察
May 23, 2013, China Association for Science secretary Shen Weichen, Provincial Party Committee and Provincial Publicity Minister Yu Hongqiu and the team to the Yunyan district Zhongtian community to have research and study

2013年5月4日，省委书记赵克志到苏宁调研
May 4, 2013, the provincial party secretary Zhao Kezhi to Suning to have research

2012年4月，贵阳市人民政府市长李再勇到贵阳市云岩区调研城市基层体制改革
April 2012, Guiyang Municipal People's Government Mayor Li Zaiyong to Guiyang City Yunyan District to research the urban grassroots system reform

2012年9月，聂雪松书记进行关于社会治安的调研
September 2012, Nie Xuesong secretary for research on social security

2012年，是全区加速发展、率先跨越、建设幸福云岩的起步之年。全区紧紧围绕省第十一次党代会、市第九次党代会和区第八次党代会明确的奋斗目标，深入贯彻落实国发2号文件精神，扎实推进生态文明城区建设，全面小康社会实现程度进一步提升。

全年地区生产总值达到441.2亿元，同比增长15.7%；财政总收入43.46亿元，同比增长20.68%；公共财政预算收入25.98亿元，同比增长26.74%；全社会消费品零售总额258.8亿元，同比增长18%；规模以上工业总产值343.32亿元，同比增长14.5%；规模以上工业增加值145.49亿元，同比增长17.5%；全社会固定资产投资300.6亿元，同比增长45%；城镇居民人均可支配收入22527元，同比增长16%；农民人均纯收入10948元，同比增长20%。

狠抓产业结构调整，努力提升经济发展速度。按照“三产立区”战略，进一步改造提升餐饮、娱乐、百货等传统优势服务业，大力发展金融、信息等现代服务业。全区三次产业结构比达到0.1：35.8：64.1，第三产业在三次产业中的比重和对经济的贡献率稳步攀升。

狠抓招商引资工作，努力扩大对外开放水平。全年共引进市外项目361个，市外实际到位资金150.2亿元、同比增长92.62%，省外实际到位资金131.13亿元、同比增长117.1%，实际利用外资5706万美元，同比增长86.6%。

2013年6月1日，杨继区长到市西商业街调研消防安全

June 1, 2013, Yang Ji mayor to City West Commercial Street Fire Safety to have nvestigation

喷水池风景

Fountain landscape

2012 is the starting year of the accelerated development of the region, the first crossing, the construction of happy Yunyan. The district closely around the province eleventh congress, city and district Ninth Party Congress Eighth Party Congress clear goal, thoroughly implement the spirit of State Issued No.2 document, push forward the construction of ecological civilization city , a comprehensive well-off society to further enhance the degree of realization.

Annual GDP reached 44.12 billion yuan, an increase of 15.7%; fiscal revenue 4.346 billion yuan, an increase of 20.68%; public budget revenues 2.598 billion yuan, an increase of 26.74%; total retail sales of social consumer goods 25.88 billion yuan, an increase of 18%; scale industrial output value of 34.332 billion yuan or more, an increase of 14.5%; above-scale industrial added value of 14.549 billion yuan, an increase of 17.5%; total fixed assets investment 30.06 billion yuan, an increase of 45%; urban residents per capita disposable income of 22,527 yuan, an increase of 16%; rural per capita net income of 10,948 yuan, an increase of 20%.

Pay close attention to industrial restructuring, efforts to improve economic development. Accordance with the "three vertical production zone" strategy to further reform and improve the catering, entertainment, department stores and other traditional advantages of service industry, vigorously develop the financial, information and other modern services. Ratio of the region's three industrial structure 0.1:35.8:64.1, the tertiary industry in the proportion of three industries and the economic contribution rate climbed steadily.

Pay close attention to investment work, efforts to expand the level of opening up. A total of 361 projects to introduce outside the city, outside the city of actual funds 15.02 billion yuan, an increase of 92.62%, foreign actual funds 13.113 billion yuan, an increase of 117.1%, the actual utilization of foreign capital $ 57,060,000, an increase of 86.6%.

延安中路

Yan'an Road

合群路夜市
Hequn road night market

永吉印务
Yongji Printing

狠抓新老城区开发，努力促进城市扩容提质。按照中心城区棚户区改造的总体安排部署，先后完成20多个棚户区改造项目的规划编制、房屋摸底和招商签约等工作；三片区开发取得有效进展。

狠抓生态文明建设，努力美化辖区环境面貌。大力巩固“创文”、“创卫”成果，深入推行社区网格化管理及环卫作业高效化运作。

狠抓科教文体工作，努力发展社会各项事业。全年共申报市级以上优秀科技项目66项，实施区级科技计划项目23个，成功申报市级科学技术奖7项，新确立两家企业为政产学研合作基地，组织两项科技成果转化项目。

狠抓民生福祉改善，努力提升人民群众满意度。进一步扩大新农合覆盖范围，提高参合人员医疗保障水平，全区参合率稳定在99%以上。

狠抓平安云岩工程，努力构建和谐稳定社会。有效防范和坚决遏制重特大安全生产事故，全年安全生产事故和死亡人数分别同比下降25%和20%。

狠抓政府自身建设，努力增强内部发展活力。按照市委、市政府关于基层管理体制改革工作的重大决策部署，撤销全区17个街道办事处，新组建25个新型社区。

此外，人事、质监、物价、民宗、档案、双拥、侨务、人防、移民、铁路护路、国防动员、人民武装等各项工作整体推进，全面发展，均取得了可喜的成绩。

永吉印务工作人员正在工作
Yongji Printing staff are working

2013年1月17日，省、市红会进宅吉社区慰问
January 17, 2013, provincial and municipal Red Cross into the Zhaiji Community to have condolences

2012年7月，云岩区首届文化旅游年活动开幕
July 2012, Yunyyan district of the first cultural tourism year activities opening ceremony

益佰制药
Yi Bai Pharmaceutical

Pay close attention to old and new city development, efforts to promote the city's expansion and quality. In accordance with the central urban shantytowns, the overall arrangements for the deployment, has completed more than 20 shantytowns project planning, housing thoroughly and investment contract etc.; three Area Development achieved effective progress.

Pay close attention to ecological civilization construction, efforts to beautify the area of environmental outlook. Vigorously consolidate "cultural town", "health town" results, in-depth implementation of community grid management and sanitation operations efficient operation.

Pay close attention to science and stylistic work, efforts to develop social undertakings. Declaration of the municipal total of more than 66 outstanding scientific and technological projects, the implementation of district-level science and technology projects 23, the successful declaration of the municipal Science and Technology Award 7, the new government established two companies for research cooperation base, organizational and technological achievements into two items.

Pay close attention to improving people's livelihood and well-being, efforts to improve people's satisfaction. To further expand the coverage of the new rural cooperative to improve the participation level of medical care personnel, the region's participation rate stabilized at 99%.

Pay close attention to safety Yunyan projects, and strive to build a harmonious and stable society. Effectively prevent and resolutely curb serious accidents in production, the annual production safety accidents and deaths were down 25% and 20%, respectively.

Pay close attention to the government itself, and strive to enhance the internal dynamism of development. In accordance with the municipal committee, municipal government on the work of grass-roots management system major decisions and plans, revocation of the region's 17 district offices, the newly formed 25 new communities.

In addition, personnel, quality supervision, price, civil cases, files, mutual support, overseas, civil defense, immigration, protect railways and roads, national defense mobilization, people's armed forces and other work as a whole to promote all-round development, have achieved encouraging results.

益康制药
Yikang Pharmaceutical

七星关区

Qixingguan District

市委常委、区委书记宫晓农
Municipal Standing Committee, party secretary Gong Xiaonong

毕节市七星关区位于贵州省西北部，是毕节市的政治、经济、科技文化和信息中心，是西南地区重要的物资集散地。全区总面积3412平方公里，辖24个镇、8个乡、6个办事处，聚居着汉、彝、白、苗、布依等23个民族，总人口148万人。境内地势西高东低，平均海拔1511米，气候温和，雨量充沛，冬无严寒、夏无酷暑，被誉为“中国十大避暑旅游城市”。

2012年，全区生产总值完成184.42亿元，同比增长17.70%；全社会固定资产投资226.85亿元，同比增长58.3%；财政总收入完成28.54亿元，同比增长32.31%；社会消费品零售总额完成52亿元；城镇居民人均可支配收入19555元，同比增长14.12%；农村居民人均纯收入5131元，同比增长16.3%。

2012年，全区粮食总产量达到41.41万吨，比上年增长22.86%，其中：夏粮13.86万吨，比上年增长14.34%，秋粮27.5504万吨，比上年增长27.65%；肉类总产量达5.9万吨，其中猪肉51465吨，牛肉2750吨，羊肉254吨；禽蛋2169吨，家禽出栏数193.1万只，猪出栏数51.46万头，牛出栏数1.31万头，羊出栏数1.49万只。农林牧渔业总产值

城区一景
One picture of the city

区委副书记、区长刘建平
District Deputy Secretary, mayor Liu Jianping

Bijie city Qixingguan District is lcated in the northwest of Guizhou Province, is the political, economic, cultural and science and technology information center in Bijie city, is the important material distribution center in southwest China. The total area of 3,412 square kilometers, jurisdiction over 24 towns, 8 townships, 6 offices, inhabited by the Han, Yi, Bai, Miao, Buyi and other 23 ethnic groups, the total population of 1,480,000 people. Lying in the territory in the East high and West low, with an average altitude of 1,511 meters, a mild climate, abundant rainfall, no winter cold, summer without heat, known as "China's ten major summer tourist city".

In 2012, the region's GDP completed 18.442 billion yuan, an increase of 17.70%; total fixed asset investment 22.685 billion yuan, an increase of 58.3%; fiscal revenue 2.854 billion yuan, an increase of 32.31%; total retail sales of social consumer goods 5.2 billion yuan; urban residents per capita disposable income of 19,555 yuan, an increase of 14.12%; rural per capita net income of 5,131 yuan, an increase of 16.3%.

In 2012, the region's total grain output reached 414,100 tons, an increase of 22.86% over last year, of which: summer 138,600 tons, an increase of 14.34% over the previous year, autumn 275,504 tons, an increase of 27.65%; meat output amounted to 59,000 tons, of which 51,465 tons of pork, 2,750 tons of beef , 254 tons of mutton; 2,169

地委委员、市委书记周荣等市领导亲临小坝镇金钟社区指导生态文明家园建设工作
Prefectural Committee member, Municipal Party Secretary Zhou Rong and other city leaders went to Xiaoba county Jinzhong community guidelines the building of ecological civilization homes

市委常委、区委书记宫晓农，区委副书记、区长刘建平，区委副书记聂忠智在区生态办、鸭池镇主要领导陪同下，到鸭池镇哈啷村就“五园新村”暨徐健生故里建设进行指导
Municipal Standing Committee, party secretary Gong Xiaonong, deputy secretary of the Party committee, mayor Liu Jianping, deputy party secretary Nie Zhongzhi is accompanied by the leaders of the area of the ecological office, Yzchi town, to Yachi town Halang village to guide the “Wuyuang new village” and Xu Jiansheng’s hometown construction

42.95亿元，比上年增长6.7%。其中：农业产值26.44亿元，林业产值0.84亿元，畜牧业产值14.6亿元，渔业产值0.08亿元，农林牧渔服务业产值0.99亿元。收购烤烟19.62万担，实现产值2.45亿元、税收0.46亿元。

2012年，全区规模工业总产值完成136.48亿元，同比增长33.10%，其中规模工业增加值完成56.34亿元，同比增长22.3%；服务业实现增加值47.47亿元，同比增长15.8%。

随着改革开放的不断深入，全区经济已进入高速发展的黄金期，现已成为西部地区最具活力的发展地区。

毕节风光
Bijie scenic

园区开工仪式
Park groundbreaking ceremony

天河夜景
Tianhe night view

tons of eggs, poultry slaughter number 1,931,000, the number of slaughter 514,600 pigs, the number of slaughter 13,100 cattle, the number of slaughter 14,900 sheep. Agriculture, forestry, animal husbandry and fishery output value 4.295 billion yuan, an increase of 6.7% over the previous year. Of which: agricultural output value 2.644 billion yuan, forestry output value 840 million yuan, animal husbandry output value of 1.46 billion yuan, fishery output value 80 million yuan, agriculture, forestry animal husbandry and fishery services output value of 990 million yuan. Acquisition of tobacco 196,200 dan, the output value of 245 million yuan, tax 460 million yuan.

In 2012, the region's scale of industrial output value of 13.648 billion yuan, an increase of 33.10%, of which the scale of industrial added value reached 5.634 billion yuan, an increase of 22.3%; service industry added value of 4.747 billion yuan, an increase of 15.8%.

With the deepening of reform and opening up, the region's economy has entered a golden period of rapid development, has become the development of the western region's most dynamic regions.

水城县

Shuicheng County

温泉公园局部鸟瞰
Aerial view of the spa park locally

天生湖
Tiansheng lake

2012年，全县生产总值增长18%以上，其中：一产增长3%以上，二产增长20%以上，三产增长10%以上；固定资产投资增长30%以上；财政总收入和地方一般预算收入分别增长25%以上；社会消费品零售总额增长18%以上；农民人均纯收入增长12%以上。全县生产总值年均增长20%，其中：一产增长3%，二产增长25%，三产增长12%；固定资产投资增长40%；财政总收入和地方一般预算收入分别增长30%。

做优做强工业经济。一是巩固和壮大煤、电、铝、建材等四大优势产业；二是积极推进煤化工、装备制造、高新技术产业发展；三是积极打造工业园区。

切实做好“三农”工作。一是抓粮食稳产增收；二是抓农业产业结构调整；三是抓龙头企业培育；四是抓农业产业园区打造，加快推进百车河现代农业产业园区建设，加快规划米箩、南开、杨梅等现代农业产业园区。

繁荣壮大第三产业。一是重点发展旅游业，以申办2013年全省旅游发展大会为契机，不断强化旅游整体服务功能，提高旅游综合效益；二是繁荣商贸流通业；三是加快发展房地产、金融、法律、中介、信息、社区服务等现代服务业。

阿勒河景区

Ale river scenic area

大峡谷

The grand canyon

In 2012, the county's GDP growth of 18% or more, including: the first industry increase of 3% or more, the second industry increase of 20% or more, the tertiary industry increase of 10% or more; fixed asset investment grew more than 30%; fiscal revenue and local general budget revenue grew more than 25%; total retail sales of social consumer goods grew by 18% or more; rural per capita net income increased more than 12%. The county's average annual GDP growth of 20%, including: the first industry increase of 3%, the second industry increase of 25%, the tertiary industry increase of 12%; fixed asset investment growth of 40%; total fiscal revenue and local general budget revenue increased by 30% .

Make the industrial economy. First, consolidate and expand the coal, electricity, aluminum, building materials and other four dominant industries; second, actively promote the coal chemical industry, equipment manufacturing, high-tech industrial development; third, is to actively build industrial park.

A really good job of "three rural" work. First, grasp the grain yield increase; second, grasp the agricultural structure adjustment; third, we must cultivate leading enterprises; fourth, grasping agricultural industrial park to build and accelerate Baiche river modern agricultural industrial park construction, accelerate the planning and rice baskets, Nankai, bayberry and other modern agricultural industrial park.

Prosperity and growth of the tertiary industry. First, focus on the development of tourism in the province's bid to host the 2013 Tourism Development Conference as an opportunity to continue to strengthen tourism overall service capabilities, improve overall efficiency of tourism; second prosperous commerce retailers; third, accelerate the development of real estate, finance, legal, brokerage, information, community service and other modern services.

玉舍海坪彝族舞蹈
Yushe Hai Ping Yi Dance

玉舍海坪彝族火把节篝火晚会
Yushe Hai Ping Yi Torch Festival campfire

全面统筹城乡发展。一是加快规划编制步伐，高起点编制规划，完成12个小城镇规划和153个村庄规划的编制工作；二是加快双水新区建设；三是加快小城镇建设，推进乡改镇工作，提高城镇化率。

加大招商引资力度。一是完善招商机制。研究制定招商引资考核及奖惩办法，进一步明确各部门、各乡（镇）争取政策性项目资金的职责，努力形成全员招商的新格局；二是提高招商实效。

全面推进项目建设。一是抓项目前期工作；二是抓开工项目建设，加快产业类、交通类、城市建设类、社会事业类、农林水类等286个项目（含续建项目）的建设步伐；三是抓项目环境优化。

加快基础设施建设。交通方面，配合水盘、杭瑞、六六高速公路建设；水利方面，积极做好2座中型水库、4座小Ⅰ型水库和8座小Ⅱ型水库的前期工作；电力方面，实施20个10千伏及以下输变电项目。

协调发展社会事业。继续实施“十大民生工程”；充分发挥“一项机制多项内容”的基层群众自治体系作用；扎实开展计划生育工作；大力发展教育、卫生、文化、体育等社会事业；继续推进保障性安居工程建设；抓好就业再就业和社会保障工作；进一步加强社会管理创新和平安创建工作。

玉舍国家森林公园
Yushe National Forest Park

米箩园区核心区观景台
Miluo Park core area of the viewing platform

水城（米箩）猕猴桃产业园区
Shuicheng(Miluo) kiwifruit industry park

Comprehensive coordinate urban and rural development. First, accelerate the pace of planning, preparation of planning a high starting point, the completion of 12 small towns and 153 villages in planning the preparation of planning; second, accelerate the construction of Shuangshui new area; third, accelerate the construction of small towns to promote the township to the town work to improve the urbanization rate.

Increase investment. First, improving the investment mechanism. Study and formulate investment appraisal and incentives and disincentives, to further clarify the various departments, townships (towns) to fight the policy responsibilities of project funds, efforts to form a full investment of the new pattern; second, is to improve the effectiveness of investment.

Comprehensively promote the project. First, grasp the project preparatory work; second, grasp the construction projects, speed up industrial class, traffic class, urban construction class, social class, forestry and water etc. 286 projects (including construction projects) the pace of building; third, grasp the project environment.

Accelerate infrastructure construction. Transport, with Shuipan, Hangrui, Liuliu highway construction; water conservancy, actively carry two medium-sized reservoirs, four type Ⅰ small reservoirs and eight Ⅱ type reservoir small preliminary work; electricity, implemented 20 10 kV and below power transmission project.

Coordinated development of social undertakings. Continue to implement the "Ten livelihood projects"; give full play to "a mechanism for several of the content" grass-roots mass self-government system function; solidly carry out family planning work; vigorously develop education, health, culture, sports and other social undertakings; continue to promote affordable housing construction; grasp employment and reemployment and social security work; further strengthen social management innovation and peace building work.

甜瓜
Melon

米箩园区蔬菜大棚
Miluo Park greenhouses

红花岗区
Honghuagang District

贵州红花岗经济开发区挂牌
Guizhou Province Honghuagang Economic Development Zone listing

遵义国际商贸城开工
Zunyi International Trade City started

老城红军街
Old Red Army Street

城市夜景
Urban Landscape

红花岗区是历史文化名城遵义的主城区，位于贵州省北部，面积624平方公里。人口66万。辖8镇8办（其中新蒲镇由新蒲新区管理委员会代管），共53个村、76个社区居委会。

2012年，全年实现地区生产总值221.49亿元，比上年同期增长17.4%。其中：一产9.32亿元，增长9.2%；二产66.08亿元，增长20.7%；三产146.09亿元，增长17.7%。全社会固定资产投资完成193.26亿元，增长68.1%。财政总收入完成20.25亿元，增长36.51%。公共财政收入完成14.03亿元，增长40.86%。城镇居民人均可支配收入、农民人均纯收入分别达到20100元、8106元，分别增长15.2%、16.3%。节能减排完成省市下达任务。三次产业结构比重调整为4.2：29.8：66。

规模工业总产值、增加值分别实现143亿元、28亿元，分别增长10.9%、24%；工业固定资产投资完成56亿元，增长55.6%。完成社会消费品零售总额128.38亿元，增长20%；旅游综合收入112亿元，增长83.4%。农林牧渔总产值实现14.61亿元，增长10.42%。旧城改造稳步推进，南部新城建设顺利进行，东部新区加快开发，开发区建设如火如荼。

Honghuagang is a historical and cultural city's main city of Zunyi, Guizhou Province, is located in the north, an area of 624 square kilometers. Population of 660,000. 8 towns eight office (where the new town of San Po Po District Management Committee escrow), a total of 53 villages, 76 neighborhood communities.

In 2012, the annual GDP of 22.149 billion yuan, an increase of 17.4% over the previous year. Where: the first industry of 932 million yuan, an increase of 9.2%; the second industry of 6.608 billion yuan, an increase of 20.7%; tertiary industry of 14.609 billion yuan, an increase of 17.7%. Total fixed asset investment of 19.326 billion yuan, an increase of 68.1%. Total fiscal revenue 2.025 billion yuan, an increase of 36.51%. Public fiscal revenue 1.403 billion yuan, an increase of 40.86%. Per capita disposable income of urban residents, rural per capita net income reached 20,100 yuan, 8,106 yuan, respectively, an increase of 15.2%, 16.3%. Energy conservation to complete assigned tasks by the provinces. Three industries the proportion of industrial structure adjustment 4.2:29.8:66.

Scale industrial output value, added value achieved 14.3 billion yuan, 2.8 billion yuan, respectively, an increase of 10.9%, 24%, respectively; industrial fixed assets investment of 5.6 billion yuan, an increase of 55.6%. Total retail sales of social consumer goods 12.838 billion yuan, an increase of 20%; tourism revenue 11.2 billion yuan, an increase of 83.4%. Animal husbandry and fishery output value of 1.461 billion yuan, an increase of 10.42%. Transformation of the old towns steadily, southern Metro got smooth construction, accelerate the development of the eastern district, the development zone construction in full swing.

佛教圣地金鼎山

Buddhist shrine Jindingshan

红花岗区第三届西南片区自行车挑战赛

Third Honghuagang Southwest Area Bike Challenge

建设中的经济开发区

Construction Economic Development

息 烽 县

Xifeng County

建设中的息烽县阳朗开磷城
Construction of Xifeng County Yanglang Kailin City

县城虎城大道“火炬广场”
County Hucheng avenue “Torch Square”

息烽县地处贵阳市北部、乌江南岸，面积1036.5平方公里，辖4镇、6乡、1个社区服务中心，有161个村13个居委会。人口26万人，有苗、布依、彝族等19个少数民族。县域交通便利，区位优势明显，川黔铁路、210国道、贵遵高等级公路穿越县境。全县旅游资源丰富，环境气候宜人，森林覆盖率达到46.91%，获得“全国集体林权制度改革百强县”、“全国生态文明先进县”、“中国绿色名县”、“全省绿化模范县”、“贵州省和谐县市”、“2011-2012年平安建设先进县”等荣誉。

2012年，息烽县抢抓国发2号文件和省、市加快县域经济发展的机遇，坚持“加速发展、加快转型、推动跨越”主基调，深入实施“科教兴县、工业强县、旅游活县、环境立县”四大战略，全力推动“三化同步”，加快生态文明建设，齐心协力、奋力拼搏，圆满完成了各项目标任务，全县经济社会健康快速发展。

息烽小寨坝镇农民安置新村
Xifeng Xiaozhaiba town resettlement of farmers new village

阳朗旅游风情小镇街景
Yanglang travel style town street

息烽60万吨合成氨厂区
Xifeng 600,000 tons of synthetic ammonia plant

息烽国际山地露营体验基地
Xifeng International Mountain camping experience base

Xifeng County is located in the northern part of Guiyang City, south bank of Wujiang river, an area of 1,036.5 square kilometers, jurisdiction over 4 towns, 6 townships, 1 community service center, there are 161 villages 13 neighborhood. Population of 260,000 people, there are Miao, Buyi, Yi and other 19 ethnic minorities. County transportation is convenient, location advantages, Sichuan, Guizhou Railway, 210 State Road, the Guizun highway and so on through the county. The county has rich tourism resources, the environment and pleasant weather, the forest coverage rate reached 46.91%, was "the collective forest right system reform hundred counties", "National Advanced ecological civilization county ", "China Green county", "the province's green model County", "harmonious cities and counties in Guizhou Province", "peace building advanced counties 2011-2012" and other honors.

息烽集中营革命历史纪念馆
Xifeng Concentration Camp Revolutionary History Memorial Hall

In 2012, Xifeng County seize the 2nd National Development files and provincial, city speed up the county's economic development opportunities, adhere to "accelerate the development, accelerate the transformation and promote across" main tone, in-depth implementation of the " science and education propers county, industrial strong county, tourism live county, county environmental legislation" four strategies, to promote the "three synchronization", to speed up construction of ecological civilization, unit together, work hard and successfully completed the mission objectives, the county's economic and social health of rapid development.

息烽循环经济磷煤精细化工工业区
Xifeng phosphorus coal circular economy fine chemical industrial zone

龙爪村女子舞龙队
Longzhua village woman dragon dance teams

西山乡水岭沟乡村旅游示范点文化广场
Xishan village Shuilinggou rural tourism demonstration cultural square

县城“西扩”的标志——永靖大道
County “westward expansion” sign - Yongjing Avenue

中国•堡子半边天文化陈列馆
China•Buzi Half of the sky Culture Exhibition Hall

发展速度明显提升，综合实力显著增强。2012年，全县完成地方生产总值84.34亿元，增长18%；全社会固定资产投资完成137.71亿元，增长61.5%。财政总收入9.6亿元，增长35.4%，公共财政预算收入完成6亿元，增长36.6%。社会消费品零售总额完成12.21亿元，增长17.5%。实现旅游总收入12.92亿元，增长9.4%。金融机构存贷款余额分别达到47.28亿元和42.94亿元，增长33.8%和21%。完成城镇新增就业8790人，增长103%。城镇居民人均可支配收入达20421元，增长16.5%。农民人均纯收入达7456元，增长15.9%，增速连续六年排全市第1位。人均GDP达39357元，突破6000美元，增长17.4%，已完成全面建成小康社会的“三个核心指标”，在全省市区县经济发展增比进位综合测评排位中，位列全市第3位，全省第12位。

青山湖秋色
The autumn of the Qingshan Lake

养龙司乡上沟水库
Yanglongsi Township Ditch Reservoir

Fair speed significantly improved, comprehensive strength has markedly increased. In 2012, the county completed GDP of 8.434 billion yuan, an increase of 18%; total fixed asset investment of 13.771 billion yuan, an increase of 61.5%. Total fiscal revenue 960 million yuan, an increase of 35.4%, the public budget revenue of 600 million yuan, an increase of 36.6%. Total retail sales of social consumer goods completed 1.221 billion yuan, an increase of 17.5%. Total tourism income of 1.292 billion yuan, an increase of 9.4%. Financial institutions deposits and loans reached 4.728 billion yuan and 4.294 billion yuan, an increase of 33.8% and 21%, respectively. Complete urban employment 8,790, an increase of 103%. Per capita disposable income of urban residents reached 20,421 yuan, an increase of 16.5%. Per capita net income of farmers reached 7,456 yuan, up 15.9%, growth for six consecutive years ranked the city first. Per capita GDP reached 39,357 yuan, breaking the $ 6,000, an increase of 17.4%, has completed a comprehensive well-off society, “three core indicators” in the economic development of the province’s city districts carry comprehensive evaluation of growth than in qualifying, the city ranked third position, the province’s 12rd.

息烽特驱家禽养殖有限公司养殖场一角
Xifeng Tequ poultry Breeding Co., Ltd breeding corner

迷人的乌江峡
The charming Wujiang Gorge

白 云 区

Baiyun District

时任省委书记、省人大常委会主任栗战书，时任省委副书记、省长赵克志，时任省委常委、贵阳市委书记李军等省、市、区领导在中泉电气听取企业发展情况汇报

When he was provincial secretary of the provincial People's Congress Chairman Li Zhanshu, when he was Provincial Committee deputy secretary, Governor Zhao Kezhi, when he was Provincial Committee and Guiyang City Party Secretary Li Jun and other provinces, municipalities and district leaders to listen in IDEC reports on the situation of enterprise development

时任贵州省委常委、贵阳市委书记李军参与元旦、春节筑城送温暖活动集中慰问活动

When he was Guizhou Provincial Committee and Guiyang City Party Secretary Li Jun involved the New Year and Spring Festival activities are concentrated fortification warmth condolences events

高新区党工委书记、白云区委书记丁雄军调研燕京啤酒项目

High-tech Zone Party Work Committee, Baiyun District secretary Ding Xiongjun research Yanjing Beer project

白云区是贵阳市的六个市辖区和新规划建设的城市中心区之一，是省级经济技术开发区，全省首批建立的20个经济强县之一，全国最大的铝工业基地和全省重要的新材料建设基地。全区面积272平方公里，下辖二乡（都拉乡、牛场乡）三镇（艳山红镇、麦架镇、沙文镇）六社区（红云社区、大山洞社区、艳山红社区、白沙关社区、铝兴社区、都新社区），56个行政村，人口27余万人。2010年被批准为“国家可持续发展实验区”，2011年被评为“全省先进开发区”。2012年全区地区生产总值达101.86亿元，增长18.1%；财政总收入15.93亿元，增长22.5%；农民人均纯收入10256元，增长15.4%；城镇居民可支配收入21796元，增长12.4%；规模以上工业总产值达260.35亿元；招商引资到位市外内资157.03亿元，实际利用外资4489万美元。

白云区的优势特点：一是区位优越。白云地处贵阳市中心地带，毗邻金阳市级行政中心，距老城区13公里，距4D级贵阳国际机场约20公里，位于贵遵和贵黄高等级公路的扇面上，是通往四川、广西、云南的重要通道。二是

白云区新貌

Baiyun District new look

高新区党工委书记、白云区委书记丁雄军、区委副书记、区长黄昌祥、区人大党组书记、人大主任张朝栋、区政协党组书记、主席卢瑞礼出席七冶建设有限责任公司共赢发展座谈会

High-tech Zone Party Work Committee, Baiyun District secretary Ding Xiongjun, deputy secretary, mayor Huang Changxiang, District People's Congress party secretary, director Zhang Zhaodong NPC, CPPCC district party secretary, chairman Lu Ruili attended Seven Metallurgical Construction Co., Ltd. and win-win development forum

区委副书记、区长黄昌祥（左）和香港俊发集团总裁赵彬（右）签署黑石头项目合作协议

District Deputy Secretary, mayor Huang Changxiang (left) and Hongkong Junfa group president Zhao Bin (right) signed a cooperation agreement of black stone

Baiyun District is one of Guiyang City six municipal districts and the new planning and construction of urban centers, is one of the provincial-level economic and technological development zone, one of the first province to establish 20 economy county, the country's largest aluminum industrial base and the province's major construction of new material base. Covering an area of 272 square kilometers, has jurisdiction over 2 townships (Dula Township, Niuchang Township) 3 towns (Yanshanhong town, Maijia town, Shawen town) 6 communities (Hongyun community, Dashandong communities, Yanshanhong mountain communities, Baishaguan communities, LVing communities, Duxing communities), 56 administrative villages, population of 270,000 people. In 2010, it was approved as "National Sustainable Development Experimental Zone", in 2011 was named "the province's advanced development zone". Region's GDP in 2012 reached 10.186 billion yuan, an increase of 18.1%; fiscal revenue 1.593 billion yuan, an increase of 22.5%; rural per capita net income of 10,256 yuan, an increase of 15.4%; disposable income of urban residents 21,796 yuan, an increase of 12.4%; above-scale industrial output value reached 26.035 billion yuan; investment in place outside the city-funded 15.703 billion yuan, the actual utilization of foreign capital $ 44,890,000.

区委常委、区政府常务副区长宋旭升与太平洋建设集团公司参加云环路通车典礼暨与太平洋建设集团投资合作框架协议签约仪式

District Committee, district government deputy mayor Song Xusheng and Pacific Construction Group Corporation to participate in the opening ceremony and cloud loop investment and Pacific Construction Group cooperation framework agreement signing ceremony

Baiyun District Advantages: First, position is superior. Baiyun is located in downtown Guiyang, adjacent to the Jinyang municipal

贵阳市白云区第十届人民代表大会第一次会议胜利召开
Baiyun District, Guiyang City, the tenth session of the first people's congress was held with victory

中共白云区委八届三次全体（扩大）会议胜利召开
Baiyun District Party committee of the Communist Party of China eight session of the three plenary (enlarged) conference was held with victory

2012年全国有色金属加工行业技术进步产业升级大会暨贵州省有色金属加工产业发展研讨会
2012 National Non-ferrous Metal Industry Conference and industrial upgrading, technological progress Guizhou Nonferrous Metal Processing Industry Development Seminar

交通便捷。210国道、贵遵高等级公路、贵阳环城高速公路、川黔铁路、贵广快速铁路和即将开工建设的环城快速铁路汇集域内，区内道路网络已经形成，32条地方公路通往全区各地。三是工业基础较雄厚。区域内聚集了中国铝业贵州分公司、中国航空工业标准件制造有限公司等一批规模大、产品技术含量高、人才富集、技术水平较高的国有大中型企业。四是开发区初具规模。自1992年成立省级经济开发区以来，经过多年的建设，完善基础设施建设，扩大招商引资力度，陆续引进了600余家各类企业，初步形成了铝及铝加工基地、贵阳（国际）新材料产业园、食品工业园、数字产业园等“一区多园”的发展态势，促进白云经济快速增长。五是城市化水平较高。由于主城区扇面不断延伸，白云区比邻城市中心城区，区位优势优越，城市化率达73.82%，并在全省率先实现了村村“八通一改一化一中心”和通乡公路“半小时白云”工程。

白云区产业分布图
Baiyun District Industrial Distribution

administrative center, 13 km from the old town, from the 4D level Guiyang International Airport is about 20 km, is located in Guizun and Guihuang highway fan, is an important channel to Sichuan, Guangxi, Yunnan. Second, the transportation is convenient. State Road 210, the Guizun highway, Guiyang city highway, Sichuan-Guizhou railway, the Guangzhou express railway and upcoming construction area around the city express railway collection, local road network has been formed, 32 local roads leading to the region country. Third, relatively strong industrial base. Region gathered Guizhou Branch of China Aluminum Industry, China Aviation Industry Standard Parts Manufacturing Co., Ltd. and a number of large-scale, high-tech products, human enrichment, high technical level state-owned enterprises. Fourth, the development zone to take shape. Since its establishment in 1992 the provincial economic development zone, after years of construction, improve infrastructure, and expand investment, have introduced more than 600 kinds of enterprises, initially formed aluminum and aluminum base, Guiyang (International) New material Industrial Park, food Industrial Park, industrial Park and other digital "one Zone various parks"development trend, and promote rapid economic growth in Baiyun. Fifth, the level of urbanization is higher. Since the main city fan continuous extension Baiyun District advantage is superior than the city near the center city, the urbanization rate reached 73.82%, and in the province to achieve the village "to change one of eight pass one center" and township roads "semi-hour Baiyun"project.

高新区白云区27个项目集中开工仪式
High-tech Zone Baiyun District 27 projects focused on groundbreaking ceremony

钟山区
Zhongshan District

区委书记付国祥（左二）陪同市委书记王晓光（左一）到贵州最高峰——韭菜坪调研
District Party Secretary Fu Guoxiang (second from left), accompanied the municipal party secretary Wang Xiaoguang (first from left) to research the Guizhou peak - Jiucaiping

区政府区长梁建向市委书记王晓光、副市长谢朝碧介绍明湖湿地公园建设情况
District government mayor Liang Jian introduced the constrction situation of Minghu wetland park to municipal Party committee secretary Wang Xiaoguang, deputy mayor Xie Chaobi

2012年，在市委市政府和区委的正确领导下，在区人大、区政协的监督支持下，区政府紧紧围绕区六次党代会的总体部署，团结带领全区人民科学发展、奋起赶超，经济社会发展取得明显成效。

全年地区生产总值完成256.76亿元，增长15.9%；财政总收入完成21.6亿元，增长30.85%；公共财政预算收入完成15.37亿元，增长39.39%；全社会固定资产投资完成262.32亿元，增长74.8%；社会消费品零售总额完成101.36亿元，增长16%；城镇居民人均可支配收入、农民人均纯收入分别为18764.1元、6779元，分别增长14.6%、17.1%。节能降耗和主要污染物排放控制在省、市要求范围以内。经济强县全省排名第七，初步测算小康实现程度达82.28%。

一年来，主要工作和成效是：

面对各地区竞相发展赶超进位的新形势，坚持把项目建设作为稳增长的根本途径，跨越发展的步伐不断加快。坚持做大做实做强投资，以更加开放的姿态筑巢引凤，坚持依法拆迁、和谐拆迁。

付国祥书记、吴仕泽常务副区长、胡宝钢副区长、潘继华副主席调研水月产业园区
Fu Guoxiang secretary, Wu Shize Deputy Mayor, Hu Baogang Vice Mayor, Pan Jihua Vice Chairman researched Shuiyue industrial park

区委书记付国祥到月照乡玉顶社区宣讲党的十八大精神
District Party Secretary Fu Guoxiang to Yuding Community Yuezhao village to preach the 18th CPC National Congress spirit

区政府区长梁建（右五）、区人大主任李明（右一）区政协主席陶贵萍（右二）到水月产业园区视察

District Government Mayor Liang Jian (fifth from right), the District People's Congress Chairman Li Ming (first from right) District Committee Chairman Tao Guiping(second from right) visits to Shuiyuet industrial park

市、区人大代表视察大河镇大箐村“四在农家”建设情况

City, district deputies inspected Daqing village Dahe town "four in the farm" construction

In 2012, under the correct leadership of the municipal committee, government and the supervision and support of the district committee, the District People's Congress, CPPCC , the district government closely around the district sixth the overall deployment congress, unite and lead the scientific development of the region's people, rise up and catch up, the economic and social development achieved remarkable results.

钟山区2013年宣传思想文化工作会议

Zhongshan District 2013 publicity of the ideological work conference

Annual GDP completed 25.676 billion yuan, an increase of 15.9%; fiscal revenue of 2.16 billion yuan, an increase of 30.85%; public budget revenue of 1.537 billion yuan, an increase of 39.39%; total fixed asset investment of 26.232 billion yuan, an increase of 74.8%; total retail sales of social consumer goods completed 10.136 billion yuan, an increase of 16%; urban residents per capita disposable income and rural per capita net income of 18,764.1 yuan, 6,779 yuan, respectively, an increase of 14.6%, 17.1%. Energy consumption and emissions of major pollutants controlled at provincial and municipal requirements range. Economic County ranked seventh in the province, preliminary estimates the degree of well-off realization of 82.28%.

Over the past year, the main work and results are:

Face the new situation of the race to catch up with the development of various regions, insist on carrying the project construction as the fundamental way to steady growth, across the pace of development is accelerating. Insist on bigger and stronger and solid investment, with a more open attitude to build home and attract investment, demolition adhere to the law, harmony demolition.

Face the ups and downs of the economic situation, adhere to accelerate the transformation of development as the main direction of development, to promote economic development of endogenous motivation significantly enhanced. Accelerating economic restructuring, and the three industries rose from 0.92:55.94:43.14 adjusted to 0.88:55.63:43.49; actively respond to industry continued to decline, downward pressure on the external economic operation situation, full service medium-sized enterprise development in the district; persevere in reform and open; accelerating the pace of building the park; strive to promote the development of cultural tourism.

The face of the new requirements of modern urban construction, adhere to the fine idea to promote the work, urban construction and

钟山区与太平洋建设集团举行座谈会
Zhongshan district held a forum with Pacific Construction Group

钟山区维护稳定工作进行专题部署
Zhongshan district thematic deployment of maintaining stability

面对跌宕起伏的经济形势，坚持把加快转变发展方式作为推动发展的主攻方向，经济发展内生动力明显增强。不断加快经济结构调整，三次产业比重从0.92:55.94:43.14调整到0.88:55.63:43.49；积极应对工业持续下滑、外部经济运行下行压力加大的形势，全力服务辖区大中型企业发展；坚持推进改革开放；加快园区建设步伐；着力推动文化旅游业发展。

面对建设现代都市的新要求，坚持以精细化理念推动工作，城市建管水平迈上新台阶。持续加大基础设施投入力度；着力打造生态文明城市。

面对农业生产条件差、地少效益低的现状，坚持把发展现代特色农业作为“三农”工作重点，城乡统筹进程不断加快。打造都市休闲观光农业；加快养殖业发展；集中力量改善村容村貌；扶贫攻坚取得新成效。

面对全区群众思和谐盼富裕奔小康的殷切期待，坚持以小财政办大民生，民生保障方面取得实实在在成效。“十大工程”、“十二件民生实事”进展顺利；千方百计扩大就业；加快推进医疗体制改革；想方设法扩保障；狠抓人口计生工作；努力探索具有钟山特色的社会管理新模式。

面对政府工作要求不断提高的新形势，坚持把务实清廉作为政府自身建设的着力点，执行力和服务能力明显提高。自觉接受监督；大力推进依法行政；加强作风建设。

钟山区政府办全体干部职工对社区老党员及计生帮扶对象进行慰问
Zhongshan district government all the staff had condolences of the old party members of the community helping object IPPF

寻找钟山最美声音、最美舞姿活动
Find Zhongshan beautiful sounds, beautiful dance activities

钟山区十五小学规划效果图
Zhongshan the fifteen primary school plan renderings

management to a new level. Continue to increase infrastructure investment; efforts to build ecological civilization city.

The face of poor agricultural production conditions, be less and less effective situation, adhere to the development of modern agriculture as the "three rural" work focus, accelerate the process of urban and rural areas. Create urban leisure agriculture; accelerate aquaculture development; concentrate on improving the village appearance; poverty alleviation got new achievements.

The face of the region's people look forward keenly await rich think fairly well-off and harmonious, adhere use small financial to do big livelihood, livelihood security has achieved tangible results. "Top Ten Project", "twelve practical livelihood" progressing smoothly; everything possible to expand employment; accelerating health care reform; find ways to extend protection; pay close attention to family planning work; efforts to explore the characteristics of the social management with Zhongshan new model.

The face of the new situation of increasing demands by the government work, adhere to the pragmatic and honest as the focus of the government itself, execution and service capacity has improved significantly. Consciously accept supervision; vigorously promote administration according to law; strengthen the work style.

钟山区集中发放30台环卫特种车到各乡镇街道
Zhongshan district issued 30 sets of centralized sanitation special vehicle to the township streets

乌 当 区

Wudang District

省、市、区领导到西南工业总部基地调研
Provincial, municipal and district leaders to the southwest industrial headquarters to have research

乌当区位于贵阳市东北部，属贵阳市新城区，面积686平方公里，辖5乡3镇、5个新型社区，76个村（场）、19个居委会，人口22.64万，居住有汉、布依、苗等33个民族。交通便利。生态环境良好。地热资源丰富，享有“林中泉城”美誉。“黔中秘境、生态乌当，一个诗意生活的林中泉城”形象深入人心。

近年来，区委、区政府团结带领全区人民突出“加速发展、加快转型、推动跨越”主基调，按照“坚持走科学发展路、加快建生态文明区”总路径，坚定不移地实施新型工业化和城镇化带动战略，扎实做好稳增长、调结构、惠民生、抓改革、促和谐的各项工作，形成了电子信息、现代制药、先进制造、新材料和特色食品加工五大工业支柱产业，全区经济社会实现又好又快发展。

经济持续较快增长，各项经济指标全面完成。2012年，全区完成地区生产总值156.57亿元，同比增长18%。全区财政总收入完成18.08亿元，同比增长28.83%；公共财政预算收入完成11.46亿元，增长30.67%；全社会固定资产投资完成161.26亿元，同比增长60.80%。全区社会消费品零售总额完成12.33亿元，增长18.10%。城镇居民人均可支配收入达21791元，增长12.72%；农民人均纯收入达9607元，增长15.30%。

鸟瞰乌当
Bird's view of Wudang

贵阳工业发展成果展乌当展厅
Guiyang Industrial Development Wudang Exhibition Hall

贵阳国家农业科技园
Guiyang National Agricultural Science and Technology Park

Wudang District is located in the northeast of Guiyang City, is a new city district of Guiyang City, an area of 686 square kilometers, jurisdiction over 5 townships 3 towns, 5 new communities, 76 villages (field), 19 neighborhood committees, population 226,400, inhabited by the Han, Buyi, Miao and other 33 ethnic groups. Convenient transportation. Good ecological environment. Rich in geothermal resources, enjoy "Spring city in the forest" reputation. "Guizhou Fam, ecological Wudang, a poetic life Lin ZSpring city in the forest" image.

In recent years, the district committee, district government to unite and lead people of the district highlight the "accelerated development, speed up transformation and promote across" the main tone, according to "stick to the road of scientific development, accelerate the construction of ecological civilization zone" main path, and unswervingly implement the new industrialization and urbanization led strategy, a solid job steady growth, adjusting structure, benefits the people's livelihood, focus on reform, and promote harmony of the work, the formation of electronic information, modern pharmaceuticals, advanced manufacturing, new materials and specialty food processing five pillar industries industry, the district to achieve sound and rapid economic and social development.

Sustained and rapid economic growth, the economic indicators completed. In 2012, the region's GDP of 15.657 billion yuan, an increase of 18%. The region's total fiscal revenue 1.808 billion yuan, an increase of 28.83%; public budget revenue of 1.146 billion yuan, an increase of 30.67%; total fixed asset investment of 16.126 billion yuan, an increase of 60.80%. The region's total retail sales of social consumer goods completed 1.233 billion yuan, an increase of 18.10%. Per capita disposable income of urban residents reached 21,791 yuan, an increase of 12.72%; rural per capita net income reached 9,607 yuan, an increase of 15.30%.

南方汇通华城楼宇中央空调调试室
South Huitong Huacheng building central air conditioning debug room

083宇光电子产品生产线
083 Yuguang electronic products production line

贵州龙食品生产线
Guizhou Dragon Food Production Line

健兴药业药品生产线
Jian Xing Pharmaceutical drug production line

黔五福猪肉食品生产线
Qian Wufu pork food production lines

创新重大项目推进体制机制，项目建设得到加强。紧紧围绕“两加一推”主基调和“三化同步”主战略，按照市“一二一”奋斗目标及“四区”发展定位，把保增长作为经济工作的首要任务，高度整合四大班子资源，组建了“领导与决策、指挥与调度、贯彻与执行”三位一体的“四区”建设重点项目统筹推进工作系统。全年56个省市区重大工程和重点项目完成投资85.81亿元。

工业经济增长较快，质量效益稳步提升，新型工业化先行区建设迈上新台阶。完成规模以上工业总产值128.82亿元，增长27.80%；工业增加值35.26亿元，增长23.80%。新增规上企业12家。新开工项目20个、建成投产项目15个、建成达产项目20个，总投资38.5亿元。

服务业蒸蒸日上，发展特色日益凸显，西南高品位休闲度假区建设得到新提升。农业经济稳步发展，基础地位更加巩固，都市型现代农业示范区建设取得新成效。城镇建设步伐加快。交通基础设施继续完善。城市形象不断提升。生态建设步伐进一步加快。教育事业成绩喜人。人口卫生事业亮点纷呈。社会保障全面给力。文体事业蓬勃发展。体制改革进一步深化。

食品工业园
Food Industrial Park

贵阳市二环四路城市带项目推介会乌当展厅

Guiyang City Second Ring Road four roads city belt projects promote will Wudang exhibition hall

南方汇通渗透膜

South Huitong permeable membranc

Innovative institutional mechanisms to promote major projects, the project construction has been strengthened. Tightly around the "two plus one push" the main tone and the "three synchronization" main strategy, according to the city "one two one" goal and the "four areas" development orientation, to ensure growth as the primary task of economic work, highly integrated four large groups of resources, the formation of the "leadership and decision-making, command and scheduling, implementation and execution" trinity "four areas" construction of key projects to promote the work co-ordination system. Yearly 56 provinces, municipalities, major projects and key projects completed an investment of 8.581 billion yuan.

Rapid industrial growth, steady improvement in quality and efficiency, new industrialization pilot area construction to a new level. Above-scale industrial output value of 12.882 billion yuan, an increase of 27.80%; industrial added value of 3.526 billion yuan, an increase of 23.80%. New regulations on business 12. 20 new projects, 15 projects put into operation, completed by the project 20, a total investment of 3.85 billion yuan.

Booming service sector, the development of specialized increasingly prominent, southwest high-grade leisure resort building get a new upgrade. Steady development of agricultural economy, more solid foundation, urban modern agriculture demonstration zones to achieve new results. Accelerate the pace of urban construction. Transportation infrastructure continue to improve. Image of the city has been increasing. Further accelerate the pace of ecological construction. Education gratifying results. Highlights trends in population health. Comprehensive social security to the force. Culture and sports career flourish. Restructuring was further deepened.

阿栗杨梅

Ali Bayberry

下坝樱桃

Xiaba Cherry

兴义市

Xingyi City

冷洞村金银花加工厂
Lengdong village honeysuckle processing plant

兴义市是我国西南地区辐射滇、黔、桂的中心城市，素有“黔桂锁钥”之称，是贵州省第四大城市，是黔西南布依族苗族自治州首府，是黔西南的政治、经济、文化、科教中心和西南地区重要的交通通信枢纽、工业基地及商贸旅游服务中心。

改革开放以来，特别是近五年来，兴义市审时度势，确立“把兴义建设成为辐射滇、黔、桂三省（区）结合部拥有100万人口的中心城市和打造全国最佳人居环境城市”之目标，坚持高起点规划、高品位设计、高标准建设、高水平管理、高效能经营原则，投资近35亿元进行旧城区改造和新城区建设。目前兴义城市建成区面积42平方公里，城市人口45万人，城镇化率47%。城市辐射带动力和产业聚集度增强，形成以房地产、汽车贸易、餐饮服务和运输物流为主的支柱产业，城乡规划信息化建设工作走在全省前列，创造出“兴义速度”。

基地示范——现代农业助农增收
The base model - modern agriculture to help farmers increase income

兴义城市新貌
Xingyi City new look

兴义山城一角
Xingyi corner of the mountain city

万峰林景区面貌一新
The scenic Wanfenglin new look

Xingyi City is the southwest China radiation of Yunnan, Guizhou and Guangxi center of the city, known as the "Guizhou-Guangxi key", is the fourth largest city in Guizhou Province, is the southwest Guizhou Buyi and Miao Autonomous Prefecture, is the southwest Guizhou political, economy, culture, science and education center and is an important transportation and communication hub, industrial base and business travel service center in southwest region.

Since the reform and opening up, especially in the past five years, Xingyi City sized up the situation, establish "Xingyi into the central city of radiation Yunnan, Guizhou and Guangxi provinces (autonomous regions) junction has a population of 1 million and build the city of the national best living environment" goals, adhere to the high starting point, high-grade design, high-standard construction, high-level management, high-performance operating principles, investment of nearly 3.5 billion yuan on reconstruction of old urban areas and the construction of the new city. At present, Xingyi city built-up area of 42 square kilometers, the urban population of 450,000 people, the urbanization rate of 47%. Cities driving force and industry aggregation enhanced, the formation of the pillar industries based real estate, automotive trade, catering and transport logistics, urban and rural planning information construction work forefront in the province, to create a "Xingyi speed".

At the same time to speed up urban construction, Xingyi City to create a civilized city, excellent tourism city, the best living environment city three working organic combine to strengthen urban management and urban greening and ecological landscape

兴义民族文化街
The Xingyi national Culture Street

街心花园夜景——兴义市新闻中心
Garden in the city at night - Xingyi City News Center

文化路夜景
Wenhua Road night

在加快城市建设的同时，兴义市把创建文明城市、优秀旅游城市、最佳人居环境城市三项工作有机结合起来，加强城市管理和城市绿化及生态园林建设，大力实施环城绿化带建设、生态园林工程和机关院落、居民小区立体绿化以及“拆围现绿、建绿”工程，让绿色透出来，让庭院靓起来。目前城区绿化率达36%，人均公共绿地7.5平方米。2006年以来，兴义先后荣获“全国双拥模范城”、“全国文化先进县市”、“全国粮食生产先进县市”、“国家地质公园”、“国家重点风景名胜区”、“中国最佳休闲旅游城市”、“中国观赏石之乡”、“布依八音之乡国家首批非物质文化遗产”、“贵州龙的故乡”、“全国民间文化艺术之乡”、“全国农业旅游示范点”、“全国工业旅游示范点”、“全国文明城市”、国家卫生应急综合示范市、中国魅力品牌城市等荣誉称号。

2012年底，全市生产总值预计实现199.61亿元，增长16.60%；财政总收入完成35.0668亿元，增长30.81%；农村居民人均可支配收入预计达到6373元，增长18.11%；城镇居民人均可支配收入预计达到19520元，增长14.80%。在小康社会23项指标体系中，多项指标已达到或接近小康目标要求。

桔山大道
Jushan Road

万峰林纳灰村夜景
The Wanfenglin Nahui village night

construction, vigorously implement the construction of green belt around the city, ecological garden project and organs courtyard, residential area three-dimensional green "demolition walls show green, green building" project, so green shone through, pretty courtyard. Urban greening rate of 36%, per capita public green space of 7.5 square meters. Since 2006, Xingyi has won the "National support model city", "National culturally advanced counties", "national food production advanced counties", "national geological park", "national key scenic spots", "China's best leisure and tourism city", "village of ornamental stones", Buyi octave township, the first national non-material cultural heritage", "Guizhou dragon hometown", "folk culture and art village", "national agricultural tourism demonstration sites", "national industrial tourism demonstration sites", "national civilized city", national health emergency demonstration city, China charm brand cities and other honorary title.

八一公园
Bayi Park

民航大道
Civil Aviation Boulevard

By the end of 2012, the city's GDP is expected to reach 19.961 billion yuan, an increase of 16.60%; total fiscal revenue of 3.50668 billion yuan, an increase of 30.81%; rural residents per capita disposable income is expected to reach 6,373 yuan, an increase of 18.11%; urban residents per capita disposable income is expected to reach 19,520 yuan, an increase of 14.80%. 23 index system of a well-off society in an all-round way, a number of indicators have reached or close to the well-off objectives and requirements.

万峰林之西峰林一角
Wanfenglin Xifenglin corner

万峰湖之红椿景点
The Wanfeng Lake toon attractions

长顺县

Changshun County

长顺惠水共建工业园签约仪式

Changshun and Huishui to build industrial park signing ceremony

长顺县城镇化建设城南新区新貌

Changshun County, south of New Urbanization new look

丹索亚刺梨庄园灌装室

Dansuo Yaci pear filling room manor

长顺县晨龙精密仪器生产车间

Changshun County Chen Long precision instrument manufacturing workshop

长顺县面积1543平方公里，辖10乡7镇、75个村民委员会、7个居民委员会。2012年末总人口25.86万人，其中少数民族15.29万人，人口较多的少数民族有布依族、苗族。全县矿产以非金属矿产为主，主要有石灰石、硅石、耐火粘土、方解石、荧石、大理石、原煤等。

2012年，全年生产总值23.4426亿元，比上年增长18.4%；三次产业比重为23.85：33.83：42.32；农林牧渔业总产值5.5911亿元，增长9.3%，工业总产值7.0928亿元，增长17.7%，其中财政总收入31828万元，增长50.7%，地方财政收入22455万元，增长71.9%；财政总支出149670万元，增长7.83%；年内固定资产投资30.9802亿元，同比增长47.1%；社会消费品零售总额6.5458亿元，同比增长16.85%；农民人均纯收入5115元，同比增长17.84%；招商引资

威远工业园区重点企业高矿重工生产车间

Weiyuan Industrial Park high key enterprises heavy mineral production workshop

威远工业园区重点企业一均电器车间

Weiyuan Industrial Park high key enterprises Yijun electrical workshop

Changshun County owns an area of 1,543 square kilometers, jurisdiction over 10 townships 7 towns and 75 village committees, 7 residents committee. By the end of 2012, the total population of 258,600 people, of which 152,900 minorities, ethnic minorities are more populous Buyi and Miao. Non-metallic mineral mining in the county, mainly limestone, silica, refractory clay, calcite, fluorite, marble, coal and so on.

In 2012, annual GDP was 2.34426 billion yuan, an increase of 18.4% over last year; three industries accounted for 23.85:33.83:42.32; agriculture forest fishing industry was 559.11 million yuan, an increase of 9.3%, industrial output value of 709.28 million yuan, an increase of 17.7%, of which the total fiscal revenue 318,280,000 yuan, an increase of 50.7%, and local revenues 224,550,000 yuan, an increase of 71.9%; fiscal expenditure 1.4967 billion yuan, an increase of 7.83%; investment in fixed assets during the year 3.09802 billion yuan, an increase of 47.1 %; retail sales of 654.58 million yuan, an increase of 16.85%; per capita net income of farmers 5,115 yuan, an increase of 17.84%; investment funds 3.621 billion yuan, an increase of 73.9%; tourism revenues 1.015 billion yuan, an increase of 46.8%.

The rural economy. Various types of agriculture funds invested 55.93 million yuan; achieve total grain production 97,524 tons, oil production 5,576 tons, meat production 16,809 tons, 46,900 mu of flue-cured tobacco acreage; forest coverage rate reached 48.2%; construction of the main agricultural products "electronic identity card", "two-dimensional code query" and other agricultural products traceability system, Changshun green shell egg, calcium Apple industrial park was included in the province's "5

果农在采摘成熟苹果

Fruit farmers are picking ripe apples

长顺县城夜景

Changshun County night view

长顺县水淹坝生态养鹅基地
Changshun County flooded dam ecological goose base

到位资金36.21亿元，同比增长73.9%；旅游总收入10.15亿元，同比增长46.8%。

农村经济。投入各类支农资金5593万元；实现粮食总产 9.7524万吨，油料总产量0.5576万吨，肉类总产量1.6809万吨，烤烟种植面积4.69万亩；森林覆盖率达48.2%；建设了主要农产品“电子身份证”、“二维码查询”等农产品溯源系统，长顺绿壳蛋鸡、高钙苹果产业园区被列入全省“5个100”工程。

工业经济。2012年，规模以上工业增加值完成5.33亿元，同比增长23%；全县民营企业已达299户，个体工商户3934户，创税2.36亿元，占财政总收入的74.2%；威远工业园区被列入全省“5个100”工程。

基础设施。全县共对接项目308个，实施各类项目126个；惠兴高速惠镇段、长顺大道一二标段、城南新区至高速公路匝道口连线等交通要道已建成通车；全年完成59处水利工程建设。

长顺县生态自然放养绿壳蛋鸡
Changshun County ecology natural restocking green shell egg hen

教育概况。全县共有小学94所，634个班，专任教师1163人，在校生19786人；初级中学19所，220个班，专任教师647人，在校生12300人；独立高级中学一所，71个班，专任教师221人，在校生4225人，2012年977人参加高考，336人录取本科院校。

卫生概况。全县卫生机构23个，其中县级医院1个，拥有床位数583个，卫生人员449人，其中卫生技术人员351人。

文化状况。全县拥有图书馆1个，藏书1.73万册，文物管理所1个，乡文化站17个，广播电视台1座，有线文播电视台1座。

社会事业。新建保障性住房350套，完成林业棚户区改造28户；城镇新增就业3522人；社会保险覆盖率达到100%；顺利通过国家计生优质服务工作检查验收，荣获“国家级计划生育优质服务先进县”称号。

黔中明珠长顺县全貌
Pearl in the middle of Guizhou Changshun County picture

长顺县潮井间歇泉景点
Changshun County Chaojing Geysers Attractions

长顺县5000年天台银杏王全景
Changshun County 5,000 years Tiantai Ginkgo King panorama

hundred" project.

Industrial economy. In 2012, above-scale industrial added value reached 533 million yuan, an increase of 23%; county reached 299 private enterprises, individual industrial and commercial households 3,934, the highest tax 236 million yuan, accounting for 74.2% of total fiscal revenue; Weiyuan Industrial Park was included in the province's "5 hundred" project.

Infrastructure. County docking project 308, the implementation of various projects 126; Huixing highspeed Huizhen Town section , Changshun Road one-two sections, new south entrance ramp to the freeway connection has been opened to traffic and other traffic arteries; Last year, completed 59 water conservancy construction.

Education Overview. County has a total of 94 primary schools, 634 classes, 1,163 full-time teachers, students in 19,786 people; Junior High School 19, 220 classes, 647 full-time teachers, students in 12,300 people; independent high school 1, 71 classes, 221 full-time teachers, students in 4,225 people, 977 people participated in the college entrance examination in 2012, 336 people admitted to colleges.

Health profiles. 23 county health agencies, including a county hospital, with 583 beds, health personnel 449 people, including 351 health technicians.

Cultural conditions. The county has a library, a collection of 17,300 books, a heritage management, township cultural stations 17, a radio and television station, a message broadcast cable television station.

Social undertakings. 350 new affordable housing units, complete forestry shantytowns 28; urban new added employment 3,522; social insurance coverage reached 100%; IPPF passed the national quality inspection and acceptance of work, won the "national advanced county family planning services" title.

国家AAAA级旅游景区——高原明珠长顺杜鹃湖
National AAAA level scenic spot - Plateau Pearl Changshun Rhododendron Lake

印江土家族苗族自治县

Yijiang Tujia and Miao Autonomous County

原省委书记栗战书在印江视察工作
Former Provincial Party Secretary Li Zhanshu had inspection work in Yinjiang

市委书记刘奇凡视察印江城镇建设
Party secretary Liu Qifan inspected Yinjiang cities and towns construction

印江土家族苗族自治县位于贵州省东北部、铜仁地区西部，地处梵净山西麓。国土面积1969平方公里，辖17个乡镇、365个村、9个居委会，总人口43.8万人，其中土家族、苗族等少数民族人口占71.2%。该县是全国科普示范县、全国法制宣传教育先进县、全国党的基层组织建设先进县、全省社会治安综合治理模范县、全省党风廉政建设先进县、省级卫生县城、省级文明县城，素有“中国书法之乡”、“中国名茶之乡” 、“中国长寿之乡”之美誉。

2012年，全县完成生产总值39.5亿元，同比增长17.3%；实现财政总收入3.41亿元，增长38.7%，其中，公共财政预算收入2.17亿元，增长40.2%；完成全社会固定资产投资58亿元，增长62.6%；城镇居民人均可支配收入达到15390元，增长18.0%；农民人均纯收入达到4396元，增长18.2%；社会消费品零售总额7.5亿元，增长15.9%；经济发展增比进位在全省综合排位从上年的47位上升到31位，提升16位。全县经济社会发展呈现出发展提速、转型加快、后劲增强、民生改善、社会和谐的良好局面，为“十二五”规划实施和全面建成小康社会奠定了坚实基础。

新农村风貌
New rural style

印江经济开发区一角
Corner of the Yinjiang Economic Development Zone

县城廉租房
County low-cost housing

Yinjjiang Tujia and Miao Autonomous County is located in the northeast of Guizhou Province, west of Tongren Prefecture, located in the western foot of Fanjingshan. Land area of 1,969 square kilometers, jurisdiction over 17 towns, 365 villages, 9 neighborhood, with a total population of 438,000, of which Tujia, Miao and other ethnic minority population accounts for 71.2%. The county is national popular science demonstration counties, the national legal publicity and education of advanced counties, the National Party's grassroots organizations advanced counties, the province's social security comprehensive management model county, honest government advanced counties in the province, the provincial health county, provincial civilized county, known as the "hometown of Chinese calligraphy", "homwtown of Chinese tea", "hometown of longevityin China" in the world.

梵净山风光

Fanjingshan scenery

土家风雨桥

Tujia Fengyu bridge

文昌公园夜景

Wenchang park at night

In 2012, the county completed GDP of 3.95 billion yuan, an increase of 17.3%; total fiscal revenue of 341 million yuan, an increase of 38.7%, which public budget revenue of 217 million yuan, an increase of 40.2%; total fixed asset investment of 5.8 billion yuan, an increase of 62.6%; per capita disposable income of urban residents reached 15,390 yuan, an increase of 18.0%; rural per capita net income reached 4,396 yuan, up 18.2%; 750 million yuan of total retail sales of social consumer goods, an increase of 15.9%; increase economic development in the province than the binary comprehensive ranking rose from 47 last year to 31, upgrade 16-bit. Economic and social development in the county showing a good situation of the speed of development, accelerate the transformation, increased stamina, improved living conditions, social harmony, laid a solid foundation for the implementation of the "12th Five-Year"plan and building a moderately prosperous society.

梵净茶园

The Fanjing tea garden

食用菌生产基地

Edible fungus production base

清 镇 市
Qingzhen City

贵阳市人大常委会副主任、清镇市委书记杨明晋致辞
Guiyang Municipal People's Congress deputy director, Qingzhen city party secretary Yang Mingjin made the speech

农业部国际交流司原司长冯玉林为红枫湖镇授牌
Ministry of Agriculture, the former director of International Exchange Division Feng Yulin award for the Hongfeng Lake Town

2012年，在贵阳市委、市政府的坚强领导下，在市人大、市政协的监督支持下，紧扣“主基调”，实施“主战略”，团结拼搏，攻坚克难，锐意进取，完成了市五届人大一次会议确定的各项目标任务。

经济继续保持平稳较快增长。全市生产总值144.16亿元，增长16.8%；财政总收入16.4亿元，增长25.8%；公共财政预算收入 9.95亿元，增长26.9%；固定资产投资241.82亿元，增长60.7%；金融机构存贷款余额分别达87.73亿元、53.82亿元，增长17.47%、16.18%。

领导调研
The leaders had research

市长李瑞陪同贵阳市领导调研清镇市经济运行情况
City Mayor Li Rui accompanied the Guiyang city leaders to have research of Guiyang Qingzhen economic operation

贵州省诚信农民建设推进大会
Guizhou Province to promote the building of farmers integrity conference

城北新区一号路奠基现场
City Beixin 1st Road groundbreaking site

In 2012, under the strong leadership of Guiyang municipal committee, municipal government and municipal party committee, support and supervision of the Municipal People's Congress, Municipal CPPCC, closely linked to the "main tone", the implementation of the "main strategy", unity and hard work to overcome difficulties and forge ahead, completed the City fifth People's Congress meeting to determine the objectives and tasks.

Economy maintained steady and rapid growth. GDP of 14.416 billion yuan, an increase of 16.8%; fiscal revenue 1.64 billion yuan, an increase of 25.8%; public budget revenue 995 million yuan, an increase of 26.9%; fixed asset investment 24.182 billion yuan, an increase of 60.7%; financial institutions, deposits and loans balance amounted to 8.773 billion yuan, 5.382 billion yuan, an increase of 17.47%, 16.18%, respectively.

"Informationization, industrialization and localization" simultaneous development accelerated. Industrial park facilities and industrial base continues to consolidate and build a coal-aluminum integration, coal-based integrated development of a good platform; relying on Vocational Education City and other industrial park construction, the central city area increased by 3 square kilometers, a population of about 20,000, opened to Jinyang bus; been listed as national modern agriculture demonstration zones and key counties for national vegetable industry.

Further promote the reform and opening up. Complete withdrawal of Qinglong Street offices to build a new community work, forming a three Administrative

签约仪式
Signing Ceremony

开工典礼
Starting ceremony

工业西区供水工程动土开工情景
Western industrial water supply project started in groundbreaking scenarios

签字仪式现场
Singing ceremony

科伦药业技术人员在生产线上紧张作业
Kelun medicine technician work on the production line in tension

“三化”同步发展步伐加快。工业园区配套设施和产业基础不断夯实，搭建了煤电铝一体化、煤电化一体化发展的良好平台；依托职教城等产业园区建设，中心城区面积增加3平方公里，新增人口约2万人，开通到金阳的公交车；被列为国家现代农业示范区和全国蔬菜产业重点县。

改革开放深入推进。完成撤青龙街道办事处组建新型社区工作，形成了三个管委会和经济开发区主抓发展、五个社区主抓服务的工作格局；招商引资市外实际到位资金110亿元，增长103.72%，实际利用外资1680万美元，增长68.34%。

人民生活进一步改善。城镇新增就业10679人；城镇居民人均可支配收入21227.2元，农民人均纯收入7953元，实际增长16.2%和15.3%。

社会管理成效显著。“两抢一盗”案件发案率下降28.7%、破案率上升39.57%，群众安全感全省测评排位前移了62位，安全感提升幅度和排位前移位次分别排全省第二位、贵阳市第一位。

建设中的翰弈汽车城
Construction of Han Yi Motor City

小城镇建设清镇市卫城镇贺龙广场
Small towns construction Qingzhen City Weicheng Town Helong Square

校园电视
Campus TV

Committees and Economic Development Zone concentrating on development, concentrating on five community service work pattern; investment outside the city of actual funds 11 billion yuan, an increase of 103.72%, the actual utilization of foreign capital $ 16,800,000, an increase of 68.34%.

Further improve people's lives. Urban new employment 10,679 people; urban residents per capita disposable income of 21,227.2 yuan, rural per capita net income of 7,953 yuan, a real increase of 16.2% and 15.3%.

Social management with remarkable results. "Robbery and Theft" case incidence rate dropped 28.7%, up 39.57% detection rate, safety of the masses of the province forward the 62 qualifying assessment, security to enhance the rate and rank advancement ranking were ranked second in the province and first in Guiyang City.

《欢乐的彝寨》舞蹈表演场景
"Happy Yi village" dance scene

合唱《醉苗乡》演出现场
Chorus "drunk Miao village" live performances

开幕式现场
The opening scene

思南县

Sinan County

县委书记胡洪成城区现场办公

County party secretary Hu Hongcheng work at the City field

县长刘云成调研现代高效农业示范园区

Magistrate Liu Yuncheng had survey of the modern and efficient agriculture demonstration park

建设中的思南山城

Construction Sinan mountain city

城北新区一角

North city new district corner

思南县位于贵州省东北部，素有“黔中首郡”之称。面积2230.5平方公里。辖27个乡（其中14个民族乡），13个镇，489个村民委员会、37个社区（居民委员会）。人口 670776人。矿产资源丰富。森林覆盖率34.8%。

经济概况：

一是综合实力大幅提升。全年生产总值60.47亿元，比上年增长17%；农牧渔业总产值31.8亿元，增长19.64%；林业总产值2.4157亿元，增长34.21%。地方财政收入5.52亿元，增长35.6%；财政总支出23.8亿元，增长21.5%。社会消费品零售总额15.98亿元，增长32%。城镇居民人均可支配收入16005元，增长25%；农民人均纯收入4342元，增长18.6%。

二是项目带动成效显著。全县完成固定资产投资110亿元，交通项目完成投资29.41亿元，水利项目完成投资1.9亿元，电力项目完成投资7236万元，产业项目完成投资52.7亿元，其他民生项目完成投资14.2亿元。争取中央和省投资项目112个，总投资11.7亿元。全县通车里程4074.73公里，2012年新修通组公路里程196.4公里。以石材产业、农特产品加工业、建筑建材业等为主的169个产业项目得以分项实施。

三是城镇建设步伐加快。规划方面，启动了规模为50平方公里的县城总规修编，完成了13个乡镇总体规划编制和100个村庄规划工作，实现了乡镇总体规划编制全覆盖。建设方面，

三桥效果图
Sanqiao renderings

中伟中央广场沿江透视效果图
Zhongwei central square Yanjiang perspective renderings

Sinan County is located in the northeast Guizhou Province, known as "the first county in Guizhou". Area of 2,230.5 square kilometers. Jurisdiction over 27 townships (including 14 townships), 13 towns, 489 village committees, 37 community (residents committee). Population of 670,776 people. Rich in mineral resources. The forest coverage rate of 34.8%.

Economy:

First, the comprehensive strength has increased significantly. Annual GDP of 6.047 billion yuan, an increase of 17% over last year; animal husbandry and fishery output value of 3.18 billion yuan, an increase of 19.64%; forestry output value of 2.4157 billion yuan, an increase of 34.21%. Local financial revenue 552 million yuan, an increase of 35.6%; fiscal expenditure 2.38 billion yuan, up 21.5%. Total retail sales of social consumer goods 1.598 billion yuan, an increase of 32%. Per capita disposable income of urban residents 16,005 yuan, an increase of 25%; rural per capita net income of 4,342 yuan, an increase of 18.6%.

温泉城效果图
Hot Springs renderings

乌江文化健康产业园效果图
Wujiang Culture Health Industrial Park renderings

Second, the project lead with remarkable results. The county invested 11 billion yuan in fixed assets, completed an investment of 2.941 billion yuan transportation projects, water conservancy projects completed investment 190 million yuan, 72.36 million yuan was invested power projects, completed an investment of 5.27 billion yuan industrial projects, other livelihood projects completed investment 1.42 billion yuan. For the central and provincial investment projects in 112, a total investment of 1.17 billion yuan. The county mileage 4,074.73 km, in 2012, through group newly built highway mileage 196.4 km. In the stone industry, agricultural products processing industry, building materials industry and other industrial projects mainly 169 to breakdown implemented.

Third, is to accelerate the pace of urban construction. Planning to start a scale of 50 square kilometers of the county master plan revision, completed 13 of township master plan preparation and 100 village planning work to achieve the full coverage of the township

福安石材项目建成投产
Fuan stone project built up and put into construction

石材生产线
Stone production line

通过将城镇基础设施建设与扶贫生态移民工程建设、新农村建设有机结合，各项重点市政工程建设加快实施，累计完成市政基础设施建设投资近15亿元，城镇化率达到35%。

四是招商引资成果显著。2012年，全县招商引资签约项目102个，协议资金206.2亿元。其中，签订正式协议89个，协议资金87.53亿元。开工项目88个，开工率98.88%。在建项目132个，到位资金51亿元，其中新开工项目88个，到位资金20亿元。投达产项目64个，其中新建项目投达产39个，续建项目25个。

五是文化旅游活力彰显。突出思南特色，继续全力打造“乌江、石林、温泉”三张旅游名片。成功举办了第一届“中国•思南乌江龙舟节”、“乌江风情•思南原创歌曲”大赛等群众喜闻乐见的文体活动。成功申报了2个省级非物质文化遗产保护项目。启动思南石林5A级旅游景区、白鹭湖4A级旅游景区创建和白鹭湖国家湿地公园、万圣山森林公园申报工作。实现旅游收入12.03亿元，同比增长47.6 %。

六是民生事业逐步改善。全县新增就业8080人，城乡居民养老保险综合参保率达90%以上。教育“三项突破”工程有序推进。医药卫生体制改革顺利推进。完成保障性住房建设2330套，农村危房改造工程7500户。顺利完成农村集体土地确权登记发证工作。

南塑包装厂生产车间
South plastic packaging plant production workshop

繁忙的南塑包装生产线
Busy South plastic packaging production line

思南县许家坝种草养畜草场
Sinan County Xu Jia Ba grass and livestock pasture

思南黄牛
Sinan cattle

master plan preparation. Construction, urban infrastructure through the construction and poor ecological migration project construction, the new rural construction combine to accelerate the implementation of key municipal engineering construction, municipal infrastructure totaled nearly 1.5 billion yuan investment, urbanization rate reached 35%.

Fourth, investment had remarkable achievements. In 2012, the county investment projects signed 102, the agreement funds 20.62 billion yuan. Among them, 89 signed a formal agreement, the agreement funds 8.753 billion yuan. Projects 88, the operating rate 98.88%. Projects under construction 132, 5.1 billion yuan of funds in place, including 88 new projects, capital in place of 2 billion yuan. Cast of 64 production projects, including the new project investment of production 39, 25 ongoing projects.

石林叠翠
Stone Forest Pinnacle

Fifth, cultural tourism activity demonstrated. Sinan prominent features, continue to create "the Wujiang River, Stone Forest, hot spring" three tourist card. Successfully held the first session of the "Sinan Wujiang, China Dragon Boat Festival", "Wujiang style • Sinan original song" contest and other sports activities loved by the masses. Declare the success of two provincial intangible cultural heritage protection projects. Start Sinan Stone Forest 5A grade scenic spot, Egret Lake 4A level scenic spots to create and Egret Lake National Wetland Park, Wansheng Mountain Forest Park reporting. Tourism revenue 1.203 billion yuan, an increase of 47.6%.

蓬勃发展的现代农业
Thriving modern agriculture

Sixth, is gradually improving people's livelihood undertakings. 8,080 new jobs in the county, urban and rural pension insurance comprehensive insurance rate of 90%. Education "three breakthrough" projects pushed in an orderly way. Medical and health system pushed smoothly. 2,330 completed construction of affordable housing units, renovation of dilapidated buildings in rural areas 7,500. Successful completion of the rural collective land ownership registration certification work.

修 文 县
Xiuwen County

县城新貌
County new look

修文县位于贵州省中部，面积1075.7平方公里，辖4镇6乡、2个社区服务中心、217个行政村，人口31.13万，有汉、苗、布依等22个民族。2012年全年实现生产总值71.24亿元，增长20.23%；完成财政总收入9.18亿元，增长29.01%。完成全社会固定资产投资145.02亿元，增长60.67%；完成城镇和农村居民人均可支配收入分别为21720元、7766元，分别增长16.02%、20.03%。

汇聚了发展共识。按照省市党代会提出的奋斗目标和“两加一推”主基调、“三化同步”主战略的要求，全县上下在抢抓机遇、自身“发力”、争取“给力”、借助“外力”发展上形成了新的共识，在创新方法、勇于担当、推动跨越上形成了新的共识，在夯实基础、挖掘潜力、聚力冲刺、后发赶超上形成了新的共识。

筑牢了跨越基础。白云至修文、金阳至扎佐、龙场至扎佐三条城市干道开工建设；扎佐工业园区升级为省级经济开发区；积极争取14个批次9000多亩建设用地指标；落实国发2号文件编制申报502个项目；扎佐镇、六广镇列入省、市示范城镇推进建设。

倡树了干事群像。四大班子成员牵头负责重大项目指挥部，班子间相互补台、相互支持、顾全大局、勇挑重担，在共谋发展中树立了新形象。

贵钢黔轮胎安置小区
The Guizhou steel Qianluntai placement cell

修文县六屯乡三寨村
Xiuwen county Liutun township Sanzhai village

2012年11月26日，龙场至扎佐城市道路建设及两侧土地整治项目开工

November 26, 2012, Longchang to Zhazuo urban road construction and both sides land remediation project started

同济堂制药有限公司

Tongjitang Pharmaceutical Co., Ltd.

Xiuwen County is located in central Guizhou Province, with an area of 1,075.7 square kilometers, jurisdiction over 4 towns, 6 townships, two community service centers, 217 administrative villages, population 311,300, Han, Miao, Buyi and other 22 ethnic groups. 2012 annual GDP of 7.124 billion yuan, an increase of 20.23%; total fiscal revenue 918 million yuan, an increase of 29.01%. In fixed asset investment 14.502 billion yuan, an increase of 60.67%; complete urban and rural residents per capita disposable income was 21,720 yuan, 7,766 yuan, respectively, up 16.02%, 20.03%.

Brought together a development consensus. In accordance with the provincial party congress goal and the "two plus one push" the main tone, "three synchronization" main strategy requirement, the county up and down in seizing the opportunity to own "force" to fight "awesome", with "external force" on the formation of the development of a new consensus, the innovative ways, the courage to play, and promote the formation of a cross on the new consensus, on solid foundation, tap potential, cohesion sprint, after catching up on the formation of a new consensus.

Build a strong span foundation. Baiyun to Xiuwen, Jinyang to Zhazuo, Longchang to Zhazuo three main urban roads to start the construction; Zhazuo industrial park upgrade provincial economic development zone; actively strive for 14 batches of 9,000 acres of land for construction indicators; implementation of the National Development NO.2 document preparation declare 502 items; Zhazuo town, Liuguang town included in the provincial and municipal demonstration towns promote the building.

Advocating and building the officer portrait. Four members of the team to take charge of major project headquarters, team sets complement each other and support each other, the overall situation, heavy responsibilities, and seek common development in establishing a new image.

贵钢项目施工现场

The Guizhou steel project construction site

洒坪乡党员创业带富示范基地

Saping village party venture with rich demonstration base

三 穗 县

Sansui County

县委书记袁尚勇（左三）、县长付乐欣（左四）到三穗经济开发区调研
County party secretary Yuan Shangyong (third from left), Magistrate Fu Lexin (fourth from left) to the Sansui Economic Development Zone to have research

省级经济开发区贵州三穗经济开发区
Provincial Economic Development Zone Guizhou Sansui Economic Development Zone

三穗县位于贵州省东部，素有“麻鸭之乡”、“斗笠之乡”的美誉。辖5镇4乡，人口22.19万，其中少数民族占65.37%。三穗自古就有“黔东要塞”和“千里苗疆门户”之称，是由湘入黔的重要通道，是黔东南州“三条精品旅游线”的中枢。

2012年，三穗坚持“两加一推”主基调，紧紧围绕构建“一城两中心三基地”（黔东重要中心城市、黔东旅游服务中心、黔东商贸物流中心，黔东产业承接基地、黔东返乡创业基地、黔东轻工产业基地）的战略定位，突出特色，发挥优势，重点实施“工业强县、城镇带县、商贸活县”主战略，全面加快经济建设和社会发展，综合实力不断增强，呈现出经济发展、社会进步、民族团结、政治稳定的良好局面。

2012年，全县生产总值完成20亿元，增长18%；财政总收入完成2.66亿元，增长44.88%；工业经济稳步发展，同年8月，产业（工业）园区经省人民政府批复升格为省级经济开发区；全社会固定资产投资完成40.9亿元，增长113.23%；农民人均纯收入达到4642元，增长17.40%。增比进位继续保持后发赶超态势，2012年在全省综合排位第41位，在全州综合排名第4位。

贵州三穗经济开发区新貌
New look of Guizhou Sansui Economic Development Zone

县城全景图
County panorama

三穗县出口创汇企业千慧服饰公司生产车间
Sansui export enterprises Qianhui apparel company production workshop

竹编艺术之乡的斗笠人家
Bamboo arts village hats homes

生态放养的三穗鸭
Sansui duck ecological stocking

Sansui County is located in eastern part of Guizhou Province, known as “duck town”, “hats town”. Jurisdiction 5 towns 4 rural towns, population of 221,900, of which ethnic minorities accounted for 65.37%. Sansui since ancient times was known as “Qiandong fortress” and “Trinidad Miao portal”, is an important gateway Hunan into Guizhou, is the Southeast states “three high-quality tourist line” hub.

In 2012, Sansui adhere to the “two plus one push” the main tone, focus on building a “one city, two central three bases” (Qiandong important urban centers, Qiandong Tourist Service Center, Qiandong trade and logistics center, Qiandong industry to undertake base, Qiandong home business base, Qiandong light industrial base) strategic positioning, highlighting the characteristics, advantages, focusing on the implementation of “industrial strong county, with the county lead towns, trade of live county” main strategy to accelerate the pace of economic and social development of comprehensive strength, showing the economic development, social progress, national unity, political stability, a good situation.

In 2012, the county’s GDP completed 2 billion yuan, an increase of 18%; fiscal revenue of 266 million yuan, an increase of 44.88%; industrial economy developed steadily, the same year in August, industrial (industrial) parks approved by the provincial people's government upgraded provincial economic Development Zone; total fixed asset investment of 4.09 billion yuan, an increase of 113.23%; rural per capita net income reached 4,642 yuan, an increase of 17.40%. The incremental ratio of carry continue to maintain growth than latecomer catch-up trend, in 2012 in the province integrated ranked No. 41 in the statewide ranking No. 4.

惠水县

Huishui County

陈敏尔省长（中）在黔南州委书记黄家培（左四），州长向红琼（左三），惠水县委书记吴丹（右一），县长万庆华（左二），陪同下到惠水天虹电缆调研

Provincial governor Chen Miner (middle) is accompanied by Qiannan party secretary Huang Jiapei (fourth from left), state governor Xiang Hongqiong (third from left), Huishui county Party committee secretary Wu Dan (first from right), county governor Wan Qinghua (second from left), to have research in Huishui Tianhong Cable

黔南州州委书记黄家培在惠水长田工业园调研

Qiannan state committee secretary Huang Jiapei had research in Huishui Changtian Industrial Park

"扬帆十八大 领航新惠水"主题培训班在中山大学开班

"Set sail 18th CPC National Congress Pilot new Huishui" theme training courses for class in Sun Yat-sen University

2012年，惠水抢抓机遇，攻坚克难，圆满完成年初确定的各项任务。发展速度在高位上运行，位次在追赶中前移，活力在开放中增强，民生在发展中改善。

经济指标实现较快增长。全年生产总值完成43亿元，增长21%。三次产业结构比重为25.3∶39.7∶35。全社会固定资产投资完成65.98亿元，增长55.02%。工业总产值完成73.53亿元，增长26.12%。社会消费品零售总额完成9.63亿元，增长16.2%。财政收入完成6.03亿元，增长50.4%。农民人均纯收入达到5521元，增长18.3%。经济发展综合测评在全省排位比上年上升6位，全州排位上升1位。

基础设施实现重大突破。惠兴高速建成通车，结束了惠水不通高速的历史。贵惠城市干道一期建成13公里，贵惠高速建设快速推进，加快了融入贵阳城市经济圈的步伐。投资3200万元扩建自来水厂，自来水供给每日达2万吨。整合资金4657万元，实施高标准农田建设3.4万亩。生态建设不断加强，森林覆盖率达到45.53%。

三化建设实现同步推进。按照州委州政府把惠水县建设成为"三化同步"示范区的要求，新型工业化、城镇化和农业产业化快速均衡推进。园区建设强力推进，省政府批准设立惠水省级经济开发区，长田工业园区被列入全省"511"示范园区和外贸转型升级示范区。城镇建设进展加快，紧扣"一年拉通骨架、两年全面铺开、五年再造新

2012年惠水第一批招商引资项目集中签约

Huishui first batch of investment projects focused on signing in 2012

贵州•惠水•珠三角招商引资答谢恳谈会

Guizhou•Huishui•the PRD investment thank association

In 2012, Huishui seize the opportunity to tackle tough, successful completion of the tasks identified at the beginning of the year. The pace of development at a high level on the run, ranking forward in catching up, the increased activity in the open, the people's livelihood improved in development.

Economic indicators to achieve rapid growth. Completion of the annual GDP of 4.3 billion yuan, an increase of 21%. Structure of three industries accounted for 25.3: 39. 7:35. The total fixed asset investment of 6.598 billion yuan, an increase of 55.02%. The completion of the total industrial output value of 7.353 billion yuan, an increase of 26.12%. Completion of the total retail sales of social consumer goods to 963 million yuan, an increase of 16.2%. Financial income of 603 million yuan, an increase of 50.4%. The per capita net income of farmers reached 5,521 yuan, an increase of 18.3%. Comprehensive evaluation of the economic development in the province ranking up six more than the previous year, a statewide ranking rose one.

Infrastructure construction to achieve a major breakthrough. Huixing Expressway opened to traffic, over Huishui unreasonable through high-speed history. Guihui city roads built I period 13 km, Huigui high-speed construction got fast forward, and to speed up the pace of integration into the economic circle of Guiyang city. 32 million yuan investment in the expansion of the water plant, water supply up to 20,000 tons per day. Integration of capital of 46.57 million yuan, the implementation of the construction of high-standard farmland 34,000 mu. The ecological construction continue to strengthen, the forest coverage rate reached 45.53%.

The construction of three promoted simultaneously. In accordance with the state government, the state commission

2012中国•贵州•惠水第四届好花红艺术节暨端午"龙游涟江"旅游文化商贸系列活动启动仪式

2012, China•Guizhou•Huishui Fourth Haohuahong Art Festival that is Dragon Boat Festival "the Longyou ripple river"tourism and cultural commerce series launch event

惠水县兴绿洲种禽基地奠基

Huishui County Xinglvzhou Breeder base foundation

惠高大道正式通车
The Huigao Boulevard official opening

惠兴高速惠水段通车
Huixing Express Huishui segment opened to traffic

城”的目标和“稳南扩北、提速扩容、产城互动、完善功能、突出特色”的思路，全力打造宜居、宜业、宜商、宜游的山水田园城市。农业产业化发展迅速。以“185工程”为载体，以结构调整为主线，坝区上设施、山区抓特色，推进农业增效、农民增收、农村发展，实现了结构调整在全州规模最大、结构最优、效益最好的目标。

民生建设实现均衡发展。坚持民生为先，着力保障和改善民生。进一步完善城乡低保、医疗保障等制度，开展低保提标工作。加快保障性住房建设。城乡居民社会养老保险试点工作顺利推进。

社会事业实现全面进步。坚持一手抓经济建设，一手抓社会事业，更加注重增强发展的协调性，努力让人民群众共享改革发展成果。以创业带动就业。加强人口计生工作，实现了年度“双降”目标，荣获“贵州省人口计生依法行政文明执法先进县”和“贵州省流动人口计划生育优质管理和服务工作合格县”称号。加强安全生产工作，实现安全生产事故起数和死亡人数“双降”目标。

项目建设实现重大进展。抢抓国发2号文件机遇，牢固树立“大招商吸引大投资、大项目支撑大产业、大产业带动大发展”的理念，积极扩大投资，全力推进项目建设。加强项目规划编制及申报，抓好项目前期工作。中央投资项目扎实推进。加大项目管理力度，强化项目推进责任制。全力推进省、州12个重大工程和重点项目建设，累计完成投资20.98亿元。

文化事业实现全面繁荣。增强文化自觉、文化自信、文化自强，着力推进文化大繁荣大发展。加强旅游工作，抓好景区建设。进一步加大民族文化的保护和传承力度。

诗意惠水
Poetic Huishui

秀美涟江——惠水
The beautiful Lian Jiang - Huishui

requirements of making Huishui County into "three synchronous" demonstration area, new industrialization, urbanization and the rapid industrialization of agriculture balanced propulsion. The construction of the park is to promote strongly, the provincial government approved the establishment of of Huishui provincial economic development zone, Changtian Industrial Park was included in the province's "511" demonstration parks, and foreign trade transformation and upgrading demonstration area. The towns construction progress accelerated, closely linked to the objectives of the "one year to pull through skeleton, two years in full swing, five year reengineering Metro" and "stable South expansion North, speed expansion, the city produced interaction, improve function, highlighting features"ideas, to build livable, desirable industry, desirable business, desirable travel landscape garden city. The rapid development of agricultural industrialization. The "185 Project"as the carrier, restructuring as the main line, and facilities in the dam area, on the mountains grasping characteristics, promote agricultural efficiency and rural incomes, rural development, realization of structural adjustment as the largest scale, structure optimal, benefit most good goal in the largest statewide.

Livelihood issues to achieve balanced development. Adhere to the people's livelihood first, to ensure and improve the people's livelihood. Further improve urban and rural low medical insurance system, carry out low insurance mentioned standard work. Speed up the construction of affordable housing. Urban and rural residents social pension insurance pilot work put smoothly.

惠水第四届艺术节——龙舟赛
Huishui Fourth Arts Festival - Dragon Boat Race

Social undertakings to achieve all-round progress. Insist on the one hand grasp economic construction, with the other hand grasp social undertakings, and pay more attention to enhance the coordination of the development, make efforts of the people share in the fruits of reform and development. Entrepreneurship to create jobs. Strengthen family planning work to achieve the goal of the year "double down", won the "Guizhou Province Population and Family Planning advanced and civilized law enforcement County"and "family planning quality management of the floating population in Guizhou Province and qualified county administration according to law" title. Strengthen production safety work, "double down" goals to achieve safe production number of accidents and deaths.

Projects to achieve significant progress. Seize the opportunity of the State NO.2 document, to firmly establish the concept of "big investment to attract large investments, large projects to support big industry, big industry driving development", actively expand investment, to promote the project construction. Strengthen project planning and reporting, a good grasp of the preliminary work of the project. Push forward projects invested by the central government. Intensify efforts to project management, strengthening project forward responsibility system. Efforts to promote the province, the state's 12 major projects and key projects, total investment of 2.098 billion yuan.

Cultural undertakings to achieve all-round prosperity. Enhance cultural awareness, cultural self-confidence, self-reliance, and efforts to promote the development of cultural prosperity. Strengthen tourism work, do a good job of scenic construction. Further increase the protection of the national culture and heritage efforts.

镇 远 县

Zhenyuan County

2012年7月29日，全国政协副主席李金华（第一排左一）到镇远县调研，州委书记李飞跃（第一排中）、州政协主席梁承祥（第二排左一）等州、县领导陪同

29 July 2012, the CPPCC National Committee Vice Chairman Li Jinhua (first from left in the first row) to Zhenyuan County to have research, accompanied by the state secretary Li Feiyue (middle in the first row), State Committee Chairman Liang Chengxiang (first from left in the second row) and other states, County leaders

2012年3月24日，原省委书记、现中央政治局委员、中央书记处书记栗战书（中）到镇远县考察，时任州委书记廖少华（右一）、州长李飞跃（右二）陪同

March 24, 2012, the former party secretary, now Politburo member of CPC Central Committee Li Zhanshu(the middle) to Zhenyuan County to have investigation, accompanied by the state secretary Liao Shaohua (the first from right), governor Li Feiyue (second from right)

2012年9月26日，县委书记刘建新（中），县委副书记、县长罗杰（右二）率县四大班子领导及县政府有关部门负责人深入贵州黔东经济开发区调研并向企业致以中秋节的慰问

September 26, 2012, the county party secretary Liu Jianxin (middle), county deputy secretary, mayor Luo Jie (second from right) led the county four team leaders and government departments responsible for in-depth research to Qiandong Economic Development Zone in Guizhou and extended condolences of the Mid-Autumn Day to the enterprises

镇远位于贵州省东部，系贵州省黔东南苗族侗族自治州下辖县。面积1878平方公里，辖6镇6乡和一个省级经济开发区，共有110个行政村、12个社区和4个居委会，人口23.8万，其中少数民族占42%，人口较多的少数民族有苗族、侗族和土家族等。

镇远主产水稻、玉米、小麦。境内主要矿产资源有铅、锌、锰、硅等，全县森林覆盖率58%。镇远历史悠久、民俗文化浓郁，是1986年国务院批准设立的首批历史文化名城之一。

镇远区位优越，交通便利，地处湘黔两省的怀化、铜仁和黔东南三地区交会处，有沪昆铁路、320国道、沪瑞高速公路过境。在建中的长沙至昆明快速铁路、思南经镇远至剑河高速公路、凯里黄平机场为镇远交通环境的进一步改善提供了广阔空间。

2012年，全县生产总值37.53亿元，同比增长18.3%；财政总收入完成6.15亿元，同比增长39.3%；城镇居民人均可支配收入达14611元，农民人均纯收入达4884元，同比分别增长20.8%和17.15%；社会消费品零售总额达8.02亿元，同比增长16.68%；金融机构个人储蓄存款余额22.4亿元，贷款余额18.3亿元，同比分别增长16.6%和14.8%。

2012年9月25日，首届中国历史文化名城“特色名菜”烹饪大赛在镇远古城文化园广场举行。图为州人大主任罗亮权（中），州人大副主任莫章海（左三）、唐斌（左六），县委书记刘建新（左五），县委副书记、县长罗杰（左二）等领导在现场参加活动并品评菜肴

September 25, 2012, the first Chinese historical and cultural city “features dishes” cooking contest was held in Zhenyuan Ancient City Cultural Park Plaza. The picture shows state director of National People’s Congress Luo Liangquan (the middle), state deputy director of National People’s Congress Mo Zhanghai (third from left), Tang Bin (sixth from left), the county party secretary Liu Jianxin (fifth from left), county deputy secretary, mayor Luo Jie(second from left), etc. leaders in the field to participate in activities and tasting dishes

2012年11月11日，2012贵州环雷公山超100公里跑国际挑战赛镇远赛区赛事成功举办

November 11, 2012, 2012 Guizhou ring Leigongshan ran over 100 kilometers of Zhenyuan Division International Challenge tournament held with success

大型舞蹈史诗《古韵镇远》演出剧照

Dance epic “rhyme Zhenyuan” performance stills

Zhenyuan located in the eastern Guizhou Province, is the county under the jurisdiction of the Miao and Dong Autonomous Prefecture Guizhou Province. With an area of 1,878 square kilometers, governs 6 towns, 6 townships and a provincial economic development zone, a total of 110 administrative villages, 12 communities and 4 neighborhood communities, population 238,000, where minorities account for 42% of the population, have more minorities Miao, Dong and Tujia and so on.

Zhenyuan production of rice, corn, wheat. Within the main mineral resources are lead, zinc, manganese, silicon, etc., the forest coverage rate of 58%. Zhenyuan owns long history, rich culture and folklore, was in 1986 the State Council approved the establishment of the first batch of historical and cultural city.

Zhenyuan has superior location, convenient transportation, located in Huaihua, Hunan and Guizhou provinces, Tongren and Southeast three areas intersect, there are Shanghai-Kunming Railway, 320 State Road, Shanghai Rui highway crossing. Under construction in Changsha to Kunming express railway, highway Sinan by Zhenyuan to the Jianhe highway, Kaili Huang Ping airport Zhenyuan further improve the traffic environment provided a broad space.

镇远县黔东循环工业园区内贵州黔东电力公司2×60万千瓦正常发电机组

Zhenyuan County, Qiandong circulation Industrial Park Guizhou Qiandong Power Company 2 x 600,000 kW normal generator normal generator

端阳赛龙舟。2011年5月，镇远赛龙舟被国务院列入“第三批国家级非物质文化遗产名录”

Dragon Boat Festival Dragon Boat Race. May 2011, Zhenyuan Dragon boat race was included in the “third batch of national intangible cultural heritage” by the State Council

2012年，全县农林牧渔业生产总值达12.84亿元，同比增长10%；粮食总产量达76315吨，比上年增长25.07%；畜牧业总产值2.7亿元，同比增长8.4%。烤烟产业是全县农业产业化的龙头，2012年，全县烤烟种植面积4.45万亩，收购烟叶10.35万担，烟农种烟直接收入达1.1亿元，产量和效益均跃居黔东南州第一位。

工业是镇远县主导产业，2012年，工业总产值达53亿元，同比增长44.33%，工业企业税收累计完成2.492亿元，同比增长31.56%。2012年，该县以冶金为代表的传统工业升级改造取得明显进展，以白酒、建材等为重点的特色优势产业逐步发展壮大，工业经济正朝着园区化、规模化、集约化方向发展，其主导地位进一步巩固。

贵州青酒集团的“洞藏青酒酿造工艺”于2007年5月29日入选第二批贵州非物质文化遗产名录。图为洞藏青酒窖藏溶洞内景

Green Wine Group in Guizhou “cave green wine brewing process” on May 29, 2007, were the second batch of intangible cultural heritage of Guizhou. The picture shows the cave cellar hole green wine interior

烟农喜获丰收

Tobacco farmers harvest

镇远自然风光秀丽、历史悠久、文化底蕴深厚。近年来，在“文化旅游兴县”战略带动下，文化旅游产业快速发展。2012年，全县共接待游客318万人次，实现旅游综合收入21.38亿元，同比增长32%。2012年，镇远古城获国家旅游局批准，升级为国家4A级旅游景区。

In 2012, the county's GDP 3.753 billion yuan, an increase of 18.3%; fiscal revenue of 615 million yuan, an increase of 39.3%; urban residents per capita disposable income reached 14,611 yuan, rural per capita net income reached 4,884 yuan, respectively, an increase of 20.8% and 17.15%; total retail sales of social consumer goods reached 802 million yuan, an increase of 16.68%; financial institutions, personal savings deposits 2.24 billion yuan, the loan balance 1.83 billion yuan, an increase of 16.6% and 14.8%, respectively.

In 2012, the county animal husbandry and fishery production value reached 1.284 billion yuan, an increase of 10%; grain output reached 76,315 tons, an increase of 25.07% over the previous year; animal husbandry output value of 270 million yuan, an increase of 8.4%. Tobacco industry is the county's leading agricultural industrialization, in 2012, the county's tobacco planting area of 44,500 acres, the acquisition of tobacco 103,500 dan, kinds of tobacco farmers direct income reached 110 million yuan, output and efficiency are ranked first in Qiandongnan state.

Industry is the leading industry in Zhenyuan County, in 2012, the industrial output value reached 5.3 billion yuan, an increase of 44.33%, industrial enterprises revenuet otaled 249.2 million yuan, an increase of 31.56%. In 2012, the county represented by the traditional metallurgical industry made significant progress in upgrading to liquor, building materials and other characteristics and advantages of focused industry gradually develop and grow, the industrial economy is moving in the park, large-scale, intensive direction, its further consolidate the dominant position.

产于镇远县金堡乡的秀地米

Produced in Zhenyuan County Jinbu village Xiudi rice

镇远特色菜之"镇远腊肉"

Zhenyuan specialties of the "Zhenyuan bacon"

产于镇远县都坪镇天印村的天印贡茶

Produced in Zhenyuan County Duping Town Tianyin Village Tianyin tribute tea

Zhenyuan owns natural scenery, long history and profound culture. In recent years, "cultural tourism prospers the county" strategy, driven by the rapid development of cultural tourism industry. In 2012, the county received a total of 3.18 million tourists trips, tourism revenue 2.138 billion yuan, an increase of 32%. In 2012, Zhenyuan Ancient City by the National Tourism Administration approval to upgrade its national 4A level scenic spots.

花 溪 区

Huaxi District

省委书记赵克志到石板农产品物流园调研

Provincial Party Secretary Zhao kezhi to the Shiban agricultural logistics park to have research

省委副书记、贵阳市委书记李军、贵阳市人民政府市长李再勇到花溪区调研

Provincial Committee,Guiyang Municipal Party Secretary Li Jun, Guiyang Municipal People's Government Mayor Li Zaiyong had investigation into the Huaxi District

新的贵阳市花溪区正式成立

The new Huaxi District, Guiyang city was formally established

花溪区位于贵阳市南部，是国家级生态示范区和省级城乡统筹示范区，是贵阳市重要的生态区、文化区、旅游区，素有“高原明珠”之美誉。总面积964.14平方公里，辖18个社区、2个镇、9个乡，160个行政村，52个居委会。年末总人口约62.9万人，常住少数民族约20.7万人，有苗族、布依族等40个少数民族，少数民族人口占总人口的32.9%。

近年来，区委、区政府紧扣发展实际和区情定位，坚持生态文明示范区建设目标，确保“生态、旅游、文化”三大定位不偏移，“生态立区、工业强区、城建扩区、科教兴区、旅游活区”五大战略不松懈。农业经济稳步发展，水利等基础设施建设有新的进展，特色农产品有新的发展，都市生态农业格局逐步形成。工业特色产业和优势产业规模不断壮大，化工、机电装备、建材、制药和食品五大主导产业提速增效。以旅游业为龙头的服务业发展提速，花溪区“中心拓展、两翼齐飞”的大物流产业布局基本形成。

辖区内的贵阳经济技术开发区，作为国家级经济技术开发区和贵州最大的装备制造产业集中区域，是贵阳目前经济发展速度最快、最具发展潜力的工业经济区域。目前，已形成了以装备制造产业、工程机械、汽车零部件、电子信息产业为主导，以新材料、生物工程、食品生产等其他高新技术产业为补充，以现代物流为配套的“多元推进、成龙配套”的多元产业发展新格局，并初步形成了横向成群、纵向成链的产业集群，是贵州目前军工技术产业、装备制造

Huaxi district is located in the south of Guiyang City, is a state-level ecological demonstration district and provincial urban and rural plan demonstration area, is an important ecological district, cultural district, tourism district of Guiyang City, known as "Pearl of the plateau". The total area of 964.14 square kilometers, administer 18 community, 2 towns, 9 townships, 160 administrative villages, 52 neighborhood committees. At the end of the year, the population of about 629,000 people, resident minority about 207,000 people, Miao, Buyi and other 40 ethnic minorities, ethnic minority population accounts for 32.9% of the total population.

贵阳国际汽车贸易城
Guiyang International Automobile Trade City

贵阳闽达钢铁有限公司棒材生产线
Guiyang Minda Iron and Steel Co., Ltd. bar production line

In recent years, the district committee, district government to the actual development and regional positioning, adhere to the ecological civilization demonstration district construction goal, to ensure that the "ecological, tourism, culture" three positioning is not offset, "ecological establish area, industrial strong area, urban expansion area, science and education prosper area, tourism alive area" five strategic is not loose. The steady development of agricultural economy, water conservancy and other infrastructure construction has new progress, characteristics of agricultural products have a new development, and gradually form a pattern of urban ecological agriculture. Industrial characteristics industry and advantages industry of the growing scale, chemical industry, mechanical and electrical equipment, building materials, pharmaceutical and food industry of five big dominant industry got speed efficiency. Speed up development of service industry in the tourism industry as a leader, the Huaxi district "central extension, the two wings in full strength" of the logistics industrial layout basically formed.

Guiyang Economic and Technological Development Zone in the area, as a state-level Economic and Technological Development Zone and Guizhou's largest equipment manufacturing industry concentrated area, is currently the fastest growing economy, the most development potential industrial area in Guiyang. At present, has been formed to the equipment manufacturing industry, engineering machinery, auto

贵阳国家经济技术开发区全景图
Guiyang National Economic and Technological Development Zone panorama

贵州花溪大学城
Guizhou Huaxi University City

贵州省大学生专场文艺演出暨花溪之夏艺术节闭幕式
Special performance of the college students in Guizhou province and Huaxi Summer Arts Festival Closing Ceremony

产业的集聚和繁荣之地，是以装备制造业以及相关的生产服务性业为主的“现代化工业强区、现代化都市新区、现代化生态示范区”。

为贯彻落实《国务院关于进一步促进贵州经济社会又好又快发展的若干意见》，该区党武乡、湖潮乡于2013年4月1日整建制委托贵安新区进行管理。2012年，根据《国务院关于同意贵州省调整贵阳市部分行政区划的批复》，将原小河区和原花溪区组建成为新的花溪区。新花溪区成立后，产业结构发生了巨大的变化。

2012年，新花溪区生产总值230.27亿元，比上年增长17.2%。其中，第一产业增加值10.19亿元，比上年增长9.0%；第二产业增加值120.33亿元，比上年增长19.4%；第三产业增加值99.75亿元，比上年增长16.0%。三次产业结构比为4.42:52.26:43.32。规模以上工业增加值94.26亿元，比上年增长24.5%。全社会固定资产投资达444.52亿元，比上年增长62.8%。实现财政总收入32.27亿元，比上年增长24.0%；公共财政预算收入19.77亿元，比上年增长33.3%；公共财政预算支出30.4亿元，比上年增长26.5%。招商引资市外实际到位资金209.03亿元，比上年增长91.2%。社会消费品零售总额89.34亿元，比上年增长18.1%；城镇居民人均可支配收入21791元，比上年增长12.7%；农民人均纯收入9396元，比上年增长14.2%。全区旅游总收入82.74亿元；旅游接待人数2261.56万人次，比上年增长46.7%。

泛舟花溪公园
Boating in Huaxi park

青岩古镇
Qingyan ancient town

parts, electronic information industry as the leading industry, with new materials, biological engineering, food production and other high-tech industries as supplement, modern logistics is a new pattern of development of multiple industry supporting the "multiple propulsion, the complete set", and initially formed a horizontal group, longitudinal chain of industrial clusters, is currently the defense technology industry, equipment manufacturing industry and prosperity of the land in Guizhou, is the equipment manufacturing industry and the production of the service industry related mainly "modern industrial strong the area, modern urban new area, modern ecological demonstration area".

To implement the "State Council several opinions on further promoting the Guizhou sound and rapid economic and social development", the Wudang Township, Huchao Township got the whole system entrust management by Gui'an new area, in April 1, 2013. In 2012, according to the "State Council approval for"Guizhou province administrative division adjustment part of Guiyang City", the original Xiaohe district and Huaxi district establish to become the new Huaxi district. After the establishment of the new Huaxi district, the industrial structure has undergone tremendous changes.

In 2012, the new Huaxi district GDP was 23.027 billion yuan, an increase of 17.2%. Among them, the first industrial added value of 1.019 billion yuan, an increase of 9%; the second industry added value of 12.033 billion yuan, an increase of 19.4%; the tertiary industry added value of 9.975 billion yuan, an increase of 16%. Three industrial structure ratio is 4.42:52.26:43.32. Above-scale industrial added value of 9.426 billion yuan, an increase of 24.5%. The total social investment in fixed assets reached 44.452 billion yuan, an increase of 62.8%. Total financial revenue was 3.227 billion yuan, an increase of 24%; public budget income was 1.977 billion yuan, an increase of 33.3%; public finance budget expenditure 3.04 billion yuan, an increase of 26.5%. Foreign capital attraction actual capital 20.903 billion yuan, an increase of 91.2%. Total retail sales of social consumer goods 8.934 billion yuan, an increase of 18.1%; per capita disposable income of urban residents was 21,791 yuan, an increase of 12.7%; per capita net income of farmers 9,396 yuan, an increase of 14.2%. The total tourism income of 8.274 billion yuan; the number of tourist reception 22,615,600 person-time, an increase of 46.7%.

花溪公园
Huaxi park

花溪国家城市湿地公园
Huaxi National City wetland park

正 安 县

Zheng'an County

2012年10月25日，全市第三季度重点项目建设现场观摩暨经济工作会议在正安县召开
October 25, 2012, the third quarter of the city's key projects construction site observation & economic work conference held in Zheng'an county

正安县地处遵义市东北部，东邻务川、凤岗，南靠湄潭、绥阳，西与桐梓和重庆南川接壤，北与道真相连。全县辖19个乡镇，152个村（社区、居委会）。2012年末总人口64.5 万人，其中农业人口57万。207、303省道穿境而过，随着黔北高速、习水至德江、遵义至绥阳高速延伸交汇该县，更将成为渝南、黔北经济文化的重要交汇区域。

2012年，按照“发挥优势、融入重庆，遵义前列、北部率先”的总要求，全力实施“新型工业、全民招商、减贫摘帽”三大攻坚，奋力抓好“工业园区、项目建设、高速公路、铝土矿开发、40万亩茶园建设及白茶之乡申报、新城区拓展”六件大事，着力转变经济发展方式，优化产

2012年9月12日，省委常委、遵义市委书记廖少华在正安调研城镇建设
In September 12, 2012, the Provincial Standing Committee, Zunyi municipal Party committee secretary Liao Shaohua had the research of the urbanization construction in Zheng'an

2012年9月12日，省委常委、遵义市委书记廖少华在正安调研野木瓜产业
September 12, 2012, the Provincial Standing Committee, Zunyi municipal Party committee secretary Liao Shaohua had the research of the wild papaya industry in Zheng'an

2012年9月12日，省委常委、遵义市委书记廖少华在正安参观尹珍博物馆
September 12, 2012, the Provincial Standing Committee, Zunyi municipal Party committee secretary Liao Shaohua visited the Yin Zhen Museum in Zheng'an

2012年6月21日，书记王忠、县长邓兆桃调研正安县城镇化建设

June 21, 2012, the secretary Wang Zhong, governor Deng Zhaotao had research of the urbanization construction in Zheng'an County

2012年6月26日，书记王忠、县长邓兆桃调研产业园区

June 26, 2012, the secretary Wangzhong, governor Deng Zhaotao had research of the industry park

2012年6月22日，书记王忠、县长邓兆桃调研新农村建设

June 22, 2012, the secretary Wangzhong, governor Deng Zhaotao had research of the new rural construction

2012年6月23日，书记王忠、县长邓兆桃调研教育工作

June 23, 2012, the secretary Wangzhong, governor Deng Zhaotao had research of the education work

2012年6月22日，书记王忠、县长邓兆桃调研正安茶产业发展情况

June 22, 2012, the secretary Wangzhong, governor Deng Zhaotao had research of the Zheng'an tea industry development situation

Zheng'an county is located in the northeastern of Zunyi city, east of Wuchuan, Fenggang, south of Meitan, Suiyang, west border of Tongzi and Chongqing Nanchuan, north with Daozhen. The county jurisdiction 19 towns, 152 villages (communities, neighborhood committees). At the end of 2012, the total population of 645,000 people, of which agricultural population of 570,000. 207, 303 provincial highway passing through the county, with Qianbei high-speed, Xishui to Dejiang, Zunyi to Suiyang high-speed extension of intersection in the county, it will become an important economic and cultural intersection region of south Chongqing, north Guizhou.

In 2012, according to "play the advantage, melted into Chongqing, the front list in Zunyi, took the lead in the forefront of the north part"the general requirements, the full implementation of "new industrial, national investment, poverty reduction ST" three tough measures, struggling to grasp the "Industrial Park, project construction, highway, bauxite exploration, 400,000 acres of tea plantations construction and white tea town declared, new city develop" six events, focus on the transformation of economic development mode, optimize the

2012年12月18日，中国白茶之乡（贵州正安）授牌仪式暨特产扶贫战略研讨会在京举行

December 18, 2012, Chinese white tea town (Guizhou Zheng'an) Ceremony & Specialty poverty alleviation strategy seminar held in Beijing

业结构；着力推进产业结构调整，培育现代农业体系；着力扩大投资，促进经济平稳较快增长。预计全年完成地区生产总值35.63亿元，同比增长17.1%；其中一产13.16亿元，同比增长10.08%；二产6.60亿元，同比增长23.5%；三产15.87亿元，同比增长18.9%；三次产业比为34.9：18.5：46.6。地方财政收入4.31亿元，同比增长42.8%；地方财政支出19.05亿元，同比增长19.7%。农民人均纯收入4546元，同比增长22.8%；城镇居民可支配收入14931元，同比增长18.75%。社会消费品零售总额13亿元，同比增长20%。金融机构年末各项存款余额58.5亿元，同比增长22%；各项贷款余额20.6亿元，同比增长21%。主体经济指标在全省综合排位预计72位，同比上升7位，实现跳出全省后10位目标；在全市排第9位，同比上升5位。

2012年7月17日，正安县召开加快发展誓师大会

July 17, 2012, Zheng'an county was convened to accelerate the development swearing meeting

2012年5月23日，正安县召开纪念胡锦涛总书记“5.23”批示精神25周年暨民营企业助推正安县域经济发展大会

May 23, 2012, Zheng'an county held in commemoration of the 25th anniversary of Hu Jintao, general secretary of the “5.23” instructions spirits and the private enterprises boost the Zheng'an county's economic development conference

2012年9月12日，正安县天赐生态科技有限公司茶叶加工等项目集中开工仪式在工业园区内隆重举行

September 12, 2012, Zheng'an county Tianci Ecological Technology Co., Ltd. tea processing and other projects focused on starting groundbreaking ceremony was held in the industrial park

2012年12月6日，务川至正安高速公路（正安段）控制性工程开工仪式在俭坪乡举行

December 6, 2012,Wuchuan to Zheng'an Expressway (Zheng'an segment) control project groundbreaking ceremony was held in Jianping Township

industrial structure; Focus on promoting the adjustment of industrial structure, develop modern agriculture system; efforts to expand investment, promote stable and rapid economic growth. Expected full-year GDP completed 3.563 billion yuan, year-on-year growth of 17.1%; among them, the frist industry of 1.316 billion yuan, year-on-year growth of 10.08%; the second industry of 660 million yuan, year-on-year growth of 23.5%; the tertiary industry of 1.587 billion yuan, an increase of 18.9%; the three industry ratio of 34.9: 18.5: 46.6. Local fiscal revenue of 431 million yuan, an increase of 42.8%; the local fiscal expenditure 1.905 billion yuan, an increase of 19.7%. The per capita net income of farmers 4,546 yuan, an increase of 22.8%; disposable income of urban residents 14,931 yuan, an increase of 18.75%. Total retail sales of social consumer goods 1.3 billion yuan, an increase of 20%. At the end of the year, financial institutions each deposit balance of 5.85 billion yuan, an increase of 22%; 2.06 billion yuan of loans, an increase of 21%. The main economic indicators in the province's comprehensive ranking is 72rd, rise 7 compared to the same period, achieve the goal of outing the last 10 in the province; in the city ranked ninth, rise 5 compared to the same period.

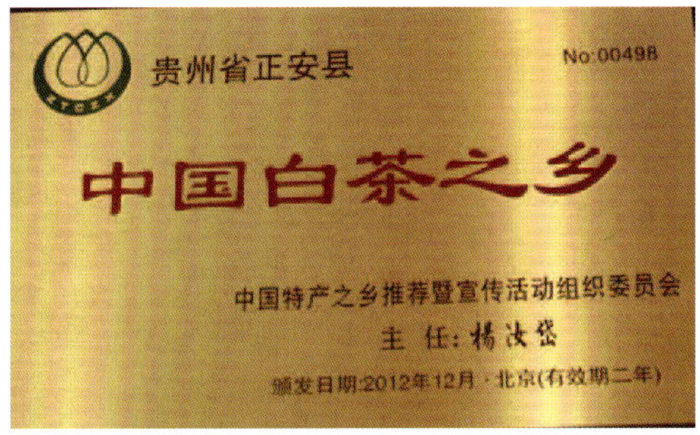

2012年12月18日，正安县荣获中国白茶之乡称号。图为牌匾
December 18, 2012, Zheng'an county won the title of Chinese white tea town. The picture is the plaque

2012年5月19日，庙塘正鑫竹业农民专业合作社荣获“全国50佳合作社”称号
May 19, 2012, Miaotang Zhengxin bamboo industry farmers professional cooperatives won the title of “national top 50 cooperatives”

2012年10月8日，正安县在新行政中心举行升国旗仪式
October 8, 2012,Zheng'an County held a flag-raising ceremony in the new administrative center

2012年11月28日，正安白茶荣获2012年度最具奢侈品潜力中国品牌荣誉称号
November 28, 2012, Zheng'an white tea won the 2012 most potential Chinese luxury brand

2012年7月10日，电影《飞扬的青春》在正安开机
In July 10, 2012, the film “the youth” got action in Zheng'an

西 秀 区
Xixiu District

2012年是西秀区在提速发展道路上的奋力赶超之年。一年来，区人民政府紧紧依靠全区人民，深入贯彻落实科学发展观，抢抓国发2号、黔党发15号文件带来的重大机遇，经济建设、城镇建设、社会建设和政府自身建设取得明显成效。

经济建设取得新进展。打响“五个攻坚战”，经济总量在全市占比提升至40%。（一）打响主体指标攻坚战，综合实力显著增强。全年完成生产总值（含开发区）139亿元，增长15.3%；全年实施项目725个（其中亿元以上项目12个），50万元以上固定资产投资完成103亿元，完成全社会固定资产投资（含开发区）152.3亿元，增速63%，首次突破百亿元大关；公共财政预算收入9.86亿元，增长36.8%；规模以上工业增加值34.45亿元，增长22.4%；社会消费品零售总额38.4亿元，增长16.2%；招商引资到位资金113.9亿元，增长182.1%。金融机构存款年末余额262.6亿元，贷款年末余额159.6亿

市委常委区委书记罗建强到项目点调研
Municipal Committee Party Secretary Luo Jianqiang researched the project points

区委副书记区长张勇率队招商引资
District deputy mayor Zhang Yong led the team to attract bid for inviting investments

区委副书记区长张勇到华西廉租房项目施工现场办公
Zhang Yong, deputy head of Huaxi District to low-rent housing project construction site office

“做文明人，创文明城”西秀区“三创”志愿者服务活动
“Do civilized people, a civilized city” Xixiu “Three constructions”volunteer service activities

“大兴学习之风　建设书香西秀”2013西秀区全民阅读活动现场会
"The study spirit, Construction of the scholarly Xixiu" 2013 Xixiu national reading activities on the spot

2013年西秀区全民阅读活动
2013 Xixiu national reading acvtivities

2012 is Xixiu district at speed on the road struggling to catch up with the development of the year. Over the past year, the district people’s government closely rely on the region’s people, thoroughly implement the scientific concept of development, seize the State Issued No.2 document, Guizhou Party document issued on the 15th brought significant opportunities, economic development, urban construction, social construction, and the government itself construction has achieved remarkable results.

Economic construction has made new progress. Started “five tough fight”, accounted for the total economy in the city increased to 40%. (A) the main indicators battle started, the comprehensive strength has markedly increased. Last year’s GDP (including Development Zone) 13.9 billion yuan, an increase of 15.3%; annual implementation of the project 725 (of which 12 projects over millions yuan), more than 500,000 yuan investment in fixed assets 10.3 billion yuan, the completion of the whole society investment in fixed assets (including Development Zone) 15.23 billion yuan, the growth rate 63%, for the first time surpassed the ten billion yuan mark; public budget revenue 986 million yuan, an increase of 36.8%; scale industrial added value 3.445 billion yuan, an increase of 22.4%; total retail sales of social consumer goods 3.84 billion yuan, an increase of 16.2%; investment funds 11.39 billion yuan, an increase of 182.1%. Financial institutions deposit balance of 26.26 billion yuan year-end, the loan balance of 15.96 billion yuan year-end, up by 22.2% and 35.92%, respectively. (B) started transportation, water conservation campaign, constantly reinforce the foundation for development. (C) started the campaign of industrial development, the development potential is growing. (D) started the agricultural adjustment battle, farmers benefit significantly. (E) started the tourism-led campaign, the tourism market vitality burst. Full annual tourists 5,580,000 passengers, tourism revenue (including Development Zone) 7.829 billion yuan, an increase of

“安顺地戏大赛”在西秀区七眼桥云峰屯堡博物馆拉开帷幕
“Anshun local drama contest”opened in Xixiu District Qiyan bridges Yunfeng tunbao museum

元，分别增长22.2%和35.92%。（二）打响交通水利攻坚战，发展基础不断夯实。（三）打响工业发展攻坚战，发展后劲不断增强。（四）打响农业调整攻坚战，农民增收效益显著。（五）打响旅游带动攻坚战，旅游市场活力迸发。全年接待游客558万人次，实现旅游总收入（含开发区）78.29亿元，增长52%。

城镇建设取得新变化。全区城镇化率达49.52%，较上年提高1个百分点。全省“满意在贵州”现场会和全市城镇化推进暨小城镇建设发展大会胜利召开。（一）城区面貌日新月异。开工新建、续建城市道路11条。（二）城镇建设同步推进。（三）城市管理更加规范。

社会建设取得新进步。全年投入12.7亿元用于改善民生，占一般预算支出的47.8%。城镇居民人均可支配收入达18680元，增长14.6%，发展成果惠及民生。（一）就业形势趋稳向好。（二）教育事业增量提质。（三）健康事业加快发展。（四）文化事业蓬勃向上。（五）科技创新取得成效。全年申请专利361件，授权155件。（六）社保网底更加牢固。城乡居民和城镇职工“五险一金”征缴及参保人数圆满完成年度目标任务，失地农就业社会保障工作走在全市前列。（七）社会管理得到加强。西秀区获全省首批、全市唯一的“省级法治县（市、区、特区）创建活动先进单位”荣誉称号。

政府自身建设继续加强。自觉接受区人大及其常委会的法律监督和工作监督，接受区政协的民主监督，办理人大代表建议136件、政协委员提案176件，满意率100%；深化行政审批制度改革，全年清理行政许可事项167项，非行政许可事项52项；坚持民主集中制，集体研究决定重大问题201个。

美丽的民族服饰
The beautiful costumes

城区一角
The corner of the city

大十字
Grand cross

贯城河
Guangcheng River

52%.

Changes made in the construction of new towns. The region's urbanization rate reached 49.52%, compared with last year increased by 1 percentage point. The province's "satisfaction in Guizhou" on the spot, and the city's urbanization to promote the development-cum- small towns development conference successfully held. (A) changing urban landscape. Start new, continued construction urban roads 11. (B) towns construction promoted simultaneously. (C) urban management more standardized.

Social construction made new progress. Annual investment of 1.27 billion yuan for the improvement of people's livelihood, accounting for 47.8% of general budget expenditures. Per capita disposable income of urban residents reached 18,680 yuan, an increase of 14.6%, the fruits of development to benefit people's livelihood. (A) the employment situation is stabilized to the good. (B) increments to mention the quality of education. (C) health industry to accelerate development. (D) vigorous cultural undertakings. (E) scientific and technological innovation to bear fruit. 361 patent applications throughout the year, authorized 155. (F) social security network at the end more solid. Urban and rural residents and urban workers "five insurance and housing fund" collection and the number of participants successfully completed the annual goals and tasks, landless agricultural employment social security work and walk in the forefront of the city. (G) social management has been strengthened. Xixiu was the first in the province, the city's only "provincial law counties (cities, districts, SAR) activities to create advanced units" the honorary title.

虹山湖
Hongshan Lake

Continue to strengthen the government itself. Consciously accept the District People's Congress and its Standing Committee Legal and work supervision, to accept the democratic supervision of the CPPCC area, handling 136 deputies, CPPCC members putting out cases 176, 100% satisfaction rate; deepen the reform of administrative examination and approval system, the annual clean-up administrative licensing matters 167, non-administrative licensing matters 52; adhere to democratic centralism, collective research decisions on major issues 201.

改造后的虹山湖
The Hongshan Lake after reconstruction

榕 江 县
Rongjiang County

2013年6月25日，黔东南州直机关百名干部“重走长征路”主题教育活动在榕江县红七军军部旧址纪念馆门前举行启动仪式
June 25, 2013, Qiandongnan organs one hundred cadres, "re-take the Long March" theme educational activities held in front of seven Red Army military site memorial ceremony in Rongjiang County

2012中国榕江萨玛节开幕式
2012 China Rongjiang Sama Festival opening ceremony

榕江县开展严厉打击毒品犯罪大型宣传活动。图为宣传队伍经过古州路场景
Rongjiang County to crack down on drug crimes major publicity campaign. The picture shows the publicity team after the ancient state road scene

榕江县面积3315.8平方公里，辖6个镇、13个乡（其中6个民族乡），3个社区、260个行政村、7个居民委员会，人口35.57万人，其中少数民族28.57万人，人口较多的少数民族有侗族、苗族、水族和瑶族。主要矿藏有锑、石煤。森林覆盖率为74.71%。榕江县是中国南方鱼米之乡、西瓜之乡、脐橙之乡、体操之乡、古榕树之乡、苗山侗水风景之乡、美食之乡、香猪香羊肉牛产地和林业大县。

坚持以经济建设为中心，改善人类生存环境，提高人民生活水平。 全年实现生产总值28.59亿元，较上年增长17.2%。农林牧渔业总产值15.17亿元，增长8.8%。工业总产值26.92亿，增长80.06%，其中500万元以上工业总产值19.7亿元，增长28.07%。财政总收入4.3亿元，增长65.21%，其中地方财政收入2.68亿元，增长

榕江县城全景
Rongjiang County panoramic

榕江县以项目带动为龙头推动扶贫攻坚战略。图为2013年葛根特色产业开发现场会
Rongjiang County project led as a leader to promote poverty alleviation strategies. The picture shows the 2013 Kudzu characteristics of industrial development on the spot

美丽的东滨江大道夜景
Beautiful night view of the East Riverside Avenue

Rongjiang County has an area of 3,315.8 square kilometers, exempted 6 towns, 13 townships (including 6 ethnic townships), 3 communities, 260 administrative villages, 7 residents of the commission, population of 355,700, of which285,700 ethnic minorities, there are more populous ethnic Dong, Miao, Shui and Yao. There are deposits of antimony, coal. Forest coverage rate of 74.71%. Rongjiang County is the breadbasket of southern China, the hometown of watermelon, the hometown of orange, the hometown of gymnastics, the hometown of the ancient banyan tree, the hometown of Miao mountain Dong village water scenery, the hometown of food, pig fragrant lamb cattle origin and forestry county.

榕江县城移民搬迁新区一角
New corner of Rongjiang County relocation

Persist in taking economic construction as the center, to improve the human living environment, improve people's living standards. Annual GDP of 2.859 billion yuan, an increase of 17.2% over the previous year. Agriculture, forestry, animal husbandry and fishery output value 1.517 billion yuan, an increase of 8.8%. Industrial output value of 2.692 billion, an increase of 80.06%, of which 5 million yuan of industrial output value of 1.97 billion yuan, an increase of 28.07%. Total fiscal revenue 430 million yuan, an increase of 65.21%, including local fiscal revenue 268 million yuan, an increase of 31.15%.

生态移民搬迁工程——摆王新区
Ecological relocation project - Baiwang new district

榕江县工业园区盛源食品公司葛根系列产品加工厂生产车间一角

Rongjiang County Industrial Park Shengyuan Foods Co., Ltd. Gegen Series food processing workshop

通村油路进侗乡

Oil road pass the village of Dong

高赧百瀑溪十里百瀑风光

Gaonan Baipu creek Baipu waterfall scenery

31.15%。财政总支出11.53亿元，增长27.31%。金融各项存款年末余额33.97亿元，增长14.58%；贷款余额28.7亿元，增长18.4%；固定资产投资41.99亿元。社会消费品零售总额9.2亿元，人均消费2586.01元。城镇居民及干部职工年均工资收入47654元，折出物价因素，实际可支配收入24235.29元。农民人均占有粮289.06公斤，纯收入5230元。乡镇企业实现产值10.5亿元，较上年增长10.5%，实现增加值2.99亿元。全社会投入扶贫资金1.23亿元。非公有制企业811户，注册资金5.87亿元。个体工商6747户，注册资金2.79亿元。农民专业合作社50户，注册资金0.2亿元。招商引资到位资金31.5亿元。旅游实现收入12.6亿元。劳务输出收入1.35亿元。国土出让收入3.55亿元。

扎实办好社会事业，促进科学发展，推动社会进步。全县有各级各类学校276所，在校在园学生儿童56977人，在职在编教职工2978人（专任教师2690人），学前、小学、初中和高中入学率分别为100%、99.4%、71.3%和57.12%。医疗卫生全年实现参合27.75万人，参合率97.5%。完成各地各类演出50场次，成功举办“2012年中国•榕江侗族萨玛节”和“2012年贵州省青少年体操锦标赛”，完成非物质文化遗产申报。农家书屋、广播电视实现全覆盖。继续推进全民素质行动计划、科普惠农计划和百万公众网络学习工程及科普示范乡镇、示范村和示范社区创建，科技项目逐步向尖端发展。

2013年榕江西瓜喜获大丰收
2013 bumper harvest watermelon in Rongjiang

瓜农喜悦运瓜忙
The farmers is busy shipping watermelon with joy

Total fiscal expenditure 1.153 billion yuan, an increase of 27.31%. Financial year-end balance of 3.397 billion yuan of deposits, an increase of 14.58%; loan balance of 2.87 billion yuan, an increase of 18.4%; fixed asset investment 4.199 billion yuan. Total retail sales of social consumer goods 920 million yuan, per capita consumption of 2,586.01 yuan. Cadres and workers of urban residents and the average annual wage income of 47,654 yuan, fold out inflation, real disposable income of 24,235.29 yuan. Farmers per capita grain 289.06 kilograms, net income 5,230 yuan. 1.05 billion yuan output value of township enterprises, an increase of 10.5% compared to last year, the added value of 299 million yuan. The whole society poverty funds invested 123 million yuan. 811 non-public enterprises, registered capital of 587 million yuan. Individual industrial and commercial 6,747, the registered capital of 279 million yuan. 50 farmer cooperatives, registered capital of 20 million yuan. Investment funds 3.15 billion yuan. Tourism revenue of 1.26 billion yuan. Labor export income of 135 million yuan. Land transfer revenue 355 million yuan.

高银弄山顶"特种养殖场"养殖的香羊
Gaoyinnong peak "special breeding factory" the breeding lamb

Solid run social undertakings, promote scientific development, promote social progress. The county has 276 schools at all levels, students in school children in 56,977 people in the garden, serving 2,978 people in total staff (full-time teachers 2,690 people), preschool, elementary, middle and high school enrollment rates were 100%, 99.4% , 71.3% and 57.12%, respectively. Health realize an annual participation 277,500, the participation rate of 97.5%. Completed 50 sessions over the various types of performances, successfully held the "2012 China • Rongjiang Dong Sama Festival" and the "2012 Guizhou Province Youth Gymnastics Championships", to complete the intangible cultural heritage declared. Farm Book House, radio and television to achieve full coverage. Continue to promote the universal quality of the action plan, preferential agricultural science learning programs and one million public network engineering and science demonstration towns, model villages and created a model community, the development of science and technology projects gradually to the tip.

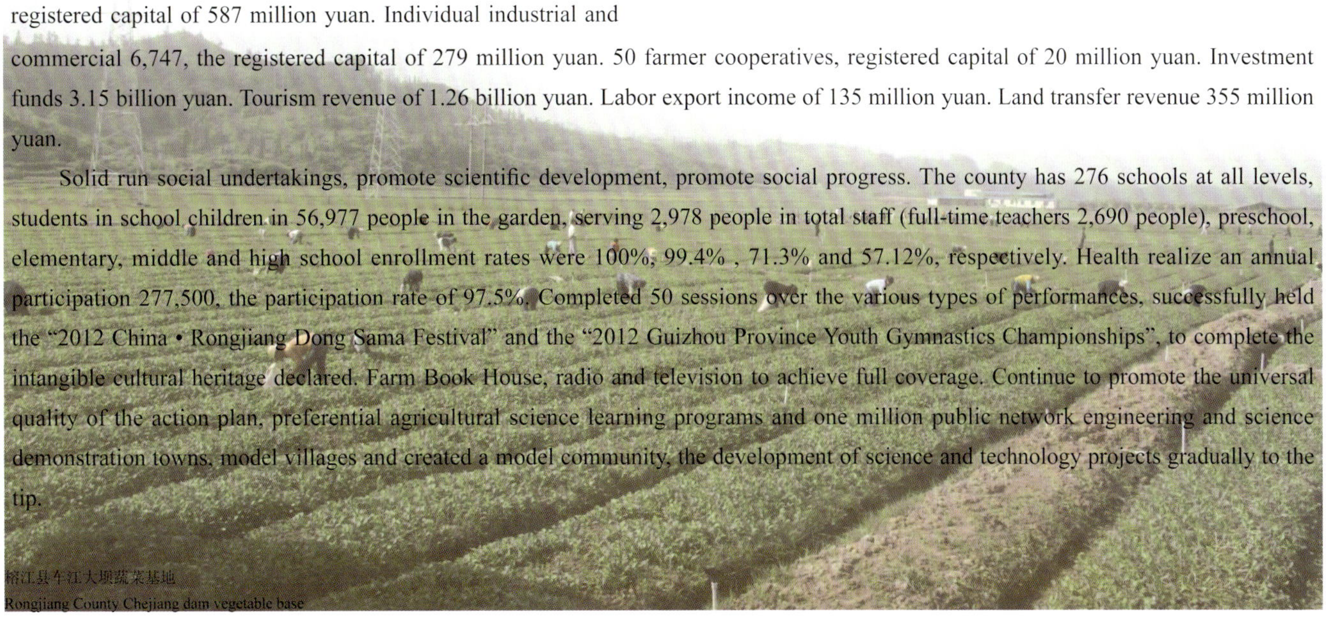

榕江县车江大坝蔬菜基地
Rongjiang County Chejiang dam vegetable base

黔西县

Qianxi County

市人大副主任、县委书记范元平在新田煤矿调研

Municipal People's Congress deputy director, the county party secretary Fan Yuanping had research in Xintian Mine

县长杨汉华到中建乡检查指导信访维稳工作

County Magistrate Yang Hanhua to inspect and guide the work of petition holding stability in Zhongjian township

县委十一届四次扩大会议通过黔西县2016年在全省率先建成全面小康的决议

Four enlarged meeting of the county through the eleventh Qianxi 2016 in the province to build a comprehensive well-off resolution

莲城、水西、文峰、杜鹃等四个街道办事处正式挂牌成立

Liancheng, Shuixi, Wenfeng, Dujuan and other four neighborhood offices formally established

黔西县位于贵州中部偏西北，是毕节市东大门。辖12个镇、13个民族乡、4个街道，有303个村委会、45个农村社区村委会、14个城市社区居委会，面积2380.5平方公里。人口90.37万人，彝、苗、白、布依、仡佬、满、水、回等18个少数民族占总人口的22.36%。

2012年是"十二五"规划承前启后的重要一年，黔西经济社会发展取得了辉煌成就。

综合实力明显提升。全县生产总值首次突破百亿元大关，达103.59亿元，比上年增长16.0%；财政收入22.22亿元，增长39.5%；全社会固定资产投资完成176.55亿元，增长68.7%；社会消费品零售总额达17.95亿元，增长14.8%；城镇居民人均可支配收入和农民人均纯收入分别达19574元和4986元，分别增长19.4%和16.6%。三次产业结构调整为13.5:45.1:41.4，经济质量和效益均明显提升。

基础设施建设全面加强。公路建设成效明显，黔织高速全线贯通，黔大高速、贵黔高速开工建设；兴修水利工程，保障农田灌溉；县城及周边地区抗旱应急水源工程全面竣工，新增恢复灌溉面积1.06万亩，烟水配套工程有序实施，解决饮水安全人口5万人；完成土地整治1.89万亩；"数字黔西"信息化建设、农村宽带提速和3G网络运用同步推进。

工业经济持续增长。全县规模以上工业总产值完成75.14亿元，比上年增长30.5%；规模以上工业增加值完成27.24亿元，增长21.2%；工业固定资产投资完成52.15亿元，增长

县城南部新区开工仪式现场
County southern new district groundbreaking ceremony site

Qianxi County is located in central-northwest Guizhou, is the eastern gate of Bijie City. Jurisdiction over 12 towns, 13 townships, 4 streets, there are 303 village committees, 45 village committees in rural communities, 14 urban neighborhood, an area of 2,380.5 square kilometers. Population of 903,700 people, Yi, Miao, Bai, Buyi, Gelo, Man, Shui, Hui and other 18 ethnic minority accounted for 22.36% of the total population.

2012 is the "Twelfth Five Year Plan" an important link between the past year, western Guizhou's economic and social development has made brilliant achievements.

Comprehensive strength has improved significantly. The county's GDP for the first time surpassed the ten billion mark, reaching 10.359 billion yuan, an increase of 16.0% over last year; fiscal revenue 2.222 billion yuan, an increase of 39.5%; total fixed asset investment of 17.655 billion yuan, an increase of 68.7%; social total retail sales of consumer goods amounted to 1.795 billion yuan, an increase of 14.8%; urban residents per capita disposable income and rural per capita net income reached 19,574 yuan and 4,986 yuan, respectively, an increase of 19.4% and 16.6%. Three industrial structure adjustment 13.5:45.1:41.4, economic quality and efficiency are improved significantly.

Overall strengthening of infrastructure construction. Marked progress in building roads, Qianzhi high-speed fully opened to traffic, Qianda high-speed, the Guiqian Expressway started construction; irrigating water conservancy to protect farmland irrigation; county and the surrounding areas and drought emergency water project completed, the new irrigation area of 10,600 mu of restoration, smoke supporting the orderly implementation of water projects to solve the drinking water safety population of 50,000 people; completion of 18,900 mu of land remediation; "digital Qianxi" information construction, in rural broadband speed and 3G networks use promoted simultaneously.

Industrial economy continued to grow. County scale industrial output value 7.514 billion yuan, an increase of 30.5% over last year; above-scale industrial added value reached 2.724 billion yuan, an increase of 21.2%; industrial fixed assets investment of 5.215 billion yuan, an increase of 15.4%. Bijie test area industries to relocate base in Qianxi and Qianxi circular economy industrial park jointly filed as a provincial economic development zone, and provincial people's government for approval.

浪漫花都•和谐人居2012大型房交会在行政中心广场举行
Romantic Huadu •harmonious living 2012 Large Housing Fair held in the administrative center of the square

水西古城奠基仪式
Shixi ancient city laid foundation ceremony

工业园区企业入驻生产
Industrial production enterprises settled in the park

花都大道
Huadu Avenue

花都民居（水西公园景观）
Huadu houses (Shuixi Park View)

龙潭路
Longtan road

15.4%。毕节试验区黔西承接产业转移基地和黔西县循环经济产业园区合并申报为省级经济开发区，并获省人民政府批准。工业园区投资完成27.04亿元，园区工业产值完成28.61亿元。

农业经济全面振兴。切实加大科技投入力度，良种覆盖、良法配套率分别达96%和98%以上；全年粮食产量达26.24万吨，加快特色农业发展步伐，初步形成一批特色农业种植、养殖示范园，农产品加工企业达16家，新建农业专业合作组织115个；全县农林牧渔业增加值达13.96亿元，增长12%。

旅游产业方兴未艾。乌江百里画廊、谷里温泉、象祠等旅游景点建设深入推进，成功承办省第七届旅发大会，实施旅发大会保障性项目22个、带动性项目34个，全年共接待游客289万人次，实现旅游综合收入19.66亿元。

城乡建设统筹推进。修订了《县城总体规划（2012-2030）》，完成了《黔西县旧城区及部分新城区控制性详细规划》等4个控规，实现城乡规划全覆盖；全年减少农村贫困人口3.42万人，完成红林、中建等7个乡“减贫摘帽”；素朴、谷里等5个幸福小镇和钟山、绿化等17个特色小城镇建设进程加快，城镇化率达41.1%（含托管区为37.5%）。

杜鹃广场演出中心一角
Horn azalea Square one corner of the performance center

永贵煤机厂
Yonggui coal machine factory

水西泰丰园大门
Shuixi Taifeng Garden Gate

Completed 2.704 billion yuan investment in industrial parks, the park completed 2.861 billion yuan of industrial output value.

Overall revitalization of the agricultural economy. Effectively increase scientific and technological input, seed coverage, good method of supporting rates were 96% and 98%; annual grain output reached 262,400 tons, to accelerate the pace of agricultural development characteristics, the initial formation of a number of characteristics of agricultural planting, breeding demonstration garden, agricultural products processing enterprises reached 16, the new agricultural cooperative organizations 115; county forestry, animal husbandry and fishery added value amounted to 1.396 billion yuan, an increase of 12%.

The tourism industry in the ascendant. Wujiang Barry Gallery, Guli springs, Elephant Temple and other tourist attractions pushed forward depth building, successfully hosted the Seventh Provincial Tourism Conference, the implementation of the Tourism Conference protection projects 22, driven projects 34, a total of 2,890,000 tourists passengers, tourism revenue 1.966 billion yuan.

Coordinate development of urban and rural construction. Revised the "county master plan (2012-2030)", complete the "Qianxi County, New Town Old Town Control and some detailed planning" and other four control regulations, to achieve full coverage of urban and rural planning; annual 34,200 rural poverty reduction people to complete the red forest, built in the other seven villages, "put off the hat of poverty reduction"; Supu, Guli and other 5 happy towns and Zhongshan, Luhua and other 17 characteristics of small towns to speed up the process of building, urbanization rate reached 41.1% (37.5% including nursery).

黔织高速——六冲河大桥雄姿
Qianzhi high-speed - Liuchonghe majestic bridge

农业园区果蔬大棚
Agricultural Park fruit and vegetable greenhouses

晴 隆 县

Qinglong County

晴隆县位于贵州省西南面，云贵高原中段，黔西南布依族苗族自治州东北角。县境南北长69公里，东西宽33公里。总面积1309.8平方公里，辖6个乡（其中1个民族乡）、8个镇、5个社区、96个行政村。2012年末总人口33.5万人。县境内主要矿藏有煤炭、黄金、锑、铅、萤石、贵翠等。森林覆盖率34.6%。

2012年，全县生产总值完成29.83亿元，增长17.2%。其中，第一产业增加值完成5.52亿元，增长10.8%；第二产业增加值完成11.60亿元，增长18.4%；第三产业增加值完成12.71亿元，增长18.5%；财政总收入实现5.12亿元，增长27.4 %；全社会固定资产投资完成36.43亿元，增长58%；社会消费品零售总额实现4.04亿元，增长15.5%；农村居民可支配收入达4088元，增长18.3%；城镇居民可支配收入达16498元，增长13%。金融机构存贷款余额分别达到29.4亿元和14.3亿元。

65号高速公路北盘江大桥
NO.65 highway Beipanjiang bridge

光照湖区风光
Light Lakes scenery

发祥煤矿煤炭资源
Faxiang coal mine coal resources

煤
Coal

光照湖一线天
The illumination Lake thin strip of sky

大厂彩玉
Dachang color jade

1980年秋，晴隆县碧痕镇笋家箐发现的茶子化石，今收藏于贵州省农科所
In the fall of 1980, Bihen town Sunjiaqing in Qinglong County found tea sub-fossil, at present it is collected in Agricultural Science Institute in Guizhou Province

Qinglong County is located in south-west of Guizhou Province, the middle of the Yunnan-Guizhou Plateau, the northeast corner of Qianxinan Buyi and Miao Autonomous Prefecture. 69 km long from north to south, 33 km wide from east to west. A total area of 1,3 09.8 square kilometers, exempted 6 townships (including 1 minority township), 8 towns, 5 communities, 96 administrative villages. By the end of 2012, the total population of 335,000 people. There are deposits of coal, gold, antimony, lead, fluorite, the emerald and so on in the county. The forest coverage rate of 34.6%.

In 2012, the county's GDP completed 2.983 billion yuan, an increase of 17.2%. Among them, the first industrial added value of 552 million yuan, an increase of 10.8%; completion of the secondary industry was 1.16 billion yuan, an increase of 18.4%; tertiary industry added value of 1.271 billion yuan, an increase of 18.5%; total fiscal revenue completed 512 million yuan, an increase of 27.4%; total fixed asset investment was 3.643 billion yuan, an increase of 58%; total retail sales of social consumer goods achieved 404 million yuan, up 15.5%; disposable income of rural residents reached 4,088 yuan, an increase of 18.3%; urban residents disposable income reached 16,498 yuan, an increase of 13%. The balance of deposits and loans of financial institutions reached 2.94 billion yuan and 1.43 billion yuan.

晴隆波尔山羊
Qinglong Boer goats

从江县

Congjiang County

省政协主席王正福看望长寿老人
Provincial CPPCC Chairman Wang Zhengfu to visit the longevity of the elderly

州委书记李飞跃到从江调研
State committee secretary Li Feiyue to have research in Congjiang

2012年8月7日，州长廖飞到从江视察贵州洛贯经济开发区
August 7, 2012, Governor Liao Fei to Congjiang inspect of Guizhou Luoguan Economic Development Zone

县委书记王之政视察香猪产业
County party secretary Wang Zhizheng inspected the miniature pigs industry

2012年，从江县围绕“稳中提速、赶超进位”发展纲领，牢牢把握主基调，按照“发展工业带城镇、弘扬文化树品牌、加快转型保民生、攻坚克难促跨越”工作思路，着力保增长、调结构、增活力、惠民生、促和谐，较好完成年初既定各项目标任务，全县经济社会呈现“速度加快、结构优化、效益提高、后劲增强、民生改善、位次前移”的良好态势。

依托“一城两区”城镇发展布局，加快城镇化、工业化进程。从江县一方面全力推进从贯一级连线公路建设，其中县城至银良段顺利建成通行，核心工程高增隧道单向掘进2.9千米，力争2013年底通车；另一方面洛贯新区路网建设全面推进，“三纵三横”城市主干道建设加快实施，2013年全线基本建成通车。

贵州洛贯经济开发区，根据“规划一片、开发一片、落地一片、成功一片”的发展思路，以北部新区8.16平方公里为2012年开发重点，从总体规划到路网建设、给排水网络建设、电力能源网络建设有序推进。启动从江洛贯新区综

县长张广渊到企业调研
Magistrate Zhang Guangyuan to business to have research

In 2012, Congjiang County around the "steady speed to catch up with the binary" agenda for development, firmly grasp the main tone, in accordance with the "development of industry with cities and towns, promote the culture and build brand, speed up the transformation of ensuring people's livelihood, to tackle tough and promote leapfrog"the work of thinking, and strive to maintain growth, structural adjustment, increase vitality, benefit people's livelihood, promote harmony, good early completion of the objectives and tasks established at the beginning of the year, the county's economic society shows faster, structural optimization, increased efficiency, increased stamina, improved living conditions, ranking forward" good momentum.

Relying on the "one city, two areas" urban development layout, speed up urbanization, industrialization process. Congjiang County, on the one hand to promote Congguan first-class connection road construction, in which the county to Yinliang successful completion of traffic, high growth core engineering tunnel-way excavation of 2.9 km, and strive to open to traffic by the end of 2013; on the other hand, Guanxin District Road the network comprehensively promote the construction, "three vertical and three horizontal" urban trunk road construction to speed up the implementation, the board basically completed and opened to traffic in 2013.

葛洲坝集团考察洛贯开发区
The Gezhouba Group test Luoguan Development Zone

贵州洛贯经济开发区正逐步成为外商投资的热土。 图为为配合洛贯经济园的建设，从江35千伏贯肇线让道重新架设施工现场
Guizhou Luoguan Economic Development Zone is gradually becoming a hot spot for foreign investment. The picture shows to meet the construction of Luoguan Economic Development Zone, Congjiang 35 kV Guanzhao line made way for re-erection of the construction site

洛贯园区加快发展动员会
Luoguan Park will accelerate the development of mobilization

从贯一级公路从江至银良段于2012年初建成通车。图为銮里村路段迷人景象
Congguan first class highway Congjiang to Yinliang segment was opened to traffic in early 2012. Pictured Luanli Village section of charming scene

连接从江老县城与洛贯工业园区的从贯一级公路核心工程高增隧道。图为隧道施工现场
Gaozeng tunnel connected Congjiang old town and Luoguan Industrial Park is Congguan first class highway core engineering. The picture shows the tunnel construction site

惠民人行铁索桥通行
The Huimin line chain bridge access

合服务中心及中学、福利院、廉租房等公共服务项目。在打牢基础设施的同时加大引资建设力度，2012年共签约项目38个，签约资金226亿元，其中合同项目28个，资金116.5亿元。签约项目建设步伐稳健。

西部山区，积极做好扶贫开发，稳步推动香猪产业化发展。2012年在宰便、加鸠等乡镇实行“整乡推进”项目实施，建设1个原种繁殖场，8个标准化规模养殖场。扶持10个乡镇、78个村、1322户的适度规模养殖户，完成圈舍建设338栋、6736间，共39113.56平方米。全年香猪出栏达20.06万头，产业总产值1.506亿元。

在继续打造岜沙、小黄、加榜梯田等旅游品牌基础上，从江县大力推进小黄、高增、占里、新安等侗文化产业园建设，挖掘和丰富民族旅游文化内涵，提高景点品位，拓展旅游空间，做大旅游买点，积极融入“桂林旅游经济圈”和“东盟国际旅游线”，以旅游带动第三产业持续快速发展。

小黄儿童合唱队获2012年全国儿童歌曲大奖赛银奖
Xiaohuang children's chorus team won the 2012 National Children's songs Grand Prix Silver

苗族芦笙节。图为大洞芦笙节热闹场面
Miao Lusheng festival. The picture shows Dadong Lusheng Festival lively scene

从江香猪广州推介会

Congjiang miniature pigs Guangzhou promotion

Guizhou Luoguan Economic Development Zone, according to "planning one area, develop one area, landing one area, success one area"the development of ideas, to northern New Area 8.16 square kilometers which is the key to develop in 2012, from the overall planning of the road network, water supply and drainage network construction, electrical energy network in an orderly way. Start Congjiang Luoguan new area multi-service centers and secondary schools, welfare, low-cost housing and other public services. Lay a solid infrastructure construction to increase efforts to attract investment construction, 38 projects were signed in 2012, signing 22.6 billion yuan of funds, which contracted 28 projects, 11.65 billion yuan of funds. The pace of construction of contracted projects promoted steadily.

香猪全席

Miniature pigs full-course dinner

Western mountain area, actively carry out poverty alleviation and development, and steadily promote the development of miniature pig industry. In 2012, implementation of the "whole village to promote" project, the construction of one of the original species breeding farms, eight standardized scale farms in Zaibian, Jiajiu and other townships. To support the 10 townships, 78 villages, 1,322 appropriate scale breeding farmers, to complete the sheds construction of 338 houses, 6,736 rooms, a total of 39,113.56 square meters. Throughout the year miniature pig slaughter up to 200,600, the total industrial output value of 150.6 million yuan.

On the basis of continuing to build the Basha, Xiaohuang, Jiabang terraces tourism brand, Congjiang County vigorously promote Xiaohuang, Gaozeng, Zhanli, Xin'an Dong cultural industrial park construction, mining and rich ethnic tourism and cultural connotations, improve attractions grade, expand the tourism space, bigger tourist buy point, actively integrate into the the "Guilin Tourism Economic Circle" and "ASEAN international tourism line", sustained and rapid development of tourism to drive the tertiary industry.

从江县城全貌

The whole picture of Congjiang county

东朗乡生态移民工程

Donglang village ecological migration project

铜仁市碧江区

Tongren City Bijiang District

贵州省委书记赵克志（左四）在碧江威顿化工视察指导工作
Guizhou Provincial Party Secretary Zhao Kezhi (fourth from left) had inspection and guidance in Bijiang Weidun chemical plant

市委书记刘奇凡（右四）在碧江经济开发区调研指导工作
Party secretary Liu Qifan (fourth from right) to guide research work in the Economic Development Zone of Bijiang

市委副书记、市长夏庆丰（右四）在碧江天龙啤酒厂调研指导工作
Deputy Secretary of Municipal Committee, mayor Xia Qingfeng (fourth from right) had research and guidance in Bijiang Tianlong brewery plant

市人大常委会副主任、区委书记陈代文（左一）在和平现代农业产业园调研
Deputy director of the Municipal People's Congress, Party Secretary Chen Daiewen (first from left) had research in Heping modern agricultural industrial park

2011年10月，经国务院批复同意，撤销铜仁地区设立地级铜仁市，原县级铜仁市改为碧江区。碧江区位于贵州省东北部，东邻湖南、北接重庆，古有“黔东各郡邑，独美于铜仁”之赞誉，今有“黔东明珠”、“黔东门户”之称号，是铜仁市政治、经济、文化、信息中心和省列“经济强县”，同时也是武陵山扶贫攻坚规划中确定的6个区域中心城市之一。全区国土总面积1012平方公里，辖13个乡（镇、办事处），总人口40万。区内聚居着汉、苗、土家、侗、仡佬等26个民族，少数民族人口占总人口的73%，具有独特的民族风情和绚丽多彩的民间文化。

碧江区历史悠久，置县历史至今已有600余年。碧江区交通便捷。铜仁凤凰机场距中心城区仅20余公里，渝怀铁路横贯全境，杭瑞、铜大高速穿境而过，所有乡（镇、办事处）均已实现油路全覆盖。碧江区资源丰富。境内矿产资源丰富，已探明可开采的矿产40余种。境内自然景观优美，文化底蕴深厚，有九龙洞国家级风景名胜区、百里锦江画廊、大明边城国家4A级景区、云林仙境国家3A级景区、天生桥景区，有国家级文物保护区东山寺、中南门古城、中国戏剧活化石傩文化博物馆、川主宫、东山古建筑群等。

区委副书记、区长杨彪（左二）在湖北产业园项目现场办公
District deputy secretary, mayor Yang Biao (second from left) in Hubei Industrial Park project site office

In October 2011, the State Council approved the revocation of Tongren Prefecture establishment of local level of Tongren City, the original county-level city of Tongren changed to Bijiang District. Bijiang district is located in the northeast of Guizhou Province, east of Hunan, north of Chongqing , ancient praise of "all counties of Qiandong, the alone beauty in Tongren", present name of "Qiandong Pearl", "Qiandong portal", is the political, economic, cultural and information center of Tongren City and province "strong economic county", is also one of the six regional central city identified in the the Wuling Mountains Poverty Alleviation planning. The whole land area of 1,012 square kilometers, jurisdiction over 13 townships (towns, offices), with a total population of 400,000. The region inhabited by the Han, Miao, Tujia, Dong, Gelo and other total 26 ethnic groups, the minority population accounted for 73% of the total population, with unique ethnic customs and colorful folk culture.

Bijiang historic home county has more than 600 years of history. The traffic is convenient in Bijiang district. Tongren Phoenix Airport is only 20 kilometers from the center city, Chongqing-Huaihua Railway run through the district, Hangrui, Tongda high-speed passing through, the township (town office) have been achieved oil line full coverage. Area resources are abundant in Bijiang. Rich in mineral resources, has proven more than 40 kinds of mineral mining. The territory of the beautiful natural landscape, rich cultural heritage, Jiulong Dong state-level scenic spots, Baili Jin Jiang gallery, the Daming Biancheng national 4A level scenic spots, Yunlin Wonderland 3A level scenic spots, Tiansheng bridge scenic, national heritage conservation area Dongshan Temple, the Zhongnan Gate ancient city, dramatic living fossil Nuo Culture Museum, Chuanzhu palace, Dongshan ancient buildings.

In recent years, Bijiang district closely around the provincial party committee and government, "two plus one push" the main strategy for the main tone and "industrialization, urbanization", seize the "the State Issued NO.2 [2012] document" and "Wuling Mountains Poverty Alleviation Planning" a pilot basis historic opportunity, vigorously implement the new-type industrialization, new urbanization, agricultural modernization and cultural tourism industry development strategy, rapid economic growth and maintain social harmony and stability. Have been named the "National Model Green County", "village of traditional Chinese Dragon Boat", "livable and appropriate business model

碧江金丰锰业生产车间
Bijiang Jinfeng Manganese production workshop

铜仁威顿化工
Tongren Weidun Chemical

和平至水源头通村公路侨梁建设“龙鱼桥”
Heping to Shuiyuantou village road building “Longyu bridge”

碧江区和平乡高标准农田水利建设项目
Bijiang Heping Township high standard of farmland water conservancy construction project

碧江城区至铜仁凤凰机场城市快速路
Bijiang urban area to Tongren Phoenix Airport City Expressway

近年来，碧江区紧紧围绕省委、省政府“两加一推”主基调和“工业化、城镇化”主战略，抢抓“国发【2012】2号文件”和“武陵山扶贫攻坚规划”先行先试的历史机遇，大力实施新型工业化、新型城镇化、农业现代化和文化旅游产业发展战略，经济快速增长，社会保持和谐稳定。相继被评为“全国绿化模范县”、“中国传统龙舟之乡”、“中国宜居宜业典范区”、“省级卫生城市”、“省级文明城市”、“省级园林城市”和“贵州省平安建设先进县”。2012年全区地方生产总值完成76.95亿元，同比增长17.2%；财政总收入完成9.12亿元，同比增长35.1%，一般财政预算收入完成6.13亿元，同比增长30.7%；全社会固定资产投资完成133.07亿元，同比增长78.1%；社会消费品零售总额完成28.18亿元，同比增长15.6%；规模以上工业总产值完成70.12亿元，同比增长28.5%；实施招商引资到位资金46.2亿元，同比增长49.4%；城镇居民人均可支配收入15911元，同比增长14.9%；农村居民人均可支配收入6310元，同比增长18.2 %。

百里锦江落鹅渡口•洪达山风光
Baili Jinjiang Luo'e ferry • Hongda mountain scenery

碧江大明边城国家4A级景区
Bijiang Daming Biancheng national 4A level scenic spots

六龙山景区小董云风光
Lilong mountain area Xiaodongyun scenery

for the area", "provincial health city", "provincial civilized city", "provincial garden city" and "Guizhou Province peace building advanced counties". In 2012, completion of the region's GDP of 7.695 billion yuan, an increase of 17.2%; total fiscal revenue of 912 million yuan, an increase of 35.1%, the general budget revenue of 6.13 billion yuan, an increase of 30.7%; total fixed asset investment of 13.307 billion yuan, an increase of 78.1%; total retail sales of social consumer goods completed 2. 818 billion yuan, an increase of 15.6%; completion of the above-scale industrial output value of 7.012 billion yuan, an increase of 28.5%; implement the investment in place capital of 4.62 billion yuan, an increase of 49.4%; per capita disposable income of urban residents was 15,911 yuan, an increase of 14.9%; rural residents per capita disposable income of 6,310 yuan, an increase of 18.2%.

三江公园一角
One corner of the Sanjiang park

黄 平 县

Huangping County

黄平县举行创建州级、省级文明县城动员大会暨万人签名仪式
Huangping County held to create state, provincial civilized town mobilize congress and rituals million signatures

黄平县位于贵州省东南部，面积1668平方公里，耕地面积1.7万公顷，辖5镇9乡、243个行政村、3个居民委员会，4个社区居民委员会。人口38.18万人，森林覆盖率41.87%。

2012年，围绕“稳中提速、赶超进位”的总体要求，深入实施“六大”发展战略，扎实推进“四项”重点工作，着力打造“五个黄平”，全县经济社会呈现出发展较快、投资增加、结构优化、民生改善、活力增强、后发赶超的良好态势。全年实现生产总值24.53亿元，同比增长17.6%；财政总收入3.21亿元，同比增长48.7%；50万元以上固定资产投资完成25.56亿元，同比增长85.2%；社会消费品零售总额实现6.57亿元，同比增长16.35%；城镇居民人均可支配收入14574元，增长18.5%；农民人均纯收入4348.5元，增长17.25%；金融机构存、贷款余额分别为36.42亿元和14.07亿元。

工业经济持续增长，全年重点以上工业增加值22659万元，比上年增长23%；城镇建设步伐加快，全县城镇化率达到25.8%；第三产业态势良好，第三产业实现增加值13.77亿元，同比增长20.5%；农业产业加速发展，全年粮食总产量89850吨，比上年增长24.42%；基础设施不断完善；民生工程扎实推进。

Huangping County, is located in the southeast Guizhou Province, an area of 1,668 square kilometers, land area of 17,000 hectares, exempted 5 towns 9 townships, 243 administrative villages, 3 neighborhood committees, 4 community residents' committees. Population of 381,800 people, the forest coverage rate of 41.87%.

In 2012, around the "steady speed, catching carry" the general requirements, in-depth implementation of the "six big" development strategy, solid progress "four projects" key work, in an effort to create "five Huangping", showing the county's economic and social development rapid increase in investment, structural optimization, improving people's livelihood, vitality, latecomer catch a good trend. Annual GDP of 2.453 billion yuan, an increase of 17.6%; fiscal revenue 321 million yuan, an increase of 48.7%; 500,000 yuan of fixed asset investment 2.556 billion yuan, an increase of 85.2%; total retail sales of social consumer goods to achieve 657 million yuan, an increase of 16.35%; urban residents per capita disposable income of 14,574 yuan, an increase of 18.5%; rural per capita net income of 4,348.5 yuan, an increase of 17.25%; financial institutions, loans were 3.642 billion yuan and 1.407 billion yuan, respectively.

Industrial economy continued to grow, the annual important industrial added value of 226.59 million yuan, an increase of 23% over last year; accelerate the pace of urban construction, the county's urbanization rate reached 25.8%; tertiary industry in good shape, the tertiary industry added value of 1.377 billion, an increase of 20.5%; accelerate the development of agricultural industrialization, the annual grain output 89,850 tons, an increase of 24.42% over the previous year; continuous improvement of infrastructure; livelihood pushed solid progress.

黄平振兴村镇银行开业庆典暨全州村镇银行建设现场会隆重举行

Huangping Zhenxing Village Bank opening ceremony cum Quanzhou village banks construction site meetings held

平 塘 县

Pingtang County

平塘上梭一座座拔地而起的保障性住房

Pingtang spindle blocks after another affordable housing

平塘县面积2815.6平方公里，辖10镇9乡（其中1个民族乡），121个村民委员会、3个居民委员会和3个社区。年末总人口32.2875万人，其中少数民族人口18.8973万人。主要矿产有煤、高岭土、方解石、花石、大理石等10余种。

2012年，全年生产总值22.6亿元，同比增长17.2%；全社会固定资产投资完成31亿元，同比增长50%；财政收入完成2.8亿元，同比增长50.1%，其中地方财政收入2.2亿元，同比增长57.8%；工业总产值完成5.2亿元；农业生产总值完成7.6亿元；社会消费品零售总额实现5.3亿元，同比增长16.6%；农民人均纯收入达到4994元，同比增长18.6%。

工业经济提速增效。至年末，投资5900万元加快通州园区建设，引进总投资达47.4亿元的盘江龙盟、安泰石材、澳华实业等16家企业入驻园区。全年招商引资项目38个，签约资金总额120亿元，到位资金25.8亿元。

农业产业结构调整明显加快。粮食实现恢复性增长，总产量达到12.3万吨。全县形成9个万亩基地和3个千亩基地。投入扶贫开发资金4850万元，实施扶贫开发项目73个。年内实现农业招商3.4亿元。

城镇化建设取得新突破。按照“以规划为先导、拉开路网、建设新城、带动老城”的思路，编制完成县城

《乡村大世界》走进平塘掌布景区

“Village World” into the Pingtang Zhangbu scenic spot

正在建设中的大射电工程

Large radio project is under construction.

大闸蟹养殖基地
Crabs breeding base

标准化的大闸蟹养殖基地
Standardized crabs breeding base

Pingtang County has an area of 2,815.6 square kilometers, jurisdiction over 10 towns 9 townships (including 1 townships), 121 village committees, 3 neighborhood committees and 3 communities. End of the year, the total population of 322,875, of which 188,973 minority population. The main mineral coal, kaolin, calcite, flower stone, marble and other 10 kinds.

In 2012, the annual GDP of 2.26 billion yuan, an increase of 17.2%; total fixed asset investment of 3.1 billion yuan, an increase of 50%; fiscal revenue of 280 million yuan, an increase of 50.1%, which the local revenue of 220,000,000 yuan, an increase of 57.8%; industrial output value of 520 million yuan; agricultural GDP reached 760 million yuan; total retail sales of social consumer goods to achieve 530 million yuan, an increase of 16.6%; rural per capita net income reached 4,994 yuan, an increase of 18.6%.

Speed efficiency of the industrial economy. To the end of the year, the investment 59 million yuan to speed up construction of the Tongzhou park , the introduction of a total investment of 4.74 billion yuan Panjing Longmeng, Antai stone material, Aohua Industrial and other 16 enterprises settled in the park. 38 investment projects throughout the year, the total funds contracted 12 billion yuan, 2.58 billion yuan of funds in place.

大闸蟹包装上市
Crabs packaging market

Adjustment of agricultural structure has accelerated noticeably. Food resumed their growth, production reached 123,000 tons. The county has formed 9 ten thousand acres of base and 3 one thousand acres of base. Poverty alleviation and development funds invested 48.5 million yuan, the implementation of poverty alleviation and development projects 73. Years to achieve agricultural investment 340 million yuan.

Urbanization achieve new breakthroughs. Accordance with the "planning for the pilot, opened the road network, construction of Metro, led the Old City" the idea, the county recently completed the preparation of detailed planning and construction of 19 township master plan. County's

生态畜牧产业发展（一）
Ecological Animal Husbandry Industry Development (one)

生态畜牧产业发展（二）
Ecological Animal Husbandry Industry Development (two)

近期建设控制性详细规划和19个乡镇总体规划。全县城镇化率达到30%。

旅游经济优势凸现。完成全县旅游开发系列策划编制，实施地质遗迹保护项目和自然遗产地保护项目。与贵州旅游投资控股（集团）公司签订投资70亿元打造平塘旅游战略合作协议。2012年共接待游客398.4万人次，旅游总收入完成28.6亿元。

基础设施不断完善。投资26亿元的独平高速公路启动建设，投资3600万元建设平塘掌布至贵定铁厂（平塘段）三级油路。实现100%乡镇通油路、100%村通公路"双百"目标。实施省、州重大工程和重点项目17个，完成投资12.1亿元。全县96个新开工和续建项目共完成投资17.9亿元。

生态建设迈出新步伐。围绕生态靓县，依托石漠化综合治理、巩固退耕还林成果专项、珠防工程和扶贫专项工程。完成卡罗河流域石漠化综合治理面积12平方公里。完成植树造林和补植补造3万亩，全县森林覆盖率达53.26%。

生态畜牧产业发展（三）
Ecological Animal Husbandry Industry Development (three)

社会管理成效显著。构建"1+12"工作机制，推进"平安平塘"建设。加快"天网工程"建设。扎实开展安全生产专项行动。积极畅通信访渠道。安全感测评排位全省19位，上升了68个位次。

社会保障不断增强。民生和社会事业财政支出达到10.03亿元。新增城镇就业人员6038人。保障性住房建成942套，农村危房改造竣工4455户。

科教文卫全面进步。引进一批良种畜禽并抓好品种改良。举办各类科技培训班，抓好农业科技特派员工作。建成广电"村村通"项目2.4万户。食品药品安全监管工作进一步加强。

规模化的玫瑰花生产基地

Large-scale production base of the rose

urbanization rate reached 30%.

Economic advantages of tourism highlights. Complete series of county tourism development plan preparation, implementation of geological heritage conservation projects and natural heritage conservation projects. With Guizhou Tourism Investment Holding (Group) Company signed invest 7 billion yuan to build Pingtang tourism strategic cooperation agreement. In 2012, a total of 3.984 million tourists trips, tourism revenue of 2.86 billion yuan.

Continuous improvement of infrastructure construction. Invest 2.6 billion yuan to start the construction of Duping Highway, 36 million yuan investment to build Pingtang Zhangbu to Guiding Tiechang(Pingtang paragraph) third level oil road. Township pass circuit to achieve 100%, 100% villages accessible by road “double hundred” target. Implementation of the provincial, state key projects and key projects 17, completed an investment of 1.21 billion yuan. The county continued construction of 96 new construction projects and a total investment of 1.79 billion yuan.

New steps were taken to ecological construction. Around the ecological beautiful county, relying on the rocky desertification control, consolidate the achievement of returning farmland to forests, Zhufang project and special aid items. Complete the Caluo river basin comprehensive harnessing desertification area of 12 square kilometers. Finish the reforestation and replanting of 30,000 mu, the forest coverage rate reached 53.26%.

通州工业园区玫瑰花基地

Tongzhou Industrial Park Rose Base

通州玫瑰花基地

Tongzhou Rose Base

The social management with remarkable results. Construction of “1+12” working mechanism, promote “peace Pingtang” construction. To speed up the “Skynet project” construction. Carry out the safety production special action. Positive smooth handling channels. Security evaluation ranking 19th in the province, with a rise of 68.

Social security constantly enhanced. The people’s livelihood and social expenditure reached 1.003 billion yuan. New urban jobs for 6,038 people. Affordable housing completed 942 sets, completed 4,455 households of rural reconstruction.

Science education culture health had comprehensive progress. The introduction of a number of livestock and poultry and grasp the variety improvement. Held various scientific and technological training, to promote agricultural science and technology correspondent. Built Radio "every village" project completed 24,000 households. Food and drug safety supervision work to further strengthen.

松桃苗族自治县

Songtao Miao Autonomous County

市政协副主席、县委书记冉晓东在推介会上作解答
Municipal CPPCC Vice Chairman, the county party secretary Ran Xiaodong at the launching conference for the answer

县长吴洋富率招商引资考察团赴福建考察招商
Magistrate Wu Yangfu led the investment delegation to Fujian visit merchants

松桃苗族自治县是全国最早成立的五个苗族自治县之一，位于贵州省东北部梵净山东麓，素有“黔东北门户”之称。辖28个乡镇，7个社区，503个行政村，面积3400平方公里，人口70.65万，其中以苗族为主的少数民族占总人口的68%。

近年来，全县抢抓国发2号文件和《武陵山片区扶贫攻坚规划》发展机遇，深入实施“环境立县、产业富县、城镇兴县、民生和县、人才强县”的发展思路，工业经济迅猛发展，农业产业化经营强势推进，城镇建设日新月异，社会各项事业取得新进展，先后被评为“省级文明卫生县城”、“全国平安建设先进县”、“全国科普示范县”。

2012年，全县地方生产总值60.14亿元，比上年增长15.1%，其中：第一产业增加值183635万元，增长9.0%；第二产业增加值200550万元，增长16.5%；第三产业增加值217239万元，增长18.9%。全社会固定资产投资完成70.07亿元，比上年增长65.9%。财政总收入完成7.32亿元，比上年增长21.9%。全年社会消费品零售总额136022万元，比上年增长15.5%。全年农村居民人均纯收入4346元，比上年增长18.1%。

矿产资源丰富。已探明具有开发价值的矿产资源有锰矿、硅矿、铅锌矿、钒矿、大理石、磷矿、石煤、石材等20余种，其中锰的远景储量达1.2亿吨，占全国总储量的八分之一，松桃素有“中国锰都”之称。钒矿储量超过1亿吨。松桃又是国家页岩气先导区之一，初步探明储量在1万亿立方米以上。

日新月异的城镇建设
Rapid urban construction

县委常委、常务副县长何支刚在全县统计工作会议上讲话
County Committee, Deputy Mayor He Zhigang made speech at the statistical work meeting in the county

松桃梵净山大道
Songtao Fanjingshan avenue

Songtao Miao Autonomous County is one of the country's oldest established five Miao Autonomous County, located in northeastern Guizhou Fanjingshan foothill, known as "Northeast Guizhou portal". Jurisdiction over 28 towns, 7 communities, 503 administrative villages, an area of 3,400 square kilometers, population of 706,500, of which the Miao ethnic minority accounted for 68% of the total population.

苗族绝技绝活：斜走大刀
Miao minority masterly skills: move diagonally broadsword

In recent years, the county seize the State Issued No. 2 Document and the "Wuling Mountain Area Poverty Alleviation Plan" development opportunities, in-depth implementation of the "environment establish the county, industry rich the county, city towns prospers the county, the people's livelihood harmony the county, talent strong the county" development ideas, the rapid development of industrial economy, industrial management of agriculture to promote a strong, rapid urban construction, social undertakings made new progress, has been named "provincial civilized health county", "National advanced County in peace building", "national science demonstration counties".

In 2012, the county's GDP of 6.014 billion yuan, an increase of 15.1% over last year, of which: the first industry 1,836,350,000 yuan, an increase of 9.0%; the secondary industry was 2.0055 billion yuan, an increase of 16.5%; The tertiary industrial added value 2,172,390,000 yuan, an increase of 18.9%. Total fixed asset investment of 7.007 billion yuan, an increase of 65.9% over the previous year. Total fiscal revenue of 732 million yuan, an increase of 21.9% over the previous year. Annual total retail sales of social consumer goods 1,360,220,000 yuan, an increase of 15.5% over the previous year. Annual per capita net income of rural residents 4,346 yuan, an increase of 18.1% over the previous year.

民族文化广场：世昌广场
Culture Plaza:Shichang square

建设中的凯迪循环经济产业园：凯迪生物质电厂
In the construction of Kaidi circular economy industrial park : Kaidi biomass power plant

太平营石榴溪村
Taiping Shiliuxi village

交通十分便捷。铜仁•凤凰机场，渝怀铁路穿境而过，迓大二级公路连接湘渝和杭瑞两条高速，公路、铁路、航空“三位一体”的交通网络正在不断优化升级。

旅游资源丰富，民族民间文化独特。松桃是“中国民间绝技艺术之乡”、“中国滚龙艺术之乡”和“贵州省苗族花鼓艺术之乡”，是“世界独生子”黔金丝猴的自由王国。境内有被列为联合国“人与生物圈”保护网成员的国家级自然保护区——梵净山，有被誉为梦幻家园的东方氧都—桃花源风光，有中国十大溶洞奇观之一——世界钟乳石密度罕见的潜龙洞，有历史悠久、神秘莫测的中国苗王城，有被文化界誉为“戏剧活化石”的苗族傩戏。

中国苗王城
Chinese Miao Town

农业生产条件得天独厚，先后被评为“全国科技进步先进县”、“全国粮食生产先进县”、“中央财政现代农业建设示范项目县”、“全国小型农田水利建设重点县”、“贵州省草地生态畜牧业产业化科技扶贫项目示范县”、“贵州省油茶发展核心示范县”。

长兴堡镇九龙新村
Changxingbao town Jiulong new [illegible]

茶叶种植产业
Tea plantation industry

五万亩百合种植
50,000 acres planted lily

商品羊养殖
Sheep farming commodity

Rich in mineral resources. Has a development value of proven mineral resources of manganese, silicon ore, lead and zinc, vanadium ore, marble, phosphate, coal, stone, more than 20 species, of which manganese prospective reserves of 120 million tons, accounting for the country's total reserves one-eighth, Songtao known as "Chinese manganese capital". Vanadium ore reserves of over 100 million tons. Songtao is one of the national shale gas pilot areas, the initial proven reserves at 1 trillion cubic meters or more.

Transportation is very convenient. Tongren • Phoenix Airport, Chongqing-Huaihua Railway passing through, Yada second-level highways connecting Xiangyi and Hangrui two high-speed, highway, railway, aviation "trinity" of transportation network is constantly upgrading.

Rich tourism resources, a unique folk culture. Songtao was "Hometown of Chinese folk arts stunt", "Chinese dragon roll art village" and "artistic hub of Guizhou Miao village", is "the world only begotten Son" Guizhou golden monkey realm of freedom. The territory is classified as UN "Man and Biosphere" protection network member National Nature Reserve - Fanjingshan, are known as oriental dream home oxygen all - paradise scenery, there is one of China's top ten cave wonders - World stalactites density rare Qianlong hole, with its historic and mysterious Chinese Miao city, there is a cultural as the "living fossil of drama" the Miao Nuo opera.

Unique conditions for agricultural production, has been named the "National Science and Technology Progress advanced county", "national food production advanced county", "central finance construction of modern agriculture demonstration project counties", "national key counties for small-scale irrigation and water conservancy construction", "Guizhou Province grass ecological animal husbandry industrialization poverty alleviation project demonstration county", "Guizhou Province Camellia development of the core demonstration counties".

万头野猪养殖场
Ten thousand wild boar farms

沿河土家族自治县

Yanhe Tujia Autonomous County

2012年6月14日，时任省委书记栗战书在沿河沙子十二盘村调研

June 14, 2012, when he was the provincial party secretary Li Zhanshu had research in Yanhe Shazi Shierpan villages

沿河土家族自治县位于贵州省东北角、乌江下游，素有“黔东北门户，乌江要津”之称。面积2468.8平方千米，辖22个乡镇、429个村、13个居民委员会、6个社区、3909个村民组，人口66万，是全国四个单一土家族自治县之一，贵州省唯一的单一土家族自治县。境内旅游资源丰富，有国家级自然保护区麻阳河、国家级风景名胜区和乌江山峡百里画廊，被文化部命名为“中国土家山歌之乡”。

2012年，沿河自治县深入贯彻党的十八大精神，抢抓国发2号文件和《武陵山片区区域发展与扶贫攻坚规划》历史机遇，以融入成渝经济区为取向，紧扣主基调、突出主战略，围绕农特产品基地县、能源输出重点县、生态旅游示范县和乌江物流港口门户城市“三县一城”发展定位和工业化、农业产业化、城镇化和旅游文化产业“三化一业”赶超途径，在狠抓大事上凝聚力量，在抢抓机遇中谋求赶超，开创了科学发展新局面，谱写了后发赶超新篇章，踏上了同步小康新征程。

2012年，全县地方生产总值48.54亿元，增长16.6%；固定资产投资78.57亿元，增长78.4%；财政总收入6.8亿元，增长27.1%；社会消费品零售总额10.56亿元，增长15.8%；城镇居民人均可支配收入14069元（预计）、农民人均收入4370.2元，分别增长19.1%和17.71%。金融机构存贷款余额分别为49.39亿元、25.19亿元，分别增长15.5%和19.3%。

县委书记张翊皓在326国道改道县城段黄家山施工现场调研

County party secretary Zhang Yihao Huang had research in 326 State Road diversions county paragraph Huangjiashan construction site

官舟现代农业园

Guanzhou modern agriculture park

县长任廷浬在坝坨新区调研

The Magistrate Ren Tingli had research in Batuo new district

山峡生态工业区

Gorge eco-industrial zone

沿河25周年县庆
Yanhe the 25th anniversary of the county celebration

Yanhe Tujia Autonomous County is in the northeast corner of Guizhou Province, downstream of Wujiang River, known as "northeastern Guizhou portal, Wujiang key locations". Area of 2,468.8 square kilometers, jurisdiction over 22 towns, 429 villages, 13 residents' committees, 6 communities, 3,909 villagers groups, population of 660,000, is the country's one of four single Tujia Autonomous Counties, only a single soil Tujia family Autonomous County in Guizhou Province. Territory is rich in tourism resources, National Nature Reserve Mayanghe, a national scenic area and the Wujiang River gorge Baili Gallery, named by the Ministry of Culture "China Tujia folk songs township".

水 中 之 城 —— 沿 河
City in the water - Yanhe

In 2012, Yanhe Autonomous County thoroughly implement the spirit of 18th CPC National Congress, seize the historic opportunity of the State Issued document NO.2 and "Wuling Mountain Area Regional Development and Anti-Poverty Plan", in order to integrate into the Chengdu-Chongqing Economic Zone orientation , closely grasp the main tone, highlighting the main strategy, around the base in the county of agricultural products, the energy output key counties, eco-tourism demonstration counties and the Wujiang logistics port gateway cities "three counties and one city" development orientation and industrialization, agricultural industrialization, urbanization and tourism and cultural industries "three one industry" catch up with ways, to pay close attention to major events and gathering strength, seeking to catch up in seizing the opportunity to create a new situation of scientific development, writing a latecomer to catch up with a new chapter, embark on a new journey of sync well-off.

In 2012, the county's local GDP of 4.854 billion yuan, an increase of 16.6%; fixed asset investment of 7.857 billion yuan, an increase of 78.4%; total fiscal revenue of 680 million yuan, an increase of 27.1%; 1.056 billion yuan of the total retail sales of social consumer goods, an increase of 15.8% ; capita disposable income of urban residents was 14,069 yuan (expected), farmers' per capita income of 4,370.2 yuan, an increase of 19.1% and 17.71%, respectively. Financial institutions, deposit and loan balances were 4.939 billion yuan, 2.519 billion yuan, an increase of 15.5% and 19.3%, respectively.

建设中的沙沱电站
The construction Shatuo power station

在建中的县城人行景观桥
Under construction the county pedestrian bridge landscape

沿河白山羊
Yanhe White goats

施 秉 县

Shibing County

施秉县云台山入选“黔东南苗岭国家地质公园主园区”

Shibing County Yuntai mountain appeared in the “National Geological Park of Southeast Guizhou Miao main park”

水龙祈雨

Rain water dragon

施秉县位于贵州省东部、黔东南苗族侗族自治州西北部，㵲阳河国家级风景名胜区的中心腹地，面积1543.8平方公里，人口16.8万人，辖4乡、4镇、64个行政村10个社区，居住着汉、苗、侗、布依等19个民族。区位优越，交通便利。

施秉资源富集，人杰地灵。年平均气温14-16℃，气候温和湿润；现有耕地35万亩，非耕地可开发利用面积30余万亩；水能资源富足，水能资源蕴藏量7.74万千瓦；矿产资源丰富；生物种类繁多；森林覆盖率达54.6%。

施秉是宜居之城。县城是一座融山、水、林、城为一体的园林式“江南小城”，533.2平方公里的国家级㵲阳河风景名胜区中有366平方公里在施秉境内。㵲阳河秀丽柔美、风光旖旎，云台山植被茂密、景象万千。民族风情浓郁古朴，杉木河清幽秀雅，激爽漂流已成为国内知名品牌，施秉因此获得了“中国漂城”的美誉。2010年杉木河景区在第三届博鳌国际旅游论坛上被授予“国家精品旅游景

山水环绕的施秉县城

Landscape surrounded Shibing county

Shibing County is located in eastern part of Guizhou Province, northwest of Miao and Dong Autonomous Prefecture, central hinterland of Wuyang national scenic area, with an area of 1,543.8 square kilometers, population of 168,000 people, exempted 4 townships, 4 towns, 64 administrative villages 10 community, inhabited by the Han, Miao, Dong, Buyi and other 19 ethnic groups. Superior location and convenient transportation.

Shibing owns rich resources, outstanding culture and location. The annual average temperature 14-16 □, the climate is mild and humid; existing 350,000 mu of arable land, development and utilization of non-cultivated land area of 300,000 mu; rich water resources, water resources reserves 77,400 kilowatts; rich in mineral resources; species variety; forest coverage rate reached 54.6%.

Shibing is a livable city. The county is a melting mountain, water, forest, garden city as one of the "southern town", 533.2 km2 Wuyang national scenic area in the territory of 366 square kilometers in Shibing. Wuyang river is beautiful soft, beautiful scenery, Yuntai mountain has lush vegetation, thousands of images. Ethnic features quaint, quiet goodly Shanmu river, Zest rafting has become well-known brands, Shibing won the "China drift city" in the world. In 2010, at the Third Boao International Tourism Forum, Shanmu river scenic was awarded the "national quality tourist attractions", Yuntai mountain scenic named "The Second China

施秉县景区示意图
Schematic Shibing County area

云台山风光
Yuntai mountain scenery

苗族刺绣
Miao minority embroidery

刻道
Engraved Road

区”，云台山景区入选“第二届中国避暑名山”和贵州十大魅力景区，并被列为“中国南方喀斯特”第二批世界自然遗产提名预选地和黔东南苗岭国家地质公园主园区。

施秉产业发展独具特色。农业产业结构调整成效显著，“两种一养”（种烟、种药和畜牧养殖）等特色农业正向规模化、产业化方向发展，并已成为推动农民增收的主导产业。现代烟草农业示范基地建设步伐加快，烤烟发展水平不断提高；中药材种植面积常年保持在6万亩左右，已发展成熟的品种有30余种，其中太子参、头花蓼、何首乌三个品种已通过国家GAP认证，太子参年产量占全国总产量的三分之一强，近年来已占半壁江山，其生产技术获得了贵州省“十一五”期间农业科技十大成就奖，施秉被誉为“中国太子参之乡”，也称“西南药城”。工业经济正努力向环保、节能、提升产品质量等方向快速发展。1999年入驻施秉县的恒盛公司，经过不断发展壮大，工业硅产能达到12万吨/年，成为国内最大的工业硅生产企业，施秉因此有“中国硅城”之称。

赛龙舟
Dragon boat race

summer mountain" and Guizhou ten charming scenic, and was listed as "South China Karst" Second World Natural Heritage nomination and Southeast Guizhou Miao preselected national Geopark main campus.

Shibing has unique industry development. Adjustment of agricultural structure with remarkable results, "two plants of a breeding" (plant of tobacco, drugs and livestock breeding species) and other characteristics of large-scale agriculture forward, the direction of industrial development, which has become the dominant industry promoting the farmers income. Modern tobacco agriculture demonstration base construction speed up, constantly improve the level of development of flue-cured tobacco; perennial planting area remained at 60,000 mu, has developed more than 30 varieties of species, including heterophylla, flower head Polygonum multiflorum three varieties have been through the national GAP certification, heterophylla annual output accounts for one-third of national output in recent years has accounted for half of its production technology won the Guizhou Province, "Eleventh Five-Year" period agricultural Science and Technology achievement Award for the top ten, is hailed Shibing "China heterophylla town", also known as "City of southwest drugs". Industrial economy is trying to environmental protection, energy conservation, improve product quality and other direction rapidly. In 1999, settled in Shibing County Hengsheng company, through continuous development and growth, industrial silicon production capacity of 120,000 tons / year, has become the largest industrial silicon production enterprises, Shibing is known as "China Silicon City".

太子参
Heterophylla

矿泉水上漂——杉木河
Mineral water on the drift - Shanmu River

册 亨 县

Ceheng County

册亨县城全景
Ceheng county panoramic

册亨位于贵州省西南部，面积2598平方公里，辖9镇5乡，2个社区，7个居委会，123个行政村，994个村民组，总人口23万，其中少数民族人口占79%，布依族占76%，建州前是全国唯一的布依族自治县。

自然资源丰富。册亨年均气温19.2℃，素有"天然温室"之称。森林覆盖率达61%，是贵州十大林业县之一，是全国无公害早熟蔬菜生产基地之一。境内矿产资源丰富，其中已探明的黄金储量23吨，锑矿储量57万吨，镁储量1260万吨。旅游资源丰富，具有山水画特质。

安居工程纳阳廉租房建设已竣工，工人正在安装通讯设备和线路
Housing projects and Nayang low-rent housing construction has been completed, workers are installing communications equipment and lines

布依文化浓郁。册亨是全国布依族人口占总人口比例最高的县，也是布依语言的第一语音区，布依文化资源丰富、底蕴深厚，被国务院命名为"布依戏之乡"。2006年，册亨的布依戏被列为首批国家级非物质文化遗产。2010年11月，成功举办了中国•册亨2010布依文化年活动，被省布依学会授予"中华布依第一县"和"布依文化

者楼镇羊场秋色
Zhelou town sheep farm autumn scene

已建成投运并过境册亨的汕昆高速

Has been put into operation and transit Ceheng of Shantou Kunming Express

册亨县城区饮用水源点坝潮水库

Ceheng county area Dianba dam reservoir of drinking water source

Ceheng located in southwestern Guizhou Province, an area of 2,598 square kilometers, jurisdiction over 9 towns, 5 townships, 2 communities, 7 neighborhood, 123 administrative villages, 994 village groups, with a total population of 230,000, of which 79% minority population, Buyi 76%, before statehood is the only Buyi Autonomous County in the whole nation.

Rich in natural resources. Ceheng average annual temperature of 19.2 ℃, known as the "natural greenhouse". Forest coverage rate reached 61%, is one of the top ten forest counties in Guizhou, the national pollution-free vegetable production bases precocious. Rich in mineral resources, which has proven reserves of 23 tons of gold, antimony ore reserves of 570,000 tons, magnesium reserves of 12.6 million tons. Rich in tourism resources, with the landscape character.

我国铁路首座湾梁桥南昆铁路板其二号大桥

China Railway First Bay Bridge Nan-kung Railway board an dits II Railway Bridge

Buyi owns rich culture. Ceheng is the highest proportion of the total Buyi population county, is the first voice Buyi language area, Buyi culture is rich in resources, deep inside, the State Council named "Buyi drama village". In 2006, Ceheng Buyi drama is listed as the first batch of national intangible cultural heritage. November 2010, successfully held China• Ceheng 2010 Buyi Culture Year activities, the provincial Buyi Society awarded "China Buyi first county" and "Buyi cultural heritage protection and research base". November 2012, Ceheng Buyi eight thousand people, "Transitions Dance" successfully won Shanghai World DSJJNS.

岩架（北盘江航运）

The ledge (Beipan River shipping)

南华糖厂全景
Nanhua sugar factory panoramic

保护与传承研究基地”。2012年11月，册亨布依族八千人“转场舞”成功获得上海大世界基尼斯之最。

经济健康发展。2012年，全县完成生产总值17.54亿元，增长15.3%；全社会固定资产投资17.26亿元，增长64.8%；全部工业增加值1.81亿元，同比增长17.1%；财政总收入2.55亿元，增长40.32%；公共财政收入1.65亿元，增长96.05%；全年财政支出12.21亿元，增长28.09%；农民人均纯收入达3960元，增长19.4%；城镇居民人均可支配收入14936元，增长19.8%；社会消费品零售总额2.1亿元，增长19.47%；金融机构各项存款余额28.19亿元、贷款余额16.8亿元，分别增长25.18%和16.92%。

社会和谐稳定。近几年来，坚持以“夯实基础、保持稳定、构建和谐、促进发展”为重点，正确处理发展与稳定的关系，努力创建“和谐库区”和“和谐工区”，“五五”普法和“平安册亨”、“无毒县”等创建活动顺利通过省级验收，全县社会和谐稳定，人民群众安居乐业，民意调查考核13项指标均名列全州第一，2011年被评为全省“十佳和谐县”、“平安铁路示范县”、“普法依法治理先进单位”。

即将点火生产的德隆水泥厂
The upcoming ignition Delong cement factory

充满发展希望。大通道的交通区位优势日益凸显，南昆铁路已建成投运，南北盘江红水河水运中通道和汕昆高速公路已经建成通航通车。随着望安高速公路的建成通车和港口的建成投用，集水路、铁路、高速公路为一体的交通枢纽基本形成，册亨将成为中国沿海和腹地紧密相连的枢纽和珠江上游的黄金水道，将成为黔西南州乃至贵州西部、攀西六盘水地区南下的“桥头堡”和前沿阵地。此外，甘蔗、林业、畜牧、蔬菜、水产五大产业基本形成。

纳盘电站机房
Napan plant room

册亨大型布依转场舞

Ceheng large Buyi transitions dance

Healthy economic development. In 2012, the county's GDP of 1.754 billion yuan, an increase of 15.3%; total fixed asset investment 1.726 billion yuan, an increase of 64.8%; total industrial added value 181,000,000 yuan, an increase of 17.1%; fiscal revenue 255 million yuan, an increase of 40.32%; public revenue 165 million yuan, an increase of 96.05%; annual spending 1.221 billion yuan, an increase of 28.09%; rural per capita net income reached 3,960 yuan, an increase of 19.4%; urban residents per capita disposable income of 14,936 yuan, an increase of 19.8 %; social retail sales of consumer goods 210 million yuan, an increase of 19.47%; financial institutions deposit balance of 2.819 billion yuan, the loan balance of 1.68 billion yuan, up 25.18% and 16.92%, respectively.

双江口风光

Shuangjiangkou scenery

Social harmony and stability. In recent years, adhere to "lay a solid foundation to maintain stability and building a harmonious development" as the focus, correctly handle the relationship between development and stability, and strive to create a "harmonious reservoir" and "harmonious work area", "55" law popularization and "peacefuk Ceheng", "non-toxic County" and other activities to create successfully passed the provincial inspection, the county's social harmony and stability, people live and work in peace, polls examination 13 indicators are ranked statewide first, in 2011 was named the province "Top Ten harmony county", "Green railway demonstration county", "advanced unit of governance according to law".

Full development of hope. A major thoroughfare traffic advantage has become increasingly prominent, Nanning-Kunming Railway has been put into operation, North and South Pan River Hongshui River waterway in the channel and the Shantou-Kunming expressway has been put into service to traffic. With the Wangan Expressway opened to traffic and the port put into use, set the waterway, railway, highway transportation hub for the integration of the basic form, Ceheng will be closely linked to China's coastal and hinterland hub and the Pearl River golden waterway, will become Qianxinan state even western Guizhou, Liupanshui area southward Panxi "bridgehead" and forward positions. In addition, sugar cane, forestry, livestock, vegetables, aquatic five industry basically formed.

冗渡双乳峰

Rongdu breasts peak

金州十八景之一——洛凡燕子洞

One of the Jinzhou 18 scenics - Luofan Yanzidong

山情水韵　魅力锦屏

Mountain Aqua　Charming Jinping

州委书记李飞跃（右一），州委副书记、州长廖飞（右三）在杨伟县长（右二）的陪同下到锦屏清江二桥建设工地调研

State committee secretary Li Feiyue (first from right), deputy secretary of state, Governor Liao Fei (third from right) accompanied by county governor Yang Wei (second from right) to the Jinping Qingjiang Er Bridge construction site to have investigation

州长廖飞（左二），州委常委、州委秘书长耿生茂（左一）在孟凡明书记（左三）的陪同下到锦屏经济开发区了解建设情况

Governor Liao Fei (second from left), State Committee Standing Committee, State Committee Secretary Geng Shengmao (first from left) accompanied by secretary Meng Fanming(third from left) to understand the construction of Jinping Economic Development Zone

原省人大常委会副主任、省苗学会会长杨光林（左二）在县人大常委会主任龙永贵（右二）的陪同下到文斗苗寨考察锦屏文书

Former deputy director of the Provincial People's Congress, the provincial seedlings Society Yang Guanglin (second from left) accompanied by the county People's Congress Chairman Long Yonggui (second from right), visit to Wendou Miao village Jinping instruments

县政协主席杨正永（左一）到三板溪库区进行水上生产安全调研

County Council Chairman Yang Zhengyong (the first from left) to research the Sanbanxi reservoir for water production safety

"鸳鸯绿浦上，翡翠锦屏中"。锦屏县因境内青水似锦、秀丽如屏而得名。全县辖7镇8乡，面积1596.9平方公里，人口22.7万人，居住有侗、苗、汉等19个民族，少数民族占总人口的88%。

锦屏风光旖旎、气候宜人，自然资源丰富，人文景观悠久，民族风情浓郁，是中国南方典型集体林区县、贵州省重点林业县，也是贵州省新批准的革命老区，被誉为"杉木之乡"、"水电之乡"、"青石之乡"、"舞龙之乡"。

锦屏围绕木材、建材、石材、电力、矿产等特色资源优势，大力发展林业、建材、石材、电力、矿产精细化加工、特色农产品"六大"产业，推进新型工业化进程；大力推进"一城两区"同城规划建设，将老县城建设成"小、特、精"的休闲度假生态县城，将新区建设成一座"大、快、强"山水林城环绕的魅力新城。

2012年，锦屏县委、县政府牢牢把握"加速发展、扩大总量、奋力赶超、推动跨越"的主基调，经济社会发展同比实现了较大增长，全县经济呈现出"总量提升、速度加快、效益较好、民生改善"的良好发展态势。

雾满山城

Full mountain fog

建设中的日产2500吨和泰水泥厂
Construction of producing 2500 tons per day Taihe cement plant

"一事一议"省级示范村隆里乡华寨
"One matter one discussion" provincial model village Longli village Huazhai

"Mandarin duck green Urakami, jade Jinping". Jinping County is named for the territory bright blue water, beautiful as screen. The county governs 7 towns 8 rural towns, an area of 1,596.9 square kilometers, population 227,000 people, living with Dong, Miao, Han and other 19, ethnic minority people account for 88% of the total population.

Jinping owns beautiful scenery, pleasant climate, abundant natural resources, cultural landscape has long history, rich ethnic customs, China's collective forest typical of southern counties, forest counties in Guizhou Province, is newly approved revolutionary base areas in Guizhou Province, known as "fir town", "water town", "bluestone town", "dragon town".

Jinping around the timber, building materials, stone, electricity, mining and other special resources to vigorously develop forestry, building materials, stone, electricity, mineral fine processing, specialty agricultural products, "six big" industries, promote the process of new industrialization; vigorously promote the "One city two areas" city planning and construction, the old county building into a "small, special, fine" eco-resort town, the new area construction as a "big, fast and strong" the charm of the landscape around forest City Metro.

隆里古城舞龙狂欢
Longli ancient city dragon dance carnival

In 2012, Jinping county committee, county government firmly grasp the "accelerated development, expanding the overall economy, struggling to catch up, and promote across" the main tone, the economic and social development to achieve greater growth year on year, the county's economy has shown a "total upgrade , faster, better efficiency, improve people's livelihood" the good momentum of development.

建设中的清水江三桥
Qingshui river San Bridge is in construction

非物质文化遗产代表作品——侗族刺绣
Intangible Cultural Heritage Representative works - Dong embroidery

经济发展明显提速，综合实力显著增强。2012年，全县生产总值完成20.2亿元，同比增长15.5%。财政总收入完成3亿元，同比增长33.4%，其中公共财政预算收入1.9亿元，同比增长38.7%。全社会固定资产投资完成25.5亿元，同比增长116.5%。金融机构存款余额34.1亿元、贷款余额11.7亿元，分别增长17.5%、17.6%。全县招商引资签约资金189.7亿元，到位资金28亿元。

基础建设不断加强，发展环境明显改善。以交通、水利为重点的基础设施建设取得历史性突破。交通建设完成投资7693万元（不含三黎高速公路）。三黎高速（锦屏段）全面进入实质性施工阶段。清江二桥、三桥建设进展顺利。“十二五”农村公路通畅工程扎实推进，实施完成70.7公里。水利建设完成投资8900万元。成功申报中央小型农田水利重点县。

木材精深加工成品车间
Deep processing of timber finished workshop

三大战略同步推进，结构不断优化升级。2012年，全县年主营业务收入500万元以上工业企业实现增加值7亿元。锦屏工业园区升格为省级经济开发区，锦屏经济开发区“三纵五横”交通骨架初步形成。启动县城“三江六岸”棚户区改造和老城区风貌整治工作，城镇化率达30%。农业实现恢复性增长，经济作物比重不断提高。旅游总收入增长29.4%。

锦屏石材
Jinping stone material

民生保障成效显著，社会事业全面发展。城镇居民人均可支配收入13610元，增长11.3%，农村居民人均纯收入4255元，增长14.1%。坚持教育优先发展战略。实施积极的就业政策。进一步健全和完善社会保障体系。全县新型农村合作医疗参合率92.4%。城乡居民各类保险综合参保率98.2%。

生态渔业合作社养殖基地
Ecological fishery cooperative breeding base

锦屏县茅坪香橘
Jinping county Maoping fragrant orange

硕果累累的油茶林
Fruitful Camellia Forest

林下养殖场
The Linxia breeding factory

Significantly accelerated economic development, comprehensive strength has markedly increased. In 2012, the county's GDP 2.02 billion yuan, an increase of 15.5%. Total fiscal revenue of 300 million yuan, an increase of 33.4%, of which the public budget revenues 190,000,000 yuan, an increase of 38.7%. Total fixed asset investment of 2.55 billion yuan, an increase of 116.5%. Financial institutions deposit balance 3.41 billion yuan, 1.17 billion yuan loan balance, respectively, an increase of 17.5%, 17.6%. County investment funds 18.97 billion yuan contract funds, in place 2.8 billion.

Continue to strengthen infrastructure construction, development environment improved significantly. In transportation, focusing on water conservancy infrastructure construction has made a historic breakthrough. Transportation construction investment 76.93 million yuan (excluding San-Li highway). San-Li highway (Jinping section) full access to the substantive construction phase. Qingjiang Er Bridge, San Bridge construction progressing smoothly. "Twelfth Five-Year" rural highway got smooth solid progress, implement complete 70.7 km. Water conservancy construction investment 89 million yuan. Declare the success of central small-scale irrigation and water conservancy key counties.

Three strategies promoted simultaneously, structural optimization and upgrading. In 2012, the county's main business income of 5 million yuan of industrial enterprises realized an added value of 700 million yuan. Jinping Industrial Park was upgraded to provincial economic development zone, Jinping economic zone "three vertical and five horizontal" traffic skeleton shape. Start the county "three rivers six shore" shantytowns and the old town style remediation work, the urbanization rate of 30%. Agriculture resumed their growth, economic crops continued to increase. Total tourism revenues increased by 29.4%.

Remarkable livelihood security, social undertakings got full progress. Per capita disposable income of urban residents 13,610 yuan, up 11.3%, per capita net income of rural residents 4,255 yuan, an increase of 14.1%. Adhere to the priority of education development strategy. Implement a proactive employment policy. Further improve and perfect the social security system. County's new rural cooperative medical participation rate 92.4%. Urban and rural residents in various types of insurance comprehensive insurance rate 98.2%.

集体林权制度改革后的乡村集体林场
After the reform of collective forest right system of rural collective farm

贵 定 县
Guiding County

发展中的贵定县
The developing Guiding county

2012年，全县围绕“加速发展、加快转型、推动跨越”主基调，实施工业强县和城镇化带动战略，着力保增长、调结构、增活力、惠民生、促和谐，经济保持平稳较快发展，社会各项事业取得新成绩。

全县实现生产总值最终核算为441084万元，比上年增长17.1%。人均生产总值19156元，比上年增长17.2%。产业结构持续优化，三次产业增加值比例调整为13.79：48.97：37.24。人均地区生产总值19156元，较上年增长17.2%。

农业经济稳步发展。工业发展继续加快。财政收支和金融较快增长。固定资产投资规模继续扩大。基础设施建设步伐加快。科、教、卫事业蓬勃发展。社会福利保障事业稳步推进，人民生活较大提高。

贵定锦绣音寨
Guiding Jinxiu Yin village

贵定云雾湖
Guiding Yuwu lake

中华第一布依寨——音寨
The Chinese first Buyi village----Yin village

In 2012, the county around “accelerate development, speed up the transformation, push forward” the main tone, the implementation of industrial county and the urbanization strategy, strive to maintain growth, structural adjustment, increase vitality, improve people’s livelihood, and promote harmony, to maintain stable and rapid economic development, various social undertakings have made new achievements.

The county realized a GDP of final accounting for 4,410,840,000 yuan, an increase of 17.1%. The per capita GDP of 19,156 yuan, an increase of 17.2%. Continue to optimize the industrial structure, the three industrial added value for the adjustment of the ratio of 13.79:48.97:37.24. The per capita GDP of 19,156 yuan, an increase of 17.2% over the previous year.

Steady development of agricultural economy. Continue to accelerate industrial development. Fiscal and financial got rapid growth. The scale of investment in fixed assets continue to expand. To accelerate the pace of infrastructure construction. Science, health, education got full development. Social welfare undertakings pushed steadily, people’s life greatly improved.

万 山 区

Wanshan District

万山位于贵州东部，面积840平方公里。辖1街道办事处，2镇6乡，70个行政村，14个居委会，人口16万人。矿产丰富，植被茂密。

2012年，全区生产总值20.80亿元，同比增长17.5%；财政总收入22650万元，同比增长49.6%；公共财政预算收入12730万元，同比增长54.2%；全社会固定资产投资37.22亿元，同比增长52.6%；社会消费品零售总额达到3.39亿元，同比增长15.3%；农民人均纯收入4229元，同比增长17.7%；城镇居民人均可支配收入15911元，同比增长14.9%。

万山谢桥新区
Wanshan Xieqiao new district

谢桥新区体育馆和游泳馆
Xieqiao new district gymnasium and swimming pool

Wanshan is located in the eastern Guizhou, with an area of 840 square kilometers. Jurisdiction of 1 district offices, 2 towns, 6 townships, 70 administrative villages, 14 neighborhood committees, population 160,000. Mineral-rich, dense vegetation.

In 2012, the region's GDP was 2.08 billion yuan, an increase of 17.5%; fiscal revenue 226.5 million yuan, an increase of 49.6%; public budget revenues 127,300,000 yuan, an increase of 54.2%; total fixed asset investment 3.722 billion yuan, an increase of 52.6%; total retail sales of social consumer goods reached 339 million yuan, an increase of 15.3%; rural per capita net income of 4,229 yuan, an increase of 17.7%; urban residents per capita disposable income of 15,911 yuan, an increase of 14.9%.

崭新的廉租住房
New low-cost housing

毕节市交通投资建设集团有限责任公司

Bijie City Transportation Investment Construction Group Co., Ltd.

六冲河大桥桥墩
Liuchong river bridge pier

毕节市交通投资建设集团有限责任公司是由原毕节市高速公路开发总公司组建而成，是中共毕节市委、毕节市政府为加快毕节市交通基础设施建设，实现试验区跨越式发展，实现省委、省政府提出的“县县通高速公路”的工作目标而组建的大型国有独资企业。公司主营业务为高速公路及其附属设施的投融资建设、经营管理。公司注册资本金10亿元人民币，现有职工50人。集团公司目标是在市委、市政府领导下，依托毕威、黔织高速公路的运营管理，积极开展资本运作，拓宽经营范围，做大做强资产池，增强对外投资能力，为推动毕节交通基础设施建设发挥积极带动作用，在试验区加速发展、加快转型、实现超常规崛起的过程中做出积极的贡献。

毕威高速天桥大桥
Bi Wei high-speed flyover bridge

Bijie City Transportation Investment Construction Group Co., Ltd. is the former Bijie City Expressway Development Corporation set up, the CPC Bijie Municipal Committee, Bijie Municipal Government to speed up the transportation infrastructure construction in Bijie City, to achieve leapfrog development experimental zone, the provincial Party committee, the provincial government proposed the “county expressway” work objectives and the formation of large-scale state-owned enterprises. The company's main business is the investment and financing construction, operation and management of expressway and its affiliated facilities. Companies registered capital of 1 billion yuan, the existing staff of 50 people. Company goal is in the leadership of the municipal party committee, municipal government, operation management based on Bi Wei, Qian Zhi expressway, and actively carry out capital operation, expand the business scope, bigger and stronger asset pool, enhance the ability of foreign investment, plays a positive role in promoting Bijie transportation infrastructure construction, and makes positive contribution for accelerating the development, speeding up the transformation, the realization process with supernormal rise in the test area.

黔织高速六冲河特大桥
Qianzhi high-speed Liuchong river special large bridge